shakespearean criticism

"Thou art a Monument without a tomb,
And art alive still while thy Book doth
    live
And we have wits to read and praise to
give."

*Ben Jonson, from the preface
to the First Folio, 1623.*

Mr. WILLIAM

SHAKESPEARES

COMEDIES,
HISTORIES, &
TRAGEDIES.

Published according to the True Originall Copies.

Martin Droeshout. sculpsit London.

LONDON
Printed by Isaac Iaggard, and Ed. Blount. 1623.

ISSN 0883-9123

Volume 36

shakespearean criticism

Excerpts from the Criticism of
William Shakespeare's Plays and Poetry,
from the First Published Appraisals
to Current Evaluations

Dana Ramel Barnes
Editor

Michelle Lee
Associate Editor

GALE

DETROIT • NEW YORK • TORONTO • LONDON

STAFF

Dana Ramel Barnes, *Editor*

Michelle Lee, *Associate Editor*

Aarti Stephens, *Managing Editor*

Susan M. Trosky, *Permissions Manager*
Kimberly F. Smilay, *Permissions Specialist*
Sarah Chesney, *Permissions Associate*
Steve Cusack, Kelly A. Quin, *Permissions Assistants*

Victoria B. Cariappa, *Research Manager*
Laura C. Bissey, Julia C. Daniel, Michele P. LaMeau, Tamara C. Nott,
Tracie A. Richardson, Cheryl L. Warnock, *Research Associates*
Alfred A. Gardner, *Research Assistant*

Mary Beth Trimper, *Production Director*
Deborah Milliken, *Production Assistant*

Mikal Ansari, *Macintosh Artist*
Randy Bassett, *Image Database Supervisor*
Robert Duncan, *Imaging Specialist*
Pamela A. Reed, *Photography Coordinator*

∞™ This book is printed on acid-free paper that meets the minimum requirements of American National Standard for Information Sciences—Permanence Paper for Printed Library Materials, ANSI Z39.48-1984.

Library of Congress Catalog Card Number 86-645085
ISBN 0-7876-1134-4
ISSN 0883-9123

Printed in the United States of America
Published simultaneously in the United Kingdom
by Gale Research International Limited
(An affiliated company of Gale Research)
10 9 8 7 6 5 4 3 2 1

Gale Research

Contents

Preface vii

Acknowledgments ix

Cumulative Index to Topics 397

Preface

S hakespearean Criticism (SC) provides students, educators, theatergoers, and other interested readers with valuable insight into Shakespeare's drama and poetry. A multiplicity of viewpoints documenting the critical reaction of scholars and commentators from the seventeenth century to the present day derives from the hundreds of periodicals and books excerpted for the series. Students and teachers at all levels of study will benefit from *SC*, whether they seek information for class discussions and written assignments, new perspectives on traditional issues, or the most noteworthy analyses of Shakespeare's artistry.

Scope of the Series

Volumes 1 through 10 of the series present a unique historical overview of the critical response to each Shakespearean work, representing a broad range of interpretations. Volumes 11 through 26 recount the performance history of Shakespeare's plays on the stage and screen through eyewitness reviews and retrospective evaluations of individual productions, comparisons of major interpretations, and discussions of staging issues.

Beginning with Volume 27 in the series, *SC* focuses on criticism published after 1960, with a view to providing the reader with the most significant modern critical approaches. Each volume is ordered around a theme that is central to the study of Shakespeare, such as politics, religion, or sexuality. The topic entry that introduces the volume is comprised of general essays that discuss this theme with reference to all of Shakespeare's works. Following the topic entry are several entries devoted to individual works. Volume 36 is devoted to the relationship between fathers and daughters in Shakespeare's plays, and provides commentary on that topic as well as on the plays *Cymbeline, Pericles* and *The Winter's Tale*.

SC also compiles an annual volume of the most noteworthy essays published on Shakespeare during the previous year. The essays, reprinted in their entirety, have been recommended to Gale by an international panel of distinguished scholars. The most recent volume, *SC Yearbook 1995,* Volume 32 in the series, was published in October 1996.

Organization of the Book

Each entry consists of the following elements: an introduction, critical essays, and an annotated bibliography of further reading.

- The **Introduction** outlines modern interpretations of individual Shakespearean topics, plays, and poems.

- The **Criticism** for each entry consists of essays that are arranged both thematically and chronologically. This provides an overview of the major areas of concern in the analysis of Shakespeare's works, as well as a useful perspective on changes in critical evaluation over recent decades. Footnotes that appear with previously published pieces of criticism are reprinted at the end of each essay or excerpt. In the case of excerpted criticism, only those footnotes that pertain to the excerpted text are included.

- All of the individual essays are preceded by **Explanatory Notes** as an additional aid to students using *SC*. The explanatory notes summarize the criticism that follows.

- A complete **Bibliographical Citation** providing publication information precedes each piece of criticism.

- Each volume includes such **Illustrations** as reproductions of images from the Shakespearean period, paintings and sketches of eighteenth- and nineteenth-century performers, photographs of modern productions, and stills from film adaptations.

- The annotated bibliography of **Further Reading** appearing at the end of each entry suggests additional sources of study for the reader. Explanatory notes summarize each essay or book listed here.

- Each volume of *SC* provides a **Cumulative Index to Topics.** This feature identifies the principal topics in the criticism and stage history of each work. The topics are arranged alphabetically, and the volume and initial page number are indicated for each essay that offers innovative or ample commentary on that topic.

Citing *Shakespearean Criticism*

Students who quote directly from any volume in the Literature Criticism Series in written assignments may use the following general forms to footnote reprinted criticism. The first example pertains to material drawn from periodicals, the second to material reprinted from books.

[1]Gordon Ross Smith, "Shakespeare's *Henry V*: Another Part of the Critical Forest," in *Journal of the History of Ideas,* XXXVII, No. 1 (January-March 1976), 3-26; excerpted and reprinted in *Shakespearean Criticism,* Vol. 30, ed. Marie Lazzari (Detroit: Gale Research, 1996), pp. 262-73.

[2]Katherine Eisaman Maus, *Inwardness and Theater in the English Renaissance* (The University of Chicago Press, 1995); excerpted and reprinted in *Shakespearean Criticism,* Vol. 33, ed. Dana Ramel Barnes and Marie Lazzari, (Detroit: Gale Research, 1997), pp. 112-17.

Suggestions Are Welcome

The editors encourage comments and suggestions from readers on any aspect of the *SC* series. In response to various recommendations, several features have been added to *SC* since the series began, including the topic index and the sample bibliographic citations noted above. Readers are cordially invited to write, call, or fax the editors: *Shakespearean Criticism,* Gale Research, 835 Penobscot Building, Detroit, MI, 48226-4094. Call toll-free at 1-800-347-GALE or fax to 1-313-961-6599.

Acknowledgments

The editors wish to thank the copyright holders of the excerpted criticism included in this volume and the permissions managers of many book and magazine publishing companies for assisting us in securing reproduction rights. We are also grateful to the staffs of the Detroit Public Library, the Library of Congress, the University of Detroit Mercy Library, Wayne State University Purdy/Kresge Library Complex, and the University of Michigan Libraries for making their resources available to us. Following is a list of the copyright holders who have granted us permission to reproduce material in this volume of *SC*. Every effort has been made to trace copyright, but if omissions have been made, please let us know.

COPYRIGHTED EXCERPTS IN *SC*, VOLUME 36, WERE REPRODUCED FROM THE FOLLOWING PERIODICALS:

Ariel, v. 13, July, 1982 for "'Here is a thing too young for such a place': Innocence in 'Pericles'," by Michael Taylor. Copyright © 1982 The Board of Governors, The University of Calgary. Reprinted by permission of the publisher and the author.—*Ball State University Forum*, v. 8, Summer, 1967. Copyright © 1967 Ball State University. Reprinted by permission of the publisher.—*Carnegie Series in English*, 1972. Copyright © 1972 by the Department of English. Reprinted by permission of the author.—*CLA Journal*, v. 19, 1975. Copyright © 1975 by The College Language Association. Used by permission of The College Language Association.—*Comparative Drama*, v. 8, 1967. Copyright © 1967 by the Editors of *Comparative Drama*. Reprinted by permission of the publisher.—*English Literary Renaissance*, v. 5, 1975; v. 16, 1986. Copyright © 1975, 1986 by *English Literary Renaissance*. Reprinted by permission of the publisher.—*English Studies*, v. 70, 1989. Copyright © 1989 by Swets & Zeitlinger B.V. Reprinted by permission of the publisher.—*Essays and Studies*, v. 31, 1978 for "Leontes' Contrition and the Repair of Nature" by Alastair Fowler. Copyright © The English Association 1978. All rights reserved. Reprinted by permission of the publisher and the author.—*Essays in Literature*, v. 15, 1988. Copyright © 1988 by Western Illinois University. Reprinted by permission of the publisher.—*Essays in Theatre/Etudes Theatrales*, v. 12, 1993 for "Imogen's Wounded Chastity," by Karen Bamford. Reprinted by permission of the author.—*Genre*, v. 3, 1970 for "The 'Comic' Mode of 'The Winter's Tale'" by Robert W. Uphaus. Reprinted by permission of the University of Oklahoma and the author.—*Iowa State Journal of Research*, v. 57, 1982. Reproduced by permission.—*Literature and Psychology*, v. 36, 1990. Copyright © *Literature and Psychology* 1990. Reproduced by permission.—*Modern Language Quarterly*, v. 46, September, 1985. Copyright © 1987 University of Washington. Reproduced by permission of Duke University Press.—*Philological Quarterly*, v. 68, 1989 for "Virago with a Soft Voice: Cordelia's Tragic Rebellion in King Lear," by Barbara Millard. Copyright © 1989 by the University of Iowa. Reproduced by permission of the author.—*PMLA*, v. 97, 1982. Copyright © 1982 by the Modern Language Association of America. Reproduced by permission of the Modern Language Association of America.—*Shakespeare Studies*, v. 1, 1965 for "Notes on Shakespeare's Cymbeline," by Charles K. Hofling. Copyright © 1965, The Council for Research in the Renaissance. Reprinted by permission of the author.—*South Atlantic Bulletin*, v. 43, 1978. Copyright © 1978 by South Atlantic Modern Language Association. Reproduced by permission.—*Studies in English Literature: 1500-1900*, v. XX, Spring, 1980 for "Cymbeline and the Imagery of Covenant Theology," by Lila Geller; v. 34, Spring, 1994 for "Speech Acts, Generic Differences, and the Curious Case of Cymbeline," by Elena Glazov-Corrigan. Copyright © 1980, 1994 William Marsh Rice University. Both reproduced by permission of publisher and the authors.—*Studies in Philology*, v. LXXV, Summer, 1978. Copyright © 1978 by the University of North Carolina Press. Reproduced by permission of the publisher.—*Texas Studies in Literature and Language*, v. 22, Fall, 1980 for "Shakespeare's Empirical Romance: 'Cymbeline' and Modern Knowledge," by Maurice Hunt. Copyright © 1980 by the University of Texas Press. Reproduced permission of the publisher and the author.—*University of Toronto Quarterly*, v. 61, Winter, 1991-92. Reproduced by permission of University of Toronto Press Incorporated.—*The Yearbook of English Studies*, v. 8, 1978. Copyright © Modern Humanities Research Association 1978. All rights reserved. Reproduced by permission of the Editor of the Modern Humanities Research Association.

Fathers and Daughters in Shakespeare

INTRODUCTION

Critics have long recognized the centrality of family relationships in Shakespeare's drama, but the shifting affections of fathers and daughters has attracted a great deal of scholarly attention only in recent decades. The focus of the critical literature has primarily centered on a few early romantic comedies, the late romances, and *King Lear*, in which daughters struggle to negotiate a passage into adulthood and marriage with their fathers' blessing, while the fathers struggle to relinquish these young women to other men—their future husbands.

Much of the reversal in critical sympathies may be attributable to the influence of feminist criticism. The earlier appraisals, dating to the 1970s and early 1980s, are typically more sympathetic to the fathers, finding the struggles between them and their daughters to be among the expected hurdles of normal family life, even if the particular plots in which they appear are atypical for Shakespeare. The later readings, however, are more likely to find a tyrannical possessiveness in excess of normal parental affection in the father's behavior—or, as the case may be, a capriciousness, coldness, or disloyalty unwarranted by the daughter's exemplary conduct. While some critics discern an incestuous desire for the daughter in the father's motivation, others see the father's possessiveness as a love corrupted by the power a patriarchal society confers on him. In these cases, the daughter takes on the aspect of a heroine, becoming the focal point of the play she inhabits.

As Shakespearean fathers came under less indulgent scrutiny, other father-daughter relationships began to attract more attention. In the most recent scholarly literature, Juliet and old Capulet, Ophelia and Polonius, and Desdemona and Brabantio move to the whims of patriarchy, willingly or not. To the extent that these daughters are helpless to change the terms of their fate, their tragedies have come to be presented as indictments of sexist oppression. The question that lies just under the surface of such analyses, then, concerns a post-modernist critical evaluation of Shakespeare, as some feminist scholars claim him to be a proto-feminist, while others assert that he remains within a tradition of patriarchy.

OVERVIEWS

Mark Taylor (essay date 1982)

SOURCE: "The Lords of Duty," in *Shakespeare's*

Darker Purpose: A Question of Incest, AMS Press, Inc., 1982, pp. 84-119.

[*In the following excerpt, Taylor focuses on the irregular control that fathers exert on their daughters in many of Shakespeare's works.*]

The plot of *As You Like It* could be described as the simultaneous movements of two daughters—one, Rosalind, toward her father, and the other, Celia, away from hers. At the beginning Rosalind and Duke Senior are apart from each other. His brother has usurped his power and banished him from the court; she has remained behind as a companion to Celia. It is an unfortunate situation, not of their own contrivance, but it raises certain questions. When we first meet the two girls Celia is trying to cheer her friend up, asking her to "be merry," Rosalind answers,

> Dear Celia, I show more mirth than I am mistress of, and would you yet I were merrier? Unless you could teach me to forget a banished father, you must not learn me how to remember any extraordinary pleasure.
>
> (1.2.2-5)

It is an understandable sadness, but why, then, did Rosalind remain behind and not accompany her father in the first place? Furthermore, she does in fact cheer up almost immediately—she starts quizzing Celia about falling in love—and when Duke Frederick banishes her as a bad influence on his daughter, it is not she but Celia who proposes they "seek my uncle in the Forest of Arden" (1.3.103)—oddly, if one considers how dependent on Rosalind Celia will become. The closer physical proximity a father and daughter enjoy, in the play, the greater is her sense of independence and initiative. Additionally, Celia provides a somewhat pathetic context for underscoring the investment fathers and daughters have in each other when she tells Rosalind, "You know my father hath no child but I, nor none is like to have . . ." (1.2.15-16).

For his part, Duke Senior has no child but Rosalind, nor none is like to have, and yet his separation from her appears to bother him not at all. In the Forest of Arden he asks Amiens and his other companions,

> Now, my co-mates and brothers in exile,
> Hath not old custom made this life more sweet
> Than that of painted pomp?
>
> (2.1.1-3)

and continues to compare their new life favorably with that lived in the court. The virtue of this life, as he says, is the absence of flatterers and false counsellors, but its distinct limitation, although he does not say so, is the absence of women, which means its inability to perpetuate itself. It is of course true that despite frequent defenses of the rural life or the life of solitude, Shakespeare's characters, like Socrates, opt finally to live in the company of other men in the city or the court.[4] In *2 Henry VI* Alexander Iden asks,

> Lord, who would live turmoilèd in the court
> And may enjoy such quiet walks as these?
> This small inheritance my father left me
> Contenteth me, and worth a monarchy.
>
> (4.10.15-18)

But after he kills Jack Cade and the King prefers him in his service, Iden says,

> May Iden live to merit such a bounty,
> And never live but true unto his liege,
>
> (5.1.81-82)

evidently quite content with his prospects at court. Duke Senior, too, is perfectly happy to have his authority restored at the end of *As You Like It,* and so we may say about his earlier praise of the solitary life that he is merely putting a good face on an unfortunate but temporary predicament. It is nevertheless strange that he should miss his daughter even less than she misses him or that he should not feel he is deserting her when she, on the verge of her maturity, might need him most.

Away from him, in any event, it falls to Rosalind not only to choose Orlando for herself but also to test his merit and honor by having him address to Ganymede the sentiments appropriate to Rosalind. When this has been done, and when the other complications that arose from Rosalind's disguise have been untangled, she can present herself equally to father and husband-to-be, saying identical words first to one, then to the other:

> To you I give myself for I am yours.
>
> (5.4.110,111)

In coordinate sentences she stresses the equality of her roles as daughter and wife by telling Duke Senior,

> I'll have no father, if you be not he,
>
> (116)

and then telling Orlando,

> I'll have no husband, if you be not he.
>
> (117)

It is quite unthinkable that the Duke should object to the way Rosalind thus limits his ownership of her, but

it is noteworthy that in distinctly dividing her roles this way, Rosalind is successful exactly where both Cordelia and Desdemona fail. Cordelia says to her father,

> Haply, when I shall wed,
> That lord whose hand must take my plight shall carry
> Half my love with him, half my care and duty.
> Sure I shall never marry like my sisters,
> To love my father all.
>
> (*King Lear,* 1.1.100-04)

And when Brabantio demands that Desdemona say "Where most you owe obedience," she answers,

> My noble father,
> I do perceive here a divided duty.
> To you I am bound for life and education;
> My life and education both do learn me
> How to respect you: you are the lord of duty;
> I am hitherto your daughter. But here's my husband;
> And so much duty as my mother showed
> To you, preferring you before her father,
> So much I challenge that I may profess
> Due to the Moor my lord.
>
> (*Othello,* 1.3.180-89)

Of course, the circumstances surrounding the three marriages differ enormously. Whereas Lear seeks, in the protestations of absolute love that Cordelia cannot give, an affirmation of the powers that he is obviously yielding to age, and Brabantio sees in Desdemona's elopement with Othello an act of something like cultural and racial treason, Duke Senior does not appear to freight his daughter with any particular emblematic value. Although they are being asked only to share their daughters, in other words, the first two fathers find in this sharing the distinct loss of something else—either personal strength or the cultural inviolability of Venice; by contrast, Duke Senior is regaining his duchy and symbolically his power at the moment he is losing exclusive title to Rosalind. That, naturally, makes her changed status much easier for him to accept. It is significant, none the less, that it no more occurs to Rosalind to seek her father's blessing than it does to Duke Senior to admonish her for proceeding so independently.

Contrasted with Rosalind, who moves toward her father in the play, Celia, in accompanying her friend into the forest, is abandoning her father. His irrational outburst toward Rosalind costs him a daughter, as does Leontes' toward Hermione (even the names Aliena and Perdita, the estranged and the lost, are not altogether dissimilar), but unlike that finally lucky father, there is no reason to suppose that Duke Frederick ever sees his daughter again. Insofar as Duke Frederick has a reason for his sudden hatred of Rosalind, it is that she draws attention away from Celia. He tells Celia,

> She robs thee of thy name,
> And thou wilt show more bright and seem
>   more virtuous
> When she is gone.
>
> (1.3.76-78)

Whether or not this contrast has been perceived by others at the court is uncertain, but it is interesting that Duke Frederick is concerned with the appearance of virtue in his daughter, not with virtue itself. In any event, he surely tries too hard to make his daughter shine. Doing so, he anticipates a later Shakespearean *mother*, Dionyza in *Pericles,* who instructs Leonine to murder Marina so that Philotea will be more honored than she is. When Cleon learns of this piece of treachery, he is outraged and denounces Dionyza as a harpy (4.3.46-48), but in one of the peculiar inconsistencies of that play, he will be both blamed and punished as if the plot has been his own. Just before their mutual recognition, Marina tells Pericles that her father had left her in Tharsus

> Till, cruel Cleon, with his wicked wife,
> Did seek to murder me,
>
>   (5.1.173-74)

and in the epilogue Gower describes how the good citizens of Tharsus had risen up against both king and queen and burned them to death in their palace:

> The gods for murder seemed so content
> To punish—although not done, but meant.
>   (Epilogue, 15-16)

Cleon is punished for Duke Frederick's sin, and more severely than Frederick himself. It would be special pleading to suggest, in this regard, that the two plays are drawn together by any common moral, but it may be observed that one extreme method fathers have of celebrating their daughters—by eliminating the competition—leads to the loss of the daughter or of the father's life.

At the end of *As You Like It,* according to Jaques de Boys (the brother of Orlando and Oliver), when Frederick was intending to kill Duke Senior,

> . . . to the skirts of this wild wood he came,
> Where, meeting with an old religious man,
> After some question with him was converted
> Both from his enterprise and from the
>   world. . . .
>
>   (5.4.153-56)

It is a very convenient conversion, for it enables Shakespeare to end his play by restoring Duke Senior's lands

to him without subjecting Frederick to any corresponding disappointment over the loss of these same lands. In Frederick's renunciation of "the world" there is an implicit surrender of the sort of control over, even interest in, Celia that he had demonstrated earlier in trying to choose her companions for her. So he is not asked to approve her marriage to Oliver, nor does he seem to be aware of it. At the same time, it is appropriate that Celia should pass from Frederick to Oliver, from one jealous usurper of a brother's prerogatives to another, from one convert to goodness to another; it is a way of finding in her husband an image of her father.

In several plays the commands of a father, at least as his daughter perceives them, are obeyed even though he is no longer alive to enforce them. Of minimal importance in *Julius Caesar,* this circumstance figures significantly in *Love's Labor's Lost, Measure for Measure,* and *The Merchant of Venice.* Until its end *Love's Labor's Lost* seems to be, like *Twelfth Night,* a play concerned with a single generation of independent young adults. It is true that the Princess of France and her ladies have come to the court of Navarre in the first place because of her father's debts to Ferdinand; but it does not appear, till the final scene, that that fact or that character has any particular pertinence other than to bring the courtiers and the ladies together. Then Marcade arrives with news of the King of France's death, and in a happy, sometimes farcical drama, "The scene begins to cloud," as Berowne says (5.2.712). The Princess and her entourage immediately prepare to depart for Paris, and Berowne and his friends, interrupted on the verge of matrimony, are left with the charge of doing good works and remaining "Remote from all the pleasures of the world" (786) so that their love may yet be requited, a year hence. Resisting the urgency felt by the Princess, the King says to her,

> Now, at the latest minute of this hour,
> Grant us your loves,

and she replies,

> A time, methinks, too short
> To make a world-without-end bargain in.
>   (777-79)

Of course, there is no world-without-end, but throughout the play its characters, especially the four young men, have acted as if there is—as if their actions are not to be contained within, and measured by, the finitude of their lives. Thus, the two main occupations in which they are engaged—the pursuit of wisdom and then the pursuit of love—are presented in perverted forms: wisdom as the most sterile trappings of scholarship and a withdrawal from life, and love as an imitation of traditional lovers' postures and a parroting of conventionally appropriate verses. The former is shown to be essentially ludicrous by its caricatured practitioners Nathaniel and Holofernes; and the latter is shown to be woefully artificial by contrast with Costard's naturally lusty chasing of Jaquenetta. Both wisdom and romance, when divorced, as it were, from the facts of life, become kinds of folly, the opposites of their true selves. Early on, the King asks,

> What is the end of study, let me know?
>
> (1.1.55)

and when Berowne can finally provide an answer to that question,

> Learning is but an adjunct to ourself,
>
> (4.3.309)

we should understand that his answer assumes some knowledge of the nature of "ourself"—that it is, among other things, a mortal organism—that they all had lacked before. We may note, equally, the contrast between the three-year period of voluntary withdrawal from the affairs of the world in act 1 and the one-year period imposed upon the men in act 5. Longaville speaks for the four (although Berowne partially demurs) when he says,

> I am resolved. 'Tis but a three years' fast.
>
> (1.1.24)

And it is this same courtier who says, when his Maria puts him off for a year,

> I'll stay with patience, but the time is long.
>
> (5.2.825)

To someone who refuses to confront the meaning of time, three years are the briefest instant; but to someone unable to ignore it, one year is long indeed.

Much credit for this transformation in attitudes must go to the King of France. Significantly, the princess's response to her father's death is directed not by any explicit statement of his will but by her sense that the pattern of artifice in which she, too, had participated, as if in a permanent design, has been shattered. She tells the men,

> We have received your letters, full of love;
> Your favors, the ambassadors of love;
> And in our maiden council rated them
> At courtship, pleasant jest, and courtesy,
> As bombast and as living to the time.
> But more devout than this in our respects
> Have we not been, and therefore met your
>   loves
> In their own fashion, like a merriment.
>
> (5.2.767-74)

In a moment she has stopped being a clever little girl and become a woman, aware of the painful burdens of life and aware, also, how these burdens make life worthwhile and change love from artifice into an expression of natural feelings. In this moment, indeed, all the characters come to man's estate. One would be hard put to find a Shakespearean father who bequeaths his daughter a more precious legacy than the King of France, who, like the man who shares his title in *King Lear,* is an indicator of the presence of real value. Contrary to the practice or the intention of some fathers, he personally confers, through his death, adulthood upon the Princess.

We have already discussed the problematic Isabella in the context of her imagined obligations to a dead father. The salient features of her personality—her general inflexibility, her desire for the most rigorous novitiate, her horror before the uses of the flesh—appear to be less a conscious response to her father's will, real or imagined, than a compensation for his loss when they were closest and she needed him most. Thus she asks the Church to be a substitute for his authority, and thus she finds the advances of Angelo particularly repugnant because her celibacy is a form of sexual fidelity to her father. This dilemma, this fixation on a lost past, is resolved by her finding in Duke Vincentio, a man we may estimate of her father's age, a fusion of supreme temporal authority in his capacity as Duke with spiritual authority in his guise as friar. He is all that she has lost in a father, and yet he is not her father, so union with him, coveted in the earlier instance, is not forbidden.

Additional light may be cast upon the problem of Isabella by a story well known to Shakespeare: the tale of the Cyprian king Cinyras who fathered on his daughter Myrrha the child Adonis (*Metamorphoses,* X). According to Ovid, it is the nubile Myrrha who conceives "unlawful love" for her father, not the other way round. This she is able to consummate, after a brief struggle with her conscience, during her mother's three-day absence at the "secret rites" of Ceres, and with the aid of her nurse who, "fynding Cinyras/Well washt with wyne" (501-02), tells him of "a pretye lasse/ In love with him" (502-03), and then dispatches Myrrha to Cinyras's dark chamber. She goes to her father several successive nights, and they enjoy each other, her identity unknown to him. Finally, in the language of Arthur Golding's translation,[5]

> Cinyras desyrous for to knowe
> His lover that so many nyghts uppon him did
>   bestowe,
> Did fetch a light: by which he sawe his owne
>   most heynous cryme,
> And eeke his daughter.
>
> (541-44)

Cinyras kills himself, and Myrrha flees to Arabia where, after being delivered of Adonis, she is changed into a myrrh tree. (Literature was not done with the poor girl, however: Dante placed *"l'anima antica di Mirra scellerata"* [XXX, 37-38] deep in his *Inferno*.)

Several features of Ovid's story are generally pertinent to this discussion. There is, for one thing, Myrrha's consciousness of the dilemma Cinyras's being her father forces upon her:

> were not Cinyras my father than, Iwis
> I myght obtaine to lye with him. But now
> because he is
> Myne owne, he cannot bee myne owne.
>
>   (374-76)

This is similar to the predicament, much exacerbated by the father's death, that hardens Isabella in her enthusiasm for the celibate life, and is resolved for her by the substitution of Duke for father. Second, the riddle that Antiochus presents to Pericles (*Pericles*, 1.1.65-72) and Pericles' words upon recognizing Marina, "O, come hither, / Thou that beget'st him that did thee beget" (5.1.196-97), passages oddly similar to each other, as we have noted, are strangely echoed in these words that the initially tormented Myrrha speaks to herself:

> Wilt thou thy fathers leman bee? wilt thou be
> both the moother
> And suster of thy chyld? shall he bee both thy
> sonne and brother?
>
>   (386-87)

The *unnaturalness* of incest in both stories is underlined by the characters' sense that it multiplies the single way one person should be, and normally is, related to another, as Hamlet, hating the "incestuous" union that has made him son to his uncle, can say, "A little more than kin, and less than kind!"

Most important, finally, is the evidence in the *Metamorphoses* that the story Ovid recounts is a clear displacement onto Myrrha of the motives and desires of Cinyras himself. It is the daughter who is said to desire her father and by deceit to seduce him; making the father an unwitting victim is the easiest way to justify his taking what he wants when the proscriptions against what he wants are so strong. Consequently, as a way of neutralizing our objections to what Cinyras does, and his own as well, Ovid has him drunk, as if that condition removes him from judgment; it is a device we saw earlier, probably used to the same purpose, in the story of the seduction of Lot by his daughters in Genesis 19. A man escapes blame for cohabiting with his daughters by the simple expedient of drunkenness. Ovid, however, is more explicit than this about Cinyras' motives. After the nurse describes the beauty of the unnamed Myrrha to Cinyras, he asks her age and is told, "shee was about / The age of Myrrha. Well (quoth he) then bring her to my bed" (504-05). This shared identity with his daughter is all it takes to fire his lust. Then, when the two are in bed together, Ovid writes, moralizingly,

> And lest this cryme of theyres
> Myght want the ryghtfull termes, by chaunce
> as in respect of yeeres
> He daughter did her call, and shee him father.
>
>   (535-37)

Cinyras goes to bed with his daughter, who pretends to be another girl so that he can pretend that other girl is his daughter. What he gets is what he wants, however much he, and the original motives attributed by the story teller, may have succeeded in disguising that fact from him; but that this success is no more than partial is shown by his suicide. Somehow knowing that what he had done is no less than what he wanted to do, he destroys himself.

The story seems to reveal Ovid working at cross-purposes with himself. It appears as if he wished to tell a story in which a man would not be culpable for incest with his daughter and thus sets the action up entirely as the daughter's practice (and as the vengeance of Venus, who cursed Myrrha because of her mother's boast that the daughter was more beautiful than the goddess); and then, in the act of telling the story, he confronts and corrects what was fundamentally dishonest in it. This correction reveals his knowledge that whatever else an act of father-daughter incest might be, it is not something truly alien to the imagination of the father. In effect, Ovid admits that the urges he had given first to Myrrha were a displacement of those of Cinyras. Correspondingly, though we know nothing about the father of Isabella other than her need for him, it is tempting to understand her whole psychic mechanism on the analogy of the motives of other Shakespearean fathers, Lear and Leontes, for instance, displaced onto their daughters.

There is nothing similarly ambiguous about the instructions left to Portia in her dead father's will in *The Merchant of Venice*, the counsel that she allow "the lott'ry that he hath devised in these three chests of gold, silver, and lead" (1.2.27-29) to determine her husband. This means that her father insists from beyond the grave that he play a part in selecting her mate. It is a tedious enterprise with which she grows easily impatient. She tells Nerissa,

> I may neither choose who I would nor refuse who
> I dislike, so is the will of a living daughter curbed
> by the will of a dead father. Is it not hard, Nerissa,
> that I cannot choose one, nor refuse none?
>
>   (1.2.21-25)

Nerissa defends the soundness of the father's device:

> Your father was ever virtuous, and holy men at
> their death have good inspirations.
>
> (26-27)

Though fidelity to her father's wishes is, as Portia says, hard, her reward—the perfect reward, in an ideal world, for an obedient daughter—is marriage to the man she had wanted all along. Doing what her father bids, Portia gets what she wants. So perfect a paradigm emerges from this situation for the harmony that results from the congruence of a father's wishes and a daughter's actions that it would be churlish to wonder whether the father's "good inspirations" are at all belied by certain unfortunate characteristics in the man she actually gets. It is significant, when Bassanio describes Portia to Antonio—

> In Belmont is a lady richly left;
> And she is fair, and fairer than that word,
> Of wondrous virtues.
>
> (1.1.161-63)

—that he mentions her wealth first, and it is equally significant that he has no compunction about letting Antonio risk death to help him out.

On the other hand, it is perhaps necessary to assert that Portia is indeed faithful to the spirit, and not the letter only, of her father's will. She employs the scheme of the three caskets to the end without any act of subversion. For over a century certain critics have maintained that Portia tips off Bassanio with the words rhyming with *lead* in the first lines of the song she chooses while he makes up his mind.:

> Tell me where is fancy bred,
> Or in the heart, or in the head?
> How begot, how nourishèd?
>
> (3.2.63-65)

John Russell Brown's commentary in the New Arden edition argues persuasively against this possibility. He points out that Portia has specifically said she will give no clues; that she believes in the efficacy of the lottery; that the themes of the play would be considerably cheapened thereby; and that in other plays "where a character *sings* a secret that he is forbidden to *speak,* the hint is very much broader than here."[6] To this I would add that Bassanio is engaged in a very serious and demanding task—choosing between a wealthy wife and perpetual bachelorhood—and since he has not been directed to listen attentively to Portia's Song, which exists as stage business for the audience's benefit while Bassanio takes the time to ponder, it is unlikely that he would allow it to interfere with his concentration.

As Portia's fidelity to the conditions of her dead father's will emphasizes the happiness that will some-

times be the result of the conjunction of a father's and a daughter's wishes, so does Jessica's disobedience provide an opposite model, showing how a daughter's happiness, as she defines it, depends upon, or can emerge from, a disjunction of values. It is not only in the relationship of Portia to her father, however, but also in that of Desdemona to Brabantio in Shakespeare's other Venetian play that we find a proper context for considering Jessica and Shylock. It is unthinkable to Brabantio that Othello can have won Desdemona without casting some spell upon her, that of her own volition she can have chosen him; but if his daughter's point of view eludes him, there is no reason to suppose that Othello's does. Brabantio could understand perfectly why Othello should wish to marry Desdemona and into the world of money and privilege that, he wrongly assumes, goes with her. His repeated references to Othello as a thief or a "foul thief" (1.2.62) make it clear that, although he abhors what Othello has done, he is not puzzled by it; it is not, in the nature of things, mysterious that a thief should take what he does not have, particularly when the acquired object is better than what he does have. That someone should aspire to more than he has is no more surprising than the belief, in the minds of those who possess wealth, in the need for vigilance to thwart the aspirations of the dispossessed. Additionally, Othello's pretensions, as Brabantio (correctly) perceives them, are not to the hand of a beautiful girl alone but also to the superior culture that she represents. He is trying to rise from a servant to a citizen of Venice, and since Venice and all things Venetian are eminently desirable (again, from Brabantio's perspective, which Othello shares) that, too, is no more surprising than that the Turks should covet Cyprus. Indeed, after the Duke tries to console Brabantio, saying,

> The robbed that smiles steals something from
>   the thief;
> He robs himself that spends a bootless grief,

Brabantio with bitter irony replies,

> So let the Turk of Cyprus us beguile:
> We lose it not so long as we can smile.
>
> (1.3.208-11)

Both Othello and the Turks are trying to usurp the very identity of Venice.

Various Shakespearean fathers object to suitors for their daughter's hands because of the inferior social or economic position of the suitors (Cymbeline, Page in *The Merry Wives,* the Duke of Milan in *The Two Gentlemen,* and others), but only in *Othello* and *The Merchant of Venice* is the alliance transcultural and transracial as well, between white and black or between gentile and Jew. If we could ask the majority of the characters in each play how successful the marriages are for the girls, they would surely hold that though Desdemona lowered herself by marrying beneath the station to which she was born, Jessica raised herself by marrying into a higher station. On pragmatic grounds, the first marriage seems a failure, the second a success, since in both cases it is the woman who joins the man, and not he her. There is, of course, no reason that Shylock, who is as proud of his racial heritage, and as bent on maintaining its purity, as the Christians are of their own, should share this view; but Jessica unquestionably earns perquisites, like entrance into the world of Belmont, that she had lacked. Or perhaps it is more accurate to say, not that she earns these perquisites, but that she purchases them with money stolen from her father.

Like Antonio and Portia when first we meet them, Jessica announces her unhappiness with her lot; but whereas the first two are made unhappy by something that has just happened, Bassanio's falling in love, or by a temporary situation, the need to wait and to see who chooses the lead casket, Jessica's unhappiness is evidently a long-term condition. She tells Launcelot,

> I am sorry thou wilt leave my father so;
> Our house is hell, and thou a merry devil
> Didst rob it of some taste of tediousness.
>
> (2.3.1-3)

There is no reason for us to doubt the legitimacy of Jessica's indictment, and Launcelot, who sees service in a Christian household as preferable to service in Shylock's, offers a kind of confirmation of Jessica's view. On the other hand, it is natural to wish for more objective evidence of conditions—hellish? tedious?—in Shylock's home than the play offers. Unless we can accept Jessica's situation as truly intolerable, and perhaps even if we do, we must regard her leaving with his gold as a terrible betrayal for any daughter. Here, as so often in the play, we must make up our minds, for less than conclusive reasons exist about the sort of man Shylock is, and then let that judgment determine subsequent judgments about everything that happens to him. It is much easier to do this in the theater, where the director will foist his decisions on us, than in the study, where almost any unambiguous view is likely to seem extreme. As a partial justification for leaving Shylock, Launcelot tells old Gobbo,

> I am famished in his service; you may tell
> every finger I have with my ribs.
>
> (2.2.98-99)

That sounds bad indeed, but Gobbo, who is "more than sand-blind, high-gravel-blind" (32-33) and cannot even recognize his son, is unable to substantiate the report. By contrast, Shylock tells Launcelot that, when he goes over to Bassanio,

> Thou shalt not gormandize
> As thou hast done with me.
>
> (2.5.3-4)

It is tempting to laugh at this hypocrisy, but we cannot be sure it is hypocrisy; it may be, rather, that Launcelot, like Jessica, simply seeks social preferment for its own sake, not because the circumstances of his life are really very bad. Again, there is Solanio's report of Shylock's outcry in the streets:

> "My daughter! O my ducats! O my daughter!
> Fled with a Christian! O my Christian ducats!
> Justice! the law! my ducats and my daughter!
> A sealèd bag, two sealèd bags of ducats,
> Of double ducats, stol'n from me by my
>   daughter!
> And jewels—two stones, two rich and
>   precious stones.
> Stol'n by my daughter!"
>
> (2.8.15-21)

which, if accurate (as it need not be), is not necessarily prejudicial to our sympathy for Shylock. Probably everyone laughs at these words and their implied equivalence of the two losses, a daughter and gold, but if the first loss should be regarded as infinitely more severe than the second, the two together still add up to everything the man owns. Furthermore, even if Solanio is providing a verbatim transcript of Shylock's words, it is unlikely that he is trying to duplicate Shylock's tone.

(Irrespective of Solanio's accuracy, however, one thing about this speech is highly significant: the pun on testicles implicit in "two sealed bags" and "two stones, two rich and precious stones." Since these bags; or stones, were stolen by Jessica, as Shylock says, it follows by corollary that he has been disembowelled, castrated, unmanned by the departure of his daughter. The point is not that this wound is present in Shylock's mind, though it may well be, but that in his words, or those of Solanio, as in those of Antigonus, there lies the association of a daughter's coming to maturity and a father's loss of sexual potency.[7])

Having lost his daughter, Shylock calls on the state for restitution. Solanio says,

> The villain Jew with outcries raised the Duke,
> With him went to search Bassanio's ship.
>
> (2.8.4-5)

Like Brabantio, Shylock believes that the power of the state will preserve a father's control over his daughter. The social insider and the social outsider are for a moment one in their appeals to external authority for buttressing of their personal authority when it is challenged within their families. The state's response to each man is ultimately the same. Though we may feel more sympathy for Desdemona than for Jessica, and though we cannot attribute the same or even similar motives to the Duke in *Othello* and the Duke in *The Merchant of Venice,* we may recognize that it is the proper business of both to allow girls to grow up, whether their fathers will or no.

Like Jessica, Hermia in *A Midsummer Night's Dream* marries the man she desires at the cost of permanent estrangement from her father; and her father, Egeus, like Shylock, is punished for his obstinacy by exclusion from the fifth act of the play. *A Midsummer Night's Dream* begins, like *Othello* and *King Lear,* with the spectacle of an old man, Egeus, enraged at the prospect of his daughter's marriage. But whereas Brabantio's anger follows from Desdemona's genuine violation of social convention, as both he and the other senators understand it, and Lear's follows from Cordelia's refusal to play the brief part he has authored for her in his harmless little love game—in terms of superficial appearances, that is, both Brabantio and Lear have a certain reasonable entitlement to their dismay—Egeus appears to lack any comprehensible basis for his quarrel with Hermia except that she is his daughter and should therefore do what he says. She wants to marry Lysander, and he would have her marry Demetrius. He blames Lysander for having

> Turned her obedience (which is due to me)
> To stubborn harshness,
>
> (1.1.37-38)

and he seeks to exert his authority against that independence of will, as if it is the only way he has of demonstrating that he occupies a needed place in the world. His is the conventional anger of the *senex iratus,* which amuses us in spite of our recognition that it has a real power to do damage and cause everlasting unhappiness. Although Egeus pretends to be crossed by Hermia, it is perhaps our impression that it is she who has been crossed, quite arbitrarily, by him. If she had fallen in love with Demetrius, then his choice for her might well have been Lysander. In any event, it is hard for him to believe that his daughter legitimately possesses a mind of her own. Like Brabantio, he denies that all is fair in love, and accuses Lysander of foul play. He tells the Duke that "This man hath bewitched the bosom of my child" (27). It is odd how these fathers denounce the natural instincts of their daughters as the supernatural powers of their daughters' lovers.

Egeus' anger and determination to keep Hermia faithful to him, though authentic emotions within himself, are hard for any reader or audience to take too seriously. One reason, as I have suggested above, is that the force of his imperative—marry Lysander or die—is immediately lessened when Theseus widens the possible consequences of disobedience:

> Either to die the death, or to abjure
> For ever the society of men.
>
> (1.1.65-66)

The curse of celibacy can always be reversed by the simple expedient of having Egeus change his mind, whenever. That is all to the good, but I think that the reader must be careful not to credit Theseus with more high-mindedness and balanced judgment than he displays. A bit earlier he had said to Hermia:

> Be advised, fair maid.
> To you your father should be as a god,
> One that composed your beauties; yea, and
>   one
> To whom you are but as a form in wax
> By him imprinted and within his power
> To leave the figure or disfigure it.
>
> (46-51)

One makes one's children, but Theseus' severe words notwithstanding, one may not then destroy a product that is unsatisfactory. Theseus is not Hermia's father, but the two men appear to belong to the same generation and class in Athens, suggesting that on certain matters one might well speak for the other. In any case, the chilling threat to "disfigure"—Theseus probably intends something like "unmake," or remove all form from the wax, but we cannot very well ignore the connotations of mutilation—recalls the similar threats of Antigonus and Polixines.

A second fact of the play that comically undercuts Egeus' determination is the alternative action that Lysander perceives. The will of Egeus, reinforced by the power of Theseus, may prevail in Athens, but Athens is not the whole world. Lysander tells the compliant Hermia that if she will accompany him to his aunt's house seven leagues distant,

> There, gentle Hermia, may I marry thee,
> And to that place the sharp Athenian law
> Cannot pursue us.
>
> (161-63)

This possibility further neutralizes the consequences of Egeus' interference.

Third, it is commonplace to observe that Egeus' preference for Demetrius is essentially preposterous, and therefore a matter that cannot worry us unduly, since the two suitors are so nearly indistinguishable.[8] This both is and is not true. Lysander and Demetrius, young Athenian noblemen, are the same age and of equivalent social rank; with either Hermia would be marrying an eligible man of her own class. Neither of them, moreover, shows any great resource of intelligence or imagination: they never understand what has happened to them in the forest or question why they have turned about in their romantic preferences as they have. That there is not much to choose between them is a probability emphasized by the decision of many directors to dress them in identical clothing. Hermia is perfectly within *her* rights to favor one over the other because—this is Shakespeare's profound comment on the nature of love—the person in love will see uniqueness where everyone else sees sameness; by definition love differentiates its chosen object from those about it.

On the other hand, Lysander has a steadfastness that Demetrius lacks. It is only under the spell of Puck that Lysander comes briefly to favor Helena over Hermia, while Demetrius had originally been infatuated with Helena, that is, before the play begins. Lysander tells Theseus, as if this history supports his claim to Hermia, that

> Demetrius, I'll avouch it to his head,
> Made love to Nedar's daughter, Helena,
> And won her soul; and she (sweet lady) dotes,
> Devoutly dotes, dotes in idolatry,
> Upon this spotted and inconstant man,
>
> (106-10)

testimony that Helena supports in her soliloquy at the end of the scene:

> For ere Demetrius looked on Hermia's eyne,
> He hailed down oaths that he was only mine.
>
> (242-43)

Such romantic fickleness, no less common than young constancy, hardly constitutes much of a sin to charge Demetrius with. There is no evidence that he came to desire Hermia only because Lysander did, as Proteus came to desire Silvia only because Valentine did in *The Two Gentlemen,* and we should not normally judge him harshly for going from one girl to another. At the same time, however, Theseus finds Demetrius' behavior objectionable. After Lysander has accused him of making love to Helena, Theseus says,

> I must confess that I have heard so much,
> And with Demetrius thought to have spoke
>   thereof;
> But, being over-full of self-affairs,
> My mind did lose it.
>
> (111-14)

It is unclear just why Theseus believes, as he seems to, that Demetrius' fickleness is a matter calling for his official adjudication or reprimand, but it is fairly certain that, though bound by the law to support Egeus' authority over Hermia, he sees Demetrius as a less honorable man than Lysander. Indeed, like a later duke, Vincentio in *Measure for Measure,* who encourages Mariana to believe there will be nothing criminal about sleeping with Angelo, Theseus seems able to promote extralegal behavior when the letter of the law suppresses natural impulse and affection. When he says,

> But Demetrius, come,
> And come, Egeus. You shall go with me;
> I have some private schooling for you both,
>
> (113-15)

he leaves Hermia and Lysander alone and gives them the opportunity, which they will seize upon, to escape into the forest. It is very likely that he is trying to see if they will dare act in their own behalf.

The scenes in the forest bear out Theseus' suspicions of Demetrius' dishonor. Although Lysander is eager to enjoy the fruits of his love before marriage (2.2.34-65), but only with the acquiescence of Hermia, Demetrius is more ominously prepared to do sexual violence to Helena, though he claims to detest her, if she will not leave him alone:

> I will not stay thy questions. Let me go!
> Or if thou follow, do not believe
> But I shall do thee mischief in the wood.
>
> (2.1.235-37)

It is perhaps significant that Shakespeare gave to this young man the name he had assigned earlier to Tamora's son, the despoiler of Lavinia in *Titus Andronicus.* It is at least arguable that Egeus' preference for Demetrius represents not merely a capricious intrusion upon Hermia's rights but a choice of the less worthy man and thus a choice contrary to the best interests of his daughter. In all events, Egeus ignores whatever these interests may be.

Although angry at Lysander when she believes that he and Demetrius, under Puck's spell, are having fun at her expense in the forest, Hermia remains constant to him, as does Helena to Demetrius, and as do most women in Shakespeare to their lovers, Cressida being a rare, though notable, exception. In her constancy Hermia prevails, for after the four young lovers have happily paired off, so that every "Jack shall have Jill," Theseus has the wisdom—if wisdom is measured by the attainment of human satisfaction—to set aside the law it is his duty to enforce. He says,

> Fair lovers, you are fortunately met.
> Of this discourse we more will hear anon.
> Egeus, I will overbear your will,
> For in the temple, by and by, with us
> These couples shall eternally be knit.
>
> (4.1.176-80)

And there the matter rests. Egeus, who does not reply, who never speaks again, is in this play of many marriages, odd man out, having lost a daughter and not gained a bride. That, perhaps, is the price he must pay for his initial irrationality; he is not even admitted to the festivities of the last act of the play.

In contrast to Shylock and Egeus, whose daughters wholly escape their control, are Lord Capulet and Brabantio, who bear direct and incontrovertible responsibility for the deaths of their daughters—fates all but preferable to their freedom. Brabantio's social motivation has already been mentioned; it is shared by Capulet though in *Romeo and Juliet,* of course, there is no question of miscegenation. When Paris first presents his suit for Juliet to her father, Capulet replies,

> Earth hath swallowed all my hopes but she;
> She is the hopeful lady of my earth.
> But woo her, gentle Paris, get her heart;
> My will to her consent is but a part.
> An she agree, within her scope of choice
> Lies my consent and fair according voice.
>
> (1.2.14-19)

It is such a moving answer, telling us that Capulet has lost other children and suggesting that therefore the congruence of his and Juliet's wills matters greatly to him—he would not force upon her his selection of a husband—that one regrets it is untrue. When Romeo is banished from Verona for killing Tybalt, Juliet grieves over the exile of her new husband, and ironically Capulet mistakes the death of Tybalt, Juliet's cousin, as the occasion of her grief. Therefore, he is more amenable to the renewal of Paris' suit:

> Things have fall'n out, sir, so unluckily
> That we have had no time to move our
>   daughter.
> Look you, she loved her kinsman Tybalt
>   dearly,
> And so did I. Well, we were born to die.
>
> (3.4.1-4)

Paris is willing to postpone his suits; but Capulet, thinking that marriage will alleviate Juliet's sorrow, presumes to offer her to Paris without her consent:

> Sir Paris, I will make a desperate tender
> Of my child's love. I think she will be ruled
> In all respects by me; nay more, I doubt it
>   not.
>
> (12-14)

Capulet does have some sense of propriety, though, and is at first reluctant to have the funeral baked meats too ostentatiously furnish forth the marriage tables. About a date for the wedding, he says,

> Well, Wednesday is too soon.
> A Thursday let it be—a Thursday, tell her,
> She shall be married to this noble earl.
> Will you be ready? Do you like this haste?
> We'll keep no great ado—a friend or two;
> For mark you, Tybalt being slain so late,
> It may be thought we held him carelessly,
> Being our kinsman, if we revel much.
> Therefore we'll have some half a dozen
>   friends,
> And there an end.
>
> (19-28)

So far Capulet sounds like a man eager to do the very best, even at the risk of raised eyebrows, for his daughter.

Though he cannot know it, his decision puts Juliet into a bind. Already wed to Romeo, she could not very well marry Paris even if she had any feeling for him. When her mother informs her of the forthcoming wedding, Juliet protests with a convincing dissimulation of her feelings:

> Now by Saint Peter's Church, and Peter too,
> He shall not make me there a joyful bride!
> I wonder at this haste, that I must wed
> Ere he that should be husband comes to woo.

This emphasis on Paris' romantic dereliction reminds us of Capulet's earlier instructions to him, which he has now set aside, that he must woo and win her. Juliet continues,

> I pray you tell my lord and father, madam,
> I will not marry yet; and when I do, I swear
> It shall be Romeo, whom you know I hate,
> Rather than Paris. These are news indeed!
>
> (3.5.117-24)

Capulet enters and learns from his wife of Juliet's obstinancy. He is enraged:

> Doth she not give us thanks?
> Is she not proud? Doth she not count her
>   blest,
> Unworthy as she is, that we have wrought
> So worthy a gentleman to be her bride?
>
> (143-46)

The reader's sympathy here cannot but be with Juliet, and not alone because he knows that she is married and understands the intensity of her and Romeo's feelings for each other. It is true in Shakespeare, as in life, that daughters legitimately "owe" their parents something for care and affection during their upbringing, however difficult this "something" is to define; but it is also true, at least in Shakespeare, that in the very moment of reminding their daughters of their debts, the fathers lose all right to have them repaid, for it is as if they have made their daughters' later submission to their wills the condition, as it were, of their earlier affection: because you will do what I tell you later on, they say in effect, I will care for you now. In thus being conditional, the early affection becomes spurious, and thus in our judgment releases the daughter from her obligations, though she will try to repay them. Capulet, like Lear, sees the beloved daughter, in her disobedience, as an unwarranted curse:

> Wife, we scarce thought us blest
> That God had lent us but this only child;
> But now I see this one is one too much,
> And that we have a curse in having her.
> Out on her, hilding!
>
> (165-69)

He would turn out his daughter rather than have her not go to the man of his choosing, the surrogate self through whose agency he retains his daughter as child and symbolically possesses her as bride. He is strengthened in his determination that Juliet wed Paris or pay a dear penalty:

> Thursday is near; lay hand on heart, advise:
> As you be mine, I'll give you to my friend;
> And you be not, hang, beg, starve, die in the
>   streets,
> For, by my soul, I'll ne'er acknowledge thee,
> Nor what is mine shall never do thee good.
> Trust to't. Bethink you. I'll not be forsworn.
>
> (192-97)

Although counseled by the Nurse to go ahead and marry Paris, Juliet decides to seek the advice of Friar Laurence.

One could be more charitable to Capulet if one had the conviction that his actions, however mistaken, were genuinely and entirely directed by his sense of what is best for his daughter. In fact, however, he is motivated by the end of personal advancement, the promise of rising in the Veronese social hierarchy. For though the Capulets, like the Montagues, may be a grand family of Verona, Paris, like Mercutio a kinsman of Prince Escalus, is royalty, and it is to this exalted station that Capulet aspires, and for the attainment of which he will happily sacrifice Juliet. When he first sets the wedding date, he envisions a discreet affair to be attended by "some half a dozen friends." Sober reflection suggests, to the contrary, that Tybalt or no Tybalt the wedding should be a magnificent event, celebrating his ascendency in the social stratosphere. He instructs a servant

> So many guests invite as here are writ,

and we imagine him handing the servant a very long list indeed, for he then says to another servant,

> Sirrah, go hire me twenty cunning cooks.
>
> (4.2.1-2)

One cannot imagine that the greatest opulence of the Renaissance required twenty cooks to cater to half a dozen guests. For her part, Juliet now pretends submission to Capulet's will, since she has learned from Friar Laurence how to be reunited with Romeo.

The causes of the tragedy that befalls this "pair of star-crossed lovers" are many: the very fact of their feuding families; the chance encounter of Mercutio and Tybalt in 3.1; Tybalt's general irascibility; the heat of the day; Romeo's clumsiness in separating Mercutio and Tybalt; his subsequent repudiation of his action as that of a coward made effeminate by beauty; the quarantine that prevents Friar John from delivering the letter; Juliet's bad luck in not awakening a few minutes earlier than she does. All of these, and others, add up to the conventional estimation of Romeo and Juliet as young lovers damned by fate. And so they are, perhaps, but their tragedy is not without human direction, for which no one deserves more blame than Lord Capulet. Were it not for his insistence that Juliet marry the man of his choosing at the time of his choosing for his own social advancement, there would be no sleeping draught, no letter to Romeo, no churchyard in Verona. It is he alone who complicates the banishment of Romeo and the grief of Juliet with the urgency of time; except for his insistence on the Thursday wedding, there would simply be no hurry to resolve problems lest happiness be lost forever. Rather than surrender his claims upon his daughter, Capulet would kill her, and he does.

If Capulet is a man eager to rise on the social scale, Brabantio is one who complacently enjoys the best position there is. He is a wealthy and respected man, a Venetian senator; it is only the extraordinary fact of Desdemona's marriage to Othello that forces us to see him more as a father, an individual, than a public official, one of a group. When Iago and Roderigo start shouting outside his window about thieves, he asks in dismay,

> What tell'st thou me of robbing? This is
>   Venice;
> My house is not a grange.
>
> (1.1.105-06)

Venice is inviolable; some things just do not happen there. There are no robberies, no social instability, no disobedient daughters, no preference of citizens for less privileged outsiders. But there is a single hint that Brabantio intuits the fragility of the system. When Roderigo tells him that his daughter is transported "to the gross clasps of a lascivious Moor," Brabantio says, unexpectedly, "This accident is not unlike my dream" (141), perhaps suggesting that on some unconscious level he has anticipated what he now abominates: Desdemona's preference for a black man over "The wealthy curlèd darlings of our nation" (1.2.68), a designation whose irony Brabantio cannot appreciate.

Shattering the still of a Venetian evening, the unthinkable has happened: the beautiful, virtuous, eminently desirable daughter's exogamous union with a black man. But Othello cannot get away with his theft, Brabantio thinks:

> The Duke himself,
> Or any of my brothers of the state,
> Cannot but feel this wrong as 'twere their own;
> For if such actions may have passage free,
> Bondslaves and pagans shall our statesmen be.
> (1.2.95-99)

In the eyes of a Venetian, a man's origins cling to him; having once been both bondslave and pagan, Othello, now neither, is not allowed to transcend adversity. That the other senators and the Duke would normally "feel this wrong as 'twere their own" appears likely; the Duke calls the elopement a "mangled matter" (1.3.173) and tells Brabantio,

> The robbed that smiles steals something from the thief,
> He robs himself that spends a bootless grief.
> (208-09)

The very sententiousness of the couplet, as often in Shakespeare, militates against its practical good sense, and the metaphor implies the Duke's acceptance of the label of robbery which had been applied at one time or another by Brabantio, Iago, and Roderigo.

Nevertheless, the Duke and the other senators have a much larger worry at hand: the purposed Turkish invasion of Rhodes or Cyprus. Therefore, when they have ascertained that Desdemona was a perfectly willing party to the courtship, a girl upon whom Othello used no enchantment, they are constrained to ignore the dangerous precedent of exogamy because, as Othello well knows, they need him. So Brabantio is frustrated in his desire to keep his daughter for one recognizably of his own kind; but he is unforgiving and in his last speech in the play says bitterly,

> Look to her, Moor, if thou hast eyes to see:
> She has deceived her father, and may thee.
> (1.3.292-93)

The words are the father's sentence of death upon his daughter, for they are heard not only by Othello,

Desdemona, Roderigo, the Duke, and the senators, but also by Iago, who will tell Othello much later,

> She did deceive her father, marrying you;
> And when she seemed to shake and fear your looks,
> She loved them most.
> (3.3.206-08)

Iago is stating as actuality what Brabantio had advanced as mere possibility, but the later statement gains authority from the former. Othello believes he does not see what is obvious to everyone else. Brabantio was wrong, of course, but it is interesting that his phraseology—"She has deceiv'd her father, and may thee"—particularly as it is echoed by Iago, tends to make equivalent the deception of a father and the deception of a husband; since the second must be a matter of sexual betrayal, the first becomes that as well. Ironically, Othello's murder of Desdemona, insofar as it is retribution for something she has really done, punishes her for the betrayal of her father. Since Brabantio's words are part of the stimulus to which Othello responds, he becomes a partner in the killing of his daughter for her sexual infidelity to him. . . . .

Notes

[4] See Plato, *Phaedrus*, 230d.

[5] *Ovid's "Metamorphoses": The Arthur Goldin Translation* (1567), ed. John Frederick Nims (New York: Macmillan, 1965).

[6] The New Arden edition of *The Merchant of Venice*, ed. John Russell Brown (Cambridge, Mass: Harvard University Press, 1955), 3.2.63 n [p. 80].

[7] On the sexual *double-entendres* of this speech, see William H. Matchett, "Shylock, Iago, and *Sir Thomas More*," *PMLA*, 92 (March 1977), p. 219. For other such uses in Shakespeare, see the entry on "Stones" in the Glossary of E.A.M. Colman, *The Dramatic Use of Bawdy in Shakespeare* (London: Longman, 1974), p. 216.

[8] See, for example, Mark Van Doren's reference to Lysander as "one of the two nonentities who are [*A Midsummer Night's Dream's*] heroes." *Shakespeare* (New York: Henry Holt, 1939; Doubleday Anchor edition, n.d.), p. 61.

Diane Elizabeth Dreher (essay date 1986)

SOURCE: "Dominated Daughters," in *Domination and Defiance: Fathers and Daughters in Shakespeare*, The University Press of Kentucky, 1986, pp. 76-95.

[*In this essay, Dreher discusses the tragic fates of Ophelia, Hero, and Desdemona maintaining that all three women are victims of patriarchal oppression*].

Shakespeare offers three examples of young women dominated by patriarchal expectations. Ophelia, Hero, and Desdemona are victimized by the traditional power structure that identifies women exclusively as childbearers, insisting on a rigid model of chastity to ensure the continuity of pure patrilineal succession. This requirement leaves women highly vulnerable. What matters is not that they are modest, chaste, and obedient, but that men perceive them as such.[1] Imprisoned in their passive situation, women cannot actively affirm or defend their honor. The more they seek to be good women, conforming to traditional expectations, the more they are victimized. Politically and psychologically, these dominated daughters remain children in their innocence, obedience, and submission to authority. Because the passive feminine ideal denies them their autonomy, they fail to resolve the crisis of intimacy, fail to become fully adult. By depicting their suffering, Shakespeare repudiates the traditional stereotype as confining and destructive, arresting young women in their growth into healthy adulthood, and in some instances even depriving them of their lives.

Ophelia: Fearful Domination

Traditionally, critics have seen Ophelia as a "pathetically weak character"[2] She has been alternately pitied and condemned for her helplessness and domination by her father. A.C. Bradley saw her as childlike, "so near childhood that old affections still have the strongest hold."[3] Critics have emphasized her innocence and dependence. "She has never been woman enough to have a mind apart from [her father]."[4] She is "young and sweet and also very passive," "pretty but ineffectual," "a timid conventional girl, too fragile a reed for a man to lean upon."[5] "Like other simple-minded daughters who lack the strength of mind to rely on themselves," she has been characterized as "a puppet in her father's hands" and "a doll without intellect."[6]

Yet while their observations are valid from one point of view, the great majority of Ophelia's critics have been "Hamlet-critics," perceiving her as he perceives her, through their regret that she does not fulfill the needs and expectations of the tormented prince of Denmark. A feminist analysis of Ophelia's behavior demonstrates that she is not the simpleminded creature she seems. Traditional readings of her character have been as superficial as nineteenth-century productions, which portrayed her as a simple, pretty girl of flowers whose mad scenes were artfully sung and danced. As Helena Faucit realized and dared to play her to a stunned audience in 1844-45, Ophelia actually does go mad.[7] There is pain and struggle beneath that sweet surface. Her misfortune merits not only our pity but our censure of traditional mores that make women repress themselves and behave like automatons.

Contrary to prevailing opinion, Ophelia is more than a simple girl, living in "a world of dumb ideas and feelings."[8] The pity of it is that Ophelia *does* think and feel. A careful examination of the text in I.iii reveals that she loves Hamlet and thinks for herself, but is forced to repress all this at her father's command, conforming to the stifling patriarchal concept of female behavior that subordinates women to their "honor," their procreative function in male society.

Torn between what she feels and what she is told to be, Ophelia is tormented by the crisis of identity. As one critic pointed out long ago, "she is not aware of the nature of her own feelings; they are prematurely developed in their full force before she has strength to bear them."[9] Caught in adolescent uncertainty between childhood and adulthood, she cannot enter the stage of intimacy and adult commitment because she does not yet know who she is. Carol Gilligan has pointed to the difficulties young women have in individuation. Raised with an emphasis on empathy rather than autonomy, girls tend to subordinate their own needs to those of others. Ophelia experiences severe role confusion in which her personal feelings are suppressed in favor of external expectations.[10]

At the beginning of the play, Ophelia is a healthy young woman with romantic feelings and a normal level of sexual awareness. This is apparent in her dismay at Laertes's warning about Hamlet; her comprehension of Hamlet's sexual innuendoes; and, finally, the sexual references that rise to the surface in her madness. As her initial liveliness in I.iii indicates, she is affectionate, expressive, ingenuous, as natural as the flowers she later embraces. In this scene, however, she comes face to face with that static and oppressive female virtue: chastity.

Both her brother and her father warn her repeatedly to defend her honor, her virginity, the fragile basis for woman's respectability and personal value in patriarchal society. They have defined her in the traditional role of nurturer and caretaker, while simultaneously devaluing that role, subordinating care to masculine power.[11] Their obsession with female chastity and the accompanying double standard reflect the patriarchal concern for legitimate issue, the demand that young women be presented as chaste vessels by their fathers to future husbands, sacrificing personal identity to their function as childbearers. Women in this sense are "womb men," reduced to walking repositories for the male seed. In order to perform their sacred function, they must remain clean, chaste, and hermetically sealed until the marriage act, which ensures the continuity of patrilineal succession for another generation. Then their husbands must see that they remain pure. It is not only

Hamlet, Laertes, and Polonius who are acutely concerned with woman's chastity. The issue looms large in *Othello,* and the preponderance of cuckold jokes among the men, even in Shakespeare's comedies, reveals their concern with legitimate issue, their underlying fears and suspicions of female sexuality.

The patriarchy upholds the traditional ideal of the sweet, innocent, and fundamentally passive young woman who obeys her father and elder brother. Their duty is to defend her honor that she may procreate only within patriarchal bounds. To a great extent, woman's reproductive function has led to her domination. The ideal of feminine virtue is static—the preservation of her chastity—while masculine virtue is dynamic, active, developmental. Men may add honor to their names by noble deeds and accomplishments, while women may only defend the small shred of honor they have, which once gone is irrevocably lost.

In his protective, masculine role, Laertes confronts his sister and warns her about the danger in her love for Hamlet:

> Then weigh what loss your honour may
>   sustain,
> If with too credent ear you list his songs,
> Or lose your heart, or your chaste treasure
>   open
> To his unmast'red importunity.
> Fear it, Ophelia, fear it, my dear sister.
>
> [I.iii.29-33]

His fearful warning later echoes in Ophelia's ears when she confronts an impassioned Hamlet in her closet. Her father warns her more abruptly: "You do not understand yourself so clearly / As it behoves my daughter and your honour" (I.iii.97-98). She is his child, his property, a vessel of procreation, no more but so. As the play progresses, Shakespeare shows us Ophelia's acceptance of this role and the tragic consequences.

At the beginning of I.iii, she is still the young and spirited girl Hamlet has loved. When Laertes maligns Hamlet's motives, calling his courtship but "a fashion and a toy in blood," Ophelia is stunned and hurt, responding, "No more but so?" (10), for she had believed in Hamlet's love. She listens to her brother's advice but knows him well enough to ask that he practice the restraint he preaches, denouncing the operative double standard and showing herself a perceptive, spirited young woman. To the young fashion plate Polonius later suspects of "drabbing" in Paris, Ophelia adds:

> But, good my brother,
> Do not, as some ungracious pastors do,
> Show me the steep and thorny way to heaven;
> Whiles, like a puff'd and reckless libertine,

> Himself the primrose path of dalliance treads,
> And recks not his own rede.
>
> [46-51]

Ophelia realizes that not all male authority figures practice what they preach. Seeing beneath appearances, she recognizes the ugly reality of hypocrisy. Although young and inexperienced, Ophelia most assuredly is not simple. She does not lack intellect, nor does she automatically take everything at face value.

But when Polonius adds his lengthy warning in the same scene, Ophelia begins to doubt herself. Her brother, then her father, has frightened and insulted her about her love for Hamlet. The two authority figures in her young life, they undermine her trust in love, making her doubt Hamlet's intentions and her own awakening sexual feelings. What had once seemed so wonderful becomes progressively more frightening. Her protestations that Hamlet has "importun'd [her] with love / In honourable fashion" and sworn to her "with almost all the holy vows of heaven" (110, 113) are met by the sordid cynicism of Polonius. As Iago poisons the mind of Othello, so do Laertes and Polonius poison Ophelia's mind, presenting a view of human sexuality that is gross, animalistic, degrading, and terrifying.[12] Hamlet's vows, they tell her, are merely a means to satisfy his lust, "springes to catch woodcocks" (116), and she has stupidly believed him, made herself his helpless prey and risked losing her honor, her very identity in patriarchal society. The image of courtship Polonius paints for her is nothing less than calculated rape.

Her dream of love lies shattered at her feet; she tells Polonius, "I do not know, my lord, what I should think" (104). According to Gilligan, moral development in women "proceeds from an initial concern with survival to a focus on goodness and finally to a reflective understanding of care."[13] Ophelia is concerned with survival in what seems a brutal, hostile world. Frightened and disillusioned, she seeks safety in the passive role assigned to women for generations. Her father tells her to stay away from the danger that Hamlet represents, and she submits: "I shall obey, my lord" (136). Her submission is not only a surrender to convention, but an act of self-preservation by a young woman for whom sexuality has become a frightening animalistic threat. Ophelia succumbs to severe security anxiety.[14] Her ensuing actions reflect a compulsive defense of her chastity in a world that appears blatantly brutal and aggressive. Ophelia's fearful withdrawal and subsequent deterioration represent an implicit accusation of a society that defines men as active sexual aggressors, condoning their promiscuity while valuing women only for their chastity which must be defended at all costs. Retreating behind the false self the patriarchy has created for her, Ophelia represses her feelings and obliterates her own reality, collapsing into a schizoid divided self and moral confusion. As R. D. Laing wrote of her: "there is no one there. She is not a person. There is no integral selfhood expressed through her actions or utterances. Incomprehensible statements are said by nothing. She has already died."[15]

Ophelia has been condemned for letting her father dominate her, for failing to "observe the fundamental responsibilities that hold together an existence."[16] But let us consider the situation from her point of view. As a young woman, she is, first of all, more inclined to defer to the wishes of others than to follow her own feelings.[17] Ophelia errs in trusting her father, but she is not the only person in the play who has taken a parent at face value. Hamlet failed to recognize his mother's moral weakness until her marriage to Claudius. Furthermore, reverence for one's parents was expected of Renaissance youth. As Harley Granville-Barker emphasized, "we may call her docility a fault, when, as she is bid, she shuts herself away from Hamlet; but how not to trust to her brother's care for her and her father's wisdom?"[18] Like Othello, Ophelia errs in trusting the wrong moral guide: in his case a friend who had shared dangers on the battlefield, in hers a father to whom convention bound her duty and obedience. Polonius's warning, seconded by her brother's, gains greater credibility. But most significant, her moral guides have not only told her how to behave; they have redefined her entire universe, inculcating in Ophelia a view of human sexuality as nasty and brutish as that which infects Othello. Ophelia sees herself in a world in which sexuality transforms human beings into beasts, with men the predators and women their prey.

If the play had offered any moral alternative, she might have been able to think more clearly and trust her love. Romantic heroines in Shakespeare's comedies defy corrupt patriarchal authority, think for themselves, and affirm their love because their moral guides or close friends uphold a nobler view of human nature. Rosalind has Celia's friendship; Portia, Nerissa's. Hermia has Helena's friendship and the example of Duke Theseus in love. Even Jessica, flawed as she is, finds a moral alternative to her father's values in Christianity and later in Portia herself. Juliet has the moral influence of the friar, who sees her marriage to Romeo as a means to greater harmony. Even the isolated and tormented Hamlet finds a friend in Horatio. But Ophelia has no one: no friar, no friend, not even a positive role model in Gertrude, the only other woman in the play. Everthing around Ophelia only confirms her father's words. Her next experience with Hamlet is a case in point. When she sees him in II.i, she runs in to her father crying, "O, lord, my lord, I have been so affrighted" (75). After she concludes her description of the disheveled Hamlet, Polonius asks, "Mad for thy love?" and her answer, "My lord, I do not know; / But truly, I do fear it" (85-86), reflects her fear and con-

fusion. No longer a romantic dream, love has become a violent and fearful thing. We know that Hamlet has confronted his father's ghost in the previous scene and that either this or his antic disposition explains his behavior. But Ophelia does not know this. The very personification of love melancholy, Hamlet rushes into her chamber in frantic disarray, grabs her by the wrist, holds her close, and stares into her eyes. He finally releases her with a sigh and backs out of the room, his eyes still riveted upon her. During all this time, not a word is exchanged. In this unfortunate encounter, Ophelia fails to give Hamlet the reassurance he seeks and confirms his suspicions about women. But for Ophelia, Hamlet's actions cannot fail to confirm what her father and brother have told her: that men's sexual passions are fearful things, transforming them into beasts. Terrified—Is he here to rape her?—she is unable to speak a word to him and runs to her father for protection.

In III.i not only Polonius but also the king and queen reinforce for Ophelia the importance of obeying her father to rescue Hamlet from the madness her love has driven him to. She succumbs to convention, becoming a puppet in their hands. But she plays her role awkwardly, revealing her inner conflict. She is understandably nervous when confronted with the violent effects of love melancholy, and her actions contradict her father's plan. Polonius has arranged this as a chance meeting with Hamlet, handing her a prayer book as a prop to ponder as she waits. But Ophelia has brought with her all Hamlet's "remembrances," and since Polonius fails to mention these, we are to assume that this is her idea. She returns the gifts with what has been called the "completely inappropriate little maxim":[19] "Take these again; for to the noble mind / Rich gifts wax poor when givers prove unkind" (100-101). To Hamlet, the gifts reveal that the encounter is not chance but contrivance, and the maxim makes no sense, for *she* has rejected him. From Ophelia's point of view, however, the maxim is quite appropriate: he had given her these gifts and promises of honorable love when he had really intended to seduce her. The prince has been unkind indeed; Ophelia feels betrayed and disillusioned. Then, in confirmation of her fears, Hamlet torments her verbally, declaring, then denying, his love. Her answer to his "I did love you once" reveals her disillusionment: "Indeed, my lord, you made me believe so" (116-17). In these lines she denies the reality of her previous perceptions; Hamlet never loved her. He had only sought to use her. This, too, he seems to confirm as he responds, "You should not have believed me; for virtue cannot so inoculate our old stock but we shall relish of it: I loved you not." She answers, "I was the more deceived" (118-21). Heartbroken, Ophelia hears the man she loves denounce her, insult her, and fall into wild ravings, the sexual nausea in his words reinforcing and confirming her own.

Her speech at the end of this encounter expresses her guilt, dejection, and despair. As Hamlet exits, raving at her, she laments:

> O, what a noble mind is here o'er-thrown!
>
> . . . . .
>
> And I, of ladies most deject and wretched,
> That suck'd the honey of his music vows,
> Now see that noble and most sovereign
>   reason,
> Like sweet bells jungled, out of time and
>   harsh;
> That unmatch'd form and feature of his blown
>   youth
> Blasted with ecstacy: O, woe is me,
> T'have seen what I have seen, see what I see!
>   [III.i.158, 163-69]

In her misery, she loves him still. This passage resonates with recognition. Rejected by her love, taken in by his "music vows," and guilty by complicity in the love that drove him to madness, she regrets what she has been and done. The devastated and emotionally exhausted Ophelia now perceives love as a poisonous dream, which attracts like honey but transforms men to beasts. Hurt, disillusioned, and troubled by her own sexual feelings, she is ashamed that her beauty has awakened such appetites in Hamlet. Claudius may not believe love has caused Hamlet's madness, but Ophelia most certainly does.

Hamlet's gross language during the play scene reinforces her impression of his lust. Insulted and humiliated by his sexual innuendoes, she keeps up a brave front, responding to him with terse formality:

> No, my lord . . .
> Ay, my lord . . .
> I think nothing, my lord . . .
> What is, my lord? . . .
> You are merry, my lord . . .
> Ay, my lord.
>
>   [III.ii.120-31][20]

Stunned into a fear of her lover and a childlike dependency on her father, Ophelia suddenly has them both removed, and even her brother is out of the country. She collapses into madness because she knows not where to turn for guidance. As one critic explained, "she was like a tender vine, growing first to the trellis of filial piety and then to that of romantic love. When these two are removed and she is left unsupported, she cannot stand alone, and falls."[21] But there is more to it. Interspersed between her songs of unfaithful lovers and dirges for dead fathers, we find this telling admission: "They say the owl was a baker's daughter. Lord, we know/What we are, but know not what we may be" (IV.v.41-43). This fragile flower has not only been deprived of her props, she also feels guilt and complic-

ity in her father's death. What emerges here is the devastating awareness of her own repressed sexuality, the shock of "what may be" in herself combined with the horrible transformations wrought by romantic love. Hamlet has desired her and she has desired him as well, loved the man who late killed her father, and, most horribly, it was her love that drove him mad. Distributing her flowers, she gives both Gertrude and herself rue, emblematic of repentance and regret.[22] In her madness, her repressed sexuality finally breaks through the conventional false self of enforced modesty, chastity, and decorum.[23] In addition to the imagery in her risqué songs, Elizabethans would have recognized the flowers she clutched to herself when she drowned as definite phallic symbols, indicative of her repressed longings.[24]

The symbolism in her drowning is itself an emblem of the inner conflict which drove her to madness. She drowns in her "fantastic garlands," woven of buttercups, daisies, nettles, and long purples, flowers that represent her innocence, pain, and sexuality, woven together here in madness as she had been unable to do in her life. Unable to combine her conflicting fears and desires into an integrated sense of self, she drowns. Encircled by this tangle of discordant meanings, surrounded by water—symbol of the unconscious[25]—gradually pulled down by her clothes, that external self which finally became too heavy to bear her up any longer, she slips beneath the surface, into madness, into death.

Hero: Slandered Innocence

Like Ophelia, Hero in *Much Ado* has been both praised and criticized for her innocence. Her passive vulnerability has inspired pity in some and boredom in others. According to William Hazlitt, Hero "leaves an indelible impression on the mind by her beauty, her tenderness, and the hard trial of her love." Others have called her "as pure and tender as a flower" or "rather a boring girl."[26] In two modern studies she has been characterized as "shadowy and silent," an ineffective heroine who lacks credibility.[27] All have found her mild and quiet, and "vulnerably passive."[28]

Hero is numinous, archetypal in her innocence, the silent woman of legend and the chaste and obedient Renaissance ideal. So silent is she that the majority of critics accord her only a passing reference, giving their attention instead to the more dynamic Beatrice, Benedick, and Claudio. In critical studies as in the play itself, Hero's role is silent and symbolic. "Throughout the courtship, misunderstandings and all, Hero herself has hardly anything to say: she is essentially a figure in the pattern whose chief dramatic function is to stand there and look beautiful."[29] In her silence and modesty, she exemplifies the perfect Renaissance woman. As an individual, she is conspicuous by her

Anthony Nicholls as Leonato and Judith Stott as Hero in Gielgud's 1955 rendering of Much Ado About Nothing.

absence. This can be better understood by noting exactly how her character functions in the text. In I.i she is present during the opening scenes but has only 1 line to Beatrice's 45. For more than 150 lines Hero simply stands there in silence. Even when her father introduces her to Don Pedro at line 103, she speaks not a word but probably curtsies dutifully. In II.i, during which she is told by her father of Don Pedro's presumed intentions, is courted by him, and agrees to help trick Beatrice into realizing that she loves Benedick, she has only 8 lines to Beatrice's 97.

Claudio falls in love with her image. In I.i he refers to her as "a modest young lady," "the sweetest lady that ever I looked on" (164,189), and determines to marry her. She is his silent goddess, his anima symbol, and the image of his dreams.[30] Unlike Beatrice, she has revealed no individuality to obscure the pure abstraction he desires in her.

The model young woman, Hero listens in silent and modest obedience to her father's instructions about her marriage in a manner Juan Luis Vives would have

applauded.[31] Her silent figure stands looking on while her father and uncle discuss her future and Beatrice dazzles with her witty exposition on marriage. All the while, Hero speaks not a single word:

> *Antonio.* [*To Hero*] Well, niece, I trust you will be ruled by your father.
>
> *Beatrice.* Yes, faith; it is my counsin's duty to make curtsy and say "Father, as it please you." But yet for all that, cousin, let him be a handsome fellow, or else make another curtsy and say "Father, as it please me."
>
> *Leonato.* Well, niece, I hope to see you one day fitted with a husband.
>
> *Beatrice.* Not till God make men of some other metal than earth. Would it not grieve a woman to be overmastered with a piece of valiant dust? To make an account of her life to a clod of wayward marl? No, uncle, I'll none; Adam's sons are my brethren; and truly, I hold it a sin to match in my kindred.
>
> *Leonato.* Daughter, remember what I told you: if the prince do solicit you in that kind, you know your answer.
>
> *Beatrice.* The fault will be in the music, cousin, if you be not wooed in good time.
>
> [II.i.55-73]

If Beatrice is the dynamic rebel who rejects the traditional woman's role, Hero is the archetypal good woman who follows it to the letter. She is "the embodiment of the courtly concept of ideal daughter and bride. Emblem of the sheltered life—crowned by beauty, modesty, and chastity—she is bred from birth for a noble alliance which will add luster to her lineage."[32] Psychologically, her character follows Erikson's description of traditional female development. She "holds her identity in abeyance as she prepares to attract the man by whose name she will be known, by whose status she will be defined, the man who will rescue her from emptiness and loneliness by filling 'the inner space.'"[33] But her obedience and archetypal purity avail her little. No matter how good or innocent she is, she cannot influence her fate. Her identity depends upon men's perceptions of her, and the illusion of doubt can quickly sully even the most virtuous reputation, leaving her no defense.

In III.i, a scene without male authority figures, Hero has a suprising 76 lines. Plotting with the other women to trick Beatrice into realizing that she loves Benedick, Hero is spirited, gregarious, and much more verbal. Apparently, she is not naturally shy or phlegmatic; her silence at other times merely reflects her breeding as a lady. Before men she is silent and deferential, while with her cousin and other women she may relax and be more herself. In III.iv, we see her again interacting with women. Dressing for the wedding, she exchanges witty banter in some 14 lines, although troubled by nervousness and forboding.

In IV.i, when exposed to public scandal in the church, she courageously affirms her innocence:

> *Hero.* O, God defend me! How am I beset!
> What kind of catechising call you this?
> *Claudio.* To make you answer truly to your
>   name.
> *Hero.* Is it not Hero? Who can blot that name
> With any just reproach?
> *Claudio.*   Marry, that can Hero;
> Hero itself can blot out Hero's virtue.
> What man was he talk'd with you yesternight
> Out at your window betwixt twelve and one?
> Now, if you are a maid, answer to this.
> *Hero.* I talk'd with no man at that hour, my
>   lord.
> *Don Pedro.* Why, then you are no maiden.
>
> [IV.i.78-88]

Not only has she been betrayed; she is powerless to exonerate herself. Regardless of what she says or does, she cannot actively prove her innocence. The staged deception of the night before has soiled the image of her chastity. Because of the dualism implicit in men's perception of women, when the shadow of doubt clouds her radiant image, she ceases to be a virgin in their eyes and automatically becomes a whore. Hero's protestations of innocence, like Desdemona's, are seen only as further proof of her guilt. Don Pedro then describes the shameful encounter at her window—as we know, an illusion. But one illusion can destroy her, so fragile is a woman's honor, so tenuous her position in man's world. Unless she is beyond suspicion, she becomes a tainted outcast.

Claudio's repudiation of her in the church may seem unduly rash, but he barely knows her. Far more shocking is her father's rejection. How quickly Leonato believes the slander about his child. Apparently, all those years in which Hero was the model daughter—chaste, silent, obedient, and submissive—have not enabled him to trust in her character.[34] Leonato sinks into anger and despair, and only Beatrice rallies to Hero's defense.

In her study *The Slandered Woman in Shakespeare*, Joyce Sexton pointed out how Hero's predicament illustrates the insidious nature of slander, an attack for which woman has no defense.[35] She cannot actively regain her honor and good name with noble deeds like a courtier who has fallen out of favor. Because of their procreative function as chaste mothers in patriarchal society, women cannot earn or acquire more honor; all they can do is behave according to patriarchal expectations. Hero is trapped by the traditional concept of virtuous womanhood, which is untenable and unhealthy. As Gilligan observed, "the notion that virtue for women lies in self-sacrifice has complicated the course of woman's development by pitting the moral issue of goodness against the adult questions of responsibility.[36] This play demonstrates how easily woman's passive virtue comes to naught and how helpless she is to defend it.

Hero's restoration, like her repudiation, is not contingent upon her actions. As a traditional woman, her identity depends upon men's perceptions of her. Fortunately, a man, Borachio, confesses, redeeming her tarnished reputation. In V.i, when Claudio discovers that Hero has been unjustly slandered, his words reveal just what she means to him: "Sweet Hero! now thy image doth appear / In the rare sembalance that I lov'd it first" (259-60). It is only her image that he loves. In V.iv the repentant Claudio receives at her father's hand another Hero. Now ceremoniously transferred from father to husband, Hero lifts her veil and reveals herself, revived, restored to life and honor. But so fragile is her identity in patriarchal society that when she fails to match men's dreams of perfection, she becomes a victim of their deepest fears and doubts. Implicit here is Shakespeare's criticism of the traditional feminine stereotype as a static and passive ideal, which represses women and makes them far too vulnerable to the oft-observed antinomy between appearance and reality.

Desdemona: Love's Sweet Victim

Alternately canonized and criticized for loving Othello, Desdemona has been praised for her devotion and censured for her sexuality, described as deceptive, proud, and manipulative or as helplessly passive. She is herself a tragic paradox. A spirited, courageous young woman, Desdemona is moved by the depth of her love to conform to a static and fatal ideal of feminine behavior. Among those critics for whom she shines as a saintly ideal, Irving Ribner said that "in the perfection of her love Desdemona reflects the love of Christ for man," and G. Wilson Knight found her a "divinity comparable with Dante's Beatrice."[37] Yet W.H. Auden observed "One cannot but share Iago's doubts as to the durability of the marriage," predicting that "given a few more years of Othello and of Emilia's influence and she might well, one feels, have taken a lover." Jan Kott, too, found her strong sexuality disturbing: "Of all Shakespeare's female characters she is the most sensuous. . . . Desdemona is faithful but must have something of a slut in her."[38]

Beyond a doubt, Desdemona is affectionate and sensual, but this does not make her a slut any more than the absence of sexuality would sanctify her. Too often her critics themselves have fallen victim to the virgin-whore complex, the false dilemma that dominates the perception of women in traditional society. A few critics have recognized the simple fact that Desdemona is both a virtuous and a passionate woman.[39]

The elopement has been cited as proof of her courage or evidence of her deceptive nature: "a measure of her determination to have a life that seems to offer the promise of excitement denied her as a sheltered Venetian senator's daughter"; "her deception of her own father makes an unpleasant impression." We may laugh at Thomas Rymer's oversimplified reading of the play as "a caution to all Maidens of Quality how, without their Parents consent, they run away with Blackamoors" and "a warning to all good Wives, that they look well to their Linnen."[40] Desdemona's critics range from the sublime to the ridiculous. Predominantly male, they have seen her as either willful and manipulative or helplessly passive: "a determined young woman . . . eager to get her own way;" her advocacy for Cassio demonstrating her desire to dominate Othello, revealing a strong case of penis envy."[41] Arthur Kirsch saw her advocacy as concern for her husband, realizing that his continued alienation from Cassio was "unnatural and injurious to them both," while Auden called this merely another demonstration of her pride: "In continuing to badger Othello, she betrays a desire to prove to herself and to Cassio that she can make her husband do as she pleases." Bradley, by contrast, found her "helplessly passive," an innocent, loving martyr:

> Desdemona is helplessly passive. She can do nothing whatever. She cannot retaliate even in speech; no, not even in silent feeling. And the chief reason of her helplessness only makes the sight of her suffering more exquisitely painful. She is helpless because her nature is infinitely sweet and her love absolute. . . . Desdemona's suffering is like that of the most loving of dumb creatures tortured without cause by the being he adores.

In a similar vein, Bernard McElroy wrote, "The inner beauty and selflessness of her character are exactly what render her most vulnerable to the fate that overtakes her." As Carol Thomas Neely observed, for traditional critics, "the source of her sainthood seems a passivity verging on catatonia."[42]

The history of Desdemona on the stage parallels these changing critical estimations. Until Fanny Kemble, Helena Faucit, and Ellen Terry endowed her with a new dynamism, Desdemona was portrayed as a pathetic girl, not a tragic heroine. In the nineteenth century her part was diminished by extensive cuts, and William Charles Macready tried to dissuade Fanny Kemble from playing it, arguing that this was no part for a great actress. Kemble persevered, creating a Desdemona who was softly feminine but also forthright and courageous. Her Desdemona, like Helena Faucit's, fought for her life in the final scene. According to Ellen Terry, most people believed that Desdemona was "a ninny, a pathetic figure," that "an actress of the dolly type, a pretty young thing with a vapid, innocent expression, is well suited to the part,"

but she felt that Desdemona was "a woman of strong character," requiring the talents of a great tragic actress.[43]

As these actresses recognized, Desdemona is a young woman who transcends any stereotype. In her courage and compassion, she is androgynous; in her boundless love and goodness she sees beyond the artificial divisions of the patriarchal hierarchy. Like Hamlet, she values people, not for their social rank, but for themselves. She has been praised for "a man's courage . . . an extreme example of that union of feminine and masculine qualities that Shakespeare plainly held essential for either the perfect man or the perfect woman."[44] Her "downright violence and storm of fortunes" demonstrate her courage and defiance of convention as well as the strength of her love (I.iii.250). She loved Othello "for the dangers [he] had pass'd," recognizing in his bold spirit a counterpart to her own, longing for adventure denied by her confining role as a Venetian senator's daughter. Othello "lov'd her that she did pity them," her feminine compassion equal to her masculine courage (I.iii.167-68).

She is by nature unconventional, a sensuous and virtuous woman in a culture that prized a cold, chaste ideal. Dynamic and courageous when the traditional feminine norm was passivity, she transcends patriarchal order and degree, reaching out in loving kindness to all. Desdemona behaved with daughterly decorum in her father's house but revealed her assertiveness and magnanimity in her love for Othello. Her enthusiastic and affectionate nature are evident in Othello's description of their courtship, especially in the Folio version. This apparently docile maiden would rush from her household chores to "devour" his stories "with a greedy ear," (I.iii.150,149). She was fascinated by this man of men and the adventurous life he led. So far was she from Brabantio's conventional "maiden never bold" (94) that she gave Othello for his pains "a world of kisses," (159) in the Folio reading far more assertive than the Quarto's "sighs."[45]

It is magnanimous woman who stands resolutely before her father and the duke in council, declaring her love for which she had defied all convention. But this young woman now places her love into the traditional perspective, speaking of her "divided duty" between father and husband in which filial obedience is transferred from one authority figure to the next. As one critic has observed, "Desdemona's description of the transfer of her feelings from her father to her husband, with its invocation of her own mother as her example, touches in almost archetypal terms upon the psychological process by which a girl becomes a woman and a wife."[46] Othello inherits the father's title, "my lord":

> My noble father,
> . . . you are the lord of duty;

> I am hitherto your daughter: but here's my
>   husband,
> And so much duty as my mother show'd
> To you, preferring you before her father,
> So much I challenge that I may profess
> Due to the Moor my lord.
>
> [I.iii.180-89]

In her elopement, Desdemona "successfully defies the Father," Brabantio himself and "the symbol of Authority and Force" he represents. Harold Goddard contrasts her to the submissive Ophelia and Hamlet, who fail to break free from paternal authority.[47] True, her love liberates her long enough to elope with Othello, but in her concept of marriage she again succumbs to the yoke of convention, adopting the traditional role inherited from her mother, a relationship in which the wife becomes her husband's submissive, obedient subject.[48] She fails to make the psychological transition to adulthood, conforming to Vives's injunction that "the woman is as daughter unto her husband."[49] As Gilligan would explain it, Desdemona's moral development is arrested at the level of altruistic self-denial. Her every action reflects a desire to demonstrate goodness over selfishness.[50] Denying her own authority, she submits to the traditional pattern, ironically out of her deep love for Othello and her desire to be the perfect wife. As she declares, "My heart's subdu'd / Even to the very quality of my lord" (I.iii.251-52).

Critics have found an echo of the traditional father-daughter relationship, pointing to Othello's age, which makes him a father surrogate, and noting that he was her father's friend before the elopement.[51] Some psychological critics have seen her choice of him as motivated by an Oedipus complex, in which she sought either to marry someone like her father or to punish her father for being faithless to her in childhood. They explain her subsequent passive behavior as "moral masochism," motivated by guilt for her incestuous urgings.[52] But one need not resort to incest and Oedipus complexes to explain Desdemona's behavior. We have seen in her love for Othello a highly idealistic strain as well as a passionate attachment, an almost religious fervor and dedication. All her young life she had longed for a heroic mission, a cause. Because she is a woman, unable to pursue her heroic ideals, she finds her cause in loving Othello, subordinating herself in her role as his wife, even as he subordinates his ego to the demands of war. It is not only Othello who "agnize[s] / A natural and prompt alacrity . . . in hardness" (I.iii.232-34). Desdemona, as well, longs for heroic commitment and sacrifice. Given the limits of her culture, she can find this only indirectly, some would say masochistically, by devoting herself to Othello.[53]

Thus we have the paradox that explains Desdemona's contradictory image. She is courageous, heroic, passive, and vulnerable. She is both extremes because of her love, which makes of her an oxymoronic "excellent wretch" (III.iii.90). On the altar of holy love she sacrifices her dynamic self to the image of her dreams, becoming not a "moth of peace" (I.ii.257) but an equally diminished shadow of herself. As she rejects the "wealthy curled darlings" (I.ii.68) of Venice, leaving her father and embracing the man of her dreams, it would seem that she has resolved for herself the crisis of identity. But in her marriage she does not commit herself with the dynamic energy that flourished in her courtship and elopement. She chooses a new identity, a controlled, ever modest and obedient self, not Desdemona but the model wife, because this is what she feels Othello deserves. She becomes a victim of the convention she embraces, a neurotic self-effacement amounting to slow suicide.[54] She, too, loves "not wisely, but too well" (V.ii.344), affirming a static ideal, a polished surface of behavior that will not withstand the tempests her marriage faces on Cyprus.

. . . [The] relation of a traditional Renaissance wife to her husband was like that of an obedient child. Although some critics censure Desdemona for failing in her wifely role, I would argue that her tragic fate stems from slavish conformity, an excess of altruism to which she sacrifices her own being.[55] After marriage, Desdemona conforms to the traditional norm for feminine behavior, as expressed by William Gouge.[56] This norm involves: "1 Acknowledgement of an husband's superioritie" and "2 A due esteeme of her owne husband to be the best for her, and worthy of honour on her part." Desdemona announces that her "heart's subdu'd / Even to the very quality of my lord" (I.iii.251-52), and in III.iv she berates herself for chiding him, even in her thoughts. Other wifely attributes are "3 An inward wive-like feare," "4 An outward reverend cariage towards her husband which consisteth in a wive-like sobrietie, mildnesse, curtesie, and modestie in apparell," and "5 Reverend speech to, and of her husband." Desdemona is gracious, poised, and respectful in her actions and speech. She refuses to speak ill of Othello after his shameful behavior in III.iv and when he strikes her in IV.i. In the former scene, she attributes his behavior to state business; in IV.ii she confesses to Emilia and Iago that she knows not what she has done to displease him but loves him still and ever will. Even when Othello comes to murder her, she behaves toward him with traditional wifely reverence.

Gouge lists "Obedience" as requirement 6. "Whate'er you be, I am obedient," Desdemona says in III.iii.89, choosing to follow his command rather than think for herself. This is also evident in her obedient departures at his command in III.iii and IV.i, and her coming at his bidding in IV.ii. Even in his jealous rages, she addresses him with love and respect. Gouge's requirement 7 is "Forbearing to doe without or against her husbands consent, such things as he hath power to order, as, to dispose and order the common goods of the familie, and the allowance for it, as children, servants, cattell, guests, journies, &c." Although some would criticize her for asking to accompany Othello to Cyprus, this request does not reflect willfulness on her part so much as an eagerness to begin married life. Most important, in asking this she does not go against Othello's wishes. Gouge also recommends "8 A ready yeelding to what her husband would have done. This manifested by her willingnesse to dwell where he will, to come when he calls, and to doe what he requireth." So attentive is Desdemona to Othello's desires and welfare that she does not even notice when she drops her hankerchief in III.iii, for she is concerned about his headache. She comes dutifully when he calls, bears his torments before Lodovico in IV.i, and seeks in every way to please him, even dismissing Emilia and retiring when her forebodings are apparent in the willow song.

Requirement 9 is "A patient bearing of any reproofe, and a ready redressing of that for which she is justly reproved." Desdemona patiently bears Othello's reproofs, although she cannot understand them and admits herself "a child to chiding" (IV.ii.114). She criticizes herself as an "unhandsome warrior" (III.iv.151) and tells Emilia that her "love doth so approve him, / That even his stubbornness, his checks, his frowns . . . have grace and favour in them" (IV.iii.19-21). Gouge also recommends "10 Contentment with her husbands present estate." Desdemona loves Othello for the dangers he has passed and accompanies him to the wars. Moreover, she even accepts his present *mental* state:

> And ever will—though he do shake me off
> To beggarly divorcement—love him dearly,
> Comfort forswear me! Unkindness may do
>   much;
> And his unkindness may defeat my life,
> But never taint my love.
>
> [IV.ii.157-61]

Gouge's final requirements are "11 Such a subjection as may stand with her subjection to Christ" and "12 Such a subjection as the Church yeeldeth to Christ, which is sincere, pure, cheerefull, constant, for conscience sake."[57] Desdemona's undying love for her husband is apparent even in her death, when she speaks not to accuse but to protect him. Her last words are: "Commend me to my kind lord: O, farewell" (V.ii.125). In her devotion, she becomes once again "the sweet and submissive being of her girlhood," adopting the pattern of neurotic compliance traditionally praised in women.[58]

Othello is the bleakest of tragedies, for although these two people love each other dearly, their love is not enough. They fail because they do not know who they are. Othello knows only what it means to be a soldier, a heroic leader who makes decisions on the battlefield, in an instant discerning friend from foe and taking violent action. Like Coriolanus, he is one of Shakespeare's warrior heroes who calls the heroic ideal into question. The same behavior that makes him a hero on the battlefield only destroys him in peacetime. Desdemona knows how to be a dutiful daughter, the traditional role she rejects in courageously following Othello and her heroic dreams. Her short-lived self-affirmation in love, however, turns to bondage in marriage. In I.iii she acknowledges the ritual transfer that makes her not her father's but her husband's chattel, surrendering her dynamic self for the passive feminine ideal. Both Othello and Desdemona err in conforming to traditional male and female stereotypes, adopting personal behavior which prevents real intimacy and trust. Desdemona's chastity becomes more important to both of them than Desdemona herself. Othello kills her and she sacrifices herself to affirm the traditional ideal. As we have seen in considering Hero, nothing the traditional woman can do will alter men's misperceptions of her. In the world of traditional male-female roles, males act and females react. Desdemona cannot change Othello's perceptions. Her loving unselfishness becomes compulsive compliance which actually prevents her from defending herself.[59]

Iago's assessment of Desdemona is correct. She attempts to please everyone, fulfilling the role of the good woman. She: "is of so free, so kind, so apt, so blessed a disposition, she holds it a vice in her goodness not to do more than she is requested" (II.iii.325-28). Desdemona's error is that of the traditional woman who lives for others, choosing goodness over selfishness.[60] In attempting to nurture everyone around her, she fails herself. She pleads eloquently to the duke about her love for Othello. In her boundless empathy, she pleads for Cassio, but characteristically woman, she cannot plead for herself. Unable to speak in her own behalf, Desdemona "becomes practically monosyllabic."[61]

Even her lie about the handkerchief can be explained as altruism. She subordinates truth to the main priority in her life, pleasing her husband. Gilligan notes how often excessively altruistic women will compromise truth to avoid hurting others. Desdemona knows the handkerchief is missing but intends to find it again without troubling Othello.[62] Emilia does not mean to hurt anyone either. She takes the handkerchief to please her own husband and had meant to return it once the work was taken out. But these small dissimulations combine in a fatal pattern.

Enslaved by the traditional ideal that not only dominates her behavior but distorts her perceptions, Desdemona sinks into passivity until in IV.ii.98 she tells Emilia she is "half asleep" in shock. Attempting to conform to "what should be," she fails to see "what is," refusing to recognize Othello's jealousy and the danger it represents. The traditional norms have given her no means of defending herself. She is told only to bear chiding with all patience and obedience, and so she does. The idealism and all-consuming nature of her love lead her into a closed-image syndrome not uncommon among battered wives: she refuses to believe all this is happening. Othello cannot really be jealous; she never gave him cause. Every shock to her system is met with a new denial, a new affirmation of her innocence and obedience in the role of perfect wife.[63] Her inability to accept Othello's jealousy is compounded by her previously sheltered life, which did not prepare her for anything like this. In loving Othello, she has risked everything, given up home, father, and country. Her identity as Othello's wife has become her *only* identity; her belief system at this point will not tolerate his rejection, which would make her a nonentity and turn her world to chaos.

A significant line early in the play is Othello's response to the street brawl: "Are we turn'd Turks, and to ourselves do that / Which heaven hath forbid the Ottomites?" (II.iii.170-71). Are we, he asks, our own worst enemies? His accusation holds true for all the principal characters in the play. Iago betrays his humanity in his murderous revenge. Cassio betrays himself by drinking to excess. Othello loses his faith in Desdemona's love, betrayed by his own insecurities. In his *anagnorisis* he acknowledges this, executing justice upon himself as he had done to the "turban'd Turk," arch enemy of the Venetian state (V.ii.353). Desdemona, too, has been an enemy to herself in slavishly following the traditional ideal of female behavior, which undermines her self-esteem.[64] Her unselfish devotion to Othello makes her a martyr to love. Desdemona's last words have been read many ways: a final act of loving kindness, a benevolent lie to protect Othello. As Emilia asks her who has done this deed and Desdemona answers, "Nobody; I myself" (V.ii.124-25), there is surely some truth in her admission. She dies upholding the impossible standard of the good woman, impossible because even though she was innocent and chaste, the man she loved failed to perceive her so.

Like Ophelia and Hero, Desdemona is in her own way a dominated daughter, a dominated woman in a patriarchal society that will not allow women to grow up, to assert themselves in their adult lives, or even to act in their own defense.[65] In her attempt to be a good wife, she loses her vitality and self-confidence, drawing her identity from her husband's perceptions. Despite her forebodings, she lies in bed waiting for him in V.ii. And as he murders her, she becomes the ultimate embodiment of the feminine ideal: silent, cold, and chaste, as beautiful as a marble statue: "Cold, cold, my girl! / Even like thy chastity" (V.ii.275-76). The

element of necrophilia in Othello's adoration of her sleeping form is no accident ("Be thus when thou art dead, and I will kill thee / And love thee after" [18-19]). Carried to its logical extreme, the traditional ideal represents a woman's denial of her thoughts and desires, her very essence, an ultimate obliteration of the self. In her death, Desdemona finally becomes the "perfect" Renaissance woman.

Notes

[1] In "Images of Women in Shakespeare's Plays," *Southern Humanities Review* 11 (1977): 145-50, Barbara A. Mowat describes the double image of Shakespeare's women, contrasting the way they are seen by their men with the way the audience perceives them.

[2] Carol Jones Carlisle, *Shakespeare from the Greenroom* (Chapel Hill: Univ. of North Carolina Press, 1969), pp. 143-44.

[3] Bradley, *Shakespearean Tragedy* (New York: St. Martin's Press, 1969), pp. 135-36.

[4] Agnes Mure MacKenzie, *The Women in Shakespeare's Plays* (Garden City, N.Y.: Doubleday, 1924), p. 218.

[5] Norman N. Holland, *The Shakespearean Imagination* (New York: Macmillan, 1964), p. 167; Bernard McElroy, *Shakespeare's Mature Tragedies* (Princeton: Princeton Univ. Press, 1973), p. 75; E.K. Chambers, *Shakespeare: A Survey* (New York: Hill and Wang, 1958), p. 187. Like Kenneth Muir, in *Shakespeare's Tragic Sequence* (London: Hutchinson Univ. Library, 1972), p. 83, I reject the view that Ophelia is "sophisticated and Hamlet's cast-off mistress." This view has been expounded by Jan Kott in *Shakespeare Our Contemporary,* trans. Boleslaw Taborski (Garden City, N.Y.: Anchor, 1966), p. 86.

[6] G. B. Harrison, *Shakespeare's Tragedies* (London: Routledge and Kegan Paul, 1951), p. 101; Rosalie L. Colie, *Shakespeare's Living Art* (Princeton: Princeton Univ. Press, 1974), p. 219; John Masefield, quoted in *Shakespeare's Critics,* ed. A.M. Eastman and G. B. Harrison (Ann Arbor: Univ. of Michigan Press, 1964), p. 180.

[7] Carlisle, *Shakespeare from the Greenroom,* pp. 136-37.

[8] George Gordon, *Shakespearian Comedy* (Oxford: Oxford Univ. Press, 1944), p. 56.

[9] Anna Jameson, *Shakespeare's Heroines* (New York: Burt, 1948), p. 139.

[10] Gilligan, *In a Different Voice* (Cambridge: Harvard Univ. Press, 1982), p. 8. Erikson, in *Identity, Youth*

and Crisis (New York: W.W. Norton, 1968), p. 87, explains that in adolescent role confusion "the young person counterpoints rather than synthesizes his sexual, ethnic, occupational, and typological alternatives and is often driven to decide definitely and totally for one side or the other."

[11] See Gilligan, *Different Voice,* p. 17.

[12] Lynda Boose noted that Laertes poisons Ophelia's mind with a "quite obscene picture of sex presented through images of military bombardment and young flowers being stroked to death," in "The Fashionable Poloniuses," *Hamlet Studies* 1 (1980): 77.

[13] Gilligan, *Different Voice,* p. 105.

[14] Her symptoms parallel those described by Horney in *New Ways,* p. 84. Irving Ribner in *Patterns in Shakespearean Tragedy* (New York: Barnes and Noble, 1960), p. 88, believes that Ophelia's "obedience to her father causes her to see love as madness and lust, to reject her fellow man in Hamlet," while I would reverse the cause and effect: her terror at the picture of sexuality Polonius presents causes her to retreat into conventionality.

[15] Laing, *The Divided Self* (London: Tavistock, 1960), p. 195.

[16] Thomas McFarland, *Tragic Meanings in Shakespeare* (New York: Random House, 1966), p. 47.

[17] Gilligan, *Different Voice,* p. 16.

[18] Granville-Barker, *Prefaces to Shakespeare* (London: Batsford, 1947), 1:212.

[19] Boose, "Fashionable Poloniuses," pp. 75-76.

[20] As Granville-Barker has noted in *Prefaces* 1:215, she seeks to deal politely with his public humiliation of her.

[21] Herman Harrell Horne, *Shakespeare's Philosophy of Love* (Raleigh, N.C.: Edwards and Broughton, 1945), p. 104.

[22] Craig and Bevington, *Complete Works of Shakespeare,* p. 933n. See also Bridget Gellert Lyons, "The Iconography of Ophelia," *ELH* 44 (1977): 69.

[23] According to Dr. Ira S. Wile, in "Some Shakespearean Characters in the Light of Present Day Psychologies," *Psychological Quarterly* 16 (1942): 62-90, quoted in Holland, *Psychoanalysis and Shakespeare,* p. 198, "her obscene language is not unknown in wards of mental hospitals—she is a victim of mania."

[24] Charlotte Otten, in "Ophelia's 'Long Purples,'" *Shakespeare Quarterly* 30 (1979): 397-402, presents evidence from Renaissance herbals identifying the "long purples" as Orchis Serapias or Satyrion Royall, both associated with the male sex organ by their names, legends, and physical descriptions.

[25] M. Esther Harding, *The 'I' and the 'Not-I'* (Princeton: Princeton Univ. Press, 1965), p. 171.

[26] William Hazlitt (1817), Georg Brandes (1895), and B.A. Young (1965), quoted in *Shakespeare: "Much Ado About Nothing" and "As You Like It": A Casebook,* ed. John Russell Brown (London: Macmillan, 1979), pp. 30-31, 42, and 228.

[27] Donald Stauffer, "Words and Actions," in Brown, *Casebook,* p. 87; and Paul and Miriam Mueschke, "Illusion and Metamorphosis," in Brown, *Casebook,* p. 130.

[28] Mueschke and Mueschke, "Illusion," p. 135; see also Arthur Kirsch, *Shakespeare and the Experience of Love* (Cambridge: Cambridge Univ. Press, 1981), p. 54.

[29] Alexander Leggatt, *Shakespeare's Comedy of Love* (London: Methuen, 1974), p. 155.

[30] Jung, "Marriage as a Psychological Relationship," 198.

[31] Vives, *Instruction,* p. 54.

[32] Mueschke and Mueschke, "Illusion," p. 135.

[33] Erikson, as described by Gilligan in *Different Voice,* p. 98; see Erikson, *Identity,* p. 266.

[34] Elmer Edgar Stoll in *Othello* (1915; New York: Gordian Press, 1967), p. 9, paralleled Othello's sudden loss of faith in Desdemona with the behavior of Leonato, who acts "as if he cherished a grudge against" his daughter. Barbara Mowat, in "Images," provides a more specific definition of this "grudge": "the fathers of Hero and Desdemona must listen as their daughters—seemingly so chaste, so perfect—are described in animalistic sexual terms: . . . Both fathers, confronted with the vision of the sweet girl-child turned lecherous animal, lash out at their own daughters and at the treachery, the terrible lust of all women" (p. 152).

[35] Sexton, *The Slandered Woman in Shakespeare* (Victoria, B.C.: English Literary Studies, 1978), pp. 39-44. In 1613 Shakespeare himself had some direct experience with the question of slander when his daughter Susannah brought action for defamation against John Lane, who had accused her of lewd conduct and adultery, as W. Nicholas Knight pointed out in "Patrimony

and Shakespeare's Daughters," *Hartford Studies in Literature* 9 (1977): 181-82.

[36] Gilligan, *Different Voice,* p. 132.

[37] Ribner, *Patterns,* p. 94; Knight, *The Wheel of Fire* (New York: Meridian Books, 1930), p. 249.

[38] Auden, *The Dyer's Hand* (New York: Random House, 1962), p. 269; Kott, *Shakespeare Our Contemporary,* p. 118.

[39] S.N. Garner, "Shakespeare's Desdemona," *Shakespeare Studies* 9 (1976): 235; R.N. Hallstead, "Idolatrous Love," *Shakespeare Quarterly* 19 (1968): 107; Marvin Rosenberg, *The Masks of Othello* (Berkeley: Univ. of California Press, 1961), p. 209; Kirsch, *Experience of Love,* p. 15; W.D. Adamson, "Unpinned or Undone?: Desdemona's Critics and the Problem of Sexual Innocence," *Shakespeare Studies* 13 (1980): 179-80.

[40] Garner, "Shakespeare's Desdemona," 243; Auden, *Dyer's Hand,* p. 268; Rymer, quoted in Eastman and Harrison, *Shakespeare's Critics,* p. 13.

[41] Harrison, *Shakespeare's Tragedies,* p. 143; Robert Dickes, "Desdemona: An Innocent Victim," *American Imago* 27 (1970): 286.

[42] Kirsch, *Experience of Love,* p. 17; Auden, *Dyer's Hand,* p. 269; Bradley, *Shakespearean Tragedy,* p. 150; McElroy, *Mature Tragedies,* p. 135; Neely, "Women and Men in *Othello*: 'what should such a fool / Do with so good a woman?' " *Shakespeare Studies* 10 (1977): 133.

[43] Rosenberg, *Masks,* pp. 135-37, 139.

[44] Harold C. Goddard, *The Meaning of Shakespeare* (Chicago: Univ. of Chicago Press, 1951), pp. 469-70.

[45] See Garner, "Shakespeare's Desdemona," pp. 239, 236.

[46] Kirsch, *Experience of Love,* p. 14. See Jung, "Theory of Psychoanalysis," pp. 168-74.

[47] Goddard, *Meaning of Shakespeare,* p. 457.

[48] As Nancy Friday observed in *My Mother/My Self* (New York: Dell, 1977), pp. 22-23, many women unconsciously imitate their mothers in their marriages, no matter how independent and assertive they have been.

[49] Vives, *Instruction,* sig. 68v.

[50] Gilligan, pp. 105, 87. See also Gayle Greene, " 'This That You Call Love': Sexual and Social Tragedy in *Othello,*" *Journal of Women's Studies in Literature* 1 (1979): 25; and MacKenzie, *Women,* p. 253, both of whom note her filial deference to him as expressed in her addressing him as "my lord." See also Harding, *Way of All Women,* p. 153, for a psychological discussion of father transference.

[51] MacFarland, *Tragic Meanings,* pp. 64-65; Kirsch, *Experience of Love,* p. 14; Stephen Reid, "Desdemona's Guilt," *American Imago* 27 (1970): 259.

[52] See Dickes, "Desdemona," pp. 281-96; Reid, "Desdemona's Guilt," pp. 259, 281.

[53] Carlisle, in *Shakespeare from the Greenroom,* p. 248, notes "a certain Joan-of-Arc quality in her nature." Horney, in *New Ways,* p. 113, and Deutsch, in *Psychology of Women,* p. 273, explained how traditional cultural norms predispose virtuous women to masochism.

[54] Horney, *Neurosis,* p. 221.

[55] Both Pitt, in *Shakespeare's Women,* pp. 50-51, and Harold Skulsky, in *Spirits Finely Touched* (Athens: Univ. of Georgia Press, 1976), pp. 240-41, find Desdemona excessively willful, while I see her behavior as a slavish attempt to conform to the contemporary image of the good wife.

[56] Both Leonora Leet Brodwin, *Elizabethan Love Tragedy* (New York: New York Univ. Press, 1971), p. 213, and Martha Andreson-Thom, "Thinking about Women and Their Prosperous Art." *Shakespeare Studies* 11 (1978): 264, see Desdemona's conformity to tradition beginning when she feels she has lost Othello's love. I see it originating in her very definition of marriage.

[57] Gouge, *Of Domesticall Duties,* sig. Alv.

[58] Bradley, *Shakespearean Tragedy,* p. 171. See Horney, *Inner Conflicts,* pp. 58-59, and *The Neurotic Personality of Our Time* (New York: W.W. Norton, 1937), p. 140.

[59] See Horney, *Inner Conflicts,* pp. 121-22, for a discussion of compulsive compliance.

[60] Gilligan, *Different Voice,* p. 132.

[61] Inga-Stina Ewbank, "Shakespeare's Portrayal of Women," in *Shakespeare: Pattern of Excelling Nature,* ed. David Bevington and Jay L. Halio (Newark: Univ. of Delaware Press, 1978), p. 224.

[62] Gilligan, *Different Voice,* p. 65. See also Lynda Elizabeth Boose, "Othello's Handkerchief," *English Literary Renaissance* 5 (1975): 360-74, for a discus-

sion of its symbolic significance. Desdemona's motives in concealing the handkerchief's loss have been variously interpreted as fear by Garner, "Shakespeare's Desdemona," p. 246, and MacKenzie, *Women*, p. 258. Robert B. Heilman, in *Magic in the Web* (1956; Westport, Conn.: Greenwood Press, 1977), p. 200, argues that Desdemona "knows" the handkerchief is missing but does not really believe this, hoping for some miracle to recover it in an irrational combination of belief and hope.

[63] See Horney, *New Ways*, pp. 271-72; and Garner, pp. 246-47.

[64] M.D. Faber, "Two Studies in Self-Aggression in Shakespearean Tragedy," *Literature and Psychology* 14 (1964): 85-87; see also Gilligan, *Different Voice*, p. 87.

[65] As Edward Snow, "Sexual Anxiety," pp. 407-8, maintains, "the tragedy of the play . . . is the inability of Desdemona to escape or triumph over restraints and Oedipal prohibitions that domesticate women to the conventional male order of things." See also Deutsch, *Psychology of Women*, p. 240; Horney, *New Ways*, p. 113.

Kirby Farrell (essay date 1989)

SOURCE: "Love, Death, and Patriarchy in *Romeo and Juliet*," in *Play, Death, and Heroism in Shakespeare*, The University of North Carolina Press, 1989, pp. 131-47.

[*Here, Farrell asserts that the intense fear of death among the characters in* Romeo and Juliet *reflects the breakdown of the patriarchal structure of Verona as well as its ability to inspire fantasies of immortality.*]

Recent criticism has tended to depict patriarchy primarily as an authoritarian institution for the regulation of society.[1] Where Elizabethan theorists praised the system for its order, we now have difficulty seeing beyond its flagrant injustices and limitations, especially its misogyny. Yet repression is not the whole picture. What made patriarchy tolerable, even valuable, to so many Elizabethans? No one in Shakespeare's Verona, for example, openly rebels against its patriarchs. Like Romeo, Juliet blames fate that she "must love a loathed enemy" (1.5.141); she desperately tries to placate her father with "chopt-logic" (3.5.149). For all their touchiness about being thought slaves, even the servants identify with—are willing to fight for—their houses. Why would individuals consistently subordinate their own desires to the will of a patriarch?[2]

The answer I read from the play is that like religion, patriarchy systematized heroic fantasies of immortal-

ity. Anxiety about death pervades *Romeo and Juliet*. The word "death" itself shows up more often here than in any other work in the canon. In the lyrical balcony scene (2.2.53-78) no less than the ominous Prologue, love is "death-mark'd." Even before Romeo's first glimpse of Juliet, as he laments Rosaline's vow of chastity, he plays at being dead: "in that vow / Do I live dead that live to tell it now" (1.1.223-24). Even then he worries that "untimely death" will overtake him (1.4.111). This "Black and portentous" dread, I shall be arguing, dramatizes the breakdown in Verona of patriarchy's ability to control people's anxiety about death, and unconsciously anticipates the dangerous consequences of that breakdown.

Patriarchy evolved from ancient systems of social order based on heroic dominance.[3] In Roman law a male child of any age "remained under the authority of his father and did not become a Roman in the full sense of the word, a paterfamilias, until the father's death. More than that, the youth's father was his natural judge and could privately sentence him to death" (Veyne, p. 27). The early Roman paterfamilias not only ruled over the family, but was priest of the family ancestor cult. In various ways this access to superhuman power persisted into the Renaissance.

Like Christianity, whose priestly fathers commonly exercised worldly as well as spiritual influence, patriarchy associated the father with the king and God: he created and validated his child's personality. As Duke Theseus formulates it to a daughter as disobedient in love as Juliet:

> To you your father should be as a god;
> One that compos'd your beauties; yea, and one
> To whom you are but as a form in wax,
> By him imprinted, and within his power,
> To leave the figure, or disfigure it.
>
> [*MND* 1.1.47-51]

Ultimately the patriarch guaranteed the psychic life of all who depended upon him. The father may be invested with maternal nurturance: "Where should the frighted child hide his head, but in the bosom of his loving father?"[4] Tasso reveals the underlying premise when he reports that he confided in his patron "not as we trust in man, but as we trust in God. It appeared to me that, so long as I was under his protection, fortune and death had no power over me" (Bradbrook 1980, p.73).

In early modern England, "in spite of all the subordination, the exploitation and the obliteration of those who were young, or feminine, or in service, everyone belonged in . . . a family group," a circle of affection, but also a likely scene of hatred (Laslett, p. 5). Patriarchal dominance was supposed to stabilize the family.

By subsuming the personalities of those dependent on him, a father or master reconciled or if need be over-rode their conflicts. His strength energized the entire family and his purpose gave it meaning. In this perspective patriarchy was a means of consolidating diverse wills into one extraordinary will and generating a communal feeling—in effect, a spell—of immortality.

The potency of that spell derived from dread as well as devotion. A patriarch could annihilate as well as make men. The prince acts to rein in his "Rebellious subjects" by threatening their lives (1.1.97). Old Capulet curses the uncooperative Juliet: "hang, beg, starve, die in the streets" (3.5.192). Servants joke anxiously about the gallows. More than mere discipline is at stake here, since one who can command death may seem to transcend it. Symbolically the patriarch appropriated the role of death himself, subjecting it to human rules. By being perfectly obedient one could hope to placate if not control death. Even unconscious anxiety about a rejection akin to death must have reinforced identification with the father.

In a system such as ancient Rome's, where "famulus" or family also meant "slave" or "servant," only self-effacement brought a share of the father's power and security. In theory, either one identified with one's master and vicariously shared his glory by lording it over inferiors, or one was dominated. Hating to be thought slaves (1.1.13) but also fearful of the executioner (5), the Capulet servants associate aggression on the master's behalf with escape from the nullity of servitude. Yet their inferiority is the creation of masters and produces volatile ambivalence in them. They summarize their situation with an ambiguity too dangerous to be consciously faced: "The quarrel is between our masters, and us their men" (19-20)—that is, not merely between houses but between masters and servants as well.

In seeking to dominate, the servants act out the submerged values of their masters. Since patriarchy is founded upon the promise of security to dependents such as women, Sampson imagines humiliating his enemy by violating his women. Likewise, he appropriates the patriarch's role as judge when he fantasizes, "I will be civil with the maids—I will cut off their heads" or maidenheads (21-23), equating rape with execution. By contrast, Romeo acts out patriarchy's benevolent generativity when he first approaches Juliet, assigning her an identity (the sun) and commanding her to arise and claim her rightful place in the order of things (2.2.3-9). These examples reflect a paradox that becomes increasingly significant the deeper we look into the play's imaginative world: that even those who seemingly oppose patriarchy internalize patriarchal values.

The marriage Old Capulet would make for his daughter helps to explain the submissiveness of dependents. By meekly wedding the paternally sanctioned Paris, making him a patriarch in his own right, Juliet would fulfill her father's will and transform herself. Lady Capulet fetishizes Paris as a book of spellbinding value that "in many's eyes doth share the glory" (91). Marrying him, Juliet too would be glorified, sharing in "all that he doth possess, / By having him, making [herself] no less" (1.3.93-94). With its connotations of worship, "glory" exactly expresses the religious assumptions underlying the patriarchal system. Compelling admiration from others, Juliet's marriage would exalt her and by extension her parents. For a dependent deference can be a means to vicarious triumph.

In Verona, however, patriarchy is under stress. The prince envisions himself protecting the city's "ancient citizens" from the turmoil of "rebellious subjects" (1.1.82, 97). A servant's spiteful taunts can provoke a full-scale brawl in the streets. At the same time romance has begun to rival patriarchy as an alternative mode of devotion and deliverance. As a result, the father's demand at least for deference, at most for total self-sacrifice, sets off a violent chain of events. Social patterns and preoccupations inherent in the patriarchal system create conflicts that make rebellion inevitable. . . .

For all their lyrical tenderness, Romeo and Juliet create their love out of the tragically conflicting materials of their own culture. In Romeo's shifting passion, for instance, the Chorus implies a struggle to inherit a father's position: "Now old desire doth in his deathbed lie, / And young affection gapes to be his heir" (2.Pro. 1-2). The lovers attempt to evade the world of the feud, yet in making love they unwittingly act out patriarchal and Christian forms. Construing love as worship, substituting the beloved for father and God, they seek apotheosis in each other.

In an imaginative world where children grow up transfixed in the aura of a protective lord or else face nullity, it is understandable that love may reproduce in a beloved the engulfing, life-giving power of godlike parents. Insofar as the polarization of power in Verona requires either continual submission or the devious homicidal assertiveness of the feud, love's mutual worship answers profound needs. For if individuals become disenchanted with absolute security and heroic aggression, as Romeo and Juliet do, they need alternative convictions to sustain them. Love is therefore counterphobic not only as any system of immortality must be, but also as a defence against the anxious demands of an ideology whose spell is no longer wholly efficacious. Mercutio makes the point in a wisecrack about play-death. Having lost Romeo after the Capulets' party, Mercutio jokes that "The ape is dead," and invokes Rosaline's "quivering thigh" to resurrect him (2.1.15-21). The jibe reduces

Romeo to a mindless animal who can only "ape" autonomy in sexual arousal.

Romeo envisions Juliet as a supernatural being, a masculine "bright angel" and "winged messenger of heaven" who overmasters awestruck "mortals" so that they "fall back and gaze on him" (2.2.26-32). At the same time, as in the gender of the angel, Romeo's vision expresses the infantile wish to be chosen by, and identified with, a majestic father. His imagination finds fulfillment in the paradox of empowering self-effacement at the heart of patriarchy. The fantasy's completion comes in Romeo's dream that Juliet has awakened him from death and ordained him an emperor, the paramount patriarchal role (5.1.9).

Juliet participates in the same fantasy when she equates orgasm and immortality in her cry,

> Give me my Romeo; and when I [Q4: he] shall die,
> Take him and cut him out in little stars,
> And he will make the face of heaven so fine
> That all the world will be in love with night.
>
> [3.2.21-24]

Like "all the world," Juliet will be subsumed as a worshipper in Romeo's apotheosis. If his transformation into stars alludes to Caesar's apotheosis as a "goodly shyning starre" in Ovid, as one editor has suggested,[8] then Juliet is envisioning an analogue to Romeo's dream that sexual love (her kiss) can revive him from death to become an emperor. By "dying" through sexuality "are happy mothers made" (1.2.12). By the same means, reciprocally, may a woman make a youth an immortal lord. In its imagination of power this fantasy is profoundly patriarchal. Like Romeo's vision of the angel, however, this celebration of all the world absorbed in the face of heaven also suggests a worshipful infant's concentration upon the all-important, life-giving face of a parent.

The lovers' mutual worship expresses a generosity, subverted or repressed elsewhere in Verona, that balances their self-destructiveness.[9] In their lovemaking Romeo and Juliet repeatedly fantasize that death-like self-effacement leads to apotheosis. Repudiating their own names (2.2.34-57), loving in darkness, they try to be invisible in hopes of escaping patriarchal control. They imagine innocent self-nullification that excuses their actual defiance of their fathers even as each casts the beloved in the role of life-giving lord.[10] When Juliet wishes Romeo were her pet bird, a "poor prisoner" (179) whose liberty she would be "loving jealous of" (181), Romeo eagerly assents. Yet Juliet declines to dominate him, protesting that "I should kill thee with much cherishing" (183).

Finally, however, the lovers' behavior is equivocal, and that doubleness makes their self-effacement perilous. Confronted by Tybalt after his secret marriage, Romeo tries to play possum, placating him. Yet his passivity allows Tybalt to use him as a screen, thrusting under his arm to kill Mercutio (3.1.103). Immediately guilt and anger overwhelm Romeo. Released, his will now turns against Juliet—"Thy beauty hath made me effeminate," he cries, "And . . . soft'ned valor's steel" (3.1.113-15)—and then, murderously, he turns against Tybalt.

In this crisis actual uncontrollable death breaks the spell of symbolic immortality, and the underlying patriarchal structure asserts itself. Defeated by Tybalt's "triumph" (122), called a "wretched boy" (130), Romeo feels overwhelmed by "black fate" (119). In reaction he tries to reassert heroic control over death by levying a death sentence on Tybalt (129). Rebelling—against the emasculating "angel" Juliet as well as the would-be master Tybalt—Romeo discharges his rage at a rival "son" and alter ego. In the complex of motives that produces the lovers' suicides this process is important. For there the part of the self that identifies with the patriarch and demands mastery finally punishes with death part of the self that for the sake of love would forgive enemies and forego worldly power in hopes of deferred rewards. The internalized father slays the weakening child.

Because the basic patriarchal structure governs even rebellion, desires for autonomy tend to call up opposite roles organized around fantasies of death and omnipotence. This split appears everywhere in Verona. When Gregory and Sampson jest about breaking the law, they promptly fantasize about slavery and execution,[11] and then in reaction about their slaughter of enemies. Similarly, the Juliet who would make Romeo outshine Caesar is also the paralyzed child who helplessly hears her parents wish her dead. If she cannot have Romeo, she vows, then "My grave is like to be my wedding-bed" (1.5.135). Protesting the ultimatum to marry Paris, she cries out to the friar:

> . . . hide me nightly in a charnel-house,
> O'ercovered quite with dead men's rattling bones,
> With reeky shanks and yellow [chapless] skulls;
> Or bid me go into a new-made grave,
> And hide me with a dead man in his [shroud]—
>
> [4.1.81-85]

Juliet's brave challenge masks a fantasy of punishing her own unconscious rage at her father, and guilt at her lover's murder of her kinsman. Lying with slain males like a child ("hide me . . . in his shroud") and a submissive paramour,[12] she would be magically undoing death with sexual fertility as in patriarchally conceived marriage. The idea of playing dead promises to resolve conflicts on more levels than she or the Friar realizes.

Exposed in his rebellion by the murder of Tybalt, the Romeo who would be an emperor (5.1.6-9) similarly abases himself, feeling himself put to death by the mere word "banishment" with which the friar, like a patriarchal judge, "cut'st my head off" (3.3.21-23). Taunted as a slave by Tybalt (1.5.55), Romeo goes to his doom in grandiose defiance of slavery, vowing to "shake [off] the yoke of inauspicious stars / From this world-wearied flesh" (5.3.111). Death and omnipotence are two faces of the same fantasy. Their dissociation contributes to the irrational violence of the feud as well as to the lovers' "mad scenes"—Romeo's tantrum on the floor of the friar's cell and Juliet's near-hallucinatory collapse as she dispatches herself with the sleeping potion.

As it happens, we can glimpse the origins of this polarization of the self in Romeo and Juliet. Headed toward the Capulets' ball, Romeo worries about "some vile forfeit of untimely death" that may overtake him before he can redeem the "despised life clos'd in my breast" through some heroic act (1.4.106-13). His imagery implies that he has mortgaged his life and will lose it since the term will "expire" before he can pay. Punning, he fears an "untimely debt" as well as "death," one that will "forfeit" his "despised life."[13] A sense of guilty inadequacy makes him expect the punishment of death or foreclosure.

In patriarchy, however, the child owes the godlike father a death inasmuch as he or she holds life at the father's will. In Theseus's summary of the doctrine, the child is "imprinted" by the father and is "within his power / To leave the figure or disfigure it" (*MND* 1.1.50-51). What is more, the child owes a debt of obedience or self-effacement, in which guilty wishes for autonomy are repressed in a symbolic death. Where patriarchy splits into the roles of the father who is a judge and the son who is a warrior, the son additionally owes this conscience figure a debt of heroic glory that may have to be paid by risking his life. Such a debt produces the self-hate in Romeo's "despised life" and helps to explain his desperate reassertion of lost "valor" in the murder of Tybalt.

Juliet's behavior also reveals an underlying psychic debt. The origin of this debt surfaces in the Nurse's account of Juliet's weaning (1.3.16-57). Though physically capable, the child angrily resisted her own independence. On the previous day her first efforts at autonomy had led to a fall that brought not parental support and further self-assertion, but a queasy joke from a surrogate father—the Nurse's husband—that a woman lives to fall. "Thou wilt fall backward when thou hast

more wit." Yet Juliet's fall implies a threat of death, especially for a child whose alter ego Susan (the Nurse's daughter) is "with God" (19).

In falling Juliet gave her "brow" "a perilous knock": the same injury she imagines inflicting on herself on waking in the monument. Trapped in the suffocating family tomb—within objectified patriarchy itself—she fears being overcome by guilty rage and dashing out her brain, seat of the self and forbidden autonomy. Moreover, she would punish herself by means of a "great kinsman's bone" (4.3.53), metonymic parental force. As in the weaning anecdote, a venture toward autonomy produces in her mental life a fall toward death, then trauma.

The Nurse's husband's joke proposes a patriarchal solution to the fall toward death. A "fall backwards" into sexually submissive marriage and motherhood will rescue the child from the terrifying "fall" toward autonomy at the cost of being able—in the joke, literally—to stand on her own two feet. Juliet consents to pay a debt/death through a marriage that will at once efface and exalt her. Girls must "fall" sexually to be redeemed by a new lord and win posterity for the family and themselves, even as young males must be willing to fall in battle to win immortalizing glory.

In this imperative of self-sacrifice lies the germ of the idea of a play-death such as Juliet acts out with the friar's potion. Her fall in a death-counterfeiting sleep would appease an outraged parental judge and lead to a resurrection from the family tomb with the banished Romeo. Making Verona new in amity, Juliet would be fulfilling a patriarchal fantasy comparable to Romeo's dream of love's resurrecting him as an emperor (5.1.6-9). The play emphasizes the pervasiveness of this fantasy in Verona. Engineering Juliet's resurrection, the friar takes a god-like role, planning literally to raise her from the grave. Uniting the lovers, aspiring to atone all Verona, he parodies Capulet's marriage plans, implicitly correcting them, as if to prove himself "the best father of Verona's welfare" (Brenner, p. 52)—one more form of patriarchal rivalry.

. . . . .

Reconstituting patriarchal forms to serve their own desires for autonomy, the lovers never openly defy their parents. Yet with the wish for autonomy comes a veiled recognition of the suffocating claims their parents make on them. The parents' will to subsume their children's identities comes unconsciously to seem to the lovers like cannibalism. The monument that embodies her family in Verona becomes to Juliet an imprisoning mouth (4.3.33-34) and to Romeo a devouring "maw," womb, and mouth (5.3.45-47). Just as the mother becomes an expression of the father's will, and the father expresses ideologically the life-giving and potentially life-withholding generativity of the mother, so the tomb conflates the parents into one ravenous orifice.

As in Lear's fantasy of the savage who "makes his generation messes / To gorge his appetite" (1.1.116-18), the threat is not merely of parental wrath or incestuous desire, but also of cannibalistic self-aggrandizement, a frantic hunger to incorporate more and more life in order to overcome death. Such aggrandizement is the more terrible for being sharply felt by the child and yet invisible. In effect, the lovers fear an infantile voracity such as a once-subsumed child, having at last come to dominate, might release against its own offspring.[14] Since monuments objectify a claim to transcend annihilating time, the "hungry" tomb expresses patriarchy's deepest and most primitive drive, the drive for survival.

We need to remember that the father's claims to mastery over death are corroborated in his role as judge and even executioner. . . . [The] father is always potentially Death himself. In this respect the prince's struggle to contain the feud is a struggle—echoed in the world outside the Elizabethan theater—to reserve for a supreme patriarch the right to command death.

At its most benign this power thrillingly confirms the lord's generosity. By conspicuously sparing the child's life, the father (or monarch) makes the love between them incalculably valuable. And so in his amorous surrender to Juliet, Romeo exults, "O dear account! my life is in my foe's debt" (1.5.18). At its most terrifying, internalized by the child, such power generates intolerable insecurity, as in Romeo's dread of the hostile stars and his suicidal sense of doom.[15]

From this standpoint the lovers' suicides reflect the dynamics of patriarchal control. To master her fate, Juliet would play a lordly role as Cleopatra does to escape Caesar: "myself have power to die" (3.5.242). Yet unconsciously, the introjected imperatives of the parental judge can make suicide a form of execution in which an alienated conscience destroys a rebellious self, as in Juliet's vision of herself dashing out her own brain with an ancestral bone, the reified will of the father. Likewise Romeo's conscience punishes him with suicidal self-hatred. Banished for his defiance, he "[falls] upon the ground . . . / Taking the measure of an unmade grave" (3.3.69-70). Angry at Juliet for his own defiance in slaying Tybalt (3.1.113-15), he turns his anger against himself, fantasizing that his own name has murdered her (102-5). With Juliet he calls down punishment on himself as Elizabethan noblemen routinely did in speeches from the scaffold professing love for the queen: "let me be put to death. / I am content, so thou wilt have it so" (3.5.17-18). And: "Come, death, and welcome! Juliet wills it so" (24). Ambiguously, however,

Juliet is also "my soul" (25), so that this execution too is internalized.

As patriarchy's internal conflicts become intolerable, its radical connection with death threatens to surface in consciousness, most insidiously in the personification of death by parent and child. Old Capulet envisions death as a young, rivalrous inheritor who has "lain with" Juliet and usurped his control over her (4.5.36). His description of his adversary of course exactly fits Romeo. In the Capulets' monument, in turn, Romeo also conceives death as a rival: a warrior-king whose "pale flag" has not yet fully "conquered" Juliet (5.3.93-96). Then the rival becomes an "amorous . . . lean abhorred monster" who will make Juliet his "paramour." Romeo imagines Juliet sexually enslaved in the "palace" of a "monster" who is also a warrior-king.[16]

This fantasy projects the long-denied dark side of the patriarchal forms in which the lovers have construed each other. Romeo dissociates from himself as Death the part of him that would be made an emperor by Juliet's kiss. In this final moment of tenderness he rejects the devouring triumphalism latent in all patriarchy. He repudiates the Death that "hath suck'd the honey" of Juliet's breath. Otherwise, loving such an emperor-Romeo, Juliet would be submitting to rape like the women Sampson fancies "ever thrust to the wall" (1.1.16). Sampson identifies with patriarchal tyranny the same tyranny that Romeo at last projects upon death and vows to resist to the end of time.

Romeo then kisses his beloved to seal "a dateless bargain to engrossing death" (5.3.115). "Engrossing" readily applies to patriarchal hegemony and competitiveness. In addition, such greedy possession calls to mind not only Romeo's imagery of the self held in forfeit, but also his vision of the tomb as a "detestable maw," a "womb of death" (45). The metaphors place the young in an engulfing parental womb that should grant, not swallow, life. The womb and the sexually enslaving monster express the parents whom the lovers love and fear and also, unknowingly, hate.[17] The spatial arrangement of Verona onstage reinforces this conflation since the monster holds Juliet in a "palace" that is in fact the Capulet monument and also, in the Elizabethan playhouse, the Capulets' house with its fortresslike walls (Gibbons, p. 74). Juliet's balcony and the lovers' first bedchamber are virtually present in Death's stronghold, as Juliet inadvertently warns Romeo: "the place [is] death, considering who thou art" (2.2.64). Just as Juliet has associated her lover with patriarchal stars (3.2.22) and a "gorgeous palace" (85), so she impulsively fantasizes about sexual violation by a patriarchal death such as Romeo imagines: "I'll to my wedding bed, / And death, not Romeo take my maidenhead" (137).[18]

Giving his own life with chivalric valor to rescue Juliet from a monster, Romeo finally plays out the warrior's debt of the son to his father. Even as he sacrifices himself in part for patriarchal values, he would "shake the yoke of inauspicious stars" (5.3.111) in a final repudiation of the fathers. It is the fatal paradox at the heart of patriarchy: that rebellion against a myth, insidiously encompassed by that myth, serves the myth. In taking his own life to defend Juliet's sexuality against the rival warrior-king Death, Romeo gives sublime new life—eschatological life—to Verona's feud.

At the close of the play, in the funerary statues the fathers decree, benevolence takes disturbing forms. Still thinking in terms of demands, Capulet vows: "This is my daughter's jointure, for no more / Can I demand." To which Montague replies: "But I can give thee more." Whereupon he boasts that he will make Juliet the golden cynosure of all true lovers: "There shall no figure at such a rate be set / As that of true and faithful Juliet" (296-304). The fathers' economic vocabulary and competition call to mind the psychic debts felt by the children, and the ominous economic term "engrossing" (115) that Romeo associates with death.[19]

Now that marriage and the sword have failed, the fathers would reconstitute their conviction of immortality by recreating their children as holy martyrs to love, "Poor sacrifices of our enmity!" (5.3.304). As icons the children will be fabricated into exemplary types. Yet there must be a difference between the golden statues and the poignant individuals we have seen. That difference is of course the basis of the play's critique of patriarchy. And in the end that difference also measures the dramatist's need to honor the structure of power outside the Globe Theater and no doubt in his own upbringing, while also enacting onstage—and in the sympathies the play evokes—a challenge to that power.

Audiences have often interpreted that challenge as a justification of romantic exaltation, even as various critics have taken it to legitimate the lovers' aspirations to autonomy. By contrast, at least one historian maintains that the original Globe audience would have felt obliged to condemn the play's disobedient children (Stone 1977). If we understand patriarchy as a system of beliefs evolved to control poisonous anxiety about death, however, these contradictory responses to the play appear in a new light. Seizing on a limited truth, each tries to protect the illusion of security at stake in the play, either by revaluing the social order (for example, by postulating its reform through love) or, more often, by repudiating patriarchal values on behalf of a substitute system of beliefs. Like the voices onstage, we too need to fortify ourselves against the prospect of annihilation.[20]

Given the danger of offending an audience, especially an audience of Elizabethan patriarchs, the play does not forcibly disenchant its myths. Instead it creates conditions in which imagination might discover itself as a tissue of beliefs. Such a recognition would momentarily at least turn the imagination against itself, showing the triumphal verities onstage and off to be as compulsive and insubstantial as dreams. In such a moment of alienation the self could begin to appreciate its dependency, even (to echo Sampson and Gregory) its enslavement. In that dizzying moment, that is, lies the possibility of change and perhaps a new ground for heroic values.

Recognition that people live by strategic fictions such as patriarchy opens up everything for negotiation and therefore provides a basis for consensual relationships and, not incidentally, the artist's own creativity. Disconnected from underlying physical forces and appetites, by contrast, a cultural fiction may be a terrifying illusion, a candle lighting fools the way to dusty death. If disenchanted, Shakespeare saw, human behavior may reduce to a fierce appetite for domination and nurture tenuously held in check by ruthless strategy: in Verona a feud, or in the imagery of the history plays a struggle between a king and ravenous wolves.

Hence Shakespeare's equivocation. Like Queen Elizabeth's regime, which revived old forms such as chivalry to disguise its innovations, he survived public life in a world of homicidal religious and political rivalry by honoring venerable cultural forms while recreating them. In one sense his genius lay in devising ways of making disenchantment healthy. His own *Romeo and Juliet* appears simply to echo Brooke's familiar, lifeless *Romeus,* although in fact it functions as a sort of pun on Brooke's story, producing a new meaning. Such a quibbling imaginative stance permitted devious self-assertion in the ostensible service of deference.

Although *Romeo and Juliet* seems to me deeply disenchanted at its core, it dramatizes the imagination's resilience in the face of annihilation. As London and Shakespeare himself survived a devastating plague in the early 1590s (a catastrophe echoed in 5.2.8-12), so the play registers the shock of mortality to a privileged system of belief. The final lines show Verona turning blasted life into art ("never was a story of more woe" [5.3.309]), as Shakespeare himself, having sensed the darkness beyond the bright dreams of culture, would go on generating fictions that engaged that darkness, including the flagrantly dreamlike late romances. In this perspective, like the lovers striving to recreate themselves in the starry gloom, the play probes the origins of belief and creativity, reshaping its anxiously conventionalized source story as that story began to reveal the dread and aspiration which are its hidden motive energy.

Notes

[1] One justly influential study finds that many of Shakespeare's plays "reveal the high cost of patriarchal values; the men who uphold them atrophy, and the women, whether resistant or acquiescent, die." See *The Woman's Part: Feminist Criticism of Shakespeare*, ed. Carolyn R. S. Lenz, Gayle Greene, and Carol Thomas Neely (Urbana: University of Illinois Press, 1980), pp. 5-6. Also see Kahn, *Man's Estate*, pp. 82-104. Peter Erickson's *Patriarchal Structures* is also primarily concerned with the representation of gender and its political implications. More disposed to see patriarchy as a comprehensive social system is Marianne L. Novy, *Love's Argument: Gender Relations in Shakespeare* (Chapel Hill: University of North Carolina Press, 1984), esp. chap. 3. Debora Shuger ("Reflections of the Father") persuasively complicates the prevailing stereotypes of the coercive patriarch.

[2] Cf. Lenz, Greene, and Neely, *The Woman's Part*: "Although women may strive to resist or correct the perversions of patriarchy, they do not succeed in altering that order nor do they withdraw their allegiance from it" (p. 6).

[3] "At the beginning of the world," Machiavelli theorized in the *Discourses*, "the inhabitants were few in number, and lived for a time dispersed like beasts. As the human race increased, the necessity for uniting themselves for defence made itself felt; the better to attain this object, they chose the strongest and most courageous from amongst themselves and placed him at their head, promising to obey him" (Schochet, *Patriarchalism*, p. 29). Schochet surveys patriarchal political theory in the Tudor period, pp.37-53.

[4] Richard Hooker, *The Works of Richard Hooker*, ed. John Keeble, 3 vols. (Oxford, 1888; reprint, New York, 1970), 3: 652 (cited in Shuger, "Reflections of the Father"). . . .

[8] See Brian Gibbon's Arden edition of the play, p. 170n. The allusion to orgasmic dying could be strengthened even further by recalling the Lord's promise to Abraham that his immortality would be in infinite progeny: "Look now toward heaven, and tell the stars, if thou be able to number them: and he said unto him, So shall thy seed be" (Gen. 15.5).

[9] Edward A. Snow discriminates two distinct modes of desire in the lovers, "exquisitely fitted to each other, but rarely meeting in the same phenomenological universe" (p. 178). Where Juliet "experiences genesis and gestation, Romeo is haunted by a sense of emptiness and unreality." His love "remains to some extent an attempt to escape from a reality he finds oppressive." See "Language and Sexual Difference in *Romeo and Juliet*," in Erickson and Kahn, *Shakespeare's "Rough Magic*," p. 179.

[10] Juliet's invocation of Phaeton suggests an unconscious appreciation of the perils of the lovers' usurpation of patriarchal reins (3.2.1-4).

[11] Since a slave must at least pretend to replace his own extirpated will with his master's, slavery can be seen as a form of playing dead in order to survive. I examine the servants' behavior in *Shakespeare's Creation*, pp. 120-21.

[12] Cf. Juliet's "O'ercovered" and "your daughter cover'd with a Barbary horse" in *Othello* (1.1.111).

[13] Romeo has mortgaged his life to "Some consequence yet hanging in the stars," and the stars themselves are associated with fathers, as Harold C. Goddard says in *The Meaning of Shakespeare* (Chicago: University of Chicago Press, 1951), 1:119. Cf. the indebtedness to a father associated with mourning in, e.g., *Twelfth Night* and *Love's Labors Lost*. Erickson notes Prince Hal's sense of guilt toward paternal figures (*Patriarchal Structures*, p. 46), and directly links Henry V to Hamlet in their common dilemma of indebtedness to fathers (pp. 63-72).

[14] I am assuming that the child has perceived the mother's own identification with the father, although in the earliest years of life the mother must have been experienced as the omnipotent and subsuming force. In an adult's unconscious, in varying ways and degrees, father and mother seem likely to have been fused. In a relevant historical context John Demos provides a useful assessment of infantile fantasies about the mother. See *Entertaining Satan* (New York: Oxford University Press, 1982), pp. 200-206.

[15] "Romeo tends to hypostatize feelings. . . . When he does imagine himself in the world rather than 'looking on' [1.4.38], it is usually by picturing himself as an object in space that is 'moved' by external forces. . . . [His] favorite metaphor is the sea-journey, with himself more often the ship than the pilot" (Snow, "Language and Sexual Difference," p. 171).

[16] "When Shakespeare makes Romeo wonder whether death keeps Juliet as his paramour . . . his words are a variation on a common notion" (Spencer, *Death and Elizabethan Tragedy*, p. 77). The "monster" Death is based on conventional imagery of the skeleton (pp. 72-77). In the play as well as in the social world from which it derives, however, that imagery is also profoundly patriarchal.

[17] A fourteenth-century English poem, "Death and Life," makes Death a devouring woman with "a marvelous mouth full of long tushes, / & the neb of her nose to her navell hanged" (quoted in Spencer, *Death and*

Elizabethan Tragedy, p. 29). "Tushes" evoke the boar-as-death in *Venus and Adonis.* The condensation of family relationships in Romeo's fantasy about death prefigures the patterns of incest and intimate strife that shadow the major tragedies and the late romances. The Capulets' monument laden with the bodies of slain suitors may anticipate the opening of *Pericles,* for example, where the palace of the incestuous tyrant Antiochus displays the severed heads of suitors who have failed to release his daughter from his thrall by answering a riddle about a devouring monster.

[18] Cf. also Juliet's vision of lying "o'ercovered" by dead men in a charnel house (4.1.85).

[19] Their own aggression exposed, the fathers behave like patriarchal sons insofar as they compulsively imagine a debt of mourning—cf. Chapters 3 and 4—that their gold statues can pay or expiate.

[20] The criticism of *Romeo and Juliet* readily reveals the compulsion to console for death. In *Coming of Age in Shakespeare* (London: Methuen, 1981) Marjorie Garber vows that "although Juliet will die young, her experiences with love, sex, pain, and loss are enough for a lifetime of adulthood" (p. 37). Cf. this Tennysonian straw ("it is better to have lived and loved than not to have lived at all") with John Lawlor's wishful encomium . . . : "It is essential . . . that we see [Romeo] grow . . . to a final maturity which outsoars all else in the play" (p. 133). Even Coppélia Kahn tries to give the lovers' force of will a quasireligious vitality: "their love-death is not merely fated; it is willed. It is the lovers' triumphant assertion over the impoverished and destructive world that has kept them apart" (Kahn, *Man's Estate,* p. 103).

COMEDIES AND ROMANCES

John A. Hart (essay date 1972)

SOURCE: "Father-Daughter as Device in Shakespeare's Romantic Comedies," in *Carnegie Series in English,* No. 12, 1972, pp. 51-62.

[*In the essay below, Hart assesses the function of the father-daughter device in Shakespeare's romantic comedies and the varied problems that arise from that relationship.*]

Father and daughter relationships recur throughout Shakespeare's romantic comedies. He takes a common and a simple family relationship, recognizable immediately to his audience as emotionally powerful, and suggests variations upon that relationship until he has worked the vein as thoroughly as he can within that genre. He begins with father-daughter as a device for expounding plot in the early comedies, *The Two Gentlemen of Verona, The Taming of the Shrew,* and *A Midsummer Night's Dream;* he develops it as a complicated contrast of ideal positions in *The Merchant of Venice;* and then in the later comedies, *Much Ado About Nothing, As You Like It,* and *Twelfth Night,* he uses it to reflect upon and undercut the positions presented in *The Merchant of Venice.*

In *The Two Gentlemen of Verona* and *The Taming of the Shrew,* father-daughter is purely plot device. In the former, conflict between the two is perfectly clear: the Duke of Milan wants his daughter Silvia to marry Thurio, an unattractive but wealthy suitor. She will have none of him; instead she loves Valentine and follows him into banishment, entirely against her father's wishes. At the end, in as sudden a flip-flop as Shakespeare ever presents, the Duke rejects Thurio as a coward and is completely won over to Silvia's choice. Father and daughter do not confront each other over their differences; the conflict becomes the cause for romantic and dramatic scenes rather than the occasion of them. It thus remains simply a device (one of several) for helping to keep the plot alive.

In *The Taming of the Shrew,* the relationship becomes a kind of framework within which the plot moves. Baptista is firm in his stand that his elder daughter Katherine should be given the chance to marry before her sister Bianca, even though the younger has all the suitors. There is in him a loyalty and a sense of propriety which neither the fractiousness of Kate nor the simpering hypocrisy of Bianca can change. In turn, they feel the authority behind their father's position, however much they chafe under it. The decree of the father is an accepted and unchanged thing upon which the real action of the play—the wooing of the girls—hinges.

At first glance the relationship between Egeus and Hermia in *A Midsummer Night's Dream* seems the same as the Duke of Milan's and Silvia's. Egeus wants his daughter to marry Demetrius; she will have no one but Lysander. But there are many ways in which variation is introduced. Egeus and Hermia face each other before a higher authority, Theseus, where the dispute is presented for decision. In this way the arguments for either side are given context, which they had not had in the earlier play. Egeus' argument is that Lysander has "filched my daughter's heart, Turned her obedience, which is due to me, To stubborn harshness" (I, i, 36-38). He implies some kind of underhandedness, some razzle-dazzle, some magic, which is the source of her behaviour. Hermia's resolution seems equally headlong and foolish. She will sacrifice everything, even her life, if she can not marry Lysander. Their plans for elopement take full account of the romance of a moonlit night and of the trials that true love will inevitably encounter but have no thought at all of her father's feelings or their own position in Athens or the harsh threats just made by Theseus.

Theseus' judgement of the case is more objective, less impassioned than either of these. In essence, he suggests that wise fathers must choose husbands for obedient daughters. When Hermia says, "I would my father looked but with my eyes," he replies, "Rather your eyes must with his judgement look" (I, i, 56-57). And his case is demonstrated by his description of the father-daughter relationship:

> To you your father should be as a god,
> One that composed your beauties—yea, and
> one
> To whom you are but as a form in wax
> By him imprinted and within his power
> To leave the figure or disfigure it.
>   (I, i, 47-51)

In the world of Theseus, which is a world of reason and law, the father is a more reliable selector of a husband for his daughter than she is. The father has concern, love, maturity, and sense to guide him, whereas the daughter has only her emotions, her love, to rely on.

The difficulty of Theseus' position is that it assumes wisdom in the father. It is not clear that Egeus has any such wisdom. The young man he chooses is no better nor worse than the one Hermia chooses. What is emphasized is the likeness, the indistinguishableness, in fact, between them. The family background, the abilities, the confusion, the behavior in the wood—all are comparable. Egeus' superior judgement is not manifest in the way the young men behave.

Yet Hermia's defiant insistence on her own choice in love does not seem much more worthy. In the wood, there are no fathers, there is no reason and law, only imagination, magic, and irrationality; but the madness among the lovers demonstrates that they are not able to choose wisely if left to themselves. Eventually, since they have help from Oberon's magic, and since Theseus, when he finds the lovers happily paired off, overrules Egeus' objections and his own former position, the conflict between father and daughter is muted and disappears. Yet the dream of that conflict lingers, for somewhere underneath all the laughter at Bottom and his company of players lies the unnoticed reminder that this playlet is the story of Pyramus and Thisbe who defy their fathers' wishes and come to grief. The conflict of father and daughter is not resolved, only shunted aside. In the final analysis, it becomes a device for furthering the action, just as Baptista's insistence on the order of his daughter's marrying had been.

With *The Merchant of Venice,* the function of the father-daughter device changes. We find two situations contrasting with one another, both involving the wishes of daughters to marry and the attitudes their fathers have towards those wishes. Because of the contrast, the device may be said to deal not so much with plot as with the essential dramatic structure of the play. For the relationship between each father and daughter determines the nature of the love each girl finds and establishes each love as opposite to the other.

Jessica's break from her father Shylock is much sharper than Hermia's had been in *A Midsummer Night's Dream.* Whereas Hermia and Lysander presumably have tried to persuade Egeus, Jessica's elopement comes like a thunderclap to Shylock. It is with a hated Christian; it is carried out with the help and knowledge of Lorenzo's friends (as Shylock sees it, probably of most of Venice); it involves her masquerading as a boy and attending the same feast her father is attending; it includes taking as many valuables from her father as she can carry. The whole incident is a monstrous insult to him, treated light-heartedly by Lorenzo and as a great joke by his friends. For the most part, Jessica echoes this cavalier attitude, yet her shame at dressing as a boy may carry with it some residue of uneasiness at the way she is treating her father. Two statements, the first words we hear her speak and her last words in her father's house suggest some possible shades of remorse or at least regret. The first of these seems like an irrelevant comment to Launcelot Gobbo: "I am sorry thou wilt leave my father so" (II, iii, 1). She is more interested in the life the young servant provides around the house than she is concerned for her father's loneliness; but it suggests a dimension of her thought, for she is already making her own plans to leave. The other statement is a repetition of her father's final words to her. He has said, " . . . shut doors after you. Fast bind, fast find" (II, v, 53-54), words which she echoes as she leaves the house: "I will make fast the doors, and gild myself With some more ducats, and be with you straight" (II, vi, 49-50). The mixture of obedience and defiance suggests at least a little confusion on her part.

We must not overdo her concern for her father. But we can justly consider what her elopement means to him. He is so isolated from Jessica, so unlike her in nature and feeling, so little aware of her as a person, that we tend to feel that he deserves the heartache her elopement brings to him. Yet the lack of concern arises simply from his complete conviction that she is the girl he thinks her to be. When he speaks his foreboding to her, when he orders her to "Lock up my doors . . . Let not the sound of shallow foppery enter My sober house" (II, v, 29, 35-36), he is expressing an attitude towards the Venetians which he expects her to share. Whatever we read into their relationship, whether Shylock is to be considered villain or persecuted alien, the failure of understanding and feeling between father and daughter, except at some uncommunicable and unrealized level, stands out. And the fact of this failure helps to define the nature of the love between Lorenzo and Jessica as we observe it in Belmont later on.

When Bassanio and Gratiano and later Portia and Nerissa rush away to Venice, Lorenzo and Jessica are left in charge in Belmont. "Lorenzo," Portia says,

> I commit into your hands
> The husbandry and manage of my house
> Until my lord's return.
>
> (III, iv, 24-26)

The husbandry and manage of the house are very undemanding. Lorenzo orders dinner and music, contemplates going inside to greet the returning owners ceremoniously, and then gives up the idea and remains out in the night with Jessica; that is complete inventory of his "manage of the house." Yet his jesting chatter with Launcelot Gobbo and the love-talk with Jessica are significant pointers to the kind of love he knows, although they are not essential to the action. Launcelot is brazen and outspoken in his jests. He delays the serving of dinner; he makes a joking accusation that Jessica ought not to have become a Christian because it "will raise the price of hogs" (III, v, 26); he dismisses with a flip remark the counter accusation of Lorenzo that he is guilty of "getting-up of the Negro's belly" (III, v, 41-42). In the midst of these jests there is an aura of permissiveness, of carelessness between master and servant, which in turn suggests little interest or talent for the "manage of the house."

In fact, Lorenzo and Jessica are completely absorbed in each other. In the outdoors of Belmont they reveal their love in several ways. They have a kinship with great lovers of the past; their understanding enables them to give a choral response when they speak of the beautiful night; they use language for play rather than for serious communication, mockingly accusing each other of faithlessness; they are mutually able to reach out to feel the harmony of the music of the spheres and to feel the rightness of themselves in relation to the music of the musicians. Private understanding, beauty, music, harmony: these are the qualities which define the kind of love Lorenzo and Jessica experience. Any man who has no music in himself is not to be trusted. Yet their love has its limitations. The lovers whose names are so beautifully dropped by them—Troilus and Cressida, Pyramus and Thisbe, Aeneas and Dido, Jason and Medea—are finally tragic lovers, having rebelled in one way or another against parents or society or the state or all three. And the love of Lorenzo and Jessica is carefully kept out of any social context. They simply yield authority to Bassanio and Portia, content to live in their own dream, scarcely aware of the strange, alienated, obsessed father with whom we as audience have had so much to do. Their love has become a love of a special and ideal kind.

The love between Bassanio and Portia stands in complete contrast. There are very formal and strict requirements imposed by Portia's father for wooing her. And although her father is dead, she accepts the conditions and will abide by them: "If I live to be as old as Sibylla, I will die as chaste as Diana unless I be obtained by the manner of my father's will" (I, ii, 116-118). She seems to run a great risk in keeping her resolution. A whole catalogue of silly suitors makes itself available to her; and although they will not all go through with the conditions necessary for choosing, two suitors try to choose correctly and fail. Both suitors—Morocco and Arragon—are unacceptable to Portia, as we learn from her relief at their failure. But it is clear that she means to abide by the terms given; if the "wrong" man chooses correctly, he wins.

At the same time, the means are perfectly safe. Portia's father, setting these bonds on her at his death, knows exactly what he is doing. The man who chooses the lead casket will possess the qualities which are perfect for her and he will be the kind of man whom she will love, will always have loved. When Theseus pronounces to Hermia the words, "Rather your eyes must with his judgement look" he is in fact saying what Portia enacts. Though her father has died, though she has committed herself to conditions which theoretically endanger her happiness, yet her father's judgment is certain and trustworthy. The risk is great but Portia lives by it and triumphs.

She has won what Jessica has abandoned: social context for her relationship with her husband. This contrast between the girls is reinforced upon Portia's return to Belmont in Act V. Jessica is bathing in the beauty of the moonlight, she is enthralled by the music she hears. For Portia, however, reactions to moon and music are opposite to this. When she enters, the moon has gone; what is apparent to her is the little candle burning in her hall. Furthermore, she regards the music as sweet but not necessarily as always so: "Nothing is good, I see, without respect. . . . How many things by season seasoned are To their right praise and true perfection!" (V, i, 99, 107-108). If she is good and right, then the music is fine; but it does not depend on whether she has music in herself. It was like that when Bassanio was choosing: music did not determine but depended on his choice.

> Let music sound while he doth make his
>   choice,
> Then, if he lose, he makes a swanlike end,
> Fading in music. . . .   He may win,
> And what is music then? Then music is
> Even as the flourish when true subjects bow
> To a new-crowned monarch.
>
> (III, ii, 43-45, 47-50)

She turns off the moon by entering; she stops the music that has been enchanting Lorenzo and Jessica. All actions turn toward her, seem almost to depend on her. She becomes again the center of the Belmont world and all things are subordinated to her and to her command. So the public Portia regains her husband and he his public reward.

Yet she and Bassanio lack the private understanding and intimacy exhibited so clearly by Lorenzo and Jessica. To Bassanio, she has always been the public Portia. When he first describes her to Antonio, it is Portia the valued prize he is thinking of:

> her sunny locks
> Hang on her temples like a golden fleece,
> Which makes her seat of Belmont Colchos'
>   strond,
> And many Jasons come in quest of her.
>   (I, i, 169-172)

He knows how to win her, by ignoring "ornament" and considering the inner qualities of the caskets; but when he wins her, it is the beauteous exterior which he is aware of, the "official" Portia. He admires the perfection of the picture he finds in the lead casket but finds that "this shadow Doth limp behind the substance" (III, ii, 129-130), that is, Portia herself. Though she is seen by Bassanio in this way, Portia is far from being mere facade. We hear her shrewd and witty comments on her suitors, we feel excitement at the approach of Bassanio and her dismay at the thought that he might choose incorrectly, we understand her attempt to communicate a sense of her girlhood and her inexperience to him:

> But the full sum of me
> Is sum of something which, to term in gross,
> Is an unlessoned girl, unschooled,
>   unpracticed,
> Happy in this, she is not yet so old
> But she may learn. Happier than this,
> She is not bred so dull but she can learn.
>   (III, ii, 159-164)

The latter part of the play demonstrates that he does not know her in the way Lorenzo knows Jessica. When she appears as a lawyer in the court of Venice, there is no recognition at all, nor afterwards when he gives her ring to the lawyer. In fact, the whole episode of the rings reinforces this. Though the end of the story deals amusingly with the problem, both Bassanio and Portia realize that he is able to recognize the Lady of Belmont but not the girl he married. The potential is there, we know. Portia has revealed herself to be a charming and fascinating woman; Bassanio, by the wisdom he shows in choosing the least ornamental casket, has demonstrated his capacity to look beyond the surface. He simply has not yet had the time to get to know her well.

Thus, each pair of lovers suggests a different kind of love. Portia and Bassanio are perfect in their social compatibility, Jessica and Lorenzo are perfect in their intimacy and understanding. In the context of the play, both love relationships arise out of the relationships of the daughter with the father. Shylock, defied by Jessica, makes impossible a love which is socially responsible; the love of Lorenzo and Jessica must be built on their own intimacy and understanding. The Duke, obeyed by Portia, makes possible a love which is publicly and socially responsible; but the love which Bassanio and Portia have has not yet had time to achieve intimacy and understanding. Each love seems an ideal, a kind of perfection of what it is, but limited to what it is.

Yet Shakespeare asks us to pause as he puts forward the father and daughter of *Much Ado About Nothing;* and he does this in two ways, one of these incidental and digressive and the other basic to the play. First of all, in a way which is incidental and causal and obviously a mistake or an earlier version or the fault of the printers, he makes us consider the absence of mothers in these plays. He raises the question which no one has ever been able to answer: whatever happened to Innogen?

She is advertised as entering with her husband Leonato and his household at the beginning of *Much Ado About Nothing;* she is also said to appear at the beginning of Act II with her husband and others among her family and guests. She is never given a line to say; she is never spoken to by any of the characters; she is never spoken about by any of them either. Occasions arise in the course of the action which might well demand her attention: her daughter Hero is wooed by a highly eligible Claudio; their marriage is arranged with the dispatch of a young man who knows what he wants; the bride is dressed for the church ceremony (will ever a mother be kept silent on such an occasion?); Hero is then denounced in public as faithless by her intended and falls into a faint, only to be denounced further by her father when she returns to consciousness. On any or all of these occasions, a mother would attend to and probably support her daughter in her joys and sorrows. But Innogen is nowhere to be found. Editors in shame and embarrassment have relegated her to a couple of footnotes and they uniformly mumble that Shakespeare left her out of the final version of the play but forgot to strike her name from the stage directions.

And indeed it may be so. For we can imagine the impulses which prompted Shakespeare both to put in a wife to Leonato and to take out a mother to Hero. For Leonato, so deferential in his behavior toward outside authority as it is represented in Don Pedro, is commanding where he can be in his family. His niece Beatrice he can control very little, nor does he show much inclination to try. But his daughter Hero he will direct and order about, for her own good, naturally:

> Daughter, remember what I told you. If the
>   Prince do solicit
> you in that kind, you know your answer.
>   (II, i, 69-71)

His role as petty tyrant would be reinforced and supported by having a timid, quiet, subservient wife. It would suggest that his word was law within his immediate family, however reliant he was on others' opinion outside that family.

But such reinforcement would not do much for the relationship between Innogen and Hero. The scene at the church would be even more awkward than it is, if both father and mother rejected their child. It is one thing to have the foolish Leonato side with the Prince against his daughter and accuse her of loose behavior. But it would be quite another to have her mother, either out of fear of Leonato or out of a comparable lack of trust in Hero, join in the accusation. And if she sided with her daughter against her husband, the picture of the happy little family doing Leonato's every bidding would be destroyed. On some such grounds, the character of Innogen may have been abandoned.

And in fact, the conceivable functions she might have in the play have been filled by other characters. Where Leonato needs support in his foolishness, it is supplied by the old man Antonio, his brother, who can be a confidant and a strong backer of Leonato's and at the same time intensify the tendencies toward folly exhibited by Leonato. He is the first to announce to his brother the Prince's plan to woo Hero; he behaves foolishly during the dance, trying to conceal his identity while Ursula mocks his age; after the church scene he appears to comfort his brother and then to outchallenge him in the quarrel with Pedro and Claudio. As part of the final reconciliation, he plays the father of a child much like Hero, who is to become Claudio's bride instead. Antonio provides support for Leonato such as Innogen might give, but he offers a dimension of humor that would not be appropriate in her.

The other function imagined for her, that of supporting her daughter when she is slandered, is more than made up for by Beatrice and the Friar. Beatrice has from the beginning established her own independence of her uncle Leonato. She would never think of marrying on his mere recommendation and she tries to persuade her cousin to be as free in her choosing. Though she is courteous and mannerly, her basic choices are going to be her own. It is easy, then, for her to insist on Hero's innocence and to utter her indignation at the accusations made by Claudio and Pedro. She does not accuse her uncle of being a dupe for believing Claudio and

not Hero; she is silent through most of the accusation scene. But her belief in Hero is never shaken and her fury at the accusers is unbounded. She is so powerful a spokesman that she needs no other character to express injustice; and Innogen's expression of the same position might be complicated by the loyalty expected toward her husband, which could in effect cause her to be silent.

The Friar also is important in clearing Hero's name and regaining her father's respect for her. He thinks of the device of declaring Hero dead, which is supposed to soften her accusers (and doesn't), but far more importantly he represents a voice to which Leonato can attend. Leonato, being the man that he is, needs to rely on an outside authority to do his thinking for him. He falls in with Pedro's proposal of Claudio as husband for Hero; he believes the accusation which Claudio makes against his daughter; and now Friar Francis persuades him of the innocence of his daughter, a conclusion which he would have difficulty coming to by himself. To imagine Innogen performing such a function would be to reconceive the kind of character Leonato is and to inject into the play a complicated marital problem that might well overshadow the rest of the action.

By positing the dramatic functions that might be performed by Innogen and by seeing how much more satisfactorily they have been taken care of by characters already in the play, we can see why Innogen seems to have been dropped from the play by Shakespeare. But the dropping of Innogen reinforces the use of the father-daughter device in the other romantic comedies I have discussed. The conflict between the "wise" father and the "emotional" daughter is simply and straightforwardly presented in each of them without the inevitable complications which a mother would introduce. And the very simplicity of the device makes it possible to resolve the conflict in a number of different, satisfactory, comic ways, culminating in the two detailed instances of *The Merchant of Venice*. Having made the Duke and his daughter Portia emerge as triumphant instances of a happy combination of father and daughter, Shakespeare proceeds to render their success ideal and improbable by the relationship suggested in the next three romantic comedies—*Much Ado About Nothing, As You Like It,* and *Twelfth Night.*

What happens, for instance, if you have a daughter who is a model from her father's point of view, only the father lacks the wisdom of a Duke of Belmont? What happens is what we find in the qualities and relationship of Leonato and Hero in *Much Ado About Nothing.*

Leonato is interested in providing for his daughter's future, but he has no such wisdom as the Duke of Belmont. He can look for a suitable son-in-law among the titled, among the favorites of the titled, among the exteriorly attractive; but he knows nothing about the interior qualities and he lacks any means of finding out. He will rejoice if Don Pedro, Prince of Arragon, is rumored seeking his daughter's hand; but he will be if it is Claudio, the Prince's protege, instead. He expects and finds an obedient response from his daughter, Hero; and she is just as compliant as ever Portia is. But the deep feeling Portia has for Bassanio is missing. She makes no protest when her father mistakenly prepares her for Pedro's wooing; she exhibits none of Portia's excitement when she accepts Claudio (although she is described as whispering in his ear); she agrees to re-accept Claudio after he has so shamefully disgraced her. There is a passivity in Hero that is a reduction to absurdity of Portia's loyalty to her father; there is a fawning before authority in Leonato that suggests that not every father has the judgment to decide properly for his daughter. The whole argument for wise fathers that had been demonstrated brilliantly in *The Merchant of Venice* comes crashing down in *Much Ado About Nothing*. In a world where facade means everything, where feeling is only tentatively and timidly present, the father and daughter roles can lead to tragedy and disgrace. The scene in the church epitomizes their pitiful dilemma. Hero, whose private feelings are either absent or never known, is condemned publicly as unfaithful by her lover. Leonato, who has placed so much reliance on the infallibility of the great Pedro and the youthful Claudio, can only join in their condemnation. Both father and daughter are helpless before the mistake, and they must be rescued by others with more resources than they. Leonato and Hero represent the bankruptcy of the "wise" father and the "obedient" daughter.

Beatrice has no father and is far better off for it. She and Benedick have a private feeling for each other which must be reconciled to their public selves by the agency of Pedro's plot to bring them together. In a sense, they are like Jessica and Lorenzo but they have no father to consider.

Rosalind and Orlando in *As You Like It* are rather like this too. Rosalind has a father for whom she mourns, when she is in Frederick's court. But when she is in the Forest of Arden, the whole world changes for everyone. She becomes not Rosalind but Ganymede playing Rosalind, and Ganymede has no father. She and Orlando can articulate private love games at their leisure, as earlier private lovers could not. Lorenzo and Jessica have their moment, but they must yield to Bassanio and Portia; Benedick and Beatrice scarcely can admit even to each other the depth of their feeling, for depth of feeling is a subject for mockery in the world of *Much Ado About Nothing*. But in a world where there is no clock and there are no jobs or duties, and the fool is not a fool but a courtier and a lover, and the Duke is without a dukedom, and there is no

possession, and the world ages with the deliberate slowness of Nature's moving, in such a world, love can be free and delightful and playful and serene. And fathers (both Rosalind's and Celia's) are forgotten about until the end when reunion takes place and seriousness in life and love resumes its role and the father and his daughter and her husband all prepare to leave the Forest.

Thus, after the triumph of the father in the Belmont world of *The Merchant of Venice,* he is given his comeuppance in the next two plays. The last of the romantic comedies, *Twelfth Night,* removes fathers altogether. Olivia's has died over a year before and Viola's long ago. The chief quality of Illyria is instability, whether from over-emotionalism (like the Duke's) or pleasure-seeking (like Sir Toby's), or puffed-up ambition (like Malvolio's). Both Olivia and Viola share in this instability, Olivia by falling in love with a girl dressed as a boy and marrying that girl's twin without knowing any better, Viola by falling in love with a Duke who doesn't know how he feels or who his love is. A steadying hand is absent. Toby, who is "consanguineous" to Olivia, assumes neither responsibility nor concern for Olivia's future, so busy is he about his fooling and his drinking; Malvolio, who would like to assume both responsibility and sovereignty, lacks the respect of anyone in Olivia's household, though he has her affection. The implication is that a wise father would have made a difference for both daughters, and that his absence places a greater burden on fortuitous circumstances to produce a happy ending.

The romantic comedies have other relationships which are explored in some such sequence—ruler and subject, master and servant, wise fool and foolish wit— but none with more delicate balance than the device of father and daughter and the varied problems arising from that relationship.

Charles Frey (essay date 1978)

SOURCE: "Shakespeare's Imperiled and Chastening Daughters of Romance," in *South Atlantic Bulletin,* Vol. XLIII, No. 4, November, 1978, pp. 125-40.

[*In the essay below, Frey examines the complex and timeless responses of daughters to familial pressures.*]

Shakespeare's plays often open with generational conflicts that point up distressing consequences of patriarchy: fathers and husbands treating children and wives as mere property or appurtenances of themselves (for example, Duke of Milan in *The Two Gentlemen of Verona,* Egeus in *A Midsummer Night's Dream,* fathers and husbands in *The Taming of the Shrew* and *The Merry Wives of Windsor,* the Capulets, Lear, Brabantio), children greedy for patrimony (Oliver in *As You Like It,* various characters in the Histories, and in *Lear* Edmund, Goneril, and Regan), or "lovers" greedy for dowry (suitors of Kate, and Portia, and Anne Fenton, Angelo in *Measure for Measure,* Burgundy in *Lear*). The elder generation often adheres, moreover, to a code of revenge or war in which it seeks to over-involve the younger generation (*Titus Andronicus, Romeo and Juliet, I Henry IV, Hamlet, Lear*), so that the procreative process becomes interrupted by misdefinitions of roles or unfortunate expectations of family loyalty and "inheritance." Sons, in particular, become tragic losers in this patriarchal overdetermin-ation of loyalties, because they are, typically, used up in fighting feuds of their fathers; the desire for primogenitural progeny becomes thwarted when the male line is forfeited in parental wars. The particular conflict between values of war (or protection of fam-ily) and love (or extension of family) shows up most clearly in tragedies such as *Romeo and Juliet* and *Hamlet.* In *Lear, Othello,* and *Macbeth,* plays shot through with sexual and familial confusion and unwholesomeness, we see the impotence of an authori-tarian, martial, aggressive, hierarchical male to enter reciprocal, fruitful relations with women or to foster life or line.

Given such often-disastrous results generated by the sys-tem of near-absolute male authority, a major issue in Shakespeare's plays often becomes: What part may women play simply to survive, and then, beyond that, what part may women play to right at least some of the wrongs of patriarchy? In what follows, I shall examine Shakespeare's evolving depictions of daughters' responses to the familial pressures outlined here. I shall consider particularly the plights and flights of daughters in Shakespeare's later plays, daughters who respond to ex-pectations of love and matrimony in surprisingly contra-dictory, complex, and modern, or perhaps timeless, ways.

To say, initially, that Shakespeare's women are to some degree victims of patriarchy is not to say that, among the range of Shakespeare's characters, one finds a dearth of spirited, sensitive, knowing, remarkably impressive women; one has but to think of Rosalind or Beatrice or Viola or Helena, or of Cordelia, Cleopatra, and Imogen. Such women manage to assert themselves, however *in spite* of the odds against them, as heroic exceptions to the more general rule of depressing male domination. Think of how often and how keenly Shakespeare con-centrates, to take the most significant theme, upon the perversity of fathers' claims to direct their daughters' destinies in marriage. We hear throughout the plays of proprietary acts and attitudes taken by fathers in re-gard to or rather disregard of their daughters:

> I beg the ancient privilege of Athens:
> As she is mine, I may dispose of her;
> Which shall be either to this gentleman,
> Or to her death. . . .
>
> (*MND* 1.1.41)

> A' Thursday let it be—a' Thursday, tell her,
> She shall be married to this noble earl.
> Will you be ready? do you like this haste?
>
> (*Rom.* 3.4.20)

> This is for all:
> I would not, in plain terms, from this time
> forth
> Have you so slander any moment leisure
> As to give words or talk with the Lord
> Hamlet.
> Look to 't, I charge you. Come your ways.
>
> (*Ham.* 1.3.131)

> Thou must to thy father, and be gone from
> Troilus.[1]
>
> (*Tro.* 4.2.91)

To the father's combined claims of legal and emo-tional interest in the daughter's marriage choice, the Elizabethans were, obviously, well-attuned. So intense, moreover, is the emotional investment of Shake-speare's fathers in their daughters' love that the thwarting of the fathers' expectations often brings forth imprecations and diatribes of surpassing bitter-ness:

> I would my daughter were dead at my foot,
> and the jewels in her ear!
>
> (*MV* 3.1.87)

> Do not live, Hero, do not ope thine eyes,
> For did I think thou wouldst not quickly die,
> Thought I thy spirits were stronger than thy
> shames,
> Myself would, on the rearward of reproaches,
> Strike at thy life.
>
> (*Ado.* 4.1.123)

> Look to't, think on't, I do not use to jest.
> Thursday is near, lay hand on heart, advise.
> And you be mine, I'll give you to my friend;
> And you be not, hang, beg, starve, die in the
> streets,
> For, by my soul, I'll ne'er acknowledge thee,
> Nor what is mine shall never do thee good.
>
> (*Rom.* 3.5.189)

> The barbarous Scythian,
> Or he that makes his generation messes
> To gorge his appetite, shall to my bosom
> Be as well neighbor'd, pitied, and reliev'd,
> As thou my sometime daughter.
>
> (*Lr.* 1.1.116)

Examples of such bitterness could be multiplied from other plays, and such multiplication would merely serve to support one's natural response and question: Why? Why do Shakespeare's fathers often hate their daughters so ambitiously, with a hate that borders on disintegration and madness? Part of the answer lies, no doubt, in the special relations between father and only or best-loved daughter. More important, I submit, is the concomitant absence, at least in the plays quoted above, of any sons.

Some of the fathers mention their reliance upon their daughters for comfort and security in old age. Thus the Duke in *The Two Gentlemen of Verona* says: "I thought the remnant of mine age / Should have been cherish'd by her child-like duty" (3.1.74), and Lear says, "I lov'd her most, and thought to set my rest / On her kind nursery" (1.1.123). Such considerations—of emotional and economic security and of political control and generational extension of line—help to dictate the father's interest in choice of the daughter's marriage partner. An absence of any sons not only may make plain the father's need for the daughter's support and thus for a congenial son-in-law, it also may turn the son-in-law into substitute son, the inheritor of family power and values. When the daughter chooses radically against her father's will, she effectively shuts him off from patriarchal domination of the son-in-law and consequent son-like extension of his power and values. In the earlier comedies, the daughter's choice does not really extend beyond the father's range. Who can tell a Lysander from a Demetrius? When the choice does extend vastly beyond the father's range, as in the case of Jessica and Shylock, the results, for the father at least, are tragic.

In the earlier comedies, the society with which we are presented at the opening does not need fundamental revision, and the daughter's choice of a partner, even if against her father's will, serves eventually to confirm existing values. In tragedies such as *Romeo and Juliet, Othello,* and *Lear,* where the order existing at the outset is often superficial, narrow, or grown archaic, the daughter marries far beyond her father's range, marries someone who challenges his sociopolitical security. Romeo's family is the age-old enemy of Juliet's family; Brabantio finds Othello repugnant as a son-in-law; France is inevitably under suspicion as rival or enemy of Lear's England, which he indeed invades later in the play. Fathers such as Capulet (though he may be on the brink of giving up the feud), Brabantio, and Lear cannot or will not think to extend their lines, given these special circumstances, through their daughters. Yet they have little alternative. Dreams they might have of patrilineal extension are shattered by their daughters' choice of marriage partners. Their resultant rage may be better understood in this light, as may its terrible consequences.

Terrible as the consequences are in terms of individual deaths, the revolts in the tragedies of daughters against their fathers' wills become essential elements in the whole process of loss and at least partial redemption that marks the tragic catharsis.[2] In Shakespeare's tragedies, as in his comedies, a daughter who defines herself *against* her father, who takes a husband, as it were, in spite of him, usually becomes associated with regenerative forces and outcomes. Where the problem, or part of it, is to break the death-dealing feud or prejudice of the father, the daughter manages to help, but in the tragedies she helps in a way that costs very dearly. Viewed in the most basic terms of patriarchal expectations, tragedies such as *Romeo and Juliet* and *Hamlet* portray fathers who employ sons to carry on their concerns, to enforce their continuing image in patrilineal succession but also to fight in the fathers' feuds. Where sons are denied to such patriarchal fathers, they may become resentful or seek substitutes. Macbeth may be analyzed usefully from this perspective. Macbeth, whose ambition to be king is threatened by Duncan's election of his son as successor, does manage to become king, but he himself has no son and remains threatened not only by Malcolm but by Banquo's line, prophesied to succeed to the throne. Macbeth becomes cast in the role of one who kills the sons of others. Unable to reach Malcolm, he attempts through hired killers to murder Banquo's son (as well as Banquo) and almost succeeds. His killers do kill, onstage, Macduff's son, and, finally, we see Macbeth himself hack down, near the end of the play, Siward's son, "Young Siward." The most significant fact about Macduff, who at last kills Macbeth, is that Macduff is "not of woman born," as if only such a person could get around Macbeth's malevolence against issue. Lear, too, has no son, but our first glimpse of him is in the act of arranging to acquire appropriate sons-in-law. He thinks to extend his line through daughters. Two of them, however, turn out to be his enemies, and the third marries France who becomes Britain's enemy, albeit in a war of "liberation." Still, as in *Romeo and Juliet,* the daughter's choice of a husband who is independent of her father's influence proves a catalyst, though a bitter one, for the changes necessary to a revitalization of the home society. Thus the tragedies rather insistently criticize the patriarch's attempt to manipulate sons or sons-in-law for his own interest.

In the Romances, these themes intensify. Here problems of sons as tragic victims of their fathers' feuds are largely eliminated (save, possibly, for the example of Mamillius in *The Winter's Tale*). In *Pericles, Cymbeline, Winter's Tale,* and *Tempest,* such sons are non-existent, lost, or killed, and only daughters are looked to for continuation of the central family. Pericles, Cymbeline, Leontes, and Prospero all have enmities in which they could tragically involve any sons of theirs, but when each such son appears to be eliminated (together with the wives of the fathers), then the relation between each father and his sole daughter becomes central. The function of each daughter is not to represent, as a son might, the father in the father's battles but rather to leave home, travel widely, perhaps marry the son of her father's chief enemy (as in *Winter's Tale* and *Tempest*), and return home to instill virtues of forgiveness and the lesson of pardon in the father. The solution for patriarchal overcontrol and quasi-incestuous inwardness thus seems to be a dramatic destruction of the progenitive center and an explosion outward through time and space that leads to regroupings at the end and visions of a wide incorporative harmony.

It seems apparent that Shakespeare in these four Romances celebrates a view of women as protectors and givers of life in a very special sense. Daughters such as Imogen, Perdita, and Miranda not only marry in ways that heal enmities but also they prove their love viable in settings that harbor lustful or permissive appetites, that is, they encounter in "nature" a rapacious Cloten or Caliban or a bawdy Autolycus but they remain chaste and eventually chasten the appetites of their true lovers. Marina, of course, chastens even the brothel. Often we see these daughters, moreover, rising from sleep and seeming death, as if to prove their miraculous power to awaken fresh life.

In all the Romances (as in other Shakespearean plays), lesser characters may be seen as representing in part components within the psyche of a central character. Each father—Pericles, Cymbeline, Leontes, Prospero—works out his emotional maturation partly through recognition of his daughter as she embodies life's powers to renew itself rhythmically and human powers to order and delay acting upon desires that else might confuse and blight themselves. Recognition of this sort is not easily won, however, and the Romances are notable for their repeated images of fathers trying to dominate their daughters as well as to learn from them. In *Pericles,* Antiochus commits incest with his daughter. Cymbeline berates Imogen and orders her locked in her chamber. Prospero admonishes Miranda to listen and to obey. In the instant before recognizing his daughter, Pericles pushes her back. Leontes, too, makes menacing gestures at the infant Perdita whom he denies is his, and later, still not knowing her, he makes in her direction a kind of romantic overture (5.1.223). All of the Romance fathers and daughters passionately interact, and it may be that dynamic which helps necessitate in psychic terms the far journey of each daughter away from home and her taking a husband in each case so clearly set apart from her father.

Despite these apparently happy solutions to problems of patriarchal domination, and though the Romance have witnessed in our supposedly liberated age a mounting tide of enthusiasm, they may be more patriarchal and patrilineal in perspective than Shakespearean interpreters have yet cared or dared to recognize. To ask the following question is to ask, in some respects, how many children had Lady Macbeth, but still: Is not the engendering of a daughter in each Romance taken implicitly as a guilty act which signals the impotence of the father or his receipt of divine displeasure? Else why should he have lost or in the course of the play lose wife and any sons he may have had? Kings need sons. When they produce daughters, in a patrilineal society, they do less than the optimum to further a secure succession. When their sons die or they produce a daughter or daughters alone, they become as vulnerable as Henry the Eighth who says, according to Shakespeare (2.4.187):

> First, methought
> I stood not in the smile of heaven, who had
> Commanded nature, that my lady's womb,
> If it conceiv'd a male-child by me, should
> Do no more offices of life to't than
> The grave does to th' dead; for her male issue
> Or died where they were made, or shortly
>   after
> This world had air'd them. Hence I took a
>   thought
> This was a judgment on me, that my kingdom
> (Well worthy the best heir o' th' world)
>   should not
> Be gladded in't by me. Then follows, that
> I weigh'd the danger which my realms stood in
> By this my issue's fail, and that gave to me
> Many a groaning throe.

In *Pericles, Cymbeline, Winter's Tale,* and *Tempest,* each leader of the state is threatened with like "issue's fail." The plays might seem to strike at patriarchal chains when they take up the device of extending a family not through sons but through a daughter's adventure in finding a son-in-law. Through this infusion of fresh male blood, the plays seem to say, a king can more truly revitalize his kingdom. And, given the English experience with Henry the Eighth and his children, the pattern of the saving daughter might well be regarded as much more than an anomolous and irrelevant residue of folktale origins of the Romances. Shakespeare could be saying, in the style of Lear's Edmund, "Now, gods, stand up for daughters!" Still, assuming that Shakespeare (who himself lost a son and, judging from the terms of his Will, looked wistfully to his daughters for continuance of his line) has raised in the Romances a kind or argument for daughters otherwise demeaned by patriarchalism, are not the daughters exalted more as potential wives and father-comforters than as persons in their own right? Marina, Imogen, Perdita, and Miranda are, to be sure, spirited and, at times, independent. Consider Marina speaking to Boult in the bawdy-house:

> Thou art the damned dook-keeper to every
> Custrel that comes inquiring for his Tib.
> To the choleric fisting of every rogue
> Thy ear is liable; thy food is such
> As hath been belch'd on by infected lungs.
> *(Per.* 4.6.165)

Or Imogen speaking of Posthumus and Cloten:

> I would they were in Afric both together,
> Myself by with a needle, that I might prick
> The goer-back.
>
> (*Cym.* 1.1.167)

Or Perdita:

> I was about to speak, and tell him plainly
> The self-same sun that shines upon his court
> Hides not his visage from our cottage, but
> Looks on alike. Will't please you, sir, be
>   gone?
> I told you what would come of this.
>
> (*WT* 4.4.443)

Or Miranda: calling Caliban "abhorred slave" to his face, breaking her father's command that she not tell her name to Ferdinand, and accusing Ferdinand of false play at chess. Despite such displays, however, the chief *function* of the daughter in each Romance is to bring home a husband and to teach or permit her father a new found love and forgiveness made possible and believable amid the restored patriarchal security. At the end of each Romance, the daughter's father explicitly rejoices over the presence of his son-in-law. Pericles says to his wife: "Thaisa, / This prince, the fair-betrothed of your daughter, / Shall marry her at Pentapolis" (5.3.70). Cymbeline says: "We'll learn our freeness of a son-in-law: / Pardon's the word to all" (5.5.421). Leontes' last act is to introduce Florizel to Hermione: "This' your son-in-law, / And son unto the King, whom heavens directing / Is troth-plight to your daughter" (5.3.149). Prospero tells Alonso of his "hope to see the nuptial / Of these our dear-belov'd solemnized" (5.1.309).

In terms of what their worlds and plays obviously expect of them, Shakespeare's daughters of Romance have done well, and Shakespeare has, in a sense, "solved" problems of over-controlling fathers and over-rebellious daughters that appeared in tragedies such as *Romeo and Juliet, Othello,* and *Lear*. In place of patrilineal succession, we have a new procreative process in which direct male issue are bypassed—perhaps as too competitive, aggressive, promiscuous, or death-dealing—in favor of virginal daughters who promise to win reinvigoration of the family through outside stock which is now more readily accepted by the fathers than it was before. The daughters themselves, however, are hardly permitted the alternative of *not* choosing a mate. To do so would be unthinkable. They must take mates to save and extend the families of their fathers, their fathers who remain so much in evidence. After working out this "solution" in the Romances, Shakespeare went on, nonetheless, to consider the matter further (as was his custom) and even to question the solution.

In *Henry VIII*, we find the familiar Romance patterns of ostracized queen, restorative daughter, and great hopes for the younger generation, but now the daughter, Elizabeth, becomes exalted in virginal radiance (5.4.32):

> Good grows with her;
> In her days every man shall eat in safety
> Under his own vine what he plants, and sing
> The merry songs of peace to all his neighbors.
> God shall be truly known, and those about her
> From her shall read the perfect ways of honor,
> And by those claim their greatness, not by
>   blood.
> Nor shall this peace sleep with her; but as
>   when
> The bird of wonder dies, the maiden phoenix,
> Her ashes new create another heir
> As great in admiration as herself,
> So shall she leave her blessedness to one
> (When heaven shall call her from this cloud
>   of darkness)
> Who from the sacred ashes of her honor
> Shall star-like rise as great in fame as she
>   was,
> And so stand fix'd.

If we compare Elizabeth to the heroines of the preceding four Romances, we find that the Romance pattern is transcended. Though the father's search for male issue remains important, is never more important than here, the daughter need now elect no husband to fulfill her function. She becomes herself a "pattern to all princes," and this, it seems stressed, is "not by blood" but by "honor," meaning, among other things, her sexual purity. Cranmer continues (5.4.59):

> Would I had known no more! but she must
>   die,
> She must, the saints must have her; yet a
>   virgin,
> A most unspotted lily shall she pass
> To the ground, and all the world shall mourn
>   her.

Praise of woman beyond or even in opposition to the supposed virtues of marriage and childbearing seems to be Shakespeare's purpose not only in his depiction of Elizabeth but also in his treatment of Katherine in *Henry VIII*. Katherine, who "failed" to give Henry the male issue he so desperately wanted, follows the lead of Buckingham and Wolsey by converting her secular fall into spiritual ascent. On her sickbed, she learns to forgive Wolsey; mediatating on "celestial harmony," she falls asleep and sees a heavenly vision that promises "eternal happiness." She asks that, when she is dead, she be used with "honor" and strewn with "maiden flowers." All this fits the general tenor of the play as it suggests the vanity of earthly pageantries, the paltriness of bodily appetites, and the insufficiency of love's whole enterprise. Reminiscent of *The Tempest*, and reaching perhaps beyond, is the strange power of *Henry VIII* to associate bodily and earthly life, especially in the getting of children, as somehow inconsequential, even petty. In its revelation of brave but diaphanous masques, of vain attempts to solidify the stage and state of earthly shows, the play is like a great finger pointing heavenward. Miranda's admirable chastity evolves toward Elizabeth's sacred virginity.

In *The Two Noble Kinsmen,* Shakespeare makes his heroine, from the outset, one of Diana's great devotees.[3] Emilia describes her affection for a childhood companion in these terms (1.3.66):

> The flow'r that I would pluck
> And put between my breasts (O then but beginning
> To swell about the blossom), she would long
> Till she had such another, and commit it
> To the like innocent cradle, where phoenix-like
> They died in perfume. On my head no toy
> But was her pattern, her affections (pretty,
> Though happily her careless wear) I followed
> For my most serious decking. Had mine ear
> Stol'n some new air, or at adventure humm'd one
> From musical coinage, why it was a note
> Whereon her spirits would sojourn (rather dwell on)
> And sing it in her slumbers. This rehearsal
> (Which, ev'ry innocent wots well, comes in
> Like old importment's bastard) has this end,
> That the true love 'tween maid and maid may be
> More than in sex dividual.

Asked later to choose as husband either Arcite or Palamon, Emilia decides, momentarily, that her "virgin's faith has fled" (4.2.46), she loves them both, but, still later, when the two kinsmen are about to fight for her hand, she prays at the altar of Diana (5.1.137):

> O sacred, shadowy, cold, and constant queen,
> Abandoner of revels, mute, contemplative,
> Sweet, solitary, white as chaste, and pure
> As wind-fann'd snow, who to thy female knights
> Allow'st no more blood than will make a blush,
> Which is their order's robe: I here, thy priest,
> Am humbled 'fore thine altar. O, vouchsafe,
> With that rare green eye—which never yet
> Beheld thing maculate—look on thy virgin,
> And, sacred silver mistress, lend thine ear
> (Which nev'r heard scurril term, into whose port

> Ne'er ent'red wanton sound) to my petition,
> Season'd with holy fear. This is my last
> Of vestal office; I am bride-habited,
> But maiden-hearted.

We could say that Shakespeare simply took his plays and themes in no special order, as they came to him. The evolution of his heroines toward virgin faith would remain, nonetheless, to be accounted for. The entire action and atmosphere of *The Two Noble Kinsmen* help account for Emilia's lack of love. Arcite and Palamon are made to seem simple-minded, outer-directed followers of Mars and Venus, respectively, but the best exposure of the post-Romance attitude occurs in two prayers which Arcite and Palamon give just before Emilia's. Arcite prays to a Mars of destruction and waste, the "decider / Of dusty and old titles," whose "prize / Must be dragg'd out of blood." Palamon prays to a Venus who commands the rage of love throughout man and woman unkind, whose "yoke / As 'twere a wreath of roses, yet is heavier / Than lead itself, stings more than nettles," who incites gross geriatric lusts, and "whose chase is this world, / And we in herds thy game." Through these debased, decadent visions of chivalric and courtly ideals, Arcite and Palamon develop further Shakespeare's critique of patriarchalism and the potential murderousness and sterility that often accompany its political, social and sexual hierarchies. Small wonder that Emilia, faced with two such votaries, chooses to remain "maiden-hearted."

Shakespeare's post-Romance has moved far beyond the paradigmatic plot of *Pericles, Cymbeline, Winter's Tale,* and *Tempest* in which the needs of a society for restoration, needs embodied in its leader, are answered by the restorative instincts of his daughter. For Emilia, as for Elizabeth the Queen, choice of a marriage partner is not dictated by a father's will or by resistance to a father's will. Remote from the dynamics of patripotestal interests, left to her own devices, Emilia displays no sense of familial drive. Lacking in evidence a father, a brother, or other male to define herself against, the daughter tends perhaps to resist marriage or to see it as specially troublesome. Countered over against Emilia, moreover, we find in *The Two Noble Kinsmen* the earlier filial pattern represented in the Jailer's Daughter whose father wants her to marry her Wooer but who loves her father's prisoner (Palamon) and even frees him from her father's prison. Irony descends again, however, as the Jailer's Daughter loses Palamon and goes mad. In this late stage in his career, Shakespeare enters a specially problematic zone in his conception of our romantic instincts and their functioning.

In the tragedies, Shakespeare's lovers—Juliet, Desdemona, Cleopatra—exercise free and vivid imaginative powers and make real, in some sense, the vigorous wide-embracing males with whom they flee, fight, and die. In the Romances, the daughters no longer display the tragic force of will that finds and loses itself in an all-consuming love. They become subordinated to the pattern of generational renewal prompted by needs of their inescapable fathers. Their husbands, too, are conceived in terms of function rather than given an independence of being. They lack, consequently, the splendid wilfulness and freedom of self-definition possessed by Romeo, Othello, and Antony. Lysimachus, Posthumus Leonatus, Florizel, and Ferdinand become, like the societies they inhabit, chastened and subdued by redemptive responsibilities their betrotheds place upon them. This is a typical pattern in such dramatic Romances as *Alcestis, The Beggar's Opera, When We Dead Awaken, The Caucasian Chalk Circle,* and *The Cocktail Party.*[4] Women are made to undertake journeys that will redeem their families and societies from some version of sterility, but the redemptive journey and return renders both husband and society strangely quiet, meditative, less lusty and more spiritual. For Antony and Cleopatra—and perhaps even for Romeo and Juliet or Othello and Desdemona—one could almost substitute Mars and Venus, their heterosexuality and the vigor of their interchange is so strong, but for Ferdinand and Miranda and other Romance couples one would prefer, at best, Apollo and Diana.

In Shakespeare's post-Romance, Diana appears to win. After the womanizing excesses of Henry the Eighth, the virgin faith and phoenix-project of Elizabeth sound persuasive, and, given the unconvincing, fatuous romanticalities of Arcite and Palamon, Emilia's chaste reserve appears appropriate. But societies are not renewed by chaste reserve, and Shakespeare, whose great subject has always been the renewal of family and society, is unlikely to settle, finally, for so sterile a solution. Emilia is made, at the end, to accept Palamon, the devotee to Venus, and, though the ending is hardly celebratory in tone, what makes the union of Palamon and Emilia acceptable, I submit, is the preceding incident of the Jailer's Daughter. Her idealizing eagerness for Palamon in part subjects him to ironic scrutiny but also in part marks the preservation in the play of an essential, sincere, and effective romantic imagination. That is, in the Jailer's Daughter and, through her in Palamon, we see that a creative passion of this romantic or romance-ic sort must be heeded and welcomed. The Jailer, Doctor, and Wooer give in to the Daughter, humor her passion, and try their best to shape her world to her liking. She responds well and takes the Wooer for Palamon. The Doctor promises, convincingly, that by these means the Daughter will in three or four days become "right again."

The Two Noble Kinsmen, then, simultaneously attacks and defends romantic imagination, attacks the moribund mythologising of Arcite and Palamon as embodied in their prayers to Mars and Venus, purges their conception of humanity as passive and powerless before secret forces of hate and love raging in the blood, even to senility. The play first substitutes Emilia set on contemplative purity and blamelessness, praying to her sacred mistress, Diana, the "constant queen, / Abandoner of revels." Then the play celebrates more positively and warmly the laughable but vital madness of the Jailer's Daughter who makes the world try to create her imagined love before her eyes. Love is thus purged and renewed. The perverse and uncreative passions must yield to shadowy cold "Diana." Emilia is never a shining vital heroine. She seems to represent a stage in the development of successively more chaste, virginal heroines away from, say, Cleopatra through the likes of Imogen, Perdita, and Miranda, to Margaret, Elizabeth (as imaged in *Henry VIII*), and beyond. But Emilia, unlike Elizabeth, does marry. And her marriage is made possible and believable, I suggest, because its aim and function are supported by the warmer eagerness of the Jailer's Daughter toward Palamon and love.

Further investigation into Shakespeare's treatment of these acts and themes might seem foreclosed at this point by the absence of any more plays to contemplate. There are, however, significant links or overlaps between *The Two Noble Kinsmen* and the Cardenio episode in *Don Quixote,* the episode upon which, almost certainly, the lost play, *Cardenio,* attributed to Shakespeare and Fletcher in a significant "blocking entry" of the Stationers' Register and acted by the King's Men in 1613, is based.[5] Cardenio falls in love with Lucinda, but Cardenio's friend Ferdinand (who had betrothed himself to Dorothea and jilted her), by a series of stratagems, contrives to marry Lucinda in Cardenio's supposed absence. Lucinda, at any rate, submits to a marriage ceremony with Ferdinand, and Cardenio, who returns just in time to spy upon the ceremony, is so horror-struck that he flees to the wilds where he meets Don Quixote and relates his misfortunes. It turns out that Dorothea, Ferdinand's betrothed, also comes to the wilds. She meets the friends of Don Quixote, and they persuade her to help them humor his madness by pretending to be a damsel in distress whom Don Quixote can aid. After elaborately playing up to Don Quixote's chivalric whims, Dorothea, Cardenio, Sancho Panza, the Barber, and the Curate bring Don Quixote to an inn where, eventually, arrive also Ferdinand and Lucinda. After the inevitable recognition, Lucinda is restored to Cardenio and Dorothea to Ferdinand. . . .

"I saw her first," says Palamon to Arcite (2.2.160) concerning Emilia. Cardenio saw Lucinda first. But both "first" lovers appear to lose out in dramatic fashion to their more active, scheming rivals. In each case the rival's intervention appears institutionally-sanctioned as when Arcite wins the battle at the pillar and is given Emilia by Theseus and, similarly, Ferdinand marries Lucinda in a church ceremony. Then there is the eventual return of the heroine to her first love but not before he is aided in each case by a mad romantic. The Jailer's Daughter frees Palamon and brings him food in the forest; Don Quixote, meeting Cardenio in the wilds, embraces him, gives him food, and vows to serve him. In each case the mad romantic's passionate desire to serve a disconsolate lover is finally gratified by friends who, through impersonations, humor the mad fancies and change the world so as to satisfy their intention.

When Palamon asserts his prior claim to Emilia, saying to Arcite, "You must not love her" (2.2.161), Arcite replies:

> I will not, as you do—to worship her
> As she is heavenly and a blessed goddess;
> I love her as a woman, to enjoy her.
> So both may love.

In *The Two Noble Kinsmen* and the conjectural *Cardenio,* the first lover is relatively passive, a worshipper of woman rather than an enjoyer. The second lover, more lusty-active, "wins" the woman but has less right and is presented with less sympathetic interiority of love. The mad romantics, the Jailer's Daughter and Don Quixote, intervene and support with intensity of conviction the worth and quest of the first lover. Both Emilia and Lucinda, moreover, are represented as rather passive and shrinking, tossed between extremes of ineffective spiritual esteem from one man and primarily physical lust from another. In each story the development of the main plot lies secretly in the hands, or minds, of the subplot characters—Jailer's Daughter and Don Quixote—who must, as it were, dream the main plot onward, substituting their creative faith, their active idealizing eagerness, for the split love of the main characters.

Both *The Two Noble Kinsmen* and the *Cardenio* story are, in one sense, satires. The state of mind that overcomes the impasse of love which is split into effete worship and Mars-like rapacity is a state of mind represented as madness, an unthinkable dedication of unified mind and heart, spirit and flesh. But behind the satire, in each case there lies, I suggest, the secret project of resuscitating the romance-ic spirit. Shakespeare, like Cervantes, may have seen ahead in his very last works to an age of satire looming up on the horizon, but he also honored, as did Cervantes, the unquenchable desire of romantic will to purge and renew itself toward some version, no matter how strangely won, of ongoing and productive love. Ever since *All's Well* and *Measure for Measure,* if not before, Shakespeare had honored the beleaguered maiden's often-instinctive retreat to Diana, to the purer precincts of that shadowy Queen, and never was this honor made more telling than in *The Two Noble Kinsmen,* but Shakespeare made Emilia—wrought even beyond Diana with impossible longings ("Were they

metamorphis'd / Both into one," 5.3.84)—yield, finally, to her fated marriage. As Emilia exits hand in hand with Palamon, there linger still the singsong cracked remarks, the deepest hopes and fears of the Jailer's Daughter:

> *Daugh.* We shall have many children. . . .
> *Wooer.*   Come, sweet, we'll go to dinner,
> And then we'll play at cards.
> *Daugh.*   And shall we kiss too?
> *Wooer.* A hundred times.
> *Daugh.*   And twenty?
> *Wooer.*   Ay, and twenty.
> *Daugh.* And then we'll sleep together?
> *Doct.*   Take her offer.
> *Wooer.* Yes, marry, will we.
> *Daugh.*   But you shall not hurt me.
> *Wooer.* I will not, sweet.
> *Daugh.*   If you do, love, I'll cry.

Shakespeare understood and made vivid, as have few artists before or since, the spirit of the maiden phoenix that flutters up periodically in women, if not in men as well, and he traced with surpassing skill the intricacies of that endless dance where daughters escape and follow, reject and recreate, their once and future fathers.

Notes

[1] See also, e.g., *Wiv.* 4.6.23; *Oth.* 1.3.192; *Lr.* 1.1.113; *Cym.* 1.2.131. Quotations are from the *Riverside Shakespeare,* ed. G. B. Evans (Boston: Houghton Mifflin, 1974).

[2] One may observe that in a tragedy where a daughter, such as Ophelia, *fails* to assert herself against her father's dictate, the sense of nature redeemed, of human nature and society revitalized, may be diminished, as when the relatively limited Fortinbras takes over at the end of *Hamlet.*

[3] Just what portion, if any, of *The Two Noble Kinsmen* John Fletcher may be responsible for is as yet undetermined. Shakespeare is generally credited with the following scenes—1.1-2.1, 3.1, 5.1.34-173, 5.3-5.4—which include the scene introducing the Jailer's Daughter and the addresses of Arcite, Palamon, and Emilia to Mars, Venus, and Diana. Paul Bertram, *Shakespeare and the Two Noble Kinsmen* (New Brunswick: Rutgers Univ. Press, 1965), argues at length that the entire play is by Shakespeare. For present purposes, I treat the play as dominated by Shakespeare's conception and handling.

[4] These plays are collected, together with *The Tempest,* in *Dramatic Romance: Plays, Theory, and Criticism,* ed., Howard Felperin (New York: Harcourt, 1973). I am indebted to Howard Felperin for this collocation and for thoughts it has fostered.

[5] In discussing *Cardenio,* I refer to the plot of the Cardenio story as contained in the first part of Cervantes' novel, translated by Thomas Shelton in 1612. The Court Chamber Account and Court (Greenwich) Account indicate that *Cardenio* was presented twice by the King's Men in 1613. E. K. Chambers, *William Shakespeare: A Study of Facts and Problems* (Oxford: Clarendon, 1930), 2.343. On 9 September 1653, the publisher Humphrey Moseley registered "The History of Cardennio, by Mr. Fletcher and Shakespeare" in the Stationers' Register. See Chambers, 1.538-42. Lewis Theobald published a play, *Double Falsehood,* in 1728, and alleged that it was based upon manuscripts of a play by Shakespeare that dealt with the Cardenio story. Opinions vary as to whether Theobald really could have adapted or did adapt his play from such a manuscript; see John Frechafer, "*Cardenio,* by Shakespeare and Fletcher," *PMLA,* 84 (1969), 501-12, and Harriet C. Frazier, *A Babble of Ancestral Voices: Shakespeare, Cervantes, and Theobald* (The Hague: Mouton, 1974). Theobald's play excludes Don Quixote.

Cyrus Hoy (essay date 1978)

SOURCE: "Fathers and Daughters in Shakespeare's Romances," in *Shakespeare's Romances Reconsidered,* edited by Carol McGinnis Kay and Henry E. Jacobs, The University of Nebraska Press, 1978, pp. 77-90.

[*In the following essay, Hoy argues that it was the psychological climate of the late romances which allowed Shakespeare to create an ideal feminine figure in the form of a daughter.*]

Behind all the fathers and daughters in Shakespeare's romances are the most affecting father and daughter he ever drew, Lear and Cordelia. Shakespeare's tragedies are the necessary prelude to the romances; the romances are inconceivable without the tragedies; and among the tragedies, *King Lear* stands out for a number of reasons, not the least of which concerns its protagonist's relation to women. Lear is a father with daughters, not a son with a mother (as in *Hamlet* or *Coriolanus*), or a husband with a wife (as in *Othello* or *Macbeth*), or a lover with a mistress who is both more and less to him than a wife (as in *Antony and Cleopatra*). Of all the possible relationships of man and woman, that of father and daughter seems finally to have been the one that moved the dramatist most, for from it he derives the mysterious rhythms of suffering and grace, of loss and restoration, that sound throughout the last four plays. The fates of Pericles and Marina, Cymbeline and Imogen, Leontes and Perdita, Prospero and Miranda, encompass patterns of error and pain and ultimate deliverance which the imagination of the dramatist obviously found comfort in contemplating, and on which all his creative energies were focused in the effort to endow the patterns with formal shape in the romances. With its poignant representation of peace after long suffering which Lear all too briefly attains with Cordelia, *King Lear* represents the beginning of the imaginative way that will lead to *Pericles, Cymbeline, The Winter's Tale* and *The Tempest.*

Cordelia is not, of course, Lear's only daughter. She has two sisters who are as false as she is true. The finality of the distinction drawn between Cordelia's faith and Goneril and Regan's treachery suggests the degree of idealization that has gone into Cordelia's creation. She is a model of the heights to which human nature can rise when actuated by a rare integrity and selflessness; Goneril and Regan are the more commonplace examples of the depths to which human nature can fall when governed by hypocrisy and greed. The ideal that Cordelia embodies cannot be sustained in the tragic world of *King Lear,* and one suspects that Shakespeare was attracted to the romance form at least in part for the freedom it gave him to create an atmosphere in which other idolized daughters—Marina, Imogen, Perdita, Miranda—could endure. But the image that Cordelia projects—of idealized virtue closed round by sinister forces—is one that persists into the romances: Marina in the brothel; Imogen at the mercy of sundry nefarious plots hatched by a scheming stepmother, a brutal stepbrother, and a deceived husband; Perdita cast out at birth to whatever chance might befall her. Only Miranda, as the consequence of her father's peculiar powers, lives in anything like security, and even she has been the object of an attempted rape by Caliban. Cordelia's role in the design of *King Lear* is paradigmatic of that of all the daughters in the last plays: they are distressingly vulnerable to a host of evils, but they are incorruptible, and they all in one way or another redeem the father figure. In *King Lear,* Cordelia is reconciled with her father, who begs her forgiveness and who is, in effect, restored to life by her ministrations in a memorable scene (IV.vii) which would comprise the play's finale if *King Lear* were a romance. As it is, the tragedy sweeps on to its catastrophe, but the sort of recognition scene Shakespeare composed for Lear is recapitulated with ever-increasing brilliance in *Pericles, Cymbeline,* and *The Winter's Tale,* where it serves as the appropriate occasion for demonstrating the daughter's redemptive powers: the restorations of Marina and Perdita to their fathers serve to restore their fathers to life after prolonged periods of mourning, even as the restoration of Imogen to her father serves to restore him to his senses after a prolonged period of foolish blindness. The finale of *The Tempest* is differently managed, as we shall see, but the redemptive quality of Miranda is affirmed from the outset of the play. Prospero calls her the cherubin who preserved him when he was exiled from his dukedom (I.ii.152-53).

Fathers and daughters had, of course, been present in Shakespeare's plays since the early years of his career, when old Baptista shrewdly made the marriage of his sweet Bianca dependent on the provision of a husband for his curst Katherina, in *The Taming of the Shrew.* Usually the fathers in early Shakespeare are the stock figures of romantic comedy, whose daughters decline to marry the suitors of their choice, as Silvia rejects Thurio in favor of Valentine in *The Two Gentlemen of Verona,* or as Hermia declines Demetrius for Lysander in *A Midsummer Night's Dream,* or as Anne Page manages to avoid Dr. Caius and win Fenton in *The Merry Wives of Windsor.* There is a tragic version of this familiar situation in *Romeo and Juliet* when old Capulet insists that his daughter, secretly wed to Romeo, should marry Paris. *Much Ado About Nothing* gives us the pathetic figure of Leonato in his indignation at the shame visited upon Hero his daughter, falsely accused of infidelity on the eve of her marriage; and in *As You Like It* we have the clever Rosalind following her father into exile in the Forest of Arden. But the relation of father and daughter does not become problematic until, inevitably, in that most problematic of plays, *Hamlet,* where we are confronted with Ophelia and Polonius. Their one scene together (I.iii) turns on the familiar subject of the man on whom the daughter has placed her love. Since her suitor is Hamlet and a prince, his intentions toward her cannot be honorable because she is not his equal; this is the line that Ophelia's brother has been taking with her when the scene begins, and it is the line that her father continues with her—in even stronger terms—in the last half of the scene, after the brother takes his leave. When she tries to state her belief that Hamlet loves her in honorable fashion, Polonius pours scorn on the notion. The "holy vows" with which the prince has "given countenance" to his declarations of love are, according to Polonius, "springes to catch woodcocks." Because he knows what young men are like, Ophelia is to be guided by his knowledge. She is, to her undoing; among the ballad stanzas that she sings in her madness is one that bears witness to what a forcible impression her father's counsel has made on her imagination: "Young men will do't if they come to't" (IV.v.60). Polonius is Shakespeare's first considerable depiction of the father as an insensitive blunderer who, persuaded of the soundness of his own judgment, is blind and deaf to all signals that he may be wrong, and impervious to the violence he may be doing in the pursuit of his own will. The type will recur in Shakespeare, though daughters will never again be as docile as Ophelia.

The next daughter whom Shakespeare drew was Desdemona, whose gentle modesty exists side by side with an independence of will and a courage to follow where love leads that surprise and disconcert her father. When she is brought into the council chamber before Othello and Brabantio, she enunciates with great clarity and force a principle of duty which places her directly in the tradition shared by daughters in the later plays:

> My noble father,
> I do perceive here a divided duty:
> To you I am bound for life and education;
> My life and education both do learn me
> How to respect you; you are the lord of duty;
> I am hitherto your daughter. But here's my
>   husband;
> And so much duty as my mother show'd
> To you, preferring you before her father,
> So much I challenge that I may profess
> Due to the Moor, my lord.
>
> (I.iii.180-89)

This is the position on which Cordelia will take her stand in *King Lear:*

> Good my lord,
> You have begot me, bred me, lov'd me: I
> Return those duties back as are right fit,
> Obey you, love you, and most honor you.
> Why have my sisters husbands, if they say
> They love you all? Happily, when I shall wed,
> That lord whose hand must take my plight
>   shall carry
> Half my love with him, half my care and
>   duty.
> Sure I shall never marry like my sisters,
> To love my father all.
>
> (I.i.95-104)

One must resist any tendency to oversimplify tragic actions as profoundly subtle as those which comprise the plots of *Othello* and *King Lear,* but in both instances the daughter's role as victim of the tragedy is unmistakably clear, and the father's share in contributing to her victimization is delicately but firmly woven into the tragic pattern. When Brabantio, Desdemona's father, says to Othello: "Look to her, Moor, if thou hast eyes to see;/ She has deceiv'd her father, and may thee" (I.iii.292-93), he is sowing a seed of suspicion that will later, under Iago's nurture, come to monstrous flower in the husband's imagination. And Lear's rejection of Cordelia is a piece of monumental folly that leads to his destruction and to hers. She is his youngest and most loved daughter, and he has no more expected to be crossed by her than Brabantio has expected his daughter to elope with a Moor. As for the daughters themselves, they leave the fathers whom they have had to disappoint in order to be themselves, and they attempt to make new lives for themselves elsewhere. But they have been enmeshed in a fate that will not finally permit this escape. Since, for purposes of the tragedy, Desdemona is first and foremost Othello's wife and only secondarily Brabantio's daughter, the implications of her death are significantly different from those which surround the murder of Cordelia, who for dramatic purposes is primarily Lear's daughter and only secondarily the wife of the King of France. The tragic spectacle which ends each play makes this clear:

Desdemona dead in the arms of her husband, Cordelia dead in the arms of her father. For all her declaration—in her speech defining her duty—to the effect that she shall never marry like her sisters, to love her father all, Cordelia after her marriage does in fact continue to love her father all; she leaves her husband to return to her father and to go about his business, and finally to die for him. Offstage, in the background to the closing scene of *Othello,* there is a dead father to Desdemona, brought to his grave through grief at her marriage, but we are concerned with him only in the moment when we hear Gratiano say that he is glad Brabantio is not alive to know of his daughter's murder (V.ii.204 ff.). For the marriage bed loaded with the corpses of Othello and Desdemona, the end of *King Lear* gives us Lear with the dead body of Cordelia in his arms, and the sad spectacle is redolent both of a father of sorrows bending over the child who has tried to save him, and a lover bending over the body of a beloved destroyed by forces he himself has unleashed.

All Shakespeare's work from *Lear* to the end of his career seems to be generated by the tension between two powerful imaginative efforts: on the one hand, to free the self from bondage to the kind of female monsters most horrifically embodied in Goneril and Regan, and on the other hand to replace the sense of female monstrosity with a sense of female purity that will have the effect of saving the imagination from despair—of sweetening it, as Lear might say, when he calls to an imaginary apothecary for an ounce of civet. The imagination at work in the romances can still produce some monstrous growths: Dionyzia in *Pericles* and the stepmother Queen in *Cymbeline* are further examples of female evil. But the romances also give us two memorable examples of women, Imogen and Hermione, who are wronged by unjust masculine suspicions, while giving us as well two extraordinary treatments of the masculine imaginations that have wronged them, namely Posthumus and Leontes, their husbands and fiercest accusers. Prior to the romances, however, all the protagonists of Shakespeare's later tragedies display a need to escape from the domination of women: Lear from Goneril and Regan, Macbeth from Lady Macbeth, Coriolanus from Volumnia, Antony from Cleopatra. The areas of tension differ widely from play to play. The shades of unrelieved evil in which Goneril and Regan are drawn make plausible the fierce tirades which Lear launches against them. There is something almost poignant in Macbeth's recognition that, in his inurement to crime, he has far outdistanced his wife, who once had to urge him to it. Coriolanus resists his mother's tutelage without ever altogether recognizing what it is that has him in its power. Antony knows that he must break his strong Egyptian fetters if he is successfully to fulfill his role as one of the triple pillars of the world, but he never manages to do so.

Lear had given us an idealized figure—Cordelia, with

her truth-telling—to counterbalance the vicious sisters, with their glozing lies, but such a figure has disappeared in all the later tragedies, at least in its female embodiment. Vestiges of what she has represented remain, notably in the person of Coriolanus, where Cordelia's refusal to compromise and her expulsion are recapitulated. The expulsion of one who speaks uncomfortable truths—or declines to speak comforting lies—is treated again in the person of Alcibiades in *Timon of Athens,* a play that is particularly interesting for what it does not contain. The idealized figure of Cordelia is obviously necessary if the imagination (either of Lear or of the dramatist who created him) is to be saved from despair; just how necessary is evident from the example of Timon, who does in fact give way to despair.

Timon of Athens is in all essential respects a womanless play; women appear in only two scenes, and it is not without significance that in their two appearances, they are brought on first (in I.ii) in a masque of Amazons led by Cupid, and later (in IV.iii) as two whores in the company of Alcibiades. The impression of women as mannish whores is a legacy of *King Lear,* where they have been fully represented as such in the persons of Goneril and Regan; it is the only impression left to the imagination of the dramatist when such an ideal of woman as that represented by Cordelia is no more. Timon the protagonist is neither father nor son, husband nor lover; he is relentlessly, irremediably alone, first in the society of his troops of seeming-friends, then in his distrust, his sense of betrayal, his misanthropy. This is especially noticeable in the dramatic treatment of Alcibiades, that prototype of the male beloved. He offers Timon his friendship, but Timon will have none of it. When in Plutarch we read of how the Athenians covered the faults of Alcibiades "with the best wordes and terms they could, calling them youthfull, and gentlemans sportes,"[1] we find ourselves back among the emotional equivocations of Shakespeare's sonnets, for example, number ninety-six, addressed to the poet's young friend and beginning "Some say thy fault is youth, some wantonness, / Some say thy grace is youth and gentle sport."

But the crucial fact about the role of Alcibiades in *Timon of Athens* is that he is determinedly kept at arm's length from the protagonist. In the play's desolate world, the idealized image of a Cordelia (destroyed at the end of *Lear*) is not likely to be revived; and the idealized image of a male beloved, however much it might once have sustained the imagination of the poet-dramatist, seems now to have outlived its usefulness. The imagination of the dramatist—to judge from the world it created in the tragedies that follow *King Lear*—is not yet capable of reviving the idealized Cordelia in the vigor and purity of Marina and Imogen, Perdita and Miranda; all it can do is dwell on the forces that drive the male protagonists who present themselves to the dramatist's vision, and the forces are all embodied in the female sex. When Shakespeare tries to ignore this fact, as he did in *Timon of Athens,* he produces a dramatic fragment from which any profound incitement to passion is lacking: an effect without a cause. In the other plays of these years (1605 to around 1607), the imagination considers the possible sensual-erotic bonds that might conceivably tie a man to a woman, and addresses itself in Lady Macbeth, Volumnia, and Cleopatra to the depiction of the woman who will be both wife and mother, who will spur the man on to surpass himself and comfort him when he fails, in whose arms he will be content to die but from whose fierce determination he will also struggle to be free, whose hold on him will in some mysterious way drive him to crime in the eyes of the world.

This is the psychological climate which produces the romances. The dramatist is engaged in a quest to free the imagination from all the shrill mistress-wife-mother figures who have inhabited the late tragedies, and to create in their place an ideal of femininity on whom the imagination can bestow its tenderest sentiments, without the distractions of sexual desire. Thus the need to make the feminine ideal a daughter. Quests are of course native to the romance form, and the dynamics of the four last plays are all directed to the revelation of a radiant young woman whose purity and integrity have the effect of bringing light to the darkness in which fathers are plunged as a consequence of the world's evil or their own folly or both. With their simplicity, courage, and healthy integrity, Marina, Imogen, Perdita, and Miranda move through their plays like redemptive graces. The impression made by these daughters is the more remarkable when we consider that the first of the romances opens with a scene in which we—along with Pericles—suddenly find ourselves in the presence of a father and daughter who are guilty of incest, the ugliest relationship that a father's love for a daughter may imply. Here, at the outset of the romances, we are confronted for just a moment with the disturbing possibilities which it will be a principal endeavor of the dramatist's art to suppress in the plays ahead. Like Pericles, the dramatist gazes at full upon the guilty love of father and daughter, and then flees; but he will never forget what he saw. The romance quest in all the four last plays will be aimed at replacing the guilty passion with a pure affection, with creating an ideal of femininity which the imagination can hover over and cherish without guilt.

The discovery of evil in the King of Antioch's incest with his daughter leaves its mark on the dramatist's treatment of father and daughter relations in everything that follows. This is particularly evident in the treatment of fathers in the romances. Each is a distinct dramatic creation and they are not to be lumped together, but no one who has studied the romances will have failed to notice the wariness with which fathers

are treated in their relations with their daughters in the first three plays. For one thing, fathers have remarkably few scenes with their daughters in *Pericles, Cymbeline,* and *The Winter's Tale.* Through most of these plays, the daughters are lost to their fathers in one way or another. Pericles' loss of Marina is presumably but one more feature of the pattern of painful adventures—which also includes loss of wife for a season—to which even so good a man as he is subject in this mutable world; his is much the least complicated case of all those on exhibit in the last plays. He has done nothing to deserve separation from his daughter. Nonetheless, they are separated until very late in the play when, sunk in years and grief, he finds her again in a scene which is clearly modeled on Cordelia's restoration to Lear. The parallels are explicit in the "fresh garments" for the long-suffering father and the music that sounds as he recognizes his daughter.

Imogen's relations with Cymbeline are more complex. He presumably loves her, but he seems bent on destroying her, perhaps from that same obscure fear of incest which causes him to try to forbid her marriage to Posthumus, bred like a son in his household. He objects to her marriage with Posthumus as strenuously as Brabantio has objected to the marriage of Desdemona and Othello. Imogen is superbly indifferent to his anger. She tells him:

> I beseech you, sir,
> Harm not yourself with your vexation,
> I am senseless of your wrath; a touch more rare
> Subdues all pangs, all fears.
>
> (I.i.133-36)

Her father has banished her husband, and that is her one concern. Long before Imogen is literally lost to her father—during that period in the last half of the play when no one but the audience knows of her whereabouts—she has been lost to him in their estrangement. He has a second wife on whom he dotes and who, with her son (the wretched Cloten), has the management of the affairs of his kingdom. Cymbeline's character consists in not seeing. For all his kingly role, he is a cipher, in the play no less than in his realm. This is evident from the long and highly elaborate final scene where the complicated plot is untangled and where the king, who might be expected to have a chief function in bringing the truth to light (as, for example, the Duke does in the final scene of *Measure for Measure*), is in the demeaning position of having to have everything explained to him. When he is told of the queen's death-bed confession, he is surprised to learn of her wickedness but sees no reason to reproach himself for not having previously suspected it:

> Mine eyes
> Were not in fault, for she was beautiful;

Mine ears, that heard her flattery, nor my
   heart,
That thought her like her seeming. It had been
   vicious
To have mistrusted her . . .

But if he sees no reason to reproach himself, he admits
that his daughter might. He continues:

            yet, O my daughter,
   That it was folly in me, thou mayst say,
   And prove it in thy feeling. Heaven mend all!
                                    (V.v.62-68)

At what ought to be an emotional high point of the
scene—the reunion of father and daughter—even
Cymbeline is not so dim as to fail to recognize that he
is playing an undignified second-fiddle. He says to
Imogen, who is locked in the embrace of Posthumus:

   How now, my flesh? my child?
   What, mak'st thou me a dullard in this act?
   Wilt thou not speak to me?
                                    (V.v.264-66)

Only then does Imogen kneel to him and ask his blessing. It is the daughter's reunion with her husband that
is the emotional high point of the scene, and the point
reinforces what is clear enough in the play as a whole:
that Imogen is first a wife and then a daughter. The
passion which she arouses is safely and conventionally
exhibited in her husband and not in her father, who
looks on uncomprehendingly.

The distancing of father from daughter is continued in
The Winter's Tale. The estrangement of the two is here
the more violent, for Leontes is literally determined to
destroy his wife's presumed bastard; he decrees the
infant Perdita's exposure to the elements. Her eventual
restoration to her father proceeds along significantly
different lines in *The Winter's Tale* from the course it
takes in Greene's *Pandosto*, Shakespeare's source. The
denouement of Greene's novel is managed as follows:
Fawnia (Perdita) is brought with her beloved Dorastus
(Florizel) into the presence of Pandosto (Leontes), and
he, not knowing the girl to be his daughter, is promptly
enflamed with a lust for her which he seeks to satisfy
in a succeeding series of alternating promises and
threats. She of course steadfastly refuses him, and when
at last her true identity is made known, the incestuous
passion he has felt for his daughter causes the already
abundant cup of his shame to run over. Greene's novel
closes:

   but Pandosto, calling to mind how first he betrayed
   his friend Egistus [Polixenes]; how his jealousy was
   the cause of Bellaria's death [i.e., the death of
   Hermione, who in the novel is not restored to life];
   that, contrary to the law of nature, he had lusted

after his own daughter—moved with these desperate
thoughts, he fell in a melancholy fit and, to close
up the comedy with a tragical stratagem, he slew
himself.[2]

It required a strong-minded dramatist to resist such a
finale as this in 1610-11, the very period when Beaumont and Fletcher were captivating audiences with the
exquisite anguish of Arbaces and Penthea, the brother
and sister in *A King and No King*. They struggle against
a passion that threatens to be bigger than they are until
they are delivered from their incipient shame by the
discovery that they are not, in truth, related. But this
is a subject which, to the imagination that produced
Shakespeare's romances, does not bear conscious thinking on, however powerful a hold it might have exercised on the unconscious workings of that imagination. Shakespeare not only suppressed all reference to
a father's incestuous love for his daughter, he declined
as well to dramatize the scene in which father and
daughter discover each other. In *The Winter's Tale* the
recognition scene takes place offstage and is recounted
by three gentlemen. The whole weight of the finale is
thus given over to the scene with Hermione's statue,
its metamorphosis to the living woman, and her restoration to her husband and daughter. Just as, for dramatic purposes, Imogen makes her principal impression as Posthumus's wife rather than as Cymbeline's
daughter, so Leontes is chiefly memorable as Hermione's conscience-stricken husband rather than as
Perdita's father.

In each of the first three romances, a scene is carefully
furnished with a father and a daughter whose reunion
is a prominent feature in the comic resolution of all
three plays. The treatment of the relationship, however, seems straitened, as if observed from a distance,
and it is never developed in terms exclusively its own.
The dramatist seems at pains to keep the full emotional weight of a play from falling on a father and
daughter's love. So Pericles and Leontes have wives
who are lost and found again, even as their daughters
are; and Imogen has a husband and Perdita a beloved
who exercise that claim on their duty of which
Desdemona and Cordelia have spoken, and which takes
precedence over duty to a father. In *Pericles,
Cymbeline,* and *The Winter's Tale,* the imagination of
the dramatist is fascinated with the relation of a father
to a daughter; it circles around the subject ever so
tentatively; it returns to it repeatedly. But it is only on
the fourth return, in *The Tempest,* that the imagination
is prepared to deal with the subject directly, to imagine
the hitherto unimaginable, to think the unthinkable.

Among the unthinkable conditions that *The Tempest* is
prepared to set before us (such as getting all one's
enemies in one's power) is a father's dream of having
his daughter entirely to himself from her infancy
through the twelve years that bring her to the verge of

womanhood, and on a desert island too. Incestuous impulses are rigorously banished, and the foreground of consciousness is occupied with the need to protect chastity from rape. Prospero's feelings for Miranda are the feelings of a father for a daughter whom he idealizes, whose innocence he would preserve against the sinfulness of the world in general, and whose chastity he would safeguard against the particular violence of men, who will do to her what he did to her mother in order to beget her. He knows his sex, as Polonius might say. It is all very poignant because it is all so natural and so hopeless. Miranda must be allowed to marry; she is ready to and she wants to. With the appearance of Ferdinand, the wheel of amorous questing has come full circle from the opening scene of the first romance to the middle scenes of this last one. Pericles, when he thought to win a beautiful lady from her father, found himself exposed to the guilty secret of their incest. Ferdinand, led into the presence of Prospero and Miranda by Ariel's music, discovers a stern father who will set him sundry tests but who is not in the end unappeasable, and a daughter whose ardor charmingly matches his own. She is spirited, and one can imagine her, if pressed far enough, roundly declaring to her father that so much duty as her mother showed to him, preferring him before her own father, so much must she now challenge that she may profess due to Ferdinand. It is to Prospero's credit, and a measure of his wisdom and his humanity, that he never forces her to say anything of the sort. Though he may not be so glad of their union as they are (as he says in soliloquy at III.i.92), he recognizes its inevitability when he recognizes Ferdinand's worthiness, and he gives it his blessing. As Prospero, when he finds his enemies repentant, is prepared to forego his natural inclination for vengeance and have mercy on them instead, so in a parallel movement, when he finds that Ferdinand has satisfactorily endured the trials he has put him to, he is prepared to forego his all-too-human inclination to keep his daughter to himself and to give her in marriage instead. He has lost his daughter, as he tells Alonso late in the play (V.i.147-48), but he is resigned to her loss for he has recognized its inevitability; Miranda was straining for her freedom every bit as avidly as Ariel was.

Part of the triumph of *The Tempest*—both the triumph dramatized in Prospero's magnanimity and Shakespeare's triumph in depicting it—resides in what the dramatist has won through to in this play: the representation of an ideal of femininity which the masculine imagination at last manages to secure for itself. Miranda is what the imagination finally succeeds in conceiving in place of the Gonerils and Regans, the Lady Macbeths and Volumnias and Cleopatras from whom, rightly or wrongly, it considers itself to have suffered. As a product of the imagination, she is very much the father's child. We hear nothing of a wife to Prospero; he has

nurtured her; she has sustained him in his moment of anguish. The imagination is here able to envision a relationship between father and daughter that is not marred on the one hand by the father's jealousy or his efforts to play the petty tyrant, nor on the other by the daughter's rebellion against or indifference to his will. Least of all is it tainted by any unnatural sexual attraction on either side. The blind and foolish fathers like Cymbeline and Leontes are replaced at last by the wise and magnanimous Prospero, even as the passionate and clamorous women of the late tragedies give way to the gentle but ardent figures of Imogen and Perdita and Miranda. The son and husband and lover of the late tragedies becomes the father of the romances, a role that he does not at first accept with perfect equanimity. Cymbeline clings to his role of husband with a vicious second wife who turns him into a doting fool, to the neglect of the best interests of his daughter. And Leontes indulges a raging jealousy on behalf of his wife, to the near destruction of their daughter. Only Prospero is set before us as a father and nothing more.

As is regularly noted in accounts of the romances, their principal figures have a way of recapitulating dramatic fates from earlier plays, but in a nontragic key. Thus both Posthumus and Leontes are Othellos who have not in fact killed their Desdemonas, and Cymbeline is a weaker Lear who has succumbed to the Goneril/Regan-like authority of his second wife, but who is ultimately delivered from the same by the not-untimely deaths of her and her son. Prospero's earlier avatar is the Duke in *Measure for Measure*: he conducts *The Tempest* as the Duke presides over the action of his play, though with a surer hand and to deeper ends. But it is the relation of both ducal figures to their play's feminine leads that is most striking. The Duke in *Measure for Measure* hovers protectingly over Isabella and presumably at the end of the play will take her in marriage, a prospect that has not always pleased audiences, however much scholars of the play may be edified by its moral-allegorical implications. Matters are more rationally—one is tempted to say more decorously—managed in *The Tempest*. Prospero's solicitude for Miranda is, appropriately, the solicitude of a father (as the Duke's solicitude for Isabella ought to be but apparently is not). And having protected and cherished the idealized figure of feminine chastity which has saved him from despair, Prospero, recognizing that Miranda can no longer appropriately be his, gives her up, along with his staff and his book.

Notes

[1] Quoted in Geoffrey Bullough, ed., *Narrative and Dramatic Sources of Shakespeare,* 8 vols. (1957-75), 6 (1966): 237.

[2] Robert Greene, *Pandosto,* in *Elizabethan Prose Fiction,* ed. Merritt Lawlis (New York: Odyssey, 1967), p. 277.

LEAR AND CORDELIA

William B. Bache (essay date 1975)

SOURCE: "Lear as Old Man-Father-King," in *CLA Journal,* Vol. XIX, No. 1, September, 1975, pp. 1-9.

[*In the following essay, Bache chronicles Lear's growth throughout the play, from his desire for a son to his acceptance of his daughter.*]

One of the genuine pleasures of reading Shakespeare comes from the vivid glimpses he gives us into the felt life of a play; that is, into the human life rendered by a play. If, however, we are not careful, Shakespeare's fine touches about human beings and their behavior trick us into making the romantic mistake of believing that these characters really lived. For Shakespeare shared with Chaucer the rare genius of being able to surprise us with shrewd insights into reality and thus to provoke our perception about reality. In part perhaps it is our delight in gossip, our relishing the hidden or unexplored or unexplained details about, for example, Desdemona or Lady Macbeth that engages us. L. C. Knights has alerted us to that danger in his excellent "How Many Children Had Lady Macbeth?" But I like to think that it is enriching to indulge our fancy about these "real" people beyond the point of gossipy concern. For if we entertain guesses or speculations, we may perceive fresh meaning, and such meaning may lead us to a deeper understanding of the human significance of a Shakespeare play.

In *King Lear,* for example, it seems evident that part of the reason that Goneril and Regan are so heartlessly cruel to their father is that they have been brought up to believe that he never loved them at all. As a king, he needed a son, a reproduction of himself, and so, when Goneril and Regan were born, he was only disappointed. In *Pride and Prejudice,* Mr. Bennet lost interest with each girl born after Elizabeth and Jane because each new birth was only another step in a mildly desperate passage to a sonless condition. As vain king, Lear would have no real interest in his first two children: he would feel the overwhelming need for a male heir. My guess would be that when Cordelia was born, Lear's wife, the queen, died. Or, at least, after the birth of Cordelia, Lear accepted the fact that he would have no son, no legitimate male heir. To the older sisters, Lear was king rather than father; to Cordelia, Lear was more father than king. In other words, the jealousy of Goneril and Regan has a sound basis: they naturally detest the favorite child and their now-doting father. Although we cannot applaud their cruelty, we can understand their loveless feeling.

It is a commonplace that Shakespeare's great tragedies are family plays: *Hamlet* is about a man who is both son and prince; *Macbeth* is about a man who is both husband and king; *Lear* is about a man who is both father and king. Each of the three plays defines man both in private, familial terms and in public, political terms: Lear is old man, father, and king. The office of king makes its particular, obsessive demands, submerging the man or the father to the office: ceremony determines action, as Henry V acknowledges to himself in the night before the battle of Agincourt. A king is flattered and lied to, presented with a view that is unreal and artificial: a king comes to live in, and to believe in, a world not consonant with reality; the image that a king projects and that his subjects perceive is a distorted one. As a matter of fact, I don't think that Lear ever fully understands what he is or what is happening to him. From beginning to end he is in some measure deluded and mistaken. I suppose that this remark is only another way of saying that Lear is always old man *and* father *and* king: his plight as old man—father—king is the subject of the action. One of the remarkable facts about the play is that it contains no mother.

King Lear begins with a seeming casualness that (such is the skill of Shakespeare) provides us with important information:

> *Kent.* I thought the King had more affected the Duke of Albany than Cornwall.
> *Gloc.* It did always seem so to us; but now, in the division of the kingdom, it appears not which of the Dukes he values most; for equalities are so weigh'd that curiosity in neither can make choice of either's moiety.

We soon discover that, since Gloucester's immediate master is Cornwall, Gloucester's "us" may even include Edmund, Cornwall, and Regan. In other words, Lear's preference for Albany was widely accepted. We gather then that Lear has overcome any preference for Albany or that, in the division of his kingdom, he has made an effort to seem as fair as possible. It seems obvious that all of the details of the public scene would have been worked out in private: Lear has been much occupied with kingly business. Like *Richard II,* Shakespeare's greatest play has as its initial scene a ceremony that is the product of careful planning and much calculation. Like Richard II, Lear intends to control response, but we first find him a public figure on a public stage, where everything is ceremonious. Everything is being stage managed, and since what Lear has planned is a performance, his fury at Cordelia and Kent is quite understandable: they are disrupting his planned, cold ceremony. All Lear wants from everyone present is the public sanction of a situation that has been, so he thinks, accepted and agreed upon by the principals in private. Why hadn't Cordelia and Kent said something earlier? What does Cordelia mean? What lurks behind Kent's untimely rudeness?

But I would also guess that Lear has been keeping his own counsel on deepest matters; in fact, I think that at the beginning Lear is a consummate politician, not a weak-minded fool. He may not and, indeed, does not understand the true feelings of Goneril and Regan, but, again, this misunderstanding is largely the result of a condition of kingship and of the demands of kingship. Lear is also a father; he is aware of his responsibilities as father. The main observation is that Lear has been striving to do whatever he can do for his daughter Cordelia, whom he does love and with whom he wants to spend the rest of his life: "I lov'd her most, and thought to set my rest/On her kind nursery." Though he is still vigorous (he hunts, for instance), Lear realizes that he is an old man. My guess is that Lear, at least at the beginning, is, like Henry IV or Henry V, a good king, a great king, and yet not greatly good. Lear does not intend to abdicate, no matter what he professes. In fact, he never intends to surrender the title of king during his lifetime, and he never does surrender it.

To be quite specific, I would imagine that after Cordelia's marriage to the Duke of Burgundy (for certainly he is the intended husband), Lear would conspire with Burgundy in order to devour France, in much the way that England conspired with Burgundy at the beginning of the fifteenth century. Then Lear and Burgundy, strengthened by the resources of a defeated France, would destroy first one son-in-law and then the other; that is to say, I think that Lear means to do away with Goneril and Regan and their husbands. The first step in this program is to separate Goneril and Regan, to separate them by putting Cordelia between them, by putting Cordelia's land between theirs. Divide and conquer. Finally, after all, Lear would have Burgundy imprisoned or killed. Although I of course rather doubt that Lear has a detailed plan of action, my guess is that Lear's main object is to destroy all of his gathered friends, who are, of course, his possible enemies; to consolidate gains after conquest; then to deliver the won world to Cordelia. But Cordelia's refusal to cooperate (her refusal to *trust* her father) and Kent's subsequent intrusion change everything. He is shaken by their behavior. What can he say? He hadn't expected that. And he can't divulge his secret plans, his real reasons, his true intentions.

Having come between the Dragon and his wrath, Kent addresses his master:

> Royal Lear,
> Whom I have ever honour'd as my King,

> Lov'd as my father, as my master follow'd,
> As my great patron thought on in my
>   prayers,—

The speech is excessive; the usually blunt Kent is professing too much. To Lear, wouldn't the speech sound as if Kent, like Bolingbroke to the king at the beginning of *Richard II,* is making a challenge and a claim under the mask of ceremony? Doesn't it look as if Kent is using the occasion, exploiting the ceremony? In other words, doesn't it seem as if Kent is really *denying* how great Lear has been as master and as patron? In any event I should like to suggest that Kent may in fact be Lear's son, his illegitimate male heir, and that it is that fact that is behind the intrusion, so Lear thinks. But, anyway, like Edmund, Kent may feel that he, Kent, has been passed over and ignored. Has Kent decided that the time has come for action? Is there a conspiracy between Kent and Cordelia? Again, a Lear, deep in strategy, would not just accept an action as being what is seemed. What does it mean? The political implications of the problem are delicate, and I want to suggest that Lear handles the difficulties and the threat in a readily understandable manner—bluntly, crudely, with an exercise of power. Lear sends Kent out of his sight: Gloucester intends to do the same thing with Edmund, we remember.

Cordelia's place with Lear is taken in I, 4, by the Fool, with whom Lear is at first avuncular ("Nuncle Lear") and then paternal ("In, boy; go first"). In a manner of speaking, the newly introduced Fool is Lear's son, a substitute for a son, a reduction from Cordelia: now that the favorite child has been cast out, the Fool is Lear's closest associate. But, immediately prior to the Fool's appearance, Kent returns, in disguise, to Lear's service; that is to say, before the Fool takes Cordelia's place in Lear's affection, the disguised Kent takes the real Kent's place in Lear's depleted retinue. Right after Lear surrenders his power and rejects his dearest child and his best servant, he gets his two "sons" back. Lear is still father—king, though in a private, restricted, special sense. To those without feeling or respect, Lear is just an old man.

In III, 4, Tom of Bedlam, the disguised Edgar, joins the rejected company of Lear, the Fool, and Kent in the tempest on the heath. Although Lear sees this seeming madman as only "unaccommodated man" and although Lear deliberately tries to become like the madman (an "unaccommodated old man"), we know that the real person is Edgar, the betrayed son, Lear's godson, the boy Lear had named. So on the heath, in the storm, Lear finds his third "son," another outcast, another "false" son emerging out of the hovel, after being discovered by the Fool. Although, again, Lear is prompted by the sight of this newcomer to emphasize his own unaccommodated manliness, it is this third son, the future Gloucester, who will become, in the last act, the good knight, the instrument of justice when, in a ceremonious trial by combat, he kills his brother, Edmund, the traitor, the false Earl of Gloucester, the creation of Cornwall in III, 7.

At the end of the third act Edgar and the Fool are left behind, and only the determined Kent remains with his master. The removal of Edgar ("Thou robed man of justice") and the Fool ("his yoke-fellow of equity") from Lear signifies a change in the world of the play. Lear sleeps. With the departure of Lear for Dover and the absence of Albany, the only king figure present at the end of the third act is Cornwall; the only father figure is the caught Gloucester. In the second act Cornwall and then Lear arrive at Gloucester's household. In the third act Cornwall takes over Gloucester's castle, usurps the place of the father, Gloucester, and then punished his host. In plucking out the eyes of Gloucester, Cornwall may be said to be plucking out the eyes of the father; that is, the holder of the office of king blinds the father.

Cornwall has his reasons for his brutal, morally shocking treatment of Gloucester, and he states them: the old man is a servant who has betrayed his master, Cornwall; the old man is a traitor to his country since he is sympathetic to France, the enemy of Britain. The false old man must be made an example of so that others will not be false. Moreover, Cornwall wants to spare the son, Edmund, the informer, from witnessing the punishment of the father, the traitor. As a matter of fact, Cornwall insists on explaining to those present why he must act as he does. In addition, the remarks of Regan, Gloucester, and the first servant push Cornwall during the trial into a loss of emotional control. He is an uneasy king, a person to whom the demands of the office are too new and too complicated. But, still, even if we are able to understand Cornwall's reasons and actions, we cannot excuse them.

At least the demands of primitive kingship seem to dictate the blinding of the guilty father, the turning of a father into an unaccommodated old man. When threatened, a king must take decisive action: because Gloucester has acted as a father might, Cornwall has acted as a king must. The first servant, who stands up to his master, Cornwall, is like Kent in that he wants to prevent the king (Cornwall) from blinding the father (Gloucester). The first servant in III, 7, intrudes upon the king's actions, just as Kent had in I, 1; that is to say, the first servant is a "true son" of Cornwall in that he wants to stop his master from behaving in a terrible manner. In other words, III, 7, can be viewed as a symbolic explanation of, or a gloss on, the initial situation: Lear as king has Lear as father bound to a chair and blinded; the blind father is then thrust out of doors as a helpless old man; the remaining two servants, like Goneril and Regan at the end of the first scene of the play, comment on the action.

Lear is always old man—father—king, but with a significant difference in the last two acts. In part the change is essential because what is done to Gloucester in III, 7, is a demonstration of what could happen to Lear if he remained behind, of what could happen to Lear if he were not taken to Dover. "I have o'erheard a plot of death upon him," Gloucester tells Kent, and it is this information that prompts Gloucester's actions. In point of fact, what may lie behind the rage of Goneril, Regan, and Cornwall in III, 7, is their frustration—Lear has escaped their power. From III, 6, to IV, 6 (for, that is, five hundred lines) Lear is not on stage; his presence as old man—father—king is lacking; his symbolic *meaning* as old man—father—king is missing. Lear does not return until he has awakened and until spring has come again and the world has awakened and changed. During the interim, the opposing forces gather and follow Lear to Dover: the main movement is both to spring and toward the slaughter at the end, to the day of final judgment. In IV, 2, Albany ("never man so chang'd") turns from Goneril, damming her unnaturalness, and extends his sympathy to the absent, badly treated Lear; after the entrance of the messenger with news of the treatment of Gloucester and of the death of Cornwall, Albany extends his sympathy to the absent, blind Gloucester. Now that Cornwall is dead and now that the king of France has gone back to his own country, Albany is the only king figure present, though both Goneril and Regan want to make Edmund king—Edmund, whose person has become the sole object of their desire.

We may put it that in III, 7, Cornwall is king; in IV, 2, Albany is king; in IV, 6, Lear, "fantastically dressed with wild flowers" (to use Capell's words), returns to the world as mad king, crowned in nature: "I am the king himself." Edgar, no longer "unaccommodated man," observes his blind father meeting the crowned mad king. Until the very end, Edgar never sees Lear when he, Lear, is other than mad; Cordelia's second view of Lear is much different from her first view. In IV, 7, the "child-chang'd father," dressed in fresh garments, is carried in on a chair to his daughter, Cordelia. Music plays. To Cordelia, Lear is "dear father" and "royal Lord." Lear calls himself "a very foolish fond old man." If Lear is primarily mad king in IV, 6, he is essentially chastened father in IV, 7: the great rage is killed in him. To Edgar Lear is primarily king; to Cordelia Lear is essentially father. Such is the sublime reunion of Lear and Cordelia that after Lear awakens to Cordelia, they are never apart, as if to emphasize the father aspect of Lear's three related roles.

Cordelia has been off stage from I, 1, to IV, 4, and perhaps we can best say that Cordelia, the child transfigured into queen, has usurped the place that Kent, the Fool, and Edgar had with Lear in the tempest in Act III. In other words, to the reborn old man—father—king is given the now-perfect offspring. From

IV, 4, on, Cordelia's only concern is her father: "He that helps him take all my outward worth." From IV, 7, on, Lear's only concern is Cordelia. As she becomes more than a daughter, Lear becomes more than old man—father—king: they become canonized by love. Her image and her example change him. As Edgar and Albany become obsessed with power and worldly justice, Cordelia and Lear, the King and his Queen, are lost in love. And the world is well lost, for Albany is, of necessity, exceedingly devious in Act V: like John of Lancaster and Westmoreland in *Henry IV, II,* Albany uses duplicity in order to trap traitors. Albany gets the letter written by Goneril to Edmund, and he keeps it hidden until the proper time. By the end, Albany, the successful son-in-law, is the main product of kingship, the chief inheritor of the "packs and sects of great ones/That ebb and flow by the moon."

When Lear reenters with Cordelia in his arms at the very end of the play, he (absent for two hundred and thirty lines) has undergone a final change. Emerging from his last trial, with the seemingly lifeless Cordelia in his arms, he once again, and now more than ever, is old man—father—king. His sudden presence prompts Albany to say, "we will resign,/During the life of this old Majesty,/To him our absolute power." And in his obsession with Cordelia, Lear sounds like an absolute ruler to these others: "you are men of stones"; "you, murderers, traitors all"; "Why should a dog, a horse, a rat have life,/And thou no breath at all?" Then with Cordelia dead, Lear sinks, and Kent delivers his master's best epitaph: "Vex not his ghost: O, let him pass; he hates him/That would upon the rack of this tough world/Stretch him out longer." like the Fool and Cordelia, Kent, now just an old man, will follow his father—king, leaving behind the cheerless Edgar and Albany, the children of a bitter world, a world now bereft of this wonderful child and this magnificent, terrifying father—king, this dead old man.

Marianne Novy (essay date 1979)

SOURCE: "Patriarchy, Mutuality, and Forgiveness in *King Lear*," in *Love's Argument: Gender Relations in Shakespeare,* The University of North Carolina Press, 1984, pp. 150-63.

[*In the following essay first delivered at the 1977 conference on Shakespeare in Performance, Novy discusses the imbalance of power between Lear and his daughters, and observes that Cordelia tries to keep her integrity by withdrawing from "the coercive 'mutuality' that patriarchy seems to demand."*]

Critics of *King Lear* have frequently noted that Lear begins with the power of the archetypal king and father; many of them have also noted that his initial lack of self-knowledge springs in part from the prerogatives of kingship.[1] It has been less observed that the play includes implicit criticism of the prerogatives of the father and an exploration of some behavior that patriarchy fosters in men and women. The apparent mutual dependence of Lear and his older daughters, following conventional patterns of male and female behavior, is deceptive. What the characters need are bonds of forgiveness and sympathy based on a deeper and less categorized sense of human connection.

Maynard Mack emphasizes the importance of relatedness in *Lear*.[2] This concern . . . pervades Shakespeare's plays. While the early comedies parallel many different kinds of mutuality, and accept them all, in tragedy mutuality is tested, and many of its varieties are found wanting. If a society is working, the principle of mutuality—or reciprocity, as the sociologist Alvin Gouldner calls it—offers its structure further justification.[3] Places in a hierarchy give reciprocal duties; the subject serves a benevolent master out of gratitude as well as obedience. However, if what the master needs of the subject includes forgiveness, this begins to call the social order into question. The emphasis on King Lear's need for forgiveness reinforces the challenge he makes to his society on the heath.

Although *Lear* is concerned with the mutuality between father and daughter, it deals with aspects of that mutuality which are also experienced by husband and wife in a patriarchal society, where the authority of fathers over their families, husbands over wives, and men in general over women are all related and analogous. Too great an imbalance in this power makes it likely that attempts at mutuality will be flawed by male coercion and female deception.

Lear's abdication scene provides a paradigm of this danger. He offers money and property in exchange for words of love.

> Which of you shall we say doth love us most,
> That we our largest bounty may extend
> Where nature doth with merit challenge.
>
> (1.1.51-53)

Of course, part of the problem with the contest is that it takes words of love as an adequate equivalent of love itself. But this is not just a problem with words; any means of expressing love may be used deceptively, and yet love requires the use of some kind of means. It is the power imbalance behind Lear's offer that makes deception both more likely and more impenetrable. Lear is really trying to coerce his daughters to a certain form of behavior; he sets up the terms and the contract. If a daughter wishes a different kind of contract, she is disowned. As king, Lear is the source of all money and property; in their dependence on him at this point the daughters resemble wives in a patriarchal marriage who can get money only by begging it from their husbands. Nora Helmer's performance in *A Doll's House* is a variant response to a similar situation. No matter how much the male depends on the female's response, if he has all the external power, the social approval, and the sole right to initiate, the mutuality is deeply flawed by coercion.

In such a situation, the obvious way for a woman to survive is to go along with the social order, as Goneril and Regan do at the beginning. In *The Taming of the Shrew*—closer to *Lear* than any tragedy or any other comedy in the large number of times the word "father" is used—this kind of survival is what Bianca practices from the beginning and part of what Kate learns by the end.[4] In a comedy we do not much mind Bianca's ability to gull Lucentio, and the ambiguity of Kate's final integration of her individuality and the social order still pleases most audiences or wins Kate more sympathy. But even that play shows in Bianca's final posture the cool self-interest that may underlie such compliance. The pretenses of Goneril and Regan have more devastating effects, but in flattering Lear they are doing a service that women are traditionally expected to do for men. Of them, as well as of his subjects, Lear could say, "They told me I was everything" (4.6.103-4).

Lear's childishness has been noted by many critics of the play, as well as the Fool and, self-interestedly, by Goneril—"Old fools are babes again" (1.3.19); but it has been less observed that the similarity between king and child is in part in their assumptions of omnipotence encouraged—for different reasons—by the flattery of those who care for them.[5] Elizabeth Janeway has explained how traditional expectations of female behavior come from nostalgia for a mother's care in childhood.[6] Lear, in wishing to "unburdened crawl toward death," wants to become a child still omnipotent in his ability to control Cordelia's "kind nursery." The illusory omnipotence of the abdicating king can be compared to the illusory omnipotence of the head of the family within his household, which the sociologists Peter Berger and Hansfried Kellner call a "play area" where he can be "lord and master."[7] Lear really is lord and master at the beginning; but in the love contest he pretends to have more power over his daughters' feelings than he actually has, and this, of course, results in the loss of power that makes the split between his wishes and reality even more glaring later on. Although at first Goneril and Regan have seemed like good mothers in their compliance and words of total devotion, now they are punitive and emphasize Lear's powerlessness, as the Fool suggests: "thou mad'st thy daughters thy mothers; . . . when thou gav'st them the rod, and put'st down thine own breeches,/ Then they for sudden joy did weep" (1.4.163-66). When Lear curses Goneril with his wish that she bear no children or a "child of spleen," it is partly because he feels that filial ingratitude such as he experiences is the worst possible suffering—but perhaps also because her behavior toward him makes him think of her as a bad mother.

The contrast between Goneril and Regan, on the one hand, and Cordelia, on the other, owes something to the traditional tendency in Western literature to split the image of woman into devil and angel, Eve and Mary.[8] Goneril and Regan are much less psychologically complex than most Shakespearean characters of comparable importance. Few of their lines carry hints of motivations other than cruelty, lust, or ambition, characteristics of the archetypal fantasy image of the woman as enemy. Shakespeare gives them no humanizing scruples like those provoked by Lady Macbeth's memory of her father. He does not allow them to point out wrongs done to them in the past as eloquently as Shylock does, or to question the fairness of their society's distribution of power as articulately as Edmund. If their attack on Lear can be seen as in part the consequence of his tyrannical patriarchy, they never try to explain it as an attack on an oppressor. Indeed, even if we follow Peter Brook's lead and imagine a Lear who knocks over tables, whose men really are a "disordered rabble," their cruelty to Lear and, even more, to Gloucester exceeds all provocation. Rather than attacking tyranny, they prefer to attack weakness, and sometimes compare those they attack to women in terms meant to be insulting. Regan says to Lear, "I pray you, father, being weak, seem so" (2.4.196). Goneril says, "I must change names at home and give the distaff / Into my husband's hands" (4.2.17-18). One of the few suggestions of psychological complexity in their characterization is this hint of a compensatory quality in their cruelty—a hatred of others they consider weak because of a fear of being weak themselves.[9] Here the play suggests that weakness, or the fear of it, can be as corrupting an influence as power. This fear of weakness is, however, a standard enough trait in the psychology of violence that it does little to individualize them.

Cordelia, by contrast with her sisters, is much less stereotyped. Shakespeare's presentation of her shows sympathy for the woman who tries to keep her integrity in a patriarchal world. Refusing pretense as a means of survival, such women often try to withdraw from the coercive "mutuality" that patriarchy seems to demand. Cordelia initially attempts to say nothing; her asides tell us her wish to "love and be silent." As she speaks further, in a mode completely alien to the love contest, her difficulties with language add to the audience sympathy with her; they make us imagine that she feels much more than she says. She describes the parent-child bond in language that emphasizes its mutuality, its elements of reciprocation and response; the possible coldness in her reference to "duties" is counterbalanced by her approximation of the marriage vow:

> Good my lord,
> You have begot me, bred me, loved me. I
> Return those duties back as are right fit,
> Obey you, love you, and most honor you.
>
> (1.1.95-98)

Cordelia looks more toward the general parental gifts
of the past than toward munificent promises for the
future; all that she anticipates is a marriage and conflicting loyalties. In Shakespearean comedy, Portia or
Rosalind can joke skeptically about professions of
absolute and exclusive love; in the tragedy, Cordelia's
refusal of hyperbole continues the challenge to Lear's
wish to be loved alone and his delight in his special
power, and it precipitates her rejection. Lear wants
more than the ordinary mutuality of parent and child,
but his ability to disown Cordelia when such ordinary
mutuality is all she will promise springs from the superior power of fathers in a patriarchal society. Lear's
rejection is total: "Better thou / Hadst not been born
than not t'have pleased me better" (1.1.233-34).

It is retributive, however shocking and disproportionate, when Lear's older daughters use the power they
receive with a coercion like Lear's own. As the Fool
says, "I marvel what kin thou and thy daughters are.
They'll have me whipped for speaking true; thou'lt
have me whipped for lying" (1.4.173-75). What Lear
criticizes in them, however, is not their general tyranny and cruelty but their lack of mutuality—their
ingratitude to him. Along with this preoccupation goes
a preoccupation with his own generosity: "Your old
kind father, whose frank heart gave all—" (3.4.20).
Perhaps this suggests something of the intent of his
gifts.

But as he experiences the sufferings of the poor and
the outcast, Lear begins to imagine less self-interested
kinds of giving. He shows concern for the Fool and
acknowledges his own responsibility for the condition
of the "poor naked wretches" he now wishes to help.
And after the fantasy trial he starts to speak of his
daughters in different terms as he moves to more general social and existential concerns: "Is there any cause
in nature that makes these hard hearts?" (3.6.75-76) In
the next scene he denounces the false mutuality that
would say "ay" and "no" to everything he said. Here
is his longest attack on women: it begins by pointing
to someone who could be Goneril or Regan as we see
them, but he does not name her, and he attacks her not
for ingratitude but for lust and hypocrisy.

> Behold yond simp'ring dame,
> Whose face between her forks presages snow,
> That minces virtue, and does shake the head
> To hear of pleasure's name.
> The fitchew nor the soilèd horse goes to't
> With a more riotous appetite.
>
> (4.6.117-22)

His words are antifeminist commonplaces of Elizabethan England, but the context suggests a basis in revulsion against pretense and sexuality in general more
than against women. A bit later he shows deeper insight about the origin of such antifeminist
commonplaces:

> Thou rascal beadle, hold thy bloody hand!
> Why dost thou lash that whore? Strip thy own
>   back.
> Thou hotly lusts to use her in that kind
> For which thou whip'st her.
>
> (4.6.157-60)

We punish others for our own faults; this is a general
phenomenon that Lear denounces here and that Shakespeare often illustrates and describes elsewhere. More
specifically, this passage implies the relationship of
such scapegoating to patriarchal society's split of human qualities, both vices and virtues, into masculine
and feminine. Patriarchal society exerts social and
psychological pressure on men to deny qualities in
themselves that would be seen as feminine and instead
to project them on to women. This analysis suggests
that Lear's disgust with women's lust is so strong because it is really disgust with himself; at the same
time, his initial expectations of Cordelia's "kind nursery" are so high because he identifies her with nurturing qualities and vulnerabilities not easily admitted by
a king whose royal symbol is the dragon.

Both textual and structural details in *Lear* support this
emphasis on projection of feminine qualities; furthermore, it is closely related to the play's concern with
connections between people. Lear's own words to
Goneril suggest something of his identification with
her:

> We'll no more meet, no more see one another.
> But yet thou art my flesh, my blood, my
>   daughter;
> Or rather a disease that's in my flesh,
> Which I must needs call mine.
>
> (2.4.215-18)

Sometimes he seems unable to recognize his daughters
as persons separate from himself: "Is it not as this
mouth should tear this hand / For lifting food to 't?"
(3.4.15-16). At other times he blames himself for begetting them, in language that again suggests revulsion
from the sexuality with which, as women, they are
linked in the imagination of Western culture: "Judi-
cious punishment—'twas this flesh begot / Those pelican daughters" (3.4.72-73). Just after Lear gags at imagining the stench beneath women's girdles, he acknowledges the smell of mortality on his own hand.

From this vision of universal guilt, Lear moves to a
vision of universal suffering, the basis for a different

kind of mutuality. He responds to Gloucester's sympathy, recognizes him, and speaks with him using the "we" of identification and common humanity.

> We came crying hither;
> Thou know'st, the first time that we smell the
>   air
> We wawl and cry. . . .
> When we are born, we cry that we are come
> To this great stage of fools.
>   (4.6.175-77, 179-80)

His use of "we" contrasts with his earlier assumption of the royal prerogative of the first person plural and with the "I" of his felt isolation; the imagery of crying makes an equally insistent contrast to his earlier stance:

> let not women's weapons, water drops,
> Stain my man's cheeks. . . .
>   . . . You think I'll weep.
> No, I'll not weep.
>   (2.4.272-73, 277-78)

And while earlier he described the alienation between himself and his daughters as like an attack by one part of his body on another, now he imagines himself giving part of his body to supply another's disability: "If thou wilt weep my fortunes, take my eyes" (4.6.173). At the same time as he acknowledges his own identity and Gloucester's, and their fellowship, he acknowledges his share in a vulnerability to suffering and a need to express it—the powerlessness of the child, and not its illusory omnipotence—which he had previously relegated to women. And the tears in his vision of all crying for their own suffering quickly become tears of compassion.

The association of tears and women is a commonplace in Shakespeare and in our culture, even though in Shakespeare at least the association is most frequently made by men who do cry themselves (Laertes, Sebastian in *Twelfth Night*). Nevertheless, it is remarkable both how often Cordelia's tears are mentioned in *King Lear*, and how the imagery strives to make them powerful rather than pathetic. Cordelia credits them with arousing France's sympathy and persuading him to help Lear (4.4.25-26); she prays that they will help restore Lear's health:

> All blessed secrets,
> All you unpublished virtues of the earth,
> Spring with my tears!
>   (4.4.15-17)

And at the climactic moment of their reunion, Lear, whose own tears "scald like molten lead" (4.7.48), touches her cheek and says, "Be your tears wet? Yes, faith" (4.7.71).[10] With Cordelia's tears, as with other aspects of her characterization, Shakespeare is suggest-

ing a kind of power different from the coercion dependent on political rank or violence; it is the power of nurturing, of sympathy, of human connection as an active force.

The physical connection of parenthood, on which Lear relied earlier in his reproaches to Goneril and Regan, has proved too often only a torment to him; in his reunions with Gloucester and, even more, with Cordelia, Lear experiences a connection—based on shared suffering—which can also be called physical insofar as it involves touching and being touched by others, weeping and being wept for.[11] This kind of sympathy underlies Cordelia's ability to restore the parent-child bond rather than simply responding with the revenge Lear expects when he says, even after he has felt her tears,

> If you have poison for me, I will drink it.
> I know you do not love me; for your sisters
> Have (as I do remember) done me wrong.
> You have some cause, they have not.
>   (4.7.72-75)

The creative power of Cordelia's compassion transcends the mechanism of revenge; nor, her words suggest, is her sympathy confined to relatives:

> Had you not been their father, these white
>   flakes
> Did challenge pity of them. Was this a face
> To be opposed against the jarring winds?
> . . . Mine enemy's dog,
> Though he had bit me, should have stood that
>   night
> Against my fire.
>   (4.7.30-32, 36-38)

But for all the universality of her sympathy, she expresses it in the context of their particular relationship: to Lear's "as I am a man, I think this lady / to be my child Cordelia," she responds "And so I am! I am!" (4.7.69-70). She is too tactful to speak of forgiveness; guilt and innocence seem irrelevant to her sympathy. But it is forgiveness that Lear needs, and finally he can ask for forgiveness instead of praise and gratitude: "Pray you now, forget and forgive. I am old and foolish" (4.7.84).

In his final vision of what their relationship would be, alone and happy together in prison, he says, "When thou dost ask me blessing, I'll kneel down / And ask of thee forgiveness" (5.3.10-11). In Shakespeare's England, Lawrence Stone tells us, kneeling to ask blessing was a common gesture of respect from child to parent, a symbol of generational hierarchy.[12] In Lear's vision, parent kneels to child. The need for forgiveness reverses hierarchies of both age and sex, and suggests their limitations.

Northrop Frye, noting the emphasis on forgiveness in Shakespeare's comedies, claims that it results from "impersonal concentration on the laws of comic form."[13] This does not, however, account for the importance of forgiveness, explicit and implicit, in a tragedy like *Lear,* and I think there are more basic reasons for the emphasis on the need for forgiveness in Shakespeare's tragedies, problem comedies, and romances. Shakespeare's plays are concerned with both power and relationship. Lear, for example, depends on power—even though he thinks he wants to give it up—and he wants love. Frequently, Shakespeare shows a man's attempt to get, preserve, or control a relationship with a woman resulting in disaster because he abuses his power. Lear and Angelo are the most obvious examples. From the problem comedies on, Shakespeare suggests that in a patriarchal society mutuality between man and woman must include the mutuality of forgiveness and repentance, because the powerful are so likely to abuse their power.

However, before the female characters forgive, the balance often shifts: Lear and Angelo lose power, Cordelia and Isabella gain some. Alternatively, like Desdemona, they forgive when their forgiveness cannot possibly promise to help them. In either case, the forgiveness is freely chosen, not coerced by dependence on their men like the apparent forgiveness of a battered wife who has nowhere else to go. When Shakespeare's tragic and tragicomic heroes receive forgiveness, they have generally given up all expectations of it. Perhaps the women's forgiveness of them comes as even more of a surprise because it avoids the distancing of such self-righteous forgiveness as Prospero's words to his unrepentant brother:

> For you, most wicked sir, whom to call
>   brother
> Would even infect my mouth, I do forgive
> Thy rankest fault—all of them.
>
>   (5.1.130-32)

Rather, their forgiveness is acceptance. Reversing the mechanism of projection and scapegoating, it implies a recognition of their own limitations as well, somewhat like the forgiveness Prospero begs from his audience: "As you from crimes would pardoned be, / Let your indulgence set me free" (Epilogue, 19-20).

However structurally important forgiveness is in Shakespeare's comedies and romances, where R. G. Hunter finds frequent affinities to the ritual stages of the sacrament of penance, it is worth noting how much more psychologically realistic and dramatically compelling are Lear's repentance and Cordelia's forgiveness.[14] Nor does *Lear* leave us with the sense of the inadequacy of forgiveness that Howard Felperin suggests in the problem comedies.[15] Cordelia's forgiveness cannot stop the political consequences of Lear's

acts, to be sure, but there is no denying the emotional power of their reunion scene.

We can never completely account for *Lear's* power to move us, of course, but it is worth considering the possibility that some of the intensity of this scene comes from an element in the play that would seem to move in an entirely opposite direction from sympathy and forgiveness—its portrayal of anger. The experience of *Lear* depends on the paradox that people are at the same time connected and separate, a paradox to which both sympathy and anger are responses. The intensity of anger may measure the intensity of feelings of loss; it also demonstrates how much sympathy is willing to forgive. Anger and sympathy are both signs of human vulnerability and relationship. In Lear's last scene his sorrow and anger at losing Cordelia merge:

> Howl, howl, howl! O, you are men of stones.
> Had I your tongues and eyes, I'd use them so
> That heaven's vault should crack.
>
>   (5.3.258-60)

As he imagines the power his emotions could have with his listeners' help in expressing them, the effect in the theater is that he is also addressing the audience. Before the intensity of his expressions of grief for Cordelia, our responses to our own losses, as well as to him, seem inadequate. We cannot heave our hearts into our mouths.

Earlier I suggested that the mutuality between characters in Shakespeare's comedies is analogous to the mutuality between actors and audience. Stanley Cavell has proposed that in *Lear* the inevitable separation between actors and audience mirrors the ultimate isolation of the characters, and all of us, from each other: we cannot stop the characters from acting wrongly, from suffering pain, just as they cannot stop each other, just as we cannot stop those closest to us.[16] Yet, although Lear cannot save Cordelia, nor she him, before this ultimate loss he does experience her acceptance. This acceptance includes tragic perception—it is combined with knowledge of his faults. It does not condescend, but it supports Lear in his own new willingness to acknowledge his limitations.

Perhaps this acceptance is a model for our relationship to Lear, and through him, to the play. Cordelia's attitude toward Lear mediates the attitude of the audience toward him. We can neither change Lear nor admire him uncritically, any more than Cordelia can, but we can join her in feeling with him. It is interesting that Shakespeare not only emphasizes his characters' capacity for sympathy, but also, in his descriptions of audiences, frequently presents sympathy as an important aspect of audience response. It may be the experience of feeling sympathy for someone we cannot change, whose faults we accept as we accept our own faults, that Shakespearean tragedy brings to its highest artistic expression, both within the play and between the play and the audience.

There is so much sympathy with Lear at the end that it seems cold to turn from feeling with him to any further analysis of the play in terms of sex-role behavior, but it is worth noting that part of the effect of the play is to impress on us the suffering created by these behavior patterns and then to show how inadequate they are. The forms of suffering in literature reflect the social structure, either directly or indirectly, and it is significant that much of Lear's and Cordelia's sufferings are related to the particular vulnerabilities of men and women in a patriarchal society, as I have shown. But when Lear enters with Cordelia dead in his arms, the visual image in itself suggests a change in him. The allusion to the pietà that many critics have seen here includes the fact that Lear is at this point taking on a posture much more characteristic of women than of men in our society—holding a child, caring for the dead. His patient watch over Cordelia, looking for a sign of life, may recall his expectation of her answer in the opening scene, but it is very different in tone. Though he still clings to some of his traditional images of male and female virtues, when he says, "Her voice was ever soft, / Gentle and low" (5.3.273-74), it is his own gentleness we see.[17] Now he would give to her in a way that would be nurturing and not coercive, but it is too late.

His suffering includes a sense of guilt for misusing his past power, but before the ultimate fact of death he feels the powerlessness that we all feel, king and subject, man and woman. At the end of the play, the surviving characters can for the most part only watch Lear's sufferings like the offstage audience, and the only acts they can perform are gestures of sympathy. All Edgar says in the concluding speech establishing his dominance is about feeling and sympathy for Lear. Thus in the sympathy that is the audience's only power we are united with the surviving characters. Cordelia's values spread beyond her and outlive her, but this is no matter for complacent intellectualization. Shakespeare probes in *King Lear* to the very heart of loss. Although here, unlike the parallel explorations of *Antony and Cleopatra* and *Othello*, the issue of sexuality as such remains mostly submerged, he shows with great depth the vulnerabilities to each other that the contrasting social roles of men and women intensify. The only consolation that he offers—and in a theater it is a significant one—is that we feel each other's loss because of our basic connection.

Notes

1 See, for example, Alfred Harbage, Introduction to *King Lear,* ed. Alfred Harbage (Baltimore: Penguin, 1970), pp. 20-21; Maynard Mack, *King Lear in Our Time* (Berkeley: University of California Press, 1972), pp. 49-51.

2 Mack, *King Lear in Our Time,* pp. 100-113. He notes that the term was earlier applied to *Lear*'s world by Enid Welsford in *The Fool: His Social and Literary History* (London: Faber and Faber, 1935), p. 258.

3 Alvin W. Gouldner, "The Norm of Reciprocity," *American Sociological Review* 25 (April 1960): 173-75.

4 Marvin Spevack, *A Complete and Systematic Concordance to the Works of Shakespeare,* 8 vols. (Hildesheim: Georg Olms, 1968-75), 4: 984-88.

5 See, especially, Norman Holland, *Psychoanalysis and Shakespeare* (New York: McGraw-Hill, 1966), pp. 216-19.

6 Elizabeth Janeway, *Man's World, Woman's Place* (New York: Delta, 1971), pp. 37-47.

7 Peter Berger and Hansfried Kellner, "Marriage and the Construction of Reality," *Diogenes* 46 (Summer 1964): 17, 7.

8 See, for example, Simone de Beauvoir, *The Second Sex,* trans. H. M. Parshley (New York: Bantam, 1961), pp. 129-85.

9 Their attack on Lear draws on the role of the old as another stigmatized group, with another set of ready-made stereotypes overlapping with some of the negative images of women. For hostility toward the old in seventeenth-century England, see Lawrence Stone, "Walking Over Grandma," *New York Review of Books,* May 12, 1977, pp. 10-16, and Keith Thomas, "Age and Authority in Early Modern England," *Proceedings of the British Academy* 62 (1976): 205-48. . . . [If] patriarchy rests on male superiority in physical strength, it ceases to favor old men. In choosing Edmund, Goneril and Regan can be seen as following this form of patriarchy, which defines manhood by capacity for violence. The Elizabethan structure of institutional power did still favor old men, and Thomas suggests that this provoked much of the hostility.

10 See Marvin Rosenberg, *The Masks of King Lear* (Berkeley: University of California Press, 1972), p. 290, for the frequency of this gesture in recent performances.

11 Cf. Paul J. Alpers, "*King Lear* and the Theory of the 'Sight Pattern,'" in *In Defense of Reading,* ed. Reuben Brower and Richard Poirier (New York: Dutton, 1962), p. 150.

[12] Lawrence Stone, *The Crisis of the Aristocracy, 1558-1641* (Oxford: Clarendon Press, 1965), pp. 591-92.

[13] Northrop Frye, "The Argument of Comedy," in *English Institute Essays,* 1948, ed. D.A. Robertson (New York: Columbia University Press, 1949), p. 62.

[14] R.G. Hunter, *Shakespeare and the Comedy of Forgiveness* (New York: Columbia University Press, 1965). Hunter discusses the dependence of the forgiveness in Shakespeare's plays on a sense of common humanity that he identifies with the medieval idea of charity as distinguished from the modern one (p. 243).

[15] Howard Felperin,   *Shakespearean Romance* (Princeton: Princeton University Press, 1972), p. 87n.

[16] Stanley Cavell, "The Avoidance of Love," in *Must We Mean What We Say?* (New York: Charles Scribner's Sons, 1969), pp. 310-53.

[17] See Carolyn Heilbrun, *Toward a Recognition of Androgyny* (New York: Harper & Row, 1973), pp. 28-34, for a discussion of Shakespeare's "androgynous ideal" and its relationship to forgiveness and the father-daughter theme.

Act IV, scene vii. Doctor, Cordelia, Lear, and Kent. By Robert Smirke (n.d.).

Barbara C. Millard (essay date 1989)

SOURCE: "Virago with a Soft Voice: Cordelia's Tragic Rebellion in *King Lear,*" in *Philological Quarterly,* Vol. 68, No. 2, Spring, 1989, pp. 143-65.

[*In this essay, Millard examines Cordelia's part in the political elements of* King Lear, *noting that her rejection of her role as daughter in favor of one typically reserved for a son results in an internal struggle to attain her identity.*]

Cordelia's silences, absences, and the highly emblematic quality of the scenes in which she appears have inspired a strong critical tradition which views the role played by Lear's youngest daughter as primarily supportive and, therefore, dramatically secondary. With so few lines, Cordelia, however revered, has yet to be recognized fully as a major character at the center of the play's action, a tragic figure who consistently plays a crucial role in the determination of events in *King Lear,* including her own death.[1] This oversight may also be due in part to our assumptions about the importance of her military action within the political sphere of the play. As one critic articulates this view, Cordelia's decision to invade Britain is "not immediate or important in the play." Consequently, the battle is perceived as only a background for Edmund's speeches,

while Cordelia "moves in shadows" as the truly patient woman and daughter.[2]

A comparison of *King Lear* with the earlier play, *King Leir,* however, emphasizes both the force and coherence of political elements in Shakespeare's play and Cordelia's central part in them. Rather than dismiss Cordelia's death as accident, the effect of Lear's tragic action, or even as poetically appropriate self-sacrifice, we might better consider the defeat of Cordelia's French forces and her subsequent death in terms of the importance of temporal structure in Renaissance drama; that is, as resulting from her decision to invade Britain, a preemptive attempt to reverse the effects of her rebellion in the first scene of the play.[3] As the play moves from the ritualistic first act to its apocalyptic conclusion, Cordelia chooses to operate in a political sphere whose demands conflict with her more personal mission to rescue Lear. The military campaign in act four is the consequence of an off-stage decision by Cordelia to postpone giving "unaccommodated" Lear the serene "place" he needs in an effort to restore the place she believes him to have lost and desire still. In this militant and righteous posture, she not only suggests the doomed *Virago* of Renaissance legends but also assumes the role of the tragic hero, by mistaking both the nature of things and the proper way to attain the necessary end—Lear's rescue or release. More significantly, Cordelia presents a tragic paradigm as a woman who first rejects the self-obliterating role of daughter/mother demanded by her father, only to be defeated later by her attempt of the heroic militant role reserved for the son/father. In changing so radically Cordelia's fate from that of the traditional Leir story, Shakespeare's play not only presents us with a more ambiguous character but also raises challenging questions, reflective of Jacobean culture, about the redemptive role of women.

1

In attempting to comprehend the gothic structure that is *Lear,* one is sorely tempted to view Cordelia as monolithic. Indeed, Paula S. Berggren has noted that most women in Shakespearean tragedy seem to split into two basic types: the good, as victims, or the evil, as monsters.[4] Yet, to see Cordelia as either sainted martyr (pathetic, timid, politically naive, misunderstood) or villain (cold, willful, insensitive, proud, unbending) is to ignore an important dramatic tension in the play. In fact, Cordelia's struggle to attain her identity while poised between political necessity in a patriarchal world and her own moral wisdom defines her tragic experience, her simultaneous movement toward retribution and atonement. Moreover, her ambiguous personality seems designed to elicit our ambivalence, our dual response. The Lear story in any of its forms demands that we recognize Cordelia's need for integrity in the love-test scene, and so too in Shakespeare's play, the tension of the first scene partly draws from our compulsion to align ourselves with the youngest, fairy-tale third child. But when we regard Cordelia as specifically a *female* child (as "our joy" and "least"), we—including many who are female, and especially, parents—tend to put her at the other end of the telescope, to see her in harsher, more traditional terms: one who betrays her identification as the loving nurse, one whose begrudging response must be an error, as later acknowledged by her tears in act four. Both Cordelia's plain truth and her "silence" in the first scene have been viewed as "manly" insofar as they are courageous, hard or untender postures (Kent is rarely criticized for his bluntness or lack of ceremony), which Lear would not expect from his most beloved daughter. That it is "pride which she calls plainness" is true, after all; that it is undesirable in any child, especially a daughter, is a paternalistic perception. From this point of view, the critic sees Cordelia's movement toward self-possession and her plea for her integrity as unladylike insubordination, a reflection of her father's pride and arrogance and a taint which is later

purged by her banishment and/or converted by the romance of marriage with France.[5]

Another look at Shakespeare's probable sources for the Lear story, however, reveals more about Shakespeare's creation of tension and ambivalent response for the audience of this first scene. The purpose of the love-test in *The True Chronicle Historie of King Leir and His Three Daughters* is to divide equally the kingdom-as-dowry so as to dispose of three unwed daughters and to maneuver Cordelia into marrying the suitor Leir favors, not Shakespeare's foreign lord but "a King within this Isle." In his own version of the scene, Shakespeare removes hints about Lear's motivation which would lend him pathos (that he is sad and distraught because his wife has died, and that he wants to live in devout contemplation), and eliminates the suggestion of naiveté which might excuse his error (that he is ignorant of the affairs and character of daughters, "For fathers best do know how to governe sonnes" [1.1.19]).[6] In *Leir,* Gonorill and Ragan are clearly revealed, in a scene before the love-test, to be carping, mean-spirited, and jealous of Cordella's beauty, so that the audience is predisposed to appreciate Cordella's disgust with their prevarication.

The most significant change is in the character of Cordelia as she appears in Shakespeare's play. The youngest daughters in the accounts of Geoffrey of Monmouth, Raphael Holinshed, and John Higgins are cryptic, riddling, and intimidated. The slightly varying answers invariably point to the issue of spiritual versus material evaluation: "Look how much you have, so much is your Value [or "woorth," or "goodes," respectively], and so much I love you." The injunction of such an answer is for the king to look within; the riddle is a key to the sisters' true avarice. In *Leir,* Cordella's reply, "What love the child doth owe the father, / The Same to you I beare, my gracious Lord" (ll. 279-80)—is yet personal as it speaks of a potentially open-ended relationship. As Shakespeare's Lear increases the demand ("more opulent") of the old men of the legends, so he receives less, in fact, nothing. As Cordella presented an expansive equation, Cordelia specifically limits hers: "I love you according to my bond, no more nor less." As Cordella, under fire from her father's wrath, reaches toward conciliation: "Deare father, do not mistake my words, / Nor my playne meaning be misconstrued; / My toung was never usde to flattery" (ll. 301-3), so Cordelia stands taller in the fire and seeks justification. Thus Shakespeare transforms his material to ask what the older stories more confidently assume, and the question is one of central importance in the later romances: What does it mean to be a royal daughter in a patriarchal society? What does it require?

To begin, Shakespeare emphasizes Cordelia's competition with her already-married sisters. That her personal dislike of her sisters noticeably influences her behavior has been frequently observed. Her first response is to them in the *aside,* "What shall Cordelia speak?" Or, rather, it is to herself; for throughout the scene, Cordelia is primarily in a conversation with herself, as the third person reference in her question indicates. Meanwhile, Goneril's and Regan's opulence places her in a competition where being last is a distinct embarrassment if not a liability: "Then poor Cordelia!" But Cordelia's concern is less with winning or losing and more with her own feelings, as her answer to herself makes clear: "And yet not so, since I am sure my love's / More ponderous than my tongue." The Quarto text presents "richer" in lieu of "ponderous," alluding to the original riddle of spiritual/material worth. The substituted "ponderous," however, combines the idea of weight with thought. Cordelia's pondering, in the exchange with her father, about the real nature of her love and their relationship leads to a dialectic in which her asides posit one answer to the question (to one half of herself and to us) and her public response posits another (to Lear and her other half). As Lear divides his kingdom, so his uncompromising demand divides Cordelia, a psychological state which endures for one reason or another until her tragic death.

At this point, the political expediency of Lear's contest—to ensure his youngest daughter's power (and his own "rest") by means of "more opulent" property and a carefully selected husband—apparently does not escape Cordelia. Neither is the task at hand beyond her. She is eloquent in her brief asides and infuriatingly articulate and precise in her replies to Lear. In fact, she has forty-six lines in the scene as compared with the earlier Cordella's eighteen, or her sisters' eleven and nine. Cordelia's famous "silence" refers not to what she does say but to what she does not say, beyond her hints in the asides (the other half of the dialectic). Rather than a helpless reply, "Nothing" is a deliberate choice, the alternative dictated by her own imperative: "Love and be silent," as well as by Lear's equation of words with reward. Whereas the Quarto text includes only Cordelia's "Nothing," the Folio adds Lear's query, "Nothing?" and its reprise, simultaneously prolonging the tension and asserting her rejection of Lear's formula.[7] Like a person indicted. Cordelia is driven by Lear's imperatives into an equally uncompromising confrontation with herself, for she cannot answer Lear's question and define their relation without defining herself. It is a perilous journey for Cordelia in so little space and time. When she speaks again, she dramatically increases the proportion of first person pronouns to second person: "Unhappy that I am, I cannot heave / My heart into my mouth. I love your majesty / According to my bond, no more nor less." When she "mends" this speech a little, the proportion is more balanced: "You have begot me, bred me, loved me. I / Return those duties back as are right fit, / Obey you,

love you, and most honor you." While the other Cordelias were teaching the father about himself, Cordelia teaches Lear about his daughter: "So young, my lord, and true."

A good deal of Cordelia's comment, of course, is an attempt to refute her sisters' hypocrisy, and in the process both define and distance herself from her siblings in the only was the social order permits, by distinguishing herself as daughter and wife: "Sure I shall never marry like my sisters, / To love my father all." By coming to realize the limits of her own personality, she finds the dimensions of her integrity. Cordelia's dramatic assertion bespeaks her claim to adulthood and emotional autonomy. Joyce Carol Oates has aptly commented on the tenor of this confrontation: "In this woman's insistence upon a moral intelligence not determined by her social role we have rebellion, the first and the most surprising of all."[8] That Cordelia's rebellion is all the more offensive to her father because she is female is suggested by Lear's invocation of the witch Hecate in his curse. That he views her violation of familial duty as destructive of the civil order as well is indicated by his "preference" for the barbarous Scythian over this "sometime daughter."[9]

However splendid Cordelia's personal realization, her achievement is shadowed by the socio-political realities of the context. The fate of Britain as well as of her father hangs suspended, and neither her courage nor her militant candor can defeat her sisters' politic skill or avert their triumph. If she lacks that "glib and oily art," she also eschews poetry. Where her sisters imagine their golden future of "grace," "health," "beauty," "felicitation," "joys," "freedom," and "honor," Cordelia withdraws from the necessity of Lear's "darker purpose" and speaks of "duty," "bond," "care," "plight," "obedience," "vicious blot," "unchaste act," and dishonor. What her sisters eloquently proclaim with impunity is what Cordelia, as "last" and "least" would have to (and does) inherit, that is, to prefer her father to "space" or "libertie" or "life" or other "love." Cordelia's language reveals to Lear and the court what he would leave unsaid, his intention to usurp her life and subsume her future to his "rest." We recognize that the political alternatives are unacceptable, Burgundy, Lear's probable choice for Cordelia's husband ("I crave no more than hath your Highness offer'd"), proves greedy and politically ambitious. Cordelia's dowry of a larger third would ensure the enmity of her sisters and guarantee the strife Lear wished to avoid. So, too, Cordelia's unconditional commitment to the perpetual "nursery" of the father she must love "all" would preclude all hope of self-possession. As it is, Cordelia reverses their positions and power and, in effect, wins her freedom and ascends a throne of moral individualism. Furthermore, her ascension to the throne of France completes an emblem of a most highly-charged and threatening political meaning for British kings and subjects. Cordelia's role as Queen of France becomes a part of her identity which no one in the play can afford to forget. Edmund's only legitimacy in the last two acts of the play is as defender of Britain against this foreign Queen.

Both Cordelia's struggle to maintain her integrity and her right to rule Britain according to Lear's design would have been her unquestioned prerogative had the "least" been more in this society, that is, male. Unlike his counterparts in the source stories, Lear never laments the lack of a son but compensates himself instead with his demand for the full measure of his daughters' feminine virtues: obedience, love, servitude. With shattering clarity the events of the play dramatize the ramifications of Lear's attempt to impose these virtues rather than encourage the development of a true sovereignty in his daughters. Gloucester's apocalyptic vision in scene two reveals that Lear has tried, in fact, to make Cordelia both daughter-mother by her personal love-pledge and son through his gift of patrimony: "and the bond cracked d'twixt son and father . . . there's son against father; the king falls from bias of nature" (ll. 111-14). Cordelia's independent stance, her rejected role as primary inheritor, and her "male" bluntness are thus put in ironic relief to Edmund's "lusty" bid to "top th' legitimate" in this juxtaposed scene.

Lear's unethical and politically dangerous experiment and its subsequent confusion—his hasty re-division of the kingdom to punish Cordelia—place him in jeopardy but not Cordelia. She has side-stepped the trap for a "better where." Her fate—to die as an invading queen—is not the inevitable consequence of this scene until, exiting, she "commits" him to the "professed bosoms" of the sisters whose "faults" and "cunning" she well knows, if "loath to call / . . . as they are nam'd." Having avoided one impossible commitment, she makes another she cannot, in her humanity, keep. Ironically, Cordelia's wish to "prefer him to a better place" suggests the scenario of the source material, his safe removal to her care in France, rather than the preemptive tragic invasion Shakespeare has her choose later when she recants this "commitment." When, in a recounted off-stage action, Cordelia's "importun'd tears" convince France to "incite" their arms in the service of her father's business, she chooses to imitate her father's impulsive act and punish her sisters, the "shame of ladies," by attempting to seize their patrimony through military offensive and return it to her father—an action personally ineffective and politically unacceptable.[10] As we shall see, one of the most terrible ironies which Shakespeare suggests in the catastrophe of this play is that in her militant posture Cordelia unwittingly participates in her sisters' destructiveness, even as she battles their inhumanity.

Cordelia's choice of a militant role in advance of the ministerial one is central to both the play's action and

its ominous theme regarding female ascendancy in conflict with patriarchal order. Having received their power through Cordelia's "default," Goneril and Regan demonstrate more obviously the dangers of female assertion and provide the context for Cordelia's actions in acts four and five. The steady descent of Goneril and Regan into "unnatural," ruthless monstrosity suggests the consequences of freeing these women from the patriarchal power which held them in check (and forced both obedience and eloquence upon demand) and the folly of allowing such daughters such "unnatural" authority. The Fool consistently chides Lear and Lear commiserates with Poor Tom, specifically, about "daughters" not children.

After the first scene of the play, Shakespeare mythically projects a situation similar to that described by Simone de Beauvoir as the fearful vision of patriarchal society. The reign of women is perceived as "the reign of irreducible duration, of contingency, of chance, of waiting, of mystery."[11] As an old dispossessed man, Lear is as vulnerable in the female realm of Nature as Cordelia is in the male-dominated settings provided for her trials: the court and the battlefield. The entire import of act three is that no man can stand in the fierce winds of a real matriarchy. Striving in his "little world of man," Lear not only identifies the storm (raw unchecked nature) with his mother-daughters but also recognizes that the support of patriarchy, Jupiter's thunderbolts, have been suborned as well: "But yet I call you servile ministers, / That will with two pernicious daughters join / Your high-engender'd battles 'gainst a head / So old and white as this" (3.2.21-24). As much as to the storm within, his own unleashed personality, Lear succumbs to two unpredictable forces of life: elemental nature and women. The movement of all the characters from dwellings, across a desolate landscape, to the field of battle and the cliffs of Dover in the last two acts of the play would seem to suggest that there is no home, no sanctuary of rest in the shifting world of female dominance. Even Cordelia who desires to provide shelter for Lear's "abused nature" can only offer the vicissitudes of the French camp.

2

Like so many other Renaissance writers, Shakespeare treats militant or Amazonian women according to whether they operate within the frame of the existing patriarchal order. Since there is no patriarchal order after Lear's abdication and subsequent madness, all his daughters' actions, however motivated, can only contribute to the chaos. Only when Albany demands authority from Goneril, and denies to Edmund that lent him by Regan (5.3.83-85), does the political turmoil begin to subside.[12] One can look at the anti-feminism of the Jacobean stage in general, and of *King Lear* in particular, as deriving from several contemporary events: male revulsion toward the threatening phenomenon of "a monstrous regiment of women" rulers and militant politicos in Europe; the recent death of the Queen, and with her the Tudor ideal of peace; and the various political plots against James I's throne, especially the Cobham plot in 1603, which attempted to overthrow the king in favor of the insubordinate Lady Arabella Stuart. One can also cite the strictures of various humanists, like Castiglione and Vives, against the teaching of martial arts and government to young ladies of the court, to explain Shakespeare's association of male disaster and psychological horror with female defiance and power. Contemporary polemicists were found of quoting the ancients, especially Juvenal: *"Quem prestare potest mulier galeata pudorem?"* (*Satires* 6.252: What modesty can you expect in a woman who wears a helmet?). However, the legend from British Celtic history of a real *Virago,* Boudicca, suggests a paradigm by which we can better comprehend Shakespeare's conception of the militant women in his plays and the necessity of their tragic fates.

Of that British stock from which the Tudors came, this queen and patriot fought gloriously against the Roman invaders of her country only to face ultimate defeat. Like Cleopatra, Boudicca had no mind to figure in a Roman triumph, and like several Shakespearean women of "manly" courage she killed herself. The Roman historian, Dion Cassius, records the Britons' deep respect and passionate mourning for her, while the Welsh Gildas exhibits contempt for "that deceitful lionness" who led a cowardly rabble army and lost the final battle.[13] This duality of response to Boudicca's legend is manifest in Tudor histories and sheds light on Cordelia's complex character. The Elizabethan humanists were noticeably influenced by Tacitus' account of a wronged woman seeking revenge in a fool-hardy manner, but one book, Petruccio Ubaldini's *The Lives of the Noble Ladies of the Kingdome of England and Scotland* (written for Elizabeth in 1588 and published in 1591), specifies a double for Boudicca. Together "Bunduica" and her double, "Voadicia," resemble the dual image of the female warrior which appears in the work of Shakespeare and his contemporaries. The "Bunduica" figure, a bold *Virago,* is noted for her military prowess which is balanced by her marvelous virtues and praiseworthy deeds.[14] We can see that image in Elizabeth I, in her white velvet dress and silver cuirass, "like some Amazonian Empress," and in the likes of Britomart, and perhaps Cordelia.[15] Edmund Spenser celebrates Boundicca in *The Faerie Queene* as the precursor of Gloriana in her courageous opposition to oppression. Like Cordelia, Spenser's heroine loses the final battle underservedly, a victim of the universal corruption "overcome in happlesse fight," yet triumphant "on death in enemies despight" (2.10.14-16).[16] On the other hand, Bunduica's double, Voadicia, suggests that Elizabethan man-woman whose thirst for vengeance leads to folly and impetuosity on the battle-

field and chaos in the civil order. She is the actual Amazon queen of unmitigated power: a Tamora or Goneril or Pucelle. And she is also a failure. The legend of Boudicca generally connects with the exempla of other emotional women of classical fame, such as Dido or Cleopatra, who fail in moments of crisis, usually as a result of their passion (Note Goneril's "I had rather lose the battle than that sister / Should loosen him and me" [5.1.18-19]). After Elizabeth's death, the legend of Boudicca becomes increasingly tarnished. By the time she appears in Milton's *History of Britain* (1670), she is not only deplorably immodest, but also responsible for the barbaric and impotent conduct of British men and the failure of the campaign. Evidence that the legend of Boudicca, used for propaganda for the monarchy of Elizabeth, was turned to anti-feminist use in the Jacobean era can perhaps be found in Fletcher's *Bonduca,* performed by the King's Men in 1610 and therefore, contemporary with Shakespeare's own interest in ancient British history evident in Lear and *Cymbeline.* Bonduca is clearly subordinated in this play to the more chivalrous and competent leader Caratach, who watches in horror the fatal consequences of her generalship. After accusing her of complicity with the devil in meddling in "men's affairs," he bids the "trifle" go home and "spin" (3.5.132-35).[17] Although many classical figures, human and divine, serve in Renaissance drama as models of female valor, Boudicca's dual identity is especially significant in the ambivalence it exposes in Renaissance culture towards militant women, an ambivalence which perhaps accounts for the incongruous juxtaposition of Cordelia's militant posture and patient resignation in acts four and five, if not for her defeat in battle. Indeed, Holinshed's account of Boudicca contains several parallels in tone and characterization with *King Lear.* Like Cordelia, Queene Voadicia moves against the Romans because of the disinheritance of her royal family and the plight of people who have been forced to endure a houseless condition of "hunger, thirst, cold. . . . " As Cordelia speaks of her sisters' treatment of Lear in contrast to that of a dog, Voadicia similarly complains of Roman cruelty "since there is no man that taketh so much as a wild beast, but at the first he will cherish it." Also like Cordelia, Voadica disclaims any motive of personal gain in her address to her troops. She comes not "to fight for her kingdome and riches," but to regain liberty and punish cruelty.[18]

That female militancy, however qualified by goodness, cannot prevail is indicated by the ironic interplay between the parallel careers of Edgar and Cordelia. Whereas Edgar, the elder, legitimate heir, can combine the dual role of "nurse" and champion—and triumph, Cordelia in her similar attempt cannot. So, too, the subconscious wish to punish the hurtful, unappreciative father can be executed with impunity and transcended by Edgar in the ritualized suicide attempt of his father.[19] Conversely, Cordelia cannot prevent the annihilation of herself and her father as a consequence of both her attempt at separation in act one and her later chivalrous action in behalf of her "aged father's right." The virtues of goodness, patience, love, forgiveness, and "nursery," ultimately celebrated in Cordelia, are manifest first in Edgar. In acts three and four, he anticipates Cordelia's part by sympathizing with and tending to Lear, first, and then to his own father. At this point in the play, the sub-plot overtakes the main plot. Edgar, together with the Fool, assumes Cordelia's function, so that when Cordelia appears, her ministration is both a reflection of and comment on Edgar's. While Cordelia evokes all the "unpublished virtues of the earth" to "spring" with her tears and be "remediated in the good man's distress," Edgar, as Poor Tom, studies and learns. "How to prevent the fiend, and to kill vermin" (4.4.15-17; 3.4.157). Finally, Edgar's ability to cope with political and moral evil through personal, death-encountering ritual succeeds where Cordelia's tears and well-intentioned war fail. While both figure forth the moral victory of filial love, Cordelia pays the higher price, and Edgar's moment of justification is ironically juxtaposed with the terrible vision of hanged Cordelia in Lear's arms.

Although Cordelia and Edgar both might be described as naive in their response to evil, Edgar imitates the imaginative procedures of Shakespeare's women in the comedies and romances. He retreats to disguise, yields to emotional distress through the persona, Poor Tom, and learns the miseries of his father "by nursing them," before asserting his right.[20] Understanding "ripeness," he abides his father's death before engaging Edmund, not on his father's business, but his own. Thus he is at one with his action; a harmonious relation exists between all his ends and purposes, harmony exists between his purposes and means. Since tragedy stems from alternatives ignored as well as choices made, we should note the alternative to Cordelia's military action which Edgar offers when he allows time to bring Gloucester to him and prompt his part. That time is the remedy for destructive male impulse in the romances is generally acknowledged. Whatever Cordelia hopes to achieve by her action, the temporal structure of the play indicates that the military campaign is precipitous and premature. Often, in *Lear,* the motive for choosing alternative behavior is not given dramatic consideration; rather, the choices themselves and the consequences of these choices are more important than the reasons for them. Thus, Cordelia, who determines in an early letter to Kent to "give losses their remedies" (2.2.171-73), determines the events of the play from the blinding of Gloucester (3.7) to the battle (5.2), when she embarks "with a force" for England.

In this point, Shakespeare's divergence from his sources is only less dramatic than in Cordelia's death itself, a fact that suggests a relation between the two events. All known sources of the story have the king escape England and undergo a healing process before the redress of political wrongs. Leir, whose life is in certain danger from assassins hired by his daughters, seeks out Cordella in France and desires military assistance of her. The political implications of Shakespeare's events are specific. Cordella, France, and the French force, in whatever combination, however deployed in the various tales, are given legitimacy, first by the *dukes'* rebellion and second by Leir's responsible advocacy. No such legitimacy attends Cordelia's and France's invasion; this invasion is anticipated as retributive (3.3.11-13) and later described as personal: her love, its "mourning and importuned tears," did their "arms incite." That the Folio text excludes the several references to the invasion, prior to Cordelia's appearance in act four, attests to the political explosiveness of the issue for an English audience.

As a woman who will do before she says, Cordelia anticipates on her father's part a desire he no longer has—to reclaim his throne and power. While there is no textual evidence to support the contention that France has political ambitions for himself, there is his hasty retreat to deny it. In attempting to gauge Cordelia's motive, certainly, one cannot discount the punitive tone regarding the two who are the "Shame of Ladies" and the final cold anger of "Shall we not see these daughters, these sisters?" But this tone is only one of several, including her expression of filial sympathy when "she heav'd the name of 'father' / Pantingly forth, as if it press'd her heart" (4.2.27-28). Cordelia accepts and would restore the role Lear defined for himself in the first scene; she endeavors to atone for her sisters' crimes by returning kingly majesty to him through military exploit, as if, to quote Lamb, "the childish pleasure of getting his gilt robes and sceptre again could tempt him to act over again his misused station."[21] Like Lear in act one, Cordelia treats Britain as her father's property. When she alludes to her dear father's business, we shiver to realize that the real business Lear must get on with is dying. Thus an exhausted old man tells Cordelia, "You do me wrong to take me out o' the grave" (4.7.45).

For his thematic purpose, then, Shakespeare not only compressed the events of Lear's rescue as they are described in the source material but also changed them so much as to risk troubling the play's audiences through the ages. Like Edgar, the Cordelias of the other versions minister to the father, providing him with shelter, comfortable rest, and restoring his confidence *before* raising troops to aid him in battle. For Cordelia, nursery and battle are simultaneous and therefore mutually defeating. Throughout act three, Lear's houseless condition suggests its remedy, the relief that Cordelia might provide. Indeed, Lear's confused question, "Am I in France?" suggests that happy alternative of the history; so too, the double edge of his reply ("Do not abuse me") to the truth of where he is suggests that to be in this hostile place, no longer "his," is both abuse and error. Shakespeare's use of dramatic contrast further conveys the inappropriateness of Cordelia's military campaign to her personal mission. The cries of a raving Lear in act three are punctuated with intelligence reports of France's maneuvers. After act three, scene four, Shakespeare never allows his characters to mention Lear's responsibility as king; rather, the mad king demonstrates all too clearly his distance from the mundane world of affairs. At the end of this sequence of "mad" scenes, Kent points to the real necessity of Lear's condition: "Oppressed nature sleeps. / This rest might yet have balm'd thy broken sinews / Which, if convenience will not allow, / Stand in hard cure" (3.6.95-98). In a scene positioned between Edgar's meeting with the blinded Gloucester and their arrival at the "cliff" site, Cordelia discusses Lear's treatment with the Doctor (or Gentleman of the Folio text). The prescription echoes Kent's emphatically: "Our foster-nurse of nature is repose. / The which he lacks" (4.4.12-13). Immediately follows the report that the British powers are on the march. Whereas Lear has learned through extremity to transcend the political world, and Edgar, to suspend it, Cordelia is trapped and destroyed by both its realities (her foreign royalty and disinheritance) and its burdens, "the darker purpose" of her surrogate male-child role, or the punishment of her sisters. Once she commits herself to her "father's business," Cordelia casts herself in the image of the redemptive Son, a role immediately recognizable for its sacrificial implications, a role from which she cannot extricate herself once she discovers her father's transformation and hears his plea to "forgive and forget." In her "male" role, she eschews the imaginative, female suberfuge practiced by Edgar and the comedies' heroines: withdrawal and disguise. When the Gentleman describes her to Kent, the image poignantly depicts her struggle to remain poised within the dual impulse: "it seem'd she was a queen / Over her passion, who most rebel-like / Sought to be king o'er her" (4.2.15-17). The rebel-like Cordelia has brought herself and her father to the cliffs of Dover, in an action parallel to that of Edgar, only to find that she has misjudged her father's business and her own, and that the fall is real. Unlike Edgar, Cordelia does not enjoy integrity of action in act four. The reality of Lear's condition places her role as champion "son" at odds with that of nursing daughter:

> O my dear father, restoration hang
> Thy medicine on my lips, and let this kiss
> Repair those violent harms that my two sisters
> Have in thy reverence made!
>
> (4.7.26-29)

As ministering daughter, Cordelia follows in the well-established tradition, dating at least from twelfth-century Arthurian romance, in which female healers tend the hero's wounds. The extension of this power to psychological healing is praised in the Renaissance by such as Anthony Gibson, in *A Womans Woorth, defended against all the men in the world:* "Even so a woman qualifies divers tempests, which wandring through a mans braines, do weaken his stronger powers untill this lawful and natural medicine be thereto applyed."[22]

That her meeting with Lear is so peaceful, joyous, and genuine in its pathos only emphasizes the incongruity of the context in which Cordelia would attempt to cure "this great breach," his "untuned and jarring senses." Accordingly, Shakespeare presents jarring visual and auditory effects to underscore the irreconcilable nature of Cordelia's divided purpose. The Doctor and the Soldiers enter the scene together, the literal means by which Cordelia hopes to "repair those violent harms" made by her sisters.[23] As a "soul in bliss" dressed in battle armor, as she should be (and rarely is), Cordelia would appear to be a travesty. The newly feminized Lear, pacifist, patient and humble, is wakened to music and comfort only to face the alarum of troops. Cordelia has done her best to create the illusion of haven, a "redeemed world," but it evaporates all too quickly in the hostile landscape of civil war. Even Cordelia's expression of sympathy to her father combines the language of nursery: "restoration," "medicine," "kiss," "repair," "reverence," "pity," "benediction"—with the terms of warfare: "violent," "breach," "challenge," "oppos'd," "warring," "dread-bolted," "terrible and nimble stroke," "perdu," "helm," "enemy."[24]

Plausibility has not been left behind in *Lear* regarding the defeat of Cordelia's forces and her death. Those in the British camp are so absorbed in preparation and the gathering of intelligence regarding the French force (5.1.51-54), that their personal affairs become muddled. But there is no discussion of strategy in the French camp where personal concerns have replaced the political. Cordelia prepares us for her tragic fate before Lear awakes. Acknowledging Kent's goodness, she predicts, "My life will be too short, / And every measure fail me" (4.7.2-3). While the gentle benedictions of Lear and Cordelia are yet fresh, the Gentleman reminds us that "the arbitrement is like to be bloody." While Edmund and Albany express their determination to repel the French and, now, English rebel forces, Cordelia in the fullness of her heart, is preoccupied with the Doctor's warning about Lear's condition: "Trouble him no more / Till further settling" (4.7.81-82). That Cordelia with Lear "by the hand" should fall into the abyss while walking the tightrope between these two poles of retribution and ministration should be no surprise. Victory for Lear and Cordelia, moreover, would present a situation as politically undesirable as Lear's proposal in act one. Whereas Cordila, in *The Mirror for Magistrates* version, "manly fought" beside her husband and her father, the spectacle of Cordelia, supporting a tottering Lear and leading forces against Goneril, Regan, Albany and Edmund is so obvious in its implication as to allow Shakespeare to omit most details of battle. The battle lost before it began, Cordelia's death at the hands of her ruthless enemy is, more likely than not, the logical outcome of principles of plot and characterization that have operated in the play.

As with another well-intentioned child, Hamlet, we can neither blame nor justify the action of Cordelia "who with best meaning . . . incurred the worst." Both France as a chivalrous prince, coming to the rescue of virtue in the first scene, and Edgar in his ritual combat with Edmund suggest analogues to Cordelia's militant stance. In ritual combat, however, Edgar accepts a higher (male) authority, submits to the gods' adjudication, and trusts to "this sword, this arm," with the result that he receives not only justice but also a confirmation of his authority. Without authority, Cordelia is indeed as a fly to whatever gods rule in the patriarchal world of Shakespearean tragedy. That Goneril ("the better soldier") and Regan are destroyed by their lusts does not provide occasion for Cordelia's rescue, but rather a fatal distraction from that purpose. Involved with the business of restoring a patriarchal order, the men in whose hands her life is suspended simply forget her.

Albany, as the eldest son-in-law and legal inheritor in scene one, finally assumes his patrimony, simultaneously with Cordelia's defeat, and yields it to Edgar, the champion son (F1). The reestablishment of patriarchal order, however, is a destructive mission for Cordelia, and an undesirable one for at least two of the three male survivors. There are those who view the return of Lear's "kingly" manhood as worth the price of Cordelia's death ("sacrifice"). Robert Egan, for example, comments, "Cordelia is in Lear's arms, more his child now than ever, and Lear is massive with the dignity of his fatherhood."[25] Does Cordelia's death free Lear? He rouses from his feebleness to kill "the slave that was a-hanging" her. As he laments the loss of her life ("dead as earth") and its mystery—that "a dog, a horse, a rat, have life," and her no breath at all—does not the "idol" of a gilded cage become finally subordinate to his assertion that his "poor Fool is hanged?" However pathetic and magnificent Lear is in his last moments, his love for Cordelia remains possessive. The quality of love remains the human value which Cordelia carries like a grail on her quest, across that tightrope of polarities. But children cannot redeem their parents, neither by loving them "all" nor by living with them forever and wearing out "packs and sects of great ones." Children can only replace their parents, as Edgar does.

Whether Cordelia's "sacrifice" is redemptive at all remains one of those critical questions to which we bring our own perspectives. Unlike Desdemona, Juliet, or Cleopatra, Cordelia is denied a triumphant death on stage with its suggestion of moral quality. Unlike

Ophelia or Lady Macbeth, she inspires no memorial description of her final moment. No recorded statement of faith or final assertion lingers after her. Her heroism is superseded by Lear's heroic boast regarding the hangman. And, unlike Hamlet, she receives no royal eulogy, no soldier's rites. Rather, Lear speaks of her as though she had died after many years as his companion and emphasizes her femininity: "Her voice was ever soft, / Gentle and low, an excellent thing in woman." If Cordelia, unlike her counterparts in the source material, never acknowledges responsibility for Lear's ordeal, neither does Lear acknowledge any responsibility for her fate now. To the contrary, Lear's perception and that of the survivors in the play is that her death was accidental, futile, and meaningless. The "men of stones," who say little else that they feel, vaguely wonder, "Is this the promised end?" and even Kent observes only that, "If Fortune brag of two she loved and hated, / One of them we behold" (5.3.283-84). Cordelia's requiem is indeed a "dull sight." The pity belongs to Lear for his loss rather than to Cordelia for hers.

Ever since Bradley, critics have found Cordelia's existence to be less important than what she *represents*. Cordelia's "No cause, no cause," inspires us to cherish her as a feminine principle of goodness, selflessness, and love. As Lisa Jardine has argued, the literary examples of "good" women from antiquity through the Christian martyrs enshrine a female hero that is defined by weakness, vulnerability, and tears, by her being *other than* manly.[26] In "gentle" Cordelia Shakespeare seems to reaffirm the traditional perspective that female sacrifice protects the sacred bonds of human society from the devastation which natural freedom would unleash. But it is Lear who calls Cordelia's imprisonment together with him a "sacrifice," not she, and it is Lear who denies her the measure of her greatness because of his total self-absorption in his sorrow. In his close reading of the last 70 lines of the play, Stephen Booth traces the pattern of testing by which Lear strains to determine Cordelia's renewed life, tests, Booth says, which echo the test "in which Cordelia could not heave her heart into her mouth" at the beginning of the play.[27] But what weighs in the balance of these tests of the looking glass and the feather is more than an ample third of the kingdom; it is, for Lear, no less than the redemption of "all sorrows / That ever I have felt" (5.3.67-68). The darkest implication here is that in her death, incurred as invading French Queen, Cordelia has failed Lear again, failed to redeem his sorrow, evaded the "sacrificial" role that he would have of her alive and in his keeping.

Like her "silence" regarding her heart in act one, her silence as she is led to prison and death assures her mystery. Her use of royal address—"We are not the first . . ."—indicates her self-possession and calm, and her acceptance of the consequence of her actions: "who with best meaning have incurred the worst." Having achieved an inner poise and freedom of spirit ("I am, I am"), she is sustained by insight and courage: "For thee, oppressed king, I am cast down; / Myself could else out-frown false Fortune's frown" (5.1.4-5). In this, the last scene in which she appears alive, Cordelia exemplifies that "manliness" in the face of death which humanists like Thomas Lupset espoused in his *Treatise of Dieying Well* (1530): "Let us then take a lusty courage of this desperation, seinge there is no remedy: lette us manfully go to it."[28] However few her lines or appearances, Cordelia's tragic stature is fully realized. Having rejected the static role that Lear would have imposed on her in act one, Cordelia goes on to create her own future, to seek retribution and the creation of a new order beyond her sisters', and eventually to achieve her own transcendence from political constraints through her reconciliation with Lear. She has in a "manly" fashion forged her own destiny and loses her life as a result of heroic risk. Like other heroic women in Shakespeare's tragedies, Cleopatra, Desdemona, or Juliet, she takes her "failure" upon herself. She does not try to evade it, but stands dignified by the truth or guilt of her free act.

Why then, in his last scene, does Shakespeare deny Cordelia the final recognition that he accords to others of his tragic women? Is it because she failed by her death to reaffirm, to redeem some hope of man in his own spiritual power? The only character who acknowledges the political reality of "the Queen's" militancy (as distinct from that of France) is Edmund who, in describing his plot and her apparent "suicide," alludes to her volition in the war and the possibility that "upon her own dispair . . . she fordid herself" (5.3.256-57). As stated, this suicidal motive evokes the legendary fate of both the Cordella whose nephews (resenting the "gynarchy") had her imprisoned, and that predecessor of British warrior queens, Boudicca. According to Holinshed, Cordella, imprisoned, followed the example of Boudicca and, "being a woman of manlie courage, and despairing to recover libertie, there she slew hirselfe."[29] Throughout the play Shakespeare suggests that the invasion is a mistake, and that such a stance is destructive of that female virtue which can redeem man through other more poetic means. Yet, as the histories and tragedies portray, patriarchy frequently isolates women and forces them to seek relief or redress in the political sphere, where they are invariably destroyed (or, in the histories, at least bereft) and their destruction can usually be legitimized. As Juliet Dusinberre comments in *Shakespeare and the Nature of Women:* "If women go to war themselves they cease to offer an alternative to the male world of politics and violence . . . ferocity in women challenges the stability of the civilized world."[30]

In Shakespeare's period of high tragedy, after 1603, the incidence of militant queens and women of "manly

courage" who desire to be "fair warriors," but who end as "unhandsome," is highly suggestive of this male anxiety. They include: Desdemona, Cordelia, Goneril, Regan, Lady Macbeth, Volumnia, and Cleopatra. Like Shakespeare's histories, the tragedies are set in the dense landscape of social and cultural history. They present women who cannot survive the aggressive tactics of patriarchal politics with any tactics of their own: either their feminine goodness and compliance is important or their female power and determination to resist or change the landscape is destructive. Prior to this period, militant women appear in a noticeable cluster only in Shakespeare's earliest plays: Queen Margaret, Joan La Pucelle, Tamora, and perhaps Kate ("I think she'll sooner prove a soldier" [2.1.145]—whereas the women of the Henriad are "good soldier-breeders" (*1 HIV* [3.1.193]). When such militant women appear in the late romances, they are evidently types of female evil, such as Dionyza or the Queen in *Cymbeline.* On the other hand, Viola's comic declaration, "I am no fighter," extends literally to the heroines of Shakespearean romance: the gods must fight for Perdita, a "poor thing" (2.3.191); Marina turns to her needlework and virtuous speech to protect her; the angelic Imogen serves as a page to the Roman general Lucius; and Miranda's "affections / Are then most humble" (1.2.484-85). Possessed of the romantic heroines' beauty, youth, gentleness, and moral commitment, Cordelia clearly lacks only the monumental "Patience" which presides over their crises.

If critical response to Cordelia's role in *King Lear* continues to fracture along the lines of blame and praise, perhaps it is because a traditional cultural perspective, to some extent, informs the play. But, more importantly, such response seems to reflect the dramatic ambiguity of Cordelia's character as manifest in the two key scenes in which she figures (the love test and reconciliation scenes). The difficulty in reconciling the rebellious and dutiful in Cordelia also derives from the dramatic question which Shakespeare poses in the first scene of the play: What does it mean to be a royal female child? What is required?—and the playwright's intuitive response: nothing and all. If there is resistance to accepting her in her dual role as loving daughter and *Virago,* it is because these realities appear to be highly incongruent in the play itself. In Lear's darkest vision, she, like all women, is a centaur underneath, capable of opposition when least expected. Female militance in *King Lear* is, after all, more devastating than the male because its effects are more personal. However virtuous, Cordelia in her militant, rebellious posture is a sister to her monster sisters and a daughter to that dead, forgotten mother who bore such daughters. A tragic queen in cuirass, Cordelia in her nursing role anticipates the heroines of the last plays, who, Shakespeare seems to suggest, can only save themselves and the sons of man through their healing power.

Notes

[1] Since Coleridge, studies of Cordelia as a tragic figure locate her decisive action only in 1.1. The argument that Cordelia's contribution to the tragic plot is limited to that scene is exemplified by Robert B. Heilman who maintains that, although Cordelia is a tragic actor because of her decision to "withdraw" in the first scene, her fate is not a central effect of the play but only meaningful as it "amplifies the tragic experience of Lear" (*This Great Stage: Image and Structure in "King Lear"* [Louisiana State U. Press, 1948], pp. 35-36, 301); and more recently by John McLaughlin when he asserts: "Cordelia is a tragic figure because the flawed life plan that prevented her from giving Lear the flattery he demanded is punished too severely" ("The Dynamics of Power in *King Lear*," *Shakespeare Quarterly* 29 [1978]: 40).

[2] Cf. John Reibetanz, *The Lear World: A Study of* "King Lear" *in Its Dramatic Context* (U. of Toronto Press, 1977), pp. 14, 31, 52.

[3] Reviewing past arguments for the dramatic justification of Cordelia's death, Susan Snyder argues that the event does not follow from the logic of the action, but is rather part of a grotesque joke (*The Comic Matrix of Shakespeare's Tragedies* [Princeton U. Press, 1979], pp. 156-59). As the debate continues, Stephen J. Lynch sees its tragic ending as an appropriate conclusion to a drama more consistently concerned with spiritual and Christian values than the earlier *Leir* play ("Sin, Suffering, and Redemption in *Leir* and *Lear*," *Shakespeare Studies* 18 [1986]: 172-74).

[4] Berggren, "The Woman's Part: Female Sexuality as Power in Shakespeare's Plays," in *The Woman's Part: Feminist Criticism of Shakespeare,* ed. Carolyn Ruth Swift Lenz, Gayle Greene, and Carol Thomas Neely (U. of Illinois Press, 1980), p. 18.

[5] See, for example, Sophia B. Blaydes, "Cordelia: Loss of Insolence," *Studies in the Humanities* 5 (1976): 15-21.

[6] All citations of source material for *King Lear* are from those texts reproduced in *Major Tragedies: "Hamlet," "Othello," "King Lear," "Macbeth,"* volume 7 of *Narrative and Dramatic Sources of Shakespeare,* ed. Geoffrey Bullough (London: Routledge & Kegan Paul, 1973). Quotations of Shakespeare's texts are from *The Complete Signet Classic Shakespeare,* ed. Sylvan Barnet (New York: Harcourt, Brace, Jovanovich, 1972).

[7] It is not my purpose here to debate the primacy of either the Q1 or F1 texts, but the Folio text is generally accepted as a corrected or adjusted version of Q1, perhaps used as prompt copy. Whether the revisions are Shakespeare's or the playing company's, they suggest a more tactful approach to the political issues of the play. Hence Q1 variants prove intriguing. Most of the variation in 1.1 concerns Lear's response to Cordelia. F1 variants change Lear's more authoritarian, formal expression in Q1 to a personal, more paternal address. For example, Q1, "Goe to, goe to, mend your speech . . . / Lest you may mar your fortunes" becomes "How, how Cordelia?. . . . Lest you may mar your fortunes."

[8] Oates, "'Is This The Promised End?': The Tragedy of *King Lear*," *Journal of Aesthetics and Art Criticism* 33 (1974): 22. Also, Marianne Novy observes: "Cordelia, by contrast with her sisters, is much less stereotyped. Shakespeare's presentation of her shows sympathy for the woman who tries to keep her integrity in a patriarchal world" ("Patriarchy, Mutuality, and Forgiveness in *King Lear*," *Southern Humanities Review* 13 [1979]: 284).

[9] Both Lynda Boose and Coppèlia Kahn discuss this scene as a variant of the wedding ceremony. See Boose, "The Father and the Bride in Shakespeare," *PMLA* 97 (1982): 325-47; and Kahn, "The Absent Mother in *King Lear*," in *Rewriting the Renaissance: The Discoures of Sexual Difference in Early Modern Europe,* ed. Margaret W. Ferguson, Maureen Quilligan, and Nancy J. Vickers (U. of Chicago Press, 1986), pp. 33-49. Kahn argues further that the renunciation of Cordelia as "daughter/wife" awakens a deeper need in Lear for Cordelia as "daughter/mother" (p. 40).

[10] In "The War in *King Lear*," *Shakespeare Studies* 33 (1980): 27-34, Gary Taylor argues convincingly against conflating the Q1 and F1 texts, especially as they present different versions of the political/military action in the last three acts. Taylor's analysis concludes that the Folio text was revised to emphasize "who leads the invasion army" and to transform a French invasion into a "rebellion."

[11] DeBeauvoir, *The Second Sex,* trans. and ed. H.M. Parshley (New York: Knopf, 1952), p. 70.

[12] Goneril significantly loses her claim to authority when Albany receives testimony of her adultery with Edmund. As Barbara Mowat observes, "Goneril and Regan are embodiments of the male anxieties about women seen in many of Shakespeare's males: in their power madness, their cruelty, their treachery they are like witches; in their lust for Edmund they are like harlots" ("Images of Women in Shakespeare's Plays," *Southern Humanities Review* 11 [1979]: 153).

[13] Quoted by Donald R. Dudley and Graham Webster in *The Rebellion of Boudicca* (New York: Barnes and

Noble, 1962), p. 113. For Dion's account, see *Dio's Annals of Rome,* trans. Herbert Foster (Troy, N.Y.: Pafraets Book Co., 1906), 5: 29-40.

[14] The OED documents the ambiguity of the term Virago as one of praise or blame in Renaissance usage, defining both "a man-like, vigorous, and heroic woman," and "a bold, impudent (or wicked) woman."

[15] The phrase is cited by Paul Johnson in *Elizabeth I: A Study of Power and Intellect* (London: Weidenfeld and Nicholson, 1974), p. 320.

[16] The reference is to *The Faerie Queene,* ed. J.C. Smith (Oxford: Clarendon Press, 1909-1910).

[17] References are to the text of *Bonduca* in Volume 6 of *The Works of Francis Beaumont and John Fletcher,* ed. Arnold Glover and A.R. Waller (Cambridge U. Press, 1908).

[18] Raphael Holinshed, *The Historie of England,* volume 1 of *Chronicles of England, Scotland and Ireland* (London: J. Johnson, 1807; rpt. New York: AMS, 1965), p. 495.

[19] See Marvin Rosenberg, *The Masks of King Lear* (U. of California Press, 1972), pp. 334-35.

[20] Devon Leigh Hodges notes that Edgar and Kent remain intact because they adopt disguises which protect their noble natures. As a "sublime truth," however, Cordelia's spirit disintegrates into "fragmented matter in order to make it visible" ("Cut Adrift and 'Cut to the Brains': The Anatomized World of *King Lear,*" *English Literary Renaissance* 11 [1981]: 210).

[21] Charles Lamb, "On the Tragedies of Shakespeare," *Lamb's Criticism,* ed. E. M. W. Tillyard (Cambridge U. Press, 1923; rpt. Westport, Conn: Greenwood Press, 1970), p. 89.

[22] Gibson, *A Womans Worth* (London: John Wolfe, 1599), B1.

[23] The Doctor becomes a Gentleman in F1 in accordance with revisions which de-emphasize the French invasion before act four. Gary Taylor makes the point that, while surgeons appeared with armies in Elizabethan drama, the Doctor in Q1 is an anomaly ("The War in *King Lear,*" p. 30).

[24] Enfans perdus, to which Cordelia's term refers, were the most "reckless and intrepid volunteers for military exploits regarded as desperate ventures, "as noted in *The Variorum King Lear,* ed. W. H. Furness (1880; rpt. American Scholar Publications, 1965), p. 300. S. L. Goldberg notes this hostile vocabu-

lary as well in *An Essay on* "King Lear" (Cambridge U. Press, 1974), p. 148.

[25] Egan, *Drama within Drama: Shakespeare's Sense of His Art in "King Lear," "The Winter's Tale," and "The Tempest,"* (Columbia U. Press, 1975), p. 55.

[26] Jardin, *Still Harping on Daughters: Women and Drama in the Age of Shakespeare* (Sussex: The Harvester Press: Totowa, N.J.: Barnes and Noble, 1983), p. 193.

[27] Booth, *"King Lear," "Macbeth," Indefinition and Tragedy* (Yale U. Press, 1983), p. 24.

[28] Lupset, *A Compendious Treatise, Teachying the Waie of Dyeing Well,* in *The Life and Works of Thomas Lupset,* ed. John Archer Gee (Yale U. Press, 1928), p. 280.

[29] Bullough, p. 319.

[30] Dusinberre, *Shakespeare and the Nature of Women* (London: Macmillan, 1975), p. 299.

ROLE OF MARRIAGE

Richard P. Wheeler (essay date 1974-75)

SOURCE: "The King and the Physician's Daughter: *All's Well That Ends Well* and the Late Romances," in *Comparative Drama,* Vol. 8, No. 4, Winter, 1974-75, pp. 311-27.

[*In this essay, Wheeler contends that, unlike the festive comedies, All's Well That Ends Well "presents an action in which parental figures are closely and actively involved in the steps that lead to marriage."*]

In his now classic formulation of "The Argument of Comedy," Northrop Frye called attention to the unusual turn Shakespeare gives the typical comic pattern in *All's Well that Ends Well*—and noted the difficulties this alteration has posed for critics:

> The normal comic resolution is the surrender of the *senex* to the hero, never the reverse. Shakespeare tried to reverse the pattern in *All's Well that Ends Well,* where the king of France forces Bertram to marry Helena, and the critics have not yet stopped making faces over it.[1]

This curious inversion of comic action is all the more remarkable in the light of Frye's suggestion that New Comedy dramatizes a "comic Oedipus situation" in which a young man (the son in the Oedipus triangle) outwits a father to win the love of a young woman. The heroine is unconsciously linked to an image of the youthful mother that a son loved and thought himself to possess as a young child. In this framework, the comic movement toward marriage builds on fantasies of triumphant return to a time in which a boy thought himself in secure and complete possession of a mother's love and the father could still be regarded as an unwelcome intruder, susceptible, at least in the child's imagination, to magical exclusion.[2]

The complex dramatic strategies in Shakespeare's festive comedies which safeguard triumphs in love relations from the contamination of familial associations deserve more extensive treatment than they may be given here. But their purpose in creating a world in which young love may prosper is neatly summed up by Rosalind in *As You Like It:* "But what talk we of fathers when there is such a man as Orlando?" In *All's Well,* however, there is a very strong emphasis on bonds that are grounded in family experience.

Unlike the festive comedies, *All's Well* presents an action in which parental figures are closely and actively involved in the steps that lead to marriage. In the late romances there is a further intensification of family bonds, as Shakespeare evolves a comic design that includes but does not turn on the fulfilment of youthful love in marriage. In this paper I will try to account for some of the difficulties posed by *All's Well* by examining one kind of relation that play has to the late romances.

C. L. Barber has provided the framework that brings this relation into focus. "In the festive comedies," argues Barber, "holiday liberty frees passion from inhibition and the control of an older generation." But in the late romances,

> the festive movement is included within a larger movement where the centre of feeling is in the older generation. The festive comedies move out to the creation of new families; *Pericles* and *The Winter's Tale* move through experiences of loss back to the recovery of family relations in and through the next generation. . . . One can put this in summary by saying that where regular comedy deals with freeing sexuality from the ties of family, these late romances deal with freeing family ties from the threat of sexual degradation.[3]

In *All's Well*, a play caught in the middle of this transition, a central action much like those of the festive comedies is brought under unique and disruptive pressures by the partial intrusion of a pattern of love and desire that is grounded in relations within a family.

Professor Barber argues that in the late romances "fulfilment for the principal figure requires a transformation of love, not simply liberation of it" *(ibid.)*.

Pericles and *The Winter's Tale* transform love relations which include hazardous, perverse trends. Repressed components in Pericles' love for a daughter and Leontes's love for a friend[4] lead to catastrophic situations of loss and betrayal. The action of these plays recovers those relations on a new plane, purified of perverse sexual longings. In *All's Well,* Shakespeare attempts to dramatize the resolution of a love situation that is in need of "transformation" without having yet fully discovered a form that goes beyond the dramatic strategies of "liberation."

Erotic fulfilment in marriage provides the main plot line moving toward comic resolution in *All's Well*, although this movement is interrupted by Bertram's disgust at "the dark house and the detested wife" the king has compelled him to accept. In "Marriage and Manhood in *All's Well that Ends Well,*"[5] I argue that Bertram's hasty flight from his marriage to Helena is an attempt to flee a sexual union that is marred by incestuous associations. Bertram's sexual longings are released in a context that for him necessarily lies outside his marriage, in what he thinks is his successful seduction of Diana in Florence. But this flight from a union marred by family ties into erotic release is forced to double back on itself when Helena substitutes her body for Diana's. This substitution lets the plot move along, but it does nothing to act on the roots of the psychological problem. Bertram's final acceptance of Helena does not build on a fundamental eradication of his aversion to her, but simply evades the forces that make her repugnant to him in the first place. With the late romances in mind, it is possible to extend this interpretation further, and to recognize more fully the role of the king in intensifying the conflicts of this play.

Shakespeare does not provide an appropriate romantic response to Helena's love for Bertram. Helena is a much loved character, however, and a very important expression of love for her is dramatized in the king. When Helena raises him from his "sickly bed," she begets in the king a love for his "preserver" that reaches far deeper than Bertram's reluctant acceptance of her as his wife. Helena's winning of the king's affection is the key part in a larger pattern in which Helena comes to occupy a position of love and hope previously held by Bertram.

When Bertram flees France and his dreaded marriage, he abdicates his place at home. Bertram makes this clear in Italy when he tries to bribe Diana into bed by giving her his father's ring, the symbol of his position in the Rousillion family tradition. At home in France, the countess makes the fact of Bertram's abdication even more explicit, and adds an important element to it. Addressing the abandoned Helena, the countess declares:

> He was my son,
> But I do wash his name out of my blood,
> And thou art all my child.
>
> (III.ii.65-67)

The starkness of the countess's shift of parental affection from Bertram to Helena is qualified a little later by her confusion—"which of them both/ Is dearest to me, I have no skill in sense/ To make distinction" (III.iv.38-40). But the pattern is clear. For the countess, Bertram the "unseasoned courtier" and the hope of the Rousillion family has become that "rash and unbridled boy" who has betrayed himself and denied his family. This devaluation of Bertram is inversely proportionate to the countess's heightened regard for Helena, who

> deserves a lord
> That twenty such rude boys might tend upon
> And call her hourly mistress. (III.ii.79-81)

Bertram forfeits his place in a loving family relation, and this place is filled by a highly idealized Helena.

This pattern is echoed in shifts of attitude in the old counsellor Lafew and in the French lords Bertram joins in Italy. But most importantly, the repudiation of Bertram as the dramatic center of love and hope and his replacement in this role by Helena take place at court. The king first receives Bertram with warmth and high hopes, seeing him, as did the countess, as a young man who promises to duplicate the merits of his dead father. But the king is outraged when Bertram refuses the hand of the woman who has brought health back to his majesty.

> Here, take her hand,
> Proud scornful boy, unworthy this good gift
> That dost in vile misprision shackle up
> My love and her desert. . . . (II.iii.149-52)

The king's anger violently compresses attitudes that will be sorted out in a very different dramatic rhythm when they reappear in Prospero's mixed response to Ferdinand. Prospero's surrender of his daughter Miranda to the young suitor he has himself chosen to be her husband is a central source of dramatic tension in *The Tempest.* Prospero achieves controlled release of his fatherly resentment of Ferdinand by imposing verbal abuse and ritual slavery upon the young man before awarding him with the "rich gift" of his daughter. A similar paternal ambivalence is concentrated in the king's demand upon Bertram, with a father's resentment compounded by the king's frustration when Bertram refuses the "good gift" of Helena. This powerful and explosive scene, in which the king plays the role of the father bestowing the daughter on an "unworthy" suitor, verifies the important shift in

family conflict that has occurred since the early scenes of the play.

All's Well opens with the creation of a symbolic family parented by the king and the countess:

> LAFEW: You [Countess] shall find of the king a husband, madam; you, sir [Bertram], a father. (I.i.6-7)

But by the second act, Helena has replaced Bertram in this family situation. Bertram, the very hope of the comic family when *All's Well* begins, has become, by the last act, a "stranger" who must justify his acceptance into the restructured family through marriage.

The late romances will build more centrally on situations very similar to the family situation that is evolved in *All's Well.* Central to the designs of these later plays is the opening up of a family that includes a strong bond of father to daughter in order to admit an outsider. The role of suitor into which Bertram is moved suggests the positions of Florizel and Ferdinand in *The Winter's Tale* and *The Tempest.* Although Bertram is a reluctant husband and Florizel and Ferdinand are quite eager to marry, their roles are parallel in certain important respects. Florizel's attempt to win Perdita from the Old Shepherd, her apparent father, is violently interrupted by the rage of his own father. Faced with disinheritance, he flees Bohemia and the angered Polixenes only to be caught in a lie in the court of Leontes, Perdita's real father. Ferdinand, in order to win Miranda, must chop wood in ritual debasement before Prospero, while being made to think his own father has perished. Like Bertram, who undergoes utter humiliation before the king in the last act of *All's Well,* each of these characters must suffer estrangement from father and home and withstand a stiff challenge to his own masculine autonomy in order to complete a marriage to the precious daughter.

Closely related to these conflicts in the late romances are the paired themes of loss and redemption. Particularly in *The Winter's Tale,* the loss of the daughter results from attitudes or actions of the father, and she must be recovered before the father may be restored to vital qualities he has lost within himself. Helena's "pilgrimage" to Florence is accepted, on the basis of the note she leaves behind, as a journey to her death. Helena's apparent death anticipates the loss of Imogen, Marina, and Perdita in the later plays. The king, in anticipation of Pericles, Cymbeline, and Leontes creates the conditions that lead to Helena's apparent death when he forces the marriage to Bertram.

A daughter's service in restoring a father to a full sense of life is also anticipated by Helena's cure of the king. But in the later plays, the recovery of the father either follows or, as in *The Tempest,* accompanies the loss or expulsion of the daughter. In *All's Well,* Helena finds the king at the edge of death, cures him of his fistula, and restores him to the vigor of his manhood. She then must undergo a symbolic death because of disturbances in her marriage to Bertram.

This ordering of the pattern of loss and recovery precludes the achievement, within the relation of the king and Helena, of the balance of reciprocated protective and creative powers that will be essential to father/daughter relations in the late romances. Leontes, "ready to leap out of himself for joy of his found daughter" (*The Winter's Tale,* V.ii.47-48), confers upon Perdita in turn her proper status as the child of a king, and makes possible her union with Prince Florizel. In *All's Well,* the king is exasperated in his attempt to balance his debt to Helena. "What should be said?" he demands of Bertram:

> If thou canst like this creature as a maid
> I can create the rest. Virtue and she
> Is her own dower; honor and wealth from me.
>   (II.iii.140-43)

Bertram's immediate answer ("I cannot love her, nor will strive to do't") is momentarily overcome only to give way to the even deeper frustration of Helena's apparent death.

Rather than "create" a worthy noblewoman, duly rewarded with the husband of her choice, the king sets Helena up to be abandoned and disgraced. It is no wonder that the king broods with such ominous force in the final scene as he attempts, clearly with little success, to forget the negation of his power caused by Bertram's flight:

> Let him not ask our pardon;
> The nature of his great offense is dead,
> And deeper than oblivion do we bury
> Th' incensing relics of it. (V.iii.22-25)

Nor is it any wonder that the king is still trying to recover his power to "create the rest" in his very last speech, when he turns to a girl of even humbler origins, the Florentine Diana, and directs her to choose, as Helena did before her, a husband from among the courtiers present: "If thou beest yet a fresh uncropped flower, / Choose thou thy husband, and I'll pay the dower" (V.iii.323-24).

The need for a central male figure to balance a debt to the creative or regenerative powers, frustrated in the king's relation to Helena, is an important feature in the design of the late romances. In the earlier comedies simple gratitude was an easier achievement for men who, like Bassanio or Orlando, are brought to positions of consummating their love by the efforts of strong women. That the investment of such a trust in the power

of women becomes a threatening feature in Shakespearean drama is made clear, however, by the fierce struggles that are fought in the tragedies as a result of erosions of male power or wisdom which result, at least partially, from relations to women.

The failure, in an intimate relation with a woman, of the capacity for trust, either through excess or through inhibition, is a theme deeply implicated in many of the tragedies. This theme is given a tentative first statement when Brutus refuses the counsel and confidence of his Portia, and continues through to the dramatization of Coriolanus as a man whose life has been shaped in every respect by his deference to the domineering power of Volumnia. Perhaps the elaborate scheme devised by Lear to justify his need for Cordelia's total love is the most appropriate example. Lear, as Stanley Cavell has shown in his brilliant essay,[6] can only accept Cordelia's love by placing it within the distorting medium of a coercive trade-off in which Lear attempts to command the love of his daughter with the gift of land and power.

This covert attempt to impose an illegitimate balance in which Lear trades something for, essentially, everything, precipitates the tragic outcome of *King Lear.* In *The Winter's Tale* and *The Tempest,* the achievement of an acceptable balance is central to dramatic movements which, like those of the tragedies, turn on the issue of trust, but which move beyond catastrophe to a restored order that includes the main characters. Leontes' banishment of his daughter follows his failure to trust his wife and his childhood friend. The multiple reunions at the end of that play dramatize the restoration of the capacity for trust as it is bolstered by an altered structure of relations. Prospero's banishment from Milan, however, follows an over-investment of trust in his brother Antonio:

>   . . . my trust
> Like a good parent, did beget of him
> A falsehood in its contrary as great
> As my trust was, which had indeed no limit,
> A confidence sans bound.
>   (*The Tempest,* I.ii.93-97)

The learned and ultimately powerful Prospero is able to recoup his will and his energy because of the strength he finds in the presence of the helpless infant Miranda, who has been banished with him.

>   O, a cherubin
> Thou wast that did preserve me! Thou didst smile,
> Infused with a fortiude from heaven,
> When I have decked the sea with drops full salt,
> Under my burden groaned: which raised in me

An undergoing stomach, to bear up
Against what should ensue.

                    (I.ii.152-58)

A balance continues through their life together on the island, Prospero providing for Minada the roles of both father and mother while sustaining himself through his love for her. Prospero's life on his island is a kind of toughened revision of Lear's dream of a prison/paradise with Cordelia, surrendered begrudgingly but necessarily and under conditions created by his own large powers, when the child becomes a woman ready to take a husband.

The issue of trust enters *All's Well,* together with the insistence that a man's power to bestow position and wealth within the social structure of life balances a woman's power to create or regenerate the vitality of life itself, when the king decides to let Helena perform her cure:

> More should I question thee, and more I must,
> Though more to know could not be more to
>   trust—
> From whence thou cam'st, how tended on—
>   but rest
> Unquestioned welcome, and undoubted blest.
> Give me some help here, ho!—If thou proceed
> As high as word, my deed shall match thy
>   deed.
>
>   (II.i.205-10)

Helena makes available to the king a renewed sense of trust that takes a man who is past hope and brings him to a new faith in life's possibilities. The king's "past-cure malady" metaphorically presents the sterility of a life that has lost touch with its own deepest emotional springs. Helena brings to this life a remedy which "oft . . . hits/ Where hope is coldest and despair most fits" (II.i.142-43). If cured by the "undoubted blest" Helena, the king will "match" her deed with one that lies within his own power.

A sense of basic trust, according to Erik Erikson, is the necessary "cornerstone" of a vital human identity, and may be deeply involved in the psychological crises of all stages of human life. Such trust, Erikson argues, is essential to the development of what becomes the "capacity for *faith*" and of what is "conducive to the vital strength of *hope*. . . ."[7] This sense of trust must create, and in turn be sustained by, an image of a "reasonably coherent world" which makes meaningful actions and relations to others feasible. Basic trust initially

> arises out of the encounter of maternal person and small infant, an encounter which is one of mutual trustworthiness and mutual recognition. This, in all its infantile simplicity, is the first experience of what in later reoccurrences in love and admiration can

only be called a sense of "hallowed presence," the need of which remains basic in man. (Erikson, p. 105)

But this first encounter, which provides the indispensable foundation for all ensuing human growth, provides the framework for the deepest psychic hazards as well. "For along with a fund of hope, an inescapable alienation is also bequeathed to life by the first stage, namely a sense of threatening separation from the matrix, a possible loss of hope, and the uncertainty whether the 'face darkly' will brighten again with recognition and charity."[8]

Shakespeare dramatizes in the recognition scenes in the late romances the recovery of this "hallowed presence" after a calamitous crisis of trust has taken a key figure beyond hope, away from the matrix that has given his life substance and coherent meaning. In *Pericles, The Winter's Tale,* and *The Tempest,* this key figure is a father. His recovery of the basic trust vital to human functioning includes a deep and compelling response to the presence of his daughter. But this recovery must be protected from hazards that accompany it within the regressive substructure of a crisis of trust, lest other essential pychological achievements be swept away. In the late romances, the power of the father to provide the daughter with protection, position, and a worthy suitor, along with his recovery of the power to function fully in the social and political dimensions of his own life, sustains for him the masculine autonomy that would be sacrificed in an overt posture of submission before his daughter's idealized presence.

But Bertram's reluctance to accept Helena for his wife in *All's Well* calls into question the enraged king's restored powers, undermines his capacity to return Helena's gift of health by providing her with a husband:

> My honor's at the stake, which to defeat
> I must produce my power.
>
>   (II.iii.148-49)

The play fails to provide the king with the means of returning fully Helena's gift with a suitable exercise of his own power. From this point on, an awesomely efficient Helena is in charge of retrieving her husband for herself.

The extreme intensity of the king's outburst at Bertram, however, suggests that there is more even than honor at the stake. The king does not relinquish Helena to Bertram; he compels him to take her, forcing the issue even after Helena has withdrawn her claim: "That you are well restored, my lord, I'm glad./ Let the rest go" (II.iii.146-47). That Bertram's resistance should provoke so strong a response suggests that the king's concern for Helena and Bertram's aversion to her are more deeply connected than at first appears. The king seems to regard Bertram as symbolic equivalent of his own restored potency, which is threatened by the young count's assertion of his right to choose a wife for himself:

> It is in us to plant thine honor where
> We please to have it grow. Check thy
> 　contempt.
> Obey our will, which travails in thy good.
> Believe not thy disdain, but presently
> Do thine own fortunes that obedient right
> Which both thy duty and our power claims;
> Or I will throw thee from my care forever,
> Into the staggers and the careless lapse
> Of youth and ignorance, both my revenge and
> 　hate
> Lossing upon thee, in the name of justice,
> Without all terms of pity.
>
> 　　　　　　　　　　(II.iii.155-65)[9]

A potential hazard in the crisis of trust, perhaps even more threatening than the risk of autonomy, derives from the origins of basic trust in a situation of infantile sexual attachment to the mother. These incestuous ties may be evoked anew by one who restores at a new level what the mothering person provided initially. Lafew provides the king's recovery at the hands of Helena with sexual undertones when he watches the newly healed monarch enter with his "preserver":

> Lustick! as the Dutchman says. I'll like a maid the better whilst I have a tooth in my head. Why, he's able to lead her a coranto. (II.iii.40-42)

A close look at the scene in which Helena proposes her cure suggests that the king's regard for his healer includes components which, because they cannot be expressed in his relation to Helena, are projected onto Bertram.

The dying king, who has been pronounced beyond hope of recovery by the "most learned doctors," at first rejects Helena's promise of a cure. It would, he asserts, discredit the dignity of his position "to prostitute our past-cure malady" to the futlie and debasing efforts of pseudo-healers. After all, he argues, "the congregated college" of physicians having failed, there is little an unlearned girl can do. Lafew, however, in his praise of Helena's medical power, has already suggested qualities that set it apart from that of the typical physician.

Before Helena is granted her first audience with the king, Lafew provides him with this enthusiastic description of her skills:

> I have seen a medicine
> That's able to breathe life into a stone,

> Quicken a rock, and make you dance canary
> With sprightly fire and motion; whose simple
> 　touch
> Is powerful to araise King Pepin, nay,
> To give great Charlemain a pen in's hand,
> And write to her a love-line.
>
> 　　　　　　　　　　(II.i.72-78)

What is remarkable about this account, beyond its concern with the miraculous nature of Helena's medicine, is the emphasis on erotic properties. The dance with "sprightly fire and motion," the power to put life in a stone, to raise "King Pepin" by mere touch, or to provide Charlemain with a "pen" with which to make love, these qualities stress the power of the medicine not only to restore but to arouse male potency.[10] Such erotic suggestions are brought fully into play when Lafew, on leaving the king alone with Helena, likens to Pandarus: "I am Cressid's uncle,/ That dare leave two together. Fare you well."

The ensuing exchange with the king and Helena, however, presents this eroticism in another mode, once removed from the openly sexual banter of Lafew. Helena brings to the king a special "receipt" bequeathed to her by her dead father, the physician Gerard de Narbon, which "he bade me store up as a triple eye,/ Safer than mine own two." After much persuasion, the king decides to test her assurance that "my art is not past power, nor you past cure." The conditions under which they agree to proceed include elements that define the nature of the king's bond to Helena.

Helena's extraordinary confidence in her curative powers, the king concludes, "must intimate/ Skill infinite, or monstrous desperate." The terms of his agreement to let her proceed account for both possibilities: "Sweet practicer, thine physic I will try,/ That ministers thine own death if I die." Helena, however, provides an even more interesting suggestion, along with her death, regarding an appropriate punishment for her should the medicine fail to heal the king. Her proposal indicates more clearly the nature of the "monstrous" possibilities entertained by the king. "Upon thy certainty and confidence/ What dar'st thou venture?" asks the king, and Helena responds:

> 　　　　Tax of impudence,
> A strumpet's boldness, a divulged shame
> Traduced by odious ballads; my maiden's
> 　name
> Seared otherwise; nay, worse of worst,
> 　extended
> With vilest torture let my life be ended.
>
> 　　　　　　　　　　(II.i.169-74)

Her willingness to risk utter degradation prompts the king to think that in Helena "some blessed spirit doth speak/ His powerful sound within an organ weak"

(II.i.174-75). Either Helena is the very ideal of young womanhood, the frail but loving organ of "some blessed spirit," embodying all that is precious in life, or she is a creature of shame, a "strumpet" deserving the notoriety of a convicted whore. And if she is successful in her cure—"Then shalt thou give me with thy kingly hand/ What husband in thy power I will command" (II.i.193-94).

The future of Helena, to be determined by her medical service to the king, is settled in terms of sexual legitimacy. Depending on her success, she will know either the fate of a prostitute or that of an honored wife. The two possible outcomes dramatize an unacknowledged sexual trend in the king's regard for Helena and the defense against that trend through idealization and projection. The recovery of the king allows the idealized version of Helena to survive the monstrous one. The forbidden sexual longings in the father/king's love are then projected into the legitimate order of marriage, but a marriage arranged by the king. The elevation of the king's regard for Helena to an idealized plane enhances the scope of his love, while the projection of the sexual component of that love onto another assures parental propriety. When Bertram is presented with this "good gift" of a wife, he becomes an agent who must complete an unconscious, unacceptable dimension that finds its way into the king's relation to Helena.

The relationship of the king and Helena introduces into *All's Well* the incestuous motive in a father's love for a daughter that will undergo transformation in the design of the late romances. Barber has demonstrated how closely the incestuous component of a father's love comes to making a disastrous intrusion into *The Winter's Tale* when Leontes looks on Perdita, not yet recognized as his daughter, with an eye that has "too much youth in't." But the ensuing action serves to redefine this longing by placing it in the larger context of Leontes's renewed relations to Perdita as daughter, to Polixenes as friend, and to Hermione as wife. The relation gains in meaning within a dramatic arrangement that allows Leontes to release his daughter to the youthful Florizel. In *The Tempest,* Prospero's love for Miranda is relieved of its tabooed dimension by the presence of the monstrous Caliban, who, as a part of his role, represents repressed components that may seek expression in a father's relation to his daughter. Because of this function served by Caliban, Prospero can confront the need to relinquish Miranda to a young husband in a context that has been dramatically insulated from much of the force of its most hazardous elements.

These actions are anticipated by the king's relations to Helena and Bertram in *All's Well.* But in *The Winter's Tale* and *The Tempest,* the dramatic movement of the whole play responds to conflicts organized by the experience of a central character, including conflicts that hinge on that character's fatherhood. The somewhat simpler action of *Pericles* helps to show the importance of this mode of ordering comic form in the late plays. *Pericles,* as Professor Barber has shown, transforms a loving motive that includes dangerous components within itself, particularly the threat of incestuously bound sexual drives. Projection is one of two principal psychological strategies for controlling those dangers dramatically, and idealization, expressed in the elevation of love to the realm of the sacred, is the other. The obstacles that obstruct the fulfilment of Pericles' quest for loving relations project those dangers in externalized form. Because they are objectified and put into external opposition to the loving motive, these dangers may be overcome as obstacles alien to the self, and the experience of love in a single character may be brought to a joyful completion. But in *All's Well,* the incestuous trend in the king's love for Helena is expressed in the attempt to compel Bertram to marry her. Their union is not dramatically separated from this dimension of longing, but is forced to include it.

In *Pericles,* the incestuous associations within the loving motive are expressed in a context that transforms them away from the sexual and "in the direction of the sacred" (Barber, p. 60) in order to restore and purify a relation within the family. Spiritual renewal in *Pericles* builds on the recovery of an infant's magical participation in benevolent powers awesomely larger than its own. The need to restore one's participation in these larger powers in a context that redefines adult relations is presented in the central importance of miracle and magic in the late romances.

Lafew provides an extensive expression of this need to immerse merely human affairs in a realm of mysterious power that encloses them in *All's Well.* In remarks that open the scene that will display for the first time the recovered king, Lafew proclaims:

> They say miracles are past, and we have our philosophical persons, to make modern and familiar, things supernatural and causeless. Hence is it that we make trifles of terrors, ensconcing ourselves into seeming knowledge when we should submit ourselves to an unknown fear. (II.iii.1-6)

But whereas the late romances achieve a design that calls out the fullest dramatic possibilities of this immersion in the miraculous, and which protects it from the psychological hazards it evokes, *All's Well* does not. Even Lafew's evocation of transcendent powers gets caught up in the burlesque of an exchange in which clownish Parolles competes with Lafew to describe the wondrous qualities of the king's cure (II iii.7-43).

The psychological base of Shakespearean comedy shifts after the writing of the festive comedies, and this shift demands a radically new form. The base of the festive comedies in fantasies of oedipal triumph calls for an action that brings together young lovers in sexual unions which evade the contamination of family ties. This action affirms and protects a faith in the fundamental compatibility and interdependence of liberated human feelings and social order. The whole festive movement is grounded in a sense of trust. But the faith that encloses the actions of these plays becomes the center of conflict in the late romances, where faith and hope are lost and then restored in an action that pivots on a crisis of trust. The base of the romances is, psychologically, "deeper." It demands a recovery of the quality of basic trust, first acquired in the earliest phases of infancy. "Primitive religions," writes Erikson,

> the most primitive layer in all religions, and the religious layer in each individual, abound with efforts at atonement which try to make up for vague deeds against a maternal matrix and try to restore faith in the goodness of one's strivings and in the kindness of the powers of the universe.[11]

This "layer" of needs for atonement and the restoration of a vital world image is expressed in the dramatic pattern of the late romances.

All's Well, caught up in this shift, is unable to absorb entirely the pressures of a changed psychological situation with dramatic strategies rooted in festive comic form. Characteristics central to the design of the late romances are present in *All's Well* as intrusions not fully integrated into its comic action. The tentative and partial shift of focus toward the older generation in *All's Well,* rather than establish a new center of feeling, blurs that center which the comic design attempts to locate in the experience of youth. Rather than a recovery of relations through a younger generation, the king's pressure on Bertram intensifies the young count's disdain for Helena to revulsion and flight. When these two young people are finally united, it is not through an action of atonement or redemption that touches the beneficent force of miraculous or magical powers basic to a vision of the world, but through the manipulations of industrious Helena. The sense of awe or wonder, evoked and then aborted in the second act in connection with the healing of the king, fails to reappear in the service of the final ordering of relations at the play's end.

I have tried to show how precisely correct Frye was when he saw that the central difficulty for *All's Well* arises when "the king of France forces Bertram to marry Helena." But this gesture does not so much signify Shakespeare's reversal of the comic pattern as his tentative step toward a new mode of comedy that will be completed and perfected in the late romances. In *All's Well* the forceful intrusion of the fatherly king into the

realm of youthful love subverts the festive comic purpose of liberation but does not achieve the characteristic purpose of the late romances, of protecting family ties from incestuous motives. The king's role in the marriage of Bertram to Helena merges a family centered love, unconsciously identical with the father/daughter bonds of the late romances, with an action leading to sexual union. Bertram's understandable flight from this union undermines the sense of a renewed social order that might have found its appropriate emblem in the newly revived king. The play's closing does not effectively restore a strong feeling for the king's power to give order to his society or to balance his debt to Helena, nor does it clear the relation of Bertram to Helena of the obstacles which have interfered with it. Our confused attempt to find our bearings in a play in which the action does not respond coherently to its own emotional springs culminates in an ending which, as A. P. Rossiter has observed, speaking for many critics of *All's Well*, "makes us neither happy nor comfortable."[12]

Notes

[1] "The Argument of Comedy," *English Institute Essays 1948*, ed. D. A. Robertson (New York: Columbia Univ. Press, 1949), p. 59. Quotations from Shakespeare in this paper are from William Shakespeare, *The Complete Works*, gen. ed. Alfred Harbage (Baltimore: Penguin, 1969). The text of *All's Well that Ends Well* is edited by Jonas A. Barish.

[2] For a more rigorously psychoanalytic consideration of this comic pattern, see Ludwig Jekels, "On the Psychology of Comedy" (1926), tr. I. Jarosy, in *Theories of Comedy*, ed. Paul Lautner (New York: Doubleday, 1964), pp. 424-31.

[3] "'Thou that Beget'st Him that did Thee Beget': Transformation in *Pericles* and *The Winter's Tale*," *Shakespeare Survey*, 22 (1969), 61. Much recent criticism "has stressed the affinities of *All's Well* with the last plays, and seen it as belonging to the main stream of Shakespearean comedy" (Barish, "Introduction," p. 365). A useful summary and extension of this criticism is presented by G. K. Hunter in the introduction to the Arden Edition of *All's Well* (London: Methuen & Co., 1957). Three recent books have further developed this trend: Larry S. Champion, *The Evolution of Shakespeare's Comedy* (Cambridge, Mass.: Harvard Univ. Press, 1970); R. A. Foakes, *Shakespeare, the Dark Comedies to the Last Plays* (Charlottesville, Va.: Univ. of Virginia Press, 1971); Alan R. Velie, *Shakespeare's Repentance Plays: The Search for an Adequate Form* (Rutherford, N.J.: Fairleigh Dickinson Univ. Press, 1972). The notes to Professor Champion's book, particularly, provide a valuable bibliography of recent work on *All's Well*. These studies have, however, largely searched for formal or thematic anticipa-

tions in *All's Well* or the late romances. My essay explores a shift in the psychological base in which Shakespeare's comic strategies are grounded.

[4] Barber's view of Leontes' relation to Polixenes enlarges an observation first made by J. I. M. Stewart, who explores *The Winter's Tale* in terms of Freud's analysis of the relations of repressed homosexuality, delusional jealousy, and paranoia (*Character and Motive in Shakespeare* [New York and London: Longmans, Green, 1949]). For a penetrating consideration of Leontes's delusional jealousy as one aspect of "a form of psychic imprisonment in which the loss of ego boundaries makes the external world *nothing but a confluence of symbols, selected according to am-bivalent wishes and fears*," see Murray M. Schwartz, "Leontes' Jealousy in *The Winter's Tale*," *American Imago*, 30 (1973), 250-73.

[5] *Bucknell Review*, 21 (1973), 103-24.

[6] "The Avoidance of Love: A Reading of *King Lear*," *Must We Mean What We Say?* (New York: Charles Scribner's Sons, 1969), pp. 267-353.

[7] *Identity: Youth and Crisis* (New York: Norton, 1968), p. 106.

[8] "Human Strength and the Cycle of Generations," *Insight and Responsibility* (New York: Norton, 1964), p. 154.

[9] The force of the king's demands on Bertram in Shakespeare's conception of the play is brought into clear relief when this passage is set against the principal source for *All's Well*, Paynter's re-telling of a Boccaccio tale in the *Palace of Plea-sure* (Geoffrey Bullough, ed., *Narrative and Dra-matic Sources of Shakespeare* [London: Routledge and Kegan Paul, 1957-], II, 389-96). In that story, when Giletta (Helena) asks for Beltramo (Bertram) in marriage,

> the king was very loth to graunt him unto her: but for that he had made a promise which he was loth to breake, he caused him to be called forth, and said unto him: 'Sir Countie, knowing full well that you are a gentleman of great honour, oure pleasure is, that you returne home to your owne house to order your estate according to your degree: and that you take with you a Damosell which I have appointed to be your wife.' (p. 391)

Paynter's king then insists, firmly but politely and perhaps even a little apologetically, that the reluctant Beltramo accept Giletta, arranges the marriage, and is never heard from again.

[10] For the sexual connotations of stone, fire, motion,

touch, [a]raise, and pen, see Eric Partridge, *Shakespeare's Bawdy* (1948; rpt. New York: Dutton, 1960).

[11] *Childhood and Society,* revised ed. (New York: Norton, 1963), p. 251.

[12] *Angel with Horns* (New York: Theatre Arts, 1961), p. 128.

Lynda E. Boose (essay date 1982)

SOURCE: "The Father and the Bride in Shakespeare," in *PMLA,* Vol. 97, No. 3, May, 1982, pp. 325-47.

[*Here, Boose explores the phases of the marriage cer-emony—separation, transition, and reincorporation—as a pattern for the father-daughter relationship.*]

The aristocratic family of Shakespeare's England was, according to social historian Lawrence Stone, "patrilinear, primogenitural, and patriarchal." Parent-child relations were in general remote and formal, sin-gularly lacking in affective bonds and governed solely by a paternal authoritarianism through which the "hus-band and father lorded it over his wife and children with the quasi-authority of a despot" (*Crisis* 271). Stone characterizes the society of the sixteenth and early seventeenth centuries as one in which "a majority of individuals . . . found it very difficult to establish close emotional ties to any other person" (*Family* 99)[1] and views the nuclear family as a burdensome social unit, valued only for its ability to provide the means of patrilineal descent. Second and third sons counted for little and daughters for even less. A younger son could, it is true, be kept around as a "walking sperm bank in case the elder son died childless," but daughters "were often unwanted and might be regarded as no more than a tiresome drain on the economic resources of the fam-ily" (Stone, *Family* 88, 112).[2]

Various Elizabethan documents, official and unoffi-cial, that comment on family relations support Stone's hypothesis of the absence of affect.[3] Yet were we to turn from Stone's conclusions to those we might draw from Shakespeare's plays, the disparity of implication—especially if we assume that the plays to some extent mirror the life around them—must strike us as significant. Shakespeare's dramas con-sistently explore affective family dynamics with an intensity that justifies the growing inference among Shakespearean scholars that the plays may be pri-marily "about" family relations and only secondarily about the macrocosm of the body politic.[4] Not the absence of affect but the possessive overabundance of it is the force that both defines and threatens the family in Shakespeare. When we measure Stone's assertions against the Shakespeare canon, the plays must seem startlingly ahistorical in focusing on what would seem to have been the least valued relationship of all: that between father and daughter.

While father and son appear slightly more often in the canon, figuring in twenty-three plays, father and daughter appear in twenty-one dramas and in one narrative poem. As different as these father-daughter plays are, they have one thing in common: almost without exception the relationships they depict depend on significant underlying substructures of ritual. Shakespeare apparently created his dramatic mirrors not solely from the economic and social realities that historians infer as having dictated family behavior but from archetypal models, psychological in import and ritual in expression. And the particular ritual model on which Shakespeare most frequently drew for the father-daughter relationship was the marriage ceremony.[5]

In an influential study of the sequential order or "relative positions within ceremonial wholes," Arnold van Gennep isolated three phases in ritual enactment that always recur in the same underlying arrangement and that form, in concert, "the pattern of the rites of passage": separation, transition, and reincorporation.[6] The church marriage service—as familiar to a modern audience as it was to Shakespeare's—contains all three phases. When considered by itself, it is basically a separation rite preceding the transitional phase of consummation and culminating in the incorporation of a new family unit. In Hegelian terms, the ceremonial activities associated with marriage move from thesis through antithesis to synthesis; the anarchic release of fertility is positioned between two phases of relative stasis. The ritual enables society to allow for a limited transgression of its otherwise universal taboo against human eroticism. Its middle movement is the dangerous phase of transition and transgression; its conclusion, the controlled reincorporation into the stability of family. But before the licensed transgression can take place—the transgression that generates the stability and continuity of society itself—the ritual must separate the sanctified celebrants from the sterile forces of social interdiction. The marriage ritual is thus a pattern of and for the community that surrounds it, as well as a rite of passage of and for the individuals who enact it. It serves as an especially effective substructure for the father-daughter relation because within its pattern lies the paradigm of all the conflicts that define this bond at its liminal moment of severance. The ceremony ritualizes two particularly significant events: a daughter and a son are being incorporated into a new family unit, an act that explicitly breaks down the boundaries of two previously existing families; yet, at the same time, the bonds being dissolved, particularly those between father and daughter, are being memorialized and thus, paradoxically, reasserted. In early comedies like *The Taming of the Shrew*, Shakespeare followed the Roman design of using the father of the young male lover as the *senex iratus*, a blocking figure to be

circumvented. The mature comedies, tragedies, and romances reconstruct the problems of family bonds, filial obedience, and paternal possessiveness around the father and daughter, the relation put into focus by the marriage ceremony. When marriage activities are viewed from the perspective of their ritual implications, the bride and groom are not joined until the transitional phase of the wedding-night consummation; before that, a marriage may be annulled. What the church service is actually all about is the separation of the daughter from the interdicting father.

The wedding ceremony of Western tradition has always recognized the preeminence of the father-daughter bond. Until the thirteenth century, when the church at last managed to gain control of marriage law, marriage was considered primarily a private contract between two families concerning property exchange. The validity and legality of matrimony rested on the *consensus nuptialis* and the property contract, a situation that set up a potential for conflict by posing the mutual consent of the two children, who owed absolute obedience to their parents, against the desires of their families, who must agree beforehand to the contract governing property exchange. However true it was that the couple's willing consent was necessary for valid matrimony and however vociferously the official conduct books urged parents to consider the compatibility of the match, fathers like Cymbeline, Egeus, and Baptista feel perfectly free to disregard these requirements. Although lack of parental consent did not affect the validity of a marriage and, after 1604, affected the legality only when a minor was involved,[7] the family control over the dowry was a powerful psychological as well as economic weapon. Fathers like Capulet, Lear, and Brabantio depend on threats of disinheritance to coerce their children. When their daughters nonetheless wed without the paternal blessing, the marriages are adversely affected not because any legal statutes have been breached but because the ritual base of marriage has been circumvented and the psychological separation of daughter from father thus rendered incomplete. For in Shakespeare's time—as in our own—the ceremony acknowledged the special bond between father and daughter and the need for the power of ritual to release the daughter from its hold.

As specified in the 1559 *Book of Common Prayer,* the marriage ritual enjoins that the father (or, in his absence, the legal guardian)[8] deliver his daughter to the altar, stand by her in mute testimony that there are no impediments to her marriage, and then witness her pledge henceforth to forsake all others and "obey and serve, love honor and keep" the man who stands at her other side. To the priest's question, "Who giveth this woman to be married unto this man?"—a question that dates in English tradition back to the York manual (*Book of Common Prayer* 290-99; 408, n.)—the father must silently respond by physically relinquishing his daughter, only to watch the priest place her right hand into the possession of another man. Following this expressly physical symbolic transfer, the father's role in his daughter's life is ended; custom dictates that he now leave the stage, resign his active part in the rite, and become a mere observer. After he has withdrawn, the couple plight their troths, and the groom receives the ring, again from the priest. Taking the bride's hand into his, the groom places the ring on her finger with the words, "With this ring I thee wed, with my body I thee worship, and with all my worldly goods I thee endow," thus solemnizing the transfer in its legal, physical, and material aspects.[9]

Before us we have a tableau paradigmatic of the problematic father-daughter relation: decked in the symbols of virginity, the bride stands at the altar between her father and husband, pulled as it were between the two important male figures in her life. To resolve the implied dilemma, the force of the priest and the community presides over and compels the transfer of an untouched daughter into the physical possession of a male whom the ceremony authorizes both as the invested successor to the father's authority and as the sanctified transgressor of prohibitions that the father has been compelled to observe.[10] By making the father transfer his intact daughter to the priest in testimony that he knows of no impediments to her lawful union, the service not only reaffirms the taboo against incest but implicitly levels the full weight of that taboo on the relationship between father and daughter. The groom's family does not enter into the archetypal dynamics going on at this altar except through the priest's reference to marriage as the cause why a man "shall leave father and mother and shall be joined unto his wife." The mother of the bride is a wholly excluded figure—as indeed she is throughout almost the entire Shakespeare canon. Only the father must act out, must dramatize his loss before the audience of the community. Within the ritual circumscription, the father is compelled to give his daughter to a rival male; and as Georges Bataille comments:

> The gift itself is a renunciation. . . . Marriage is a matter less for the partners than for the man who gives the woman away, the man whether father or brother who might have freely enjoyed the woman, daughter or sister, yet who bestows her on someone else. This gift is perhaps a substitute for the sexual act; for the exuberance of giving has a significance akin to that of the act itself; it is also a spending of resources.[11] (218)

By playing out his role in the wedding ceremony, the father implicitly gives the blessing that licenses the daughter's deliverance from family bonds that might otherwise become a kind of bondage. Hence in *A Midsummer Night's Dream,* a play centered on marriage, the intransigent father Egeus, supported by the king-father figure Theseus, poses a threat that must be converted to a blessing to ensure the comic solution. In *Love's Labor's Lost,* the sudden death of the Princess' father, who is likewise the king-father figure for all the French ladies, prevents the necessary blessing, thus cutting sharply across the movement toward comic resolution and postponing the happy ending. In plots constructed around a daughter without a father, the absent father frequently assumes special dramatic prominence. This absence felt almost as a presence may well contribute to the general unease and unresolved tensions emanating from the three "problem plays," for Helena, Isabella, and Cressida are all daughters severed from their fathers.

Within the father-daughter plays, the daughter's association of father with husband is so strong that even when a woman as independent as Rosalind or Viola first thinks about the man she will eventually marry, her thoughts immediately call to mind her father. Her movement toward conjugal love unconsciously resuscitates a mental movement back to the father to whom she will remain emotionally as well as legally bound until the ritual of marriage transfers her loyalties from one domain to the other. The lack of narrative logic in the association emphasizes its subconscious quality. When Viola first hears the governor of Illyria named, she responds: "Orsino! I have heard my father name him. / He was a bachelor then" (*TN* 1.2.28-29). When Rosalind meets Orlando she instantly tells Celia, "The Duke my father lov'd his father dearly," making a connection that Celia pointedly questions in her response, "Doth it therefore ensue that you should love his son dearly?" (*AYL* 1.3.29-32). Once inside Arden Forest—ostensibly on a journey to find her father—Rosalind pays scant attention to her purpose, instead asking Celia, "But what talk we of fathers, when there is such a man as Orlando?" (3.4.38-39). But at the conclusion of the play, when Rosalind prepares to become Orlando's wife, she seeks out her father as the necessary figure who must ritually enable her to do so. Whereas she can freely don male clothing and shift her identity back and forth between Rosalind and Ganymede without the assistance of ritual, marriage is not merely the transposition of assumed roles but the actual transition from daughter to wife. And the movement must be ceremonialized through its distinct, sequential phases. Having spent the play testing various roles and disguises, Rosalind at the end chooses a fixed identity as wife; but that identity depends on her first having re-entered the role of daughter. To be incorporated into a new stasis, she must have one from which to be separated; she must be reunited as child to her father before she can be joined to her "child's father" (1.3.11). Thus in ritual language she repeats the vow of incorporation first to her father and then to Orlando: "To you I give myself, for I am yours" (5.4.116, 117). The play itself becomes paradigmatic of the ritual movement that concludes it: Rosalind's search to be reunited with her father metamorphoses into a journey to be united with the husband who replaces and supersedes him. And instantly on completion of the ceremony, having first been rejoined with his daughter and having then fully performed the father's formulaic role, Duke Senior is miraculously reinstated in his dukedom, regaining the paternal authority over his domain that he had lost at the same time as he had lost that over his daughter. In *King Lear* and *The Tempest,* Shakespeare uses the same pattern, making the King's ability to govern his state depend on his ability to enact his ritual role as father. In *Lear,* however, the dual restitution of paternal roles that concludes the two comedies is reversed into an opening scene staging the dual divestiture of daughter and kingdom.

In tragedies like *Lear, Othello,* and *Romeo and Juliet,* the father's failure to act out his required role has a special significance, one that we can best apprehend by looking not at the logic of casual narrative progression but at the threat implied by the violation of ritual. Even when marriage is sanctified by the presence of a priest, as it is in *Romeo and Juliet,* the absence of the father becomes crucial. In *Romeo,* the significance is dramatically projected through ritual structures in which Capulet repeatedly "gives away" his daughter without her consent and Juliet is repeatedly "married" without the blessing of her father, a father who ironically has been "a careful father" in choosing a harmonious match compatible with the best interests of the daughter he obviously cherishes.

At the same moment as Romeo and Juliet consummate their wedding upstairs, downstairs the father figuratively gives his daughter's hand to the Count Paris. Although Capulet earlier tells Paris, "My will to her consent is but a part" (1.2.17), he now presumes his paternal authority: "I think she will be rul'd / In all respects by me; nay more, I doubt it not" (3.4.13-14). Here, at the structural center of the play, where Romeo and Juliet are momentarily joined only to be separated until death reunites them, Shakespeare has drawn on inverted marriage ritual as the vehicle for the tragic peripeteia. Scenes 4 and 5 of act 3 dramatize two phases of the matrimonial rite, featuring two bridegrooms: the one downstairs to whom the father gives his consent and the one upstairs with whom the daughter consummates hers. While the separation ritual of scene 4 is legitimizing Paris as bridegroom, the incorporation rite of scene 5 is legitimizing Romeo; both young "grooms" consequently come to the Capulet monument to lie with Juliet, both convinced of their right to claim her. In these two scenes, disjunct phases of the rite of passage are enacted in isolation. But although each scene includes a groom, each is missing a crucial figure— either the father or the bride—and a crucial sequence, the daughter's transition from one male domain to the other. The juxtaposition obviously increases the tension of the narrative by making us aware, as Romeo

and Juliet celebrate their union, of the unexpected threat that will irrevocably separate them, a threat emphasized by the lovers' intuition of a growing darkness that invades the ecstasy of their morning aubade (3.5). The threat that they metaphorically imagine as darkness is to us, however, a great deal more specific. Specifically, it is Juliet's father, who comes, as we know he will, to invade his daughter's bridal chamber, assert his paternal prerogative to invalidate her right to choose a future, and conclude that, since she is his property, he has the ineluctable right to dispose of her as he will: "And you be mine, I'll give you to my friend; / and you be not, hang, beg, starve, die in the streets" (3.5.191-92). The central conflict in the play, projected in microcosm through these two scenes, mirrors the archetypal conflict in the daughter's life. The altar ritual likewise mirrors it, for the threat to the marriage and the daughter's future is always embodied in the person of the father, the character propelled into the role of tragic nemesis in *Romeo and Juliet* by the substructuring logic of marriage ritual.

After the crucial scenes in act 3, the remainder of *Romeo* progresses as a series of inverted and disordered epithalamia.[12] When the priest, the groom, and the musicians organized by old Capulet enter Juliet's chamber to take the bride to church, Capulet finds that she has already been wedded and the festival has gone on without him. He can thus only lament that "Death is my son-in-law, Death is my heir, / My daughter he hath wedded" (4.5.38-39) and that "All things that we ordained festival / turn from their office to black funeral" (4.5.84-85). In a parody of the father's due expectations on entering the bridal chamber the morning after a wedding, Capulet exclaims when he discovers Juliet's bleeding body lying with her husband:

> . . . O wife, look how our daughter bleeds!
> This dagger hath mista'en, for lo his house
> Is empty on the back of Montague,
> And it mis-sheathed in my daughter's bosom!
> (5.3.202-05)

The play ends in a final reversal, concluding with the scene that should traditionally have preceded the wedding: the two fathers bargaining over the bridal portion, Capulet initially asking for Montague's "hand" as all he feels able to demand as a widowhood entitlement for his "daughter's jointure" (5.3.297); Montague insisting that "I can give thee more / for I will raise her statue in pure gold" (298-99); and Capulet countering with his matching offer of as rich a statue for Romeo.[13] Appropriately, this play, so controlled by the problems of time and timing, ends with the ritual elements scattered out of sequence and the fathers participating in a futile attempt to validate the spousals retroactively, finally playing out their correct but now untimely paternal roles as reciprocal gift givers vying to give countergifts that surpass each other in sumptuousness (see Lévi-Strauss).[14] The barrenness implicit in their action is projected on stage through the subtext of parodic ritual.

The famous "nunnery scene" in *Hamlet* is another such inverted marriage ceremony, furnished as it is with the couple themselves and with the bride's father and the figure of state authority secreted where they can overhear the vows. Ophelia, who even holds the prayer book that the bride traditionally carries, is dramatically positioned between her concealed father on the one side and Hamlet on the other. But instead of the groom's awaiting the entrance of the bride and her father, the hidden father and the nervous Ophelia await Hamlet; instead of having the groom give the bride a ring, this scene inverts the model by having Ophelia return Hamlet's gifts, which she says she has "longed long to redeliver" (3.1.93). The awkward phrase is an appropriate one. For the scene presents, not a deliverance of a daughter to a new family, but a redeliverance to her father. When Hamlet suddenly demands of Ophelia "Where's your father?" (129), he is essentially asking her to choose, to declare just where her obedience and service, her love and honor, are bound. In her response, "At home, my lord" (130), not only does she lie but, more importantly, she chooses: through the very words she desperately seizes on, she indicates her own inability to break away from the weighty bonds of home and father. In making such a choice Ophelia violates the ritual. And Hamlet responds in savage parody by giving her the dowry she has indeed received from Polonius: to be as chaste as ice and as pure as snow and yet not escape calumny. He then shatters the mock ceremony with his injunction that there shall be no more marriages. When Ophelia later sings her bawdy songs and distributes her symbolic flowers with an insight born of derangement, thoughts of her father and Hamlet entangle in her mind like the fantastic garlands she wears. To both the unfaithful Gertrude and herself she gives rue. She also gives Gertrude a daisy, symbolic of dissembling; but, as she says, she has no violets to give away, for these flowers of faithfulness "wither'd all when my father died" (4.5.184). The fidelity that should have been given to Hamlet is inextricably entwined with thoughts of her father, the male from whom she has never ritually transferred her obedience or her loyalty.

Through the use of ceremonial substructures, Shakespeare invokes a sacramentality, a context of sacredness, for a certain moment and space within the play. Such structures temporally and spatially set the ritualized moments away from the undifferentiated profane events of the drama. But once a ritual has been invoked, has in effect drawn a circle of archetypal reference around the moment and space, any events from the nonsacramental surrounding world that interrupt or counter its prescribed direction take on special, portentous significance.[15] By interrupting or converting the invoked ritual to parody, such profane invasions rupture its sacramental context. Ritual structure is explicitly invoked, for example, in *Othello* 2.2, a twelve-line scene staged only to allow a "Herald" to proclaim that "every man put himself into triumph" for "the celebration of [Othello's] nuptial." When next Iago—earlier identified by Brabantio as a "profane wretch" (1.1.114) and by Desdemona as "a most profane and liberal counsellor" of "lame and impotent conclusion" (2.1.163, 161)—then converts the epithalamion outside Othello's chamber into a drunken, violent rout that interrupts the bridal pair within, our intuition of an ominous significance attached to the action derives from a half-conscious awareness of ritual violation. The matter is not one of direct casuality. No one is reductively to infer, for example, that Othello murders his wife because the revelers got drunk or that Romeo and Juliet come to a bad end just because her father did not participate in the wedding. Shakespeare's inverted rituals are a matter, rather, of violated sacramentality, the transgression of a sacred enclosure, the disruption of a hallowed sequence by incongruous actions penetrating from the profane world.

When Shakespeare wants to create a heightened aura of harmony, he will periodically blend ritual references, incorporating our associations with the "rite of May" and "Saint Valentine" into the festival already evoked by the title of *A Midsummer Night's Dream*. Conversely, to intensify a tragic moment, he will—rather than blend ceremonial structures—bring two incompatible rituals into collision, most frequently those of wedding and funeral.[16] When the technique works, the consequent explosion infuses the scene with the energy released by the violation of two sacred spheres, each shattered by its convergence not with something of a lesser energy but with something of equal sacred intensity. In *Romeo* we often encounter dual ritual references, as in Lady Capulet's line "I would the fool were married to her grave" (3.5.140). Such merely verbal references only allude to ritual structures without actually invoking them; Lady Capulet's juxtaposition of incompatible ceremonies serves as a tragic foreshadow. In scenes from other plays, however, the collision of modes incipient in the words is converted to a presentational dramatization. One of the finest examples of this collision of rituals is Ophelia's funeral.

Hamlet 5.1 begins as a scene of profaned ceremony: an inverted funeral of maimed and truncated rites presided over by a "churlish priest" who refuses the brother's plea for traditional ceremonies, instead asserting that "Shards, flints, and pebbles should be thrown on her," for "We should profane the service of the dead / To sing a requiem" (230-31, 236-37). Through Gertrude's action of strewing flowers, returning them as it were to Ophelia, the ritual moment is suddenly expanded to present us with an image associated not only with funerals, but with weddings:

I hop'd thou shouldst have been my Hamlet's
    wife.
I thought thy bride-bed to have deck'd, sweet
    maid,
And not have strew'd thy grave.

(5.1.243-45)

The double context harkens back to one of the major disturbances of the play. It echoes the paradigm of colliding sacred rituals already alluded to in Hamlet's bitter description of the conjunction of his mother's marriage and his father's funeral feasts, where "the funeral bak'd meats / Did coldly furnish forth the marriage tables" (1.2.180-81). The coincidence of the two ceremonies desecrates the ritual sacramentality of each. This collision of significations is enjoined when Laertes, playing out his role as his sister's natural guardian, leaps into her grave to assert the seemingly unchallengeable primacy of his bond (5.1). But his claim of authority is challenged and the sullied funeral recast into the bizarre image of a superimposed parodic wedding when Hamlet, fulfilling the role earlier defined by his mother, steps forward to this mock altar to assert his own claim to Ophelia's body. Again the tableau at the altar is invoked as the two claimants struggle over possession of the mock bride, Laertes refusing to relinquish the "fair and unpolluted flesh" of his sister (239) and Hamlet asserting that "Forty thousand brothers / Could not with all their quantity of love / Make up my sum" (269-71). The stage image of the two men competing for possession of Ophelia's shrouded body is the more suggestively dual in ceremonial reference when we recall the wedding custom—alluded to in Robert Herrick's "Nuptial Song on Sir Clipsby Crew and His Lady"—of sewing the bride up in a white sheet before laying her on the flower-strewn bed to await the groom's entrance.[17] The violent rivalry of the two competing claimants pulling the sanctified body back and forth between them reflects the structural principle underlying the scene: the violent collision of two mutually exclusive rituals, funeral and wedding, each struggling to claim the sacramentality it unwittingly pollutes by its own parodic enactment, the two competing claims forced by simultaneity into the fusion of energies that releases the scene's dramatic explosion.

In *Othello,* the father-daughter rupture is dramatized as a structural parody of the church service. As in most of the father-daughter plays, the father here is apparently a widower with only one child, a daughter whom he loves possessively and has denied to several suitors. When he is awakened in the first scene by Iago's vividly pornographic pictures of "your daughter cover'd with a Barbary horse," "your daughter and the Moor . . . making the beast with two backs," "your daughter . . . in the gross clasps of a lascivious Moor" (111-12, 115-17, 122, 126), Brabantio's odd response, "This accident is not unlike my dream, / Belief of it op-

presses me already" (142-43), suggests the repressed voyeurism of the father's incestuous projection seeping into the unconscious world of his dreams. In his brief moment alone on stage, the father speaks of the isolated sense of loss that his subsequent rage and denial attempt to supplant: " . . . gone she is; And what's to come of my despised time / Is nought but bitterness" (160-62). Although Brabantio voices a bitterness that has been purged from Prospero's response in a later play, both men express an unassuageable emptiness. Like that other Venetian father Shylock (who also tries to lock his daughter inside his house), Brabantio sets off through the city streets determined to reclaim his stolen treasure before it has been "possessed" by the claimant he has never authorized. Instead of using either the ritual archetype of the father's bringing the bride to the altar or the folktale pattern of the groom's kidnapping her from her father's fortress, Shakespeare here stages an inverted model, with the father storming the groom's quarters and attempting to recapture the bride.

Brabantio's action dramatizes the emotional and psychological problem that the marriage ritual seems implicitly designed to control and prevent. For consciously or unconsciously, overtly or implicitly, the father of the bride in most of Shakespeare basically wants, like Brabantio, to retain, withhold, lock up, and possess his daughter. Prevented by law, custom, and ritual injunction from taking any of these actions, the only satisfaction available to him is to arrogate to himself the choice of her husband, most often insisting on someone she does not want, lest a desired husband usurp the father's primary position in the daughter's life. But in spite of the paternal preference for Cloten over Posthumus Leonatus, Burgundy over France, Demetrius over Lysander, Paris over Romeo, or Saturninus over Bassianus, Shakespeare always stages the defeat of the father's choice, in both comedy and tragedy.

Brabantio's defeat in the Duke's chamber is played out against the set sequential movement of the church ceremony. Hoping to persuade the Duke that there are impediments to the marriage, Brabantio alleges that "Sans witchcraft" Desdemona could not "fall in love with what she fear'd to look on" (1.3.64, 98). He is here alluding to a specific impediment recognized by canon law as an *impedimentum dirimens,* one that, if proved, would indeed prevent a marriage or could nullify it retroactively. Specifically, Brabantio is claiming the impediment of *vis et metus,* or a condition of fear, duress, and constraint overruling the will—a general category that included the more specific accusation of witchcraft.[18] The Duke's rejoinder to Brabantio, "To vouch this is no proof" (106), reflects the appropriate procedure for such a charge, for an alleged impediment would prevent a marriage only when accompanied by substantive proof (Wheatly 491, *Rathen* 34-35).

When Othello then refutes the charge of coercion by denying that he seduced Desdemona by any "indirect and forced courses" (111), the Duke accepts the validity of Othello's story and gently advises Brabantio to "Take up this mangled matter at the best" (173). But the sadly stubborn father orders Desdemona to tell the congregation "Where most you owe obedience" (180). Desdemona answers with what is essentially the recitation of her wedding vow to obey and serve Othello, forsaking all others, including her father:

> I do perceive here a divided duty:
> To you I am bound for life and education;
> My life and education both do learn me
> How to respect you; you are the lord of duty;
> I am hitherto your daughter. But here's my
>   husband;
> And so much duty as my mother show'd
> To you, preferring you before her father,
> So much I challenge that I may profess
> Due to the Moor, my lord.
>
>   (1.3.181-89)

The nine-line passage is rhetorically arranged to reflect the "divided duty" of the bride poised at the altar. Its structure is a balance of two separate sentences, each one made up of four and one-half lines, the structural "volta," or difficult turn, from father to husband occurring at the midpoint of the fifth and longest line, the full stop in midline reflecting the attempt to terminate one status and begin a new one. The important fifth line is given added weight through alliteration, which emphasizes the turn to "husband." Following this transition, the terms "lord" and "duty" are transferred from the first to the second rhetorical domain of the passage. In the final line, which conveys Desdemona's determination through its brevity and its emphatically monosyllabic construction, the "duty" in question metamorphoses to "due," the proscriptive stasis of "duty" in the first line converting to the vitality of "due" in Desdemona's concluding speech-act pledge. Desdemona's response accords with the ritual; Brabantio's parodies it. Instead of presenting his daughter as a consecrated gift, the possessive and now dispossessed father hurls her across the stage at Othello with the words

> I here do give thee that with all my heart
> Which but thou hast already, with all my
>   heart
> I would keep from thee.
>
>   (1.3.193-95)

The Desdemona-Brabantio scene and the Lear-Cordelia confrontation, two versions of the same ritual model, have obvious similarities.[19] The opening scene of *King Lear,* however, is infused with the additional tension of colliding, incompatible ritual structures: the attempt of the man who is both king and father to substitute the illegitimate transfer of his kingdom for the legitimate one of his daughter.

In *King Lear,* the father's grudging recognition of the need to confer his *daughter* on younger strengths while he unburdened crawls toward death should be understood as the basal structure underlying his divestiture of his kingdom. Lear has called his court together in the opening scene because he must at last face the postponed reckoning with Cordelia's two princely suitors, who "Long in our court have made their amorous sojourn, / And here are to be answer'd" (1.1.47-48). But instead of justly relinquishing his daughter, Lear tries to effect a substitution of paternal divestitures: he portions out his kingdom as his "daughters' several dowers," attaching to Cordelia's share a stipulation designed to thwart her separation. In substituting his public paternity for his private one, the inherently indivisible entity for the one that biologically must divide and recombine, Lear violates both his kingly role in the hierarchical universe and his domestic one in the family. Nor is it accident—as it was in *Hamlet* 5.1—that brings these two incompatible rituals into collision in *Lear* 1.1. It is the willful action of the king and father, the lawgiver and protector of both domain and family, that is fully responsible for this explosion of chaos.

Yet of course Lear's bequest of his realm is in no way an unconditional transfer of the kingdom from one rulership to another. Instead, Lear wants to retain the dominion he theoretically casts off and to "manage those authorities / That he hath given away" (1.3.17-18). Likewise, the bequest of his daughter is actually an attempt to keep her, a motive betrayed by the very words he uses. When he *dis*claims "all my paternal care" and orders Cordelia "as a stranger to my heart and me / Hold thee from this for ever" (113, 115-16), his verb holds to his heart rather than expels from it the daughter he says is "adopted to our hate" (203), another verbal usage that betrays his retentive motives. His disastrous attempts to keep the two dominions he sheds are structurally linked through the parodic divestiture of his kingdom as dowry. In recognition of the family's economic interest in marriage, the terms of sixteenth-century dowries were required to be fully fixed before the wedding, thus making the property settlement a precondition for the wedding (see n. 13).[20] But Lear the father will not freely give his daughter her endowment unless she purchases it with pledges that would nullify those required by the wedding ceremony. If she will not love him all, she will mar her fortunes, lose her dowry, and thus forfeit the symbolic separation. And yet, as she asserts, she cannot marry if she loves her father all. The circularity of Lear's proposition frustrates the ritual phase of separation: by disinheriting Cordelia, Lear casts her away not to let her go but to prevent her from going. In Lévi-Strauss' terms, Lear has to give up Cordelia because the father must obey the basic social rule of reciprocity, which has a necessarily communal effect, functioning as a "distribution to undo excess." Lear's refusal is likewise communal in its effect, and it helps create the universe that he has "ta'en too little care of."

Insofar as Burgundy's suit is concerned, Lear's quantitatively constructed presumption works. Playing the mime priest and intentionally desecrating the sacramental ritual question he imitates, Lear asks the first bridegroom-candidate:

> Will you, with those infirmities she owes,
> Unfriended, new adopted to our hate,
> Dow'r'd with our curse, and stranger'd with
>   our
>   oath,
> Take her, or leave her?
>
>   (1.1.202-05)

Burgundy's hedged response is what Lear anticipates—this suitor will gladly "take Cordelia by the hand" only if Lear will give "but that portion which yourself propos'd" (243, 242). Shrewdly intuiting that France cannot be dissuaded by so quantitative a reason as "her price is fallen," Lear then adopts a strategy based on qualitative assumptions in his attempt to discourage the rival he most greatly fears. Insisting to France that

>   For you, great King
> I would not from your love make such a stray
> To match you where I hate; therefore beseech
>   you
> T'avert your liking a more worthier way
>
>   (208-11)

Lear tries to avoid even making the required ritual offer. By calling his own daughter "a wretch whom Nature is asham'd / Almost t'acknowledge hers" (212-13), Lear implies by innuendo the existence of some unnatural impediment in Cordelia that would make her unfit to marry and would thus prevent her separation. Effectively, the scene presents an altar tableau much like that in *Much Ado,* with a bride being publicly pronounced unfit for marriage. In *Lear,* however, it is the father rather than the groom who defames the character of the bride, and his motives are to retain her rather than to reject her. In this violated ceremony, the slandered daughter—instead of fainting—staunchly denies the alleged impediments by demanding that her accuser "make known / It is no vicious blot . . . No unchaste action, or dishonored step, / That hath deprived me of your grace and favor" (226-29). And here the groom himself takes up the role implicit in his vows, defending Cordelia's suborned virtue by his statement that to believe Lear's slanders would require "a faith that reason without miracle / Should never plant in me" (222-23). The physical separation of the daughter from the father is finally achieved only by France's

perception that "this unpriz'd precious maid . . . is herself a dowry" (259, 241); France recognizes the qualitative meaning of the dowry that Burgundy could only understand quantitatively.

In Cordelia's almost archetypal definition of a daughter's proper loyalties (1.1.95-104), Shakespeare uses a pun to link the fundamental predicament of the daughter—held under the aegis of the father—to its only possible resolution in the marriage troth: "That lord whose hand must take my plight shall carry / Half my love with him" (101-02), says Cordelia. When France later addresses his bride as "Fairest Cordelia, that art most rich being poor, / Most choice forsaken, and most lov'd despis'd" (250-51), he echoes the husband's traditional pledge to love "for richer, for poorer" the daughter who has "forsaken all others." And France himself then endows Lear's "dow'rless daughter" with all his worldly goods by making her "queen of us, of ours, and our fair France" (256-57). His statement "Be it lawful I take up what's cast away" (253) even suggests a buried stage direction through its implied allusion to the traditional conclusion of the *consensus nuptialis* as explained in the Sarum and York manuals: the moment when the bride, in token of receiving a dowry of land from her husband, prostrates herself at her husband's feet and he responds by lifting her up again (*Rathen* 36, Legg 190, Howard 306-07).

The visual and verbal texts of this important opening scene allude to the separation phase of the marriage ritual; the ritual features are emphasized because here, unlike the similar scene in *Othello,* the daughter's right to choose a husband she loves is not at issue. Because the ritual is sacred, Cordelia dispassionately refuses to follow her sisters in prostituting it. Lear, in contrast, passionately destroys his kingdom in order to thwart the fixed movement of the ritual pattern and to convert the pattern's linear progression away from the father into a circular return to him.[21] The discord his violation engenders continues to be projected through accumulating ritual substructures: in a parody of giving his daughter's hand, Lear instead gives her "father's heart from her" (126); in a parody of the ring rite, Lear takes the golden round uniting king and country and parts it, an act that both dramatizes the consequences of dividing his realm and demonstrates the anguish he feels at losing his daughter to a husband.

Once Lear has shattered the invoked sacred space by collapsing two incompatible rituals into it, he shatters also all claims to paternal authority. From this scene onward, the question of Lear's paternal relation to his daughters and his kingdom pervades the drama through the King's ceremonial invocations of sterility against the daughters he has generated and the land he has ruled. In the prototype of a harmonious wedding that concludes *As You Like It,* Hymen—who "peoples every town"—defines Duke

Senior's correct paternal role as that of the exogamous giver of the daughter created in heaven:

> Hymen from heaven brought her,
> Yea, brought her hither,
> That thou mightst join her hand with his
> Whose heart within his bosom is.
>
> (5.4.112-15)[22]

Hymen characterizes the generating of children as a gift from heaven, an essential spending of the self designed to increase the world. By contrast, Lear's image of the father is the "barbarous Scythian, / Or he that makes his generation messes / To gorge his appetite" (1.1.116—18). The definition is opposite to the very character of ritual. It precludes the possibility of transformation, for the father devours the flesh he begets. Here, generation becomes primarily an autogamous act, a retention and recycling of the procreative energies, which become mere extensions of private appetite feeding on its own production. The unnatural appetite of the father devouring his paternity is implicit even in the motive Lear reveals behind his plan to set his rest on Cordelia's "kind nursery" (124), an image in which the father pictures himself as an infant nursing from his daughter. The implied relationship is unnatural because it allows the father to deflect his original incestuous passions into Oedipal ones, thus effecting a newly incestuous proximity to the daughter, from whom the marriage ritual is designed to detach him. And when this form of appetite is thwarted by France's intervention, Lear effects yet another substitution of state for daughter: having ordered Cornwall and Albany to "digest the third" part of his kingdom, he and his gluttonous knights proceed to feed off it and through their "Epicurism and lust / Make . . . it more like a tavern or a brothel / Than a grac'd palace" (1.4.244-46). Compelled by nature to give up his daughter, he unnaturally gives up his kingdom; when his appetites cannot feed on her, they instead devour the paternity of his land.

The father devouring his own flesh is the monstrous extension of the circular terms of Lear's dowry proposal. The image belongs not only to the play's pervasive cluster of monsters from the deep but also to its dominant spatial pattern of circularity. Within both the narrative movement and the repeated spatial structure inside the drama, the father's retentive passions deny the child's rite of passage. When Cordelia departs from the father's realm for a new life in her husband's, ostensibly fulfilling the ritual separation, the journey is condemned to futility at its outset, for Cordelia departs dowered with Lear's curse: "Without our grace, our love, our benison" (1.1.265). Although the bride and groom have exchanged vows, the denial of the father's blessing renders the separation incomplete and the daughter's future blighted. Cordelia, like Rosalind, must therefore return to be reincorporated with her father

before she can undergo the ritual severance that will enable her to progress. She thus chooses father over husband, returning to Lear to ask his blessing: "look upon me, sir, / And hold your hand in benediction o'er me" (4.7.56-57). In lines that indicate how futile the attempt at incorporation has been when the precedent rites of passage have been perverted, Cordelia asserts, "O dear father, / It is thy business that I go about" (4.4.23-24), and characterizes her life with France as having been one of constant mourning for the father to whom she is still bound.

Shakespeare rewrote the source play *Leir* to make Cordelia remain in England alone (rather than with France at her side) to fight, lose, and die with her father, a revision that vividly illustrates the tragic failure of the family unit to divide, recombine, and regenerate. The only respite from pain the tragedy offers is the beauty of Lear's reunion with Cordelia, but that reunion takes place at the cost of both the daughter's life and the future life of the family. And for all the poignancy of this reunion, the father's intransigence—which in this play both initiates and conditions the tragedy—remains unchanged: it is still writ large in his fantasy that he and his daughter will be forever imprisoned together like birds in a cage.[23] At the end of the play, excluding any thought of Cordelia's new life with France, Lear focuses solely on the father-daughter merger, which he joyfully envisions enclosed in a perpetuity where no interlopers—short of a divine messenger—can threaten it: "He that parts us shall bring a brand from heaven, / And fire us hence like foxes" (5.3.22-23). The rejoining is the precise opposite of that in *As You Like It*. To Rosalind's question, "if I bring in your Rosalind, / You will bestow her on Orlando here?" Duke Senior responds, "That would I, had I kingdoms to give with her" (*AYL* 5.4.6-7, 8). In the Duke's characterization of Orlando's newly received endowment as "a potent Dukedom" (5.4.169), the implied fertility of both kingdom and family in ensured through the father's submission to the necessary movement of ritual. In *King Lear,* the father who imagined that he "gave his daughters all" extracts from his daughter at the end of the play the same price he demanded in the opening scene—that she love her father all. The play's tragic circles find their counterpart in its ritual movements. Cordelia returns to her father, and the final scene stages the most sterile of altar tableaux: a dead father with his three dead daughters, the wheel having come full circle back to the opening scene of the play. Initially barren of mothers, the play concludes with the death of all the fathers and all the daughters; the only figures who survive to emphasize the sterility of the final tableau are Albany, a widower, and Edgar, an unmarried son.

In Shakespearean tragedy, the cost demanded of the daughter is appallingly high. No matter how wrongheaded the inflexible father may be, the child who severs herself from him—even from allegiance to his impossible demands—becomes guiltlessly agentive in the wrack of the original family and tragically incapable of creating a new one. Such images of amputation and sterility are implicit in Gratiano's address to the dead young wife of Othello:

> Poor Desdemon! I am glad thy father's dead.
> Thy match was mortal to him, and pure grief
> Shore his old thread in twain.
>
> (*Oth.* 5.2.204-06)

Even Juliet, the most determinedly independent of all the daughters of tragedy, never considers what would seem to be the most practical solution to Romeo's banishment, that is, leaping over Verona's walls and going with him to Mantua. Instead, Juliet tries to effect a resolution that—even at the symbolic cost of her own life—will reunite her with her husband inside the structure of the Capulet family tomb. If the alternatives thus posed are equally unattractive, the dilemma thereby created is quintessentially Shakespearean: the "unresolvably problematic sense of experience" that raises questions we can "neither ignore nor answer" (Rabkin 29, 31) but affords no easy answers.

In *The Merchant of Venice,* Shakespeare gives us two versions of the daughter's solution to the repressive demands of the father. In each, the father follows the folktale motif of trying to lock up his daughter and retain her for himself. Portia's physical self has been symbolically locked up inside a lead casket by her dead father's "will," a term that suggests the father's desire to maintain both legal and physical possession of her. Jessica, meanwhile, is literally locked up inside her father's house—a house that becomes, through Shylock's calling it "my sober house" and its casements "my house's ears" (2.5.36, 34), an anthropomorphic refiguration of the father himself.

In this play, each father's determination to lock up his daughter sets up the test by which the daughter defines herself. While more theologically oriented readings have seen Jessica as a nominative figuration of the House of Jesse and her flight from Venice to Belmont as a symbol for the transition from Old to New Testament law, an allegorical interpretation of Shakespeare's characters that did not allow for the possibility of irony would end up making Gratiano—surely the most graceless figure in the play—an emblem of a theological concept he seems as incapable of representing as does Jessica. While biblical allusion is clearly important in *The Merchant,* we must remember that Shakespeare is writing drama, not theological allegory. Jessica serves as a dramatic foil to Portia; against Portia's relationship with both her wealthy father and her impoverished suitor we are implicitly invited to measure Jessica's. And inasmuch as the play gives us two specific test objects—the caskets and the rings—that en-

able Portia to engineer her transition from filial to conjugal bonds, they should likewise be understood as test objects that measure the success of Jessica's rite of passage.

To escape the repressive will of her father, Jessica climbs out the casement windows carrying "a casket" full of Shylock's jewels and money, gilding herself with her father's ducats and essentially selling herself to a Lorenzo who seems as interested in the acquired ducats as in the daughter who stole them. Jessica's theft here is dual. From the symbolic house of the father she simultaneously steals both herself and her father's fortune, leaving the House of Shylock empty in every sense. When in court the defeated Jew states:

> Nay, take my life and all, pardon not that:
> You take my house when you do take the
>   prop
> That doth sustain my house; you take my life
> When you do take the means whereby I live
>
> (4.1.374-77)

the voice that speaks is not only the miser's. It is also the father's.

Shylock's daughter, who defies all the structures and denies the bond—a term fundamental to the tragic plot of the play—ends up symbolically disavowing the sanctity of the conjugal bond of her own heredity, a point that receives comic allusion through Launce's hope "that you are not the Jew's daughter" and Jessica's response, "That were a kind of bastard hope indeed; so the sins of my mother should be visited upon me" (3.5.11-14). In purchasing her escape to an imagined freedom, the daughter sells her mother's "ring" and her father's "stones," symbolic representations of the female and male generative organs. And in figuratively delegitimizing herself, the daughter reciprocally disinherits and defiles the father in a way that alludes to the Old Testament family laws of Shylock's faith. For in the same chapter of Leviticus that ostracizes any sons of Aaron who have "cuttings in their flesh" as being polluted before the Lord and states that if the "daughter fall to playe the whore, she polluteth her father," it is also written that any man who may "haue *his* stones broken" is defiled and shall not "come nere to offer the sacrifices of the Lord" (21.5, 9, 20, 21).[24] The Old Testament precedent suggests that in demanding a pound of Antonio's flesh, Shylock is calling for a retributive defilement against the man who has spat on Shylock's Jewish gabardine, broken the legal bond, and furthermore—at least in Shylock's mind (see 2.7.1-10)—joined with the other Christians in severing Shylock's flesh. For "my daughter," Shylock tells us, "is my flesh and blood" (3.1.37). The precedent also makes Solanio's metaphoric use of "stones" a cruelly appropriate means of mocking Shylock's anguish over Jessica's disavowal of a heritage that to her father is "rich and precious." Behind Solanio's gleeful mimicry of the comic hoarder ranting in the streets for his stolen ducats lies the figure of the tragic father castrated by his daughter and disinherited from the future:

> A sealed bag, two sealed bags of ducats,
> Of double ducats, stol'n from me by my
>   daughter!
> And jewels, two stones, two rich and precious
>   stones,
> Stol'n by my daughter!
>
> (2.8.18-21)[25]

What Jessica buys in return for the symbols of her parents' procreative act is a monkey, a grotesque imitation of the infant human form. And in act 5, scene 1, she is left singing a moonlight duet with Lorenzo that—beneath the beauty of its lyrical surface—uneasily equates their love to that of Troilus and Cressida, Pyramus and Thisbe, Aeneas and Dido, and Jason and Medea, all ominous archetypes of bonds somehow shattered in conjunction with attempts to invalidate family or cultural allegiances. Lorenzo's line "In such a night / Did Jessica steal from the wealthy Jew, / And with an unthrift love did run from Venice" (5.1.14-16) unwittingly suggests a poverty implicit in Jessica's purchase on the night of her gilded stealth. The daughter who meant to discard her paternity is furthermore left with an ironic dependence on her father's money, a fortune obtained not by legacy but by robbery, as Lorenzo unwittingly suggests in his joke about acquiring "thieves for wives" (2.6.23). The final bitter irony of Jessica's stolen dowry comes at the end of the play, when Lorenzo describes the second seized fortune they will get from Shylock as "manna" dropped from heaven. The reference echoes Portia's courtroom paean to the quality of mercy and simultaneously alludes to the sustenance that the Old Testament Father freely gave the children of Israel as they wandered in the wilderness en route from bondage to freedom in the Promised Land. Jessica's attempt to make the transition from filial to conjugal bonds by means of theft is, in its ritual implications, as unsuccessful as Shylock's attempt to lock up and possess his treasure, the family treasure that is ultimately the daughter herself.

In contrast to Shylock, Portia's father has not conflated his ducats and his daughter but has understood that his true treasure is Portia. What he has locked up inside the casket is not his jewels but his daughter's "counterfeit," the image of the family fortune. In the riddle game the successful suitor will be the one who values Portia enough to choose not the gold or silver she brings with her as dowry but the lead casket that requires him to "give and hazard all." What France recognizes as true of Cordelia is likewise true of Portia: she is herself a dowry.

Like Jessica, Portia chafes against the restrictions of this bond. With a quibble on her use of "will," she laments:

> O me, the word choose! I may neither choose who
> I would, nor refuse who I dislike; so is the will of
> a living daughter curb'd by the will of a dead father.
> Is it not hard . . . that I cannot choose one, nor
> refuse none?
>
> (1.2.22-26)

But, unlike Jessica, Portia does not try to ensure her happiness by throwing away the filial bonds—any more than she will ensure Antonio's freedom by denying Shylock's claim or by overturning the legal structure outright. Instead, she characteristically works out a solution that amounts to fudging a bit. She resolves the strictures of institutional bonds by readjusting them to her own will, thus achieving a sort of independence within the given structures. In the marriage riddle, she must passively rely on the base natures of the suitors themselves to cause them to choose wrongly. But she does—without actually disobeying her father—manage to guide Bassanio's choice by first telling him to "pause a day or two / Before you *hazard*" (3.2.1-2; my italic) and then giving him a hint that she gave no previous suitor, in the form of the music and the song whose end lines rhyme with the word "lead."

To attribute to Portia a conscious complicity in directing Bassanio's choice is not to demean her integrity. Rather, it is to do justice to her role as the daughter-heroine of comedy who must play a part in shaping her own future. While the death of the father does free a male heir like Petruchio to choose an independent future, it does not likewise free the heiress richly left in Belmont. Nor for that matter does the marriage ritual allow even the fatherless daughter to walk independently down the aisle and give herself away; fatherless or not, she is always a property to be bequeathed by some figuratively paternal authority. And to resolve the potentially unacceptable alternatives symbolically posed by the paternal structures surrounding her, the daughter-heroine of comedy must often resort to disguise, either literal or figurative. Since Portia, as she says, can neither "choose one, nor refuse none," she must subtly find a way to lead the suitor she first silently chooses to choose her. Faced with the predicament dramatized in the marriage ceremony, she enacts the archetypal resolution frequently defined in folktale romance. Led to the altar, "given" to the husband by the father before she herself is ever asked to acknowledge that she will "take this man," she must either acquiesce to her father's will or violate the ritual by refusing—unless she can ensure by contrivance that the hand to which she is transferred is the one she herself has already chosen. In mythic terms, the daughter escapes her father's castle not by climbing out of its casements but by symbolically throwing down the key to the suitor she chooses. Like Rapunzel, who lets down her hair, Portia directs Bassanio to discover the key that will unlock "Portia's self" from confinement. Jessica—like Desdemona, a daughter inside tragedy—chooses to escape at the cost of violating the family house and all it represents; Portia also "chooses," but in a way that leaves the structure intact for the future.

And unlike Jessica, who in selling her mother's betrothal ring rejects the value of the conjugal bond it represents, Portia insists on the value of her ring and on the family ties it symbolizes. When Bassanio gives away her ring at Antonio's request, here acceding to the demand that his friend's love be "valued" 'gainst your wive's commandment" (4.2.450), the act is not one that Portia dismisses lightly. At the end of the play, having first induced Bassanio to repeat his vows of faith, Portia puts Antonio into the role of surrogate priest and bonded witness to the sanctity of those vows. By acting as Bassanio's "surety," Antonio figuratively takes out a bond once again for Bassanio; only this bond guarantees the validity of Bassanio's marriage at the pledge of Antonio's soul rather than, as previously, of his flesh: "I dare be bound again, / My soul upon the forfeit, that your lord / Will never more break faith advisedly" (5.1.251-53).[26] In a further mimesis of the ceremonial pledge to "love, honor and keep" the recipient of the ring, Portia makes Antonio the priest, giving him the ring and telling him to give it to Bassanio with the instructions to "bid him *keep* it better" (5.1.255; my italic). The comedy thus ends with a correct ritual enactment, which resolves the threat to union implied by Bassanio's transfer of Portia's ring.

Not only in *The Merchant of Venice* but frequently throughout the canon, Shakespeare draws on ritual substructures for the conclusions of his plays. Within these patterns, tragedy ends with an emphasis on broken or inverted ritual designs; comedy ends with the scattered elements of ritual regrouped and correctly enacted. And in the four late romances—plays in which oracular prophecies and the sudden descent of divine beings constantly reshape the linear narrative—the shattered human world, through obsessive reenactments of broken rituals, strives to recapture what has been lost and thus to reconnect itself with the sacred world of its origins. The design closely approximates Mircea Eliade's description of the ritual process as humanity's attempt to effect the "myth of the eternal return." Within these late plays, the declining world of inflexible paternal authority rediscovers a redemptive teleology through the ritualized reclamation of that particular bond which could only be viewed as a liability to the family's prospects for economic and patrilineal prosperity. In *The Winter's Tale,* the murderous wrath Leontes directs against his innocent wife and daughter is punished by the immediately conjunctive death of the son he imagines will carry his lineal posterity. Only when he comes to value "that which has been lost"—

the daughter Perdita, who is a matrilineal rather than a patrilineal extension—is Leontes allowed the partial restitution implicit in his adoption of Florizel. And even this compensation is made possible only through the return and affirmation of the hitherto unvalued daughter.

In *Pericles,* another play in which redemption depends on reclaiming the lost female child, a riddle game and caskets again serve as ritual structures through which the father-daughter relation is expressed. The Prince of Type, perceiving the horrible truth that explains how Antiochus can be "father, son, and husband mild" to his own daughter (*Per.* 1.1.68), flees from this daughter, whom he calls a "glorious casket stor'd with ill" (77). Parallel to Lear's barbarous Scythian who gorges on his own generation, the daughter in Antioch is "an eater of her mother's flesh" (130); both are autophagous and monstrous images of generative consummation perverted into degenerative consumption. Antiochus' daughter is a type of living death. While Portia was the family jewel inside the lead casket, the life locked into the symbolically maternal container by the "will" of her dead father, this daughter is the casket itself, containing inside her the deadly ill of the father's incestuous generation.

As D. W. Harding aptly points out, whether or not Shakespeare wrote this opening of *Pericles,* the events at Antioch "have a sharply defined significance for the broad topic of the relation between father and daughter, since they ask us to contemplate, and decisively reject, the possibility of incest" (59). The background story of Antioch, which Gower narrates at the beginning of the play, is a mirror of that leading up to Pericles' recognition of Marina in act 5. Gower tells of a great king who

> unto him took a peer,
> Who died and left a female heir,
> So buxom, blithe, and full of face
> As heaven had lent her all his grace;
> With whom the father liking took.
>
> (1.21-25)

While yet oblivious to the deadly perversion in Antioch, Pericles had thanked Antiochus for having "taught / My frail mortality to know itself, / . . . For death remembered should be like a mirror" (1.1.41-42, 45); once aware, he calls the princess a "Fair glass of light" from whom his "thoughts revolt" (76, 78). Yet this scene has still another mirror, one that frames the other two and reflects the unnatural reality of the relationship: the mirror of ritual enactment. The scene features a father, a bride, and a groom and parodies the appropriate and expected progression of a marriage ceremony. Instead of enacting the father's role of bringing in and giving away his bridal-decked daughter to a waiting husband, Antiochus demands—while music plays—

"Bring in our daughter, clothed like a bride / For embracements even of Jove himself" (6-7). The father has here positioned himself in the groom's role to receive and embrace this daughter, who is clothed *like* a bride but is not one, and he embraces her in the incongruous person of Jove the father. Instead of relinquishing her to a husband's hand, Antiochus warns the daughter's suitor to "touch not, upon thy life, / For that's an article within our law" (87-88). Here, the daughter's necessary search for a husband to supplant the father, the successful metamorphosis of love in *As You Like It,* is prevented by the insidious bond of "kindness," culminating in the relationship of unnatural kin and kind semantically alluded to in the princess' riddle: "I sought a husband, in which labor / I found that kindness in a father" (66-67).

Although the rest of the play can rightly be called a flight from incest, years later Pericles is aroused from his silent apathy only by the sight of an unidentified young woman who reminds him suddenly of his dead wife, the triggering association that lies at the heart of the father's incestuous love for his daughter. Having spent the play fleeing the punishment of recognizing the father's ugly secret in Antioch, he finds himself, now a father, aroused to life by his own daughter. But having once looked into the deadly mirrors of the first scene, Pericles can go on to reject the implicit seductiveness of the situation reflected in his own response to Marina.

In this play, which is characterized by a highly symbolic, mythic set of connections, the lust between Antiochus and his daughter is condignly punished by fire from heaven, which consumes them. The punishment meted out to Pericles throughout the play has no such obvious cause, and it seems in fact so basically causeless that it makes him appear almost Job-like. The implicit "cause," however, is rooted in the matter of Antioch that begins and ends the play and that Pericles' actions unconsciously mirror. Pericles, mistakenly presuming his wife dead, had thrown "her overboard with these very arms" (5.3.19), abandoning the woman who, locked up in a casket, at that moment gave birth to the daughter whom he ultimately finds in the brothel in Mytilene. Symbolically, this action reflects the same choice that the father in Antioch made. Such a choice discards the conjugal bond and the treasure of legitimate family generation, which here, as in *The Merchant of Venice,* is represented by the emblematic womb-tomb of casket-coffin.

Only after Pericles, having wandered for years, comes full circle back to face the terrifying secret from which he had fled can he release Marina from the brothel in which he finds her; and only after the father has freed his daughter from the structure to which the image of his own desire has symbolically consigned her can the husband again move forward in his own life. At the end of the play Pericles sets off again to reestablish the legitimate order of the family by reclaiming the lost treasure that is rightly his. In recovering Thaisa and asking her to "come, be buried / A second time within these arms" (43-44), Pericles effects the reclamation and rebirth of the family "fortune," here reversing his earlier act of throwing it away in a coffin.

Through the daughter's return—and only through her return—can the king in both *Pericles* and *The Winter's Tale* proceed to recover the mother, whom the daughter resembles yet who symbolically "died" in conjunction with the daughter's birth. In both plays the physical presence of the daughter exerts a unique, enormously evocative power over the father, initially attracting him in a way that is definably incestuous. Yet from this attraction and from it alone springs the force of regeneration incipient in all the father-daughter relationships, even the tragic ones. The spiraling inwardness of Leontes' and Pericles' paternal narcissism leads both of them to the threatened incestuous moment. But the recognition obtained in this frightening instant generates an impulse to create life anew, the exogamous impulse that compels the father to relinquish his daughter and bring back to life the abandoned mother. The final scene of each play moves into a markedly mythic structure to enact what becomes a dual progression of the ritual passage, the separation of daughter and father leading to the incorporation of the daughter into a new union, simultaneous with the reincorporation of the father into the one he had cast away. As opposed to the sterile circularity of the violated ritual in *King Lear,* the structure of these plays returns to its origin so that the family can be recreated through the redemption of the ritual now correctly enacted. The recreation is made possible by the daughter's regenerating both the mother and the father who generated her. She becomes, in Pericles' words, the force "that beget'st him that did thee beget" (5.1.195).

The father-daughter relation in *The Tempest,* the last of the romances, is somewhat similar, in that Miranda, like Perdita and Marina, is the force that preserves her father. Here, however, there is no mother for Prospero to rediscover when he at last gives up his daughter and abandons his island. Instead of the miraculous reunion with a lost daughter as the force that suddenly resuscitates life, *The Tempest* shows us a father who has never lost his child and whose concern for her welfare has always given him his will to live. And of all the Shakespearean fathers of daughters, Prospero is undoubtedly the most successful in enacting his proper role. His purpose, much like that defined by Hymen in *As You Like It,* has always been to educate, discipline, and nurture Miranda so that he can set her free, as he does Ariel. Prospero understands the need to play the father's mock role as the barrier to young love, the need to make Ferdinand realize the value of his daughter through laboring to earn her lest "too light winning / Make the prize light" (1.2.452-53). He also understands the need for the daughter to choose her husband over her father, a choice that Desdemona and Cordelia could not make their fathers accept. When he commands Miranda not to talk with his prisoner or reveal her name, he is purposely acting to fulfill both roles. While Lear casts Cordelia away so that he can keep her, Prospero ties Miranda to him so that she will disobey his commands and initiate the required transition of loyalties from father to husband. Yet, for all his awareness, Prospero turns aside from watching Miranda and Ferdinand play out the parts he himself has written for them and makes the pained comment "So glad of this as they I cannot be" (3.1.92).

Shakespeare shows us that it is no easier for Prospero to give up Miranda, even to a husband he himself has chosen, than it was for poor Brabantio to relinquish Desdemona. Throughout the play Prospero remains disproportionately preoccupied with tormenting thoughts of his daughter sexually possessed by another male, an obsession that has its analogue in Brabantio's dream. Hence the father lectures Ferdinand—the future son-in-law whom old Prospero never manages to like very much—that

> If thou dost break her virgin-knot before
> All sanctimonious ceremonies may . . . be
>   minist'red,
> . . . barren hate . . . and discord shall
>   bestrew
> The union of your bed with weeds so loathly
> That you shall hate it both.
>
> (4.1.15-22)

And hence he sets Ferdinand to work hauling logs, doing the labor that Caliban refused to do, thereby domesticating Ferdinand's energies in a way that could never reform the uneducable lust of Caliban. In his betrothal gift to Miranda and Ferdinand, the dowry masque he evokes out of the powers of his mind, Prospero includes the rainbow goddess Iris, the emblematic fertility of Ceres, and the archetypal wife-consort Juno. Significantly, from this vision the father banishes Venus and her son, turning them back on their way to the celebration, where he fears they would have done "some wanton charm upon this man and maid, / Whose vows are, that no bedright shall be paid / Till Hymen's torch be lighted" (4.1.95-97).

The forces of erotic chaos that Prospero hoped to banish from his daughter's prothalamion are, however, not so easily vanquished. For before the masque has ended, Prospero realizes that Caliban and his confederates are on their way, and the very thought of the would-be rapist abruptly dissolves the insubstantial pageant into thin air.

In *The Tempest,* Prospero essentially overcomes his incestuous desire to retain his daughter imprisoned on his island. He recognizes his own repressed but monstrous wishes in confessing that Caliban, who would people the island with Calibans, is a "thing of darkness I / [must] Acknowledge mine" (5.1.275-76). Caliban, the monster of *The Tempest,* whose name suggests an anagram for "cannibal," refigures the incestuous, self-consumptive desires imaged in Lear's "barbarous Scythian" and in the "monstrous lust" between Antiochus and his daughter in *Pericles.* He is also a force on whose nature nurture will not stick. And so while daughter and father are simultaneously released from the enchantment of living together forever isolated on an island controlled by the father's shaping fancies, Caliban must remain enslaved on it. Their release and their ability to return to the natural order of civilization are made possible only by the arrival of Ferdinand, who comes—like the prince of the fairy tale—to take the bride away from her father's fortress and lead her out into generative space and time.

The end of *The Tempest* leaves us with a father who has learned what nature requires of him: the father must take part with his nobler reason against his fury and let his admired Miranda go. Yet doing so leaves Prospero with the lonely emptiness apparent in his confession to Alonzo: "I / Have lost my daughter . . . In this last tempest" (5.1.147-48, 153). As in *Pericles* and *The Winter's Tale,* the ritual dissolution of the father-daughter bond is dramatically realized; but in this final play the relationship gains added depth through the exploration of the central paradox always inherent in its resolution. Here, we are not left entirely with the "brave new world" imagined by Miranda and in some respects promised to the reclaimed families of the two earlier romances. For Shakespeare goes beyond the happy ending to show us the pain and loss bequeathed to the isolated father who has acted out the required rite of separation. For while at first glance the church ceremony might seem only to dramatize the transfer of a passive female object from one male to another, in reality it ritualizes the community's coercion, not of the bride, but of her father. Ultimately, it is he who must pay the true "bride price" at the altar and, by doing so, become the displaced and dispossessed actor. As the celebratory reunification that concludes Shakespeare's comedy begins in the final scene, it is therefore left up to Prospero to complete the demands dictated by his role and—like every father of every bride—retire from the scene to seek out his seat in the congregation. Thus Prospero concludes the ritual and the play with his only remaining expectation:

> to see the nuptial
> Of these our dear-belov'd solemnized,

And thence retire me to my Milan, where
Every third thought shall be my grave.

(5.1.309-12)

Notes

[1] Stone accounts for the drama and poetry of the sixteenth and early seventeenth centuries by modifying his "rather pessimistic view of a society with little love and generally low affect" to allow for "romantic love and sexual intrigue . . . in one very restricted social group . . . that is the households of princes and great nobles" (*Family* 103-04). This qualification does not extend to his view of parent-child relationships.

[2] Stone also points out that the high infant-mortality rate, "which made it folly to invest too much emotional capital in such ephemeral beings," was as much responsible for this lack of affective family ties as were any economic motives (*Family* 105). For Stone, paternal authority—not affection—was the almost exclusive source of the family's coherence. Furthermore, the domestic patriarchy of the sixteenth century was not merely a replica of family structures inherited from the past but a social pattern consciously exploited and reinforced by the state to emphasize the injunctions of obedience and authority; nor was it replaced until absolute monarchy was overthrown (see *Family* 151-218). Meanwhile, because of the prevalent child-rearing practices, the maternal impact was relatively insignificant, hence not nearly so important to the psychological process of maturation; in Stone's estimate, our familiar "maternal, child-oriented, affectionate and permissive mode" of child rearing did not emerge till about 1800 (*Family* 405). During the Elizabethan era, the upper-class practice of transferring a newborn infant immediately to a village wet nurse, who nurtured the child for two years, substantially muted any maternal influence on child development and no doubt created an inestimable psychological distance between mother and child. Stone cites the strained and formal relationship between Juliet and Lady Capulet as vivid testimony of the absence of affective mother-child bonds that results from such an arrangement (106); in the Capulet household, it is even left up to the nurse, not the mother, to remember Juliet's birthday. Yet Stone does not measure the relationship between Juliet and her father against his hypothesis of the absence of affect. Old Capulet is indeed the authoritarian dictator of Stone's model, but he is also a "careful father" who deeply loves his child. Instead of being eager to have her off his hands, Capulet is notably reluctant to give up the daughter he calls "the hopeful lady of my earth" (1.2.15; all Shakespeare quotations are from the Evans ed.); his bull-headed determination to marry her to Paris following Tybalt's death is born, paradoxically enough, from the deeply rooted affection that Stone's hypothesis excludes.

[3] As Christopher Hill suggests in his review of Stone's *Family,* much of the evidence used could well imply its opposite: "The vigour of the preachers' propaganda on behalf . . . of breaking children's wills, suggests that such attitudes were by no means so universally accepted as they would have wished" (461). Hill and others have criticized Stone for asserting that love and affection were negligible social phenomena before 1700 and for presuming throughout "that values percolate downwards from the upper to the lower classes" (Hill 462). Because of the scope and importance of Stone's subject, his book has been widely reviewed. As David Berkowitz comments, "the possibility of endless symposia on Stone's vision and performance looms as a fashionable activity for the next half-dozen years" (396). Hill's review and the reviews by Keith Thomas and John Demos seem particularly well balanced.

[4] One could chart the new emphasis on the family by reviewing the Shakespeare topics at recent MLA conventions. The 1979 convention featured Marriage and the Family in Shakespeare, Shirley Nelson Garner chairing, as its Shakespeare Division topic and also included a related special session, The Love between Shakespeare's Fathers and Daughters, Paul A. Jorgensen chairing. Before becoming the division topic, the subject had been examined in special sessions for three consecutive years: 1976, Marianne Novy chairing; 1977, John Bean and Coppélia Kahn chairing; and 1978, Carol Thomas Neely chairing. Special sessions continued in 1980 and 1981, with Shirley Nelson Garner and Madelon S. Gohlke as chairs. A parallel phenomenon has meanwhile been taking place in sixteenth-, seventeenth-, and eighteenth-century historical scholarship, which Hill explains by saying that " . . . the family as an institution rather suddenly became fashionable, perhaps as a by-product of the women's liberation movement" (450).

Most of the work on fathers and daughters in Shakespeare has been done, as might be expected, on the romances. See the essays by Cyrus Hoy, D. W. Harding, and Charles Frey. Of particular interest is the Schwartz and Kahn collection, which was published after I had written this paper but which includes several essays that express views related to my own. See esp. David Sundelson's "So Rare a Wonder'd Father: Prospero's *Tempest,*" C. L. Barber's "The Family in Shakespeare's Development: Tragedy and Sacredness," and Coppélia Kahn's "The Providential Tempest and the Shakespearean Family."

[5] Margaret Loftus Ranald has done substantial work on the legal background of marriage in Shakespeare plays. I have found no marriages (or funerals) staged literally in the plays of Shakespeare or of his contemporaries. Although, for instance, the marriage of Kate and Petruchio would seem to offer a rich opportunity for an indecorously comic scene appropriate for *The Taming of the*

Shrew, the action occurs offstage and we only hear of it secondhand. Nor do we witness the Olivia-Sebastian marriage in *Twelfth Night.* Even the fragment of the botched ceremony in *Much Ado* does not follow the liturgy with any precision but presents a dramatized version of it. This omission—apparently consistent in Elizabethan and Jacobean drama—may have resulted from the 1559 Act of Uniformity of Common Prayer and Divine Service in the Church, which stipulates sanctions against "any persone or persones whatsoever . . . [who] shall in anye Entreludes Playes Songes, Rymes or by other open Woordes, declare or speake anye thing in the derogation depraving or despising of the same Booke, or of any thing therein conteyned" (1 Elizabeth 1, c. 2, in *Statutes* 4:355-58). Given the rising tempo of the Puritan attack on the theaters at this time, we may reasonably infer that the omission of liturgy reflects the dramatists' conscientious wish to avoid conflict. Richmond Noble's study corroborates this assumption (82). Of the services to which Shakespeare does refer, Noble notes that the allusions to "distinctive features, words, and phrases of Holy Matrimony are extremely numerous" (83).

⁶ Van Gennep built his study on the work of Hartland, Frazer, Ciszewski, Hertz, Crowley, and others who had noted resemblances among the components of various disparate rites. His tripartite diachronic structure provides the basis for Victor W. Turner's discussions in the essay "Liminality and Communitas" (*Ritual Process* 94-203).

⁷ The church canons of 1604 seem to have confused the situation further by continuing to recognize the validity of the nuptial pledge but forbidding persons under twenty-one to marry without parental consent; this ruling would make the marriage of minors illegal but nonetheless binding for life and hence valid (Stone, *Family* 32). Until the passage of Lord Hardwicke's Marriage Act in 1753, confusion was rife over what constituted a legal marriage and what a valid one. In addition to bringing coherence to the marriage laws, this act was designed to protect increasingly threatened parental interests by denying the validity as well as the legality of a religious ceremony performed without certain conditions, including parental consent for parties under twenty-one (Stone, *Family* 35-36).

The concern for parental approval has always focused on, and in fact ritualized, the consent of the bride's father. In 1858, the Reverend Charles Wheatly, a noted authority on church law, attributed the father's giving away his daughter as signifying the care that must be taken of the female sex, "who are always supposed to be under the tuition of a father or guardian, whose consent is necessary to make their acts valid" (496). For supportive authority Wheatly looks back to Richard Hooker, whose phrasing is substantially harsher. Hooker felt that the retention of the custom "hath still this vse that it putteth we men in mind of a dutie

whereunto the verie imbecillitie of their [women's] nature and sex doth binde them, namely to be alwaies directed, guided and ordered by others . . ." (215).

Even though the validity of a marriage was not vested in parental consent, "the Protestants, including the Anglicans, considered the consent of the parents to be as essential to the marriage as the consent of the bride and bridegroom" (Flandrin 131). Paradoxically, "both Church and State claimed to be supporting, at one and the same time, freedom of marriage and the authority of parents" (Flandrin 132). The ambiguity arose because the child was obliged, under pain of mortal sin, to obey the parent. Technically, the child was free to choose a marriage partner, but since the church never took steps against the prerogatives of the father, the notion of choice was problematic.

⁸ Given the high parent mortality rate, a number of brides necessarily went to the altar on the arms of their legal guardians. Peter Laslett notes that in Manchester between 1553-1657 over half of the girls marrying for the first time were fatherless (103), but some historians have criticized his reliance on parish registers as the principal demographic barometer.

⁹ The groom's pledge suggests the wedding ring's dual sexual and material symbolism. Historically, the ring symbolizes the dowry payment that the woman will receive from her husband by the entitlement of marriage; it apparently superseded the custom of placing tokens of espousal on the prayer book (see *Book of Common Prayer* 408). It also signifies the physical consummation, a point frequently exploited in Renaissance drama and also implied by the rubrics in the older Roman Catholic manuals, which direct the placing of the ring. The Martène manual specifies that the bride is to wear it on the left hand to signify "a difference between the estate and the episcopal order, by whom the ring is publicly worn on the right hand as a symbol of full and entire chastity" (Legg 207). *The Rathen Manual,* which follows the Use of Sarum, contains a rather charming piece of folklore widely believed through the eighteenth century. It, too, allusively suggests the sexual significance of the ring: "For in the fourth finger there is a certain vein proceeding to the heart and by the chime of silver there is represented the internal affection which ought always to be fresh between them" (35-36; see also Wheatly 503). Even after the priest took over the ceremonial role of transferring the bride's hand from her father's to her husband's, he did not also become the intermediary in transferring the ring from the groom's keeping to the bride's finger. Such an incorporation of duties might seem logical were it not that this part of the ritual simultaneously imitates and licenses the sexual act.

The English reformers retained both the symbol of the ring and the groom's accompanying pledge to "worship" his wife's body, a retention that generated consideration attack from the more radical reformers. The controversy over this wording occupies the major portion of Hooker's defense of the Anglican marriage rite (see also Stone, *Family* 522, on the attempts in 1641 and 1661 to alter the wording of the vow from "worship" to "honor"). Hooker justifies the husband's "worship" as a means of transferring to the wife the "dignitie" incipient in her husband's legitimizing of the children he now allows her to bear. She furthermore receives, by this annexation of his worship, a right to participate in his material possessions. The movement of the vow, from sexual to material pledge, thus sequences a formal rite of passage, a pattern alluded to in Hooker's phrase, "the former branch hauing granted the principall, the latter graunteth that which is annexed thereunto" (216).

[10] The ceremonial transfer of the father's authority to the husband is acknowledged by the Reverend John Shepherd in his historical commentary accompanying the 1853 *Family Prayer Books:* " . . . the ceremony shows the father's consent; and that the authority, which he before possessed, he now resigns to the husband" (Brownell 465). By implication, however, the ceremony resolves the incestuous attraction between father and daughter by ritualizing his "gift" of her hand, a signification unlikely to be discussed in the commentary of church historians. When first the congregation and next the couple are asked to name any impediments to the marriage, there are, Wheatly says, three specific impediments the church is charging all knowledgeable parties to declare: a preceding marriage or contract, consanguinity or affinity, and want of consent (483). The final act of Ben Jonson's *Epicoene* enumerates all the possible legal impediments that might be subsumed under these three.

The bride's father, by virtue of his special prominence in the ritual, functions as a select witness whose presence attests to the validity of the contract. The Friar in *Much Ado* asks Hero and Claudio whether they "know any inward impediment why you should not be cojoin'd" (4.1.12-13). Leonato dares to respond for Claudio, "I dare make his answer, none," because, 'as father of the bride, he presumes to have full knowledge that no impediment exists. When he learns of Hero's supposed taint, the rage he vents over the loss of his own honor is the more comprehensible when we understand his special position in the ceremony as a sworn witness to the transfer of an intact daughter.

[11] The sections on the celebration of "Festiuall daies" and times of fast that precede Hooker's defense of the English "Celebration of Matrimonie" are especially helpful in understanding Elizabethan ritual, for in these sections Hooker expands his defense of the Anglican rites into an explanation of, and rationale for, the whole

notion of ritual. Having first isolated three sequential elements necessary for festival—praise, bounty, and rest—he goes on to justify "bountie" in terms remarkably compatible with the theories of both Bataille and Lévi-Strauss on the essential "spending-gift" nature of marriage. To Hooker, the "bountie" essential to celebration represents the expression of a "charitable largenesse of somewhat more then common bountie. . . . Plentifull and liberall expense is required in them that abounde, partly as a signe of their owne ioy in the goodnesse of God towards them" (292, 293). Bounty is important to all festival rites, but within the marriage rite this "spending" quality incorporates the specific idea of sexual orgasm as the ultimate and precious expenditure given the bride by her husband, a notion alluded to in Bataille and one that functioned as a standard Elizabethan metaphor apparent in phrases like "Th' expense of spirit" (sonnet 129) or Othello's comment to Desdemona, "The purchase made, the fruits are to ensue; / That profit's yet to come 'tween me and you" (2.3.9-10). The wedding ceremony ritualizes this notion of bounty as the gift of life by having the father give the groom the family treasure, which the father cannot "use" but can only bequeath or hoard. The groom, who ritually places coins or a gold ring on the prayer book as a token "bride price," then fully "purchases" the father's treasure through his own physical expenditure, an act that guarantees the father's "interest" through future generations. This money-sex image complex is pervasive and important in many of Shakespeare's plays. The pattern and its relation to festival are especially evident in Juliet's ecstatic and impatient speech urging night to come and bring her husband:

> O, I have bought the mansion of a love,
> But not possess'd it, and though I am sold,
> Not yet enjoy'd. So tedious is this day
> As is the night before some festival.
>
> (3.2.26-29).

In another context, this pattern enables us fully to understand Shylock's miserly refusal to give or spend and the implications of his simultaneous loss of daughter and hoarded fortune. His confusion of daughter and ducats is foreshadowed when he recounts the story of Jacob and equates the increase of the flock through the "work of generation" to the increase of money through retentive "use." To Antonio's question, "Or is your gold and silver ewes and rams?" Shylock responds, "I cannot tell, I make it breed as fast" (*MV* 1.3.95-96).

[12] McCown discusses the use and inversion of epithalamic conventions in Juliet's address to the night (3.2.1-31). My article "Othello's Handkerchief" analyzes the handkerchief in terms of Elizabethan wedding customs. For examinations of epithalamic traditions in Renaissance poetry, see also the works by Virginia Tufte and R. V. LeClercq.

[13] The bride was expected to bring with her either property or a substantial cash sum as her "dowry." In the sixteenth and early seventeenth centuries, this money usually went directly to the father of the groom, who often used it as a dowry to marry off one of his own daughters. In return, the groom's father guaranteed the bride an annuity, called a "jointure," to provide for her if she survived her husband (see Stone, *Family* 88-89, and Ranald 69). In the closing moments of *Romeo and Juliet,* Shakespeare creates an irony of pathos by referring to this custom. Juliet has in truth "survived" her husband by dying after him; the "jointure" that old Capulet here requests from the groom's family on behalf of his daughter is the dowry that has been crucially missing throughout the play, the cessation of enmity represented in Capulet's demand for his "brother Montague's hand." The terms of the dowry and jointure settlements were fixed before the wedding and were often made public during the ceremony by the priest's asking the groom, immediately following the ring rite, "What shall the morwyn gift be?" (*Rathen* 2, 36). In the York and Sarum manuals the question was what "dower" the woman should receive from her husband (see Howard 1:306-07). The significance of these negotiations as a precondition of the wedding is evident in *The Taming of the Shrew,* where Petruchio delineates Kate's jointure to her father even before he begins his otherwise unorthodox wooing and where the choice of Bianca's husband clearly rests entirely on which suitor can ensure the shrewd old Baptista the largest jointure for his daughter.

[14] In his famous *Essai sur le Don* (1923), Marcel Mauss concludes that exchange in primitive societies involves not so much economic transactions as reciprocal gifts. Building on these conclusions, Lévi-Strauss analyzes exogamy and the prohibition of incest as substantially identical rules of kinship that reflect a reciprocal gift system based on the condition of surpassing sumptuousness. He stresses that the idea of a mysterious advantage attached to reciprocal gifts is not confined to primitive society but is inherent in our own notion of the father "giving away" the bride (52-62). The parodic dowries concluding *Romeo and Juliet* reflect the same reciprocity of escalating generosity.

[15] Hooker also makes the point that the sacramentality invoked by ritual is profaned when festival celebration overflows the measure or when the form of ceremony becomes parodic. Hooker asserts that the festivals of the "Israelites and heathens," though they contained the necessary elements, "failed in the ende it self, so neither could they discerne rightly what forme and measure Religion therein should obserue. . . . they are in every degree noted to haue done amisse, their Hymnes or songs of praise were idolatrie, their bountie excesse, and their rest wantonnesse" (294). On the use of ritual as the human means to recover the sacred dimension of existence, see Eliade:

Driven from religious life in the strict sense, the *celestial sacred* remains active through symbolism. A religious symbol conveys its message even if it is no longer consciously understood in every part. For a symbol speaks to the whole human being and not only to the intelligence. . . . Hence the supreme function of the myth is to "fix" the paradigmatic models for all rites and all significant human activities. . . . By the continuous reactualization of paradigmatic divine gestures, the world is sanctified. (129, 98-99)

Unquestionably, the late C. L. Barber's study is the best book to date on the relation of Shakespeare's plays to underlying patterns of ritual.

[16] Hooker also stresses the necessary separation of festival and fast, celebration and mourning, for "as oft as joy is the cause of the one and grief the welspring of the other, they are incompatible" (212); "Seeing therefore all things are done in time, and many offices are not possible at one and the same time to be discharged, duties of all sortes must haue necessarily their seuerall successions and seasons . . ." (197). When Theseus bids Philostrate call forth the nuptial revels, he directs that mourning be banished—"Awake the pert and nimble spirit of mirth; / Turn melancholy forth to funerals" (*MND* 1.1.13-14). Likewise Spenser, acting as his own poetic master of revels in *Epithalamion,* ritually banishes all evil spirits, sounds of mourning, or other activities that would counter the mood of marriage celebration. This felt imperative governing the segregation of ritual activities underlies Shakespeare's strategic use of colliding ritual structures.

[17] Robert Herrick, who gave us detailed pictures of May Day customs that did not survive in later generations ("Corinna's Going A-Maying"), also recorded a number of now forgotten Elizabethan wedding customs, including that of shrouding the bride in her wedding sheets:

> But since it must be done, despatch, and sew
> Up in a sheet your bride; and what if so
>   It be with rock, or walls of brass
>   Ye tower her up, as Danae was,
>   Think you that this
> Or hell itself a powerful bulwark is?
>   I tell ye no; but like a
> Bold bolt of thunder he will make his way,
>   And rend the cloud, and throw
>   The sheet about like flakes of snow.
>   (141-50)

[18] The divorce trials of Henry VIII provide a wealth of information on the conditions recognized as impediments to marriage, since of course Henry at one time or another tried nearly every legally acceptable means to extricate himself from his numerous marriages. The

accusation that he had been "seduced and constrained by witchcraft" was one he considered leveling at the hapless Anne Boleyn. After all—Richard III had succeeded in nullifying (at least temporarily) his brother Edward IV's marriage to Henry's grandmother, Elizabeth Woodville, and the marriage between Humphrey, Duke of Gloucester, and Eleanor Cobham had been annulled on the same grounds. These details are included in Henry Ansgar Kelly's highly informative study (241-42). See also *Church and the Law of Nullity,* which notes that the impediment of *vis et metus* remained unchanged by the Reformation (58).

[19] C. L. Barber also notes the ritual connection: "*Lear* begins with a failure of the passage that might be handled by the marriage service, as it is structured to persuade the father to give up his daughter. Regan and Goneril, though married, pretend to meet Lear's demand on them in all-but-incestuous terms. Cordelia defends herself by reference to the service" (in Schwartz and Kahn 197).

[20] *Measure for Measure* provides the most dramatic testimony to the importance of fixing the dowry provisions before the wedding. Although Juliet is nearly nine months pregnant and although she and Claudio believe themselves spiritually married, they have not legalized the wedding in church because of still unresolved dowry provisions.

[21] Alan Dundes points out the psychological dimensions of various folktale types underlying a number of Shakespeare's plays; significantly, the central figure in the folktale is usually the daughter-heroine. The theme of incest, which Freud himself recognized as a powerful undercurrent in *King Lear,* is manifest in the folktale father who demands that his daughter marry him; Shakespeare transforms the overt demand into a love test requiring that she love her father all (358). In Dundes' interpretation, the more obvious father-daughter incest wish is actually an Electral daughter-father desire that has been transformed through projection. Dundes also lists other discussions of the father-daughter incest theme in *King Lear* (359).

[22] Hymen's verses emphasize the religious sense of the marriage ritual. In this context the genetic father is only a surrogate parent, appointed by the heavenly parent to act out the specific role of bequeathing the daughter to a new union; Hymen himself functions as the mythic priest, the agent authorized by heaven to oversee the transfer. Wheatly's notes reflect this same sense of the religious meaning of the roles played by father and priest: " . . . the woman is to be given not to the man, but to the Minister; for the rubric orders, that the minister shall receive her *at her father's or friend's hands;* which signifies, to be sure, that the father resigns her up to God, and that it is God, who, by His Priest, now gives her in marriage . . ." (497).

[23] See Barber's essay in Schwartz and Kahn, esp. pp. 198-221. Barber additionally provides a striking iconographic association, noting the image of Lear with Cordelia in his arms as being effectively "a *pietà* with the roles reversed, not Holy Mother with her Dead Son, but father with his dead daughter" (200).

[24] *Geneva.* Deuteronomy 23.1 contains a similar text that the 1611 King James Bible translates as "He that is wounded in the stones, or hath his priuie member cut off, shall not enter the Congregation of the Lord." "Stones" is not only an Old Testament term but Elizabethan cant for testicles (Partridge).

[25] When Iago shouts to Brabantio, "Look to your house, your daughter, and your bags! Thieves, thieves!" (*Oth.* 1.1.80-81), his innuendo is the same as Solanio's.

[26] A similar incident took place in connection with Shakespeare's own marriage when Anne Hathaway's father appointed two friends to guarantee the wedding (Schoenbaum 78-79). The bond for Shakespeare's marriage, dated 28 Nov. 1582, is an extant record. The sureties who purchased it were named later as "trusty" friends in the will of Richard Hathaway, Anne's father. That the bond mentions no spokesmen for Shakespeare's family has generated a number of suspicions, including Sir Sidney Lee's feeling that it was taken out to prevent a reluctant bridegroom from evading his obligation to marry the pregnant bride. Schoenbaum, however, thinks that it was customary for the bondsmen to be friends of the bride's family, to ensure an unmarried heiress protection from fortune-hunting suitors. If so, then Shakespeare would seem to be flouting tradition in his conclusion to *The Merchant of Venice,* for the bondsman here is clearly a friend of the groom's.

Works Cited

Barber, C. L. *Shakespeare's Festive Comedy.* Princeton: Princeton Univ. Press, 1959.

Bataille, Georges. *Death and Sensuality: A Study of Eroticism and the Taboo.* 1962; rpt. New York: Arno, 1977.

Berkowitz, David. *Renaissance Quarterly* 32(1979): 396-403.

The Book of Common Prayer, 1559. Ed. John E. Booty. Charlottesville: Univ. of Virginia Press, 1967.

Boose, Lynda E. "Othello's Handkerchief: 'The Recognizance and Pledge of Love.'" *English Literary Renaissance* 5(1975):360-74.

Brownell, Thomas Church, ed. *The Family Prayer Book; or,* The Book of Common Prayer *according to the Use of the Protestant Episcopal Church*. New York: Stanford and Swords, 1853.

The Church and the Law of Nullity of Marriage. Report of a commission appointed by the archbishops of Canterbury and York in 1949. London: Society for Promoting Christian Knowledge, 1955.

Demos, John. *New York Times Book Review,* 25 Dec. 1977, 1.

Dundes, Alan. "'To Love My Father All': A Psychoanalytic Study of the Folktale Source of *King Lear.*" *Southern Folklore Quarterly* 40(1976): 353-66.

Eliade, Mircea. *The Sacred and the Profane*. Trans. Willard R. Trask. New York: Harcourt, 1959.

Evans, G. Blakemore, ed. *The Riverside Shakespeare*. Boston: Houghton, 1974.

Flandrin, Jean-Louis. *Families in Former Times: Kinship, Household and Sexuality*. Trans. Richard Southern. Cambridge: Cambridge Univ. Press, 1979.

Frey, Charles. "'O sacred, shadowy, cold, and constant queen': Shakespeare's Imperiled and Chastening Daughters of Romance." *South Atlantic Bulletin* 43(1978):125-40.

The Geneva Bible. 1560; facsim. rpt. Madison: Univ. of Wisconsin Press, 1961.

Harding, D. W. "Father and Daughter in Shakespeare's Last Plays." *TLS,* 30 Nov. 1979, 59-61.

Hill, Christopher. "Sex, Marriage and the Family in England." *Economic History Review,* 2nd ser., 31(1978):450-63.

Hooker, Richard. *Of the Lawes of Ecclesiasticall Politie*. 1594; facsim. rpt. Amsterdam: Theatrum Orbis Terrarum, 1971.

Howard, George Elliott. *A History of Matrimonial Institutions*. London: T. Fisher Unwin, 1904.

Hoy, Cyrus. "Fathers and Daughters in Shakespeare's Romances." In *Shakespeare's Romances Reconsidered*. Ed. Carol McGinnis Kay and Henry E. Jacobs. Lincoln: Univ. of Nebraska Press, 1978, 77-90.

Kelly, Henry Ansgar. *The Matrimonial Trials of Henry VIII*. Stanford, Calif.: Stanford Univ. Press, 1976.

Laslett, Peter. *The World We Have Lost*. 2nd ed. 1965; rpt. London: Methuen, 1971.

LeClercq, R. V. "Crashaw's Epithalamium: Pattern and

Vision." *Literary Monographs* 6. Madison: Univ. of Wisconsin Press, 1975, 73-108.

Legg, J. Wickham. *Ecclesiological Essays*. London: De La More Press, 1905.

Lévi-Strauss, Claude. *The Elementary Structures of Kinship*. Trans. James Harle Bell. Ed. John Richard von Sturmer and Rodney Needham. Paris, 1949; rpt. Boston: Beacon, 1969.

McCown, Gary M. "'Runnawayes Eyes' and Juliet's Epithalamion." *Shakespeare Quarterly* 27(1976): 150-70.

Noble, Richmond. *Shakespeare's Use of the Bible and The Book of Common Prayer*. London: Society for the Promotion of Biblical Knowledge, 1935.

Partridge, Eric. *Shakespeare's Bawdy*. 1948; rpt. New York: Dutton, 1969.

Rabkin, Norman. *Shakespeare and the Problem of Meaning*. Chicago: Univ. of Chicago Press, 1981.

Ranald, Margaret Loftus. "'As Marriage Binds, and Blood Breaks': English Marriage and Shakespeare." *Shakespeare Quarterly* 30(1979):68-81.

The Rathen Manual. Ed. Duncan MacGregor. Aberdeen: Aberdeen Ecclesiological Society, 1905.

Schoenbaum, S. *William Shakespeare: A Compact Documentary Life*. Oxford: Oxford Univ. Press, 1975.

Schwartz, Murray M., and Coppélia Kahn, eds. *Representing Shakespeare: New Psychoanalytic Essays*. Baltimore: Johns Hopkins Univ. Press, 1980.

The Statutes of the Realm. London: Record Commissions, 1820-28; facsim. ed. 1968.

Stone, Lawrence. *The Crisis of the Aristocracy: 1558-1660*. Abridged ed. London: Oxford Univ. Press, 1971.

————. *The Family, Sex and Marriage in England: 1500-1800*. New York: Harper, 1977.

Thomas, Keith. *TLS,* 21 Oct. 1977, 1226.

Tufte, Virginia. *The Poetry of Marriage*. Los Angeles: Tinnon-Brown, 1970.

Turner, Victor W. *The Ritual Process: Structure and Anti-Structure*. Chicago: Aldine, 1969.

Van Gennep, Arnold. *The Rites of Passage*. Trans. Monika B. Vizedom and Gabrielle L. Caffee. 1908; rpt. London: Routledge and Kegan Paul, 1960.

Wheatly, Charles. *A Rational Illustration of* The Book of Common Prayer *according to the Use of the Church of England*. Cambridge: Cambridge Univ. Press, 1858.

FURTHER READING

Blechner, Mark J. "King Lear, King Leir, and Incest Wishes." *American Imago* 45, No. 3 (Fall 1988): 309-25.

Analyzes the changes Shakespeare made to the source of *King Lear* in order to demonstrate his interest in the father-daughter incest motif.

Coursen, H. R. "Lear and Cordelia." *Cahiers Elisabethains* 40 (October 1991): 11-20.

Reviews several productions of *King Lear* that exist on tape, focusing in particular upon the relationship between Lear and Cordelia.

Godard, Barbara. "Caliban's Revolt: The Discourse of the (M)Other." In *Critical Approaches to the Fiction of Margaret Laurence,* edited by Colin Nicholson. London: Macmillan, 1990, pp. 208-27.

Argues that the mother is a figure of subversion in *The Tempest* and in Margaret Laurence's fiction.

Hansen, Carol. "Authority of the Father." In *Woman as Individual in English Renaissance Drama: A Defiance of the Masculine Code*. New York: Peter Lang, 1993, pp. 11-26.

Examines the parameters of masculine power as it is reinforced by social institutions, focusing primarily on the relationship between Lear and Cordelia to show how that power can be subverted.

Harding, D. W. "Shakespeare's Final View of Women." *Times Literary Supplement,* No. 4002 (November 30, 1979): 59-61.

Assesses the late romances as focused on the task of creating positive images of womanhood.

Leventen, Carol. "Patrimony and Patriarchy in *The Merchant of Venice*." In *The Matter of Difference: Materialist Feminist Criticism of Shakespeare,* edited by Valerie Wayne. New York: Harvester Wheatsheaf, 1991, pp. 59-80.

Historicizes the relationship of the women of *The Merchant of Venice* and money.

Mazzon, Gabriella. "Shakespearean Thou and You Revisited, or Socio-affective Networks on Stage." In *Early Modern English: Trends, Forms and Texts,* edited by C. Nocera Avila, N. Pantaleo, and D. Pezzini. Catania, Italy: Schena Editore, 1992, pp. 121-36.

Studies father-daughter relationships in *Othello, Hamlet,* and *King Lear* by tracing the use of formal and affectionate pronouns.

McEachern, Claire. "Fathering Herself: A Source Study of Shakespeare's Feminism." *Shakespeare Quarterly* 39, No. 3 (Autumn 1988): 269-90.

Contends that the valuing of brides as commodities results in an emotional conflict for the fathers in *Much Ado About Nothing* and *King Lear*.

Melchiori, Barbara. "Still Harping on My Daughter." In *English Miscellany,* edited by Mario Praz. Rome: British Council, 1960, pp. 59-74.

Analyzes the incest motif in the late romances.

Neill, Michael. "Unproper Beds: Race, Adultery, and the Hideous in *Othello*." *Shakespeare Quarterly* 40, No. 4 (Winter 1989): 383-412.

Argues that Desdemona becomes the object of the racial fear and sexual revulsion that mark the unspoken shame of society, both Elizabethan and modern.

Ravich, Robert A. "A Psychoanalytic Study of Shakespeare's Early Plays." *The Psychoanalytic Quarterly* 33, No. 3 (1964): 388-410.

Analyzes father-daughter relationships in the early plays from a Freudian perspective and proposes an analysis of Shakespeare himself on that basis.

Stallybrass, Peter. "Patriarchal Territories: The Body Enclosed." In *Rewriting the Renaissance: The Discourses of Sexual Difference in Early Modern Europe,* edited by Margaret W. Ferguson, Maureen Quilligan, and Nancy J. Vickers. Chicago: The University of Chicago Press, 1986, pp. 123-42.

Argues that Desdemona's fate in *Othello* is entwined with issues of class.

Wilcockson, Colin. "Father-directors, Daughter-performers in Shakespeare." *Critical Survey* 3, No. 2 (1991): 134-41.

Explores the analogy between the roles of director and actress on the one hand and father and daughter on the other to expose the effects of differences in power on relationships, focusing on *Much Ado about Nothing, Hamlet,* and *King Lear*.

Cymbeline

For further information on the critical and stage history of *Cymbeline*, see *SC*, Volumes 4 and 15.

INTRODUCTION

Traditional scholarship on *Cymbeline* has treated such questions as the genre of the play, its relation to other Shakespeare plays, its historical background, and what many critics consider to be its inconsistent structure. While twentieth-century criticism continues to address these themes, modern scholars have also focused on issues such as the relation of language to drama, the influence of myth and psychology on Shakespeare's works, and the role of women and their relationships to various male figures.

Increasing attention has been given to the character of Imogen. Some critics, such as E. A. M. Colman, have studied Imogen's portrayal as it is revealed through her language and the language of those around her. Colman has examined the syntax in *Cymbeline*, concluding that although Imogen is portrayed as a clearsighted character, her speech reveals that she is unaware of the constraints placed upon her by her father, family, and society. Refuting earlier criticism castigating Shakespeare's dialogue as faulty, Maurice Hunt has argued that Shakespeare carefully crafted the dialogue to accompany the dramatic structure of the play. Coburn Freer has also analyzed the play's language, contrasting the characters of Imogen and Iachimo by comparing their speeches. While Iachimo is "the master of [his] speeches," using words to confirm his self-regard and the opinions he has of others, Imogen's speeches help her discover her own ideals and find her role in society.

Imogen's relationships with Cymbeline and other male characters is a theme often studied in current scholarship on *Cymbeline*. Charles K. Hofling, for example, has explored Shakespeare's own background and assesses its influence on the main characters of the play and their interrelationships. Building on the earlier psychohistorical work, he suggests that the relationship and final reconciliation of Cymbeline and Imogen reflects Shakespeare's own relationships with his mother and daughter. Other scholars have focused more explicitly on the father-daughter relationship between the characters of Imogen and Cymbeline. John P. Cutts has argued that Cymbeline, while appearing to be dominated by his wife, is actually in control of the plot and characters of the play and acts vicariously through Imogen, whose behavior and values end up mimicking his.

The father-daughter relationship in *Cymbeline* has also been explored in terms of another theme undertaken by modern scholarship, that of the discrepancy between man's inner nature and outward appearance. Joan Hartwig has contended that Cymbeline's position as king serves to force people into unnatural behavior. Thus Posthumus' behavior contradicts favorable reports of him, and Cloten becomes a parody of Posthumus in speech and physical characteristics. Imogen, as the king's daughter, becomes a pawn who has a deeper understanding than any of the other characters, but must behave in ways that conform to the inverted world Cymbeline has created. Many modern critics have addressed similar themes, concluding that the dramatic structure, language, and characterization of the play are more complex than earlier criticism allowed.

OVERVIEWS

Joan Hartwig (essay date 1972)

SOURCE: "*Cymbeline*: 'A Speaking Such as Sense Cannot Untie'," in *Shakespeare's Tragicomic Vision*, Louisiana State University Press, 1972, pp. 61-103.

[*In the essay below, Hartwig contends that while* Cymbeline *is characteristic of Shakespeare's tragicomedies, it has an unprecedented complexity stemming from shifting perspectives and the juxtaposition of reality and illusion.*]

To move from *Pericles* to *Cymbeline* is to move from majestic simplicity to bewildering complexity. *Cymbeline* has three basic plot lines, but each of these has many subsidiary plots and their interweaving is more intricate than the two plot lines in *Pericles*. First, there is the suit for the hand of Imogen, which includes Iachimo's "wager" and Cloten's "revenge" as well as Posthumus' banishment and return. A second plot concerns the lost sons of Cymbeline and their abductor-guardian Belarius; and the third is the separation and reunion of Britain and Rome. Furthermore, the chorus of *Pericles*, so artlessly open in the figure of Gower, becomes more integrated into the dramatic action in

Cymbeline, although the choral speeches remain artificially obvious. For example, the Gentlemen of the opening scene supply the necessary background of Posthumus' lineage, the marriage of Imogen and Posthumus, and the earlier loss of the king's sons in set speeches that do not try to disguise their expository function (I.i.29-64).[1] Shakespeare has joined several conventional frameworks in *Cymbeline,* too, making the play more complicated in terms of audience expectations than *Pericles.* The earlier play is built primarily upon the romantic legend of a wandering hero who discovers that life's adversities have a benevolent purpose. *Cymbeline* also uses the romantic convention of the young hero banished from his homeland who finally returns to claim his heritage; but, in addition, *Cymbeline* incorporates the conventions of the history play and of the pastoral. Each of the three main plots, in fact, is a vehicle for one of these conventions: the romantic plot of New Comedy revolves about the Posthumus-Imogen relationship; the history play concerns the Britain-Rome controversy; and the pastoral conventions manifest themselves in the situation of Cymbeline's lost sons. Aside from this fusion of traditional expectations, characterization is more complex in *Cymbeline* than in *Pericles.* Posthumus fails to sustain his trust in Imogen and he suffers for his weakness; whereas Pericles suffers without committing a sin. Because Posthumus errs, his heroic nature undergoes serious qualification. The censure which his lapse of faith and subsequent order for Imogen's murder incur is somewhat allayed, however, by the presence of Cloten who becomes a parodic surrogate for Posthumus both in life and in death. The interweaving of this triad of characterizations (Posthumus-Imogen-Cloten) is much more subtle and complicated than anything in *Pericles.*

Despite its greater complexity, *Cymbeline* resembles *Pericles* in its tragicomic action. Even though the main characters have a more intricate dramatic relationship, both Posthumus and Imogen undergo a reduction to "nothing" similar to Pericles' apathy before the restorative vision. Their settled sense of the world is dislocated and they rebuild their perspectives to include a much larger world than they had previously known. *Cymbeline* has also a great stress on artifice, and the mingling of tragic and comic "pleasures" has the same kind of effect as in *Pericles.* The sense of wonder in the final scene differs in several respects, but it is achieved through the double awareness of the characters and of the audience, all of whom are simultaneously involved in and removed from the staged illusion. *Cymbeline,* thus, shares with *Pericles* the chief characteristics of Shakespeare's tragicomic vision, but it displays a greater complexity of materials used to create that vision.

The discrepancy between man's true nature and his outward appearance, a theme developed to some ex-

tent in *Pericles,* becomes the dominant concern in *Cymbeline.* In the opening scene, the Gentlemen announce the problem: "You do not meet a man but frowns" (I.i.1). Cymbeline's anger is reflected in the faces of his subjects, but they are secretly glad that Imogen has married Posthumus rather than Cloten.

> But not a courtier,
> Although they wear their faces to the bent
> Of the king's looks, hath a heart that is not
> Glad at the thing they scowl at.
>
>   (I.i.12-15)

This is the first of many dissembling countenances, but an important one. The king and his subjects do not feel the same way about the marriage of Imogen and Posthumus. Discord in the kingdom results from the enforced separation of the marriage partners. The harmony which a royal marriage of the king's only remaining child should effect is broken by the king's banishment of Posthumus; the dissembling looks of his lords, who are aware of Posthumus' superiority to Cloten, are a sign of the split between king and kingdom. The First Gentleman evaluates Imogen's two suitors candidly:

> *First Gent.* He that hath miss'd the princess is a thing
> Too bad for bad report: and he that hath her
> (I mean, that married her, alack good man,
> And therefore banish'd) is a creature such
> As, to seek through the regions of the earth
> For one his like; there would be something failing
> In him that should compare. I do not think
> So fair an outward, and such stuff within
> Endows a man, but he.
> *Sec. Gent.*   You speak him far.
> *First Gent.* I do extend him, sir, within himself,
> Crush him together, rather than unfold
> His measure duly.
>
>   (I.i.16-27)

This hyperbolic praise is immediately suspect, as the Second Gentleman indicates, but the arresting aspect— and a point that makes the praise hyperbolic—is that Posthumus seems as good within as he is outwardly fair. Such an evaluation is high praise indeed in a world which has grown used to discrepancies between the inner natures and outward appearances of men.

As the First Gentleman continues to present the history of Posthumus' lineage and birth, the Second Gentleman becomes so convinced that he must "honour him, / Even out of your report" (54-55). By this point, the death of Posthumus' father between his conception and birth and the death of his mother giving him birth have established Posthumus symbolically as the figure upon whom the life-from-death theme centers in the play. Posthumus' fame is known not only in Britain but in Rome as well. The guests in Philario's house speak of Posthumus' reputation in less worshipful tones (I.v) and so provide a balance for the hyperbole of the opening scene.

> *Iach.* Believe it sir, I have seen him in Britain; he was then of a crescent note, expected to prove so worthy as since he hath been allowed the name of. But I could then have look'd on him without the help of admiration, though the catalogue of his endowments had been tabled by his side and I to peruse him by items.
>
> *Phil.* You speak of him when he was less furnish'd than now he is with that which makes him both without and within.
>
> *French.* I have seen him in France: we had very many there could behold the sun with as firm eyes as he.
>
> *Iach.* This matter of marrying his king's daughter, wherein he must be weighed rather by her value than his own, words him (I doubt not) a great deal from the matter.
>
> *French.* And then his banishment.
>
> *Iach.* Ay, and the approbation of those that weep this lamentable divorce under her colours are wonderfully to extend him; be it but to fortify her judgement, which else an easy battery might lay flat, for taking a begger without less quality.
>
> (I.v.1-23)

Iachimo's doubt that Posthumus could be as worthy as his reputation makes him seem characterizes Iachimo more than it does Posthumus; even so, his doubt polarizes the First Gentleman's assurance and suggests that the truth lies somewhere between the two evaluations. Philario's use of the word "furnish'd" suggests that acquiring the king's daughter in marriage has increased Posthumus' appearance of worth to match his inner nature. Iachimo immediately picks up the point and turns it to Posthumus' disadvantage, a comment which increases the distance between Philario's open-natured hospitality and Iachimo's capacity for distorting appearances. Still, the idea of Imogen as a furnishing carries preparative weight for the wager which follows. In agreeing to test Imogen's pure spirit, Posthumus unwittingly gives evidence that he views her as an object to be possessed rather than as a person to be known by her own identity. The wager which symbolizes his limited perspective fits appropriately into a scene which qualifies his good report. From this point, the central action in the play concerns Posthumus' growing inwardly to match his noble outward appearance.

Posthumus' reported worth is entwined with Imogen's esteem of him in both of these scenes. Iachimo's recognition that Posthumus' marriage to the king's daughter weighs greatly in his favor (I.v.14-25) echoes the First Gentleman's most convincing proof of Posthumus' worth:

> To his mistress,
> (For whom he now is banish'd) her own price
> Proclaims how she esteem'd him; and his
>   virtue
> By her election may be truly read
> What kind of man he is.
>
> (I.i.50-54)

As heir apparent, Imogen's "price" is absolute without the additional force of her own worthy nature to support her value. As she herself recognizes, the fact that she is the only heir to the throne makes her price more important than her desires are.

> Had I been thief-stolen,
> As my two brothers, happy: but most
>   miserable
> Is the desire that's glorious. Bless'd be those,
> How mean soe'er, that have their honest wills,
> Which seasons comfort.
>
> (I.vii.5-9)

> 'Mongst friends?
> If brothers: [*Aside*] would it had been so,
>   that they
> Had been my father's sons, then had my
>   prize
> Been less, and so more equal ballasting
> To thee, Posthumus.
>
> (III.vii.47-51)

Both of these speeches express Imogen's wish to realize her true nature—always in conjunction with Posthumus—together with her understanding that her role as Cymbeline's daughter forces a discrepancy between her inner and outward natures. The latter speech occurs when she has disguised her appearance in order to seek Posthumus. She knows that he has ordered her murder, but she also knows that her identity is merged with his. Her recognition that she is, against her will, a pawn in Cymbeline's world, which is also the world she has to live in, pathetically underlines the use of her as an object in the wager between Iachimo and Posthumus. Her reputation, however, is the thing wagered upon, not her inner nature, although Posthumus assumes there is no difference. The outward Imogen is all that Posthumus knows as yet, but insofar as her inner nature depends upon him, the inner Imogen is inextricably limited by her "report." She must give the lie to her appearance, finally, in order to save the value of her real identity from destruction.

The wager grows out of a circumstance similar to one that Posthumus had encountered during earlier travels in France. He had, on a former occasion, been about to duel in defense of his lady's honor when a Frenchman, who is now a guest in Philario's house, had persuaded the two rash men to desist. Posthumus' testiness on the subject is immediately apparent when he bristles at the Frenchman's implication that the matter was too slight to risk death over. Iachimo, quick to notice Posthumus' vulnerability, inquires further into the cause of the proposed duel, and cynically avows that perfection in ladies is a state unknown in this world. Posthumus takes the bait and is drawn into the wager easily enough, despite his statement that his lady's virtue "is not a thing for sale, and only the gift of the gods" (I.iv.87-88). Philario protests with the voice of reason that the wager rose too suddenly and should be left to "die as it was born" (125), but Iachimo pushes and Posthumus bends, putting up the ring which he has sworn he would wear on his finger "while sense can keep it on" (I.ii.49). Obviously his reason has given way to his pride of purchase for that which cannot be bought.

The ignobility of encouraging a test of Imogen's virtue does not occur to Posthumus, and he is only aware of how his own sense of honor has been pricked by Iachimo's boasts. Posthumus' lack of insight becomes even clearer to the audience, however, in the scene which soon follows where Iachimo actually tests Imogen's virtue. When he first views her, Iachimo perceives that he may be in for a real test of his own power of deception.

> [*Aside*] All of her that is out of door most
>   rich!
> If she be furnish'd with a mind so rare,
> She is alone th' Arabian bird; and I
> Have lost the wager.
>
> (I.vii.15-18)

There is a verbal as well as conceptual parallel in this evaluation which recalls Philario's comment that Posthumus is more furnished now with that "which makes him both without and within" (I.v), and the meaning of Philario's statement is enhanced by this elaboration. Imogen has a mind as rare as her beauty and being so "furnish'd" she can supply Posthumus with what he may lack in making the inner and outward man the same. That she is more nearly concordant in her inner and outer natures is clear from the manner in which she resists Iachimo's testimony that Posthumus has been false to her in Rome. When Iachimo encourages her to revenge Posthumus' infidelity by allowing him to her bed, Imogen recognizes his utter baseness.

> Away, I do condemn mine ears, that have
> So long attended thee. If thou wert
>   honourable,
> Thou wouldst have told this tale for virtue,
>   not

> For such an end thou seek'st, as base, as
>   strange.
> Thou wrong'st a gentleman, who is as far
> From thy report as thou from honour, and
> Solicits here a lady that disdains
> Thee, and the devil alike.
>
> (I.vii.141-48)

Imogen does not hesitate, when her reason distinguishes Iachimo's lies, to discount them as in any way affecting Posthumus' real nature. Posthumus, on the other hand, does not even demand all the evidence that Iachimo has collected to condemn Imogen of infidelity. Her assurance of his goodness and his assurance that she has been false are a measure of the distance that he has yet to travel before he is in fact worthy of her.

When Iachimo shows the stolen bracelet which Posthumus had given Imogen at his departure and which signified her fidelity, just as the diamond ring which Posthumus had put up for the wager signified his, Posthumus immediately assumes the worst has happened.

> Here, take this too;
> [*Gives the ring.*
> It is a basilisk unto mine eye,
> Kills me to look on't. Let there be no honour
> Where there is beauty: truth, where semblance:
>   love,
> Where there's another man. The vows of
>   women
> Of no more bondage be to where they are
>   made
> Than they are to their virtues, which is
>   nothing.
> O, above measure false!
>
> (II.iv.106-13)

Philario persuades him to ask for more than this circumstantial evidence, advising patience, but when Iachimo swears he "had it from her arm" Posthumus again relaxes into ignoble doubt. Philario, acting Posthumus' part in defense of Imogen, forces Iachimo to give further evidence of Imogen's guilt and Iachimo reveals his knowledge of the mole under her breast. Despite the seriousness of the consequences of his belief in Iachimo's lies, Posthumus' eagerness to accept them without even reasonable questioning places him in a foolish position, so that when he returns at the end of the scene to deliver his diatribe against women, his excess spills over from a tragic to a comic effect. Posthumus, the fool, does not measure consistently with the image of his worth built up at the play's beginning.

Cloten, the true fool, makes Posthumus' deficiencies as a romantic hero even more apparent when he dons

Posthumus' clothes and parodies Posthumus' violent speech with a diatribe of his own (IV.i). Yet by his very violence, which is more gratuitous than Posthumus' bitter reaction to Iachimo's lies, Cloten takes some of the censure away from Posthumus. In fact, Cloten repeatedly "protects" Posthumus' characterization as he absorbs criticism through his excessive and parodic actions. Their characters regularly qualify each other, either in the report of others or in Cloten's conversation, yet they never appear onstage together. In the first scene, during the Gentlemen's discussion of Imogen's choice, the First Gentleman says bluntly enough that Cloten "is a thing / Too bad for bad report" (I.i.16-17). And after Posthumus has appeared onstage and departed, Cymbeline berates Imogen for her choice. She replies with some force that "I chose an eagle, / And did avoid a puttock" (I.ii.70-71). In the wake of Posthumus' noble report and noble appearance, Cloten's report suffers comic diminution. Pisanio adds another facet to Cloten's already clownish characterization when he tells the Queen and Imogen of how Cloten detained the banished Posthumus by drawing upon him. Pisanio states that if Posthumus had not played, but fought, Cloten would have suffered injury. Imogen's anger at Cloten's indecorous action flares.

> Your son's my father's friend, he takes his
> part
> To draw upon an exile. O brave sir!
> I would they were in Afric both together,
> Myself by with a needle, that I might prick
> The goer-back.
>
> (I.ii.96-100)

Imogen's scorn for Cloten, which never alters while he lives, expresses itself through comparative means. She implies, as the First Gentleman has, that to yoke Cloten and Posthumus in the same breath, or worse, to join them in any comparison, is an act that disturbs reason. No real comparison is possible: the eagle resembles the puttock only in species.

Thus introduced, Cloten appears onstage with two Lords, who make their distaste for him farcically clear.

> *First Lord.* Sir, I would advise you to shift a shirt; the violence of action hath made you reek as a sacrifice: where air comes out, air comes in: there's none abroad so wholesome as that you vent.
> *Clo.* If my shirt were bloody, then to shift it. Have I hurt him?
> *Sec. Lord.* [*Aside*] No, faith: not so much as his patience. . . .
> *Clo.* I would they had not come between us.
> *Sec. Lord.* [*Aside*] So would I, till you had measur'd how long a fool you were upon the ground.
> *Clo.* And that she should love this fellow, and refuse me!

> *Sec. Lord.* [*Aside*] If it be a sin to make a true election, she is damn'd.
>
> (I.iii.1-7, 21-27)

To tell a prince that he smells bad is a grievous breach of decorum, yet Cloten fails to comprehend it. His refusal to change his shirt unless it were bloody characterizes his oblivious offensiveness. He cannot sense much in the way of social delicacy and he comprehends nothing of the way he affects others. The broadness of the Second Lord's jests is another measure of how far Cymbeline has inverted the proper order of his kingdom and forced a division between appearance and reality. A comic butt is hardly a match for a princess of Imogen's rare understanding.

The next scene in which Cloten and his pair of Lords appear (II.i) reveals further his bad temper at losing, this time at the game of bowls. To express his anger, Cloten has broken his bowl over a spectator's head. Through his comments on the observance of decorum, Cloten shows himself to be even more stupid and childish than he has seemed already. In attempting to observe proper form, Cloten creates self-parody, and, as always, he is oblivious to the foolish impression he makes. "I had rather not be so noble as I am," he says, annoyed because his inferiors refuse to fight with him. He considers it "fit I should commit offence to my inferiors" and inquires if it is "fit I went to look upon" the stranger, Iachimo, who has come to court. The Second Lord again toys with him in some rather broad punning, assuring Cloten that it would be impossible for him to "derogate" himself by any action. The soliloquy which this Lord remains onstage to speak, however, suggests the more serious attitude that informs the disgruntled courtiers' comic dissembling.

> That such a crafty devil as is his mother
> Should yield the world this ass! a woman that
> Bears all down with her brain, and this her
> son
> Cannot take two from twenty, for his heart,
> And leave eighteen. Alas poor princess,
> Thou divine Imogen, what thou endur'st,
> Betwixt a father by thy step-dame govern'd,
> A mother hourly coining plots, a wooer
> More hateful than the foul expulsion is
> Of thy dear husband, than that horrid act
> Of the divorce, he'ld make. The heavens hold
> firm
> The walls of thy dear honour, keep unshak'd
> That temple, thy fair mind, that thou mayst
> stand,
> T' enjoy thy banish'd lord and this great
> land!
>
> (II.i.54-67)

The soliloquy acts also as a bridge from the low comedy to the awe-inspiring scene in Imogen's bedchamber, where Iachimo gathers signs of her beauty to use in his deception of Posthumus. The divinity which the Second Lord attributes to Imogen is immediately confirmed by Iachimo's description of what he sees: "Though this a heavenly angel, hell is here" (II.ii.50). The admiration which the Second Lord and Iachimo express for Imogen's nature and outward beauty finds its terms in a theological vocabulary. To the Second Lord, Imogen is "divine," and he prays that the "heavens" will protect her honor and the "temple" of her mind. Iachimo describes her very breath as "perfume," an incense for the "chapel" which her chamber seems to him. His own monstrous purpose frightens him as he commits the sacrilege of plundering a shrine. Although he fails to realize that he alone creates the "hell" which "is here," he perceives the monstrous contrast between Imogen, "a heavenly angel," and the lie he intends to give of her.

This awed use of a theological vocabulary to describe the perfections of the human Imogen complements the punning use of it in earlier scenes. Both Imogen and the Second Lord indulge in theological punning in the scenes which reveal their repugnance for Cloten. This word play reverberates against a system of values that involves more than a local crisis in Cymbeline's kingdom: the values concern the spiritual nature of man himself. When Imogen resists her father's advancement of Cloten, Cymbeline accuses her of heaping age upon him when she should repair his youth. She responds that she is senseless of his wrath because "a touch more rare / Subdues all pangs, all fears."

> *Cym.*   Past grace? obedience?
> *Imo.* Past hope, and in despair, that way past
>   grace.
>
>   (I.ii.66-68)

Again, when Imogen questions Pisanio about Posthumus' departure, she says, "if he should write, / And I not have it, 'twere a paper lost / As offer'd mercy is" (I.iv.2-4). And when she laments her lack of free choice, Imogen creates a tenth Beatitude: "Bless'd be those, / How mean soe'er, that have their honest wills, / Which seasons comfort" (I.vii.7-9).[2] Her loss of Posthumus—though at this point only through physical banishment rather than through his betrayal of spirit, which occurs later—she regards at least metaphorically as a loss of heavenly grace and the possibility of redemption. When the Second Lord jestingly concurs that "if it be a sin to make a true election, she is damn'd" (I.iii.26-27), he pinpoints two problems of perspective. First, according to Cymbeline's inverted order, Imogen is damned—by her choice to live outside of Cymbeline's grace, and by his choice for her to be besieged by Cloten. Second, Imogen herself has substituted Posthumus for the ultimate values her soul can achieve. He is her source of grace, the means to her redemption. She learns, in the course of the play, how great a risk she incurs by this substitution for her

own sense of being, and she too finds a more inclusive referent for her own identity. The final goal of romance conventions proves insufficient for her as well as for Posthumus. Such serious issues are only implied by the theological vocabulary, and they are contained by their punning usage. Taken with absolute seriousness, they would push beyond the delicate balance of tragicomedy; but their inclusion through the rhetoric of comedy provides a reminder that Shakespeare's tragicomic vision is firmly anchored in meaningful issues. The use of a theological vocabulary and the spiritual concerns which it implies deepen the characterizations of both Imogen and Posthumus in marked contrast to the surface characterization of Cloten.[3]

In the very next scene, following Iachimo's enchanted description of the sleeping Imogen, Cloten impatiently says, "If I could get this foolish Imogen, I should have gold enough" (II.iii.7-8). His reduction of Imogen to a foolish girl and to an object of barter comically qualifies his own powers of perception; at the same time, it comments upon the use of Imogen as an object of barter by Cymbeline, by Posthumus, and by Iachimo. All three of these men are drawn into a comic conflation with Cloten at this moment of his imperception. His attempt to "penetrate" Imogen with a morning song further demonstrates his superficial level of understanding. The contrast between the boorish Cloten and the delicate task of the music to appeal to Imogen on his behalf illustrates how art itself can be violated. The aubade has an ideal artistic purpose, to celebrate the morning and love, and its use by appropriately noble romantic characters (such as Romeo and Juliet) realizes its conventional beauties; but used by Cloten, it becomes "too much pains / For purchasing but trouble" (II.iii.89). That it fails is not the fault of the music, as Cloten would interpret it, but the fault of those who promote the music in hopes that it will have an aphrodisiac effect on the "stern" Imogen (II.iii.37).[4] This scene modulates the tone between the bed-chamber scene, in which Imogen is described in terms of divinity, and her confrontation with Cloten in which she expresses her distaste for him in vitriolic terms; but it is also a criticism of the improper uses of art.[5] The harmony of art results from appropriate human motivations, and perversion here as well as in other actions characterizes Cloten's ineffectual malice.

So far is Cloten from achieving success with his music that Imogen "vouchsafes no notice" (II.iii.41). Still, on the advice of the Queen, Cloten pursues Imogen to her chamber, parodically repeating Iachimo's earlier pursuit of her. Imogen's strained tolerance breaks under Cloten's persistence in his suit and his denigration of Posthumus.

> *Imo.*   Profane fellow,
> Wert thou the son of Jupiter, and no more
> But what thou art besides, thou wert too
>   base

To be his groom: thou wert dignified
  enough,
Even to the point of envy, if 'twere made
Comparative for your virtues to be styled
The under-hangman of his kingdom; and
  hated
For being preferr'd so well.
Clo.   The south-fog rot him!
Imo. He never can meet more mischance than
  come
To be but nam'd of thee. His mean'st
  garment,
That ever hath but clipp'd his body, is
  dearer
In my respect, than all the hairs above thee,
Were they all made such men.
                                              (II.iii.125-37)

Cloten grasps the insult of "the mean'st garment" and repeats it several times throughout the remaining action of the scene while Imogen directs Pisanio to search for her missing bracelet. Cloten's sense of injury irritates Imogen so much that she offers to satisfy him with a duel. He replies with a threat to tell her father and she leaves, obviously in disgust. Cloten remains onstage to say, "I'll be reveng'd: / 'His mean'st garment!' Well."

With all the power of his one-track mind, Cloten pursues his revenge by wearing Posthumus' garments—though not his meanest ones.[6] After several scenes in which he appears, comically, as counselor to the king advising him to defy Rome, and as wretched lover in the Catullian fashion (III.v.71-81), he directs Pisanio to bring him some of Posthumus' garments. Cloten ruminates to himself:

> She said upon a time (the bitterness of it I now belch from my heart) that she held the very garment of Posthumus in more respect than my noble and natural person; together with the adornment of my qualities. With that suit upon my back, will I ravish her: first kill him, and in her eyes; there shall she see my valour, which will then be a torment to her contempt. He on the ground, my speech of insultment ended on his dead body, and when my lust hath dined (which, as I say, to vex her I will execute in the clothes that she so prais'd) to the court I'll knock her back, foot her home again. She hath despis'd me rejoicingly, and I'll be merry in my revenge.
>
>   (III.v.132-50)

The brutality of his intentions for the first time outweighs the comedy of his position and his departure for Milford-Haven sets a real threat into motion. The expression of his enthusiasm to gain his revenge (III.v.159-60) echoes Imogen's eager departure for the same place, where she deludedly thought she would find her loving husband (III.ii.49). Both Imogen and Cloten rush to their imagined fulfillment with energy that finds its answer in death: for Imogen, only in seeming, but for Cloten, in actuality.

From this point on, Cloten and Imogen are symbolically linked because they are both disguised: Cloten wears Post humus' clothes and Imogen wears those of a page. The changes in appearance create odd confusions, but for the audience the inner natures of the characters never alter. Imogen in her soliloquy before the cave of Belarius and the two brothers is very much herself, despite her altered situation (III.vi). She has learned a new perspective—"I see a man's life is a tedious one"—but her reflections on the shifting values of her world show her to be absorbing new experience with her characteristically full understanding. Two scenes later Cloten, alone on the same bare stage near the cave, offers his soliloquy of malice and revenge. He is still puzzling over the problem of why Imogen prefers Posthumus to him: "The lines of my body are as well drawn as his; no less young, more strong, not beneath him in fortunes, beyond him in the advantage of the time, above him in birth, alike conversant in general services, and more remarkable in single oppositions; yet this imperseverant thing loves him in my despite. What mortality is!" (IV.i.10-16). Imogen's poetic contemplation of possible deception even in poor folk who only give directions (III.vi.8-14) suggests a complexity of perception that renders Cloten's simple assurance comic. In prose, he speaks also of directions he has been given: "the fellow dares not deceive me" (IV.i.27). Her sensitivity to ambiguity in appearances and his oblivion to it join them in a parodic duet which culminates in their common burial.

Having befriended Belarius and the two brothers, Imogen remains behind in their cave while they go out to hunt. Because she feels sick, she takes the sleeping potion that has found its devious way to her from the Queen. No sooner has Imogen retired to the cave than Cloten enters, also feeling "faint" (IV.ii.63). Belarius recognizes him and fears that he must be accompanied by others from the court. Guiderius tells the other two to look for Cloten's "companies" and takes on the irate prince alone. Their exchange is humorous more than foreboding and Cloten manages to seem typically pompous and foolish. Their dialogue (IV.ii.74-100) insists on comparisons, not only between Cloten and his adversary, Guiderius, and between Cloten and Posthumus, whose clothes he wears, but also between what Cloten claims to be—a prince—and what he is—a fool. A few lines later the fool is beheaded, but his power to elicit laughter remains in his "report." Cloten has found concord between his inner and outer natures only as a dead fool. Horror is impossible, even in response to the spectacle of Cloten's head severed from its body. When Guiderius explains the battle, the audience can only nod at the appropriateness of Cloten's end; he had found nothing so "fit" at court.

Gui.   With his own sword,
Which he did wave against my throat, I
   have ta'en
His head from him: I'll throw't into the
   creek
Behind our rock, and let it to the sea,
And tell the fishes he's the queen's son,
   Cloten,
That's all I reck.

                    (IV.ii.149-54)

The severed head floating down the "creek" to the sea is strongly reminiscent of the "Death of Orpheus" in Ovid's *Metamorphoses* (XI, 50 ff.), but with a parodic diminution. Cloten's association with music in the presentation of a morning song to Imogen establishes his perversion of the art. His death and dissolution in this mock-heroic conclusion, which he himself predicted would be Posthumus' fate at his own hands (IV.i.17-18), is an appropriate ending for the fool whose sole effect has been to invert. Cloten, the anti-Orpheus, in death fulfills the purpose he vainly attempted to realize in his life: that is, he assumes the outward nobility he has always claimed he possessed. Without his head, which when attached testified to his lack of reason, Cloten actually differs little from the "noble" Posthumus.

Imogen, upon waking next to the headless body of Cloten dressed in Posthumus' garments, assumes that this is in fact her murdered husband.

    The dream's here still: even when I wake it is
    Without me, as within me: not imagin'd, felt.
    A headless man? The garments of Posthumus?
    I know the shape of's leg: this is his hand:
    His foot Mercurial: his Martial thigh:
    The brawns of Hercules: but his Jovial
        face—
    Murder in heaven! How?—'Tis gone. . . .
    . . . Damn'd Pisanio
    Hath with his forged letters (damn'd Pisanio)
    From this most bravest vessel of the world
    Struck the main-top!
                (IV.ii.306-12, 317-20)

Imogen's confusion of Cloten's body with that of her husband's seems offhand to be an outrageous flaunting of probability.[7] Yet the shock of identification of two polarized figures, the fool and the hero, forces the audience to puzzle over its plausibility. Suddenly, all the pretenses to real distinctions which depend on outward form have been exploded. Posthumus, without the distinction of rational perception and rational control of his appetites, might very well be a Cloten. The missing head symbolizes the vast difference between them, yet Posthumus has already displayed his capacity for unreason in response to Iachimo's lies about Imogen.

The identification of Cloten and Posthumus has been very carefully and pointedly prepared for by Cloten's insistence that there was little physical difference between them. And though the audience tends to disregard the validity of Cloten's insistence upon this point, when the identification occurs, we immediately recognize its truth and proceed to evaluate its implications. It is not, as some critics claim, evidence of Imogen's stupidity, but instead it is a device to enforce the essential perception that outward seeming and inner being have a complex relationship which formulas of any kind tend to oversimplify. The Posthumus of noble and worthy report exists until he is subjected to a test of faith; however, that "noble" Posthumus is not destroyed because he fails the test. The identity of outer and inner worthiness is still possible, but it has to be achieved through adversities that challenge the character's potential worth to awaken and to realize itself.

The death of Cloten and Imogen's confusion of his headless body with Posthumus provide a symbolic and dramatic link to the next appearance of Posthumus onstage.[8] Cloten has become a surrogate victim for Posthumus and in his death has absorbed much of the blame which otherwise would still attach to Posthumus' figure. Imogen's lament over what she thinks is Posthumus' body and her bathing her cheeks in his blood (IV.ii.330) cleanses the figure of Posthumus of the worst of his blame, so that when he enters soon thereafter (V.i) the audience is prepared to accept his own lament with sympathy. The fact that Posthumus carries a bloodsoaked handkerchief, sent to him by Pisanio at his command as evidence of Imogen's death, links his lament with Imogen's visually and symbolically. They are both deceived by surrogate victims, but the reality of death makes clear to each of them what true values the other held for them. The evidences of infidelity, which have convinced them that each has been deceived by the other, no longer weigh significantly in their feelings. The more substantial values of their union have clarified themselves and symbolically prepare them for their ultimate reconciliation. With the death of Posthumus, Imogen confronts "nothing." In reply to Caius Lucius' question "What art thou?" she says, "I am nothing; or if not, / Nothing to be were better" (IV.ii.366-67). And Posthumus dedicates himself to "die / For tree, O Imogen, even for whom my life / Is, every breath, a death" (V.i.25-27). Their former identities have been tested by crisis and the surfaces of their natures have been shattered, so that they must rebuild themselves out of core substance.

At this point Posthumus too dons a disguise in order that his true nature will not be hampered by his outward appearance.

    I'll disrobe me
  Of these Italian weeds, and suit myself
  As does a Briton peasant: so I'll fight

Against the part I come with: so I'll die
For thee, O Imogen, even for whom my life
Is, every breath, a death: and thus, unknown,
Pitied, nor hated, to the face of peril
Myself I'll dedicate. Let me make men know
More valour in me than my habits show.
Gods, put the strength o' th' Leonati in me!
To shame the guise o' th' world, I will begin,
The fashion less without, and more within.

                              (V.i.22-33)

The pointed reversal of the final couplet can hardly be missed. Whereas in the first scene of the play the appearance of nobility was the starting point in both Posthumus' report and actions—that is, his actions were directed toward supporting his outward guise—now he will act from inner nobility and force the outward fashion to coincide with the inner man. As in the "rusty armour" episode in *Pericles,* base appearance will henceforth be associated with noble action and change the "guise o' th' world."

Posthumus is not the only one to suggest that the world's habit of equating noble appearance with noble action is misleading. The two sons of Cymbeline in their wild and savage environment have acted so gently toward Imogen that she remarks: "These are kind creatures. Gods, what lies I have heard! / Our courtiers say all's savage but at court; / Experience, O, thou disprov'st report!" (IV.ii.32-34). The valiant brothers and Posthumus come together in the battle scene to save Cymbeline from the Romans and together with Belarius they are the talk of the British soldiers (V.iii.84-87) and of the court group.

   Cym. Stand by my side, you whom the gods
        have made
   Preservers of my throne: woe is my heart,
   That the poor soldier that so richly fought,
   Whose rags sham'd gilded arms, whose
        naked breast
   Stepp'd before targes of proof, cannot be
        found:
   He shall be happy that can find him, if
   Our grace can make him so.
   Bel.   I never saw
   Such noble fury in so poor a thing;
   Such precious deeds in one that promised
        nought
   But beggary and poor looks.
                              (V.v.1-10)

Posthumus has obviously enacted his new principle effectively. He has placed his appearance and his reality under question, and the attempt to reconcile discrepancies no longer begins with the outward form but with inner valor.

The multiplicity of perspectives in the play finds expression concomitantly with the particular verbal stress-

es on outward and inner natures. Posthumus' awakening from his dream of ancestors and of Jupiter is the dramatic peak of his character's development, and his speech joins together these two complementary themes: the shifting perspectives through which man views the world, and the outward-inner discordancy of human nature. He awakes to find a tablet on his breast, left there by Jupiter "wherein / Our pleasure his full fortune doth confine" (V.iv.109-10).

      A book? O rare one,
   Be not, as is our fangled world, a garment
   Nobler than that it covers. Let thy effects
   So follow, to be most unlike our courtiers,
   As good as promise.

But then he reads the riddle.

   'Tis still a dream: or else such stuff as
        madmen
   Tongue, and brain not: either both, or nothing,
   Or senseless speaking, or a speaking such
   As sense cannot untie. Be what it is,
   The action of my life is like it, which
   I'll keep, if but for sympathy.

                              (V.iv.133-51)

Posthumus' disgust stems from self-loathing, so that when he prays that the book be as noble within as its cover indicates,[9] he is speaking out of his own bitter self-recognition that he has failed to live up to his noble report. His soliloquy which opens Act V expresses his profound sense of guilt and his resolution to dedicate himself to peril, and the three scenes which lead up to his vision of familial shades and of Jupiter increase his despairing self-censure. Aware that he does not deserve reprieve, Posthumus nonetheless hopes that the vision's promise is not false, like the false courtier he has been. The riddle which the "rare book" contains does, in fact, promise his ultimate redemption, and, though he cannot decipher its conceits, he determines to allow it time to fulfill its promises. At least, he will no longer actively seek death.

The lines following his reading of the riddle reveal that Posthumus is undergoing a strenuous shift in perspective. First of all, the dream vision has brought the supernatural realm into direct contact with the natural, suggesting that, though invisible to the normal eye, the two realms may interweave more closely and more frequently than man has assumed. Posthumus suspects that his waking is a continuation of the dream, just as Imogen had suspected when she awoke from her sleeping potion ("The dream's here still" [IV.ii.306]). If not a dream, the content of the riddle is stuff that madmen speak without reasoning about it. But Posthumus recognizes that it is "either both"—a dream merging with reality—"or nothing." The words and reason are at odds, just as the actions of Posthumus' life—being preserved in battle and now promised redemption—are at odds with reason. Because he cannot extract from evident action the causes and their effects, Posthumus accepts on faith that which he cannot rationalize. His bewildering change in perspective has suspended his ratiocinative impulses and it forces him to act out of "sympathy," which need not be defined, but only felt. Had he been true to his "sympathies" for Imogen in the first place, rather than allowing Iachimo's lies to distort the meaning of appearances, Posthumus would not have needed to learn what he now has learned through deprivation.

The limitations of human vision are under question throughout *Cymbeline*. To a certain extent, reality depends upon the person who perceives it, and habitual attitudes tend to narrow the individual's vision. In order to achieve a truer perspective of a world which cannot be contained in one fixed point of human view, it becomes necessary to look at the world from different places. Thus, Posthumus sees one reality when he looks from his place of "noble" courtier, but he sees another reality from the position of British peasant. Or again, when he assumes that Imogen is dead at his command, he sees only a man's world where consequences of action seem to be controlled by the man who directs that action. But after his dream vision that incorporates supernatural power and motive into the natural world, Posthumus can see the possibility of his actions being redeemed.

In *King Lear* (IV.vi.11-24, 69-74) Edgar creates a larger world for the blind Gloucester by convincing him that he has survived a fall from a cliff although he remains on the same spot.[10] Edgar tells him, "Thy life's a miracle" (55), a point Gloucester has been unable to "see" until he has viewed his life from more than one perspective. Edgar's speeches emphasize that reality is relative to the position from which it is viewed at the same time they stress the limitations of a single point of view. In *Cymbeline* there are similar speeches.

When Imogen questions Pisanio about the departure of Posthumus (I.iv), she berates him for not having pressed his vision to its limits.

> *Imo.*   Thou shouldst have made him
> As little as a crow, or less, ere left
> To after-eye him.
> *Pis.*   Madam, so I did.
> *Imo.* I would have broke mine eye-strings,
>   crack'd them, but
> To look upon him, till the diminution
> Of space had pointed him sharp as my
>   needle:
> Nay, followed him, till he had melted from
> The smallness of a gnat, to air: and then
> Have turn'd mine eye, and wept.
>
> (I.iv.14-22)

Imogen tries to move beyond the limitations of the human eye in keeping the reality of Posthumus within her necessarily fixed perspective. Of course, this speech is hypothetical, since she was unable to say a proper farewell in the haste of Posthumus' departure. But her intensity, even in hypothesis, points up her sense that the reality of their love depends on their perception of it. And truly enough, when Posthumus ceases to hold his perception of Imogen's goodness and loyalty, the lapse destroys the reality of their love. In terms of the play, however, ultimate reality does not depend on man's perception of it, and his turning away does not actually diminish the nature of what remains unperceived. Thus, Imogen's goodness remains real despite the fact that Posthumus ceases to perceive it.[11] The action of his life then becomes a motion toward renewed perception, toward achieving a perspective that contains more than man typically is able to see.

Belarius, too, knows the difference that the position of the human eye makes in the perception of reality. He speaks this caution to his "sons," who are unaware of their noble birth and who long for worlds they have not yet known:

> Now for our mountain sport, up to yond hill!
> Your legs are young: I'll tread these flats.
>   Consider,
> When you above perceive me like a crow,
> That it is place which lessens and sets off,
> And you may then revolve what tales I
>   have told you
> Of courts, of princes; of the tricks in war.
> This service is not service, so being done,
> But being so allow'd.
>
> (III.iii.10-17)

Reality depends on perception, but human vision, being limited, may not see all that there is to be seen. Certainly, this has been the case with Cymbeline's banishment of Belarius. Still, Belarius himself has tried to limit the boys' perspective to the world outside of court, giving them only his bias for perceiving that other world. The boys are aware of this, and their desire to expand their vision emphasizes the narrowness of Belarius' well-intended protection of them from the deceptions of the court world. Guiderius says,

> Out of your proof you speak: we poor
>   unfledg'd,
> Have never wing'd from view o' th' nest;
>   nor know not
> What air's from home. Haply this life is best
> (If quiet life be best) sweeter to you
> That have a sharper known, well
>   corresponding
> With your stiff age; but unto us it is
> A cell of ignorance, travelling a-bed,

A prison, or a debtor that not dares
To stride a limit.

(III.iii.27-35)

The limitations of "country" can be as narrowing for human nature as the limitations of "court." There is little doubt that extending the boundaries of both worlds is the action which the play recommends.

The imagery which Guiderius uses to express his desire for expanded vision—the vision that birds have but that man can only imagine—reiterates a pattern of images that is significant throughout the play. Of the various birds cited, the eagle supposedly has the keenest and most resilient vision, being able to look unblinkingly at the sun without damage to its eyes.[12] Imogen likens Posthumus to an eagle early in the play (I.ii.70), but the Frenchman at Philario's house warns that Posthumus' vision may be as limited as that of other men: "I have seen him in France: we had very many there could behold the sun with as firm eyes as he" (I.v. 11-13). Posthumus turns his gaze from the sun which, in the Platonic terms that seem operative here, is truth itself. But there are other eagles in the play which inform the association of Posthumus with the noble bird: Jupiter descends to the stage "sitting upon an eagle" (V.iv) and the Roman soothsayer, Philarmonus, has a vision the night before the battle in which "Jove's bird, the Roman eagle, wing'd / From the spongy south to this part of the west, / There vanish'd in the sunbeams, which portends / (Unless my sins abuse my divination) / Success to th' Roman host" (IV.ii. 348-52). For a while it seems as if the soothsayer's divination has been abused, but at the conclusion of the play, the truth of the vision returns to focus.

> The fingers of the powers above do tune
> The harmony of this peace. The vision,
> Which I made known to Lucius ere the
>   stroke
> Of yet this scarce-cold battle, at this instant
> Is full accomplish'd. For the Roman eagle,
> From south to west on wing soaring aloft,
> Lessen'd herself and in the beams o' the sun
> So vanish'd; which foreshow'd our princely
>   eagle,
> Th' imperial Caesar, should again unite
> His favour with the radiant Cymbeline,
> Which shines here in the west.

(V.v.467-77)

More than a political harmony, the eagle's disappearance into the sunbeams signifies as well the return of Posthumus to the truth of Imogen's goodness. The world which his experience of loss and renewal has revealed to him is one in which the perspective contains the eagle's view: the earth beneath and the heavens into which he soars.

As in *Pericles,* this wider perspective is achieved partially through the blend of modes: tragic threats are contained to an extent by comic presentations, and comic resolutions are qualified by tragic impulses which remain operative. When Iachimo tries to seduce Imogen with his lies about Posthumus' infidelity (I.vii), the threat of evil is real enough, but his presentation of the bad report is comic. Immediately after Imogen welcomes him, Iachimo leaps into a suddenly intense consideration of the madness of men who cannot distinguish between "fair and foul." Imogen is puzzled by his abrupt soliloquy and inquires, "What makes your admiration?" Iachimo, however, seems carried away by the pleasure of making conceits and dwells on images of lust and depravity until Imogen can only surmise that he is ill. Realizing that he is making no progress through this oblique approach, Iachimo sends Pisanio away on a pretext and gains a more intimate audience with Imogen. She changes the subject (so she thinks) to Posthumus' health, and this gives Iachimo his cue. He proceeds to insinuate very bluntly that Posthumus has been making merry with too much boldness in Italy. Iachimo is still building his attack by circumlocution, and Imogen impatiently asks him to come to the point: "I pray you, sir, / Deliver with more openness your answers / To my demands" (87-89). Circling closer to his point, Iachimo waxes prolix with the revelation:

>   Had I this cheek
> To bathe my lips upon: this hand, whose
>   touch
> (Whose every touch) would force the
>   feeler's soul
> To th' oath of loyalty: this object, which
> Takes prisoner the wild motion of mine eye,
> Firing it only here; should I (damn'd then)
> Slaver with lips as common as the stairs
> That mount the Capitol: join gripes, with
>   hands
> Made hard with hourly falsehood
>   (falsehood, as
> With labour): then by-peeping in an eye
> Base and illustrous as the smoky light
> That's fed with stinking tallow: it were fit
> That all the plagues of hell should at one
>   time
> Encounter such revolt.
> *Imo.*   My lord, I fear,
> Has forgot Britain.

(I.vii.99-113)

Imogen's restraint in judging Posthumus from Iachimo's report reveals her emotional maturity, and her composure in the face of slander underlines Iachimo's feverish exhilaration in creating his lies. Iachimo's excitement causes him to push too far, however. When he suggests that Imogen "revenge" herself by taking him to bed, she calls out for Pisanio and denounces Iachimo severely, proudly assuring him that he is unworthy even to speak to her on the subject of Posthumus. Iachimo beats a clever retreat and admits that he was merely testing Imogen's affection, and, reversing the content of his prolixity, he eulogizes Posthumus.

Iachimo's pride in his own craftsmanship leads him beyond his goal. The evil which he is dealing in becomes subordinated by the comedy of the audience's seeing the manipulator being manipulated by the art of his craft.[13] The theatricality of the scene—in Iachimo's "feigned soliloquy"[14]—and in Imogen's melodramatic. "What ho, Pisanio!" which she repeats to a servant who never appears—stresses the artifices that are conventional in seduction scenes which involve a subtle villain and a virtuous heroine. Except in melodrama, however, these conventions are not advertised, and it is interesting to note what makes this scene tragicomic rather than melodramatic.

First, the stress on artifice symbolically restates Iachimo's purpose. He, like the playwright, is working with fiction and trying to convince his audience that the fiction is real. Unlike the playwright, Iachimo is here an ineffectual artificer. Second, Imogen reveals her own human frailty in so readily accepting Iachimo's trumped-up excuse that he was testing her. She is flattered that she has passed the test and never considers his impertinence in testing her at all. She is also as flattered by his praise of Posthumus as she had been insulted by his denigrations a moment earlier. Further, she agrees to keep Iachimo's trunk in her bedchamber as an excessive gesture of apology for having suspected Iachimo at all. The virtuous heroine of melodrama would never show such human frailties.

The scenes in which Iachimo tries to convince Imogen and Posthumus of each other's infidelity are parallel, but the results are opposite. Because Iachimo fails to seduce Imogen, we have a momentary hope that he will also fail to pervert Posthumus' imagination. The bedchamber scene (II.ii) intervenes, however, and qualifies this comic expectation. Iachimo's admiration for Imogen's heavenly beauty briefly offsets the power of his evil intentions; at the same time, her beauty magnifies the ugliness of the "evidence" he will use to convince Posthumus. The comedy of Iachimo's failure to realize his plan contains the greatest part of his evil threat in the earlier scene, but the comedy exists conjoined to the tragic potential of the bedchamber scene. These two scenes create a tragicomic expectation—that is, opposite expectations held simultaneously—for Iachimo's approach to Posthumus (II.iv). When Posthumus succumbs, he weights the effect on the tragic side, but the ease with which he falls and the bombastic soliloquy with which he ends the scene readjust the balance. This blend of impulses, and the dramatic relationship of the comic scene to the one in which

Iachimo's plan succeeds sustain the comic scene at a level more complex than melodrama.

The Queen is another advocate of evil in the play, more evil in purpose than Iachimo, and therefore excluded from the redemptive conclusion. Her plans which give the impetus to the larger actions of the play are evil in design and selfish in their ends: she wants the power of the crown to continue hers into the next generation. She apparently has Cymbeline well in control, but she wants to insure Imogen's cooperation by marrying her to Cloten. The Queen sets two of the three main plots into motion by convincing Cymbeline to advance Cloten as a suitor to Imogen and to refuse tribute to Rome; and she then functions dramatically to absorb Cymbeline's guilt. His speech on hearing of her death and of her deceptions is moving (V.v.62-68), especially when viewed under the larger construct of the inner-outward discrepancy in human nature which has deceived others in the play. Effective to purge evil from the renewed world at the play's end, the Queen demonstrates throughout the play the manner in which the threat of evil can remain operative even as it is contained in comic representation.

The anxiety which might accompany the Queen's vicious plans to poison Pisanio, and perhaps even Imogen, whom Pisanio serves, is displaced at the same moment it is created (I.vi). The physician Cornelius presents the Queen with a small box containing what she thinks are "poisonous compounds." He asks her what use she plans for them and she dissembles—a habit she has already announced (I.ii.34-37). Pisanio enters and the Queen descends upon her first prey, taking him aside while Cornelius lets the audience know that he has fooled her "with a most false effect: and I the truer, / So to be false with her" (I.vi.43-44). Her actions from this point are comic since she is unaware that her dissembling has been met with even craftier dissembling.[15]

Nonetheless the Queen's evil purposes cannot be contained only by Cornelius' deception. She shows her power again when she persuades Cymbeline to deny the tribute to Rome (III.i). This threat, even as it is being shaped in her speech, is diminished by the interruption of Cloten, who wishes to second his mother and to terminate her argument. The business of state is no doubt tedious for Cloten. Yet Cymbeline's terse "Son, let your mother end" (III.i.40) injects a comic pattern which qualifies the otherwise serious matter. The Queen's speech, which out of context might be heard as an altogether commendable eulogy of Britain, is thus diminished and placed by Cloten's "second" and the king's reprimand.

The Queen's threats of evil are contained by the comic means through which she is circumvented: in these two instances by Cornelius and by Cloten. Even in her last effort, her death, she can hardly be taken too seriously because of the manner in which Cornelius reports her confession. He begins in a straightforward enough way: "With horror, madly dying, like her life, / Which (being cruel to the world) concluded / Most cruel to herself. What she confess'd / I will report, so please you" (V.v.31-34). Cymbeline encourages him to continue and the matter-of-factness of Cornelius' enumeration of her confessions is comic: "First, she confess'd she never lov'd you. . . ." The list grows so long that whatever effect of surprise might have been generated at the beginning is lost in the disproportion of the number of confessions the Queen had to make (Cornelius' report of her confession requires twenty-two lines, aside from Cymbeline's choric rejoinders). But the cap of the comedy occurs almost two hundred lines later when Imogen is accusing Pisanio of having tried to poison her. Cornelius steps forward with part of the confession he had forgot.

> O gods!
> I left out one thing which the queen
>   confess'd,
> Which must approve thee honest. "If Pisanio
> Have," said she, "given his mistress that
>   confection
> Which I gave him for cordial, she is serv'd
> As I would serve a rat."
>
>   (V.v.243-48)

This intrusion after the matter of the Queen had been satisfactorily completed demolishes the last shred of seriousness which her characterization might have sustained. Like her son Cloten's, the Queen's evil plans and even her death have been contained in comedy.

The threat of evil is not the only effect which is offset by comic presentation. The sense of awe engendered by grand things—appropriate to tragedy but too overbearing for tragicomedy—is counterbalanced as well by comic characterization. For instance, the pastoral situation of Belarius and the two brothers in an idealized formulation would be entirely good and polarize an entirely bad situation at court. But the pastoral formula is no more sufficient than any other single formula is to represent the world of Shakespeare's last plays. Therefore Belarius has his own guilt to counterbalance the unjustly maligned nobility of his character. He stole Cymbeline's sons from their proper place in the world and he has insisted on limiting their experience according to his own necessities. His recurrent eulogies for their inherent nobility are awesome in implication but self-conscious in their execution. The sons' retention of nobility in motive and action despite savage surroundings is an impressive fact and it elicits admiration (especially from Imogen), but Belarius' repetition of this point in five speeches of the last three acts and even twice in the same scene exaggerates the situation.[16] Excessive emphasis on the convention of

princes disguised as commoners draws the artifice itself into central focus; and this comic stress balances the wonder of a pastoral situation where mountaineers behave more nobly than courtiers.

The dream vision is another scene (V.iv) which inspires a sense of awe in the characters who participate in the admirable events. But the audience is not asked to share this sense of awe with Posthumus—or with Imogen and Belarius in the case of the noble brothers—at least not fully. Wonder is much greater in the dream vision scene because ghosts and a divinity actually appear onstage. To emphasize the spectacular quality of this wonder Jupiter even descends on an eagle. Of course, the self-consciousness of this artifice generates amazement of a sort that nullifies the wonder which a god's visitation should create within the illusion of the play. That is, the audience marvels at the mechanical strategy which lowers Jupiter to the stage more than it marvels at the descent of a god into a man's world. Aside from the mechanical ingenuity, the characterization of the god and his relationship with the ghosts displace much of the awe an audience might feel within an unbroken illusion. His first words to these suppliant shades are a reprimand.

> No more, you petty spirits of region low,
> Offend our hearing: hush! How dare you
>   ghosts
> Accuse the thunderer, whose bolt (you
>   know)
> Sky-planted, batters all rebelling coasts?
>   (V.iv.93-96)

Jupiter's characterization is comic and he descends primarily to show how silly it is to doubt that he is controlling everything. The shades are awed and so is Posthumus, but the audience can appreciate the comic quality of these characters' previous doubt because the audience has been pushed to a distance that creates a more sensible perspective on such things. The self-conscious artifices have pointed all along to a controller of the play's incidents, and it is less of a surprise to the audience than to the characters to discover that, true enough, Jupiter has kept these "mortal accidents" under his Jovial eye with the purpose of making his gifts "the more delay'd, delighted."

The final scene is a tour de force in every critic's evaluation, and I shall not attempt to imitate those who have counted twenty-four separate denouements in it.[17] It is easier to distinguish the moments in which the tragicomic perspective shifts all these revelations into the same sphere—that inclusive container that allows the audience to see through the delightful artifices into the more profound meanings which the play has created. The resolutions progress with dramatic skill. The battle is just past, and the final scene opens with Cymbeline's praise of those who rescued him. After the report of the Queen's confession and death which holds the movement in stasis, Lucius and his train of Romans enter, catching up the gap in the dramatic progress. This forward, halting, and catch-up procedure becomes the pattern for the rest of the scene. Lucius presents Imogen-Fidele to Cymbeline and asks that the page be spared. Cymbeline becomes intrigued with the familiar features of his daughter disguised as a page and Fidele then moves into the director's position. The result of the long sequence of revelations which Imogen's inquiry about Iachimo's diamond ring sets off is the reconciliation of all domestic factions to a national harmony. Cymbeline describes it thus:

> See,
> Posthumus anchors upon Imogen;
> And she (like harmless lightning) throws her
>   eye
> On him: her brothers, me: her master hitting
> Each object with a joy: the counterchange
> Is severally in all. Let's quit this ground,
> And smoke the temple with our sacrifices.
> [*To Belarius*] Thou art my brother; so we'll
>   hold thee ever.
>
>   (V.v.393-400)

But domestic harmony is not enough, and Imogen reminds her father about Lucius and the international problem that remains to be solved. Through Posthumus' forgiveness of Iachimo, Cymbeline takes his example and pardons the entire company. Posthumus then presents Jupiter's riddle and the soothsayer interprets it according to the revelations which have just been made. The union of the British and the Roman nations at a level that surpasses the insularity expressed in the orginial refusal of tribute (III.i) is an expansion of vision for all parties concerned. It is in large a recognition which Imogen had made in small when she was forced to don a disguise and look for a new way of life. At that time she had said to Pisanio:

> *Imo.*   Why, good fellow,
> What shall I do the while? Where bide?
>   How live?
> Or in my life what comfort, when I am
> Dead to my husband?
> *Pis.*   If you'll back to th' court—
> *Imo.* No court, no father, nor no more ado
> With that harsh, noble, simple nothing,
> That Cloten, whose love-suit hath been to
>   me
> As fearful as a siege.
> *Pis.*   If not at court,
> Then not in Britain must you bide.
> *Imo.*   Where then?
> Hath Britain all the sun that shines? Day?
>   Night?
> Are they not but in Britain? I' th' world's
>   volume

> Our Britain seems as of it, but not in't:
> In a great pool, a swan's nest: prithee think
> There's livers out of Britain.
>
>   (III.iv.128-41)

The narrowness that fixed positions give to man's perspective has been supplanted by the eagle's overview. The marvelous resolution of the "history" part of the play in which both sides win fits into the larger scheme of action in which man finds that his free choice accords with Providential design. The reunion of Britain and Rome joins traditional authority and present independence. Cymbeline freely chooses, following Posthumus' example of forgiveness, to bring his kingdom back into harmony with a larger order.[18]

Yet *Cymbeline* is obviously more than a history play; it is a romantic comedy in which the young lovers are thwarted by parental hostility, are forced into a pastoral world where their values adjust themselves to the reality of their plight, and, through shedding of their disguises, are returned to each other under the blessing of a substantially benevolent father. But this romance has some odd quirks in its pattern. There is the "wager" plot of Iachimo, the "revenge" plot of Cloten, the "poison" plot of the Queen, the unintentional disguise of the princely brothers, not to mention the international war. The "romantic" resolutions in the final scene go awry in more than one of their typical formulations; however, all of the irregularities are logical conclusions of what the play has previously set in motion.

Aside from the counterbalancing report of the Queen's death and the enormity of her confession, the first thing that disturbs the patness of the resolution scene is the thwarting of Lucius' expectation that Imogen-Fidele will plead for his life as the favor Cymbeline has offered. Lucius generously says, "I do not bid thee beg my life, good lad, / And yet I know thou wilt." But when Imogen asks for a different "boon," Lucius is obviously surprised. The boon is Iachimo's explanation of how he happens to be wearing the ring she had given to Posthumus. Iachimo, at the center of attention, makes the most of his theatrical opportunity. He announces first that he is glad of the chance to confess and to deliver up his guilt for judgment because "a nobler sir ne'er lived / 'Twixt sky and ground" than the Posthumus he has wronged. His hyperbole of praise recalls the opening scene, in which Posthumus also received such praise—but Posthumus has traveled a vast distance between the two speeches. As Iachimo has displayed in his earlier scene of revelation with Imogen (I.vii), he is fond of rhetorical embellishment and hesitation and now he indulges in them to their limits. Cymbeline becomes impatient with him, as Imogen had earlier, and in vain asks him to "come to the matter." But Iachimo pushes his speech to the limit of prolixity, enjoying his own skill, until he sees Posthumus advancing—at which point he breaks off.

Posthumus becomes almost as involved with the art of his lamentation as Iachimo had been in the art of his revelation, and when Fidele interrupts, Posthumus resentfully strikes the page: "Shall's have a play of this? Thou scornful page, / There lie thy part." This is comic at the same time it is serious. It reveals that Posthumus has learned humility in some areas and not in others; but the astounding revelation that his action causes— the identification of Imogen—creates another "speaking such as sense cannot untie." Cymbeline cries, "Does the world go round?" and Posthumus, "How comes these staggers on me?" Reality, Posthumus discovers again, is not easy to recognize.[19] His first error had been to mistake Iachimo's lies about Imogen as truth. Now he mistakes Imogen's gesture of comfort as an attempt to upstage him. All fixed positions are made to shift their ground.

Much like Thaisa in *Pericles,* Imogen awakens from the blow in a second return to life, but she again mistakes the causes of what she sees and accuses Pisanio of treachery. The doctor steps forward and comically remembers that the Queen's confession covered this too, and things seem restored to harmony momentarily. Imogen embraces Posthumus but Cymbeline interrupts their enraptured gazing upon each other.

> How now, my flesh, my child?
> What, mak'st thou me a dullard in this act?
> Wilt thou not speak to me?
>
> (V.v.264-66)

Cymbeline, too, wants a part in the action of this theatrical performance. This desire, like so many of the other impulses expressed in this scene, is both comic and serious in a symbolic way. It is comic because the king must ask to be included in the party; but it is also symbolic of his passivity in the past, allowing the Queen to direct him to evil actions which have verged on destroying his kingdom's harmony. He prompts Imogen to an emotional recognition by telling her "Thy mother's dead." But when she says she is sorry, he responds, "O, she was naught." His childlikeness in wanting to matter is touching if unkinglike. The reminder nonetheless recalls the disappearance of Cloten and this leads to the discovery of Guiderius' guilt in slaying Cloten, and so on, until Cymbeline finally comments: "O rare instinct! / When shall I hear all through?" When all is finally made clear, Posthumus presents the puzzle of his riddle, and even in the deciphering of its meaning, the soothsayer includes a little comic pedantry.

> The piece of tender air, thy virtuous daughter,
> Which we call *mollis aer*; and *mollis aer*
> We term it *mulier*: which *mulier* I divine
> Is this most constant wife, who even now,
> Answering the letter of the oracle,

> Unknown to you, unsought, were clipp'd about
> With this most tender air.
>
> (V.v.447-53)

Cymbeline agrees that "this hath some seeming." Serious matters are constantly undergoing dislocation by comic perspectives which the characters cannot seem to refrain from creating by their human gestures. These gestures keep the resolution from being patent and suggest that the lesson the characters have learned may not be as fully effective as a formulaic resolution would provide. The characters have not been delivered from their human weaknesses even though they have gained new powers of vision. This retention of their human quality forces their renewed play-world to re-encounter the pressure of actuality, and this keeps the play in touch with the lives of the audience.

The complexities of *Cymbeline*'s plot and the self-consciousness with which the characters live their parts push the play beyond the limitations of conventions and formulas into a sphere where boundaries are not so well defined. The characters' growing awareness of the reality contained in illusion and the illusion involved in the actual is a microcosmic development of what the audience experiences in the same kind of recognition. Perspectives multiply bewilderingly for those who participate in life's action, but a controller of these perspectives always reminds the actor that the control is operative even when the power of reason cannot decipher its purpose. In the case of the play's audience, it is the playwright. But the powers of divinity and creativity mingle in the analogy, and the world into which the audience moves from the theater is a world which seems infused by complexities and controlling powers like those in the play they have just watched.

Notes

[1] Other examples are Cornelius' speech to explain his substitution of a sleeping potion for poison (I.vi.33-44) and the Second Lord's recapitulation of what is wrong with the kingdom (II.i.54-67).

[2] Compare the poetic rhythms of the Beatitudes from Christ's Sermon on the Mount, Matt. 5:3-11.

[3] Imogen's application of the theological terms *grace* and *mercy* to Posthumus underlines the dramatic irony created by his lack of generosity. Posthumus' want of Patience and his learning to delay judgment constitute the poles of his spiritual journey. Concerning the theme of Patience and the education of the human spirit, see Robert G. Hunter, *Shakespeare and the Comedy of Forgiveness* (New York and London, 1965), Chap. I.

[4] See Eric Partridge's note under "penetrate" in *Shakespeare's Bawdy* (New York, 1960), 163. The word *penetrate* has special meaning in Renaissance theories of music as well as a sexual implication. For discussion, see Gretchen L. Finney, "Ecstasy and Music in Seventeenth-Century England," VIII (1947), 175 ff.; and James Hutton, "Some English Poems in Praise of Music," *English Miscellany,* II (1951), 20 ff.

[5] Richmond Noble, *Shakespeare's Use of Song* (London, 1923), 130-35, makes several perceptive points about this aubade. He suggests that because of the limitations of his theater Shakespeare used the morning song as a means to transform night into dawn. Noble does not consider the possibility of the indoor lighting advantages of the second Blackfriars theater which the King's Men had leased by the probable dates of composition of *Cymbeline*. For further comments on the song, see J. M. Nosworthy, Arden edition, *Cymbeline* (London, 1964), Appendix C, 220-22.

[6] The intricate irony of the parodic relationship between Cloten and Posthumus manifests itself here. When Posthumus puts on the clothes of a British peasant to fight the invading Romans (V.i.23-24), he is most worthy of Imogen's praise. He is most noble when dressed in his "mean'st garment."

[7] Harley Granville-Barker, *Prefaces to Shakespeare,* Second Series (3 vols.; London, 1927-36), II, 246-47, points out that the "emphasizing of the artifice . . . does much to mitigate the crude horror of the business, to bring it into the right tragi-comic key."

[8] Some critics, of whom Nosworthy is typical, feel that Posthumus' long absence from the stage is not overcome successfully by his return in Act V: his appearance is not integrated into the dramatic flow of events (Arden edition, 152 n.). However, Posthumus' physical absence from the stage has been more than balanced by the fact that he has been the central focus of almost all the other characters' thoughts and actions (with the exception of those of the Roman ambassador and party). In addition, the death of Cloten brings Posthumus onstage in effect, even though by substitution.

[9] The discrepancy between man's appearance and his true nature is often pointed by the trope of the book and its cover in Shakespeare. See, for examples, *Romeo and Juliet,* III.ii.83-84; *Pericles,* I.i.15-16, 94-95; and *Henry VIII,* I.i.122-23. In *Cymbeline,* Jupiter's book is a particularly appropriate literalization of the trope, since it occurs at the climax of a play which stresses the difference between inner nature and outward appearance.

[10] Cf. Alvin Kernan, "Formalism and Realism in Elizabethan Drama: The Miracles in *King Lear,*" *Renaissance Drama,* IX (1966), 59-66.

[11] Similarly, in *The Winter's Tale,* Hermione's goodness is not actually diminished by Leontes' distorted perception of her; however, the context in which her goodness can be meaningful disappears until Leontes' vision is renewed.

[12] See James Edmund Harting, *The Birds and Shakespeare* (London, 1871), 24, who cites various authorities on the extraordinary vision of eagles: "The opinion that the eagles possessed the power of gazing undazzled at the sun, is of great antiquity." See also Edmund Spenser's use of the idea in *The Faerie Queene* (I.x.47): "Yet wondrous quick and persant was his spright, / As Eagles eye, that can behold the Sunne." In the *Physiologus,* the eagle is a symbol of man's power to renew his vision in Christ because the bird climbed to the sun and supposedly burned off the old feathers and the dull film from his eyes (the "old man"); see *Physiologus,* trans. James Carlill, in *The Epic of the Beast* (London, n.d.), 209-10. There may be something of this tradition behind the use of the eagle in *Cymbeline,* which refers more frequently to the eagle than any other of Shakespeare's plays.

[13] On this point and others in my general argument, cf. Arthur C. Kirsch, "*Cymbeline* and Coterie Dramaturgy," *ELH,* XXXIV (1967), 285-306.

[14] This is Edward Dowden's phrase. See Arden edition, 35 n. 32.

[15] Granville-Barker, *Prefaces to Shakespeare,* II, 246, makes the same point and adds, "We must be interested in watching for the working out of the trick played upon her." Barbara Mowat's comments on this scene, "*Cymbeline:* Crude Dramaturgy and Aesthetic Distance," in George Walton Williams (ed.), *Renaissance Papers, 1966* (Durham, N.C., 1967), 41-43, are also similar in their conclusions.

[16] Belarius' speeches are the following: III.iii.79-107; IV.ii.24-30; IV.ii.169-81; IV.iv.52-53; V.v.348-53.

[17] See Nosworthy's note on p. 172 of the Arden edition.

[18] William B. Thorne, "*Cymbeline:* 'Lopp'd Branches' and the Concept of Regeneration," *Shakespeare Quarterly,* XX (1969), 143-59, discusses the ritualistic aspects of the regeneration of Cymbeline through his sons with a nationalistic focus that broadens a reading of the play as "history."

[19] As Anne Righter points out, *Shakespeare and the Idea of the Play* (London, 1964), 195.

Maurice Hunt (essay date 1980)

SOURCE: "Shakespeare's Empirical Romance: *Cymbeline* and Modern Knowledge," *Texas Studies in Literature and Language,* Vol. 22, No. 3, Fall, 1980, pp. 322-42.

[*In this essay, Hunt refutes early criticism of Shakespeare's convoluted language as a major fault in the play, arguing that the playwright's dialogue deliberately relates to the dramatic structure and tone.*]

"In narration," Dr. Johnson memorably observed in his *Preface* (1765), Shakespeare "affects a disproportionate pomp of diction and a wearisome train of circumlocution, and tells the incident imperfectly in many words, which might have been more plainly delivered in few. . . . Not that always where the language is intricate the thought is subtle, or the image always great where the line is bulky; the equality of words to things is very often neglected, and trivial sentiments and vulgar ideas disappoint the attention, to which they are recommended by sonorous epithets and swelling figures."[1] Dr. Johnson's famous indictment includes a certain obtuseness of expression on Shakespeare's part as well as the implied violation of neoclassical principles of decorum. "It is incident to him to be now and then entangled with an unwieldy sentiment, which he cannot well express, and will not reject; he struggles with it a while, and if it continues stubborn, comprises it in words such as occur, and leaves it to be disentangled and evolved by those who have more leisure to bestow upon it" (p. 73). Critics are only beginning to investigate the possibility that Shakespeare's crabbed, convoluted, and tumid verse at times reflects a similarly embroiled, darkly skeptical world view. In other words, the obscure manner in which certain dramatic characters occasionally speak might not always be regarded as one of the playwright's major "faults." Considered from another perspective, their language can be an aesthetic index to a less-than-harmonious dramatic world which Shakespeare has carefully constructed.[2] This relationship between language and dramatic design figures centrally in the following analysis of *Cymbeline.* Shakespeare's notorious "fault" of style has a special relevance in this Last Romance, where contemporary, empirical variations are played upon certain received themes about knowing. The themes constitute the dominant Renaissance epistemological scheme. Posthumus' erroneous knowledge of Imogen, new acts of knowing induced by art and patient suffering in Wales, and the revelation of divine providence make up a recognizable Christian-Humanist progress of mind.[3] The celebrated uniqueness of *Cymbeline* derives, in large part, from Shakespeare's unorthodox treatment of one orthodox Elizabethan design.[4]

The two Gentlemen at Cymbeline's court who initiate the dramatic action do not merely neglect the equality of words to things; the dictum is flagrantly controverted in their speech. First Gentleman's remark is perhaps the most cryptic opening speech in Shakespearean drama:

> You do not meet a man but frowns. Our bloods
> No more obey the heavens than our courtiers
> Still seem as does the King.[5]
>
> (I. i. 1-3)

Evidently Cymbeline's courtiers appear differently than does Cymbeline himself. A peculiar disobedience involving "blood" pervades the court, but its cause and nature remain obscure to the audience. Since the courtiers wear frowns, the viewer is tempted to believe at this early moment that the King acts otherwise than troubled. Nothing in the Gentleman's next speech violates this possible expectation.

> His daughter, and the heir of's kingdom, whom
> He purposed to his wife's sole son—a widow
> That late he married—hath referred herself
> Unto a poor but worthy gentleman. She's wedded,
> Her husband banished, she's imprisoned. All
> Is outward sorrow, though I think the King
> Be troubled at very heart.
>
> (ll. 4-10)

The viewer now comprehends the several reasons for the pervasive unhappiness at court, but he still does not definitely know how the inwardly vexed Cymbeline "seems." Consequently he remains without a key for unlocking the thought of the ambiguous opening statement. Only upon a restatement does First Gentleman's primary meaning become apparent.

> But not a courtier,
> Although they wear their faces to the bent
> Of the King's looks, hath a heart that is not
> Glad at the thing they scowl at.
>
> (I. i. 12-15)

The Gentleman thus simply means that the courtiers are grieved outwardly, as Cymbeline is; unlike him, however, they are inwardly joyous over Imogen's and Posthumus' wedding.

Some viewers of this play might argue that contrivance in the Gentlemen's speech is unavoidable: initial dialogue between minor Shakespearean characters rapidly introduces several major dramatic issues, and generally sets the tone. The courtier's turgid language, requiring fifteen lines of verse to clarify a rather uninvolved truth about appearances and emotional realities, could represent, nevertheless, the variety of writing that Dr. Johnson regretted.[6] First Gentleman alters his original remark until words more accurately convey his thought. This procedure can be called empirical in the most general sense: the truth issues from a repeated modification of a given fact. Instead of being deduced from an authoritative utterance, the truth is gradually induced from a primary, ambiguous saying. This stylistic phenomenon, by which Shakespeare regularly unravels his knotted poetry, certainly is not unusual in his plays. It in fact uniformly characterizes his dramaturgy as much as it marks everyday conversation between people. What distinguishes *Cymbeline* is the place that this natural phenomenon, involving Shakespeare's idiosyncratic style, finds within a larger portrayal of speech and meaning.

During their discussion of Imogen's and Posthumus' exceptional natures, the two Gentlemen dramatize a special restriction within speech. They suggest that a rarity cannot be voiced in words without inadvertent slander. Although he cannot boast of material riches, Posthumus, according to First Gentleman,

> is a creature such
> As, to seek through the regions of the earth
> For one his like, there would be something failing
> In him that should compare. I do not think
> So fair an outward and such stuff within
> Endows a man but he.
>
> (I. i. 19-24)

Impressed, Second Gentleman observes, "You speak him far" (I. i. 24). First Gentleman in turn disagrees, but instead of coining more spectacular terms, as the viewer might expect, he rather obscurely says,

> I do extend him, sir, within himself;
> Crush him together rather than unfold
> His measure duly.
>
> (I. i. 25-27)

The Gentleman's statements, not the admittedly colorless words within them, constitute Posthumus' eulogy. His latter utterance implies that no words or syntax can wield matter more magnificent than themselves. The most well-meaning praise of Posthumus' virtue appears inadequate when spoken. The dramatic problem is not that hyperbole fails ridiculously, as it did in *Troilus and Cressida;* nor that the hero lacks excellence; nor that his genuine worth is artificially divided into outer and inner qualities. The difficulty lies in the fact that his virtue, as the Gentlemen imagine it, is so unparalled that speech cannot authentically represent it.

To emphasize a verbal insufficiency, Shakespeare makes the idiom in which First Gentleman casts his belief that he cannot describe Posthumus' virtue labored and somewhat disparaging to the hero. Any idea of Posthumus' excellence is lost in the perplexing accordianlike effect of the lines quoted above. When the viewer hears them spoken rapidly in the theater, Posthumus' value suddenly expands with the word "extends," just as quickly contracts in the phrase "Crush him together," and abruptly increases again in the word "unfold" and the remainder of the passage. The speech anticipates Polixenes' tortuous attempt in *The Winter's Tale* to forge normal words, by themselves insufficient to convey his gratitude to Leontes, into an original image of thanks, Metaphysical in its arithmetic ingenuity (*WT* I. ii. 1-10). Specific lines later in the play nicely describe the viewer's feeling that there is a vast difference between Posthumus' virtue and First Gentleman's lame representation of it. Iachimo tells the company in Rome that Imogen's marriage to Posthumus "words him, I doubt not, a great deal from the matter" (I. iv. 16-17).[7]

The unintentional slander, which results from imperfect ways of speaking, creates the opportunity for the more conventional type of slander that pervades *Cymbeline.* Iachimo's poisonous infection of Posthumus' faith is made possible by a radical problem in speaking that gives the Italian the means to realize his jealous plot. He capitalizes upon the disparities between Posthumus' incomparable idea of Imogen and the alien words and jewel by which the protagonist struggles to make it understandable. A Frenchman in Philario's house begins the chain of events that leads to the wager when he recalls that Posthumus once praised Imogen in language as grand as the members of the present gathering have used to extol their mistresses. Then Posthumus believed that his beloved was

>   more
> fair, virtuous, wise, chaste, constant, qualified,
> and less attemptable, than any of the rarest of
> our ladies in France.
>
> (I. iv. 63-66)

Upon Iachimo's ridicule of such hyperbole, Posthumus maintains that her virtue and his opinion have not altered with time. Attentive to the form of the Briton's praise, Iachimo calls attention to the making of comparisons, which becomes a source of trouble in the present dispute:

> As fair and as good—a kind of hand-
> in-hand comparison—had been something too
> fair and good for any lady in Brittany.
>
> (I. iv. 75-77)

The insult is double. To Iachimo's mind, Posthumus has "outspoken"—overshot—Imogen's value, even though the comparisons by which he expresses it make up a common epithet. His sarcastic phrase, "a kind of hand-in-hand comparison," suggests that "as fair and as good" is a predictable formula: one cliché draws forth the other.

Pressing Posthumus to believe that he can easily lose everything related to his love, Iachimo says,

> Your ring may be stol'n too. So your
> brace of unprizable estimations, the one is
> but
> frail and the other casual. A cunning thief,
> or
> a that-way-accomplish'd courtier, would haz-
> zard the winning both of first and last.
>
> (I. iv. 98-102)

In the passage the word "unprizable" chiefly means "inestimable," but it also has overtones of "worthless." When a "that-way-accomplish'd" courtier can with carnal purposes use Posthumus' well-meant words in his courtship of any woman, they by implication can- not be unique ways of expressing Imogen's rarity—or the rarity of any woman, for that matter. Such words are public property available to any base fellow. Voicings of them infrequently reveal speakers' good and evil motives. Thus they remain imprecise symbols. The problem is essentially that which Francis Bacon describes in *The New Organon* (1620).

> There are also Idols formed by the intercourse and association of men with each other, which I call Idols of the Market-Place, on account of the commerce and consort of men there. For it is by discourse that men associate and words are imposed according to the apprehension of the vulgar. And therefore the ill and unfit choice of words wonderfully obstructs the understanding. . . . For men believe that their reason governs words; but it is also true that words react on the understanding; and this it is that has rendered philosophy and the sciences sophistical and inactive. Now words, being commonly framed and applied according to the capacity of the vulgar, follow those lines of division which are most obvious to the vulgar understanding. And whenever an understanding of greater acuteness or a more diligent observation would alter those lines to suit the true divisions of nature, words stand in the way and resist the change.[8]

While Bacon is asserting that precise philosophic and scientific inquiry can never be conducted through com- mon language, his generalizations about the leveling effects of speech do apply to *Cymbeline*.[9] Words are generally formed in such popular senses and define things by such broad lines that they cannot in the play convey singular truths.[10]

Many of the memorable details of the second wager scene drive home this point. The rich tapestry woven with the story of Cleopatra's meeting on the Cydnus with Mark Antony, a chimney-piece of chaste Diana bathing, the roof worked with golden cherubims, and the andirons wrought into two winking Cupids are marvelous pieces of art in Imogen's bedchamber that Iachimo never saw "so likely to report themselves" (II. iv. 83). So lifelike is this compelling art that only motion and breath are lacking. The tapestry and and- irons unfortunately have latent erotic values that inten- sify the notion of sensuality that Iachimo is attempting to implant in Posthumus' imagination.[11] More impor- tantly, Iachimo hopes by minutely describing these objects to convince Posthumus that he has passed the night with Imogen, gazing upon these beauties amid his sport:

> Sir, my circumstances,
> Being so near the truth as I will make them,
> Must first induce you to believe.
>
> (II. iv. 61-63)

But his account of the fine features of these art objects is not conclusive proof of his wife's adultery in Post- humus' opinion. Iachimo might have heard a vivid narration of them in either Britain or Rome, and not been struck by a first-hand viewing. Referring to the chimney-piece of Diana, Posthumus says,

> This is a thing
> Which you might from relation likewise reap,
> Being, as it is, much spoke of.
>
> (II. iv. 85-87)

Because they can be counterfeited, the art objects for- feit their veridical power. This judgment applies not only to the slanderous use to which Iachimo would put them, but also to their communicative value in general. Their meanings are transferable. The tapestry's re- sidual moral about erotic love, for example, is essen- tially caught in Iachimo's remark that "Cydnus swell'd above the banks, or for/ The press of boats or pride" (II. iv. 71-72).[12] The art objects lose their inspirational force when their meanings can substantially be con- veyed by Iachimo's narration. An inferior medium of expression can in effect approximate their specialness, without communicating the conviction that only they themselves directly can.

The report of the beautiful art in Imogen's bedchamber thus reiterates in small the basic problem of knowing that the wager scenes more generally set. Unique val- ues are lost when they are expressed through lessen- ing mediums. Imogen can be known truly only in terms of Imogen; she is her own precious self-refer- ent. She is, after all, on a different plane of value than the diamond ring and bracelet to which she is reduced in the course of Posthumus' and Iachimo's wrangling. At the beginning of the debate, Iachimo seizes upon Posthumus' diamond ring as a metaphor for his belief that Imogen is not the perfect woman:

*Act III, scene vi. Imogen, Belarius, Guiderius, and Arviragus.
Frontispiece to the Hanmer edition by H. Gravelot (1744).*

                           If she went
before others I have seen as that diamond
  of
yours outlusters many I have beheld, I
  could not
but believe she excelled many; but I have
  not
seen the most precious diamond that is, nor
  you the lady.
                         (I. iv. 77-82)

By dwelling upon the ring, Iachimo encourages Post-
humus to equate Imogen's worth with an inappropri-
ate object, just as Iago did when he insinuated that
Desdemona's handkerchief was symbolic of her honor.
At this point Iachimo does not succeed in getting
Posthumus to identify Imogen with the diamond:

> *Post.* I prais'd her as I rated her: so do I my
>   stone.
> *Iach.* What do you esteem it at?
> *Post.* More than the world enjoys.

Iach. Either your unparagon'd mistress is
  dead, or she's outpriz'd by a trifle.
Post. You are mistaken. The one may be
  sold or given
if there were wealth enough for the purpose
or merit for the gift; the other is not a
thing for sale, and only the gift of the gods.
                     (I. iv. 83-91)

After Iachimo has returned from Britain with his evidence, Posthumus uses the diamond ring as a metaphor for Imogen's honor. He thus makes the association that Iachimo contrived in the first wager scene.
Concerning Iachimo's success, he asks, "Sparkles this
stone as it was wont, or is't not/ Too dull for your
good wearing?" (II. iv. 40-41). In his mind, Imogen's
chastity now gives luster and hence worth to the ring.
Rather than properly being on another value level, her
chastity has become synonymous with the diamond.
Now Iachimo insists that Imogen and the ring cannot
be equated: "If I had lost it,/ I should have lost the
worth of it in gold" (II. iv. 41-42). Upon her discovery that her bracelet is missing, Imogen said, "I hope
it be not gone to *tell* my lord/ That I kiss aught but
he" (II. iii. 152-53). Once a material object expresses
values, those values are subsequently known chiefly in
terms of the object. Because Imogen's chastity has
come to be esteemed as a material article (a ring),
another material article (a bracelet) appropriately proclaims her reputed adultery. Just as nurture cannot
supply the words, nature cannot provide the metaphorical objects that would express without slander
Posthumus' idea of Married Chastity.

Posthumus finally knows Imogen in the last stage of
his wager by the most common romance device: a
mole significantly shaped like a star—a pentangle.
That is a traditional figure of divinity that the hero
does not credit because he no longer desires to believe that his wife is the gods' creation.[13] The necessity of speaking in iron conceptions lesser than his
golden intuition causes Posthumus initially to tarnish
his idea of Imogen. Like Cordelia, who also could
not find words "fit" for her devotion, he should have
loved and courageously remained silent before Iachimo's taunts. Posthumus' infected will reveals itself
after his erected wit cannot sustain his heavenly idea.
Enraged, he declares,

                    Let there be no honour
Where there is beauty; truth, where
  semblance; love
Where there's another man! The vows of
  women
Of no more bondage be to where they are
  made
Than they are to their virtues, which is
  nothing!
                     (II. iv. 108-12)

Posthumus in this passage sets an important condition for later scenes of the play. "Fair-and-good" comparisons have not been able to indicate how Imogen's inner truth and outward beauty are integral. The unique binding of her virtues into a transcendent whole occurs in Wales during Arviragus' elegy. In the Welsh mountains, Shakespeare presents new ways of knowing that do not slander a remarkable idea in its expression.

Enduring adversity, Imogen, disguised as Fidele, takes the drugs that Cornelius substituted for the Queen's poison, and so appears dead to her brothers and Belarius. In his elegy for her, Arviragus depicts her beauty by means of a Renaissance pastoral convention:

> With fairest flowers,
> Whilst summer lasts and I live here, Fidele,
> I'll sweeten thy sad grave. Thou shalt not lack
> The flower that's like thy face, pale primrose; nor
> The azur'd harebell, like thy veins; no, nor
> The leaf of eglantine, whom not to slander,
> Outsweet'ned not thy breath. The raddock would
> With charitable bill (O bill, sore shaming
> Those rich-left heirs that let their fathers lie
> Without a monument!) Bring thee all this;
> Yea, and furr'd moss besides, when flowers are none,
> To winter-ground thy corse.[14]
>
> (IV. ii. 218-29)

Natural flowers unequivocally express Arviragus' idea of Imogen's beauty: the primrose communicates the loveliness of her face, the harebell that of her veins, and the eglantine leaf that of her breath. The eglantine is not slandered; her breath's sweetness is no more nor no less than the leaf's. There is no question in the elegy of competition between words and intuitions. Elevated thought smoothly becomes elevated artistic speech without slander. Nor are words and things antagonistic; a flower inspires Arviragus to eloquence. Barren winter, however, mars Arviragus' art. Transient summer blossoms and the speaker's impermanent residence make the flowers' testimonial power ultimately relative. Late in the play, nevertheless, Imogen suggests that Wales is a realm of true speech. Discovering her companions' identity, she declares,

> O, never say hereafter
> But I am truest speaker! You call'd me brother
> When I was but your sister, I you brothers
> When we were so indeed.
>
> (V. v. 375-78)

Given the wager scenes, Arviragus' dramatization of that notion has a special relevance.[15]

Primarily, however, experience expands the understanding in Wales. Mountaineers can be "kind creatures," Imogen learns:

> Gods, what lies I have heard!
> Our courtiers say all's savage but at court.
> Experience, O, thou disprov'st report!
> Th' imperious seas breed monsters; for the dish
> Poor tributary rivers as sweet fish.
>
> (IV. ii. 32-36)

In Wales, Imogen is instructed in faithful love. Once her husband has accused her, she too easily believes that some Italian whore has betrayed him (III. iv. 51-52). Faithful Pisanio is not so credulous. Shakespeare introduces Pisanio into *Cymbeline* partly as a measure of loyalty revealing that the main characters' faith is not ideally strong. The good servant correctly suspects that

> It cannot be
> But that my master is abus'd. Some villain,
> Ay, and singular in his art, hath done you both
> This cursed injury.
>
> (III. iv. 122-25)

Imogen, on the contrary, believes that "some Roman courtesan" has, and Pisanio must repeat, "No, on my life" (III. iv. 126). By comparison, her view is not so complimentary to her husband. Although she never loses her love for him, once in Wales Imogen continues to doubt Posthumus' faith. Imogen pardons the two beggars who give her false directions to Milford Haven. Poor people may be driven by need; Posthumus' great lies of love have no imaginable cause (III. vi. 9-15). And she would change her sex to be the rustics' companion since she thinks that her husband has broken his vow (III. vi. 88-89).

When Imogen adopts the alias Fidele as part of her masculine disguise, she indicates that her experience in Wales involves her faith. After Guiderius proves himself the best woodsman during the deer hunt, he becomes the lord of a feast at which Arviragus and Belarius play the cook and servant, respectively. Imogen acts the role of their housewife, dutifully cutting their root diet into letters for an alphabet soup that symbolizes the nature she would given them (IV. ii. 45-51). By this experience her wifely faith, which has been thrown into question, is practiced and strengthened. Her faith is therefore not reaffirmed by any miraculous means. Suffering Posthumus' imagined death teaches her how much she loves him. When Imogen thinks that Cloten's trunk is her husband's, Jupiter is doing much more than perversely demonstrating that love is at the mercy of ocular knowledge. In contrast to the depraved experimenter, the Queen, who poisons her soul by her noxious testing of animals, Jupiter probes mortals relentlessly to discover their spiritual mettle. His trials always have this humane end. Imogen learns that her husband's supposed infidelity is a minor evil compared with his ultimate loss. She thus experiences the play's educative dynamic: a greater grief displaces an extreme sorrow. Imogen does not feel Cymbeline's anger concerning her forbidden meeting with her husband because Posthumus' banishment is more painful. In her words, "a touch more rare / Subdues all pangs, all fears" (I. i. 135-36). That misery becomes nothing when she learns that Posthumus believes that she is a strumpet and has ordered her execution, and that grief, which appeared definitive, in turn becomes trivial when she thinks that Posthumus is dead. This process of emotional displacement gives force to Jupiter's precept: "Whom best I love I cross; to make my gift,/ The more delay'd, delighted" (V. iv. 101-02). The ethical rationale for painful deception given earlier by Cornelius in this instance can stand for that of the divine physician, Jupiter. Cornelius has justified his substitution of a harmless drug for the Queen's poison:

> there is
> No danger in what show of death it makes,
> More than the locking up the spirits a time,
> To be more fresh, reviving. She is fool'd
> With a most false effect; and I the truer
> So to be false with her.
>
> (I. v. 39-44)

By suffering adversity, Imogen understands that her consummate joy is Posthumus' well-being and is consequently prepared for her reunion with him.

Thus when the Roman Lucius demands that she identify the body upon which she is stretched, Imogen speaks of her husband in the noblest terms:

> Richard du Champ. (Aside) If I do lie and do
> No harm by it, though the gods hear, I hope
> They'll pardon it.
>
> (IV. ii. 377-79)

Giving her husband a knight's name, Imogen confers upon him the honor that his deeds in battle will soon show that he deserves. Lying for necessity discovers Imogen's revived love as well as the truth of Post–humus' character. Lucius suggests that such devotion is an extreme example of faith. Learning her assumed name, Fidele, he pronounces, "Thou dost approve thyself the very same:/ Thy name well fits thy faith, thy faith thy name" (IV. ii. 380-81). In other words, in Wales Imogen's persona gradually becomes part of her; so much so that her assumed name is the major instance in the play of a word that absolutely expresses an idea.[16] Because Imogen's role as Fidele entails the tentative acceptance and probing of new ideas, her Welsh experience is in part experimental. Imogen's experimental role provokes the original use and examination of words: certain terms lose their social encrustations and regain an evocative clarity of meaning—Shakespeare's interest in the process resembling Baconian concerns.

Not only does it augment knowledge, the experience of suffering in *Cymbeline* also corrects the conventional sounding ideas characters repeatedly utter. In passage after passage the characters interpret dramatic events by means of *sententiae*. As Pisanio, for example, watches Imogen react to the letter directing him to murder her, he construes her grief in terms of a Renaissance commonplace of slander:

> What shall I need to draw my sword? The
> paper
> Hath cut her throat already. No, 'tis slander,
> Whose edge is sharper than the sword, whose
> tongue
> Outvenoms all the worms of Nile, whose
> breath
> Rides on the posting winds and doth belie
> All corners of the world. Kings, queens, and
> states,
> Maids, matrons, nay, the secrets of the grave
> This viperous slander enters.
>
> (III. iv. 34-41)

A character in *Cymbeline* often begins with one interpretation of an event, catches himself up when he realizes that the interpretation does not precisely fit his situation, and qualifies his first idea with additional ones. So Pisanio first believes that Posthumus' vengeful letter has undone Imogen, disagrees with himself in the second line of the passage, and then portrays the slander that has struck her, quarreling with himself for greater clarity one last time in the penultimate line.[17] While the process appears to be one of greater specification, in reality the effect is usually the opposite. The qualifying ideas lead the speaker away from a complex dramatic situation into a conventional world where distinctions are blurred. Sententious ideas often become corrupting interpretative frames of reference that prevent the incidents of this Last Romance from being understood purely in their own terms. In this case, the criterion for slander is exacting to an Olympian degree. *Only* a bird in hand is, strictly speaking, worth two in the bush. Any experience in which one actually holds something which can potentially be possessed in abundance naturally is bound to have dimensions which the saying about birds and bushes cannot encompass. Thus any saying has only one context for the most precise understanding: the original one that bred it, of which it in turn gives the clearest interpretation. Any other application suffers from the distortions of metaphor. When Cornelius reports the Queen's death, Cymbeline finds some consolation in the saying that bad news best becomes a physician and that, while medicine can prolong life, death will also seize the doctor one day (V. v. 27-30). Such common knowledge works against the King's eventual understanding of the courageous virtue the physician Cornelius showed when he removed the deathly drugs from the chest that the Queen gave Pisanio. Belarius curtails inquiry into Imogen's "death" by apostrophizing melancholy (IV. ii. 203-09); Cymbeline into the Queen's evil by moralizing Woman (V. v. 47-48); Lucius into Imogen's failure to plead for his life by reflecting upon the falsity of boys and girls (V. v. 106-07), and so on. Sententious stereotypes in *Cymbeline* impede understanding so that the astute viewer must reflect upon the limitations of preconceived, deductive knowledge. "The subtlety of nature is greater many times over than the subtlety of the senses and understanding," Bacon noted; "so that all those specious meditations, speculations, and glosses in which men indulge are quite from the purpose."[18]

Posthumus' response to Jupiter's epiphany is a central illustration of the general problem discussed above. After his frustrated efforts at verbalizing Posthumus' virtue, First Gentleman asserted that Imogen's act of choice best declares it: "By her election may be truly read/ What kind of man he is" (I. i. 53-54). The mortal flaws noted in Imogen's married faith call into question that ultimate standard. Thus it is by the mysterious election of the gods, signified by Jupiter's conferral of the dream-vision and tablet, that Posthumus' excellence can finally be understood truly. When he awakens in prison, Posthumus does not appear to realize this fact, for he first construes the vision in terms of an idea that sounds like a courtly truism. Dejected, he says that

> Poor wretches that depend
> On greatness' favour, dream as I have done;
> Wake, and find nothing.
>
> (V. iv. 127-29)

Such an idea is an interpretative mental set which threatens to keep Posthumus from giving any importance to the dream-vision. But he chides himself before it is dismissed by a commonplace:

> But, alas, I swerve!
> Many dream not to find, neither deserve,
> And yet are steep'd in favours. So am I,
> That have this golden chance and know not
> why.
>
> (V. iv. 129-32)

Posthumus' remorse for his rash command for Imogen's death has helped forge a new humility. Immediately before the dream-vision, he entreats the gods: "For Imogen's dear life take mine" (V. iv. 22). Genuine modesty and penitence offer a better context for

appreciating the dream-vision and tablet than any court idea. The hero understands one of the play's most crucial events by means of his own special punishment for proudly testing his wife. In the manner of an empiricist he lucidly interprets his experience in terms of the unique context out of which it emerges. Concerning the oracle, Posthumus announces,

> Be what it is,
> The action of my life is like it, which
> I'll keep, if but for sympathy.
>
> (V. iv. 149-51)

He thus retains the arcane tablet about a lion's whelp embraced by tender air that will be the sole proof that Jupiter has assisted the characters from despair to happiness. Only the most tenuous idea of correspondence, of "sympathy," between an enigmatic life and an obscure riddle prevents Posthumus from throwing the tablet away. He here exercises well the instinct for comparison that he employed in pride during the wager scenes.

The several discoveries and stories of the last scene of *Cymbeline* reveal their experiences to the characters in terms of those experiences themselves. The totality of experience in the play is transparently set forth in successive narrations without the alien commonplaces that, as frames of reference, might misrepresent events and warp their true meanings. In detail and vigor narration must approximate experience as well as narrative permits. By means of Iachimo's protracted story of his intrigue (V. v. 153-208), Shakespeare rather elvishly makes this point. The dramatist desires to lay words to the very curve of experience. Iachimo's eccentric words, imaginative ellipses, and digressive detail so catch and repeat the very form of his betrayal experience that they draw the spellbound Posthumus out of his part as a Roman soldier into a compulsive reenactment of his sin when the story reaches that stage. In his true identity, he rehearses his former hatred for his wife by unknowingly striking Imogen when she would quiet his guilty ravings. A lively narrative so purely recreates an experience that the hero is catapulted into the spirit of the latter. Iachimo's episodic narrative, however, in one respect works against art's peculiar value. While one standard for art is the mimicry of life, Shakespeare implies in this episode that, when the principle is rigorously observed, art in effect duplicates experience—losing the special powers of enlightenment that come from the aesthetic reorganization and distortion of life.[19] The dramatist forces his audience, as well as his characters, to consider how art without strong inherent artistic valuation has relevance beyond itself.

Without the interpretive perspective Jupiter's oracle provides, narratives of the characters' actions in *Cymbeline,* no matter how vital or truthful, would as a whole stand bare, made up of wonderful accidents that may have no greater significance. Shakespeare in this Last Romance especially focuses upon the human yearning for the imposed design that makes episodic experience meaningful. Upon hearing of his Queen's evil plot against him, Cymbeline protests that

>   Mine eyes
> Were not in fault, for she was beautiful;
> Mine ears, that heard her flattery; nor my heart,
> That thought her like her seeming. It had been vicious
> To have mistrusted her.
>
>   (V. v. 62-66)

According to a Christian view, man does not viciously mistrust the eyes' and ears' report because he knows that any evil carried unintentionally by them is somehow part of a benign scheme. And if his senses report apparent evil, he gives the report the most charitable interpretation because he knows that divine Providence is forwarded mainly by such an attitude. In all other surviving versions of the wager story, the villain persuades an old woman to conceal him in a chest in the heroine's bedchamber.[20] Imogen without question accepts Iachimo and his chest into her safekeeping after he has debased Posthumus and her marriage and acted churlishly toward her. By the dramatic adaptation, Shakespeare emphasizes Imogen's martyrlike trust that her eyes and ears tell her of no real evil. The deeds that her charity prompts in this case are necessary links in the chain of painful events that creates her permanent happiness. She, however, has no intuition of her destiny when she openly receives obnoxious Iachimo.

Thus Imogen and Cymbeline deserve credit when they give sensuous knowledge the most charitable constructions, for when they do they have no reason to believe that mortal charity is fulfilling step-by-step a celestial plan. So that they do not have to remain creatures of blind faith, the specific knowledge of Jupiter's providence is redemptive for the characters of *Cymbeline*. The oracular tablet is the dramatic raison d'être for Jupiter's epiphany, and that, we saw, depends for significance upon earthly experience. Writing in *The History of the World* (1614), Sir Walter Raleigh observes that

> The example of Gods universall Providence is seene in his creature. The Father provideth for his children: beasts and birds and all livings for their young ones. If Providence be found in second Fathers, much more in the first and Universall: and if there be a naturall loving care in men, and beasts, much more in God, who hath formed this nature, and whose Divine love was the beginning, and is the bond of the Universall.[21]

The characters of *Cymbeline* similarly deduce Jupiter's providence retrospectively, from their experiences.[22] Understanding divine Providence by means of natural events and earthly creatures reveals a seventeenth-century shift in interest from heavenly to terrestrial affairs. According to Wilbur Sanders, "the implication seems to be that these matters can be legitimately discussed on the naturalistic plane."[23] The oracle becomes comprehensible when its terms are experienced in the last scene—acted out before the Roman Soothsayer, Philarmonus. Only then can this Sage decree that the riddle is fulfilled: King Cymbeline is the lofty cedar whose lopped branches, grafted to him again, are his lost sons. "Leo-natus" Posthumus is the lion's whelp, and

> The piece of tender air, thy virtuous daughter,
> Which we call *mollis aer,* and *mollis aer*
> We term it *mulier;* which *mulier* I divine
> Is this most constant wife, who even now
> Answering the letter of the oracle,
> (*To Posthumus*) Unknown to you, unsought, you were clipp'd about
> With this most tender air.
>
>   (V. v. 446-52)

Philarmonus can venture this etymology of "wife," one well-established in Shakespeare's day and even then recognized to be somewhat strained, because he has seen Imogen in the joyful act of embracing her husband.[24] That is a triumphant gesture of love that inspires Posthumus to say, "Hang there like fruit, my soul,/ Till the tree die!" (V. v. 263-64). This composite image nicely conveys his charitable idea of the bond between man and wife, a bond so strongly empathetic that Posthumus would change nature's pattern and make the nourished as important as the nourisher—the fruit as important as the tree. Posthumus fashions from the existential moment as original symbol by which he conceives of his love, expressing by the act his new capacity for unselfishness. As has happened previously, a well-told tale moves its auditors to act out its consequences. The acting in this case does not take the form of a cliché, but originally grows out of experience to give birth to a rich visual metaphor. Posthumus' image suggests an inversion of the Christian symbol for the experience of sin, and therefore a prelapsarian purity for the lovers. Those who are jarred from construing life in terms of preconceived metaphors, and can patiently wait for each action to dictate its own context for understanding, find their happiness when they discover that their experiences have assumed the form of a unifying holy metaphor.

Still, Shakespeare will not let us leave the theater underestimating the virtues of experience. It holds the key to the right reading of Jupiter's other, equally ambiguous revelation: the Soothsayer's dream-vision, in which

> Jove's bird, the Roman eagle, wing'd
> From the spongy South to this part of the
>   West,
> There vanish'd in the sunbeams.
> (IV. ii. 348-50)

Philarmonus naturally first thought that the vision predicts victory for the Roman host. By his Western flight, Jupiter's bird is glorified. But after the British defeat the Roman legions and peace reigns, he detects that it foretells that imperial Caesar, the winged eagle, shall again unite with "radiant" Cymbeline in the West (V. v. 470-76). An equivocal vision thus gains true meaning only when the Soothsayer can retrospectively see that experience fulfills it, however roughly, for there is still some tension in the interpretation. Rome is absorbed within Britain ("vanish'd in the sunbeams") in the Soothsayer's definitive reading, while it is tiny Britain's immersion, signified by the paying of the tribute, within the greater Roman Empire that makes possible the Peace of Augustus. Divine Ideas are never directly or easily divulged in this play, but remain far-removed mysteries confirming Shakespeare's conservative attitude toward celestial knowledge.[25] In the final ingenious operation of Philarmonus' mind upon the hard facts of experience, we see one last time Shakespeare's irrepressible empirical method.

Notes

[1] *Johnson on Shakespeare,* ed. Arthur Sherbo, Yale Edition of the Works of Samuel Johnson (New Haven, Conn.: Yale Univ. Press, 1968), VII, 73-74.

[2] For the critical investigations, consult Richard Fly, *Shakespeare's Mediated World* (Amherst: Univ. of Massachusetts Press, 1976), esp. pp. ix-xv, 27-52; and T. McAlindon, "Language, Style, and Meaning in *Troilus and Cressida,*" PMLA, 84 (1969), 29-43. Both Fly and McAlindon draw upon Una Ellis-Fermor, *The Frontiers of Drama* (London: Methuen, 1964). Ellis-Fermor was perhaps the first Shakespearean scholar to assume a discordant dramaturgy.

[3] In the last two Books of *Paradise Lost,* the Archangel Michael teaches Adam that his passage from error through suffering to an epiphany of Providence will be archetypal for mankind until the Last Judgment. Refer to Stanley Eugene Fish, *Surprised by Sin: The Reader in Paradise Lost* (New York: St. Martin's Press, 1967), pp. 286-331. The progress of mind is explicit in the *Faerie Queene.* The Redcross Knight's exposure to Errour has symbolic value at the beginning of his mission to slay the dragon threatening Una's kingdom: Adam's Original Sin is reenacted whenever the knight proudly judges by misleading appearances. His errors aptly lead to his imprisonment in Orgoglio's castle. After his purification in the House of Holiness, how-

ever, the knight has an elect vision of the Heavenly Jerusalem (I. X. xlxi-lxviii). In one general sense, then, the dramatic movement of *Cymbeline* is generic.

[4] Another approach partly concerned with dramatic ways of knowing in *Cymbeline* is Douglas L. Peterson, *Time, Tide, and Tempest: A Study of Shakespeare's Romances* (San Marino, Calif.: Huntington Library Press, 1973), pp. 108-50. Peterson hopes to demonstrate that, in his Last Romances, Shakespeare creates a "radically new mode of tragicomedy which, by appropriating the improbable fictions of romance, allowed him to celebrate the restorative power of the good and to affirm in the face of growing Jacobean skepticism and despite all appearances to the contrary, a morally coherent universe" (p. 4). That good triumphs at the conclusion of *Cymbeline* is indisputable. That the play's universe is morally coherent is not so readily observable. That good triumphs "in the face of growing Jacobean skepticism" forms the subject for a lively debate. In my view, the Last Romances frequently derive their power and appeal from a complex, even skeptical, dramatization of humanist commonplaces about Fortune, Constancy, and Virtue. Without his unique perspective, Shakespeare in his final phase risks becoming a dramatic Spenser. According to Peterson, epistemology in the Last Romances derives from a binary opposition: Fortune's slave is deceived by the surfaces of the phenomenological world, beyond which he cannot (will not) pierce, while the faithful believer in Occasion, the Restorative Cycle behind Mutability, and Redemptive Love abides illusion, confident of Providence (pp. 4-14). In my opinion, ways of knowing in the Last Romances are more dynamic, often involving the spoken word.

[5] All quotations are from *The Complete Works of Shakespeare,* ed. George Lyman Kittredge (Boston: Ginn, 1936).

[6] "This passage is so difficult," Johnson in fact wrote about the Gentleman's opening lines, "that commentators may differ concerning it without animosity or shame." To Johnson's mind, the lines are "a licentious and abrupt expression." (Sherbo, VIII, 874).

[7] Derek Traversi in *Shakespeare: The Last Phase* (Stanford: Stanford Univ. Press, 1964) notices a "complexity of expression" in the Gentlemen's dialogue which he believes points to "a deep-seated dislocation of natural feeling" (pp. 44-46). More precisely, problematic speech and feeling play back and forth in the Gentlemen's dialogue, dislocating each other.

[8] *The Works of Francis Bacon,* eds. James Spedding, Robert Ellis, and Douglas Denon Heath (London: Longmans, 1875), IV, 54-55, 61.

[9] "In the sixteenth century, it was assumed that defects in man brought about confused speech; in the

seventeenth century, it became widely held that confused speech brings on many of the defects in man" (Margreta De Grazia, "Shakespeare's View of Language: An Historical Perspective," *SQ,* 29 [1978], 381). According to De Grazia, Bacon first inverted the relationships described above. Shakespeare's Baconian point of view and his emphasis upon experiential knowledge in *Cymbeline* have been discussed by Geoffrey Hill, " 'The True Conduct of Human Judgment': Some Observations on *Cymbeline,*" *The Morality of Art,* ed. D. W. Jefferson (London: Routledge and Kegan Paul, 1969), pp. 24, 27-30.

[10] Shakespeare's preoccupation with this subject—the manner by which society's verbal currency, public words, debases unique private values expressed therein—has been treated by Sigurd Burckhardt, *Shakespearean Meanings* (Princeton, N.J.: Princeton Univ. Press, 1968), esp. pp. 22-46, 260-84; and by James L. Calderwood, "*Love's Labour's Lost*: A Wantoning with Words," *SEL,* 5 (1965), 317-32; and "*Coriolanus;* Wordless Meanings and Meaningless Words," *SEL,* 6 (1966), 211-24. Calderwood has expanded his linguistic thesis in *Shakespearean Metadrama* (Minneapolis: Univ. of Minnesota Press, 1971), pp. 58-84.

[11] For another account of how each allusion to the art objects "contributes to the establishment of Iachimo's character and ironically signals the futility of his schemes," see R. J. Schork, "Allusion, Theme, and Characterization in *Cymbeline,*" *SP,* 69 (1972), 212-13.

[12] Shakespeare thus denies the popular humanist aesthetic: *ut pictura poesis.* The significant meanings of painting and poetry cannot be re-created by the sister art. In *Cymbeline,* a painting is not a picture of poetry; nor does poetry comprise a painting. "Such and such" are the bedchamber's paintings; "there the window; such/ Th' adornments of her bed; the arras, figures—/ Why, such and such; and the contents o' th' story" (II. ii. 25-27). Iachimo's notation, as the word "such" denotes, could not be more mundane. For the *ut pictura poesis* tradition, consult Rennselaer W. Lee, *Ut Pictura Poesis: The Humanist Theory of Painting* (New York: Norton, 1967).

[13] See, for example, *Sir Gawain and the Green Knight,* II. 619-64. The pentangle's divinity has been explained by J. A. Burrow, *A Reading of Sir Gawain and the Green Knight* (London: Routledge and Kegan Paul, 1965), pp. 187-79. Both Iachimo and Posthumus in their ignorance regard Imogen's mole as a "stain" (II. iv. 138-41).

[14] The flower portrait of the heroine occurs, for example, in Achilles Tatius' *Clitophon and Leucippe,* trans. William Burton (Oxford: B. Blackwell, 1923), p.

19; and Robert Greene's *Menaphon,* ed. G. B. Harrison (Oxford: B. Blackwell, 1927), p. 25.

[15] In *Shakespeare's Wordplay* (London: Methuen, 1965), M. M. Mahood asserts that Shakespeare in the course of his career moved from a skeptical belief that words have no inherent magic to a conviction of their "immense connotative powers," best heard in Prospero's evocative speeches (p. 181). I would argue that Shakespeare in his final period employs extraordinary speech because the multiple nuances of words frequently fail to convey special meanings.

[16] This is an epistemological convention of Renaissance pastoral. Characters in this genre personify human qualities in order to learn them better through role playing. Consult Walter R. Davis, *Idea and Act in Elizabethan Fiction* (Princeton, N.J.: Princeton Univ. Press, 1965), pp. 28-54.

[17] For some time, the unusually conceited style of this late play has been a special critical problem. See Harley Granville-Barker, *Prefaces to Shakespeare* (Princeton, N.J.: Princeton Univ. Press, 1965), II, 114; Wolfgang Clemen, *The Development of Shakespeare's Imagery,* (Cambridge, Mass.: Harvard Univ. Press, 1951), pp. 208-09; and Derek Traversi, *Shakespeare: The Last Phase,* p. 69. I am interested in discrediting the latter writers' assumption that the late Shakespeare reverted to conceits because he had not yet forged a dramatic style to express his new romance vision. The quality of the verse in *Cymbeline* is deliberately meant to express the quality of the characters' ideas. They speak conceitedly because they think conceitedly, until corrected by experience.

[18] *The New Organon,* p. 48.

[19] Shakespeare's tongue-in-cheek dramatization of Iachimo's confession may anticipate his humorous method in *The Tempest* where, perhaps provoked by a Jonsonian claim that he always violated the Unities, he has Prospero in such detail narrate crucial events prior to the circumscribed action of the play that Miranda almost dozes off.

[20] *The Decameron,* The Tudor Translations (New York: AMS Press, 1967), XLII, 209-10; and *Cymbeline,* New Arden Edition, ed. J. M. Nosworthy (London: Methuen, 1955), pp. 201-02.

[21] *Ralighes' History of Y^E World* (London: W. Stansby, 1617), p. 18.

[22] Prior to the last plays, Shakespeare negatively portrays knowledge given retrospectively by action. Hardened by crime, Macbeth states, "Strange things I have in head, that will to hand, / Which must be acted ere they may be scann'd" (III. iv. 139-40). Macbeth's

earlier, cowardly desire that his eye wink at the hand's bloody deeds is justly fulfilled. Fragmented by sin, he now must await the deed that plunges him further into guilt in order to know himself. And when Volumnia requests Coriolanus to beg votes in the marketplace, he refuses: "Lest I surcease to honour mine own truth/ And by my body's action teach my mind/ A most inherent baseness" (III. ii. 121-23). The continuity between Coriolanus' thoughts and actions is usually ragged—so much so that his lack of self-control destroys him in Corioli. Unlike that of these tragic heroes, the knowledge given retrospectively by action is not harmful for the characters of *Cymbeline*. Providence, we learn, oversees their world.

[23] *The Dramatist and the Received Idea* (Cambridge: Cambridge Univ. Press, 1968), p. 117.

[24] The etymology apparently was coined by Isidore of Seville. Consult J. A. K. Thomson, *Shakespeare and the Classics* (London: G. Allen and Unwin, 1952), p. 135. T. W. Baldwin notes the seventeenth-century criticism of it in *William Shakspere's Small Latine and Lesse Greeke* (Urbana: Univ. of Illinois Press, 1944), I, 719-20.

[25] One need only recollect Lorenzo's eloquent judgment in *The Merchant of Venice* that we could intuit divine harmony, but for our "muddy vesture of decay" (V. i. 58-65).

Joan C. Marx (essay date 1980)

SOURCE: "The Encounter of Genres: 'Cymbeline's' Structure of Juxtaposition," in *The Analysis of Literary Texts: Current Trends in Methodology,* edited by Randolph D. Pope, Bilingual Press/Editorial Bilingüe, 1980, pp. 138-44.

[*In the following essay, Marx examines the structure of* Cymbeline *in terms of its juxtaposition of different genres.*]

Dr. Johnson dismissed *Cymbeline* as "unresisting imbecility," and only slightly politer versions of his opinion held sway until the 1930's when Shakespeare's last plays (*Pericles, Cymbeline, The Winter's Tale, The Tempest*) were first considered as a group and admired for their optimistic romantic vision, their reconciliations of kingdoms and families, of man and a beneficent Providence.[1] Yet *Cymbeline* is still regarded as the group's bewildering poor relation. E. M. W. Tillyard, one of the first supporters of the late plays, viewed *Cymbeline* as a mixture of disparate elements which blurred and ran together in a "welter of unreality," and after seeing a 1974 Royal Shakespeare production, Frank Kermode suggested that we no longer know what structure the first audience ever found in

the play: "the loss of some code . . . [can] make something that was originally well formed look like an untidy mess."[2]

It is not my purpose to argue that a minor Shakespearean drama has the power and beauty of a major play, but rather, by employing the method of genre criticism, to suggest that *Cymbeline*'s structure is quite different from what it has been assumed and that a clearer perception of this structure will make the play livelier and more coherent than modern critiques and productions allow.

As a drama whose plot elements include the machinations of a wicked stepmother Queen, the lustful pursuits of a court fop, the Welsh mountain life of two kidnapped princes, Jupiter's descent from the sky, the hero's testing in an Italian jealousy plot like *Othello's,* the princess' disguise as a pageboy, and the invasion of Britain by Imperial Rome, *Cymbeline* gives cause to those who find it a mixture of disparate elements. Yet I will argue that the play has seemed inchoate because its actual structure consists in juxtaposition, in unmediated and sharp contrast not only of characters but of scenes. These scenes are so distinct in nature and so discretely rendered that we are justified in calling them bits of different genres. It has been the attempt to blur these different genres—among them fairytale, satire, Italian intrigue, chronicle, and pastoral romance—into a uniform whole which has created the sensation of welter. For *Cymbeline*'s energy and coherence lie in the contrast of its different genre worlds.

As a technique, juxtaposition is common to all Shakespeare's plays: the Porter's sleepy muttering of Hell after Duncan's murder, Antony's majestic declaration, "Kingdoms are clay," just after Philo scoffs at him as a strumpet's fool." These are only two among countless instances in the plays when a new action or view supplies a fresh and striking context to the scene before. But to find juxtaposition serving as a play's major structural device, as it does in *Cymbeline,* is rarer; we see it in *Love's Labour's Lost* and *As You Like It,* two plays where there is almost no plot action and the energy and sense of movement are largely created by thrusting together contrasting characters and scenes.[3] What makes *Cymbeline* remarkable is that, unlike the other two plays which use juxtaposition as their structure, it also has plot events to move its characters from one action and place to another, from Wales to Italy.

Let me describe *Cymbeline*'s structure more precisely by comparing two moments in *Cymbeline* and *As You Like It,* a comparison which will help to make clear *Cymbeline*'s contrasts of genres and the abruptness of those contrasts. In both plays, characters with different, discrete styles are allowed to interact, Touchstone with Corin in Arden and Cloten with Guiderius in Wales, and our pleasure lies in hearing the encounter of their styles.[4] In *As You Like It,* Corin asks, "And how like you this shepherd's life, Master Touchstone?" and Touchstone replies:

> In respect that it is solitary, I like it very well; but in respect that it is private, it is a very vile life. Now in respect that it is in the fields, it pleaseth me well; but in respect it is not in the court, it is tedious (III.ii.15-18).[5]

Then Touchstone asks in turn for the shepherd's "philosophy," and, hearing that he has never been to court, pronounces him "damn'd." So in *Cymbeline* when the courtly Cloten and the pastoral Guiderius meet in the Welsh mountains, they too question each other, though this time it is the pastoral figure who has the best of it. Cloten demands, "What slave art thou?"; Guiderius returns, "What art thou?" Cloten responds with a puff of his garments, "Know'st me not by my clothes?" But Guiderius only laughs at "the tailor . . . thy grandfather."

However, the encounters of *As You Like It,* its contrasts of characters, take place within a unified whole; the play establishes the likeness of its two worlds, court and forest, and it rings with a single tone. *Cymbeline* uses none of the same techniques to establish one mellow world; instead, its juxtaposition is like a force of gravity, pulling together objects of unlike mass as the play speeds towards its end.

In *As You Like It,* the forest's special tone of leisure and civility silvers the air. Touchstone and Corin stroll together,/stroking out their differences without a spark of acrimony, rather with a pleasure in the parley. Touchstone pricks at Corin's descriptions of country manners with "Instance, briefly; come, instance," and when Touchstone pronounces, "You are damn'd," the shepherd counters, "For not being at court: Your reason." They are gracefully fencing in the manner of Lyly's characters, who rejoice in their debates, even though, unlike Lyly's characters, they have wide differences in viewpoint.

Moreover, though the court's ingratitude separates it from the forest, Arden shares its civility of style and manner with the court, as Orlando's exaggerated fears of the alien "desert" help to make clear. After charging the Duke's feast with drawn sword, he appeals to the desert inhabitants by whatever touch of civilization they may have known, if they have been "where bells have knoll'd to church," and his appeal calls forth the ceremonious echoes of the Duke, his reply that he has "with holy bell been knoll'd to church." Their shared language, these echoes in themselves, are the sign of their shared manners.[6]

Cymbeline, on the other hand, is not blended into such a whole. When Cloten and Guiderius encounter each other, they clash together as two very different qualities; their encounter lacks the light tone, the civil play, that mediates between Touchstone and Corin. Since Cloten and Guiderius see each other, challenge, and then duel, they are bound to give the effect of division, but their language further reveals their isolation.

> Gui.   Say what thou art:
> Why I should yield to thee.
> Clo.   Thou villain base,
> Know'st me not by my clothes?
> Gui.   No, nor thy tailor, rascal,
> Who is thy grandfather; he made those
>   clothes,
> Which, as it seems, make thee.
>   . . . . .
> Clo.   To thy further fear.
> Nay, to thy mere confusion, thou shalt
>   know
> I am son to th' Queen.
> Gui.   I am sorry for't; not seeming
> So worthy as thy birth.
> Clo.   Art not afeard?
> Gui. Those that I reverence, those I fear—the
>   wise:
> At fools I laugh, not fear them.
>   (IV.ii.80-97)

Unlike Orlando, Cloten keeps expecting that the pastoral world will be like the court. But whereas Orlando's tentative claims were reassuringly echoed, knolling bell to knolling bell, Cloten's terms are neatly opposed. His clothes mean nothing to Guiderius and to his "I am the son to th' Queen," comes "I am sorry for't; not seeming / So worthy as thy birth."

The two characters step forward from quite different worlds, which they seem to pull behind them. We recognize these two worlds, for each has earlier occupied whole scenes: there have been short scenes of Cloten, the court dandy and fool, bowling and swearing (I.iii, II.i, II.iii), other scenes of Guiderius and his fellows in Wales, bowing to the sun and returning from the hunt (III.iii, III.vii). And in these scenes Cloten and Guiderius have set and controlled the tone of the scenes in a way that single characters in *As You Like It,* touchstone and Corin, for example, never have.

Indeed in *Cymbeline* we are watching the extraordinary confrontation of two genres, the comic butt of satire, Cloten, and the hero of pastoral, Guiderius, meeting at swordpoint, each gesturing in the most conventional terms of his genre and finding his mirror image responding. The foolish satire butt is flaunting his elegant clothes, the sign of rank, a moment made for a satiric commentator who could flay the world that allows such a discrepancy between worth and birth. Guiderius, solidly noble in the simplest of clothes, completely ignores the flap of Cloten's clothing and as simply as he is dressed, declares his allegiance to moral categories that discard social rank: "Those that I reverence, those I fear—the wise." As the hero of the pastoral romance, his worth is completely consistent with his birth, but he has been temporarily divested of social recognition.

In fact, the question with which Guiderius judges Cloten, "Art thou 'so worthy as thy birth'?"—a demand that moral worth equal social rank—is fundamental to both pastoral and satire. The two genres are mirror images of each other,[7] each asking the same question but from polar perspectives. Thus the encounter makes us perceive the difference and likeness between two genre worlds, their fundamental values and the relationship of those values.

Since Cloten and Guiderius step forward from distinctly different, neatly opposed worlds, and there is no mediation between them, they seem, as we have said, to pull those worlds behind them; it is as if their two genres have clashed. This effect of the abrupt juxtaposition of qualitatively different worlds is typical and essential in *Cymbeline*. Cloten and Guiderius' particular encounter is uncommon only in that this effect arises from the meeting of two characters. For, although there are other such meetings, such as that of Roman Lucius and pastoral Fidele, the Italians and the British knight, the play is constructed so that unmediated juxtapositions are usually felt between two scenes rather than two characters.

Typical of *Cymbeline* is the opening of the play with the First Gentleman's lament of Posthumus' banishment, a sorrow stirred by the absolute value of Posthumus' person and character: "I do not think/So fair an outward and such stuff within/Endows a man but he." All the court is of his mind, he says, although the King and Queen mistakenly preferred Cloten, "a thing/Too bad for bad report" as the bridegroom. When the scene shifts to Rome, again it opens with a discussion of Posthumus, his marriage, his banishment: "We had very many there [in France] could behold the sun with as firm eyes as he." Surely, Iachimo suggests, his banishment has been a sentimental temptation to excuse his ordinary character and the princess' mistake. Rome sounds quite different, cynical, shaded, doubting. Philario's protest only underlines the way in which the opinion of the First Gentleman and all the British court is being reshaped: "You speak of him when he was less furnished than now he is with that which makes him both without and within." In effect Philario has already accepted a modified judgment of the young Posthumus. We seem to have shifted worlds—the same man, the same issues, but quite differently received.

Or the worldly travelers of the Italian novella, visiting Philario with their talk of thieves, accomplished courtiers, reputation, and the sale of "ladies' flesh," with-

draw from the stage, and we hear, "While yet the dew's on ground, gather these flowers." It is the stepmother Queen in her garden, preparing to make her fairytale poisons. Or Cloten chatters crudely of "fingering" and "penetration" in a morning of court satire which follows Iachimo's midnight, hushed veneration of "Cytherea." The pastoral hunters withdraw and the Roman senators appear. Posthumus rages offstage at the climax of the Italian plot swearing his revenge on Imogen, and the state council of a chronicle scene begins. Or there will be two scenes not immediately juxtaposed but borne together by their similarity: Iachimo adores Imogen at midnight in the sensuous Ovidian mode; her body creates the aura of a "chapel" around her in which he worships the rubies of her lips, the eyelids "azure lac'd." Then Belarius, in daylight, moves toward the cave and finds Imogen, and he too marvels; he sees "an angel," an "earthly paragon."

Thus *Cymbeline's* juxtaposition causes different worlds, fairytale Britain and Italianate Rome, pastoral Wales and the Roman Empire, to meet up without attempting to mitigate, indeed exploiting, their differences. Each supplants the other in the play's progress, and since these shifts are not ruled by one tone or set of attitudes, as were the juxtapositions in *As You Like It,* each new scene demands that the audience choose its viewpoint, or at least recognize its tone and attitude, as a new alternative.

For as the play thrusts these different genres together, we are made to recognize the differences in their perspectives. Both the Queen and Iachimo love secrecy, poison, intrigue, but the power of the Italian indirection is much greater than the lucid fairytale evil. The Queen fools only her husband; Imogen and the entire court perceive her "dissembling courtesy" immediately. Therefore, when the Italian courtiers leave the stage and the Queen appears with her poison in the garden, we are right to feel that this is a "morning" evil, much easier to take and less threatening than a shrug which assumes women unfaithful and their infidelity indiscernable, than the bitter distillation of gossip and resentment in Rome.[8] Or we see that the moral pillars, the clear, absolute judgments of a thing too good, a thing too bad, of the fairytale opening are simply not part of the structure of the Italian novella world. There is no idealizing in that cynical world—with one exception. Shakespeare endows Iachimo with the Ovidian tongue to intensify our vision of the Italian marvelling before the body, the one unguarded adoration allowed in the Italian novella genre. Belarius is struck by the same beautiful body, but his pastoral romance admiration is for the spirit he sees. In his genre, the body declares the spirit.[9] Posthumus' angry refusal to continue to "pay tribute" to Imogen and his fervid wish that men no longer be dependent on women are part of his proud insistence on independence; after sorrowing at his fierce, mistaken anguish on Iachimo's return, we cannot help but question the national independence proclaimed by the Queen in the council scene which follows.[10] Yet in the chronicle genre complete independence is a possibility for nations as it can never be for the lovers of a novela.

If the play is produced with each scene played distinctly, each genre given its due, we will be able to mark *Cymbeline's* structural continuities and the play of values against one another: the repetition of the first scene, the versions of idealizing, the visions of indirect evil. The Queen and her doctor can both be played as fairytale figures; there is no need to make this stepmother "sultry" or to muffle the perfect click with which Cornelius, the good servant, supplies missing, needed information to the finale.[11] But on the other hand, their clear absolutes of good and evil belong to their particular genre: there is also no need to blur other genres in the play to accord with theirs, to suppress Iachimo's wonder at Imogen's beauty, for example, as the 1974 Royal Shakespeare did, or to choreograph the chronicle battle, or to cut out Cloten's small-minded, static scenes of court satire.[12] Granville-Barker's notion of "artlessness" which "displays art," perceptive and important as it is, has proved a particular critical temptation to stir all the genres of the play together.[13] The recent Royal Shakespeare production, for instance, concentrated on the play as a self-conscious "fictional construct"[14] and, to dramatize this focus, used Cornelius as a presenter figure throughout it to smooth out all disjunctures and difficulties. According to Frank Kermode, Cornelius would continually call to the audience "by means of interpolated speeches, winks, shrugs, and leers," to make them recognize that "the whole thing is actually meant to be naive or absurd."[15] The result—the play appeared "an untidy mess."

Cymbeline is a play which consists of our looking out from one genre to another and our learning to recognize their different visions, to feel the air of their different worlds. It is a minor Shakespearean play because each of the genres remains simple, its plot and characters stereotyped, but acted as it is written, the play offers bare, exciting glimpses of genres' essential and differing values, and these views juxtaposed form a clear and lively whole.

Notes

[1] Samuel Johnson, "*Cymbeline*," *Samuel Johnson: Notes to Shakespeare,* ed. Arthur Sherbo, 3:2 (Los Angeles: Univ. of California, 1958).

[2] E. M. W. Tillyard, *Shakespeare's Last Plays* (London: Chatto and Windus, 1938), p. 76; Frank Kermode, "*Cymbeline* at Stratford," *TLS* (5 July 1974), p. 710. For other examples, see Arthur Kirsch on the play's

lack of "coherency," in "*Cymbeline*" and Coterie Dramaturgy," *ELH* 34 (1967), pp. 285-306; Emrys Jones on its "central fumbling"; Murray Schwartz's judgment that it is "unsatisfying drama," in "Between Fantasy and Imagination: A Psychological Exploration of *Cymbeline*," *Psychoanalysis and Literary Process,* ed. Frederick Crews (Cambridge, Mass.: Winthrop Pub., 1970), p. 283.

[3] Harold Jenkins, "*As You Like It,*" *Shakespeare Survey 8* (1955), rpt. in *Shakespeare: Modern Essays in Criticism,* ed. Leonard F. Dean (New York: Oxford Univ. Press, 1957), pp. 108-27.

[4] *Ibid.,* pp. 125, 121. "Encounter" is Jenkins' term.

[5] All Cymbeline quotations are from the Arden edition, ed. J. M. Nosworthy (Cambridge, Mass.: Harvard Univ. Press, 1955). All other references to Shakespeare's plays will be to the edition of Peter Alexander: *William Shakespeare: The Complete Works* (London: Collins, 1951).

[6] From a lecture by Donald Friedman, Univ of California, Berkeley, 1964.

[7] Northrop Frye similarly remarks on a mirroring of irony and romance in *Anatomy of Criticism* (New York: Atheneum, 1957), pp. 162 ff.; satire and pastoral are their respective sub-genres.

[8] *Shakespeare and the Comedy of Forgiveness* (New York, Columbia Univ. Press, 1965), p. 151.

[9] See Edmund Spenser's *The Faerie Queene,* III, v, p. 35 and VI, ix, pp. 11 ff. for other examples of this convention.

[10] D. R. C. Marsh discusses this relationship of isolation between the two scenes in *The Recurring Miracle* (Pietermaritzburg: Univ. of Natal Press, 1962), pp. 50 ff.

[11] Joan Miller played a "sultry" Queen in the Straford 1957 production, according to J. C. Trewin, *Shakespeare on the English Stage 1900-64* (London: Barrie and Rockliff, 1964), p. 238. J. R. Brown discusses the laughter Cornelius' pat timing can cause in *Shakespeare's Plays in Performance* (London: Edward Arnold Ltd., 1966), p. 108.

[12] Frank Kermode reported Iachimo's exchange of "turbulence" for "banter" in the bedroom scene, in "*Cymbeline* at Stratford," *TLS* (5 July 1974), p. 710. The Old Vic staged a battle with "eurhythmic movement" in 1932, according to J. C. Trewin, *Shakespeare on the English Stage 1900-1964,* p. 140, and Derek Traversi wishes there were fewer Cloten scenes in *Shakespeare: The Last Phase,* p. 58. In contrast, James

Edward Siemon suggests the need for all the court satire scenes by pointing out neat parallels between Cloten's actions and Posthumus', in "Noble Virtue in *Cymbeline*," *Shakespeare Survey* 29 (1976), pp. 55-61.

[13] "*Cymbeline*," *Prefaces to Shakespeare*, II, p. 94.

[14] From the program note.

[15] "*Cymbeline* at Stratford," p. 710.

Ann Thompson (essay date 1991)

SOURCE: "Person and Office: The Case of Imogen, Princess of Britain," in *Literature and Nationalism*, edited by Vincent Newley and Ann Thompson, Liverpool University Press, 1991, pp. 76-87.

[*In this essay; Thompson studies the character of Imogen, concentrating on her inner conflict between personal desires and royal duties.*]

In his British Academy lecture of 1970, *Person and Office in Shakespeare's Plays*, Philip Edwards explored the relationship between self and professional role, private and public being, asking whether the role-theory of 1960s sociology (as exemplified by the work of Erving Goffman) was appropriate to a discussion of Shakespeare's plays. Rejecting as anachronistic the cynical (but currently fashionable) assumption that the private self is always estranged from the public self and that the latter must inevitably be a falsification of the former, he differentiated between two Shakespearean models:

> I argue, then, that Shakespeare presents two views of man; one, in which there is a continuum of the person and his public activities, an amalgam so complete that it is impossible to distinguish what a man is from what he is accustomed to do; the second, in which there is an autonomous and plastic self, urging itself forward and adapting to the various moulds available to it, in such a way that we are always aware of the separateness of the person and his office.[1]

Richard II and King Lear represent the first view, 'the idea of unity of being, in which the person and his office, the private and the public being, are coextensive and inseparable',[2] while Prince Hal represents the second view, 'the idea of an adjustable and compliant self, which can change when it is necessary from companion to king, and keep a certain detachment from either activity'.[3] The first view, it is observed, is most often associated with tragedy, or tragical history:

> It is strange that the condition of unified being is usually shown as something unattainable, or

discarded, or destroyed. Lear and Richard throw a pearl away, richer than all their tribe. Hamlet is denied that office which alone could define him and make him a whole man: there is never the 'doing' which can complete his 'being', so during the whole play he is a soul without a body, like a ghost.[4]

By contrast, it is implied that the second view is associated with comedy, or comical history, but the lecture does not have room for an exploration of comedy as such; nor does it consider any female characters. *Person and Office* was a brilliant lecture, which I was privileged to attend as a postgraduate student. Reading it now, while wrestling with the multiple problems of *Cymbeline* for a projected edition, I have found it productive to ask what does happen if the person in question is a woman and the genre tragicomedy.

Imogen is clearly defined by her office as Princess of Britain. She is described by the First Gentleman in the play's opening scene as the king's daughter 'and the heir of's kingdom' (I.i.4).[5] He does not name her in this scene, but refers to her twice as 'the princess' (I.i.16, I.i.69), a title which is used frequently by other characters as the action proceeds. Posthumus calls her 'my queen' in the first Act (I.ii.23, I.ii.30, and as reported by Pisanio at I.iv.5), and even Cloten admits she is 'royal' (III.v.71). Her very name, first mentioned by herself at I.ii.45, associates her with the ancient British nobility—that is if we assume it should be 'Innogen', the name of the wife of Brutus, legendary founder of Britain.[6] When Thomas D'Urfey adapted *Cymbeline* during the Restoration he retitled it *The Injured Princess, or the Fatal Wager*,[7] and the actress Helena Faucit, writing at the height of nineteenth-century 'Imogenolatry', likewise suggested that *Imogen, Princess of Britain* might be a better title for Shakespeare's version.[8] It has been widely claimed, both by performers and by critics, that Imogen has a regal bearing (perhaps most obviously in her contemptuous treatment of Iachimo in I.vii and Cloten in II.iii, and in her assurance of Pisanio in III.iv that she will go through with her adventure in male disguise 'with / A prince's courage'); even George Bernard Shaw, who wanted Ellen Terry to separate the 'real woman' in Imogen from the 'idiotic paragon', insisted that she was 'a natural aristocrat'.[9]

Imogen identifies herself with her country when she comments sadly in response to Iachimo's false reports of Posthumus' behaviour in Rome, 'My lord, I fear, / Has forgot Britain' (I.vii.112-13),[10] and this identification is made by other characters, notably by both Posthumus and Iachimo in Act V. Posthumus remarks in soliloquy:

> I am brought hither
> Among th'Italian gentry, and to fight

Against my lady's kingdom: 'tis enough
That, Britain, I have kill'd thy mistress:
   peace,[11]
I'll give no wound to thee.

                  (V.i.17-21)

In the next scene, Posthumus, in his disguise as a
poor soldier, *'vanquisheth and disarmeth'* Iachimo who
rationalizes his defeat by saying

             I have belied a lady,
The princess of this country; and the air on't
Revengingly enfeebles me.

                  (V.ii.2-4)

Only once is it suggested that Imogen is not a true
princess at all, when Iachimo urges her to reciprocate
Posthumus' supposed infidelity:

                Be reveng'd,
Or she that bore you was no queen, and
   you
Recoil from your great stock.

              (I.vii.126-28)

While the play does not seriously question Imogen's
legitimacy, it does require her to give up her kingdom,
to separate herself from her office. Her wicked step-
mother-Queen consciously plots her elimination, explaining 'She being down, / I have the placing of the
British crown' (III.v.65-66), but more powerful forces
are at work. From the very beginning we are alerted to
the narrative inevitability of Imogen's displacement
when, in response to the question 'Is she sole child to
the King?', the First Gentleman says

            His only child.
He had two sons (if this be worth your
   hearing,
Mark it) the eldest of them at three years old,
I'th'swathing-clothes the other, from their
   nursery
Were stol'n; and to this hour no guess in
   knowledge
Which way they went.

               (I.i.56-61)

What auditor or reader is so naive as not to realize that
if missing children are mentioned in the first scene of
a play they will be found before the last one? We
know, before we even meet her, that Imogen is sched-
uled to be superseded by her brothers. (Whether they
in fact preceded her in birth is not absolutely clear, but
as males they would in any case take priority.) This
might be expected to be an unhappy experience for
her: as Philip Edwards has noted, 'The pain of being
superseded is the subject of much of Shakespeare's
work',[12] but Imogen is a tragicomic heroine rather
than a tragic hero and the play insists on the rightness,

even the desirability, of her dispossession. When her
brothers, the true heirs, first appear in III.iii, we are
assured of their natural, princely qualities by their
foster-father Belarius, who remarks in soliloquy 'How
hard it is to hide the sparks of nature!' (III.iii.79) and
describes how the royal blood manifests itself, especially in 'This Polydore, / The heir of Cymbeline and
Britain' (III.iii.86-87). He repeats this point in further
speeches (IV.ii.169-81 and IV.iv.50-54), and the young
men finally get a chance to prove their worth by their
heroic actions in the battle in V.ii. Jupiter himself
predicts their restoration to their proper position in the
'tablet' he leaves with Posthumus in V.iv. (138-45).

Imogen, meanwhile, is presented as something of an
heiress *manquée* in so far as she does not actually
perform the duties of her office. She is in disgrace at
the beginning of the play and literally absent from her
official role for large stretches of it. Although in court
at the time, she does not take part in the reception of
the delegacy from Rome in III.i, nor in the burst of
defiant, patriotic rhetoric which issues from the Queen,
Cymbeline and even Cloten in that scene. Cymbeline
comments on her absence later (III.v.30-32), but seems
to miss merely her emotional supportiveness (he calls
her 'The great part of my comfort' at IV.iii.5), whereas
in political and military matters he relies on 'the counsel of my son and queen' (IV.iii.27). She runs away
from court, and expresses her determination never to
return to it even before Pisanio discloses his plan for
her survival (III.iv.108-09, 133-36). When he tells her,
'If not at court, / Then not in Britain must you bide'
(III.iv.136-37), she responds sharply:

   Hath Britain all the sun that shines? Day?
     Night?
   Are they not but in Britain? I'th'world's
     volume
   Our Britain seems as of it, but not in't:
   In a great pool, a swan's nest: prithee think
   There's livers out of Britain.

              (III.iv.138-42)

This slighting reference to her own country is the
more remarkable given that the notion of Britain as 'a
world beyond the world' occurs elsewhere in this text
and in other texts of the period as a wholly positive,
even sentimental saying.[13] And although Imogen does
not in fact achieve her ambition to leave Britain, she
finally reappears before her father as the follower and
attentive servant of his chief enemy.

Moreover, she is at best a reluctant heiress. In her
opening scene she voices an escapist fantasy—

           Would I were
   A neat-herd's daughter, and my Leonatus
   Our neighbour-shepherd's son!

               (I.ii.79-81)

and in her soliloquy in I.vii she both reminds us of her own false position as heir and envies her disinherited brothers:

> Had I been thief-stolen,
> As my two brothers, happy: but most
>   miserable
> Is the desire that's glorious. Bless'd be
>   those,
> How mean soe'er, that have their honest
>   wills,
> Which seasons comfort.
>
> (I.vii.5-9)

When she eventually meets 'Polydore' and 'Cadwal' in Wales she wishes that they were really her brothers:

> would it had been so, that they
> Had been my father's sons, then had my
>   prize
> Been less, and so more equal ballasting
> To thee, Posthumus.
>
> (III.vii.48-52)

In some ways she seems to fit more comfortably into the pastoral world than do the young men who feel frustrated and imprisoned by it (III.iii.27-44): she takes to the simple life of the cave, enhancing and domesticating it with her singing and her 'neat cookery' (IV.ii.48-49), and seems almost to have become a part of nature, a bird or a flower, by the time of her supposed death (IV.ii.197-203).

While it is not apparent to Imogen as it is to us that her brothers are going to be found, she has her own reasons for wishing to shed her role as royal heiress. These are of course, as my last three quotations from the play demonstrate, related to her marriage: like other Shakespearean heirs such as Hamlet and Florizel, her capacity to 'carve for herself' is restricted. While it seems from Gertrude's words at Ophelia's grave that Laertes was wrong to think that a marriage between Hamlet and his sister would have been thought unsuitable, and Florizel's marriage to Perdita can be saved by the discovery that she is a king's daughter after all, Imogen's marriage to Posthumus can only be saved by the discovery that she is not the real heir.[14]

Imogen's problem is quite simply that she is 'worth more' than her husband, a point which is constantly emphasized throughout the play. Posthumus himself is acutely conscious of it in I.ii when he remarks that even her parting gift to him is more valuable than his to her:

> As I my poor self did exchange for you
> To your so infinite loss; so in our trifles
> I still win of you.
>
> (I.ii.50-52)

Other characters see him from the same perspective, as when Iachimo suggests that his virtues have been overestimated:

> This matter of his marrying his king's daughter,
> wherein he must be weighed rather by her value
> than his own, words him (I doubt not) a great deal
> from the matter.
>
> (I.iv.12-15)

Cymbeline deplores the lowliness of Imogen's choice, calling Posthumus 'Thou basest thing' (I.i.56) and telling his daughter

> Thou took'st a beggar, wouldst have made my
>   throne
> A seat for baseness.
>
> (I.i.72-73)

Cloten articulates the view that the difference in worth is so great that the marriage can simply be set aside:

> The contract you pretend with that base
>   wretch,
> One bred of alms, and foster'd with cold
>   dishes,
> With scraps o'th'court, it is no contract, none;
> And though it be allow'd in meaner parties
> (Yet who than he more mean?) to knit their
>   souls
> (On whom there is no more dependency
> But brats and beggary) in self-figur'd knot,
> Yet you are curb'd from that enlargement,
>   by
> The consequence o'th'crown, and must not
>   foil
> The precious note of it; with a base slave,
> A hilding or a livery, a squire's cloth,
> A pantler; not so eminent.
>
> (II.iii.112-23)

Even Pisanio, shocked by Posthumus' unjust accusations against Imogen, comments

> O my master,
> Thy mind to her is now as low as were
> Thy fortunes.
>
> (III.ii.9-11)

This inbuilt disparity seems a significant factor in the extraordinary turn of events whereby Posthumus, unlike every other Shakespearean hero in his position, is ultimately prepared to forgive his wife for her supposed adultery. In two major soliloquies he stresses that she is *still* worth more than he is even though she is, as he thinks, guilty of what is taken elsewhere in the canon to be the worst crime a woman can commit. In V.i he first repents having given orders for her murder, saying

> You married ones,
> If each of you should take this course, how
>   many
> Must murder wives much better than
>   themselves
> For wrying but a little?
>
> (V.i.2-5)

She is still 'The noble Imogen' (10) and her infidelity a 'little fault' (12); he assures the gods that 'Imogen is your own' (16) and that he himself is 'more worth your vengeance' (11). This theme is continued three scenes later when he implores the gods

> For Imogen's dear life take mine, and though
> 'Tis not so dear, yet 'tis a life; you coin'd it.
>
> (V.iv.22-23)

One way in which the play redresses this balance is to emphasize Posthumus' virtues or 'inner worth' to a quite extravagant extent. He is described as a paragon by the First Gentleman in the opening scene (I.i.22-53), and Imogen herself insists on his superiority in justifying her choice (especially when she compares him with Cloten); like her brothers he proves himself in battle in the last Act, and he is endorsed by the ghosts of his own family and by Jupiter in V.iv. The effect is at times almost suggestive of a split personality, as when Iachimo swings from describing Posthumus 'vaulting variable ramps' in Rome to declaring that 'He sits 'mongst men like a descended god' (I.vii.134, 169), or again in the last scene when the praise—

> the good Posthumus
> (What should I say? he was too good to be
> Where ill men were, and was the best of all
> Among'st the rar'st of good ones)
>
> (V.v.157-60)

—seems at odds with the actual behaviour being described. This division in the character is further emphasized by the way that both Iachimo and Cloten seem to be surrogates for Posthumus, expressing and enacting the darker side of his feelings towards Imogen.

But while Posthumus must be built up, Imogen must also be brought down. Cloten, angered in particular by her contemptuous comparison of him with Posthumus, wants to humiliate her as well as to rape her:

> when my lust hath dined . . . to the court I'll knock her back, foot her home again. She hath despised me rejoicingly, and I'll be merry in my revenge.
>
> (III.v.143-47)

Her male disguise does not give her the greater scope and freedom afforded to earlier Shakespearean hero-ines. Pisanio tells her she must display 'a waggish courage' and be 'Ready in gibes, quick-answer'd, saucy, and / As quarrelous as the weasel' (III.iv.159-61), evoking our memory of Rosalind as Ganymede, but Imogen/Fidele is characterized rather by silence and timidity. The cave-dwellers respond immediately to her 'feminine' qualities despite her disguise and install her as their 'housewife' (IV.ii.45), while her increasing feebleness and passivity turn into illness and apparent death. Although we know during the very moving funeral speeches and dirge in the later part of IV.ii that she is not really dead (we have after all been assured by Cornelius that what he has given the queen is not a mortal poison but merely a drug which will 'stupefy and dull the sense awhile' (I.vi.37)), there is a level on which Imogen has to die as an heiress in order to be re-born as a wife. Even after reviving from this 'death', she has to undergo the traumatic (and humiliating) experience of mistaking the headless body of Cloten for that of her husband, and she tells Lucius who finds her, 'I am nothing; or if not, / Nothing to be were better' (IV.ii.367-68). She continues to display her 'feminine' qualities as his 'nurse-like' servant (V.v.88) until she is finally restored to (or put in) her place at the cathartic moment when Posthumus hits her hard enough for Pisanio to think he has killed her (V.v.229-31).

Much has been made of the emphasis on revitalization and reunion at the end of the play. On the political level, Philip Edwards argued in *Threshold of a Nation* that we should finally see Britain and Rome as partners rather than Britain superseding Rome in its imperial role:

> the play is not talking about the succession of empires but about the only true form of empire, which is when vassalage is removed, and union is a contract freely entered into.[15]

He has reiterated this idea in his most recent book on Shakespeare:

> In both *Henry V* and *Cymbeline* there is an idea of empire in which, though one country is dominant, the image of the alliance is marriage and not serfdom.[16]

Marriage is not after all in this play or in this period an *equal* partnership: *Cymbeline* has gone to some trouble to show that a marriage in which the wife 'outweighs' her husband too much is in fact a misalliance.

The reunion of Posthumus and Imogen and the restoration of Cymbeline's heirs go together, as the twice-read 'tablet' insists, but the negative consequence for Imogen is pointed out immediately by Cymbeline: 'O Imogen, / Thou hast lost by this a kingdom.' She replies, 'No, my Lord; / I have got two worlds by't' (V.v.373-75). These lines have very rarely been cut in performance, even in those versions which most radically abbreviate and alter the last scene.[17] They were much quoted and admired by Victorian 'Imogenolaters', who saw the heroine's character exemplified in this magnanimous reply, remarking that 'This sweet soul knows no low ambitious promptings' and that she 'loses without a pang the heirship to a kingdom'.[18] It was indeed an important element in their idealization of her that she should be so prepared to give up her public office, so much the model wife in her unselfishness and self-sacrifice. Modern feminist critics are, as one would expect, less enthusiastic about this outcome. Marilyn L. Williamson, for example, who subtitles her chapter on the Romances 'Patriarchy, Pure and Simple', comments:

> The power of women in these plays is strictly procreative and conciliatory: even the spunkiest of them has no desire for political authority, especially if it disturbs her husband's equilibrium.[19]

In *Cymbeline* even the procreative function is finally transferred to men as the king describes himself as 'mother to the birth of three' (V.v.370) and the Soothsayer looks forward to the 'issue' of the King's male heirs (V.v.458).

So in the case of Imogen, one must conclude, the division between person and office is presented as entirely right and proper. Neither authentic nor happy in her role as heir to the kingdom, she can only be fulfilled by dwindling into 'this most constant wife' (V.v.450). A modern response may, however, find room for uneasiness at some of the strategies employed to bring her down to this level, and at the insistence on defining royal power as male, both in the post-Elizabethan period of the play's composition and in the Victorian period when it was so extravagantly popular.

Notes

[1] Philip Edwards, *Person and Office in Shakespeare's Plays,* Annual Lecture of the British Academy (London, 1970), p. 15.

[2] Ibid., p. 13.

[3] Ibid., p. 15.

[4] Ibid., p. 15.

[5] All *Cymbeline* quotations are from the New Arden text, ed. J. M. Nosworthy (London, 1955).

[6] I do accept 'Innogen', which has been proposed by a number of critics and editors, most notably by Emrys

Jones in 'Stuart *Cymbeline'*, *Essays in Criticism,* 11 (1961), pp. 84-99. This version of the name first appeared in an edited text in the Oxford *Complete Works,* ed. Stanley Wells and Gary Taylor (Oxford, 1986), and was used on stage in the London National Theatre production in 1988. I am, however, retaining the incorrect form 'Imogen' here since it is used by the Arden editor (against his better judgement: see his note on I.ii.0. SD) and by all the critics I cite.

[7] This version was printed in 1682 and probably performed in that year, though D'Urfey claims in the epilogue to have made the adaptation nine years previously. It supplanted Shakespeare's original on the stage until 1744 or 1746.

[8] Helena Faucit, Lady Martin, *On Some of Shakespeare's Female Characters* (London, 1885), p. 209. Faucit was much acclaimed for her performances as Imogen. While the other chapters in her book are headed simply 'Ophelia', 'Portia' and so forth, she herself uses the title 'Imogen, Princess of Britain' for this one.

[9] *Ellen Terry and Bernard Shaw: A Correspondence,* ed. Christopher St John (New York, 1931), p. 36. (Shaw's letter is dated 6 September 1896.)

[10] It is remarkable that out of 26 usages of the word 'Britain' in the Shakespeare canon, 23 occur in *Cymbeline.* This has been related to the topical issue of the desire of James I to unite England and Scotland as 'Great Britain'. See Emrys Jones as cited in n.6 above; Philip Edwards, *Threshold of a Nation* (Cambridge, 1979), pp. 87-94; and Leah S. Marcus, '*Cymbeline* and the Unease of Topicality', in *The Historical Renaissance,* ed. Heather Dubrow and Richard Strier (Chicago, 1988), pp. 134-68.

[11] The Oxford *Complete Works* reads 'mistress-piece' here, an emendation suggested by Staunton in 1873 (*Athenaeum,* 14 June), but not hitherto adopted by any edition. It would of course help to emphasize my point.

[12] *Nationalist Theatres: Shakespeare and Yeats,* University of Liverpool Inaugural Lecture (Liverpool, 1976), p. 19. See also his *Shakespeare and the Confines of Art* (London, 1968) p. 5 and *Person and Office,* pp. 16-17.

[13] See Philip Edwards, *Threshold of a Nation,* p. 88.

[14] It is curious, in this context, that George Bernard Shaw's *Cymbeline Refinished* was not performed at Stratford as originally intended in 1937 because it was thought to allude to the abdication of Edward VIII. This topical reference was more obvious because Shaw made Polydore/Guiderius refuse to become crown

prince partly on the grounds that he would be 'Not free to wed the woman of my choice'.

[15] *Threshold of a Nation,* p. 93.

[16] *Shakespeare: A Writer's Progress* (Oxford, 1986), p. 124.

[17] A partial exception is the version by William Hawkins, performed in 1758-59 and published in 1759, in which these lines are followed by the decision of 'Palador' to share the kingdom with his brother Cadwal and to give Imogen the 'moiety' previously intended for Cloten.

[18] See Anna Jameson, *Shakespeare's Heroines* (London, 1897), p. 199; Louis Lewes, *The Women of Shakespeare,* tr. Helen Zimmern (London, 1895), p. 340; William Winter, typescript of a commentary prepared for Viola Allen's acting version (1905), Folger Library (*Cymbeline,* Folio 1), p. ix.

[19] *The Patriarchy of Shakespeare's Comedies* (Detroit, 1986), p. 154.

CYMBELINE AND IMOGEN

Charles K. Hofling (essay date 1965)

SOURCE: "Notes on Shakespeare's Cymbeline," in *Shakespeare Studies,* Vol. 1, 1965, pp. 118-36.

[*In the following excerpt, Hofling explores "the psychological relationship of* Cymbeline *to its author" and notes important similarities between Shakespeare's personal relationships (such as that with his daughter Susanna) and the play.*]

Cymbeline has been called "Shakespeare's most recapitulatory play." It is of interest to note certain of the echoes of the great tragedies in *Cymbeline.* This interest is heightened by the recognition that at least one such echo is obviously conscious and deliberate, a circumstance which raises the likelihood that a number of others were introduced in the same manner. *King Lear* and, to a slightly lesser extent, *Othello* are the plays of which the echoes appear to be the clearest and most significant. Not only is a father-daughter relationship of great importance in *Cymbeline,* as in *Lear,* but there is considerable correspondence in details of the situation. Cymbeline, like Lear, is an early British king; like Lear he is quick-tempered; like Lear, he trusts the wicked and rejects the loyal. Imogen, like Cordelia, is the third child of her father; like Cordelia, she is warm-hearted and sincere; she loves her father, but will not permit him to dominate her to the loss of her own self-respect. Like Lear, Cymbeline is influ-

enced by an immoral woman, an influence which is to the detriment of himself and the heroine. Like Lear, Cymbeline becomes separated from all three of his children. As in *Lear,* there is in *Cymbeline* a reconciliation between father and virtuous daughter.

Echoes of *Othello* are scarcely less striking. The one which is unmistakably deliberate is the name of the principal villain. Iachimo is literally "little Iago." Although the personality of Iachimo is not merely an echo or repetition of that of Iago, there are manifest similarities, such as the misogyny, the shrewdness, and the dishonesty. The entire "wager-plot" in *Cymbeline* is closely analogous to the main plot of *Othello.* In both instances, the villain manages so effectively to misrepresent a faithful wife as to rouse murderous rage in a previously loving husband. There is even a correspondence in certain smaller details of the situation. For example, in both *Othello* and *Cymbeline* the heroine has married against her father's wishes a man whom the father considers socially inferior. In both plays the villain uses a piece of the heroine's personal property to clinch his argument. In both plays the article was originally given the wife by her husband and then stolen from her by the villain or his agent.

This brief review does not begin to exhaust the list of echoes of previous writings to be found in *Cymbeline,* a list which includes material from *Romeo and Juliet, Hamlet, Macbeth,* and *Coriolanus,* as well as some of Shakespeare's non-dramatic poetry, but it is of almost equal interest to realize the close relationship of *Cymbeline* to the other romances: *Pericles, The Winter's Tale,* and *The Tempest.* In the first part of each play a father loses a daughter through his own poor judgment and instinct-ridden behavior. A considerable portion of the action in each play is devoted to the suffering and/ or remorse following from this estrangement. In the end, the child is reconciled with the father and becomes an instrument of a more general reconciliation. Since *Cymbeline* is the first of these plays (apart from *Pericles*), one might reasonably expect to be able to make out certain psychological implications regarding the author with particular clarity. In a general way, these links with other plays before and after it attest to the psychological significance of *Cymbeline.* More specifically, some of the links enable one to postulate certain psychological developments in the author, a matter which can only be discussed, however, after a glance at the characterization of Imogen.

One of the several telling arguments which have been advanced against the old idea that the romances gave evidence of Shakespeare's failing powers is that the dramatist never showed a firmer grip on characterization than is revealed at times in these last plays. *Cymbeline* furnishes a number of examples of this strength in characterization, of which the most outstanding is Imogen. In the opinion of a number of critics, Imogen has but one rival among Shakespeare's women—Cleopatra—in the richness of her portrayal. Other critics feel that she has no rival.

In expressing a woman's point of view, Margaret Webster[3] writes: "Imogen is she whom every woman in love would wish to be, free-generous, sane, miraculously happy in the expression of her love. Over and over again she puts feeling into words so just that she seems to express the emotion for all time." Goddard has pointed out that Imogen, "like Hamlet, is an epitome, uniting in herself the virtues of at least three of Shakespeare's types: the naive girl (in boy's costume part of the time), the queenly woman, and the tragic victim. It is as if the poet had consciously set out to endow his heroine with the finest traits of a dozen of her predecessors: 'from every one The best she hath, and she, of all compounded, Outsells them all.'"[4]

Examples of the intensity and beauty of Imogen's love are frequent in her speeches. Her first words to Pisanio after the banishment of Posthumus (Act I, Scene iii) are typical.

> I would thou grew'st unto the shores o' th'
>   haven,
> And question'dst every sail: if he should
>   write
> And I not have it, 't were a paper lost
> As offer'd mercy is.

At times, when speaking of Posthumus, as a little further on in this same scene, Imogen shows a fresh and youthful quality reminiscent of Juliet.

> I did not take my leave of him, but had
> Most pretty things to say. Ere I could tell
>   him
> How I would think on him at certain hours
> Such thoughts and such, or I could make
>   him swear
> The shes of Italy should not betray
> Mine interest and his honor, or have
>   charg'd him
> At the sixth hour of morn, at noon, at
>   midnight,
> To encounter me with orisons, for then
> I am in heaven with him; or ere I could
> Give him that parting kiss which I had set
> Betwixt two charming words, comes in my
>   father
> And like the tyrannous breathing of the
>   north
> Shakes all our buds from growing.

It is of importance to realize that Imogen is not a paragon—certainly not just a paragon—but a young woman of very human qualities. She has married without her father's consent, a rather serious offense in Elizabethan days, and as Granville-Barker says, "has been a clandestine wife for some while . . . under Cymbeline's very nose, which shows . . . some ability in deception." Moreover she speaks out to her father at times with a forthrightness verging on disrespect.

>   I beseech you, Sir,
> Harm not yourself with your vexation:
> I am senseless of your wrath.

Imogen is capable of humor, as in the "shes of Italy" line in the long speech quoted above; of gracious courtesy, as in her reception of Iachimo, thinking him her husband's friend, and of flashing anger, as in response to Iachimo's attempt at seduction: She can be free with contempt, as in speaking to the foppish and and cowardly Cloten. She is no unreal, superhuman tower of strength: given the cruel shock of finding, as she supposes, Posthumus beheaded, she sinks, after her initial, near-hysterical outburst, into a dazed state. To the Roman's question, "What art thou?" she can answer only, "I am nothing: or if not, Nothing to be were better."

Perhaps most significantly of all, Imogen is *capable of hope*. To a certain extent one may ascribe Imogen's belief that matters will eventually work out well for herself and for Posthumus to a realistic appraisal of certain strengths in his character and in her father's, but one is still left with the question of what enables her to maintain this appraisal in the face of very adverse circumstances. To perceive the crucial significance of this quality of hope, one must consider what is technically the central scene of the play, Act III, Scene iv, toward the end of which Imogen rallies from near-despair and achieves an attitude of hope which sustains her throughout the rest of the play. It is the outcome of this scene which determines that the play is to be a tragi-comedy and not a tragedy. Imogen and Pisanio are on the road to Milford Haven, when Pisanio breaks down and shows the princess the letter he has received from his master, Posthumus.

> *Imo.* (Reads.) "Thy mistress, Pisanio, hath played the strumpet in my bed. . . . I speak not out of weak surmises, but from proof as strong as my grief and as certain as I expect my revenge. . . . Let thine own hands take away her life. . . ."
>
> *Pis.* What shall I need to draw my sword? The paper hath cut her throat already.

Imogen's first reaction is pure anguish. This is quickly succeeded by honest anger.

> *Imo.* False to his bed! What! is it to be
>   false
> To lie in watch there and to think on him;
> To weep 'twixt clock and clock; if sleep
>   charge nature,

To break it with a fearful dream of him,
And cry myself awake? That's false to's
  bed, is it?

This hostility is temporarily "directed inward," as Imogen expresses the wish for Pisanio to carry out his order; but not entirely so, even in this moment of great stress; a certain amount of honest self-respect remains (as well it may in view of the largely unambivalent character of her love for Posthumus).

Imo.   Do his bidding; strike.
Thou mayst be valiant in a better cause,
But now thou seem'st a coward.
Pis.   Hence, vile instrument!
Thou shalt not damn my hand.
Imo.   Why, I must die;
And if I do not by thy hand, thou art
No servant of thy master's. Against self-
      slaughter
There is a prohibition so divine
That cravens my weak hand. Come, here's
  my heart,
(Something's afore't,—soft, soft! we'll
  no defense)
Obedient as the scabbard. What is here?
      [Draws the letters from her bosom.]
The scriptures of the loyal Leonatus,
All turned to heresy? Away, away,
Corruptors of my faith! you shall no more
Be stomachers to my heart.

Pisanio is unwilling to carry out his commission, but suggests that Imogen play for time, and the heroine quickly picks up the suggestion. When Pisanio advises her to return to her father, Imogen is too proud to accede, but she continues actively thinking of possible plans.

Pis.   If you'll back to th' court—
Imo. No court, no father; nor no more ado
With that harsh, noble, simple nothing,
That Cloten, whose love-suit hath been to
  me
As fearful as a siege.
Pis.   If not at court,
Then not in Britain must you bide
Imo.   Where then?
Hath Britain all the sun that shines?
  Day, night,
Are they not but in Britain? I' th' world's
  volume
Our Britain seems as of it, but not in't
There's livers out of Britain.

Pisanio then hits on the plan of Imogen's dressing like a boy and joining the expedition of Caius Lacius, a move which is likely to bring her eventually to Rome and the vicinity of Posthumus. Imogen accepts this idea with fortitude and hope.

Imo. There's more to be consider'd; but
  we'll even
All that good time will give us. This attempt
I am soldier to, and will abide it with
A prince's courage.

So it is the emotional health, and particularly the capacity for hope, in Imogen which, at this decisive point, makes the difference between tragedy and comedy. Imogen adopts none of the courses which would lead to a morbid outcome: submission to her father and step-mother, marriage to Clothen, suicide, revenge on Posthumus. Instead she is amenable to the one course which gives eventual promise of a healthier outcome.

This matter of hope warrants further consideration, but to round out this sketch of Imogen's personality, two other incidents should be noted. The diffuse material of Act IV, involving events at the mountain retreat of Belarius and the young princes, does not contribute appreciably to the portrayal of Imogen's personality. It is almost solely concerned with the romantic-narrative aspects of the play. The last scene of Act V, however, yields significant glimpses of Imogen. The first of these occurs when Imogen notices the ring she had given Posthumus on the finger of Iachimo. She asks a boon of the king that Iachimo be required to give an explanation of the circumstance. Dazed, shaken and heartbroken as she has been rendered by the horrendous events in Act IV, Imogen retains the strength to resume her goal-directed behaviour as soon as she realizes that somehow Posthumus is still alive. Then, in the final surge of relief after Iachimo has confessed and Posthumus has recognized her, Imogen speaks three charming lines, playful, affectionate, and sensual all at once, which complete the portrayal of her personality.

Imo. Why did you throw your wedded lady
  from you?
Think that you are upon a lock, and now
Throw me again.

II

Having reviewed briefly the position of the play among Shakespeare's works, its connections with some of the other plays, its complicated plot, and the personality of its leading character, we may now consider the difficult task of exploring the psychological relationship of *Cymbeline* to its author and, in particular, the continuity of development between the psychological status of the author of *Coriolanus* and that of the author of *Cymbeline*. To this effect, it may be well to note at the outset Shakespeare's biographical data at the period of his life just before and during the presumed time of writing of *Cymbeline*.

1. On June 5, 1607, Shakespeare's older daughter, Susanna, married John Hall, a Puritan physician of Stratford, eight years older than she.

2. February, 1608. A daughter was born to this union.

3. September, 1608. Shakespeare's mother died.

4. Late in 1608 or early in 1609 *Coriolanus* was written.

5. During 1609 the *Sonnets* were published.

6. Late in 1609 or in 1610, *Cymbeline* was written.

7. In September, 1610, Shakespeare retired to Stratford, occupying the house he had previously purchased, New Place, which had once been the home of Sir Hugh Clopten, one of the town's most distinguished former citizens.[5]

To this list should be added several other items of a biographical nature having a possible bearing on the significance of *Cymbeline*. For example, it is clear that the period of twenty years was of particular significance in the life of Shakespeare being (approximately) the length of time that he lived in London as an actor and playwright. Twenty years was also the approximate length of time between the postulated critical period in Shakespeare's early childhood (see Ella Sharpe's work, discussed in the following section) and the known critical period in his young adult life, at which he left home and went to London.

Another biographical feature of possible relevance is the likelihood that Shakespeare and Anne Hathaway lived as man and wife for some little time before their wedding (possibly having a "pre-contract").

It may also prove of interest that there were important similarities—or identification points—between Shakespeare and his daughter Susanna. Susanna was in fact, spoken of as being very like her father, "witty above her sex."[6] Like his daughter, Shakespeare had married a person eight years older than himself and with Puritan leanings. (The latter circumstance is a possible reason for Anne not accompanying her husband to London and becoming a part of his life in the theater.)

Finally, while Shakespeare was not literally one of three children—his mother having borne eight—yet there were situations within the family in which a *sense* of being one of three children must have assumed significance. Shakespeare was the third child of the family, yet, for awhile, the only child, since the two elder had died in infancy. Then, during a highly significant developmental period—age five to age seven and one-half—Shakespeare was one of three living children in

the family. It is also true that he, himself, had three children, the boy Hamnet, and two daughters.

If we return to *Cymbeline,* certain correlations between the foregoing biographical material and events depicted in that play become interesting to the student of psychology. The theme of reunion and reconciliation so prominent in the final comedies and especially striking in *Cymbeline* does tend to reflect events in the poet's own life. In the play, no fewer than five characters—Imogen, Posthumus, the two princes, and Cymbeline—in effect "share" certain experiences with Shakespeare. Like the princes, Shakespeare returns home after twenty years: indeed, he comes home to what amounted to a palace, one of the finest houses in town. But more importantly, we may observe the shape of family-relationships. Shakespeare's own childhood situation offers certain similarities to the composition of Imogen's family, and, as far as the poet's later life is concerned, his romance with Anne is reminiscent of the relationship between Imogen and Posthumus. The drama is marked, too, by the absence, through death, of one mother and the current death of another, and we are perhaps reminded that Shakespeare's career, being obviously marked by an absence from his own mother, is to a certain extent affected by her death in that this is followed by a decision to return to Stratford. Finally, we have suggested Imogen as somewhat atypical in that her existence as a composite of womanly types is not characteristic of Shakespeare's other figures.

Other parallels can be found, but these are perhaps sufficient to show that *Cymbeline,* unlike many of the other plays, presents matters of some basic concern to Shakespeare's own emotional life, no matter how removed from his work we may assume an artist to be. For the events of this period of the dramatist's life are such as to emphasize his relationships with significant women. There are the death of his mother, the marriage of his daughter, the return to his wife, and even—through the publication of the Sonnets—some reminiscence of his relationship (whether real or only in fantasy) with the "dark lady."

Before going further with the attempt to discern what Shakespeare may have been revealing about himself in the play *Cymbeline,* it may be well to return for a moment to a consideration of the psychological truism presented [earlier in the essay], namely, that any extended effort a person makes is in some measure characteristic of him. Modern depth psychology teaches that all creative writing is in some measure a projection of certain facets of the author's personality. The view is that one cannot create realistically except out of one's self, that one cannot, to be more specific, create a fictional character of vitality and significance except insofar as something within one's own personality is in resonance with the strivings and the defenses of the character. On this view, one might say of Shakespeare (or any other great writer) that any given work—let us say, to take an extreme case, *Love's Labor's Lost*—expresses the emotional conflicts of its author. There is, I should think, truth in such a statement, but it involves an over-simplification so great that the attendant error exceeds the truth. In the productions of a great master, such as Shakespeare, one can find expression of essentially all of the fundamental conflicts of which human beings are capable. If all of these conflicts had been of personal importance to Shakespeare, his mind would have been not one of the most highly organized the world has ever seen, but quite disorganized. Thus, one is led to the conclusion that it is possible for a very great artist to create entertainingly, beautifully, realistically, without being *deeply* involved in a personal way. On the other hand, when it is a matter of his greatest masterpieces, the case appears to be different quantitatively. Without knowing anything of Shakespeare's personal life, most persons would surmise that the creation of *Hamlet* arose out of more moving personal experiences of the author than did *Love's Labor's Lost*. And indeed, a study of Shakespeare's life gives some evidence to support such a contention.

Three plays which seem particularly to belong together psychologically and to reflect a developmental sequence in the author are *King Lear, Coriolanus,* and *Cymbeline*. Some of the evidence for postulating a significant relationship between *King Lear* and *Cymbeline* has been given [earlier in the essay]. Initially the reasons for suspecting a significant psychological relationship between *Coriolanus* and *Cymbeline* were that the two plays were (barring *Pericles*) written in quick succession within a short time of the death of Shakespeare's mother and that they lie, so to speak, on either side of a point which marks striking changes in Shakespeare's *genre* of expression and in his personal life.

I do not propose to offer here a psychoanalytical investigation of *Lear*. This has been done, however, with great technical competence by Ella Freeman Sharpe.[7] Taking Miss Sharpe's essay at face value—which is surely the wisest course, in view of her undoubted integrity—one finds that the validity of its speculations is attested by its author's being able to deduce, solely from a careful reading of *Lear,* that Shakespeare had been, for a while, an only child, that one of his siblings had been born when he was about two years of age, and that another sibling had been born at a time when he was able to walk about the neighborhood independently. In *King Lear,* Miss Sharpe finds evidence of reactivation in Shakespeare, at the time of writing the tragedy, of intense conflicts from his early childhood, conflicts which involved what a psychoanalyst would call "pre-oedipal strivings," i.e., strivings for gratifications of the sort of paramount importance

to a child below the age of three years. In the reactivation, these conflicts are, of course, considered to have been completely unconscious.

In *Coriolanus,* as I have pointed out in an earlier essay,[8] the principal conflicts of the protagonist are at an early oedipal level. Insofar as this circumstance may be taken to indicate a similar shift in the author's principal conflicts at the time, one may say that, if there has been an emotional retreat of the sort suggested by Miss Sharpe, it has begun to be reversed. If the ideas offered previously are accepted, then one may add that the psychological healing was accompanied by a certain amount of personal insight. What is relatively certain is that the writing of *Coriolanus* was shortly followed by a definitive change in the author's literary productions and style of personal living. While the destructive mother figure occupies the center of the stage for a large portion of the time in *Coriolanus,* there are clear glimpses of a wholesome woman figure in the person of Virgilia. Although in the play Virgilia is the wife of Coriolanus, nevertheless her significance as a mother figure is unmistakable (through interaction with her son as well as in her having partially reversed the effects of Volumnia's personality on Coriolanus).

Cymbeline may be considered the third term in a series of which *Lear* and *Coriolanus* are the first and second terms, with the series being thought of as reflecting changes in the psychological position of the author.

In examining *Cymbeline* from this point of view, the most conspicuous factor is surely the characterization of Imogen. This portrayal is not only rich but almost completely unambivalent. Moreover it is not appreciably touched by the effects of psychological defenses in the author; that is to say, it is not sentimental, not rigid, not idolatrous. It might be called an oedipal or post-oedipal portrait, in the sense that such an image of a woman is characteristically held only by a man of considerable personal maturity. Its richness appears to indicate that the portrait was drawn from marked breadth and depth of experience, probably involving the four women figures in Shakespeare's life mentioned [earlier in the essay].

At first consideration, one might think that, although rich and genuine, the characterization of Imogen as an ideal woman is incomplete since specifically maternal features are not included. This is, however, only partially true. It is a well-known fact of human psychology that emotions and attitudes—particularly if they are to some extent repressed—of a woman toward her father or of a man toward his mother are frequently revealed in emotions and attitudes experienced toward a child of the same sex as the parent in question.

> *Lear*. When were you wont to be so full of songs, sirrah?

Michael Gwynn as Lucius, William Squire as Cloten, Wynne Clark as the queen, Leon Quartermaine as Cymbeline, and Timothy Bateson as dwarf to the queen. Act III, scene i.

Fool. I have used it, nuncle, ever since thou mad'st thy daughters thy mother, for when thou gav'st them the rod, and puttest down thine own breeches . . .

Miss Sharpe is of the opinion that Shakespeare expressed deep-seated, largely unconscious feelings about his mother through the characterization of Lear's three daughters. The close parallels between *Cymbeline* and *Lear,* and the fact that *Cymbeline* was written rather soon after Shakespeare's mother's death, suggest to me that the same process of substitution is in operation in this play. On this view, the reconciliation of Cymbeline and Imogen is not only one of father and daughter but also of son and mother. The son, as it were, forgives the mother, and the mother reaffirms her loyalty to the son.

This line of thought suggests a closer look at the relationship between Shakespeare and his daughter, Susanna, and invites speculation upon it. In view of the documented resemblance between them, it is a

reasonable inference that the bonds were strong despite the infrequency of contacts during Susanna's later childhood and adolescence. On the other hand, it seems likely that there was some basis for negative feelings in Shakespeare toward his daughter, partly conscious and partly unconscious. Clearly the playwright had some reason for irritation toward Susanna for her marrying Doctor Hall, inasmuch as he was a Puritan and therefore strongly opposed to the theater. To speak of unconscious factors, it is a permissible inference that there was some old resentment toward Susanna for having been born at all, thus terminating the idyllic phase of Shakespeare's relationship with Anne, for having begun to reconstitute the situation which Shakespeare, according to Miss Sharpe's analysis, found so difficult in his own early childhood, namely the advent of rivals for the affection of the woman figure in his life. At least one knows that Shakespeare left his home for London shortly after the birth of his second and third children. (The conscious rationale for a young man's going to London to seek his fortune is, of course, in no sense contradictory to the idea that Shakespeare's leaving Stratford was also running away, since it is quite possible to run to something and away from something else at the same time.)

Yet these negative feelings must clearly have been counterbalanced by some other force or forces during the period in which the ideas for *Cymbeline* were germinating. Again it is possible to speak of conscious and unconscious factors. It seems reasonable to surmise that Shakespeare was thinking in terms of a male heir at this time. Indeed, all of the elaborate provisions of his will seem to have been designed with the purpose of seeing that his wealth would be concentrated in the hands of such an heir. With Anne well past the age of childbearing, it was to Susanna or Judith that he must look for such an heir, and Susanna was the elder and his favorite. (The will makes it quite clear that if Susanna has a son, he will become Shakespeare's heir.) Further, it seems reasonable to assume that this child-to-be was thought of by Shakespeare as his own (consciously, in a figurative sense; unconsciously, in a literal sense), and that the wish for a child by daughter had become fused unconsciously with the common oedipal wish for a child by mother.

Susanna had shown herself to be fertile and doubtless was delighted with her father's intentions with respect to her son-to-be. Thus there was every reason for the relationship between father and daughter to become increasingly cordial and mutually pleasant.

There seems little reason to doubt that, in addition to the psychological forces just mentioned, Shakespeare's mastery over the feelings of bitterness and near-despair which were given expression in *Lear* was fostered by, as well as expressed in, a favorable trend in his relationship with Anne, his wife. (Anne may well have been one of the sources of the "queenly" characteristics of Imogen.)

Here again one should consider both conscious and unconscious factors in the situation. To think first of conscious factors, one must recall something of Anne's position. Like Shakespeare's mother, Anne was of a highly respectable background, having come from a family of landowners. There seems to have been something dignified about Anne which made her quite suitable as a wife to one who aspired to become and did become a member of the gentry. While her leanings toward the Puritan faith produced a definite incompatibility with her husband during the years when he was an actor in London, this factor must have faded markedly in significance with Shakespeare's acquisition of property and status in Stratford, and may well have become inconsequential by the time now in question, when he had become established as a gentleman resident of Stratford.

It would have been only natural for Anne to have been appreciative of the mounting evidence of Shakespeare's intention to reestablish himself in Stratford and to give up the stage. Her positive feelings may well have been gratifying to Shakespeare and so, no doubt, was her continuing loyalty, a virtue highly prized by the author of the *Sonnets*.

On an unconscious level, the mother-transference which seems to have caused difficulty to Shakespeare in the early years of the marriage may now have become a source of gratification. The conflicts mobilized by the advent of the children would have quieted since they were no longer in childhood or adolescence. Shakespeare may well have come to feel reinstated as Anne's first concern. Then, too, the transference would have been somewhat diluted at this point, with Susanna being its partial recipient.

III

Up to this point, in the consideration of certain psychological sequences in Shakespeare, the person, only material deriving from a study of the characterization of Imogen (in relation to biographical data) has been utilized. To supplement the line of thought which has been developed, one may now turn to a consideration of certain aspects of the plot of *Cymbeline* together with a look at certain of the other figures in the story.

First, the plot of the wager and the slandered lady. The action of this portion of the play primarily involves Imogen, Posthumus, and Iachimo. The names of the two male characters are surely significant. The name, "Iachimo," clearly represents a conscious and deliberate attempt to call to mind the villain, Iago from the tragedy, *Othello*. The name, "Posthumus," clearly represents a conscious and deliberate effort to call to mind the parentless state of this protagonist.[9] The latter circumstance is completely irrelevant to the action of the play,—but *Shakespeare* became parentless with the death of his mother at the beginning of the pivotal period which saw the writing of *Coriolanus* and *Cymbeline*. (Mary Shakespeare died in September, 1608. The plays were written in the period of late 1608 to early 1610.)

The choice of the name, "Iachimo," has a superficial explanation, no doubt valid so far as it goes: the wish to remind the audience of the highly successful villain in the highly successful play, *Othello,* and thereby to increase the interest in the action to follow. On the other hand, the question of the similarity in names merges with the question as to the similarity in plot between this portion of *Cymbeline* and the Othello-Iago-Desdemona action in Othello, and this leads into deeper waters.

It has been postulated that if one wishes to study *Othello* from the point of view of a series of projections of its author's conflicts, it is appropriate to consider Othello and Iago as two aspects of a single personality, with Iago representing certain unquenchable hostile and homoerotic id forces and Othello the struggling ego. It is not possible to draw a tight analogy between the Othello-Iago-Desdemona plot and the Posthumus-Iachimo-Imogen plot because of the enormous shift in importance in the heroine of the latter plot. On the other hand, one can go so far as to say that this portion of Shakespeare's message in *Cymbeline* is that, given time and hope, the disruptive id forces (which destroyed Othello) can be brought under control.

The significance of the time element is shown in one of Shakespeare's modifications of the plot as found in his source. Unlike the situation in Boccaccio—and unlike that in *Othello*—Posthumus has time for his ego to assert itself before tragedy has occurred. On returning to England, Posthumus repents of his instructions to Pisanio *while still under the impression of Imogen's guilt*. The message further implies that hostility need not be quenched in revenge, not even in being shown to be groundless, but by the ability to love.

The significant element of hope (together with a healthy aggressivity) is, of course, principally manifested not in Posthumus but in Imogen. Put Imogen in Desdemona's place and the tragedy of *Othello* would not have occurred. Put her in Cordelia's place and the tragedy of *Lear* would not have occurred. If one considers the characters of *Cymbeline*, like those of *Othello* and *Lear*, from the standpoint of their being projections of strivings and attitudes of their creator, one may say—on the basis of the portrayal of Imogen alone—that Shakespeare's bitterness and near-despair have been vanquished by hope.

To summarize and rephrase what has been said of the implications to be found in the character of Imogen and the action in which she is involved, one may begin by saying that she is consciously represented as both a wife and a daughter. Both husband-wife and father-daughter reconciliations are thus represented in the last scene. These correspond to Shakespeare's renewed gratifying relationships with wife and daughter. Unconsciously (for the dramatist), Imogen, like Cordelia, represents a mother. This facet of the situation corresponds to Shakespeare's being able (unconsciously) to forgive and be reconciled with his memory representations of his mother.

Imogen is taken back to the palace; Shakespeare installs Anne in New Place and deeds it to Susanna. Reduction in a sense of guilt, reconciliation, and hope for the future are all linked.

What has thus far been worked out appears internally consistent and consistent with the facts that are known.

It is possible, however, to view the central portion of the play in a more speculative way, one which touches deeper layers of the poet's unconscious. In this view, the figure of Imogen is, perhaps, best considered as one with whom Shakespeare is identified. We have noted that the pivotal point of the play is Act III, Scene iv. Actually, it would be more nearly correct to speak of a pivotal area, since the fourth scene is surrounded by two others, the third and sixth, which supplement it and, taken in sequence with it, furnish the basis for the reconciliations in the final scene of the play. These three scenes take place in the Welsh hills in and around the secret cave. It is necessary to view these scenes in a more symbolic fashion than much of the rest of the play to appreciate fully their significance. When, however, one takes such a view, the material is seen to be fully consonant with the interpretations previously derived from the play.

In effect, one may say that the descending or tragic component of the action is arrested during this sequence of scenes and the successful (in this sense, comic) resolution of the difficulties begins or is prepared for. The setting of the cave strongly suggests that an unconscious reference is being made to the mother's womb. From the cave issue the two young princes—sibling figures. It seems a reasonable inference that Shakespeare was here unconsciously symbolizing the critical periods in his life when he was in danger of experiencing a pathogenic regression.

There seem to have been three such periods. The most recent was the potential regression discussed by Miss Sharpe (and others) as being in relation to the writing of the great tragedies. The intermediate one was the occasion of Shakespeare's going from Stratford to London following the birth of his second and third children. The original occasion may well have followed the birth of Shakespeare's sister, Joan (the second sibling to succeed him). The idea of these scenes' representing a regression is reinforced by the circumstance that, in a sense, they involve a turning back of the clock by twenty years. Belarius and the princes are, so to speak, figures of the past.

The important new element represented in these scenes—as contrasted, say, with the message of *Lear*—is that love appears at the critical moment for Imogen (and, by inference, in Shakespeare's view of life at this time). Love reigns in the primitive surroundings of the cave. It affects Imogen, the princes, and Belarius. In other words, Shakespeare seems now to have succeeded in getting through the (psychic residuals of the) stressful periods of his early childhood, detected by Miss Sharpe in *Lear*, back to (the psychic residuals of) a still earlier period, rock bottom, at which there were love and reason for hope, and to have succeeded in reversing the regression through this knowledge. With the reversal, the love and hope begin to infiltrate later periods, bringing with them the possibility of a reconciliation between Shakespeare and sibling figures and between Shakespeare and his offspring.

One thus returns to the key element of hope. Indeed, if one were to epitomize the significance of the play, *Cymbeline,* insofar as it is a representation of its author's psychological position, one could scarcely do better than to say that it is his fullest expression of an unambivalent picture of woman and of the power of hope. Furthermore, one is led strongly to suspect that the two expressions are here (as usually) dynamically connected. St. Paul says, "Faith is the substance of things hoped for, the evidence of things not seen," and where—if he is fortunate—does everyone first find this faith but in the ministrations of a woman, a mother, whose availability to her small child does not cease when she leaves the room?

Thus the meaningful sequence, *Lear, Coriolanus, Cymbeline,* is completed. In *Lear* the good woman (mother figure) is visualized but is ineffectual (Cordelia); in *Coriolanus,* she is partially effective (Virgilia); in *Cymbeline,* she is fully effective (Imogen). One is led to postulate that there were two sets of factors which contributed to Shakespeare's achievement of this final position. The first is surely the self-induced catharsis of the writing of the tragedies, beginning with *Julius Caesar* and ending with *Coriolanus.* In Miss Sharpe's words, "The poet is not Hamlet. Hamlet is what he might have been if he had not written the play of *Hamlet.*" One is inclined to agree that "The massive cycle of the tragic plays gives the impression of a renewed attempt to master every phase of development."[10] In the writing of the great plays there was an element of regression, but it was truly what psychoanalysts call a "regression in the service of the ego," that is to say, a controlled regression which is ultimately of value to the whole personality. The regression achieved its purpose by reason both of the poet's marvelous endowment and of the fact that the first years of his childhood were, by and large, happy and successful ones.

Hand in hand with the reassertion of ego control—favored by it and fostering it—went the second set of factors, the real-life developments referred to previously in this paper. As Dover Wilson put it, "Wordsworth recovered by falling in love a second time with the Lake Country; Shakespeare by falling in love a second time with Stratford." To this should be added that it was not merely Stratford that was effective, but circumstances involving the women figures in Shakespeare's life: the death of his mother, the loyalty of Anne, and the coming of age and marriage of Susanna.

The immediate (psychological) effect of the death of Shakespeare's mother is, perhaps, not known, but a proximal effect was exemplified in the writing of

Coriolanus and a later effect in the writing of *Cymbeline.* An effective mourning must have contributed toward halting the poet's regression and fostering—in combination with other events—a return to a more mature orientation. Shakespeare's early childhood strivings were not fully abandoned but were attenuated and merged into strivings more nearly capable of fulfillment in the real world. At the same time, circumstances in that world were developing to bring some fulfillment and the promise of additional fulfillment.

Notes

[3] Margaret Webster, *Shakespeare without Tears* (Cleveland, 1955), p. 271.

[4] H. C. Goddard, *The Meaning of Shakespeare* (Chicago, 1951), pp. 635-636.

[5] For these well-known facts, see Chambers, I, 86 f.; 555 ff.; II, 4 ff.

[6] Chambers, II, 12.

[7] E. F. Sharpe, "From *King Lear* to the *Tempest,"* *Collected Papers on Psychoanalysis* (London, 1950).

[8] "An Interpretation of Shakespeare's *Coriolanus,"* *American Imago,* XIV (1957), pp. 407-435.

[9] See *NED,* "posthumous," meanings *a-c.*

[10] Sharpe, "The Impatience of *Hamlet,"* in *Papers.*

CLASSICAL ALLUSIONS

Joan Carr (essay date 1978)

SOURCE: "*Cymbeline* and the Validity of Myth," in *Studies in Philology,* Vol. LXXV, No. 3, July, 1978, pp. 316-30.

[*In the following essay, Carr maintains that Shakespeare sought to explore the effects of myth on the human pysche in* Cymbeline *through his allusions to stories of death and resurrection.*]

The complex plot of *Cymbeline* incorporates a large number of situations paralleled in myths and folk tales, often with bizarre twists that suggest Shakespeare is composing a playful, sophisticated *scherzo* on archetypal themes. However, the theatrical experimentation in this play is not merely playful or self-indulgent. *Cymbeline* is a probing, often rueful questioning of the mythic habit of thought and of its ability to make sense of the human condition. Its fully psychologized, warmly human heroine is forced to live and act in a capricious fairytale world so that her flesh-and-blood reactions may serve as a skeptical probing of the consoling power of myth.

For example, the motif of beheading is perhaps the most grotesque of the play's many variations on the resurrection myth. In a scene which piles up macabre incidents, the reawakened Imogen, whose drugged body has been mourned as dead by her long-lost brothers, embraces the headless body of the brutal Cloten, mistaking it for that of her husband. Dismemberment is sometimes a prelude to resurrection in myths, and Cloten's beheading duly precedes Imogen's "resurrection" from her death-like trance as well as the much later "resurrection" of Posthumus, whose corpse she thinks she is embracing. But the sensationalism of this scene strikes many critics as gratuitous and hence un-Shakespearean.[1] To be sure, the coming to life of the "statue" of Hermione in *The Winter's Tale* is similarly theatrical and sensational; yet the scene recapitulates so much of the play's meaning that it is wonderfully moving. On the other hand, Imogen's grief seems to result from a cruel and pointless practical joke, as apparently pointless as the beheading of Cloten's corpse.

But despite the cruel shock to Imogen, the headless corpse is thematically relevant to the play because it is meant to recall myths about dying and resurrected gods and heroes, such as the orthodox type of Christ the Redeemer or such well-known pagan figures as Osiris, Dionysus, or Proserpina. The mythic figure that Shakespeare has specifically in mind here is Orpheus, whose death and dismemberment are closely paralleled in the strange circumstances of Cloten's death. For example, Guiderius says of the head he has just severed:

> I'll throw't into the creek
> Behind our rock, and let it to the sea,
> And tell the fishes he's the queen's son,
> Cloten.
>
> (IV.ii.151-3)[2]

Guiderius has no apparent motive for this strange action. He returns shortly thereafter, announcing that he has "sent Cloten's clotpoll down the stream, / In embassy to his mother," when "solemn music" is heard. The younger brother Arviragus thus announces that he has just discovered the apparently dead body of Fidele, whom the brothers promise to strew with flowers. The ceremony reminds us of the flower-strewing in classical pastoral elegy; in fact, both the "solemn music" that announces the discovery of Fidele's corpse and the most famous of English pastoral elegies, Milton's *Lycidas,* can help tell us why Shakespeare wants Cloten's head thrown in a creek. In Milton's monody

for the drowning of a fellow-poet, he reminds us that not even the Muse of epic poetry, Calliope, could prevent the furious Bacchantes from ripping apart her son, Orpheus:

> Whom Universal nature did lament
> When by the rout that made the hideous
>   roar,
> His gory visage down the stream was sent,
> Down the swift *Hebrus* to the *Lesbian* shore.
>
> (60-3)

Since Cloten cannot be saved in remote Wales by his sorceress-mother and his gory visage is sent downstream while music plays offstage, Shakespeare must be thinking of Orpheus the divine musician. Furthermore, like Milton after him, Shakespeare draws Orpheus' death into the context of pastoral elegy by having Fidele mourned beside the headless Cloten.

The allusion is appropriate, for, like the classical flower-strewing with its hint of springtime renewal, Orpheus' death was regarded in the Renaissance as an allegory of continuity and regeneration.[3] When Orpheus' head, protected by Apollo, was recovered from the sea by the Lesbians, along with his harp that kept on playing though its master was dead, they enshrined both and were ever afterward rewarded with the gift of song.[4] Thus both Shakespeare and Milton suggest possibilities of resurrection in the midst of a lament over early death. Yet whose resurrection is Shakespeare hinting at? Is it simply that of Imogen-Fidele, who will soon recover from her potion? Cloten will also be in a sense resurrected. Since his body is clothed in Posthumus' garments, Imogen mistakes the headless body for her husband's, who will be "resurrected" for Imogen when he is reunited with her in the last act. In a play whose most central theme is spiritual regeneration, these stagey resurrections are obviously symbolic, and the strange transformation of the oafish Cloten into an Orpheus figure is part of the imagistic pattern.[5]

The reason for this bizarre identification is that, in an Orpheus-like regeneration, the chastened Posthumus will be returned to Imogen in Act V after he has purged himself of the violence and brutality of his now defunct *alter ego,* Cloten. Notice that Shakespeare does all he can in this scene to make us identify Posthumus with Cloten. He is not only wearing Posthumus' clothes and is mistaken for him by Imogen, but their strong physical resemblance, at least below the neck, is also strangely emphasized by Imogen herself:

> I know the shape of's leg: this is his hand:
> His foot Mercurial: His Martial thigh:
> The brawns of Hercules: but his Jovial
>   face—
> Murder in heaven! How?—'Tis gone,
>
> (IV.ii.309-12)

A wife should know her own husband's body, but there are even stronger reasons to equate Cloten with Posthumus. The audience must shudder to see poor Imogen embracing the body of the man who had recently boasted how he would rape and abuse her:

> He [Posthumus] on the ground, my speech of insultment ended on his dead body, and when my lust hath dined (which, as I say, to vex her I will execute in the clothes that she so prais'd) to the court I'll knock her back, foot her home again.
>
> (III.v.141-6)

Elsewhere he plans to rape her and "spurn her home to her father" (IV.i.18-19).

Yet Posthumus, whom Imogen thinks she is embracing, is hardly preferable to Cloten, since he is trying to have his wife murdered. At one point Posthumus even wallows in practically the same revenge fantasy that Cloten imagines:

> O, that I had her here, to tear her limb-meal!
> I will go there, and do't, i' th' court, before
> Her father. I'll do something—
>
> (II.iv.147-9)

Both Cloten and the raging Posthumus wish to beat up and publicly humiliate the woman who is the object of Posthumus' love and at least of Cloten's libido. As such, Cloten seems to be a grotesque projection, and yet not all that much of an exaggeration, of the very worst elements in Posthumus' nature. By doubling Posthumus' viciousness onto the repulsive Cloten, Shakespeare deliberately strains our ability to feel heartened by Imogen's loving forgiveness. If, with the best will in the world, we follow her example of trust, will we not also end up embracing a monster?

Throughout the play's early scenes Cloten also serves as a parody of the chivalry that characterizes Posthumus' attitude toward Imogen. When departing from his wife, he speaks of her as "queen," "mistress," and swears his "loyalty." He is also conventionally eager to defend her honor in Rome. Cloten, a determined courtier, observes the same forms of courtly wooing, yet they cover a bestiality that shows through in a manner both comic and disturbing. The morning serenade that Cloten has sung outside Imogen's window is as refined as a medieval French tapestry. In contrast are Cloten's remarks on the song. His sexual puns are as crudely physical as those of DeFlores when he handles Beatrice-Joanna's glove:

> Come on, tune: if you can penetrate her with your fingering, so: we'll try with tongue too: if none will do, let her remain: but I'll never give o'er. . . .
>
> (II.iii.13-15)

> [I]f this penetrate, I will consider your music the better: if it do not, it is a vice in her ears which horse-hairs, and calves'-guts, nor the voice of unpaved eunuch to boot can never amend.
>
> (II.iii.26-9)

This scene, like *Othello* and Sonnet 129, presents the paradox of eroticism; it can contain both delicate idealism and animal appetite. However, an even wider polarity between the angelic and the bestial is presented in Posthumus' sexual feelings toward Imogen. In Act I he all but kneels before her as a goddess. Later he can imagine his goddess mounted by a full-fed German boar or can scream that he'd like to tear her to pieces. Cloten's sexual sadism sums up the viciousness in Posthumus. Yet the brute is so much a part of Posthumus' nature and of the nature of human eroticism that it takes miracles, stagey ones to be sure, to banish Cloten and his influence from the play. In both Cloten and Posthumus the root of their desire to maim Imogen's body is sexual. This violent coexistence of tenderness and cruelty within erotic relationships serves in this play, and in others as well, as a metaphor for the problematic nature of all personal and social relationships, either sexual or non-sexual. Thus Shakespeare refurbishes an old tale about trouble between lovers to explore our capacity to survive the cruel paradoxes of the human condition, and even to redeem ourselves.

The death and dismemberment of Cloten signal a great spiritual change within Posthumus. The very next time we see him after Imogen falls upon the dead body, he has fallen into repentant grief for the murder he thinks he has committed. His remorse is all the more remarkable because he still believes that Imogen has committed adultery, and his attitude parallels the Christian doctrine of forgiveness: "Love your enemies, do good to them that hate you":

>   You married ones,
> If each of you should take this course, how many
> Must murder wives much better than themselves
> For wrying but a little? . . .
>   Gods, if you
> Should have ta'en vengeance on my faults, I never
> Had liv'd to put on this: so had you saved
> The noble Imogen, to repent, and struck
> Me, wretch, more worth your vengeance.
>
> (V.i.2-II)

This rebirth of love in Posthumus, a love which forgives freely, makes a new man of him, very different from the Cloten-like old man. Cloten, whose name suggests a clod of earth, and Posthumus, whose name suggests something beyond the earthly, recall St. Paul's distinction between the old man of earth, flesh, and sin, and the new man of the spirit. Even Cloten's angry preoccupation with Posthumus' meanest garment, which Imogen professed to love better than Cloten's whole person, is part of this nexus of imagery. When he dies in his rival's clothes, Cloten in effect becomes Posthumus' "meanest garment," that is, the Pauline "body of death," enslaved to passion and sin. Yet this dichotomy is not expressed in exclusively Christian terms, not only because of the Orpheus allusion, but also because the act which makes this transformation possible is presented in terms of myths, pagan or otherwise, and of fertility rites, rather than in terms of the spirit and the inner conscience. There is no psychological preparation for the great change in Post humus, and considering the usual attitude toward adulterous wives in Renaissance society, the change is indeed tremendous. If we look for any cause of Posthumus' regeneration, it must be not through psychological analysis but through consideration of the mythic, folkloric aspect of Cloten's dismemberment, which signals the demise of the bloodthirsty, unregenerate Posthumus, and of the quasi-death and resurrection of their intended victim, Imogen.

The mythic parallel to Imogen's situation is that of the divine scapegoat or, what Shakespeare probably had more nearly in mind, those Greek mythical heroes such as Adonis who die and come to life again as flowers. Note that Imogen's meeting with her lost brothers in Wales does much to impart to the three of them a semi-divine aura. For example, Shakespeare uses pieces of legendry in pristine, naive form to convey a sense of numinous forces: Belarius marvels at the unexpected taste for war and heroism that reveals the brothers' "princely" nature despite their rustic upbringing; the brothers are miraculously restored to the king their father precisely when they reach heroic maturity in battle; and they profess eager, intuitive loyalty to the stranger whom they do not yet know to be their royal sister. These demigods not only repeatedly describe Imogen-Fidele in terms of flowers, suggesting that she is a fertility figure, but also as a "fairy" and "angel" (III.vii.14,15) whose physical body is incorruptible:

> With female fairies will his tomb be haunted,
> And worms will not come to thee.
>
> (IV.ii.217-18)

Above all, Shakespeare makes an almost Wordsworthian connection between the exiled royal family and a nature that is divine because of qualities remote from pastoral prettiness and commonly identified in the eighteenth century with the "sublime." The poetry of the Welsh scenes often suggests nature's fearsomeness, austerity, and indifference:

> When we shall hear
> The rain and wind beat dark December? How

> In this our pinching cave shall we discourse
> The freezing hours away? We have seen nothing:
> We are beastly: subtle as the fox for prey
> Like warlike as the wolf for what we eat. . . .
>
> (III.iii.36-41)

The harsh, elemental life of nature has imparted to these princes an aura of superhuman strength and freedom. Similarly, Imogen's wanderings in the wild identify her, as in most myths of wandering, with a world alien to and more permanent than that of human mortality.[6]

But pointing out mythic allusions can only begin to tell us what Shakespeare is trying to accomplish.[7] He is not, I believe, merely playing with "mouldy tales," as Ben Jonson, like many of his more modern critics, might have accused him of doing.[8] I believe Shakespeare is examining what myth does to the human psyche and that he does so largely through Imogen, the only really developed character in the play. She is neither a type like Cloten the Brute nor Iachimo the Schemer, nor an Everyman figure like Posthumus, who is, to paraphrase Dostoyevsky, the battlefield on which God and the Devil are fighting. Her reactions to the play's situations, compounded as they are of the tag-ends of legend, folktale, and romance, are fully human, so much so that Arthur Kirsch has called her a Shakespearean heroine in a Fletcherian world.[9] In fact, Imogen's reactions to what tough-minded critics like Samuel Johnson call *Cymbeline's* absurdities are at the center of the play's meaning. The play does not simply celebrate regeneration; it profoundly, even ruefully, examines what it means to accept those patterns of regeneration that mankind eagerly incorporates into its value-systems. The world of the play is absurd because it violates the probabilities of representational realism; yet the world of our personal experience is, in absolute terms, as absurdly capricious as even the wildest romance. Posthumus speaks of Jupiter's oracle as being the stuff of madmen, a "senseless speaking," but adds, "Be what it is, / The action of my life is like it" (V.iv.149-50). Any one of us might sincerely utter that speech. Thus Shakespeare postulates a world no more absurd intrinsically than our own, but different in its surprising conformity to those myths whereby we attempt to explain or even control the random flux of experience. Shakespeare gives full humanity to a Proserpina-type to examine if such consoling legends have human validity. The play ends with the *Pax Augusta* and allusions to the imminent birth of Christ in far-off Palestine,[10] but this *coda* is part of the play's mythic pattern, with finally as tenuous a relationship to the world of private experience as the play's soothsayers, magic potions, and identifying birthmarks.

Yet the central mythic incident of the play, the one which, if anything, propels Posthumus' almost Christian repentance, penance, and salvation, is imbued with the full force of the Shakespearean type of psychological realism. I refer to Imogen's awakening to discover what she thinks is the headless body of her husband. The scene is a most cavalier violation of verisimilitude, but assuming that a human being can be so strangely deluded, Imogen's feelings are convincing and entirely consistent with the woman as we know her. She concludes that the man before her has been murdered, wrongly but understandably assumes that Pisanio the servant is the murderer and has forged Posthumus' instructions to kill her, and then falls on the body in a frenzy of grief. I have already referred to the sensationalism of this scene and to the *frisson* the audience must feel in watching Imogen embrace the body of the man who intended to beat and rape her. But poor Imogen is even more abused (though we do not notice it so strongly) in supposing that Posthumus is innocent of any intent to murder her. Her explaining away of his guilt seems so natural in a loving wife that it scarcely surprises us; but the fact is, Imogen's desperate clinging to the body of her would-be rapist is a precise symbolic representation of her relationship to Posthumus at this point in the play. She not only forgives her victimizer, indeed to the point of believing his crime is non-existent, but loves him with the full force of erotic passion. Is Shakespeare, then, merely reducing Christian love and forgiveness to a kind of vulgar sexual sado-masochism?

This conclusion, I believe, misses Shakespeare's almost agonizing sense of life's ironies. *Cymbeline* may be a pretty, optimistic fable on the surface, but of all the regenerative females of the late plays—Marina, Thaisa, Perdita, even Hermione—none seems to feel as much ordinary human pain while playing that role as does Imogen. When Hermione at her trial reminds us that she is the Emperor of Russia's daughter, we have an alienation effect, a reminder that we are witnessing an old tale. When Imogen, forced to become a homeless wanderer, complains of hunger, weariness, and the malicious misdirections given to strangers, and then (a most telling psychological detail) awakes from a frightening nightmare in which she can never walk far enough to reach Milford Haven, she seems an ordinary helpless woman rather than a fairy-tale princess. Furthermore, as intense as her mental and physical suffering may be, she is also repeatedly placed in situations in which she mistakes or does not realize some grave danger to herself, as when Iachimo steals her bracelet while she is sleeping or when she hastily concludes that Posthumus did not want her murdered. Of course, we can justify the cruelties of the plot by arguing that Imogen's sufferings make her a redemptive scapegoat who, after being victimized by the husband and father whom she loves, somehow purges them of hatred and revenge. Furthermore, Shakespeare seems to emphasize a concept most evident in Judaeo-Christian versions of the scapegoat myth, namely, that the

sacrifice is redemptive because the victim selflessly loves its victimizer, whether it be fallen mankind in the story of the Crucifixion or the Creator of mankind in the story of Job or of Abraham and Isaac. Thus we see the point of Shakespeare's fashioning a scapegoat myth out of a folktale about a loving wife persecuted by her husband. The real point, however, is that Shakespeare, by adding this erotic dimension with its latent and undignified sado-masochism, is questioning whether ordinary human love, such as that between a man and a woman, can contain the redemptive possibilities implied in scapegoat legends. The mean tricks that Shakespeare deliberately seems to be perpetrating on his heroine draw the absolutes of myth into a more problematical realm.

It is no accident that, as F. D. Hoeniger suggests, some Hardyish god seems to be at work in the play.[11] Repeatedly, Shakespeare forces us to ask whether Imogen's love and loyalty are not wasted or, what is worse, whether scapegoats like her are not merely the ignorant, obedient playthings of some wanton god who is killing them for his sport.[12] That is why Imogen is often placed in situations where she must act blindly or where her danger is worse than what she suspects. That is also why she has so many enemies in this play: an irate, autocratic father, a wicked-witch stepmother, the brutish suitor Cloten, the scheming Machiavel Iachimo, and finally a jealous husband. In fact, a list of Imogen's victimizers reads exactly like a catalog of standard literary and folklore villains, so much that taken together they seem to be composite aspects of a single force of evil.

Consider also that a case can be made for treating Iachimo, like Cloten, as an aspect or extension of Posthumus. Cloten is a type of brute appetite and violence, while Iachimo is a type of egotistic intellectual cunning, and he very much acts as Posthumus' agent. One might object that Posthumus wants him to fail, but, as Homer Swander plausibly argues, Shakespeare makes us question Posthumus' motives for testing Imogen in the first place.[13] Iachimo thus acts as an instrument of Posthumus' will, and the magnificent scene in Imogen's bedroom has much of the symbolic atmosphere of that of her ritual death and resurrection. For instance, like Posthumus and Cloten, Iachimo is Imogen's would-be bedfellow; thus his hovering menacingly over the half-naked, sleeping woman intensifies, as when Imogen ignorantly embraces the body of Cloten, a sense of her vulnerability, both sexual and otherwise. So do Iachimo's allusions to Tarquin softly pressing the floor rushes and to the moment when Philomel gave up in the tale of Tereus. Imogen's inertness even suggests the posture of a willing victim. Iachimo's describing her as a goddess, "Cytherea," and in terms of flowers, with a body like a "fresh lily" and a mole "cinque-spotted: like the crimson drops / I' th' bottom of a cowslip" (II.ii.15, 38-9), gives her the aura of a nature deity, and the whole scene subtly suggests a religious sacrifice: "[B]e her sense but as a monument, / Thus in a chapel lying" (32-3).

Note also that Iachimo's type of eroticism is in keeping with his symbolic function in the play. In contrast to Cloten's lumpish carnality, his attempt to seduce Imogen is through entirely verbal and intellectual means. Even the sexual menace of the bedchamber scene is achieved through Iachimo's revelry in physical restraint. He kisses Imogen just once—but only to compare the soft flesh of lips with "Rubies unparagon'd." Indeed, the exquisite delicacy of Iachimo's paean to Imogen's beauty depends on the metaphorical transformation of her body into the non-human, even the intangible. Her physical parts are compared with lilies, cowslips, windows, perfume, light, and the blue of the sky. This speech is the verbal distillation, filtered through Iachimo's fanciful brain, of the erotic idealism Posthumus displayed in Act I, just as Cloten represents an intensification of his sexual brutality. Finally, the carnal knowledge of which Iachimo later boasts to Posthumus was never anywhere but in his head. Iachimo may have temporarily despoiled Imogen's honor, but it was purely an intellectual rape.

Thus through Iachimo Imogen becomes the victim of Posthumus' murderous rage, and like Posthumus Iachimo comes to repent. Indeed, it is as though the self-seeking intellectual will finally yields to the redeemed spirit. I won't label Cloten, Iachimo, and Posthumus, id, ego, and superego, as though they were the Brothers Karamazov. But in this play the individual natures and interrelationships of the victimizers are clearly derived from allegory. For example, Posthumus' forgiveness of Iachimo in the play's final scene is the immediate signal for Cymbeline to free the Roman captives he intended to kill and to pay the tribute exacted by Augustus Caesar, just as Joseph and Mary paid Augustus Caesar's world tax in Bethlehem. In allegorical terms, once Imogen the divine scapegoat loves and forgives her persecutors, it is easy for the play's villains to show the same generosity. Because their relationships are so often purely allegorical, the play's victimizers seem different in kind from their more complexly and fully characterized victim, Imogen. This disjunction among character types emphasizes the loneliness and uncertainty of her situation. Some critics complain that Posthumus' characterization seems pallid next to Imogen's and that even after his purgation he seems not quite satisfactory as a husband.[14] This inadequacy is part of the play's nexus of meaning and has nothing to do with Posthumus' worth considered in the abstract, for he represents mankind fallen and then redeemed. But the husband with whom our convincingly humanized scapegoat-figure is rewarded has emerged from a world of myth and wish-fulfillment that just barely touches actuality. The suffering of the scapegoat is fully realized, but the redemption that gives the scapegoat myth its meaning is not quite so palpable.

An incident in the final scene that is quite as bizarre as Imogen's embracing of Cloten's headless corpse recapitulates, quite self-consciously, this problematic view of redemption through sacrifice. Posthumus is in another passion of grief because he has learned from the contrite Iachimo that Imogen, whom he thinks he murdered, was innocent. Imogen runs forward to reveal herself but gets struck down by her husband, who cries: "Shall's have a play of this? Thou scornful page, / There lie thy part" (V.v.228-9). There is no reason for Posthumus to start kicking Imogen around again, this time physically, except that, as his allusion to plays and play-acting suggests, it has been his role throughout this mythologizing drama to play the deluded victimizer while it has been Imogen's role to play his victim. So they go at it again, Posthumus as blind to what he is doing as ever, and Imogen once more playing her scapegoat's part with all the loving earnestness she has shown before:

> Why did you throw your wedded lady from
>   you?
> Think that you are upon a rock, and now
> Throw me again.
>
> (261-3)

She realizes by now that Posthumus did want her killed, and, true to her role of sacrificial victim, implies that he can try to kill her again if he wants to. She is of course happily certain that he will not, but Posthumus' beautiful reply to her suggests all the irony of the scapegoat's situation: "Hang there like fruit, my soul, / Till the tree die." In tying herself to Posthumus, Imogen is depending on the mortal and transient, like the fruit that draws its sustenance from a tree that will not live forever. The play's peaceful conclusion depends on such a willingness to accept the limits of being human, just as Imogen puts up bravely with all the indignities the play forces upon her. George Bernard Shaw declares himself undelighted to learn that "Imogen is so dutiful that she accepts her husband's attempt to have her murdered with affectionate docility." He adds, "I cannot share these infantile joys."[15] Shaw does not give Shakespeare credit for himself seeing and, through his dramaturgy, exposing his play's joy as infantile, that is, a product of the childlike faith that Paulina wakens in Leontes rather than of reasoned reflection. Yet the world of myth reveals wherein the most sophisticated of us are children, and when we try to affirm, as do *Cymbeline* and the late plays, our faith in life, we can understand Shakespeare's fascination with naive old tales.

Notes

[1] This judgment is eloquently argued by Harley Granville-Barker, *Prefaces to Shakespeare* (Princeton, 1946), vol. I, 539-42.

[2] Line citations from *Cymbeline* refer to the Arden edition, ed. James Nosworthy (1955; rpt. London, 1969).

[3] See Caroline W. Mayerson, "The Orpheus Image in *Lycidas*," *PMLA,* LXIV (1949), 189-207. For a thorough account of the allegorical and Christian tradition, see John Block Friedman, *Orpheus in the Middle Ages* (Cambridge, Mass., 1970).

[4] Friedman quotes the account of the Hellenistic poet Phanocles, p. 9.

[5] It is of course typical of more recent criticism to regard the last plays as works about renewal and regeneration and to draw *Cymbeline* into that context. See, e.g., William Barry Thorne, "*Cymbeline:* 'Lopp'd Branches' and the Concept of Regeneration," *SQ,* XX (1969), 143-9. To G. Wilson Knight, *Cymbeline is* "mainly a historical play," (*The Crown of Life* [London, 1947], p. 129).

[6] Wanderers in myths tend to have been either visited by the gods (Psyche, Io, Bellerophon, Kundry, the Wandering Jew) or to be demigods themselves (Herakles, Theseus).

[7] For more mythological allusions, see R. J. Schork, "Allusion, Theme, and Characterization in *Cymbeline*," *SP,* LXIX (1972), 210-16.

[8] This judgment is explored, with great sympathy to the play, by Frank Kermode, *William Shakespeare: The Final Plays* (London, 1963), pp. 22-8.

[9] Arthur Kirsch, "*Cymbeline* and Coterie Dramaturgy," *ELH,* XXXIV (1967), 299.

[10] See Northrop Frye, *A Natural Perspective* (New York, 1965), pp. 66-7.

[11] F. D. Hoeniger, "Irony and Romance in *Cymbeline*," *SEL,* II (1962), 223.

[12] Granville-Barker believes that the play has bludgeoned Imogen beyond recovery.

[13] Homer Swander, "*Cymbeline* and the 'Blameless Hero,'" *ELH,* XXXI (1964), 259-70.

[14] Knight and Granville-Barker, trying to fit Posthumus into a psychological type, treat him as the stolid-but-dependable Briton, a kind of bluff Victorian John Bull somehow wedded to a fairy princess and conned by a sleazy foreigner.

[15] "Foreword," *Cymbeline Refinished,* in *Bernard Shaw: Collected Plays with Their Prefaces,* vol. 7 (London, 1974), 182-3.

Karen Bamford (essay date 1993)

SOURCE: "Imogen's Wounded Chastity," in *Essays in Theatre / Études Théâtrales,* Vol. 12, No. 1, November, 1993, pp. 51-61.

[*In the essay below, Bamford compares the plot and role of Imogen to the classical legend of Lucretia.*]

In act 2, scene 2 of *Cymbeline*—for many viewers no doubt one of the most memorable moments in the play—Iachimo emerges from a trunk and moves toward the sleeping Imogen. As he does so he compares himself to the ravisher of the legendary Lucretia: "Our Tarquin thus / did softly press the rushes, ere he waken'd / the chastity he wounded" (2.2.12-14).[1] The allusion is significant: it points to an analogy between Imogen and Lucretia that goes far beyond their common vulnerability to a sexual predator.

The story of Lucretia—the Roman wife whose suicide liberated her nation—was widely known in the period and exercised a powerful influence on Jacobean drama. Heywood's adaptation of Livy, replete with bawdy songs, drums and trumpets, proved a popular triumph at the Red Bull in 1608. Around the same time the Lucretia story emerged covertly in a series of Italianate tragedies performed by the King's Men: *The Revenger's Tragedy* (1606), *The Second Maiden's Tragedy* (1611) and Fletcher's *Valentinian* (c. 1612). It is, I suggest, in the context of these plays that we should read *Cymbeline*—produced around 1609 (Nosworthy xiv-xvii), the year after Heywood's *Rape of Lucrece.*

Iachimo's specular violation of Imogen, which strongly recalls the rape of Shakespeare's Lucrece, points to larger affinities between *Cymbeline* and the classical legend. Like her Roman prototype Imogen is persecuted by a lustful male (Cloten) who represents the corrupt government; her suffering proves redemptive for a diseased polity; and a final climactic battle marks the regeneration of the community. By connecting the wager plot derived from Boccaccio[2] with British history—that is, by making the wife of Boccaccio's tale the heiress presumptive to the British throne—Shakespeare invests the heroine's suffering with national, political significance. Like Lavinia—an earlier Lucretia figure—Imogen embodies the state.

Imogen's marriage sets her apart from the other young heroines of Shakespeare's romances and connects her with Lucrece. As Granville-Barker remarks, "married chastity . . . is the chief theme of the play," and "Imogen is its exemplar" (2: 153). Her marriage is highly irregular, however—a secret contract quickly severed by paternal wrath—and Posthumus implies that it may not have been consummated:

Me of my lawful pleasure she restrain'd,
And prayed me oft forbearance: did it with
A pudency so rosy, the sweet view on't
Might well have warm'd old Saturn; that I
   thought her
As chaste as unsunn'd snow.

                 (2.4.161-65)

The logic of the wager plot requires, of course, that Posthumus know Imogen's bedroom and the "cinque-spotted" mole. Like the time scheme of *Othello,* however, Imogen's sexual status is ambiguous.[3] The play directs us to view her as both wife and virgin, a duality reflected in the pictures of "Proud Cleopatra" and "Chaste Dian" which decorate her chamber. In her virginal aspect Imogen is—like Spenser's Amoret[4]— an unravished bride, wedded but not bedded, and as such she is the focus of intense erotic excitement and anxiety.[5]

Four men, including her husband, father, and step-brother, persecute Imogen, and from the beginning the threat of sexual coercion looms. The play's emphasis is thus far less on the opposition between good and evil political groups (tyrannical Tarquins / oppressed Romans), than on the extended suffering of the heroine, upon whose integrity, literally and figuratively, the future of the commonwealth depends. The anonymous Second Lord draws our attention both to Imogen's perilous position and her national significance:

      Alas poor princess,
Thou divine Imogen, what thou endur'st,
Betwixt a father by thy step-dame govern'd,
A mother hourly coining plots, a wooer
More hateful than the foul expulsion is
Of thy dear husband, that horrid act
Of the divorce, he'ld make. The heavens hold
   firm
The walls of thy dear honour, keep
   unshak'd
That temple, thy fair mind, that thou mayst
   stand,
T'enjoy thy banish'd lord and this great
   land!

                (2.1.55-64)

This summary also underlines the political parallel between Cymbeline's court, Tarquin's, and the Rome of the Andronici. In each case an ambitious queen is the root of all evil; in each case that queen's son threatens the innocent heroine.[6]

The Second Lord's fervent prayer occurs ironically in the interval between Iachimo's failure to seduce Imogen (1.7) and his successful invasion of her bedroom (2.2). The Lord's use of the traditional analogy between a building and the female body ("the walls of thy dear

honour") points to the significance of the next scene. Immediately after his prayer we see Imogen in her room, commending herself to the gods as she prepares to sleep. Her prayer, unconsciously echoing the Second Lord's,[7] emphasizes her vulnerability. Iachimo's penetration of her room—figuratively, "the walls" of her "dear honour"—follows directly.

Unlike his sources Shakespeare treats the bedroom scene erotically. Indeed he comes as close as he can to actually staging the rape he narrates in *Lucrece.* It is, as many critics have noted, a theatrical tour-de-force. Unlike the reader of the source tales, Shakespeare's audience is ignorant of the villain's scheme. We are surprised by Iachimo's appearance and probably apprehend a physical assault. Iachimo himself arouses expectations of a rape by comparing his movements to Tarquin's. Like Shakespeare's Tarquin, Iachimo hovers hungrily over the sleeping woman, excited by her unconscious beauty.[8] The violation is more than just specular: the text seems to indicate a kiss ("That I might touch!/But kiss, one kiss! Rubies unparagon'd,/ How dearly they do't" [16-18]),[9] as well as the symbolic theft of the bracelet. The audience's response to this scene will depend largely on the extent to which each member identifies with the passive woman and/or the active man. Here, as in *Lucrece,* Shakespeare exploits the peculiar excitement and/or horror that emerges from the encounter between male predator and unconscious female victim.

Imogen is not, of course, Lucrece; Iachimo does not "enjoy" her "dearest bodily part." Nevertheless, the difference between Tarquin's crime and Iachimo's is, in one sense, negligible: Iachimo has access to Imogen's body without her consent, and thus—because he can prove this access publicly—he "steals" her honour, just as a rapist "steals" the chastity of the woman he rapes. In terms of the wager-plot, the effect of an actual rape would be the same as that of the lesser, specular violation: Iachimo could prove his intimate knowledge of her body in the same way, and Imogen would be the same faithful wife and unconsenting victim. She would not, however, be chaste and, according to the conventions governing chastity in Jacobean drama, the consequences of this would be tragic: Imogen would have to die—either by her own hand or another's.[10] Because she remains technically pure, a comic ending is possible: with her "honour" restored to her, Imogen can resume her marriage with Posthumus. (The difference between Lucrece's fate and Imogen's highlights the essentially physical nature of chastity: the chaste woman is the one who is vaginally penetrated only by her husband.) Imogen's visual violation by Iachimo, like her subsequent mock-death, is thus a tragic-comic device. It is a rape that is not a rape. It allows Shakespeare to exploit theatrically the eroticism of *Lucrece* without sacrificing his heroine and a happy ending.

The mock-rape also ensures, on one level, a blameless heroine. Since Imogen is asleep throughout the scene, she enjoys a manifest innocence that Lucrece has to prove by her suicide. Nevertheless this episode does affect our perception of her. Neely observes that Iachimo's "salacious desires contaminate their object," while Imogen's "inert chastity, as he describes it, invites assault" (182). I think she is right. Imogen is degraded by Iachimo's objectifying gaze—in spite of the "reverence" of his courtly rhetoric—and, just as Shakespeare's verse shows us a Lucrece whose beauty makes her complicit in Tarquin's assault, so here the text constructs an Imogen whose beauty is provocative. Two other small signs suggest that Imogen, on some level, shares responsibility for Iachimo's successful access to her body. In her bedtime prayer Imogen asks for protection from "fairies and tempters of the night" (9)—not from "all perils and dangers of this night" as *The Book of Common Prayer* puts it (64), but from *tempters*.[11] A tempter is "one who . . . tempts or entices to evil" (OED 1). This suggests that Iachimo comes to her in bed, as the devil came to the legendary St. Justina, as a figure of sexual templation;[12] that in fact he represents her desire. Secondly, Iachimo tells us that Imogen has been reading the "tale of Tereus" and that "the leaf's turn'd down / Where Philomel gave up." In his Arden edition, Nosworthy glosses "gave up" as "yielded, succumbed" and by this reading Iachimo implies Philomel's shared responsibility for her rape: she "gave up"—yielded or succumbed—as if to a pressing invitation to sexual pleasure. These two verbal signs—Imogen's fear of "tempters," and Iachimo's allusion to the yielding Philomel—frame the violation of Imogen and subtly direct us to see her as complicit in Iachimo's guilty desires.[13]

Although Imogen's unconsciousness throughout the scene ensures her technical innocence, it also works against her. Unlike the legendary Justina, who wrestles with the devil, or even Shakespeare's Lucrece, who challenges Tarquin rhetorically, morally and emotionally, Imogen is entirely passive. She lacks the dignity conferred by action. She lacks even the dignity of consciousness. She is utterly unaware of what is happening to her, and—in spite of our anxiety for her—this ignorance distances her from the audience. We know too much, she knows too little. Imogen becomes, for the length of the scene, merely a victim, and her victimization is our spectacle.

Iachimo's bedroom victory determines Imogen's fate. From this point she is subject to a progressive degradation which ends only with her rescue by Lucius (4.2). In his early morning visit—with its ironic aubade for her night with Iachimo—Cloten takes up the theme of assault in another key: eroticism gives way to the crude bawdy of his puns ("if you can penetrate her with your fingering, so: we'll try with tongue too" [2.3.13-14]). Iachimo's slanderous description of Imo-

gen's "adultery" continues her degradation. Even though we know that Iachimo is lying about Imogen's surrender, his narrative powerfully creates—for us as well as for Posthumus—the thing it describes, her body:

> under her breast
> (Worthy her pressing) lies a mole, right proud
> Of that most delicate lodging. By my life,
> I kiss'd it, and it gave me present hunger
> To feed again, though full.
>
> (2.4.134-38)

His speech constructs Imogen here, just as in her bedroom, as the object of his lust. Since in this second description he casts her as his willing partner, he also creates a false, promiscuous Imogen.[14] Posthumus, credulous and angry, creates in turn a grotesque caricature of this "Imogen," a pornographic cartoon in which she is reduced to an orifice for Iachimo's lust:

> O, all the devils!
> This yellow Iachimo, in an hour was't not?
> Or less; at first? Perchance he spoke not, but
> Like a full-acorn'd boar, a German one,
> Cried "O!" and mounted . . .
>
> (165-69)

Posthumus's initial cry of vengeance—"O, that I had her here, to tear her limbmeal! / I will go there and do't, i' th' court, before / Her father" (2.4.147-49)—foreshadows Cloten's plan to rape Imogen and then "knock her back" to her father's court. In both cases the imagined violence is conceived theatrically, as a public display of sexual dominance—in particular, as a demonstration of manhood to Cymbeline, who has been a father to both young men. In the event, Posthumus elects to murder Imogen by proxy. Clearly the death he orders is not simply the execution of an adulteress: it is a lust-murder, a form of sexual aggression.[15] As his surrogate, Cloten pursues Imogen dressed in Posthumus's clothes, acting out their shared desire for a violent sexual revenge.[16] Cloten also pays the penalty for Posthumus's signal lapse in faith. It is he, still dressed as Posthumus, who dies a violent death; and it is thus his body that Imogen mistakenly grieves over, clasping it in a bloody embrace (4.2.295-332).

This extraordinary misidentification has caused critics some difficulty. Granville-Barker calls it "dramatically inexcusable":

> It is a fraud on Imogen; and we are accomplices in it. . . . Imogen herself is put, quite needlessly, quite heartlessly, on exhibition. How shall we sympathize with such futile suffering? And surely it is a faulty art that can so make sport of its creatures.
>
> (2: 178)

More recently Michael Taylor, acknowledging our probable discomfort with this scene, has attempted to defend its dramatic propriety:

> [H]owever much . . . we would like to spare Imogen and ourselves her necrophiliac embrace, we can hardly fail to notice that it seems in some respects no more than fitting that she should suffer such an indignity, the like of which would be unimaginable for Marina and Perdita. . . . Although we may flinch from its painful accumulation of detail, in a powerful way the indignity to Imogen satisfies expectations aroused in us during the course of Shakespeare's treatment of the wager story in *Cymbeline,* bringing to a suitably grotesque climax an element of punitive behaviour in relationships and towards the self . . .
>
> (98)

Taylor is right to note the episode's propriety: it is, as he says, "a suitably grotesque climax" to Imogen's progressive humiliation. I believe he errs, however, in concluding that it is part of "a pattern of erotic punishment in which both lovers suffer for the naivety of their expectations" (105). This implies a symmetry to the lovers' experience. Their suffering, however, is not equivalent, nor equally deserved. Imogen suffers far more, and far more visibly than Posthumus: her pain is, as Granville-Barker puts it, "on exhibition." It is caused, moreover, not by her own "sexual frailty," as Taylor implies (105), but by her husband's. This attempt to rationalize Imogen's ordeal ignores the extent to which—in spite of the defiling eroticism of the "rape" scene with its suggestion of her complicity—the play insists on her purity,[17] almost, indeed, her divinity. As Pisanio declares, "She's punished for her truth; and undergoes, / More goddess-like than wife-like, such assaults / As would take in some virtue" (3.2.7-9)

Like Lucrece, Imogen is a holy victim, and like her bears a strong resemblance to the legendary virgin martyrs. In addition to being chaste, beautiful, and well-born, she is persecuted by her father for refusing a marriage, and punished for a sexual crime she did not commit.[18] Our sense of Imogen as beleaguered virgin is strengthened by a change Shakespeare makes to the traditional wager plot. While in the sources the villain does not even try to seduce the heroine, Iachimo does attempt a seduction—an attempt Imogen calls an "assault" (1.7.150). Like Castiza in *The Revenger's Tragedy,* she repulses her assailant angrily, disdaining him "and the devil alike" (148).

Such language—the language of the morality plays—surrounds Imogen and her persecutors. To the Second Lord, the Queen is "a crafty devil" (2.1.51) and Imogen "divine" (2.1.56). For Iachimo in her chamber, Imogen's sanctity compels acknowledgement: "I lodge in fear," he cries, "Though this a heavenly angel, hell is

here" (2.2.49-50). Indeed, Iachimo's emergence from the trunk at midnight strongly suggests a devil unloosed at the witching hour, as his fearful retreat on the stroke of three enacts the demon's return to the hell-mouth.

One of the most arresting religious images is Imogen's early description of Posthumus as her "supreme crown of grief" (1.7.4). As Michael Taylor points out (101), the lovers' situation scarcely explains this extravagant language. It is, however, prophetic of Imogen's approaching ordeal. It suggests the crown of thorns—a symbol of Christ's passion—as well as the crown he bestows on his brides, the Virgin Mary and the virgin martyrs. It is thus highly appropriate for Imogen, the virgin wife whose marriage becomes a species of martyrdom.

Imogen's spirited virtue prompts her vocal defiance of both her father (1.2.64-81) and Cloten (2.3.123-35), and her flight from the prison of Cymbeline's court. Once she learns that Posthumus believes her unfaithful, however, this spirit deserts her. She becomes a Patient Grissill, sanctified by her willingness to suffer. In contrast to the heroine of the source tales, who pleads with her husband's servant for her life, Imogen invites the death Posthumus has commanded. Indeed, she asks for execution repeatedly before Pisanio can unfold his plan to save her.[19] Religious imagery underlines her sacrificial role ("Prithee, dispatch," she urges, "the lamb entreats the butcher" [3.4.97-98]).[20] Though Pisanio prevents Imogen's physical death, the text makes it clear that she suffers a spiritual death here, symbolized by her subsequent burial. As Pisanio puts it, "What shall I need to draw my sword? the paper / Hath cut her throat already" (33-34).

At this point in the source stories the resourceful heroine, bent on survival, escapes in disguise, and by her efforts rises to a position of power and influence. Finally she organizes the triumphant denouement which restores her to her identity and honour. By contrast, the pathetic Imogen stumbles about the Welsh wilderness, at the mercy of the kindly inhabitants, the noble Romans, and an apparently capricious Fortune, which allows her first to be "buried" alive and then to mistake Cloten's headless body for Posthumus's. When at length the denouement does occur, it is, as the vision of Jupiter insists, in fulfillment of a divine not human design.[21]

In the microcosm of the royal family, Britain's decay is manifest in the persecution of Imogen, the heir apparent, and, on a national level, in the refusal of tribute to Rome. Symbolically Imogen's suffering and "death" atone for the sins of her family and country. There is also a direct practical connection between her ordeal and their rejuvenation. The first sign of that renewal is Guiderius's defeat of Cloten (4.2), and it is

Imogen who unwittingly brings Cloten to Wales and his well-deserved death. Guiderius, equally unwitting, avenges the sexual threat to his sister and rids his country of a tyrant.[22] The second stage in Britain's recovery is the climactic battle which brings the princes out of hiding to save their father's life and kingdom.[23] Again, Imogen's martyrdom acts as a hidden cause of that victory, and thus of the final reunion: Posthumus, who helps the princes in their spectacular feat (5.3), is there to fight for Imogen and atone for her "murder":

> 'tis enough
> That, Britain, I have kill'd thy mistress: peace,
> I'll give no wound to thee: therefore, good heavens,
> Hear patiently my purpose. I'll disrobe me
> Of these Italian weeds, and suit myself
> As does a Briton peasant: so I'll fight
> Against the part I come with: so I'll die
> For thee, O Imogen . . .
>
> (5.1.19-26)

Posthumus's heroism is thus a form of religious service, an act of devotion to the wife he believes he killed. Finally, the recognition scene recapitulates Imogen's sacrificial role in the rejuvenation of her family/ country: when she, as Fidele, attempts to comfort Posthumus, he strikes her angrily to the ground (5.5.229). Her fall prompts the chain of revelations which leads to the restoration of the princes and Britain's peace with Rome.[24]

Heywood's *Rape of Lucrece* celebrates a political order in which women are finally irrelevant: the heroine's perfunctory suicide in act 4 is displaced by the fifth-act heroics of the regenerate Romans and a valiant Tarquin. *Cymbeline,* however, offers a far more disturbing vision of gender and politics. Imogen's heroism is central to the play, but it is the heroism of the beaten wife. She is punished not—as Pisanio claims—for her truth, but for her beauty, her sexuality. Cruelly victimized, she "undergoes more goddess-like than wife-like" the assaults of her husband, who sends Iachimo to seduce her and Pisanio to kill her. The "divine Imogen" is the apotheosis of Patient Grissill— a tragi-comic Lucrece whose "wounded chastity" redeems both family and country.

Notes

[1] All citations of *Cymbeline* are from Nosworthy's Arden edition.

[2] *Decameron,* the ninth novel of the second day. The English prose tale *Frederyke of Jennen,* translated from the Dutch, was also a source for the wager plot. Both are reprinted in Bullough 8:50-78. For Shakespeare's

use of his sources see also the Arden xvii-xxviii, Sexton 61-76, and Swander's "Blameless Hero."

[3] For this reason Imogen's virginity has been the subject of critical contention. Gesner argues that the marriage must be a "handfasting, an old form of the irregular or probationary marriage" (102) and as yet unconsummated, but Kirsch disagrees (148). There is no way to resolve the dispute: Shakespeare withholds all information on the lovers' history.

[4] Amoret is abducted from her wedding feast by the "vile Enchauntour Busyran" (*Faerie Queene* 4.1.3) to endure captivity and multiple threats to her chastity.

[5] Imogen shares this ambivalent status with other sexually threatened heroines on the Jacobean stage: for example, Marston's Sophonisba, the Lady in *The Second Maiden's Tragedy,* and Castabella in *The Atheist's Tragedy.* The peculiar excitement and anxiety generated by Imogen's anomalous position extends beyond the play to its critical reception, and may partly account for the cult of Imogen which flourished in the nineteenth century (see below, n. 9).

[6] The role of Cecropia and Amphialus in *The Countess of Pembroke's Arcadia* presents another parallel. Sidney even transfers most of the guilt for the sexual threat to Philoclea from the son to the mother (see, for example, Cecropia's speech at bk. 3, ch. 17 [532-34]).

[7] Imogen's prayer ("To your protection I commend me, gods" [2.2.8]) also echoes that of Heywood's Lucrece as she goes to bed ("love unto thy protection I commit / My chastitie and honour to thy keepe" [*Dramatic Works* 5:220]).

[8] Miola lists many close verbal parallels between *Lucrece* and *Cymbeline,* including the imagery of siege and invasion, the walled fortress and sacred temple, locks, treasures, flowers and even the "azure" colour of the heroines' veins (52-53). Curiously, Miola also compares Iachimo and Tarquin to the latter's advantage:

> Iachimo fancies himself another Tarquin and Shakespeare delights in fostering the illusion. All the while, however, the disparity between the brutal rape and the sneakily malicious note-taking comes into effect. Tarquin violates Lucrece, her household, family and city; Iachimo merely plays a cheap trick.
>
> (53)

[9] In his 1886 edition, Ingleby reacts violently to the suggestion that Iachimo actually kisses Imogen: "Capell's vulgar interpretation is too monstrous to need refutation. Shakespeare could not have intended the

profligate Italian to sully the purity of Imogen's lips. He does not kiss her" (59).

[10] A possible tragic variation would be a wasting sickness, like the one that kills Penthea in *The Broken Heart,* or that which consumes, at much greater length, Richardson's Clarissa. A comic variation would be Imogen's marriage to Iachimo although her prior marriage to Posthumus, of course, precludes this "happy" ending.

[11] Nosworthy notes the liturgical echo without comment (49).

[12] According to de Voragine's *The Golden Legend*(5: 166-72), a series of devils try to move Justina to lust. After two minor devils fail, the prince of devils, in the shape of a girl, nearly succeeds in persuading the saint to give in to her carnal desires: "the hart of the virgin was smitten with evil thoughts, and was greatly inflamed in desire of the sin of the flesh, so that she would have gone thereto, but then the virgin came to herself . . ." (168). Finally, the devil

> transfigured him in the likeness of a fair young man, and entered into her chamber, and found her alone in bed and without shame sprang into her bed and embraced her, and would have had a done with her. And when she saw this she knew well that it was a wicked spirit, and blessed her as she had done tofore, and he melted away like wax.

> (168)

[13] In the B.B.C. production Elijah Moshinsky picked up and magnified the suggestion of Imogen's complicity:

> Iachimo so disturbs Imogen, who may or may not be pure, that she in a sense has a nightmare about the presence of Iachimo which we know, objectively, to be true. . . . On television you get the opportunity of actually making the scene like her nightmare . . . we do all the filmic techniques of close-up and time-lapse and silhouettes and menacing shots and the suggestion of his nakedness, so he has a rather potent sexual force.

> (B.B.C. *Cymbeline* 17)

Iachimo's evil, Moshinsky observes, "actually depends on having made the other person guilty. The removal of the bracelet is in fact a rape. It's an extraordinary scene, the rhythm of it is so sexual" (23). Robert Lindsay concurs:

> I think the trunk scene is very pornographic. . . . He's excited, he's been in this trunk for hours, he's hot and sweaty and he gets out and he can do anything he wants; and Imogen is dreaming about being raped. . . .

> (24)

Robin Phillips's 1986 production at Stratford, Ontario enhanced the pornographic aspect of the bedroom scene. According to Roger Warren,

> Innogen [sic] seemed in greater danger than she has seemed in any other modern production, especially when Giacomo [sic] drew the bedclothes completely off her and straddled her before kissing the mole on her breast. . . . As she twisted and turned, she appeared very disturbed. . . . This graphic staging implied much more strongly than Moshinsky's that the near-rape was an externalizing of her nightmare. It also carried another suggestion. Giacomo wore jodhpurs, which gave the additional impression of 'riding' her in the sexual sense; and as her body twisted and buckled beneath his, the distinction between near-rape and actual rape began to seem very thin. . . . Innogen seemed much more soiled than usual, far more than in the television version, for all Lindsay's nakedness.

> (*Cymbeline* 91)

[14] Cf. the false Una that enrages Spenser's knight (*Faerie Queene* 1.1.36-2.6) and the pseudo-Amoret in Fletcher's *The Faithful Shepherdess* who provokes Perigot to wrath by her loose behaviour (3.1.243-318; *Dramatic Works* 3). Like Posthumus, Perigot attempts to kill his betrothed and nearly succeeds twice (3.1.318, 344 and 4.4.162).

[15] Siemon observes:

> In its particular details Posthumus's plan differs from Cloten's, although the degree of distinction one allows depends upon one's readiness to take as a phallic symbol the sword which is to be the instrument of Posthumus's revenge. At the least, both respond with violence to sexual humiliation and just as Shakespeare places the scenes of humiliation back to back, so he puts together the scenes in which the plans for violent revenge are most fully stated. The invitation to compare is patent, and the comparison shows the disintegration of Posthumus's character as a process by which he adopts Cloten's manners and some, at least, of his morals.

> (59)

[16] Siemon, Kirsch, 154-59, and Warren, "Virtuosity and Complexity," are particularly good on the relationship between Posthumus and Cloten.

[17] If, as seems likely, Shakespeare wrote "Innogen" rather than "Imogen," the heroine's name expresses her essential purity. See Warren, *Cymbeline* viii.

[18] For the unjust punishment of sexual crimes in hagiography, see, for example, the legend of St. Marine (*Golden Legend*3: 226-28). Jardine relates this motif to the Grissill legend and identifies it as one of "the

saving stereotypes of female heroism" in the Renaissance (182-83).

[19] At 3.4.54, 65-66, 68, 72, 75, 79, 97, 102.

[20] Ann Thompson notes the similarity between Imogen in this scene and Ovid's Philomela, who when she "sawe the sworde, she hoapt she should have dide, / And for the same hir naked throte she gladly did provide" (*Metamorphoses* 6. 705-6, Golding's translation; Thompson 24). The connection strengthens the sense of Posthumus's attack on Imogen as a form of sexual aggression, like Tereus's assault on Philomela.

[21] Sexton cites as an analogue to *Cymbeline* a French miracle play, *Miracle d'Oton, Roi d'Espagne,* which makes similar use of a wager plot: there the Virgin reveals the truth and effects a happy ending (62-73). Sexton observes that Imogen and the heroine of the French play "suffer with strength and dignity, but their helplessness is emphasized. They are exhausted and heartsick" (73).

[22] Since the wicked Queen dies of a "fever with the absence of her son" [4.3.2], we may credit Guiderius and Imogen with that death as well.

[23] Cymbeline graphically insists on their national significance when he calls the unknown heroes, "the liver, heart, and brain of Britain, / By whom . . . she lives" (5.5. 14-15).

[24] The role of the heroine in Greene's *James IV* presents an interesting analogue. There the lustful King of Scotland attempts to have his wife murdered. Disguised as a boy, the Queen flees to the forest with a faithful retainer, and is wounded. Providentially she survives to reconcile her husband with her father, the King of England, and prevent national disaster.

Works Cited

Bergeron, David M. "Sexuality in *Cymbeline.*" *Essays in Literature* 10 (1983): 159-68.

The Book of Common Prayer, 1559. Ed. J. E. Booty. Washington, DC: Folger, 1976.

Brownmiller, Susan. *Against Our Will.* 1975. New York: Bantam, 1976.

Bullough, Geoffrey, ed. *Narrative and Dramatic Sources of Shakespeare.* 8 vols. London: Routledge, 1957-75.

De Voragine, Jacobus. *The Golden Legend.* Trans. William Caxton. 7 vols. London: Dent, 1931.

Donaldson, Ian. *The Rapes of Lucretia.* Oxford: Clarendon P, 1982.

Fletcher, John. *The Dramatic Works in the Beaumont and Fletcher Canon.* 8 vols. General ed. Fredson Bowers. Cambridge: Cambridge UP, 1966-92.

Ford, John. *The Broken Heart.* Ed. Brian Morris. New Mermaids. London: Benn, 1965.

Gesner, Carol. *Shakespeare and the Greek Romances.* Lexington: UP of Kentucky, 1970.

Granville-Barker, Harley. *Prefaces to Shakespeare.* 4 vols. 1930. Ed. M. St. Clare Byrne. London: Batsford, 1963.

Greene, Robert. *James the Fourth.* Ed. J. A. Lavin. New Mermaids. London: Benn, 1967.

Heywood, Thomas. *Dramatic Works.* Ed. R. H. Shepherd. 6 vols. 1874. New York: Russell, 1964.

Jardine, Lisa. *Still Harping on Daughters.* Brighton: Harvester, 1983.

Kirsch, Arthur. *Shakespeare and the Experience of Love.* Cambridge: Cambridge UP, 1981.

Marston, John. *The Selected Plays of John Marston.* Ed. MacDonald P. Jackson and Michael Neill. Cambridge: Cambridge UP, 1986.

Miola, Robert S. "*Cymbeline:* Shakespeare's Valediction to Rome." *Roman Images.* Ed. Annabel Patterson. Selected Papers From the English Institute, 1982, n.s., n. 8. Baltimore: Johns Hopkins UP, 1984. 51-62.

Neely, Carol Thomas. *Broken Nuptials in Shakespeare's Plays.* New Haven: Yale UP, 1985.

The Second Maiden's Tragedy. Ed. Anne Lancashire. Revels Plays. Manchester: Manchester UP, 1978.

Sexton, Joyce H. *The Slandered Woman in Shakespeare.* English Literary Studies. Victoria: U of Victoria, 1978.

Shakespeare, William. *Cymbeline.* Literary Consultant: John Wilders. B.B.C. TV Shakespeare. London: B.B.C., 1983.

———. *Cymbeline.* Ed. J. M. Nosworthy. Arden Shakespeare. 1955. University Paperback. London: Methuen, 1980.

———. *Cymbeline.* Ed. C. M. Ingleby. London, 1886.

———. *The Poems.* Ed. F. T. Prince. Arden Shakespeare. 1960. University Paperback. London: Methuen, 1969.

———. *Titus Andronicus*. Ed. Eugene M. Waith. Oxford Shakespeare. Oxford: Clarendon P, 1984.

Sidney, Sir Philip. *The Countess of Pembroke's Arcadia*. Ed. Maurice Evans. Harmondsworth: Penguin, 1977.

Siemon, James E. "Noble Virtue in *Cymbeline*." *Shakespeare Survey* 29 (1976): 51-61.

Spenser, Edmund. *The Faerie Queene*. Ed. A. C. Hamilton. London: Longman, 1977.

Swander, Homer D. *"Cymbeline* and the 'Blameless Hero'." *ELH* 31 (1964): 259-70.

———. *"Cymbeline:* Religious Idea and Dramatic Design." *Pacific Coast Studies in Shakespeare.* Ed. W. F. McNeir and T. N. Greenfield. Eugene: U of Oregon P, 1966. 248-62.

Taylor, Michael. "The Pastoral Reckoning in *Cymbeline." Shakespeare Survey* 36 (1983): 97-106.

Thompson, Ann. "Philomel in *Titus Andronicus* and *Cymbeline." Shakespeare Survey* 31 (1978): 23-32.

Tourneur, Cyril. *The Atheist's Tragedy.* Ed. Irving Ribner. Revels Plays. London: Methuen, 1964.

———. *The Revenger's Tragedy.* Ed. R. A. Foakes. Revels Plays. London: Methuen, 1966.

Warren, Roger. *Cymbeline.* Shakespeare in Performance. Manchester: Manchester UP, 1989.

———. "Shakespeare's Late Plays at Stratford, Ontario." *Shakespeare Survey* 40 (1988): 155-68.

———. "Theatrical Virtuosity and Poetic Complexity in *Cymbeline." Shakespeare Survey* 29 (1976): 41-49.

LANGUAGE AND IMAGERY

E.A.M. Colman (essay date 1974)

SOURCE: "The Language of Sexual Revulsion," in *The Dramatic Use of Bawdy in Shakespeare*, Longman Group Limited, 1974, pp. 112-42.

[In this excerpt, Colman suggests that the dark bawdiness of Cymbeline *places it in the tradition of* Othello,

King Lear, and Timon, *of Athens, rather than with the other Shakespearean romances.]*

From most critical viewpoints, *Cymbeline* fits tidily into the place that chronology gives it, among Shakespeare's last plays. Recent editors have hazarded guesses of 1608 or 1609 as its most probable time of composition,[22] and it has long been regarded as a companion piece to its close successor or contemporary, *The Winter's Tale.* Like both *The Winter's Tale* and *Pericles,* it has a plot that belongs in the romance genre, and many of its underlying concerns—loyalty, chastity, separation, remorse, reconciliation—are shared with *The Tempest* also. So far as its use of bawdy is concerned, however, *Cymbeline* belies this grouping. Its affinities are with *Othello, Lear* and *Timon,* plays in which the sexual elements are rarely funny and often sinister. Perhaps the dark implications of *Cymbeline's* bawdy can best be brought out by a survey of its functions for each of the three characters to whom most of it belongs—Iachimo, Posthumus and Cloten.

It has become a commonplace of *Cymbeline* criticism that Iachimo is no Iago. He has been said to lack both the sense of purpose and the steady malignity of the earlier villain: 'there is something fantastic about the fellow,' wrote Granville-Barker, 'and no tragically-potent scoundrel, we should be sure, will ever come out of a trunk.'[23] That is true so far as it goes. Iachimo does partake of the grotesque quality that characterises much of this whole play. But to stress his sub-tragic stature is beside the point. Like the Queen, the King's sons and Belarius, Iachimo *as a character* is a stock figure, yet his scheming comes close to being as vicious as Iago's, both in style and in result. When he sets out to incite jealousy, first in Posthumus and later in Imogen, his mode of suggestiveness is exactly Iago's: 'You may wear her in title yours; but you know strange fowl light upon neighbouring ponds. . .

If you buy ladies' flesh at a million a dram, you cannot preserve it from tainting' (I.iv.84, 130). And he uses another Iago-like technique when he makes sudden, unnerving lurches into bawdy exaggeration:

> O dearest soul, your cause doth strike my heart
> With pity that doth make me sick! A lady
> So fair, and fastened to an empery,
> Would make the great'st king double, to be partnered
> With tomboys hired with that self exhibition
> Which your own coffers yield! with diseased ventures
> That play with all infirmities for gold
> Which rottenness can lend nature! such boiled stuff
> As well might poison poison!
>
>   I.vi.117

The decisive difference, I would suggest, is not between Iachimo and Iago but between the royal Imogen and naive Desdemona. While both heroines serve as the embodiment of wifely loyalty, Imogen's loyalty is of a more mature order than Desdemona's. The effect of this difference on the tonality of the entire play can be felt when Imogen rounds on Iachimo to answer him with princely vigour.

So far so good, one might feel, were it not for the King's hostility to his daughter. Clearsighted though she is, she cannot know what Shakespeare allows us in the audience to know—that she is already encircled by people who are, in one way or another, her enemies. So the trunk plot succeeds, and Imogen's next indirect assailant is Posthumus himself.

Posthumus speaks no bawdy lines in the play until after becoming convinced that Imogen has committed adultery. He then falls victim to a typically Jacobean sexual nausea.

>   No, he hath enjoyed her.
> The cognizance of her incontinency
> Is this: she hath bought the name of whore
>   thus dearly.
>
>   . . . . .
>
>   Never talk on't;
> She hath been colted by him.
>
>   II.iv.126

The misogynous soliloquy that ends Act II has been censured as wild and disintegrating.[24] Certainly the lines show bathos and a measure of incoherence, but it is a literal rather than emotional incoherence, and, as with *Cymbeline* as a whole, the disparities and absurdities are part of the point. Life is a disparate business, and Imogen's tough, resourceful struggle with it forms an extended contrast with Posthumus's easy disillusion. His rant is the outpouring of a mind temporarily unhinged by that disillusion. Further, as we in the audience well know, Posthumus is entirely wrong about Imogen, who still is 'As chaste as unsunned snow'. Shakespeare accordingly lessens our empathy with the hero by making his fulminations bawdily absurd.

>   O, all the devils!
> This yellow Iachimo in an hour—was't not?
> Or less!—at first? Perchance he spoke not, but,
> Like a full-acorned boar, a German one,
> Cried 'O!' and mounted; found no opposition
> But what he looked for should oppose and she
> Should from encounter guard.
>
>   II.v.13

The distancing of Posthumus can be seen on a larger scale in what seems at first glance to be a major dislocation in the structure of the play: we are not shown the hero's recovery from his Act II state of bitterness. He simply disappears for two whole acts, and by the time we meet him again in V.i he is calm, repentant and on the point of seeking death as punishment for having had Imogen murdered. Yet in leaving a gap in Posthumus's story, Shakespeare has been less careless than he may seem. His primary interest—the play's primary interest—is in Imogen, and the progress of the action after Posthumus's second-act tirade encourages us to relate everything to her rather than to him. What we then see is resilient and chaste womanhood sustaining a long series of attacks—from Cymbeline and his Queen, from Cloten and Iachimo, from Posthumus, and from the deceptiveness and chanciness of life itself.

With Cloten, as with Iachimo, and even with Posthumus in his wager-taking, the threat is specifically directed against Imogen's chastity. Cloten makes an interesting comparison with one Armenio, his counterpart in *The Rare Triumphs of Love and Fortune,* a play of the early 1580s on which *Cymbeline* seems to be based. Of the two, Cloten has much the bawdier turn of mind, so that the total share of lubricity is altogether larger in the economy of Shakespeare's play than in *Love and Fortune.* This shambling lecher at court represents no less a danger to Imogen's safety than does Iachimo. So closely do their separate schemes interlock, indeed, that it often seems impossible that she can escape, despite the spasmodic hopes held out in some quasi-choric speeches from the Second Lord and Pisanio (II.i.54-63, III.v.157-62, IV.iii.36-46). Emblematically, Imogen's bedside reading is the story of Tereus, a tale of rape and multilation: 'here the leaf's turned down,' notes Iachimo, 'Where Philomel gave up.' As he returns fearfully to his claustrophobic hiding-place he looks again towards Imogen and adds: 'Though this a heavenly angel, hell is here.' The words take on a double truth, because they have barely died away before Cloten arrives on stage, ready to reel off coarse jokes to his hired musicians.

> Come on, tune. If you can penetrate her with your fingering, so. We'll try with tongue too. . . . If this penetrate, I will consider your music the better; if it do not, it is a vice in her ears which horsehairs and calves' guts, nor the voice of unpaved eunuch to boot, can never amend.
>
>   II.iii.13,28

The peculiar vileness of Cloten's *double entendres* comes from their being delivered as monologues rather than in the course of any conversational cut and thrust. Shared between two or more speakers his innuendos would pass as harmless chatter. Flowing uninterruptedly from the black holes of a single mind, they acquire a quality of sniggering gaucheness. On the stage Cloten can take on a certain pathos, not unlike that of Middleton's somewhat similar creation The Ward in *Women Beware Women*. But despite occasional flashes of authorial pity, neither Shakespeare nor Middleton leaves any doubt about the hideous threat that such a creature would represent in the role of lover. Cloten amounts to more than 'that harsh, noble, simple nothing' whom Imogen describes, and when he conceives his plan for raping her it becomes only too easy to imagine his being able to succeed. He is—to adapt another of Granville-Barker's phrases—an educated Caliban.

It is all the more disconcerting, consequently, when Imogen, reviving from deathly unconsciousness outside Belarius's cave, finds Cloten as her headless 'bedfellow' and mistakes him for Posthumus. This weird occurrence bears out in action Imogen's own aphorism, 'Our very eyes / Are sometimes, like our judgements, blind.' But if that were all, Shakespeare's far-fetched stage situation would be a crazily elaborate way of making so ordinary a point. What should be borne in mind as well is the lingering influence of the obsequies that so shortly preceded Imogen's awakening. When Belarius, Guiderius and Arviragus strewed their flowers over the pair of bodies, male and female, the funeral rites merged into marriage symbolism; and that makes it surprisingly easy to imagine now, with Imogen's help, that her pursuer Cloten and her husband Posthumus have mysteriously merged their identities. 'Thersites' body is as good as Ajax', / When neither are alive.' At the risk of over-schematising the play, one might envisage Cloten as a satanic 'shadow' of Posthumus in much the same way as Wagner in *The Ring* sees Alberich and Wotan as two aspects of the same power-figure.[25] In all superficial ways Cloten and Posthumus are utterly unlike, yet both have sought Imogen's love, only to turn on her in hate.

Happily this uncanny identification of hero and villain is no more than an illusion, a stage trick. Cloten will stay dead, while Posthumus—his name presages it—survives to be reunited with Imogen:

> Why did you throw your wedded lady from
>   you?
> Think that you are upon a rock, and now
> Throw me again.
>
>   V.v.261

Our instinctual certainty that he will never again reject her represents a double victory for the wifely ideal that she embodies.[26] Like Lear, Posthumus has emerged from sick revulsion into a new world of sanity and forgiveness, and Imogen has at the same time escaped the clouds of hostile, bawdy sexuality that hung about her for so long. In the face of an opposite that was

dangerous as well as mocking, ideality has been doubly affirmed.

. . . . .

As an end-note to this chapter, a word or two about *Pericles,* which comes strikingly close to *Cymbeline* in feeling and not far ahead of it in date (*c.* 1607/8). The widely held opinion that Shakespeare did not write the play's first two acts need not concern us here, since it happens that these acts, at least in the form in which they have reached us via the Quarto of 1608, introduce no bawdy. On discovering the incest between Antiochus and his daughter, Pericles shows disgust, but not the hysterical kind of disgust that finds expression in gross terms. The play then continues free of verbal indecency—even in II.i, the fishermen's scene—until IV.ii, by which time we are well inside the segment generally accepted as Shakespeare's.

The three brothel scenes, IV.ii, v and vi, have often been compared with the underworld scenes of *Measure for Measure,* but again *Cymbeline* makes the apter parallel. For Marina as for Imogen, the situation is one of virtue-in-danger, and it is presented here with an archetypal simplicity of outline. The physical and moral degradation threatening Marina is boldly dramatised in the utter dejection of the Pander and his troop when they first appear:

> BAWD We were never so much out of creatures. We have but poor three, and they can do no more than they can do; and they with continual action are even as good as rotten. . . . The stuff we have, a strong wind will blow it to pieces, they are so pitifully sodden.
>
> PANDER Thou sayest true; they are too unwholesome, o' conscience. The poor Transylvanian is deal that lay with the little baggage.
>
>   IV.ii.7,18

Insistence on the deadly physical corruptiveness of the brothel can be heard again in the discussion of Monsieur Veroles, 'the French knight that cowers i'th'hams' (IV.ii.104), and yet again in the breezy arrival of Lysimachus:

> LYSIMACHUS How now! How a dozen of virginities?
> BAWD Now, the gods to bless your Honour!
> BOULT I am glad to see your Honour in good health.
> LYSIMACHUS You may so; 'tis the better for you that your resorters stand upon sound legs. How now! Wholesome iniquity have you, that a man may deal withal and defy the surgeon?
>
>   IV.vi.19

Such an emphasis heightens suspense over Marina's fate, while at the same time eliminating even for the

Act II, scene ii. Iachimo and Imogen. Frontispiece to the Rowe edition (1709).

umph. Marina's success is all the more important to the moral design of the play because it represents the outcome of a head-on collision of values, with the miseries and cruelties of the brothel neither evaded nor laughed aside. *Pericles,* for all its vagaries of structure and narrative line, can thus claim the merit of providing, in this fourth act, a convincing objective correlative for what in *Timon* was an arbitrary and weakly motivated disgust. It confirms Shakespeare as being firmly in command again of the measured idealism that had helped to shape the final dispensations of *Hamlet, Othello* and *Lear.* It focuses sharply on the fact that sex can be both shameful and ugly, but it also focuses on the kind of callousness that makes it so—a poison for which antidotes are possible. Finally, looked at from the point of view of Shakespeare's developing technique in the dramatic use of bawdy, *Pericles* shows the farthest swing of the pendulum away from the casual scurrilities of his very early comedies.

Notes

[22] J.M. Nosworthy in New Arden *Cymbeline* (1955), pp. xiv-xvii; and C. Maxwell in New Cambridge edn (1960), pp. xi-xii.

[23] Harley Granville-Barker, *Prefaces to Shakespeare* (1963 edn, 4 vols), ii, 146.

[24] By Nosworthy, *op. cit.,* p. lxvi.

[25] Schwarz-Alberich and Licht-Alberich. See Ernest Newman, *The Wagner Operas* (2nd edn, 1961), p. 554; and Robert Donington, *Wagner's 'Ring' and its Symbols* (1963), p. 187.

[26] I assume that martial rejection is what Imogen is talking about when she says, smilingly, 'Throw me again.' If, on the other hand, she meant 'throw me to the floor' (as in wrestling)—a possibility that tempted Edward Dowden into conjectural emendation of FI's 'Rock' to 'lock'—she would be giving the play its last, and most domestic, bawdy joke.

[27] An edition of *The Pattern of Painful Adventures* was published in London in 1607. An earlier edition, possibly *c.* 1594, is reprinted in Bullogh, vi, 423-82.

Lila Geller (essay date 1980)

SOURCE: *"Cymbeline* and the Imagery of Covenant Theology," in *Studies in English Literature: 1500-1900,* Vol. XX, No. 2, Spring, 1980, pp. 241-55.

[*In the essay below, Geller examines the religious imagery and covenant-contract theology found in* Cym-

most hard-boiled of audiences any risk of her being thought priggish. Comparison between this part of the play and its source material, the thirteenth and fourteenth chapters of Lawrence Twyne's novel *The Pattern of Painful Adventures,*[27] shows the dramatist making the most of the brothel-keepers' cold-bloodedness but playing down Twyne's suggestion that their trade is rich. The new stress falls rather on their depraved lust.

> BAWD Boult, take her away; use her at thy pleasure. Crack the glass of her virginity, and make the rest malleable.
>
> BOULT An if she were a thornier piece of ground than she is, she shall be ploughed.
>
> IV.vi.141

Consequently when Lysimachus and the two Gentlemen of IV.v are brought 'out of the road of rutting' and even Boult has been won over to gentleness by Marina's persuasion, virtue has gained a multiple tri-

beline, *noting that "each of* Cymbeline*'s main plots revolves about a covenant or contract."*]

In a stimulating disclaimer of F. R. Leavis' *caveat* that in *Cymbeline* "the organization is not a matter of strict and delicate subservience to a commanding significance, which penetrates the whole, informing and ordering everything—imagery, rhythm, symbolism, character, episode, plot—from a deep centre,"[1] Robert Hunter finds such a "deep centre" in "Christianity, with the doctrines of repentance and regeneration at its center."[2] Working from that orientation, he elevates Posthumous to the central role in the drama and convincingly discusses the wager plot, but he has little to say about the rebellion against Rome or the lost princes plot. I would contend that a more precise center can be located in a related aspect of Christianity, covenant-contract theology, a theology with strong social and political overtones. Each of *Cymbeline*'s main plots revolves about a covenant or contract; the Imogen-Posthumous plot involves the covenant (sacrament) of marriage and the covenant (wager) that replaces it, and the political rebellion plot involves the breach of covenants between the Britons and Romans. Even the subsidiary lost princes plot is related to the covenant theme in that it is motivated by the breach between Cymbeline and Belarius, a schism between king and loyal subject which evokes some examination of the idea of the social contract between ruler and ruled.

The imagery of the play underlines the basic unity. As a number of critics have observed, though overtly pagan, *Cymbeline* contains perhaps the greatest amount of religious imagery of Shakespeare's romances.[3] The other dominant body of imagery found in the play centers about the world of business—buying, selling, contracts.[4] The idea of the religious covenant underlies both bodies of imagery and forms their common factor.

Covenantal thinking has roots in early church theology, is re-emphasized in early Protestant thinking, and again becomes central in Puritan theology.[5] The idea of the covenant is usually, though not always, linked with the image of Britain as a second Israel, as a specially chosen people. In examining the nature of the covenant each group that adopts the concept seems to find it necessary to establish the antiquity and primacy of its own religion; this is accomplished by verifying the validity of the original covenants made between God and man, then demonstrating the deviation of intervening groups from the contract and the subsequent renewal in the body of the new church. Thus, to the early Christian writers, latter-day Jews fall away from the covenant of Abraham and Moses, and the early Christians receive the promise; to the early Protestants, the Roman Catholics fall away from apostolic Christianity, which then becomes the direct inherit-

ance of the Protestants; subsequently, to the Puritans, the Anglican Church will appear as deviant from apostolic Christianity as the Catholic Church had seemed to the early Protestants and the Puritans will claim the right of immediate descent.[6]

To have been impressed by patterns of thought that see history in terms of the descent of the covenant, Shakespeare need not have been inordinately interested in theological writing or been particularly attentive at crucial sermons. For medieval Christian writers history was Christian history, and though the origins of secular history long predate the seventeenth century, the tenacity of the religious view of history through the time of *Cymbeline* is attested to by the publication of John Speed's massive *Theatre of the Empire of Great Britaine* in 1611 with its reaffirmation of the providential view of history.[7]

Christian ecclesiastical history properly begins with Eusebius in the third century. In his rendition of the rise of Christianity Eusebius sees all of history to the birth of Christ as Christian prehistory.[8] He gives very special emphasis to the pre-Mosaic patriarchs of God's first covenants, regarding that early era as one of true religion, while that of Mosaic Judaism seems a deviation from the pure patriarchal religion.[9] Christianity is, to him, substantially the same as patriarchal Judaism, and is a renewal of the basic covenants.

Eusebius also works the history of Rome into Christian prehistory by seeing it as fulfillment of Old Testament prophecy. The prosperity of Rome was essential to the effective spreading of Christianity by the apostles. Thus the Pax Augustus is part of God's preparation for the incarnation. The arguments that lead to Eusebius' acceptance of the necessity of the Roman Empire are commonly repeated in Renaissance histories. Stow is typical when, in making the usual comment about the reign of Cymbeline (Cunobelinus) being largely noteworthy because it encompasses the birth of Christ, he says, "When Caesar Augustus the second Emperoure, by the will of God had stablished most sure peace throughe the Worlde, our redeemer Iesu Christe, verye God and man, was borne."[10]

For Gildas, the earliest extant British historian, the Romans have much the same significance as they do to Eusebius. They are treated sympathetically as the civilized peacemakers, against whom the Britons were wrong to revolt.[11] Britain is specifically equated with Old Testament Israel when Gildas deals with the Briton-Saxon conflict, which is a test of the fidelity of the Britons to God.[12] The defeat of the Britons is punishment for their sins, a direct result of their breaking of God's covenant. Spenser gives literary expression to this association of Britain's fortunes and misfortunes as part of God's system of reward and punishment.

For th'heauens haue decreed, to displace
The Britons, for their sinnes dew
  punishment,
And to the Saxons ouer-give their
  gouernment.
Then woe, and woe, and euerlasting woe,
Be to the Briton babe, that shalbe borne,
To liue in thraldome of his fathers foe;
Late king, now captiue, late lord, now
  forlorne,
The worlds reproch, the cruell victors
  scorne,
Banisht from princely bowre to wasteful
  wood:
O who shal helpe me to lament, and mourne
The royall seed, the antique Troian blood,
Whose empire lenger here, then euer any
  stood.[13]

But in countless commonplace writers we see the same analogies carried to modern examples; the saving of England by the destruction of the Spanish Armada is compared to the saving of Israel by the passage through the Red Sea; the prosperous state of England under Elizabeth is compared to the state of Ninevah just before its destruction.[14]

Bede accepts Gildas' account of the sinfulness of the Britons, but not Gildas' equation of them as the new Israel. For him the Saxons (who accepted the Roman version of Christianity) work better as the chosen people, replacing "sin-stained Britons."[15] Later, with the coming of Protestantism, we see many shifts in the old Israel-new Israel equations, depending on which religion is to be discredited. Bede's sixteenth-century translator, Thomas Stapleton, a Catholic, prefixes a list of forty-five differences between the primitive church and the reformed religion to show the identity of his faith (and Bede's) with the "original."[16] He is obviously defending his church against the kind of arguments early Protestants drew from Eusebius to prove their religion identical to that taught by the apostles in the time of Christ. One R. V., for example, takes this line, considering the faith as pure up to the coming of Austen with his "romish rites."[17] John Foxe takes basically the same position, that the true church in England began with the apostles, was pure to Austen, and only began to re-emerge with Wycliffe.[18] In *Christ Iesus Triumphant* Foxe implies the concept of successive churches falling away from their covenants, being scourged or afflicted by God as a result of their deviation, and being replaced by a church more faithful to the original covenant; his three examples of God's scourging of his favorites to enable them to suffer so as to achieve wisdom are the commonwealth of the Israelites, the church of Rome (which he considers to have been "good" only under persecution and to fall off in prosperity), and the church of England in its afflictions after Edward VI.[19]

Though the providential view of history is a rather long-standing one, the revival of the concept of the chosen nation and the increasing identification of Britain as the second Israel in the early decades of the seventeenth century must be interrelated with complex social, political, and economic motivations. However that may be, this emphasis is one that grows steadily throughout the first decade of the seventeenth century with the growth of covenant theology.

Much has been made of *Cymbeline*'s particularly Stuart qualities.[20] Its specific brand of nationalism conveys the confidence that brought historians to link England's prosperity with God's promises and the special situation of England. Speed refers back to Eusebius and other early Christian church historians for confirmation of the special promises to be found in the Old Testament and New being fulfilled in Britain. Isaiah (66.19) prophesies "The Iles a farre off which had not heard of his [Christ's] fame should be converted, and have his glorie to them declared among the Gentiles."[21] This event occurred the very morning of Christ's ascent, Speed maintains, citing Gildas, inasmuch as in Romans (10.18) "the Apostle himselfe saith, that the sound of the Gospell went thorow the earth, and was heard unto the ends of the world; which his saying cannot more fitly bee applied to any other Nation then unto us of Britaine, whose Land by the Almightie is so placed in the terrestriall globe, that thereby it is termed of the ancient, The Ends of the Earth, and deemed to be situated in another world."[22] The examples of British pre-eminence in things Christian are too many to enumerate; suffice it that "the saying of the Psalmist [Psalm 2.8] [is] accomplished, that God would give his sonne Christ the Heathen for his inheritance, and the Ends of the Earth (the proper attribute of this our Britaine) to be his possession. And the successe in Historie most apparently sheweth these parts (by an especiall prerogative) to be Christs Kingdome."[23] It is in the person of James especially that "most properly is performed that propheticall promise made unto the Church of Christ [i.e., Anglican Church] that Kings should become her nursing Fathers."

Of course writers with more Puritan leanings than those of Speed could interpret the idea of the covenant in ways far less supportive of the monarchy. Though James was delighted with the reasoning that made him God's anointed vice-regent on earth, answerable only to God, he certainly did not countenance those aspects of covenant thinking which were later to be expanded as a basis for limiting the rights of monarchy, the contract made between the all powerful and the less powerful by which the all powerful voluntarily subjected himself to conditions. The political idea of the covenant, especially the double covenants of works and of grace, becomes central to the thinking of a certain strain of English Puritans; in America it becomes the basic tenet of all New England Puritan theology.[24]

What should be clear from the preceding discussion and examples is that the idea of the covenant is indigenous to Christian thought but varies largely in the degree of emphasis it receives. Though associated with the Puritans, the covenant idea is not unique to that group. It is possible neither to look at isolated quotations from a theologian's work and state his denomination, nor to scan a dramatist's imagery and pinpoint his religious doctrines. Shakespeare's use of covenant imagery might suggest, however, the growing interest in the issues it involves.

Though few regard Cymbeline as the leading character of the play, we may well begin our discussion with him, for he links the three main actions of the play in that he initiates the events with which they are concerned: the exile of Posthumous, leading to the wager plot; the rebellion against Rome; and the casting off of Belarius, leading to the lost princes plot. As has frequently been noted, the reign of Cymbeline was not especially noteworthy, and the critics have been quite correct, I believe, in assuming that Shakespeare chose this reign primarily because the birth of Christ occurred during it. To understand the unity of the play, though, we must note not only the birth of Christ during this period, but the emphasis of almost every chronicler available to Shakespeare that the universal peace of the Romans was a prerequisite to the Incarnation. Without the chronicles we would be rather hard pressed to assess the significance of the Roman component of the play.

The original agreements between the Romans and the Britons made during the reign of Cassibelan, always called covenants in the chronicles, entail a payment of tribute to the Romans that is rarely described as particularly onerous.[25] Several of the chronicles, including Holinshed, mention that Cymbeline had been reared as a Roman gentleman (cf. *Cymbeline,* III.i.70-72), was "romanizing" Britain by the introduction of coins stamped with his image in the Roman manner, and was indeed on such favorable terms with the Romans that he was probably not even expected really to pay the tribute.[26] Most place the rebellion against Rome in the reign of Guiderius. Shakespeare's deviation from the scanty chronicle histories does little to make Cymbeline a more interesting character; rather, it makes him more errant. The errors of the following generation are thrown back onto Cymbeline, and his act of defiance against the noble Roman ambassador Lucius, emissary of the peace-maker Augustus Caesar, seen in the light of Christian history, becomes less the act of a patriot than the misplaced egoism of a ruler mindless of Providential plan. In *Cymbeline* the kind of patriotic speech that would grace the mouth of a John of Gaunt is the verbiage of the depraved queen (III.i.15-34). The nationalism of the play is expressed not in terms of defying foreign rule in the year one, but in voluntarily submitting to the power of Rome as a sign that

Britain is returned to the piety that accords with God's plan and that will lead to the fulfillment of promises that its audience could see effected. The unforced allegiance to Rome at the end of the play, coupled with lauding of the rightful gods, suggests an England returned to its fundamental faith.

In addition, of course, the whole question of Roman significance is influenced by the Trojan associations of the Britons to which we have seen Spenser alluding. The idea that Rome and Britain might be congenitally linked has of course no part in Eusebius' or Gildas' interpretation of the significance of Rome. Only after Geoffrey of Monmouth's time had English writers need to concern themselves with acceptance or rejection of the Brutan legends. Holinshed, for one, continues to retell the tale. The Brutan legend does not figure directly in the play; indirectly it forms another arena for the theme of fall from potential, as the degenerate Britons betray their Trojan inheritance by fleeing from the Romans until they are redeemed by the outcasts of their society, revitalizing symbols of past and future.

Cymbeline's actions up to the end of the play are in error. The error with regard to the Romans becomes fully evident only at the end of the play, but the errors regarding his close associates are apparent from the start. He seems to be alone in his disregard for Posthumous' merits and his over-regard for those of his Queen and her son. In the midst of the play we discover that his error regarding Belarius had lost him his sons. He also errs badly in his dealings with his daughter, but these errors are not really part of the covenant-breaking theme of the play, for to make a true covenant there must be some element of freedom in the making of the conditions, a prerequisite manifestly lacking in the parent-child bond.

The most powerful evocations of the covenant theme are reserved for the Posthumous-Imogen relation. Their marriage is a sacrament, or covenant, suggestive of the covenants of the Israelites with God when they are in His grace. Posthumous early in the play is identified as the son of Leonatus, and the emphasis on this identification is assured later by the prophecy of Jupiter (V.iv.138) referring to the lion's whelp, a prophecy regarding the union of Posthumous and Imogen in relation to Britain's happiness. The lion image suggests the tribe of Judah, an emblem of the Old Law and the tribe considered to be in Mary's lineage (Romans 1.3).[27]

Posthumous' complex and changing moral position with regard to his covenant with Imogen echoes some of the complexity of the covenant idea itself. The idea of the double covenant had changed by the turn of the century: for earlier Christians the covenant of works refers to the whole law of the Old Testament which is replaced by the covenant of grace, belief in the New Testament, which forms the entire basis for salvation. Later we see the term covenant of works applied to the covenant made with Adam only, with intimations of the covenant of grace seen in God's sign of the rainbow to Noah and confirmed by the covenant of grace with Abraham. The Christian faith then is seen as entire from the time of Abraham, who is assumed to have envisioned Jesus, and grace is extended earlier to those who believed Christ had come. One can see this doctrine summarized in a pamphlet based on the writing of Dudley Fenner, who has been credited with being the first Englishman fully to articulate this position.[28] The difference between the Law and the Gospel is that the Law alone would provide salvation if man could perfectly obey it, but the Gospel gives even imperfect man the power to perform the Law, if he has faith. Thus the covenant of grace does not abrogate the Law, but supplements it.[29]

Posthumous, in his covenantal relation to Imogen, is like the Old Testament "Christian," the pre-Christian Christian whose covenant of works is supplemented by a covenant of faith. Imogen epitomizes the faithful wife, as her later adoption of the name Fidele underscores. The figures are not schematically allegorized, but Imogen is surrounded by images associating her with the related notions of faith, grace, and divinity.[30] Posthumous' problems in keeping his covenant simulate those of the Christian in covenant with God.

The inequality of the match between Posthumous and Imogen is as apparent as that between man and God. Man no more deserves God's favor than Posthumous deserves Imogen's allegiance. Like the Old Testament covenant of works, valuable and necessary in itself, but obsolete without the addition of faith, Posthumous is of a line now dead, though once honorable in its own right, and he derives his honor not from his birth, what he is, but from his works, his actions, which can never be noble enough in his social environment to make him a match equal to Imogen. Rather, he is chosen; Imogen freely "elects" him to be her spouse (I.i.53; I.iii.25). Though he confesses himself "her adorer, not her friend" (I.v.66), it is her willing acceptance of him, her recognition of his native virtues that gives him value equal to a king's daughter, as she binds herself to observe the contracts and covenants of marriage.

And their marriage clearly is a contract.[31] Images of buying and selling are constantly played about their arrangement. "Her own price / Proclaims how she esteem'd him" (I.i.51-52). Imogen protests, he "overbuys me / Almost the sum he pays" (I.ii.77-78). The exchange of tokens at parting seems like the earnest of a contract, one with unequal terms, as Posthumous suggests when Imogen entrusts him with her valuable ring in exchange for his bracelet. "As I my poor self did exchange for you / To your so infinite loss; so in our trifles / I still win of you" (I.ii.50-52).

As with the errant Israelites, or virtuous English primitive Christians whose true covenant was broken by the sophistries of Roman Catholicism, Posthumous is not always faithful to his covenant. Away from Imogen he debases the covenant he has made with her by wagering about Imogen's "bond of chastity," securing the wager with the very ring he had promised to keep till death. He is seduced from his bond by Iachimo, truly seduced, for while he thinks he is defending or exalting Imogen, he gives up the ring and enters into inferior covenants with Iachimo which replace in priority those with Imogen. The wager is a covenant—this is emphasized several times:

> Let there be covenants drawn between's
>
> (I.v.140)

> Your hand, a covenant
>
> (I.v.162)

> If you keep covenant
>
> (II,iv,50)

The sense of the true Christian religion being seduced by Roman Catholicism is reinforced by the Italianate setting of the scene of Posthumous' fall. This Rome seems to have no part of the virtuous pagan Rome that spawns Lucius, a Roman who will protect Imogen for her basic goodness (even without knowledge of her true person), a Rome that is the ethical nurturer of the true faith.

Imogen's faith is tested by Iachimo and his "Italian brain" (V.v.196). She maintains her purity while Posthumous succumbs to the same kind of circumstantial evidence that had so long ago caused Cymbeline to condemn Belarius. His letters, taken as the testament of their love, become deceptive lures to her place of assassination, "scriptures . . . turn'd to heresy," "corrupters of . . . faith" (III.iv.82-84). The old testament becomes worthless without the faith of the new. Pure in her faith, Imogen remains pure in her works.

Posthumous' falling away from his covenants is double: first in faith, in his failure to believe in his beloved's truth despite appearances, secondly in works, in his arranging for her murder. Remorse for the murder comes quickly, but it is long before the initial faith is restored. Returned to Britain, Posthumous debates with himself the nature of bonds. That of a servant to a master now seems conditional: "Every good servant does not all commands; / No bond, but to do just ones" (V.i,6-7). Posthumous' conversion back to faith seems to be along a road of actions. True, he is internally changed between his hysterical outbreak at the end of Act II and his reappearance in the play in Act

V. The first dramatized action indicative of his inward change is his external change of dress, casting off "Italian weeds" in favor of the dress of the humblest Briton. His second action indicates a more internal reformation, when he overcomes Iachimo and leaves him. In Act II his injuries caused him to fall back on a code of vengeance, death for dishonor. Here a code of mercy prevails. The disarming of Iachimo operates on more than one level, for his repentance starts at the point of his loss to the unknown "carl." We see in operation what a seventeenth-century audience would perceive as Old Testament justice modified by New Testament mercy.

Posthumous' soliloquy in the jail cell regarding the nature of repentance and forgiveness is a plea to God to make a new contract with him, to "Take this audit" (i.e., his less worthy life in exchange for Imogen's) and to "cancel these cold bonds" (V.iv.27-28). Posthumous sees himself as morally bankrupt, and God, as do human brokers, must content Himself with receiving back only a portion of His investment. The dream of his ancestors, with the vision of Jupiter explaining the afflictions of Posthumous, emphasizes the providential thrust of the romance. Chosen by God as he is chosen by Imogen, his birth and his marriage are divinely overseen. His afflictions, God's scourging of the chosen people when they fall from his worship, will eventually make him happier and perfect his union with faith, "Fidele." Imogen is cheered similarly by Lucius: "Some falls are means the happier to arise" (IV.ii.403). The book of prophecy which Posthumous discovers in the jail cell foretells the union of Posthumous, the "lion's whelp," with the tender air, the inheritance of Israel with the holy spirit, and with it the flourishing of the true faith in a united Britain, all of which is effected in the last scene.

While the princes are not personally involved in the making and breaking of covenants, they too have a role in the pattern of religious prophecy and fulfillment that underlies the play. The thematic integration of the lost princes plot into the play as a whole assumes perhaps greater importance than it otherwise might because this subplot links rather lightly to the two other plot strands. To be sure, the princes are involved in both the rescue of Imogen and the rescue of Britain, but it would not have been difficult to bring these plots to a happy conclusion without the princes' intervention. The play is half over before the princes make their first appearance, an appearance prepared for by not more than a half-dozen line summary of their history some two and a half acts earlier.

We cannot well account for the appearance of the princes on the basis of carry-over from the chronicle materials, for Shakespeare disposes of the children of Cymbeline freely. Imogen is not mentioned historically as a child of Cymbeline, and is generally taken as a

Shakespearean invention who owes her name to the Innogen cited in Holinshed (whose ultimate source was Geoffrey of Monmouth) as the wife of Brute. Guiderius and Arviragus are mentioned prominently, but only in their capacities as kings, never as princes, and their childhood abduction is totally ahistorical. As kings they are important in the rebellion against Rome, and Arviragus sometimes figures in discussions of the implanting of the Christian religion in British soil, though Lucius is generally credited with being the first Christian king.[32]

When we look at the thematic patterns of the Shakespearean romances as a group, we see that the princes fit as easily into some of Shakespeare's more general thematic concerns as they do into those of this particular play, for it is clear that they reflect the theme of the exposure of the innocent child, usually as a result of the sins of the elders, that is also seen in the perils of Marina, Predita, and Miranda. They, with Imogen, are scattered members of the royal family that must be restored to unity for a satisfactory comedic resolution to the play. They additionally provide examples of the ease with which nobility surfaces despite inadequate environment or training. Perhaps they are less dramatic an example than Marina, for they do have the guidance of Belarius, although he assures us that he has taught them nothing, that their virtue is "rare instinct." However, their instinctive virtue, combined with their native piety, has an additional significance in this play which the virtue of the displaced nobles does not convey in the other romances.

There is more than a bit of suggestion that the princes are like the sylvan precursers of the true religion in Britain, the Druids, in the wooded setting of their religious observance and their pre-Christian burial rites for the supposed Fidele. Their chanting because of unwillingness to distort like "priests and fanes that lie" (IV.ii.242), and their scorn of those who "worship dirty gods" (III.vii.28), suggest the purity of their native religion.

Though the writers of England's ecclesiastical history differ somewhat as to the significance of the Druids (according to whether they wish to prove or disprove the establishment of Christianity in England by Rome), all accept at least part of what was believed to have been Druid theology as significant in the early conversion of England to the true faith. Their belief in the immortality of the soul did not win the Druids as much credit as it might otherwise have done since it was coupled with a belief in transmigration of souls, but their belief in one god was seen as extremely significant.[33] Camden quotes Origen:

> The Britans with one consent embraced the Faith,
> and made way themselves unto God by meanes of

the Druidae, who alwaies did beat upon this article
of beleefe, That there was but one God.[34]

The unusual instinctive religious insight of the Druids is
acknowledged in the prevalent legend that they prophesied the virgin conception and built churches for the
worship of the mystery long before the birth of Mary.[35]

Perhaps the treatment of Imogen by her unrecognized
and unrecognizing brothers owes something to the
receptiveness of the Druids to the Christian religion.
We have already noted some of the many places in the
play where she evokes a sense of New Testament divinity. Her brothers immediately perceive Imogen as
"an angel," as "divineness / No elder than a boy!"
(III.vi.43-44). Her needs take priority over any other
obligations the boys have previously acknowledged,
and while Belarius' acceptance of the boys' altered
allegiance as a miracle may refer only to the wonder
of their instinctive virtue, or be a foreshadowing of
the revelation of the blood relationship, it is difficult to
understand even a fraternal relationship being allowed
such unusual precedence if nothing more is implied.

Guiderius and Arviragus display a rough, unsentimen-
tal justice, unconcerned with the demands of civility,
in their contact with Cloten, who expects to be acknowledged by his clothes or possessions. Guiderius
responds with the contempt due to those who, as
Arviragus phrases it, "worship the dirty gods" of "gold
and silver." In contact with Imogen, however, their
pagan aspect is seen in its most spiritual manifestation,
and they see her as the lily that her purity suggests
(IV.ii.201). But as do some of the fallen characters of
the play, the princes feel themselves in bondage, not
the bondage of error or sin, but the bondage of isolation, of separation from the fulfillment of their full
potential. Like Spenser's "Briton babe," they too have
been "Banisht from princely bowre to wasteful wood"
because of the sins of their elders. In their wooded
setting they are given the opportunity to show their
recognition of virtue, and in the convenient battle with
the Romans they are able to display their latent courage and strength, but total fulfillment of their potential
can only come with their reabsorption into the civilized center of Britain, a rejuvenated court purged of
error, cognizant of the validity of the contractual relationships between its members. Though the boys may
have felt their exile a bondage, they had been strengthened by their trials, and without being subject to court
corruption they were enabled to grow vigorously, to
be able to add the needed strength of new growth to
the stock of the old cedar in fulfillment of the prophecy. Their regrafting is again part of the specifically
British form of the faith that is to come from the
merger of the true revealed religion with native piety.

Thematically, the princes' involvement in the covenant
theme through their participation in the fulfillment of

prophecy integrates their story into the play, but what
brings their plot into the clearest parallel with the other
plot strands is that their isolation results from Cymbeline's violation of covenant between ruler and loyal
subject inherent in the degradation of Belarius. But
Belarius' relationship to Cymbeline is ambiguous. Belarius is represented throughout as a virtuous character,
high minded, lofty in ideals, a noble guardian for the
princes. Nevertheless, though he is a patriot, his motivation in stealing the boys is not to provide uncorrupted leadership for the nation later, but to punish
his king for his wrongful banishment of a noble servant.

> I stole these babes,
> Thinking to bar thee of succession as
> Thou refts me of my lands.
>
> (III.iii.101-103)

His participation in the same misfortune as Imogen's
in being maligned by villains "whose false oaths prevail'd / Before my perfect honour" (III.iii.66-67) of
course develops sympathy for him. Nevertheless, Belarius is clearly in as great an error as the king, for
whatever the basis of the contract between king and
subject, Cymbeline's breach could no more justify
Belarius' actions than Imogen's supposed fall could
justify Posthumous' arranging for her murder. Though
Belarius questions the obligation entailed in the covenant between king and loyal subject when the agreement has been violated, Shakespeare does not here
show the interest in exploring this political theme that
he does in the earlier chronicle plays, especially *Richard II*. In this play the king's errors are redressed not
through retaliation but by forgiveness and reaffirmation of the ordained covenants that regulate each central relationship within the play.

It is the idea of the covenant that integrates the actions
and themes of the play. All fundamental relationships—
that of Britain to world history, that of king to country, that of husband and wife—are seen as based on
the analagous relation of man to God within the covenant that leads to man's salvation. As the covenantal
history of mankind reveals a rhythm of covenant, failure,
forgiveness, and reaffirmation of the covenant, so are
these rhythms recurrent in the play. The emphasis is
always on the strong sense of purpose that dominates
action and theme, the motion from uncertain and tentative relationships to firmly accepted and validated
ones that will lead to the fulfillment of God's promises. Britain had to accept its role in world history by
submitting to Roman domination so that Christ could
be born. By accepting its covenant with Rome, it prepared the way for the fulfillment of the promises of
God for the prosperity of His chosen people.

Within the context of this movement we see the imperfectly bonded double covenants of Posthumous and

Imogen refined in the crucible of suffering. If Posthumous is more closely associated with the covenant of works and Imogen with the covenant of grace, nevertheless it is the perfect union of the two into the double covenant of works and grace that associates them with the figure of the redeemed pre-Christian Christian who anticipates the new dispensation. The princes' intuitive allegiance with Imogen and their readiness to convert to her cause is suggestive of the inherent conformity of the native British religion to the Christianity towards which it prepares the way. Pagan, Old Testament, and New—one religion follows the other in a pre-ordained plan that insures that even what may appear to be random errant behavior is turned towards strengthening of the bond. At the end of the play we find Cymbeline acknowledging tribute to Rome, and viewing the Queen's and Cloten's deaths as just retribution for her wicked dissuasion (V.v.463-66); Cymbeline accepts the privations suffered by Belarius as atonement for his sin of retaliation and welcomes him back as brother (V.v.400); and the family reunion is perceived as part of the prophecy that brings together Posthumous, Imogen, and the two princes to renew old Cymbeline's line, "whose issue / Promises Britain peace and plenty." There is freedom in the willing acceptance of bonds, as the motion to proceed towards the temple to laud the gods suggests. Temporal as well as spiritual bonds will be redeemed, Cymbeline gratefully promises:

> All o'erjoy'd,
> Save those in bonds, let them be joyful too,
> For they shall taste our comfort
>
> (401-403).

Freedom comes from willing acceptance of covenantal bonds, and in this romance of redemption, even those whose bonds are unwillingly imposed may learn to accept them as a covenant.

Notes

[1] F. R. Leavis, "The Criticism of Shakespeare's Late Plays: A Caveat," *Scrutiny,* 10, no. 4 (April 1942): 340.

[2] Robert G. Hunter, *Shakespeare and the Comedy of Forgiveness* (New York: Columbia Univ. Press, 1965), p. 176.

[3] Robin Moffet, "*Cymbeline* and the Nativity," *SQ,* 13, no. 2 (Spring 1962): 207-18, explores this topic and cites many predecessors.

[4] J. M. Nosworthy, *Cymbeline,* Arden edn. (London: Methuen & Co., 1955), p. lxxi. All *Cymbeline* citations are taken from this text. Hunter, p. 146, notes the conjunction of images in another context.

[5] Leonard J. Trinterud, "The Origins of Puritanism," *Church History,* 20, no. 1 (1951): 37-57; William A. Clebsch, *England's Earliest Protestants, 1520-1535* (New Haven: Yale Univ. Press, 1961), especially ch. 10, "Tyndale's Rediscovery of the Law," and ch. 11, "Tyndale's Theology of Contract."

[6] A particularly clear expression of this interpretation of history is to be found in Robert Rollock, *A Treatise of God's Effectual Calling,* trans. from Latin by Henry Holland (London: 1603), pp. 6 ff.

[7] The Christian view of history is chronicled in C. A. Patrides, *The Phoenix and the Ladder* (Berkeley: Univ. of California Press, 1964).

[8] Eusebius Pamphilus, *The Auncient Ecclesiasticall Histories of the First Six Hundred Yeares After Christ,* trans. Meredith Hanmer (London: 1577). See especially I, v.

[9] Robert W. Hanning, *The Vision of History in Early Britain: from Gildas to Geoffrey of Monmouth* (New York: Columbia Univ. Press, 1966), p. 24. For an interesting example of how the idea of depraved Judaism persists in the seventeenth century, but is varied according to temporal perspectives, see A[lexander] R[oss], *A View of the Jewish Religion* (London: 1656), pp. 12, 427. To Ross the Mosaic religion is valid, that of the "foolish Rabbi's," Maimonides, corrupt.

[10] *The Chronicles of England* (London: 1580), p. 35.

[11] *The Epistle of Gildas,* trans. from Latin (London: 1638), pp. 8-10.

[12] Gildas, p. 60; see Hanning, p. 55.

[13] *The Faerie Queene* (London: 1590), III.iii.41-42.

[14] O[liver] P[igge], *Meditations Concerning Praiers to Almightie God for the saftie of England* (London: 1588), p. 30; Stephen Batman, *The New Arrival of the three Gracis, into Anglia* (London: [1580]), f. B4ᵛ. Thomas Lodge and Robert Greene, *A Looking Glasse for London and England* (London: 1594) makes a similar comparison in the play's closing lines.

[15] Hanning, p. 70.

[16] *The History of the Church of England* (Antwerp: 1565).

[17] *The Olde Fayth of Greate Brittaygne and the new Learnyng of Inglande* (London: c. 1549), f. a₄.

[18] *Ecclesiastical History* (London: 1576), "Acts and Monuments," p. 107.

[19] (London: 1579), pp. 23-24. Also see "Acts and Monuments," p. 32, for Foxe's adoption of Gildas' scourge concepts.

[20] J. P. Brockbank, "History and Histrionics in *Cymbeline*," *ShS*, 11(1958): 42-48; Emrys Jones, "Stuart *Cymbeline*," *EIC*, 11, no. 1 (January 1961): 84-99.

[21] John Speed, *Theatre* (London: 1611), p. 202.

[22] Speed, p. 203.

[23] Speed, p. 205.

[24] Perry Miller, *The New England Mind: The Seventeenth Century* (New York: Macmillan Co., 1939), pp. 447, 476.

[25] Richard Broughton, *The Ecclesiasticall Historie of Great Britain* (London: 1633), p. 2; Stow, *Annales of England* (London: 1592), p. 23.

[26] Raphael Holinshed, *Chronicles* (London: 1587), bk. 3, p. 32; Speed, p. 189. Another favorable association of the Romans with religion occurs in William Attersoll's derivation of the word "sacrament" in *The New Covenant or A Treatise of the Sacraments* (London: 1614), p. 14, where the theological sense of the word is taken to be a metaphoric extension of the soldier's oath of the Romans, called a sacrament.

[27] Naseeb Shaheen, "The Use of Scripture in *Cymbline*," *ShakS*, 4(1968): 294-315, lists extensive Old and New Testament parallels in *Cymbeline*, but does not feel that they form any consistent allegorical pattern. Among the references to Posthumous he cites the Lion of Judah passages and relates the upbringing of Posthumous at Cymbeline's court to Moses raised by Pharoah, though he more prominently stresses associations with Christ.

[28] *The Sacred Doctrine of Divinitie Gathered out of the Worde of God* (London: 1599), bk. 2, ch. 13, pp. 30-31 (very irregular pagination). Trinterud, pp. 48-49, gives special emphasis to Fenner in his summary of the development of the double covenant idea, citing his *Sacra Theologia* of 1589.

[29] John S. Coolidge, *The Pauline Renaissance in England* (Oxford: The Clarendon Press, 1970), ch. 5, "The Covenant of Grace," fully explicates these ideas. See especially pp. 102-103. Donald Joseph McGinn, *The Admonition Controversy* (New Brunswick: Rutgers Univ. Press, 1949), ch. 8, "The Old Law vs. the New," sees the difference in interpreting the New Testament as an extension of rather than an abrogation of the Old Testament as the core of the differences between Cartwright and Whitgift. McGinn associates (p. 127) Cartwright and the Puritans alone with the "chosen people" idea, but I hope I have demonstrated that the Puritans were not alone in connecting Britain with the Israelites.

[30] Though when taken out of context we find several images surrounding Posthumous that would exchange the god/adorer relation between him and Imogen, it should be noted that the idea that Posthumous is "like a descended god" comes from the mouth of the deceptive Iachimo.

[31] The comparison of God's covenant with man to the marriage covenant is not unusual in theological literature. Cf. John Cotton, quoted in Miller, p. 413, who extends the analogy to include not only the covenant of marriage, but that of friendship and that of prince and people.

[32] John Hardyng, *Chronicle* (London: 1543), ch. 48, maintains that Joseph of Arimathea converted Arviragus to Christianity and gave him a shield of arms on which was painted a cross of goules, and all of this "long afore sainct George was gotten or borne."

[33] Broughton, pp. 242-46; Speed, p. 204.

[34] William Camden, *Britain, or a chorographical description . . .* , trans. Philemon Holland (London: 1610), p. 68.

[35] Broughton, p. 9; Speed, p. 204.

Coburn Freer (essay date 1981)

SOURCE: "*Cymbeline*," in *The Poetics of Jacobean Drama*, The Johns Hopkins University Press, 1981, pp. 103-35.

[*In the following essay, Freer contends that the motives, self-regard, and development of the three main characters—Imogen, Iachimo, and Posthumus—can be traced through the imagery and syntax of their speeches.*]

When Iachimo first meets Imogen, he recognizes, with the quickness which he alone seems to possess in this play, that she looks like all that Posthumus had claimed her to be:

> If she be furnish'd with a mind so rare,
> She is alone th' Arabian bird; and I
> Have lost the wager.
>
> [1.7.16-18][1]

In an instant he conceives a daring plan whose purpose we grasp a few moments later. As Imogen reads Posthumus's introductory note, Iachimo launches into a wildly exaggerated "Elizabethan world-picture":

What! are men mad? Hath nature given
　them eyes
To see this vaulted arch, and the rich crop
Of sea and land, which can distinguish
　'twixt
The fiery orbs above, and the twinn'd
　stones
Upon the number'd beach, and can we not
Partition make with spectacles so precious
'Twixt fair and foul?

[1.7.32-38]

We know this is not Iachimo's usual manner because his earlier speeches in the wager scene, though in prose, were nowhere near as obscure metaphorically, nor was his initial aside in this scene.[2] He is trying to see if Imogen has "a mind so rare," although his approach is only partly successful; Imogen's mind is not as rare as her soul, but she *is* smart enough to reply that she does not understand him:

What makes your admiration? . . .
What is the matter, trow? . . .
　　　　What, dear sir,
Thus raps you? Are you well? . . .
　　　　I pray you, sir,
Deliver with more openness your answers
To my demands.

[1.7.38, 47, 50-51, 87-89]

As Iachimo's speeches go on, they reveal the poets' "dark wit" as well as a general nastiness quite odd for a wooer:

　　　　　　　apes and monkeys,
'Twixt two such shes, would chatter this
　way, and
Contemn with mows the other. Nor i'the
　judgement:
For idiots in this case of favour, would
Be wisely definite: nor i' th' appetite.
Sluttery, to such neat excellence oppos'd,
Should make desire vomit emptiness,
Not so allur'd to feed.
　　　　. . . The cloyed will—
That satiate yet unsatisfed desire, that tub
Both fill'd and running—ravening first the
　lamb,
Longs after for the garbage.

[1.7.39-46, 47-50]

Before offering any specific details about Posthumus's alleged infidelity, Iachimo has made a great imaginative leap,[3] and begun with weirdly illustrated generalizations about unfaithful lovers. The prosody of the passage—which consists of two speeches, interrupted by Imogen's extrametrical "What is the matter, trow?"—shows Shakespeare's habit, common in the later verse, of allowing some of the nominally stressed

syllables to carry almost as little weight as the nominally unstressed syllables;[4] *and* and *would,* at the ends of the second and fourth lines, are conspicuous examples, as is

Should make desire vomit emptiness.

The diphthong in the second syllable of *desire* almost adds another syllable, putting only the briefest space before the sudden lurch into the verb and its object. The effect is astonishing in its larger context too, because up to this point the pauses in Iachimo's lines have occurred earlier and earlier; this last pause before *vomit* then occurs later and with more violence than anyone could have expected. The rhythms of the verse are one of Iachimo's chief means of seeming in a state of "admiration," and the technique is now allied, still without specific charges, to images of labor, dirt, and disease:

　　　　　　　Had I this cheek
To bathe my lips upon: this hand, whose
　touch
(Whose every touch) would force the
　feeler's soul
To th'oath of loyalty: this object, which
Takes prisoner the wild motion of mine eye,
Firing it only here; should I (damn'd then)
Slaver with lips as common as the stairs
That mount the Capitol: join gripes, with
　hands
Made hard with hourly falsehood
　(falsehood, as
With labour): then by-peeping in an eye
Base and illustrous as the smoky light
That's fed with stinking tallow. . . .
　　　　　　　A lady
So fair, and fasten'd to an empery
Would make the great'st king double, to be
　partner'd
With tomboys hir'd with that self exhibition
Which your own coffers yield! with diseas'd
　ventures,
That play with all infirmities for gold
Which rottenness can lend Nature! Such boil'd
　stuff
As well might poison poison!

[1.7.99-110, 119-26]

The imagery seems to take off on its own, without any overt plan, as a cheek becomes a basin, lips become stairs, hands develop apparently psychosomatic calluses, and eyes smoke like the wicks of poor candles. There is a strictly logical contrast with Iachimo's first speech on order, but in terms of poetic style, and the way the imagery functions, the two speeches fit together and complicate his tone marvelously. In his unrelenting pressure against the expected iambic pattern,[5] in the frequent and irregularly spaced pauses, the syntactic units broken across line-ends, the bizarre diction, and the zigzagging in ideas from ideal to real and back, Iachimo mystifies Imogen while suggesting some truth just out of reach.

One thing is certain: if Iachimo were trying to seduce Imogen, he could not have chosen a method less likely to succeed. She would have to have the interpretive quickness of a Coleridge even to know she is being propositioned; she does not understand Iachimo until line 137, when he finally mentions her bed. Deliberately astounding and incomprehensible—there would be no reason to doubt that Shakespeare conceived of Iachimo as a pupil of Marino—Iachimo's verse style is calculated to put Imogen on her guard. He knows what he is doing: as he had told Posthumus earlier, "I am the master of my speeches" (1.5.137). If (and this is his long shot) she is quick enough to understand him but does not feel the need to remain faithful to Posthumus, he may win the wager directly; if she cannot understand him until he becomes explicit, and then rejects him, he can appeal soberly to her own sense that the confusion is now past. And sure enough, when he reveals that it was all just a plot to test her, he returns to smooth and flat blank verse. His earlier use of the astounding style becomes a way of affirming his ethical conventionality now:

> O happy Leonatus! I may say:
> The credit that thy lady hath of thee
> Deserves thy trust, and thy most perfect
>   goodness
> Her assur'd credit. Blessed live you long!
> A lady to the worthiest sir that ever
> Country call'd his; and you, his mistress,
>   only
> For the most worthiest fit. Give me your
>   pardon.
>
>   [5.7.156-62]

Now the good honest fellow, when he goes on to praise Posthumus his poetic manner becomes naive and clumsy, full of "unintentional" rhymes and tongue-twisting stumbles, standing with his poetic feet together:

> He sits 'mongst men like a descended god;
> He hath a kind of honour sets him off,
> More than mortal seeming. Be not angry,
> Most mighty princess, that I have
>   adventur'd
> To try your taking of a false report, which
>   hath
> Honour'd with a confirmation your great
>   judgement
> In the election of a sir so rare,
> Which you know cannot err.
>
>   [1.7.169-76]

In this, his most sincere voice, Iachimo abandons imagery altogether, straightens out his syntax, and smooths his meters. As surely as Jaques in *As You Like It,* he knows when he is hearing blank verse, and he knows that his verse style also has a special relation to the problems at hand.[6]

By this time Iachimo realizes that if he plays fairly he has lost the wager, and the next time we see him, climbing out of the trunk in Imogen's bedroom, we might expect some nominal anguish. But there, although Iachimo is speaking only to himself, questions of sincerity or moral intent seem even more irrelevant than they might have in his first speeches:

> The crickets sing, and man's o'er labour'd
>   sense
> Repairs itself by rest. Our Tarquin thus
> Did softly press the rushes, ere he waken'd
> The chastity he wounded. Cytherea,
> How bravely thou becom'st thy bed! fresh
>   lily!
> And whiter than the sheets! That I might
>   touch!
> But kiss, one kiss! Rubies unparagon'd,
> How dearly they do't: 'tis her breathing that
> Perfumes the chamber thus.
>
>   [2.2.11-19]

The first two sentences set the hypnotic tone (for Iachimo's own benefit) through the alliteration of metrically stressed key words (*sing-sense, repairs-rest*), the suggestion of internal rhyme (*thus/rushes; softly/chastity/bravely/lily/dearly; waken'd/wounded*), the many sibilants, the enjambment, and the varied caesurae that keep the steady iambics from falling into a singsong. Until the last two lines there are no reversed initial feet to disturb the pickup of a steady beat at the start of each line. In the apostrophe to Imogen, the alliteration becomes stronger (*bravely/becom'st/bed*) just as the tension in the meter also curves to a peak, with four end-stopped lines and pressures in each against the last two feet. The style matches perfectly Iachimo's fascination with Imogen's place in an imagined setting. The Victorian critics who flew into rhapsodies over Imogen forgot that at least her appearance is actually Iachimo's creation, and Iachimo is very aware of his own role in the creative process.[7] No one else in the play goes into such ecstasies over her beauty—certainly not her husband, and her brothers are more taken by the way she trims vegetables. Her beauty is Iachimo's creation: one might append, as a gloss on the whole scene, Wallace Stevens's poem "So-and-So Reclining on Her Couch." Too much of the passage reflects upon itself for it to be a lyric cri de coeur; the opening line alludes to the way he worked upon Imogen earlier, and comparison of himself to "our Tarquin" only underscores the differences between the two—the rapist physical and the rapist imaginary. Even his kiss is qualified, for himself and for us, by the way he lays on the imagery of touch, sight, and sound, in a remote kind of self-titillation. As the visual images become steadily more ingenious, they receive a conscious termination:

> The flame o' th' taper
> Bows toward her, and would under-peep her
>   lids,
> To see th'enclosed lights, now canopied
> Under these windows, white and azure lac'd
> With blue of heaven's own tinct. But my
>   design.
> To note the chamber: I will write all down:
> Such, and such pictures: there the window,
>   such
> Th'adornment of her bed; the arras, figures,
> Why, such, and such; and the contents
>   o'th'story.
>
> [2.2.19-27]

The conventional prettiness of a partly cloudy sky (Imogen's blue and white eyelids) hiding the sun (her eyes) is immediately distanced by his melodramatic return to his task: "But my design." Abandoning pauses, parallels, and images, his colorless "such, and such" recreates, in its own quick irregular rhythms, the indifference of the rapid notetaker; the alternation of metric expansion and density satisfies us that three hours elapse during the scene. As he removes the bracelet, Iachimo then returns to the language of an overheated sonneteer:

> On her left breast
> A mole cinque-spotted: like the crimson
>   drops
> I'th'bottom of a cowslip. Here's a voucher,
> Stronger than ever law could make; this
>   secret
> Will force him think I have pick'd the lock,
>   and ta'en
> The treasure of her honour.
>
> [2.2.37-42]

The much-admired natural detail raises a number of questions. Some readers have seen in this and similar passages a Shakespeare "reverting" to the style of his earlier work, particularly the poems, but the remembered passages must be the critic's and not the artist's; what mature poet sits down to reread, much less imitate, his earlier poetry? One can readily imagine, though, an accomplished poet looking at a slightly faded mode and seeing in it some ways of shaping fresh material, in this case a poetic voice unlike any he had created before.[8] If we wished to understand Iachimo better, we could begin with these "Elizabethan" passages, for curiously enough, some of these delicious details never find their way into the temptation of Posthumus. Consider that mole, for example. In the source for this

scene, the prose tale *Frederyke of Jennen,* the heroine was identified by a black wart on her arm. Shakespeare's shift to the spotted mole is important because of its effect on Iachimo, who never tells Posthumus the mole is spotted and never uses on him the simile of the flower. Iachimo is describing Imogen for his own pleasure, and that pleasure has its origins less in sexual desire than in the use of a poetic style, tried out for effect upon himself alone.

Self-regard is fundamental to Iachimo's character, and after the passage just quoted he turns again, as if to catch his own image in a mirror:

> No more: to what end?
> Why should I write this down, that's riveted,
> Screw'd to my memory?
>
> [2.2.42-44]

Iachimo's nervous reflection upon his own memory comes out in short, irregularly stressed clauses, and the next detail is an even greater step back from "literature":

> She hath been reading late,
> The tale of Tereus, here the leaf's turn'd
>   down
> Where Philomel gave up.
>
> [2.2.44-46]

A master's stroke, that: the Elizabethan best-seller has put the heroine to sleep at the very height of the narrative. It is a fine satiric touch that leads nowhere, another detail that Iachimo never mentions. But it tells us much about the limits of Imogen's romantic imagination, while it distances still further Iachimo's Elizabethan manner.[9]

It would be pointless to object that none of Iachimo's verse leads to self-knowledge, for he is not in search of any self that can be detached from the pleasures of his different voices. His self-depiction involves no reaching after recognition:

> Swift, swift, you dragons of the night, that
>   dawning
> May bare the raven's eye! I lodge in fear;
> Though this a heavenly angel, hell is here.
>
> [2.2.48-50]

Possibly these lines contain a backward glance to *Romeo and Juliet, Macbeth,* or even Marlowe's *Faustus;* but Iachimo's "hell is here" involves no probing of his own depths, if he has them; few villains on the Jacobean stage are less tormented than Iachimo.

The care that Shakespeare has put into Iachimo's surface may be seen by comparing him with the villain in *Frederyke of Jennen.* John of Florence hardly thinks at all, but goes straight to his work; he speaks only once, when he sees that unfortunate wart on the heroine's arm: "O good lorde! What great fortune have I. For now have I sene a pryvy token, wherby he shall byleve me that I have had my pleasure of his wyfe; and so I shall have the money of hym."[10] In his simpleminded declaration John shows no concern for the effect of the deception upon himself, whereas that is almost entirely Iachimo's concern. Iachimo has, after all, undertaken the wager not to make a profit but to prove that human nature is not fixed: "I make my wager rather against your confidence than her reputation" (1.5.107-8).[11] If Iachimo had to acknowledge that there really *is* one woman true and fair, he would have to revise his ideas on human nature in particular and the universe in general.[12] His own pleasure in his poetic style will hold off that knowledge until act 5.

Returning to Rome, Iachimo springs the trap on Posthumus in a casual, almost unconcerned way. He knows he has legitimately lost the wager, and points out as much to Posthumus:

> my circumstances,
> Being so near the truth, as I will make them,
> Must first induce you to believe.
>
>   [2.4.61-63]

Creating a fiction, he half expects to be exposed; when he shows Posthumus the bracelet and Posthumus says "May be she pluck'd it off/To send it to me," he asks nervously "She writes so to you? Doth she?" (2.4.104-5). Suppose Imogen had not been asleep as Iachimo thought? Letting him go back to Posthumus with an explanatory letter would be the best way to set up a punishment, and Iachimo has an anxious moment after his sketches of Imogen's room. But except for the description of the mole, Iachimo scores his telling points briefly and with no poetic heightening: "By Jupiter, I had it from her arm," "Will you hear more?," "I'll be sworn," "I'll deny nothing" (2.4.121, 141, 143, 146). Taking over the deception for himself, Posthumus does not even require much elaboration on the mole:

> under her breast
> (Worthy her pressing) lies a mole, right proud
> Of that most delicate lodging. By my life,
> I kiss'd it, and it gave me present hunger
> To feed again, though full.
>
>   [2.4.134-38]

Iachimo's mind is still fabricating (he moves the mole from *on* her breast to *under* it, thus requiring a more intimate perusal), but if he can deceive Posthumus without using his battery of lyric detail, so much the better: It is a greater victory against the upstart notions of confidence and constancy.

Posthumus reaches his own impasse at the same time as Iachimo, although his path to it is less connected with Iachimo's than it might seem at first. From the beginning of the play, Posthumus has a tone entirely different from Iachimo's mimic facility. He speaks in a manner direct and unaffected at its best, but abrupt and inconsiderate at its worst. His farewell to Imogen is a model study in curtness:

> Should we be taking leave
> As long a term as yet we have to live,
> The loathness to depart would grow. Adieu!
>
>   [1.2.37-39]

Posthumus's wooden stance is apparent in the unvaried rhythms, the unintended rhyme of *leave/live,* and his tendency to package his syntax in units that coincide with line-ends. The rigidity of the final product is emphasized by its lack of imagery. As Imogen complains affectionately, "Were you but riding forth to air yourself,/Such parting were too petty" (1.2.41-42); she passes over his rather brutal suggestion that they might spend the rest of their lives saying goodbye.

When imagery does appear in Posthumus's first speeches, it usually jars in the context, with reverberations that Posthumus does not hear and cannot control:

> Write, my queen,
> And with mine eyes I'll drink the words you
>   send,
> Though ink be made of gall.
>
>   [1.2.30-32]

As Nosworthy says, this is more the language of Troilus parting from Cressida;[13] both lovers place all their emphasis upon their own experience: Posthumus stresses, for example, not the beauty of Imogen's words but the bitterness of his own reading, in a metaphor quite as strained as one of Troilus's. Posthumus's reserve originates partly in his desire not "to be suspected of more tenderness/Than doth become a man" (1.2.25-26); the stiff rhythms of his verse thus reflect his coolness as well as his conviction of his own merits. It is not surprising that when Cymbeline commands him to leave, he can manage only a farewell that suggests his own priggish self-concept: "The gods protect you,/And bless the good remainders of the court!" (1.2.60).

Posthumus's combination of reserve and self-regard appears even more strongly in the wager scene. Although conducted entirely in prose, this scene tells us much about the development of Posthumus's poetry. The clumsiest member of the group at Philario's, Posthumus tries the witty and graceful Roman manner, but takes himself so seriously that he is easily thrown off balance; he invites antagonism by being alternately deferential and obtrusive. It is a wonder that Philario puts up with him; as we see later, he is the sort of nightmare guest we have all come close to having, who makes fulsome apologies for imposing (thus ignoring a long friendship), but at the same time makes virtually no plans to leave until he is carried out feet first:

> in these fear'd hopes,
> I barely gratify your love; they failing,
> I must die much your debtor.
>
> [2.4.6-8]

No other gentleman in the play (including in that term Philario, Lucius, Belarius, and Cornelius) goes to such lengths to emphasize his unworthiness as does Posthumus in the early scenes of the play. In the wager scene he says with typical extravagance to the Frenchman, "I have been debtor to you for courtesies which I will be ever to pay, and yet pay still" (1.5.34-35). This shows the ambivalence of Posthumus's submission: the last time they met, the Frenchman had separated Posthumus from quarreling with another Frenchman, again over Imogen's virtues.[14] Despite Posthumus's protestations of indebtedness now, he still believes the fight was worth it: "Upon my mended judgement (if I offend not to say it is mended) my quarrel was not altogether slight" (1.5.44-46). The elaborately apologetic manner does not conceal a repetitive insistence upon his own rectitude (*not* upon Imogen's), and the conspicuous self-esteem that is part of Posthumus's public manner must be fairly evident in order for Iachimo's sarcasm in this scene to have effect:

> *Iach.* Either your unparagon'd mistress is dead, or she's outpriz'd by a trifle.
>
> *Post.* You are mistaken: the one may be sold or given, or if there were wealth enough for the purchase, or merit for the gift. The other is not a thing for sale, and only the gift of the gods.
>
> *Iach.* Which the gods have given you?
>
> *Post.* Which by their graces I will keep.
>
> [1.5.77-84]

Posthumus is not quick enough to rally off Iachimo's claim that the woman is dead, or else the world would be enjoying her; instead he depersonalizes Imogen as "the other," "a thing," "a gift." Posthumus's final retort is of course intended to be ironic, but at the moment it has an offensively complacent ring to it.

Posthumus's public self-regard gives his speedy rejection of Imogen a great psychological validity. In one sense, Posthumus *needs* to believe that Imogen is false because of the large claims he has made upon himself. In public he is the self-confident and competent courtier; in private, he is intensely conscious of his own deficiences. Imogen notes after he had left that

> When he was here
> He did decline to sadness, and oft-times
> Not knowing why.
>
> [1.7.61-63]

Posthumus knows that Imogen has married beneath her station, and also knows of the gossip that says "his virtue / By her election may be truly read" (1.1.52-53). He tells Imogen himself that "I my poor self did exchange for you / To your so infinite loss" (1.2.50-51); even at the start of act 5 he asks, "how many / Must murder wives much better than themselves" (5.1.3-4). His continued protests about his inadequacy become a chewing on the sore gum, a more or less socially acceptable way of favoring his tic; they also help explain why he wants to, why he must, reject Imogen. He is a character born guilty; as his name constantly reminds us, he has already been the cause of one woman's death. His own consciousness of his failings and his distinct sense of being Imogen's inferior are attitudes he must shake, and by suspecting her of being unfaithful, that whole great weight can be canceled, that sense of perpetual obligation removed.[15] One could call it a form of projection, Posthumus's sexual jealousy being a reflection of his own sense of unworthiness, but a formulation like this would not imply the liberating health, the full love, that finally comes out of this particular sickness.

Many details in this outline can be clarified by a careful reading of Posthumus's poetry, especially the scene of the deception and the soliloquy immediately following. Immediately before the deception Posthumus and Philario have been talking about the Roman-British political situation, and Posthumus has been holding forth in a manner more pompous than usual:

> I do believe
> (Statist though I am none, nor like to be)
> That this will prove a war. . . .
>
> [2.4.15-17]

Into this conversational desert comes Iachimo, and for a brief moment Posthumus's verse flourishes with imagery:

> The swiftest harts have posted you by land;
> And winds of all the corners kiss'd your sails,
> To make your vessel nimble.
>
> [2.4.27-29]

Agreeing to Iachimo's initial statement that Imogen is fair, Posthumus begins by saying that she is

> therewithal the best, or let her beauty
> Look through a casement to allure false hearts,
> And be false with them.
>
> [2.4.33-35]

As he thinks of what she can do with her beauty if it prove false, the rhythms become uncertain and groping, the first sign of the crack-up:

> Look through a casement to allure false
>   hearts,
> And be false with them.

The image of the prostitute at the window is strangely uncalled-for, as if Posthumus expects (or wants) to lose the wager; a fond husband might reassert his belief in his wife's constancy at this point. Iachimo's arrival, and with it the prospect of Imogen's infidelity, seems to have stimulated Posthumus's poetic imagination as conversation with Philario could not. Now when Posthumus reasserts the terms of the wager, the imagery begins to fade and the rhythms once more strain against the iambic pattern:

>   If you can make't apparent
> That you have tasted her in bed, my hand
> And ring is yours. If not, the foul opinion
> You had of her pure honour gains, or loses,
> Your sword, or mine, or masterless leave
>   both
> To who shall find them.

> [2.4.56-61]

The meter becomes impacted at two points crucial to meaning:

> Her pure honour gains

and

> Masterless leave both.

The logical and metrical ambiguity of *both* is a brilliant touch; both swords *and* both lovers will have to go their separate ways.

When Posthumus concedes the wager and gives Iachimo the ring, his verse runs out of imagery altogether and becomes quite uncertain in its meters:

>   The vows of women
> Of no more bondage be to where they are
>   made
> Than they are to their virtues, which is
>   nothing.
> O, above measure false! . . .
> 'Tis true, nay, keep the ring, 'tis true: I am
>   sure
> She would not lose it: her attendants are
> All sworn, and honourable:—they induc'd
>   to steal it?
> And by a stranger? No, he hath enjoy'd
>   her:
> The cognizance of her incontinency

> Is this: she hath bought the name of
>   whore, thus dearly.

> [2.4.110-13,123-28]

Mentally Posthumus is wobbling among concepts that are never defined or given concrete form in imagery.[16] His mingled dogmatism and distrust are echoed in his ambivalent rhythms, which fall into iambics but take an unusual number of light endings, often combined with reversed initial feet in the lines immediately following. The speech sounds off-balance, tilting unpredictably as it struggles to approach an orderly rhythmic pattern. The first major rift in Posthumus's control appears in the last line quoted above, and from that point on he is unable to control the movement of his mind and voice. His first soliloquy is a bravura passage for his wildly dislocated style:

> Is there no way for men to be, but women
> Must be half-workers? We are all bastards,
> And that most venerable man, which I
> Did call my father, was I know not where
> When I was stamp'd. Some coiner with his
>   tools
> Made me a counterfeit: yet my mother seem'd
> The Dian of that time: so doth my wife
> The nonpareil of this. O vengeance,
>   vengeance!
> Me of my lawful pleasure she restrain'd,
> And pray'd me oft forbearance: did it with
> A pudency so rosy, the sweet view on't
> Might well have warm'd old Saturn; that I
>   thought her
> As chaste as unsunn'd snow. O, all the
>   devils!
> This yellow Iachimo, in an hour was't not?
> Or less; at first? Perchance he spoke not, but
> Like a full-acorn'd boar, a German one,
> Cried "O!" and mounted; found no
>   opposition
> But what he look'd for should oppose and
>   she
> Should from encounter guard.

> [2.4.153-71]

The imagery that tumbles out now is radically mixed and only barely under rational control. Coining and tools, sun and snow, the "yellow Iachimo" and the "full-acorn'd boar"—it is as if Posthumus's belief in Imogen's infidelity had released a flood of images, the sheer quantity of which he could not have managed before. As for the imagery itself, one recent reader describes the passage as "Othello reorchestrated,"[17] but that is to miss the point: Othello never does come up with an image of Desdemona in flagrante delicto; Iago plants these images, and Othello never reaches the loquacious sort of verbal rage that Posthumus soars into here. The passage on the boar would make us think of Othello only if we forgot who was speaking.

Here imagery is a function of characterization, and it matters greatly that these lines come from a mind that has been terse and generally abstract up to now. And graphic as the imagery is, it is still as notable for what it leaves implied as for what it pictures directly. Imogen's "pudency so rosy" in having restrained Posthumus of his "lawful pleasure" has occasioned some comment,[18] but the thought is clear enough: Posthumus thought that she was reluctant because of her chastity, but now that she has been proved to be lustful, her restraint must have had some other motive. That epithet "full-acorn'd"[19] would seem to imply a fear on Posthumus's part that he has been unable to satisfy Imogen sexually.

Horrified by what he sees in this welter of images, Posthumus returns to abstractions, running through a catalog of vices:

> Could I find out
> The woman's part in me—for there's no
>   motion
> That tends to vice in man, but I affirm
> It is the woman's part: be it lying, note it,
> The woman's: flattering, hers; deceiving,
>   hers:
> Lust, and rank thoughts, hers, hers:
>   revenges, hers:
> Ambitions, coveting, change of prides, disdain,
> Nice longing, slanders, mutability;
> All faults that name, nay, that hell knows,
> Why, hers in part, or all: but rather all. For
>   even to vice
> They are not constant, but are changing
>   still;
> One vice, but of a minute old, for one
> Not half so old as that. I'll write against
>   them,
> Detest them, curse them: yet 'tis greater skill
> In a true hate, to pray they have their will:
> The very devils cannot plague them better.[20]
>   [2.4.171-86]

The great agitation of rhythms in this passage is expressive, in that it mirrors Posthumus's racing mind; at the same time it is also functional, in that it positively blocks any realization on his part that these are his own vices, too. The purpose of the speech can be unfolded in part from the last line, which has a curious history in the Variorum. Many editors have tried to justify dropping it, and thus have the soliloquy end neatly with a couplet. However, the thought is not complete without the last line, and Posthumus is hardly in any state of mind to be thinking—or rhyming—precisely. By concluding with a line that is falling in rhythm and has an extra light syllable at the end, Posthumus emphasizes the triteness and bathos of the curse, which is only a variant on "This hurts you more than it does me." He is enjoying the pleasures of his

own rant, just as Iachimo in his long soliloquy enjoyed the pleasures of his own lyricism. In more than one sense, Shakespeare has freed Posthumus through the shifts in his imagery and rhythmic intention.

From the standpoint of technique, the most significant element in the passage is its use of pauses, which will take on a major role in Posthumus's characterization. Posthumus seems continually to break off, qualify, or chop at what he has just said, and he always does this by an abrupt shift in rhythm. Someone who is distraught does not automatically speak blank verse with a great many pauses; the verse might just as well tumble out in long gushes. Of all the other characters in the play, only one speaks in short bursts like this, and that is Cloten. (If we did not notice Cloten's choppy habit of speaking, Belarius later points to "the snatches in his voice / And burst of speaking" [4.2.105-6].) It is appropriate that Posthumus should assume the accents of Imogen's archpest, for at this point both men want to shame and humiliate her. The resemblance between them is later stressed, of course, by the scene in which Imogen discovers Cloten's headless body. There, surveying all his anatomy with a wifely eye, she is convinced he is Posthumus, and it is possible that the two parts were played by the same actor, for Cloten and Posthumus never appear in a scene together.[21] Given their physical identity the doubling would have been natural, and the stylistic resemblances between their manners of speech at this point reveal Shakespeare's understanding of Posthumus's degradation.

After this speech, his own impasse, Posthumus drops out like Iachimo, not reappearing until act 4;[22] like Iachimo's, Posthumus's style has obvious limitations, and Shakespeare has done all he wants to within them for now. The relationship between Iachimo and Posthumus is also designed to be dropped by the middle of the play, freeing the stage for the development of Imogen and the subplot of Belarius and the two sons. But there is finally more than a little Shakespearean humor in Posthumus's departing to become a satiric poet, this man who knows himself so little and whose verse is stiff and preoccupied when not raging. The humor is like that in Imogen's being put to sleep by Ovid. At least we *saw* her asleep over the book, but the extent of Shakespeare's interest in satiric poetry is evident in the way that Posthumus has to write it and speak it all offstage.

With Posthumus and Iachimo safely stowed until the last act, Shakespeare begins to develop Imogen and her own unique idiom. His problem with her character is simple: how can he make health and balance appealing as verse, without lapsing into a stiff pattern of correctness? To describe her in a negative way, Imogen has none of the tendencies toward self-regard that we saw in the two men, even though she has a fertile romantic imagination. She enjoys experience itself, yet unlike many mental travelers, she is constantly weighing and judging. We have already noted her gentle admonition to Posthumus upon his stiff and ungenerous goodbye; consider also her miniature of Posthumus's departure:

> I would have broke mine eye-strings, crack'd
> them, but
> To look upon him, till the diminution
> Of space had pointed him sharp as my
> needle:
> Nay, followed him, till he had melted from
> The smallness of a gnat, to air: and then
> Have turn'd mine eye, and wept.
>
> [1.4.17-22]

The point overlooked by many readers is that she did *not* see him leave; this is all a superbly evoked and conscious creation. The rhythmic structure of the passage as a whole shows Imogen's organizing intelligence, because the lines gather to the actual point of Posthumus's disappearance; the rhythms build to that delicate line with two strong stresses, spaced and surrounded by pauses, evoking the almost tangible *feel* of an object isolated in immense space. Perhaps a four-stress scansion would indicate best the balance of tensions in Imogen's mind:

> The smallness of a gnat # to air # and then . . .

Imogen is more aware of her own dependence upon words than is any other character except Iachimo; as she says in this same scene, "I did not take my leave of him [Posthumus], but had/Most pretty things to say" (11.25-26); she had even planned her parting kiss to appear "Betwixt two charming words" (1.35). And not long after Posthumus has left, she rebuffs Cloten, telling him "You put me to forget a lady's manners,/ By being so verbal" (2.3.104-5). She knows from the first that words have a potency and value that should not be used lightly.

Imogen's attitude toward her own poetry is especially evident in her first long speech, in which she plans with Pisanio to go to Milford Haven. Here we see her interest in sensation, not for its own sake, as is the case with Iachimo, but rather as a means of understanding her own ideals and ultimate desires. Always sampling and testing, she often moves toward a tentative and aphoristic phrasing, which further restrains her essentially plain style:

> You good gods,
> Let what is here contain'd relish of love,
> Of my lord's health, of his content: yet not
> That we two are asunder; let that grieve him;
> Some griefs are med'cinable, that is one of
> them,
> For it doth physic love: of his content,

> All but in that! Good wax, thy leave: blest
> be
> You bees that make these locks of counsel!
> Lovers
> And men in dangerous bonds pray not alike:
> Though forfeiters you cast in prison, yet
> You clasp young Cupid's tables. Good news,
> gods!
>
> [3.2.29-39]

The first unusual and unexpected stress on *relish,* and then the final shift onto *pray,* keeps us from any feeling that she might be repeating a formula. Savoring her own excitement at the letter, she nonetheless realizes that separation from Posthumus could be a way of purifying and strengthening both their loves. Her interest in the sensation of the moment is not purchased at the expense of her judgment.

She can immerse herself in sensation when she wants to, for after she has read Posthumus's letter, she releases a glorious passage of huddle-duddle, in broken syntax and rhythms. Halfway through, she even gives the style a name:

> O, for a horse with wings! Hear'st thou,
> Pisanio?
> He is at Milford Haven: read, and tell me
> How far 'tis thither. If one of mean affairs
> May plod it in a week, why may not I
> Glide thither in a day? Then, true Pisanio,
> Who long'st, like me, to see thy lord; who
> long'st
> (O let me bate) but not like me: yet long'st
> But in a fainter kind. O, not like me:
> For mine's beyond beyond: say, and speak
> thick,
> (Love's counsellor should fill the bores of
> hearing,
> To th'smothering of the sense) how far it is
> To this same blessed Milford.
>
> [3.2.49-60]

"Thick speech": this is the closest Imogen ever comes to indulging herself in a stylistic romp for its own sake, yet she still knows exactly what she is doing. After talking then about the time it takes to get to Wales, she concludes,

> But this is foolery:
> Go, bid my woman feign a sickness, say
> She'll home to her father; and provide me
> presently
> A riding-suit; no costlier than would fit
> A franklin's housewife.
>
> [3.2.74-78]

Recovering her balance, weighing and judging again (as in the wit of her last remark), she knows well what her strengths and temptations are; but the game of style is not one of them, and it is left to the men.

Where Imogen is deeply tested, however, is in her discovery of Posthumus's real intent in sending her to Milford Haven. The temptation would be for her to reject Posthumus in turn, and to emphasize the self-lessness of her own devotion. Instead she goes into a deeper understanding of their relationship, though at first her reaction is the healthy one, simple anger:

> False to his bed? what is it to be false?
> To lie in watch there, and think on him?
> To weep 'twixt clock and clock? If sleep
>   charge Nature,
> To break it with a fearful dream of him,
> And cry myself awake? That's false to's
>   bed, is it?
>
> [3.4.41-45]

After running through some charitable but realistic explanations—the first being that Posthumus was betrayed by "some jay of Italy" (3.4.50)—she starts to generalize about men, as Posthumus did about women. There is a great difference in their two approaches:

> so thou, Posthumus,
> Wilt lay the leaven on all proper men;
> Goodly and gallant shall be false and perjur'd
> From thy great fail.
>
> [3.4.62-65]

Imogen's interest is in the way men are regarded, and her point of view is much more sophisticated than Posthumus's; he was less concerned with attitudes than with what he took to be objective truth about the evil of women. Imogen's self-concern, when it appears, involves no stylistic adornment. She acknowledges the facts of her family and her former suitors, then admits that her disobedience to her father might figure in Posthumus's estimate of her (actually they do not; he cannot reason that far past himself). At the same time she avoids self-pity, thinking exactly and turning her verse with care. Notice in particular the firm stressing of the verbs here:

> I grieve myself
> To think, when thou shalt be disedg'd by
>   her
> That now thou tirest on, how thy memory
> Wilt then be pang'd by me.
>
> [3.4.94-97]

Hardly thick speech. The dominant terms all concern physical appetite (*disedg'd, tirest,* a term from falconry meaning "to tear", and *pang'd*); the metaphor of eating returns later, when she says of Posthumus "Now I think on thee,/My hunger's gone" (3.6.15-16). Imogen's critical sense applies to herself as well as to Posthumus; she sees the interdependence of their love and more, that Posthumus tried to use her as if she were a commodity, and that she accepted that role. In the speech above, her meters tie her thoughts together, rising on *myself* and *disedg'd,* then coming down on *tirest;* all have the sibilant and thin *e*-sound, shaped by frontal consonants, physically giving the sense of her exactness; the darker vowel and nasals in *pang'd* prolong that word and allow time for us to grasp the realization behind it. However much her consciousness may be manipulated in some scenes, here it is demonstrably full.

Imogen's attitudes continue to grow after this; otherwise Shakespeare would have sent her off sooner to wait for act 5, as he did with Iachimo and Posthumus. Her further characterization is again most easily described in negatives. She does not cease to consider and discriminate; she does not lose her sense of humor or her ironic view of herself. Even under the stress of her pastoral trials,[23] she retains her essentially critical mind:

> To lapse in fulness
> Is sorer than to lie for need: and falsehood
> Is worse in kings than beggars. My dear
>   lord,
> Thou art one o'th' false ones! Now I think
>   on thee,
> My hunger's gone; but even before, I was
> At point to sink, for food.
>
> [3.6.12-17]

The thought of Posthumus can relieve hunger, but only for about three lines. Because of the rhythmic flexibility-within-order of these lines we feel no doubt of Imogen's fundamental balance and sanity. Even in circumstances like these she has no tendency to rant, and her accusation of Posthumus is brief, though it swells the line with two elisions: "Thou art one o'th'false ones! Now I think on thee, . . ." Though firm, the accusation needs only light control, and even when she is surprised by the aristocratic mountaineers, she says to herself, with light but pointed emphasis,

> 'Mongst friends?
> If brothers: would it had been so, that they
> Had been my father's sons, then had my
>   prize
> Been less, and so more equal ballasting
> To thee, Posthumus.
>
> [3.7.47-51]

Here she uses her present experience to understand better her bond to her husband, and the fine metrical shading in the last two and a half lines emphasizes her growing knowledge. Had Cymbeline not had only one child to dote upon, her defection would not have been so heinous: because she would have been prized less,

Posthumus would have seemed a more suitable husband. The wonderful thing about the lightness of the meters here is that it keeps us from feeling even a trace of condescension in her attitude. That her meditation is addressed to Posthumus shows that she has now understood more fully his own sense of shamed insufficiency.[24]

It is necessary to insist upon the depth of Imogen's awareness here if we are to regard her next scene, in which she discovers Cloten's headless body, as something besides a grotesque joke at her expense. Most immediately, her concern over Posthumus when she meets her brothers helps to prepare us for her anguish in the next scene: just as she begins to understand why he has rejected her, she discovers him dead. Her speech over the corpse also gives us something by which to judge Posthumus's later speech, in which he thinks he has killed Imogen and reached a new self-understanding. Not just a lament, these lines show her thinking forcefully, admitting and discarding first one set of possibilities and then another. When she believes she may be having hallucinations, the rhythms are accordingly tentative.

> If there be
> Yet left in heaven as small a drop of pity
> As a wren's eye, fear'd gods, a part of it!
> The dream's here still: even when I wake it is
> Without me, as within me: not imagin'd, felt.
> [4.2.303-7]

She comes out of her concentration in an alexandrine, which prolongs the moment of balance between dream and waking; what follows is not an elegy (that comes later) but a passage of mental discovery and fabrication, more important than mourning, in which Imogen convinces herself that Pisanio was hired by Cloten to deceive her and Posthumus both. Appropriately enough, the next passage is more excited than anything else that Imogen speaks in the play; often putting extra syllables in a line, her voice gains in urgency, the biggest jump occurring as she suddenly imagines the conspiracy of Cloten and Pisanio:

> Pisanio,
> All curses madded Hecuba gave the Greeks,
> And mine to boot, be darted on thee! Thou,
> Conspir'd with that irregular devil, Cloten,
> Hast here cut off my lord. To write, and read
> Be henceforth treacherous! Damn'd Pisanio
> Hath with his forg'd letters (damn'd Pisanio)
> From this most bravest vessel of the world
> Struck the main-top!
> [4.2.312-20]

Of all the plausible explanations for things, it is surprising that Cloten should pop in here, for there were others in the play besides Cloten who disliked Post-

humus. Why does she think of him? One cannot go so far as to conclude that Imogen subconsciously loved Cloten, in the manner of Beatrice and DeFlores in *The Changeling;* the point of the confusion is that without their reason—that is, their heads—men may have much in common.[25] No opportunity is lost to identify Cloten with Posthumus; when Imogen concludes that Pisanio forged Posthumus's letters and led her to Wales where Cloten could kill Posthumus, she calls out Cloten's very name as she embraces the corpse: "This is Pisanio's deed, and Cloten,—O!/Give colour to my pale cheek with thy blood" (4.2.329-30). This parody of unselfish forgiveness removes some responsibility from Posthumus; in a narrow sense, he was no more responsible for his deception in the first place than Cloten was for his noble appearance.

Imogen has been a measured speaker before, but now her verse leaps at every crucial point in her fiction of Pisanio and Cloten; in the passage quoted above, she stresses Pisanio's name two different ways in two consecutive lines. Distraught as she is though, her own impulse to live is never threatened in these lines; at the end she even thinks directly of "those/ Which chance to find us" (4.2.331-32).[26] When she goes with Lucius, she never once suggests or implies that she will not continue living. Having none of Posthumus's tendencies toward self-deception, she never can become intoxicated by the theme of honor.

Imogen's knowledge runs deeper than she herself realizes, for one side effect of her speech on Cloten-Posthumus is to qualify the dirge ("Fear no more the heat o' th' sun") that her brothers had just spoken.[27] As elsewhere in the play, the lyrical moments in an Elizabethan style are all followed by more grotesque passages in a mode we usually think of as Jacobean: Iachimo's reverie over the sleeping Imogen is tinged by his own posturing, not to mention his dastardly intentions; and the short song "Hark, hark" of act 2 is surrounded by vulgarities from the ineffable Cloten.[28] (This song and the dirge are so familiar that quotation should be unnecessary.) In a lesser artist, the practice would seem like a failure of nerve, an unwillingness to risk the lyric description of nature without the addition of an ironic context. Here the juxtaposition implies that the lyric response is an unsatisfactory mirror of the world in which it appears; in each case the lyric moment fails to describe with even momentary accuracy the situation before it. Iachimo is not so taken with Imogen's beauty that he repents of his vile behavior; "Hark, hark" has only the most perversely idealized connection with Cloten's desires; and the dirge cannot account for the way that Imogen and Posthumus are still alive, or the fact that the only dead body present is Cloten's, and he is hardly a "golden lad."[29]

In terms of the play's poetic, two provisional conclusions emerge. The coherent lyrical manner cannot resist the thick speech, which Iachimo, Posthumus, and Imogen all employ to disastrous effect at one time or another. However, the lyric moments do give the audience a way of evaluating the fineness of the characters' sensibilities. We recognize the nobility of Guiderius and Arviragus as much by their dirge as by their martial zeal, and we find Iachimo disturbing not because he is a cad simple but because he can recreate Imogen's beauty and still do evil deeds in spite of this ability. (If Shakespeare were not interested in Iachimo's lyricism he could just as easily have made him a two-dimensional Don John.) Poetry of the pretty sort makes nothing happen; yet in this play as in few others, it is our chief means of understanding *why* things happen.[30]

Posthumus's second soliloquy begins act 5 and announces that his rehabilitation is to be one of the main subjects of the act. Since we last saw him, he has schooled his voice; he now speaks neither woodenly, as in his early private moments with Imogen, nor in the erratic and inflated manner of his first soliloquy. Somehow he has found a plain and spontaneous tone:

> Gods, if you
> Should have ta'en vengeance on my faults,
>   I never
> Had liv'd to put on this: so had you saved
> The nobel Imogen, to repent, and struck
> Me, wretch, more worth your vengeance. But
>   alack,
> You snatch some hence for little faults;
>   that's love,
> To have them fall no more.
>
> [5.1.7-13]

On one level Posthumus is still confused: he has not forgiven Imogen, but only wishes she had lived to repent, which he would do his best to encourage by his own death, an added punishment for her. His sense of responsibility is still woolly, since he blames first Pisanio and then the gods for Imogen's death, going on to note "my faults" without the unpleasant bother of any precision: his saying that the gods have snatched her hence is the excellent foppery of the world.

None of this accounts for the tone of the passage, which could hardly have come from Posthumus's vow to write invective.[31] The diction and syntax of the lines are plain; in most lines a long phrase leads out, followed by a short phrase that in turn draws the sense into the next long phrase. With his thoughts thus linked, even though his imagery is sparse, Posthumus has none of the close-lipped constriction that had marked his style in the early scenes. As important as the syntax and line-endings, however, is the new freedom in his meters. Abandoning the heavy iambics of his first speeches and the jumble of his first soliloquy (just as he also abandons the abstractions and surreal imagery

that went with these), Posthumus is now moving into cadences, patterns repeated from line to line. They appear in the lines quoted above, and continue as he resolves to reform and sacrifice himself:

> I'll disrobe me
> Of these Italian weeds, and suit myself
> As does a Briton peasant: so I'll fight
> Against the part I come with: so I'll die
> For thee, O Imogen, even for whom my life
> Is, every breath, a death: and thus,
>   unknown,
> Pitied, nor hated, to the face of peril
> Myself I'll dedicate. Let me make men know
> More valour in me than my habits show.
> Gods, put the strength o' th' Leonati in me!
> To shame the guise o' th' world, I will
>   begin,
> The fashion less without, and more within.
>
> [5.1.22-33]

Most of these lines contain a similar rhythmic pattern, descended from that in Posthumus's early speeches; it consists of two phrases separated by a pause, each pause containing two strong stresses, . . . [and] a sort of extended pair of iambs. . . . Posthumus's vow to retreat into anonymity and fight to the death may be a somewhat limited program for building character, but the new poetry in his voice suggests that he will grow into a larger attitude.[32] Posthumus is at last beginning to sound like someone who is educable, a condition that none of his earlier speeches had suggested. The play shows a division between the poetic characters of Posthumus, who is reluctant either to let his poetic style grow or to trust it; of Imogen, who uses it to deepen her understanding; and of Iachimo, who regards it as an end in itself.

Posthumus's lingering desire not to relinquish his claims on himself has a parallel in his own family history. Because his father, Sicilius Leonatus, lost his first two sons in wars, he despaired even while his wife was pregnant with Posthumus. He was "fond of issue," the gentleman in act 1, scene 1, tells us, but not, apparently, fond enough of his wife or the child his wife was carrying. Like Posthumus, he was unable to grow out of the past and into a future. It is precisely this ability that we have seen in Imogen. Both Posthumus and Imogen began in similar circumstances: Posthumus's brothers died before he was born, and Imogen's brothers were kidnapped before she was born.[33] As we have seen, she is aware of the burden this puts upon her in relation to her father, but she is still able to direct and control her own feelings of insufficiency toward Cymbeline. The great discrepancy between Imogen's and Posthumus's resources is evident most of all in Posthumus's suicidal plan for dealing with his loss.

Posthumus's description of the battle (which follows the soliloquy and Iachimo's perfunctory confession that he has "belied a lady"—a knavish pun) might seem at first to be exposition and little else. Its style shows, however, that Posthumus has begun to open his closed mind. Like the soliloquy in act 5, scene 1, this descriptive speech shows a great resourcefulness in imagery and metric. The battle has had a decisive influence on Posthumus; one of its chief effects has been to remove his tendency to speak abstractly in a frozen rhythmic pattern—what might be called the rigidity of a virtue shaped only by a sense of shame. Now, with more positive accomplishments to his credit (the defense of his country—in other words, his mother) he can move beyond that shame to a final acceptance of his own limits.

The battle itself is a metaphor for the change in Posthumus. What happens to the Britons is nothing less than a total change of personality; cowards before, they become all the more valiant by having grown out of cowardice: "having found the back-door/Of the unguarded hearts, heavens, how they wound!" (5.3.45-46). For a speech describing such a reversal in character, a stylistic upheaval would be appropriate; and one sign of Shakespeare's craft in this play is that he has developed the character of Posthumus in such a way as to make the speech dramatically plausible. In some ways the speech is closer to the huff-snuff that was still popular on some Jacobean stages than it is to narrative poetry circa 1610:

> [these three] with this word "Stand, stand,"
> Accomodated by the place, more charming,
> With their own nobleness, which could have
>   turn'd
> A distaff to a lance, gilded pale looks;
> Part shame, part spirit renew'd, that some,
>   turn'd coward
> But by example (O, sin in war,
> Damn'd in the first beginners) 'gan to look
> The way that they did, and to grin like lions
> Upon the pikes o' th' hunters.
>
> [5.3.31-39]

The imagery is thoroughly conventional and almost Spenserian in its formal qualities; there are no unexpected juxtapositions, and the heroic scale is insisted on throughout, with the harts, lions, and eagles. Later the losers even flee like chickens in the approved epic manner. Archaism is just the point in a description that extols old-fashioned values.

At the same time, as with Iachimo's Elizabethan speeches over the sleeping Imogen, the style has the late Shakespearean tint, so that we never fear we might be listening to Hamlet's player. The enjambments, for example, contain reversals of a sort seldom found in earlier Elizabethan narrative:

> three performers are the file when all
> The rest do nothing. . . .
> their own nobleness, which could have
>   turn'd
> A distaff to a lance. . . .
>
> [5.3.30-31,33-34]

In each case the focus suddenly moves from an agent to the things worked upon. By means of such shifts, and the metrical sophistication, the speech creates the effect of an older rhetoric viewed through a refracting prism; in this remodeling of heroic narrative, the dramatist holds up an ideal and emphasizes its distance at the same time. Self-conscious the manner may be, yet it is not merely Shakespeare's self-consciousness but that of Posthumus as well. He knows he is close to parody of the heroic style, admitting at the end that one could "vent it for a mockery" (5.3.56).

This enlargement of Posthumus's awareness leads directly to his final repentance: within fifteen lines of his battle speech he delivers his last soliloquy, forgiving Imogen for her alleged lapse. Now he has come around to a language at once fully conscious, plain, and spontaneous:

> Most welcome bondage; for thou art a way,
> I think to liberty: yet am I better
> Than one that's sick o' th' gout, since he
>   had rather
> Groan so in perpetuity than be cur'd
> By th' sure physician, Death; who is the
>   key
> T' unbar these locks. My conscience, thou
>   art fetter'd
> More than my shanks and wrists: you good
>   gods, give me
> The penitent instrument to pick that bolt,
> Then free for ever.
>
> [5.4.3-11]

The metric organization of the speech, like its logic, conveys a sense of directed energy rather than disorganized, line-by-line tension. The stress pattern identifies *bondage* with *liberty*, each taking more weight than the other words in its line. An extended comparison then flows over three line-ends to make a double pause around *Death*; the next firm stress falls on *key*, and then in one short pause he is back where he began, the locks he now wears. The unexpected weight on *my conscience* helps emphasize that the word here carries its double meaning of awareness as well as moral sense. (Jupiter, when he enters, is much more interested in Posthumus's knowledge than he is in his moral development.) Posthumus's formal repentance that follows is convincingly personal, because the rhythms are broken around each of the three stages of penitence, that is, sorrow, repentance, and satisfaction:

> Is't enough I am sorry? . . .
> Gods are more full of mercy. Must I
>   repent, . . .
> Desir'd more than constrain'd: to satisfy,
> If of my freedom. . . .
>   [5.4.11,13,15-16]

The natural and unforced displacements reveal a man without affectation and pretense; his self-knowledge is complete enough that he seems neither impatient for his recognition nor humbly frozen. He ends in the firm cadences we heard before:

>   and so, great powers,
> If you will take this audit, take this life,
> And cancel these cold bonds. O Imogen,
> I'll speak to thee in silence.
>   [5.4.26-29]

Finally his educated voice coalesces with his awakened moral sense; his development is substantially complete, and he has achieved it by himself, before the intervention of Jupiter.[34]

Editors since Pope and Johnson have had a low opinion of the speeches by the spirits in Posthumus's dream, but their poetic and dramatic relevance has been so well established in recent years that there is no need to repeat what has already been said by G. Wilson Knight and others.[35] Briefly, the characters of Posthumus's mother, father, and brothers all speak (as one sign of their great age) in stanzas of fourteeners, with short two-stress codas. This dated form suits both their age and their lack of poetic sophistication; the rustic simplicity of the generation just past has always been a cherished fiction. Jupiter answers the spirits in alternately rhymed, stolidly Senecan couplets, half in imperatives; most of the speech is heavy-handed and sententious—both desirable qualities in this case, for he would be a very shallow monster indeed if he descended speaking light verse. In Jupiter's speech as in the speeches of the spirits, the poetic technique is consistent with that in the rest of the play, since the play's verse repeatedly gestures toward conventions and styles outside the experience of the character himself. In this play the poetic style of any given character is liable to become something without himself as within, something other than what he literally seems to be on the stage. All of the characters—including Jupiter and the spirits—are ventriloquists, particularly at the crucial moments in the play.

Posthumus's manner of speaking does not change greatly after the vision; as in his second soliloquy, the metaphors are vivid but not mixed, and the flexibility of his metric remains unimpaired. Like Imogen when she thought she had discovered that Posthumus was dead, he trusts what he sees, accepts the inexplicable without irritation or impatience:

Peggy Ashcroft as Imogen.

> 'Tis still a dream: or else such stuff as
>   madmen
> Tongue, and brain not: either both, or
>   nothing,
> Or senseless speaking, or a speaking such
> As sense cannot untie. Be what it is,
> The action of my life is like it.
>   [5.4.146-50]

That calm is tested in the final scene, which is so full of peripeteia—twenty-four, in all—that the reader is apt to ask, with Posthumus, "How comes these staggers on me?" Yet as far as the three principals are concerned, the plotting still remains an extension of character. Imogen naturally feels no necessity to come forward and explain why she is not dead; nor does Posthumus, who is still dazed after the battle, and although he sees Iachimo early in the scene, before Iachimo confesses, he remains beyond all thought of revenge or recrimination.[36] Perhaps Shakespeare's cleverest dovetailing of plot and character, however, appears in the way that the restoration of Posthumus's moral sanity is finally revealed in his striking Imogen. There would be every reason for him to suppose that the page (as Imogen appears to be) was one of

Iachimo's cohorts; no one else present would have understood the significance of Iachimo's ring. The blow that Posthumus strikes is the sort of unequivocal response he should have made to Iachimo's taunts in the first place.

The elements of *cuisine opera* in Posthumus's final confession should not blind us to the real alterations that have occurred in his mind and speaking voice; these appear, once again, in his extraordinary line to Imogen, after the confusion has been cleared away:

> Hang there like fruit, my soul,
> Till the tree die.
>
> [5.5.263-64]

"The tree" is the body, their one body, and the appropriately strong rhythm suggests anything but melting abandon; it is also very distant from the abstract and rhythmically mechanical phrases Posthumus spoke at the beginning. This sentence, one of the few he has after the concluding revelations, shows that his imagery and verse style have become means of understanding, not simply techniques for concealment or decoration.

But it is Iachimo's development that shapes and controls the act; the conclusion of the romantic plot itself is one side of Iachimo's development. After Posthumus disarms him, Iachimo claims to know the reason for his own weakness, but his final confession gives the lie to that. If Shakespeare is to play fair with Iachimo, he cannot let him change; he has been out of sight since the play's initial action, and there would be no middle term for his growth. The growth of Posthumus is dramatically justifiable because of Imogen's exploration of Posthumus's problems. She supplies the middle term for his growth, and through her we realize that all—all!—Posthumus has to do in order to come around is to identify the reason for his rejecting her. If we accept Imogen's judgment of him, we must accept that all he needs is enough time and aggravation, neither of which requires that he be onstage. Iachimo is another matter, and because we gain no insights into his character in the middle of the play, we are reluctant to believe that he has changed at the end.

If we ignore Cymbeline's two half-line interruptions, Iachimo's confession is the longest speech in the play (ll. 153-209); it obviously fascinated Shakespeare, even if it does not do the same for many modern critics.[37] So elaborate that it seems more an aria than a speech,[38] it lets all of Iachimo's old habits reappear, in a form more highly polished than before. Imogen may have invalidated Iachimo's ideas about human nature, and he may claim to be in a state of neurasthenic collapse, but he still has the pleasure of his poetic creation to fall back on. (That pleasure,

incidentally, revives him long before Posthumus gets around to forgiving him.)

Iachimo's self-conscious tone is signaled early, as he calls for Cymbeline's attention, and then requests first aid:

> *Iach.*   Wilt thou hear more, my lord?
> *Cym.* All that belongs to this.
> *Iach.*   That paragon, thy daughter,
> For whom my heart drops blood, and my
>   false spirits
> Quail to remember—Give me leave! I faint.
>
> [5.5.146-49]

How finely absurd: the character with the most presence in the play about to faint; Cymbeline thinks Iachimo is dying, although he has suffered no worse in battle than acute embarrassment. Far from quailing or drooping, any one of Iachimo's lines above would show his old control returning. It is as if Shakespeare wanted to try the instrument one more time, showing a reassertion of self in poetic rather than psychological terms (as in the tragedies); it would have been an easy matter to have unraveled the story circumstantially rather than poetically, as Shaw's revision showed. Iachimo's baroque tone seems highlighted by the salubrious and self-congratulatory atmosphere of the British victory:

> Upon a time, unhappy was the clock
> That struck the hour: it was in Rome,
>   accurst
> The mansion where: 'twas at a feast, O,
>   would
> Our viands had been poison'd (or at least
> Those which I heav'd to head) the good
>   Posthumus
> (What should I say? he was too good to be
> Where ill men were, and was the best of all
> Amongst the rar'st of good ones) sitting sadly,
> Hearing us praise our loves of Italy
> For beauty, that made barren the boast
>   swell'd
> Of him that best could speak.
>
> [5.5.153-63]

As before, his rhetoric employs interminable interruptions, shifts in tone, striking of poses, and sudden intrusions of unexpected and racy metaphors. Beyond these there is also the prosodic luxuriance that we associate with Iachimo; against the dominant iambics he often slides into trochaics at the beginning of lines ("Those which I heav'd to head," "What should I say?" "Hearing us praise our loves"), which the frequent light endings reinforce. This sense of being suspended between two ways of thinking is typical of Iachimo; his manner insists upon the listener's concentration, because the heavy internal rhymes and alliterations often link contraries, as in *poison'd/Post-humus* or *beauty/barren* and *boast/best*. Iachimo extends his matter as far as he can, offering paradox and logical redundancy in metrically exotic settings: "beauty that made barren the swelled boast," or "Fairness, which strikes the eye" (5.5.168). . . . Raising the tension by enlarging one basic pattern, he goes on to ransack his full magazine of effects, and he does not use the same rhythms and pauses in any two lines of the speech.

Critics who complain about Iachimo's interruptions can join Cymbeline, who responds just as Iachimo wants: "I stand on fire./Come to the matter" (5.5.168-69). Iachimo proceeds economically for a few lines but then, in spite of himself, slides back to more extreme variations, gross images formed in grosser vowel contrasts:

> This Posthumus
> Most like a noble lord in love and one
> That had a royal lover, took his hint,
> And (not dispraising whom we prais'd,
>   therein
> He was as calm as virtue) he began
> His mistress' picture, which, by his tongue,
>   being made,
> And then a mind put in't, either our brags
> Were crak'd of kitchen-trulls, or his
>   description
> Prov'd us unspeaking sots.
>
>   [5.5.170-78]

When Iachimo comes to "his mistress' picture" he can no longer restrain himself, and sails off into a longer line that introduces the most telling distortion of all. Claiming to be a defender of Italian womanhood, he reveals that his real concern was—as we knew all along—to show how well *speaking* really could be done.

For someone listening closely this is the heart of the matter, but Cymbeline, with his usual brash irrelevance, exclaims, "Nay, nay, to th' purpose" (5.5.178), and Iachimo then begins his last and fullest display of artistry. He describes, at about equal length, the wager, his British interlude, and his deception of Posthumus; the transitions are marked with unusual deliberation, and show Iachimo's conscious organization of his material. Although as he speaks he is surrounded by people, his prime audience remains himself, and many of the details in the speech would be comprehensible to Iachimo alone. At first he leans toward self-justification, impugning Posthumus's integrity while claiming to uphold it, but then he makes some surprising turns:

> Your daughter's chastity (there it begins)—
> He spoke of her, as Dian had hot dreams,

> And she alone were cold: whereat I, wretch,
> Made scruple of his praise, and wager'd
>   with him
> Pieces of gold, 'gainst this (which he then
>   wore
> Upon his honour'd finger) to attain
> In suit the place of's bed, and win this ring
> By hers and mine adultery: he, true knight,
> No lesser of her honour confident
> Than I did truly find her, stakes this ring,
> And would so, had it been a carbuncle
> Of Pheobus' wheel; and might so safely,
>   had it
> Been all the worth of's car.
>
>   [5.5.179-91]

According to this version, the reference to Diana's "hot dreams" seems to be a metaphor from Posthumus, while Iachimo's picture of himself as a miserable outcast ("I, wretch") who had small reservations ("made scruple") bears little resemblance to the Iachimo we saw. There is also that preposterous detail of "his honour'd finger." The humanized digit must be related to Imogen's "right proud" mole, and in both cases the detail ends up diminishing its object rather than enlarging it. These distortions accompany some most distracting imagery: the gold coins, the finger, the bed, the diamond, the rubies of the sun and the imagined wheel they form—all shift and move as if they were props in an animated display. The rhetorical uses of meter are especially evident in the contrast between "I, wretch" and "he, true knight"; *whereat* holds back the expected two stresses that would finish the line, then deposits them both on *I, wretch;* Iachimo then lands firmly on *scruple* and *wager'd,* but gives *him* almost no weight at all, as if Posthumus were an ignorant accessory. The wager then unfolds in two lines of alliteration, consonance, and unexpected pauses, becoming regular again at *attain* and stressing even more heavily *win this ring,* as if to emphasize his own preoccupation with the symbol itself. Posthumus's confidence and Imogen's honor are described, by contrast, in unvaried iambics, but when Iachimo describes the ring for a third time, the meters loosen again; as the ring becomes a celestial gem, the line slows to take up the slack of a missing stress:

> And would so, had it been a carbuncle.

Plunging through to a flourish, he pauses briefly on *wheel,* but (sign of his gallantry) he does not mention Imogen, instead moving quickly over two pauses with unstressed syllables before each (*and might so safely, had it / . . .*), then making her honor even more remote by the emphasis of the open vowels at the end: *All the worth of's car.*

The speech takes some odd turns for a confession, endorsing and sympathizing uncertainly in the verse and imagery; but this is only the start. The second (and slightly longer) section concerns the scenes in Britain, and the description here is notable for not containing one image, in contrast to the description of the wager; the cosmic scale is gone too, with its deities and myths. In this colorless atmosphere Iachimo's meters almost dissolve as he describes his encounter with Imogen; it would be hard to tell where to place stresses in either of the full lines here:

> I was taught
> Of your chaste daughter the wide difference
> 'Twixt amorous and villainous. Being thus
>   quench'd
> Of hope, not longing. . . .
>
> [5.5.193-96]

Because we already know the story and its ending, the main focus for the audience is the sheer evasiveness with which Iachimo's style can work upon a matter for simple narrative. To us, all of this seems only a buildup for the deception of Posthumus, yet when Iachimo comes to that, he drops it flatly, saying that he is subtle but hardly showing his trade secrets:

> I return'd with simular proof enough
> To make the noble Leonatus mad,
> By wounding his belief in her renown,
> With tokens, thus, and thus: averring notes
> Of chamber-hanging, pictures, this her bracelet
> (O cunning, how I got it!) nay, some marks
> Of secret on her person, that he could not
> But think her bond of chastity quite crack'd,
> I having ta'en the forfeit.
>
> [5.5.200-208]

Metrically regular with no suggestion of ambiguity (there is only one light ending, and not until the end does Iachimo change the initial foot), the speech comes out as a quick, simplified view of the event. Elisions in *simular* and *Leonatus* speed the first two lines along, the "evidence" is swept up in enjambed lines that allow minimal pausing (*notes/bracelet/marks*), and the conclusion is enjambed as well, as if it were inevitable: *he could not/But think.* Iachimo tactfully avoids pointing out that Posthumus wanted to doubt Iachimo even before Iachimo had presented all his "evidence."

For us the main question is why the poetic organization of Iachimo's speech heightens the account of the wager, lowers the tone of his encounter with Imogen, and finally dismisses what was psychologically the most important part of all, the deception of Posthumus. We seem to run very quickly into questions about the nature and mode of Iachimo's dramatic existence. If self-justification were Iachimo's dominant motive, he could have done much better than he does: he could have presented Posthumus in a much less favorable light merely by telling the truth. One might explain the emphases of his speech as partly the result of habit, or partly the operatic occasion at hand, the stage having, by conservative estimate, twenty-one people on it at the moment.

But more than either of these, Iachimo seems to be led on by the variety and delight of his own voice, and in this he remains thoroughly consistent. As we saw earlier, many of the details he alludes to would be appreciated or understood by himself alone: his self-distanced longing for Imogen, his knowledge that his attempt to seduce her was instant theater for her benefit, his ingenious way of getting into her room. These details, unstated but hinted at, suggest that Iachimo is highly conscious of what he is doing at that moment. Similarly, the intricate organization and rich poetic texture of his confession satisfy him as a poet and justify his self-depiction as an "Italian brain," although none of this is of much interest to the uncouth Britons, who are "on fire" to follow the mere narrative.[39]

Certainly of the three characters whose poetic development we have followed, Iachimo is the least changed at the end.[40] This comes across well on the stage; in the 1974 Royal Shakespeare Company production of the play, there was barely restrained laughter in the audience when Posthumus forgave Iachimo, not so much because of Posthumus's earnest boy-scout manner—"Live/And deal with others better"—as because Iachimo so obviously finds his own performance of more interest than anyone else's forgiveness.[41] No one could believe in his reformation on the basis of his five-line repentance:

> now my heavy conscience sinks my
>   knee,
> As then your force did. Take that life,
>   beseech you,
> Which I so often owe: but your ring first,
> And here the bracelet of the truest princess
> That ever swore her faith.
>
> [5.5.414-18]

By offering the ring and bracelet after asking for death, instead of before, Iachimo gallantly leaves the emphasis upon Imogen's endurance, just as his request for death follows a generous reference to Posthumus's force (which no gentleman would use now on a captive). Like the exaggeration and pathos of "so often," it all goes with the conspicuously falling rhythms, which add to the precious atmosphere; of the eight disyllabic words in the passage, seven have the stresses on the first syllables. Whatever truth the speech contains (Is he repentant, or is he angling for a reprieve?) must finally lie in its poetry and not in its sentiments.

Having begun with Iachimo, we will find him the best place to end; he is the one character whose stylistic variation does not lead him out of himself. But that may be a misplaced criterion with Iachimo in any case: the notion that there is one "sincere" self back of all the masks becomes the final illusion. Trying on one voice after another, he is the play's chief poetic ventriloquist, and because the play is a romance, he can be spared in order to exhibit his villainy fully at the end, now neutralized and harmless to the community. Iachimo is a kind of living nightmare through which the other characters have traveled; if their transformations are to seem convincing, he will have to be alive and present at the end, not simply dead, or worse, silenced.

Notes

1 Unless otherwise noted, all quotations are from the Arden edition, ed. J. M. Nosworthy (London: Methuen, 1969). Act, scene, and line numbers for quotations are cited hereafter in the text.

2 The passage has occasioned a clutch of emendations it would be tiresome to discuss; Nosworthy rightly rejects them all. None of the critics and editors in the Variorum seem to have realized that Iachimo's obscurity is intentional and functional.

3 In a brilliant note to line 36, Nosworthy remarks that Iachimo is seeing things "as it were through the eye of God." There may be a biblical parallel in this passage (Matt. 10:30), but like the many others in the play, it does not seem to fit into a coherent scheme. See Naseeb Shaheen, "The Use of Scripture in *Cymbeline*," *ShS* 4 (1968):294-315; cf. Hugh M. Richmond in "Shakespeare's Roman Trilogy: The Climax of *Cymbeline*," *SLitI* 5 (1972):130.

4 The metrical characteristics of Shakespeare's later verse have been set out by Percy Simpson in "Shakespeare's Versification: A Study in Development," in *Studies in Elizabethan Drama* (Oxford: Clarendon Press, 1955), pp. 64-88, and by Frank Kermode in his Introduction to the Arden edition of *The Tempest* (London: Methuen, 1958), pp. lxxvii-lxxxi.

5 Again I would refer the reader to Dorothy L. Sipe, *Shakespeare's Metrics,* YSE no. 166 (New Haven: Yale University Press, 1968).

6 Arthur C. Kirsch suggests in *Jacobean Dramatic Perspectives* (Charlottesville: University Press of Virginia, 1972), that "when he is attempting to seduce Imogen, Iachimo becomes so intoxicated with his own verbal extravagance that he subverts his own intentions" (p. 64). This seems to ignore the self-consciousness that permeates all of Iachimo's speeches; at the least, it makes him a rather dull fellow. Granville-Barker says that these speeches reduce Iachimo to a "slavering, lascivious fool" (*Prefaces to Shakespeare*

[London: Batsford, 1946] 3:132, but this view is inconsistent with Granville-Barker's view of Iachimo's intelligence and vanity.

7 Iachimo (not Posthumus and not, certainly, Cymbeline) is the most complex character in the play and has attracted some splendid actors—Henry Irving, Laurence Olivier, Ian Richardson. Despite this obvious clue as to the center of the play, the character still has not attracted many critics.

8 Nosworthy's Arden edition is especially useful for the way it collates echoes of Shakespeare's other work, but when he says of one speech, for example, that "powerful images of *Macbeth* and *Antony and Cleopatra* have intruded here" (p. lxiii), *here* should be understood as the critic's mind rather than Pisanio's; similar thinking governs terms like *revert* (p. lxix). Unfortunately, the citation of parallels does not tell us why Shakespeare wrote as he did in the play at hand. A more helpful approach might be to get back of the imagery, following Frank Kermode's suggestion that Shakespeare's state of mind in *Cymbeline*—difficult, tortuous, ironical"—resembles that in the sonnets (*Shakespeare, Spenser, Donne* [New York: Viking, 1971], p. 232). William Barry Thorne has remarked some of the parallels between *Cymbeline* and the rest of the canon, but his concern is with situation rather than with verbal echoes; see "*Cymbeline*: 'Lopp'd Branches' and the Concept of Regeneration," *ShQ* 20 (1969):143-59.

9 R. J. Schork has discussed some of the ironies of the allusion in "Allusion, Theme, and Characterization in *Cymbeline*," *SP* 59 (1972):210-16. However, Schork takes the ironies pretty much at face value, and does not comment on the way they are distanced by the action (e.g., Imogen's lack of interest) or by the self-conscious Elizabethanisms. An acceptance of Shakespeare's distance from his allusions is implicit in Jan Knott's study of "Lucian in *Cymbeline*," *MLR* 67 (1972):742-44.

10 Quoted by Nosworthy in Arden edition, p. 196. John also steals three jewels from the heroine's chamber, but Iachimo is unconcerned about such rewards. By making Iachimo the brother of a great duke, Shakespeare effectively removed the old motivation. Besides Nosworthy's remarks in the Arden, there are discussions of the play's sources by Kenneth Muir in *Shakespeare's Sources* (London: Methuen, 1957), pp. 231-40, and F. P. Wilson, in *Shakespeare and Other Studies* (Oxford: Clarendon Press, 1969), pp. 130-42. The most thorough study (with all the documents) is that by Geoffrey Bullough in *Narrative and Dramatic Sources of Shakespeare* (London: Routledge and Kegan Paul, 1975), 8:3-111.

11 Karl F. Thompson, in *Modesty and Cunning: Shakespeare's Use of Literary Tradition* (Ann Arbor: Uni-

versity of Michigan Press, 1971), rightly says that Iachimo wants to "discredit and destroy faith in idealized love" (p. 150); but it seems doubtful that in his first encounter with Imogen he is "test[ing] her susceptibility to the frailties traditionally ascribed to those unworthy of love" (p. 152).

[12] Iachimo's values have been mapped by Derek Traversi in *Shakespeare: The Last Phase* (London: Hollis and Carter, 1954), pp. 49-53, although Traversi does not account for Iachimo's odd fondness for the lyric mode.

[13] See Nosworthy's Introduction to the Arden edition, p. 8.

[14] Cf. Homer Swander's "*Cymbeline* and the 'Blameless Hero,'" *ELH* 21 (1964): 259-70. Swander has noted that this past quarrel, one of Shakespeare's first additions to his sources, helps establish the weakness of Posthumus's judgment. Swander is also specific on the way Shakespeare has elevated Posthumus above the conventional figure of the "virtuously boastful" husband.

[15] As will be apparent, I cannot accept Bertrand Evans's view: "Highly circumspect, Posthumus fell victim because Iachimo's evidence was undeniable" (*Shakespeare's Comedies* [Oxford: Clarendon Press, 1960], p. 262). Iachimo's evidence is eminently deniable, as Philario points out. No rational man would doubt his wife on the basis of Iachimo's story, and further, Posthumus believes Imogen guilty before he has even heard it all.

[16] *Cognizance* may be an image, however; see Nosworthy's note to this line in the Arden edition.

[17] W. Gordon Zeeveld, *The Temper of Shakespeare's Thought* (New Haven: Yale University Press, 1974), p. 239.

[18] See, e.g., E. M. W. Tillyard, *Shakespeare's Last Plays* (London: Chatto and Windus, 1938), p. 31, and Clifford Leech, *Shakespeare's Tragedies and Other Studies in Seventeenth-Century Drama* (London: Chatto and Windus, 1950), p. 134.

[19] Hough-Lewis Dunn glosses the term in "Shakespeare's *Cymbeline*, 2.5.15-17," *Expl* 30 (1972), item 57.

[20] The Folio hyphenates "Nice-longing" in line 178; this places the metrical stress upon the first word. I have used the Folio's lineation; most editors relineate at *knows* and *vice,* although it is suitable that at the end of his catalog Posthumus should be in a state of frenzy, which the length of the alexandrine mirrors; because of the choppy pauses it is hard to accept J. C.

Maxwell's statement in his New Cambridge edition that the line is "very lumbering" (Cambridge: At the University Press, 1960), p. 167.

[21] It has been suggested that the parts of Cloten and the First Gaoler were doubled (see Julia Engelen, *SJH* [1927], pp. 138-40, and W. M. Keck, *ShAssocBul* [1935], pp. 68-72), but in view of the close physical resemblance between Cloten and Posthumus the doubling of this pair seems more likely. There would be only one rapid costume change between scenes 3 and 4 of act 2, but given the parallels between the scenes—each ends with the character going out vowing to get vengeance upon Imogen—the change might be suggestive; and anyway, Posthumus has at least one other rapid change, the one into and out of his peasant grab. In *The Organization and Personnel of the Shakespearean Company* (Princeton: Princeton University Press, 1927), T. W. Baldwin proposed that Burbage played Posthumus to Armin's Cloten (pp. 238, 394); even if this guess is correct—and there are some problems with it—the imaginative connections between the two characters' minds are still established through their speech.

[22] Granville-Barker feels that the disappearance and return of Posthumus was a botch on Shakespeare's part (*Prefaces*, 3:76), although he devotes little study to the character or his verse. Though an appreciative reader of individual scenes, Granville-Barker never asks in this essay if a character's accents change, or if they bear any relation to the structure of the whole; thus Iachimo's verse, for example, remains "merely decorative" (3:92) or "a new Euphuism" (3:112-16). Granville-Barker sees the verse as prompted by the dramatic needs of the moment rather than by the larger development of a character; his hit-or-miss attention seems designed to illustrate his claim that the plotting and emotional pressure do not support the tension of the verse (3:118). More recently, Roger Warren has viewed the style of *Cymbeline* as a sequence of charged passages, which comment upon the apparent simplicity of the scenic structures ("Virtuosity and Complexity in *Cymbeline*," *ShS* 29 [1976]:41-49; a fuller study along these lines, with many acute insights into the changing depths of the verse, is R. A. Foakes's chapter on *Cymbeline* in *Shakespeare's Last Plays* (Charlottesville: University of Virginia Press, 1971), pp. 98-118.

[23] Because I am concerned chiefly with the central triangle of Imogen, Posthumus, and Iachimo, I have not discussed the pastoral themes of the play; these have been treated by Hallett Smith in *Shakespeare's Romances* (San Marino, Calif.: Huntington Library, 1972), Douglas Peterson in *Time, Tide, and Tempest* (San Marino, Calif.: Huntington Library, 1973), and Thomas MacFarland in *Shakespeare's Pastoral Comedies* (New Haven: Yale University Press, 1972). Es-

pecially valuable are the late Rosalie Colie's comments in *Shakespeare's Living Art* (Princeton: Princeton University Press, 1974), pp. 292-302.

[24] Jackson Cope studies the relation of this scene to Posthumus's dream later, and to similar moments in *The Taming of the Shrew, A Midsummer Night's Dream, Pericles,* and *The Tempest;* see *The Theater and the Dream* (Baltimore: Johns Hopkins University Press, 1973), pp. 239ff.

[25] From the neck down, Cloten must be as handsome as Posthumus, and not just on Imogen's testimony; Lucius describes the corpse as "a worthy building" now in ruins (4.2.355). For the relation of this disguise to others in the play, see John Scott Colley, "Disguise and New Guise in *Cymbeline*," *ShakS* 7 (1973):233-52. Colley remarks "how different is the reality of a Cloten from the reality of a Posthumus" (p. 249); but the reality here seems to be that the body before Imogen is in no sense different from Posthumus's (save for being dead). Cf. Robert Grams Hunter, *Shakespeare and the Comedy of Forgiveness* (New York: Columbia University Press, 1965), p. 158. An essay enlarging on the visual identification of Cloten and Posthumus is Joan Hartwig's "Cloten, Autolycus, and Caliban: Bearers of Parodic Burdens," in *Shakespeare's Romances Reconsidered,* ed. Carol McGinnis Kay and Henry E. Jacobs (Lincoln: University of Nebraska Press, 1978), pp. 91-103.

[26] G. Wilson Knight has some wise comments on Imogen's endurance and self-awareness; see *The Crown of Life* (London: Methuen, 1965), pp. 154-156. With all his concern for values, Knight still never loses track of Imogen's function in the drama. The same cannot be said for another study of her endurance, Charles K. Hofling's "Notes on Shakespeare's *Cymbeline*," *ShakS* 1 (1965): 118-36. Hofling sees Imogen as an illustration of Shakespeare's own mother-transference; she is a figure with whom Shakespeare personally identified, thus halting his own regression.

[27] In "The Spoken Dirge in Kyd, Marston, and Shakespeare: A Background to *Cymbeline,* (*N & Q,* n.s. 11 [1964]: 146-47), G. K. Hunter notes that the speaking of the dirge represents the "unvarnished sincerity" of the youths; however, the context of the dirge also comments on the theatrical convention. D. R. C. Marsh makes an extended analysis of the dirge, showing its relation to the play's major themes; see *The Recurring Miracle: A Study of "Cymbeline" and the Last Plays* (Pietrmaritzburg: University of Natal Press, 1962), pp. 82-85.

[28] The contrasts between these songs and their contexts have been discussed by Evans in *Shakespeare's Comedies,* pp. 258-59; see also Peter J. Seng, *The*

Vocal Songs in the Plays of Shakespeare (Cambridge: Harvard University Press, 1967), pp. 214-18.

[29] For the distance between what Imogen sees and what we see, Evans uses the term "discrepant awareness," although to stress its occurrence throughout the play he assumes that neither we nor Shakespeare's audience would be familiar with any versions of the calumniated wife story, or with any of the characters as representative types; see *Shakespeare's Comedies,* pp. 245-89. Barbara A. Mowat, in numerous remarks throughout *The Dramaturgy of Shakespeare's Romances* (Athens: University of Georgia Press, 1976), offers an analysis that builds upon the audience's different levels of awareness and their knowledge of the fables in the background.

[30] Lurking behind *Cymbeline* is, of course, *Philaster;* one helpful note on the stylistic differences between the two plays is Kenneth Muir's "A Trick of Style and Some Implications," *ShakS* 6 (1970): 305-10.

[31] The growth of a lyrical style is a private thing, and Shakespeare seldom shows it happening; in *King Lear,* e.g., Cordelia also learns a sweeter style offstage, but Shakespeare does not emphasize the arbitrariness of this by having her say that she will go to France and write satire.

[32] In *The Poetry of Shakespeare's Plays* (London: Duckworth, 1954) F. E. Halliday says that "we neither know nor care much about" Posthumus, one of Shakespeare's "shadowy or scarcely credible creations, important only as they work out the story and speak the poetry, stock figures who do not really determine the action" (p. 173). On the contrary, Posthumus's poetry *is* "the action"; realizing this, one can see also the limitations of Tillyard's statement that the changes of style have "little apparent reason for their occurrence" (*Shakespeare's Last Plays,* p. 75). More plausible is Maynard Mack's analysis of the way the late Shakespearean hero reaches and passes through his own antithesis ("The Jacobean Shakespeare," in *Jacobean Theatre,* ed. John Russel Brown and Bernard Harris, Stratford-upon-Avon Studies no. 1 [London: Arnold, 1960], esp. pp. 33-41). The shifts in style that Posthumus undergoes are directly related to his moral growth.

[33] The boys were three and two when Belarius took them; Belarius does not know that Cymbeline had a daughter, and Cymbeline is surprised that the three have met.

[34] A point made also, from a quite different perspective, by Douglas Peterson in *Time, Tide, and Tempest,* p. 142.

[35] The first reasoned argument in favor of the authenticity of the vision came from E. H. W. Meyerstein,

"The Vision of *Cymbeline*," *TLS*, 15 June 1922, p. 396; other landmarks include Shaw's Foreword to *"Cymbeline" Refinished* (1945) and G. Wilson Knight's overwhelming demonstration in *The Crown of Life*, pp. 168-202. Hardin Craig has some brief remarks in "Shakespeare's Bad Poetry," *ShS* 1 (1948): 55; Nosworthy extends some of these in his Introduction to the Arden edition, pp. xxxv-xxxvi. J. C. Maxwell, editor of the New Cambridge edition, concurs that the vision is probably Shakespeare's, although Dover Wilson has a strongly dissenting Preface.

[36] The ingenuity of the play's end has distracted many readers from the very real development of Posthumus, which has occurred prior to the divine intervention; thus it is hard to agree with Arthur Colby Sprague and J. C. Trewin, who say that "if the idea of a supernatural—providential—guidance is given to the happy ending, then we may be willing to accept what otherwise . . . seems over-plotted, or too pat" (*Shakespeare's Plays Today* [Columbia, S.C.: University of South Carolina Press, 1970], p. 44). As Peterson points out, we have seen more than either the Soothsayer or Cymbeline, and we know how Posthumus has transformed himself into an agent of renewal: "The heavens have intervened . . . but only after human agents have taken the initiative" (*Time, Tide, and Tempest*, p. 147).

[37] Knight, Traversi, and Marsh, for example, finish off Iachimo with only a sentence or a clause, assuming that his exposure is the essential thing; but since the information in Iachimo's speech is all familiar, we can safely say that Shakespeare's interest lay in the manner in which it is presented. Similar difficulties occur in an approach to the play via the pastoral; neither Peterson nor Colie, for example, sets up a critical vocabulary that can deal with Iachimo. Whatever the merits of Shaw's ideas about the vision, he did realize that Iachimo has a deep relation to the ongoing concerns of the play's world, as is evident in his revision of the ending. Still believing that Imogen has slept with Iachimo, Posthumus nonetheless forgives her cheerfully, and asks—to her great disgust—if she would like to have Iachimo come live with them.

[38] Northrop Frye has a tactful discussion of "arias" and operatic theatricality in the late plays; see *A Natural Perspective* (New York: Oxford University Press, 1965), pp. 23 ff.

[39] Shakespeare's final concern with Iachimo perhaps should qualify F. D. Hoeniger's suggestion that at the end of the play "mockery yields to vision, the world of appearance to the world of reality" ("Irony and Romance in *Cymbeline*," *SEL* 2 [1962]: 220). A related group of readings of the play that seldom if ever acknowledge the existence of Iachimo, much less his role at the end, are those determined to see it as a Stuart allegory. The most challenging of these is that

offered by Frances A. Yates, in *Shakespeare's Last Plays: A New Approach* (London: Routledge and Kegan Paul, 1975), pp. 41-61; Bernard Harris takes a similar yet more speculative line in "'What's past is prologue': *Cymbeline* and *Henry VIII*," in *The Later Shakespeare*, Stratford-upon-Avon Studies no. 8 (London: Arnold, 1966), pp. 202-33. Persuasive as these arguments are in themselves, they still ignore characterization and verbal texture, which have a great impact upon the audience and may supply levels of meaning that comment upon the historical themes.

[40] Hugh M. Richmond, reading the play as a study in Christian history, feels that Posthumus reforms Iachimo at the end. See "Shakespeare's Roman Trilogy: The Climax in *Cymbeline*," p. 136.

[41] As Frank Kermode said in his review of the RSC production at Stratford, "the part of Iachimo is tense with oppositions between what he says and what he does" (*Cymbeline* at Stratford," *TLS*, 5 July 1974, p. 710). Kermode objected, incidentally, to Richardson's edited Iachimo at Stratford; but it should be noted that by the time the RSC brought the play to London, all of Iachimo's extravagant lines to Imogen had been restored.

Elena Glazov-Corrigan (essay date 1994)

SOURCE: "Speech Acts, Generic Differences, and the Curious Case of *Cymbeline*," in *Studies in English Literature: 1500-1900*, Vol. 34, No. 2, Spring, 1994, pp. 379-99.

[*In this essay, Glazov-Corrigan explores the unique relationship in* Cymbeline *between words and actions, maintaining that linguistic analyses such as Speech Act theory are useful tools for understanding Shakespeare.*]

Cymbeline, one of the most unwieldy of Shakespeare's plays, exhibits a sprawling plot, an overwhelming number of characters, a striking lack of coordination between these characters and their language,[1] and a last act invariably challenging at every performance with "its twenty-four . . . dénouements,"[2] much hated by Bernard Shaw. [3] This essay seeks to show that a striking correspondence exists between the language of the play, "so curiously mixed in [its] style of composition,"[4] and the lack of coordination at every other level of the play. My main argument is that the hidden mechanism for this lack of unity is to be found in the play's use of language. It is also in *Cymbeline's* language, unsuitable for either tragedy or comedy, that one must seek an explanation of its genre. Some basic tenets of Speech Act theory will be invaluable in this analysis, although the essay will also isolate the limitations involved in the application of Speech Acts to the literary text. In view of these difficulties, I shall propose a new avenue of inquiry, namely, the exploration of the relationship between speech acts and the generic characteristics of drama itself.

Speech Acts and Shakespeare Scholarship

There are at least two main reasons for heuristic uncertainty regarding the application of Speech Acts to Shakespearean scholarship. Even if one disregards John L. Austin's initial placement of performative utterances outside the domain of drama (viewed by him as unreal or pretended speech)[5] and accepts Searle's definition of artistic discourse as "a serious illocutionary intention" (i.e., a real textual order for actors to pretend and for readers to imagine),[6] still the main obstacle to the application of Speech Acts resides in the fact that a strict classification of speech utterances is impossible to uphold.

The basis for differentiation was established by Austin's initial distinction between *constatives* (statements which can be either true or false) and *performatives* (utterances in which saying something counts as doing something) and also in his alternative classification of *locutionary acts* (certain sentences with sense and reference roughly equivalent to meaning), *illocutionary acts* (utterances which invite a response, e.g., warning, suggesting), and *perlocutionary acts* (utterances which achieve their goal in the moment of being employed, e.g., misleading, surprising, deterring). It became clear nonetheless to Austin and subsequent investigators not only that in communication acts merge into each other,[7] but also that these distinctions are context-oriented,[8] and, as other theorists have shown, socially and politically determined.[9] In other words, *no strict rules of grammar or social reality* can adequately explain or measure the progression of language from a binding order to mere suggestion and then to the neutral communication of information.

What then can be the need for Speech Act theory in literary criticism? The major relevance of Speech Act theory to drama remains indisputable: in drama words generate action, or rather a plot unfolds out of a series of Speech Acts,[10] and "the action rides on a train of illocutions."[11] Thus, the attractiveness of Speech Acts still consists in their central concern with language as action, a concern which coincides with a direction of inquiry central to literary theory, namely, a view of literary language as a generative principle of the artistic work as a whole rather than its secondary characteristic. Nevertheless, once the parallel directions and correspondences of pragmatic linguistics and literary theory are accepted, one immediately encounters a second very real obstacle: the above-mentioned lack of clear rule-tested classifications becomes further complicated by a genuine uncertainty about the practical applicability of even the initial classification to the literary text.

While in theory the view of language as a generative principle of fiction promises a shift from a static view of "'characters' represented by their 'diction'" to an examination of "interpersonal forces responsible for carrying forward the narrative dynamic,"[12] in reality this enterprise is locked into a laborious and often sterile cataloguing of multiple utterances.[13] The result has been that in almost two decades the application of Speech Acts to Shakespeare has not escaped Stanley Fish's pessimistic conclusion concerning the integration of Austin's theory and Shakespeare's text, a conclusion drawn from Fish's study of the Speech Acts in *Coriolanus*: "while a Speech Act analysis of such texts will always be possible, it will also be trivial (a mere list of the occurrence or distribution of kinds of acts); while it is the condition of intelligibility that makes all texts possible, not all texts are about those conditions. *Coriolanus* is about those conditions, and it goes the theory one better by also being about their fragility."[14] In other words, Fish suggests that since commands, oaths, promises, and pleadings often fail in Shakespeare's plays, their investigation and cataloguing are ultimately futile.

Speech Acts and Genre: Tragedy and Comedy

It is remarkable that in this conclusion Stanley Fish misses the central discovery of his own analysis: the correspondence between the play's two striking failings, the failure of its protagonist to persuade Roman citizens and the failure of the play itself to secure the effect of tragic action (cf. "it is questionable whether or not it is a true tragedy, or even in the usual sense, a drama").[15] *Coriolanus* refuses to plead; he wants only to command, but as a general among civilians he is surrounded by a democratic Rome which by definition refuses to grant perlocutionary force to the hero.[16] Since the sociopolitical situation of civil obedience necessary for the tragic hero is absent from Coriolanus's Rome, the play becomes a depository of the characteristics constituting an alienation from the tragic genre and an abandonment of the central word-mode which nourishes tragedies, that is, the illocutionary utterance with perlocutionary force which, in fact, becomes a binding perlocution, a command which must be carried out, and which, of course, Coriolanus cannot employ.

Viewed in this light the application of Speech Acts to genre permits the reader to enter into new levels of metadrama in Shakespeare. When the binding command of the protagonist is isolated as a form-creating generic characteristic, its prescriptive unconditional goal reflects the necessary character of the tragic effect, namely, tragic pathos, the arousal and purgation of pity and fear, the only cathartic effect that tragedy seeks, prescribes, and fulfils and which Lear articulates best:

> Howl, howl, howl! O, [you] are men of
>   stones!

Had I your tongues and eyes, I'd use them
   so
That heaven's vault should crack.
(V.iii.258-60)[17]

The prescriptive language of the tragic protagonists and the necessary and predetermined effect of the genre reflect each other and in Speech Acts both come under the heading of perlocutionary force.

Indeed, the consensus among Speech Act theoreticians who have ventured into Shakespearean scholarship is to regard tragedy as the purest form of the performative as well as one of the most intense forms of the perlocutionary act.[18] The significance of these observations becomes clear when they are considered in the context of the genre as a whole, a genre whose delineations are so precise that they have hardly changed since Aristotle first gave them description in his *Poetics:* single, rarely a double plot; a protagonist larger than life and of the highest social status; a man deserving sympathy and even admiration, but possessing a tragic flaw, which in turn effects a reversal of fortune, tragic *peripeteia.*[19]

Moreover, as already indicated in the case of *Coriolanus,* the structure of the genre cannot change without an alteration of its effect on the audience, for the organization of this genre ensures that the force behind the binding language of the tragic protagonist is his political power, and his words are literally heavier and weightier than those of any other character. Whether he communicates in either locutionary or illocutionary acts (whether he is informing or ordering), his words, in fact, have perlocutionary power; his thoughts and intentions are to be obeyed. The movement of tragedy inevitably consists in the depiction of how the protagonist's words construct the universe and then become entrapped by their own performative reality. Moreover, the protagonist's linguistic domination, *hubristic* by necessity, is not the folly of a petty tyrant, but a characteristic of his social state.[20] As Mark Antony observes about Caesar's state: "When Caesar says, 'Do this,' it is perform'd" (I.ii.10). The world such power constructs, however, will always be short of the Divine, always marred by human imprecision, or *hamartia,* which causes the character's downfall. Tragedy, therefore, is a depiction of the destruction implicit at the very foundation of autocratic, aristocratic power. The linguistic reality of the text reflects the downfall of authorized perlocutionary acts in the inevitable fall of the protagonist whose every word is a command simply by the very nature of his status. Viewed in this light, language ceases to be the genre's external characteristic, but becomes its dynamic centre, and genre instead appears as an outward manifestation of an utterance's unveiling into act.

It becomes significant in terms of the alteration within the genre that when compared to their tragic predecessors, Shakespeare's tragedies exhibit an additional characteristic: his protagonists give vows and the ensuing tragic action customarily unveils and dramatizes the determinism evoked in the moment of swearing rather than of command.[21] Hamlet swears thrice to the ghost of his father. Lear seals his fate by banishing Kent for the latter's opposition to the royal vow. Lady Macbeth calls upon demonic power to assist her in the unhesitating execution of the intended murder; Othello swears to Iago that he shall visit a horrifying punishment upon Desdemona; and Coriolanus binds himself by an oath to plead like a beggar: "I will not do't, / Lest I surcease to honor mine own truth" (III.ii.120-21). The introduction of oaths as a dominant illocutionary/perlocutionary force into the tragic genre is a specifically Shakespearean characteristic: the shift to *commissive* illocutions (committing the speaker himself to a certain course of action) from *directives* as a main focus of drama results in an important shift in action.[22] While in Greek tragedies the powerful protagonists bind others to the execution of their will and in so doing bind themselves, in Shakespeare tragic characters bind themselves and then discover that they have thereby bound others.[23] The emphasis shifts from a political and religious spectacle to a psychological one; *hamartia* as an error in judgment becomes an inner defect, a flaw of the overall character.[24]

Furthermore, the dominant patterns of tragic utterance provide an insight into the hidden dynamism of other genres. In Shakespeare's early history, *Richard III,* for example, Queen Margaret's curses (I.iii.187-302) already play this double role of action-initiator and indicator of genre: they literally prescribe action as they call for the death of her enemies, all of whom, including Richard himself, are much more powerful than the destitute queen. Here in the very manner of these curses' utterance—"Poor breathing orators of miseries / Let them have scope" (IV.iv.129-30)—one finds a mirror of the play itself and its contrast to tragedy: their speaker is powerless and, thus, calls upon a supernatural effect of hate and misery to help victims destroy the victor. The employment of curses in *Richard III* underscores their difference from the role of oaths/ commands in the tragedies as both initiators and indicators of action. Curses (and in Shakespeare's histories all deposed or injured characters curse), while prescribing and predetermining action, put emphasis not upon the fall of the word-utterer but upon those who are cursed. Curses, therefore, admit the social inferiority and relative unimportance of the utterer's fate and include an ever-widening circle of other characters and fates, whereas oaths shift the focus back to the speaker as an initiator and major participant in the unfolding action. Thus, if tragedy is a study of *hubris,* or of autocracy destroying itself, the histories examine and include the binding and deconstructing power of marginalia, which finds its symbolic expression in the supernatural and seemingly marginal intrusion of curses.

Nevertheless, the histories and tragedies employ a language that binds and binds unconditionally. Their plots are inevitably striking for the irreversibility of the unified progression from intention to deployment, from word to act. In contrast to this perlocutionary imprisonment of life by language, the comedies concern themselves with depicting and celebrating unauthorized decodings of language, with the multiplicity of fracturing and misadventure that occurs on the journey of the word into its incorporation into act. Keir Elam's recent study of the application of Speech Acts and Language Games (Wittgenstein's notion) to the language of comedies shows that the basic design of comic dialogues is the construction of linguistic impediments to the progress of customary linguistic decoding. When, for example, Benedick and Beatrice in *Much Ado about Nothing* (or Petruchio and Katherina in *The Taming of the Shrew*) insult each other, the comic effect of their insults or "flyting" springs not merely from their intention to misrepresent each other's words in a wilful fashion, but also from the multiplicity of unauthorized interpretations and unauthorized diversions found in this manner. The merry-making of comedy, therefore, operates as a growing circle of unauthorized decodings and corruption of words, a craft at which Clown Feste in *Twelfth Night* declares himself to be a master: "I am indeed not her fool, but her corrupter of words" (III.i.35-36).[25] The design of unauthorized decodings progresses from a single interchange into a series of unauthorized effects, and also into the very design of Shakespeare's comedy as a whole; the multiplicity of unauthorized miscomprehensions is reflected in comedy's multiplotted convolutedness, its complex and again multileveled sociopolitical reality,[26] its surfeit of characters, and ultimately the multiple marriages celebrated at the end of so many plays.

Still, the freedom of misreadings offered by a comic genre represents only a superficial contrast to the perlocutionary force of tragedies and histories, for comedy seeks and secures the effect of laughter with the same perlocutionary force of intention, as tragedy seeks *pathos* and most of the histories a royal demise. In other words, a jester cohabits with a king, sharing with him the space of perlocutionary intention.

Specifically in the tragedies, however, where all are eventually encompassed by common woe and where the perlocutionary power of oaths and commands charges language with hidden determinism, Shakespeare dramatizes in a focused manner the reality and the consequences of the imprisonment of action and of characters by linguistic utterance.[27] This is not to say that the protagonists have no choice, but rather to propose that they are presented as abandoning this

choice, choosing to succumb to the power of words, and then finding themselves entrapped.[28] In other words, perlocutions transmit their capacity for control to locutions and illocutions and literally imbue them with a sort of sinister prefigurement to action which reduces all discourse to perlocutionary inevitability. When Juliet, for example, muses upon meeting Romeo, "If he be married, / My grave is like to be my wedding-bed" (I.v.134-35), she uses a constative utterance, but as the play unfolds, this utterance proves to be performative; the world of the play is created according to the laconic design of her observation. Similarly when Gloucester explains to Regan his assistance in the king's disappearance "Because I would not see thy cruel nails / Pluck out his poor old eyes" (III.vii.56-57), he too inadvertently initiates his own blinding scene. Here language dictates life, and tragedy discloses the reality of the social world ruled by perlocutionary intentions.

The overwhelming power of tragic language and spectacle imprisons actions and reactions, arrests life and freedom, and finds its ultimate fulfillment when the animate characters become the most static of all objects—corpses upon the theatrical floor. The heaviness of language and its implicit malice are frequently counterpointed in tragedies by a distrust of language's role altogether, by the desire to negate the force of what is simply "words, words, words" (*Hamlet* II.ii.192). When at the closing of Shakespeare's tragic period the word-shy Coriolanus greets his wife with the only tender words of the play, "My gracious silence, hail" (II.i.175), he articulates a constant subtheme of Shakespeare's tragedies—a preference for silence, be it Hamlet's refusal to be played upon as a flute, Cordelia's stubborn reticence, Edgar's postponement of the revelation of his identity, or even Iago's mysterious last words.

This surfacing theme of choice between a language which overdetermines and entraps, on the one hand, and determined silence, on the other, emphasizes the auto-reflective nature of Shakespeare's tragic craft and testifies to a resistance to the propagation of language which strips choice and freedom from those who enter the threshold of the speaker's world. A bitter self-irony is strikingly disclosed in *Timon of Athens* where the predominant theme of linguistic bankruptcy indicates a full-fledged state of artistic impasse, as is declared by Timon's servant: "That what he speaks is all in debt: he owes / For ev'ry word" (I.ii.198-99). Furthermore, *Pericles,* the first of the romances, forcefully reenacts the attraction of silence implicit in the tragedies, when King Pericles chooses not to speak in the face of his life's great disasters.[29] The king's silence is defeated by Marina only at the end of the play. Pericles' resumption of speech is counterpointed by an announcement that a more joyous performance is about to begin and that, furthermore, it will reinterpret Pericles' long sufferings:

Before the people all . . .

. . . . .

perform my bidding, or thou livest in woe;
Do't, and *happy,* by my silver bow!
                    (V.i.243-48; emphasis added)

Cymbeline, therefore, coming upon the heels of *Pericles,* is thematically introduced and prefigured as a juxtaposition to tragedy.

"It is . . . as if something had been given up and resigned,"[30] observed B. Ivor Evans of the language of the romances, and this observation can equally be applied to the language and every other feature of *Cymbeline.* Indeed, the means by which Shakespeare habitually develops either his tragic or his comic actions are emphatically left behind. The social superiority of the hero is no longer a focus for action, since otherwise Cloten, and not Leonatus Posthumus, would have found himself in the role of the play's protagonist. Nor is there any place for comic flyting, since the lovers are separated for most of the play. Most significant, perhaps, is the carefully staged confusion regarding the performative power of the main speeches, all of which are invariably misplaced: the vicious fool, Cloten, for example, recites the soliloquy about the power of gold (II.iii.66-76) "in an accomplished blank verse, and in tones that might echo those of Timon or Lear."[31] "The silken smooth" villain Jachimo speaks fifty or so lines (II.ii.11-50) in "the finest language . . . [with] a hypnotic fascination beyond any other passage in Shakespeare";[32] and Imogen's heartbreaking lament over the body of her husband is pronounced over the body of Cloten (IV.ii.295-332)! Lack of coordination enters into every aspect of the play, and it seems as if no new constructive pattern follows upon the ostensible abandonment of the earlier, so successfully deployed artistic forms. It is at this juncture that an examination of the play's locutionary, illocutionary, and perlocutionary acts helps to uncover the linguistic *figura* which serves in *Cymbeline* as a hidden vehicle of generic form-creation.

Locutionary Acts in Cymbeline

A good example of a locutionary act is a description, and central to *Cymbeline*'s gallery of portrayals is that of Posthumus, presented at the beginning of the play in a manner "that must have puzzled nine playgoers out of ten,"[33] for it sets up a mutual interdependence between Leonatus's external appearance and his inner qualities, as if both are measurable, tangible items: after seeking "through the regions of the earth" it becomes unlikely that "so fair an outward and such stuff within / Endows a man but he" (I.i.20-24). Once the measurable correspondence between the superior inner and outer qualities has been established, it is immediately

canceled as insufficient, but canceled in such a manner that the language of external appearance is still propagated:

I do *extend* him, sir, within himself,
Crush him *together* rather than *unfold*
His *measure* duly.

                    (I.i.25-27; emphasis added)

Even Imogen's portrayal of her husband treats human qualities in terms of solid objects, or monetary values, while undercutting this correspondence with an uncertain "almost": "A man worth any woman; overbuys me / Almost the sum he pays" (I.i.146-47). The implicit cancellation and yet employment of the referential field of physical evidence plays more than a passing role: it is a first trace of the new linguistic direction which becomes more and more prominent as *Cymbeline*'s plot unfolds, and both Leonatus and Imogen are literally weaned (albeit in painful fashion) from this manner of comparing human qualities with material objects. Jachimo, an initiator of the protagonists' misunderstanding and subsequent misfortune, is, in fact, irritated precisely by Posthumus's reputation, as constant and permanent as any inanimate object or monetary value: "He was then of a crescent note. . . . But I could then have look'd on him without the help of admiration, though the catalogue of his endowments had been tabled by his side, and I to peruse him by items" (I.iv.1-7).[34] Thus Jachimo, by proposing to measure Imogen's virtue solely by his ability to acquire her bracelet, literally ruptures this referential dependence of human qualities on objects. As a result, when Leonatus confronts the ensuing chaos of his life, he is insistent that no external objects are to be employed to measure his new state: "I will begin / The fashion: less without and more within" (V.i.32-33). When he finally relents and accepts an external signifier—"this label on my bosom" (V.v.430), this new description is ostensibly confused, an illogical prophecy which attracts him through "sympathy":

Or senseless speaking, or a speaking such
As sense cannot untie. Be what it is,
The action of my life is like it.

                    (V.iv.147-49)[35]

Even when the soothsayer unfolds the meaning of the prophecy, the dislocation between utterance, on the one hand, and its sense and reference, on the other, is not eliminated: all the etymological roots which the soothsayer offers are, in fact, false derivations.[36]

Thus, none of Posthumus's descriptions, neither the original eulogy nor the final and adequate "label," can be regarded as *bona fide* locutionary or constative utterances. The portrayals fail as locutions because their referential field is undermined as soon as it is established. They fail as constatives because their truth value remains uncertain. When Leonatus at the end of the play dismisses Jachimo's high praise of himself and of his "noble" intention to wager Imogen's honor (V.v.170), Leonatus's self-deprecation—"villain-like, I lie" (V.v.218)—proves to be equally wrong, since from the vantage point of this new high moral perspective he still does not recognize his Imogen ("The temple / of virtue was she" [V.v.220-21]) in the young page who tries to quieten him. Descriptions in terms of valuable material objects prove neither true nor false, for the protagonists are both better and worse than the cardboard figures of high eulogies.

Leonatus's descriptions are only a sampling in a much broader and persistent pattern of a language which no longer "name[s] things directly"[37] and which flees a clearly established field of reference. Imogen's brothers, for example, have two names—their birth names and the names acquired while they lived in nature. When the two realities are brought together, the identities of the two princes remain in a state of permanent tension between two states, two styles, two fathers (V.v.347-403), to which Imogen testifies "I have got two worlds by't" (V.v.374) and accepts Bellarius as her second father. The identities of all protagonists can only be caught in a state of transition: they are literally "not born for bondage" (V.v.305). Nosworthy points to *Cymbeline*'s enigmatic and yet consistent pattern of attaching the names of birds to the main characters,[38] and even this curious device strengthens the overall sense of the dynamism of every description. Thus, language does not merely reject its own equation with static objects, and the parallel equation between human beings and the objects thus evoked, but it itself is depicted as originating in this equation and literally escaping from it into act, just as Posthumus's "label" becomes a prophecy and not a description.

This pattern of flight from identification with static appearance is challenged in the play only in the figures of its two unredeemed villains: the queen and Cloten. These two exceptions, however, are instructive in that they prove the overall pattern rather than refute it. The queen's dedication of her life to a perfect semblance of virtue should have been a warning to the king of her duplicity even though "it had been vicious / To have mistrusted her" (V.v.65-66), for the perfect incarnation of virtue has to be rejected for its very perfection. Moreover, if the queen pretends that her nature is like her appearance, Cloten, her son, believes that appearances determine nature. Thus, the famous scene where he speaks about the power of gold (II.iii.63-76) only *appears* to contradict his character; in reality, it summarizes the whole nature of his world. The discovery that men are ruled by riches, that their every act is best expressed as a function of soulless beings—such a discovery could have crushed Shakespeare's tragic characters; but for Cloten it is simply a statement of the rule that governs his world. More-

over, this complete identification on Cloten's part with the world of static appearances explains why Imogen's statement that she prefers Posthumus's garments to Cloten (II.iii.132-36) is taken by him as a straightforward insult to his being. What is crystallized in the queen and Cloten, therefore, goes so far against every other pattern of description, that with their deaths the idea that a material counterfeit can represent the whole of reality is expelled from the play altogether.

The central descriptions of *Cymbeline* consistently refuse to be static in a manner which sharply contrasts with those of the tragedies and comedies. As a rule in tragedy constative utterances were clearly defined and were also threatening in their uncanny ability to become irrefutable inanimate objects, to create a sinister world of intentions and solidified thoughts. Thus, Macbeth's "dagger of the mind" becomes a dagger in the hand, Othello's jealous ramblings cannot rest until Desdemona is silenced, and Leontes' spirited wife turns into a stone statue after his investigation of the evidence in the court scene. By contrast in *Cymbeline,* locutions are never finalized within a static reference: the undercutting of any hard and fast identification between word, human subject, and static object keeps all descriptions perpetually in transition. Perhaps, Arviragus's determination to use even the "green world" as his point of departure and not as his identity operates in the play as a symbol of a new artistic program which visits the craftsman in his old age, wherein he perceives static objects not as a final tangible reality but as a bondage from which flight originates:

> What should we speak of
> When we are old as you? When we shall hear
> The rain and wind beat dark December . . .
>
> . . . . .
>
> Our valour is to chase what flies. *Our cage*
> *We make a choir,* as doth the prison'd bird,
> And sing our bondage freely.
> (III.iii.35-44, emphasis added)

In other words, there is no demarcation line in the world of *Cymbeline* between locution and illocution, constative and performative, because the initial state of locutionary utterance is already moving; the audience observes the words as fleeing, as turning into action, even if they may appear to be in need of rest.[39]

Illocutionary and Perlocutionary Acts in Cymbeline

The blurred line between illocutionary and perlocutionary acts constitutes the very heart of drama, since drama invariably concerns itself with the double effect of the spoken word upon both the characters and the observing audience. *Cymbeline* in this regard is a striking play, for the only effect upon the audience deduced so far is that of confusion and, thus, a complete contrast to the precision of the tragedies.

Furthermore, since the relationship between words and things is constantly undercut in this romance, one may suspect that the link between words and actions is more synchronized, more streamlined. Even a casual glance at the play, however, discovers that this is hardly the case. In fact, none of the usual arsenal of illocutions or perlocutions—promises, lies, commands, oaths—displays even a vestige of what appeared in tragedy to be the irreversible progression of words into acts. On the other hand, and herein resides the complexity of the new employment of language, it is also impossible to deduce that all such progressions are thereby ruptured or deferred.

For example, the promises of *Cymbeline* are strikingly ambivalent: they are neither fulfilled, nor failed. When, for example, the play's lovers are separated, Posthumus promises to "remain / The loyall'st husband that did e'er plight troth" (I.i.95-96) and to keep Imogen's ring as a sign of truce. In his very next scene, Posthumus gives the ring away to Jachimo (I.iv), but he does *not* thereby break his own trust; rather he demonstrates his total confidence in its reality. His subsequent order to Pisanio to kill Imogen is again both a break and a continuation of his promise to "plight troth," for in his wife's murder he intends to wipe away her dishonor. The journey between word and action is a simultaneous rupture and yet fulfillment.

Similarly ambivalent is the fate of false reports, as Bellarius's paradoxical escape indicates. Falsely accused of being a traitor to the king, Bellarius knows himself to be innocent. However, if he is to remain loyal, he must be obedient to Cymbeline's order and thus be executed. Yet, in order to avoid a traitor's punishment, Bellarius in fact commits treachery: he escapes from the kingdom and steals the king's sons, whom he thereby saves from certain death at the hands of the queen. In treachery honest and in honesty treacherous, Bellarius proves the false report to be truthful by preventing it from ever taking effect.

In a similar way, the commands of the play reinforce the ambivalence of the emerging design, for they simultaneously display and yet prevent their own consequences. Cymbeline's first appearance in the play is accompanied by a frightful order to Posthumus to leave and to return only if he is ready to die (I.i.125-27); Leonatus breaks the command and returns to Cymbeline, but he does this *in search of death in battle*. A similar pattern is disclosed in Cymbeline's orders to the queen to ensure Imogen's death,[40] and even in Leonatus's command to Pisanio to kill his mistress. Pisanio's refusal to obey orders is paradoxically a sign

of his loyalty and true obedience, whereas the queen's attempt to poison her stepdaughter is a profoundly treacherous act.

Only the play's oaths, perhaps, do not strike the audience as utterances which result in an ambiguous effect. Nevertheless, this very lack of ensuing ambiguity is balanced by the incorporation of ambiguity into the act of giving vows, for in *Cymbeline* all oaths *without exception* are used to promote evil ends or to deceive. Thus, Bellarius states that he was defamed in the eyes of Cymbeline by a false oath (III.iii.65-68). Moreover, the two villains, Cloten and Jachimo, prove to be the only swearers. Cloten's attachment to oath is underlined in all his scenes: "When a gentleman is dispos'd to swear, it is not for any standers-by to curtal his oaths" (II.i.10-11), and his central wicked act, the attempted rape of Imogen, is replete with oaths:

> Lord Cloten,
>
> . . . . .
>
> With his sword drawn, foam'd at the mouth, and swore
>
>   [A]way he posts
> With unchaste purpose, and with oath to violate
> My lady's honor.
>
>   (V.v.274-85)

If Cloten's swearing is the reflex action of a sinister character, Jachimo uses oaths specifically in order to arrive at a wicked end. It seems particularly poignant in view of Shakespeare's long fascination with oaths that Jachimo's swearing is a decisive detail that finally persuades Posthumus of Imogen's unfaithfulness (II.iv. 121-29). It is no coincidence, therefore, that Pisanio's greatheartedness is revealed when he forgoes oaths and proves forsworn to Posthumus (III.ii.11-23).

Thus, the ambivalence of the incorporation of words into acts is curiously a consistent feature of the play: these acts both testify to the control of words and yet undermine this control. To put this another way, a similar pattern exists in the journey from word to action (in illocutions and perlocutions), as from word to thing (locutions): the straightforward path is broken and yet a kind of interdependence is still enacted. In fact, the action stretches the initial significance of the word into an extended space of simultaneous fulfillment and rupture. Only oaths seem to be beyond this manner of expansion: in their search for perlocutionary control they are demoted in *Cymbeline* explicitly to negative characters.

There can hardly be, therefore, a more dissimilar pattern between the employment of illocutionary and perlocutionary utterances in the tragedies and in *Cymbeline*. If in tragedy the word determines and imprisons action, in *Cymbeline* action is at least as powerful as word: for action initiates the reevaluation, expansion, and even reinterpretation of words. The association between Cloten and oaths is particularly significant in this context, for here Shakespeare embodies his most pessimistic nightmare in the complete fool. Whereas tragic action, directed by a given vow, progresses in an unmistakable design, this dependence of action on word is suspended in *Cymbeline*. This suspension is effected in such a manner that the action can rewrite the word's significance, can, indeed, pull this significance at once in two opposite directions, and yet can stop short of refusing these words and acts their mutual interdependence.

When confronted with such a deployment of language, the audience, almost against its own will, is drawn into the same confusion as the play's protagonists. This curious ambivalence of language makes the spectators almost sympathize with the villain Jachimo, or dislike the heroic Posthumus, and suppress laughter at Imogen's grief. In the terms of Speech Act theory, one may suggest that Shakespeare explores a perlocutionary utterance against its grain, moving not towards the pole of direction and control, but towards its potential to produce resistance to its command, while, nevertheless, employing obedience. The audience's struggle with the pull of language draws it into an enactment of the central dilemma of the play—into a new relationship between language and action.

In fact, this consideration of the audience's perspective uncovers an additional Speech Act, whose role is both central in *Cymbeline* and yet almost imperceptible. Bertrand Evans observes that in contrast to Shakespeare's other nontragic plays the audience in *Cymbeline* is given no figure which presides over the action: *"no force to our knowledge while action continues—* watches Jachimo as Vincentio and Prospero watch Angelo and Caliban."[41] Evans's insight is marred by a curious omission, for while it is true that no character presides over the plot, it is incorrect that "no force" is present: each time the audience's awareness of future events is as insubstantial as that of the heroes, the situation is invariably accompanied by a prayer. Posthumus prays for the safety of his marriage when he is forced by Cymbeline to leave Imogen (I.i. 115-17); the second lord prays most emphatically for Imogen's honor (II.i.62-65) just prior to Jachimo's emergence from the trunk (an occasion upon which Evans bases his view). Pisanio calls upon the power of heaven to intervene during Cloten's chase after Imogen (III.v.160-61). He restates his belief that "the heavens still must work" (IV.iii.41) just prior to the battle when all the major characters confront their unmasked vulnerability. And, of course, in the prison scene where

Posthumus awaits his death, all the preceding prayers are gathered in the prayer of the spirits. Jupiter's answer—

> No more, you petty spirits of region low
> Offend our hearing; hush! . . .
>
> . . . . .
>
> No care of yours it is, you know 'tis ours.
>   (V.iv.93-100)

—shows both that prayers *do disturb* the heavenly gods and that the gods are constantly involved in human affairs.[42] This means that in terms of the construction of *Cymbeline*, there is a force which presides over the characters' fate and is exhibited (inconspicuously everywhere except in its culmination in the Jupiter scene) and communicated to the audience at those moments of highest danger—and this force, in terms of Speech Acts, is the perlocutionary force of prayer.

The inconspicuous nature of prayers in *Cymbeline* provides further insight into the specific nature of the perlocutionary control which they possess. Jupiter's confirmation of their effective power ("offend our hearing") is reminiscent of Queen Margaret's belief in *Richard III* that her curses "ascend the sky, / And there awake God's gentle-sleeping peace" (I.iii.286-87). While it is evident that a similar principle is at work, the difference in these perlocutions is profound. Curses, and in this they foreshadow both oaths and commands, *determine* the pattern of action they initiate in the moment of their utterance, whereas this mutual determination of word and action is canceled in *Cymbeline* as the romance pushes acts and utterances as far apart as the dramatic action can permit.

In fact, the prayers of the play are a literal incorporation of that indeterminate distance between word and action which is performed in *Cymbeline*. All the play's prayers refrain from dictating the action, from articulating or predetermining the pattern which they call forth. In contrast to the anguish of separation from Imogen, Posthumus simply asks the gods to help him keep his wife, and Pisanio in a similar manner prays for Imogen's protection: "Flow, flow, / You heavenly blessings, on her!" (III.v.160-61). The prayer of the spirits is, of course, a simple call for help. The action which such prayers initiate, therefore, is not predetermined or controlled: the inner elasticity of the utterance is reflected in the puzzling design of its incorporation. Prayers, therefore, play the role in *Cymbeline* which in tragedies is executed by oaths and commands (or in *Richard III* by Margaret's curses), and the difference between these perlocutions is enacted in the difference between the plays' overall emotional timbre and, of course, the more general construction of genres. If oaths and commands accelerate the execution of the action they prescribe, prayers unfold the connection between word and act into a prolonged time-frame as well as into as into an enigmatic and unexpected design. Moreover, if oaths and commands concentrate action in the hands of the protagonists, prayers employ every peripheral response and action. In fact, if in tragedy the successful fulfillment of its major perlocutions can be witnessed only by a small number of characters, action as an answer to prayer runs a natural and seemingly unfocused course of developing the potential of each character. The correspondence between prayer and action can become clear only when the limitation of a single vision is replaced by a mosaic of many testimonies, unwieldy with "its twenty-four dénouements."

This new relationship of the word's unveiling into act dramatized in *Cymbeline* profoundly influences two subsequent plays: in *The Winter's Tale* and *The Tempest* this dramatic technique is developed further and cast into a more active mode. If *Cymbeline* discovers a Speech Act which in its enactment incorporates the participation of all the play's characters within the boundaries of the natural, or probable, unfolding of each different temperament, then *The Winter's Tale* transforms this deployment of language into a double movement: the demise of oaths and commands is mirrored in the stripping of the tyrant Leontes of his verbal powers, whereas the second part of the play grants verbal control to his servants Camillo and Paulina whose proclaimed role is not to impose, but to synchronize: in Camillo's words, "Omit / Nothing may give us aid" (IV.iv.624-25). Prospero's verbal magic reenacts prayer's potential to incorporate all elements both central and peripheral, but Prospero's spells cast the passive character of *Cymbeline*'s prayers into an active mode. The magic of his island is such that it *commands* lovers-to-be to be in love, revelers to revel, traitors to commit treachery and then lose all sense of their inner world, and those capable of repentance to repent. However, the control which Prospero's spells impose is not a control of external design or will, but an acceleration of the natural unfolding of what is originally only a potential. Thus, Prospero's magic borrows from *Cymbeline* a sense of the natural rather than the social perlocution, and from the tragedies an understanding of dramatic perlocution as a temporal acceleration of its unveiling, which produces as a result a much crisper romance than the unwieldy *Cymbeline*.

One may regard *Cymbeline*, therefore, as an experimental play, which dramatizes the relationship between words and deeds in a manner never again repeated in Shakespeare. Paulina is emphatic that no prayer will get Leontes out of his predicament (III.ii.210-14), and Prospero closes his play by indicating that the acts of prayers lie alongside the province of his craft. As an artist still, he consoles his weak, disrobed self that this

word-mode is the only utterance which can assist the journey from word-magic to everyday reality, for there prayers are as potent as the spells of his beloved island (Epilogue.15-20). In contrast to the two earlier genres, *Cymbeline*'s prayers as form-creating utterances have power but no authority; they cannot control or yet be disobeyed. *Cymbeline,* then, does provide a dramatic alternative both to tragedy and to comedy: to the former because the play's prayers direct action without subduing it and to the latter because devoid of authority they cannot initiate unauthorized patterns of enactment. In this, *Cymbeline* becomes a careful and fully worked out dramatic draft for the subsequent plays, for it disperses the habitual direction of the verbal drama and in so doing finds a new pattern of performance and even permits the poet to redefine his view of his own craft.

The employment of Speech Act theory in Shakespearean scholarship, therefore, can assist in touching the very axis of language's role in dramatic form-creation. The journey from word to deed and the relationship between utterances are as variable as human experience and often as enigmatic. In fact, the history of pragmatic linguistics seems to follow the progression of Shakespeare's work with genre: the initial belief that utterances have clear demarcation lines is found after the first excitement to be too restrictive and is slowly replaced by a vision of their interpenetration and mutual co-dependence. What Shakespeare's tragedies and comedies show most specifically is that if the demarcation between the Speech Acts is sought for and upheld with all possible strictness, the perlocutions isolated as separate reality will subdue all other acts, freezing the world within their autocratic structure. Shakespeare's work with language indicates how the strictness of linguistic divisions and the patterns of their interpenetration can reflect and even generate disaster, imprisonment, doom, fate, happiness, joy, and wonder. In the final analysis, his plays emphasize not so much the purity of speech acts as the levels and characteristics of their mutual influence and interpenetration by enacting them in dramatic forms. As Speech Act theory reorganizes itself according to its employment in communication and sets itself into the context of the social paradigms of the speakers and their interlocutors, it may venture with profit into the world of Shakespeare's plays. Thus, as one traces the transmutations between locutions, illocutions, and perlocutions in the comedies, tragedies, and romances, the emerging theoretical design shows not only what Speech Acts can do for Shakespeare, but what Shakespeare can do for Speech Acts.

Notes

[1] J.M. Nosworthy summarizes critical opinions about "occasions when the characters' portrayal seems in-

consistent or even contradictory" (Introduction to the Arden edition of *Cymbeline* [London: Methuen, 1955], pp. lxiii-lxxii). For a more recent discussion see J. Gillies, "The Problem of Style in *Cymbeline,*" *SoR* 18, 3 (November 1982): 269-90.

2 This is the opinion of a theatrical company of 1909 quoted with approval by Roger Rees ("Posthumus in *Cymbeline,*" *Players of Shakespeare: Essays in Shakespearean Performance by Twelve Players with the Royal Shakespeare Company,* ed. Philip Brockbank [Cambridge: Cambridge Univ. Press, 1985], p. 150).

3 On Shaw's revision of *Cymbeline* and for the mockery of the last scene, see Ruby Cohn, *Modern Shakespeare Offshoots* (Princeton: Princeton Univ. Press, 1976), pp. 334-36.

4 James Sutherland, "The Language of the Late Plays," *More Talking of Shakespeare,* ed. J. Garret (London: Longmans, Green and Co., 1959), p. 151.

5 John L. Austin, *How To Do Things with Words* (Cambridge, MA: Harvard Univ. Press, 1962), p. 22.

6 John R. Searle, *Expression and Meaning: Studies in the Theory of Speech Acts* (Cambridge: Cambridge Univ. Press, 1979), p. 75.

7 Austin, pp. 55, 88; see the account of Austin's revisions in de Souza Filho, *Language and Action: A Reassessment of Speech Act Theory* (Amsterdam: John Benjamin, 1984), pp. 17-55; see also Manfred Bierwisch, "Semantic Structure and Illocutionary Force," *Speech Act Theory and Pragmatics,* ed. John R. Searle (Boston: Reidel, 1980), pp. 1-35.

8 John R. Searle, "The Background of Meaning," *Speech Act Theory and Pragmatics,* pp. 221-32.

9 de Souza Filho, pp. 146-47.

10 Ross Chambers, "Le Masque & le miroir: Vers une théorie relationelle du théatre," *Etudes littéraires* 13, 3 (December 1980): 397-412, 401.

11 Richard Ohmann, "Literature as Act," *Approaches to Poetics,* ed. S. Chatman (New York: Columbia Univ. Press, 1973), pp. 81-107, 83.

12 See Keir Elam's summary of the application of speech act theory to dramatic discourse, *Shakespeare's Universe of Discourse: Language-Games in the Comedies* (Cambridge: Cambridge Univ. Press, 1984), p. 7.

13 For a similar assessment, see Elam, p. 89.

14 Stanley Fish, "How to Do Things with Austin and

Searle: Speech-Act Theory and Literary Criticism," *MLN* 91, 5 (October 1976): 983-1025, 1025.

15 Fish, p. 1024.

16 Considerable disagreement exists among Speech Act theoreticians about whether to regard the utterance which secures an intended effect by verbal means as illocutionary with perlocutionary force (Searle's position) or perlocutionary (Peter Strawson and H.P. Grice). This essay sides with the latter position, although it is clear that the ensuing dilemma is far from settled. Therefore, when in doubt (as in the case of oaths) I will refer to the utterances as illocutionary / perlocutionary. On the background to this disagreement, see *The Philosophy of Language,* ed. John R. Searle (Oxford: Oxford Univ. Press, 1971), and the latest forceful restatement of the argument in *Speech Act Theory and Pragmatics,* particularly the essays by Bierwisch (n. 7 above) and Steven Davis, "Perlocutions," pp. 37-56, who emphasize the importance of accepting the perlocutionary utterances as a verbal conventional act.

17 All quotations from Shakespeare will be given parenthetically in the text and are taken from *The Riverside Shakespeare,* ed. G. Blakemore Evans (Boston: Houghton Mifflin, 1974).

18 Ohmann, pp. 87-90; Elam, pp. 200, 230-31.

19 Aristotle, *Poetics,* trans. and ed. S.H. Butcher (London: Macmillan, 1917), chaps. 6-13.

20 On the relationship between the action of Greek drama and the political significance of the protagonist's status, see P.O. Cleirigh, "Political Anachronisms in the Pattern of Power in Sophoclean Drama" (Ph.D. diss., Cornell Univ., 1975).

21 Frances Shirley first observed a tangible connection between the frequent use of oath by the protagonists and the tragic intensity of the action, and observes, for instance about Othello, "One wonders if Othello would have been able to complete the killing, had he not taken a vow" (*Swearing and Perjury in Shakespeare's Plays* [London: George Allen and Unwin, 1979], p. 118).

22 The oaths which the protagonists of Greek drama give are usually peripheral to the action whereas their commands constitute the focus of action (e.g., Creon's oath in *Antigone,* lines 300-310).

23 The downfall of the king's commands and of his language as a manipulator of others was dramatized by Shakespeare not so much in the tragedies as in the histories. See James L. Calderwood, *Metadrama in Shakespeare's Henriad: Richard II to Henry V* (Ber-

keley: Univ. of California Press, 1979) and Joseph A. Porter, *The Drama of Speech Acts: Shakespeare's Lancastrian Tetralogy* (Berkeley: Univ. of California Press, 1979). The latter work is very insightful in connecting Speech Acts to the wider issue of genre in the histories.

[24] In support of the meaning of *hamartia* as an error in judgment, "ignorance combined with the absence of wicked intent," and not a character flaw, see Brian Vickers's discussion of the history of the interpretations of "hamartia" (*Towards Greek Tragedy: Drama, Myth Society* [London: Longman, 1973], pp. 4, 44 n.1).

[25] Elam, p. 308.

[26] Camille Slights, "The Unauthorized Language of *Much Ado About Nothing,*" *Elizabethan Theatre XII* (1993): 113-33.

[27] Lack of consensus among theorists with regard to illocutionary/ perlocutionary distinction prevents Elam from considering the possibility that the secured effect of laughter indicates a perlocution: "Perlocutionary success is not, generally speaking, a fruitful source of comic plotting in Shakespeare" (Elam, p. 231). On the resulting inconsistency of his conclusions, see Joseph A. Porter, "Speech Act Theory Abused," *SQ* 36, 4 (Winter 1985): 505-507.

[28] On the entrapment of the protagonists by action, see James L. Calderwood, *If It Were Done: Macbeth and Tragic Action* (Amherst: Univ. of Massachusetts Press, 1986).

[29] Cf. Elena Glazov-Corrigan, "The New Function of Language in Shakespeare's *Pericles:* Oath Versus 'Holy Word,' " *ShS* 43 (1990): 131-40.

[30] B. Ivor Evans, *The Language of Shakespeare's Plays* (Bloomington: Indiana Univ. Press, 1952), p. 176.

[31] R.A. Foakes, "Character and Dramatic Technique in *Cymbeline* and *The Winter's Tale,*" in *Studies in the Arts,* ed. Francis Warner (Oxford: Clarendon Press, 1968), pp. 116-30, 120.

[32] Bertrand Evans, *Shakespeare's Comedies* (Oxford: Clarendon Press, 1960), p. 255.

[33] Sutherland, p. 145. On the difficulty of this opening speech see also Maurice Hunt, "Shakespeare's Empirical Romance: *Cymbeline* and Modern Knowledge," *TSLL* 22, 3 (Fall 1980): 322-42.

[34] In the last scene of the play, Jachimo confesses that he was also irritated by Posthumus's bragging about Imogen's permanence of virtue "as Dian had hot dreams / And she alone were cold" (V.v.180-81).

[35] See also Leonatus's new understanding of the insubstantial value of external appearance in V.iv.22-25.

[36] David Solway, "Intoxicated Words: Language in Shakespeare's Late Romances," *Sewanee Review* 95, 4 (Fall 1987): 619-25.

[37] Solway, p. 620.

[38] Nosworthy, pp. lxxii-lxxiv.

[39] See Sutherland's suggestion that Shakespeare in *Cymbeline* is tired (p. 155).

[40] On the correspondence between the king's order and the queen's use of mineral poison, see Solway, pp. 619-20.

[41] Bertrand Evans, p. 253.

[42] Without observing the presence of the prayer pattern in the play, Richard P. Knowles emphasizes that the appearance of Jupiter "is the surfacing of a control that we have both sensed and wanted" ("The More Delay'd, Delighted: Theophanies in the Last Plays," *ShakS* 15 [1982]: 271-72).

FURTHER READING

Baxter, John. "*Cymbeline* and the Measures of Chastity." In *The Elizabethan Theatre XII*, pp. 135–55. Toronto: P. D. Meany, 1993.

> Maintains that while Shakespeare wrote *Cymbeline* in the romance genre, he used tragic elements for his dramatic purpose, particularly to reveal his view of marital chastity.

Colley, John Scott. "Disguise and New Guise in *Cymbeline.*" In *Shakespeare Studies: An Annual Gathering of Research, Criticism, and Reviews*, Vol. VII, edited by J. Leeds Barroll, 1974, pp. 233-52.

> Suggests that the plot development of *Cymbeline* was more easily understood in Elizabethan times, when audiences viewed costuming and the use of guises as important tools of characterization.

Cutts, John P. "Cymbeline." In *Rich and Strange: A Study of Shakespeare's Last Plays*. Washington State University Press, 1968, pp. 26-50.

> Asserts that the characters in *Cymbeline* live in a dream world made up of artificial relationships, such as that between Cymbeline and Imogen.

Evans, Bertrand. "A Lasting Storm: The Planetary Romances." In *Shakespeare's Comedies*, pp. 220-315. Oxford: Oxford University Press, 1960.

Argues that *Cymbeline* is Shakespeare's finest play, considering its manipulation of dramatic devices and complex hierarchy of discrepancies.

Lewis, Cynthia. "'With Simular Proof Enough': Modes of Misperception in *Cymbeline.*" *Studies in English Literature, 1500–1900* 31, No. 2 (Spring 1991): 343–64.

Expands previous critical scholarship addressing the theme of misperception in *Cymbeline*. Lewis argues that Shakespeare presents a hierarchy of misperception in which the type of deceit itself reveals insights into each character's motives and intellectual state.

Richmond, Hugh M. "Shakespeare's Roman Trilogy: The Climax in *Cymbeline.*" *Studies in the Literary Imagination* V, No. 1 (April 1972): 129-39.

Argues that Shakespeare structured the play as a historical and fictional commentary on the coarseness and inadequacy of pre-Christian law and behavior.

Schork, R. J. "Allusion, Theme, and Characterization in *Cymbeline.*" *Studies in Philology* LXIX, No. 2 (April 1972): 210–16.

Contends that Iachimo's and Imogen's allusions to classical myth and history are important contributions to the dramatic structure of the play, revealing their characters and hinting at plot developments.

Simonds, Peggy Muñoz. "'No More. . .Offend Our Hearing': Aural Imagery in *Cymbeline.*" *Texas Studies in Literature and Language* 24, No. 2 (Summer 1982): 137-54.

Describes the dual function of aural imagery in *Cymbeline*. Simonds argues that while auditory means often cause the major characters in the play to make mistakes, sound also plays an important redemptive role.

————. "The Marriage Topos in *Cymbeline*: Shakespeare's Variations on a Classical Theme." *English Literary Renaissance* 19, No. 1 (Winter 1989): 94–117.

Analyzes Shakespeare's appropriation of historical and religious marriage symbolism and imagery in *Cymbeline*.

Thompson, Ann. "*Cymbeline*'s Other Endings." In *The Appropriation of Shakespeare: Post-Renaissance Reconstructions of the Works and the Myth*, edited by Jean I. Marsden. New York: Harvester Wheatsheaf, 1991, pp. 203-20.

Discusses the numerous variations on the ending of the play, suggesting that the richness of the text has allowed a wealth of interpretation.

Ziegler, Georgianna. "My Lady's Chamber: Female Space, Female Chastity in Shakespeare." *Textual Practice* 4, No. 1 (Spring 1990): 73–90.

Maintains that in his plays Shakespeare examines sixteenth-century northern European patriarchal society and its proscribed domestic space and societal roles for women.

Pericles

For further information on the critical and stage history of *Pericles*, see *SC*, Volumes 2 and 15.

INTRODUCTION

Likely composed and first performed in the years 1606-08, *Pericles* is a tale of loss and reconciliation between father and daughter, based upon the classical legend of Pericles of Tyre. Despite the considerable age of this folk story—Ben Jonson once called it a "mouldy tale"—scholars have identified the primary sources that Shakespeare probably used to compose his drama as John Gower's *Confessio Amantis* (1385-93) and Lawrence Twine's *The Patterne of Paynfull Adventures* (1576). Since the recognition of these and other sources of the work, much scholarly interest in the play has been devoted to the question of its authorship. While contention still exists, the majority opinion seems to favor the theory that Shakespeare collaborated with another author, who is said to have written the somewhat inferior first two acts of *Pericles*, while Shakespeare himself is generally credited with having composed the last three acts of the play. Further areas of twentieth-century critical inquiry have included an exploration of the relationship between Pericles and his daughter Marina as well as the characterization of both, and discussions of the play's imagery and treatment of sexual motifs, especially regarding the theme of incest that pervades the work.

Critical observations on the authorship of *Pericles* and its lesser quality typically originate from the corruption of the text as part of the 1609 quarto version of Shakespeare's works and its exclusion from the more reliable First Folio edition (1623). Still, many scholars, including Kenneth Muir, have located significant evidence of Shakespeare's authorship in the work's language and imagery. Muir and others have observed that the play represents a departure for Shakespeare, and is a transitional drama that bridges the gap between the great tragedies of his middle period, such as *Hamlet* and *King Lear,* and his later plays, including *The Winter's Tale* and *The Tempest*. Overall the work has been seen as less complex and less realistic than either group, with more simplified characters and a thinner plot. Other commentators, while accepting Muir's conclusions for the most part, have nevertheless observed the literary richness of *Pericles*. Andrew Welsh has noted the unifying theme of tradition in the play, and traced its classical, medieval, and folklore sources in the appearance of riddles, the Seven DeadlySins, and knightly emblems. Ruth Nevo, taking a psychoanalytic approach to the drama, has outlined its symbolic power as a dream-fantasy which meditates on the repressed subjects of death and incest.

The characters of Pericles and Marina have also attracted the attention of modern scholars. Their assessments have offered a reevaluation of the prince as a patient sufferer and analyzed the play's themes of suffering, loss, repentance, and reconciliation between father and daughter. As for Marina's character, critical estimations have typically emphasized her chastity and purity. Michael Taylor has noted the juxtaposition of innocence and wisdom in Marina, while Nona Fienberg has associated her with the value of "moral discourse." Both critics have observed that her character stands in opposition to the darker aspects of the play, including the incestuous relationship between Antiochus and his daughter, and the degradation of the brothel where she finds herself in Act IV.

Shakespeare's use of imagery in *Pericles*, especially as it applies to the motifs of sexuality and incest, has also provided additional topics for modern critics of the play. Alexander Leggatt has commented on the riddle of incest and Antiochus's illicit relationship with his daughter, arguing that the fear of deviant sexuality informs the drama throughout. Anthony Lewis has seen the prevalent imagery of eating in *Pericles* as an indication of the play's theme of sustaining and nourishing oneself and others. Several commentators, including Mary Judith Dunbar and W. B. Thorne, have argued that through its symbolic devices the play presents a unified poetic, moral, and comic vision. For Thorne, the oppositions in the play, between generations and between loss and reconciliation, form the dramatic structure of the work and represent an evolution of Shakespeare's earlier comedies. Overall, these assessments of the mechanics of *Pericles* have demonstrated a small critical shift in the evaluation of a play that was popular in Shakespeare's time, but has since fallen into relative disregard. However, while scholars acknowledge that the work suffers from certain flaws, most agree that it offers an abundance of form and a quality of language that surpasses its weaknesses of character and incident.

OVERVIEWS

Kenneth Muir (essay date 1960)

SOURCE: *"Pericles,"* in *Shakespeare as Collaborator,* Barnes & Noble Inc., 1960, pp. 77-97.

[In the following essay, Muir surveys the text of Pericles, *locating evidence of Shakespeare's authorship in the language, imagery, and thematic qualities of the work.]*

Whether we accept Mr Philip Edwards' view that the difference between the first two acts of the play and the remainder is due to the differing skill of two reporters, or assume that Shakespeare based his play on the work of another dramatist, making few alterations in the opening acts and completely rewriting the last three, we may agree that the text given in the Quarto is a bad one, and almost certainly reported. But the two theories have different editorial implications. Those who believe that [George] Wilkins' novel [*The Painfull Adventures of Pericles, Prince of Tyre*] is based on an earlier play which Shakespeare revised should be less ready to accept readings from the novel into the text of the last three acts of the play than those who regard Wilkins' novel as a kind of rival report. On the other hand, those who think that Wilkins was reporting Shakespeare's play ought to have the courage of their convictions and print the Lysimachus-Marina dialogue almost as given in the novel. In any case we may assume that the text of the play is so poor that it is only a garbled version of what Shakespeare actually wrote. Whole lines and parts of lines have been omitted by reporters or compositors, and others have been so corrupted that not even the most confident textual critic can hope to restore them. On the other hand, there are speeches, and even whole scenes, where little emendation is required, and which appear to be so accurate that Hardin Craig could believe that they must have been printed from Shakespeare's foul papers.

Although, as I have argued, Shakespeare was probably using an old play as his main source, it was his usual custom to consult more than one source.[1] Wilkins made extensive use of Twine's version of the Apollonius story in *The Painfull Aduentures of Pericles,* and it is not unlikely that Shakespeare made use of it too. It was readily accessible in the 1607 reprint, but it is impossible to prove that Shakespeare consulted it. He would certainly have referred to Gower's *Confessio Amantis.* It is probable that Shakespeare himself was responsible for the re-naming of the main characters; and, as I have suggested elsewhere,[2] he may have taken Marina from the story of the Mexican girl who became interpreter to Cortes and who was baptized under that name. She had been born the daughter of a chief, and on her father's death she had been sold to some Indians by her own mother, so as to ensure the succession of her son by her

second husband. Years later, while acting as interpreter to Cortes in the province in which she was born, she was seen and recognized by her mother and half-brother, who were terrified that she would take vengeance on them. But Marina, either moved by their tears or taking her newly acquired religion seriously, forgave them and made them presents. This story of a princess, who was sold into slavery by her mother and step-father and who forgave her mother and the son for whom the crime had been committed when she had them in her power, would have appealed to Shakespeare while he was writing the plays of the last period. The story resembles the plot of *The Tempest* in one respect, and the plot of *Pericles* in others. Unfortunately the full story is not known to have been published in Shakespeare's lifetime. The brief version given by Francisco Lopez de Gomara (whose *Historie of the Conquest of the Weast India, now called new Spayne* appeared in translation in 1578) lacks the touch of maternal treachery and the sequel of filial forgiveness. The stealing of the child, her name, and her gift of the tongues would be somewhat tenuous links with *Pericles;* but Shakespeare may have come across a published version of the story nearer to the one outlined above, and have been reminded of the Mexican Marina when he read of Dionyza's treatment of Apollonius' daughter, of the seizure of the girl by pirates, and of her escape from the brothel by means of her various accomplishments, as Marina earned a Spanish husband by her gift of the tongues. The name Marina, moreover, would strike Shakespeare as appropriate for one who was born at sea.

Ben Jonson referred to *Pericles,* in a moment of pique, as 'a mouldy tale'—a hit, presumably, not merely at the antiquity of the Apollonius story, but at its naïvety. It consists of a series of events linked together only by the fact that they illustrate the operations of fortune in the life of the hero. There is no integral connexion between Apollonius' wooing of the daughter of Antiochus and the later episodes of his marriage, the loss of his wife and daughter, and his final reunion with them. Apollonius happens to meet his bride when he leaves Tyre for fear of the wrath of Antiochus. Even if Shakespeare had dramatized only the second part of the story—the separation of his hero from his wife and daughter and his ultimate reunion with them—he would not have been able to imbue it with the kind of significance to be found in *Cymbeline* or *The Winter's Tale.* Posthumus loses his wife, and Leontes his wife and children, through their own fault; and they earn the restoration of their lost ones by their penitence. The misfortunes which befall Pericles can hardly be said to be due to his own sins, though it has been suggested that he was paying for his inability to recognize until too late the evil hidden beneath the fair exterior of Antiochus' daughter. It is possible, however, that an attempt by Shakespeare to impose significance on his material has been blurred by the corruption of the text.[3] In Act II, Scene IV Simonides informs Thaisa's suitors that she will not marry for at least twelve months:

One twelve moons more she'll wear Diana's
  livery.
This by the eye of Cynthia hath she vow'd,
And on her virgin honour will not break it.

We are not told definitely whether Simonides is speaking the truth. His words immediately after the departure of the suitors—'So, they are well despatch'd'—suggest, perhaps, that he has invented the vow to rid himself of the suitors so as to leave the field free for the favoured Pericles. Whether the vow was an invention or not, it is worth noting that Diana is mentioned several times in the Shakespearian parts of the play and once, as Lucina, in the first scene. (Lucina, incidentally, was Twine's name for Thaisa.) Pericles prays to Lucina during his wife's labour—

  Divinest patroness, and midwife gentle
  To those that cry by night—

and his prayer is rejected. When Thaisa is restored to life, her first words are addressed to the same goddess—'O dear Diana!' Assuming that she will never see Pericles again—why is not explained—she decides to put on a vestal livery and serve as priestess in the temple of Diana at Ephesus. Gower, as chorus, speaks of Diana as Marina's mistress. Pericles vows 'by bright Diana' to leave his hair 'unscissored'. Marina, appropriately, prays to Diana in the brothel; and in the last act Diana appears to Pericles in a vision, telling him to visit her temple at Ephesus. He promises to obey 'Celestial Dian, goddess argentine'. The last scene takes place in the temple. In his address to the goddess, Pericles describes his child as wearing yet Diana's 'silver livery'; and, after his wife has been restored to him, he declares:

  Pure Dian, bless thee for thy vision! I
  Will offer night-oblations to thee.

It looks as though Shakespeare intended Thaisa's time in the temple to be a means of expiating the sin of taking the name of the goddess in vain, and that his intentions have been partially hidden by the corrupt text.[4] But the trials which Pericles and his family undergo are also a means of testing them; and their final reunion is in accordance with Jupiter's pronouncement in *Cymbeline*—

  Whom best I love I cross; to make my gift
  The more delay'd, delighted—

an echo, no doubt, of the scriptural 'Whom the Lord loveth, He chasteneth'.

It has often been observed that in the plays of the final period the characters are much less complex, less realistic, than they had been in the great tragedies and comedies of Shakespeare's middle period. They are

not merely simplified: they tend to be puppets, unable to control their own destinies. Although Hamlet speaks of the 'divinity that shapes our ends', Malvolio declares that 'all is fortune', Kent exclaims that 'it is the stars that govern our condition', Edmund acknowledges that 'the wheel has come full circle', Macbeth comes to think that life is 'a tale told by an idiot', and Othello asks despairingly 'Who can control his fate?', we recognize in all those plays that fate works through character. In *Cymbeline* and *The Winter's Tale,* although human evil and weakness are equally apparent, these do not produce their logical results, since the action of the play appears to be controlled by the gods.[5] Mr T. S. Eliot has suggested that Shakespeare in his last plays makes us feel not so much that his characters are creatures like ourselves, as that we are creatures like his characters, 'taking part like them in no common action of which we are for the most part unaware'. The characters are 'the work of a writer who has finally seen through the dramatic action of men into a spiritual action which transcends it'. A similar idea is expressed in the well-known lines in *Murder in the Cathedral:*

  Neither does the actor suffer
  Nor the patient act. But both are fixed
  In an eternal action, an eternal patience
  To which all must consent that it may be
    willed
  And which all must suffer that they may will
    it
  That the pattern may subsist, for the pattern
    is the action
  And the suffering, that the wheel may turn
    and still
  Be forever still.

But although Shakespeare might see some such pattern in the story of Apollonius—the converting of the wheel of fortune into the wheel of Providence—the difficulty remained of imposing a strictly dramatic unity on such an episodic story. Shakespeare had read Sidney's amusing account of a dramatic treatment of this kind of material:

You shall have *Asia* of the one side, and *Affricke* of the other, and so manie other under Kingdomes, that the Player when he comes in, must ever begin with telling where he is, or else the tale will not be conceived. Now you shall have three Ladies walke to gather flowers, and then we must beleeve the stage to be a garden. By and by we heare newes of shipwreck in the same place, then we are to blame if we accept it not for a Rock. Upon the back of that, comes out a hidious monster with fire and smoke, and then the miserable beholders are bound to take it for a Cave: while in the meane time two Armies flie in, represented with four swords & bucklers, and then what hard hart wil not receive it for a pitched field.

Now of time, they are much more liberall. For ordinarie it is, that two yoong Princes fall in love, after many traverses she is got with child, delivered of a faire boy: he is lost, groweth a man, falleth in love, and is readie to get an other childe, and all this in two houres space: which howe absurd it is in sence, even sence may imagine: and Arte hath taught, and all aunciant examples justified . . . But they will say, how then shall we set foorth a storie, which contains both many places and many times?

Sidney answers that a tragedy is not tied to the laws of history, that events can be reported by a *Nuntius,* and that

if they will represent an Historie, they must not (as *Horace* saith) beginne *ab ovo,* but they must come to the principall poynte of that one action which they will represent.

In the choruses of *Henry V* Shakespeare seems to be apologizing for not taking Sidney's advice; andFather Time, in *The Winter's Tale,* asks the audience to impute it not a crime that he disobeys the unity of time and slides over sixteen years. In *Pericles* Shakespeare uses the device of Ancient Gower, whether borrowed from an earlier play or suggested to Shakespeare by his reading of *Confessio Amantis.* Although the Gower choruses would not satisfy a modern student of Middle English, they do suggest, with remarkable skill, the general atmosphere of Gower's garrulous masterpiece. His rudimentary art, with its monotonous octosyllabic lines, its neutral diction, its rare imagery, and its pervasive moralizing, appealed to the simple curiosity of its readers. They asked, 'What happened next?' The causal relationship between one incident and the next and the psychology of the characters were equally unimportant. Incident followed after incident, with a running commentary designed to point the appropriate morals. Shakespeare has caught the manner to perfection, even though he cannot refrain from an occasional touch of better poetry. He doubtless recalled Chaucer's epithet for Gower—'moral'—when he penned the last lines of the play:

In Antiochus and his daughter you have
  heard
Of monstrous lust the due and just reward:
In Pericles, his queen, and daughter, seen,
Although assail'd with fortune fierce and
  keen,
Virtue preserv'd from fell destruction's
  blast,
Led on by heaven, and crown'd with joy at
  last.
In Helicanus may you well descry
A figure of truth, of faith, of loyalty;
In reverend Cerimon there well appears
The worth that learned charity aye wears . . .

The naïvety of Gower's chorus provides a suitable framework for the play. Shakespeare was asking his audience to listen to the story in an unsophisticated frame of mind, forgetting for the time being the kind of intelligent response they would make to *King Lear* or *Twelfth Night,* and adopting rather the simpler and relaxed attitude suitable to a play like *Mucedorus* or *The Rare Triumphs of Love and Fortune.* It is said that the tale of Apollonius is still told by professional story-tellers in the villages and round camp-fires in the Lebanon. A good thing, we are told, is the better for being ancient:

Et bonum quo antiquius, eo melius.

It was presumably because he wished to suggest the unsophisticated way in which the story should be received that the producer of *Pericles* at the Memorial Theatre, Stratford-upon-Avon, in 1958, hit upon the ingenious idea of turning a Middle English poet, Gower, into a Negro boatswain, and provided him with an audience on the stage of simple-minded seamen who followed the story with open-eyed wonder. But it should, of course, be borne in mind that when a sophisticated audience is asked to respond in an unsophisticated way it does so with some ambivalence. When Mr Eliot, for example, introduces into *Murder in the Cathedral* verse apparently imitated from *Everyman,* the effect on an audience is complex. It does not react in a purely unsophisticated way, but with a mixture of simplicity and sophistication.

When all allowances have been made for textual corruption, it is apparent that both character and incident in *Pericles* have been deliberately simplified. The characters are either very good or very evil. The daughter of Antiochus in the first act, though surpassingly beautiful,

    clothed like a bride
For the embracements even of Jove himself,

is entirely evil. The mouldering remains of her former suitors which tell Pericles

with speechless tongues and semblance pale,
That without covering, save yon field of
  stars,
Here they stand martyrs, slain in Cupid's
  wars;
And with dead cheeks advise thee to desist
From going on death's net,

inform the audience that they are watching a romantic and unrealistic play, set in a remote and unreal world. It is a world where murderers carry out their orders with the minimum of fuss, as when Antiochus orders the assassination of Pericles:

Thaliard, behold here's poison and here's
  gold;
We hate the Prince of Tyre, and thou must
  kill him.
It fits thee not to ask the reason why,
Because we bid it. Say, is it done?

Thaliard replies laconically: 'My lord, 'tis done.' Even in the Shakespearian part of the play, where 'Leonine, a murderer' is endowed with some scruples, these are felt to be a tribute to Marina's beauty and goodness rather than a means of humanizing Leonine:

  I will do't; but yet she is a goodly creature.

The scene between Cleon and Dionyza is almost a parody of scenes between Albany and Goneril or between Macbeth and his wife. Dionyza, like the hypocritical and devilish Queen in *Cymbeline,* has no redeeming characteristics: she is a picturesque and melodramatic villain.

On the other side of the moral fence, the good people are perfectly good—Helicanus is a perfect counsellor, Marina is a paragon, Cerimon is a type of aristocratic learning, benevolence, and wisdom. Only with Lysimachus is there any doubt. He has to be fundamentally decent to enable him to marry Marina; but he has to be something of a rake to enable him to be a prospective client in the brothel. Most of Shakespeare's audience would not have worried about this; and they would cheerfully assume that he had been converted, as even Boult is converted, by Marina's purity. But Shakespeare himself seems to have had a twinge of uneasiness on the matter, and he throws in a hint at the end of the brothel-scene that Lysimachus, like Duke Vincentio in *Measure for Measure* or a modern social scientist, was making a study of the red-light district for reputable motives:

  Had I brought hither a corrupted mind
  Thy speech had altered it . . .
  For me, be you thoughten
  That I came with no ill intent; for to me
  The very doors and windows savour vilely.

These lines are difficult to reconcile with the way Lysimachus is greeted by the Bawd as an old customer, and we have to assume either that Lysimachus is whitewashing himself to Marina or that Shakespeare belatedly realized that Lysimachus as he had depicted him was not a suitable husband for her.[6]

There are no lines in the first two acts which are certainly Shakespeare's, though there are a number which could be his. It is a thrilling moment in the theatre when at the beginning of Act III the voice of Shakespeare is heard, indubitable and potent, with a tempest at sea to match the storm in *King Lear:*

Thou god of this great vast, rebuke these
  surges,
Which wash both heaven and hell; and
  thou that hast
Upon the winds command, bind them in
  brass,
Having call'd them from the deep! O, still
Thy deaf'ning dreadful thunders; gently
  quench
Thy nimble sulphurous flashes!—O, how,
  Lychorida,
How does my queen?—Thou stormest
  venomously:
Wilt thou spit all thyself? The seaman's
  whistle
Is as a whisper in the ears of death,
Unheard.

The whole scene is palpably Shakespearian, and this is evident in spite of the misprints, the mislineations, and one obvious omission in the Quarto. On the whole, the reporter has done his work surprisingly well, better than one could expect from existing methods of shorthand.[7] A later speech in the same scene exhibits both the colloquial ease and the magical phrasing of Shakespeare's last period:

  A terrible childbed hast thou had, my dear;
  No light, no fire. Th'unfriendly elements
  Forgot thee utterly; nor have I time
  To give thee hallow'd to thy grave, but
    straight
  Must cast thee scarcely coffin'd, in the ooze;
  Where, for a monument upon thy bones,
  And aye-remaining lamps the belching whale
  And humming water must o'erwhelm thy
    corpse,
  Lying with simple shells.

This is not the first storm in the play, and the recurrence of tempest imagery even in the early acts made Wilson Knight suspect that Shakespeare was revising an early play of his own. At the beginning of Act II Pericles had been wrecked on the shore of Pentapolis, the sole survivor; and his speech may derive any Shakespearian quality it may be thought to possess from the acquaintance of its author with Shakespeare's earlier plays:

  Yet cease your ire, you angry stars of
    heaven!
  Wind, rain and thunder, remember earthly
    man
  Is but a substance that must yield to you;
  And I, as fits my nature, do obey you.
  Alas, the sea hath cast me on the rocks,
  Wash'd me from shore to shore, and left me
    breath
  Nothing to think on but ensuing death.

The opening lines of this speech are reasonably effective; but the last three are a sad anti-climax, whether due to the inefficiency of the reporter or to the uncertain mastery of the author. In itself the speech can hardly be regarded as a proof that Shakespeare was himself the author of the original *Pericles*. Some account of a storm was demanded by the story at this point in the play, and any author would have had to provide it.

The scene in which Thaisa is restored, though reported less accurately than the scene in Marina's birth, is equally authentic in its conception. Cerimon, of whom Pericles later remarks—

> The Gods can have no mortal officer
> More like a god than you—

is a character of wisdom and nobility, who seems to embody the essential spirit of the plays of Shakespeare's last period. In some ways he resembles Prospero, though he lacks the touch of asperity and disillusionment of that character. He speaks in verse which is worlds away from the crudity of that used in the first two acts of the play:

> I held it ever,
> Virtue and cunning were endowments greater
> Than nobleness and riches: careless heirs
> May the two latter darken and expend,
> But immortality attends the former,
> Making a man a god. 'Tis known, I ever
> Have studied physic, through which secret
>   art,
> By turning o'er authorities, I have,
> Together with my practice, made familiar
> To me and to my aid the blest infusions
> That dwell in vegetives, in metals, stones;
> And I can speak of the disturbances
> That nature works, and of her cures; which
>   doth give me
> A more content in course of true delight
> Than to be thirsty after tottering honour,
> Or tie my treasure up in silken bags,
> To please the fool and death.

This self-portrait prepares the way for the 'resurrection' of Thaisa, which is accompanied by music, as Lear's had been and as Hermione's was to be. Thaisa bequeaths to death her dumbness, and Cerimon uses the jewel imagery which is taken up and developed in the last act of the play:

> Behold,
> Her eyelids, cases to those heavenly jewels
> Which Pericles hath lost, begin to part
> Their fringes of bright gold; the diamonds
> Of a most praised water do appear,
> To make the world twice rich.

So Cerimon, in the last scene, tells Pericles:

> I op'd the coffin,
> Found there rich jewels;

and Pericles is reminded of Thaisa when he sees his daughter in the ship:

> Her eyes as jewel-like
> And cased as richly.

This imagery is appropriate to a play which is concerned with the finding of that which was lost, and we may suspect that it was suggested, like the pearl and the chrysolite in *Othello,* by the Gospel parable of the pearl of great price.

The first of the Marina scenes (IV. I) contains a flower passage comparable to similar ones in *The Winter's Tale, Cymbeline,* and *The Two Noble Kinsmen,* a superb example of tempest imagery—

> Ay me! poor maid,
> Born in a tempest, when my mother died,
> This world to me is like a lasting storm,
> Whirring me from my friends—

and one or two passages which well suggest Marina's crystalline innocence; but there are other passages of stumbling verse which appear to be corrupt. The feebleness of the following lines and the awkward internal rhyme are presumably the ruins of a genuine Shakespearian speech:

> My father, as nurse says, did never fear,
> But cried 'Good seamen' to the sailors,
>   galling
> His kingly hands hauling ropes,
> And clasping to the mast, endured a sea
> That almost burst the deck.

The prose of the brothel scenes is sometimes masterly (e.g. in IV. ii.) but, as we have seen, the verse of Act IV, Scene VI is fragmentary, and less sustained than the verse-fossils contained in Wilkins' novel. It is not till the first scene of Act V, in which Pericles is reunited to his daughter, that Shakespeare's imagination seems to be again working at full pressure, unless the weakness of the Marina-Lysimachus scene is due to the failure of the reporters rather than to that of the poet.

In the restoration scene,[8] tempest imagery is again used, but now no longer expressing hatred and discord—

> Lest this great sea of joys rushing upon me
> O'erbear the shores of my mortality,
> And drown me with their sweetness.

Once again, as in *King Lear,* the restoration is accompanied by music, first by Marina's lost song, and then by the music of the spheres; it is followed by Pericles' demand for fresh garments and by the appearance of Diana in a vision—the first theophany in Shakespeare's works.[9]

The quality of the scene may be illustrated by a single image.[10] In *Twelfth Night* Viola speaks of the love-sick maid who

> sat like Patience on a monument,
> Smiling at grief.

A similar image is used in this scene in *Pericles* with even greater dramatic force. The hero, meeting his daughter after many years of suffering, sees in her face the signs of her suffering and of ordeals bravely borne. He then uses the following image:

> Yet thou dost look
> Like Patience, gazing on Kings' graves, and
>   smiling
> Extremity out of act.

This wonderful image suggests all that Marina has undergone and all that Pericles himself has endured. It suggests that Marina is a king's daughter; it suggests her courage and patience in adversity—pursued by a murderer, captured by pirates, and sold to a brothel. Pericles is to be reborn; Thaisa is to be restored to him from the sea; and the whole family is to be reunited in an earthly resurrection. This is the situation in the play, and the image is exquisitely appropriate to it. The theme of the play is the restoration of the lost and the conquest of death by love—in so far as the theme of one of Shakespeare's plays can be expressed in abstract terms. This theme, this particular scene, its antecedents and its sequel, and the face of the girl imagined by the poet called up the inevitable image which is not merely a symbolic description of Marina but also helps to create the vision of the play.

Journeys that end in lovers' meeting, scenes in which brother and sister, husband and wife, or parents and children meet again after long separation, when each believed the other dead, were frequent episodes in Elizabethan fiction—and in the Greek Romances on which they were sometimes based—and they have always been effective on the stage, whether in Greek tragedy or Latin comedy. Two of Euripides' most effective scenes are the meeting of Iphigenia and Orestes in Tauris and the restoration of Alcestis to her husband. Even the reunion of Egeon and his wife in *The Comedy of Errors* is a moving scene in a play which is largely farcical; the silent reunion of Isabella and Claudio is a little-recognized master-stroke in *Measure for Measure;* and the meeting of Viola and Sebastian in *Twelfth Night* is a touching climax to that

play. The meeting of Pericles and Marina surpasses all these. Its effectiveness, and the effectiveness of the whole play, is due partly to Shakespeare's creation of a kind of myth which he could set up against the changes and chances of this mortal life. He is calling in a new world to redress the balance of the old, a new world in which the designs of evil men are frustrated and in which everything comes right in the end—the beautiful queen is not really dead, the beautiful princess is saved from murder and rape and the contamination of the brothel, and the hero, after more trials and tribulations than are normally the lot of man, is rewarded with unforeseen and unimagined happiness. Shakespeare is aware that his story is too good to be true, but such fables are a criticism of life as it is, and (as some think) a statement of faith. In a pagan setting he creates what is virtually an immortality myth.

The misfortunes that befall Pericles are undeserved, and the restoration to him of his wife and child is due to the inscrutable workings of Providence. In the plays which followed Shakespeare set out to eliminate accident, and to infuse the restoration theme with ethical meaning. This could be done only by replacing the workings of an arbitrary providence by the operations of sin and forgiveness. Leontes' jealousy causes the death of Mamillius, and apparently of Hermione also, the loss of Perdita, and estrangement from Polixenes. But the two kings are reconciled through the marriage of their children; and when Leontes by his penitence has earned forgiveness, Hermione is restored to him. In *Pericles* Shakespeare had dealt at length with the finding of the lost daughter and only cursorily with the reunion of husband and wife. In *The Winter's Tale* the emphasis is reversed. The father-daughter recognition takes place off stage, and Shakespeare concentrates on the reunion of Leontes and Hermione—because Leontes has sinned chiefly against her and needs her forgiveness before the play can end in reconciliation. In *Cymbeline* Imogen forgives Posthumus for his attempted murder, and their reconciliation does not require a marriage of children to cement it. In *The Tempest* Shakespeare concentrates on the act of forgiveness itself. In *The Winter's Tale* and *Cymbeline* the hero is the sinner; in *The Tempest* the hero is sinned against, and the betrayal had taken place sixteen years before. By this means Shakespeare eliminated the break of sixteen years which occurs in both *Pericles* and *The Winter's Tale.* The advantages are not all on one side; and the French critic who remarked that Shakespeare finally succeeded in obeying the unity of time by eliminating action altogether was not without some justification. The looser structure of *The Winter's Tale* is necessary to the particular effects at which Shakespeare was aiming; and the yet looser structure of *Pericles* is the only way by which the story of Apollonius could be put on the stage.

In recent years there has been a revival of interest in the play, heralded by T. S. Eliot's exquisite *Marina* and by Wilson Knight's eloquent reassessment in *The Crown of Life,* and exemplified by productions at the Old Vic and Birmingham and by two at Stratford. One Stratford production omitted the first act, and the liberties taken in the other seemed to indicate a lack of confidence in the play's ability to appeal to a modern audience. But at Birmingham the audience was captivated throughout the performance; and this was yet another indication that Shakespeare knew better than his critics, and better even than modish producers, that he had hit on precisely the right form for the material he was dramatizing, and that we have no right to deplore the taste of the groundlings who were enthusiastic when the play was first performed.

Notes

[1] Cf. K. Muir, *Shakespeare's Sources* (1957), *passim.*

[2] *English Studies,* XXXIX (1958), pp. 74-5.

[3] Cf. *N.Q.* (1948), p. 362.

[4] To judge from the Wilkins novel, Shakespeare did not find the broken vow motivation in the source-play.

[5] The following paragraphs are based on a lecture given at Wayne State University, Detroit, to be published in a volume entitled *Last Periods.*

[6] The verse in Lysimachus' speech is so bad that we may suppose that the text is corrupt. In Wilkins' novel, as we have seen, Lysimachus says 'and for my parte, who hither came but to haue payd the price, a peece of gold for your virginitie'. Possibly this more nearly represents the correct text—it is, it will be noticed, in verse—but it is surely more likely that Shakespeare altered his source at this point with the object of presenting Marina a more presentable husband.

[7] In the above speech the Quarto prints *The god* for *Thou god, then storme* for *Thou stormest,* and *Unheard* is attached not to *whisper* but to the word *Lichorida* which follows. These errors might well be due to the compositor rather than to the reporter. Although we have no good text with which to compare that of the *Pericles* quarto, it would appear to be far more accurate in this scene than (say) the bad quarto of *Hamlet.*

[8] The reader may be referred to the chapter in Derek Traversi's *Shakespeare's Last Period* and to the masterly analysis by G. Wilson Knight in *The Crown of Life.*

[9] The appearance of Hymen in *As You Like It* is in a masque performed by human actors.

[10] This paragraph is based on a passage in my article 'The Future of Shakespeare' (*Penguin New Writing* 28).

Andrew Welsh (essay date 1974)

SOURCE: "Heritage in *Pericles,*" in *Shakespeare's Late Plays,* edited by Richard C. Tobias and Paul G. Zolbrod, Ohio University Press, 1974, pp. 89-113.

[*In the essay below, Welsh cites four "heritages" operating in* Pericles: *the archaic tale itself, the importance of riddles, the seven capital sins, and the appearance of the "flourishing emblem."*]

It's an old tale, told age after age in language after language. It was probably first told to eastern Greeks by a romance written no later than the third century A.D. The Greek romance has been lost, but a Latin proseversion made sometime between the third and the sixth centuries A.D. carried the tale throughout Europe, and many manuscripts of this popular version still survive. The Latin version entered Godfrey of Viterbo's twelfth-century *Pantheon* and the fourteenth-century collection of tales *Gesta Romanorum.* The tale was told in most of the vernacular languages of Europe as well, and versions of it have been found in Old English, Provencal, French, Italian, Spanish, Portuguese, German, Danish, Swedish, Dutch, Polish, Russian, and Hungarian.[1] In the twentieth century it has been found in oral tradition in Modern Greek, told as a folktale in the islands and on Asia Minor, sung as a ballad by wedding processions in Crete.[2] Chaucer knew the tale, and Gower, and Sidney. And Shakespeare. Like any traditional story, it changed often through many retellings: names were changed, incidents dropped out and other incidents were attracted from other stories, thematic meanings or moral lessons were developed and then forgotten or misunderstood by the next story-teller. Manuscripts of the many variant versions proliferated and then were damaged, surviving only in fragments. Time, with its anonymous accidents, was always to be counted among the many authors of this tale, and these conditions remain when we try to focus on a particular version of it in England at the beginning of the seventeenth century. The play *Pericles, Prince of Tyre* was from its first appearance attributed to Shakespeare, but it was not included in the First Folio. All texts of the play are based on a quarto published in 1609, badly printed and full of mistakes. The quarto, in turn, was based on seriously corrupt reported copy, perhaps pirated from a performance of the play. No other play of Shakespeare's has such an unreliable textual base.[3] To what extent it is in fact a play of Shakespeare's has been clouded as well, and at different times the play has been regarded as one of his early works, as a work that was composed at two periods of his life, as a play by someone else that Shakespeare partially revised, and as a collaboration in which Shakespeare wrote the last half. Yet the tale survives.

And that is the point: of all the plays, the hand of Shakespeare has suffered the most obliteration in this one, and of all the plays this one is based on a story that has in its own right shown an amazing vitality through its long history. It was no obscure incident from English or Roman history to which Shakespeare turned in this first of his four romances, but an old, fantastic tale that had pleased many and pleased long. Its enduring vitality, critics have speculated, may have been the main reason for Shakespeare's attraction to it just at the time he was leaving the great tragedies behind and searching out new forms for his late plays. This tale, so close to the traditional motifs of folktales, brought to him basic, archaic patterns of the story-telling imagination. From them he could expand into the themes that resonate more and more in his late plays, themes which involve the spreading out of time through long journeys and many incidents during which people age and learning becomes much more of a ripening than a catastrophic tragic recognition. The ways in which the tale's thematic concerns of loss and recovery, fathers and daughters, tempests and music, death and rebirth become the central themes of the late plays have been followed by such critics as G. Wilson Knight, Derek Traversi, and Northrop Frye, among others.[4] In addition to these major themes, however, there are other elements, smaller ones associated with different periods in the tale's long tradition, that Shakespeare also inherited and put to use. They are like the armor that Pericles recovers from the sea after his shipwreck—"part of mine heritage," he calls it[5]—something passed on to him by his father, known by a certain mark, a little rusty now, perhaps, but helpful and even necessary for him to accomplish the prize. Some small heritages that this centuries-old tale passed on to Shakespeare, and what he did with them, are my subject. There are four of them that I shall look at, and each one was put to new use by Shakespeare. Throughout most of the play they remain submerged, but in the central recognition scene between Pericles and Marina these external heritages of the tale's long tradition are gathered up by Shakespeare and used within the play in such a way that the theme of heritage—something passed on from one generation to another—itself becomes one more of the play's central themes.

The first heritage is the tale itself, the old story that carries the sense of being told by one generation to another. For fourteen hundred years the tale had been told as a narrative rich in incidents extending over many places and a long period of time. The incidents themselves show the tale's closeness to the motifs offolktales and popular literature—the riddle-tests,

shipwrecks, banquet scenes, disguised or unknown princes, abductions of virgins by pirates, lost children, recognition tokens and remarkable reunions that story-tellers have always used, from prehistory up through the novels of Sir Walter Scott and James Fenimore Cooper. Shakespeare's first problem must have been in deciding how to change the manner or mode of the tale, in Aristotle's terms, from narrative to drama. He solved the problem by respecting the tale and keeping the older narrative mode importantly present in the play in the figure of Gower. There is no character quite like Gower in any other Shakespeare play. The Prologues in *Henry V* and *The Winter's Tale* perform the same necessary function of turning over the hour glass, but Gower's part in *Pericles* goes far beyond—and behind—this. He has usually been seen as a classical chorus in the play, or as an illusion-breaking stage manager, but when he steps forward to begin the tale he tells us very simply who he is:

> To sing a song that old was sung,
> From ashes ancient Gower is come,
> Assuming man's infirmities,
> To glad your ear, and please your eyes.
>
> (I.Cho.1-4)

He is the ancient story-teller whose job it is to pick up this echoing tale from the even more distant past and to pass it on. As the narrator who spins out a tale of voyages and marvelous incidents, he represents a tradition that goes back to Homer standing forward and beginning a story about a man who wandered far and saw much in his sea travels. When Gower begins, he is making a claim for attention not on behalf of himself but on behalf of the old tale. He goes on to say that

> It hath been sung at festivals,
> On ember-eves and holy-ales.
>
> (I.Cho.5-6)

The tale belongs to festival times, story-telling times, and we should remember this if we find it a bit naive in places. It is meant to entertain us, not with its realism but with its truth: "The purchase is to make men glorious" (I.Cho.9). In an Elizabethan version of his rough old language, Gower then begins the tale, pointing to the long line of story-tellers behind him: "I tell you what mine authors say" (I.cho.20). Shakespeare, or whoever is the author of this passage, is also pointing back here to the long tradition behind him, a tradition that includes the poet John Gower himself, whose *Confessio Amantis* (1393) is one of the play's two known sources. In the *Confessio*, John Gower had in turn pointed back to the long tradition behind his version, the twelfth-century *Pantheon* and other "olde bokes."[6] As a character in the play, Gower embodies an important meaning that this old tradition represents: the very survival of the tale, in spite of centuries of accidents and changes in its transmission, is a conquest of devouring time by the human imagination. Just as the story-teller within the play controls time and space—

> Thus time we waste, and long leagues make
>   short;
> Sail seas in cockles, have and wish but
>   for't;
> Making, to take our imagination,
> From bourn to bourn, region to region.
>
> (IV.iv.1-4)

—so as one in a long line of story-tellers the poet Gower has conquered time with the story itself.

Within the play, the conquest over time by the human spirit is a meaning that Pericles must find; without this, the final reunions hardly pay him back for the fourteen years of wandering, loss, and sorrow that he has suffered. The meaning is found by bringing the external sense of the continuing tradition of the old tale into the play itself. Twice, the telling of the story is used as an element of the plot, in both cases as a recognition device that brings about a restoration and a triumph over the long years of separation and loss. The retelling of the story within the story was a conventional feature of Greek romance, but this tale is nearly unique in using it as a recognition device. It is used in the earliest surviving versions of the tale, and Shakespeare kept this heritage as an important working element of his play, a recognition device more powerful than Pericles' ring or any other token. When Marina tells her story to Pericles in the harbor of Mytilene, the tale is both a means by which the father recognizes the daughter and a means by which the daughter restores the father to new life. Later, when Pericles retells his story in the temple of Diana at Ephesus, the telling is once more a means of recognition and restoration, this time for the lost husband and the lost wife and for the lost mother and the lost daughter. What is recognized through the tellings, we must believe, is that time has brought not merely suffering and loss but also ripening and regeneration. With this recognition, one generation is able to look to the next: Pericles' last words in the play look forward to the marriage of Marina and to the continuation of the story. If we listen to other versions of the story, such as Book VIII of Gower's *Confessio Amantis* or Laurence Twine's novel *The Patterne of painefull Adventures* (1576)—Shakespeare's other main source for the story—we can see the tale's sense of its own tradition raised to a further power, looking back at itself as it set out on its long journey. Gower tells us that the citizens of Ephesus had gathered at the temple of Diana to see the great king, and when they heard his story from his own lips they began to tell it over and pass it on,

> And al the toun thus sone it wiste.
> Tho was ther joie manyfold,
> For every man this tale hath told
> As for miracle, and were glad,

and Twine tells us that "when report heereof was spread abroad, there was great joy throughout all the Citie of Ephesus, and the report has blowen about in everie place."[7] They are the first of the many story-tellers who, like Gower, have assumed the responsibility of making the tale's hopeful recognition of the possibilities of restoration part of the human heritage.

In addition to the tale's hope for the triumph of the human spirit over annihilating time, another characteristic of the original romance was passed on to Shakespeare. The story had always been a sea tale, a story of voyages and tempests and shipwreck. G. Wilson Knight has pointed out that Shakespeare's imagination, from *The Comedy of Errors* onwards, had been attracted to tempests and sea-voyages, and that in choosing the story of *Pericles* he found a new structure for his last plays that was based on "his most instinctive symbol" (*The Crown of Life*, p. 36). A sea tale poses another particular problem for a dramatist, yet Shakespeare kept this characteristic of the tale as a powerful and important element throughout the play. The sea is always there for Pericles, and he finally becomes lost in it. At first, following the almost casual advice of Helicanus to "go travel for a while" (I.ii.106), Pericles turns to the sea as an escape from the wrath of Antiochus—

> So puts himself unto the shipman's toil,
> With whom each minute threatens life or
>   death.
>
> (I.iii.23-24)

It saves him by taking him to his false hosts in the city of Tharsus. The next time he uses the sea as an escape he is shipwrecked and loses everything. Later, in a second tempest, Pericles loses his wife Thaisa in childbirth, and it is the law of the sea that she must go overboard. Pericles' lines at her sea burial are the occasion for one of Shakespeare's finest elegies:

> A terrible childbed hast thou had, my dear;
> No light, no fire: th'unfriendly elements
> Forgot thee utterly; nor have I time
> To give thee hallow'd to thy grave, but
>   straight
> Must cast thee, scarcely coffin'd, in the
>   ooze;
> Where, for a monument upon thy bones,
> And e'er-remaining lamps, the belching
>   whale
> And humming water must o'erwhelm thy
>   corpse,
> Lying with simple shells.
>
> (III.i.56-64)

Years later the child born during the tempest, Marina, is captured on the sea shore by pirates who take her back to the sea on their ship. Finally Pericles, who believes that she is dead, inexplicably rushes back onto the sea that has brought him such painful losses. There he is a victim of a third tempest which, in Shakespearean fashion, is both external and internal:

> He bears
> A tempest, which his mortal vessel tears,
> And yet he rides it out.
>
> (IV.iv.29-31)

Pericles, Thaisa, and Marina are all lost to the sea—Pericles twice, the second time by a kind of suicide. Yet the sea gives back too: Pericles is saved after his shipwreck by three fishermen, three men of the sea, and the sea returns the lost armor. It pays for Thaisa's death with the birth of a daughter, a "fresh-new sea-farer" whom Pericles—in one of the most striking changes in the tale made by Shakespeare—names "Marina." Thaisa's coffin, like Ishmael's in another sea tale, is cast up by the sea onto the shores of Ephesus, where Cerimon revives her. Marina's abduction by pirates who come off the sea saves her from the murderer Leonine, and the third tempest that wracks Pericles and his ship drives him to the harbor of Mytilene on the feast day of Neptune and to Marina who restores him. As critics have noticed, the sea in this play is "the mask'd Neptune" that has the essential ambiguity of Fortune: it brings both loss and restoration, dealing indifferently with human beings without regard for their virtues or vices. The world of *Pericles,* however, is not a Lear universe, and Shakespeare was careful to keep another original element of the old tale in the figure of the goddess Diana, who by the end of the play has become the story's controlling deity. As the chaste goddess she is Marina's patron saint; as the cult-goddess of Ephesus she provides a haven for sea-buried Thaisa; as the bright "goddess argentine" associated with the moon there may be the suggestion that she brings Pericles help in the form of some control over the sea's indifferent blows—not control over the deep-sea tempests that have battered him, but at least a knowledge that applies to the shores and harbors where most of the human life in this tale is lived, transition zones whose tidal rhythms follow the moon's own rhythms of death and rebirth.

A second heritage that the tale brought to Shakespeare came not from the original Greek romance but from the early Latin version made sometime between the third and sixth centuries A.D., the *Historia Apollonii Regis Tyri.* During this early Latin period echoes of Virgil, Ovid, and Roman comedy appeared in the tale, and at some point ten literary riddles composed by Symphosius in the fourth or fifth century were also brought into the story. They are asked by Marina (or

Tharsia, as she is known in the *Historia*) when she comes on board the ship in the harbor of Mytilene, and they are part of her attempt to heal Pericles (Apollonius). Before we look at this scene, however, we should recall the important riddle that begins the play.

Pericles at the court of Antiochus finds himself in an old folklore situation: like Oedipus, he faces a riddle for which he must find the answer or lose his life. It is, moreover, a double-edged riddle, for if he does give the answer he will still lose his life. In the *Historia,* Antiochus himself is the speaker of the riddle, which is convincingly difficult: *Scelere vehor, materna carne vescor, quaero fratrem meum, meae matris virum, uxoris meae filium; non invenio* ("I am carried along by crime, I feed on my mother's flesh, I seek my brother, my mother's husband, my wife's son, and I do not find him").[8] The answer turns on the various in-law relationships that Antiochus and his daughter have created by their incest, and this riddle tests Pericles' skill much more than the relatively transparent one given in the play:

> I am no viper, yet I feed
> On mother's flesh which did me breed.
> I sought a husband, in which labour
> I found that kindness in a father.
> He's father, son, and husband mild;
> I mother, wife, and yet his child:
> How they may be, and yet in two,
> As you will live, resolve it you.
>
> (I.i.65-72)

In addition to simplifying the riddle, the play makes one other small change: the answer depends on realizing that the speaker of the riddle is not Antiochus but his daughter, a change that emphasizes Marina's very different use of riddles and her very different relationship to her father.

Pericles' skill with riddles was itself a heritage passed on to his daughter. Like her musical skill and her other graces, Marina's cleverness with riddles is a birthmark by which she is recognized. The skill is much more obvious in the older versions of the tale, but it still survives in Shakespeare's play through submerged allusions, as when Marina diverts an attack on her virginity (something Antiochus' daughter could not do) by asking Boult an enigmatic question, "What canst thou wish thine enemy to be?" (IV.vi.157), or when Gower tells us that in addition to educating the young ladies of Mytilene in music, dance, and needlework, she was also outwitting the city's scholars with riddles they could not answer: "Deep clerks she dumbs" (V.Cho.5). In the Latin *Historia,* when Marina comes to heal Pericles, she first sings to him: he thanks her, gives her gold, and sends her away. She comes a second time and asks him her ten riddles. Pericles easily finds the answers: 1) the wave and fish, 2) the river-reed, 3) a ship, 4) a bath, 5) an anchor, 6) a sponge, 7) a ball, 8) a mirror, 9) wheels, and 10) the steps of a ladder (Haight, pp. 168-70). He then asks her again to leave, and it is only after he strikes her and she cries out her story that he recognizes her. Although it is tempting to notice that half of the riddles are connected with sea imagery, in the *Historia* they remain obvious interpolations that contribute very little to the progress of the scene. This is also true in Shakespeare's two sources: Gower tells us that Marina asked the riddles, but he does not give them, while Twine keeps three of the original ten—the sea, a ship, and a bath. Shakespeare, then, finished a job begun a thousand years before when he made Marina's riddles an integral part of the recognition scene (V.i). Groping his way out of his isolation, Pericles sees a woman standing before him; to find out who she is he questions her, asking first about her parentage and birthplace:

> What countrywoman?
> Here of these shores?

She answers with a riddle based on the condition of her birth at sea:

> No, nor of any shores;
> Yet was I mortally brought forth, and am
> No other than I appear.

He next asks her where she now lives, and she answers, "Where I am but a stranger." To this apparent contradiction she adds a further ambiguity:

> from the deck
> You may discern the place.

She is pointing toward the land, where she obviously lives but which, she says, is not her home; something else in the scene, however, is pointing in another direction. As the recognition and Pericles' restoration proceed, he asks her to sit by him, to tell him her story and her name. She answers this time not with puzzles but with a simplicity that resolves all ambiguities:

> My name is Marina.

She could be pointing toward the sea now. When the riddles of her birth and her presence in Mytilene are finally resolved, Pericles embraces the final recognition with a return of his old skill:

> O, come hither,
> Thou that beget'st him that did thee beget;
> Thou that wast born at sea, buried at
> Tharsus,
> And found at sea again.

"Thou that beget'st him that did thee beget" cannot but recall the riddle of Antiochus' daughter, but this is a "restored" version of that riddle. At the beginning of the play the riddle's deception overshadowed all, and the ugly incest it concealed presented Pericles with the first of many false appearances that were to plague him. The daughter of Antiochus, Pericles learned, was a "glorious casket stor'd with ill" (I.i.78), the music she entered with was false music, and her "graces" (I.i.14) were equally false. Marina's riddle skill, however, is used not to conceal but to reveal. She is as she says, "No other than I appear," and, like her other heritage, the gift of music, her riddles are not deceptions but healing graces. The situation concealed by the riddle of Antiochus' daughter has led to the destruction of Antiochus and his daughter, but the "birth" riddles of Marina and Pericles express a resurrection of both the daughter, "buried at Tharsus, And found at sea again," and of the father. Where the first riddle marked a corrupt father-daughter relationship, Pericles, begotten by his daughter, uses a riddle to mark the restoration of a healthy father-daughter relationship in which he can do what Antiochus could not do: give away his daughter to a husband. Pericles, the riddle shows, has engendered a future, whereas Antiochus, like the cannibalistic parents in famine-stricken Tharsus, has devoured his future.

The tale's long passage through the Middle Ages brought with it another heritage known by its mark in Shakespeare's play, the tradition of the seven capital sins. Originating with the early desert fathers, the scheme of the capital sins was developed by Gregory the Great and Thomas Aquinas into an important element of medieval Christian theology and—more importantly for our purposes—medieval Christian iconology.[9] It was known and used by Dante, Langland, Chaucer, and Spenser, and John Gower organized the tales in his *Confessio Amantis* according to the sin each tale exemplified. In Gower's order, the seven sins are Pride, Envy, Wrath, Sloth, Avarice, Gluttony, and Lust. The last sin was understood as excessive or illicit sexual desire, and it was under "Lust" that Shakespeare found in the *Confessio* the long story that became *Pericles,* placed there by Gower because of the unlawful love of Antiochus and his daughter—the "foul incest" (I.i.127) and "heinous capital offence" (II.iv.5) that opens the play. The sins were called "capital" sins not in the sense that they were the most serious sins (as in "capital punishment"), but because they were considered to be the fountainheads (*capita*) from which all other sins spring. Antiochus' incest, Pericles knows, will easily lead to wrath and then to homocide (a sin of wrath, in the medieval classification), once Antiochus is aware that the first sin has been uncovered:

> One sin, I know, another doth provoke;
> Murder's as near to lust as flame to smoke.
> (I.i.138-39)

This is not to say that *Pericles* is a medieval Christian play. Gower's external framework of the seven capital sins and his reading of the Pericles story as an example of incest were not explicitly adopted by Shakespeare, but the entire artistic tradition of the sins could not help but influence this play which, on one level, reads like a psychomachia of the virtues and vices. The tradition remains beneath the surface in Shakespeare's play, integrated like the other heritages of the tale into the plot, diction, and imagery, but it is nevertheless present. T. S. Eliot sensed this, and his poem "Marina," based on the play, brings the capital sins to the surface again, each sin associated with an animal in good medieval fashion.

References to the sins occur throughout the play, but there are three scenes in particular in which the author brings the medieval tradition to the surface. The corresponding passages in the play's two principal sources, we note, make no such use of the capital sins. The first scene is at Tharsus before the arrival of Pericles; the governor, Cleon, and his wife, Dionyza, are recounting to each other the pitiful state of their city, contrasting it with its former prosperity:

> A city on whom plenty held full hand,
> For riches strew'd herself even in her
>   streets;
> Whose towers bore heads so high they
>   kiss'd the clouds,
> And strangers ne'er beheld but wond'red at;
> Whose men and dames so jetted and
>   adorn'd,
> Like one another's glass to trim them by—
> Their tables were stor'd full to glad the
>   sight,
> And not so much to feed on as delight:
> All poverty was scorn'd, and pride so great,
> The name of help grew odious to repeat.
>   (I.iv.22-31)

This is not a picture of a prosperous city, but a city wallowing in pride, vainglory, wasteful gluttony, sloth, lack of charity (the contrary virtue of envy, in Gower) and, in general, a sense of *luxuria* and "superfluous riots" (I.iv.54). This pride has had its fall, but it is in the same city that another capital sin later arises, "That monster envy" (IV.Cho.12) that leads to the attempted murder of Marina. The capital sin is once again the source of other sins: envy breeds wrath in Dionyza, who sends Leonine, "The pregnant instrument of wrath" (IV.Cho.44), to commit homocide.

If Tharsus is a city of pride, gluttony, and envy, a society of avarice is the subject of the little allegory overheard by Pericles on the shores of Pentapolis. Patch-breech, a fisherman, tells his head fisherman that he marvels at "how the fishes live in the sea." The master answers,

> Why, as men do a-land: the great ones eat up the little ones. I can compare our rich misers to nothing so fitly as to a whale: a' plays and tumbles, driving the poor fry before him, and at last devours them all at a mouthful. Such whales have I heard on a'th' land, who never leave gaping till they swallow'd the wholeparish, church, steeple, bells, and all. (II.i.28-34)

"A pretty moral," observes Pericles in a play full of pretty morals.

The moral of a later scene, however, is less pretty. From primitive religion onwards the concept of sin has been associated with disease, and through the Middle Ages specific correspondences were made between particular capital sins and particular diseases. In English literature, the sin of lust had been associated with a wounded foot in the *Ancren Riwle,* with dropsy in the Northern Homily Cycle MS., with leprosy by Gower in the *Mirour de l'omme,* and with venereal disease by Spenser in Book I of the *Faerie Queene.* Shakespeare darkened the comedy of the brothel scenes in *Pericles* with images of disease, emphasizing the inevitable associations of lust with the rotting, wasting effects of syphilis. By the conventions of this kind of romantic tale, the abducted virgin must pass through the trials of not simply any brothel, but the lowest of the low, and there is a feeling in the play that the brothels of Mytilene, like the brothels of Veracruz, were proverbial. The three girls of the brothel, the Bawd complains, are "rotten" with disease and "sodden" from attempts to control the disease with sweat tubs. The language of this scene brings out a sense of decay and disintegration behind the comedy:

> *Bawd.* What else, man? The stuff we have, a strong wind will blow it to pieces, they are so pitifully sodden.
> *Pandar.* Thou sayest true; there's two unwholesome, a' conscience. The poor Transylvanian is dead, that lay with the little baggage.
> *Boult.* Ay, she quickly poop'd him; she made him roastmeat for worms. (IV.ii.17-23)

In her attempts to encourage Marina, the Bawd tells her that she will live in pleasure, "taste gentlemen of all fashions" and "have the difference of all complexions" (IV.ii.74-76), but all that the scene shows of these gentlemen is a Transylvanian dead from the disease, a Frenchman weak in the legs from it, and a Spaniard whose slavering mouth and premature heat also show suspicious signs of disease as well as of lust. Even Lysimachus, as a customer, is aware of the dangers in the pleasures of the brothel ("How now, wholesome iniquity, have you that a man may deal withal, and defy the surgeon?"—IV.vi.23-25); it is a "sty," Marina tells him, where "Diseases have been sold dearer than physic" (IV.vi.97). The scenes show that the brothel deals not in pleasure but in disease, and into this situation Marina comes anticipating her later role as a healer. She wreaks havoc by treating not the symptoms of the disease but the cause, converting the men who visit her from vice to virtue. Chastity triumphs over Lust, and we see two of the customers abandoning the girls of the brothel for healthier pursuits—they are going to hear the vestal virgins sing.

The clear definitions of morality in the play often lend themselves to simple conflicts of Virtue and Vice, such as a figure representing Chastity conquering the contrary Vice of Lust. If this is a common pattern in medieval literature, it should still be remembered that conflicts between figures representing the seven capital sins and figures representing contrary virtues were meant to represent a complex conflict within a man's soul. The most important use Shakespeare made of this heritage was in the situation of Pericles, who lost himself at sea. Although the play brings us to an understanding of Pericles' condition, it has been difficult to find the terminology to describe it. Helicanus, in the play, calls it "melancholy" (V.i.219), a traditional medieval term with precise meanings. Pericles had in fact suffered from "dull-ey'd melancholy" (I.ii.3) when he returned to Tyre from Antioch, and again at the banquet in Pentapolis where Simonides comments that his shipwrecked guest "doth sit too melancholy" (II.iii.54). In both cases, however, Pericles could talk, hear, see, remember the past and plan for the future; his melancholy was a long way from the depths of his later condition. It is also worth noting in passing that there was a tradition, persisting in Englandup until the twelfth century, of an eighth capital sin, *tristitia,* or sadness. It was later incorporated into the scheme of seven capital sins by making it (as in Gower) a sin of *acedia*—which meant spiritual as well as physical sloth, a drying up of the spirit. Both melancholy and sadness tell us something of Pericles' condition, but neither is a sufficient concept for a state which seems to me best described as despair, the sin pictured by Giotto's "Last Judgment" as a woman hanging herself, and by a capital on the Ducal Palace in Venice as a woman thrusting a dagger into her own throat (Bloomfield, pp. 103-4).

The apparent death of Marina breaks Pericles, and he responds to it with a kind of spiritual suicide. Even his appearance becomes that of a corpse: shut up in the mausoleum of his tent, speechless, sightless, his clothes unchanged, his hair and nails grown out to macabre length. John Arthos has described Pericles' state as "apathy," a state that he falls into "when, believing Marina dead, through some stubborness he grows dumb, rejecting in life everything but sorrow."[10] I would recommend instead that Pericles' apathy should be understood in the root sense of the word, that he is insensible to everything, *including* sorrow. Unable to bear any further blows, he has deliberately taken the extreme course of suicide; by inflicting upon himself a death of the spirit, he has isolated himself from further pain. Arthos' point of view does receive some support from Helicanus in the play, who says that Pericles eats only enough to "prorogue his grief" (V.i.26), but Helicanus, we have seen, is an unreliable diagnostician. To him, Pericles is simply undergoing another bout of melancholy, and he does not realize the accuracy of the corpse appearance that Pericles has assumed.

Although despair had been incorporated by the medievals into the scheme of the seven capital sins as another sin of *acedia,* it also belonged to another tradition, a group of sins known as the "unforgivable" sins against the Holy Spirit—"unforgivable" because these were sins that by their very nature put obstacles in the way of forgiveness. Pericles' spiritual suicide has erected the walls of a tomb about him, walls which, Lysimachus realizes, can only be breached by the artillery of Marina's "grace"—now understood in all the meanings of that word.

> She, questionless, with her sweet harmony
> And other chosen attractions, would allure,
> And make a batt'ry through his deafen'd
>   ports,
> Which now are midway stopp'd.
>
>   (V.i.44-47)

In the Christian scale, despair was a sin even more serious than the incest of Antiochus or the murderous envy of Dionyza. In Middle English it was called *wanhope*; it sins against the virtue of hope by abandoning hope and rejecting the possibility of any help from within or without. How close Pericles was to the total and final isolation of despair is seen only as the walls that he had built around himself come down one by one. First to fall are the walls built around his senses, entombing them away from a world that had become an unbearable sequence of sorrows. The gift of music was another heritage that Pericles had passed on to his daughter, and in the recovery scene Marina first approaches him with a song. There is no immediate response, but when she approaches him again he breaks the long dumbness of his voice with bestial snarls and pushes her away: life returns first on the most primitive level, and like a provoked animal he snaps at the provoker and retreats back into his hole. She begins her story by telling of her parentage, and fragments of her voice break through the walls around his hearing. As he mumbles the fragments over, we see life stumbling and groping its incoherent way out of a long isolation:

> My fortunes—parentage—good parentage—
> To equal mine—was it not thus? what say
>   you?

Sight returns next, and he looks at her. As he does, another wall begins to crack: "You're likesomething that—" But he breaks off. The strongest wall has been built around the painful memories in his own mind, and he pushes back this momentary resurgence of the past. When Marina speaks again, however, answering his question with her birth-riddle, the implications of the riddle, the beauty of her voice, and her resemblance to his lost wife bring him to a full confrontation with the memories he has walled out of consciousness:

> I am great with woe
> And shall deliver weeping. My dearest wife
> Was like this maid, and such a one
> My daughter might have been: my queen's
>   square brows;
> Her stature to an inch; as wand-like
>   straight;
> As silver-voic'd. . . .

After her story is told and Pericles realizes that she is his daughter, he recognizes Helicanus and cries out,

> O Helicanus, strike me, honour'd sir!
> Give me a gash, put me to present pain,
> Lest this great sea of joys rushing upon me
> O'erbear the shores of my mortality,
> And drown me with their sweetness.

He can feel pain again, and even invites it—both to convince himself that she is not a dream of his "dull'd sleep" and to remind himself that pain and sorrow alloy the human life to which he has returned. The sensation of "present pain" marks the falling of the final wall as the corpse emerges from the tomb, revived by a power of Marina's that has reached even deeper than Cerimon's recovery of Thaisa.

All of the heritages of the old tale that crop up at different points in the play—the telling of the tale, the riddles, the tradition of the capital sins—are fused in the magnificent recognition scene between a father and a daughter, a scene about heritages. This is true of the newest heritage in the tale as well, a heritage from the flourishing emblem book tradition of Renaissance Europe. Images derived from emblems have been found throughout Shakespeare's work, and in this play Simonides praises the knights at his banquet with an explicit reference to the emblems and heroic devices that appeared on the title pages of books:

> To place upon the volume of your deeds,
> As in a title-page, your worth in arms,
> Were more than you expect, or more than's
>   fit.
>
> (II.iii.3-5)

It has been known for a century that the devices of the knights in the tournament scene of Act II, a scene

not in either of the play's sources, were drawn from emblem books. Henry Green showed that three of the six devices that the knights presented to Thaisa were adapted from Claude Paradin's *Devises Heroïques* (1551; English translation, 1591), two of them appearing also in Geoffrey Whitney's popular *A Choice of Emblemes* (1586), and that sources for two more can be found in other emblem books.[11] Only for the device of the sixth knight, Pericles, has no source been found. The devices consist of an emblematic image and a motto, or "moral," and they are presented to Thaisa in this order (II.ii):

> First Knight: the device is "a black Ethiop reaching at the sun," and the motto is *Lux tua vita mihi* ("Thy light is life to me")
>
> Second Knight: the device is "an arm'd knight that's conquer'd by a lady," and the motto *Piùe per dolcezza che per forza* ("More by gentleness than by force")
>
> Third Knight: the device is "a wreath of chivalry," the motto *Me pompae provexit apex* ("The crown of the triumph has led me on")
>
> Fourth Knight: the device is "A burning torch that's turned upside down," the motto *Qui me alit, me extinguit* ("Who feeds me extinguishes me")
>
> Fifth Knight: the device is "an hand environed with clouds, Holding out gold that's by the touchstone tried," and the motto is *Sic spectanda fides* ("Thus is faithfulness to be tried")
>
> Sixth Knight: the device is "A wither'd branch, that's only green at top," the motto *In hac spe vivo* ("In this hope I live")

These are not heraldic coats of arms representing the noble lineages of the knights, but devices which each knight designed himself to express his purpose. Mario Praz reminds us that the device does not look back to the past of family glories, but to the knight's own future: the device, or *impresa,* "is nothing else than a symbolical representation of a purpose, a wish, a line of conduct (*impresa* is what one intends to *imprendere,* i.e. to undertake) by means of a motto and a picture which reciprocally interpret each other."[12] Thus Thaisa, asked by her father "to entertain The labour of each knight in his device" (II.ii.15), is reading in the devices not only the knight's artistic accomplishments but also the various lines of conduct each knight sees himself following in the attempt to win her hand. All of the knights are suitors for Thaisa's love: the tournament is part of the labor they have undertaken to win that love, and the devices show their conceptions of that love.

The first knight's device of life dependent on the sun is an emblem of (in the modern sense) necessity; it expresses to Thaisa his view that love is essential to life. The second knight's device, a knight conquered by a lady, views love as conquest, while the third knight's device, the wreath of chivalry, views love as honor. The device of the fourth knight is a torch extinguished by the wax that fed it (cf. the dying fire in Sonnet 73, "Consum'd with that which it was nourish'd by"), and it sees love as paradox. The fifth knight's device is an emblem of faith, expressing this knight's view of love as faith. The device presented by the sixth knight, Pericles, is of course an emblem of hope. Earlier in the play Pericles, the prince of Tyre, had referred to his position as the head of a state as

> no more but as the tops of trees
> Which fence the roots they grow by and
> defend them.
>
> (I.ii.31-32)

Now his roots and support have withered and he is nothing but a shipwrecked man, his only heritage the rusty armor that he wears. His only experience with love also withered at the court of Antiochus. Of all the knights, he in particular can only look forward. The device he presents, a withered branch green only at the top, expresses love as hope. His hope does blossom, we see, for he wins the tournament and he wins Thaisa, but fourteen years later, when Pericles again needs this device, he has lost it. His despair (*wanhope*) is an abandonment of hope and an abandonment of any purpose directed toward the future, yet he is recovered by his future, the fruit of his past hope, in the figure of Marina. Emerging from his self-made tomb, Pericles sees Marina as an emblematic statue, the figure of Patience on a king's tomb—an image, it has been shown, that is also a heritage from the emblem books (Hoeniger, p. 147n):

> yet thou dost look
> Like Patience gazing on kings' graves, and
> smiling
> Extremity out of act.
>
> (V.i.137-39)

Even over a tomb Patience will wait, refusing to believe that time brings only loss and annihilation to human life. The extremities of despair and suicide, the smiling figure shows, are shortsighted acts that forget the future, that forget the emblem of hope and the promise of rebirth in the withered branch. The figure is his daughter, Pericles learns, and she has recovered him with the gifts—"graces"—of word, music, and hope that are her heritages from him.

In the epilogue spoken by Gower at the end of the play, Shakespeare brings together the first and the last heritages of the tale. Gower had begun the play with an emblematic motto for the tale itself, keeping it in another language as the emblematists always felt the motto should be: *Et bonum quo antiquius eo melius*

("And the older a good thing is, the better it is"— I.Cho.10). Now the story-teller steps forward one last time and turns his whole story into an emblem:

> In Antiochus and his daughter you have
> heard
> Of monstrous lust the due and just reward.
> In Pericles, his queen and daughter, seen,
> Although assail'd with fortune fierce and
> keen,
> Virtue preserv'd from fell destruction's
> blast,
> Led on by heaven, and crown'd with joy at
> last.
> In Helicanus may you well descry
> A figure of truth, of faith, of loyalty.
> In reverend Cerimon there well appears
> The worth that learned charity aye wears.

We are reminded that it is an old tale, that it all happened long ago. The long temporal narrative is seen at the last transformed into Gower's emblematic tableau, complete with figures of the Virtues and Vices. As Charles Olson said of Melville's great sea tale, time is here pushed back so far it turns into space,[13] and the space waits for the next story-teller and his audience to enter. In this last flourish, the dramatist has transformed Gower himself into an emblem as well, the figure of the scholar-poet as an emblem of the old tale, its many heritages, and its triumphs over time by the human imagination laboring in faith and hope and love to engender a future.

Notes

[1] Peter Goolden, ed., *The Old English* Apollonius of Tyre (London: Oxford Univ. Press, 1958), p. xii; Elizabeth Hazelton Haight, *More Essays on Greek Romances* (New York: Longmans-Green, 1945), p. 178. Ben Edwin Perry, however, argues in *The Ancient Romances* (Berkeley and Los Angeles: Univ. of California Press, 1967), pp. 294-324, that this romance is unique in being the creation of a Latin author.

[2] R. H. Dawkins, "Modern Greek Oral Versions of Apollonius of Tyre," *MLR,* 37 (1942), 169-84.

[3] F. D. Hoeniger, ed., *Pericles,* New Arden Shakespeare (London: Methuen, 1963), pp. xxiii-lii.

[4] G. Wilson Knight, *The Crown of Life: Essays in Interpretation of Shakespeare's Final Plays* (1947; rpt. London: University Paperbacks, 1965); Derek Traversi, *Shakespeare: The Last Phase* (Stanford, Calif.: Stanford Univ. Press, 1955); Northrop Frye, *A Natural Perspective: The Development of Shakespearean Comedy and Romance* (New York: Columbia Univ. Press, 1965).

[5] II.i.122; all citations from *Pericles* are taken from the New Arden edition by F. D. Hoeniger.

[6] *CA* VIII.271-72, 1152; citations from Gower are taken from *The English Works of John Gower,* ed. G. C. Macaulay, E.E.T.S., Nos. 81-82, 2 vols. (London: Kegan Paul-Trench-Trübner, 1901).

[7] Gower, *CA* VIII.1864-67; Twine, *The Patterne of painefull Adventures,* in *Narrative and Dramatic Sources of Shakespeare,* ed. Geoffrey Bullough, VI (London: Routledge and Kegan Paul, 1966), 474.

[8] P. Goolden, "Antiochus's Riddle in Gower and Shakespeare," *RES,* NS 6 (1955), 246-47, quotes the riddle and works it out ingeniously.

[9] For the background of the tradition and its appearances in medieval English literature see Morton W. Bloomfield, *The Seven Deadly Sins* (Michigan State Univ. Press, 1952).

[10] "*Pericles, Prince of Tyre*: A Study in the Dramatic Use of Romantic Narrative," *SQ,* 4 (1953), 266.

[11] *Shakespeare and the Emblem Writers* (1870; rpt. New York: Burt Franklin, n.d.), pp. 156-86.

[12] *Studies in Seventeenth-Century Imagery,* 2nd ed., Sussidi Eruditi, 16 (Rome: Edizioni di Storia e Letteratura, 1964), p. 58.

[13] *Call Me Ishmael* (San Francisco: City Lights, 1947), p. 14.

Ruth Nevo (essay date 1987)

SOURCE: "The Perils of Pericles," in *The Undiscover'd Country: New Essays on Psychoanalysis and Shakespeare,* edited by B. J. Sokol, Free Association Books, 1993, pp. 150-78.

[*In the following essay First published in 1987, Nevo presents a psychological overview of* Pericles, *focusing on the work's chaotic symbolism and dream-like aspects.*]

A thing which has not been understood inevitably reappears; like an unlaid ghost, it cannot be laid to rest until the mystery is solved and the spell broken.

Sigmund Freud, 'Little Hans'

Pericles, first of Shakespeare's four romance narratives of vicissitude, loss and restoration, is usually regarded as the most tentative, fumbling or inchoate of the four, or not entirely Shakespeare's at all. Critics have been made unhappy not only by a text probably transcribed in part from memory, but also by the Gower narrator's laboured tetrameters, the jerky tempo of frame narration and dramatized episode, the curiously 'phlegmatic' or 'passive' character of the protagonist, and the outlandish events. It is only, it is widely felt, in Act III, with the death of Pericles' wife and the birth of his daughter, that the true Shakespearian fire breaks forth from the flint.

It is certainly a very weird play. Severed heads, more storms and shipwrecks than most readers can confidently count, the miraculous preservation of persons alive under water or dead and unburied on land, a denouement which mixes, if not hornpipes and funerals, at least brothels and betrothals, and a remarkably accident-prone protagonist. 'Most critics', says Ernest Schanzer,

are agreed that, while Acts III, IV and V are substantially Shakespeare's, Acts I and II are not. The questions to be asked, therefore, are: Who is the author of Acts I and II? And how did the non-Shakespearean first two acts come to be joined to the Shakespearean last three acts? (1965, p. xxi)

I would like to ask quite other questions of this text, which seems to me, so far from being fractured, to possess a degree of unity bordering on the obsessive. I shall hope to show that a reading *of,* rather than round, *Pericles'* strangenesses, a reading attentive to the oneiric dimension of its symbolism and the dream-like aspects of its representations, will give the play a rather different specific gravity than is usually attributed to it, and will enable us to find it, once again, convincing. 'Till the closing of the theaters in 1642,' Ernest Schanzer tells us, '*Pericles* seems to have been one of Shakespeare's greatest stage successes' (p. xli). I would like to return the presently undervalued *Pericles* to the canon, finding it, precisely because it is closer to primary process, more anomalous, 'crude', absurd, strange, a representation of elemental and universal fantasy of great power.

The story of Pericles is impossible, of course. So, André Green reminds us, is the tragedy of Oedipus. 'How can the life of a single man pile up such a set of coincidences?' (1979, p. 18) He continues: 'It is not for the psycho-analyst to answer; but rather for the countless spectators of *King Oedipus* who might say, with Aristotle, "a convincing improbability is preferable to what is unconvincing even though it is possible".' What is 'convincing'? Green's answer is implicit in his account of his project: 'The aim of a psycho-analytic reading is the search for the emotional springs that make the spectacle an affective matrix in which the spectator sees himself involved and feels himself not only solicited but welcomed, as if the spectacle were intended for him.' It is with the identification of this matrix, and with the investigation of the symbolic activity which allows us access to it, that I shall be engaged.

The questions I would ask, then, emerge from the following reflections. It is not in dispute that the father/daughter theme in the play is its dominant concern, repeated time after time and, in the reunion scene, treated with an admirably expressive pathos, not granted, for example, to Rosalind's father, or Hero's, who also have their lost daughters returned to them. Why then is the axis of the play's action skewed? It is after all the story of Pericles, but Pericles does not become a father until Act III. At the peak of his fortunes his hard-won wife is snatched from him, his newly-born daughter left motherless in his charge. Then indeed he rages against the storm in language reminiscent of Lear, man of sorrows, and daughters. But the child is immediately abandoned to the care of foster parents. And what of his role up to that point? Is it really a kind of marking time, or fragments of a cobbled-together or corrupt text, or the work of an inferior collaborator? Or rather a chapter in what Coppélia Kahn sees as Shakespeare's lifelong pursuit of 'a dramatic and psychological strategy for dealing not only with our common ambivalence toward our families but specifically with the male passage from being a son to being a father' (1980, p. 217)? This is useful for the situating of Pericles in the life cycle of sons; but when she continues, 'He found it [the strategy] through the romance, in one of its typical patterns of action that I shall call "the providential tempest" . . . this pattern is that of a journey . . . the individual's passage from emotional residence within the family to independence and adulthood' (p. 218), I believe her invocation of the archetypal symbol of the journey blinds her to a false distinction. 'Independence and adulthood' is surely not the opposite, but rather the authentication and clarification of 'emotional residence within the family'. Do we, in other words, ever 'reside' elsewhere than within the family? The 'providential tempest' in the story of Pericles will, I believe, reward closer examination, as will the role of the son in the triad father, daughter, suitor which appears again and again in the play.

Pericles is tragicomedy *comme il fault* according to Renaissance theory, which demanded both extreme peril and happy solution; and Pericles' saga of preposterous and totally fortuitous misfortunes can be moralized without difficulty into a vision of longsufferingness (Barker, 1963), princely excellence (Schanzer, 1965) and the wondrous ways of a mysterious Providence. In this, I suggest, traditional criticism is swallowing the bait of secondary revision which camouflages, or is even itself blind to, the insights that it nevertheless makes available. Traditional criticism characteristically judges the responses of characters to the events which happen to them in terms of ethical, theo-

logical or didactic value systems, or interprets them methodically by means of allegory. It is therefore flustered by the gaps, awkwardnesses, inconsequentialities, archaisms it encounters in a text. Indeed, unless we can read in 'the progressive, educative "official" plot' the threatening 'repetitive process obscurely going on underneath or beyond it' (Brooks, P., 1980, p. 511), we will very probably find 'no solution to the problems of *Pericles*' (Edwards, 1976, p. 41), no alternative to the dismissal of *Pericles* as a mere blueprint, or rehearsal, for the greater plays to follow.

T.S. Eliot once said that 'meanings' in poetry were like the meat the burglar throws to the house-dog to keep him quiet while it gets on with its proper business. He was, perhaps, paraphrasing Freud, who remarked, drily, that 'it is the much abused privilege of conscious activity, wherever it plays a part, to conceal every other activity from our eyes' (1900b, p. 774). We need to cap these gnomic sayings with the programmatic Lacan, who, intent on that 'other activity', that 'proper business', says, 'every unsuccessful [verbal] act is a successful, not to say "well turned", discourse . . . and exactly in the right quarter for its word to be sufficient to the wise' (1966, p. 58). The passage of interpretation from signifier on the stage—perhaps odd or crude to the rationally disciplined eye—to signified of 'that other scene'—and 'Is it not that the theater is the best embodiment of that "other scene", the unconscious? It is that other scene' (Green, 1979, p. 1)—requires a reading 'wise' to the 'tentacular network' of the normally forgotten or repressed, for, and I quote Green again, 'in the long succession of signifiers in linked sequence which constitutes the work, the unconscious signified rises . . . from the gulf or absence in which it resides . . . not in order to express what has to be said, but in order to indicate, by veiling it, what needs to be hidden' (1979, p. 28). 'Every literary narrative', says Geoffrey Hartman, 'contains another narrative . . . discontinuous and lacunary' (1978, p. 102). In order for 'the outward movement of the plot to become an inward movement of the mind' (Skura, 1980b, p. 212) it is this other narrative that we must attempt to pursue.

One cannot do better than to begin at the beginning, for this is a play which begins with a bang. The presenter, Gower, puts the audience in complete possession of the ugly facts, and the quite extraordinary circumstances in which the young pretender to the hand of the Syrian princess makes his suit. There is a riddle to be explicated and the cost of failure to do so is graphically depicted by a gruesome row of severed heads: the remains of previous contenders in this risky enterprise. This is not an inviting scenario. It is, as the audience knows, a classic double-bind: if he solves the riddle he falls a prey to Antiochus' rage at being discovered. If he doesn't, he dies. Freudian symbologists will immediately identify a castration fantasy. Traditional criticism has chosen to ignore or play down any such specificity in the threat, repressing its terrors and regarding it simply as a rather melodramatic launching pad for Pericles' adventures. It is, for example, simply 'by the discovery of hidden evil', according to Traversi, that Pericles is 'driven . . . to abandon his first dream of felicity' (1969, p. 265).

Traditional criticism, in fact, has not taken the opening quite seriously. If we do take it, and the fantasy that it represents, seriously, however, if we decide not to detach so startling an opening from its unconscious moorings, we will at once discover a great deal else that suddenly figures in Pericles' responses, much as Napoleon's hat will suddenly emerge from among the leaves of a tree, in the children's puzzle game used by Leclaire and Laplanche as a model for the absent presence of unconscious representations (Skura, 1980b, p. 204). Note, for example, the timbre, and the content, of Pericles' opening speech at his first sight of the beautiful daughter of Antiochus, 'apparelled like the spring' (I,i,12), in whose face, it seems, 'sorrow were ever ras'd, and testy wrath/ Could never be her mild companion' (17-18). Conventional enough, no doubt, on the face of it, these praises, but not every young lover admires in his mistress the absence of attributes (sorrow, wrath) not usually associated with youth and love at all. More is to come. Where Antiochus likens his daughter to the golden apples of the Hesperides, defended by 'death-like dragons' (27, 29), Pericles associates the gratification of his desire with the dangerous and forbidden fruit whose eating is the source and origin in Genesis of sexual guilt, and of death:

> You gods, that made me man, and sway in
>   love,
> That have inflam'd desire in my breast
> To take the fruit of you celestial tree
> (Or die in th'adventure), give me your helps
> As I am son and servant to your will . . .
>
> (19-22)

What, in this context, can we make of the homiletic meekness with which he turns to Antiochus:

> Antiochus, I thank thee, who hath taught
> My frail mortality to know itself,
> And by those fearful objects to prepare
> This body, like to them, to what I must;
> For death remembered should be like a
>   mirror,
> Who tells us life's but breath, to trust it
>   error.
> I'll make my will then, and as sick men do,
> Who know the world, see heaven, but
>   feeling woe,
> Gripe not at earthly joys as erst they did . . .
>
> (41-55)

Is this not, Christian-stoical though it may seem, somewhat cold for an ardent lover? Is there not the trace of more than a conventional *contemptus mundi* here? A dyspepsia, a melancholy, a lassitude of the will to live and love? This young lover, it seems, is preternaturally ready to envisage his own body in the image of an (already) severed head, preternaturally ready to 'make his will . . . as sick men do'. He bequeaths, he says, his 'riches to the earth from whence they came;/ But [his] unspotted fire of love' to the Princess (52-3). The odd splitting and the opposition draw attention to an unspoken tension within the rhetoric. The riches that he bequeaths to Mother Earth can only in the context be his body—rich to him as to any man—and it is this body that stands in opposition to the 'unspotted' fire of love. It, therefore, by implication, is what is spotted. The sense of carnal taint is the stronger for the evasive displacement. This suggestion of a sexual anxiety in Pericles' deference to the father of his hoped-for bride magnetizes the apparently banal figures of speech in Antiochus' warning: 'because thine *eye/* Presumes to reach, all the whole *heap* must die . . . / Yon . . . princes/ Tell thee, with speechless *tongues* . . . / And with dead *cheeks* advise thee to desist' (32-9 *passim;* my italics). The body imagery speaks a subtle and menacing sexuality, at once desire and threat.

It is upon this textual ground, so to speak, that the seed of the riddle falls. We, of course, know the answer to the riddle because we have been told of the incest; and for that reason we may miss its central symbolic import, its own crucial condensation. Let us recall it:

> I am no viper, yet I feed
> On mother's flesh which did me breed.
> I sought a husband, in which labour
> I found that kindness in a father.
> He's father, son, and husband mild;
> I mother, wife—and yet his child.
>
> (64-9)

The riddle, it will be noticed, is a riddle because it introduces a third, complicating term into the incest relation between father and daughter: the absent mother. Antiochus is father and husband to his daughter quite literally. How is he her son, she his mother? The expression 'feeding [like a viper] upon mother's flesh' is metaphorically tenable for the daughter whether taken to mean simply 'taking that which belongs to my mother', or whether relayed through the prior metaphor which makes man and wife one flesh (cf. *Hamlet,* IV, iii,52). Shakespeare's innovation was to make the implied speaker the daughter rather than Antioch as in older versions of the tale.[1] There is a moment during which the solution of the riddle hovers indeterminately between father and daughter: the viper might pick up the previous Eden associations and so keep the riddle's 'I' within the feminine orbit, or it might be

Patrick Wymark as Boult and Geraldine McEwan as Marina in Tony Richardson's 1958 production.

phallic and so masculinize the whole grotesque image. That Pericles himself is the reader of the riddle, hence our conduit to it, is important in this respect, especially in the theatre. There is a certain double-take, therefore, in the deciphering of the riddle. The daughter feeds upon her mother's rightful possession—her own father; but Antiochus too can be said to feed upon mother's flesh—the issue of the mother who is (or was) his own wife. Antiochus is father and husband to his daughter literally but it is only by trope that he is her son, she his mother. It is just this metaphorical condensation that the riddle performs, making Antiochus' daughter/wife his surrogate mother: 'he's father, *son,* and husband mild' (my italics).

The riddle is constructed like a dream as Freud expounded the dream work. It is the dream work methodized: condensation, displacement, representation in pictorial image all cunningly tricked out by secondary revision into the form of the conventional riddle. The absurdities, or catachreses, are instantly penetrated by Pericles, as if the enigma were to him transparent. As

indeed it is. 'All love the womb that their first being bred' (I,i,107), he says, summing up the meaning of the King's evil; but how is this the meaning? Philip Edwards says, 'This puts the incest the wrong way round, son and mother' (1976, p. 145) and suggests textual corruption. Is it not possible that 'the wrong way round' is the right way up, the essence of the matter, a parapraxis if you will, or slip of the text—the desire of the mother being shared, in unconscious complicity, by these two mirror-image oedipal contenders?

The traumatic experience at Antioch precipitates Pericles' return home, causes his subsequent flight, hence his first shipwreck, hence his arrival in Pentapolis and so forth; but its function as casual event in a linear series does not exhaust its significance. Indeed, we can read the play's events as causing the Pericles story, but we can also read the Pericles story as motivating the events. Drama is peculiarly the art of the present tense, but in its present, as in all presences, is contained the unrecognized past, the other 'uncensored draft' of the history (Lacan, 1977, p. 51). As psychoanalysis teaches us, 'What is forgotten is recalled in acts.' Lost to conscious memory the past reproduces itself as an unmastered force in the present. We 'follow' the fable unfolding before us 'with cunning delays and ever-mounting excitement' (Freud, 1900b, p. 363) as a tissue of surprises, as if their end were undetermined; at the very same time we move backwards through a retrospective succession of partial recognition scenes. We move back and forth in a shuttle which enables us to find relationships between the end towards which we progress and the beginning to which we return ('to know the place for the first time'). Drama, the supremely metaleptic art, resembles, as Freud observed, the 'remembering, repeating and working through' of psychoanalysis more than any other form of narrative.[2]

Interestingly, in *Pericles,* because of the narrator Gower, the dual textual functions of relating and enacting are separated. Gower is the only continuous narrator/presenter in Shakespeare. Like the chorus in *Henry V* or Time in *The Winter's Tale,* but unlike other mediating or parabastic figures, he *only* addresses the audience, never the dramatis personae.[3] This has the effect of distancing or framing the events, and creating a split in the audience between empathetic participation and critical awareness somewhat as in the Brechtian alienation effect. Only here, since Gower is a character accompanying the whole play, and since the historical Gower has already told the story before in the *Confessio Amantis,* the effect is of a *mise-en-abyme,* a telling within a telling. What is shown and what is told seem fairly arbitrary. Events (some of which wehave ourselves witnessed) are recapitulated, other events are anticipated in narrative discourse; a nodal change-producing occurrence is mimed; further events, unrepresentable practically speaking, like the storms and shipwrecks, are reported. Gower's punctuation of the sequence of direct dramatic enactment by alternating narration and dumb-show foregrounds the question of selection and deletion in narration itself; for that matter the question of the authentic as against the authenticated—the re-told. The Gower figure offers his tale to the audience 'for restoratives'; he steps out on stage between the audience and the dramatis personae; he interferes. He constantly requests his audience to conjure up for themselves events anticipated or recapitulated: 'In your imagination hold/ This stage the ship' (III, Chorus, 58-9). I suggest that we can regard him as a kind of threshold figure—indeterminately analyst and censor, a mediator both vehicle and obstacle. It is as if either the unconscious of the text, like an analysand, strove to communicate a deeper, more inward substance, but was constrained by some inner resistance to offer a processed or prepackaged version. Or, as in Peter Brooks's notion of 'the erotics of form' (1987), as if the text was leading us on with pre-images to some anticipated consumma-

tion or resolution, yet delaying progress by returns and repetitions. We are sensitized by Gower's mediation to levels of consciousness, and to functions of the telling. Gower remembers, and recounts the story; Pericles re-enacts it; and the re-enacting itself, *en abyme,* is a compulsive repetition.

What Antiochus thus triggers in Pericles, by way of the condensations of primary process fantasy, is we intuit, a repetition of himself, an unconscious recognition. Antiochus is his uncanny double; and the progress of the play is the haunting of Pericles by the Antiochus in himself, the incest fear which he must repress and from which he must flee. For Pericles, who, it will be recalled, referred to himself as 'son' to Antiochus (I,iv,24,27), already at the outset is, as we have seen, in the grip of the oedipal guilt which Freud, in *The Ego and the Id,* characterizes as 'the pure culture of the death instinct . . . [which] often enough succeeds in driving the ego into death, if the latter does not fend off its tyrant in time by the change round into mania' (1923, p. 394). Pericles is indeed very nearly driven into death or mania as the play proceeds, but we are not, I submit, to see this as a matter of contingent circumstance alone. Rather, to understand *Pericles* is to see that the Pericles figure—the Periclean fantasy—is always already death-driven.

Let us once more attend to the drama's text as it proceeds with its articulation of the fantasy it both veils and reveals. The predicament presented in Act I, scene i, produces a delayed action, like a time bomb. Pericles abandons his courtship, of course, flees Antioch, and goes back home to Tyre; but there he falls into an inexplicable melancholy. He is surrounded by courtly pleasures; his thoughts have 'revolted' against the 'sweetest flower' once, but no longer, desired; danger is at a distance, in Antioch, and yet he can find no peace.

> Why should this change of thoughts,
> The sad companion, dull-ey'd melancholy,
> [Be my] so us'd a guest as not an hour
> In the day's glorious walk or peaceful
>   night,
> The tomb where grief should sleep, can
>   breed me quiet?
>
> (I,ii,1-5)

Why, indeed? On the face of it he does have a plausible reason for fear, and for the flight he decides upon. The long arm of the King, whose secret he discovered, will surely pursue him and

> With hostile forces he'll o'erspread the land,
> And with [th'ostent] of war will look so
>   huge,
> Amazement shall drive courage from the
>   state,

Our men be vanquish'd ere they do resist,
And subjects punish'd that ne'er thought
    offence.

                                    (I,ii,24-8)

The apparent plausibility of this argument must strike us as disingenuous. Its worst-case reasoning is exaggerated, unnerved. It is surely odd for a prince so avidly to envisage defeat, and critics have been properly dismayed at such strangely unrulerlike behavior. How can we account for it? The speech continues thus:

Which care of them, not pity of myself—
Who [am] no more but as the tops of
    trees,
Which fence the roots they grow by and
    defend them—
Makes both my body pine and soul to
    languish,
And punish that before that he would
    punish.

                                    (29-33)

The disavowal of self-pity suggests its presence, and we note the insistence on the notion of punishment (as opposed for example to revenge or retaliation). Why so much punishment? What crime has been committed (by Pericles) that his thoughts should be so full of punishment? What, moreover, in this deviant syntax, is the subject of the first 'punish' in line 33? It is, or it should be, 'care of them', which precedes the embedded subordinate clause. 'Care of them', however, requires a third person verb. The absence of such a form derails the syntax at that point and generates a search for a possible alternative. If we read 'punish' as an infinitive (correlative to 'to languish') our alternative subject becomes 'soul'. Thus: 'Care of them makes my body pine, and my soul to languish and to punish that (myself) before he (Antioch) does.' Pericles needs the remonstrances of his loyal and candid counsellor (51-124) to crystallize the decision to set sail from Tyre, and to justify the decision as the action of a noble Prince ready to remove himself, a *casus belli*, from the scene; but the packed syntax reveals to us that it is a self-inflicted punitive suffering from which he flees. Why? A powerful potential enemy is an ostensible reason for his flight. That that potential enemy is an intimidating father-figure, law-maker, and beheader, possessed of a (significantly nameless) daughter/mother/bride—'an O without a figure' (*Lear* I,iv,193)—is suggestive of preliminary conditions; but the immediate precipitating source of his dread—an archaic energy at work like Hamlet's old mole—is specific: it is that *he has uncovered* the King's terrible secret. The primal scene of the play—Act I, scene i—triggers a primal-scene fantasy for Pericles, which powers thenceforth his guilt-stricken, haunted drivenness.[4]

But his sallying forth is not only fugue. At all events, as it turns out, it acquires major value and virtue through the role of feeder and saviour he is enabled to play in famine-stricken Tarsus. There, Cleon reports, once fastidious palates now beg for bread, man and wife draw lots to decide who shall die first, there is scarcely strength left to bury the dead, and

Those mothers who, to nousle up their
    babes,
Thought nought too curious, are ready
    now
To eat those little darlings whom they
    lov'd.

                                    (I,iv,42-4)

These are dismaying, and resonant, images to appear in the description of the plight of Tarsus.[5] And he is not permitted to remain a saviour for long. These devouring mothers mark the oscillation of longing and fear, fight and flight which is the rhythm of Pericles' wayfaring. The next phase of the action is introduced by Gower again recounting the initiating incest story, and by his dumb show, in which bad news is delivered of pursuit from Tyre. Act II opens with Pericles' address to the elements when he finds himself cast up upon the shore at Pentapolis after the wreck of his escape ship.

Bred on the thunderous eloquence of Lear we may find these lines at first somewhat threadbare; but it is a speech worthy of remark in several respects.

Yet cease your ire, you angry stars of
    heaven!
Wind, rain, and thunder, remember earthly
    man
Is but a substance that must yield to you;
And I (as fits my nature) do obey you.
Alas, the seas hath cast me on the rocks,
Wash'd me from shore to shore, and left
    [me] breath
Nothing to think on but ensuing death.
Let it suffice the greatness of your powers
To have bereft a prince of all his fortunes;
And having thrown him from your wat'ry
    grave,
Here to have death in peace is all he'll
    crave.

                                    (II,i,1-11)

Pericles has every cause for distress at this point—'All perishen of man, of pelf, / Ne aught escapend but himself' (II, Chorus, 35-6)—but it will be noticed that there is no reference in his lament to the loss of the ship, or the sailors, nor any reference to the trauma of the wreck itself; nor for that matter is there any rejoicing or thanksgiving, however qualified, regarding his own escape. It is a total submission, a capitulation, that he expresses, and the powers to whom he capitulates are given, by the nature and the configuration of the imagery, a distinctly familial cast; the paternal, wrathfully punitive sky elements which it is 'his nature' to obey; the maternal ocean from which he has emerged. We note the casting upon rocks, immediately displaced by the rocking motion ('wash'd me from shore to shore') suggesting a cradle, or womb; but he is a castaway upon this rocky shore, breathless and bereft, and it is a 'wat'ry grave' from which he has been thrown. The passage is indissolubly ambivalent: whether he wishes or fears this womb/grave is impossible to determine—the condensation is, precisely, a compromise formation. The parent-child configuration gives a particular tinge to the melancholy he expresses, the deep depression, the dispirited craving for death. We discern the backward drift of an unresolved, unnamed preoccupation. We perceive the stance of a son whose rebellious rage against a parental couple—sky-father and sea-mother—has turned inward against himself.

This is the first of the play's sea journeys, which mark the pendulum swing of desire and dread, outgoing and withdrawal in the psychodrama which we follow. The play enacts its complex fantasy by repeated emergings from the sea, repeatedly foiled by the sea tempests themselves—a collusion of both parental figures in a rejecting fury. Pericles is dogged by mischance, but do not these chances as Freud said 'reflect the destiny which has decreed that through flight one is delivered over to the very thing that one is fleeing from'? That the sea, Pericles' constant refuge, and betrayer, giver and taker, destroyer and restorer, is a powerful presence in the play, has escaped no interpreter but its import has been found bewildering. 'The unlikelihood of the events,' says Philip Edwards,

> the lack of cause-and-effect in the plot, make the play a presentation of images which, while individually they expand into wide and general meanings, yet as a whole sequence withdraw from asserting how things run in this world. We are offered ideas or propositions about love and suffering and chastity, and the relation of them to a divine will, but we are not offered a clue to any meaning lying in the progression of events. The sea, therefore, remains a mystery. (1976, p. 31)

Yet his own description of 'the sea of life, the flow of unaccountable circumstances in which we drift' contains more of the clue he seeks than, it seems, he realizes: 'The sea threatens and comforts, destroys and rebuilds, separates and unites' (p. 17). Archetypal symbol of vicissitude in human life—yes; but 'oceanic', it will be recalled, was Freud's term for those fantasies of merging, union and dissolution which are rooted in yearnings for the primal symbiosis of infant

and mother; and it is not without relevance to remember the interesting image used by the melancholy wandering Antipholus in *The Comedy of Errors*: [6]

> He that commends me to mine own content,
> Commends me to the thing I cannot get:
> I to the world am like a drop of water,
> That in the ocean seeks another drop,
> Who, falling there to find his fellow forth
> (Unseen, inquisitive), confounds himself.
> So I, to find a mother and a brother,
> In quest of them (unhappy), ah, lose myself.
> (I.ii.33-40)

The mere identification of a symbol is no more than is available in any dictionary of symbols. Simply to name is to vivisect, as Freud himself warned (though he often sinned himself in this respect (see Freud, 1900b, pp. 496-529), failing to distinguish between hallucinatory infantile visual symbolization and subtly complex verbal derivatives). The sea has been with us, and in our iconologies, for a very long time, but there is a pre-Freudian and a post-Freudian way of attending to symbols. In 1899, in his Notes to *The Wind among the Reeds*, Yeats speaks of 'some neo-platonist [who] describes the sea as a symbol of the drifting indefinite bitterness of life'; in 1932, in his Notes to *Fighting the Waves*, 'a German psychoanalyst', he says, 'has traced the "mother-complex" back to our mother the sea—to the loneliness of the first crab or crayfish that climbed ashore and turned lizard' (Yeats, 1899, p. 66; 1932, p. 571). Yeats makes my point. What the play *Pericles* wonderfully captures, obsessively reiterates, is, indeed, the rhythm of vicissitude in human life, the rhythm of maturation: separation, dispossession, return, under the cross of guilt, where three roads meet. The original loss, or lack, or absence, psychoanalytic theory tells us, is always the same; but its individual manifestations are always different, for it is through an endlessly varied chain of displaced signifiers that we strive, in language, to reconstitute the ever-receding, forever lost state of undifferentiated wholeness that was the bliss, and the fate, of the speechless infant.

Yeats's note treats evolutionary biology with considerable poetic licence, but let us, adopting his metaphor, pursue the adventures of our 'lizard'. It is the sequence of his recovery at this point which is particularly worth remarking.

Pericles climbs ashore at Pentapolis, and meets fishermen who have acerbic and foolish-wise things to say about the inequalities of the worldly world, where 'the great ones eat up the little ones' (II,i,28) like whales, who would swallow all, 'parish, church, steeple, bells, and all' (34). The Third Fisherman caps this parable with his own: 'when I had been in his belly, I would have kept such a jangling of the bells, that he should never have left till he cast bells, steeple, church, and parish up again' (40-3). What the 'whale', or sea, casts up is in fact the dripping Pericles: 'What a drunken knave was the sea to cast thee in our way!' (58)

Ancient paradigms have suggested themselves as models for the wanderings and sufferings of Pericles, in particular Ulysses, and the long-suffering Job; but in the light of the imagery in which the fishermen's observations are cast, Jonah would seem to be no less suitable a candidate (see Nathan, 1956). Not that these figures need be mutually exclusive. Texts wander about the world in each other's company, as we know, no less than romance protagonists. But, it will be remembered, Jonah too fled from commitment, sank deeper and deeper into withdrawal during his three days aboard— a fugue which culminated in the belly of the whale— and was spewed forth to take up his mission again willy-nilly. Once again it is such derivatives of the primal oral infantile fantasies of eating and being eaten which lend support to the theory of 'the other story', the repressed or censored draft. Pericles' first response to the fishermen's questions is that of a passive victim—mere tennis ball (like Bosola) to the waters and the wind; 'a man throng'd up with cold' (73), he envisages death and imagines his own burial; but when the good King Simonides is referred to, and the joust that he plans, at which suitors will 'tourney for the love of his fair daughter', Pericles regains a will to live. 'Were my fortunes equal to my desires,' he says, 'I could wish to make one there' (111-12). Whereupon, hey presto, what should emerge from the sea in the fisherman's net but—his dead father's armour! This is a blessing, obviously, since it provides Pericles with the means to pursue honour, and a bride, at the court of Pentapolis; but for this purpose any treasure chest, or for that matter any suit of armour from the sunken ship would have served. Pericles' father's armour is talisman and symbol as well as blessing. Bequeathed in the father's will, it defended the father as the latter hopes it may defend his son. In the dream language of condensation, wearing it, blessedly belched forth out of the sea, Pericles both is, and is safe from, his dead father. He 'becomes' his father, legitimately, even obligatorily, as he sets forth upon his second courtship adventure.

In *Pericles* the psychomachia—the motivations at war within the protagonist, the bonds and bindings, the desires and fears which constitute for him his impossible choice—is not explicit, not immediately to be perceived. We are listening with the third ear, catching the unspoken filtering into discourse in the underhand ways the unspoken has of speaking. Ostensibly what Pericles contends with is the weather, the ocean, the winds and the waves, or competing knights at a tourney; but consider the scene of the tourney, or rather the scene which, significantly, takes the place, and at some length, of any staged combat.

The actual tourney, which takes place off stage, is prefaced by a procession of the contender knights each bearing a shield with an emblematic device and an explanatory Latin tag. On the face of it, and at the level of the represented world of the fable, what we are presented with here is simply a piece of chivalric decoration. We may entertain ourselves (as do the courtiers—the hermeneutic game of emblems was very popular in the seventeenth century) checking the match of tag to enigma, wondering what riddle will come next and what Pericles' contribution will be. The emblem game consisted of pictorializing epigrams or sententiae of extreme and uncontextualized generality: 'a black Ethiop reaching at the sun . . . *Lux tua vita mihi*' (II,ii.20-1); 'a hand environed with clouds,/ Holding out gold that's by the touchstone tried . . . *Sic spectanda fides*' (36-8); and so on. The connection between image and idea was often enough conventional, but the game became popular and interesting, worth playing indeed, in so far as the images were derived from the motto by rebus-like or arcane associations of one kind or another, or by what we would call today 'free' association. The resemblance to the techniques of dream, here as in the first riddle, is again striking: condensation, displacement, pictorialization and secondary revision; and we have a context—threatening parental figures, an imagery of bodily injury, menace and engulfment, which, if not repressed by readers, will magnetize the whole semiotic environment.

We can read the knights, minimally identified and all identical in aim, as essentially all one knight—projections of Pericles himself. We can read these images as mirrors in which Pericles reads himself, or as signifiers given meaning in Pericles' dream. The anomalies, paradoxes or absurdities at the level of the signifier solicit *our* interpretation; the ulterior signifieds, his. The devices are all configurations of ambivalence, the repressed unconscious fear concealed by the decorous mask of the mottos' secondary elaboration which expresses the conventional devotions and tribulations of courtly desire. Thus, while *'Lux tua vita mihi'* suggests an appropriate knightly ardour, the Ethiop in the emblem is (also) a black, or blackened, or shadowed Icarus, an overweening son against the sun. The armed knight that is conquered by the lady bears the unexceptionably courtly message: *'Piu per dolcezza che per forza'* (27), but this could be taken literally (as is the way of dreams) as referring to an actual conquest by a woman, and so articulates ambivalent wishing and fearing. In the symbology of dreams, crowns and wreaths, metamorphoses of that most fertile of all figures, the circle, are genital displacements upwards (see Willbern, 1980, pp. 244-64). The burning torch turned upside down, to show that 'beauty hath his power and will,/Which can as well inflame as it can kill' (34-5), has for motto *'Qui me alit, me extinguit'* ('Who feeds me puts me out')—again a thralldom of desire and dread, which plugs, with splendid over-determination, into oral, filial and sexual anxieties. The image of the hand holding out gold from amidst clouds to be tested by the touchstone (36-7) is surely very strange and obscure unless we can see an (anal)ogy to infantile anxieties about producing and withholding, while the 'country knight's' own phallic device, a withered branch with a green tip (43), once again marvellously symbolizes an irresolvable ambivalence of hope and fear.

Pericles, despite his rusty armour, wins the tourney and Thaisa's heart; and Simonides, good king, not bedazzled by outward show, recognizes the inner worth of his impeccably courteous future son-in-law: but is it courtesy, or a humility bordering upon a surrender-ing self-abasement? Perhaps the most revealing mo-ment in these scenes is the melancholy knight's own aside immediately after his victory at the tourney. A triumphant winner at this point, what he says is as follows:

> [Yon] king's to me like to my father's
>   picture,
> Which tells [me] in that glory once he was;
> Had princes sit like stars about his throne,
> And he the sun for them to reverence . . .
> Where now his [son's] like a glow-worm in
>   the night,
> The which hath fire in darkness, none in
>   light.
>
> (II,iii,37-44)

At the point of winning his fair bride Pericles' self-estimation has, strangely, never been lower, nor his guilty self-abasement more explicit. If we reverse the son/sun homonym, moreover, the tempting/frightening possibility of usurping the father-figure comes again into view: 'And he the son for them to reverence . . . / Where now his sun's like a glow-worm in the night.' Danger—of supplanting the father—is inherent in suc-cess. That which is dangerous—*pericoloso*—is em-bedded in Pericles' name.[7] Moreover the play reiter-ates its obsessions in other figures besides Pericles. Simonides, despite his acceptance of the match, is not immune to paternal jealousy.

> By Jove, I wonder, that is king of thoughts,
> These cates resist me, he but thought
>   upon.[8]
>
> (28-9)

This pang of resentment is at once dissimulated as a testing of his daughter's feelings for 'but a country gentleman' who has 'done no more than other knights have done' (33). Scene iii concludes with the utmost amity on his part towards Pericles, yet scene v repeats the whole premarital testing sequence, with Simonides acting out a Brabantio-like rage towards Pericles—

'Thou hast bewitch'd my daughter and thou art/ A villain' (II,v,49-50)—and a blocking father's tyranny to his daughter:

> I'll tame you; I'll bring you in subjection.
> Will you, not having my consent,
> Bestow your love and your affections
> Upon a stranger?
>
> (75-8)

Whether we read Simonides' dissembling as simply for the purpose of testing Pericles' character, or as an acting out of his own fatherly ambivalence ('Nay, how absolute she's in't, / Not minding whether I dislike or no!' (19-20)) is immaterial. The question is how this unwilling son will respond to Simonides' assault. Pericles' initial response is to abase himself, to disavow all aims or claims to Thaisa's hand, to plead like a scolded child. Yet suddenly, at the charge of treachery, he rises to defend his honour at sword's point.

Pericles, it would seem, is a kaleidoscopically waver-ing character. He oscillates between listlessness and energy, withdrawal and outgoingness, defence or flight and attack. He seeks a wife, a family. He is a respon-sible king. He can rouse himself to courageous action despite his diffidence, as we have seen, and phonemic ambiguities (son/sun) may serve as cover for a con-siderable urge to self-assertion. Yet he withdraws, gives up, wanders away, evades, or is foiled. What happens to him is invariably what he fears, not what he hopes, as if the elements conspire with a self-fulfilling proph-ecy. The chorus which opens Act III images sexual fulfillment, achievement, but at once comes terrible reversal. Pericles loses his wife in a tempest at sea as his daughter is born. In terms of tragic structure this is as it should be: a fall from a height of power and prosperity. But the constant repeat or reiteration of such events is itself a message which solicits our attention. These vicissitudes of fortune can be read, at one level, simply as such. Ostensibly they represent the turn of Fortune's wheel, now up, now down, testing Pericles' powers of endurance with its muta-tions; but if, at a level more covert, the sea is a dis-placed signifier of the maternal oceanic, then Pericles' tale is very easily retold. 'If what Freud discovered and rediscovers with a perpetually increasing sense of shock has a meaning,' says Lacan,

> it is that the displacement of the signifier determines the subjects in their acts, in their destiny, in their refusals, in their blindnesses, in their end and in their fate, their innate gifts and social acquisitions notwithstanding, without regard for character or sex, and that, willingly or not, everything that might be considered the stuff of psychology, kit and caboodle, will follow the path of the signifier. (1972, p. 60)

Pericles travels out and away and back. He cannot escape, cannot cut the umbilical cord, and cannot resolve the later oedipal guilt. The sea is indeed his beloved enemy, as the sun-father is his envied and hostile rival. Antiochus represents at the outset the threatening father-figure, and whatever person Pericles seeks is a symbolic personage representing the mother, lost and forbidden. It is therefore always by the incest fear that he is haunted. Derivatives of these primal constellations erupt in language and situation throughout: the very name he gives his daughter is the name of the sea.

It is as such a haunting fantasy, I think, that we can read the report of Helicanus in Tyre of the exposure of Antiochus' incest with his daughter (it is the third time we have been told of it) and of their terrible fate. This report is apparently arbitrarily intercalated between the two scenes in which Simonides plays the role of a threatening father, rather as in a film when shots from another time and place are interpolated into a sequence to represent an image in the mind. Seated in a chariot with his daughter:

A fire from heaven came and shrivell'd up
Those bodies, even to loathing; for they so
    stunk,
That all those eyes ador'd them ere their fall
Scorn now their hand should give them
    burial.

(II,iv,9-12)

The blocking father and the incestuous daughter are dead, indeed, but their nightmare image continues to haunt; the shrivelled bodies stink to high heaven, unburied, preserved mysteriously as images of fear and horror and loathing as yet unexorcized.

The nightmare is the obverse of the oceanic dream; the prohibition of its siren lure. It is the tempests at sea, with their lightning and thunder, that repeatedly overthrow him. It is perhaps not without significance that Pericles' address to the storm recalls that of Lear, who would have set his rest upon Cordelia's 'kind nursery'.

    O, still
Thy deaf'ning dreadful thunders, gently
    quench
Thy nimble, sulphurous flashes! . . .
. . . [Thou] storm, venomously
Wilt thou spet all thyself?

(III,i,4-7)

The jealous, tempestuous sea takes Thaisa, yet once again the sea spews its victims (Pericles himself, or his wife, or his daughter) forth, in the struggle to be born again. The mortal combat between Thanatos and Eros is given in the second part of the play with a verbal felicity and resonance to which no critic can fail to respond. Consider the peculiarly evocative speech in which he consigns Thaisa to the waves, which contains within its compassion ('A terrible childbed hast thou had, my dear;/No light, no fire' (56-7)) the Jonah death-wish, the great desire to be, at last, at peace, beneath the 'humming water' and 'the belching whale', 'lying with simple shells' (62-4). (On shells see Bachelard, 1964, chapter 5.)

The recovery of Thaisa in Act III, scene ii is manifestly a compensatory birth or rebirth fantasy: out of the chest/coffin emerges a sweet-smelling 'corse'. Why does the play need a birth fantasy, and a nourishing father (in the life-giving physician Cerimon: 'hundreds call themselves/Your creatures' (III,ii,44-5)) when it has the real birth of Marina?; and how can we account for his leaving the babe, that 'fresh new seafarer' (III,i,41), to be reared by Cleon and Dionyza while he retreats into the monkish garb of a Nazirite? The tragic reversal of Act III, culminating in the tempest which kills Thaisa, is transformed by amazing happenstance into a happy reunion, with the sea giving up its 'dead' and a reconstituted, benign family configuration replacing the monstrous union of the first act. However, this comic resolution is due to happenstance only in terms of the 'official' or exterior plot. If we read 'the repetitive process obscurely going on underneath or beyond it' (Brooks, P., 1980, p. 511), expressing itself indirectly through the very means which veil it, much of great interest becomes apparent.

The recovery of Thaisa, belched forth from the sea, is a rebirth fantasy in the text, to which we, the audience, are privy, but in the progress of the fable her loss at sea represents regression in Pericles. As his abandonment of his baby daughter to the care of others also indicates, he is still not enfranchised, not ready to accept fatherhood, still haunted by the spectre of incest. Lear, as the Fool tells him, made his daughters his mother; Pericles cannot permit himself to love his daughter, lest he desire her—and when he dares, it is too late.

Years later, he 'again thwart[s] the wayward seas . . . /To see his daughter, all his live's delight' (IV,iv,10-12) and to bring her home. He finds her, as he believes, in her grave. That Pericles will suffer grievously over this loss hardly needs explanatory comment, but Gower's comment points interestingly to the relation between mourning and melancholia which was in due course (three hundred years and a decade later) to become a Freudian theme. 'He swears', Gower informs us, 'Never to wash his face, nor cut his hairs;/ He [puts] on sackcloth, and to sea. He bears/ A tempest, which his mortal vessel tears,/ And yet he rides it out' (27-31). Tempest-tossed, death-possessed, he has become fixed in the mortified posture which acts out the wish to die that is born of the conviction that he deserves to die.

The play's remedial and recognitive last two acts will tell us that what Pericles needs is not the return of his wife or the birth of a child but a rebirth for himself. Not until Pericles' lost and found daughter 'beget'st himthat did [her] beget' (V,i,195), as he puts it, is the tempest which his mortal vessel tears at last stilled. But is it? And how shall we integrate into our reading the grotesqueries of Mytilene?

The 'absolute' Marina, it will be recalled, is done away with by her jealous foster mother—a figure who reappears as Imogen's stepmother in *Cymbeline,* and, as the witch Sycorax, lurks in the background of Prospero's island. Her own daughter is put in the shade, so she feels, by Marina's surpassing excellence in the womanly arts and virtues. Cleon protests, but is overborne by his Goneril-like queen. This weak and recessive father cannot save his step-daughter from the assault of the dominant mother, since he is undermined by Dionyza's taunts of cowardice. Is Cleon, proxy father for Pericles, also his masochistic self-image? 'In the dream,' André Green reminds us, 'when the dreamer's representation becomes overloaded, the dreamer splits it into two and sets up another character to represent, separately, one or more of his characteristics or affects' (1979, p. 2).[9] This will prove a useful principle with which to approach the next phase of the play.

Act IV, which follows the adventures of the fatherless Marina (orphaned also of her faithful old nurse), is, it will be noticed, quite conspicuously full of surrogate parental or quasi-guardian figures including the brothel 'family'—the pandar, his bawd wife and their servant Boult—and Lysimachus himself, who, though his age is never mentioned, seems, as governor of the city, authority-figure and Marina's patron, more a father than a lover until their betrothal. It is also conspicuously full of imminent rape. Leonine expects the rescuing pirates to ravish Marina; the brothel 'family', for whom Marina's virginity at first presented itself as a commercial asset, are later intent upon disabusing themselves of her 'peevish' intractability ('We must either get her ravish'd or be rid of her . . . she would make a puritan of the devil' (IV,vi,5-9)); the two gentleman customers are put by her 'quirks, her reasons, her master-reasons, her prayers, her knees' (8) 'out of the road of rutting forever' (IV,v,9) and the disguised governor Lysimachus is—what? unmanned? derailed? converted? (we shall return to Lysimachus presently) by what the Bawd calls Marina's 'virginal fencing' (IV,vi,57).

The classic recourse, in psychoanalytic theory, of the maternally fixated libido is a debased sexual object—prostitute or courtesan. The transformation of Marina into such a figure liberates sexual fantasy, the brothel scenes providing a screen through which the deeply repressed sensuality of Pericles can find release. Thus the remedial fourth-act exorcism-through-exacerbation which characterizes Shakespearian comedy can be seen to be effected through the brothel scenes.[10] Pericles, himself absent from the stage, a monk in his mourning and his melancholy, is replaced by these fantasized figures, whose bawdy eroticism can be allowed free play within the constraining limits, or off-limits, of Marina's charismatic chastity. What strikes us in the sexual metaphors here is that they are sadistic, rather than comic. The overriding theme is not reciprocal sexual play, cheerfully spilling over into verbal play as in the early comedies, or in Mercutio's jesting, nor even the wry consequences of sexual play in the form of venereal-disease punishment which is also usual in Shakespeare. The overriding theme is simply defloration, and the metaphors are fantasies of injury, force, mutilation or cannibalism too threatening to amuse. They at once titillate and alienate by appeals to a voyeurism or sadomasochism not veiled but provoked by the euphemism or metaphor: 'Marry, whip the gosling, I think I shall have something to do with you. Come, you're a young foolish sapling, and must be bow'd as I would have you' (IV,ii,86-8); 'if I have bargain'd for the joint—Thou mayst cut a morsel off the spit' (130-1); 'For flesh and blood, sir, white and red, you shall see a rose' (IV,vi,34-6); 'Boult, take her away, use her at thy pleasure. Crack the glass of her virginity, and make the rest malleable . . . And if she were a thornier piece of ground than she is, she shall be ploughed' (141-5).

The brothel sequence fulfills its exorcist function despite, or within, the control of secondary revision. The drama's seductive fable ensures that the physical act, through the wit, wisdom and self-possession of Marina, the protective bounty of Lysimachus and the good offices of Boult, does not in fact come about. The wholebrothel sequence takes something of the form of a protracted, though in the end frustrated, initiation ritual: 'My lord, she's not pac'd yet, you must take some pains to work her to your manage,' says the Bawd (IV,vi,63-4); she is to be initiated into 'our profession' (7). This, because it is parody of a sort, serves as a species of legitimization; even the commercialization of sex does this. One notes that it is this theme which is made to yield the Shakespearian humour of Boult's final grumbling protest at Marina's excoriation of his trade: 'What would you have me do? Go to the wars, would you? where a man may serve seven years for the loss of a leg, and have not money enough in the end to buy him a wooden one?' (171-3); but read at the level of primary process Marina is a depersonalized sex object for the release of deeply repressed and traumatized libido.

It is at this point that we can take up two nagging questions that have troubled the critics. Why, it is asked, does Thaisa, retrieved from a watery grave by Cerimon, become a vestal in Diana's temple instead of setting forth in search of her husband? 'The plot of romantic fiction will have it so', says Hallett Smith (1974, p. 1481). It is the answer, not the question that, I suggest, is naive. If we read, not the plot of romance narrative, but the plot of 'the other scene', we can see that it is necessary for both Marina's parents to be sexually in abeyance, neutralized, while the screen fantasies of the brothel scenes are taking place. The psychic burden is shifted, so to speak, to the shoulders of the surrogate figures. It is upon similar lines that we can address the second nagging question: What was Lysimachus doing in the brothel in the first instance?

The text is poker-faced. We cannot make out whether he is caught out in a visitation the like of which it is his custom to make—he is certainly familiar enough to and with Boult—and subsequently converted by Marina's spirited virtue; or whether he is covertly investigating—what?—the state of morality in the stews of his city? 'I came with no ill intent' (IV,vi,109), he says. Then with what intent did he come? This unsolved mystery is more serious than it seems because it puts into question his relation to Marina, making this brothel-betrothal seem a rather hugger-mugger affair, to say the least. This problem too cannot be solved by appeal to comic genre conventions such as marriages all round or sudden conversion and the like because, first, too much emotional interest is invested in protagonist figures for us to be content with mere plot devices to round off a play. In the second place it is never made clear whether Lysimachus was in need of conversion or not. He remains therefore a split character, indeterminately ravisher and protector. This split, or anomaly, is our clue. For if the dream burden has been displaced to other figures in the way Green describes, and we can read Lysimachus as a representation, or extension of Pericles, then the split in Lysimachus is the unconscious split in Pericles. If therefore, the archaic turbulence of ambivalent desire and dread has been played out in the fantasy, and Marina has been saved by a fatherly figure (and/or a brotherly figure if we see Boult as her immediate saviour), when the young girl is brought to the ailing King, in Act V, to warm him back to life there is a double indemnity against the threat of incest. Pericles and Marina are safe and the way is clear for rebirth and restoration.

When the reunion occurs therefore it is truly miraculous—thaumaturgic. The King's grief has brought him to the point of death; now his healing is enacted before us. His initial resistance as he pushes Marina away, her resemblance to Thaisa, the gradual dawning of his recognition, the reluctance to believe lest it not be so, the fear of too great joy:

> O Helicanus, strike me, honoured sir,
> Give me a gash, put me to present pain,
> Lest this great sea of joys rushing upon me
> O'erbear the shores of my mortality,

> And drown me with their sweetness. O, come hither,
> Thou that beget'st him that did thee beget . . .
>
> 　　　　　　　　　　　(V,i,190-5)

these draw their power not only from finely observed human behaviour, but from our intuition of the entrenchedness of defence and repression that has had to be broken through. We must love, said Freud, in order not to fall ill. The pleasure we feel is the measure of the depth of the need, and the deprivation:

> My dearest wife was like this maid, and such a one
> My daughter might have been . . .
> 　　. . . another Juno;
> Who starves the ears she feeds and makes them hungry,
> The more she gives them speech.
>
> 　　　　　　　　　　　(V,i,107-14)

We witness the paradigmatic moment of the late romances which, in Barber's felicitous formulation, 'free family ties from the threat of sexuality', whereas the early comedies had freed sexuality from the ties of family (1969, pp. 59-67). 'Thou that beget'st him that did thee beget' is, as Barber notes, the secular equivalent of Dante's theogony: 'Virgine madre, figlia in tua figlio', and is 'the rarest dream that e'er dull'd sleep/ Did mock sad fools withal' (V,i,161-2).

Here, clearly, the play cannot remain. For a totality of psychic value in one beloved figure—mother and daughter at once—reproduces the spectre of Antioch. The play offers us a solution to this impasse in the recovery of Thaisa, and the betrothal of Marina to Lysimachus. There is even a separate kingdom available for both the generations, since the recent death of Thaisa's father leaves the throne of Pentapolis vacant for the parental couple.

And yet there is an unresolved indeterminacy in the text which makes it possible to read the ending of *Pericles* not as a mandala closure but as a dizzying return to square one. Consider the strange ambiguities of Pericles' final speech to the restored Thaisa:

> 　No more, you gods, your present kindness
> Makes my past miseries sport. You shall do well
> That on the touching of her lips I may
> Melt, and no more be seen. O, come, be buried
> A second time within these arms.
>
> 　　　　　　　　　　　(V,iii,39-43)

Eros? Thanatos? Can we say? To die upon a kiss was a common Renaissance metaphor for consummation;

but how shall we read these words? Does the text crumble to its own deconstruction at the end, with nothing resolved or exorcized, but all to be done again? I turn once more to André Green. 'We shall often feel a renewed disappointment', he says, 'faced by [the text's] refusal to take us anywhere except to the point of origin from which it took its own departure' (1979, p. 23). Is this the case in *Pericles*? And is it disappointment that we feel? Or is this refusal simply a sign that the play has put us in touch with the familiar ghosts—the desires and the terrors—that habitually haunt our minds?

Notes

¹ P. Goolden ('Antiochus's riddle in Gower and Shakespeare', *Review of English Studies,* n.s., Vol. 6, No. 23, 1955, p. 251) reviews the history of the riddle from the Latin prose *Apollonius,* where involuted in-law relations provide the clues, through Gower's Middle English version to Shakespeare's adaptation in *Pericles.* He notes that Shakespeare's innovation allows for simplification; he ignores, however, the oddity that catches our attention. R. E. Gajdusek ('Death, incest and the triple bond', *American Imago,* Vol. 31, 1974, pp. 109-30) has recourse to a Jungian Triple Goddess both for the riddle and the play which he reads as a mythical contest between the feminine (all-devouring) and the masculine (separative) principles. DrRivka Eifferman, in the course of a seminar on Psychoanalysis and Literature held at the Hebrew University Centre for Literary Studies in 1985, suggests the possibility that 'All love the womb that their first being bred' could paraphrase as 'All love the daughter that they first [in their youth] raised', thus providing a literal solution to the riddle and obviating recourse to the unconscious.

² The riddle contains metalepsis in Quintillian's sense: the metonymical substitution of one word for another which is itself figurative. But I am using the term in the sense made familiar in narratology: transpositions of past and present, foreboding and retrospection. Both senses offer paradigms for the psychoanalytic process.

³ For an account of levels of representation in Shakespeare—the use of choric figures, plays-within-plays, actors acting actors, on-stage audiences and other parabastic devices, see Aviva Furdi ('The play with a play within the play', Ph. D. dissertation, Hebrew University, 1984). See also the interesting earlier account of 'multi-consciousness' given by S. L. Bethell (*Shakespeare and the Popular Dramatic Tradition,* Staples Press, 1944).

⁴ See F. D. Hoeniger's Arden edition (1963) for an account of the textual problems in this passage. I am

indebted to Dr Rivka Eifferman for the primal-scene insight.

⁵ Alan B. Rothenberg ('Infantile fantasies in Shakespearean metaphor: (I) the fear of being smothered', *Psychoanalytic Review,* Vol. 60, No. 2, 1973, p. 215) notices the image of maternal devouring in I,v,41-3, and points out that in the 1609 and 1611 Q texts of *Pericles* 'nousle' (to nurse) is spelled 'nouzell' (our 'nuzzle'—to thrust the nose into). The composite neatly condenses feeding and projective threat, mother and child.

⁶ *The Comedy of Errors,* derived from the same literary source as *Pericles*—the popular fifth-century *Apollonius of Tyre*—is evidently a younger oedipal fantasy in which the threatened father, Egeus, is rescued by his son. See Freud on rescue fantasies in 'Family romances' (1909, in *The Standard Edition of the Complete Psychological Works of Sigmund Freud,* edited by James Strachey, 24 vols. Hogarth, 1953-1973, Vol. 9, pp. 235-41).

⁷ I am grateful to Dr Paul Gabriner for suggesting this onomastic possibility.

⁸ This difficult line has been glossed in many ways. The 1609 Q text has 'not', which is followed by Hoeniger's Arden edition (1963), and by Ernest Schanzer in the Signet edition (1965). Philip Edwards' emendation (*Shakespeare and the Confines of Art,* 1976) is 'but', which makes good sense for the reading here advanced. Edwards suggests that the aside be given to Thaisa, which however would destroy the repartee effect of her 'Juno' to Simonides' 'Jove'.

⁹ As Robert Rogers says, 'Whenever decomposition (splitting, doubling or multiplication of personae) takes place in narrative, the cast of characters is never quite as large as it would appear to be' (*A Psychoanalytical Study of the Double in Literature,* 1970, p.63).

¹⁰ In Nevo (*Comic Transformations in Shakespeare,* 1980) I have attempted to develop a cathartic, or 'exorcist' theory of comic form.

FATHERS AND DAUGHTERS

Michael Taylor (essay date 1982)

SOURCE: "'Here is a thing too young for such a place': Innocence in *Pericles,*" in *Ariel,* Vol. 13, No. 3, July, 1982, pp. 3-19.

[*In this essay, Taylor explores the difference between the quality of Pericles' innocence and Marina's.*]

I

In Shakespeare's plays the corrupt often confuse innocence with stupidity. Swayed by their reductive view of human nature (innocent and simplistic itself) these confident, pragmatic observers of human behaviour cannot acknowledge the possibility that any sensible person can (or should) act beyond his or her immediate self-interest. Such a stance helps to explain why Shakespeare's evil-doers are so sure of their intellectual superiority over their innocent victims, so certain that their interpretation of the world exposes its essential, shabby truth. In Dionyza's jeering tone in *Pericles,* for instance, as she lords it over her ineffectual husband, can be heard echoes of many of Shakespeare's antagonists to virtue, ranging from the maledictions of Richard III to the urbane mockery of Antonio and Sebastian in *The Tempest.* And what, among other things, these scoffers have in common—what Dionyza parades most contemptuously—is a confirmed aversion to the idea that some kind of beneficent supernatural power is at work in the world's affairs. With Iago they believe that it is in themselves that the innocent are thus or the wily thus. And Dionyza is at her most sardonic when she equates Creon's moral compunctions with mere superstition:

> Be one of those that thinks
> The petty wrens of Tharsus will fly hence
> And open this to Pericles.
>
> (IV.iii.21-23)[1]

Dionyza of course speaks here truer than she knows. In a romance like *Pericles* the "petty wrens" could well be the romancer's agents of fatal disclosure. Equally unwittingly, Dionyza's contemptuous injunction betrays the appalling innocence of the morally infantile. Her supercilious view of what she considers to be a pathetic example of moral credulity is like the naiveté of Lady Macbeth who believes her husband's horror at the murder of Duncan to be regressive and unmanly. Lady Macbeth deplores Macbeth's scruples as childishly frivolous, the product of cowardice or an unhinged fancy; but when she at last realizes fully what Macbeth has fully realized all along, the revelation drives her mad. In *Pericles* Dionyza remains steadfast in her determination to do away with Marina despite her having infinitely less reason to murder her daughter's closest friend than even Macbeth has to murder his guest, kinsman and king; and if we were to take Dionyza as seriously as she takes herself then she might well be considered more truly "fiend-like" than the woman so famously described by Malcolm. Just *how* seriously, though, are we meant to respond to Dionyza's operatically villainous pursuit of the unspeakable? Many critics think it preposterous to take Dionyza any more seriously than the fabulous ogres of fairytale. They argue that Dionyza's naiveté in her murderous intentions towards Marina, along with the states of

consciousness of many of the play's other characters, cannot be profitably discussed in terms other than those of mere baffled acknowledgement—the equivalent of the unbaffled acknowledgement we give to the Dionyzas of macabre fairy tales. Philip Edwards, for one, takes this position: "The good are good and the bad are bad. Changes of moral state (Dionyza, Lysimachus, Boult) are as uncomplicated and unconvincing as the moral states themselves."[2]

Although we may agree that Dionyza's moral state is uncomplicated, it does not seem to me to be at all unconvincing, and it may even be slightly more opaque than Edwards would allow. Indeed, I would argue that it is vital for us in *Pericles* to respond as fully as possible to the moral inadequacy of Dionyza's innocent view of affairs especially as it occurs in Shakespeare's section of the play—the last three acts—where it is rendered with all the vigour of the mature artist writing at his most persuasive. We need to respond, that is, to the casual horror of her encouragement of Leonine, "'Tis but a blow, which never shall be known" (IV.i.2), or to the even more inappropriate encouragement of "but be / A soldier to thy purpose" (IV.i.7-8). The absurdity (and unpleasantness) of this particular injunction—coupled with Dionyza's cruel joke about Marina's virtue—"The fitter then the gods should have her" (IV.i.10)—is underscored by Marina's entrance at this point (as the Stage Direction makes graphic): *"Enter Marina, with a basket of flowers."* This is not the first time in the play that one kind of innocence has confronted another. Shakespeare seems to have taken the hint for a series of encounters between the two different kinds of unawareness[3] from whoever wrote the play's opening scene where an innocent Pericles confronts the grotesque naiveté of the incestuous relationship between Antiochus and his unnamed daughter. It may be that the relationship strikes the spectator as naive rather than simply unpleasant (though it is that too) because the author of this opening scene has failed to raise the level of the writing above the vapidly melodramatic. At all events, it is hard to repress our incredulity when Antiochus' daughter (whose incestuous union with her father has already been the subject of Gower's moral outrage) indicates that Pericles has captured her heart: "Of all 'sayed yet, mayst thou prove prosperous! / Of all 'sayed yet, I wish thee happiness!" (I.ii.60-61). Equally infantile and even more monstrous is Antiochus' justification for dispatching Pericles: "For by his fall my honor must keep high" (I.i.150).

The falsely innocent appearance of Antiochus' daughter—"apparelled like the spring" (I.i.13) in Pericles' infatuated words—and her corrupt childish mind prefigure Dionyza's "angel's face" (IV.iii.47) hiding her naive, false heart. Like Lady Macbeth Dionyza pours scorn on her husband's human kindness, such as it is. The brief scene in which she does so—Act IV, Scene iii—is particularly telling because there's really no need for us to return to Tarsus except to experience once more, and even more chillingly, the distance between Dionyza and the rest of humanity, here represented by her unremarkable husband, Cleon. Not unexpectedly she has immense contempt for Cleon's stricken conscience, which she perversely interprets as betraying a lack of natural affection on his part for their daughter, Philoten, who, because of Marina, was "held a mawkin, / Not worth the time of day" (IV.iii.34-35). As a consequence she can only regard the murder of Marina in monstrously innocent fashion "as an enterprise of kindness / Performed to your sole daughter" (IV.iii.38-39). She dismisses Cleon's scruples in the same superior way that Lady macbeth had dismissed Macbeth's. "Why are you foolish? Can it be undone?" (IV.iii.1) she asks—as Lady Macbeth had asked—and, like her also, accuses her husband of being childish: "I think you'll turn child again" (IV.iii.4). She is particularly scornful of a possible claim to innocence on his part:

> Who can cross it?
> Unless you play the pious innocent
> And for an honest attribute cry out
> "She died by foul play."
>
> (IV.iii.17-19)

More in keeping perhaps with Dionyza's disconcerting sense of values is the 1609 quarto reading of the second line, "Unless you play the impious innocent," which Philip Edwards restores in his New Penguin edition of the play describing it as a "bold oxymoron."[4] I doubt whether "pious" should be "impious" considering the awkwardness then of "honest attribute" in the line that follows, but it's certainly not out of character for someone who regards the murder of Marina as an "enterprise of kindness" to think contrition a sacrilegious response to it.

II

Opposed to the impious innocence of Dionyza's views is its educated counterpart (educated morally, that is) embodied in Marina, the victim of Dionyza's wickedly infantile pieties. Like the other four romance heroines (even Miranda), she owes something in her make-up to her counterparts in the earlier romantic comedies, although none of the romance heroines has quite her predecessor's remarkable ease of manner, especially in erotic matters. What Marina lacks in conservatory sophistication she makes up for in militancy: her chastity has iron in it, forged no doubt in the production of Shakespeare's tragic heroines whose plays follow and shatter the bright dream of the world as we would like it.[5] With the partial exception of her mother and Cerimon, there is no-one else like Marina in the play, and, although there has been some controversy over the interpretation of Pericles as heroic sufferer, it seems to me to be undeniable that his innocence has little of the energy of his daughter's in both the non-Shakespearean and Shakespearean sections of the play. In this Pericles also resembles (in even more muted fashion) the heroes of Shakespeare's romantic comedies who often seem flat-footed in the adroit presences of the women with whom they are romantically entangled.

Marina's first words bely the pathos of her flowery, tear-stained entrance: "No, I will rob Tellus of her weed, / To strow thy green with flowers" (IV.i.14-15). Has someone (Dionyza perhaps) told her not to pick flowers for Lychorida's grave? Or is it simply that Shakespeare wants Marina's opening lines to convey immediately (though mysteriously) the defiant resolution that invariably stiffens her tender feelings? Vehement (the *in medias* "No" suggests the press of impassioned argument), belligerent and active, Marina in her metaphor transforms an archetypally innocent act into an aggressive one as she strips the Roman goddess of her flowery dress to bedeck her nurse's grave. And in the ensuing dialogue between Marina and Dionyza's hired murder, Leonine, Shakespeare continues to balance tender sentiment with youthful bravado in everything Marina says. She obsessively reverts to her stormy birth, expatiating on the heroic exploits of her father "galling / His kingly hands haling ropes" (IV.i.54-55). Marina's ecstatic admiration for the notion of royalty galled, of a prince buckling to it in egalitarian confusion, anticipates our own admiration for her later capacity to withstand vulgar siege. What she most relishes in the story of her father (a detail new to us, incidentally) springs from a vital instinct for participation, a form of *noblesse oblige* that the romances encourage.

Marina's militancy sits well with her fundamental innocence and occasional naiveté: we never feel that the two conditions constitute awakward incompatibilities. In this she resembles a host of Shakespeare heroines but the one most immediate to her is her mother Thaisa, though she is frequently overlooked in critical discussion perhaps because she appears mainly in the first two acts of *Pericles,* those clearly not written by Shakespeare. Something of the same resilience of spirit, however, grounded in a similarly constituted moral sense, can be perceived in the way in which Thaisa woos Pericles—in pale imitation perhaps of the self-assurance of those predecessors in the romantic comedies I have already mentioned. In *The Winter's Tale* Shakespeare conveys the sophisticated warmth of Perdita's mother, Hermione, in similar (though far more dazzling) fashion: both daughters come from mothers whose cheerful and sinless sensuality (to use S. L. Bethell's fine phrase)[6] has something of the same effect on putative lover and husband that Marina has on Philoten: they become mawkins, viciously so in Leontes' case, in contrast to the insouciant women. Pericles' dealings with Thaisa and her father, Simonides, in the

last scenes of the second act, could not be more remote from his previous unpleasant experience with
Antiochus and his daughter. We are obviously intended
to see the relationship between father and daughter in
Pentapolis as a paradigm of the healthy devotion that
Pericles imagined to exist between the play's first father
and daughter in Antioch.

In other words, however perfunctorily handled, there
seems to have been some attempt in the first two acts
of *Pericles* to contrast opposing kinds of innocent
behaviour: the outspoken innocence of the truly sinless
person, on the one hand, unafraid to acknowledge the
promptings of a legitimate sensuality, and the perverted innocence of corrupt natures, on the other,
whose persistent need for instant gratification marks
them as chronic moral adolescents. What Shakespeare
takes from these first two acts, then, to revitalize inhis
own manner in the last three, is not only the underlying notion that a truly innocent response to the world's
dangers and enticements is a radical expression of the
integrity of the self but also the equally modern-sound-
ing notion that the most chilling manifestation of evil
appears in characters who have no understanding of
the enormity of their conduct.

III

One of the rules of reality that, in her radical innocence, Thaisa blithely breaks—one that Antiochus'
daughter of all Shakespeare's daughters should have
broken (if we may continue to think of her as one of
Shakespeare's daughters, seeing as she only appears
in the first two acts)—is the one demanding filial
obedience, in Shakespeare's earlier comedies a convention at first impossible to circumvent as the heroines of *A Midsummer Night's Dream, As You Like It*
and *Much Ado About Nothing* discover to their cost.
Not for them the possibility of Beatrice's advice to
Hero in *Much Ado* to "make another cursy, and say,
'Father, as it please me'" (*Much Ado,* 2.1.47-48): they
must either obey their fathers or abandon home and
civilization for a time as do the lovers in *A Midsummer
Night's Dream* and Rosalind and Celia in *As You Like
It*.[7] Apart from the way in which Katherine treats her
father (and everyone else) in *The Taming of the Shrew*,
I cannot think of another Shakespeare daughter (to
continue to think of her as such) who rules the roost
in quite Thaisa's manner—with her father as a more
than willing accomplice. Fortunately, his feelings for
Pericles fall only a little short of hers: for both of them
in everything he does Pericles belies the shabbiness of
his trappings, pointing to an inner worth far superior
to that revealed by the other knights competing for
Thaisa's favour. Nothing could be more romantically
conventional: in these situations the leaden casket always conceals the chooser's rich rewards. By their
instinctive recognition of Pericles' innate nobility,
Simonides and Thaisa put themselves on the side of

the forces conspiring in romance to bring about—no
matter how belatedly—the establishment of the just
and healthy society.

In Shakespeare's section of the play, when Thaisa
learns what has happened to Pericles—or rather what
she thinks has happened to him—she retreats from the
world's perturbations, unjoyously putting on a "vestal
livery" (3.4.9). It's a signally strategic retreat: Shakespeare cannot afford to have another active woman
competing with Marina for our admiration. But the
play's design is sufficiently careful for us to see this
particular withdrawal as one in a network of advances
and retreats whose distribution tells us something vital
about the quality of innocence needed to push back
the forces of darkness. Howard Felperin perceives a
connection between Thaisa's renunciation of the world
and Pericles' increasing passivity in the face of its
hardships: both "withdraw from the pain and flux of
the Earthly City into a decidedly medieval asceticism."[8]

Nothing could be less ascetic in contrast than Marina's
uninhibited response to the pain and flux of the earthly
city, even when that city may very well be one of the
ancient world's earthliest—Mytilene. It is here that
Marina undergoes the severest assaults on her innocence as the management of the brothel attempts to
force her to become their star attraction. Wry intimations of their inevitable failure in dealing with what
John Danby calls the "invincible virgin-mind"[9] occur
even before they encounter her. In a grimly comic
conversation among the three Bawds, Pander complains that the brothel's reliance on its "pitifully sodden" (IV.ii.18) merchandise—so ravaged as to make
their clients "roast meat for worms" (IV.ii.23)—of-
fends his professional pride. What is needed to restore
the brothel's credibility—they all agree—is new and
healthy (and preferably virginal) blood, no matter what
the cost. In this commercial context, Pander's glib
use of the term "conscience" can only be viewed as
a comic misappropriation; but a little later there seems
to be something genuine in his fleeting concern for
their standing *sub specie aeternitas:* "the sore terms
we stand on with gods will be strong with us for
giving o'er" (IV.ii.32-33). We might see in this admission some kind of comic, crippled yearning for the
benefaction that Marina brings in her role as harbinger
of the fresh new world. However mutated, Pander's
is a dream of innocence.

In these scenes, where Marina's radical innocence
triumphs, the play is extremely affecting—hilarious and
moving in equal measure. Against all odds, Marina not
only retains her virtue but has a profoundly disturbing
effect upon the brothel's habitués who find themselves exposed for the first time to the power of evan-
gelistic purity in the face of which their worldliness
crumbles. A brief discussion between two unnamed
customers that constitutes Act IV, Scene v, makes

clear the devastation wreaked on the brothel's clientele. As Felperin points out, behind both rueful, half-comic acknowledgements of her power lies the myth of Proserpine: "The underlying myth employed by Shakespeare is that of a figure of innocence transported to a realm of darkness, where she eventually becomes its ruler."[10]

IV

One of the most astute essays on *Pericles,* "Heritage in *Pericles*" by Andrew Welsh, takes as its point of significant departure the fact that the play's plot is as old as the hills, and so popular as to be constantly retold in countless variations, in language after language.[11] Welsh observes that Shakespeare's use of Gower as a story-telling intermediary insistently draws our attention to the tale as something inherited from an ancient past, revived and made significant repeatedly by the writers of the day. The great age of the tale "is a conquest of devouring time by the human imagination" and we should be alive to its external, articulate seniority in our response to the form it finds in Shakespeare: "The meaning is found by bringing the external sense of the continuing tradition of the old tale into the play itself."[12] The continuing tradition of the old tale exploits a number of profound simplicities, not least that of an unchanging human nature: men as they always have been—to revert to the Bawd's fundamental understanding of her clients' hearts and minds. Yet the romances also reveal the extent to which human beings seem perennially to hunger for some kind of deifying experience, as though an essential constituent of their human nature were a yearning to transcend its only too humanly defining limitations: in *Pericles* "at a level deeper than the laughter . . . the idea of purification, the *possibility* of it in this climate of easy-going, casual sexual gratification."[13]

All four romances make much of the possibility of purification, of a renewal of innocence, latent in human nature, the heritage ultimately of God's gift of free will to mankind. When Gower says that the purchase of *Pericles* is to make men glorious we sense behind this proud boast not only a prediction about the revitalization of the play's characters and society but also the ancient claim for the power of art "to lead and draw us to as high a perfection, as our degenerate soules, made worse by theyr clayey lodgings, can be capable of."[14] While it may not be possible to number Pericles among the play's degenerate souls we can hardly fail to notice the difference in the quality of his innocence from Marina's. The innocence that matters, Marina's, flourishes amid the bustle of the world's doings. From the play's beginning—however ineptly written those first two acts—Pericles fluctuates between rashness and a kind of stricken despair. When he discovers the incestuous relationship between father and daughter he shrinks into a melancholy pru-

dence, convinced of his own helplessness in the courts of powerful kings: "Who has a book of all that monarchs do, / He's more secure to keep it shut than shown" (I.i.95-96). There is a hint of collusion in the alacrity with which he accepts his role as the blind mole thronged by man's oppression: prudent, cynical, defeated, he succumbs to what he conceives to be an immitigable Jovian authority whose power leaves him no choice but to become, like Antiochus' daughter, corruption's silent accessory. Intentional or not on the part of whoever wrote these opening scenes, his jingles on self-preservation expose his lack of dignity:

> It is enough you know; and it is fit,
> What being more known grows worse, to
>   smother it.
> All love the womb that their first being bred.
> Then give my tongue like leave to love my
>   head.
>
> (I.i.106-09)

Howard Felperin goes so far as to see Pericles' response to the difficulties of his situation as a minor fall from grace and innocence: " . . . his recognition of the incest writ large in the riddle is presented as a kind of fall, if only from innocence into knowledge, and his play too will be concerned with redemption."[15]

Pericles' disturbing stoicism takes another form in the second act. Forced to flee from Tarsus, he puts to sea again only to be shipwrecked by the storm that is ubiquitous in these romances, destiny's agent for significant change—in this case, permitting Pericles to be washed ashore at Pentapolis to marry Thaisa. His response to nature's buffeting parallels his response to the savagery of human authority; no King Lear, he submits to the judgement of the elements:

> Wind, rain, and thunder, remember earthly
>   man
> Is but a substance that must yield to you;
> And I, as fits my nature, do obey you.
>
> (II.i.2-4)

Later, in Shakespeare's half of the play, after Thaisa's apparent death in a second storm, he voices again in plangent monosyllables his disturbing fatalism:

> Could I rage and roar
> As doth the sea she lies in, yet the end
> Must be as 'tis.
>
> (III.iii.10-12)

As he says: "We cannot but obey / The powers above us" (III.iii.9-10), just as we cannot but obey those considerably less elevated. Despite the miraculousness of Pericles' first escape, he chooses to brood on his imminent death (as he imagines), close enough for him to refer to himself in the third person in yet another line of soporific monosyllables as though soul and body were already disjoined: "Here to have death in peace is all he'll crave" (II.i.11). Fortunately, his peace is rudely shattered by the arrival of the three fishermen whose robust good humour serves to make more obvious Pericles' insufficiency. Whoever constructed these opening scenes at least knew the value of such organic and discreet commentary.

It takes more than the miracle of his own survival, however, and more than the heartiness of the three fishermen, to reanimate Pericles. It takes, in fact, what he perceives as an impressively symbolic miracle—the fishing up of his father's armour, bequeathed to him on his father's death with the usual solemn injunctions about its superior efficacy. Pericles throws off his sluggishness only in response to this most obtrusive of interventions on the part of the guardian spirit of romance; and we can hardly fail to contrast the necessity for such a literal provision of armour—the miraculous armour of romance fiction—with the spiritual armour provided by her own strength of character on which Marina can only rely. No armour—spiritual or material—can help Pericles withstand the catastrophe of Marina's apparent death (despite his not having seen her for fourteen years)—an event so dire as to overwhelm the expression of human individuality itself, his capacity for speech, so that we never hear from his own lips the extent and degree of his suffering but witness it partially in expressive dumb-show: "*Pericles makes lamentation, puts on sack-cloth, and in mighty passion departs*" (IV.iv.22 S.D.). When we next meet him "hirsute and atrabilarian, upon the barge"[16] he has retreated deep within himself, silent, comatose. Our sympathy for his sufferings should not obscure the sustained contrast between him and Marina—brought to a focus in the fifth act in their therapeutic confrontation. As Andrew Welsh argues, Pericles has throughout responded to his misfortunes in a perilously defeated manner and here "he has deliberately taken the extreme course of suicide; by inflicting upon himself a death of the spirit, he has isolated himself from further pain."[17] Welsh's conclusion is that Pericles suffers from what the Middle Ages often thought to be the eighth cardinal sin: Tristitia, or a despairing, enervating sadness.

V

In *Pericles* and *The Winter's Tale* great store is laid by the ability to know the world in all its deceptiveness, an ability which requires education, knowledge and experience as much as any intuitive awareness. Much to their chagrin, Marina usually understands her corrupt teachers only too well: in her responses to them she exemplifies the educated evangelism that Calvin thought essential for the practising Christian, "The Christian profession requireth us to be children, not in understanding, but in malice."[18] A child in malice, a

wise adult in understanding: a formidable combination in Marina who, in her moral superiority, resembles Cerimon, the quasi-magical director of what J. P. Brockbank calls the "miraculous first-aid post of Ephesus."[19] In Cerimon innocence and knowledge find their ideal representative, though Shakespeare, anxious to keep his paragon lawfully human, begins with an admission of Cerimon's human limitations as a doctor. "There's nothing can be minist'red to nature / That can recover him" (III.ii.8-9) he advises the Servant of one who is about to die. Having, as it were, established Cerimon's human credentials, Shakespeare can then afford to stress the attributes whose purchase makes Cerimon glorious: philanthropic, ascetic, loving, Cerimon has become an institution in Ephesus. And, speaking in the lofty style of one who knows his own worth, Cerimon (whose name also suggests "sermon" as well as "ceremony") makes explicit the important connection between knowledge and morality:

> I hold it ever
> Virtue and cunning were endowments
>   greater
> Than nobleness and riches. Careless heirs
> May the two latter darken and expend;
> But immortality attends the former,
> Making a man a god.
>
> (III.ii.25-30)

Virtue and cunning make a man a god, or a woman a goddess: in this play transformations devoutly to be wished, for it is this god-like combination which enables the play's society to rid itself finally of the original Antiochan curse. In the last two acts Marina's intellectual accomplishments—her learned abilities—vie with her beauty and virtue for awed compliment. Gower tells us that she

> hath gained
> Of education all the grace,
> Which makes her both the heart and place
> Of general wonder.
>
> (IV Cho. 8-11)

"Grace" and "wonder," powerful words in Shakespeare's romances, invest "education" with a profound spiritual significance, and Marina's harrowing of Mytilene's sinners anticipates the persuasive evangelism of Perdita in *The Winter's Tale* whose influence, according to the Servant, could easily spawn another cult of the virgin (V.i.106-09).

The religious importance of knowledge in *Pericles* and *The Winter's Tale,* and the devastation false knowledge can cause, reflects a widespread assumption among seventeenth-century English intellectuals, largely Anglican in persuasion and liberal by inclination, of the efficacy of the mind in all matters, even in those pertaining to faith and belief. Herschel Baker's important book, *The Wars of Truth,* places this reverence for knowledge in a long and respectable tradition:

> The great Thomistic assumption of a rational God revealed in a rational universe and comprehensible by rational man found repeated restatement in the seventeenth-century—mainly from those Anglican apologists for the *via media* between paths of faith and knowledge, but also from Puritans trying to mitigate the harsh voluntarism of Calvinism.[20]

Marina's mockery of Mytilene's brothel-keepers or Cerimon's dignified justification of the enquiring mind would be well understood by Baker's seventeenth-century Anglican apologists for rationality; and one can image someone like Hooker, had he lived to attend a performance of one of Shakespeare's romances, applauding the sweet combination of innocence and understanding that the play advocates, aspecially as his *Laws of Ecclesiastical Polity* mocks anti-intellectualism generally, and Puritan antiintellectualism specifically, for the naiveté of thinking reason "an enemy unto religion, [and] childish Simplicity the mother of ghostly and divine Wisdom."[21]

As an artist, Shakespeare, like Henry James, recognized the aesthetic value of the conjunction of Hooker's contraries: reason and childish simplicity. Gower's Chorus introducing Act V praises Marina's talents even more fervently than at the beginning of Act IV. Singer, dancer, composer, scholar ("Deep clerks she dumbs"), and innocent craftswoman, Marina overflows with accomplishments; like Paulina and Perdita in *The Winter's Tale* she's someone who rivals nature in the golden work of creation and renewal. Her skill and her innocence combine in the first scene of the fifth act to "allure" Pericles back to life, although Lysimachus, with perhaps his own experience in mind, does justice in his military metaphor to the iron determination behind the allurement:

> She, questionless, with her sweet harmony
> And other chosen attractions, would allure,
> And make a batt'ry through his deafened
>   parts,
> Which now are midway stopped.
>
> (V.i.45-48)

Marina's assault succeeds in restoring Pericles' desire to speak which he uses, at least initially, to give vent to his wondering admiration for the miraculous creature so unexpectedly come his way; in the course of which he speaks the play's most famous lines:

> Yet thou dost look
> Like Patience gazing on kings' graves and
>   smiling
> Extremity out of act.
>
> (V.i.138-40)

In his Arden edition of the play, F. D. Hoeniger notes that most commentators fail to see the obvious inspiration for the image in carved figures of Patience on tombs; and he also enlarges the usual interpretation of "smiling / Extremity out of act (i.e., suicide)" to "smiling extreme calamity out of existence (i.e., making it melt away), whatever the dictionaries say."[22] Nothing could be more eloquent, from our point of view, than the way this bride of quietness smilingly cures man's infirmities. Although both statue and personification, Patience takes on here the active humanity necessary to repair the workings of extremity, the difference between merely "gazing on," and "smiling . . . out of." (I can't think of any famous statue, incidentally, that has been given the humanity of a smile.) What Pericles chooses to praise in these lines is an active, uncloistered patience—though he himself, as we have seen, was much more inclined passively to gaze, especially on the deeds of kings, than to smile extremity out of act.

Marina once more smiles extremity out of act when she forces her father to forego the comfort of hisself-induced narcotic state. When he recognizes her as his child he is overcome by a "great sea of joys" (V.i.194) and thinks of her as the creator of his happiness: "Thou that beget'st him that did thee beget" (V.i.197)—an innocent reordering of the incestuous dependency of Antiochus on his daughter, and imbued with Christian feeling as Philip Edwards notices: "The paradox is the ancient paradox of Christianity, in which God the father becomes the son of his own daughter, a virgin."[23] And it is at this rhapsodic moment that Pericles hears "heavenly music" (V.i.234) falls into a "thick slumber" (V.i.235) and has his vision of Diana—the whole experience justifying the way in which Edwards ties together intellect, innocence and the supernatural in the play: "in the depth of their learning [Cerimon, Marina] or in the strength of their innocence [they] have the power to change others, to revive and recreate them, and their power suggests divine help."[24]

Mysteriously aiding, Diana commands Pericles to journey to her temple at Ephesus, there to recount the story of his troubled life before a congregation that includes Cerimon and Thaisa, now the High Priestess of Diana's church. Like Gower, Pericles must tell the tale that will purchase for him the glory that "Makes my past miseries sports" (V.iii.41), a minor penance surely, but a highly appropriate one for a man who from the beginning at Antioch has retreated further and further into the extremity of his quietism. It is this terrible spell that Marina breaks, and Pericles' revitalization and reuniting with his wife and daughter climax Shakespear's presentation of Marina as divinely and formidably innocent. The play, therefore, as J. P. Brockbank remarks, "smiles extremity out of act,"[25] but it could never have done so without Marina and the gift of innocence at her bestowal. She is never too young for all the places that need her. The three romances that follow *Pericles* also smile extremity out of act, and also depend upon militant innocence for being able to do so; but only *The Winter's Tale* has the bold, confident sweep of *Pericles*. The other two achieve the same new-born state, if indeed they quite do so, in a much more ambiguous manner. But for this we should be just as grateful as we are for the way in which *Hamlet* and *Measure for Measure* challenge the felicity of *As You Like It* and *Twelfth Night*.

Notes

1 References to Shakespeare are from *The Complete Pelican Shakespeare,* ed. Alfred Harbage (Baltimore, Maryland: Penguin Books, Inc., 1969).

2 *Pericles,* The New Penguin Shakespeare (Harmondsworth, Middlesex: Penguin Books, Inc., 1976), p. 14.

3 Marina with Dionyza and Leonine; Marina with Lysimachus; Marina with Boult and co. The wooing of Pericles by Thaisa (abetted by her father) looks forward to the relationship between Leontes and Hermione in *The Winter's Tale*. Neither woman keeps her innocence at the expense of her sophistication: both men have the kind of innocent unawareness that blinds them to the reality of what is going on around them. In the case of Leontes, of course, such ignorance is disastrous.

4 Edwards, p. 176.

5 Howard Felperin notices in the romances how Shakespeare draws upon the experience of the tragedies, the "harshest cacophonies of the tortured soul" *Shakespearean Romance* (Princeton, New Jersey: Princeton University Press, 1972), p. 63.

6 *The Winter's Tale: A Study* (London: Staples Press, 1947), p. 31.

7 Northrop Frye sees the way in which these comedies begin as part of a larger comic pattern where an irrational society blocks for a time the legitimate desires of some of its leading citizens whose refusal to submit to such tyranny constitutes the revitalizing process. He notes: "All four of the romances introduce a hostile father or father figure who descends from the *senex iratus* of New Comedy." *A Natural Perspective*(New York: Columbia University Press, 1965), p. 74.

8 "Shakespeare's Miracle Play," *SQ* 18 (1967), 370.

9 *Poets on Fortune's Hill* (London: Faber and Faber, 1952), p. 99.

10 Felperin, "Shakespeare's Miracle Play," p. 370.

11 Andrew Welsh, "Heritage in Pericles," in *Shakespeare's Late Plays: Essays in Honor of Charles Crow,* edited by R. C. Tobias and P. G. Zolbrod (Athens, Ohio: Ohio University Press, 1974), pp. 89-113.

12 Welsh, p. 93.

13 Edwards, p. 21.

14 Sir Philip Sidney, *An Apologie for Poetrie,* ed. E. S. Shuckburgh (Cambridge: Cambridge University Press, 1905), p. 13.

15 *Shakespearean Romance,* p. 149. Cf. W. B. Thorne who thinks that Pericles is tainted by Antiochus' sin, "*Pericles* and the 'Incest-Fertility' Opposition," *SQ* 22 (1971), p. 47. Both critics probably owe a debt to Wilson Knight who describes Pericles' venture at Antioch as a "plunge into sin and death closely associated with ravishing desire." *The Crown of Life* (New York: Barnes and Noble, 1961), p. 38.

16 Philip Brockbank, "*Pericles* and the Dream of Immortality," *SS* 24 (1971), p. 113.

17 Welsh, p. 106. Cf. John Arthos who talks of Pericles in terms of an apathy which is a "kind of desperation." "*Pericles, Prince of Tyre*: A Study in the Dramatic Use of Romance Narrative," *SQ* 4 (1953), p. 261.

18 John Calvin, *Concerning Offenses* (London, 1567), Sig. B3v. Quoted in R. M. Frye, *Shakespeare and Christian Doctrine* (Princeton, N.J.: Princeton University Press, 1963), p. 74.

19 Brockbank, p. 113. Cf. Felperin who writes: "Cerimon is clearly a desendant of the miracle-play Christ," "Shakespeare's Miracle Play," p. 369.

20 (London: Staples Press, 1952), p. 29.

21 2 vols., Everyman's Library (London: Dent, 1963), Book 2, p. 311.

22 *Pericles,* ed. F. D. Hoeniger (London: Methuen, 1963), p. 147.

23 Edwards, p. 188.

24 Edwards, pp. 20-21.

25 Brockbank, p. 116.

Frederick Kiefer (essay date 1991-92)

SOURCE: "Art, Nature, and the Written Word in *Pericles,*" in *University of Toronto Quarterly,* Vol. 61, No. 2, Winter, 1991-2, pp. 207-25.

[*In the following essay, Kiefer explores the thematic links of art/nature and father/daughter in* Pericles.]

As a metaphor the book of nature elucidates the realms of art and nature in Shakespeare's late plays, especially *Pericles*. Although the metaphor may not explicitly appear in *Pericles,* the written word does, and it takes a variety of forms, including a riddle, an impresa, a message in a coffin, an inscription on a tomb. Each of these artful constructions describes or applies to one or another young woman who, by her appearance, evokes the personification of nature herself. Nature, then, is evoked both as a person and as an artifact evincing aesthetic design.[1] Together, these two formulations reveal more than either alone. The juxtaposition of written material and nubile woman achieves what the debate over flowers in *The Winter's Tale* or the argument over painting and poetry in *Timon of Athens* achieves: it clarifies the subtle relationship between art and nature, suggesting that, here at least, co-operation rather than strife prevails.

If the courtly world that Pericles discovers at Antioch seems artificial in the extreme, it is because everyone present has agreed to participate in a ritual whose bizarre nature is accentuated by its long-standing practice. In seeking marriage to the daughter of King Antiochus, Pericles enacts a ceremony performed many times before. The skulls of other prospective suitors stare down at him, and he will join their number if he fails a test administered by the king—the solving of a riddle. Despite the high stakes and the simmering sexual tension, the characters behave in studied fashion; passions are sublimated, proprieties observed.

The use of a riddle contributes to the stylization of the action.[2] By presenting a truth enigmatically, a riddle usually defies immediate comprehension; it requires the challenger to pause and ponder—in this instance the relationship between the 'I' of the riddle and someone else.[3] The playwright specifically indicates such a lull by the fifteen line aside of Pericles, following his recitation of the riddle, as he realizes the meaning and expresses it to himself. The theatrical effect of the riddle, then, is to slow down the action almost as soon as it has begun. The characters seem frozen for a moment, and, as a result, the sense of strangeness is prolonged.

Even when the action resumes, it has an oddly formal quality, for, however shocked Pericles may be by his recognition of incest, he is as indirect in dealing with Antiochus as the king has been with him. Pericles' strategy takes advantage of the protocol dictating an elaborate politesse. If he publicly discloses what he knows, he risks death at the hands of a man who sees him not as a future son-in-law but rather as a sexual rival. Hence Pericles preserves a bland exterior despite a seemingly desperate situation. And he manages to extricate himself, ironically, by capitalizing on the manner of the king's challenge. That is, Antiochus has presented the riddle in written form to Pericles. Now, taking his cue from what the king has just given him, Pericles employs a metaphor involving the written word: 'Who has a book of all that monarchs do,/ He's more secure to keep it shut than shown' (I.i.94-5).[4]

This metaphoric book not only signals the king that Pericles has deduced the riddle's meaning but also complements the literal words of that riddle by subtly implicating the king's daughter in wrongdoing. Presumably she is part of the 'book of all that monarchs do' since her relationship to her father is the (largely) unspoken issue of the scene. The metaphor is doubly apt because she has already been likened to a book earlier when Pericles admired her beauty: 'Her face the book of praises, where is read / Nothing but curious pleasures' (lines 16-17). The fact that both father and daughter are compared to books in the same scene and by the same character suggests an underlying similitude.

That a riddle should be required to explain the nature of a tie binding father and daughter illustrates something important about this play: that some familial relationships may be discerned only with difficulty. Ordinarily we think of kinship as being readily apparent to the observer; a child, for instance, resembles its parents, while husband and wife indicate their relationship by their demeanour. In *Pericles* a character may perceive the obvious and natural bond, as Pericles does when he beholds the king and his daughter. But ascertaining the other bond between father and child, unusual and secret, is more problematic. And elsewhere in the play, discovering even the most basic relationship may require what is needed here: the explanation of the written word.

Appropriately, the written word is present in yet another form in the opening scene, though one not so easily read: the book of nature.[5] It is implicit in the figure of the king's daughter, whose dramatic presentation seems almost to evoke a tableau vivant. Following her entry, she stands still; nothing in the script, at least, requires her to move. Moreover, she has neither soliloquy nor aside with which to reveal her feelings; she speaks only two lines in the entire scene, a mere expression, dictated by circumstance, of good will towards her suitor. Although at the centre of the action, she is curiously remote. More the outline of a character than a character, she lacks even the individualizing feature of a name. Her identity is established not by what she herself says but rather by what others say about her, and through their remarks she comes to bear a double association. First, she resembles nature in that she embodies (apparently) vitality and sensuality. Introducing her, Antiochus cites her most salient feature, her physical beauty: 'Nature this dowry gave' (line 9). In keeping with her appearance, she seems to promise fertility too. Pericles likens her to the season of the year heralding fruitfulness: 'See where she comes, apparelled like the spring' (line 12). Her beauty is such that it leads to the formulation of a second comparison. Using a metaphor belonging as much to the realm of art as of nature, Pericles calls her face 'the book of praises' (line 15). That the same woman should evoke both nature as woman and as artifact containing the written word is consistent with a culture that can personify nature as a woman and also imagine nature as a book. It is consistent too with the world of a play that defines a woman's identity by means of the written word (the riddle).

Although the personality and disposition of the king's daughter are shrouded by her nearly complete silence and by a public behaviour of inflexible decorum, she nevertheless creates a vivid image, one that lingers in the mind's eye. Indeed, the image will, with variations, recur in the subsequent dramatic action, at divers times and places. As here, the audience will behold a young woman who appears in the company of her father, who embodies simultaneously the natural and the artificial, and whose identity is revealed through the written word.

When Pericles flees Antioch, he takes with him his memory of the woman he so recently sought in marriage. Arriving in Pentapolis, he must experience a sense of *déjà vu*, for he discovers a situation eerily reminiscent of that which he left behind. He finds another young woman, also a king's daughter. And again she seems an embodiment of nature. Just as Antiochus personified nature when he spoke of his daughter, saying, 'Nature this dowry gave' (I.i.9), so Simonides personifies nature when he says that his daughter Thaisa 'Sits here like beauty's child, whom nature gat / For men to see, and seeing wonder at' (II.ii.6-7). The king speaks these words on an occasion that pays tribute to nature's fruitfulness—a 'triumph,' or tournament, celebrating the anniversary of Thaisa's birth. And her role at the subsequent banquet underscores her association with nature as generative force: she presents to the victorious Pericles a wreath made, presumably, of green leaves (II.iii.9-11).

While not herself an artist, Thaisa becomes an interpreter of art through the action she performs at the tournament, one which, incidentally, has no precedent in either of the play's chief narrative sources, John Gower's *Confessio Amantis* and Lawrence Twine's *The Patterne of Painfull Adventures*.[6] Thaisa assumes the task of describing designs which decorate the knights' shields at the tournament. Those shields are paintedwith imprese, Renaissance formulations combining picture with written word; typically these served as coats of arms, symbolizing a family's identity. Thaisa

gives an account of each in turn, receiving shields from the knights' pages, inspecting them, and finally returning them to the pages. Five times Thaisa performs this ritual, enumerating the designs and reading aloud the Latin of the accompanying mottoes.

The sixth (and last) of the designs, unlike the others, is presented directly by the hand of the knight. Thaisa tells her father:

> He seems to be a stranger; but his present
>   is
> A withered branch, that's only green at top;
> The motto: *'In hac spe vivo'*. (II.ii.42-4)

In the motto, which means 'In this hope I live,' Simonides perceives a particular relevance for his daughter: 'A pretty moral: / From the dejected state wherein he is, / He hopes by you his fortunes yet may flourish' (lines 45-7). The impresa may have a still more profound application than even the king realizes, for as Douglas L. Peterson observes, 'The hope in which Pericles "lives," and which leads to eventual victory, is in the living though seemingly dead branch that represents the family of whom he is the only survivor.'[7] Interpreted in these terms, the green branch betokens nature as life and fertility, hence the issue of the future marriage between Thaisa and Pericles—their child Marina. The branch thus evokes a genealogical tree, a symbol long used to represent a family's lineage.[8]

In her own desire to marry, Thaisa identifies herself with vitality and fruitfulness, qualities that signal her allegiance to nature. Her intention of taking Pericles as her husband, however, is expressed in unusual form: she writes a letter to her father. In another play this might strike us as improbable, but not here. As F. David Hoeniger comments, 'The unlikelilihood of a daughter who lives in the same palace as her father communicating with him that way is consistent with the nature and spirit of the story.'[9] Hoeniger does not go on to explain specifically how Thaisa's action is 'consistent,' but his judgment seems correct. For one thing her writing is in keeping with what the audience witnessed earlier at Antioch: the use of a written message to set forth the bond existing between a man and a woman. We do not know for certain that Antiochus' daughter is the author of the riddle, but the personal pronouns of the riddle refer to her, and the incestuous relationship described is unquestionably hers.[10] Now at Pentapolis, as earlier at Antioch, a character turns to the written word when seeking to express a sexual relationship.

Thaisa's action is consistent in another sense as well—in the theatrical effect that it achieves. Just as Antiochus' riddle presented Pericles with a *fait accompli*, so too does Thaisa's letter; it reflects the unyielding quality of her decision. Had she expressed in conversation her desire to marry Pericles, she might have been subject to importuning or imprecation. By casting her decision in written form, she forecloses any effort to change her mind. Her readers within the play confront a page which hears no plea, observes no body language, feels no emotion. Consequently, the dramatic emphasis falls where it did in the play's opening scene: on the reader, as first Simonides peruses the letter and then Pericles does the same. Along with the king, we watch and listen as Pericles studies, comprehends, and reacts. Though the use of soliloquy and aside, the playwright focuses on Pericles' emotional response and mental processes. Here, as at Antioch when he read the riddle, we are made to feel Pericles' sense of peril, which leads him to blurt out, 'O, seek not to entrap me, gracious lord' (II.v.45).

Thaisa's letter is also in keeping with the figurative language at her father's court. Following the tournament, Simonides addressed his knights, praising their accomplishment:

> Knights,
> To say you're welcome were superfluous.
> To place upon the volume of your deeds,
> As in a title-page, your worth in arms,
> Were more than you expect, or more than's
>   fit,
> Since every worth in show commends itself.
>   (II.iii.1-6)

Thaisa, of course, hears these words, for she is present as 'queen of the feast,' and, following Simonides' speech, she turns to Pericles, bestowing on him the victor's wreath. The letter that she subsequently writes complements the metaphor and simile applied to Pericles and the other competitors. Her letter befits a dramatic world wherein a person witnesses public feats and imagines the title page of a volume,[11] infers private conduct and imagines 'a book' of deeds (I.i.94). For Thaisa and her father, as for Pericles, action and the written word, whether literal or figurative, are one.

Thaisa's letter is consistent with the dramatic action in still another way as well, for additional instances of silent reading on Pericles' part both precede and follow his perusal of the letter. At the beginning of act II, Gower's speech breaks off for this dumb show:

> Enter at one door Pericles talking with Cleon; all the train with them. Enter at another door a Gentleman with a letter to Pericles; Pericles shows the letter to Cleon; Pericles gives the Messenger a reward and knights him. Exit Pericles at one door and Cleon at another.

The letter that passes from hand to hand has been written by Helicanus to warn Pericles, now on the isle of Tharsus, of danger from emissaries of King Antiochus. Later, at the beginning of act III, Gower reappears and we watch a dumb show curiously similar to the first:

> Enter Pericles and Simonides, at one door, with attendants. A messenger meets them, kneels, and gives Pericles a letter. Pericles shows it Simonides; the Lords kneel to him. Then enter Thaisa with child, with Lychorida, a nurse. The King shows her the letter; she rejoices. She and Pericles take leave of her father, and depart. . . .

This dumb show duplicates, in essential respects, the previous one.[12] Again Pericles enters with another man, receives a letter, shows it to his companion, and departs with the purpose of immediately undertaking a voyage. In both instances the travel has implications for Thaisa. Shipwrecked, in act II, Pericles meets and marries her; buffeted by a violent storm, in act III, Pericles suffers her loss. The dumb shows dramatize the moment when these developments are set in motion by delivery of the letters. And these deliveries visually bracket Pericles' experience at Pentapolis.

The similarity between the dumb shows points to an important feature of the play's dramaturgy: although the action of *Pericles* may be episodic and the changes in locale abrupt, the play contains an extraordinary number of parallels and correspondences, many of them visual. For example, when Pericles arrives in Pentapolis, he finds himself in a world resembling Antioch. Again a widowed king presides over a court. Again a nubile daughter attends the king. Again Pericles beholds the woman on a ceremonial occasion. And again that woman seems the embodiment of nature. These resemblances not only lend coherence to the disparate materials of the story but also suggest that we are witnessing something archetypal.[13] Despite evident incongruities in the textually ragged script of *Pericles,* perhaps the result of collaboration or of the playwright's adapting the work of another writer, the play is coherent in performance. The audience sees that behind and beyond the particular incidents of Pericles' adventures is a pattern, transcending time and place, of the relationship between father and daughter: Antiochus and his daughter; Simonides and his; Pericles and his.[14] In the persistence of this pattern we behold nothing less than an expression of nature herself. Evenwhere there is a departure from the norm, as when Pericles confronts an instance of incest, we are made to feel the fundamental strength of the nature that has been violated, and we share the characters' sense of relief when nature reasserts herself through the destruction of those who betray her purposes, especially the impulse to be fruitful.

So powerful is the nature that animates humanity that she is capable of affirming herself under even the most dire of circumstances, indeed, even in the face of death. Thus amid the storm which threatens to destroy Pericles' ship, the nurse brings word that Thaisa has succumbed during childbirth. In the arms of that nurse, however, is the continuation of life and the potential for future fertility: 'Here's all that is left living of your queen: / A little daughter' (III.i.20-1). Like the other daughters who have appeared in previous episodes, this one is aligned with nature, for when Pericles looks upon the infant girl, he says, 'Poore inch of Nature.' At least this is what he says in George Wilkins's *The Painfull Adventures of Pericles Prince of Tyre* (1608), a narrative probably based on the play about Pericles that was performed by Shakespeare's company.[15] For more than a century, scholars have recognized these words as almost certainly Shakespearean.

The promise of a resurgent nature is here, as elsewhere, closely identified with the written word. When the sailors insist that the body of Thaisa be consigned to the waves, Pericles resolves to write a message that will be enclosed in his wife's coffin: 'Bid Nestor bring me spices, ink and paper' (III.i.65). With the subsequent discovery of the coffin, Pericles' words are read aloud:

> 'Here I give to understand,
> If e'er this coffin drives a-land,
> I, King Pericles, have lost
> This queen, worth all our mundane cost.
> Who finds her, give her burying,
> She was the daughter of a king.
> Besides this treasure for a fee,
> The gods requite his charity!'
>
> (III.ii.68-75)

The message proves crucial to both Pericles and his daughter, for it justifies the extraordinary efforts of the physician Cerimon to revive this woman. Without it, the discoverers of the coffin would not know that the body belongs to the wife and daughter of kings. Her restoration, then, and her eventual reunion with husband and daughter depend upon the identity which the written word discloses.

In its revelation of a woman's identity, the message in the coffin recalls another communication—the riddle read aloud by Pericles in the play's opening scene:

> I am no viper, yet I feed
> On mother's flesh which did me breed.
> I sought a husband, in which labor
> I found that kindness in a father.
> He's father, son, and husband mild;
> I mother, wife—and yet his child.
> How they may be, and yet in two,
> As you will live, resolve it you.
>
> (I.i.64-71)

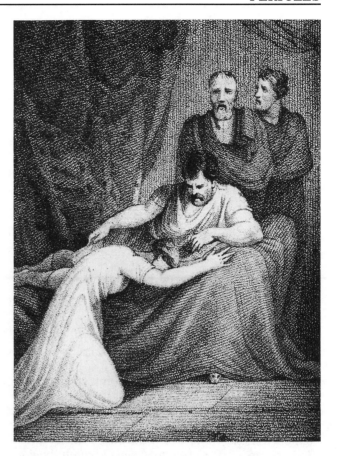

Act V, scene i. Marina, Pericles, Helicanus, and Lysimachus. By Porter (1800).

The content of the riddle and of Pericles' message is similar in that both describe a sexualrelationship, and the woman in each instance is the daughter of a king. In addition, the riddle and message consist, stylistically, of similar verse: eight lines in four couplets. And the high proportion of monosyllables in both gives to each the same staccato rhythm. Thus although Pericles' message in the coffin may strike us as singular and strange, it has about it a familiar quality.

Why should the message in Thaisa's coffin recall, by its form and content, certain features of the riddle? Through this resemblance the playwright contributes to the air of stylization, of patterned action, of recollection and anticipation that characterizes the play. One message takes the place of another just as one woman takes the place of another just as one relationship takes the place of another. With this substitution nature's continuity is reasserted. Thaisa's return to life, thanks to the efforts of the physician, represents not just an individual's triumph over death but also a larger restoration. When she revives, Cerimon says not that Thaisa awakes but rather that *nature* awakes: 'Gentlemen, this queen will live. Nature awakes, / A warmth breathes out of her' (III.ii.92-3).

Not only is the power of nature reasserted but so too the efficacy of art. For Cerimon identifies his physician's skill with what he calls 'secret art':

> 'Tis known, I ever
> Have studied physic; through which secret art,
> By turning o'er authorities, I have,
> Together with my practice, made familiar
> To me and to my aid the blest infusions
> That dwells in vegetives, in metals, stones;
> And can speak of the disturbances
> That nature works, and of her cures. . . .
>
> (III.ii.31-8)

His art, then, depends upon his study: 'I heard of an Egyptian / That had nine hours lien dead, / Who was by good appliance recovered' (lines 84-6). Or, as George Wilkins writes, perhaps in words that more closely approximate the original words of the playwright, 'I have read of some Egyptians, who after foure houres death, (if man may call it so) have raised impoverished bodies, like to this, unto their former health.'[16] In the revival of Thaisa, we witness the exercise of art as well as the resilience of nature. What allows nature to realize fully the potential for continued life and future growth is the written word—in the form of Pericles' message, a carefully constructed artifact that justifies the application of Cerimon's art; and in the form of Cerimon's reading, which provides the technique of his life-saving art.

The significance of the written word to the relationship of art and nature underlying this episode is elucidated by a passage in George Puttenham's *Arte of English Poesie* (1589):

> In some cases we say arte is an ayde and coadjutor to nature, and a furtherer of her actions to good effect, or peradventure a meane to supply her wants, by renforcing the causes wherein shee is impotent and defective, as doth the arte of phisicke, by helping the naturall concoction, retention, distribution, expulsion, and other vertues, in a weake and unhealthie bodie.[17]

That the author of a treatise on poetry should enlist the analogy of a physician mending a body may seem odd until we reflect on the way that the written word mediates between art and nature. For a culture that conceived of nature as a book and thus of nature as possessing inherent artistry, the analogy would seem less strange. If nature is a book, then art may co-operate with and reinforce the excellence of that book. Art can minister to nature because there is in nature something amenable to art. In the written word, which constitutes the contents of a book, art and nature converge. Peter Paul Rubens gives pictorial form to this convergence in a design used for the title page of *De Symbolis Heroicis* (Antwerp 1634) by Sylvester Pietrasanta (or Petrasancta).[18] It depicts nature as a multibreasted woman with flowers in her hair, and holding a laurel wreath. Opposite her stands Mercury, caduceus in one hand, representing art. He hands to the personification of talent, standing between himself and nature, a pen and brushes so that the heroic devices contained in the volume may be recorded. (Mercury's representation, incidentally, recalls his ancient association with the invention of the alphabet.)[19] Between art and nature is a stone altar, inscribed with the author's name and with the title of the book. The written word thus quite literally occupies the space where art and nature are conjoined.

The co-operation of art and nature informs the climactic meeting of Pericles and the young woman who is his daughter. Even before that point, Marina is identified with nature. As an adult, she makes her first appearance carrying a basket of flowers (IV.i.12). In the brothel, moreover, she is specifically associated with nature's bounty; the Bawd tells Boult, 'When nature fram'd this piece, she meant thee a good turn' (IV.ii.139-40). And Boult evokes Marina's initial appearance with flowers when he advertises her beauty to Lysimachus: 'For flesh and blood, sir, white and red, you shall see a rose, and she were a rose indeed' (IV.vi.34-5). By aligning Marina with nature, the playwright identifies her with the other young women who have preceded her onstage. We recall that Pericles, seeing Antiochus's daughter, spoke of tasting 'the fruit of yon celestial tree' (I.i.21). We recall too that Pericles' device at the tournament—a branch green at top—was presented to Thaisa. And now at Mytilene, Marina applies to herself a vegetative metaphor evocative of a family tree: 'My derivation was from ancestors / Who stood equivalent with mighty kings. / But time hath rooted out my parentage' (V.i.90-2).

Although Marina's natural beauty is her most salient characteristic, she is also herself an artist. Gower says that she successfully limns the natural world:

> Deep clerks she dumbs, and with her neele composes
> Nature's own shape of bud, bird, branch, or berry,
> That even her art sisters the natural roses.
>
> (act V chorus, 5-7)

And when Pericles describes Marina, he does so in terms that specifically connote artistic creation:

> My dearest wife was like this maid, and such a one
> My daughter might have been. My queen's square brows,

Her stature to an inch, as wand-like straight,
As silver-voic'd, her eyes as jewel-like
And cas'd as richly. . . .

(V.i.107-11)

The language, particularly 'silver-voic'd,' 'jewel-like,' and 'cas'd,' befits a work of art, something made of natural materials for aesthetic delight; a jewel, after all, is typically fashioned of a precious metal which provides the setting, and of a gem shaped by the cutter's skill. The appellation 'jewel-like' also identifies Marina with the woman who gave birth to her. We recall that Pericles encloses jewels in Thaisa's coffin; and when Thaisa revives, Cerimon speaks of her as though she were herself a jewel: 'behold / Her eyelids, cases to those heavenly jewels / Which Pericles hath lost, begin to part / Their fringes of bright gold' (III.ii.97-100).[20] When Pericles, at Mytilene, calls Marina 'jewel-like,' he is not, of course, suggesting that her appearance is the result of Boult's contrivance; she has not been gussied up with precious stones or make-up. Rather, her natural beauty is such that it evokes in the beholder the language of art.

It is precisely because she conflates the natural and the artistic that Marina can minister successfully to Pericles, who is described as her 'kingly patient' (V.i.71). Lysimachus, governor of Mytilene, addresses her as though she were a physician, when he urges her to help the ailing Pericles:

If that thy prosperous and artificial feat
Can draw him but to answer thee in aught,
Thy sacred physic shall receive such pay
As thy desires can wish.

(V.i.72-5)

'Physic' epitomizes her participation in both nature and art, for that term, deriving from a Greek word meaning 'knowledge of nature,' can signify 'natural science, the knowledge of the phenomenal world,' according to the *OED,* and also 'the art or practice of healing, the healing art.' In so far as Marina possesses knowledge of nature, she is capable of acting as physician, performing what Lysimachus calls an 'artificial feat.' Unlike Cerimon, she relies not on learning but rather upon an intuitive sympathy with nature, which Lysimachus alludes to when he calls her 'of a gentle kind and noble stock' (V.i.68). Hers is, then, not a power *over* nature so much as it is a power achieved *through* nature.

Although Marina is not a professional physician, she goes about her task in much the same way that Cerimon did when he sought to revive Thaisa. Confronting an inert and seemingly dead body, isolated from its surroundings by a coffin, Cerimon instructed his servant, 'The rough and woeful music that we have, / Cause it to sound, beseech you' (III.ii.88-9). The music has the effect of evoking Thaisa's latent vitality, re-estab-

lishing her link with the phenomenal world.[21] Now in Mytilene, Marina confronts a man whose self-absorbed silence is deathlike and whose isolation is expressed by the curtain behind which, apparently, he lies or sits.[22] Lysimachus hopes that Marina, 'with her sweet harmony' (V.i.45), may restore Pericles; and Marina, 'train'd / In music's letters' (act IV chorus, 7-8), sings to him, hoping to accomplish what Queen Katherine's song in *Henry VIII* achieves: 'In sweet music is such art, / Killing care and grief of heart' (III.i.12-13). Here in *Pericles* music may not immediately succeed in banishing the patient's 'Grief of heart,' but that music begins the process of re-establishing his relationship to his surroundings, a relationship that attains its most sublime form when he hears the music of the spheres (V.i.229). As a maker of music Marina imitates the creator himself, who brings order and proportion out of his multifarious creation. In the words of Godfrey Goodman, praising God: 'O excellent Artist, that could so sweetly tune nature to make such a melody, where there is such a concent and agreement on every side; the parts to the whole, the whole to the parts, each to it selfe, all to the Maker! here is neither sound, nor voice to the eare, yet a most sweet and delectable harmony, a musicke of nature.'[23]

As physician Marina balances graceful solicitude with a certain detachment; she is characterized by extraordinary poise. Even though her effort initially seems ineffectual, as Pericles pushes her away following her song, she remains serene. When Pericles says, 'thou dost look / Like Patience gazing on king's graves, and smiling / Extremity out of act' (V.i.137-9), he describes the courteous though reserved demeanour that compels admiration. Like Antiochus' daughter and Simonides' daughter earlier, this daughter of Pericles has the composure and restraint befitting someone of noble ancestry.

In the comparison of Marina to a statue on a tomb, Pericles implicitly likens her to a work of art. Missing from the comparison, though, is any reference to what one usually sees on such a monument—an inscription. This absence points to something that earlier scenes may lead us to expect: the representation of the written word in some literal form, shaped by the writer's art and used to define the identity of a woman whose beauty evokes the personification of nature. The written word, however, has already been employed to describe Marina. For earlier, when Pericles, supposing his daughter dead, visits her tomb, he reads an inscription that has been written 'In glitt'ring golden characters' (IV.iii.44). Gower presents the text:

'The fairest, sweetest, and best lies here,
Who withered in her spring of year.
She was of Tyrus the King's daughter,
On whom foul death hath made this
    slaughter.

> Marina was she call'd, and at her birth,
> Thetis, being proud, swallowed some part o'
>   th' earth.
> Therefore the earth, fearing to be
>   o'erflowed,
> Hath Thetis' birth-child on the heavens
>   bestowed;
> Wherefore she does, and swears she'll
>   never stint,
> Make raging battery upon shores of flint.'
>
> (IV.iv.34-43)

Reading this epitaph and seeing the tomb are what trigger Pericles' passion, which is presented in a dumb show:

> Enter Pericles at one door with all his train; Cleon and Dionyza at the other. Cleon shows Pericles the tomb; whereat Pericles makes lamentation, puts on sackcloth, and in a mighty passion departs.
>
> (IV.iv.22)

This pantomimic action has the effect of fixing the moment powerfully in our minds. And coming near the conclusion of act IV, the dumb show precedes, with the intervention of the brothel scene, the meeting of Marina and Pericles in the first scene of act V.

As Pericles and Marina confront one another, they evoke, by sight, sound, and speech, a much earlier meeting—that in the play's opening scene when Pericles gazes upon Antiochus' daughter. Again Pericles beholds a young woman who is as beautiful as she is poised. Again music accompanies their meeting: instrumental music earlier, at Antiochus' direction; song here, followed by the music of the spheres. Again there is talk of physic: earlier 'Sharp physic,' in the words of Pericles, referring to the last lines of the riddle; now, 'sacred physic,' in the words of Lysimachus, referring to Marina's power. And again there is a riddling quality to the conversation, in the replies of Marina.[24] When Pericles asks her, 'What country-woman? / Here of these shores?' (V.i.102-3), she answers, 'No, nor of any shores, / Yet I was mortally brought forth, and am / No other than I appear' (lines 103-5). Similarly, when Pericles asks where she lives, she replies elliptically, 'Where I am but a stranger. From the deck / You may discern the place' (lines 114-15). Throughout this conversation Pericles seeks to discover who the woman really is. This time no literal message is available to help him. But he has a clue in the very features of her face. Scrutinizing her, Pericles figuratively reads her countenance and moves towards the answer: 'thou lookest / Like one I lov'd indeed' (V.i.124-5).

The recognition of Marina leads within moments to Pericles' vision of the goddess Diana. Like many pre-vious incidents, the theophany may seem sudden—no deities have appeared in any earlier scene. And yet, as elsewhere, the action is not entirely without precedent. In fact, from the opening lines of the play Diana has been present in the characters' minds.[25] Under her name Lucina,[26] Diana is invoked by Antiochus when he speaks of his daughter's birth; by Simonides when he tells Thaisa's suitors that she will continue to 'wear Diana's livery' (II.v.10); by Pericles (again under the name Lucina) when his wife gives birth to their daughter; by Thaisa herself when she is revived by the physician and cries, 'O dear Diana' (III.ii.104); by Pericles, who swears 'By bright Diana' (III.iii.28) when he leaves his daughter at Tharsus; and by Marina who, in the brothel, says, 'Diana aid my purpose!' (IV.ii.148). Since so much of the dramatic action hasoccurred under the aegis of the goddess, there is a logic to her appearance and to her instructions that Pericles journey to her shrine at Ephesus and recapitulate his story there. After all, she has been involved, in some way, with virtually every turn of his fortunes.

Pericles' journey to Ephesus is consistent too with the very meaning of the goddess whose temple he visits. Although she is the goddess of chastity, Diana is also frequently depicted amid the world of external nature, hunting in a forest. Hence her customary implement is the bow, along with quiver and arrows. Diana's other principal symbol, the crescent moon, points to a still more profound association with nature.[27] She is identified with cyclicity, with natural rhythms, whether of the moon, tide, or human body. Hence she is a deity associated with childbirth and nurturing and, thus, with nature herself. In some Renaissance representations, Diana's identity with nature is unmistakable. Her statue at Villa d'Este in Tivoli, created about 1565-72, presents her as a multibreasted herm,[28] as do Renaissance books of mythography. Vincenzo Cartari's chapter on Diana includes a picture of a multibreasted figure and, beneath, a caption that begins, 'Imagine della dea Natura.'[29] Giordano Bruno, moreover, in his *Heroic Frenzies* identifies Diana with 'the world, the universe, the nature which is in things.'[30] As a symbol of nature, Diana rightly presides over the reunion of Pericles, Marina, and Thaisa at Ephesus. For at the moment that husband and wife, mother and daughter, and father and daughter are reunited after so many years, we feel nature's essential stability, permanence, and capacity for renewal. It is this that Pericles celebrates when, in his joy, he says, 'Pure Dian, / I bless thee for thy vision, and will offer / Night-oblations to thee' (V.iii.68-70).

Diana's shrine, legendary for its splendour, provides the appropriate site for the culmination of Pericles' story in another way as well, for the goddess is the recipient of the written word. In Lawrence Twine's *Patterne of Painefull Adventures,* the narrator reports that, following the hero's reunion with his family, he applied his vacant time to his booke, and hee wrote the whole storie and discourse of his owne life and adventures at large, the which he caused to be written foorth in two large volumes, whereof he sent one to the Temple of Diana at Ephesus, and placed the other in his owne library. Of which historie this is but a small abstract. . . .[31]

The history befits a narrative in which the written word, in its various forms, has proved so important. Like Lawrence Twine, the author of the play too associates divinity with the written word.[32] When Cerimon opens Thaisa's coffin and finds a message, he calls upon the twin brother of Diana: 'A passport too! / Apollo, perfect me in the characters!' (III.ii.66-7). Later, in the reunion scene, this same physician appears at Diana's shrine bearing 'letters of good credit,' with news of Thaisa's father. And Gower makes explicit the connection between Diana and the artistry of the written word when he relates that in childhood Marina 'would with rich and constant pen / Vail to her mistress Dian' (act IV chorus, 28-9).[33]

Although the Pericles of the play neither records the story of his adventures with pen and ink, nor sends an account to Diana's shrine, the presenter of the dramatic action, Gower, possesses Pericles' story in written (or printed) form. We know this because the title page of George Wilkins's *Painfull Adventures of Pericles Prince of Tyre* is adorned with a woodcut showing 'what Gower probably looked like on stage during the play's first performance.'[34] In the illustration Gower stands beside a lectern on which is set an open book, presumably a book containing Pericles' story. It seems likely that in performance the actor playing Gower would lift that book from the lectern and refer to it during his summary of Pericles' experience. (This seems especially likely when Gower reads aloud the inscription on Marina's monument.) That book would, along with Gower's presence, serve a theatrical purpose, emphasizing the antiquity of the events dramatized, the psychic distance separating past and present, the remoteness of the actual events from the lives of the spectators. The book would also suggest that Pericles' wondrous adventures have a discernible shape and purpose. Turbulent and disorderly as individual episodes of tempest and passion may seem, they manifestcoherence when viewed collectively in the written words of a book. To stand back from the immediacy of events, as Gower does and as he invites us to do, is to recognize the pattern that Lawrence Twine names in the very title of his book about Pericles, a pattern that finds its genesis in an artful nature.

Notes

[1] The art-nature topos has been discussed by Edward William Tayler, *Nature and Art in Renaissance Litera-*

ture (New York: Columbia University Press 1964), and by Leonard Barkan, *Nature's Work of Art: The Human Body as Image of the World* (New Haven: Yale University Press 1975). For nature as book, see Ernst Robert Curtius, *European Literature and the Latin Middle Ages,* trans Willard R. Trask, Bollingen Library (1953; New York and Boston: Harper and Row 1963), 319-26.

[2] Stylized action in *Pericles* takes various forms: the ritual at Antiochus' court; the tournament, with its ceremonial presentation of imprese; the banquet at Pentapolis, with its accompanying dance; the solemn reunion at Diana's temple; and the dumb shows.

[3] In 'Puzzle and Artifice: The Riddle as Metapoetry in "Pericles," ' *Shakespeare Survey* 29 (1976), 11-20, Phyllis Gorfain comments: 'We may consider the riddle a false artifice, for its end is deception, not revelation' (13). Every riddle, however, may be considered to display 'false artifice' in the sense that the riddle seeks to delay recognition of the truth. Moreover, whatever Antiochus' purpose, the riddle does in fact bring about a revelation. Therefore, I think that it would be more accurate to say that the riddle represents true artifice, but that the relationship it represents is, of course, perverted.

[4] *The Riverside Shakespeare,* ed G. Blakemore Evans et al (Boston: Houghton Mifflin 1974).

[5] In *Antony and Cleopatra,* a play entered in the Stationers' Register together with Pericles on 20 May 1608, the soothsayer says, 'In nature's infinite book of secrecy / A little I can read' (I.ii.10-11).

[6] Gower's *Confessio Amantis* was written c 1383-93. David Bevington, in *Shakespeare: The Late Romances* (New York: Bantam 1988), notes that Lawrence Twine's work was registered in 1576 but exists today 'only in two editions from about 1594-1595 and 1607' (115).

[7] *Time, Tide and Tempest: A Study of Shakespeare's Romances* (San Marino: Huntington Library 1973), 85.

[8] Does this branch appear as a picture or is it a real piece of wood? G. Wilson Knight, in *The Crown of Life: Essays in Interpretation of Shakespeare's Final Plays* (London and New York: Oxford University Press 1947), suggests that the branch is 'probably the actual thing, not merely a device' (47). Mary Judith Dunbar, in ' "To the Judgement of Your Eye": Iconography and the Theatrical Art of *Pericles,*' in *Shakespeare, Man of the Theater,* ed Kenneth Muir, et al (Newark: University of Delaware Press; London and Toronto: Associated University Presses 1983), 86-97, accepts Knight's suggestion: 'Having no shield he has had to make his own device, probably from a natural branch'

(90). If Knight and Dunbar are correct in their supposition, one wonders where precisely the motto would appear: could it have been written on a piece of paper and then attached to the branch? Whatever the materials, scholars have failed to discover an exact pictorial antecedent for Pericles' device. Henry Green, in *Shakespeare and the Emblem Writers* (1870; New York: Burt Franklin n.d.), comments: 'The sixth knight's emblem is very simple, natural, and appropriate; and I am most of all disposed to regard it as invented by Shakespeare himself to complete a scene, the greater part of which had been accommodated from other writers' (182). F.D. Hoeniger, editor of the New Arden *Pericles* (London: Methuen 1963), agrees with Henry Green: 'No source for this motto has been found; it may well have been invented by the playwright' (56). However, Alan R. Young, in 'A Note on the tournament Impresas in *Pericles*,' *Shakespeare Quarterly* 36 (1985), 453-6, proposes that Shakespeare may have turned for this detail 'to an impresa that Sidney had invented for one of his own appearances at aWhitehall tournament' (454). For analogues of Pericles' branch in the visual arts, see Gerhart B. Ladner, 'Vegetation Symbolism and the Concept of Renaissance,' *De Artibus Opuscula XL: Essays in Honor of Erwin Panofsky,* ed Millard Meiss (New York: New York University Press 1961), 1:303-22.

[9] 'Gower and Shakespeare in *Pericles*,' *Shakespeare Quarterly* 33 (1982), 473.

[10] P. Goolden, in 'Antiochus' Riddle in Gower and Shakespeare,' *Review of English Studies,* n.s. 6 (1955), 245-51, observes that the playwright departs from his sources by having the 'I' of the riddle refer to the daughter instead of the father.

[11] James O. Wood, in 'The Running Image in *Pericles*,' *Shakespeare Studies,* 5 (1969), 240-52, observes that Simonides' book metaphor 'led the author to invent the indispensable bibliographical term (surprisingly, not recorded by the *OED*), *title-page*.' Wood comments, 'This matches happily Shakespeare's invention (see *OED*) of the companion term, *title-leaf* (2H4, I.i.60)' (243).

[12] Joan Hartwig, in *Shakespeare's Tragicomic Vision* (Baton Rouge: Louisiana State University Press 1972), observes: 'Gower's explanation of all the dumb shows in *Pericles* is so extensive that one wonders why the first two are necessary. Since the letters' contents are explained anyway, the visual elaboration seems excessive. Ostensibly they present little more than the reading of a letter, which hardly merits the attention of this special dramatic form. For example, Simonides enters reading a letter in II.iv, the content of which he makes known in a soliloquy (15 ff.). The pantomime, on the other hand, removes the scene from the realistic level and insists on its symbolic potentials' (37).

[13] In *The Secular Scripture: A Study of the Structure of Romance* (Cambridge, Mass, and London: Harvard University Press 1976), Northrop Frye comments, '*Pericles* . . . seems to be a deliberate experiment in presenting a traditional archetypal sequence as nakedly and baldly as possible' (51).

[14] To these three sets of fathers and daughters we may add Cleon and Philoten. This daughter does not actually appear as a character onstage, but she is described by Gower (act IV chorus, 15-40).

[15] For evidence that Wilkins's narrative was based upon a dramatized account of Pericles' story, performed by Shakespeare's company, see Nancy C. Michael, 'The Relationship between the 1609 Quarto of *Pericles* and Wilkins's *Painful Adventures*,' *Tulane Studies in English* 22 (1977), 51-68. The Shakespearean quality of the words spoken by Pericles when he sees his daughter was first noted by John Payne Collier, in *Shakespeare's Library: A Collection of the Plays, Romances, Novels, Poems and Histories Employed by Shakespeare in the Composition of His Works,* 2nd ed (London: Reeves and Turner 1875), 240. The suggestion has been widely accepted. In his edition of Wilkins's *Painfull Adventures of Pericles Prince of Tyre* (Liverpool: University Press of Liverpool 1953), Kenneth Muir says that the passage beginning with the words 'Poore inch of Nature' seems to preserve a Shakespearean phrase, omitted by accident from Q' (xii). Similarly, J. C. Maxwell, in his edition of *Pericles* (Cambridge: Cambridge University Press 1956), says that the words 'belong to the Shakespeare original' (146). James G. McManaway concurs in his Pelican edition of *Pericles* (Baltimore: Penguin 1961), 121. Philip Edwards, in the New Penguin *Pericles* (Harmondsworth: Penguin 1976), restores the four words to the text (at III.i.34 of his edition), but places them within square brackets. The 'reconstructed text' of *Pericles,* included in *William Shakespeare: The Complete Works,* gen ed Stanley Wells and Gary Taylor (Oxford: Clarendon Press 1986), restores Pericles' four words (scene xi, line 34) and omits brackets.

[16] *The Painfull Adventures of Pericles Prince of Tyre,* in *Narrative and Dramatic Sources of Shakespeare,* ed Geoffrey Bullough, 8 vols (New York: Columbia University Press 1957-75), 6:522. G. Blakemore Evans,in the Riverside edition of *Pericles,* writes of Cerimon's statement about Egyptians, 'eds. have felt that the text here is corrupt and that Wilkins preserves something close to the original' (1514). Evans then quotes the words that Wilkins ascribes to Cerimon, and he concludes, 'the blank verse movement of Wilkins' prose is obvious.'

[17] *The Arte of English Poesie,* ed Gladys Doidge Willcock and Alice Walker (Cambridge: Cambridge University Press 1936), 303.

[18] Reproduced by J. Richard Judson and Carl van de Velde, *Book Illustrations and Title-pages,* Corpus Rubenianum Ludwig Burchard 21, 2 vols (London and Philadelphia: Harvey Miller-Heyden and Son 1978), 2:fig. 234.

[19] A pictorial rendering of Mercury's connection with the written word appears in an anonymous Florentine engraving of about 1460. In the lower section of the print, the artist illustrates various human activities over which Mercury, who rides across the sky in his chariot, presides. In the foreground two seated scholars examine books piled on a table. See *Children of Mercury: The Education of Artists in the Sixteenth and Seventeenth Centuries* (Providence: Brown University Press 1984), 8.

[20] Those jewels in the coffin may remind some spectators of the powerfully restorative effects which gems were believed to exert on the human body. Paracelsus, for instance, speaks of 'the first entities of gems, which, indeed, by their primal essence most powerfully reinstate the whole body in its pristine powers, cleanse it from all its impurities, and renovate and restore it none otherwise than the fire changes lead into purest glass.' See *The Hermetic and Alchemical Writings of . . . Paracelsus the Great,* trans Arthur Edward Waite (1894; Boulder: Shambhala 1976), 2:132.

[21] In *Touches of Sweet Harmony: Pythagorean Cosmology and Renaissance Poetics* (San Marino: Huntington Library 1974), S.K. Heninger writes: 'Music is capable of increasing or diminishing the passions of the human soul by affecting its harmony, and there are numerous examples of the emotional effects of music, Biblical as well as classical. David calmed the anguish of Saul by playing on the lyre and singing, and Timotheus by his music aroused Alexander from feasting to warfare. The source of this tradition for music's power is likely to have been Pythagoras' school made popular through Plato' (103). In a discussion of Marsilio Ficino's interest in the occult, John S. Mebane (*Renaissance Magic and the Return of the Golden Age: The Occult Tradition and Marlowe, Jonson, and Shakespeare* [Lincoln and London: University of Nebraska Press 1989]), suggests the efficacy of music as a restorative to the human body and soul: 'music imprints itself on the air, and consequently it can mingle freely with the *spiritus* which lies within the human ear. The harmoniously ordered forms are in motion, as are actual celestial influences, and they communicate that patterned movement, through the *spiritus,* to the soul' (31).

[22] Richard Hosley has suggested to me that the action preceding Helicanus' words, 'Behold him' (V.i.36), may have consisted of the drawing back of a curtain, revealing Pericles recumbent on a chaise longue, or day bed. The chaise may then have been either thrust or carried out onto the stage from the discovery space. That Pericles is probably behind a curtain is suggested by Lysimachus' question, 'May we not see him?' (line 31), and by Helicanus' ensuing remark, 'Behold him.' That Pericles is probably reclining is suggested both by the overall situation—he has been incommunicado for three months and has eaten little—and by his words to Marina later in the scene, 'Come sit by me' (line 141). Still later, as Pericles hears the music of the spheres, he says, 'Let me rest' (line 235), and Lysimachus adds, 'A pillow for his head' (line 236).

[23] *The Creatures Praysing God: or, The Religion of dumbe Creatures* (London 1622), 22.

[24] Phyllis Gorfain observes that Marina's reply, at V.i.103-5, 'encapsulates her autobiography in the form of an oppositional riddle' (15), which 'contains at least two comments on a hidden referent; they oppose each other by contradicting laws of logic, natural form, or causality' (15n1).

[25] In the New Arden *Pericles,* F.D. Hoeniger notes: 'The goddess is referred to only twice in Gower and in Twine, but about a dozen times in the play, which may be significant' (4). Marion Lomax, in *Stage Images and Traditions: Shakespeare to Ford* (Cambridge: Cambridge University Press 1987), writes of Hoeniger's remark: 'This would seem to be an enormous understatement,' and Lomax goes on to observe, 'it seems that Shakespeare carefully deprived the play of an active mother-figure. Until the end, none of the characters have such a guardian—the role is supplied by Diana, who plays a central part throughout' (82). Lomax provides an extensive and insightful analysis of Diana in the play.

[26] For the conflation of Diana and Lucina, see Cicero, *De Natura Deorum,* trans H. Rackham, Loeb Classical Library (1933; Cambridge, Mass: Harvard University Press; London: William Heinemann 1961), 189-91.

[27] In *1 Henry IV,* Falstaff alludes to Diana's familiar associations when he tells Prince Hal, 'Let us be Diana's foresters, gentlemen of the shade, minions of the moon, and let men say we be men of good government, being govern'd, as the sea is, by our noble and chaste mistress the moon' (I.ii.25-9).

[28] Reproduced by Barbara von Barghahn, *Age of Gold, Age of Iron,* 2 vols (Lanham, New York, London: University Press of America 1985), 2:fig 290. Such representations are based on classical statues. The Palazzo dei Conservatori, on the Capitoline hill in Rome, contains an ancient statue of the multibreasted Diana of Ephesus, whose body is decorated with the heads

of various animals and whose head is surmounted by a tower.

[29] *Le Vere e Nove Imagini de gli Dei delli Antichi* (1615), ed Stephen Orgel (New York and London: Garland 1979), 109. Similarly, a ceiling decoration in the Palazzina Marfisa d'Este (Ferrara), painted at the end of the sixteenth century, depicts Diana as a symbol of fertility, her front covered with the same assemblage of breasts. Reproduced by Ranieri Varese, *Ferrara: Palazzina Marfisa* (Bologna: Calderini 1980), 21, fig 95.

[30] *The Heroic Frenzies*, trans Paul Eugene Memmo, Jr (Chapel Hill: University of North Carolina Press 1964), 225.

[31] In *Narrative and Dramatic Sources of Shakespeare*, ed Bullough, 6:481.

[32] Robert Grams Hunter, in *Shakespeare and the Comedy of Forgiveness* (New York and London: Columbia University Press 1965), observes that 'In this use of the theophany, Shakespeare is returning to a romance tradition older than that of his immediate predecessors in the romantic drama' (138). Hunter cites *The Rare Triumphs of Love and Fortune and Sir Clyomon and Sir Clamydes*. Interestingly, the written word figures in the theophanies of both plays. Divine intervention in *Pericles, Cymbeline,* and other late romances is usefully discussed by Richard Paul Knowles, ' "The More Delay'd, Delighted": Theophanies in the Last Plays,' *Shakespeare Studies* 15 (1982), 269-80. Finally, Stephen Dickey, in 'Language and Role in *Pericles,'* *English Literary Renaissance* 16 (1986), 550-66, notes that the intersection of art and nature 'often makes for a supernatural moment in the romances' (561). Dickey makes this remark in a paragraph dealing with the invocation of Diana's name in *Pericles.*

[33] In ' "Deep clerks she dumbs": The Learned Heroine in *Apollonius of Tyre* and *Pericles,'* *Comparative Drama,* 22 (1988-9), 289-303, Elizabeth Archibald claims that Marina's skills, including her 'writing poetry to Diana,' are 'stereotypically feminine' (295). Although weaving and needlework, also ascribed to Marina,may fall under this rubric, and although devotion to Diana may be more commonly feminine than masculine, I can find no justification in this or any other Renaissance play for calling writing a specifically feminine activity. The men in *Pericles* who write include Pericles, Helicanus, and, presumably, Cleon, author of the inscription on Marina's tomb. We may add Antiochus to this list, if he is the author of the riddle. Moreover, both Pericles and Simonides use figurative language involving the written word.

[34] F. David Hoeniger, 'Gower and Shakespeare in *Pericles,'* 463.

IMAGERY AND SEXUALITY

Gerald J. Schiffhorst (essay date 1967)

SOURCE: "The Imagery of *Pericles* and What It Tells Us," in *Ball State University Forum,* Vol. VIII, No. 3, Summer, 1967, pp. 61-70.

[*In the essay below, Schiffhorst surveys the varied imagery of* Pericles, *offering it as evidence that the play was either entirely written or emended throughout by Shakespeare.*]

Critical attention to the imagery of Shakespeare's *Pericles* has been almost negligible, and commentators have often been content to dismiss the play as only in part Shakespeare's. Recent scholarship has indicated that the differences between the first two and the last three acts are due either to two separate reporters involved in the transmission of the text or to the likely possibility that Shakespeare, basing the play on the work of another dramatist, made a few alterations in the first two acts but completely rewrote the last three. Concludes Kenneth Muir: "There are no lines in the first two acts which are certainly Shakespeare's, though there are a number which could be his."[1] It is my purpose to suggest that, although the imagery of *Pericles* cannot compare in richness with that of the great plays, it spans the whole breadth of Shakespeare's imaginative material and presents a more rewarding poetic experience than is often thought possible; and, what is more important, that the number, types, and efficacy of the images and clusters in the first two as well as the last three acts point to work that seems indisputably Shakespearean. Imagery is hardly a foolproof basis for discussing questions of authorship, but it can provide us here with a new and meaningful look at Shakespeare in the process of revision.

The images of *Pericles* can, in general, be said to conform to the basic Shakespearean patterns as established by Caroline Spurgeon and others.[2] The following discussion will concern itself with each of these general types of images: those concerned with nature and those concerned with daily life and customs. I am also indebted to the work of Edward Armstrong,[3] who has divided the wealth of Shakespeare's images into two fundamental thematic categories—those dealing with life and death, which are clues to all of the poet's associations. Thus light, love, warmth, and harmony are manifestations of life; whereas hatred, darkness, evil, and fear are aspects of the other half of the dichotomy. With relatively little difficulty, the images of *Pericles* can be seen as clear and often salient examples of the basic preoccupations of Shakespeare's imagination.

I

Turning first to the clusters of images, the result of the associative processes of Shakespeare's mind, we are initially surprised to find so many in the first half of the play and so few in what is usually said to be more authentically Shakespearean. The eight passages discussed below are the most obvious examples of seemingly Shakespearean poetic associations. The following speech of Antiochus may be less rich in scope than other cluster patterns, but the juxtaposition of so many images of life and death is inescapable.

> Before thee stands this fair Hesperides,
> With golden fruit, but dangerous to be
>   touched;
> For death-like dragons here affright thee
>   hard.
> Her face, like heaven, enticeth thee to view
> Her countless glory, which desert must gain;
> And which without desert because thine eye
> Presumes to reach, all the whole heap must
>   die.
> Yon sometimes famous princes, like thyself,
> Drawn by report, advent'rous by desire,
> Tell thee, with speechless tongues and
>   semblance pale,
> That without covering save yon field of
>   stars,
> Here they stand martyrs, slain in Cupid's
>   wars;
> And with dead cheeks advise thee to desist
> For going on death's net, whom none resist.
>   (I. i. 27-40)[4]

The use of such terms as "fair," "golden," "countless glory" indicates the superficial virtues of the speaker's daughter; and the distinction between appearance and reality is manifest by the terms which follow: "dangerous," "death-like dragons," and the other words signifying death. The use of "eye" at line 32 not only connotes the common association of hollow eye sockets with death but is also in keeping with a common device (see also *Macbeth*, II. i. 49) involving the use of eyes to suggest an awareness of evil; it is as if Shakespeare associated the sense of vision with the perception of sin or evil beneath a deceptive veneer. The "semblance pale" and the "field of stars" are in keeping with the cold quality of fear ("affright") and of death. Thus we have a statement not only of the danger which awaits the wooer but also of the ineluctable connection between sin and death.

When Pericles reveals in the following soliloquy that he has discovered the truth about Antiochus and his daughter, we have a similar combination of images connoting sin and death, but the dualism is more obvious:

> Sharp physic is the last: but, O you powers
> That give heaven countless eyes to view
>   men's acts,
> Why cloud they not their sights perpetually,
> If this be true, which makes me pale to read
>   it?
> Fair glass of light, I love you, and could
>   still
> Were not this glorious casket stored with ill.
> But I must tell you, now my thoughts
>   revolt;
> For he's no man on whom perfections wait
> That, knowing sin within, will touch the
>   gate.
> You are a fair viol and your sense the
>   strings.
> Who, fingered to make man his lawful
>   music.
> Would draw heaven down and all the gods
>   to hearken,
> But being played upon before your time,
> Hell only danceth at so harsh a chime.
>   (I. i. 72-85)

Here heaven's "countless eyes" clearly indicates the awareness of evil, and the "glorious casket storedwith ill" is a graphic example of the appearance-reality dichotomy. The allusions to music indicate the tendency of Shakespeare's mind to swing from sin to chaos ("my thoughts revolt") and as a loathsome disease to its complete opposite; yet, by the end of the speech, the perfection of music, too, is sullied: "Hell only danceth at so harsh a chime." The various theological terms ("heaven," "sin," "lawful") indicate more than a mere physical conception of sin, however; and the images of light, jewels (casket), and music as foils to the expression of evil are striking.

A few lines later, the sin-death correlation is again apparent when Pericles says to Antiochus:

> For vice repeated is like the wand'ring wind,
> Blows dust in others' eyes, to spread itself;
> And yet the end of all is bought thus dear,
> The breath is gone, and the sore eyes see
>   clear
> To stop the air would hurt them. The blind
>   mole casts
> Copped hills towards heaven, to tell the
>   earth is thronged
> By man's oppression; and the poor doth die
>   for 't.
> Kings are men's gods; in vice their law's
>   their will;
> And if Jove stray, who dares say Jove doth
>   ill?
> It is enough you know; and it is fit,
> What being more known grows worse, to
>   smother it.

All love the womb that their first being
   bred,
Then give my tongue like leave to love my
   head.

                              (I. i. 96-108)

Here we are moving from scandal to evil in general
and finally to death. The references to "eyes," "ill,"
"die," "vice," and "smother" juxtaposed with "air" and
"breath," plus "dust" (cf. "dusty death," *Macbeth,* V.
v. 23), all indicate the evil-death theme. The three
references to eyes and the mention of "womb" denote
the typically Shakespearean association of death with
hollowness, and the dualistic use of "love" in such a
passage is note worthy. The "sore eyes," "blind mole,"
"poor worm" images suggest the inevitable connection
between sin and disease and remind us of the unifying
blindness imagery here. Images of man's oppression
and insignificance are also used effectively as a sharp
and surprising contrast to what follows: "Kings are
earth's gods."

The final speech of Pericles at the close of the same
scene indicates still other variations on the same theme:

   How courtesy would seem to cover sin,
   When what is done is like an hypocrite,
   The which is good in nothing but in sight!
   If it be true that I interpret false,
   Then were it certain you were not so bad
   As with foul incest to abuse your soul;
   Where now you're both a father and a son,
   By your untimely claspings with your child,
   Which pleasure fits an husband, not a
      father;
   And she an eater of her mother's flesh,
   By the defiling of her parents' bed;
   And both like serpents are, who, though
      they feed
   On sweetest flowers, yet they poison breed.
   Antioch, farewell! for wisdom sees, those
      men
   Blush not in actions blacker than the night
   Will shun no course to keep them from the
      light.
   One sin, I know, another doth provoke;
   Murder's as near to lust as flame to smoke:
   Poison and treason are the hands of sin,
   Ay, and the targets to put off the shame:
   Then, lest my life be cropp'd to keep you
      clear,
   By flight I'll shun the danger which I fear.

                              (I. i. 121-42)

The use of "bed," "eater," "soul," "feed," and the
pervasive idea of imminent death comprise the major
portion of what Armstrong calls the kite image cluster.[5] Despite the absence of any bird references, there
are clear indications of every other part of the cluster:

bed, death, spirits (soul), and food (because of the
frequent Shakespearean association of kites with car-
rion). The connection between love and food, especially between loathsome food and evil, and the flow-
ers-serpent dualism, are treated below. Another use of
dualism is the mention of "light" in the line following
"blacker than night." "Sin," "sees," "sight," "murder,"
"smoke," "poison," "danger," "fear," "lust," "flame,"
"treason," and the military "targets" (shields) are all
indicative of various aspects of death or sin, which
are conceived in terms of red ("blush" and "flame")
and black ("night" and "smoke").

The opening speech of the following scene involves an
interesting progression from sorrow to the inevitable
evil and death which have been haunting Pericles:

   Why should this change of thoughts,
   The sad companion, dull-eyed melancholy,
   Be my so used a guest as not an hour
   In the day's glorious walk, or peaceful
      night,
   The tomb where grief should sleep, can
      breed me quiet?
   Here pleasures court mine eyes, and mine
      eyes shun them,
   And danger, which I feared, is at Antioch,
   Whose arm seems far too short to hit me
      here;
   Yet neither pleasure's art can joy my spirits,
   Nor yet the other's distance comfort me.
   Then it is thus: the passions of the mind.
   That have their first conception by mis-
      dread,
   Have after-nourishment and life by care;
   And what was first but fear what might be
      done,
   Grows elder now and cares it be not done.

                              (I. ii. 2-15)

(Lines from *Richard II,* II. ii. 70, are remarkably similar to the above, not only in the grief-womb combination but also in the mention of eyes, which appear a
few lines later:

   Why should I welcome such a guest as
      grief . . .
   Some unborn sorrow, ripe in fortune's
      womb.)

Eyes are mentioned in the above passage three times,
and the picture of the inescapable sorrow leads directly to the "tomb where grief should sleep," thus
giving us two more images of death. "Sad," "danger,"
"fear," and "mis-dread" also contribute to the theme.
The second half of the death pattern, the womb imagery, emerges with "passions," "conception," "after-
nourishment," "breed," "grows," and "care." There is
possibly no more pervasive or striking use of dualism

in Shakespeare than the womb-tomb correlation, which enables the poet to suggest death by employing images of birth.

The discussion of famine in Tharsus between Cleon, Dionyza, and the others (I. iv. 34-70) includes a number of fairly obvious images of death in terms of hunger, eyes, hollowness, teeth, and mouths. The following words indicate the proliferation of such imagery here: "mouths," "starved," "hunger's teeth," the empty houses, "hollow eyes," "die," "weeping," "misery," "burial," and "sorrow." The use of summer, the season of plenty, as a measurement of time is ironic as is the combination of "stuffed" with "hollow vessels" in the same line.

The conversation between Pericles and the fishermen at II. i. 28-51 is noted by Armstrong[6] as a singular example of the association between two dissimilar king images: the drone, the king of insects, appearing with the whale, the king of the sea. More important thematically is the way in which the drone, a robber like death, the swallowing whale with its Jonah overtones, and the hollow references contribute to the pervasive suggestion of death: "mouthful," "belly," "belfry," "bells," "devours," "gaping."

The dualism in the following passage is effective in its reflection of the good and bad aspects of time:

> THAISA: To me he seems like diamond to glass.
> PERICLES: Yon king's to me like to my father's picture,
> Which tells me in that glory once he was;
> Had princes sit, like stars, about his throne,
> And he the sun, for them to reverence;
> None that beheld him but, like lesser lights,
> Did vail their crowns to his supremacy:
> Where now his son's like a glow-worm in the night.
> The which hath fire in darkness, none in light:
> Whereby I see that Time's the king of men;
> For he's their parent and he is their grave,
> And gives them what he will, not what they crave.
>
> (II. iii. 36-47)

Images of light ("sun," "diamond," "fire," "lights") lead to those of darkness, Shakespeare making it clear that the two, like good and evil, are inextricably mixed: the "glowworm in the night" and the "fire in darkness" are perfect images for this concept and lead directly to the key idea—that time, a king like the sun,

is both a joy and a sorrow. Thus the dualism in the imagery both reflects and heightens the significance of Shakespeare's thought.

Marina enters in the fourth act with a basket of flowers, but she speaks of death:

> No, I will rob Tellus of her weed,
> To strew thy green with flowers; the yellows, blues;
> The purple violets, and marigolds,
> Shall as a carpet hang upon thy grave,
> While summer-days doth last. Ay me! poor maid,
> Born in a tempest, when my mother died
> This world to me is as a lasting storm,
> Whirring me from my friends.
>
> (IV.i. 14-21)

There is no inconsistency here between the beauty of the flowers and the mention of death and evil; for not only does the dualism serve as an effective foil to the tempest imagery, but imagery of death predominates from the first line. The connection between death and robbery has been noted above, and the references to the decorated "green" (grave), the purple violet of mourning, and fading summer, together with the storm and wind allusions (cf. *The Winter's Tale,* IV, iv. 119 ff.), indicate that beauty and tragedy often go hand in hand.

II

Individual images may provide less striking or convincing clues to Shakespeare's hand, but collectively they form an impressive series of parallels. As is evident from a study of Spurgeon's work, flowers occupy the most prominent place in the "growing things" category of nature imagery; and it is not surprising that, next to the twenty-three images in *Pericles* based on trees, plants, and fruit, flowers should be dominant here, as they are in *Cymbeline;* for when Marina exclaims, as we have just seen, "No, I will rob Tellus of her weed. . . ." we are reminded of *Cymbeline*'s "With fairest flowers . . . I'll sweeten thy sad grave." (IV. ii. 218-20) Life seen as a flower is common in Shakespeare (see *As You Like It,* V. iii. 29: "Life was but a flower in springtime"); thus we have "life's flower" in Cerimon's speech at III. ii. 101. The reference to the chaste Marina as a "never-plucked" flower at IV. vi. 42 has several parallels, notably *Othello,* V. ii. 13.

One of the most important images of the play, Pericles' chivalric symbol of "A withered branch that's only green on top" (II. ii. 43), is a striking representation of the play's theme of hope and endurance in spite of difficulty. The analogy between men and plants when Helicanus says to Pericles,

How dare the plants look up to heaven,
  from whence
They have their nourishment?

(I. ii. 55-56)

reminds us of the garden scene in *Richard II* (III. iv. 29-107), though it is also important as an example of the common "sun as king" image. Several other images derived from growing and farming are relevant here. Lysimachus refers to the "seeds and roots of shame and iniquity" (IV. vi. 87); and, in the same scene, Marina is discussed as a "thornier piece of ground" (1. 46) which should be plowed. And, much earlier, Gower speaks of wit as "ripe" (Prol. I. 12). In short, the diversity of the references to growing things seems to be in keeping with Shakespeare's work as a whole.

Poetic use of the sea, another main subdivision of nature as material for imagery in the plays, is represented plentifully, in keeping not only with the presence of the sea in the plot materials but also with the imagery of the late romances (notably *The Tempest*) as a whole. In addition to numerous personifications of the sea noted below and several commonplace references to life or the world as a sea (e.g., II. i. 48-49), we have the image of the body as a ship, resembling *Cymbeline,* I. iii. 14:

> He bears
> A tempest, which his mortal vessel tears,
> And yet he rides it out.
>
> (*Pericles,* IV. iii. 87-89)

The sea as an image of trouble ("I leap into the seas" at II. iv. 45) bears a significant relation to the theme of the play and reminds us of *Hamlet's* "sea of troubles" (III. i. 59). The image of an overflowing river, emphasized by Spurgeon, appears twice here, at IV. iv. 40, and in these effective lines at II. iv. 25-26:

> . . . our griefs are risen to the top,
> And now at length they overflow their
>   banks.

In the same connection, storm, wind, and weather images are particularly vivid and significant, not only because of their integral relation to the plot and theme, but because of parallels with other plays.[7] A tempest as indicative of discord on the personal or political level is used effectively at I. ii. 98 and at IV. iii. 87-89, both of which are similar to Lear's "tempest in my mind" (III. iv. 12). Similarly, Marina laments that "This world to me is like a lasting storm" at IV. i. 20 (cf. *Romeo and Juliet,* III. ii. 64). In addition to several images based on spring (I. i. 12 and IV. iv. 35) and on winter, the reference to Thaisa as lovely "As a fair day in summer" (II. v. 36) seems to be closest to sounding Shakespearean (see Sonnet XVIII) and is based on the connection between love and light (day).

The sun and stars dominate the "celestial body" imagery, as is usual in Shakespeare. There are three references to the sun as a king (II. iii. 40), but the use of stars is more common. "Yet cease your ire, you angry stars of heaven!" says Pericles in an effective speech at II. i. i; but stars are used more frequently as images of light (II. iii. 39 and V. iii. 80) or of fate (V. iii. 9).

Birds and their movement are a primary aspect of Shakespeare's nature imagery, and birds figure more prominently in *Pericles* than any other animals. Their appearance only in the second half of the play tends to support the view[8] that the last three acts alone represent Shakespeare's work. The image of a ship as a duck in line 49 of the Prologue to Act III resembles *Othello,* II. i. 190; and a nightingale appears in the fourth act (Prol., 26). A few lines later, we have the dove and crow as contrasting birds of good and evil, thus exemplifying Armstrong's thesis that the crow is indicative of death. In the same speech (1. 47) we have an interesting example of Shakespeare's concern both for the speed of time and for the flight of birds (see also IV. vi. 102-103 and V. ii. 15: "in feathered briefness"). The goose, Armstrong tells us, is an erotic image; and the use of the "gosling" in the brothel scene (IV. ii. 85) is very fitting. The "petty wrens" (IV. iii. 23) as small, annoying creatures (see *King Lear,* IV. vi. 114 and *Macbeth,* IV. ii. 9) are employed here as a unique but graphic symbol of rumor. The eagle as a common indicator of kingship is used in reference to Cleon at IV. iii. 48.

Other important animal references include the analogy between men and fish; the imagery underlying the speeches of the fishermen at II. i is parallel to *The Tempest,* III. ii. 30 and to *Henry IV, Part II,* I. 1. 200. The whale (II. i. 30), the king image, is used here to represent rich men, as in *Henry IV, Part II,* IV. iv. 40. The "belching whale" appears at III. i. 62, as in *Troilus and Cressida,* V. v. 23. In addition to several reptile and insect images, the use of the worm to indicate human depravity (I. i. 102; see *The Tempest,* III, 1. 31) or evil in general (V. i. 59) is noteworthy. An interesting example of the mixture of good and evil in the world occurs when Pericles says, "his son's a glowworm in the night" (II. iii. 43), which parallels *Hamlet,* I. v. 90. Among the poet's other uses of animals to denote human oppression, insignificance, or bestiality is the picture of man as a "blind mole" (I. i. 100), an epithet appearing also in *The Winter's Tale* and *The Tempest.* The connection between a "spaniel" (IV. vi. 126) and an annoying or base creature is common in Shakespeare (cf. *Julius Caesar,* III. i. 43).

Among the domestic images the use of mirror imagery for various purposes seems typically Shakespearean, both "the glass of fashion" (*Hamlet,* III. i. 155) suggested at I. iv. 27 and the surprisingly well-developed images at I. i. 45-46, which present a clear example of the Shakespearean conception of life as a breath and of death as the mirror which proves this to us.[9] These lines,

> death . . . should be like a mirror,
> Who tells us life's but breath, to trust it
> error. . . .

are similar to Lear's poignant scene with the dead Cordelia (V. iii. 261-63). This concept of death as a mirror is a good example of what Armstrong calls dualism, that is, that Shakespeare's "imagination constantly swings from an image to its contrary."[10] Thus a mirror, instead of reflecting life, suggests death. Such an apparently mature and characteristic image so early in the play, together with much of the other striking poetry, would seem to indicate Shakespeare's hand very definitely in the first part of *Pericles*. A mirror is also used, as in *Measure for Measure* (II. iv. 125-26), in connection with light and virtue; thus the Bawd tells Boult to "crack the glass of her virginity." (IV. vi. 144)

There are two other more limited groups of domestic images which can be noted here, appearing as they do both early and late in the play: the images of fire and of jewels. There are at least five instances of the former, one occurring in the opening scene of the first act (1. 138) when Pericles says, "Murder's as near to lust as flame to smoke." The playwright apparently connected smoke with murder (*Macbeth*, I. v. 52: "Come, thick night, and pall thee in the dunnest smoke of hell.") and with passion ("love is a smoke. . . ." *Romeo and Juliet*, I. i. 196). The line can also be seen in connection with the natural association of evil with darkness as discussed below. Salient examples of the three primary uses of jewel imagery, to suggest a reputation, love, or one's eyes, are found scattered throughout the play. Spurgeon[11] has noted the frequent association of a jewel with a spotless reputation (see *Richard II*, I. 1. 180), an analogy appearing three times in *Pericles;* Marina's chastity is called a jewel at IV. vi. 156. "You shall like diamonds sit around his crown" (II. iv. 55) is called unShakespearean by Spurgeon,[12] yet it resembles a similar crown and light image at II. iii. 39 as well as *Macbeth*, V. viii. 86. Diamonds, which appear seven times in *Cymbeline*, suggest love when Thaisa says, "To me he seems like diamond to glass." (II. iii. 36) They also occur as tears (III. ii. 108) as they do in *The Merry Wives of Windsor* (III. iii. 59). One of the most characteristic and memorable uses of jewels, though not mentioned by Spurgeon, is to suggest eyes (see *King Lear*, I. i. 271); both references here mention eyelids as "cases to those heavenly jewels" (III. ii. 106); and we have "Her eyes as jewel-like and cased so richly." (V. i. 112) A more oblique reference is Pericles' analogy between the daughter of Antiochus and a "glorious casket stored with ill" (I. i. 25); the casket or box of

jewels is well employed here to connote the distinction between appearance and reality, and it mirrors the use of caskets in *The Merchant of Venice* (III. ii). The fact that Thaisa is coffined with jewels (III. i. 66) echoes Clarence's dream in *Richard III* (I. iv. 28) of jewels "All scatt'red in the bottom of the sea."

Those images concerning metals are generally similar in function to the jewel references. This parallel is particularly apparent when Dionyza says that Marina's life and reputation will live in "glitt'ring golden characters" (IV. iii. 44); cf. the "golden letters" of *King John*, III. i. 85. Here the brightness of the metal indicates light and life—an ironic linking, for Marina is thought to be dead. A similar use of dualism occurs in the characteristic "golden slumber of repose" at III. ii. 23; see *Henry IV, Part I*, II. iii. 44. Marina is called "silver-voiced" (V. i. 111), an image similar to *Romeo and Juliet*, IV. v. 130. And Diana is termed the "goddess argentine" in the same scene. In one of the most vivid of the speeches describing the tempest—both literally and figuratively—Pericles calls upon the "god of this great vast" to bind the winds "in brass" (III. i. 3), thus recalling the gusts loosed from "their brazen caves" in *Henry VI, Part II* (III. ii. 89).

Turning to ideas and emotions relating to the life-death antithesis as discussed by Armstrong,[13] we can see a number of characteristically Shakespearean associations. His conception of love as hot or as food or as swift and uncertain is obvious from a study of *Pericles* alone. At I. i. 53, Pericles refers to his "unspotted fire of love" for Antiochus' daughter; and the chivalric symbol of the burning torch (II. ii. 32) indicates, saysSimonides, that love can "inflame as it can kill." When Dionyza orders Leonine to murder Marina, she reminds him not to let love "inflame too nicely" (IV. i. 6) nor to let pity "melt thee" (1.7). The connection of love with food also appears throughout the play. Pericles refers to love as "the fruit of yon celestial tree" (I. i. 21); a few lines later, he is told that love is the "golden fruit" of "this fair Hesperides" (27-28). In the same scene, the incestuous relationship is referred to as one of feeding (1.64). Thaisa speaks of Pericles as "my meat" at II. iii. 32. References to lust as food in the brothel scenes are common; and the allusion to Marina as one who "starves the ears she feeds, and makes them hungry" (V. i. 114) bears strong resemblance to Cleopatra, who "makes hungry/Where most she satisfies." (*Anthony and Cleopatra*, II. ii. 242-43) The destructive and uncertain course of love, so emphasized in *Romeo and Juliet* and in *Troilus and Cressida*, is seen here in the mention of lovers as "martyrs, slain in Cupid's wars." (I. i. 38)

Images of light (including those based on the heavens, days, and lamps) are also plentiful. "Her face, like heaven," says Antiochus about his daughter (I. i. 30; see *Anthony and Cleopatra*, V. ii. 79: "Her face was as the heavens."). In the same scene, he refers to "our daughter, clothed like a bride" (1. 6); the white-light-love connections are obvious and resemble *Measure for Measure,* III. i. 84. A little later, Pericles calls the daughter, "Fair glass of light." (1. 76) "Heavens make a star of him," says Pericles, referring to Simonides at the end of the play (V. iii. 80); similar images of light related to stars (as well as to jewels and metals) have already been mentioned.

There are, as would be expected, many more images at the opposite extreme in *Pericles;* typical conceptions of death as sleep, as hollow, or as destructive, together with numerous images of evil as black or as a disease, are plentiful. The connection between darkness and sin or evil is apparent when Pericles refers to "actions blacker than the night" (I. i. 136); in the next scene, we have "as black as incest" (1.76), his "bed of blackness" (1.89), and a picture of evil as all-encompassing night:

> Under the covering of a careful night,
> Who seemed my good protector. . . .
>
> (II. 81-82)

Another level of meaning is added to the frequent association of evil and darkness when Lysimachus refers to sexual intercourse as "the deed of darkness" (IV. vi. 29; cf. *King Lear,* III. iv. 89).

References to evil in terms of disease or decay are common here as they are generally in Shakespeare and appear both at the beginning and end of the play. There are references to sin as a "sharp physic" (I. i. 72); and there are several analogies to medicine and doctors. The description of whores as "rotten" and "pitifully sodden" (see *Troilus and Cressida,* III. i. 44) are relevant here as is Marina's admonition to Boult to "empty old receptacles . . . of filth." (IV. vi. 176-77)

The connections of sin or evil with food and smell confirm Shakespeare's physical rather than spiritual conception of sin. The archetypal association between evil and serpents is dominant in the imagery of the opening scene ("I am no viper," I. i. 64); and, a few lines later, Pericles, reflecting on the incestuous relationship, says,

> And both like serpents are, who though
>   they feed
> On sweetest flowers, yet they poison breed.
>
> (I. i. 132-33)

A similar use of dualism (serpents-flowers) is seen in "Look like the innocent flower, but be the serpent under it." (*Macbeth,* I. v. 66-67) Boult assures the Bawd that "thunder shall not so awake the bedsof eels" (IV. ii. 141-42) as his hawking of Marina's virtues in the streets. The use of worms in this connec-

tion has been noted; and Marina's description of the brothel as "this sty" (IV. vi. 98) is important here as well as for its resemblance to Hamlet's remark (*Hamlet,* III. iv. 94).

The speed and destructive power of time are graphically presented in *Pericles.* In the opening prologue, line 16, "taperlight" can be seen not only in the life-light connection but also as indicative of the speed of time (cf. *Macbeth's* "Out, out brief candle!" V. v. 23). Time appears as "winged" in the Prologue to Act IV, as a "feathered briefness" later. "Time hath rooted out" (V. i. 93-95) indicates, in an effective nature image, the destructive power of time; but, as usual, time is seen by Shakespeare as both good and bad, as the powerful breeder and destroyer of men; no passage is more clearly indicative of this conception:

> . . . Time's the king of men,
> He's their parent, and he is their grave. . . .
>
> (II. iii. 45-46)

A similar personification of time occurs in *Troilus and Cressida,* III. iii. 174. Other personifications, of virtues, cities, emotions, and natural phenomena, are often rich but, of course, too numerous to mention.

III

The images which have been discussed are of significance not only for their intrinsic beauty and/or effectiveness but also for what light they shed on the authenticity of Shakespeare's hand in the work. The first two acts may often lack that indefinably Shakespearean quality, yet there are numerous images there, many of which reappear later in the play. The many striking passages and the apparent clusters of images (all of which relate to some aspect of the sin-death correlation) early in the play also serve to corroborate the thesis that Shakespeare had a much more profound connection with the first two acts of *Pericles* than is generally recognized. It seems probable that the poet revised an earlier play and that the revision was more thorough in the last three acts.

The unity of the play's authorship is also attested to by the many parallels occurring throughout the play, especially with such late works as *Macbeth, Troilus and Cressida,* and *Anthony and Cleopatra,* as well as by the similarity in imagery (tempests, music, jewels, flowers) between this play and *The Tempest, The Winter's Tale,* and *Cymbeline.* Critics are generally agreed that the play contains many clear examples of Shakespeare's late style.

Thus it seems difficult not to disagree with Spurgeon's conclusion that the imagery of *Pericles* throws "grave doubts on its authorship,"[14] and with her cursory treatment and dismissal of the imagery as "flat, general, uninteresting, and unShakespearean."[15] On the contrary, the imagery of *Pericles* conforms in large measure with the characteristically Shakespearean patterns and modes of association.

Notes

[1] Kenneth Muir, *Shakespeare as Collaborator* (New York, 1960), p. 88.

[2] Caroline F. E. Spurgeon, *Shakespeare's Imagery and What It Tells Us* (Cambridge, 1935); see also John E. Hankins, *Shakespeare's Derived Imagery* (Lawrence, 1953) and Wolfgang Clemen, *The Development of Shakespeare's Imagery* (London, 1953).

[3] Edward A. Armstrong, *Shakespeare's Imagination* (Lincoln, 1963).

[4] Quotations from *Pericles* follow the edition by J. C. Maxwell (Cambridge, 1956): quotations from the other plays are taken from *The Complete Plays and Poems of William Shakespeare,* edited by W. A. Neilson and C. J. Hall (Boston, 1942).

[5] Armstrong, *op. cit.,* pp. 11-16.

[6] *Ibid.,* p. 29.

[7] See G. Wilson Knight, *The Shakespearean Tempest* (Cambridge, 1935).

[8] See William T. Hastings, "Shakespeare's Part in *Pericles,*" *Shakespeare Association Bulletin,* XIV (1939), 67-85.

[9] Spurgeon, *op. cit.,* p. 184.

[10] Armstrong, *op. cit.,* p. 108.

[11] Spurgeon, *op. cit.,* p. 241.

[12] *Ibid.,* p. 291.

[13] Armstrong, *op. cit.,* pp. 42-49.

[14] Spurgeon, *op. cit.,* p. 291.

[15] *Ibid.*

Mary Judith Dunbar (essay date 1981)

SOURCE: "'To the Judgement of Your Eye': Iconography and the Theatrical Art of *Pericles,*" in *Shakespeare, Man of the Theater,* edited by Kenneth Muir, Jay L. Halio and D. J. Palmer, University of Delaware Press, 1983, pp. 86-97.

[*In this essay originally presented in 1981 at the second Congress of the International Shakespeare Association, Dunbar examines the stage imagery of* Pericles, *maintaining that the "visual presentation in* Pericles *is integral both to the intellectual design of the play and to its theatrical art."*]

Pericles' quest involves a fresh exploration of a problem central to classical, medieval, and Renaissance thought: what is the relation of fortune to the gods and to human virtue? This problem, as ancient as the *Odyssey* to which *Pericles* is related in the literary tradition, is richly depicted in Renaissance visual arts which deepen our understanding of verbal and visual images in the play.[1] Iconographical analysis, including awareness of the context of dramatic language and situation, suggests that *Pericles* is not, as some critics have thought, "purely spectacular," or "pictures more than drama."[2] Visual presentation in *Pericles* is integral both to the intellectual design of the play and to its theatrical art.

In *Pericles* images with analogues in the visual arts are part of the verbal and conceptual design of the play; some become fully developed visual stage images.[3] In Shakespeare's images analogous to those in nondramatic visual traditions, we see his theatrical art. In his drama, visual images are modified by their intricate relation to fluid, temporal dramatic moments as well as to language; words and dramatic situations are not only the context for stage images but help to create their meaning.[4] Thus what, especially in emblem books, is sometimes static and simplified, becomes kinetic and complex; what is often designed to be recondite, Shakespeare is careful to clarify for the audience; what are often simply visual commonplaces become subtly changed and charged, in dramatic context, with fresh force.

Even when the dramatist gives verbal life to images with analogies in the visual arts without making them a full part of the visual art of the play, he adapts traditional images creatively to specific dramatic contexts. The shipwrecked Pericles uses a metaphor that occurs, for example, in Renaissance emblems: human beings are tennis balls in the hands of the gods or of fortune.[5] But instead of the familiar comparison of the earth to the court for fortune's tennis, the court is the sea. Pericles, his garments wet, presents himself as

> A man whom both the waters and the wind,
> In that vast tennis court, hath made the ball
> For them to play upon.[6]

More important to an understanding of Shakespeare's theatrical art are those images that are not only verbal but are very closely related to visual presentation on stage. The simplest of these are stage properties; the most remarkable, which reveal Shakespeare's stagecraft in the late plays, are complex stage images composed not only of properties, but of costumes, groupings of actors, gestures, and moments of action.

Death's Heads at Antioch

The opening scene at Antioch is a striking example of the use of symbolic stage properties: death's heads are presented to our eyes. They form the central image that defines Antiochus' court; the language suggests that these skulls of suitors for Antiochus' daughter are visible throughout the scene (probably affixed to part of the stage or to a stage property).[7] These properties are a theatrical use of the *memento mori* tradition and of allegorical traditions that link lust and death.

The viewer is given an ironic perspective that Pericles lacks, since Gower has told the audience of the incest between Antiochus and his daughter before Pericles enters. The daughter is unnamed; she is important as stage image. When we see her juxtaposed to the death's heads we already know what Pericles sees only later, that she is a "glorious casket stor'd with ill" (1. 1. 78). Even viewers who have little familiarity with iconography can sense a connection between lust and moral death because of the stage picture. Awareness of the common tradition of moral allegory linking lust and death would enrich their perception. Antiochus warns Pericles

> Before thee stands this fair Hesperides,
> With golden fruit, but dangerous to be
> touch'd;
> For death-like dragons here affright thee
> hard.

> [1. 1. 28-30]

With the aid of a dragon, the Hesperides, daughters of evening, guarded the garden containing the golden apples Hercules plucked. Shakespeare uses the classical story in the manner of Renaissance moral allegory, and connects the story to the theme of Hercules at the Crossroads, which was widely used in the Renaissance to symbolize the choice between the way of lust and the way of virtue. There is a woodcut, for example, of Hercules' choice in Sebastian Brant's *The Ship of Fooles* (1570?).[8] A young knight lies at the fork of a road which divides two ways: the broad path leads to a figure of a woman with death behind her, his skull by her head.

Ironically, Antiochus himself, for his own ends, suggests that Pericles should see the death's heads as symbolic images, which "with dead cheeks advise thee to desist" (1. 40). Pericles' reply shows his desire to understand the image:

> For death remember'd should be like a
> mirror,

> Who tells us life's but breath, to trust it
> error.

> [1. 1. 46-47]

Pericles sees the death's heads as a *memento mori,* and his couplet sounds like a quotation, as if he is a young man remembering his emblem book. Though he has the words, he misapplies their meaning. For the point of the *memento mori* tradition as represented by Peacham's emblem of a death's head in *Minerva Britanna,* for example, is that faced with one's mortality, one should steer a course toward heavenly joys, and attempt to live wisely.[9] Pericles draws a witty but wrong conclusion: he places heaven in the lady (1. 1. 48-54). The courtly parody of religious language is our clue. It is only when he solves the incest riddle and learns that Antiochus' "courtesy" covers "sin" (1. 1. 122) that Pericles chooses rightly.

The scene at Antioch uses symbolic properties for specific dramatic ends. Such properties establish Antioch as a court of death: a place where spectacle is used to conceal truth, where natural love is parodied by its opposite, incest, where the heroic and chivalric code is misapplied. Pentapolis is its exact opposite.

Fortuna and Ars

The stage image confronting the viewer near the beginning of act 2 is of the storm-beaten Pericles.[10] Pericles himself is a figure of the suffering caused by storms of fortune. He cries to the "stars of heaven," which he feels are "angry" (2. 1. 1). But at the same time, the audience has the perspective given them by Gower the moment before Pericles' entrance: fortune "threw him ashore, to give him glad" (2. Ch. 38). This dramatic juxtaposition suggests the ambiguity of fortune in a fresh use of an iconographical commonplace: a ship in a storm is used to explore the problem of fortune, including mutability and the relation of chance to virtue and to the gods. In Whitney's *A Choice of Emblems,* for example, a ship in a storm is the picture to the motto *Res humanae in summo declinant* (p. 11); Whitney cites Ovid: "*Passibus ambiguis fortuna volubilis errat.*" Shakespeare's use of this tradition is complex: the scene not only portrays the destructive instability of fortune, but hints that we are about to see its benign aspect.

To the figure of the shipwrecked Pericles is quickly juxtaposed a brief but moving stage image: a fisherman gives his gown to the cold, nearly naked Pericles. The stage picture speaks of charity. Its resonance would be richer for an audience familiar with the representation in visual art of charity: a person giving a garment to clothe another.[11] By stage gesture, the viewer sees one of the ways bad fortune can become benign: through a specific human virtue in action.

The dramatist suddenly presents a third stage image relevant to the problem of fortune and human action: "*Enter Second and Third Fishermen, drawing up a net*" (first quarto). In their net they recover part of Pericles' heritage: the armor of his father. The action makes clear that this gift of "Fortune" (2. 1. 120) could not have happened without the skill of the persistent men who fish despite the storm. The dramatist gives concrete theatrical form to a traditional visual representation of hope and of the skill that can overcome ill fortune.[12]

Pericles, to "rise" (2. 1. 165), seizes the occasion of the tournament at Pentapolis about which he now hears. The dramatic timing suggests the ancient antithesis . . . sometimes stated in the Renaissance as *fortuna* and *ars*.[13] Pericles shows courageous virtue in choosing this occasion as the right moment to act and to try hisskill, or art, of arms.

Imprese on the shields of the knights who sue for Simonides' daughter at Pentapolis are designed to show the moral purpose of each.[14] The important thing is not to claim sources for these *imprese* but to see how they are used in the dramatic context: the playwright creates a telling contrast of "outward show" (2. 2. 47) and inward worth. Motto and picture on the shields of the first four knights play upon the Renaissance love of what Mario Praz calls "that new-fangled wonder which was the perfect device": they are framed as ornate courtly conceits.[15] The fifth device is framed with serious wit: the "gold that's by the touchstone tried." It may be significant that Thaisa's reading of the motto "*Sic spectanda fides*" is timed to occur just before the moment Pericles enters; but the fundamental point is the contrast between richly costumed knights and the ill-furnished Pericles in rough garb with a piece of rusty armor. Having no shield he has had to make his own device, probably from a natural branch; having no page, he would present his device himself directly to Thaisa. Her description assists the audience in perceiving the image:

> A wither'd branch, that's only green at top;
> The motto, *In hac spe vivo*.
>
> [2. 2. 42-43]

Even a viewer who has no familiarity with iconography can see the fundamental meaning of the image: despite his "wither'd" state and fortune, Pericles hopes for renewal. The dramatist is careful to clarify the *impresa* further by Simonides' interpretative comment:[16]

> A pretty moral;
> From the dejected state wherein he is,
> He hopes by you his fortunes yet may
>   flourish.
>
> [2. 2. 44-46]

It is perhaps fitting that no exact parallel to Pericles' device has yet been found in books of devices, *imprese,* and emblems, because the very purpose of the scene is to contrast fashionable and elaborate courtly devices to a simpler one that Pericles must invent. The invention, however, is drawn from a widespread tradition. The dry and verdant tree or branch recur in classical and Christian iconography to relate natural (vegetative) reflowering and human renewal; in some instances, the image indicates the renascence of a noble family, despite death and time, through the growth of children.[17] In the motto he gives Pericles, the dramatist fuses these concepts with another that is crucial in the play at this point: hope. Hope in his renascence counters the longing for death Pericles experiences after shipwreck and impels him to continue the quest that he began at Antioch, to renew his lines of life by marriage.

Grief and Patience

Pericles' quest seems to him to have ended in total loss when, believing his wife dead, he is confronted with his daughter's tomb (4. 4); his lineage now seems forever eradicated. A dramatic function of the dumb show of Pericles at the tomb is that its visual heightening helps us hold a sharp image in our minds: Pericles himself as a figure of grief.[18] The stage picture is clear in the directions of the first quarto: ". . . *Pericles makes lamentation, puts on sackcloth, and in a mighty passion departs.*" The ancient image of sackcloth is often used in the context of lamentation and mourning, as when Jacob thinks Joseph is dead (Gen. 37:34), or where Job expresses his extreme suffering (Job 16:15). Gower gives the verse to the picture of the dumb show: "See how belief may suffer by foul show!" (4. 4. 23).

Pericles becomes a symbolic figure also because of the language Gower uses to describe him. In a striking change from the two main sources of the play, which emphasize the literal storm Pericles meets as he sails from Tharsus,[19] the play stresses a highly metaphoric one.

> He bears
> A tempest, which his mortal vessel tears,
> And yet he rides it out.
>
> [4. 4. 29-31]

It is primarily a tempest of the mind and soul; it tears his body—which is identified in the compressed language with his ship.

When we next see Pericles, we are presented with the most powerful stage image of his suffering in the play: Pericles, on shipboard and in sackcloth, dumb with grief. The probable blocking (Pericles seated or reclining up stage and all on stage looking toward him),

Pericles' silence, the pauses, and Helicanus' word *mortal*—all make the figure Pericles presents when discovered to the audience on stage and to us symbolic in force:

> *Hel.*   Behold him. This was a goodly
>   person,
> Till the disaster that, one mortal night,
> Drove him to this.
>
>   [5. 1. 35-37]

Helicanus' language is not only finer than most emblem verses but is in the context of Pericles' particular grief; his words thus give the audience a vivid experiential awareness. At the same time, his language gains in symbolic force by functioning, in part, like verse to a pictorial emblem: he makes an explicit comment on the stage picture. There is thus the suggestion, with no overly emphatic moralizing, that Pericles' particular experience of the suffering caused by the radical contigencies of fortune, so stricking when it happens to a "goodly person," could be the lot of anyone.

Pericles' "distemperature" (5. 1. 27) is a paralyzing "melancholy" (5. 1. 219) that makes him unable to act in adversity as the moralistic verse of emblem makers often advised—as a skillful pilot, or one who has hope as his anchor.[20] Helicanus stresses the need for recovery (5. 1. 53). Gower has made us aware of the ripe occasion of Pericles' meeting with Marina; his ship has been "driven before the winds" to Mytilene at the very time the "city striv'd/God Neptune's annual feast to keep" (5. Ch. 16-17).

The setting of Pericles' encounter with Marina is one Gower asks us to hold in our imagination: "Of heavy Pericles, think this his bark" (5. Ch. 22). Not all visual images in *Pericles* are—or can be—represented to the viewer's eye on stage; indeed it is part of Gower's role to play upon the problem of representation in drama. But Gower's language can make the stage itself symbolic. That Marina and Pericles are on shipboard reinforces the awareness that each has lost a place in the world and has been "toss'd from wrong to injury" (5. 1. 130) subject to that mutability of fortune that emblems and other visual arts often symbolize by a ship in a storm. Marina has earlier reflected, in emblematic terms, "This world to me is as a lasting storm" (4. 1. 19); she now tells Pericles that she is bound by "wayward fortune" and "awkward casualties" (5. 1. 89-94).

After Marina comes on shipboard, the inner state of separation from others and from each other Pericles and Marina both experience is suggested visually in the physical positioning on stage: Pericles, seated, in sackcloth, apart; Marina, standing away from him after he has pushed her back (1. 83). This blocking helps

to create a stage image closely related to Pericles' words at the next moment. He is amazed at what he sees:

>   thou dost look
> Like Patience gazing on kings' graves, and
>   smiling
> Extremity out of act.
>
>   [5. 1. 137-39]

The conceptual patterns of the play and its visual design are united here in a moment when a verbal image is strongly intimated by what we see on stage. This dramatic moment is not built on a simple one-to-one equivalence of verbal and visual images. Greater complexity occurs in part because of the dynamic, fluid situation in which Pericles is still testing the truth of what he sees and hears. His moving declaration of the qualities Marina seems to figure forth is filled with wonder, yet he is not fully certain she is, as she says, "No other than I appear" (5. 1. 105). His declarations are surrounded by questions—until he at last hears her say her name, Marina (5. 1. 142).[21] There is symbolic intimation[22] here rather than a simple equation of verbal and visual also because of the metaphorical richness of the phrase "king's graves," when applied to Pericles' state, and because the simile "Like Patience" is used suggestively in the moment of Pericles' quickened perception, not as a mere label for Marina. In this dramatic context, personification heightens, rather than reduces, Marina's character. It gives her added symbolic force, while the stage image is rooted in the particularities of the situation: Pericles' own severe melancholy (especially as shown by his initial stony silence) has been deathlike; Marina has endured in the face of her own grief, and has undertaken the task of restoration for Pericles in his.

The stage image Shakespeare creates at this moment of action has many analogues in the visual arts. W. S. Heckscher thinks the image of patience in *Pericles* may be more closely related to monumental tomb sculpture than to two-dimensional representation.[23] Whether or not there are specific types of "inspiration" for Shakespeare's images, it is important, for audience response, that Shakespeare use a widespread tradition. And it is a tradition, as Heckscher documents, in which the visual arts are related to a field of ideas including *Fortitudo* and *Patientia* as virtues that oppose *Melancholia-Tristitia-Acedia*; this is a central field of ideas used throughout *Pericles*.

The heightened moment when Marina's qualities suggest the inward virtue of Patience to Pericles is not only evidence of Shakespeare's fresh use of a familiar tradition but also of his mastery of visual craftsmanship in the late plays. The stage image in *Pericles* is founded on a freer and more forceful use of the commonplace of patience and her monument than Shakespeare gives to Viola: "She sat like patience on a monument/Smiling at grief" (2. 4. 113-14). And in *Twelfth Night* the verbal image is not strongly related to a stage image: in *Pericles,* the verbal image has a strikingly suggestive context in the visual composition on stage.

Stage images that draw on iconographical motifs are a recurrent feature of Shakespeare's plays; their centrality in *Pericles* suggests Shakespeare's emphasis, in the romances, on symbolic form. Stephen Orgel points out that visual experience in Shakespeare's late plays is integrally related to wonder "as the means to reconciliation and the restoration of losses."[24] In addition, visual experience is made thematic in *Pericles*: there is a recurrent problem of how we are to know truth from the appearance of things, and how we are to believe when faced repeatedly with the kind of deception Pericles met at Antioch and Tharsus.

Toward the end of the play, spectacle is used to intimate an ideal order beyond the flux of particulars, an order glimpsed only at rare moments. At such a "right time" Pericles is given the theophany of Diana. At Ephesus, when we see Pericles reunited to Marina and Thaisa, the gods themselves seem makers of spectacle.[25] The final tableau, which includes the figures of Cerimon and Helicanus, suggests how the gods work: through specific human virtues in action.

The epilogue invites us to see the characters, and the action of the play itself, as symbolic.

> In Antiochus and his daughter you have
>   heard
> Of monstrous lust the due and just reward.
> In Pericles, his queen and daughter, seen,
> Although assail'd with fortune fierce and
>   keen,
> Virtue preserv'd from fell destruction's blast,
> Led on by heaven, and crown'd with joy at
>   last.
> In Helicanus may you well descry
> A figure of truth, of faith, of loyalty.
> In reverend Cerimon there well appears
> The worth that learned charity aye wears.
>   [Epilogue, ll. 1-10]

Although these rhymed couplets are less moving than the final stage tableau, Gower's epilogue is appropriate to a play in which visual presentation is so closely related to moral vision. Throughout *Pericles,* speaking pictures have been presented "to the judgement of your eye" (l. Ch. 41).

Notes

[1] I am indebted to Mary Davison's work, "The Metamorphoses of odysseus: A Study of Romance Iconography from the *Odyssey* to *The Tempest,*" (Ph.D. diss., Stanford University, 1971), for information on this subject. I am also grateful to Peter M. Daly of McGill University, in a privately circulated paper, "Shakespeare's Eye: Iconographical and Emblematic Effects in the Plays: A Review of Recent Scholarship," for a critique of the term *emblem* in dramatic criticism that helped in my revision of this paper, and to Alan R. Young of Acadia University for his skillful leadership of the seminar "Shakespeare's Eye" at the Second Congress of the International Shakespeare Association, in which participants considered the difficult problem of relating terms from art history to dramatic criticism.

[2] See, for example, critical comments in F. D. Hoeniger, ed., *Pericles*. The Arden Shakespeare (London: Methuen, 1963), p. lxxvii.

[3] *Stage imagery* is defined as follows by Martha Hester Golden [Fleischer] in *The Reader's Encyclopedia of Shakespeare,* ed. Oscar James Campbell and Edward G. Quinn (New York: Cromwell, 1966):

> Stage imagery is created by the persons, properties, and actions visible and audible on stage when a play is in production. Its function is analogous to that of the allegorical picture in the emblem books of the Renaissance: to present the essential truth for instantaneous comprehension by the eye; while the dialogue, like the emblem book's verses, explicates and elaborates the image for the benefit of methodical, discursive reason.

I accept this definition in part but agree with John Doebler that it "seems to make all stage action symbolic"; and I also query the emphasis upon static presentation. See Doebler, *Shakespeare's Speaking Pictures* (Albuquerque: University of New Mexico Press, 1974), p. 7. Furthermore, the analogy to the emblem book tradition has limitations; emblems often create an ingenious image *not* for "instantaneous comprehension" but to force thought by wit.

[4] I am grateful to Inga-Stina Ewbank for her emphasis on the crucial importance of language in relation to other elements in Shakespearean theater in her paper "The Word in the Theater," published in the present collection. See also her "'My name is Marina': The Language of Recognition," in *Shakespeare's Styles: Essays in Honour of Kenneth Muir,* ed. Philip Edwards, Inga-Stina Ewbank, and G. K. Hunter (Cambridge: At the University Press, 1980), and her "'More Pregnantly than Words': Some Uses and Limitations of Visual Symbolism," *Shakespeare Survey* 24 (1971): 13-18.

[5] There is a clear example in Peacham, *Minerva Britanna* (London: Wa. Dight, 1612), p. 113, *Sic nos Dij.*:

a hand in the heavens strikes a ball onto an earth drawn to resemble grids of a tennis court.

[6] *Pericles* 2. 1. 59-61. All references to *Pericles,* unless otherwise indicated, are to The Arden Shakespeare, ed. F.D. Hoeniger.

[7] The death's heads are probably already on stage when Gower speaks—see I. Ch. 40—and can remain throughout the exchange between Pericles and Antiochus—see l. 1. 40, 44. They could be borne away when Antiochus exits (l. 121); they may remain until Pericles' exit (l. 143) or even throughout the exchange between Antiochus and Thaliard (1b).

[8] Hallett Smith, *Elizabethan Poetry: A Study in Conventions, Meaning, and Expression* (Cambridge, Mass: Harvard University Press, 1968), pp. 293-99, gives references to the story of Hercules' choice from Hesiod through its representation in Renaissance art and literature. I am indebted to Doebler's *Shakespeare's Speaking Pictures,* pp. 22-29, 98, and 192-93 nn. 2-3, for his references to this theme in another context and for the representation of the woodcut from Sebastian Brant, *The Ship of Fooles,* trans. Alexander Barclay, 2d ed. (London, 1570?), fol. 239v. Mario Praz notes that Brant's very frequently translated and edited *Narren Schyff* (1494?) is not, strictly speaking, an emblem book. See *Studies in Seventeenth-Century Imagery,* 2d ed., enl. (Rome: Edizione di storia e letteratura, 1964), p. 286.

[9] See the verse to Peacham's emblem with the motto *Nec metuas nec optes,* p. 8. Peacham's marginal notes to this emblem refer to James I's *Basilicon Doron* (London, 1603), Bk. 1, p. 17. James links his advice to live so that one is ready for death to the "vertue of true Fortitude." Fortitude is a virtue central to *Pericles.* The *memento mori* tradition is also clear in Geoffrey Whitney, *A Choice of Emblems* (Leyden: Christopher Plantyn, 1586), p. 229, and is documented by Roland Mushat Frye, "Ladies, Gentlemen, and Skulls: *Hamlet* and the Iconographic Tradition," *Shakespeare Quarterly* 30 (1979): 15-28.

[10] "Enter Pericles wette" is the stage direction of the 1609 first quarto. References in my paper to the first quarto are to the facsimile reprint introd. by P.Z. Round (London: C. Praetorius, 1886).

[11] See Douglas Peterson, *Time, Tide and Tempest* (San Marino, Calif.: Huntington Library, 1973), p. 83 and p. 106 n. 14, who refers to a figure of *caritas* in Adolph Katzenellenbogen, *Allegaries of the Virtues and Vices in Medieval Art* (New York: Norton, 1964), p. 76. Lawrence J. Ross, "Art and the Study of Early English Drama," *Research Opportunities in Renaissance Drama* 6 (1963): 35-47, notes (p. 44) that by the time of the Renaissance there was an established tradition that

singled out clothing the naked "as the symbol of the idea of Charity itself." I have noticed a representation of clothes being given for those in need in Bruegel's engraving "Charity," in his series of the Seven Virtues. See reproduction in H. Arthur Klein, *The Graphic Worlds of Peter Bruegel the Elder* (New York: Dover, 1963), p. 229.

[12] See Davison, "The Metamorphoses of Odysseus," pp. 169-70, for the suggestion that the spectacle of fisherman hauling in their nets is used in this scene to "express the older Homeric tradition that a virtuous man can exercise his virtue, skills, and foresight to overcome worldly misfortune." Dramatic timing when the armor is discovered suggests that Shakespeare also balances this view in the scene with the one she cites in the proverb "Quod ars negat, Fortuna praestat," used by Jean Cousin in *Le Livre de Fortune* (1568), Plate 157, for a scene of fishermen bringing in fish with a net. A fisherman fishes in a raging sea in Bruegel's engraving of "Hope." See reprint in Klein, *The Graphic Worlds of Peter Bruegel the Elder,* p. 225.

[13] See Edgar Wind, "Platonic Tyranny and the Renaissance Fortuna: On Ficino's Reading of Laws IV 709 A-712 A," in Millard Meiss, ed., *Essays in Honor of Erwin S. Panofsky* (New York: New York University Press, 1961), I: 491-92. See also Rudolph Wittkower, "Chance, Time and Virtue," *Journal of the Warburg and Courtauld Institutes* 1 (1937-38): 313-21.

[14] Praz, *Studies in Seventeenth Century Imagery,* p. 58, gives a cogent definition of courtly devices: "For the device is nothing else than a symbolical representation of a purpose, a wish, a line of conduct (*impresa* is what one intends to *imprendere,* i.e., to undertake) by means of a motto and a picture which reciprocally interpret each other."

[15] Ibid., p. 57. Henry Green, *Shakespeare and the Emblem Writers* (London: Trübner, 1870), is sometimes naive in his attempt to locate sources for these *imprese;* we can, however, identify analogues. The devices of the third, fourth, and fifth knights can be closely paralleled in *The Heroicall Devises of M. Clavdivs Paradin,* trans. P. S. (London: William Keamey, 1591), as well as in other sources. The respective references to Paradin are: sig. V3, p. 309; sig. Z3, p. 357; sig. 03, p. 213. The devices of the fourth and fifth knights can also be paralleled in Whitney, *A Choice of Emblems,* pp. 183 and 139 respectively. The second device, as cited by Green, *Emblem Writers,* p. 165, can be seen in a somewhat similar form in Corrozet's *Hecatomgraphie* (1540), Emblem 28. There is no close known parallel to the first device, although the motto is also that of the Blount family (see Green, *Emblem Writers,* p. 160).

[16] Peterson, *Time, Tide, and Tempest*, pp. 84-85, comments on Pericles' emblem and motto: "The meaning of the symbol and its accompanying moral were misread by Simonides." But Simonides' comment is perfectly suited to the action and in any case *implies* the reading that Peterson suggests: "the living though seemingly dead branch that represents the family of whom he is the only survivor."

[17] I am indebted to Gerhart B. Ladner, "Vegetation Symbolism and the Concept of the Renaissance," in Meiss, ed., *Essays in Honor of Erwin S. Panofsky*, 1:303-22, for his excellent article that discusses these concepts in another context.

[18] William S. Heckscher, "Shakespeare in His Relationship to the Visual Arts: A Study in Paradox," *Research Opportunities in Renaissance Drama* 13-14 (1970-71):5-17, discussing *Pericles*, notes (pp. 41-42; 67, n 29) that in scholastic thought *tristitia* (a mixture of sorrow and despair) was seen as part of the sin of *acedia*. But since, as he says, "sloth" or *acedia* was identified in Christian theology with loss of faith in the mercy of God, I have not emphasized *acedia* and have stayed as close as possible to the language used in the text. The word *despair* is not used; Shakespeare uses *sorrow* (4. 4. 25); *grief* (5. 1.26,29,87); *griefs* (5. 1. 131); *woe* (5. 1. 105); *distemperature* (5. 1. 27); and *melancholy* (5. 1. 219).

[19] See the two most widely recognized immediate sources of *Pericles*, John Gower's *Confessio Amantis*, Bk. 8, ll. 1600-1601, and Lawrence Twine's *The Patterne of Painefull Adventures*, chap. 11, p. 540, in Geoffrey Bullough, *Narrative and Dramatic Sources of Shakespeare*, vol. 6 (London: Routledge, 1966).

[20] My argument here differs substantially from Peterson's, *Time, Tide and Tempest*, pp. 52 and 81, although in many other respects I greatly admire his analysis of *Pericles*.

[21] I am indebted to Inga-Stina Ewbank, in "'My name is Marina,'" for her valuable emphasis on a conditional quality in the exchanges between Pericles and Marina up to 1. 142 of the recognition scene; for stressing, in "'More Pregnantly than Words,'" that Shakespeare does not set up a merely illustrative relationship between words and visual images; and for her exploration of these points in a fresh way in her paper "The Word in the Theater." See note 4, above. For his vivid realization that Pericles continues to test what he sees and hears, I am also grateful to Paul Whitworth, in an interview (15 March 1975) he gave me about his performance as Pericles in the then-current Oxford University Dramatic Society production.

[22] John B. Bender, "Affinities between Jacobean Masques and Plays," *Research Opportunities in Renaissance Drama* 17 (1974):9-12 suggests a distinction between the way symbolic intimation (the term is his) in plays, as opposed to statement in Masques, was influenced by iconography.

[23] Heckscher, "Shakespeare in His Relationship to the Visual Arts," pp. 36-56.

[24] "The Poetics of Spectacle," in *New Literary History* 2 (Spring 1971): 382-83.

[25] I am indebted to Samuel Lee Wolff's *The Greek Romances in Elizabethan Prose Fiction* for this idea; he points out that Heliodorus, in the *Aethiopica*, for example, conceives of his story "as a series of theatrical spectacles arranged by superhuman agency" (p. 183). . . . See Wind, "Platonic Tyranny and the Renaissance Fortuna," pp. 491-92.

Alexander Leggatt (essay date 1987)

SOURCE: "The Shadow of Antioch: Sexuality in *Pericles, Prince of Tyre*," in *Parallel Lives: Spanish and English National Drama 1580-1680*, edited by Louise and Peter Fothergill-Payne, Bucknell University Press, 1991, pp. 167-79.

[*In the following essay first presented at an International Conference in 1987, Leggatt describes the specter of incest that hangs over all of the sexual relationships in* Pericles.]

When incest appears in Jacobean drama it is generally treated as a fundamental violation of nature, a criminal passion that horrifies even those who are in its grip. Arbaces in *A King and No King* is driven temporarily mad when he believes he has conceived an incestuous desire for his sister; Ferdinand in *The Duchess of Malfi* will not admit his desire even to himself. Isabella in *Women Beware Women* will sleep with her uncle only when told he is not her uncle; when she learns the truth she murders the woman who deceived her. The love of brother and sister in *'Tis Pity She's a Whore* is made the vehicle for Giovanni's defiance of all conventional values, including religion; and Anabella finally recoils from what they have done. The treatment of incest in *Pericles* appears to fit this pattern. In the play's first scene Pericles comes to the city of Antioch to win the King's daughter by the romantic device of answering a riddle; and he discovers that the beautiful princess he wants to win is having an incestuous affair with her father. This represents a fundamental violation of both sexual and family ties, a violation that is put right later in the play by images of healthy courtship and sexual love, and of normal family relations. This is, in fact, one of the binding themes of this somewhat episodic play. To touch for a moment on the question of authorship: few believe *Pericles*

Act III, scene ii. Thaisa, Cerimon, and Gentlemen.
From the Rowe edition (1709).

to be entirely Shakespeare's; the writing is so incon-sistent, not just in quality but in kind. There is, on the other hand, no general agreement about the identity of the other author, or authors, or about the nature of Shakespeare's involvement. To most critics the first two acts seem like hackwork, while in the last three they hear the voice of Shakespeare. Yet while no one can deny the power of the third-act storm sequence, there are passages of flat writing in the scenes that follow, and there are subtle and haunting passages earlier—including, I think, the opening scene in Antioch. The play does not seem to me fully coherent: there is some unassimilated political commentary, for example. But it explores sexual themes at least in a way that I find thoughtful, sensitive, and imaginative—in outline, if not always in execution. I would like to examine this aspect of the play, and for the sake of convenience I will call the author Shakespeare.

In most respects the treatment of the incest theme that begins the play is clear and straightforward. The

violation involved in incest is so deep that it taints other areas of life. The riddle Pericles must answer shows a scrambling of relationships and a loss of identity, and we note that Antiochus's daughter has no name:

> I am no viper, yet I feed
> On mother's flesh which did me breed.
> I sought a husband, in which labour
> I found that kindness in a father.
> He's father, son, and husband mild;
> I mother, wife, and yet his child.
>
> (1.1.65-70)[1]

The image of cannibalism recurs later in the play, in the famine that draws the mothers of Tharsus to eat their own children (1.4.42-44). Gower, in his role as chorus, tells us that incest "Was with long use account'd no sin" (chorus 1, 30). As in Jonson's *Sejanus,* with the loss of moral values words lose their meanings. The fact that Antiochus has named his city after himself indicates a Tamburlainian arro-gance, a refusal to accept the human community that controls individual wills. He orders Pericles' murder with the words, "It fits thee not to ask the reason why: / Because we bid it." (1.1.158-59). Recoiling from his discovery, Pericles uses an image of music turned to discord: "Hell only danceth at so harsh a chime" (1.1.86). All the values violated here are put right in later scenes. Against the arrogant tyranny of Antiochus, we hear the plain, frank speech between prince and counsellor in the relations of Pericles and Helicanus. In Pentapolis Pericles meets a good king, Simonides, with a fair daughter, Thaisa, whose beauty this time is not deceptive. In place of the riddle, Pericles proves himself in a tournament. Simonides, as Prospero will do more seriously later, briefly acts the role of the heavy father, as though to exorcise through comedy the memory of Antiochus. Point by point, the sequence in Pentapolis gives a benevolent form of the images that were violated at Antioch (Flower 1975, 33-34). So, later in the play, does Pericles' reunion with his lost daughter Marina, in a scene that depends on establishing true names and true identities: "Is it no more to be your daughter than / To say my mother's name was Thaisa?" (5.1.208-9). Even the scrambling of relationships becomes a benevolent paradox (Barber 1969, 61) when Pericles addresses his daughter as "Thou that beget'st him that did thee beget" (5.1.195). The harsh chime, the discordant music of Antioch, is countered by true harmony in later scenes. Pericles entertains the court of Pentapolis with music, leading Simonides to compliment him: "Sir, you are music's master" (4.5.30). Marina, we are told, "Sings like one immor-tal" (chorus 5, 3), and on her reunion with her father Pericles hears what he thinks is the music of the spheres. (It is an interesting touch that, while Helicanus and Lysimachus do not hear it, Marina remains silent on the subject; such enigmatic silences at important moments will become a key device in *The Tempest*.)

So far all this is as we would expect. The incest of Antiochus and his daughter is, like the jealously of Leontes in *The Winter's Tale,* a threat that the rest of the play counters. Because of the play's episodic structure we do not feel the pressure of that problem throughout, as we do in much (though not all) of *The Winter's Tale;* but the echoes in language and situation are clear enough to show that the Antiochus episode is not just an arbitrary way to start the hero's adventures but an appropriate introduction to the play as a whole. Yet the development of the play's themes from this opening scene is not perhaps so straightforward as I have made it sound. There are some elusive undercurrents that, I think, broaden and complicate the play's vision. In what follows I will be dealing largely in hints and suggestions; and I think Shakespeare *wants* them to be hints and suggestions, no more. Some of the points to which I will call attention are actually stronger and more disturbing in other versions of the story—Gower's *Confessio Amantis,* Twine's *The Pattern of Painful Adventures,* and Wilkins's *The Painful Adventures of Pericles Prince of Tyre.* Shakespeare has toned them down. But he has not suppressed them altogether.

To begin with, there are suggestions that what Pericles experiences in Antioch is not just a quick, horrified glance at somebody else's sin, but an initial encounter with sexualty itself, including his own sexuality, an encounter that leaves him repelled and shaken. If this is so, then *Pericles* makes an appropriate transition from Shakespeare's dark comedies—which, as Kenneth Muir (1979, 103) has observed, are concerned withsex where his romantic comedies are concerned with love—into the final romances, with their broader concern with marriage and the ties of family. G. Wilson Knight (1965, 73-74) has suggested that the abstraction of the play's characterization makes it seem the life story of an Everyman figure. In that pattern, the scene in Antioch is the hero's sexual initiation, one that goes badly because his first encounter is with the dark side of sexuality. He greets Antiochus's daughter with an innocent celebration of her beauty:

> See where she comes apparell'd like the
>   spring,
> Graces her subjects, and her thoughts the
>   king
> Of every virtue gives renown to men!
> Her face the book of praises, where is read
> Nothing but curious pleasures.
>
> (1.1.13-17)

In that last reference to "curious pleasures" the spring-like freshness of the opening is replaced by something a little more jaded and sophisticated. Though Antiochus

compares his daughter to the apples of Hesperus, guarded by dragons—the dead knights who have preceded Pericles—Pericles' desire "To taste the fruit of yon celestial tree / Or die in the adventure" (1.1.22-23) suggests rather the apple of Eden. The threat of death that accompanies his wooing reminds us of the traditional linking of sex and death, a point to which I will return. In both respects Pericles is undergoing a loss of innocence: "Antiochus, I thank thee, who hath taught / My frail mortality to know itself" (1.1.42-43). He determines "to prepare / This body, like to them, to what I must" (1.1.44-45). As a man about to undergo a deadly ordeal, and as a prospective bridegroom, he is venturing his body, and the two ventures go together.

Wilson Knight's observation (1965, 38) that the hero's "plunge into sin and death is . . . associated with ravishing desire" may be stronger in tone than the writing of the scene will justify, but there are, I think, suggestions that Pericles is undergoing a kind of fall, not so much sinning himself as becoming aware of the existence of sin. He recoils from the discovery:

> Fair glass of light, I lov'd you, and could
>   still,
> Were not this glorious casket stor'd with ill.
> But I must tell you, now my thoughts
>   revolt;
> For he's no man on whom perfections wait
> That, knowing sin within, will touch the
>   gate.
> You are a fair viol, and your sense the
>   strings,
> Who, finger'd to make man his lawful music,
> Would draw heaven down and all the gods
>   to hearken;
> But being play'd upon before your time,
> Hell only danceth at so harsh a chime.
>
> (1.1.77-86)

The sexual suggestion of the word "gate" will be unmistakable in the jealous ravings of Leontes; but it is clear enough here. Together with the reference to fingering it suggests not just Pericles' horror at incest but a queasy apprehension of, and recoil from, sexuality itself. In this light, the final punishment of Antiochus and his daughter is significant:

> A fire from heaven came and shrivell'd up
> Their bodies, even to loathing; for they so
>   stunk,
> That all those eyes ador'd them ere their fall
> Scorn now their hand should give them
>   burial.
>
> (2.4.9-12)

Like the putrefied core Hector finds inside the armor in *Troilus and Cressida,* this suggests a disgust with the body itself, a disgust echoed later in the brothel in Mytilene, whose employees "with continual action are even as good as rotten" (4.2.8-9).[2]

Pericles himself has not literally sinned. But in the allegorical mode the play occasionally touches, to encounter sin in another character is to entertain the possibility of sin in oneself. Some critics have seen Pericles' flight from Antiochus as a kind of penance (Thorne 1971, 47), though not everyone agrees, and at the literal level there is not much support for this reading. Helicanus offers it as a public explanation for the prince's flight: " . . . doubting lest he had err'd or sinn'd, / To show his sorrow he'd correct himself" (1.3.21-22), and this at least allows a shadow of the idea into the play. A stronger clue is Pericles' account of his own state on his return to Tyre: "Here pleasures court mine eyes and mine eyes shun them" (1.2.7). In retreating from Antiochus he may not be just saving his subjects from the tyrant but trying to retreat, in his own mind, from the dark knowledge Antiochus represents. When he comes to Pentapolis it is as though he is beginning his life over again; he is cast up on its shores as unaccommodated man, "bereft . . . of all his fortunes" (2.1.9). In this state he is allowed a fresh start, a new and healthier sexual initiation. It is significant that, while he comes to Antioch with no background that we know of, he begins his stay in Pentagolis by recovering his father's armor from the sea— the first reference in the play to his father. And he recovers his father in another way, in his recognition of Simonides: "Yon king's to me like to my father's picture" (2.2.37). In *As You Like It,* Rosalind recovers her father in the forest and then sets about her affair with Orlando. There is the same pattern here: courtship begins from the base of a secure background in one's own family. And it may be significant that the Pentapolis sequence ends with the full recovery of Pericles' lost identity as Prince of Tyre.

And yet Pericles himself does not seem altogether secure. He is wary of Simonides, in whom he sees a potential Antiochus: "'Tis the king's subtlety to have my life" (2.5.44). There is something a little priggish in his denial of interest in Thaisa: he claims he "never aim'd so high to love your daughter, / But bent all offices to honour her," adding, "never did my actions yet commence / A deed might gain her love or your displeasure" (2.5.47-48, 52-53). Is this proper courtesy or needless caution? Simonides and Thaisa seem to take it as the latter. The association of sex with eating, which takes a dark form in the cannibalism of incest, is more cheerful in Thaisa's frank desire for Pericles:

> By Juno, that is queen of marriage,
> All viands that I eat do seem unsavoury,
> Wishing him my meat.
>
> (2.3.30-32)

When he tries to play the gentleman, she will have none of it:

> PERICLES. Then as you are as virtuous as fair,
> Resolve your angry father, if my tongue
> Did e'er solicit, or my hand subscribe
> To any syllable that made love to you.
> THAISA. Why, sir, say if you had, who takes offence
> At what would make me glad?
>
> (2.5.66-71)

She herself had pretended reluctance when her father urged her to talk to the strange knight, but thispretence did not last. Simonides' eagerness for the match makes him sound like a cleaned-up Pandarus: "It pleaseth me so well, that I will see you wed; / And then, with what haste you can, get you to bed" (2.5.91-92).[3] Pericles' experience in Pentapolis is not just that of a hero who finds and wins his bride; it is also that of a cautious young man whose girl friend has to tell him it's all right to touch her and who makes the even more astonishing discovery that her father approves.

Yet the sexual anxiety created in Antioch may not have been completely disposed of. At the end of *Cymbeline,* another play in which there is a certain recoil from the body, Imogen tries to embrace Posthumus and, not knowing her, he flings her away, earning the rebuke, "Why did you throw your wedded lady from you?" The equivalent moment in *Pericles* comes when Marina approaches her father. Neither knows the other's identity. She is about to restore him to life, but his first greeting to her is a subhuman noise, "Hum, ha!" (5.1.83), to which editors generally add some such stage direction as "pushes her back," an addition justified by dialogue later in the scene. Her rebuke, "if you did know my parentage, / You would not do me violence" (5.1.99-100), suggests that the push is far from gentle. In Gower and Wilkins he strikes her in anger; in Twine, he kicks her in the face, drawing blood (Bullough 1966, 414; 466-67; 543). Shakespeare has toned down the violence, but it is still a startling and disturbing moment. While Lear at first shrinks away from the new life offered by Cordelia, Pericles lashes out at his daughter. In *The Winter's Tale* Shakespeare almost obliterates the problem of father-daughter incest that ends the source novel, Greene's *Pandosto*—almost, but not quite, for on first seeing her, before he knows her identity, Leontes finds his daughter Perdita rather too attractive (Melchiori 1960, 63-64). It may be that what surfaces when Pericles pushes Marina away is an old, instinctive fear that goes back to his encounter with Antiochus—who at one point, by the way, evidently flings down the riddle in a gesture that anticipates Pericles' flinging away Marina (1.1.57 SD; see Arden note). Seen in this light, Pericles' desire to leave Marina in Tharsus and his determination not to cut his hair till she is married may not be just arbitrary plot developments. They may suggest a desire to submit to an ordeal and a period of separation till his daughter is safely out of his reach. This recoil from the possibility of incest makes a direct link with the play's opening; but if, as I suggested, that opening expressed a fear of sexuality itself, then it is proper to notice that Marina is not the only woman Pericles flings away. Though the staging of the storm scene does not make this altogether clear, Pericles later says of Thaisa, "I threw her overboard with these very arms" (5.3.19). Even so Prospero will drown his book in the sea, getting rid of something that is potent, desirable, and dangerous. Thelma N. Greenfield (1967, 53) has rebuked Pericles for giving in too quickly to the sailors' demand, accusing him of lack of faith.[4] It may be that the problem runs deeper than that. And it may not just be arbitrary plotting when Thaisa herself declares:

> since King Pericles,
> My wedded lord, I n'er shall see again,
> A vestal livery will I take me to,
> And never more have joy.
>
> (3.4.7-10)

Like Pericles when he abandons Marina, she makes a decision that looks arbitrary but may suggest, by its very arbitrariness, an instinct to reject human involvement.

The relations of Pericles with Thaisa and with Marina are healthy, normal, and attractive. But they may be touched by shadows from Antioch—not just the crime of incest but the fear of an inherent corruption in all sexuality. The brothel scenes in Mytilene show the other side of the coin. Lysimachus is the converse of Pericles. The one comes to win a beautiful princess and finds an unnatural sinner; the other comes to do business in a brothel and finds a beautiful princess. And there is, I think, not much doubt that he *has* come to do business: the sly comedy of the Bawd's line, "Here come the Lord Lysimachus, disguis'd" (5.6.15-16),suggests that he is a regular customer whose disguise has long ceased to fool anybody (Flower 1975, 39). His manner is brisk and cynical: "How now! How a dozen of virginities?" and his first reaction to Marina is, "Faith, she would serve after a long voyage at sea" (5.6.19; 42). But as Pericles' innocent romanticism at Antioch may be touched by sensuality, so Lysimachus's cynicism has a nervous rattle; it is a little defensive, as though the man is half ashamed and keeping up his spirits. In his dialogue with Marina he is delicate to the point of being mealy-mouthed, and she challenges him to be honest and speak plainly:

> LYSIMACHUS. Now, pretty one, how long
>   have you been at this trade?
> MARINA. What trade, sir?

> LYSIMACHUS. Why, I cannot name't but I
>   shall offend.
> MARINA. I cannot be offended with my trade.
>   Please you to name it.
>
> (4.6.65-70)

Impressed by her virtue, he recoils from his own corruption to the point of claiming it never existed: "Had I brought hither a corrupted mind, / Thy speech had alter'd it" (4.6.103-4). It is a puzzling moment; and Wilkins's version of the scene, in which Lysimachus admits that he *was* corrupt and has now reformed, is much more logical. This version is adopted into the play in the new Oxford edition (10.127-36; Bullough 1966, 536). But the sheer illogic of the text as usually printed makes its own point: Lysimachus is trying to rewrite his life, and there may be more than just wishful thinking involved. When he declares, "I came with no ill intent; for to me / The very doors and windows savour vilely" (4.6.109-10), he may be telling part of the truth, in that he is now fully awake to feelings he was already aware of but never before acted on.

This is the man who will be Marina's husband. As in the Pentapolis sequence, the fixing of their relationship is accompanied by Marina's recovery of her parents. But the striking paradox is that Lysimachus finds a pure bride in a brothel, while the aggressively virginal Marina finds in a regular brothel customer her future husband. Love has pitched his mansion in the place of excrement. We may at first think that the brothel, like the court of Antioch, represents the dark side of sex, and so, up to a point, it does. (In performance the connections can be emphasized by the doubling of parts, as in the 1986 Stratford, Ontario, production in which Nicholas Pennell played both Antiochus and Boult.) But as there is unexpected corruption in Antioch, so there is unexpected innocence in the brothel. C. L. Barber (1969, 63) has called the brothel sequence a "comic exorcism of gross sexuality," and in fact the nature of its comedy is quite unexpected. We were prepared for a melodrama in which a helpless, innocent girl was threatened with a fate worse than death. In fact the helpless, innocent girl not only looks after herself quite nicely, thank you, but reduces her persecutors to laughable futility. Two of her customers stagger away, dazed and sheepish:

> 2. GENTLEMAN. . . . Come, I am for no more
>   bawdy-houses. Shall's go hear the vestals
>   sing?
> 1. GENTLEMAN. I'll do anything now that is
>   virtuous; but I am out of the road of
>   rutting forever.
>
> (4.5.6-9)

Boult and the Bawd throw up their hands at her ultimate outrage:

BOULT. Worse and worse, mistress; she has
    here spoken holy words to the Lord
    Lysimachus.
BAWD. O abominable!

(4.6.132-34)

The comedy turns in more than one direction. It is not just that Marina's tormentors are so helpless against her; that would suggest that the power of darkness they represent is so feeble it can be laughed off as not worth worrying about. There is also something self-mocking in the images of virtue triumphant, as though Marina's power is not quite real, not quite believable. And if some of the mockery touches chastityitself there may be a reason: as the Bawd complains of her new employee, "She's able to freeze the god Priapus, and undo a whole generation" (19. 13). Virginity is all very well but, as Benedick insists, the world must be peopled.

Marina's virginity and the brutal couplings of the brothel represent extremes, and each extreme is comic. The solution is the licensed sexuality of marriage. But sex itself remains an ambiguous force. Pericles wooing Thaisa was as reluctant to admit what he was doing as is Lysimachus when he comes to the brothel. In Wilkins's novel the storm in which Pericles' daughter is born and in which he loses his wife occurs not when he is going back to Tyre, but when he is going back to Antioch, to claim its kingship (Bullough 1966, 517-18). It is as though Antioch represents some dark fear at the heart of sexuality, and the storm that sunders the family is in some way connected with it. Perhaps in the story of Pericles Shakespeare is allegorizing the notion (which of course he would not have seen formulated) that, as our first sexual feelings are incestuous, so our sexuality thereafter is never free of the taint of incest. Perhaps. But once again I think the fear runs deeper than the fear of incest. Pericles is pursued from Antioch not just by the thought of a sexual taboo violated, but by a killer, the hired assassin Thaliard. As Pericles puts it, "Murder's as near to lust as flame to smoke" (1.1.139). Leonine, another hired killer, starts Marina on the path that leads her to the brothel. And in the brothel itself the danger persists: "The poor Transylvanian is dead, that lay with the little baggage. . . . She quickly poop'd him; she made him roast-meat for worms" (4.2.20-23). Antiochus, as we have seen, initiates Pericles not just into the dark mystery of sex but into the knowledge of death. His daughter comes "apparell'd like the spring" on to a stage decorated with severed heads:

    Before thee stands this fair Hesperides,
    With golden fruit, but dangerous to be
      touch'd;
    For death-like dragons here affright thee
      hard.

(1.1.27-30)

The encounter in bed about which Simonides is so jocular leads to the pain of childbirth in a storm, where "The lady shrieks and well a-near / Does fall in travail with her fear" (chorus 3, 51-52). In bringing new life Thaisa apparently dies. Recalling his loss, Pericles shows how his imagination is haunted by the pain of childbirth: "I am great with woe / And shall deliver weeping" (5.1.105-6). In his reunion with Thaisa, Pericles welcomes his new life as a kind of death, telling the gods,

              You shall do well,
  That on the touching of her lips I may
  Melt and no more be seen. O come, be
    buried
  A second time within these arms.

(5.3.41-45)

And Marina declares, "My heart / Leaps to be gone into my mother's bosom."

Whether feared or longed for, death is the constant companion of love. Shakespeare has already treated this theme in *Romeo and Juliet* and *Antony and Cleopatra*. One reason for the connection is that the procreative instinct is at once an answer to, and a reminder of, our mortality. And in the Christian tradition—until recently, at least—even wedded sexuality was never altogether free of a sense of sin: "Behold I was shapen in wickedness: and in sin hath my mother conceived me" (Psalm 51). In *The Tempest* Prospero celebrates the betrothal of Ferdianand and Miranda with vision of the ordered fertility that marriage represents. The vision is broken when Prospero remembers "that foul beast Caliban"—who, we recall, tried to rape Miranda, driven by an instinct to people the isle with Calibans. When Prospero subjects Ferdinand to an ordeal before he can win Miranda, he gives him Caliban's job of piling logs, as though his purpose is to test the Calibanin him.

From Caliban's attempt to rape Miranda to the vision of Ceres, *The Tempest* connects our sexuality to our bond with nature. And nature, in these last plays, is not just the "great creating nature" we hear of in *The Winter's Tale*. Even in that play, the force that produces daffodils that come before the swallow dares produces also a storm and a devouring bear. In *Pericles,* Cerimon evokes the benevolent and curative powers of nature in language that recalls Cordelia. He has studied

           the blest infusions
  That dwells in vegetives, in metals, stones;
  And can speak of the disturbances that
  Nature works, and of her cures.

(3.2.35-38)

But we notice that he also sees nature as ambiguous, like Friar Laurence, who can see poison and medicine in a single flower. Using fire and music, he brings Thaisa back to life. But he tells a servant who comes to him for help:

> Your master will be dead ere you return;
> There's nothing can be minister'd to nature
> That can recover him.
>
> (3.2.7-9)

Nature can help us, but not forever; after a certain point she gives us up. Pericles, noting how Simonides resembles his dead father, may be said to have cheated time by finding a new father; but in the same speech he compares his father's glory with his own dejected state and concludes, "I see that Time's the king of men; / He's both their parent, and he is their grave" (2.3.45-46). Even a moment of recovery is touched by the thought of loss.

At several points the play refers to the arbitrary whims of Fortune, especially in the storm sequences: " . . . fortune, tir'd with doing bad, / Threw him ashore, to give him glad (chorus 2, 37-38); " . . . fortune's mood / Varies again" (chorus 3, 46-47). But this is a mechanical idea, mechanically stated. The puzzle of human life is conveyed more powerfully when Pericles addresses his seemingly dead queen. He evokes not Fortune but the mystery of birth and death in a natural world that is at once beautiful and terrifying, bound up with man yet finally indifferent to him:

> A terrible childbed hast thou had, my dear;
> No light, no fire: th'unfriendly elements
> Forgot thee utterly; nor have I time
> To give thee hallow'd to thy grave, but
>   straight
> Must cast thee, scarcely coffin'd, in the
>   ooze;
> Where, for a monument upon thy bones,
> And e'er-remaining lamps, the belching
>   whale
> And humming water must o'erwhelm thy
>   corpse,
> Lying with simple shells.
>
> (3.1.56-64)

Pericles speaks here of the natural world that surrounds us, whose elements we need for our comfort, even our survival; and he senses that this world ultimately goes its own way, indifferent to us. Not just indifferent, either, but overwhelmingly remote, capable of bearing down and destroying us without a moment's thought. But there is another, and perhaps greater mystery, in the power we carry in our own bodies. We need that power too, for our happiness and for the survival of our kind. But there is something in it that frightens us. And so we invent rules and codes to give ourselves the illusion that we control it. We moralize it, we separate it into right and wrong. But in the

moralizing of sex in this play there is something shadowy and unreal: the guilt we sense but cannot literally justify in Pericles when he flees from Antioch, the purity Lysimachus claims in the brothel. Marina's chastity and the corruption of her employees seem equally artificial. The proper relations of husband and wife, father and daughter, are touched by thoughts of Antiochus and his daughter; and the play's final marriage begins in a brothel. It is as though all the play's characters are adrift on the same sea. The relations of Antiochus and his daughter are, from any civilized perspective, a horror that the rest of the play should counter and suppress. That is our first impression, it remains the dominant one, and I do not wish to dislodge it. But from another point of view, harder to analyze, harder to see clearly, and harder to accept, the play seems to suggest that power Pericles first meets in Antioch is the power that will haunt him all his life.

Notes

[1] All references to *Pericles* are to the Arden edition by F.D. Hoeniger (London: Methuen, 1963).

[2] Flower (1975, 39) connects the fire that consumes Antiochus and his daughter with the pox that is endemic to the brothel.

[3] Stephen Dickey (1986, 559) calls Simonides' joking "a redirection of Antiochus' paternal lust into more proper channels: Simonides accepts rather than exploits his daughter's sexuality."

[4] According to the Quarto (and most editors), Cerimon declares, "They were too rough / That threw her in the sea" (3.2.81-82). For "rough" Malone conjectured "rash" and his reading is adopted in the "reconstructed" Oxford text (1986, 12.77).

Works Cited

Barber, C. L. 1969. "'Thou that beget'st him that did thee beget': Transformation in *Pericles* and *The Winter's Tale*." *Shakespeare Survey* 22:59-67.

Dickey, Stephen. 1986. "Language and Role in *Pericles*." *English Literary Renaissance* 16:559.

Flower, Annette C. 1975. "Disguise and Identity in Pericles, Prince of Tyre." *Shakespeare Quarterly* 26:30-41.

Greenfield, Thelma. 1967. "A Re-Examination of the Patient Pericles." *Shakespeare Studies* 3:51-61.

Knight, G. Wilson. 1965. *The Crown of Life*. London: Methuen.

Melchiori, Barbara. 1960. "'Still Harping on My Daughter.'" *English Miscellany II:* 63-64.

Muir, Kenneth. 1979. *Shakespeare's Comic Sequence.* New York: Barnes and Noble.

Narrative and Dramatic Sources of Shakespeare. 1966. Edited by Geoffrey Bullough. London: Routledge and Kegan Paul.

Shakespeare, William. 1986. *The Complete Works.* Edited by Stanley Wells and Gary Taylor. Oxford: Clarendon Press.

Thorne, William B. 1971. "*Pericles* and the 'Incest-Fertility' Opposition." *Shakespeare Quarterly* 22:43-56.

Anthony J. Lewis (essay date 1988)

SOURCE: "'I Feed on Mother's Flesh': Incest and Eating in *Pericles*," in *Essays in Literature,* Vol. XV, No. 2, Fall, 1988, pp. 147-63.

[*In the essay below, Lewis focuses on the thematic implications of the relationship between sexuality and eating in the imagery of* Pericles.]

The problems which have, historically, plagued critics of *Pericles* stem not so much from its doubtful origins—its exclusion from the First Folio and the attendant questions of authorship—as from the sense that the play is, finally, meaningless. For Ben Jonson *Pericles* was "a mouldy tale,"[1] all the more exasperating for its considerable popularity on the stage. But for more recent commentators the play is less an old familiar story than a mish-mash, a repository filled with the stuff of romance but jumbled in a way that defies understanding. Though the play is occasionally read as a myth of death and re-birth, as a dream, as an allegory of patience in suffering, or for its affinities with *King Lear* and with Shakespeare's earlier comedies and later romances, the typical refrain has to do with *Pericles'* apparent incoherence. Perhaps collaboration simply did not work, the argument seems to run, and *Pericles* is no more than a series of familiar and often fascinating incidents adding up to an incomprehensible totality.[2]

What I would like to argue in the following essay, however, is that *Pericles* enacts one theme: the personal, familial, and governmental obligation to nourish self, relations, and citizens. Taking my cue from the curious definition of incest as cannibalism in Antiochus' riddle in Act I, and using the recent work of social scientists, I read the play's persistent analogy between sexuality and eating habits as a vivid and terrifying illustration of the ways in which hu-

man beings respond to the need to sustain themselves and to nurture others.

I

It is fitting that the action of so intractable a play as *Pericles* should begin with a riddle. Though the meaning of the puzzle with which the King of Antioch challenges suitors to his daughter is transparent, "significant interpretation of this key incident is lacking, and intriguing problems remain unexplored":[3]

> I am no viper, yet I feed
> On mother's flesh which did me breed.
> I sought a husband, in which labour
> I found that kindness in a father.
> He's father, son, and husband mild;
> I mother, wife, and yet his child:
> How they may be, and yet in two,
> As you will live, resolve it you.
>
> (I.i.65-72) [4]

What scholarship has done is locate sources and analogs for the play, and therefore for the riddle. P. Goolden, in particular, has traced its evolution from the Latin prose of *Apollonius of Tyre,* through the Eighth Book of John Gower's *Confessio Amantis,* to *Pericles,* noting significant changes including a shift in the riddle's speaker, from the father in *Apollonius of Tyre* to the daughter in *Pericles.*[5] But what Goolden does not discuss—and what editions of the play routinely ignore—is the tacit definition of father/daughter incest which the riddle provides: "I feed on mother's flesh." Like the "sexual cannibals"[6] biologists describe in the world of insects, an incestuous daughter, the riddle tells us, is one who devours her mother.

Identifying incest in particular as a kind of devouring is, in fact, at least as old as the Pericles (Apollonius) story itself, and is used, in one form or another, in every extant version of the tale. In *Apollonius of Tyre* the riddle includes "*maternam carnem unescor,*"[7] "I feed on my mother's flesh." The King in Gower's *Confessio Amantis,* described as one who "devoureth/ His owne flesh," declares in the riddle, "I ete, and have it not forlore/ My moders flesshe." In Lawrence Twine's *The Patterne of Painfull Adventures* which, with the *Confessio Amantis,* is generally recognized now as a source for *Pericles,* the King states in the riddle, "*I eate my mothers fleshe.*"[8] George Wilkins' *The Painfull Adventures of Pericles Prince of Tyre,* an analog to Shakespeare's play, uses virtually the same phraseology as *Pericles,* "I am no viper, yet I feede/ On mothers flesh, that did me breede . . ."[9]

Shakespeare's play insists on identifying incest with eating, for when Pericles describes the incestuous couple later in the first scene he repeats this curious definition and echoes the language of the riddle:

Where now you're both a father and a son,
By your uncomely claspings with your
    child,—
Which pleasures fits a husband, not a
    father;
And she an eater of her mother's flesh,
By the defiling of her parent's bed;
And both like serpents are, who though
    they feed
On sweetest flowers, yet they poison breed.

                   (I.i.128-34)

The reference to serpents in lines 133-34, which describe feeding in literal terms, echoes the definition in lines 131-32, which describe the Princess in metaphorical terms. Although the analogy between the incestuous couple and serpents is somewhat ambiguous, what is clear is the linking of sexuality of feeding habits, a linkage emphasized by the "feed/breed" rhyme. Although serpents eat healthful, even "sweet" foods, flowers, they produce "poison," just as the incestuous king and his daughter use the sweetness of sexual love to "breed" the poison of incest. The allusion to serpents, however, amplifies the description of the incestuous couple in yet another way, for folk wisdom had it "that vipers at birth eat their way out of the mother's body," a notion F. D. Hoeniger believes derives from Herodotus and other classical sources.[10] Thus, serpents were simply thought to be thanklessness incarnate, a sense clear in Lear's rage at Goneril, "How sharper than a serpent's tooth it is/ To have a thankless child!" (I.iv.288-89), as well as in Cleopatra's ironic reference to the asp that kills her as "my baby at my breast . . ." (V.ii.309). Thought to be cruel offspring, serpents became, by analogy, symbols of cruel parents as well; Geoffrey Whitney describes Medea and "all dames of cruell kinde" as tyrants to their own young, "serpentes seede" "that tender not theire frute."[11] Referring to an incestuous couple as "serpents" thus reinforced a sense of the two as hideously ungrateful devourers of their own.[12]

To describe the Princess of Antioch's incest as devouring and, in particular, as cannibalism, was to use an image familiar to readers and audience in the seventeenth century as a time-honored indication of evil. After all, the Bible had presented original sin in the homiest of ways, the King James Version of Genesis simply stating that Eve "tooke of the fruit thereof, and did eate, and gaue vnto her husband with her, and hee did eate."[13] Medieval and Renaissance dramatic tradition had established hell's demons as fierce eaters of the sinful, and it is hardly necessary to rehearse here the history of so popular an image. As Emile Male notes,"almost all thirteenth-century representations of the Last Judgment show an enormous mouth vomiting flames";[14] and from *The Castle of Perseverance,* with its devils prancing into Hellmouth, to Doctor Faustus, a hero "glutted" with learning[15] who must "taste the

smart of all" (V.ii.127) even as he himself is devoured, to Jacobean tragedy, where vengeance can be described as "thou terror to fat folks,"[16] eating and cannibalism are familiar metaphors for perverse human behavior, conveying a rich history of religious, economic, and social connotations.[17]

Shakespeare himself had, of course, much before *Pericles,* used similar images and references, and Ruth Morse is, I think, correct in seeing "consistent and coherent imagery of animals and eating . . . from the beginning to the end" of his career.[18] The "blood-drinking pit" (II.iii.224) into which Quintus and Martius fall in *Titus Andronicus* has a "mouth" (II.iii.199) and is a "fell devouring receptacle" (II.iii.235). Romeo describes the vault of the Capulets as a devouring animal,

Thou detestable maw, thou womb of death,
Gorg'd with the dearest morsel of the earth,
Thus I enforce thy rotten jaws to open,
And in despite I'll cram thee with more
    food.

                  (V.iii.45-48)

And when the wheel turns in *Richard III,* "prosperity begins to mellow/ And drop into the rotten mouth of death" (IV.iv.1-2). Shakespeare found such imagery an especially effective way of delineating character and of clarifying issues in his more mature plays. In *The Merchant of Venice,* for example, where direct references to the eating of human flesh abound, attitudes toward food are used as a method of separating Shylock from the Christian community and of identifying him as one with special dietary restrictions. It is Shylock who refuses to eat with other Venetians, preferring, as Leslie Fiedler puts it, the "explicitly cannibalistic," wishing to "feed" (III.i.54) his revenge on Antonio's pound of flesh. Shakespeare clearly implies through such images that usury is a kind of cannibalism, and perhaps alludes as well, as Fiedler suggests, to "anti-Semitic child-murder" stories such as that told by the prioress in *The Canterbury Tales.*[19] Morse, who discusses the image in general, observes that in the early histories, *Macbeth,* and *Timon of Athens,* eating, cannibalism, and the body politic are related to one another.[20] In *Coriolanus,* too, as Janet Adelman has shown, Shakespeare uses images of food, eating, and cannibalism to define central issues and to describe the psychological, indeed, pathologically, complex relationship between Volumnia and her son.[21] Adelman argues that "the image of the mother who has not fed her children enough" (p. 130) is at the center of the play, and that "in this hungry world, everyone seems in danger of being eaten" (p. 136).[22]

Cannibalism was a familiar plot element found not only in Medieval and Renaissance drama, but also in Shakespeare's classical and folk sources, as well as in traveller's tales. In the mid-sixteenth century Montaigne used recent reports of cannibalism among isolated tribes in the new world as a way of pointing to what he saw as degeneracies among his compatriots in "Of Cannibals," an essay which goes so far as to praise that practice for its naturalness. Similar tales, no doubt, lie behind Othello's report of having seen the Anthropophagi, "the Cannibals that each [other] eat" (I.iii.143). Arthur Golding's edition of Ovid's *Metamorphoses,* which popularized the stories from Greek and Roman mythology, uses eating as a metaphor for greed and lust throughout, and offers stunning instances of cannibalism, often linked with infanticide and incest. For example, Tereus' rape and mutilation of Procne, his wife Philomela's sister, is avenged by the women's killing and cooking his son, Itys. Tereus "fed/ And swallowed downe the selfesame flesh that of his bowels bred,"[23] and later, having been told the precise nature of his fare, this descendant of Mars tried "To perbrake up his meate againe, and cast his bowels out" (VI.839). Much the same tone is taken in the last book of the *Metamorphoses,* when Pythagoras not only lectures on the inappropriateness of eating flesh, but also argues that metamorphosis implies that the human spirit—indeed, the souls of relatives—may residein the bodies of animals. He begins by decrying carnivorousness in general, lamenting, "Oh, what a wickednesse/ It is to cram the mawe with mawe, and frank up flesh with flesh" (XV.95-96), but quickly moves to the central point, "That whensoever you doo eate your Oxen; you devowre/ Your husbandmen" (XV.156-57). Repeatedly we are counseled not to "nourish blood with blood" (XV.195), not to eat the "bodyes which perchaunce may have the spirits of our brothers,/ Our sisters, or our parent," (XV.511-12), not, "Thyesteslyke," to "furnish up our boordes/ With bloodye bowells" (XV.515-16). In similar fashion, Seneca, to whom the English Renaissance dramatists turned both for stylistic examples and for exciting plot, re-wrote his Greek models so as to highlight the violent, and abounds, quite specifically, in instances of child abuse. In *Thyestes* Seneca combines infanticide with cannibalism in Atreus' killing of his brother's children and Thyestes' unwitting dining on them. This "Thyestean feast" is echoed in *Titus Andronicus,* in Tamora's eating meat pies made from her sons, a meal "Whereof their mother daintily hath fed,/ Eating the flesh that she herself hath bred" (V.iii.61-62). Familial cannibalism is also suggested in symbolic ways in Shakespeare, for example in Queen Margaret's offering to York a handkerchief dipped in his young son's blood in *3 Henry VI.* Wearing a paper crown, grieving Rutland's death, York can only protest,

> O tiger's heart wrapp'd in a woman's hide!
> How couldst thou drain the life-blood of the
>   child,
> To bid the father wipe his eyes withal,
> And yet be seen to wear a woman's face?
>   (I.iv.137-40)

Given the enormous popularity of images relating to eating and cannibalism both in Shakespeare's works and in those of his sources and contemporaries, it might seem unnecessary to gloss lines in *Pericles* which define incest as familial cannibalism, a child's devouring a parent or a parent's devouring a child. After all, common sense supports the notion that incest destroys one relationship in favor of another, removing parent or child, consuming, in a sense, one family member and replacing him or her with another. And yet, it is only here in *Pericles* that Shakespeare equates cannibalism specifically with incest, as his sources had done before him for millennia. The tenacity with which the metaphor has remained in all versions of the Pericles story attests to something more than simply the regressive pull of literary tradition. In spite of common sense and the ubiquity of eating and cannibalism as metaphor for evil, Shakespeare's definition of incest in particular as a kind of devouring remains refractory. What logic, if any, lies behind the apparently traditional association of incest and eating, and how, if at all, does this startling definition illuminate central issues in this puzzling play?

II

Psychologists and anthropologists have long noted a relationship involving social groupings, sexual mores in general, and those having to do with eating. Erich Neumann generalizes that "sexual symbolism is still colored by alimentary symbolism,"[24] while Robin Fox sums up the connection between food and sexuality simply by declaring, "whatever else humans do, one can be sure that they will classify and make rules about kin and the food supply, confuse the two, and be anxious about the whole process. . . ."[25] In "Taboos on Eating and Drinking" in *The Golden Bough,* Sir James G. Frazer mentions in passing tribal customs prohibiting women from eating with—or even observing—men who are eating or drinking, and prohibiting opposite-sex food preparation.[26] Similarly, Christiane Klapisch-Zuber has shown that in fifteenth-century Italy social relations were often defined by eating arrangements, for "blood relatives customarily are together under the same roof and made this sharing into a right,"[27] and that "a uno pane e uno vino" (sharing food and drink), was an expression "often used by the taxpayers and the scribes . . . to describe families" (p. 36). Her study shows as well how questions of familial bloodlines were related to those of eating in parents' reactions to a wet nurse's pregnancy. If the man who impregnated the nurse were unknown or of questionable socialstanding, her pregnancy was often considered a development fraught with dire consequences for the infant who might ingest debased milk (p. 159). The prevalence of "alimentary separation of the sexes" in primitive societies is noted by Laura and Raoul Makarius,[28] who explain that "the notion of sharing food establishes the primitive notion of kinship quite as much as does the idea of a common lineage" (p. 43). The authors point out that

> there are many facts to prove that, although as a rule men fear the danger inherent in all women, they particularly dread the establishment of a food bond with those women who are—or will become—their sexual partners, illustrating the fundamental incompatibility that exists in the primitive mentality between sexual union and the sharing of food. (p. 48)

Freud, who cited Frazer's studies as well as those of W. Robertson Smith in the final section of *Totem and Taboo,* thought "it probable that the totemic system . . . was a product of the conditions involved in the Oedipus complex."[29] That is, for Freud the symbolic devouring of the father through the totem animal was intimately related to incest prohibitions and to laws governing exogamy. Julia Kristeva, building on Freud, sees a relationship between food and sexual intercourse which has to do with a social unit's perceptions of its ability to thrive. "In a number of primitive societies religious rites are purification rites whose function is to separate this or that social, sexual, or age group from one another, by means of prohibiting a filthy defiling element."[30] Food, like sexual intercourse, may be debased and is thus "liable to defile," to bring one into contact with "the other" that "penetrates the self's clean and proper body" (p. 75). Ingesting food that is considered unclean or impure can bring on disease and death; similarly, illicit sex can destroy an individual or a nation for it too crosses established boundaries. Oedipus, "through murder of the father and incest with the mother interrupted the reproductive chain" and was responsible for "the stopping of life" (p. 85), a defilement of the human social condition. Because defilement is "incest considered as transgression of the boundaries of what is clean and proper" (p. 85), both feeding and sexuality contain the potential for disrupting personal and social integrity with sterility, disease, and death.

The connection between sexual intercourse and eating habits was addressed more directly in a recent issue of the *Journal of the Polynesian Society* devoted to questions of incest in Polynesia and Micronesia. Anthony Hooper notes that "eating blood" "is a literal gloss of the Tahitian phrase *'amu toto,'* which denotes, among many other things, 'incest',"[31] while J. L. Fischer, Roger Ward, and Martha Ward observe that one of the "two most common Ponapean terms given as translations for the English word 'incest'" is "*li-kengkeng-enih-mat,* literally, 'rotten corpse eater'."[32] In the same issue, David Labby finds a close link between eating and incest based less on psychological than on economic determinants.[33]

In an attempt to discern the reasoning behind the Yapese identification of incest as cannibalism, Labby points out that the Yapese word for incest, *"ku'w,"* "also referred to a variety of large sea bass which was notorious for its voraciousness and huge mouth. It would engulf all fish, even its own offspring, perhaps even a man. People who committed incest, it was said, were similarly voracious, consuming their own kin in a sort of sexual cannibalism" (p. 171). Labby develops the analogy between incest and cannibalism by pointing to the similar ways in which the incestuous and cannibals consume themselves: "As the cannibals appear to survive by eating off themselves, by self-consumption, rather than by working the land and receiving food from it in exchange, so incest attempts to perpetuate the clan by sexual self-consumption rather than through the cultural exchange with other groups" (p. 174). For Labby it is clear that when food production and exogamous reproduction are perverted into cannibalism and incest, a culture's ability to survive is impaired if not destroyed. Thus, for the Yapese, "incest was ultimately 'cannibalistic,' a denial of culture, of exchange, or work, a kind of survival through self-consumption" (p. 179).

I offer the conclusions of anthropologists not as a way of suggesting that "all people" reason or experience the world alike, or that the folklore of Pacific islanders is somehow the same kind of material as English dramatic literature of the seventeenth century. My point is not that cultures are simply interchangeable and that all stories are analogous, but rather that the idea of sustenance, which links the sexual and the alimentary in Yapese oral history, helps us to see a similar binding of healthful sexuality and licit eating, and of cannibalism and incest, in *Pericles.* For the Yapese, eating and sexual intercourse, both necessary in order for the individual and the society as a whole to survive, are fundamentally alike in that food is sustenance and reproduction is sustaining. In *Pericles* Antiochus and the Princess seek to sustain themselves through self-consumption, perverting the socially acceptable means of propagating their family as fully as if they nourished themselves by eating human flesh.

The idea of sustenance thus provides a nexus, and helps to explain Shakespeare's linking cannibalism and incest. That he understood the notion of sustenance as the common denominator between eating and sexual intercourse is clear from *Pericles,* as we shall see, as well as from other sources. For example, in *Measure for Measure,* when Isabella tells Claudio that Angelo will save his life if she agrees to sleep with him, her imprisoned brother begs, "Sweet sister, let me live" (III.i.132). Isabella calls him a "faithless coward" and a "dishonest wretch" (III.i.136), asking rhetorically,

> O dishonest wretch!
> Wilt thou be made a man out of my vice?

Is't not a kind of incest, to take life
From thine own sister's shame?

                     (III.i.136-39)

Here again we find incest coupled with the idea of sustenance, for to "be made a man" and "to take life" are to sustain life. J. W. Lever, one of few editors to gloss these lines, interprets Claudio's desire to live as incestuous "since through Isabella's shameful intercourse her own brother would be 'born' again."[34] For Lever, the accent is clearly on the relationship between Isabella and "her own brother," and it is certainly the conjunction of siblings and sexuality here that prompts the notion of incest. Yet Claudio's behavior is "a kind of incest" not only because he encourages his sister's sexual intercourse, but also because he attempts "to take life," that is, to live, to sustain himself, in a grossly inappropriate manner, in this instance, through his "sister's shame." The distinction between the two ways of reading the line— either emphasizing the relationship between brother and sister, or emphasizing the inappropriateness of "taking life" in a shameful way—is more than simple hairsplitting. *Pericles,* which begins with incest (and abounds in images of devouring and cannibalism), is quite self-consciously about sustenance, about the ways in which people nourish themselves, propagate the species, and protect their families, friends, and nation. Like a morality play, *Pericles* presents side by side a variety of examples of good and bad nurturing, and uses images of eating as the medium through which we must interpret the action.

III

When Ben Jonson used *Pericles* as a prime example of a "mouldy tale," "stale/ As the shrieve's crust, and nasty as his fish,"[35] he was doing no more than hoisting the play with its own petar, for images of eating are pervasive in *Pericles.* "I feed/ On mother's flesh," the riddle's metaphor, is but one—and not the first—in a series of literal and figurative references to devouring. Although Caroline Spurgeon concluded that "*Pericles* alone of the romances has no sign of any running 'motive' or continuity of picture or thought in the imagery,"[36] the play in fact presents an almost obsessive chain of images and actions having to do with eating, food, vomiting, starving, and nourishment. From Pericles' description of his determination to win the Princess of Antioch as "an inflam'd desire in my breast/ To taste the fruit of yon celestial tree" ([I.i.21-22], the first of many which imply cannibalism), to his description later of his daughter Marina as one "Who starves the ears she feeds, and makes them hungry/ The more she gives them speech" (V.i.112-13), *Pericles* uses the gustatory for a variety of purposes, though most often as a way of indicating sexual desire. That is, as in the riddle, where a kind of eating (cannibalism) describes a kind of sexuality (incest), so in the play as a whole the

alimentary is used to define the sexual. Indeed, in *Pericles* a scheme of moral values relating to sexuality and nurturance is indicated primarily by right and wrong sorts of appetite, food, and eating. The two activities— eating and propagating—form an apt metaphorical duo, for both, as we have seen, are natural and sustaining activites from which we "take life."[37]

Like most Shakespearean comedies, *Pericles* identifies love with plenty, and the play has its fair share of feasts and celebrations which use eating and drinking as signs of communal celebration. The happy recognitions of the fifth act, for example, begin with Gower's telling us that Pericles' ship arrived in Mytilene as that city "striv'd/ God Neptune's annual feast to keep" (V.Cho.16-17). Earlier, when the fishermen discover Pericles ashore near Pentapolis after the shipwreck, they offer him food and clothing, promising that "we'll have flesh for holidays, fish for fasting-days, and moreo'er puddings and flap-jacks. . . . " (II.i.81-83). Their gracious sharing with him is echoed later, after Pericles defeats competitors at the tournament at Pentapolis, when Simonides, his host, entertains the contestants with a lavish banquet, enjoining them to be happy, "for mirth becomes a feast" (II.iii.7).

But eating and drinking in *Pericles* always suggest more than simple celebration, and the speed with which literal references to eating become figurative characterizes Shakespeare's use of language in this play. For example, the banqueting at Pentapolis takes on a less innocent coloration, and seems less the simple sign of community, when Thaisa offers Pericles wine in language which suggests transubstantiation, or a totemic sacrifice:[38]

> *Thai.* The king my father, sir, has drunk to
>   you.
> *Per.* I thank him.
> *Thai.* Wishing it so much blood unto your
>   life.
>
>   (II.iii.75-77)

The threatening aspect of the father, which Pericles had witnessed to his horror in Antioch, seems to reappear in Pentapolis. Here, however, the King's words are part of the language of courtesy, and though they suggest the carnivorous, and perhaps cannibalism, they merely indicate Simonides' hospitality. Many of the metaphors in the play, however, perhaps taking their cue from the riddle, do suggest cannibalism in fairly direct ways. Thaisa, "queen o'th' feast" (II.iii.17), is so taken with Pericles that she loses her appetite for the foods offered by her father to his guests:

> By Juno, that is queen of marriage,
> All viands that I eat do seem unsavoury
> Wishing him my meat.
>
>   (II.iii.30-22)

Pericles had wanted to "taste" the Princess of Antioch, who was herself "an eater of her mother's flesh," and now Thaisa wishes Pericles her "meat." The identification of people with food, the reduction of human beings to comestibles, is this play's way of indicating human desire and the intensity and quality of relationships. What *Pericles* makes equally clear, however, is the difference between the kinds of eating and sexuality which are licit and sustaining, and those forms which are not. Thaisa and Simonides stand as corrective examples against which Pericles and the audience can measure the perversely sustaining habits of Antiochus and his daughter.

Clearly, the banquet scene at Pentapolis uses images of food and eating to indicate community values and the healthfulness of Simonides' court, though its language toys with the idea of cannibalism, using such gruesome images for positive effects, much as *The Merchant of Venice,* for example, uses pecuniary imagery to define Portia's worth. But if cannibalism is occasionally used playfully in *Pericles,* as a sign of one's ultimate deliciousness (as in popular songs and rhymes where little girls are "sugar and spice"), this play in general is full of less innocuous examples. In terms of the play's dominant, and perhaps sole, image pattern, it is significant that it is fishermen who discover a bedraggled Pericles on the shore after his shipwreck (II.i). When one marvels "how the fishes live in the sea" (II.i.26-27), another responds,

> Why, as men do a-land: the great ones eat up the little ones. I can compare our rich misers to nothing so fitly as to a whale: a' plays and tumbles, driving the poor fry before him, and at last devours them all at a mouthful. Such whales have I heard on a' th' land, who never leave gaping till they swallow'd the whole parish, church steeple, bells, and all. (II.i.28-34)

Once again, as in the riddle, an inappropriate *modus vivendi* is illustrated through the agency of a metaphor having to do with eating. In this case, the fishermen, who sustain themselves in a socially acceptable way—by catching and eating what they need—point to "our rich misers," comparing them to whales and calling them whales "a' th' land." The natural order in the ocean, where the big eat the small, is simply an unpleasant fact of life for the fishermen. But Shakespeare, who moralizes in *Pericles* as nowhere else,[39] uses nature as a way of commenting on the impropriety, the obscenity, of what a later era would call social Darwinism, where "the great ones eat up the little ones," on a world where power is appetite, "And appetite, an universal wolf/ . . . / Must make perforce a universal prey/ And last eat up himself" (*Tro.,* I.iii.121-24). Thus, *Pericles,* which begins with child devouring parent, that is, the little (like young snakes) eating the great, soon expands the metaphor to include

the more familiar horror of the great devouring the little. This scenario recalls Labby's analysis of the Yapese identification of cannibalism with incest: the huge sea bass "would engulf all fish, even its own offspring, perhaps even a man. People who committed incest, it was said, were similarly voracious, consuming their own kin in a sort of sexual cannibalism." The vehicle of the metaphor, devouring, is the same in Labby's example and in *Pericles;* and the tenor, incest in the former, human greed in the latter, are both unacceptable—because ultimately self-defeating—methods of sustenance.

Storms in the natural world are associated in this play with the excesses of overeating and drinking, and lead, as we might expect, to the riots associated with vomiting. "What a drunken knave was the sea to cast [i.e., vomit] thee in our way!" chide the fishermen when they find Pericles (II.i.57); the north "disgorges" (III.Cho.48) the tempest that splits Pericles' ship and brings on Thaisa's labor; the sea has its "belching whale" (III.i.62), and later "belches" Thaisa's coffin upon shore (III.ii.56) when its "stomach" is "o'ercharg'd" (III.ii.54). Shakespeare uses a similar set of images throughout the brothel scenes, and equates prostitution with gluttony and cannibalism, much as he does the immorality of miserliness in the fisherman's lament in II.i. The whores are "unwholesome" (IV.ii.19), "rotten" (IV.ii.9), and are killing off the customers, one of whom was made "roast-meat for worms" (IV.ii.22-23). The Bawd needs "fresh ones" (IV.ii.10) to replace the "sodden" [i.e., "stewed"] (IV.ii.18) women who remain in the business. Marina is instructed in her new duties by the Bawd, her "herb woman" (IV.vi.84), so that "she may not be raw in her entertainment" (IV.vi.51-52) in a house where the "doors and windows savour vilely" (IV.vi.110). When she proves intractable, causing the profession to "stink afore the face of the gods" (IV.vi.135-36), Boult tries to force her. Marina defends herself by telling the pander's servant that his

> food is such
> As hath been belch'd on by infected lungs.
> (IV.vi.167-68)

The connection between Boult's trade and the condition of his food is clear enough, I think, to most audiences. Marina's point, an elaboration of the terms of the riddle—where eating is used to describe sexuality—is that a debased profession and a shameful way of earning money, that is, of "taking life," to borrow *Measure for Measure*'s phrase again, is the same as sustaining oneself on diseased food. The physical is used to illustrate the moral, all the more telling an approach given the real danger in seventeenth-century Europe of ingesting bad food or of contracting a disease and infecting one's lungs.[40]

Although Marina is told she will "taste gentlemen of all fashions" (IV.ii.74-75), and that "Men must feed" her (IV.ii.88), most descriptions in these scenes suggest that it is she who will be cannibalized and become food for the men. Such a substitution—Marina for rotten meat—underscores the horrific nature of her life in the brothel. The virgin, Western literature's pre-eminent sign of moral healthfulness,[41] is to be used, indeed, consumed, by those corrupt natures who ordinarily eat diseased flesh. When Boult "cried her through the market" (IV.ii.90), "There was a Spaniard's mouth water'd" (IV.ii.97-98). Boult himself argues that he is entitled to sleep with her; after all,

> if
> I have bargain'd for the joint,—
> *Bawd.* Thou mayst cut a morsel off the spit.
> (IV.ii.129-30)

The Bawd tells Marina her chastity "is not worth a breakfast in the cheapest country under the cope" (IV.vi.122-23), and then calls her "my dish of chastity with rosemary and bays!" (IV.vi.150-51). The reduction of people to "morsels" suggests the horrors of fairy tales, where caged children are fattened, sleeping children have their throats cut, and young girls are simply devoured by hungry animals. Marina's treatment, however, quite self-consciously conflates sexual abuse and physical abuse in a way fairy tales do not, implying that she will be cannibalized as a graphic way of indicating rape. Thus, like the riddle, the brothel scenes describe illicit sexuality and moral turpitude by calling attention through their imagery to appetite and rapacity. The assumption inherent in such an approach seems to be that the easiest way for an English audience of the seventeenth century to comprehend the ghastliness of sexual abuse is via the more familiar horrors of hunger, disease, and the sicknesses attendant on gluttony.

To understand the connection between eating and propagating in *Pericles* is to appreciate the equal importance of both elements which comprise the central metaphor. Thus, although *Pericles* begins with a glaring instance of perverse sexuality, and emphasizes its perversity by offering both the salutary example of Simonides' and Thaisa's healthy father/daughter relationship, as well as the vivid portrayal of Marina's sexual abuse in the brothel, the play pays quite as much attention, in the final analysis, to food, eating, starvation, and appetitive excesses. Indeed, I.iv, which describes Pericles' relieving the starving masses in Tharsus, does so in terms which lead us back to Antiochus' riddle as directly as do the brothel scenes. If the Princess of Antioch is a child who feeds "on mother's flesh," and Marina a child who is threatened with being eaten, at least figuratively, it is only Pericles' fortuitous arrival which prevents the children of Tharsus from being devoured in fact. Pericles brings Cleon and

Dionyza "corn to bake your needy bread,/ And give them life whom hunger starv'd half dead" (I.iv.95-96), forestalling desperate attempts by mothers to cannibalize their young. The citizens of Tharsus, Knight tells us, are "brought low by savage hunger; brought, that is, to realize its ultimate dependence; brought up against basic fact; such fact as is the natural air breathed by the admirable fishermen of Pentapolis."[42] Cleon comments on the dreadful family situations in Tharsus,

> Those palates who, not yet two summers
>   younger,
> Must have inventions to delight the taste,
> Would now be glad of bread, and beg for
>   it;
> Those mothers who, to nuzzle up their
>   babes
> Thought nought too curious, are ready now
> To eat those little darlings who they lov'd.
> (I.iv.39-44)

This description of the state of mind of the mothers in Tharsus is an ironic reversal of the terms of the riddle. Though it mirrors the horror with which the play opens, it is but the most direct—and one of the earliest—in a long series of allusions to eating in general, and to cannibalism in particular. *Pericles* begins by defining incest as a kind cannibalism, and then proceeds to describe societies divided into the starving and the over-fed, in which the great eat the little, "the poor fry" are devoured by the whale and "the whole parish" by the gluttons on land. From its grotesque initial metaphor *Pericles* moves quickly and inexorably to a world where cannibalism is a real possibility. The vehicle of the riddle's metaphor achieves a life of its own, and an outrageous comparison suddenly describes the precise social conditions in which some characters actually live. The grotesqueries of fairy tale are thus validated early on in the world of *Pericles,* where it is entirely likely that a daughter will be "an eater of her mother's flesh," but also that parents will devour "those little darlings whom they lov'd." All may become foodstuffs.

How one "takes life" is thus quite clearly the focus of this play. Are we, *Pericles* seems to ask, to sustain ourselves by using our children? Are children to thrive by consuming their parents? Ought one prostitute others, or gobble up the small fry, or devour the parish as a way of carving one's place in "this breathing world" (*Richard III,* I.i.21)? If Robert Wiemann is correct in concluding that the vitality of Elizabethan and Jacobean theater derives primarily from its ability to reflect the "heterogeneous ideas and attitudes"[43] born in an age of "economic expansion and national awakening" (p. 161), an age in which "[o]lder conceptions of honor were confronted by the new pride of possession, hatred of usury by the fervor for gold, the idea of service by the idea of profit, deeply rooted community consciousness by passionate individualism" (p. 169), then it is not at all surprising that *Pericles* emphasizes a human obligation to imitate nature in nurturing our own. The universe in which the characters in *Pericles* move describes both ends of its "Great Chain of Being," not so much in terms of their hierarchical relation to one another, as in terms of nurturance and familial and governmental responsibility. What Morse says of images of ingestion in Shakespeare in general clearly applies to his use of such images in *Pericles:*

> A complex series of moral observations is conveyed by describing characters as eating like animals, eating food which is only appropriate to animals, or even eating what animals themselves might refuse. At the extreme, the worst eating is cannibalism, the worst cannibalism is that which occurs within the family. By virtue of the double metaphor of the state as both like a human body and like a parent, the worst kind of family-cannibalism is treason.[44]

In *Pericles* Shakespeare repeatedly stresses the importance of a natural and proper relation between parent and child, citizen and country, man and God. Though images of eating and food form the heart of his approach to the subject of nourishment and sustenance, in this play there are as well a series of fairly direct references to nurturance and generation. Pericles assumes that "All love the womb that their first being bred" (I.i.108), for, as Helicanus tells us, even the "plants look up to heaven, from whence/They have their nourishment" (I.ii.56-57). We learn that it is the earth "From whence we had our being and our birth" (I.ii.113-14), and that "Time's the king of men;/He's both their parent, and he is their grave . . ." (II.iii.45-46). Appropriately, Thaisa sits by her father "like Beauty's child, whom Nature gat" (II.ii.6), for "princes are/ A model which heaven makes like to itself" (II.ii.10-11).

Antiochus is not the only character to exploit the common understanding that "All love the womb that their first being bred," that strong will protect weak as parents their children and children their parents. When Marina's nurse, Lychorida, dies, Dionyza counsels Pericles' child, "Do not consume your blood with sorrow:/ Have you a nurse of me!" (IV.i.23-24). Pericles, who had assumed years earlier that he left Marina "At careful nursing" (III.i.80) with Dionyza, could hardly anticipate that queen's perverse understanding of "nursing":

> *Cle.*   What canst thou say
> When noble Pericles shall demand his child?
> *Dio.* That she is dead. Nurses are not the
>   fates,
> To foster it, not ever to preserve.
>
>   (IV.iii.12-15)

Just as the example of Simonides and Thaisa serves to balance the perverse example of Antiochus and his daughter, so the ultimate cohesiveness and loyalty among Pericles and his wife and daughter balance the selfishness of Cleon and Dionyza.

Perhaps "*Pericles* might be called a Shakespearian morality play," as Knight suggests,[45] primarily because "correspondences emerge"[46] as the action advances. Surely, two of the clearest parallels have to do with Marina, not so much as a reincarnated Thaisa, as most critics would have it, but rather as a benign, healthy, and natural version of the Princess of Antioch. More fully than Thaisa, Marina stands as an exemplar of a right relation between a daughter and her parents, in part because the circumstances of her birth seem to echo rather than contradict Antiochus' relationship with his daughter. That is, just as the Princess of Antioch "takes life" by devouring her mother, so Marina "takes life" at the expense of her mother, who (seemingly) dies as she is born. Pericles is told that his daughter is a "piece" (III.i.17) of his queen, "all that is left living" (III.i.20) of his wife. Though Marina is innocent of wrongdoing and the Princess a "Bad child" (I. Cho.27), *Pericles* describes a world where, by accident or design, children place parents in the gravest danger. We have seen as well, however, that the reverse is equally true, that children are likely to be abused by parents, by all adults, for the children of Tharsus are finally thought of as food, and Marina herself is dreadfully abused in the brothel at Mytilene.

It is in the play's last act that the apparent potential for destruction in both parents and children is finally defused. Here, father and daughter rescue one another, and then go on to reclaim a wife and mother who had long been thought dead. Pericles redeems from the brothel the daughter whom he had left with the most unmaternal Dionyza in Tharsus, and Marina revives the father whom she had rendered bereft by the fact of her birth. The ways in which father and daughter are mutually dependent, connected not only by the undeniable facts of biology but by family history as well, are captured in Pericles' call to Marina,

>   O, come hither,
> Thou that beget'st him that did thee
>   beget. . . .
>
>   (V.i.194-95)

Pericles acknowledges that as parent and child and he and Marina take life from one another, he as her biological father, and she as the agent of his spiritual rebirth. Child and parent, each to the other, Pericles and Marina in the fifth act exemplify that healthful relationship which is so cruelly debased in the play's opening act. Gorfain argues that "Pericles's paradox [ll. 194-95] inverts the roles of father and daughter without consuming maternity and creativity"[47]; indeed, his paradox points to "the thing that is most emphasized in the feminine figures—their power to create and cherish life, their potential or achieved maternity."[48] As the play ends we are drawn back to that other paradox, the riddle which points to sterility and death; as Peterson suggests, "We have seen that the dialectical terms of process—a love that sustains, restores, and renews and a love that corrupts and destroys—are represented throughout the play by characterswho are simple exemplars."[49] The Princess of Antioch, "an eater of her mother's flesh," destroys the parent who begat her and, in fact, sustains herself by "feed[ing]/ On mother's flesh which did me breed." Marina, sustained by her parents, indeed, taking life as her mother dies, reciprocates, begetting a father whose revival implies and impels the resurrection of her mother. Thaisa is told that Marina is "flesh of thy flesh" (V.iii.46), and hears her daughter declare, "My heart/ Leaps to be gone into my mother's bosom" (V.iii.44-45). The disparate units of Pericles' family are reintegrated, "flesh" joins rather than feeds on flesh, and the family becomes a self-sustaining entity comprised of parents and child who nourish and nurture one another.

Notes

[1] George Parfitt, ed. *Ben Jonson: The Complete Poems* (New Haven: Yale Univ. Press, 1982), p. 283.

[2] Hazlitt objected to "the far-fetched and complicated absurdity of the story" ("Characters of Shakespear's Plays," *The Complete Works of William Hazlitt,* ed. P.P. Howe [London: J. M. Dent, 1930], p. 357), and quoted Schlegel, who felt that "Shakespeare here handled a childish and extravagant romance of the old poet Gower, and was unwilling to drag the subject out of its proper sphere" (p. 355). For Larry S. Champion (*The Evolution of Shakespeare's Comedy* [Cambridge: Harvard Univ. Press, 1970]) the play's startling events "entertain for their own sake, not because they arouse interest in what happens to a certain character or how he is affected" (p. 97). Similarly, James G. McManaway (ed. *The Complete Pelican Shakespeare* [Baltimore: Penguin, 1969]) writes *Pericles* off as a play with "striking incidents selected from a long romance with small regard for causality" (p. 1260), and Hallett Smith (ed. *Pericles,* in *The Riverside Shakespeare,* gen. ed. G. Blakemore Evans [Boston: Houghton, 1974]) claims that "From any realistic point of view, the spectacular scenes of *Pericles* are of course utter nonsense" (p. 1481).

[3] Phyllis Gorfain, "Puzzle and Artifice: The Riddle as Metapoetry in 'Pericles'," *Shakespeare Survey,* 29 (1976), 11.

[4] References to *Pericles* are from the New Arden, ed. F. D. Hoeniger (London: Methuen, 1963); those to

other plays by Shakespeare are from *The Riverside Shakespeare.*

[5] "Antiochus's Riddle in Gower and Shakespeare," *Review of English Studies,* N.S., 6 (1955), 245-51.

[6] Stephen Jay Gould, *The Flamingo's Smile* (New York: W. W. Norton, 1985), p. 55.

[7] *Historia Apollonii Regis Tyri,* ed. A. Riese (1893; rpt. Stuttgart: Teubner, 1973), p. 6.

[8] Geoffrey Bullough, ed., *Narrative and Dramatic Sources of Shakespeare,* VI (London: Routledge and Kegan Paul, 1966), pp. 377, 379, 428.

[9] Bullough, p. 498. The earliest extant version of the Apollonius story, *Historia Apollonii Regis Tyri* (see note 7), a late Latin prose romance, is thought to have been based on earlier Greek models. Thomas Hagg (*The Novel in Antiquity* [Berkeley: Univ. of California Press, 1983]) discusses the enormous popularity of *Apollonius of Tyre* (pp. 147-53), which exists as well in Latin verse fragments, and appears in Old English, Old French, Byzantine Greek, and Middle High German, as well as in numerous Renaissance versions. For a discussion of its genesis, provenance, and affinities with earlier Greek literature, see Philip H. Goepp, 2nd, "The Narrative Material of *Apollonius of Tyre,*" *ELH,* 5 (1938), 150-72. For its affinities with modern Greek oral narrative, see R. M. Dawkins, "Modern Greek Oral Versions of Apollonios of Tyre," *Modern Language Review,* 37 (1942), 169-84.

[10] Hoeniger, p. 12. Allusions to serpents as devourers of their mothers abounded in the Renaissance. See, for example, Jonson's *Poetaster:* "Out viper, thou that eat'st thy parents, hence" (*The Complete Plays of BenJonson,* ed. G. A. Wilkes, II [Oxford: Oxford Univ. Press, 1981], V.iii.291).

[11] Henry Green, *Shakespeare and the Emblem Writers* (New York: Burt Franklin, n.d.), p. 191.

[12] If serpents helped Shakespeare to describe in pictorial terms the cannibalism implicit in the riddle, they also suggested incest in more direct terms, for one of the examples which the *OED* uses to define "incestuous," Sylvester's *Du Bartas* (1591), seems to assume in its description of usury a relationship between incest and serpents: "You City-Vipers, that (incestious) joyn/ Use upon use, begetting Coyn of Coyn!" The reptilian, incest, and devouring are, of course, linked in Milton's *Paradise Lost* when Satan attempts to make his way through the gates of hell. The fallen angel is stopped by his daughter, Sin, the "Snaky Sorceress" (II.724), half woman, half serpent, and by Death, her son (and brother) begotten by her father. Milton makes clear the irony in the impending battle between Satan

and Death in Sin's plea, "O Father, what intends thy hand . . . / Against thy only Son?" (II.727-28). Interestingly, Merritt Y. Hughes (ed. *Paradise Lost* [New York: Odyssey, 1962]) points out that John Gower had personified "Sin as the incestuous mother of Death in the *Mirrour de l'Omme*" (p. 51).

[13] William Aldis Wright, ed. *The Authorised Version of the English Bible,* I (Cambridge: Cambridge Univ. Press, 1909), Gen.III 6.

[14] Emile Male, *The Gothic Image,* trans. Dora Nussey (New York: Harper & Row, 1958), p. 379.

[15] Christopher Marlowe, *Doctor Faustus,* ed. John D. Jump (Cambridge: Harvard Univ. Press, 1962), Cho. 24.

[16] Cyril Tourneur, *The Revenger's Tragedy,* ed. R. A. Foakes (Cambridge: Harvard Univ. Press, 1966), I.i.45.

[17] The traditional association of evil and the torments of hell with cannibalism is most clearly seen in the visual arts. For example, Fra Angelico's "Last Judgment" (Florence), painted ca. 1430, divides the netherworld into eight chambers. In the various rooms sinners eat at a table, are cooked in a large pot, are stewed in an even larger pot—in the center of which the devil tears them to bits with his teeth—and devour themselves in what appears to be an orgy of cannibalism and self-mutilation. Occasionally, as in the literature of the period, artists commented on social injustice through depictions of universal gluttony or starvation. See, for example, Peter Brueghel's drawings "Big Fish Eat Little Fish," "The Poor Kitchen," and "The Rich Kitchen."

[18] Ruth Morse, "Unfit for Human Consumption: Shakespeare's Unnatural Food," *Shakespeare-Jahrbuch* (1983), 148.

[19] Leslie Fiedler, *The Stranger in Shakespeare* (New York: Stein and Day, 1972), pp. 111, 119.

[20] Morse, p. 126, et passim.

[21] Janet Adelman, "'Anger's My Meat': Feeding, Dependency, and Aggression in *Coriolanus*," in *Representing Shakespeare,* ed. Murray M. Schwartz and Coppelia Kahn (Baltimore: Johns Hopkins Univ. Press, 1980), pp. 129-49.

[22] See Gail Kern Paster, "To Starve with Feeding: The City in *Coriolanus*," *Shakespeare Studies,* 11 (1978), 123-44, on "the thematic link between animal imagery and the images of food and eating which recur throughout the play" (p. 136). It is likely that the enormous popularity of images having to do with eating, starving, and related subjects, whether familiar and reassuring or gruesome, may in fact partly be accounted for in the social history of the period. At the beginning of her essay Adelman suggests that popular protests and riots against food shortages may have provided real impetus to Shakespeare, who "shapes his material from the start [in *Coriolanus*] to exacerbate those fears in his audience" (p. 129). Robert Darnton, who has written extensively on pre-Revolutionary French cultural history (*The Great Cat Massacre and Other Episodes in French Cultural History* [New York: Random House, 1984]), feels strongly the shaping influence of economic constraints on popular literature, and argues that the cannibalism, infanticide, and incest of 18th-century French fairy tales find their origin in the living conditions of the masses: "to eat or not to eat, that was the question peasants confronted in their folklore as well as in their daily lives" (pp. 31-32). Indeed, at least one critic thinks the "famine relief" (Graham Anderson, *Ancient Fiction* [London: Croom Helm, 1984], p. 105) in *Apollonius of Tyre* (echoed in *Pericles,* I.iv) speaks directly to a crucial social issue. Anderson believes that "romantic motifs are related to the kind of realities of ancient life that are at least familiar in a sophisticated Western culture" (p. 100).

[23] John Frederick Nims, ed. *Ovid's Metamorphoses: The Arthur Golding Translation* (New York: Macmillan, 1965), VI.824-25.

[24] Erich Neumann, *The Great Mother,* trans. Ralph Manheim, 2nd ed. (Princeton: Princeton Univ. Press, 1974), p. 172.

[25] Robin Fox, *The Red Lamp of Incest* (New York: E. P. Dutton, 1980), p. 182.

[26] Sir James G. Frazer, "Taboo and the Perils of the Soul," *The Golden Bough,* 3rd ed. (London: Macmillan, 1919), pp. 116-19.

[27] Christine Kapisch-Zuber, *Women, Family, and Ritual in Renaissance Italy,* trans. Lydia Cochrane (Chicago: Univ. of Chicago Press, 1985), p. 92.

[28] Laura and Raoul Makarius, "The Incest Prohibition and Food Taboos," *Diogenes,* 30 (1960), 46.

[29] Sigmund Freud, *Totem and Taboo,* trans. James Strachey (London: Hogarth, 1957), p. 132.

[30] Julia Kristeva, *Powers of Horrors,* trans. Leon S. Roudiez (New York: Columbia Univ. Press, 1982), p. 65.

[31] Anthony Hooper, "'Eating Blood': Tahitian Concepts of Incest," *The Journal of the Polynesian Society,* 85 (1976), 227.

[32] J. L. Fischer, Roger Ward, and Martha Ward,

"Ponapean Conceptions of Incest," *The Journal of the Polynesian Society,* 85 (1976), 200.

[33] David Labby, "Incest as Cannibalism: The Yapese Analysis," *The Journal of the Polynesian Society,* 85 (1976), 171-79.

[34] *Measure for Measure,* ed. J. W. Lever (London: Methuen, 1966), p. 75.

[35] George Parfitt, ed. *Ben Johson: The Complete Poems* (New Haven: Yale Univ. Press, 1982), p. 283.

[36] *Shakespeare's Imagery* (Cambridge: Cambridge Univ. Press, 1935), p. 291.

[37] W. B. Thorne, "*Pericles* and the Incest-Fertility Opposition," *Shakespeare Quarterly,* 22 (1971), 43-56, reviews scholarship which sees *Pericles* as a play about the opposition between young and old, fertility and sterility, themes related to nurturance.

[38] See Freud, pp. 140-46.

[39] On Shakespeare's overt moralizing in *Pericles* see G. Wilson Knight, *The Crown of Life* (Oxford: Oxford Univ. Press, 1947), pp. 32-75, and Maurice Hunt ("A Looking Glass for *Pericles,*" *Essays in Literature,* 13 [1986], 3-11), who discusses the play's "strong roots in Miracle drama" (p. 3). Goepp discusses the "didacticism" (p. 170) of *Apollonius of Tyre.*

[40] See William H. McNeill, *Plagues and Peoples* (New York: Doubleday, 1976), Ch. 5.

[41] Northrop Frye, *The Secular Scripture* (Cambridge: Harvard Univ. Press, 1976), discusses the meaning of virginity in romance literature in Ch. 3.

[42] Knight, pp. 48-49.

[43] Robert Weimann, *Shakespeare and the Popular Tradition in the Theater* (Baltimore: Johns Hopkins Univ. Press, 1978), p. 169.

[44] Morse, p. 126.

[45] Knight, p. 70.

[46] Douglas L. Peterson, *Time Tide and Tempest* (San Marino: The Huntington Library, 1973), p. 83.

[47] Gorfain, p. 15.

[48] C. L. Barber, "'Thou That Beget'st Him That Did Thee Beget': Transformation in 'Pericles' and 'The Winter's Tale,'" *Shakespeare Survey,* 22 (1969), 61. Marianne Novy writes, "Here, as when Pericles ap-

plies imagery of pregnancy and childbirth to himself earlier in the scene, the interchange of sexes suggests that the distinction between male and female experience has become less important than a sense of general human vulnerability and of the interdependence between generations" (*Love's Argument* [Chapel Hill: Univ. of North Carolina Press, 1984], p. 175).

[49] Peterson, p. 88.

CHARACTERIZATION

Nona Fienberg (essay date 1982)

SOURCE: "Marina in *Pericles*: Exchange Values and the Art of Moral Discourse," in *Iowa State Journal of Research,* Vol. 57, No. 2, November, 1982, pp. 153-61.

[*Here, Fienberg discusses the economic metaphors of* Pericles *in relation to Marina's character, arguing that by selling moral discourse instead of her body "Marina acknowledges the market system, yetremains uncorrupted by it."*]

In his essay, "Of Truth" (1625), Francis Bacon distinguishes between "theological and philosophical truth" and the truth of "civil business." While he further distinguishes between the poets, whose harmless lies give pleasure, and the merchants, who lie "for advantage," both stand in the second category of the truth of civil business, since both participate in the nascent spirit of capitalism of seventeenth-century London. A spokesman for his economic world, Bacon frames his essay with a cynical portrayal of truth in the marketplace: "Truth may perhaps come to the price of a pearl, that showeth best by day; but it will not rise to the price of a diamond or carbuncle, that showeth best in varied lights. A mixture of a lie doth ever add pleasure."[1] But if the world of civil business where even truth has its price informs his essay, Bacon grants us, in the heart of the essay, a vision of truth "in varied lights," the spiritual truth that does not change with market prices: "Certainly it is heaven upon earth to have a man's mind move in charity, rest in providence, and turn upon the poles of truth."[2] Bacon's simultaneous complicity in the world of economic values and vision of a "heaven on earth" provides an analogy to the complexity of Shakespeare's vision in *Pericles.* In the play world, Pericles' lost daughter Marina, while initially subject to the selfish, mutable truth of civil business, ultimately triumphs over the marketplace. Through her mastery of the linguistic act Marina not only controls audience response to her value, but also shapes her own destiny. Through

Marina's eloquence, *Pericles* becomes a celebration of action carried out in a spirit of charity.

In her 1976 article, Phyllis Gorfain argues for the structural importance of Gower's role as mediator: "the patience he urges in enduring the narrative parallels the virtue with which the heroes bear temporal dangers."[3] But Gorfain's discussion of the analogical structure of the play does not fully account for Marina's structural function in Acts Four and Five. C. L. Barber also cannot accommodate, in *Pericles,* the "strange comical scenes in the brothel" to his vision of the transformations which help humans to approach divinity.[4] Nevertheless, the play insists in a number of ways on the importance of Marina's brothel experience. First, Gower carefully frames the scenes, bidding his audience to bear Pericles' daughter's "woe and heavy well-a-day/In her unholy service" with "patience."[5] Second, our most extended encounter with Marina occurs when she is in the brothel, where she is sold by pirates after escaping from the grasp of a paid murderer. We learn there most fully her inherent value when she contrives to escape from the contract of prostitution by creating a market for her discourse. The third way the play suggests the importance of the brothel experience is a more mysterious one. In the fifth act recognition scene between father and daughter, as Pericles slowly and painfully solves the enigma of Marina's identity, her brothel experience forms no part of their dialogue. Instead, as Marina relates it, the pirates, who sold her into presumed prostitution, are transformed from cruel profiteers into benevolent rescuers. Pericles learns the lesson of her inner worth through the example of her moral discourse.

Act Four and particularly Marina's role in it serve as the thematic and structural pivot between two contrasting economies, that which values women as a commodity to exploit and that which values their wholeness and integrity. In the debased economy of Antiochus' court, the king himself exploited his daughter as a sexual object. When Act Four begins, Marina has reached puberty, the marriageable, that is, marketable, age in Renaissance England. Dionyza, her surrogate mother, plots to have her killed in order to enhance the marriage value of Philoten, her own daughter. As long as praises are, as Gower says, "paid as debts" (IV.i.34) to Marina, Philoten's worth suffers. Abandoned at the seaside to the savage Leonine, whose only incentive to murder is profit, Marina is powerless to save herself. Once the pirates capture her, however, she enters a world where the debased economy implicit in Antiochus' and Dionyza's courts becomes explicit. In the brothel, Marina challenges the truth of civil business with her spiritual truth; she sets her value system against their market economy.

The pirates' cries as they seize Marina declare how they value her. One calls, "A prize, a prize!" (IV.i.93);

another claims his share in the profits, "Half-part, mates, half-part" (IV.i.94). They treat her as they would gold, silver, ivory, or pearls, purely as coin in the marketplace. When they sell Marina into the brothel, they drive a hard bargain but gain their price, "one thousand pieces" (IV.ii.51). In the world of Pander, Boult and Bawd, such objectification of women becomes even more reductive. The three take inventory, find that their stock in trade is low, and determine to replenish it. Pander's complaint pertains to quantity, "We lost too much money this mart by being too wenchless" (IV.ii.4-5), while Bawd's assessment concerns quality, "The stuff we have, a strong wind will blow it to pieces, they are so pitifully sodden" (IV.ii.18-20). By reducing a girl or young woman to a "wench" and further diminishing her to fabric to be worked, blown upon, or sold, they reveal the moral bankruptcy of their commerce. But as long as the accounting remains general, an audience can be amused by the spectacle of a brothel's financial concerns. The reductive language they apply both to their "goods" and their customers is itself richly metaphorical and solidly Anglo-Saxon: "Ay, she quickly poop'd him, she made him roast-meat for worms" (IV.ii.24-25). Until Marina enters this world, its moral emptiness matters less than its linguistic richness.

Marina, however, insists on the bond between the inherent value of a person and the moral content of language. In her dialogue with Bawd, for example, the term "woman" is at issue:

> *Mar.* Are you a woman?
> *Bawd.* What would you have me be, and I be not a woman?
> *Mar.* An honest woman, or not a woman.
> (IV.ii.82-85)

To Marina, the word contains a moral value, as a woman expresses wholeness and integrity. To Bawd, a woman's value lies in her use. When she instructs Boult to cry their wares in the marketplace, she describes Marina by means of a *blazon*: "Boult, take you the marks of her, the color of her hair, complexion, height, her age, with warrant of her virginity, and cry, 'He that will give most shall have her first.' Such a maidenhead were no cheap thing, if men were as they have been" (IV.ii.57-61). In effect, Bawd shatters Marina into pieces, hair, height, complexion, age, maidenhead, in order to recover their one thousand piece investment. Such a process continues the violent assaults on Marina threatened by Leonine and the pirates. Bawd breaks her up into parts, with an aggressive, appropriative purpose.[6] In that economy, Marina's sense of her integrity as a "woman" constitutes a danger.

Yet, in the brothel, Marina herself learns how to use her exchange value in a way quite at odds with what her masters intended. She finds, that is, another commodity to trade. Instead of selling the virginity for which she can gain a greater prize, she creates a market for her moral discourse. Through the art of her speech, moreover, she transforms the brothel customers into generous spirits. While we do not see her transform the two Gentlemen leaving the brothel, we hear them attest to her powers:

> *1. Gent.* Did you ever hear the like?
> *2. Gent.* No, nor never shall do in such a
> place as this, she being once gone.
> *1. Gent.* But to have divinity preach'd
> there! did you ever dream of such a
> thing?
>
> (IV.v.1-5)

Although Gower has just warned us that we must watch Marina in her "unholy service," presumably her performance of a postitute's part, we see, in contrast, a "holy service." Marina has preached divinity so convincingly that the Gentlemen determine to "hear the vestals sing."

The testimony of the two Gentlemen prepares us for the more complex encounter between Marina and Lysimachus, the Governor of Mytilene. If she has opened the Gentlemen's ears to the worth and beauty of the Vestals' song, she educates the Governor's ears to her moral discourse. When Lysimachus enters her company, he calls her a "creature of sale" (IV.vi.78), expecting to pay for his sexual pleasure. Moreover, he addresses her in prose speeches appropriate to the setting. Marina, however, both confounds his expectations that he is meeting an object for sexual exploitation and counters his prose with her poised, imaginative verse. When he leaves her company, he communicates in the verse appropriate to his own social position, to his inherent nobility, and to his teacher, Marina.

To effect such a conversion and to reveal her value she uses an integrated myth of her own identity:

> For me,
> That am a maid, though most ungentle
> fortune
> Have plac'd me in this sty, where since I
> came,
> Diseases have been sold dearer than
> physic—
> That the gods
> Would set me free from this unhallowed
> place,
> Though they did change me to the meanest
> bird
> That flies i' th' purer air!
>
> (IV.vi.95-102)

Through this myth of mysterious origins, present alienation, providential intercession and metamorphosis,

Marina tames the rude Lysimachus. Despite its brevity and general outline, the myth describes accurately her subjection to a debased society and a corrupt economy. Without revealing her origins directly, she implies her worth in references to "ungentle fortune" and her moral and social superiority to "this sty." In addition, the central broken verse, "That the gods" looks syntactically in two directions. At first, it seems to complete the thought begun with "For me/That am a maid . . ." suggesting that she is a maid for whom the gods intend a nobler fate. Yet the syntax shifts unexpectedly into her wish to become "the meanest bird." In the listener's mind, the implied contrast remains between true nobility and apparent debasement. Her further complaint that in the brothel buyers purchase diseases instead of physic implies an additional contrast between that debased exchange and the medicinal value in her true discourse.

Lysimachus does not merely declare his transformation through the moral speech of Marina, he shapes his new measure of himself as a man and a governor into the measure of blank verse. He completes the unfinished last line of her myth with his praise:

> I did not think
> Thou couldst have spoke so well, ne'er
> dreamt thou couldst.
> Had I brought hither a corrupted mind,
> Thy speech had altered it.
>
> (IV.vi.102-05)

Yet her story also commands a high exchange value. Because Lysimachus learns of Marina's integrity through her myth, he values her not in pieces, but, he says, as "a piece of virtue" (IV.vi.111). Nonetheless, he presses coin on her, "Hold, here's gold for thee" (IV.vi.105) and "Hold, here's more gold for thee" (IV.vi.113). Just as he would have paid for the sexual pleasure he expected to purchase, Lysimachus pays for his pleasure in her narrative. Indeed, he may pay more for Marina's myth of selfhood and her redefinition of his moral role than he would have paid for a "creature of sale."

Ironically, the moral discourse which earns a good price resembles the skills Bawd so wanted her protégée to learn. Appropriately using the rhetorical figure of *gradatio,* in which one word is exchanged for another of greater value in a climactic sequence, Bawd tutors Marina in the strategy of earning a high price for her favors, "to weep that you live as you do makes pity in your lovers; seldom but that pity begets you a good opinion, and that opinion a mere profit" (IV.ii.116-21). To Bawd, the tears serve merely as counters in a commercial transaction, like the pieces into which she shatters Marina through the *blazon.* Indeed, in the account of the conversation between Lysimachus and Marina provided in George Wilkins' *The Painfull Aduentures of Pericles Prince of Tyre* (1608), the governor accuses her of using her tears as "some new cunning, which her matron the Bawde had instructed her in, to drawe him to a more large expence."[7] As he later affirms, however, Marina's tears signify her integrity and her identity. When Pericles seeks to understand the mysterious origins and source of power of the maid who has made him weep, he asks Lysimachus what he knows of her (V.i.183-84). The Governor's response:

> She never would tell
> Her parentage; being demanded that,
> She would sit still and weep.
>
> (V.i.187-89)

proves her value to Pericles. To "tell," in this instance, suggests to estimate the value of as well as to narrate. In the pun, Lysimachus glances at the bond between true discourse and inherent worth.

But before Marina exploits the riches in silence, she uses her eloquence to assume control over her role in the brothel. When Boult vows to rape her, he speaks of the act as a robbery, threatening "To take from you the jewel you hold so dear" (IV.vi.154) and hoping to subject her through violence to the brothel's market economy. But Marina, who failed to tame Leonine, now tames this savage. She determines both her persuasive strategies and the commodities she will sell. First, she engages Boult in a dialogue where she controls the terms. She asks a riddle, "What canst thou wish thine enemy to be?" (IV.vi.158). The answer that Boult is his own enemy emerges from the truth-telling portrait Marina paints of him, "Thou art the damned doorkeeper to every/Custrel that comes inquiring for his Tib" (IV.vi.165-66). Then, she slips Boult some money, echoing Lysimachus, "Here, here's gold for thee" (IV.vi.172). Finally, she convinces him that she can support the brothel through singing, dancing, and embroidery. The combination of moral discourse and financial considerations persuades Boult. In this exchange, Marina acknowledges the market system, yet remains uncorrupted by it. Gower celebrates her new role as both an aesthetic success, a happy reconciliation of nature and art, and an economic triumph, a profitable enterprise:

> . . . pupils lacks she none of noble race,
> Who pour their bounty on her; and her gain
> She gives the cursed bawd.
>
> (V.Gower.8-10)

Like the art of the narrator of the play, Gower himself, Marina's arts now have exchange value. Although she still gives the brothel all her gold, she has retained the chastity which serves as a synecdoche for her inner value as well as her value in the marriage market.

The greatest test of Marina's ability to exert the power of moral discourse occurs in the recognition scene (V.i.) when she and her father reunite. Faced again with a version of man's savage nature, in a Pericles whose grief has made him barbaric, unwashed, and devoid of language, Marina civilizes him. In contrast to *The Tempest,* where Miranda only wishes she were "any god of power," while Prospero draws his family to his shore and teaches a savage to speak, here Marina draws Pericles to Mytilene and teaches him language. The medicinal value of truth is applied to a Pericles wounded by the world's deceptions, especially the falseness possible in speech. When the Governor brings Marina on board Pericles' ship, he raises the question of the value of her powers, "Thy sacred physic shall receive such pay / As thy desires can wish" (V.i.73-74). It is on this question of the source of Marina's value and the nature of rewards in this world that the recognition scene turns.

While Marina participated in the money and commodity-based economy of Myteline, she was called a rose, "pretty one," "a maidenhead," and "mistress" but was bereft of her name. On board Pericles' ship, however, where value resides not in the mutable "truth of civil business," but in the more stable qualities of inherent gentility and noble parentage, naming becomes crucial to Marina's revelation of her true nature. Like the Gentlemen, Lysimachus, and Boult, Pericles is prepared to objectify Marina, to handle her roughly, even violently. But just as Marina has brought others from complicity in the debased economy of the brothel, so she teaches Pericles a more charitable understanding of their relationship. His first words after his long silence brokenly shift between the world of civil business and that of more lasting truths, "My fortunes—parentage—good parentage—/ To equal mine—(V.i.97-98). But when he lauds her as "Thou that beget'st him that did thee beget" (V.i.195), he attests to Marina's creative function and the spiritual dimension of her powers. In this suggestive formula, he replaces the commercial motive "to get" with the theological truth of the relationship between God, the Son, and the Word associated with the verb "to beget."[8]

To effect such a transformation, Marina's strategy consists not only in what she tells Pericles but in what she conceals from him. Even after she reveals, "My name is Marina" (V.i.142), she stalls. Three separate times she threatens to withhold her story:

> Patience, good sir!
> Or here I'll cease.
>
> (V.i.144-45)

and,

Act I, scene i. The riddle scene in Antioch. Shakespeare Memorial Theatre production (1958).

> You said you would believe me,
> But not to be a troubler of your peace,
> I will end here.
>
> (V.i.150-52)

and again,

> You scorn. Believe me, 'twere best I did
>   give o'er.
>
> (V.i.166)

By drawing attention to what she veils, the art of her telling resembles what Barthes describes as "narrative striptease" and is analogous to the Bawd's lesson on how to exchange tears for gold.[9] But Marina has translated the brothel's corrupt system of exchange into a true equivalence between moral discourse and inner worth. Just as she chooses not to squander her chastity, so she retains for herself the value of her brothel experience. Thus, in her narrative, the pirates who sold her into prostitution "came and rescued me; / Brought me to Meteline" (V.i.174-75). There she interrupts herself with a question, "But, good sir, / Whither will you have me?" (V.i.175-76). By means of such strategies of withholding and interrogation, Marina draws Pericles into a dialogic process of the discovery of truth. She bases her truth on the fixed, immutable sources of her being, as the solidity of the repetition of her parents' names suggests:

> I am the daughter to King Pericles,
> If good King Pericles be.
>
> (V.i.178-79)

and,

> Is it no more to be your daughter than
> To say my mother's name was Thaisa?
> Thaisa was my mother, who did end
> The minute I began.
>
> (V.i.209-12)

With the listing of the three names, Marina, Pericles, and Thaisa, she has told the sum of her identity. Yet the conditional "if" and the interrogative "is it" in Marina's naming call upon Pericles to complete her strange affirmations through his own response.

Once she has opened the Gentlemen's ears to the song of Vestal Virgins, Lysimachus' ears to verse, and Pericles' ears to the music of the spheres and Diana's message, Marina herself withdraws into virtual silence for the rest of the play. The action of the play, however, celebrates the transformations her moral discourse has effected. Pericles generously proclaims first that Lysimachus will gain Marina in marriage, and then, freely and unpredictably, that, "Our son and daughter shall in Tyrus reign" (V.iii.82), while he and Thaisa will reign in Pentapolis. The "pay" her "sacred physic" thus gains has indeed a material dimension. But Shakespeare has undertaken, through Marina, to dramatize the possible action of truth in the world of civil business. In the variety and power of her moral discourse, she embodies that active truth which Bacon describes in his essay:

> . . . yet truth, which only doth judge itself, teacheth that the inquiry of truth, which is the love-making or wooing of it, the knowledge of truth, which is the presence of it, and the belief of truth, which is the enjoying of it, is the sovereign good of human nature. (p. 48)

Just as Marina's art transforms her listeners into generous spirits, so Gower's tale transforms his audience. When the audience enters the theater, it too participates in Francis Bacon's world of civil business paying for the mixture of lie that gives pleasure. But we applaud the concluding vision of "heaven on earth" like that of which Bacon dreamed in a spirit of charity.

Notes

[1] Francis Bacon, *A Selection of His Works,* ed., Sidney Warhaft (Indianapolis: The Odyssey Press, 1965), p. 47.

[2] Bacon, p. 48.

[3] Phyllis Gorfain, "Puzzle and Artifice: The Riddle as Metapoetry in *Pericles*," *Shakespeare Survey,* 29 (1976), 19.

[4] C. L. Barber, "'Thou that beget'st him that did thee beget': Transformation in *Pericles* and *The Winter's Tale*," *Shakespeare Survey,* 22 (1969), 59-69.

[5] William Shakespeare, *Pericles* in *The Riverside Shakespeare,* ed., G. Blakemore Evans (Boston: Houghton Mifflin, 1974), IV.iv.49-50. All subsequent act, scene, and line references will be to this edition and will follow in the text.

[6] Nancy Vickers, "Diana Described: Scattered Woman and Scattered Rhyme," *Critical Inquiry,* 8 (1981), 26-81.

[7] George Wilkins, *The Painfull Aduentures of Pericles Prince of Tyre* in *The Riverside Shakespeare,* p. 1515, notes to IV.vi.79-116.

[8] The *OED* quotes Tindale, 1534, 1 John v.1, "Every one that loveth him which begat, loveth him also which was begotten of him," and Golding, 1587, De Mornay, vi. 71, "God . . . begate the Sonne or Word equal to himselfe."

[9] Roland Barthes, *S/Z,* trans., Richard Miller (New York: Hill and Wang, 1974), pp. 113-14.

Stephen Dickey (essay date 1986)

SOURCE: "Language and Role in *Pericles*," in *English Literary Renaissance,* Vol. 16, No. 3, Autumn, 1986, pp. 550-66.

[*In this essay, Dickey analyzes the characters of Pericles and Gower and the peculiarities of their dramatic and metadramatic relationships.*]

Criticism of *Pericles* traditionally has been attracted either to its textual difficulties or to its position as apprentice romance. Partially deprived of Shakespeare's authorship, disowned by the First Folio, its quarto bad, the bastard *Pericles* has provoked numerous speculations about its parentage of collaboration, adaptation, or revision. Otherwise, the play is valued chiefly for its transitional place in the canon, where Shakespeare turns from tragedy to romance.[1] Thus *Pericles* appears as an abbreviated *King Lear,* ending with reunion and reconciliation but without death, or as a trial run through the still evolving romance paradigm, the "rhythm of pain, endurance, and joy."[2] Either way, of course, attention is deflected from the play itself, as drama, and from the behavior of its characters. Even discussions of the play that do not subsume it under larger schemes of analysis omit critical attentions that are routinely focused on any play.[3] Peggy Ann Knapp speaks for many when she claims that the romances "will not bear and do not need" an analysis of "subtle and dynamic shiftings of motive and impulse," arguing further that to give "every event in a play like *Pericles* a full psychological justification robs the play of its romance aura."[4]

But the characterization of Gower and Pericles complicates the play by illuminating its romance aura of improbability with glimmers of psychological motivation and self-conscious action. For the world of the play functions on two levels. One is the province of Gower, who is chorus, apologist, and guide, himself a revived stage manager for the revival of this production. The other is that of Pericles, who is the hero of the story Gower shows us. Gower's several appearances are dramatic events in their own right, however, particularly as the play aligns the attitudes of Gower to his artistic presentation with the attitudes and responses of Pericles to his own life in the play. By examining the relationship of Gower, who is *Pericles'* character, to Pericles, who is Gower's character, the plot gains intrinsic significance as something more than a vehicle for myth, and the characters grow to something more than ciphers who achieve meaning only as their types recur in other plays. To look below the surface of their words is to discover idiosyncrasy and individuality that make any discussion of romance typology a drastic oversimplification.

"To sing a song that old was sung, / From ashes ancient Gower is come, / Assuming man's infirmities, / To glad your ear and please your eyes" (1.Cho. 1-4): Gower's return to life is made possible by art, the demands of performance, and by its appropriateness to the ensuing play. "Gower's reincarnation gives the initialimpulse to the play's theme of loss and restoration."[5] Yet his oddly pessimistic formulation of what it means to return to life also anticipates other themes; namely that, in the world of *Pericles,* life is generally a series of painful adventures, storms at sea, treacherous hosts, and random disasters that upset expectations of prosperity. Gower's insinuation that it should "glad" us to have him assume "man's infirmities" offers a psychological insight on which much of the play is grounded, and on which Gower's counterpart, Pericles, bases his self-conception as that of a patient, long-suffering, virtuous man.

Gower proceeds, in effect, to flatter the audience by glancing at its courtly predecessors, all the while addressing the theme of restoration, of the beneficent efficacy of art:

> It hath been sung at festivals,
> On ember-eves and holy-ales;
> And lords and ladies in their lives
> Have read it for restoratives.
> The purchase is to make men glorious,
> *Et bonum quoantiquius, eo melius.*
> If you, born in those latter times,
> When wit's more ripe, accept my rhymes,
> And that to hear an old man sing
> May to your wishes pleasure bring,
> I life would wish, and that I might
> Waste it for you like taper-light.
>
> (1.Cho. 5-16)

But as Gower offers further praise to the audience, by way of apology for his outmoded, unfamiliar verse

and for his archaic story, his humility quietly sharpens a double edge. The characteristically medieval deference to authority, evident in "I tell you what mine authors say" (1.Cho. 20) and in his Latin praise of tradition, contradicts his flattery of the present. If "wit's more ripe" now, why insist "the older the better?" The pains Gower takes (and suffers) in telling his story from the past to the present compose a gesture of generosity that pointedly calls attention to the personal cost involved.[6] His intense self-consciousness as entertainer creates a pose of humility and selflessness calculated to force the audience into an apparently superior position from which it can seem to itself to accept or dismiss him. In fact, this pose of modesty seems to be generated more from self-assurance than from any genuine humility before a sophisticated contemporary audience. Gower's covert arrogance courts a martyr's role so that it may, in turn, boast that role. His production at this point takes on the air of a sacrifice of himself to his art, a sacrifice, curiously, of death to life, of the ease of the grave to the trouble of existence.

Critics have called sometimes contradictory attention to the metadramatic effects of the obsolete, quaint, and gnomic language of Gower's choruses but have overlooked its immediate characterizing force.[7] Gower's instinct for cliché betrays his readiness to pass moral judgement that seeks to establish deceptively simple boundaries between right and wrong. That Gower guides our reaction by his vocabulary of absolute morality may be seen, again, as a function of the concealed arrogance of his stance toward the audience. His verse talks down to us with fairy tale simplicity and sing-song condescension:

> This king unto him took a peer,
> Who died and left a female heir,
> So buxom, blithe, and full of face
> As heaven had lent her all his grace;
> With whom the father liking took,
> And her to incest did provoke—
> Bad child, worse father, to entice his own
> To evil should be done by none.
>
> (1.Cho. 21-28)

Gower's moral certitude and his arrogance in the guise of humility appear in another character, Pericles, who is involved differently, but not necessarily more intimately, in the plot. If Gower's attitudes are, at bottom, aesthetic and didactic, Pericles' are existential: that is, on stage Gower is concerned with his production and audience; in the plot Pericles is concerned with his life and the proper moral shape he desires for it. Yet that life soon takes the shape of a contrived performance, as Pericles endures, or perhaps invites, his several trials and misfortunes, and as he attempts to invest his experience with the dignity of suffering.[8]

Pericles begins his life in the play in an awkward enough situation, even without knowing of his intended bride's incest: a young man meeting for the first time his prospective father-in-law. Add to this the strange gamble of marriage and death riding on a riddle's answer, and the situation becomes a suitor's nightmare. When revelations of incest follow, the essentially comic predicament goes ludicrously haywire. Already on uneasy social grounds about this meeting with Antiochus, Pericles begins with an awkwardly self-conscious speech whose rhyme quickly falters, the main effect of which is that of a rehearsed performance:

> See where she comes, apparelled like the
>   spring,
> Graces her subjects, and her thoughts the
>   king
> Of every virtue gives renown to men!
>
> Her face the book of praises, where is read
> Nothing but curious pleasures, as from
>   thence
> Sorrow were ever ras'd, and testy wrath
> Could never be her mild companion.
> You gods that made me man, and sway in
>   love,
> That have inflam'd desire in my breast
> To taste the fruit of yon celestial tree
> (Or die in th'adventure), be my helps,
> As I am son and servant to your will,
> To compass such a boundless happiness!
>   (1.1.12-24)

Having got past the obligatory set piece of praise and divine invocation, which strives obliquely to deflect Pericles' own responsibility in the matter of his love, he must fall into a more spontaneous dialogue with a man who knows his part well, having performed it as many times as there are heads on spikes. Pericles ventures little more than noncommittal aphorism in response: "For death remembered should be like a mirror, / Who tells us life's but breath, to trust it error" (1.1.45-46). Furthermore, he makes a Gower-esque gesture of generosity that is obligatory more than ungrudging and that reveals Pericles' main motivation to be merely the appearance of virtue, the abiding by formalized superficial codes of behavior without a clear understanding of them except that "virtue gives renown to men." As Gower says about his play, "The purchase is to make men glorious" (1.Cho.9):

> I'll make my will then, and as sick men do,
> Who know the world, see heaven, but
>   feeling woe,
> Gripe not at earthly joys as erst they did;
> So I bequeath a happy peace to you
> And all good men, as every prince should
>   do.
>   (1.1.47-51)

Of course, Pericles' language here also attempts to remind Antiochus of the moral demeanor he should exhibit as king. It is an advance plea for mercy should Pericles fail to solve the riddle on which his life and wife depend. And when we recall his plight, we can hardly blame him for playing it safe, for resorting to convention and tritely smooth observation. Language here is security, and Pericles deploys language—with its communicative obverse, silence—in this way throughout the play. Likewise, Gower's language of simplistic moral judgment seems justified by the ostentatiously malign Antiochus. Gower starts us off with an easy one, and, surrounded by the skulls that are the consequences of Antiochus' peculiar requirements for his daughter's courtship, he assures himself of our concurrence. Concealed by the extremity of the first situation, though, is the fact that throughout the play these responses of Gower and Pericles are characteristic no matter what their predicament, no matter what the moral issue. Gower's depiction of dramatic situations, when not simply a narrative of intervening events, is marked by cliché and sharply drawn moral distinctions. Pericles' response to the situations of his life is consistently marked by aphorism and concern for action that announces the lonely virtue of its performer.

Both Gower and Pericles are full of rote wisdom, and both are self-consciously superior to their audiences. Smugly exhorted by Antiochus' daughter to win her hand, Pericles offers a self-portrait that sorts well with his opinion of what "every prince should do" and with his self-congratulatory suspicion that he is the only prince to behave fully in this manner: "Like a bold champion I assume the lists, / Nor ask advice of any other thought / But faithfulness and courage" (1.1.61-63). Having figured out the riddle by dint of attributes wholly other than those he enlists in his aid, Pericles again launches an address to the gods, and again casts about for a suitable aphorism or moral conclusion:

> But O you powers!
> That gives heaven countless eyes to view
>   men's acts
> Why cloud they not their sights perpetually,
> If this be true which makes me pale to read
>   it? . . .
> But I must tell you, now my thoughts
>   revolt,
> For he's no man on whom perfections wait
> That, knowing sin within, will touch the
>   gate.
>   (1.1.72-80)

Pericles, concerned primarily with his own purity as a "man on whom perfections wait," extricates himself from Antiochus' bargain by making it clear he knows the answer and refusing to disclose it. To this end, he trots out several more bits of wisdom: "For vice repeated is like the wand'ring wind, / Blows dust in others' eyes, to spread itself / . . . The blind mole casts / Copp'd hills towards heaven, to tell the earth is throng'd / By man's oppression, and the poor worm doth die for't" (1.1.96-102). Indeed, though persuasively intricate, the latter observation is so far-fetched as to be virtually irrelevant. Rather than chalking this up to authorial incompetence or incomplete revision, it is perhaps more illuminating to see this as an extreme example of Pericles' habitual speech-making, in turn a symptom of his perception of life and of his self-appointed role as victim.[9] One critic remarked that Pericles "shows himself a creature of formulae . . . his virtues are as bloodless as they are noble and fastidious," and another notes "Pericles' tendency to rely on wit and to retreat in the face of odds greater than himself."[10]

One of the things Pericles constantly retreats from is the task of governing. Like ancestor Lear and descendent Prospero, Pericles, if not actually incompetent as a ruler, does relinquish political power for psychological leverage over other characters.[11] To be sure, he rescues Tharsus from famine, but this is nothis kingdom, and the gesture, however commendable, is a bribe for asylum in his flight from Antiochus.[12] Pericles wastes no opportunity to renege on his duties as prince of Tyre, and, at the end with family intact, consigns Marina and Lysimachus to that realm, resolving with Thaisa to "spend our following days" (5.3.81) in her land, Pentapolis.[13]

His first abdication of responsibility occurs directly after returning from the abortive courtship in Antioch. Lord Helicanus rebukes those who would attempt to give specious cheer to Pericles:

> They do abuse the King that flatter him,
> For flattery is the bellows blows up sin,
> The thing the which is flattered, but a spark
> To which that blast gives heat and stronger
>   glowing;
> Whereas reproof, obedient and in order,
> Fits kings as they are men, for they may err.
>
>   (1.2.38-43)

In fact, this kind of talk is itself flattery of the most persuasive sort. Its aphoristic shape inevitably appeals to Pericles, who commends the kneeling Helicanus for being "no flatterer" (1.2.61). Pericles then narrates his escapade in Antioch and confides his fear of retributive war to Helicanus, who is ready with advice:

>   Antiochus you fear,
> And justly too, I think, you fear the tyrant,
> Who either by public war or private treason
> Will take away your life.
> Therefore, my lord, go travel for a while,
> Till that his rage and anger be forgot,

> Or till the Destinies do cut his thread of life.
> Your rule direct to any; if to me,
> Day serves not light more faithful than I'll
>   be.
>
>   (1.2.102-10)

Helicanus' motives may seem questionable here beyond the extenuations of textual corruption.[14] Not only does he endorse Pericles' fears, but he enhances them by suggesting the additional possibility of "private treason." He introduces the idea of Pericles' departure and hastily volunteers his services as replacement, barely tempering his offer by the word "if."[15] The scene affords Pericles an excuse for quitting his rule while maintaining that it is done in the best interests of his subjects, as an example of "princely charity" (1.2.100). The scene is conspicuously a charade, with the two principals cuing each other toward a conclusion desirable to both. And the conclusion for Pericles is exile, a predicament that lends itself to the appearance of suffering and of the patience Helicanus counsels.[16]

Having fled to Tharsus, Pericles is prodded to still further travels by an alarmist message from Helicanus that plays on the fears of vengeance Pericles has professed. In describing Pericles' subsequent flight from Tharsus and his first storm at sea, Gower resorts to his customarily extreme vocabulary:

> And he, good prince, having all lost,
> By waves from coast to coast is toss'd.
> All perishen of man, of pelf,
> Ne aught escapend but himself;
> Till Fortune, tir'd with doing bad,
> Threw him ashore, to give him glad.
>
>   (2.Cho. 33-38)

And so, the humorously concise stage direction: "Enter Pericles, wet," into a scene that parodies his own aphoristic inclinations in the rough accents of three fishermen. Overhearing their struggle to fashion significant analogies between fish and men, Pericles is, predictably, appreciative. "A pretty moral" (2.1.35), he allows, to one who "can compare our rich misers to nothing so fitly as to a whale: 'a plays and tumbles, driving the poor fry before him, and at last devour them all at a mouthful. Such whales have I heard on a'th'land, who never leave gaping till they swallow'd the whole parish, church, steeple, bells, and all" (2.1.29-34). Pericles begins to explain his situation, but the fishermen curtail his self-conscious, alliterative pomposity:

> *Per.* May see the sea hath cast upon your
>   coast—
> *2. Fish.* What a drunken knave was the sea
>   to cast thee in our way!
>
>   (2.1.56-58)

"Cast," of course, also has the sense of "vomit," further denying Pericles the dignified entrance he desires.

The blunt fisherman soon hauls ashore Pericles' armor, and bends over backwards to impart yet another marine analogy: "Help, master, help! here's a fish hangs in the net, like a poor man's right in the law; 'twill hardly come out" (2.1.116-18). The essential comedy of the scene is further shown by the response of the fisherman who is mystified by Pericles' expression of gratitude to Fortune and his lengthy re-enactment of his father's dying bequest of the armor: "What mean you, sir?" (2.1.135). Withdrawing from his reverie, Pericles speaks more to the point and asks for his armor back, as well as some additional trappings, that he may appear respectably before the king. Not surprisingly, Pericles resists explicit plans of courtship. When asked if he will tourney for the king's daughter, Pericles, who has been through one such trial, replies merely, "I'll show the virtue I have borne in arms" (2.1.145), a remark that unwittingly reveals again his abiding concern with the appearance of virtue. And when, in rusty armor, Pericles displays his device of "a withered branch" (2.2.43), he reveals as well his equation of virtue with ostentatious suffering.

The scenes in Pentapolis parallel and revise the scene in Antioch. Simonides' ribald jesting with Pericles and the other knights, though a strained attempt to join the younger crowd, nevertheless represents a redirection of Antiochus' paternal lust into more proper channels: Simonides accepts rather than exploits his daughter's sexuality. Pericles' initial response to Simonides' game of parental disapproval is a fastidious defense of his own propriety, a denial of interest in courtship, even though the fishermen had told him that the function of the tournament was partly to this end. But after Antioch, we can hardly blame Pericles for being a reluctant groom.

Indeed, the characterization of Pericles through his self-conscious inactivity is reinforced dramatically: his potentially heroic actions are insistently suppressed by the play or are drowned out by Gower's narrative hurdy-gurdy throughout the first two acts, marking them for many critics as the work of an incompetent dramatist squandering his material. Pericles' wit in riddles (1.1), his high repute in Tharsus and survival of the shipwreck that beaches him at Pentapolis (2.Cho.), his victorious tourneying (2.2), and his musicianship (2.5) are reduced to report, pushed off stage, or otherwise slighted. Yet such treatment both follows from Pericles' initial refusal to admit his actions are his own and foreshadows the extraordinary self-suppression of Act 4, Pericles' total avoidance of any action and his retreat to silence.

While Gower is hardly silent, a new attitude is audible in the lengthy chorus that begins Act 3 as Gower presents a dumb show and informs us of the wedding night of Pericles and Thaisa, the necessity of his return to Tyre, and the storm-wracked journey. Most obviously, Gower refrains from overt moral interpretation and sticks to narrative. He now entrusts more imaginative responsibility to play and audience, thereby enhancing his own role as provider of vital narrative information. He becomes more the storyteller, less the quaint old man. Before the dumb show, he advises:

> Be attent,
> And time that is so briefly spent
> With your fine fancies quaintly eche:
> What's dumb in show I'll plain with speech.
>   (3.Cho. 11-14)

And at the end of his speech his deference includes an advertisement for the necessity of his contribution:

> And what ensues in this fell storm
> Shall for itself itself perform.
> I nill relate, action may
> Conveniently the rest convey,
> Which might not what by me is told.
>   (3.Cho. 53-57)

Gower's unusually blunt analysis of the requirements of stagecraft has dramatic justification within the development of the play. It signals an onslaught of event, an acceleration of the story and, thereby, a more strenuous demand for necessary information. Gone are the leisurely excursions into moral analysis, even when the issues seem cut and dried. His diction, except for an occasional archaism, is familiar, as if his reincarnation had proceeded yet another stage, from life to contemporaneity. On the second level, that of Pericles and the plot, a like change ensues with the beginning of Act 3. The prince's meanderings grow more purposive, even if his fundamental motivations remain concerned with appearance and role-playing. As Gower more sharply defines his role as chorus, so Pericles commits himself with a vengeance to no vengeance at all, to the status of permanent victim, recipient of fortune's whim.[17] Pericles' willful passivity is clear, too, in his response to the sailors who wish his wife Thaisa, apparently dead in childbirth, thrown overboard, a sacrifice to their nautical superstitions. One critic opposed to the traditional reading of the "patient" Pericles cites this episode as typical of "Pericles' lack of faith and his hasty withdrawal from threatening situations," mannerisms he demonstrates at Antioch, Tyre, Tharsus, and now at sea.[18]

Yet another dealer in commonplaces is Cerimon, the agent of Thaisa's revival, a man esteemed for generosity and medical know-how, who is wealthy enough to afford sentiments such as:

I hold it ever
Virtue and cunning were endowments
   greater
Than nobleness and riches. Careless heirs
May the two latter darken and expend;
But immortality attends the former,
Making a man a god. 'Tis known, I ever
Have studied physic . . .

. . . . .

. . . which doth give me
A more content in course of true delight
Than to be thirsty after tottering honor,
Or tie my pleasure up in silken bags,
To please the fool and death.

(3.2.26-42)

Yet when the chest bearing Thaisa's body washes ashore, his first response belies his leisurely self-portrait: "What e'er it be, / 'Tis wondrous heavy. Wrench it open straight. / If the sea's stomach be o'ercharg'd with gold,/ 'Tis a good constraint of fortune it belches upon us" (3.2.52-55). Like Gower's and Pericles', Cerimon's initial, calculated self-presentation is eventually exposed as something both less and more than that, as a self-serving social maneuver and as proof of an unexpected complexity of characterization and motivation in the play.

Cerimon restores Thaisa to life with "air" (3.2.91), that is, music and oxygen, the pun combining the worlds of art and nature whose intersection so often makes for a supernatural moment in the romances. Her waking words invoke Diana: an ambiguous oath indeed. In her dispensation as goddess of childbirth, Diana is appropriate to Thaisa's last conscious memory. But Diana is also goddess of chastity, and might well be invoked in retrospective wish-fulfillment by Thaisa, whose motherhood was nearly fatal. Either way, Diana's newest votaress is Thaisa, whose possibly hasty assumption that she will never again see Pericles represents a noticeable intrusion of the requirements of plot. And, indeed, Gower's next chorus speaks of "our fast-growing scene" (4.Cho. 6) as he assumes a greater narrative burden than before.

In the meantime, Pericles has also sworn by Diana an oath of strange resolve. Leaving Marina at Tharsus, Pericles tells Dionyza:

Till she be married, madam,
By bright Diana, whom we honor, all
Unscissor'd shall this hair of mine remain,
Though I show ill in't.

(3.3.27-30)

Whatever the reason, Pericles typically emphasizes the personal cost involved in his sacrifice: until his daugh-

ter weds he will "show ill." Later, upon hearing the false report of Marina's death, Pericles embellishes his original oath and "swears / Never to wash his face, nor cut his hairs" (4.4.27-28). Such a vow is made possible by Pericles' supposition that inactivity betokens sincere martyrdom. For he merely lets happen what will happen, hair grow and face soil, expending no effort to stop it. Although his grief is genuine, it is the prolonged proclamation of that grief, the display of the self-appointed role of sufferer as Pericles' appearance speciously asserts selflessness, that marks his characteristic experience in the world of the play. Pericles acts on the same psychological assumptions that inform the Bawd's advice to Marina about the necessity of role-playing: "You must seem to do that fearfully which you commit willingly, despise profit where you have most gain. To weep that you live as ye do makes pity in your lovers; seldom but that pity begets you a good opinion, and that opinion a mere profit" (4.2.116-21).

Furthermore, according to Helicanus, Pericles "for this three months hath not spoken / To any one, nor taken sustenance / But to prorogue his grief" (5.1.24-26).[19] Pericles, whose platitudes are respected by men, including himself, demonstrates his grief by retracting that princely office, speech, he was proudest of, imagining it the hardest deprivation for him and for others who cannot now profit by his hackneyed lore. Silence is therefore Pericles' most conspicuous gesture of suffering, and it is the loudest expression of the role he has sought all along, that of Fortune's tennis ball (2.1.60), the pure recipient of disaster. Indeed,Gower consigns Pericles to "bear his courses to be ordered / By Lady Fortune" (4.4.47-48). His passivity and willful trust in accident, however, is a decision grounded in narcissism without self-confidence. By repeatedly committing himself to the desires of others, his kingdom to the control of others, Pericles establishes for himself a martyr's role in many ways analogous to that constructed by Gower toward the audience. But where Gower patronizes by his simplistic morality and conventional invocations of the audience's assistance, Pericles patronizes by his silence.

This silence of Pericles and this idiom of Gower are but two uses of language by which the speaker forges a role for himself. Marina, alive and residing unwillingly in a brothel, exercises a third, unassailably persuasive speech that not only preserves her virtue but reforms those who assault it. Although Pericles' language seeks to demonstrate his virtue, it is without the fabulous efficacy of his daughter's. One gentleman leaving Marina's lectures in the brothel claims with comically exaggerated finality, "I'll do any thing now that is virtuous, but I am out of the road of rutting for ever" (4.5.8-9): he has learned to act as Pericles instinctively does, with conspicuous displays of virtue.

The brothel scenes function parodically as another courtship, the third of the play, for among the patrons of the brothel is Lysimachus, lord of Mytilene, who eventually marries Marina. In this case, the suitor is not, as Pericles had been twice before, fastidious about his virtue—at least not until Marina's arguments deter him, after which he tells her, "I did not think / Thou couldst have spoke so well, ne'er dreamt thou couldst" (4.6.102-03). Lysimachus attempts, not very deftly, to disown his previous inclinations:

> Had I brought hither a corrupted mind,
> Thy speech had altered it. Hold, here's gold
>   for thee . . .
> For me, be you thoughten
> That I came with no ill intent, for to me
> The very doors and windows savor vilely.
>   (4.6.104-10)

The speculation that a sermon is here missing from the text itself misses the point of Marina's use of language.[20] Her words are miraculously effective—a prerogative of romance, but also of dramatic purpose in this play as an example of successful verbal achievement of virtue of a kind that eludes Pericles, who changes no one. As such, Marina's language contrasts with that of Gower and Pericles who use language in the attempt to garner either compassion or praise.

Marina's words to Lysimachus and Boult elicit pity and cooperation, and her words to Pericles, who in his grief has refused all communication, elicit speech. Their mutual recognition is brought about chiefly by a comparison of their various sufferings. Pericles is at first testy about this competition: "Tell thy story; / If thine, considered, prove the thousand part / Of my endurance, thou art a man, and I / Have suffered like a girl" (5.1.134-37). Pericles' restoration to language begins in his grief-stricken silence and gropes slowly toward intelligibility from "Hum, ha!" (5.1.83), to the elliptical and fractured "My fortunes—parentage—good parentage—/ To equal mine—was it not thus? What say you?" (5.1.97-98), to a series of genuine interrogatives, really the first significant non-rhetorical questions Pericles asks in the play. His language is to some extent reformed by Marina's presence, purified of needless proverbial observation by his surpassing joy.

As identities come clear, the bliss of discovery and recovery is too strenuous for Pericles, and he retreats to sleep. The ensuing appearance of Diana, like virtually every supernatural event in Shakespeare's romances, is most immediately pertinent as characterization of the mortal involved than as testimony to a beneficent, divinely ordered cosmos.[21] Pericles' previous oath, to "show ill" until Marina's marriage, had been sworn to Diana, and now it is no coincidence that Diana's particular instructions fully correspond with Pericles' desire to display his sufferings:

> Before the people all,
> Reveal how thou at sea didst lose thy wife.
> To mourn thy crosses, with thy daughter's,
>   call
> And give them repetition to the life.
>   (5.1.243-46)

Indeed, that Pericles seems to have fallen asleep just before Diana's entry suggests why she so thoroughly represents his dream of his own necessary performance in the world of the play; Diana is as much Pericles' vision, hope, and creation as he is her votary.

Ordered to Ephesus, Pericles first approves Lysimachus as suitor for Marina: "You shall prevail, / Were it to woo my daughter, for it seems / You have been noble towards her" (5.1.261-63). This, however, is a question that had not yet been raised, and is a further revision of the earlier scenes of courtship. In foisting off his daughter, however, Pericles dissembles nothing, unlike Antiochus in his malignity or Simonides in his male jocularity and manipulative zeal. By instigating this marriage, Pericles here accelerates his situation to an artificially comic conclusion, offering a reason—the seeming nobility of Lysimachus—that would appeal more to him than to Marina. She herself is audibly silent in the matter of her wedlock. Indeed, Marina speaks but once more in the play, and then it is to herself, regarding her mother: "My heart / Leaps to be gone into my mother's bosom" (5.3.44-45).

Gower's language grows less conspicuous through the play as we accustom ourselves to his appearances, as his idiom begins to accord with that of the other characters, and as the burden of narration usurps the opportunity for editorial comment. Forced increasingly to provide factual background, to apologize for the play in standard ways, and to enlist the audience's imaginative aid, Gower is not permitted many of his earlier idiosyncrasies and impositions of moral judgment. Only in the epilogue can Gower insist once again upon the moral lessons of his story:

> In Antiochus and his daughter you have
>   heard
> Of monstrous lust the due and just reward.
> In Pericles, his queen and daughter, seen,
> Although assail'd with fortune fierce and
>   keen,
> Virtue preserv'd from fell destruction's
>   blast,
> Led on by heaven, and crown'd with joy at
>   last.
> In Helicanus may you well descry
> A figure of truth, of faith, of loyalty.
> In reverend Cerimon there well appears
> The worth that learned charity aye wears.
>   (5.3.85-94)

This operation of retributive justice is clean, neat, and conspicuously artificial, available only in plays whose moral can be unpacked so thoroughly by such a spokesman.[22] For the benefit of an audience Gower regards as in need of this moral instruction, he has tried to present the story of a character who views life much as Gower views his own artistic enterprise: conventionally and proverbially. Like Pericles', too, Gower's behavior is generated by his self-image as one with superior moral insight who must oversimplify for the sake of his audience; hence the resort to black and white morality and to cliché, the way Pericles adheres to adage. Both view themselves as long-suffering, and both construe virtue chiefly as displays ofpatience, generosity, martyrdom—in short, self-sacrifice. Both, in turn, wield this kind of virtue in the worlds of plot and stage that they inhabit. And in both characters, such qualities are never free of self-interest nor of a certain condescension that in the case of Pericles is directed to his fellow characters, in that of Gower, to the audience.

The moral and emotional impulses at work in the play are therefore much more complicated than either character or chorus admits, and the struggle of their language (or lack of it) to achieve the safety of a specious moral and emotional clarity through trite aphorism (or utter silence) betrays this complexity.[23] At one point Gower tells us to attend to the characters: "Like motes and shadows see them move a while" (4.4.21). Significantly, this request precedes a dumb show, where action must be self-evident without the aid of words, and it implies as well as anything the necessity of language to these characters' existences as something more than the motes and shadows we reduce them to if intent only on a symbolic reading. Shakespeare's language not only creates Pericles and Gower, but also shows them in some sense creating their own roles, prince and poet.

Notes

[1] All references to *Pericles* are from *The Riverside Shakespeare,* gen. ed., G. Blakemore Evans (Boston, 1974).

[2] G. Wilson Knight, *The Crown of Life* (New York, 1966), p. 31.

[3] Derek Traversi, *Shakespeare: The Last Phase* (London, 1954), p. 35, finds that "plot . . . exists in *Pericles* as a function of imagery."

[4] Peggy Ann Knapp, "The Orphic Vision of *Pericles,*" *Texas Studies in Literature and Language* 15 (1974), 618.

[5] Joan Hartwig, *Shakespeare's Tragicomic Vision* (Baton Rouge, La., 1972), p. 34.

[6] Richard Hillman is correct to note "the Chorus' spiritual generosity, his willingness to interrupt his 'final pes.'" (In "Shakespeare's Gower and Gower's Shakespeare: The Larger Debt of *Pericles,*" *Shakespeare Quarterly* 36 [1985], 437.) My point is simply that Gower makes certain we cannot possibly avoid noting it, and that therein lies a central characterizing trait.

[7] A sampling follows: Northrop Frye, *A Natural Perspective* (N.Y., 1965), pp. 31-32: "He reminds us that this is a play, and the effect of the reminder is to shatter the framework of the play and lead us inside it . . . He stands for the authority of literary tradition; he is himself dependent on still older sources, and he is there to put us in as uncritical a frame of mind as possible." F. W. Brownlow, *Two Shakespearean Sequences* (Pittsburgh, 1977), p. 120: "His presence, the limitations of his simple speech, and his homely moralizings keep the illusionary characters firmly within the time and place of the stage." Kirby Farrell, *Shakespeare's Creation* (Amherst, 1975), pp. 193-94: "Gower's assemblage of cliches creates more mystery and uncertainty than it dispels. . . . He characteristically construes reality in cliches."

The romances in general are noted to be thematically reflexive, in some sense about their own art, and Gower's manipulation of dumb show, his very presence, and especially his diction keep this issue squarely before us by insisting on the artificiality of the play. This point, however, can suffer overemphasis, as all plays in a way announce their own artifice in production.

[8] See Annette C. Flower, "Disguise and Identity in *Pericles, Prince of Tyre,*" *Shakespeare Quarterly* 26 (1975), 31: "All of Pericles' experience in the play consists of playing parts, adopting the postures and pointsof view which allow him to adjust to circumstance, and to learn." Of course, whether he learns anything, or what it may be that he learns, are other questions.

[9] More often, the "mole" passage is simply felt to be an isolated fragment of Shakespearean revision. As a response to style and tone, this suggestion is plausible. As a response to Pericles' characterization, it is unnecessary, for Pericles' self-conception is evident throughout. As Michael Taylor notes, there is "a hint of collusion in the alacrity with which [Pericles] accepts his role as the blind mole thronged by man's oppression: prudent, cynical, defeated, he succumbs to what he conceives to be an immitigable Jovian authority," in "'Here is a thing too young for such a place': Innocence in *Pericles,*" *Ariel* 13 (1982), 12.

[10] Farrell, p. 194 and Thelma N. Greenfield, "A Reexamination of the 'Patient' Pericles," *Shakespeare Studies* 3, ed. J. Leeds Barroll (Dubuque, Iowa, 1967), p. 52.

[11] Unfortunately for Pericles, though, he hardly has the audience of either Lear or Prospero, and his self-denial matters little to anyone else in the play. It is perhaps this peculiar isolation of the hero that leads criticism of *Pericles* away from the issues of characterization and motive that are better marked in *King Lear* and *The Tempest*.

[12] Flower, p. 32: "The rescue of Tharsus . . . demonstrates magnanimity when it is easy for Pericles to be magnanimous."

[13] W. B. Thorne points out that Pericles' "own speech, in which he likens himself, as King, to the 'tops of trees,/ Which fence the roots they grow by and defend them' (1.2.31-32), begins the association of Pericles with the concept of the scapegoat and the noble figure who takes upon himself the dangers and sins of his community." "*Pericles* and the 'Incest-Fertility' Opposition," *Shakespeare Quarterly* 22 (1971), 50. It should be stressed, however, that it is Pericles himself who assigns this role, assuming here, as throughout the play, the role of the virtuous sufferer. The whole speech (1.2.1-33) represents an imposition of private fear on the whole society as it disguises Pericles' own escapism as the duty of a conscientious prince.

[14] 1.2 is famously corrupt as Pericles' lords bid him farewell before they seem to know of his decision to leave. In a sense, of course, it makes for an entirely appropriate joke by the play on a hero who is always in the process of leaving and who could turn up anywhere within "the four opposing coigns / Which the world together joins" (3.Cho. 17-18).

[15] Farrell, p. 197, has written perceptively about this scene: "Offering up his life to indict flattery, Helicanus takes a role Pericles has yearned to play. In addition, however, their scene enacts a fantasy of achieving power through self-effacement." Also, see John P. Cutts, *Rich and Strange: A Study of Shakespeare's Last Plays* (Pullman, Wash., 1968), p. 28: "Pericles only vaguely acknowledges the possibility of fault 'when all, for mine, if I may call offense, / Must feel war's blow' (I.ii.92-93), and then carries on as an offended innocent for the rest of his days."

[16] Indeed, as Marilyn French points out, "Pericles continues to flee long after there is any need to fear Antiochus." *Shakespeare's Division of Experience* (New York, 1981), p. 294.

[17] One critic has termed Pericles "Shakespeare's only entirely will-less hero," an appraisal only superficially accurate. Pericles is will-less because he chooses to be. Bertrand Evans, *Shakespeare's Comedies* (Oxford, 1960), p. 237.

[18] Greenfield, p. 53.

[19] Beyond its primary sense of "prolong," the word "prorogue" has a specific political usage, "to discontinue a session of government," that makes it appropriate to the politician's vocabulary of Helicanus. Moreover, the etymology ("to ask publicly," that is, also, "to extend a term of office") suggests that Pericles' office *is* suffering and silence and not the more conventional governing duties of a prince. The root emphasis on speech (*rogare*) subverts Pericles' role as silent, private mourner and suggests that his grief is in the nature of a public request. Silence, too, can communicate, can beg, and can beg questions.

[20] Gerard A. Barker, "Themes and Variations in Shakespeare's *Pericles*," *English Studies* 44 (1963), ed. R. W. Zandvoort, p. 406: "Shakespeare has to strike out most of Marina's argument, since Lysimachus does not need conversion." This misses the comic tone of the scene established by Lysimachus' uncomfortable nervousness as he backs off and by the incompetence that makes for the Bawd's sardonically offhand remark: "Here comes the Lord Lysimachus disguis'd" (4.6.16-17). Inga-Stina Ewbank is more accurate in describing "that mixture of lechery and mealy-mouthedness which Lysimachus exhibits." In "'My Name is Marina': The Language of Recognition," in *Shakespeare's Styles: Essays in Honour of Kenneth Muir*, ed. Philip Edwards, Inga-Stina Ewbank, and G. K. Hunter, (Cambridge, 1980), p. 116.

[21] Bertrand Evans' assertion, p. 242, dismantles itself by showing how strained must be any such Goweresque confidence in a morally ordered world: "In *Pericles* it is necessary for us to spell out, from scanty signs and dubious manifestations, the existence and character of an invisible and benevolent controlling force."

[22] Alexander Leggatt terms Gower's last speech "a self-satisfied catalogue of wickedness punished and virtue rewarded." *Shakespeare's Comedy of Love* (London, 1974), p. 260. Gower is the first critic of *Pericles*, and a most reductive critic at that.

[23] Kenneth J. Semon, "*Pericles*: An Order Beyond Reason," *Essays in Literature* 1 (Spring, 1974), 17: "The world of *Pericles* is morally inscrutable. . . . Gower . . . tries and fails to impose a moral on those actions."

FURTHER READING

Brockbank, J. P. "'Pericles' and the Dream of Immortality." *Shakespeare Survey* 24 (1971): 105-16.
    Examines the sources of *Pericles* and its theme of death as illusion.

Fawkner, H. W. "Miracle." In *Shakespeare's Miracle Plays: 'Pericles,' 'Cymbeline,' and 'The Winter's Tale,'* pp. 13-56. London: Associated University Presses, 1992.

Analysis of *Pericles* informed by the metaphor of "muteness" and "contrasting masculine and feminine principles."

Flower, Annette C. "Disguise and Identity in *Pericles, Prince of Tyre*." In *Shakespeare Quarterly* 26, No. 1 (Winter 1975): 30-41.

Examines the motif of disguise in *Pericles* and investigates its relation to the play's themes of reconciliation and restoration.

Gajdusek, R. E. "Death, Incest, and the Triple Bond in the Later Plays of Shakespeare." *American Imago* 31, No. 2 (Summer 1974): 109-58.

Explores mythic, religious, and archetypal elements of *Pericles*.

Glazov-Corrigan, Elena. "The New Function of Language in Shakespeare's *Pericles*: Oath Versus 'Holy Word'." *Shakespeare Survey* 43 (1991): 131-40.

Contends that *Pericles* represents a departure from the tragedies in terms of Shakespeare's use of language and its powers of persuasion.

Gorfain, Phyllis. "Puzzle and Artifice: The Riddle as Metapoetry in *Pericles*." *Shakespeare Survey* 29 (1976): 11-20.

Structuralist analysis of *Pericles* which emphasizes the ritual nature of Antiochus's riddle and defines the riddle's importance in relation to themes of incest and kinship.

Greenfield, Thelma N. "A Re-Examination of the 'Patient' Pericles." *Shakespeare Studies* III (1967): 51-61.

Characterizes Pericles as a type of the "wise and learned" rather then the "patient" man.

Helms, Lorraine. "The Saint in the Brothel; Or, Eloquence Rewarded." *Shakespeare Quarterly* 41, No. 3 (Fall 1990): 319-32.

Traces classical sources of Marina's character.

Hunt, Maurice. "A Looking Glass for *Pericles*." *Essays in Literature* XIII, No. 1 (Spring 1986): 3-11.

Observes that Thomas Lodge and Robert Greene's *A Looking Glass for London and England* represents a contemporary precedent for *Pericles* as a morality/miracle play.

Jordan, Constance. "'Eating the Mother': Property and Propriety in *Pericles*." In *Creative Imitation: New Essays on Renaissance Literature in Honor of Thomas M. Greene*, edited by David Quint, Margaret W. Ferguson, G. W. Pigman III, and Wayne A. Rebhorn, pp. 331-53. Binghamton, N. Y.: Medieval & Renaissance Texts & Studies, 1992.

Explores the Jacobean political and cultural subtexts of *Pericles*.

Preston, Claire. "The Emblematic Structure of *Pericles*." *Word and Image* 8, No. 1 (January-March 1992): 21-38.

Maintains that *Pericles* is structurally and thematically unified by its emblematic qualities.

Stockholder, Kay. "Sex and Authority in *Hamlet, King Lear* and *Pericles*." *Mosaic* XVIII, No. 3 (Summer 1989): 17-29.

Argues that in *Pericles*, *King Lear*, and *Hamlet*, Shakespeare "was entrapped in the attitudes toward sexuality and women with which his protagonists struggle."

Thorne, W. B. "*Pericles* and the 'Incest-Fertility' Opposition." In *Shakespeare Quarterly* 22 (1971): 43-56.

Maintains that *Pericles* represents an extension of the comic vision found in Shakespeare's earlier comedies.

The Winter's Tale

For further information on the critical and stage history of *The Winter's Tale*, see *SC*, Volumes 7 and 15.

INTRODUCTION

Twentieth-century criticism of *The Winter's Tale* has varied widely in emphasis, reflecting the broad scope of topics suggested in the play. Since Victorian times, commentators have struggled to define the genre of the play because of the unique two-part structure. While some modern critics, such as Northrop Frye, have praised Shakespeare for achieving unity and balance in the two parts, controversy still surrounds the general design of the play. For example, Charles Hieatt has contended that a two-part view of the play represents only a portion of a larger, more complicated scheme; he focuses instead on the influence of humans over their own destiny, a principle which unifies the individual segments. Joseph Lenz has divided the play into three sections, "each associated with a specific genre and each reflecting one means by which closure can be attained." Howard Felperin has praised the "imaginative environment" constructed by Shakespeare out of the conventions of older dramatic traditions, which, he maintains, can support the lifelike characters of *The Winter's Tale*.

The relationship of Perdita and Leontes is often explored in modern criticism. Many commentators, including Patricia Southard Gourlay, have viewed Perdita's return to the Sicilian court as the key to Leontes's new life. Similarly, Bruce Young has commented that Perdita is consistently "associated with divine regenerative power and is even described as a life-giving goddess." Scholars have also focused on her role in Leontes's redemption; Robert Watson has asserted that "only Perdita's return can rouse into life the latent nature in Leontes's and Hermione's artificial poses."

Another topic of particular interest to critics is the genesis of Leontes's jealousy, which has resulted in two primary positions: that Leontes is not jealous until Hermione convinces Polixenes to stay, a position held by Rene Girard; and that Leontes's jealousy is simmering from the onset of the play, then finally erupts. Several critics, such as Martha Ronk, have also compared Leontes to another jealous Shakespearean character, Othello. Ronk argues that the sixteen-year gap in time "offers Leontes an experience denied Othello . . . . [He] is allowed time to settle and be still." Lawrence

Wright has discussed yet another approach to this topic: the distinction between "the inception of Leontes's jealousy and the start of the tragi-comic disruption."

OVERVIEWS

Northrop Frye (essay date 1962)

SOURCE: "Recognition in *The Winter's Tale*," in *Essays on Shakespeare and Elizabethan Drama*, edited by Richard Hosley, University of Missouri Press, 1962, pp. 235-46.

[*In the following essay, Frye examines the dramatic contrast found in* The Winter's Tale, *focusing on the differences between the human arts—music, poetry, and magic—and the power of the gods and nature, as well as the truths these elements reveal.*]

In structure *The Winter's Tale*, like *King Lear*, falls into two main parts separated by a storm. The fact that they are also separated by sixteen years is less important. The first part ends with the ill-fated Antigonus caught between a bear and a raging sea, echoing a passage in one of Lear's storm speeches. This first part is the "winter's tale" proper, for Mamillius is just about to whisper his tale into his mother's ear when the real winter strikes with the entrance of Leontes and his guards. Various bits of imagery, such as Polixenes' wish to get back to Bohemia for fear of "sneaping winds" blowing at home and Hermione's remark during her trial (reproduced from *Pandosto*) that the emperor of Russia was her father, are linked to a winter setting. The storm, like the storm in *King Lear*, is described in such a way as to suggest that a whole order of things is being dissolved in a dark chaos of destruction and devouring monsters, and the action of the first part ends in almost unrelieved gloom. The second part is a tragicomedy where, as in *Cymbeline* and *Measure for Measure*, there is frightening rather than actual hurting. Some of the frightening seems cruel and unnecessary, but the principle of 'all's well that ends well' holds in comedy, however great nonsense it may be in life.

The two parts form a diptych of parallel and contrasting actions, one dealing with age, winter, and the jealousy of Leontes, the other with youth, summer, and the love of Florizel. The first part follows Greene's

Pandosto closely; for the second part no major source has been identified. A number of symmetrical details, which are commonplaces of Shakespearian design, help to build up the contrast: for instance, the action of each part begins with an attempt to delay a return. The two parts are related in two ways, by sequence and by contrast. The cycle of nature, turning through the winter and summer of the year and through the age and youth of human generations, is at the center of the play's imagery. The opening scene sets the tone by speaking of Mamillius and of the desire of the older people in the country to live until he comes to reign. The next scene, where the action begins, refers to Leontes' own youth in a world of pastoral innocence and its present reflection in Mamillius. The same cycle is also symbolized, as in *Pericles,* by a mother-daughter relationship, and Perdita echoes Marina when she speaks of Hermione as having "ended when I but began." In the transition to the second part the clown watches the shipwreck and the devouring of Antigonus; the shepherd exhibits the birth tokens of Perdita and remarks, "Thou mettest with things dying, I with things new-born." Leontes, we are told, was to have returned Polixenes' visit "this coming summer," but instead of that sixteen years pass and we find ourselves in Bohemia with spring imagery bursting out of Autolycus's first song, "When daffodils begin to peer." If Leontes is an imaginary cuckold, Autolycus, the thieving harbinger of spring, is something of an imaginative cuckoo. Thence we go on to the sheep-shearing festival, where the imagery extends from early spring to winter evergreens, a vision of nature demonstrating its creative power throughout the entire year, which is perhaps what the dance of the twelve satyrs represents. The symbolic reason for the sixteen-year gap is clearly to have the cycle of the year reinforced by the slower cycle of human generations.

Dramatic contrast in Shakespeare normally includes a superficial resemblance in which one element is a parody of the other. Theseus remarks in *A Midsummer Night's Dream* that the lunatic, the lover, and the poet are of imagination all compact. Theseus, like Yeats, is a smiling public man past his first youth, but not, like Yeats, a poet and a critic. What critical ability there is in that family belongs entirely to Hippolyta, whose sharp comments are a most effective contrast to Theseus's amiable bumble. Hippolyta objects that the story of the lovers has a consistency to it that lunacy would lack, and everywhere in Shakespearian comedy the resemblance of love and lunacy is based on their opposition. Florizel's love for Perdita, which transcends his duty to his father and his social responsibilities as a prince, is a state of mind above reason. He is advised, he says, by his "fancy":

If my reason
Will thereto be obedient, I have reason;
If not, my senses, better pleased with madness,
Do bid it welcome.

Leontes' jealousy is a fantasy below reason, and hence a parody of Florizel's state. Camillo, who represents a kind of middle level in the play, is opposed to both, calling one diseased and the other desperate. Both states of mind collide with reality in the middle, and one is annihilated and the other redeemed, like the two aspects of law in Christianity. As the Gentleman says in reporting the finding of Perdita, "They looked as they had heard of a world ransomed, or one destroyed." When Leontes has returned to his proper state of mind, he echoes Florizel when he says of watching the statue,

No settled senses of the world can match
The pleasure of that madness.

The play ends in a double recognition scene: the first, which is reported only through the conversation of three Gentlemen, is the recognition of Perdita's parentage; the second is the final scene of the awakening of Hermione and the presenting of Perdita to her. The machinery of the former scene is the ordinary *cognitio* of New Comedy, where the heroine is proved by birth tokens to be respectable enough for the hero to marry her. In many comedies, though never in Shakespeare, such a *cognitio* is brought about through the ingenuity of a tricky servant. Autolycus has this role in *The Winter's Tale,* for though "out of service" he still regards Florizel as his master, and he has also the rascality and the complacent soliloquies about his own cleverness that go with the role. He gains possession of the secret of Perdita's birth, but somehow or other the denouement takes place without him, and he remains superfluous to the plot, consoling himself with the reflection that doing so good a deed would be inconsistent with the rest of his character. In *The Winter's Tale* Shakespeare has combined the two traditions which descended from Menander, pastoral romance and New Comedy, and has consequently come very close to Menandrine formulas as we have them in such a play as *Epitripontes.* But the fact that this conventional recognition scene is only reported indicates that Shakespeare is less interested in it than in the statue scene, which is all his own.

In *Measure for Measure* and *The Tempest* the happy ending is brought about through the exertions of the central characters, whose successes are so remarkable that they seem to many critics to have something almost supernatural about them, as though they were the agents of a divine providence. The germ of truth in this conception is that in other comedies of the same general structure, where there is no such character, the corresponding dramatic role is filled by a supernatural being—Diana in *Pericles* and Jupiter in *Cymbeline.* *The Winter's Tale* belongs to the second group, for the return of Perdita proceeds from the invisible providence of Apollo.

In *Pericles* and *Cymbeline* there is, in addition to the recognition scene, a dream in which the controlling divinity appears with an announcement of what is to conclude the action. Such a scene forms an emblematic recognition scene, in which we are shown the power that brings about the comic resolution. In *The Tempest,* where the power is human, Prospero's magic presents three emblematic visions: a wedding masque of gods to Ferdinand, a disappearing banquet to the Court Party, and "trumpery" (4.1.186) to entice Stephano and Trinculo to steal. In *The Winter's Tale* Apollo does not enter the action, and the emblematic recognition scene is represented by the sheep-shearing festival. This is also on three levels. To Florizel it is a kind of betrothal masque and "a meeting of the petty gods"; to the Court Party, Polixenes and Camillo, it is an illusion which they snatch away; to Autolycus it is an opportunity to sell his "trumpery" (4.4.608) and steal purses.

An emblematic recognition scene of this kind is the distinguishing feature of the four late romances. As a convention, it develops from pastoral romance and the narrative or mythological poem. The sheep-shearing festival resembles the big bravura scenes of singing-matches and the like in Sidney's *Arcadia,* and *The Rape of Lucrece* comes to an emblematic focus in the tapestry depicting the fall of Troy, where Lucrece identifies herself with Hecuba and Tarquin with Sinon, and determines that the second Troy will not collapse around a rape like the first one. In the earlier comedies the emblematic recognition scene is usually in the form of burlesque. Thus in *Love's Labours Lost* the pageant of Worthies elaborates on Don Armado's appeal to the precedents of Solomon, Samson, and Hercules when he falls in love; but his appeal has also burlesqued the main theme of the play. The allegorical garden episode in *Richard II* represents a similar device, but one rather different in its relation to the total dramatic structure.

In any case the controlling power in the dramatic action of *The Winter's Tale* is something identified both with the will of the gods, especially Apollo, and with the power of nature. We have to keep this association of nature and pagan gods in mind when we examine the imagery in the play that reminds us of religious, even explicitly Christian, conceptions. At the beginning Leontes' youth is referred to as a time of paradisal innocence; by the end of the scene he has tumbled into a completely illusory knowledge of good and evil. He says:

> How blest am I
> In my just censure, in my true opinion!
> Alack, for lesser knowledge! How accurs'd
> In being so blest!

Or, as Ford says in *The Merry Wives,* "God be praised for my jealousy!" The irony of the scene in which

Leontes is scolded by Paulina turns on the fact that Leontes tries to be a source of righteous wrath when he is actually an object of it. Hermione's trial is supposed to be an act of justice and the sword of justice is produced twice to have oaths sworn on it, but Leontes is under the wrath of Apollo and divine justice is his enemy. The opposite of wrath is grace, and Hermione is associated throughout the play with the word grace. During the uneasy and rather cloying friendliness at the beginning of the play Hermione pronounces the word "grace" conspicuously three times, after which the harsh dissonances of Leontes' jealousy begin. She also uses the word when she is ordered off to prison and in the only speech that she makes after Act 3. But such grace is not Christian or theological grace, which is superior to the order of nature, but a secular analogy of Christian grace which is identical with nature—the grace that Spenser celebrates in the sixth book of *The Faerie Queene.*

In the romances, and in some of the earlier comedies, we have a sense of an irresistible power, whether of divine or human agency, making for a providential resolution. Whenever we have a strong sense of such a power, the human beings on whom it operates seem greatly diminished in size. This is a feature of the romances which often disappoints those who wish that Shakespeare had simply kept on writing tragedies. Because of the heavy emphasis on reconciliation in *Cymbeline,* the jealousy of Posthumus is not titanic, as the jealousy of Othello is titanic; it expresses only a childish petulance about women in general: "I'll write against them, Despise them, curse them." Similarly Leontes (as he himself points out) falls far short of being a somber demonic tyrant on the scale of Macbeth, and can only alternate between bluster and an uneasy sense of having done wrong:

> Away with that audacious lady! Antigonus,
> I charg'd thee that she should not come about me.
> I knew she would.

This scaling down of the human perspective is in conformity with a dramatic structure that seems closely analogous to such Christian conceptions as wrath and grace. But the only one of the four romances in which I suspect any explicit—which means allegorical—references to Christianity is *Cymbeline.* Cymbeline was king of Britain at the birth of Christ, and in such scenes as the Jailer's speculations about death and his wistful "I would we were all of one mind, and that mind good," there are hints that some far-reaching change in the human situation is taking place off-stage. The play ends on the word "peace" and with Cymbeline's promise to pay tribute to Rome, almost as though, as soon as the story ended, another one were to begin with Augustus Caesar's decree that all the world should be taxed.

No such explicit links are appropriate to *The Winter's Tale,* though it is true that the story does tell of a mysterious disappearing child born in the winter who has four father-figures assigned to her: a real one, a putative one who later becomes her father-in-law, a fictional one, Smalus of Libya in Florizel's tale, and a shepherd foster-father. This makes up a group of a shepherd and three kings, of whom one is African. The first part of *The Winter's Tale* is, like *Cymbeline,* full of the imagery of superstitious sacrifice. Leontes, unable to sleep, wonders if having Hermione burnt alive would not give him rest. Antigonus offers to spay his three daughters if Hermione is guilty, though he would prefer to castrate himself. Mamillius, whom Leontes thinks of as a part of himself, becomes the victim necessary to save Leontes, and the exposing of Perdita is attended by a sacrificial holocaust. Not only is Antigonus devoured by a bear, but the ship and its crew were "Wrecked the same instant of their master's death and in the view of the shepherd; so that all the instruments which aided to expose the child were even then lost when it was found." In contrast, the restoring of Perdita to her mother is an act of sacramental communion, but it is a secular communion, and the "instruments" aiding in it are the human arts. The main characters repair to Paulina's house intending to "sup" there, and are taken into her chapel and presented with what is alleged to be a work of painting and sculpture. Hermione, like Thaisa in *Pericles,* is brought to life by the playing of music, and references to the art of magic follow. Art, therefore, seems part of the regenerating power of the play, and the imagination of the poet is to be allied with that of the lover as against that of the lunatic.

Apart from the final scene, at least three kinds of art are mentioned in the play. First, there is the art of the gardener who, according to Polixenes' famous speech, may help or change nature by marrying a gentler scion to the wildest stock but can do so only through nature's power, so that "the art itself is nature." This is a sound humanist view: it is the view of Sidney, who contrasts the brazen world of nature with the golden world of art but also speaks of art as a second nature. Sidney's view does not necessitate, but it is consistent with, his ridiculing of plays that show a character as an infant in one act and grown up in the next, and that mingle kings and clowns in the same scene. It is also the view of Ben Jonson who, recognizing a very different conception of nature in Shakespeare's romances, remarked good-humoredly that he was "loth to make nature afraid in his plays, like those that beget tales, tempests, and such-like drolleries." We note that Polixenes' speech entirely fails to convince Perdita, who merely repeats that she will have nothing to do with bastard flowers:

> No more than, were I painted, I would wish
> This youth should say 'twere well, and only
> 　therefore
> Desire to breed by me. . . .

—a remark which oddly anticipates the disappearance of the painted statue of Hermione into the real Hermione. It also, as has often been pointed out, fails to convince Polixenes himself, for a few moments later we find him in a paroxysm of fury at the thought of his own gentle scion marrying the wild stock of a shepherd's daughter. Whatever its merits, Polixenes' view of art hardly seems to describe the kind of art that the play itself manifests.

Secondly, there is the kind of art represented by Julio Romano, said to be the painter and sculptor of Hermione's statue, a mimetic realist who "would beguile Nature of her custom, so perfectly is he her ape." But it turns out that in fact no statue has been made of Hermione, and the entire reference to Romano seems pointless. We do not need his kind of art when we have the real Hermione, and here again, whatever Romano's merits, neither he nor the kind of realism he represents seems to be very central to the play itself. The literary equivalent of realism is plausibility, the supplying of adequate causation for events. There is little plausibility in *The Winter's Tale,* and a great deal of what is repeatedly called "wonder." Things are presented to us, not explained. The jealousy of Leontes explodes without warning: an actor may rationalize it in various ways; a careful reader of the text may suspect that the references to his youth have touched off some kind of suppressed guilt; but the essential fact is that the jealousy suddenly appears where it had not been before, like a second subject in a piece of music. "How should this grow?" Polixenes asks of Camillo, but Camillo evades the question. At the end of the play Hermione is first a statue, then a living woman. The explanations given do not satisfy even Leontes, much less us. He says:

> But how, is to be question'd; for I saw her,
> As I thought, dead, and have in vain said
> 　many
> A prayer upon her grave.

As often in Shakespeare, further explanations are promised to the characters, but are not given to the audience: Paulina merely says, "it appears she lives."

Thirdly, though one blushes to mention it, there is the crude popular art of the ballads of Autolycus, of which one describes "how a usurer's wife was brought to bed of twenty money-bags at a burden." "Is it true, think you?" asks Mopsa, unconsciously using one of the most frequently echoed words in the play. We notice that Shakespeare seems to be calling our attention to the incredibility of his story and to its ridiculous and outmoded devices when he makes both Paulina and the Gentlemen who report the recognition of Perdita speak of what is happening as "like an old tale." The magic words pronounced by Paulina that draw speech from Hermione are "Our Perdita is found," and Paulina has previously said that the finding of Perdita is "monstrous to our human reason." And when one of the Gentlemen says "Such a deal of wonder is broken out within this hour that ballad-makers cannot be able to express it," we begin to suspect that the kind of art manifested by the play itself is in some respects closer to these "trumpery" ballads than to the sophisticated idealism and realism of Polixenes and Romano.

My late and much beloved colleague Professor Harold S. Wilson has called attention to the similarity between Polixenes' speech and a passage in Puttenham's *Arte of English Poesie* (1589), which in discussing the relation of art and nature uses the analogy of the gardener and the example of the "gillyvor."[1] Puttenham also goes on to say that there is another context where art is "only a bare imitator of nature's works, following and counterfeiting her actions and effects, as the Marmoset doth many countenances and gestures of man; of which sort are the arts of painting and carving." We are reminded of Romano, the painter and carver who is the perfect "ape" of nature. The poet, says Puttenham, is to use all types of art in their proper place, but for his greatest moments he will work "even as nature her self working by her own peculiar virtue and proper instinct and not by example or meditation or exercise as all other artificers do." We feel that Puttenham, writing before Shakespeare had got properly started and two centuries earlier than Coleridge, has nonetheless well characterized the peculiar quality of Shakespeare's art.

The fact that Leontes' state of mind is a parody of the imagination of lover and poet links *The Winter's Tale* with Shakespeare's 'humor' comedies, which turn on the contrast between fantasy and reality. Katharina moves from shrew to obedient wife; Falstaff from the seducer to the gull of the merry wives; the King of Navarre and his followers from contemplative pedants seeking authority from books to helpless lovers performing the tasks imposed on them by their ladies. Similarly when Florizel says that his love for Perdita

                         cannot fail but by
The violation of my faith; and then
Let nature crush the sides o' th' earth together
And mar the seeds within! . . .

—he is supplying the genuine form of what Camillo describes in parallel cosmological terms:

                you may as well
Forbid the sea for to obey the moon,
As or by oath remove or counsel shake
The fabric of his folly, whose foundation
Is piled upon his faith.

Puttenham begins his treatise by comparing the poet, as a creator, to God, "who without any travail to his

divine imagination made all the world of nought." Leontes' jealousy is a parody of a creation out of nothing, as the insistent repetition of the word "nothing" in the first act indicates, and as Leontes himself says in his mysterious mumbling half-soliloquy:

Affection, thy intention stabs the centre!
Thou dost make possible things not so held,
Communicat'st with dream—how can this be?
With what's unreal thou coactive art,
And fellow'st nothing.

A humor is restored to a normal outlook by being confronted, not directly with reality, but with a reflection of its own illusion, as Katharina is tamed by being shown the reflection of her own shrewishness in Petruchio. Similarly Leontes, in the final scene, is "mocked with art," the realistic illusion of Romano's statue which gradually reveals itself to be the real Hermione.

In the artificial society of the Sicilian court there are Mamillius, the hopeful prince who dies, and the infant Perdita who vanishes. In the rural society of Bohemia there are the shepherdess Perdita who is "Flora Peering in April's front," and Florizel who, as his name suggests, is her masculine counterpart, and the Prince Charming who later reminds Leontes strongly of Mamillius and becomes Leontes' promised heir. Perdita says that she would like to strew Florizel with flowers:

        like a bank for love to lie and play on,
Not like a corse; or if, not to be buried,
But quick and in mine arms.

The antithesis between the two worlds is marked by Polixenes, who is handed "flowers of winter" and who proceeds to destroy the festival like a winter wind, repeating the *senex iratus* role of Leontes in the other kingdom. But though he can bully Perdita, he impresses her no more than Leontes had impressed Hermione. Perdita merely says:

I was not much afeard; for once or twice
I was about to speak and tell him plainly
The selfsame sun that shines upon his court
Hides not his visage from our cottage but
Looks on alike.

There is a faint New Testament echo here, but of course to Perdita the god of the sun would be Apollo, who does see to it that Polixenes is out-witted, though only by the fact that Perdita is really a princess. As always in Shakespeare, the structure of society is unchanged by the comic action. What happens in *The Winter's Tale* is the opposite of the art of the gardener as Polixenes describes it. A society which is artificial in a limited sense at the beginning of the play becomes at the end still artificial, but natural as well. Nature provides the means for the regeneration of artifice. But still it is true that "The art itself is nature," and one wonders why a speech ending with those words should be assigned to Polixenes, the opponent of the festival.

The context of Polixenes' theory is the Renaissance framework in which there are two levels of the order of nature. Art belongs to human nature, and human nature is, properly speaking, the state that man lived in in Eden, or the Golden Age, before his fall into a lower world of physical nature to which he is not adapted. Man attempts to regain his original state through law, virtue, education, and such rational and conscious aids as art. Here nature is a superior order. In poetry this upper level of nature, uncontaminated by the sin and death of the fall, is usually symbolized by the starry spheres, which are now all that is left of it. The starry spheres produce the music of the spheres, and the harmony of music usually represents this upper level of nature in human life.

Most Shakespearian comedy is organized within this framework, and when it is, its imagery takes on the form outlined by G. Wilson Knight in *The Shakespearean Tempest* (1932). The tempest symbolizes the destructive elements in the order of nature, and music the permanently constructive elements in it. Music in its turn is regularly associated with the starry spheres, of which the one closest to us, the moon, is the normal focus. The control of the tempest by the harmony of the spheres appears in the image of the moon pulling the tides, an image used once or twice in *The Winter's Tale*. The action of *The Merchant of Venice,* too, extends from the cosmological harmonies of the fifth act, where the moon sleeps with Endymion, to the tempest that wrecked Antonio's ships. In *Pericles,* which employs this imagery of harmony and tempest most exhaustively, Pericles is said to be a master of music, Cerimon revives Thaisa by music, Diana announces her appearance to Pericles by music, and the final recognition scene unites the music and tempest symbols, since it takes place in the temple of Diana during the festival of Neptune. Music also accompanies the revival of Hermione in the final scene of *The Winter's Tale*. All the attention is absorbed in Hermione as she begins to move while music plays; and we are reminded of Autolycus and of his role as a kind of rascally Orpheus at the sheep-shearing festival: "My clown . . . would not stir his pettitoes till he had both tune and words; which so drew the rest of the herd to me that all their other senses stuck in ears. . . . No hearing, no feeling, but my sir's song, and admiring the nothing of it." Here again Autolycus seems to be used to indicate that something is being subordinated in the play, though by no means eliminated.

In another solstitial play, *A Midsummer Night's Dream,* the cosmology is of this more conventional Renaissance kind. In the middle, between the world of chaos symbolized by tempest and the world of starry spheres symbolized by music, comes the cycle of nature, the world of Eros and Adonis, Puck and Pyramus, the love-god and the dying god. To this middle world the fairies belong, for the fairies are spirits of the four natural elements, and their dissension causes disorder in nature. Above, the cold fruitless moon of Diana, whose nun Hermia would have to be, hangs over the action. While a mermaid is calming the sea by her song and attracting the stars by the power of harmony, Cupid shoots an arrow at the moon and its vestal: it falls in a parabola on a flower and turns it "purple with love's wound." The story of Pyramus is not very coherently told in Peter Quince's play, but in Ovid there is a curious image about the blood spurting out of Pyramus in an arc like water out of a burst pipe and falling on the white mulberry and turning it purple. Here nature as a cycle of birth and death, symbolized by the purple flower, revolves underneath nature as a settled and predictable order or harmony, as it does also in a third solstitial play, *Twelfth Night,* which begins with an image comparing music to a wind blowing on a bank of violets.

But in *The Winter's Tale* nature is associated, not with the credible, but with the incredible: nature as an order is subordinated to the nature that yearly confronts us with the impossible miracle of renewed life. In Ben Jonson's animadversions on Shakespeare's unnatural romances it is particularly the functional role of the dance, the "concupiscence of jigs," as he calls it, that he objects to. But it is the dance that most clearly expresses the pulsating energy of nature as it appears in *The Winter's Tale,* an energy which communicates itself to the dialogue. Such words as "push" and "wild" (meaning rash) are constantly echoed; the play ends with the words "Hastily lead away," and we are told that the repentant Leontes

> o'er and o'er divides him
> 'Twixt his unkindness and his kindness; th'
> one
> He chides to hell and bids the other grow
> Faster than thought of time.

Much is said about magic in the final scene, but there is no magician, no Prospero, only the sense of a participation in the redeeming and reviving power of a nature identified with art, grace, and love. Hence the final recognition is appropriately that of a frozen statue turning into a living presence, and the appropriate Chorus is Time, the destructive element which is also the only possible representative of the timeless.

Note

[1] "'Nature and Art' in *Winter's Tale* 4.4.86 ff.," *SAB,* 18 (1943), 114-20.

Robert W. Uphaus (essay date 1970)

SOURCE: "The 'Comic' Mode of *The Winter's Tale*," in *Genre,* Vol. III, No. 1, March, 1970, pp. 40-54.

[*In the essay below, Uphaus discusses the role of language in establishing the integration of tragic and comic perception in* The Winter's Tale.]

There are some striking affinities between tragedy and comedy, not the least of which is their mutual concern with perception. Both kinds of plays represent actions whose fulfillment, in diverse ways, is the fulfillment of feeling. (Susanne Langer has said that feeling is the intaglio image of reality, and I see no reason to argue against this point.) Both kinds of plays frequently challenge the meaning and, ultimately, the seriousness of the universe we live in, and for this reason alone the problems of tragedy are as easily accommodated, though less easily solved, in the comic form. Both kinds of plays also work within well-defined conventions and are built on a similar dramatic paradox: their image of reality heightens and intensifies as a tighter control or artifice is exerted on the play's subject.

Yet tragedy and comedy do not share a similar permissiveness, for they do not share a similar awareness of the nature of play. Tragedy, almost of necessity, represses the kind of knowledge that comedy thrives on—the knowledge that human vitality has a way of righting the inevitable wrong. Mistakes, the subject of both dramatic forms, lead to an inevitable degradation in tragedy while in comedy they bring about a fellowship of mutual remembrance. Much of this has to do with a primary structural difference: unlike tragedy, comedy is less dependent on one character's perception, which is usually all-encompassing, than on a multiple revelation of human possibility. This difference in accommodation of perception may be stated in another way: where tragedy deals with the disintegration of a head of a family, or of a head of state, comedy plays, sometimes very seriously, with a *threatened* disintegration of state which culminates, however, in an integration of feeling or festivity. This integrative element in *The Winter's Tale*—the subject of my paper—may be largely explained by a discussion of the play's unique mode of perception.

If comedy is the after-hours of tragedy's curfew, it is truant in the sense that it hangs around and plays in spite of the evening's menace. And its chief source of play is language, frequently the language of tragedy. This may be seen by looking at *The Winter's Tale,* a play strikingly built on the separation of tragedy and comedy, and by gauging the way the interaction of language and theme reveals this play's distinctive mode of perception.[1] The integrative element of Shakespearean comedy usually involves the purgation of a kind of language, and such a purgation is always rein-forced by the presentation of a representative kind of dramatic event that is itself the reciprocal of the vying sets of language. And yet it is quite a distance from the recollection of identity (a theme common to Shakespeare's early comedies) to the redemption of the "world," which is the path *The Winter's Tale* travels. Certainly, like many of the early comedies, *The Winter's Tale* deals with the disjunction between feeling and fact, but the conversions in this play require a distinctive mode of perception, one that goes beyond the external fact (though it is occasioned by it) and moves more tellingly into the realm of inner being. And this mode of perception, established through a pattern of remembrance, is nowhere better evident than in the play's first scene.

In a scene of less than fifty lines the representative forces of Sicilia and Bohemia are openly revealed, and the play's imagery is inconspicuously established. One of the keys to the play and to this scene is "difference," a matter investigated and finally torn asunder by the play's universalizing impulse. Archidamus immediately alludes to the presence of difference—"You shall see, as I have said, great difference betwixt our Bohemia and your Sicilia." The difference is more than just a climatic one, but it is not until a few lines later that the presence of difference is internalized. Difference characterizes the tentativeness of Polixenes' and Leontes' friendship; having grown together in innocence, they have been separated by kingly responsibilities:

> Since their more mature dignities and royal necessities made separation of their society, their encounters, though not personal, have been royally attorneyed with interchange of gifts, letters, loving embassies, that they have seemed to be together, though absent: shook hands, as over a vast; and embraced as it were from the ends of opposed winds.

> (I. i. 26-32)[2]

It is interesting to observe that one aspect of ceremony (e.g., "royally attorneyed") is meant to overcome separation, yet the ceremony itself is evidence of the separation. Ceremony is used in these diverse ways throughout the play. Part of the play's pattern of remembrance—shaped, to a great extent, by the image of the "vast," together with the multiple functions of ceremony—appears in the last three lines of the play. Everyone, we are told, will "answer to his part / Performed in this wide gap of time since first / We were dissevered." The theatrical terms—"part," "performed"—are, of course, another aspect of ceremony.

Two other motifs related to the "vast" also appear in this scene: the revivifying power of sons and the proper regard of utterance. Of Mamillius, we are told that he is "a gallant child; one that, indeed, physics the subject, makes old hearts fresh." This medicinal power is mentioned still again, first by Polixenes:

He makes a July's day short as December,
And with his varying childness, cures in me
Thoughts that would thick my blood.

                      (I. ii. 169-71)

And later, in a new variation, Paulina assumes this function:

                      . . . I
Do come with words as medicinal as true,
Honest as either, to purge him of that humor
That presses him from sleep.

                      (II. iii. 35-38)

Shakespeare's use of language as purgation is as old as *The Taming of the Shrew,* but the range of implication here is considerably more varied. This is almost immediately apparent when we notice the connections between language as remedy and the dependence of such remedy on the truthfulness of expression—"medicinal as true / Honest as either." Shakespeare has evidently suspended the wit-combats of the earlier comedies, a form of excess meant to effect "remedy," and replaced them with a form of plain statement counterpointing the excess of "sick" people. Buttressed by some powerful disease imagery, health becomes less a pose than a real, almost tragic issue. Archidamus gives the linguistic formula for health, and by implication the index to illness, when he says to Camillo, "I speak as my understanding instructs me, and mine honesty puts it to utterance." (In this regard, it is well to recall Edgar's comment at the end of *King Lear:* "Speak what we feel, not what we ought to say.") The point is, something other than honesty puts Leontes' language to utterance.

Act I, scene ii dramatizes the divergence of language hinted at in I. i. Each dramatic occasion—Leontes' request of Polixenes to remain, Polixenes' resistance, Leontes' request of Hermione to intervene and her eventual intervention, and finally Leontes' jealousy—is supported by a corresponding rift in language. The exterior "vast" of separation seeps down into Leontes' language, and he becomes estranged by his own perverted suspicion. His initial request begins innocently enough, but the play's early attentiveness to language indicates the possibility of serious conflict:

LEONTES.   Tongue-tied, our Queen?
  Speak you.
HERMIONE. I had thought, sir, to have held my
  peace until
You had drawn oaths from him not to stay.
  You, sir,
Charge him too coldly. Tell him you are sure
All in Bohemia's well. . . .
LEONTES.   Well said, Hermione.
HERMIONE. To tell he longs to see his son
  were strong;

But let him say so then, and let him go;
But let him swear so, and he shall not stay. . .

                (I. ii. 27-31, 33-36)

"Tongue," "speak," "tell," "charge," "say," "swear"—these frequent references to language underlie the play's rhythm of events. It would be difficult to call all of this deception comic, for the source of conflict is language *in toto,* rather than wit alone. Leontes quickly associates language with the highest human events—his own marriage—and therefore as his suspicion grows he subverts all human discourse. To Hermione he says, "thou never spok'st / To better purpose" (with the exception of her marriage vow), only now he associates her purpose with the destruction of that vow. For the moment, then, it is the play's intention to "stab the center."

This sudden reversal of trust in turn brings about a mistrust of the "real." Leontes rejects his wife, his friends, his children—all in the name of "play." Where play in the earlier comedies is linked with the verbal, with dexterity of identity and enhancement of event, play now challenges the universe; it perverts the memory of human goodness and sullies human belief. Play intensifies suspicion where formerly it mediated mistrust:

Go play, boy, play: thy mother plays, and I
Play too—but so disgraced a part, whose issue
Will hiss me to my grave; contempt and
  clamor
Will be my knell. Go play, boy, play.

                (I. ii. 187-90)

The pun on "issue" distorts the revivifying powers of children; their innocence is corrupt because they reflect the memory of events gone sour; memory is brought to focus through suspicion:

         Physic for't there's none;

                (I. ii. 200)

Know't
It will let in and out the enemy,
With bag and baggage. Many thousand
  on's
Have the disease, and feel't not. How now,
  boy!

                (I. ii. 204-7)

Leontes links birth, once symbolic of innocence, with disease. Act I closes, however, with an effective counterpoint to Leontes' suspicion—the assertion of trust. Camillo implores Polixenes to flee the diseased kingdom, and for evidence he urges truth unverified as the only requirement: "Be not uncertain / . . . I / Have uttered truth; which if you seek to prove / I dare not stand by" (I. ii. 442-45).

Except for the important introduction of Paulina, Act II pretty well mirrors the design of Act I. The issues of language, belief, knowledge, play, disease, are all present, though the use of language seems to receive the thematic nod. Paulina is another in the long line of Ladies of the Tongue, yet her thematic function carries associations far exceeding the possibilities of a Kate or Beatrice. Indeed, as the "vast" widens and the characters are further separated from one another, Paulina becomes the character who perpetuates the play's pattern of remembrance: the re-creation of the past, and ultimately the regeneration of Leontes, is left almost entirely up to her. And, although Paulina dates back to Shakespeare's early use of "practicers," she performs a mediating function rather unlike any other in the earlier comedies: on her the redemption of the "world" and the final sanctity of art depend.

The three scenes of Act II successively trace out the play's pattern of illness and correspondingly they allude to the play's pattern of regeneration through memory. Scene i, centered around Leontes' repudiation of Hermione, abounds with references to the perversion of reason: "In my just censure, in my true opinion! / Alack, for lesser knowledge" (II. i. 37-38); "All's true that is mistrusted" (II. i. 48); "You smell this business with a sense as cold / As is a dead man's nose; but I do see't and feel't" (II. i. 151-52); "What, Lack I credit" (II. i. 157)—and this pattern of suspicion culminates in Leontes' final assertion that

> Our prerogative
> Calls not your counsels, but our natural
>   goodness
> Imparts this. (II. i. 163-65)

which is a perversion of Archidamus' opening statement (I. i. 19-21): "Believe me, I speak as my understanding instructs me, and as mine honesty puts it to utterance."

Scene ii works toward the redemptive power of Paulina's speech, itself established through her continual association with nature (particularly the cycle of Perdita's birth and Hermione's "death"). Paulina's medicinal powers, her power to evoke memory as a remedy to suspicion, lie of course in language—"If I prove honey-mouthed, let my tongue blister" (II. ii. 32); and far more conclusively:

> Tell her, Emilia,
> I'll use that tongue I have; if wit flow from't
> As boldness from my bosom, let's not be
>   doubted
> I shall do good. (II. ii. 50-53)

Her ability to mediate the play's "tragic" conflict is unquestioned: "Do not you fear—upon mine honor, I / Will stand betwixt you and danger" (II. ii. 64-65). Act II, scene iii is built around two crucial and mutually interpenetrating speeches. Presenting herself as Leontes' "physician" and his most obedient "counsellor," Paulina attempts to purge Leontes of suspicion, only to experience an explicit dramatization of the "vast":

> . . . I
> Do come with words as medicinal as true,
> Honest as either, to purge him of that humor
> That presses him from sleep.
> LEONTES.   What noise there, ho?
> PAULINA. No noise, my lord, but needful
>   conference . . .
>
>   (II. iii. 35-39)

There is an evident distinction between "needful conference" and "noise," and it is the space separating the two views that Paulina directs her comments to. She has the unenviable task of mediating a potentially tragic conflict within a comic mode. Paulina is a practicer, but she is not Cassandra, nor is she, as Leontes thinks, "a most intelligencing bawd." Perhaps the following speech, seen against the background of Shakespeare's earlier comedies will explain why the first three acts are "tragic" though not tragedy:

> PAULINA.   . . . for he,
> The sacred honor of himself, his queen's,
> His hopeful son's, his babe's, betrays to
>   slander,
> Whose sting is sharper than the sword's; and
>   will not
> (For as the case now stands, it is a curse
> He cannot be compelled to't) once remove
> The root of his opinion, which is rotten
> As ever oak or stone was sound.
>
>   (II. iii. 82-89)

All the elements of tragedy are here—honor, curse, diseased perception. But there is no "plague," for Leontes' disease is centripetal not centrifugal. Leontes' tragic uncertainty may appear to shake the "world," so to say, but Paulina's assurance—as unwavering "as oak or stone was sound"—more than compensates for a potentially tragic disillusionment.

Paulina, then, brings us back to language, the source of this play's and the earlier comedies' mode of perception and illusion. In betraying his family to "slander," Leontes joins his predicament, at least in form, with Claudio's repudiation of Hero in *Much Ado About Nothing*. And the comic formulation of remedy in *The Winter's Tale* is similar to that of the earlier comedies: like Hero in *Much Ado,* Hermione will "die to live," and like Kate in *The Taming of the Shrew,* Leontes will be "killed in his own humor." Though the comic resolution of *The Winter's Tale* is a good deal more resonant, Leonato's explanation of Hero's "resurrection" in *Much Ado* aptly formulates the conditions for Hermione's reappearance: "She died, my lord, but whiles her slander lived."

Act III is almost exclusively taken up with three forms of ceremony, embodying, as they do later, the conjunction of diverse events into one pure and all-encompassing reconstruction of memory. The divine, the secular, and the natural are the three forms of ceremony; and each takes its substance from the dramatization of the "vast." The oracle is the divine, and Cleomenes' description of the island—"delicate," "most sweet," "fertile"—anticipates the later pastoral qualities of Perdita and Florizel. At the same time Cleomenes' and Dion's language in III. i. in some ways anticipates the reverence of V. ii. and V. iii. The tribunal in III. ii. dramatizes the "vast" by pointing to the diseased disjunction of feeling and fact. Certain of his accusation, Leontes dismisses Hermione's resistance, and she immediately recognizes the source of her estrangement; "and / The testimony on my part no other / But what comes from myself, it shall scarce boot me / To say, 'not guilty'" (III. ii. 22-25). Acknowledging Leontes' rejection of honesty, Hermione reasons in much the same manner as Friar Francis does of Hero's predicament in *Much Ado:* "To me can life be no commodity." However, the nature of Hermione's appeal clearly differentiates the depths of *The Winter's Tale* from *Much Ado.* For in *The Winter's Tale,* the source of conciliation must be in "powers divine." Apollo will be Hermione's judge; so the appeal is to a higher principle of "reality." Moreover, the disjunction between feeling and fact is, for the moment, absolute:

> HERMIONE. You speak a language that I
>   understand not.
> My life stands in the level of your dreams,
> Which I'll lay down.
> LEONTES.   Your actions are my dreams.
> You had a bastard by Polixenes,
> And I but dreamed it. As you were past all
>   shame—
> Those of your fact are so—so past all truth;
>   (III. ii. 78-83)

As with Paulina, so with Hermione: they both, in Leontes' view, speak "noise."

Soon Hermione and Mamillius perish, with a suddenness as startling as Leontes' initial fit of jealousy. Yet with their "deaths" the tragic action exhausts itself: one vein has been mined, one set of purposes has been realized. But Leontes' perceptions to this point are as fool's gold to the rich vein of human experience that Paulina uncovers. Twice in the first three acts Leontes makes an important request. The first—asking his wife to detain Polixenes—brings about his "tragedy," and

the second, made of Paulina, greatly affects, in a far deeper way than he appreciates, the restoration of life:

> I have too much believed mine own suspicion.
> Beseech you tenderly apply to her
> Some remedies for life. Apollo, pardon
> My great profaneness 'gainst thine oracle.
>   (III. ii. 148-51)

Hermione "dies," a necessity for the revitalization of life, and Paulina at once purges memory and promotes a reconstruction of the past through the resources of language. Correspondingly, the references to speech abound: "I have deserved / All tongues to talk their bitt'rest" (III. ii. 213-14), "Say no more" (III. ii. 214), "th' boldness of your speech" (III. ii. 216), "Thou didst speak but well" (III. ii. 230). Indeed, Paulina's use of speech is so well established that her medicinal language no longer requires utterance, for Leontes' memorialization of his own past through the ritual reenactment of guilt becomes a symbolic expression of Paulina's medicinal language.

Act III, scene iii dramatizes the modulation of tragic illusion to comic perception through the reenactment of death. The scene pulls away from the secular, the logic of tribunals, and immerses itself in the natural. Perdita's desertion awakens the life impulse, for she is not so much deserted as planted in the earth, there to awaken, without memory, into pure time. Destiny in the guise of Fortune prevails; accident awakens life. Even when the bear kills Antigonus, there is no evidence of malignity but rather a natural purpose doused with some humor—"They [the bears] are never curst but when they are hungry." The dark side of death is illuminated by the comic mode of perception; great creating nature is beneficent as well: "Heavy matters, heavy matters! But look thee here, boy. Now bless thyself; thou met'st with things dying, I with things new born." The tone of "heavy matters, heavy matters" aptly commands the remainder of the play, shaping the perspective necessary for the blossoming of human feeling. The "savage clamor" of the tempest, to some extent an analogue to the tragic, quickly subsides with Perdita's awakening into life; she is the birth of the floral.

With Paulina absent, Act IV sustains the play's pattern of remembrance through the presentation of new memory as it merges with the old. Camillo and Polixenes talk about the old, as do Perdita and Florizel about the new, but their conversations remain smaller instances of the play's dramatization of memory. The Bohemia scenes to a large extent parallel the events of Sicilia, with the notable addition of Autolycus. The play, having now digested death in III. iii., reworks old memories within an evident comic mode, and Autolycus is one aspect of that impulse. He is the new practicer, but it is interesting to see how he is separated from any significant encounter (save one) with the "high" plot. He is rightly submerged, though his presence is continually felt; his impulse is fundamental to the comic mode, but it is, nevertheless, the very impulse that comedy must master. His presence mirrors, to a degree, the play's sense of transformation: Autolycus' forays on society stand in effective relief with Leontes' more serious pillages on human integrity. The two men amount to diverse aspects of disorder, aspects of the Dionysian if you will, and the play, we should recall, steadfastly moves toward an Apollonian assertion of the primacy of form. Autolycus, then, is one part of the re-creation of memory, but Act IV provides many additional instances.

Time is fundamental to the play's reconstruction of remembrance. Sixteen years have passed, sixteen years for things to change; and some things have changed. For one thing, there is a list of new characters. Yet in another sense the situation remains the same. Time refers to "that wide gap," which is a clear allusion to the "vast" of the first three acts; and this allusion in turn leads us to a reconsideration of Archidamus' initial comment in the play (I. i. 3-4): "You shall see, as I have said, great difference betwixt our Bohemia and your Sicilia." Obviously the theme of "difference" remains a vital issue, performing diverse functions, some ironic. There are at least two possible uses of "difference": difference between and difference within. There are several differences between Bohemia and Sicilia: they are separated by the sea (geographic difference), and one is temporarily more peaceful than the other (social and psychological difference). There is yet another difference between Bohemia and Sicilia, for they are in conflict with one another, though at the time of Archidamus' comment this was not so. Finally, and more fundamentally, there is *not* (ironically) a great difference between the two countries because the same differences within Bohemia occur within Sicilia.

Memory, then, is dramatically established and revivified through the recapitulation of former events. Bohemia *becomes* Sicilia. Act IV scene ii opens with Polixenes' imploring a wistful Camillo to remain, just as Leontes and Hermione earlier begged Polixenes to stay. Yet for Polixenes the remembrance of Sicilia is still divisive: "Of that fatal country Sicilia, prithee speak no more, whose very naming punishes me with . . . remembrance." Having said this, he then asks for his son, dramatically a displaced memory of Mamillius, and a note of suspicion is heard. In fact, his suspicion is so familiar to Leontes' (in form) that Shakespeare invests his speech with one of Leontes' images. At the height of his jealousy, Leontes said:

> I am angling now,
> Though you perceive me not how I give line.
> (I. ii. 180-81)

And now Polixenes:

> That's likewise part of my intelligence; but,
> I fear, the angle that plucks our son thither.
> (IV. ii. 48-49)

But there remains a significant difference of commitment, one indicative of the play's modulation from the tragic to the comic. Polixenes carries out his plan in disguise, comedy's special form of illusion, so no serious loss of identity is involved. Furthermore, before Polixenes finds his son and before he can go through the gestures of suspicion, Shakespeare presents Autolycus' use of disguise (IV. iii.). Here we have a new variation of the theme of theft, an analogue, in other words, to Leontes' and Polixenes' accusations: Autolycus traffics in "sheets," his form of prize, and not in wives, daughters, and sons. In the one instance disguise effects theft; in the other case it confirms theft (e.g., Polixenes' jealousy). But the point is, in Bohemia disguise governs all.

The subject of disguise carries over into IV. iv., unquestionably the most important scene in Bohemia. Disguise is viewed as at once indicative of difference and symbolic of transformation. First Perdita is fearful and chides Florizel:

> Your high self,
> The gracious mark o' th' land, you have obscured
> With a swain's wearing;
> (IV. iv. 7-9)

and later she says (IV. iv. 17) "To me the difference forges dread." Then the language of transformation accumulates, tracing a unifying line from the divine to the natural. Of the god's transformations, Florizel observes:

> Their transformations
> Were never for a piece of beauty rarer,
> Nor in a way so chaste . . .
> (IV. iv. 31-33)

and Perdita, still aware of opposition, remarks "that you must change this purpose, / Or I my life" (IV. iv. 38-39). It is, of course, the latter possibility which occurs, again through disguise: "sure this robe of mine / Does change my disposition" (IV. iv. 134-35). And the line of transformation through disguise culminates with the convergence of high and low plot. Autolycus and Florizel exchange garments, signifying, perhaps, both the dexterity of the comic mode and the fertility of the "world." At least Autolycus would have it so:

> What an exchange had this been without boot! What a boot is here, with this exchange! Sure, the gods do this year connive at us, and we may do anything extempore. (IV. iv. 678-82)

Fortune "drops booties" in more than one mouth and in more than one way. There is Perdita for the high plot and Autolycus for the low plot: flowers for one, gold for the other.

The most important re-enactment of memory, however, occurs with Polixenes' attempted interference with Florizel and Perdita. Now in Bohemia the roles and reversed: Polixenes, not Leontes, plays the jealous father, and Florizel and Perdita play youthful versions of Leontes and Hermione. All the issues of speech, reason, counsel and remedy reappear, save that the play this time is better prepared to absorb the conflict. Polixenes urges "Reason my son / . . . hold some counsel / In such a business," but the former theme of separation, mirroring the division between feeling and fact, still obtains:

> FLORIZEL. Mark our contract.
> POLIXENES.   Mark your divorce . . .
> (IV. iv. 421)

This time, though, love commands an affirmative avowal. Florizel honors love as steadfastly as Leontes has repudiated it; he is as certain of his own identity as he is of his own faith: "What I was, I am" (IV. iv. 468). It is especially important to notice how Shakespeare associates the memory of Polixenes and Leontes with the urgency of Florizel's vow. The very thing that Leontes and Polixenes are unable to accomplish, Florizel does with ease. He reaffirms the sanctity of one form of ceremony—the constancy of love-and in doing so he rejects a form of reason and counsel. Contrary to Leontes' and Polixenes' madness, Florizel's madness, to borrow from Emily Dickinson, is "divinest sense." But Florizel does ask the counsel of Camillo, who like Paulina effects a mediating and medicinal experience: "Camillo—/ Preserver of my father, now of me, / The medicine of our house—how shall we do?" (IV. iv. 589-91).

Overall, Act V presents the miracle of transformation spoken of in IV. iv. The play moves through the purgation of language (V. i.) and advances experience into the realm of the ineffable (V. ii., V. iii.). With the return to Bohemia, the drama abounds with redemptive language. Cleomenes speaks of Leontes' "saintlike sorrow" and his being "redemmed"; and Leontes' who has been urged to "forgive" himself, later says "sorry" to Florizel several times. However, the antagonism between Paulina and Leontes (III. ii.) reappears, except this time the conflict is softened by the bittersweet remembrance of the past. Responding to Paulina's reminder that he "killed" Hermione, Leontes says "it is as bitter / Upon thy tongue as in my thought" (V. i. 18-19), and yet he realizes that Paulina "hast the memory of Hermione." Now, having purged Leontes' language Paulina becomes the oracle; her recommendation to Leontes about marriage closely resembles the oracle's

edict: "That / Shall be when your first queen's again in health / Never till then." But memory is pushed into an even higher realm, one beyond speech where madness is "divinest sense" (IV. iv. 486-88). Though Leontes welcomes Florizel "as is the spring to th' earth" (displacing, in other words, the "winter" of the past), he is afraid that his former madness will re-emerge with Florizel's appearance:

>   Sure
> When I shall see this gentleman, thy speeches
> Will bring me to consider that which may
> Unfurnish me of reason.
>   (V. i. 120-23)

But the play's final appeal rests with the restorative power of remembrance: Leontes becomes the advocate of Florizel's love and arbitrates what he formerly repudiated—the union of father and son, a motif as old as life.

Language, the center of Leontes' disease, has been cleansed, and with this purgation there occurs in V. ii. the celebration of a new level of perception. Reason is set aside; the limitations of language are dramatized; the way for belief—assent *without* proof—is prepared. The miraculous converges with the ineffable:

> They seemed almost, with staring on one another,
> to tear the cases of their eyes. There was speech in
> their dumbness, language in their very gesture; they
> looked as they had heard of a world ransomed, or
> one destroyed.
>   (V. ii. 12-17)

Later in this scene the Third Gentleman asks the Second, "Did you see the meeting of the two kings?" and when he answers "no," the Third Gentleman replies, "Then have you lost a sight which was to be seen, cannot be spoken of." Still later the Third Gentleman continues, "I have never heard of such another encounter, which lames report to follow it, and undoes description to do it." All this amounts to a preparation for the highest madness, enacted through Hermione's "resurrection"—namely, the perception of the unity of being.

Looking back, one can trace this ever-widening perception of transformation by charting a line beginning with the divisions of language, seen at first as an aspect of the "unreal," later modulated by the introduction of art, and finally explicitly presented through its dramatic reciprocal—the resurrection of Hermione. In the first instance (I.ii.) the division is all too evident:

>   Thy intention stabs the center.
> Thou dost make possible things not so held,
> Communicat'st with dreams—how can this be?—
> With what's unreal thou coactive art,
> And fellow'st nothing. (I. ii. 138-42)

In IV. iv. the mediating function of art, its power to "make possible things not so held," is presented; and art is clearly able to overcome the opposed forces that Leontes' suspicion cannot contain:

> You see sweet maid, we marry
> A gentler scion to the wildest stock,
> And make conceive a bark of baser kind
> By bud of nobler race. This is an art
> Which does mend Nature, change it rather; but
> The art itself is Nature.
>
> (IV. iv. 92-97)

Finally, in V. iii. Leontes, stunned by Hermione's re-emergence into life, concludes:

> No settled senses of the world can match
> The pleasure of that madness. Let't alone.
>
> (V. iii. 72-73)

Art *is* nature, for Hermione's statue lives. The "vast" no longer exists.

One more comment about the play and then I will "Let 't alone." In a sense, the conclusions to *Much Ado* and *The Winter's Tale* are similar. The rebirth of Hero and Hermione is dependent on the purgation of language. We are told about Hero, "She died, my lord, but whiles her slander lived"; and early in *The Winter's Tale* (I. ii, 94) Hermione utters a similar formulation: "Our praises are our wages." Yet the mode of perception in *The Winter's Tale* is different, in that, as one character says, "Every wink of an eye some new grace will be born." In a word, where the earlier comedies tentatively establish the need for a belief beyond understanding, *The Winter's Tale* uncovers the articulate silence of the peace that passes all understanding.

Notes

[1] My approach to Shakespeare's use of language in *The Winter's Tale* partly grows out of my essay on Chaucer, "Chaucer's *Parlement of Foules:* Aesthetic Order and Individual Experience," *TSLL* (Fall 1968), pp. 349-58.

[2] All textual references are to Frank Kermode's edition of *The Winter's Tale* (New American Library, 1963). Although I have refrained from citing secondary sources in this essay, I would like to express my special indebtedness to the work of C.L. Barber, Northrop Frye, G. Wilson Knight, Susanne Langer, and D.A. Traversi.

Stanton B. Garner, Jr. (essay date 1985)

SOURCE: "Time and Presence in *The Winter's Tale*," in *Modern Language Quarterly,* Vol. 46, No. 4, December, 1985, pp. 347-67.

[*In the following essay, Garner analyzes* The Winter's Tale *in terms of two temporal aspects—the change and consequences of time, and the moment unaffected by it—and extends his discussion to the interpenetration of these aspects during the statue scene.*]

Literally as well as figuratively, Time stands at the center of *The Winter's Tale,* giving strikingly emblematic stage life to a theme that had resonated in Shakespeare's imagination since the sonnets and the earliest plays, through the often turbulent drama of the playwright's middle years, and into the romances, those strangely fabulous works that play variations on all that came before. The confusions of Syracuse and Illyria sort themselves out in the movements of time; Richard of Gloucester and Macbeth draw back to seize time's promise; an aging poet reminds his younger friend—still in its graces—of time's quiet ravages: "That time of year thou mayst in me behold / When yellow leaves, or none, or few, do hang. . . . "[1] Though time constitutes an organizing motif in Shakespeare's nondramatic work, as this last example makes clear, its presence is structurally more central to the world of the plays, where characters must confront dramatic time—its threats as well as its opportunities—as it unfolds in the present, and where actors must navigate through the temporal movement of performance. In drama, time is a theme by necessity, for in the medium of performance it stands as an inescapable backdrop to dramatic action, as well as a fundamental condition of theatrical life.

The Winter's Tale—with its memories, fond and bitter, its plans and prophecies, its tales and ballads, and its striking leap of sixteen years—reveals this temporal background with a prominence and self-consciousness unusual even in Shakespeare. In keeping with the other pairs that serve to organize this dramatic diptych (Sicilia and Bohemia, youth and age, Nature and Art, rosemary and rue), *The Winter's Tale* presents the experience of time in terms of a duality—one that edges into paradox. On the one hand, man lives in the present, a moment so complete in its immediacy that it seems to escape time entirely. This experience of the Now, and all its apparent eternity, infuses Polixenes' description of the childhood innocence that he and Leontes shared:

> We were, fair queen,
> Two lads that thought there was no more
>   behind
> But such a day to-morrow as to-day,
> And to be boy eternal.
>
> (I.ii.62-65)

His lines subvert the very idea of time, for the words "behind," "to-morrow," and "to-day" work upon each other in such a way that their distinctions, which underlie the notion of temporal succession, blend and dissolve, warping past and future into the seemingly boundless expanse of the present, opening the moment into eternity.

For all its apparent timelessness, however, this Edenic state is a memory, telescoped into what Prospero calls "the dark backward and abysm of time," in part by the very tense through which it is articulated. The stage presence of Leontes and Polixenes, both adults, constitutes a pressing visual reminder of Time's hourglass, where the present is barely an instant, gone before it can be grasped. As Time boasts,

> I witness to
> The times that brought them in; so shall I do
> To th' freshest things now reigning, and make
>   stale
> The glistering of this present, as my tale
> Now seems to it.
>
>   (IV.i.11-15)

His speech recalls the temporal world of the sonnets, where existence is subject to the ironies of mutability as it plays its movement from "glistering" to "staleness"—a world where "every thing that grows / Holds in perfection but a little moment" (Sonnet 15, lines 1-2). From this vantage point, time confronts man with the fact of change and with the inevitability of consequence, since action, in the temporal realm, always has outcomes, foreseen or unforeseen: "I, that please some, try all, both joy and terror / Of good and bad, that makes and unfolds error . . ." (IV.i.1-2). The contrast is pronounced: if the present in *The Winter's Tale* is the realm of an almost prelapsarian joy, time is the province of memory and anticipation, nostalgia and eagerness, regret and foreboding.

This duality of man's experience—immediate and temporal—is highlighted during the course of *The Winter's Tale,* most pointedly in the play's second half, where characters are forced to come to terms with time's changes and consequences. But the sixteen-year gap signaled by Time's appearance is only one of many instances in which temporal change dramatically and ironically counterpoints the present. Down to the level of individual lines, like those fondly spoken by Polixenes, the play displays a temporal intricacy rivaled, perhaps, only by Shakespeare's other romances. As William Archer noted early this century, Shakespearean drama is generally characterized by little exposition:[2] unlike the drama of Sophocles or Ibsen, its action lies largely within a present that moves forward to its culmination. But the past bears on the present of the play through a number of subtler inclusions: the childhood of the two kings; the courtship of Hermione; the Old Shepherd's wife; the man who "Dwelt by a churchyard," frozen in Mamillius' "sad tale" (II.i.25-32); numerous moments of story and remembrance. This layering of past on present, and present on past, becomes more pronounced as the very stage moment

in which the characters move is set against the broader passage of years. As *The Winter's Tale* progresses, in other words, it acquires—like *Pericles, Cymbeline,* and *The Tempest*—a temporal double vision strangely reminiscent of the opening lines of a fourth-century Chinese poem: "Swiftly the years, beyond recall. / Solemn the stillness of this fair morning."[3]

But Shakespeare's investigation of the relationship between the present and its temporal contexts is not restricted to the play's dramatic world; it extends, as well, to his audience's temporal experience of the play in performance—an experience that significantly parallels, in its duality, the experience of the play's characters. Drama unfolds in time, unmediated by the authorial "voice" of literary narrative, and it accordingly places specific demands on audience comprehension of its developing action. For one thing, spectators must impose coherence on the stage events they witness—locate the present within a specific framework of "dramatic time," construct a past out of planted clues, and project possible outcomes to complete this temporal whole. At the same time, like dramatic characters, spectators are faced—during performance—with a stage present which is actual, changing, always somewhat outside the temporal structures created to enclose it. Shakespearean drama is built, in part, out of the tension between these two poles of the audience's theatrical experience: in the irony with which we watch a stage event, aware of all its contexts and consequences, and—often most powerfully—in those moments when the stage reveals itself with an immediacy beyond such frameworks of comprehension. Lear howls blankly over the dead Cordelia, Feste fills the theater with the music of his lute—at these points the stage acquires a momentary autonomy, a presence slightly beyond time, which lasts until the audience returns the moment to its temporal outlines.

As a medium that fuses narrative with physical actuality, the theater engages the twin experiences of time and presence in unusually strong counterpoint. It is not surprising, therefore, that *The Winter's Tale*—Shakespeare's most explicit treatment of time—should manipulate these experiences, not only in its dramatic action, but also in its theatrical effect. As Inga-Stina Ewbank rightly observes, "while in *The Winter's Tale* time has largely disappeared from the verbal imagery, it is all the more intensely present as a controlling and shaping figure behind the dramatic structure and technique."[4] In general, close study of Shakespearean structure and technique—and of the ways in which these dramatic elements shape response—demonstrates how fully his plays ground thematic issues within the theatrical experience, and how essential this experience is to dramatic meaning. This article will trace Shakespeare's dramaturgical balancing, in *The Winter's Tale,* of time's rhythms with a dramatic and theatrical present that can never be fully "staled." In doing so, it will suggest that this strange but powerful play forges clear experiential links between the dramatic action on stage and the stage's "action" on its audience.[5]

When Time exits from the middle of *The Winter's Tale,* he leaves a dramatic world disrupted by his passage. For the play's characters, time's impact is concentrated in "that wide gap" (IV.i.7) between the dramatic present and the events of the first three acts, a span during which, as Time informs us, Leontes has continued to mourn "Th' effects of his fond jealousies" (18) and during which Perdita and Florizel have grown up. The past, though, bears differently upon different characters. Those who have lived through it—the members of the now older generation—have hardened themselves against time by maintaining a sharp remembrance of its losses, a remembrance that they are nonetheless powerless to erase. Camillo misses Sicilia and still feels bonds of loyalty to Leontes, whose "sorrows" remain so tangible that Camillo calls them "feeling" (IV.ii.7-8). Polixenes, too, lives in memory, burdened with a past that refuses to fade:

> Of that fatal country Sicilia, prithee speak no more, whose very naming punishes me with the remembrance of that penitent (as thou call'st him) and reconcil'd king, my brother, whose loss of his most precious queen and children are even now to be afresh lamented. (20-25)

Time, for these three, only fixes the memory of what has been lost, and in these losses the past seems more real than the present which has taken its place.

Polixenes, however, has more recent concerns to temper his bitterness. Shifting from friend to father, he urges Camillo to accompany him on a mission to discover the cause of his son's disappearance from court. The scene likewise shifts, and before the two arrive at the Shepherd's cottage the stage is given to Perdita and Florizel, who demonstrate a markedly different sense of past and present. Neither is burdened by the events at Sicilia, and both show an attitude toward their more immediate pasts unlike that of their elders. Perdita says nothing of her early years as a shepherdess, and Florizel hides the signs of his past by donning rustic clothes. To Perdita's concern over his father's disapproval of their match, he replies by affirming a love outside such threat and its consequences, modulating between the languages of present and future:

> To this I am most constant,
> Though destiny say no. Be merry, gentle!
> Strangle such thoughts as these with any thing
> That you behold the while. Your guests are
>   coming:
> Lift up your countenance, as it were the day
> Of celebration of that nuptial, which
> We two have sworn shall come.
>
> (IV.iv.45-51)

Both are characterized by this forward-gazing anticipation, conceiving of the future as a never-ending continuation of the present, free of change, with "such a day to-morrow as to-day." In their innocence they dwell on this present and on the sounds, objects, and gestures that constitute it. Florizel's description etches Perdita within the moment:

> Each your doing
> (So singular in each particular)
> Crowns what you are doing in the present
>   deeds.
> That all your acts are queens.
>
> (143-46)

Perdita, more the realist, nevertheless allows hope to "strangle such thoughts." "O Lady Fortune," she exclaims, "Stand you auspicious!" (51-52).

When Polixenes and Camillo enter disguised and the sheep-shearing scene gets under way, the stage contains a mixture of attitudes toward time and its relationship to the present. On the one hand, it presents the lovers, with their sense of the immediate and their vision of possibility; on the other, it presents the king and counsellor, aged by time and scarred by its memories, their awareness of consequence a potential threat to Perdita and Florizel. By this point in the play, though, the audience has had its own experience of dramatic time shifted and modulated, through techniques more subtle than the mere passage of years. Theatrical versions of immediacy and temporality are counterpointed throughout the play's development—often in sharp juxtaposition, as we can see if we review the audience's comprehension of dramatic time in the first three acts. There is, for instance, the play's beginning, in which the stage image of friendship between Polixenes and Leontes—the present's version of the past's innocence—is abruptly dispelled by the King's distorted jealousy. William H. Matchett points out sexual ambiguities in the lines between Polixenes and Hermione and claims that the audience is made to feel suspicious (pp. 94-98), but these ambiguities are subliminal and largely recollected, if at all, in light of Leontes' misinterpretation of them.[6] Vastly more pronounced is our sense of their "timeless" friendship—of which Archidamus has said "I think there is not in the world either malice or matter to alter it" (I.i.33-34) and of which Polixenes has described the childhood origins. The initial stage interaction between the characters does little to dispel these accounts: gracefulness and compliment characterize the beginning of the scene, and the "gestural dialogue" of hands that Charles Frey discerns throughout the play (pp. 134-38) here expresses bond and affection. When Leontes' *"tremor cordis"* does appear, it constitutes an intrusion of dissonance into the scene's easiness, and the stage present becomes abruptly shadowed by the disturbing threat of consequence: "I am angling now, / Though you perceive me not how I give line" (I.ii.180-81). The words "angling" and "line" are revealing, for it is the essence of Leontes' jealousy to form imaginary connections between people and between incidents, quickly generating a web of misperception and suspicion that includes even Mamillius and Camillo. As Leontes begins to act on these misperceptions, consequences multiply with rigorous inevitability, and the stage present becomes increasingly pressured by a network of events, imaginary as well as real.

One of the most remarkable features of the developing Sicilia sequence is its tightness and autonomy; omitting Perdita's survival, it could stand by itself, brief but complete. Its incidents are relentlessly forward-moving and continuous. For one thing, the narrative line of Leontes' jealousy and its effects is—to an extent unusual even in Shakespearean tragedy—unrelieved by breaks. Hermione's exchange with Mamillius constitutes only 32 lines, and the scene in which Cleomines and Dion describe their visit to Delphos is shorter still (22 lines). Far from serving as self-contained interruptions, both are themselves interrupted, and swallowed up, by the omnivorous main action: the former by Leontes' entrance, the latter by a reminder of the proclamations against Hermione. For another thing, incidents and details are introduced and linked with a high degree of narrative continuity. Shakespeare changed the source material of *Pandosto* to increase the "probability" of the story's incidents,[7] and he did so, in part, by tightening its plot connections: whereas Greene's young prince Garinter dies suddenly, for instance, Shakespeare's Mamillius sickens and dies specifically out of grief concerning his mother's situation. This tight sense of antecedents and consequences focuses audience attention even more closely on the unfolding narrative sequence, on dramatic time in its actual and potential outlines.

The sequence concludes with a pronounced note of closure, heightened by the rapidity with which its final events take place. The oracle's tersely declarative pronouncements reveal the truth concerning the preceding actions, a truth which the audience and all the characters save Leontes have known. Entering with news of Hermione's death, Paulina condemns his folly by outlining the consequences of his misconceived actions on Polixenes, Camillo, his abandoned daughter, Mamillius, and Hermione: "O, think what they have done, / And then run mad indeed—stark mad!" (III.ii.182-83). Her speech rings with summary force and—together with Leontes' heartbroken resolve to bury his wife and son in a single grave, to display an account of the "causes of their death" (237), and to visit it every day for the rest of his life—it gives the sequence of the play's Sicilian first half what J. H. P. Pafford has called "a Miltonic close fitting for the end of a tragedy" (p. lv).[8]

"The King shall live without an heir, if that which is lost be not found" (III.ii.134-36). A strand remains incomplete—an opening, as it were, in the closed sequence of action and its consequence which the audience has followed for over two acts. With Antigonus' entrance in III.iii, the narrative line continues. But the audience's temporal comprehension of the play's events and its orientation toward the stage and its actions shift in two important ways. First, attention no longer centers on the inevitable triumph of truth and the stripping away of a central character's delusion. Throughout the Sicilian sequence, the audience has had a kind of Olympian distance from Leontes' jealousy, secure in its awareness of the actual state of events. The audience, in other words, stands in the position of superior awareness that Bertrand Evans considers one of the characteristic dramatic principles of Shakespearean drama;[9] and although its awareness is far from complete, the audience's understanding of temporal outlines is more closely aligned to that of Time than to that of any of the action's participants. Once the truth is revealed, though, subsequent action becomes open-ended: although the oracle's pronouncement suggests further resolution, this final clause is cast as a riddle and contains no details as to how the resolution might be achieved. Uncertainty, therefore, replaces inevitability; the outcome of events becomes less determinate, less subject to rigorously constrained consequence. Evans's ironic awareness is replaced by uncertainty, and the audience, like Perdita, is left in the wilderness—a wilderness, in this case, of the stage and its unpredictability.[10]

Second, the coherent narrative of the first part is replaced by a remarkable sequence of incidents, each of which is characterized by a striking immediacy, and all of which stand in sharp juxtaposition to each other. Immediacy is achieved partly through a dazzling array of "theatrical" effects—effects of sound, movement, and spectacle that display the stage at its most physical. Such effects are strikingly absent from the Sicilian sequence of the play's first half. Although the earlier sequence is characterized, as Daniel Seltzer points out, by numerous examples of "intimate stage business" between characters,[11] there is nothing to compare with the storm effects (suggested by the text), the bear, the sound of hunting horns, or the archaic staginess of Time's entrance. The immediacy of the sequence's incidents is heightened by their almost Brechtian juxtaposition: the mixture of tones and effects gives each a kind of discontinuous autonomy on stage, and this sudden, unprepared-for variety—following the vastly more streamlined narrative of the first half—forces abrupt, disorienting shifts in audience response.

Matchett observes that this sequence wrenches us "from our response to the plot and the action to a wider perspective. . . . Challenging our awareness, it opens us to fresh experience" (p. 101). He discusses this shift in terms of the art/nature opposition, but his observations apply still more valuably to the basic level of audience attention that this sequence engages. On this level, the sense of "fresh experience" is a result of elements that draw attention away from broader temporal outlines and heighten the autonomy of individual stage moments, much as the storm scene does to the dramatic world of *King Lear*. Such "fresh experience" in Shakespearean drama (and in drama generally) is that experience uniquely available in the theater: an experience of a stage present existing in its own right, intruding itself into the very "tales" that dramatists make it tell. When Time stands forward to signal the leap of years, in other words, he addresses an audience that is already undergoing its own experiential leap—from comprehension and irony to bewilderment and surprise—in the face of a stage turned strange and new.

As with the graceful present of the play's first scene, this scenic presence is dispelled, distanced. The couplets of Time's soliloquy telescope the seacoast sequence into the past and return the audience to the play's main narrative line. But this line, with its rigid chain of consequence, has been weakened by the appearance of incidents and stage elements outside its projected outcomes, and the theatrical moment in all its presence and autonomy looms large in time's subsequent developments. Indeed, the stage is now set for one of the longest scenes of stage presence in all of Shakespeare: the "sheep-shearing" scene. Interestingly, this scene is introduced three times—by Time, by Polixenes and Camillo, and by Autolycus—and each introduction contributes a "timelessness" to the scene. The first two are usually viewed as "connective" scenes, linking past and present, and indeed (as we have seen) each does include references to the play's first half. Oddly, though, these references are less conjunctive than disjunctive: Time's reference to Leontes, after all, is offered to take "leave" of him (IV.i.17), and Polixenes finally urges Camillo to "lay aside/the thoughts of Sicilia" (IV.ii.51-52). Both scenes look ahead to Florizel and Perdita, and both do so, in part, by distancing the past. The result is that the sheep-shearing scene bears few reminders of the Sicilian past. Even the Bohemian past is made less consequential to the scene: Shakespeare omits the marriage plans that Greene's Egistus made for his son Dorastus and has Polixenes visit the Shephered's cottage as much from curiosity as from suspicion.

The third introduction to the sheep-shearing scene also introduces one of its main participants. Despite the number of critical attempts to integrate Autolycus into the play's thematic structure,[12] this stage rogue continues to baffle the play's readers (while delighting its spectators). He is introduced later (IV.iii) than probably any other major Shakespearean character, yet he plays no part in the play's concluding scene. He becomes almost a *genius* of the Whitsun pastoral, yet he was once a member of Florizel's retinue—a detail introduced so casually (between stanzas of a song) that

it risks being missed. But if we put aside attempts to incorporate Autolycus into the play's thematic framework and concentrate instead on his stage presence, his *dramatic* function in the play (and in the sheep-shearing scene in particular) becomes clearer. In a play that counterpoints modes of time and presence, Autolycus represents life (and drama) at their most theatrically immediate.

Speaking to the Clown in a self-dramatizing third-person, Autolycus characterizes himself as a figure of Protean identity:

> I know this man well; he hath been since an ape-bearer, then a process-server, a bailiff, then he compass'd a motion of the Prodigal Son, and married a tinker's wife within a mile where my land and living lies; and, having flown over many knavish professions, he settled only in rogue. Some call him Autolycus. (IV.iii.94-100)

On stage he displays a similar fluidity of roles, moving between them with an improvisational randomness that suggests his opportunism and delight in mischief. Like the Vice figures of earlier morality drama—or like Ben Jonson's comic knaves—he plays upon the moment, and the impulsiveness of his actions makes them strikingly self-contained. His major contribution to the main plot (discovering the Old Shepherd's secret and deciding to act on it) originates largely out of whim: "Though I am not naturally honest, I am so sometimes by chance" (IV.iv.712-13). Moreover, his incessant acting and his tumbling prose are charged with a vibrant self-assertiveness that draws attention away from more serious matters and toward himself. His wonder at the rustics' response to his ballads—"No hearing, no feeling, but my sir's song, and admiring the nothing of it" (IV.iv.612-13)—captures much of the distracting effect of his stage presence as a whole. Like the wares he hawks, Autolycus himself is largely an "unconsider'd trifle" (IV.iii.26), "inconsequential" in the strictest sense.

His appearance before and during the sheep-shearing scene, then, contributes to its self-contained immediacy: along with the shepherds' dance which precedes him and the "Saltiers" who succeed him, his presence during the scene—with his "ribbons of all colors i' th' rainbow" (204-5), songs and ballads, and other antics—provides some of the play's most frenetic stage activity. Even before Autolycus' entrance as ballad-monger, this scene has drawn characters and audience alike into an experience of less consequential timelessness. Among the characters, the past is suspended almost by consent: as we have seen, Polixenes and Camillo dismiss memories of Sicilia, and Perdita and Florizel "strangle" thoughts of his superior rank. Time and its effects (as well as its threat) remain present during the scene, especially in the disguised visitors, but the emphasis is on the moment, and even age is brought within its domain. Matching Florizel's "time-less" admiration, Camillo tells Perdita: "I should leave grazing, were I of your flock, / And only live by gazing" (109-10). Polixenes, too, participates in the festival atmosphere to an extent not generally acknowledged in discussions of the scene; his famous debate with Perdita concerning the "streak'd gillyvors"—for all its potential allusion to Perdita's station and its implications—is largely playful, a quality more evident in the theater than in the text, and one that tends to undercut threat. Moreover, when later in the scene the Clown remarks, "My father and the gentlemen are in sad talk" (310), Polixenes is "refreshed" enough by the entertainment to request the Saltiers. It would be a mistake to claim that Polixenes "forgets" his mission, even temporarily, but it would also be a mistake to neglect the extent to which even he surrenders to his disguise and submits to the scene and its diversions. Both visitors could, with truth, join Perdita in her confession: "Methinks I play as I have seen them do/ In Whitsun pastorals. Sure this robe of mine / Does change my disposition" (133-35).

It is important to stress that the audience, too, is offered a "fresh experience" of the stage present, one that tends to subsume awareness of time and its consequences. Francis Berry claims that the audience, remembering the play's first half, "frames" the sheep-shearing scene and modifies its response to the lovers "in the light of their parents' . . . experience."[13] But pictorial metaphors such as this are misleading, since the theater is a temporal, as well as a spatial medium: earlier moments are rapidly distanced in performance, and memory often requires explicit reminders if it is to "frame" the stage present with past action. Such reminders are few, and the audience's awareness of threat is subordinated, in large part, to the scene's compelling immediacy—an immediacy heightened by the timeless love of Perdita and Florizel, by Autolycus' antics, and by a gracefulness of gesture that finds its natural culmination in dance. The audience may never completely abandon its apprehensive detachment from the lovers, but we must not underestimate how much the stage draws all who watch into its easiness.

With the exit of the dancing Saltiers, however, and Polixenes' interruption of the festivities, the audience is abruptly returned to an awareness of consequence and the claims that time exerts on the present. If Leontes' earlier attack of jealousy is painful because of the idyllic picture we have been given of his childhood friendship with Polixenes, the latter's remark to Camillo—"'Tis time to part them" (344)—is even more chilling, because we have been given an extended stage version of such carefreeness. Polixenes' subsequent explosion, like Prospero's truncation of his wedding masque, completes the disillusionment for the audience and for Perdita and Florizel, returning the audience to its awareness of consequence as it returns the

lovers to the realities of their disparate stations. Perdita tells Florizel,

> Beseech you
> Of your own state take care. This dream of
> mine
> Being now awake, I'll queen it no inch farther,
> But milk my ewes, and weep.
>
> (447-50)

Just as Time makes "stale" the "glistering" present, so Polixenes' rage makes the festival timelessness seem itself a dream.

When Camillo persuades the lovers to sail to Sicilia, the audience returns one last time to the play's broader narrative outline, reassuming a more privileged distance concerning events. But, relieved of the tragic irony of the first three acts, the audience now enjoys a new perspective of comic irony. Possessed of the secret of Perdita's recovery, the audience watches the characters—each of whom lacks at least one piece of information—move toward a reconciliation with romance inevitability. All converge on Sicilia—Florizel with Perdita, Polixenes with Camillo, Autolycus with the rustics and their secret. Audience attention centers on the logic of events, which unfolds with a neatness both providential and artistic; time, "that makes and unfolds error," begins to right the situation, and the audience is allowed the omniscience to appreciate its workings. Anticipation runs high, looking forward to a reconciliation that will redeem the present from the apparent irrevocability of the past, awaiting the wonder on the part of the characters when the apparently miraculous is disclosed.

It is part of the dramaturgical brilliance of *The Winter's Tale* that these expectations are at once fulfilled, unfulfilled, and more than fulfilled. On the one hand, the Gentlemen who report the reunion between Leontes and Perdita underscore the miracle of the encounter, calling it "so like an old tale, that the verity of it is in strong suspicion" (V.ii.28-29). On the other hand, despite the attempt of Nevill Coghill to defend the effectiveness of these messenger speeches (p. 39), if there is any clear *scène à faire* in the play, the disclosure of Perdita's identity is it, since, in fulfilling the oracle's prophecy, it gives Leontes an heir, Florizel a wife, and Perdita a royal family. The reunion effects a reconciliation between age and youth, past and present, Sicilia and Bohemia. Such a scene, the audience expects to *see;* ironically, the messenger scene is disappointing precisely because *The Winter's Tale* is not a tale, but a play, and a play's most powerful moments are stage moments. The very quality of the reunion which "lames report to follow it, and undoes description to do it" (57-58) is that quality of immediacy which the stage provides. We want the scene to be a dramatic present, not deflected into a narrative past.[14]

The usual justification for the messenger scene is that the reunion is described to lend focus to the final scene, but this explanation underestimates both the disappointment of the former and the theatrical coup of the latter. For the audience, there is no play beyond this reunion; at least this is what the earlier scenes have indicated. The oracle's only prophecy concerns the lost child, as does Time's anticipation of the play's second half:

> What of her ensues
> I list not prophesy; but let Time's news
> Be known when 'tis brought forth. A
>   shepherd's daughter,
> And what to her adheres, which follows after,
> Is th' argument of Time.
>
> (IV.i.25-29)

In terms of the audience's expectations since the shipwreck, Perdita's return represents the projected end of the narrative movement, and the audience has anticipated it as final. To extend the play beyond this promised conclusion is to press stage action, once again, beyond the apparent confines of plot.

We have been studying *The Winter's Tale* in terms of two interrelating experiences: that of time, understood through its effects of change and consequence, and that of the moment, experienced as something seemingly beyond these effects. We have explored, too, how the play represents a complex dramaturgical manipulation of temporality as it is experienced within performance—drawing attention away from narrative outlines into the stage present, distancing the present by the perceived intrusion of time and its effects. In the play's own vocabulary, occasioned by Perdita's gift of "rosemary and rue" to the disguised king and counsellor, we have been exploring the interacting rhythms of something like "Grace and remembrance" (IV.iv.76) and the ways in which Shakespeare builds these rhythms into the play's dramaturgy and stagecraft. The statue scene, justly praised as one of the culminations of Shakespeare's art, represents the play's crowning interpenetration of these two poles of temporal experience.

As in *The Tempest,* the final reunion of this play is orchestrated by a master of ceremonies in command of the secrets behind all events. When Paulina reappears with Leontes in the fifth act, however, she does so, not as a provider of second chances, but as a spokesman for memory, keeping fresh the remembrance of an apparently irretrievable past and feeding its hold on the present with almost unpleasant insistence. Cleomines appeals to Leontes to "Do as the heavens have done, forget your evil, / With them, forgive yourself" (V.i.5-6), and Dion urges him to consider his heirless kingdom; but Paulina, who "hast the memory of Hermione . . . in honor" (50-51), pressures his conscience with the claims of the past:[15]

> Were I the ghost that walk'd, I'ld bid you
>   mark
> Her eye, and tell me for what dull part in't
> You chose her; then I'ld shriek, that even
>   your ears
> Should rift to hear me, and the words that
>   follow'd
> Should be "Remember mine."
>
> (63-67)

After sixteen years, in other words, she appears as a rather grim spokesman for time's irrevocability. To the servant's praise of Perdita's beauty, Paulina laments:

> O Hermione,
> As every present time doth boast itself
> Above a better gone, so must thy grave
> Give way to what's seen now!
>
> (95-98)

Her lines deny the possibility that loss can ever be replaced, or that the present can in any way heal the past. At the same time, unknown to Leontes and to the audience, these lines are half-truths, since the play's conclusion will dramatize a transcendence of memory and a better "present" that will fill time's grave. In their paradoxical truths and untruths, Paulina's lines anticipate the transformation of time that structures the statue scene itself.

This transformation is seamless in its movement from one temporal vision to the other. Leontes' initial response to the statue unveiled before him is one of acute "remembrance" of a past so cunningly recreated in stone that its image is resurrected, with equal vividness, in memory: "O, thus she stood, / Even with such life of majesty (warm life, / As now it coldly stands), when first I woo'd her!" (V.iii.34-36). The statue, in short, confronts Leontes with the past and with his responsibility for its loss, while paradoxically bringing it so vividly into the present that this loss seems to vanish. As he continues to gaze, the harsh line between past and present blurs, shading the memorial presence of the statue into the living presence of Hermione. In a word that reverberates throughout the scene, time's apparent irrevocability is "mocked" by a reappearance that seemingly occurs outside time's laws, and memory is both dissolved and brought to life in the face of the present's revelation. With this dramatic stroke, Shakespeare steps beyond Aristotle, whose third form of anagnorisis bears striking resemblance to the statue scene:

> The third kind of recognition is through memory: we see one thing and recall another, as a character in the *Cyprians* of Dicaeogenes saw the picture and wept, or the recognition scene in the lay of Alcinous, where Odysseus listens to the bard and weeps at his memories, and this leads to the recognition.[16]

Act V, scene iii. Camillo, Leontes, Paulina, Florizel, Polixenes, Perdita, and Hermione. Frontispiece to the Rowe edition (1709).

speare withholds a narrative detail the revelation of which transforms both the outcome of the play and the significance of what has preceded it.

That the play hinges on such a deception is, by now, a commonplace in criticism of *The Winter's Tale*. But, like many Shakespearean commonplaces, its implications for audience response, and Shakespeare's manipulation of this response, remain imperfectly understood, even though (as this article has tried to suggest) dramaturgical decisions invariably adjust the audience's relationship with the developing stage action. Most obviously, the audience is forced into a collective experience which mirrors that of the stage characters, and chiefly that of Leontes, whose discovery constitutes the scene's focus. Like Leontes, the audience is initially forced into its own moment of remembrance. It matters little at what point the audience realizes that Hermione is alive; when the statue shows signs of life, the audience scans its memories, recalling the play's earlier scenes, trying to find the connections that could justify a development so beyond expectation. Hermione explains to Perdita that she remained in hiding to await the fulfillment of the oracle's prophecy, but this detail—like all others in the closing scene—is subsumed in the moment itself, luminous in its freedom from expectation. In place of the ironic superiority over characters that audiences usually enjoy during such dramatic reconciliations, Shakespeare creates a theatrical experience that we have no word for, an experience that constitutes the *opposite* of irony, for in this instant, as the statue becomes that which it has commemorated, the present is suddenly vastly *more* than we thought—fuller and richer, freed from irony's frameworks.

By setting the statue scene outside the audience's comprehension of plot and time, in other words, and by making the stage action, literally, beyond the anticipation that has sought to contain it, Shakespeare allows the stage itself, one last time, to assume a heightened autonomy and presence. As in the sheep-shearing scene, attention is directed toward individual objects, movements, and gestures, carefully orchestrated by dramatic speech highlighting the particular.[17] Polixenes' "The very life seems warm upon her lip" (66) and Leontes' "The fixure of her eye has motion in't" (67) recall, in their specificity, Autolycus' ribbons, the "flow'rs of winter," and (most tellingly) Florizel's admiration of Perdita's movements:

> When you do dance, I wish you
> A wave o' th' sea, that you might ever do
> Nothing but that; move still, still so,
> And own no other function.
>
> (IV.iv.140-43)

Ewbank writes of this scene:

> Speeches are short, the diction plain, the language almost bare of imagery: as if Shakespeare is anxious

Recognition in *The Winter's Tale,* by contrast, moves beyond memory into the miraculous—it occurs when what is seen actually *becomes* what is recalled.

Paulina commands the statue to "Strike all that look upon with marvel" (100), and the final brilliance of Shakespeare's stagecraft in *The Winter's Tale* lies in the audience's inclusion in the striking marvel of this scene. The stage reconciliation that the audience was denied in V.iii takes place, but the disclosure that makes it possible—Hermione's survival—comes as a revelation for the audience as well as for the characters. The earlier image of Hermione falling to the stage floor, Paulina's confirmation of her death, Leontes' plans to bury her, and Antigonus' ghostlike dream-apparition (recalling "visitors from the dead" elsewhere in Shakespeare), all establish the queen's death as a dramatic reality for the audience, breaking sharply with Shakespeare's usual practice (in plays such as *Twelfth Night* and *Pericles*) of making his audience confidants to all secrets and partners to all contrivance. Much more in the manner of Beaumont and Fletcher, Shake-

not to distract attention from the significance of action and movement. . . . An unusual number of speeches are devoted just to underlining the emotions and postures of people on-stage, as in Paulina's words to Leontes: "I like your silence, it the more shows off Your wonder." (p. 97)

This shift of emphasis away from language and toward gesture is heightened by the audience's own attention on the actress playing Hermione, as it watches for signs of breathing and movement, trying to detect the gesture that will reveal whether or not Hermione lives. The final discovery of *The Winter's Tale,* then, lies in a surrender to the moment; and for the audience, this involves surrender to the stage moment, a moment in which the most riveting activity is pure gesture; outlined, almost pictorially, within the stage's stillness, and to which the most appropriate response is rapt attention and "wonder." Indeed, so self-contained is this moment in its theatrical immediacy that, with the accompanying music, gesture approaches the expressive fluidity of dance.

It is easy to see why the play's conclusion has tempted critics toward Christian interpretations of the play—especially in light of Paulina's reference to redemption from death and her pronouncement that "It is requir'd / You do awake your faith" (94-95), and in light of the word "grace," which recurs throughout the play like a musical motif.[18] Though strictly Christian frameworks are hard to attach to the play as a whole, the final scene is indeed charged with an almost religious sense of grace as something freely given, beyond desert. Hermione's reappearance provides characters and audience with a development beyond the apparent consequence of events as the play has suggested them, with "the experience of restoration after total loss" (Matchett, p. 106). In this sense, the scene is beyond time, or at least beyond time as it has constituted a reality in the minds of characters and audience alike. If time participates in the play's denouement, it is less the stock figure of the play's middle than a force of mystery, always outside comprehension's grasp, revealing itself in the miracles of the present. For the audience, grace is born in the "wink of an eye" (V.ii.110), when the stage action severs itself from rigorous connection with the "dramatic time" which has ruled for much of the play.

In the midst of its transformations, however, such grace is never completely free of remembrance. The first four acts have presented grace in terms of freshness, innocence, and simple gracefulness: Hermione has been called "a gracious innocent soul" (II.iii.29), and Perdita was first described as "now grown in grace / Equal with wond'ring" (IV.i.24-25). This grace, like the youth of Polixenes and Leontes, is timeless because it has not yet been subjected to change and consequence. The grace of the final scene, however, is richer because more dearly bought, and the passage of time out

of which it emerges leaves traces to spark remembrance. For one thing, the scene contains reminders of irreversible change. Hermione has grown old: "Hermione was not so much wrinkled, nothing / So aged as this seems" (28-29). And while Perdita has found a mother, she has also acquired a history, which, like Prospero's narration to Miranda in Act I of *The Tempest,* marks her emergence into a world that contains, among other things, time and its changes.

Also present are reminders of consequences not rescued from time. Paulina recalls the dead Antigonus with moving regret, and Leontes' decree that she should marry Camillo does not fully dispel this awareness of "wither'd" loss (133). Similarly, the scene lacks Mamillius, who actually *was* buried. Although he is never explicitly mentioned in the final scene, he has been mourned as recently as V.i, and his absence leaves the reunited family vaguely incomplete. While Florizel serves as a replacement for Mamillius, he is also a reminder of his loss. In other words, with its image of a world ransomed from time, the play's conclusion resolves the plot, but it nevertheless remains marked by the memory of that which time has destroyed.

In the play's closing lines, Leontes alludes to "this wide gap of time, since first / We were dissever'd" (154-55). Shakespeare's investigation of time in *The Winter's Tale* has left the audience with both poles of its temporal experience in balance. The audience has seen, in the end, that time's effects are inescapable, since action, for all the world's miracles, does have consequences. Nor can one escape the reality of change in a sublunary world ruled by mutability's "staling" hand. Whitsuntide must end: Perdita and Florizel enter the cycle of the generations, and Autolycus, after his appearance in the penultimate scene, simply vanishes. Nonetheless, through Shakespeare's manipulation of the stage and its possibilities, the audience feels the rigor of time open, again and again, into a stage presence always slightly beyond time's changes and consequences. Sicilia gives way to the wilderness of Bohemia; Polixenes, in spite of his age and station, succumbs in part both to the festival's liveliness and Perdita's charm. Most of all, in the play's final stroke, the audience discovers that, when it tries to predict time's outlines and outcomes, it risks amazement—that the present can mock, not only consequence, but comprehension as well.

Notes

[1] Sonnet 73, lines 1-2. Quotations from Shakespeare are taken from *The Riverside Shakespeare,* ed. G. Blakemore Evans (Boston: Houghton Mifflin, 1974).

[2] "In sum, then, it was Shakespeare's usual practice, histories apart, to bring the whole action of his plays within the frame of the picture, leaving little or noth-

ing to narrative exposition" (*Play-Making: A Manual of Craftsmanship* [New York: Dodd, Mead, 1912], p. 98).

[3] T'ao Ch'ien (A.D. 365-427), in *A Hundred and Seventy Chinese Poems,* trans. Arthur Waley (New York: Alfred A. Knopf, 1919), p. 116; quoted (with slight inaccuracy) and discussed in William Empson, *Seven Types of Ambiguity* (London: Chatto and Windus, 1930), pp. 30-32.

[4] "The Triumph of Time in 'The Winter's Tale,'" *REL,* 5, No. 2 (1964): 84.

[5] Investigating this connection brings us into the company of those critics who have already begun to explore this play's dramaturgy and stagecraft: Nevill Coghill, "Six Points of Stage-Craft in *The Winter's Tale,*" *ShS,* 11 (1958): 31-41; William H. Matchett, "Some Dramatic Techniques in 'The Winter's Tale,'" *ShS,* 22 (1969): 93-107; Barbara A. Mowat, *The Dramaturgy of Shakespeare's Romances* (Athens: University of Georgia Press, 1976); and Charles Frey, *Shakespeare's Vast Romance: A Study of "The Winter's Tale"* (Columbia and London: University of Missouri Press, 1980). *The Winter's Tale* has made itself available to some of the finest "theatrical" readings in Shakespearean criticism, perhaps because (as we have long sensed) its dramatic effects depend, more than those of other plays, on its realization in performance. The statue scene alone has been an important school for such readings.

[6] Shakespeare, after all, makes the relationship between Hermione and Polixenes much less "ambiguous" than Greene did in *Pandosto,* where Bellaria, "willing to shew how unfainedly she loved her husband, by his friends entertainment, used him likewise so familiarly, that her countenance bewrayed how her mind was affected towards him: oftentimes comming her selfe into his bedchamber, to see that nothing shuld be amisse to mislike him" (*The Descent of Euphues: Three Elizabethan Romance Stories,* ed. James Winny [Cambridge: Cambridge University Press, 1957], p. 69). For a discussion of ways in which this question has been addressed in productions of *The Winter's Tale,* see Dennis Bartholomeusz, *"The Winter's Tale" in Performance in England and America, 1611-1976* (Cambridge: Cambridge University Press, 1982), esp. pp. 229-32.

[7] See Stanley Wells, "Shakespeare and Romance," in *Later Shakespeare,* Stratford-upon-Avon Studies 8 (London: Edward Arnold, 1966), pp. 66-67; and J. H. P. Pafford, ed., *The Winter's Tale,* The Arden Shakespeare (London: Methuen, 1963), p. lxiv.

[8] Though Mowat disputes the claim of critics such as E. M. W. Tillyard that the first three acts constitute the equivalent of Shakespearean tragedy (pp. 5-21), it is nonetheless striking how dramaturgically similar this concluding scene is to the tragedies, and how many devices it borrows from them: the stage configuration of assembled characters grouped around a *locus* of suffering, commemoration of the tragic events in the form of narrative, the ironic counterpointing of knowledge and loss.

[9] *Shakespeare's Comedies* (Oxford: Clarendon Press, 1960), pp. vii-ix.

[10] It is also significant, in this regard, that Shakespeare here abandons Greene's narrative, which has helped structure the events of the play's first half, and moves into his own dramatic material, though the theatrical implications of this shift into unfamiliarity would be more strongly felt by the play's original audience.

[11] "The Staging of the Last Plays," in *Later Shakespeare,* p. 137.

[12] One of the most extensive thematic studies of Autolycus' role within the play is Lee Sheridan Cox, "The Role of Autolycus in *The Winter's Tale,*" *SEL,* 9 (1969): 283-301.

[13] "Word and Picture in the Final Plays," in *Later Shakespeare,* p. 93.

[14] To a much lesser extent, the reunions between Leontes and Polixenes and between Leontes and Camillo are also "obligatory," and these too are merely reported.

[15] In this role, she anticipates Ariel, who likewise scourges memory in his "ministers of Fate" speech to Alonso, Antonio, and Sebastian:

> But remember
> (For that's my business to you) that you three
> From Milan did supplant good Prospero,
> Expos'd unto the sea (which hath requit it)
> Him, and his innocent child. . . .
> (*The Tempest* III.iii.68-72)

[16] *Poetics* 16.1454b-55a, in *Aristotle: On Poetry and Style,* trans. G. M. A. Grube (New York: Liberal Arts Press, 1958), p. 33. For Grube's "Antinous," I have substituted the more familiar "Alcinous;" see S. H. Butcher, *Aristotle's Theory of Poetry and Fine Art with a Critical Text and Translation of "The Poetics,"* 4th ed. (1907; rpt. New York: Dover, 1951), p. 59.

[17] For a discussion of the ways in which Shakespeare uses specific notations in the text to control the theatrical realization of the statue scene, see Jörg Hasler, "Romance in the Theater: The Stagecraft of the 'Statue Scene' in *The Winter's Tale,*" in *Shakespeare: Man of the Theater,* ed. Kenneth Muir, Jay L. Halio, and D. J. Palmer (Newark: University of Delaware Press, 1983), pp. 203-11.

[18] See S. L. Bethell, *"The Winter's Tale": A Study* (London: Staples Press, [1947]); and Roy Battenhouse, "Theme and Structure in 'The Winter's Tale,'" *ShS*, 33 (1980): 123-38.

LEONTES AND PERDITA

Patricia Southard Gourlay (essay date 1975)

SOURCE: "'Oh My Most Sacred Lady': Female Metaphor in *The Winter's Tale*," in *English Literary Renaissance*, Vol. 5, No. 3, Autumn, 1975, pp. 375-95.

[*Here, Gourlay traces Shakespeare's use of female metaphors in the play to explore elements of Leontes' own nature, and asserts that he opposes dark masculinity with the qualities of love, art, and nature represented by the three principal women.*]

Early in *The Winter's Tale*, while all is still compliment and courtesy, Polixenes describes the innocent idyll he and Leontes shared as boys. He says to Hermione:

> O my most sacred lady,
> Temptations have since then been born t'us, for
> In those unfledged days was my wife a girl;
> Your precious self had then not crossed the eyes
> Of my young playfellow.[1] (I. ii.77—81)

When Polixenes makes his little joke, no one, least of all the gracious Hermione, takes exception to his comic aspersion on women, accompanied as it is by the honorific address, "sacred lady." Polixenes rightly takes for granted that his audience shares his own assumptions about the perfection of his childish friendship and recognizes in it the metaphor of a prelapsarian Eden. Only indirectly does he suggest that woman is the cause of Adam's fall. Yet Polixenes' courtly teasing introduces the complex theme of "femaleness" which Shakespeare expands to major importance in this play.

The identification of women with sexual temptation, the ready analogy to Eve in the garden, is a commonplace. It reflects a conception of women's nature deeply rooted in Shakespeare's society. That society is, of course, masculine, with male and female roles, in general, conventionally defined. Because men rule, the "masculine" values are power, law, and reason; a man is hardheaded, disciplined, practical, as well as honorable.[2] Weakness is "womanish," as are those elements of their own nature that the men deny or repress. With some encouragement from Aristotle, St. Paul, and the Christian fathers, male smugness can shade off easily into fear and even abhorrence of sexuality and then of women. Sexual guilt can be displaced by blaming women as tempters; Eve's seduction of Adam is an archetypal

expression of such attitudes. At the other extreme, women can be idealized by Neoplatonic philosophers and courtly lovers, adored as repositories of those ideal qualities not accommodated in the "real" world of men.

Renaissance treatment of the goddess Venus typifies this uncomfortable polarity, which Shakespeare turns so adroitly to his dramatic purpose. In most Renaissance mythography Venus' province seems to be mere sexuality.[3] Golding, in the Preface to his translation of the *Metamorphoses*, declares that Venus stands allegorically for "such as of the fleshe too filthie lust are bent."[4] A favorite myth is Venus' seduction of Mars; she is commonly seen as corrupting his "inner virtus" by her female arts.[5] Shakespeare himself draws on these familiar associations fairly often. So Adonis accuses Venus as "sweating lust" in *Venus and Adonis*, though Shakespeare makes her pleasures appealing to the reader as well as to Adonis. Most particularly, the Romans in *Antony and Cleopatra* express their disapproval of Cleopatra and her influence by comparing her to Venus.[6] Cleopatra "unmans" the Mars-like Antony by her mysterious sexual magic. At the same time, the Venus/Mars myth is associated with Eve's responsibility for Adam's fall; Cleopatra is the "serpent of old Nile," who brings about the "fall of Antony."

In his use of both the Venus and Eve myths Shakespeare invites from us a double response. Venus has another face in the mythography of the age, deriving very largely from the Neoplatonists. She often stands for the Neoplatonic concept of ideal love, for that beauty which draws men to the good. In Neoplatonic astrology, Venus is the moderating force who softens the harsher influences of Mars. Her sexuality becomes not merely lust, but a fertile and creative principle. Botticelli paints her in his *Primavera* as the beneficent Venus, reflected in the three Graces, presiding over the earth's flowering, suggestive of the Virgin herself. Botticelli's Venus may, as Frances Yates indicates, have magical properties as a talisman "to draw down the Venereal spirit from the star, and to transmit it to the wearer or beholder of her lovely image."[7]

In *Antony and Cleopatra*, Shakespeare also reflects a beneficent side to Cleopatra's femaleness, as well as a destructive one. He balances the flat Roman condemnation of Cleopatra with a life-giving Venus/Cleopatra who transcends the Roman conception of her; their hostility and fear reflect more upon themselves than upon her. Suggesting an identification of Cleopatra's femaleness with imagination—in fact, with art—Shakespeare suggests the hollowness and sterility of the Roman world. If, like Eve, Cleopatra causes Antony's fall, yet as artist she re-creates the fallen Antony by her imagination, as Sidney's poet re-creates the lost golden world.[8]

When he writes *The Winter's Tale*, then, Shakespeare has already used "femaleness" to imply the limitations of a masculine world. Introducing the theme into pastoral romance, Shakespeare finds a form singularly suited to his theme and his method. Walter Davis, in his account of Elizabethan fiction, credits medieval romance writers with turning Greek romance to serious purposes by adding moral questioning to a mode previously innocent of it.[9] In the Renaissance, Sidney particularly develops the philosophical potential of fictional romance by giving it a strong Neoplatonic bias. In his *Defence of Poesie,* Sidney has described the poet's art as leading men to the divine Idea as the courtly lover's lady leads him to ideal beauty. In the *Arcadia,* Sidney offers the reader the "golden world" which his poetic theory describes as the end of art. His heroes experience ideal value in a pastoral paradise and return to the "real" world of action enriched by that encounter. The *Arcadia,* as Davis puts it, is "a speculation about the possibility of reaching perfection in this life."[10]

Greene's *Pandosto,* which Shakespeare adapts to his purpose for *The Winter's Tale,* is not itself a serious philosophical romance. Shakespeare, however, gives its gratuitous improbabilities mythic significance. The pastoral Eden is offered as an alternative to the fallen world; now that ideal world is associated with femaleness, and the actual world with what the masculine social order takes for its truth. Like Theseus in *A Midsummer Night's Dream,* Leontes speaks for that order, but he does not typify it. Rather, his conduct makes explicit the worst assumptions of his society. His despairing cynicism is the extreme form of Polixenes' gentlemanly misogyny. Like Othello, his claim to justice and his perversion of law and reason to support his madness suggest the dangerous possibilities in his masculine social order. To Leontes' dark vision Shakespeare opposes the ideal qualities represented in the play by the three women, Hermione, Paulina, and Perdita, who suggest the subversive and creative power of love, art, and nature. In *The Winter's Tale* they triumph totally over Leontes' "reality."

Leontes' court seems idyllic in the opening scene, as Camillo and Archidamus vie in courtesy. Its defects, however, are suggested rapidly, as Shakespeare develops and expands the few hints of sexual hostility he finds in Greene. At the same time he offers the first hints of that idealization which treats the three women, damned by their husband-father-king, as near-divinities. The tension develops slowly, beginning with protestations of love: friend to friend, husband to wife. Yet below the smiling surface, Shakespeare already suggests the polarization between male and female and makes the connection between the fallen world and female frailty in Polixenes' joking reference to the women as "temptations." (Only later are we to recognize that, at a deeper level, Polixenes means what he says: in Act III he will denounce Perdita, blaming her as seducer of his son, in terms as brutal as Leontes' own.)

In her initial appearance Hermione is already identified for the first time with that highest of Neoplatonic qualities, grace. She answers Polixenes' teasing accusation by calling on "grace to boot" (I.ii.80). When Leontes reminds her of her earlier "good deed," she says, "Would her name were Grace," and then, a shade more seriously, she comments, "'tis Grace indeed." Her playing with the word, even as she exemplifies the quality, also implies the story's pattern: the grace she brings Leontes will save him from the consequences of his justice.

Leontes' jealous fit comes upon him very suddenly here, to the consternation of literal-minded critics. But Shakespeare is deliberately manipulating appearance. We are reminded of the deceptiveness of social forms: Leontes' sudden seizure suggests a reality that his social mask conceals. He does not need an Iago to subvert his truth; the destroyer is entirely within.

To achieve his effect Shakespeare discards the perfectly good motivation Greene provides for the king in *Pandosto.* Pandosto falls prey to jealousy, after observing a continuing and extraordinary intimacy between his wife and his friend; he considers in terms quite appropriate to romance "that Love was above all lawes and, therefore, to be staied with no law; that it was hard to put fire and flax together without burning. . . . He considered with himself that Egistus was a man and must needes love, that his wife was a woman, and therefore, subject unto love, and that where fancy forced, friendship was of no force."[11] As the wronged husband, Pandosto is remarkably sympathetic to the claims of love; he distributes blame for its temptations about equally between his friend and his wife.

Shakespeare's treatment of the issue is more significant. Leontes has been silent during the exchange between Polixenes and Hermione. When he speaks of his courtship, he gives perhaps a first hint of the attitudes behind his gallantry:

> Why, that was when
> Three crabbed months had soured themselves
>   to death
> Ere I could make thee open thy white hand
> And clap thyself my love. Then didst thou utter
> "I am yours forever."
>
> (I.ii.101-05)

The intensity of feeling suggested by his diction belies the lightness of his tone. He thinks in terms of conquest and possession: "I could *make* thee" . . . "*clap* thyself *my* love" . . . "*yours* forever." Of course this is conventional lovers' language, but Shakespeare insists on Leontes' possessiveness a touch more than necessary, thereby implying the egotism in his love. Hermione's innocent answer ironically lends itself to Leontes' poisoned imaginings:

'Tis Grace indeed.
Why, lo you now, I have spoke to the purpose
    twice;
The one for ever earned a royal husband,
Th'other for some while a friend.

(ll. 106-09)

While Leontes still holds her hand, she extends the other to Polixenes; the innocent gesture only feeds his jealousy. He recognizes the possibility of innocence in her behavior, but he moves from his awareness that appearance can deceive to a certainty that it does so:

This entertainment
May a free face put on, derive a liberty
From heartiness, from bounty, fertile bosom,
And well become the agent. 'Tmay, I grant.
But to be paddling palms and pinching fingers,
As now they are, and making practiced smiles
As in a looking glass. . . .

(ll. 111-17)

His diction here and in the speeches that follow makes plain his disgust with all sex, which comes to symbolize for him the human condition itself. The sexuality he loathes in himself may be displaced to Hermione, but there it is out of his control. He cannot fully own her; neither can he trust her. His conversation with Mamillius is especially revealing. His son is his "copy"; they are "almost as like as eggs." In Mamillius, he sees that other self who played innocently with Polixenes. When he doubts his son's paternity, he doubts both love and the very possibility of innocence. Sexuality is as dangerous as a dagger:

Looking on the lines
Of my boy's face, methoughts I did recoil
Twenty-three years, and saw myself
    unbreeched,
In my green velvet coat, my dagger muzzled,
Lest it should bite its master and so prove,
As ornaments oft do, too dangerous.

(ll. 153-58)

Even the question, "Will you take eggs for money?," restates the thesis that the wise man is an empiricist who knows "true" value.

As Leontes moves rapidly from his general distrust of women's truth—"Women say so, that will say anything" (ll. 130-31)—faith seems to him mere stupidity, like the rustics' acceptance of Autolycus' lies. Like Othello, he chooses a negative certainty rather than the ambiguity of appearances; then he makes a law of it. His distrust includes all women and extends even to his probably uneasy audience, required to participate in his suspicions:

And many a man there is, even at this present,
Now, while I speak this, holds his wife by
    th'arm,
That little thinks she has been sluiced in's
    absence
And his pond fished by his next neighbor, by
Sir Smile, his neighbor. . . .

(ll. 191-95)

Again his emphasis is on his property; Hermione is the "gate" he cannot guard. Like Pentheus in Euripides' *Bacchae,* he reveals in his imagery of restraint that he has objectified his own feelings in the person to be controlled:

No barricado for a belly. Know't,
It will let in and out the enemy
With bag and baggage. Many thousand on's
Have the disease and feel't not.

(ll. 203-06)

Hermione is merely another "belly"; sexuality is the "enemy" and a "disease"; to destroy Hermione is to heal himself.

By the time he reveals his suspicion to Camillo that Hermione is "slippery" and a "hobby-horse," the suspicion is fact. Unless it is, he says, then there is no truth at all:

Why, then the world and all that's in't is
    nothing,
The covering sky is nothing, Bohemia nothing,
My wife is nothing, nor nothing have these
    nothings,
If this be nothing.

(ll. 292-95)

When Camillo contradicts him, he insists, as if his absoluteness is proof, "It is: you lie, you lie." His truth is, he believes, a hardheaded "reasoning" man's assessment of reality; so he credits superior intelligence for perception of the truth to which others are blind: " . . . Not noted, is't, / But of the finer natures, by some severals / Of head-piece extraordinary?" (ll. 224-26). It follows, then, that he will use his civil power to stamp out those who disagree, who accept ambiguity. Camillo is a "mindless slave" if he can "at once see good, and evil, inclining to them both." Camillo knows Leontes' is a "diseased opinion," but he accepts the order of things: "I must believe you, sir." He will not do Leontes' bidding, but neither will he defy him openly, because he accepts his place as subject in Leontes' order, as he shares Leontes' masculine assumptions in general. His departure merely confirms Leontes' own certitude: "How blest am I / In my just censure, in my true opinion" (II.i.37-38). Again, like Othello, he identifies certainty with truth, so that only what is worst can be true: "All's true that is mistrusted" (l. 48).

Accusing his wife, Leontes can exercise his royal power to prevent any defense of her: "He who shall speak for her is afar off guilty / But that he speaks" (ll. 103-04). The few who speak for Hermione are quickly silenced by command. Her strongest defender is Antigonus, who dares to tell Leontes he is "abused." Yet even he offers a curiously inverted defense: if any woman is honest, then Hermione is. Such a position makes explicit the implications which have been there all along, and Antigonus states them clearly: "For every inch of woman in the world, / Ay, every dram of woman's flesh is false, / If she be" (ll. 137-39). It is a sign of the schism between their worlds that even the best disposed of the men think of women generically rather than individually. Antigonus' offer to geld his daughters if Hermione is guilty, so they will not "bring false generations," points ironically to the conclusion Leontes has already made: there is no woman who is not corrupt. Even Antigonus will, after all, accept the ugly mission his king gives him. Later, he even seems to accept the idea of Hermione's guilt after she appears to him in his sleep (III.iii). Though she comes "in pure white robes, / Like very sanctity" (ll. 21-22), he misinterprets his dream, deciding the baby is Polixenes', and that the child is punished for its mother's "fault."

Having put down all dissent, Leontes now rests his "truth" absolutely in his own sovereignty:

> Our prerogative
> Calls not your counsels, but our natural
>   goodness
> Imparts this, which if you—or stupefied
> Or seeming so in skill—cannot or will not
> Relish a truth like us, inform yourselves
> We need no more of your advice.
>
>   (ll. 163-68)

The men who serve him have no real choice. Shakespeare has neatly defined in their response to Leontes the fault in their social order. They cannot know Hermione's value for sure, because it cannot be demonstrated empirically. Neither can they assert that value in defiance of their king. So Shakespeare invents a female character to do it for them.

Paulina has no counterpart in Greene nor, apparently, in any other possible source for the play. Unlike Antigonus and Camillo, Paulina refuses to know her place. She asserts Hermione's goodness in defiance of Leontes' vilification; she keeps alive Hermione's memory, and, by implication, the possibility of her goodness; she serves ultimately as the agent by whom Leontes recovers what he has lost. She is subversive woman, truth-teller and, finally, artist, whose truth challenges Leontes' masculine order.

Shakespeare presents Paulina first as a negative female stereotype, a comic scold. Leontes tries to dismiss her as a shrew, a mere "Dame Partlet," but we recognize almost immediately the difference between his appraisal of her and her real quality. From the start, the lines of battle are clearly drawn between two kinds of power: Paulina's female tongue versus Leontes' masculine rule.

Before she takes his new-born infant to Leontes, Paulina declares: "He must be told on't, and he shall. The office / Becomes a woman best; I'll take't upon me. / If I prove honey mouthed, let my tongue blister . . ." (II.ii.31-33). When the jailer tries to stop her from visiting Hermione, he uses the diction of Leontes' "commandment," which Paulina satirizes when she asks, "Is't *lawful,* pray you, / To see her women?" (ll. 11-12). The jailer worries that she has no "warrant," but she has already promised "I'll use that tongue I have" (l. 53).

Paulina's "tongue" is emblematic for "words," in this case for the truth which cannot be coerced. Like the poets', Paulina's can be a "truth-telling tongue." It expresses other perceptions than Leontes' self-deceptive and cynical "truths," which are, in fact, as Hermione declares, "dreams."

To Leontes, Paulina is a noisy "Dame Partlet" who will not be "ruled" by her king, much less by her husband who, Leontes contemptuously charges, "dreads his wife" (II.iii.79). Again Leontes extends his loathing from one woman to the whole sex: his baby is a "bastard" and a "brat"; Paulina is a "bawd" and a "hag," "Dame Margery, you midwife." Most significantly, Paulina is a "crone" and a "mankind witch."

When Paulina keeps talking, Leontes falls back on force. He has "charg'd" Antigonus to keep Paulina out; he now commands his servants to "force her hence," to "push her out." Antigonus should be hanged because "thou wilt not stay her tongue." She shall be "burn't," presumably as a witch. He thinks his tyranny is merely assertion of his rightful male authority. The violence of his reaction suggests the degree to which his world is shaken by Paulina's refusal to play the part assigned to her. It is her tongue that frightens him, because he cannot stop it by his civil power. He calls her "a callet / of boundless tongue" and offers to hang Antigonus, a more pliant subject, because he can't "stay her tongue." When he punishes Antigonus, it is for his inability to stop his "lewd-tongued wife."

Paulina challenges simultaneously both Leontes' power and his "truth." Of course Leontes is mad, like Othello, but Shakespeare suggests in him a madness to which even a paragon of rationality like Octavius or Theseus may be liable. Paul Siegel sees in Leontes a classical tyrant whose passion has conquered his reason. Leontes' passions, he says, "make him dash the social order to pieces."[12] But Shakespeare shows no conflict between reason and passion taking place in Leontes; the conflict is between Leontes the king and the subversive

Paulina. Leontes' society is not "dashed to pieces." Leontes' alienation from his wife is, in fact, symptomatic of his society's alienation from the qualities the women metaphorically represent.

For the men in the play, women in general seem to be on trial in the person of Hermione. For the audience, however, Leontes' masculine world itself is on trial; the very foundations of its truth are in question. "The spider in the cup" defines Leontes' sour and narrow conception of a fallen world of "fact," to which the only response is force. Hermione's "grace" offers the play's alternative to Leontes' harsh vision of reality. "Grace" suggests a wide range of qualities, all of them displayed by the queen: feminine charm and beauty, the Christian grace which transcends Leontes' narrow justice, and Neoplatonic divine "grazia." Hermione is always "the gracious Lady," a "gracious innocent soul," Leontes' "gracious dam," remembered as "tender as infancie and grace."

Leontes has seen Hermione's grace only as her charming "entertainment"; even that superficial grace has seemed a means to deceive him, disguising lust with the "free face" of "entertainment," to "derive a liberty / from heartiness." But Hermione's social grace is a reflection of her spiritual quality, evidenced in her response to Leontes' accusations. She declares, "This action I now go on / Is for my better grace" (II.i.121-22). Leontes' accusation tests and enriches that "grace," providing the occasion for a dramatic display of it at many levels.

Hermione's grace manifests itself in Acts I and II as gentleness and mercy. More concerned for Leontes than for herself, she forgives him repeatedly. He does "but mistake" in his accusations (II.i.81). She worries "how this will grieve you" and finds in her prison the consolation that she does not deserve it. Even speaking in her own defense, she does not reproach Leontes directly; she only declares that condemnation on "surmises" would be "rigor, not law"[13] (III.ii.113). She wishes her father could be present to see her, "Yet with eyes / Of pity, not revenge" (ll. 120-21). "Pity, not revenge": those are among the last words Shakespeare gives her before her "death." Her merciful quality is especially striking in contrast with Leontes' demand for punitive justice.

Hermione's grace, even in the first half of the play, acquires a generalized sanctity with strong Neoplatonic implications. Shakespeare takes time for Cleomenes and Dion to discuss the "sweet air" of Apollo's precincts, and Dion is impressed by the "celestial habits" and "reverence of the grave wearers" (III.i.6-7), as if he were describing a procession of participants in the mysteries. Hermione's own grace is associated with Apollo's powers when Cleomenes and Dion hope the issue of their visit will be "gracious." Later, Antigonus

will see her in his dream wearing "pure white robes / Like very sanctity," (III.iii.21-22) as if she were an initiate. When she reappears in Act V, it will be in this same ambiguous blending of Neoplatonic and conventional Christian divinity.

Hermione is, in her unrealistic perfection, both symbol and talisman for that value which Leontes has shut out of his world. His "reason," "justice," and power enforce his "truth": he lives in a fallen world of "fact," in which women's falseness is both a cause and a symptom. But this play is romance, not tragedy. In the golden world of romance, the "truth" of the artist is triumphant; Paulina asserts and enforces that truth in defiance of Leontes. So when the oracle speaks in Act II, the play turns itself completely around. Paulina has so far been the "truth-telling tongue," insisting on Hermione's worth. She has also offered her truths as antidote to Leontes' sick imagination. Forcing her way to him, she has told the guard:

> I come to bring him sleep. 'Tis such as you
> That creep like shadows by him and do sigh
> At each his needless heavings, such as you
> Nourish the cause of his awaking. I
> Do come with words as medicinal as true. . . .
>
> (II.iii.33-37)

She sees herself as his "physician," trying vainly to persuade him to "remove / the root of his opinion, which is rotten" (ll. 88-89).

When Hermione dies, Leontes reverses himself completely and submits to Paulina's caustic healing. Shakespeare shows the change in stages. When the oracle is revealed, Leontes first declares its truth too is "mere falsehood"; only the prince's death persuades him of his "injustice." Even when Hermione faints, he smugly thinks he can undo the harm like a Claudio or a Cymbeline: "I'll reconcile me to Polixenes, / New woo my queen, recall the good Camillo . . ." (III.ii.153-54). Only Paulina's histrionic announcement of Hermione's death brings him up short. Now he accepts her wildest reproaches. Paulina's "apology" for her anger causes some confusion among the critics, but it seems clear enough when read as irony. Paulina seems to emphasize the "I," contrasting herself with Leontes, when she says, "All faults *I* make, when *I* shall come to know them, / *I* do repent" (III.ii.217-18; my italics). "I have showed too much / The rashness of a woman" pointedly emphasizes the rightness of her woman's anger compared to Leontes' masculine "rashness" disguised as reason. When she tells him,

> Do not receive affliction
> At *my* petition. I beseech you, rather
> Let *me* be punished, that have minded you
> Of what you should forget
>
> (ll. 221-24; my italics),

she is in fact reminding him of his earlier pattern of action. Her subsequent persistence in keeping his memory of his misdeeds fresh indicates that this disclaimer is ironic. Each promise she makes not to mention Leontes' victims is, of course, a deliberate reminder of them.

"Take your patience to you, / And I'll say nothing," would be entirely out of character for Paulina if we took it at face value. As an ironic summing up, it is more a threat than a promise. So Leontes acknowledges when he says, "Thou didst speak but well / When most the truth, which I receive much better / Than to be pitied of thee" (ll. 230-32). Their exit together, which marks the end of this first section of the play, points to their future relationship. Leontes' "Come and lead me to these sorrows" refers not only to the bodies of his wife and son, but also to his future penance, dictated by Paulina. When they reappear in Act v, Leontes—who mocked Antigonus' failure to rule his wife—will himself be her subject.

Leontes' education by Paulina represents a marked departure from Greene's Pandosto, whose repentance is conventionally shallow. Pandosto builds his wife the obligatory "rich and famous" tomb with a self-accusing epitaph, and he makes his daily visits there to "bewaile his misfortune." His character, however, is quite unchanged. When the fleeing couple are unmasked, he reviles Fawnia in terms as harshly anti-feminine as any in Shakespeare's play: "Thou disdainfull vassal, thou currish kite, assigned by the destinies to base fortune . . . how durst thou presume, being a beggar, to match with a Prince: By thy alluring lookes to inchant the sonne of a King to leave his owne countrie to fulfill thy disordinate lusts. . . ."[14] Before this denunciation, he has already shown himself as tyrannical as Leontes in his cruelty to Dorastus and in his amorous attempts on Fawnia herself. Even after the happy reconciliation, he "fell into a melancholie fit, and to close up the Comedy with a Tragicall stratageme, he slewe himselfe. . . ."[15]

Shakespeare's Leontes, schooled by Paulina, cannot behave like this, because Shakespeare's romance has its own rules which transform the stratagems both of comedy and of tragedy. But Shakespeare borrows the attack of father upon daughter from his source and assigns it instead to Polixenes. Shakespeare makes Polixenes' misogyny as savage as Pandosto's. When he confronts the girl his son loves, he says: "And thou, fresh piece / Of excellent witchcraft, who of force must know / The royal fool thou cop'st with . . ." IV.iv.415-17). Leontes has already expressed his fear of Paulina's female powers by calling her a witch. Now Polixenes calls Perdita a "knack," an "enchantment," who has seduced Florizel and against whose sexuality his son must be protected:

> if ever henceforth thou
> These rural latches to his entrance open,

> Or hoop his body more with thy embraces,
> I will devise a death as cruel for thee
> As thou art tender to't.
>
> (IV.iv.430-34)

So the theme of sexual hostility is repeated in this second part of the play. Leontes and Hermione are reflected in Polixenes and Perdita. Like Leontes, Polixenes blasts the joy of a gathering with accusations and threats of death, enforcing his will by civil power. As Hermione's worth has been asserted by Paulina, so Florizel contradicts Polixenes' devaluation of Perdita. But because he is a lover in the golden world of pastoral, Florizel already knows what Leontes must learn the hard way: like poets and madmen, he sees in his lady the value to which the kings are blind. Florizel's estimate of Perdita is also ours; like Hermione, she is presented to us in terms of her symbolic qualities. The diction and imagery used for mother and daughter are in both cases strongly suggestive at once of the Virgin and of the Neoplatonic Venus, whose love leads the way to truth.

From the first, Perdita is presented to us pictorially; Hermione herself will be a living icon in her reappearance. In Perdita, Shakespeare suggests the Venus Genetrix who "gives life and shape to the things in nature and thereby makes the intelligible beauty accessible to our perception and imagination."[16] Her resemblance to Botticelli's *Primavera* is interesting. Edgar Wind has suggested that the *Primavera* and *The Birth of Venus* are companion pieces celebrating iconographically the two Neoplatonic aspects of Venus, the "natural" and the "celestial";[17] they are also rather neatly suggested in Perdita and Hermione. The richly suggestive fertility symbolism surrounding Perdita has been discussed by many critics. The outcast "brat" returns as a goddess-queen, ruling in nature. Presiding over the sheep-shearing, she seems to Florizel "no shepherdess but Flora, / Peering in April's front" IV.iv.2-3). She is "most Goddess-like pranked up"; all her "acts are queens" and even Camillo declares her "Queen of curds and cream." She declares her full alliance with "great creating nature" when she scorns the gillyflowers.

Gifted with the courtly lover's sight, Florizel explicitly spurns the values of the sublunary world where his father exercises power. When he pledges his faith to Perdita, he declares he would not prize empire, beauty, "force and knowledge / More than was ever man's" (IV.iv.367-68) without Perdita's love. Later, put to the test, he renounces his right of succession; he is "heir to my affection."

As Leontes is later to choose "madness" over the "real" world's reason, Florizel tells Camillo he is "advised" by his love: "If my reason / Will thereto be obedient, I have reason; / If not, my senses, better pleased with madness, / Do bid it welcome" (ll. 475-78). Shakespeare uses his theatrical metaphor here to emphasize the rightness of Florizel's evaluation. Although Perdita seems to the realistic observers, shepherds and kings alike, to be a shepherdess playing a queen, she is in fact to be revealed as a true queen, in defiance of appearances.[18] Like the other women in the play, she is more, not less, than she seems.

When the lovers arrive at Leontes' court, Perdita's value is evident to everyone. She is praised now in quasi-religious terms: "This is a creature, / Would she begin a sect, might quench the zeal / Of all professors else, make proselytes / Of who she but bid follow" (v.i.106-09). She is a "woman / More worth than any man" (ll. 111-12). When he receives the couple, Leontes calls Perdita a "goddess" and "a paragon." He is not merely honoring her royalty. Even when told she is a shepherd's daughter, he is "sorry" that "Your choice is not so rich in worth as beauty / That you might well enjoy her" (ll. 212-14). The term "worth" seems to imply a distinction between the narrow "worth" of high birth and wealth and Perdita's worth in Leontes' eyes. The same distinction is suggested when Florizel asks Leontes to intercede for him with his father, who will grant him "precious things, as trifles"; Leontes answers: "Would he do so, I'd beg your precious mistress / Which he counts but a trifle" (ll. 222-23).

The consolations Perdita brings her father are nature's own. Her innocent sexuality is life-creating; it is the antidote to her father's barrenness. When Perdita returns, Leontes welcomes back into his world the creative and fertile power of Venus. Such consolations, however, require us to transfer our affections from the old, which is lost, to the new which takes its place.

Greene's *Pandosto* is subtitled "The Triumph of Time." Curiously, Greene goes on to explain his subtitle in terms of Time as Revealer: it shows how "Truth may be concealed yet by Time in spirit of fortune it is most manifestly revealed." Yet in the novel there is no mention of Time, and mere "Fortune" gets credit for the reunion of father and daughter. Shakespeare introduces the quaint figure of Father Time himself as "Chorus" for the second half of the play. His Time, however, unlike Greene's, is both threatening and comical. As Destroyer and Creator, he boasts:

> it is in my power
> To o'er throw law and in one self-born hour
> To plant and o'erwhelm custom. Let me pass
> The same I am, ere ancient'st order was
> Or what is now received. I witness to
> The times that brought them in. So shall I do
> To the freshest things now reigning, and
>   make stale

The glistering of this present, as my tale
Now seems to it.

                                   (IV.i.7-15)

Perdita's recovery is a demonstration of his powers, working through the cycle of nature.

But Shakespeare goes far beyond Greene in his plot by giving us Hermione's restoration; it is not a gift of Time but a defiance of it. In IV.i he has his fun with Time, both as a fusty theatrical device and as a character. In the last act, time in general is mocked, as are those temporal powers exercised by men. Paulina exercises the power of the artist to confute time, both in preserving Hermione's memory and in restoring her to life.[19]

As Act V opens, Paulina is still reproaching Leontes for Hermione's death. Paulina's persistence serves to keep Hermione both a real and an ideal presence. As Leontes says, "Whilst I remember / Her and her virtues, I cannot forget / My blemishes in them, and so still think of / The wrong I did myself . . ." (v.i.6-9). While she keeps Leontes repentant, Paulina is defying time, and rejecting the solace it can offer. So Cleomenes complains of her bluntness: "You might have spoken a thousand things, good lady, that would / Have done the time more benefit and graced / Your kindness better" (ll. 21-23). But for Hermione's restoration to have meaning, Hermione must be irreplaceable. No second wife will do, nor can even Perdita make up for her loss.

The courtiers hope Leontes will "forgive himself" and marry again. When Perdita arrives and the servant praises her, he declares he has "almost forgot" Hermione, and promises Paulina that Perdita "will have your tongue too." But Paulina's bitter tongue continues to insist on Hermione's unique value. In the celebration of Perdita, therefore, Paulina stands a little apart. She is skeptical and even jealous, on Hermione's behalf, of any praise of Perdita. So she asserts Hermione's greater worth: "Not a month / 'Fore our queen died, she was more worth such gazes / Than what you look on now" (ll. 224-26). She holds out for the reconciliation impossible in nature, the return of Hermione herself. Of course her obstinacy serves the purposes of the plot. More than that, her "magic" takes precedence over nature; the effect of Perdita's return is subsumed in the dazzling and mysterious resurrection of Hermione. . . .

Notes

[1] All textual references are to *The Winter's Tale,* ed. Baldwin Maxwell (Baltimore, 1956).

[2] Theseus, king of Athens in *A Midsummer Night's Dream,* is representative of these "masculine" attributes; appropriately, he rejects the lovers' tale of their "dream" experiences in the wood as "more than cool reason

ever comprehends" (v.i.6). Hippolyta, the wife he has won by conquest, does not agree.

[3] R. K. Root, *Classical Mythology in Shakespeare* (New York, 1965), p. 115.

[4] *Shakespeare's Ovid Being Arthur Golding's Translation of the Metamorphoses,* ed. W.H.D. Rouse (London, 1961), 1. 68.

[5] Robert P. Miller cites this interpretation as typical of "standard patterns of conflict" between the sexes, to be found also in Adam and Eve, Samson and Delila, Alcido and Rinaldo in *Gerusalemme Liberata,* and Verdant and Acrasia in *The Faerie Queene.* See "The Myth of Mars' Hot Minion in *Venus and Adonis,*" *ELH,* 26 (1959), 473.

[6] I.i.1-13; II.ii.191-204.

[7] *Giordano Bruno and the Hermetic Tradition* (London, 1964), pp. 77-78. See also Edgar Wind, *Pagan Mysteries in the Renaissance* (New Haven, Conn., 1958), pp. 100-10.

[8] The relationship between Sidney's poetic theory and the more familiar concept of Cleopatra as artist is discussed by Phyllis Rackin, "Shakespeare's Boy Cleopatra, the Decorum of Nature, and the Golden World of Poetry," *PMLA,* 87 (1972), 201-11.

[9] *Idea and Act in Elizabethan Fiction* (Princeton, N.J., 1969), p. 26.

[10] P. 62.

[11] *Life and Complete Works in Prose and Verse,* ed. Alexander Grosart (1881-86; rpt. New York, 1964), IV, 237-38.

[12] "Leontes a Jealous Tyrant," *RES,* 1 (1950), 302-07.

[13] The phrase comes from the queen in Greene's *Pandosto;* she, however, defends herself aggressively, attacking the king and herself demanding an embassy to the oracle (p. 256).

[14] Greene, p. 314.

[15] P. 317.

[16] Erwin Panofsky, *Studies in Iconology* (1939; rpt. New York, 1962), p. 142.

[17] Wind, pp. 100-20.

[18] Ann Righter discusses Shakespeare's use of this theatrical metaphor in *Shakespeare and the Idea of the Play* (London, 1964), pp. 192-201.

[19] Compare the poet's claim in Sonnet 81: "And tongues to be your being shall rehearse / When all the breathers of this world are dead."

Robert N. Watson (essay date 1984)

SOURCE: "Ambition and Original Sin in *The Winter's Tale,*" in *Shakespeare and the Hazards of Ambition,* Harvard University Press, 1984, pp. 222-79.

[*In the excerpt below, Watson discusses the physical and spiritual reunification of the natural and artificial worlds of* The Winter's Tale; *including Perdita's rejection of the dead world of Sicily and her role in the redemption of Leontes' ambitious identity.*]

Redemption and the Bohemian Garden

Immediately after Leontes resigns himself and his country to wintry stagnation, the scene shifts to an entire new world. The first three lines after his despairing vow tell us that we are in wild Bohemia, under an open sky, and tossed by swiftly changing weather. The shift of locale from one country to another is only the geographic aspect of this scene's highly complex transition, which is an exhilarating but frightening release from physical, spiritual, and temporal claustrophobia. The forces of nature Sicilia imprisoned and slandered lie waiting here in ambush, and attack the courtier Antigonus as the hapless emissary of that artificial world. Antigonus is carrying some dangerous baggage: his own version of Leontes' dream-induced doubt about Perdita's legitimacy (3.2.82-84; 3.3.16-46), and a ludicrously overcivilized notion of the workings of fallen nature. Taking up Perdita to begin the mission Leontes spitefully assigned him, Antigonus says,

> Come on, poor babe.
> Some powerful spirit instruct the kites and
>   ravens
> To be thy nurses! Wolves and bears, they say,
> Casting their savageness aside, have done
> Like offices of pity.
>
> (2.3.185-89)

Such handsome notions do not apply, as the young shepherd mentions, when the creatures are hungry (3.3.130-31). A real bear soon enforces a more realistic idea of its character on the emissary, despite his distinctly Sicilian protest, reported by the young shepherd, that "his name was Antigonus, a nobleman." The bear, not impressed, then "mock'd him" and consumed him (3.3.96-101).

The brutality of the scene raises for the audience a question that has troubled Christian minds over the centuries: "But how did man so lose his mastery over creation that irrational animals can devour him?

[Augustine's] answer is that the present state of mankind is the consequence of sin. In paradise it had been totally different, and man's forfeited powers will be restored to him at the time of the resurrection."[49] The devouring of Antigonus by the bear, like the devouring of Leontes by the wild beast within him, is fallen nature's appropriate (if harsh) response to the presumption of paradise. Antigonus is truly "gone for ever" (3.3.58), and Leontes will be trapped in a barren ritual until the babe spared by the bear returns from Bohemia, first to symbolize, then to inspire, the redemptive resurrection of Hermione. On the Bohemian shore, Antigonus has only a very marginal understanding of the regenerative force he holds in his arms. He expresses the hope that the money and documents he leaves with the child will "breed thee" (3.3.48), whereas her breeding will depend more on the kindly nature of the shepherds than on such civilized Sicilian artifacts. The shepherds soon arrive to bury Antigonus and nurture this "Blossom" (3.3.46) who receives from his death a new life.

The figure of Time itself follows this transitional scene, and speaking (like Duncan and Malcolm) in terms of "growth" and "planting," propels us into Bohemia's ongoing natural life. When Leontes accused Hermione and Polixenes of "wishing clocks more swift; / Hours, minutes; noon, midnight" (1.2.289-90), he simply meant that they eagerly awaited each night's adulterous pleasure; but in the context of his other implicit denials of time, we may infer on a secondary level that he was accusing them of accelerating time itself, thereby compromising the roles of boy eternal and eternal host by which he claimed immortality. As long as he holds his wife's seduction responsible for bringing sexuality into his garden, he may as well also hold it responsible for the intrusion of time. But his effort to deny and even overthrow Father Time proves as futile as the earlier filial rebellions, and the ambitious figure again sees even his normal patrimony threatened when the father retakes authority. When the figure of Time requests that we "imagine me, / Gentle spectators, that I now may be / In fair Bohemia," the phrasing implies more than a change of setting. Time itself, as the character of Leontes' crime invited, and as the character of his penance indicates, has virtually ceased to exist in Sicilia. With his wife's "death," Leontes, like Macbeth, disappears into a series of meaningless "to-morrows," and renewal takes place only outside his kingdom, among his more "natural" enemies.

But the transition to Bohemia is not simply a renaissance of nature; it is the first step in a rapprochement between nature and artifice. The second half of the play points less to the abandonment of custom and civility than to the redemption of those notions by rediscovering their foundations. By the same token, the tragic portrayal of an ambitious identity destroyed gives way to the romantic portrayal of an ambitious

identity saved by the recovery of its hereditary basis. The choral figure of Time, the most conventional sort of theatrical artifice, serves to introduce the drama of nature. Time's boasted ability "To plant and o'erwhelm custom" resubordinates social habit to a regenerative process, and his offer to "give my scene such growing / As you had slept between" provides a dramatic transition by the very forces of maturation and restfulness that distinguish the new locale from the old. The self-defeating manners of Leontes' overextended hospitality stand in grim contrast to the basic hospitality of the shepherds, which is a spontaneous response to Perdita's real human needs. At the sheep-shearing festival, guests are greeted with flowers and food rather than prolonged encomia, and the hosts worry more about buying and preparing the meal than they do about "customary compliment."

The language of the play similarly supports the ethical pattern, regaining health as it regains contact with literal meanings. The rhetorical absurdity of the first scene, where the metaphors clash with their forgotten literal meanings, prepares the social absurdity of the second scene, where good manners, out of touch with their basic purpose, clash with the underlying human sentiments. The overpopulation of dead metaphors in Sicilian speech foreshadows and helps create the ghost-town of Leontes' penance. Ernest Schanzer points out that Polixenes' "poetic embroideries" comparing himself and Leontes to "twinn'd lambs" yield later in the play to the shepherds' practical discussions of real sheep, and that the figurative references to planting and growing in the first half of the play "reappear in the second half on a more literal level in the horticultural debate between Perdita and Polixenes."[50] The same rule may be applied to images of birth: "issue" is generally used metaphorically early in the play (2.2.43; 2.3.153; 3.1.22), but from the moment Antigonus arrives in Bohemia (3.3.43) to the final reconciliation (5.3.128), the term tends to refer to actual human offspring.

The play now appears to be systematically divided into two opposing camps:

Sicilia	Bohemia
city	country
art	nature
ceremony	spontaneity
social artifice	human nature
figurative language	literal language
age	youth
linear time	cyclical time
dreams	senses/sleep
acts 1-3	act 4

Such a chart reveals the range of levels on which Shakespeare creates the contrast we feel. And if Shakespeare had permitted Bohemia to wage a vengeful war to free Sicilia from its withered tyrant, the right hand column marching against the left, we would have a play strongly resembling *Macbeth* in its ethical pattern and symbolic action. But Shakespeare's last plays tend to resolve, by miraculous reconciliations, the same sorts of divisions and conflicts that prove fatal in plays written only a few years earlier. The romances find ways to defuse the tragic threats of usurpation, political naiveté, premature death, incest, and the illusion of adultery; and *The Winter's Tale* defuses the subtler threat of moral idealism that defeated Coriolanus. As families in the romances ultimately reunite after a long and hazardous separation, so do the two sets of values charted above, and so, therefore, do the adopted and hereditary identities.[51] Without the natural Bohemian basis, artificialities—manners, morals, language, marriage—become monstrosities. But with that basis, they become the "art / That Nature makes" which Polixenes defends so strongly (4.4.91-92), facets of the world's beauty, such as gillyvors, which only human endeavor can incite nature to produce.

The first scenes in Bohemia establish the opposed terms, and alert us to the need for a combination, by showing us a starkly natural world that is refreshing after three acts in Sicilia, but not altogether desirable in itself.[52] The depredations of the storm on the crew, the bear on Antigonus, even Autolycus on the clown, remind us that natural law can be as capricious and tyrannical as ceremonial law. Where Sicilia denies the forces of time, sexuality, and mortality, Bohemia is obsessed by them. The old shepherd's first speech begins by lamenting the misbehavior accompanying puberty, and ends with the deduction that Perdita is the product of heated fornication; he then calls his son over to "see a thing to talk on when thou art dead and rotten" (3.3.59-81). Sin and death are on the son's mind too. Seeing the gold left with Perdita, he tells his father, "if the sins of your youth are forgiven you, you're well to live" (3.3.120-21); he then talks about the drowning of the mariners, the eating of Antigonus, and the obligation to bury what is left of him. The figure of Time itself appears next, followed by Camillo's complaint that "It is fifteen years since I saw my country; though I have for the most part been air'd abroad, I desire to lay my bones there." Polixenes resists this plea with a similarly morbid figuration: "'Tis a sickness denying thee any thing; a death to grant this" (4.2.2-6). Their conversation then turns to the illicit sexual motives that have apparently been drawing Florizel away from the court. Autolycus begins the following scene by singing about seasons, flowers, animals, and "tumbling in the hay," worrying about the prospect of hanging rather than about any "life to come."

By the time we arrive at act four, scene four, we may therefore be ready to regret the abandonment of the moral struggle that felt so oppressive in Sicilia. At the sheep-shearing festival, the chain of being seems to lie in a chaotic heap on the grass. Perdita speaks casually and publicly of Florizel's "Desire to breed by me" as

if they belonged to some lower order of creation (4.4.103). Conversely, when she describes a flower closing at night and opening in the morning wet with dew, her wording fairly drips with overtones of human seduction and subsequent regrets: "The marigold, that goes to bed wi' th' sun, / And with him rises weeping" (4.4.105-06). Florizel's remarks show even less respect for hierarchies and solemnities:

> Apprehend
> Nothing but jollity. The gods themselves
> (Humbling their deities to love) have taken
> The shapes of beasts upon them. Jupiter
> Became a bull and bellow'd; the green Neptune
> A ram and bleated; and the fire-rob'd god,
> Golden Apollo, a poor humble swain,
> As I seem now. Their transformations
> Were never for a piece of beauty rarer,
> Nor in a way so chaste, since my desires
> Run not before mine honor, nor my lusts
> Burn hotter than my faith.
> *Perdita*   O but, sir,
> Your resolution cannot hold when 'tis
> Oppos'd (as it must be) by th' pow'r of the King.
> (4.4.24-37)

She means that his intention to marry her must yield to his ceremonial duties, but his speech should also make her fear that his resolution to respect her chastity "cannot hold when 'tis / Oppos'd (as it must be)" by the appetitive power that Bohemia embodies. The speech is laden with Freudian slips, most prominently the entire comparison of his disguise to those of various gods who descended from higher stature only long enough to seduce or rape maidens and then abandoned them. Perdita should think carefully about her own image of the marigold, which is left weeping after the sun takes her to bed. Florizel hastens to cover his tracks in the second half of his speech, but the lurking pun on "chaste" and the image of his desires not running before his honor only further remind us of Apollo's destructive pursuits of mortal maidens. At the same time, his diction may remind us of Christ as a much purer sort of deity whose love led him to humble his shape and walk among his inferiors. that better sort of love, and the Incarnation by which it answers man's Fall from Grace, are far beyond the ken of the Bohemians, who are celebrating a merely natural sort of regeneration. Their innocent ignorance of the need for Grace prepares us to appreciate the Christian aspects of Hermione's mock-incarnation, just as Leontes' willful ignorance of the Fall's impact on nature prepares us to appreciate the natural aspects of Hermione's survival.

The excesses that disturb the harmony of the sheep-shearing festival and prevent the marriage are opposite to the ones that disrupt the Sicilian court and its central marriage. The faults in Florizel's language and behavior are negatives of the same faults in Leontes, and may therefore serve to redress the imbalance. The young man's desire to eternize Perdita's graceful youth bears some resemblance to Leontes' determination to remain "boy eternal" with Polixenes:

> When you speak, sweet,
> I'd have you do it ever; when you sing,
> I'd have you buy and sell so; so give alms;
> Pray so; and for the ord'ring your affairs,
> To sing them too. When you do dance, I
>   wish you
> A wave o' th' sea, that you might ever do
> Nothing but that; move still, still so,
> And own no other function. Each your doing
> (So singular in each particular)
> Crowns what you are doing in the present
>   deeds,
> That all your acts are queens.
>
> (4.4.136-46)

However greatly they differ in pleasantness and mental health, Florizel and Leontes alike become so entranced by a mundane representation of grace that they forget the need for otherworldly Grace. Natural affection can no more assure such perpetuation than ceremonial manners can: only the combination of the two, resulting in legitimate procreation, can perpetuate the youth and beauty of humankind. But if Florizel commits a version of the error that ruined Leontes' marriage—a neglect of the rule of Ecclesiastes, that each thing has its own time and season—his image of eternity as "A wave o' th' sea" suggests an awareness that this world offers eternity only through cyclical renewal and not through stasis. There may be no new thing under the sun, but each new wave or babe reproduces a former one as if it were new again—as the blossom Perdita reproduces her mother's lily-like betrothal. Perdita is playing three overlapping roles in this scene: she is partly a new bride, the symbol of human regeneration, partly Flora, the goddess of vegetative renewal (4.4.2), and partly Proserpina, the figure who connects the cyclical human escape from death with the cyclical return of vegetation. While playing these roles, she necessarily perceives death as only a normal and unthreatening counterpart to sexuality, and is utterly unshaken by the idea of Florizel's flower-strewn "dying," in either sense (4.4.129-32). So Florizel may be half-consciously acknowledging something essential and redemptive about Perdita, in the very sort of praise that represented Leontes' half-conscious decision to overlook the essential mortality of those closest to him.

In the last two lines of his speech, Florizel implies that physical "acts" take precedence for him over the ceremonial heritage of royalty—a heritage dismissed as "dreams" three times in this scene. Where Leontes dreams of rampant appetitive nature (3.2.82), the shepherd predicts (with inadvertent acuity) that the hidden princess Perdita will bring Florizel "that / Which he dreams not of," and the hidden prince Florizel promises Perdita "more than you can dream of yet" (4.4.179-80, 388). When her royal marriage seems doomed, Perdita announces, "This dream of mine / Being now awake, I'll queen it no inch farther" (4.4.448-49). The natural and sexual values the Sicilians repress, and the ceremonial and hierarchical values the Bohemians repress, surface exactly where a psychoanalyst would expect repressed material to surface: in their respective dreams.

Perdita consistently represses the artificial on behalf of the natural, inverting her father's errors in the process. Florizel refuses to buy her any of Autolycus' finery, because "She prizes not such trifles as these are. / The gifts she looks from me are pack'd and lock'd / Up in my heart" (4.4.357-59). This is an admirable alternative to the hollowly gift-laden way love was formerly exchanged between the two royal families (1.1.24-31). Furthermore, if David Kaula is correct in claiming that Autolycus' trumpery represents Catholic relics and indulgences,[53] then Perdita's emphasis on gifts of faith is an admirable alternative and an appropriate corrective to her father's implicit belief in the saving power of worldly ornamentation. But the Puritanical mistrust of ornament can be carried too far, even in defense of nature. In expressing this same strict preference during the debate about the gillyvors, Perdita commits an inverted version of the error her father committed in rejecting her. He banished her as a "bastard," apparently because unrefined nature had a part in her making. She banishes these "blossoms" (the name Antigonus gave her) from her "garden" (the name the Sicilians gave the place where Leontes perceives the adultery) because she considers them adulterated by the artificial part of their creation. She desires such a mixture "No more than were I painted I would wish / This youth to say 'twere well, and only therefore / Desire to breed by me" (4.4.101-03). Cosmetics, revealingly popular with the women of the Sicilian court (2.1.8-15), may represent an ethical danger analogous to the other Sicilian excesses. As Ben Jonson writes, the thicker the lady is painted and ornamented with "th' adulteries of art," the safer it is to assume that underneath "All is not sweet, all is not sound."[54] In fact, Paulina characterizes Leontes' jealousy as that sort of extravagance: "Here's such ado to make no stain a stain / As passes coloring" (2.2.17-18).

But meretriciously painting over one's faults differs crucially from eliciting one's natural beauty by artificial additions, just as denying one's fallen nature differs crucially from nurturing one's remaining virtues by sensible social customs. By showing Perdita and Leontes overlooking these distinctions, *The Winter's Tale* urges us to remember them. The sheep-shearing scene evokes and then shatters the supposition that keeping in touch with agricultural nature corresponds to keeping in touch with hereditary nature. In the pastoral setting that Renaissance writers often used to espouse a primitivist ethic, Shakespeare compromises the apparent primitivist ethic of several earlier plays. Here human life and legacy can be as badly disrupted by a pure obedience to nature as by the pursuit of artificial ambitions. The dark undertones of *Macbeth* and *Coriolanus,* which resemble Florentine philosophy in suggesting that mere submission to nature is itself unnatural for human beings, become forthright and redemptive toward the end of *The Winter's Tale.* As Pico's *Oration* suggests, God's gift to Adam of choice and self-consciousness authorizes us to improve on our original nature, if such a thing can be said to exist at all; the same legacy of free will that permitted original sin to occur remains with us as an obligation to virtue. To respect our heritage is to battle our hereditary frailties.

Shakespeare hints at this paradox by making Florizel necessarily deny his royal patrimony in pursuing an exclusively natural passion, just as Leontes must deny his fallen patrimony to pursue a strictly artificial purity. As his ambush by the unconsidered guilt of Adam's accident renders Leontes a wild-acting "feather for each wind that blows" (2.3.154), so Florizel describes his father's intervention as "th' unthought-on accident" that "is guilty / To what we wildly do" as "flies / Of every wind that blows" (4.4.538-41). The verbal echoes where there is little parallel in meaning are Shakespeare's invitation to associate the two incidents. In fleeing the constraints that are, Polixenes would tell them both, hereditary theirs, Leontes and Florizel perform desexualized versions of the ambitious man's Oedipal crime, and briefly lose their procreative hopes as a result. Both attempt to defy and even replace their limiting fathers: Adam, who forbids Leontes to ignore his natural impulses, and Polixenes, who forbids Florizel to obey them. Where Leontes imagines himself as something like Adam, Florizel imagines himself as his own "heir" and as King of Bohemia, promising Perdita, "Or I'll be thine, my fair, / Or not my father's; for I cannot be / Mine own, nor anything to any, if / I be not thine" (4.4.42-45). Obviously he would not be much without beings his father's as well: Shakespeare's plays are full of characters who become nullities, not "anything to any," by thus defying paternal authority. After the paternal force—this time the father himself—confronts him and forbids the marriage, Florizel reasserts this claim, but he sounds as if he were trying to reassure himself that his identity is still intact, like a man feeling himself after a bad fall: "Why look you so upon me? / I am but sorry, not afeard; delay'd, / But nothing alt'red. What I was, I am" (4.4.462-64). Fruitful marriage in Shakespeare generally requires a dutiful filial identity;[55] Florizel's loving promise effectively invites disaster to befall his engagement.

Florizel's narrow devotion to natural values also determines the type of disaster that will occur. Where Leontes' devotion to artificial values caused the venge-

ful return of the old Adam within him, along with brute sexuality and mortality, Florizel's father spies on him from behind a theatrical artifice, then attacks him on behalf of ceremonial royalty. Polixenes bursts from behind his mask, threatening to punish in kind what he sees as Perdita's crime against decorum and his son's crime against succession:

> Mark your divorce, young sir,
> Whom son I dare not call. Thou art too base
> To be acknowledg'd. Thou, a sceptre's heir,
> That thus affects a sheep-hook!
> . . . . .
> I'll have thy beauty scratch'd with briers
> and made
> More homely than thy state. For thee, fond boy,
> If I may ever know thou dost but sigh
> That thou no more shall see this knack (as never
> I mean thou shalt), we'll bar thee from
> succession,
> Not hold thee of our blood, no, not our kin,
> Farre than Deucalion off.
>   (4.4.417-31)

In threatening to avenge these offenses, Polixenes virtually recommits them. Perdita's beauty is actually the proper representation of her royal birth; and forbidding her father's wish "To die upon the bed my father died, / To lie close by his honest bones" (4.4.455-56) can hardly serve the hereditary order. In the last part of his tirade, Polixenes makes the same sort of ethical error in disavowing his son—an act reminiscent of Leontes' disowning of Perdita—as his son made in disavowing him. This speech only serves to escalate the conflict in Florizel, who now echoes his father's parenthetical threat—"he shall miss me (as, in faith, I mean not / To see him any more)" (4.4.494-95)—and simultaneously (like Macbeth) sets the entire process of generation *against* his hereditary obligations. If he leaves Perdita at his father's command, "Let nature crush the sides o' th' earth together, / And mar the seeds within! Lift up thy looks. / From my succession wipe me, father, I / Am heir to my affection" (4.4.478-81). He cannot be heir to his natural affection any more than Leontes could be heir to his artificial affectations; his phrase recalls such failures of ambition to supplant heredity as Richard III's promise to make Tyrell "inheritor of thy desire," and Volumnia's announcement that she has seen in Coriolanus "inherited my very wishes."

Camillo repeatedly interrupts Florizel's oaths with pleas for reason and reconsideration, as he did Leontes' tirades earlier. Throughout the play Camillo is the good and steady advisor, retaining the balance between natural and artificial values that is lost in the two kingdoms he serves, and leading an exodus to the opposite when the imbalance precipitates a crisis. The parallels between these two hasty departures suggest graphically the play's mistrust of both extremes. The first follows

Leontes' plea that Polixenes stay yet longer away from his homeland; the second follows Polixenes' similar appeal to Camillo, against similar objections. The Sicilian crisis emerges when Leontes watches his wife and friend embrace, and murmurs, "'Tis far gone" (1.2.218); the Bohemian crisis surfaces when Polixenes watches Florizel and Perdita embrace, and whispers, "Is it not too far gone? 'Tis time to part them" (4.4.344). Intriguingly, Camillo is given a soliloquy on both occasions to weigh his choices, and each time his decision to flee to the other kingdom is based on a perfect balance of principled Sicilian philanthropy and pragmatic Bohemian self-serving:

> If I could find example
> Of thousands that had struck anointed kings
> And flourish'd after, I'ld not do it; but since
> Nor brass nor stone nor parchment bears not
>   one,
> Let villainy itself forswear't.
>
>   (1.2.357-61)

> Now were I happy if
> His going I could frame to serve my turn,
> Save him from danger, do him love and honor,
> Purchase the sight again of dear Sicilia.
>
>   (4.4.508-11)

Camillo is therefore precisely the counselor this couple needs in its struggle to convert natural affection into a ceremonial bond. He prescribes for them a theatrical ploy which both literally and symbolically assists their effort to reach Sicilia and there achieve marriage. Echoing the phrase "royally attorney'd" that typified the overceremonious marriage of the two kingdoms at the start of the play (1.1.27), Camillo promises to have the couple "royally appointed, as if / The scene you play were mine" (4.4.592-93). Perdita sees that "the play so lies / That I must bear a part," and Florizel adds, "Should I now meet my father, / he would not call me son." (4.4.655-58). Camillo thus helps interrupt generational continuity, but only for the sake of curing such a breach. By giving them roles and disguises—they are not "like themselves" in the interim, as both Florizel and Leontes note (4.4.588, 5.1.88-89)—Camillo corrects their excessive naturalism, using the same theatrical device that led to their wedding's postponement. Such a correction symbolically qualifies them for entrance into Sicilia, where life has become the poor player's meaningless and monotonous hour upon the stage, just as it practically permitted their escape from Bohemia. Like the statue of Hermione, they are nature smuggled back into the dead kingdom under an artificial guise. The dramatic metaphor that haunted ambition in the earlier plays now serves as a corrective, bringing back the procreative order in a form the self-alienated king and kingdom can assimilate. As the Bohemian ships hastily set sail, they set a course back from the destructive extremes.

The new garments therefore disguise the young people's natures only for the purpose of restoring them to their fathers and their ceremonial identities. The notion that garments can lastingly change one's social standing, implicit in Lady Macbeth's and Volumnia's metaphors and evident in the period's sumptuary laws, here is located only in the clowns, where it can be pleasantly satirized. As Perdita's nobility shows through her peasant trappings, so Autolycus' baseness is evident even to the gullible Bohemians: the old shepherd concludes, "His garments are rich, but he wears them not handsomely" (4.4.731-50). Autolycus gains his revenge two scenes later, when the shepherds absurdly insist that their expensive new "robes" are themselves "gentlemen born" and make their wearers such. At the same time, the shepherds take their metaphorical greeting by the royal family as "brother" and "father" literally, a humorously disarming version of Leontes' overly literal reading of "customary compliment" earlier in the play. The shepherds' mistake also playfully disarms the ambitious "family romance" of earlier plays, in which people claimed to be part of an exalted lineage to which their original birth gave them no right. To have been "gentlemen born . . . any time these four hours" is, as Autolycus suggests, entirely ridiculous (5.2.125-45). But it is ridiculous in a way that distances the characteristic errors of ambition from the main characters' redemptive reunion.

We arrive back in Sicilia shortly before the first Bohemian ship, and we quickly recognize how badly Sicilia needs the reunion. The repetitive cycle of Leontes' mourning has not forestalled aging, and the Sicilian lords, worried about "his highness' fail of issue," open the scene by urging him to remarry:

> *Cleomines* Sir, you have done enough, and
>   have perform'd
> A saint-like sorrow. No fault could you make
> Which you have not redeem'd; indeed paid
>   down
> More penitence than done trespass. At the last
> Do as the heavens have done, forget your evil,
> With them, forgive yourself.
>
>   (5.1.1-6)

Paradoxically, this assurance that Leontes' penance has eradicated all his earlier faults actually indicates that those faults still infect the Sicilian court. The diction is relentless in its theological implications, which are all too similar to those of earlier remarks underestimating the residual burden of original sin. Cleomines credits his king with "saint-like" conduct that has already "redeem'd" every conceivable "fault," that has actually outweighed his primal "trespass." Such forgiveness belongs only to heaven, according to Elizabethan doctrine, but this speech makes Leontes a co-executor of God's elective Grace.[56] Cleomines' plea that Leontes "forget your evil" is another example of Sicilia's careless diction concerning innocence: he simply means that Leontes should now put his mistreatment of Hermione out of his mind, but his phrase reminds us that he mistreated her because he was determined to forget his evil in a more general sense.

But, under Paulina's guidance, Leontes is no more susceptible to his former sort of presumption than he is to his lords' entreaties for a new marriage. He tells Cleomines that his childlessness is the rightful punishment for his violation, and when Paulina reminds him that the mortal sin which destroyed his marriage is permanent in its effects, he accepts that the wages of his error is death, though that fruit is "bitter / Upon thy tongue as in my thought" (5.1.6-19). The reward for this new-found humility is the return of the lost regenerative flowers, Perdita and Florizel, a counterpart to the destructive return of "the seeds of Banquo" and those of Duncan to Macbeth's Scotland. In greeting the young couple, Leontes carefully acknowledges his own sinfulness and his kingdom's diseased mortality:

> The blessed gods
> Purge all infection from our air whilest you
> Do climate here! You have a holy father,
> A graceful gentleman, against whose person
> (So sacred as it is) I have done sin,
> For which the heavens, taking angry note,
> Have left me issueless; and your father's bless'd
> (As he from heaven merits it) with you,
> Worthy his goodness.
>
> (5.1.168-76)

Like the Sicilians discussing innocence earlier in the play, like Caliban dreaming of the heavens in *The Tempest* (3.2.140-43), Leontes is groping with the darkened outlines of a Christian revelation, but unable yet to see it face to face. Instead, he displaces onto Polixenes the characteristics of the Christian God, the "sacred," "graceful" and "holy father" whose "goodness" actually "merits" every conceivable "blessing," and "against whose person" Leontes has "done sin." The theological emphasis of this passage is far too persistent to be accidental, and what it suggests is Leontes' growing recognition of his more abstract sin, though he cannot yet recognize its real character or its real victim.

Leontes' first words to the young couple suggest that his moral convalescence in other areas is similarly encouraging but incomplete:

> Your mother was most true to wedlock, Prince,
> For she did print your royal father off,
> Conceiving you. Were I but twenty-one,
> Your father's image is so hit in you
> (His very air) that I should call you brother,
> As I did him, and speak of something wildly
> By us perform'd before. Most dearly welcome!

> And your fair princess—goddess! O! alas,
> I lost a couple, that 'twixt heaven and earth
> Might thus have stood, begetting wonder, as
> You, gracious couple, do; and then I lost
> (All mine own folly) the society,
> Amity too, of your brave father, whom
> (Though bearing misery) I desire my life
> Once more to look on him.
>
> (5.1.124-38)

The first sentence acknowledges that a child's physical resemblance to the husband proves the wife's fidelity—precisely what Leontes refused to believe, in his deep mistrust of the senses, at Perdita's birth. The last six lines submit "wonder" to the process of "begetting," and credit both to the "grac[e]" expressed in the couple's bodily nobility. The final few lines clearly contrast with the Sicilians' former denial of time, suffering, and death, specifically as displayed in their patriotic but unrealistic attitude toward Mamillius: "They that went on crutches ere he was born desire yet their life to see him a man" (1.1.39-41). Faced with Florizel, Mamillius' parallel in age and role (1.2.163-72; 5.1.115-23), Leontes hopes only to survive in pain long enough to see the boy's father, not the boy's own maturity. Certainly the Leontes who declares himself "a friend" to the young couple's "desires" at the end of the scene accepts human sexuality better than the man who furiously rejected the idea that he could have fathered Perdita.

The middle part of his speech, however, indicates that Leontes' education on these points is not yet complete. He perceives Perdita as a "goddess"—what her costume at the sheep-shearing had made her—and places the couple "'twixt heaven and earth." As he displaces his earlier godly role more humbly but still wrongly onto Polixenes, so he displaces his role as an immortal inhabitant of Eden onto this pair; good and lovely as they may be, they are not Adam and Eve any more than he and Hermione were. The hard-won generational distinction threatens to collapse in Leontes' impulse to embrace young Florizel as if he were the young Polixenes. Though for the moment Leontes keeps this impulse safely in the subjunctive, as Polixenes did his "not guilty" plea, we sense its appeal to him.

Later in the scene, the time-denying impulse returns and conquers him in a parallel case of substitution, a case clearly designed to make us morally mistrustful of such a tendency:

> *Florizel*   Beseech you, sir,
> Remember since you ow'd no more to time
> Than I do now. With thought of such affections,
> Step forth mine advocate. At your request
> My father will grant precious things as trifles.
> *Leontes* Would he do so, I'ld beg your
>   precious mistress,

Which he counts but a trifle.
Paulina   Sir, my liege,
Your eye hath too much youth in't. Not a
   month
Fore your queen died, she was more worth
   such gazes
Than what you look on now.
Leontes   I thought of her,
Even in those looks I made.

                                       (5.1.218-28)

As plausible and sufficient as this reply may seem, it reveals the dangerous absurdity of a moral idealism that leads toward incest; indeed, in Shakespeare's source, the Leontes-figure tries to seduce his unrecognized daughter, and threatens her with rape when she resists him. Even with his only son dead, Leontes finds himself in a sort of Oedipal struggle, because his desire to be "boy eternal" leads him to desire a girl-eternal version of his wife.

The same problem recurs when, on seeing the statue, Leontes protests,

> Hermione was not so much wrinkled, nothing
> So aged as this seems.
> *Polixenes*   O, not by much,
> *Paulina* So much the more our carver's
>   excellence,
> Which lets go by some sixteen years, and
>   makes her
> As she liv'd now.
>
>   (5.3.28-32)

He still tends to prefer the version of Hermione that time-denying art would conventionally strive to create, rather than the version nature would have created had she survived. But art and nature are so thoroughly interwoven in the symbolic presentation that Hermione and Perdita form a web of integrated identity, a safety net through which he cannot fall, because "the art itself is Nature," to use Polixenes' earlier formulation (4.4.97). The human Perdita is praised as static art, and only the supposed statue shows nature's progress. Where Macbeth could reunify himself neither by resolute advance nor by tedious retreat, Leontes finds a saving integration of natural and artificial identities every way he turns.

But only Perdita's return can rouse into life the latent nature in Leontes' and Hermione's artificial poses. Leontes declares the young couple "Welcome hither, / As is the spring to th' earth," and a servant calls Perdita "the most peerless piece of earth, I think, / That e'er the sun shone bright on" (5.1.151-52, 94-95). Paulina immediately chides the servant for forgetting Hermione "As every present time doth boast itself / Above a better gone," but Perdita is rightly time's choice to replace Hermione. The servant's poem, which Paulina bitterly reminds him had declared that Hermione "'had not been, / Nor was not to be equall'd,'" was merely a typical piece of Sicilian art, emptily flattering the royal family with the illusion that it could overcome time. The very fact that the poem has itself been refuted by time is the most fitting commentary on it.

As the transplanting of Bohemia's flora restores Sicilia's natural foundation and thereby ends its unnaturally prolonged winter, the fantastic "winter's tale" regains a reality that allows it to progress toward a happier season. The stories of destructive and redemptive nature are repeatedly described as "like an old tale" (5.2.27-29, 61; 5.3.116-17), but they are also described in words that associate them with the procreative miracle that allows them to be true. The report that Leontes has "found his heir" is "Most true, if ever truth were pregnant by circumstance," and the story of Paulina's statue gives hope that "some new grace will be born" (5.2.29-31, 110-11; cf. 132). The play's ethical pattern forbids it to win its audience with unnatural events, as Autolycus' ballads about unnatural births and diets do. Instead, the restoration of naturally-born children and natural appetites makes the reunions so wonderful "that ballad-makers cannot be able to describe it" (5.2.24-25). The elements of fantasy and artificiality persist in these closing scenes, but in a form that allows Shakespeare to show they are actually part of a natural reality whose scope and worth (as in *Macbeth*) have been badly underrated, and whose miracles are so frequent and ubiquitous that we tend to overlook them. The characters on stage disable our suspicions that this is all merely an old tale or a magical conjuration, by echoing those suspicions and then putting them aside as the miracle of nature unfolds.

Act five, scene two, returns the linguistic arts to their natural basis, and prepares us for the statue's reconciliation of art and nature, by the way it describes the reunion of Sicilia with its Bohemian exiles. The play has moved from the courtiers' dangerous assumption, in the opening scene, that flowery language could fully embody their kings' mutual affection, to concessions by two Sicilian gentlemen that their words cannot adequately describe the wordless expressions of the kings' reunion (5.2.9-19, 42-58). Natural feeling, once smothered by ambitious language, is here protected from language by a double wall of humility. The Third Gentleman reports the next reunion in terms that suggest the convergence of artificial elements of identity with natural ones: he speaks of "unity in the proofs," which include Hermione's garment and Antigonus' letters as well as "the majesty of the creature in resemblance of the mother; the affection of nobleness which nature shows above her breeding; and many other evidence [that] proclaim her with all certainty, to be the King's daughter" (5.2.30-39). The association of nobleness with nature, and of majesty with hereditary physical appearance, suggests that the false distinctions that disrupted Bohemia are disappearing along with those that disrupted Sicilia.

In closing his description of the reunion scene, the Third Gentleman furthers our impression that art is being reincorporated into nature, by remarking that "Who was most marble there chang'd color" (5.2.89-90). This grand metaphor, like those of the play's opening speeches, will soon become much more literal than its speaker can anticipate; but this time the literal level provides reconciliation rather than "separation" (1.1.26). Four lines later, he informs us that the court have all gone to see the statue of Hermione, "a piece many years in doing and now newly perform'd by that rare Italian master Julio Romano, who, had he himself eternity and could put breath into his work, would beguile Nature of her custom, so perfectly he is her ape." This description recalls Leontes' promise in the preceding scene not to remarry "Unless another, / As like Hermione as is her picture, / Affront his eye," which will only be "when your first queen's again in breath," when the work of art becomes again a work of nature (5.1.73-84). But Julio Romano's potentially Promethean powers are kept safely in the subjunctive here, like Polixenes' earlier speculations on escaping original sin, or Leontes' recent ones on ignoring generational time. The Sicilian court has learned that cultural endeavors alone, however skillfully refined, can provide neither eternity nor natural life to inhabit it. The Gentleman adds, "Thither with all greediness of affection are they gone, and there they intend to sup" (5.2.102-03). The hearty affections and appetites that were Bohemia's great merits have returned to cold, abstemious Sicilia.

Paulina promptly puts this new naturalness to the test—a sort of Rorschach test—by presenting the statue for evaluation in a radically cultural and ceremonial context. The setting as well as the occasion encourage distant reverence rather than human interaction. We are not only in Sicilia but in a chapel, not only in a chapel but in an art gallery within that chapel, with the theater's own discovery-space curtain probably hiding the statue itself. This is typical of the benevolent misleadings performed by Shakespeare's comic heroines, such as Rosaline and Portia and Rosalind, who test the results of their educational programs under the most trying circumstances available, to be sure that the romantic maturity of a Berowne, Bassanio, or Orlando will last. Paulina wants the audience in general, and Leontes in particular, to acknowledge the beneficent natural basis for even the most artificial-seeming of phenomena. Before revealing the statue, she assures him that it "Excels whatever yet you look'd upon, / Or hand of man hath done" (5.3.16-17), which is a beautifully equivocal clue. It encourages and then forbids him to view the statue as a superhuman creation of human art; it forbids and then encourages him to view it as the divinely created woman he has known.

At first, in their eagerness for reunion with Hermione, Leontes and Perdita nearly fail the test: they choose the artificial basis for reunion, making themselves into companion statues instead of eliciting the statue's living humanity. Leontes says he feels "more stone than it," and observes Perdita "Standing like stone with thee" (5.3.37-42). When Perdita and Leontes yield in turn to a natural desire to kiss the statue, Paulina restrains them by asserting again—in hopes of curing entirely—the delusion that this woman is a work of static and cosmetic art rather than nature, and should be treated as such. These warnings challenge father and daughter to appreciate the "art / That Nature makes." Perdita, who earlier preferred natural to cosmetic colors, here has trouble telling the difference (5.3.46-48). Leontes asks,

> What fine chisel
> Could ever yet cut breath? Let no man
>   mock me,
> For I will kiss her.
> *Paulina*   Good my lord, forbear.
> The ruddiness upon her lip is wet;
> You'll mar it if you kiss it; stain your own
> With oily painting. Shall I draw the curtain?
>   (5.3.78-83)

By kissing the statue, Leontes would not turn into a painted companion-piece; he would return fully to life, as her conjugal companion.

Leontes has earned such a transformation essentially by wishing for it. He no longer views conjugal relations as a mutual staining and marring, and retracts his implicit foolish wish for a pure, cold, unchanging version of his wife. Instead, like King Lear holding the dead Cordelia, he insists that a single breath of life in her would surpass all that human art can achieve, however fine its chisel. By insisting on staying with the statue, insisting that the curtain not fall on this imitation of life, Leontes makes the crucial choice for a living Hermione over an elegantly artificial one:

> *Paulina*   I'll draw the curtain.
> My lord's almost so far transported that
> He'll think anon it lives.
> *Leontes*   O sweet Paulina,
> Make me to think so twenty years together!
> No settled senses of the world can match
> The pleasure of that madness. Let't alone.
> *Paulina* I am sorry, sir, I have thus far stirr'd
>   you; but I could afflict you farther.
> *Leontes*   Do, Paulina;
> For this affliction has a taste as sweet
> As any cordial comfort.
>   (5.3.68-77)

An appetite for life has replaced Leontes' life-denying madness of the first act, typified by the transition from the poisoned "cordials" he imagines drinking and serving Polixenes to this sweet and salutary one. He finds a value in affliction, a use for adversity, and leaves his "settled senses of the world" to restore Hermione's life rather than (as earlier) to destroy it. In making this choice for the statue, and in fondly making his visitors represent his lost children, he in effect wills his family back into existence; and he thereby becomes the natural self he "might . . . have been" that would have saved him from losing his family in the first place (5.1.176-78).

But to maintain the play's moral pattern, Shakespeare must emphasize that these fantasies come true because they have a basis in nature, and not solely because of Leontes' life-affirming imagination. He takes the trouble to explain that Paulina "hath privately twice or thrice a day, ever since the death of Hermione, visited that remov'd house" where the statue is lodged, and where the royal family now retreats "to sup" (5.2.103-07). We may infer in retrospect, after the statue awakens, that Paulina brought Hermione meals—a significant inference, because the play often uses eating as a symbol or synecdoche of ongoing natural life. From this perspective, it is dangerously wrong to indulge in the fantasy (as some critics do) that Hermione has essentially "come back to life. We do not, that is to say, seek to explain the impossible away. Instead, we gladly accept the impossibility for the sake of the symbolic pattern."[57] Shakespeare's didactic pattern, like Paulina's, demands natural explanations that dispel the tempting illusion of impossibility. Northrop Frye suggests that "in *The Winter's Tale* nature is associated, not with the credible, but with the incredible: nature as an order is subordinated to the nature that yearly confronts us with the impossible miracle of renewed life."[58] What we must remember is that the appearance of a new generation is finally as miraculous a phenomenon as the survival and reappearance of the old. As the witches induced Macbeth to forfeit regenerative nature in favor of supernatural tricks, so Shakespeare's and Paulina's plays lead us, together with Leontes, to overlook temporarily the miracle of "great creating Nature" (4.4.88) in our fascination with the apparent miracle of art, the enlivened statue. Only if our values shift in retrospect, and we come to respect food and shelter and human patience as the necessary basis for such impressive art, have we shared in Leontes' successful education.

Paulina therefore insists repeatedly that no one mistake her awakening of the statue for the black arts. She intends to restore the very sort of regenerative order that witchcraft subverted in Macbeth's Scotland, and were she to recreate Leontes' family by conjuration, she would contradict the lesson in obedience to nature. If supernatural Grace is at work here, and for complete salvation it must be, a sort of prevenient grace arising from nature rather than descending from above it must also contribute.[59] So Paulina declares that she is not

"assisted / By wicked powers," that hers is not "unlawful business," and that her "spell is lawful" (5.3.90-105). If this is magic, it is magic of an allowed sort, and therefore similar to the play's allowed sort of ambition. The only kind of magic generally considered lawful in the Renaissance was "intransitive," intended not to impose on nature but rather to elicit the best qualities already inherent in people or objects.[60]

Earlier Leontes had demanded that Paulina be burnt as "A mankind witch" (2.3.68) for her efforts to make him acknowledge his paternity of Perdita. Now, confronting him with another instance of natural survival and his human kinship, Paulina is understandably fearful that it will again be dismissed as witchcraft. When he first sees that statue, Leontes clearly demonstrates the threat to Paulina's project:

> O royal piece,
> There's magic in thy majesty, which has
> My evils conjur'd to remembrance, and
> From thy admiring daughter took the spirits,
> Standing like stone with thee.
>
> (5.3.38-42)

The living Hermione is here portrayed as a conjurer who revives past evils, steals people's spirits, turns them to stone as if she were a Medusa, and uses magic to simulate majesty—hardly a generous description of a woman who is standing passively, displaying the natural majesty of her birth. When the same majestic nature wins Florizel's heart for Perdita, Polixenes errs in strikingly similar terms, calling her an "enchantment" and a "fresh piece / Of excellent witchcraft" (4.4.434, 422—23).

Both women might well complain to the kings (as Othello does to the Senate at 1.6.169) that a noble nature is the only witchcraft they have used; but the very fact that they are thus accused demonstrates how easily the blessings of nature can be mistaken for strayings from nature. Since Eve, women have been accused of witchcraft merely for eliciting an amoral sexual impulse that men fear and deny in their own nature. Only when Leontes can make himself reach lovingly out for Hermione does he correct these characteristic errors:

> *Paulina*   Nay, present your hand.
> When she was young, you woo'd her; now, in age,
> Is she become the suitor?
> *Leontes*   O, she's warm!
> If this be magic, let it be an art
> Lawful as eating.
>
> (5.3.107-11)

Paulina is reminding us, as she reminds Leontes, of the courtship that took place exactly a generation ago, when at last he clasped Hermione's flower-like hand in marriage (1.2.102-04). That cycle of winter and spring has repeated itself, yielding the nubile "Blossom" Perdita, and Leontes has regained the ability to appreciate such miracles of nature. His fond embrace of Hermione contrasts sharply with his earlier disgust at physical expressions of affection, and his endorsement of eating contrasts with his earlier revulsion from food and drink, which in him as in Coriolanus evinced an effort to deny his bodily frailties. . . .

Notes

[49] Rondet, *Original Sin*, p. 115, cites *De Genesi contra Manichaeos*, I, 29; PL col. 187.

[50] Schanzer, "The Structural Pattern," p. 95.

[51] C. L. Barber, *Shakespeare's Festive Comedy* (Princeton: Princeton University Press, 1959), discusses a similar dialectical pattern in the earlier comedies.

[52] Philip M. Weinstein, "An Interpretation of Pastoral in *The Winter's Tale*," *Shakespeare Quarterly* 22 (1971), 97-101, discusses Bohemia as a flawed but corrective counterpart to Sicilia.

[53] David Kaula, "Autolycus' Trumpery," *Studies in English Literature* 16 (1976), 287-303.

[54] The words are from Clerimont's song in *Epicoene*, 1.1.91-102. John Byshop, *Beautifull Blossomes . . . from the best trees of all kyndes* (London, 1577), pp. 21-24, warns against the delusive appeal of elaborate clothing and cosmetics. Arthur O. Lovejoy, *Essays in the History of Ideas* (Baltimore: Johns Hopkins University Press, 1948), p. 330, notes Tertullian's warning against betraying God as the "Author of nature" by coloring one's garments. See also Erasmus on *Fucus* in the *Praise of Folly*.

[55] See Burgundy's rejection of the newly disowned Cordelia, *King Lear*, 1.1.206. Thomas F. Van Laan, *Role-Playing in Shakespeare* (Toronto: University of Toronto Press, 1978), pp. 37 and 170, observes that the paternal interventions blocking marriage in *Midsummer Night's Dream* and *Romeo and Juliet* bring familial identity dangerously into conflict with personal identity. Near the end of Sidney's *Arcadia*, Euarchus resembles Polixenes in denying his disguised son and nephew any special rights as princes, and instead condemning them for allowing sexual passions to displace them from their royal roles into false, degrading identities and circumstances.

[56] Roland M. Frye, *Shakespeare and Christian Doctrine* (Princeton: Princeton University Press, 1963), p. 243, points out that Cleomines is guilty of claiming, on behalf of his king, "sufficient contrition," a claim Luther characterized as inherently "presumptuous."

[57] Janet Adelman, *The Common Liar* (New Haven: Yale University Press, 1973), p. 167.

[58] Northrop Frye, "Recognition in *The Winter's Tale*," in Muir, p. 197.

[59] Van Laan, *Role-Playing*, p. 114, suggests that the redemptive power in the romances usually rests in someone who has remained strictly faithful to her "true identity" as a human being, "and this suggests that the magic depends in part on some sort of collaboration . . . that, perhaps, the fidelity in some way 'earns' the divine intervention." By accepting her own mortal identity and humanity's mortal limitations, Paulina can succeed in the sort of semi-Pelagian project Leontes mishandled, and repair the damage caused by his denials.

[60] D. P. Walker, *Spiritual and Demonic Magic from Ficino to Campanella* (London: Warburg Institute, 1958), p. 32 and passim.

Bruce W. Young (essay date 1992)

SOURCE: "Ritual as an Instrument of Grace: Parental Blessings in *Richard III, All's Well That Ends Well*, and *The Winter's Tale*," in *True Rites and Maimed Rites: Ritual and Anti-Ritual in Shakespeare and His Age*, edited by Linda Woodbridge and Edward Berry, University of Ilinois Press, 1992, pp. 169-200.

[*In this excerpt, Young discusses the significance of the parental blessing in* The Winter's Tale—*both the offering and the denial—and its function in conveying grace.*]

The parental blessing was one of the most important and pervasive rituals of Renaissance England.[3] Indeed, it seems to have been peculiar to England during the Renaissance.[4] It goes back at least to the fourteenth century, and probably much earlier; and it appears to have been practiced by Catholics and Protestants, Puritans and non-Puritans, with little variation in form or meaning into the early seventeenth century.[5] In "well-ordered" households the ritual took place daily, morning and evening, with each child kneeling before its parents, both father and mother, and saying (to quote William Perkins), "Father I pray you bless me, Mother I pray you bless me" (469), or words to that effect.[6] Each parent would respond to the request by calling on God to bless the child and using one or both hands to signify the conferring of the blessing.

Renaissance writers describe several different forms of the blessing, suggesting that the precise gesture used may have varied from person to person or from time to time. Richard Hooker, the great Anglican theologian, refers to the *"imposition of handes"* (2:321). This would mean the placing of one or both hands on the head of the child who is kneeling before the parent. The same gestures are described by an eighteenth-century traveler visiting England, with the added information that children may kiss the hands that have blessed them (César de Saussure, A *foreign view of England in the Reigns of George I. and George II.* [1902], quoted in Legg 168). Another possible form of blessing, supported by pictorial and literary evidence, is the holding of one or both hands *above* the head of the recipient, not actually on it (see Whitforde, sig. D4ᵛ).

The child's kneeling to receive the blessing was in part a recognition of the parent's superior authority and maturity and an expression of respect for the parent's age, status, and (in some cases) virtue and wisdom. By kneeling, children—and this apparently included the adult children of aging parents—also acknowledged the parent as one of the sources of their own being and identity.[7] The ritual thus symbolized and affirmed the intimate connection, physical, spiritual, and emotional, between parent and child and brought to mind the duties of both: the parent's duty to educate, nourish, love, and discipline the child; the child's duty to love, honor, obey, and (when necessary) care for the parents. Though subordination—that is, location at a lower point in a hierarchical system—was certainly one of the notions conveyed by the child's kneeling, this subordination did not necessarily imply unconditional submission to a parent's wishes; it certainly did not mean that the child's agency and identity were entirely subsumed within those of the parent.[8]

Besides its symbolic, social, and emotional functions, kneeling served the practical function of enabling the parent to conveniently place hands on the child's head. The child's kneeling also effectively stationed the parent between the child and the heavens as a kind of quasi-priestly intermediary ready to bestow heavenly influence on the child. That is how Richard Hooker depicts the parent's role in giving a blessing, which he compares both with blessings described in the Bible and with blessings given in his own time by ministers. In these various blessings, someone with a special "callinge" and "dutie" to act for the good of others is able, through prayer, to *"blesse"*—that is, "to obteine the graces which God doth bestowe" (2:321). Besides viewing the parental blessing as a sacred act, involving heavenly grace, Hooker also sees it as a sign of the parent's feeling of responsibility and love for the child and of the connection between them. The *"imposition of handes,"* he says, betokens "our *restrayned desires* to the partie, whome wee present unto God by prayer" (2:321). The hands serve as an instrument for conveying heavenly power that will bless the child, but they also allow physical contact between parent and child and thus enable the blessing to serve as an expression of parental affection. Affection is also expressed by the child's kissing the parent's hands, an action that is sometimes made explicit in Shakespeare's depiction of the ritual.[9] . . .

In *The Winter's Tale,* a parental blessing takes place in the climactic scene—perhaps the most prominent appearance of the ritual in the Shakespearean canon—and its function is emphatically to convey grace. *Grace,* as a host of critics have perceived, is a crucial word and a crucial concept in *The Winter's Tale.* F. C. Tinkler, for instance, asserts that "Grace and Graciousness" are the "keynote of the play" (345). The concept, though not the word, occurs in the play's short first scene. When Archidamus, one of Polixenes' courtiers, laments that Bohemia can never adequately repay the hospitality he and his fellow courtiers have received in Sicily, Camillo responds, "You pay a great deal too dear for what's given freely" (I.i.17-18). The idea is repeated in the last scene, when Paulina tells Leontes that his visit to her "poor house" is "a surplus of [his] grace, which never / [Her] life may last to answer" (V.iii.6-8). *Grace* here means "bounty," "generosity"; it refers to giving that expects no repayment, that is motivated solely by a desire for another's good. Such "grace" is an expression of good will, of a desire to bless, of the value placed on others for their own sake, not for what they can give in return.

Perhaps the most memorable occurrences of the word *grace* are in act I, scene ii, where the word is repeated three times within twenty-five lines. The word takes on a different sense with each appearance, but the effect of the scene is to associate and even mingle these several senses. In its first appearance, when Hermione exclaims, "Grace to boot!" it means heavenly influence. In context—Polixenes has just suggested that he and Leontes have fallen from their childhood innocence—the word brings to mind the divine influence needed to regenerate sinful hearts and redeem humankind from their fallen state. Nineteen lines later, playfully asking Leontes to tell her on what previous occasion she spoke well, Hermione uses the word *grace* as a personal name, with the meaning of "virtue," applied to this earlier good deed ("O, would her name were Grace!"). When he identifies the deed—her offer of herself to him as wife—she says, "'Tis Grace indeed." *Grace* here means graciousness and generosity, as well as virtue, all these meanings being implied by the words Leontes quotes her as having said years before: "I am yours for ever" (I.ii.80, 99, 100, 105).

We shortly learn that Leontes doubts Hermione's gracious offer at the very moment he remembers it. Yet Hermione soon makes it clear, if it has not been clear before, that she is the play's most powerful figure of grace. Even when she defends herself most vigorously, she retains the abundant good will that marked her first responses to false accusation: "you, my lord, / Do but mistake"; "How will this grieve you, / When you shall come to clearer knowledge"; "I never wish'd to see you sorry, now / I trust I shall" (II.i.80-81, 96-97, 123-24). Generous, virtuous, associated with "great creating Nature" and with the divinely endowed power to give life, Hermione (like the women of *All's Well That Ends Well*) has the power to bless and redeem.[26] She is so close to ideal, in fact, that we may find it hard to accept her as a real human being. Yet what helps make her believable and appealing is that, though associated with sanctity and grace, she is vulnerable and human as well. She is capable of playful joking and camaraderie and can talk openly, though chastely, of sexual matters. Throughout the play she is associated with the concrete processes of life—pregnancy, childbirth, and her own warm, bodily presence. She is physically affectionate, so much so that her physicality threatens Leontes and arouses his suspicions. And though she may sometimes seem close to perfect, she, like other humans, requires grace—that is, blessing from a source outside herself. Having fallen out of "grace"— that is, out of favor—with her husband (III.ii.47), she trusts in "pow'rs divine" and holds that the unjust treatment she is receiving will be for her "better grace" (III.ii.28,II.i.122). She thus acknowledges not only her less than perfect humanity, but her dependence on other human beings and on the favor and providential care of heaven.

Grace is responsible in several senses for the restoration of happiness in the final scene. Leontes has undergone a fundamental change of heart and has, according to Cleomines, been forgiven by the heavens (V.i.1-6). Divine grace has also been at work in the restoration of Perdita and her betrothal to Florizel (V.i.35-36, V.iii.150-51). Paulina's whole project, culminating in this scene, may be viewed as a work of grace, even in its harsher aspect of confronting Leontes with his misdeeds and provoking his repentance. Though the heavens do not literally restore Hermione to physical life, they aid in restoring her to life within her family. The "grace" with which the play ends is thus not a state of purely isolated personal virtue, but a condition that requires the blessing of the gods and that depends on generous, trusting relationships with other human beings. Hermione is now restored to her husband's favor (i.e., "grace")—as he, having undergone a far more radical change, is to hers. Though she does not yet speak to him, she "hangs about his neck" and has apparently offered her hand before he gives his. She gives every evidence of being now, as Leontes remembers her, "as tender / As infancy and grace" (V.iii.105-12, 26-27).

The word *grace* is also associated with Perdita. She is "grown in grace / Equal with wond'ring" ("grace" here suggesting "beauty," "virtue," "graciousness," and "gracefulness") (IV.i.24). She and Florizel are a "gracious couple," "gracious" (as Leontes's words make clear) suggesting qualities that beget "wonder" and even approach divinity (V.i.131-34). Perdita, product, we are told, of "good goddess Nature," is the most radiant example of the sanctity and divinity infused from heaven into the human world (II.iii.104). But Perdita is more than merely "radiant": she is passionate, plain-spoken, even stubborn. She is associated with fertility and the forces of nature. Indeed, the "grace" with which she is endowed includes these forces and has come to her by natural means. Grace in its various senses has come to her especially from her mother, acting in co-operation with "great creating Nature" (IV.iv.88), an entity which in turn is the "instrument" or "handmaid" of the gods.[27]

Another instrument of grace, also associated closely with Hermione and Perdita and combining the human with the divine, is the parental blessing. Unlike *Richard III* and *All's Well That Ends Well,* where the blessing ritual is most prominent near the beginning, *The Winter's Tale* does not actually present the ritual until the climactic closing scene. Indeed, the preceding action may be viewed from one angle as a series of failed blessings, lost or incomplete opportunities that find their fulfillment at the end of the play. The first such opportunity is offered in act II, scene iii, when Paulina presents a newborn daughter to Leontes and "commends it to [his] blessing" (line 67). Instead of taking the child in his arms and praying for divine protection—as Henry VIII does in giving the newborn Elizabeth her first father's blessing (*H8* V.iv.10-11)—Leontes refuses to acknowledge the child as his, and even threatens its life. His horror of being linked with "another's issue" leads him to imagine seeing Perdita grow up to "kneel / And call [him] father," as if requesting a blessing (*WT* II.iii.155-56). In other words, he imagines—and again rejects—another opportunity to bless his child.

After sixteen years of separation from her, Leontes is again given the opportunity to bless his daughter. He blesses her unwittingly in act V, scene i, when he welcomes her and calls her "goddess" (lines 130-31); and a formal blessing doubtless takes place as part of the reunion described in act V, scene ii.[28] But the fulfillment of these allusions to the blessing ritual is reserved for the last scene, and there the ritual is performed by Perdita's mother, not by her father.

The first hint of the blessing comes early in the scene when Perdita kneels before what appears to be a statue of her mother and says:

> And give me leave,
> And do not say 'tis superstition, that
> I kneel, and then implore her blessing. Lady,
> Dear queen, that ended when I but began,
> Give me that hand of yours to kiss.
>
> (V.iii.42-46)

The reference to superstition, especially joined as it is here with kneeling before a "statue," may reflect the anxiety felt by some during the seventeenth century as to whether kneeling for a parental blessing might be among the "reliques of Popish . . . superstition" (Ames

Act IV, scene iv. Old Shephard, Florizel, Perdita, Clown, Polixenes, and Camillo. Frontispiece to the Hanmer edition by Francis Hayman (1744).

94).[29] But surely the primary associations Perdita's words and gestures should evoke are the filial love and reverence of a daughter for her mother as she kneels for a mother's blessing. Besides the kneeling, the idea of kissing a parent's hand would also suggest love and reverence to an audience familiar with the ritual, which often included such a gesture.

Later in the scene, as the statue apparently comes to life and it becomes clear that this is the living Hermione, Paulina tells Perdita, "kneel / And pray your mother's blessing," and then says to the mother: "Turn, good lady, / Our Perdita is found." Hermione's words indicate that she is now giving a parent's blessing: "You gods, look down / And from your sacred vials pour your graces / Upon my daughter's head!" (V.iii.119-23). The power of this blessing comes partly from the words used: the rhythms, the imagery, the word "grace" with all the meanings it has accumulated through the course of the play—beauty, gracefulness, virtue, favor, graciousness, generosity, forgiveness, and unconditional love. The blessing's power comes also from the ges-

tures used: the kneeling of Perdita, Hermione's lifting of her hands to appeal for heaven's graces (a gesture not specified by the text or by editors, but surely appropriate), and her placing of her hands at the same time on or above her daughter's head to symbolize the bestowal of those graces on her and to affirm the bond newly created between her daughter and herself.

Besides the gestures, the words of the blessing would also have been familiar and resonant to an early audience. Despite the pagan context, Hermione's appeal to the heavens to bestow graces on her daughter closely resembles the words some Renaissance parents used in blessing their children. According to Peter Erondell, a parent might say, "I pray the strong Almightie God to increase his graces in you, and to blesse you," or "I pray God to blesse you all my Children, and to increase his graces in you" (sig. E7ᵛ, P5ᵛ)—words close to Hermione's "pour your graces / Upon my daughter's head!" The emotions associated with the blessing ritual are heightened in *The Winter's Tale* by the long separation between mother and daughter that is now ending. But even here Shakespeare is drawing on a concept familiar to his contemporaries. Besides its daily practice with children living at home, the blessing ritual also served to mark a child's reunion with a parent after separation. Hugh Rhodes, writing in the sixteenth century, advised:

> When that thy parents come in syght,
> 　doe to them reverence:
> Aske them blessing if they have
> 　bene long out of presence.
>
> (73)

"Long out of presence" is a weak understatement if we are thinking of the separation of Perdita and Hermione. Yet the very flatness of Rhodes's verses reveals, by contrast, how *The Winter's Tale* lifts to mythic height what would have been a common experience for many of the play's first viewers.

We can guess at the experience of these first viewers by remembering that this ritual, taking place on stage at a moment of thematic and emotional climax, was one most of them had taken part in daily as children and still performed daily as parents. Such viewers must have seen in this parental blessing a striking combination of the wonderful and the ordinary. The blessing ritual would thus have helped give the scene the effect suggested by the Friar's words in *Much Ado About Nothing:* "Let wonder seem familiar" (V.iv.70).

Despite its familiar features, though, this blessing at the end of *The Winter's Tale* is not entirely ordinary. For one thing, the role of the child is emphasized more strongly here than in many other occurrences in Shakespeare and, undoubtedly, in contemporary life. As a result, in this play the offering of grace, the conveying of divine power, does not go in one direction only, from parent to child. Just as, during the "wide gap of time," Paulina and Leontes reversed the usual sovereign-subject relationship, so the younger generation prove in some ways to be the teachers and healers of their parents. Mamillius "makes old hearts fresh" (I.i.39); young Florizel, Polixenes tells us, "with his varying childness cures in me / Thoughts that would thick my blood" (I.ii.170-71). Perdita especially is associated with divine, regenerative power and is even described as a life-giving goddess of the spring (IV.iv.1-3; V.i.131, 151-52). With these allusions to children's restorative power in the background, it is difficult not to see in the ritual blessing of the last scene a reciprocal act: Hermione calls for heavenly grace to descend upon her daughter, yet Perdita conveys grace—love, regenerative power—in return. It is as if Perdita, especially now that Hermione can see and touch her, brings the resurrection of her mother to completion, giving birth to the woman who bore her.[30]

Another feature of the blessing in *The Winter's Tale* that, at least to a degree, reverses expectations is the fact that it is given by Perdita's mother, not her father. It is not that fathers' blessings were privileged over mothers'; the evidence suggests strongly that they were not. Yet, with both parents alive and especially given Leontes's failure to bless Perdita as an infant, we might expect to see both a mother's and a father's blessing—as indeed we do in *Pericles*.[31] The foregrounding of the mother's blessing in *The Winter's Tale* is doubtless in part a matter of dramatic construction: the second of two climactic blessings might seem anticlimactic. Yet it is likely that this foregrounding has thematic significance as well. The presence of a mother's blessing in the last scene probably has something to do with the association of both the ritual and women with grace. Indeed, all three of the plays emphasized here present women as possessing special kinds of creative or transforming power. All three also offer a picture of women's solidarity with each other and of their contrast with "graceless" men. Especially in *The Winter's Tale,* the parental blessing functions as a means one woman has of expressing her solidarity with another. And in the other plays it serves as an instrument women use to instruct and influence men.[32]

These plays thus join with other historical evidence in calling into question one of Lawrence Stone's central assertions: that parental blessings functioned mainly to reinforce patriarchal power, whether this is taken to mean a parent's power over a child or a man's power over a woman. Though Shakespeare probably emphasizes the role of children and women more than many of his contemporaries would have done, he is nevertheless drawing on common features of the blessing ritual: their performance by both women and men and their use to express love as well as—even much more than—difference in status. Stone's connection of the

blessing with "the utter subordination of the child" (*Family* 171) and Coppélia Kahn's description of it as an "extreme" expression of patriarchal power (16) hardly seem accurate reflections of Shakespeare's use— or his contemporaries' experience and understanding— of the custom.

Notes

Indeed, a careful review of Shakespeare's plays and of other evidence from the period makes it clear that, for almost everyone, the parental blessing was an unusually positive act. Associated with ancient biblical precedents, it was believed to convey heavenly influence that could regenerate and sanctify. The parental blessing was also an affirmation of the bond linking parent and child and of the generosity and good will that ideally characterized this bond. Because parents are conduits through which heavenly influence is made available, and because for Shakespeare children too may serve as conveyers of such influence, the blessing links heaven and earth. Specifically, in *The Winter's Tale* the parental blessing serves as an image of what has happened through the whole course of the play, what happens most clearly as the play closes: from their sacred vials, the gods are pouring "grace" in all its senses into the world of human life. . . .

[3] For a fuller discussion of the ritual and its place in Shakespeare and in Renaissance family life, see my article "Parental Blessings in Shakespeare's Plays," and Houlbrooke, 31, 41, 145, 168, 188.

[4] Such is the report of contemporary observers from France and Italy. See, for instance, Erondell, sig. E7^v, E8^v ("I mervaile verie much that French-men . . . doe not make [children] aske their parentes blessing"), and the Venetian ambassador's report in *Calendar,* 451 (describing this "admirable custom of [England], well worthy of imitation"). Note also Fynes Moryson's claim that the custom was practiced "in no other kingdom that I know" (quoted in Scott 53) and John Donne's question, "Children kneele to aske blessing of Parents in England, but where else?" (9:59).

[5] Fourteenth-century evidence for the custom is found in *The Good Wife.* In some form, it may have been practiced throughout Europe during the Middle Ages (see Weiser 139). For examples of non-European and non-Christian versions of the blessing ritual, see Crawley, 4-6.

[6] For other descriptions of the blessing and the words used, see Becon, fol. 519^v, 524^v; Erondell, sig. E7^v, E8^v, P5^v; Stapleton, 12; and Stubbes, sig. C4.

[7] See Becon, fol. 524^v ("bow[ing] the knee" to ask for a blessing is one way of showing "honorable reverence toward [parents], as parsons representing the

majestie of God"); Cleland, 178 ("The bowing of the knee declareth that we submit our selves to him [before whom we bow], & that we wil not remaine equal, but wil humble, and make our selves inferiour"); and Shakespeare's Prince Hal in *2 Henry IV* IV.v.146-48 (kneeling is a "prostrate and exterior bending" that witnesses a "most inward true and duteous spirit"). It appears that during the sixteenth and early seventeenth centuries the practice of kneeling before parents was commonly maintained into adulthood. In the early 1500s Sir Thomas More, on seeing his father, "would goe to him, and reverently kneelinge downe in sight of all, aske him blessing" (Ba. 59). In the seventeenth century, the adult Nicholas Ferrar similarly knelt for his mother's blessing (Wordsworth 201). In 1622 the Venetian ambassador reported seeing Londoners kneel in public places, "no matter what their age," to ask a parent's blessing (*Calendar* 451).

[8] Even on an issue so crucial as a child's potential marriage partner, the consistent advice of moralists was that, though a parent's advice and consent should be sought, the child's wishes must always be respected. The legal requirement was that, "without Consent [i.e., of the bride and groom] there cannot be any Matrimony" (Swinburne 51). Shakespeare presents the same position in *Romeo and Juliet* (I.ii.16-19), *The Winter's Tale* (IV.iv.404-10), and elsewhere. Of course, both in Shakespeare and in Renaissance life outside the theater, parents sometimes exceeded their proper authority. (See my article "Haste, Consent, and Age at Marriage.")

[9] For example, *The Winter's Tale* V.iii.118. Note also the kissing of parents in *Two Gentlemen of Verona* II.iii.26, 28; and the parent's kissing a child while blessing her in *Henry VIII* V.iv.9-11. . . .

[26] Besides the insistent association of Hermione with grace (see I.ii.233, 459, II.ii.19, II.iii.29, III.ii.198), note other references to her as a quasi-divine figure: for example, "most sacred lady" (I.ii.76), "spotless / I' th' eyes of heaven" (II.i.131-32), "her sainted spirit" (V.i.57), "There's magic in thy majesty" (V.iii.39).

[27] For a discussion of this concept, which goes back to the Middle Ages and beyond, see Tayler, 74.

[28] Besides the fact that the blessing ritual accompanies similar father-daughter reunions in other late plays (*Per.* V.i.213; *Cym.* V.v.264-66), the actions and physical contact described in *The Winter's Tale* suggest at the very least an appropriate setting for a parental blessing (V.ii.13-14: "There was . . . language in their very gesture"; 53-54: "then again worries he his daughter with clipping her").

[29] Compare Paulina's later reference to "unlawful business" (line 96).

[30] The situation echoes a phrase in *Pericles:* "Thou that beget'st him that did thee beget" (V.i.195). A few lines later Pericles gives a blessing to this daughter who "beget[s] him." These parallels between *The Winter's Tale* and *Pericles* suggest that the reciprocally life-giving relationship between parent and child, symbolized by the blessing ritual, is a deliberate, significant element in both plays. Something very similar takes place in *Lear:* Cordelia asks to be blessed by a father who is kneeling to her; later Lear, on his way to prison, says, "When thou dost ask me blessing, I'll kneel down / And ask of thee forgiveness" (IV.vii.56-58, V.iii.10-11). The motif of the life-giving child also occurs in *Titus Andronicus* I.i.166 (Titus Andronicus calls his daughter "the cordial of mine age") and *The Tempest* V.i.

[31] See V.i.204-13, 223, V.iii.44-48. See also *Henry VIII* IV.ii.131-38 and V.iv.9-11. In plays other than *The Winter's Tale* in which only one parent gives a blessing—for example, the mother in *Richard III, King John, All's Well,* and *Coriolanus;* the father in *Titus Andronicus, Lear,* and *Cymbeline*—the lack of symmetry may be explained by the absence (usually through death) of the other parent.

[32] Women's solidarity is also expressed in a blessing of sorts the Countess of Rossillion gives Helen (*AWW* I.iii.253-54). Non-Shakespearean representations of women's solidarity, expressed through a mother's blessing, may be found in the fourteenth-century poem *The Good Wife* and the seventeenth-century dialogue *The French Garden* (Erondell sig. E7ᵛ, E8ᵛ). A number of sources also represent mothers instructing their children, including sons (see Joceline; Leigh; Breton).

Works Cited

Erondell, Peter. *The French Garden.* 1605. Menston, Eng.: The Scolar Press, 1969.

Kahn, Coppélia. *Man's Estate: Masculine Identity in Shakespeare.* Berkeley: University of California Press, 1981.

Legg, J. Wickham. *English Church Life from the Restoration to the Tractarian Movement.* London: Longmans, Green, 1914.

Perkins, William. *A Treatise of the Vocations or Callings of Men.* 1603. In *The Works of William Perkins.* Ed. Ian Breward. Appleford, Eng.: Sutton Courtenay, 1970.

Rhodes, Hugh. *The Boke of Nurture, or Schoole of Good Maners.* 1577. In *Manners and Meals in Olden Time.* Ed. Frederick J. Furnivall. EETS OS 32. 1868. New York: Greenwood, 1969.

Stone, Lawrence. *The Crisis of the Aristocracy 1558-1641*. Oxford: Clarendon Press, 1965.

————. *The Family, Sex and Marriage in England, 1500-1800*. New York: Harper and Row, 1977.

Tinkler, F.C. "The Winter's Tale." *Scrutiny* 5 (1937): 344-64.

Whitforde, Richard. *A Werke for Housholders*. 1533

JEALOUSY

René Girard (essay date 1987)

SOURCE: "Jealousy in *The Winter's Tale*," in *Alphonse Juilland: D'Une Passion L'Autre*, edited by Brigitte Cazelles and René Girard, Anma Libri, 1987, pp. 39-62.

[*In the following essay, Girard interprets the jealousy of Leontes in terms of "mimetic desire," suggesting that the motive for Leontes' jealous behavior is based on his belief that he influenced Hermione to love Polixenes in a sort of imitation of his fondness for his friend.*]

The most monstrous jealousy in Shakespeare is not that of Othello but of Leontes, the hero of *The Winter's Tale*. With no villain at his side to poison his mind, the king of Sicilia comes close to destroying his entire family. His victims are completely innocent and selflessly devoted to him. This Othello without an Iago is Shakespeare's last representation of jealousy, his most uncompromising and, in my opinion, his greatest. But posterity has judged otherwise. Othello rather than Leontes has always been the great symbol of jealousy in the theater of Shakespeare.

The traditional critics appreciate the sinister quality that emanates from Leontes after he becomes jealous. They find him excellent as a madly suspicious tyrant, but unconvincing as a portrayal of jealousy. They do not understand why he becomes jealous; they find him "insufficiently motivated."

One line in the very first scene, I believe, is relevant to this objection. When the curtain rises, Camillo of Sicilia and Archimadus of Bohemia are discussing the friendship of their two kings:

> CAMILLO.
> Sicilia cannot show himself over-kind to Bohemia. They were trained together in their childhoods, and there rooted betwixt them then such an affection, which cannot choose but branch now. Since their more mature dignities and royal necessities made

separation of their society, their encounters, though not personal, have been royally attorneyed with interchange of gifts, letters, loving embassies, that they have seemed to be together, though absent; shook hands, as over a vast; and embraced, as it were, from the ends of opposed winds. The heavens continue their loves!

> ARCHIMADUS.
> I think there is not in the world either malice or matter to alter it.

> (I.i.21-32)

Unlike the thoughtful Camillo who prays for the continuation of the beautiful friendship. Archimadus sees no need for supernatural help. The bond is so strong, he believes, that it should endure forever. As we hear this, we realize, of course, that the friendship is doomed. The prophecy smacks of human pride; a friendship presented as indestructible at the outset of a play must be about to be destroyed. The amazing concord of the friends is an obvious prelude to their still more amazing discord.

Archimadus' prophecy must be false, but not entirely false, however. The terms in which it is couched are too specific to be meaningless.

Malice is what a villain can do to disturb a harmonious relationship, the wiles of an Iago for instance. *Matter* means all seemingly rational grounds for quarreling that two close friends may have, conflicts of passion, interest, prestige, power, whatever you will as long as it seems sufficient to legitimate the end of a friendship.

The words *malice* and *matter* cover everything that the traditional critics would regard as appropriate "motivation" for the jealousy of Leontes, everything that would make them happy if they could find some of it in *The Winter's Tale*.

They do not find any. In the entourage of Leontes, there is no one who wants to mislead him and flatter his jealous passion. Camillo's wife, Paulina, displays as much heroic persistence on behalf of truth and justice as Iago on behalf of deception and evil. Many courtiers do not dare contradict the king, but she puts them to shame and, thanks to her, their embarrassed silence also points to the truth. Leontes is painfully aware that no one around him shares his mad belief.

There is a religious oracle in the play and it, too, proclaims the truth. Every fact that Iago manages to distort or keep away from Othello is prominently displayed in front of the deluded husband. The play is devoid of *malice* and it is devoid of *matter* as well. Both Leontes and Polixenes are happily married and Shakespeare gives no indication that Hermione might be sexually attracted to Polixenes or Polixenes to her. Not one equivocal word passes the lips of either character, not one ambiguous glance is exchanged. Both friends are at peace with one another. Their kingdoms have no common borders. Neither one covets the possessions of the other. The play has no political *matter*.

This complete absence of *malice* and *matter* makes *The Winter's Tale* stand out as a unique exception. Shakespeare is obviously aware of the fact. All his plays until then were abundantly supplied with at least one of the two ingredients demanded by the critics. This is especially true whenever jealousy plays a prominent role. The women are invariably innocent, but the jealous hero is not really guilty either; next to him there is a villain who provides him with a convenient excuse for his violence. This is not only true of *Othello* but also of *Much Ado About Nothing,* a comedy in which Don John plays the role of the slanderer, and also of *Cymbeline* in which the part goes to Posthumus' own rival, Iachomo.

Even if the lack of *malice* and *matter* could be regarded as a fault from a dramatic standpoint, it cannot be an ordinary fault if Shakespeare himself planned it deliberately. The line of Archimadus resembles too much the "lack of motivation" bemoaned by the traditional critics not to allude to the same reality. These critics were wrong when they treated the whole matter in a purely negative fashion, as something to be censored rather than understood. And their modern successors will also be wrong as they rush into the void created by the absence of *malice* and *matter* with some "critical theory" of their own choosing, some kind of psychoanalytical scheme for instance. Shakespeare obviously had his own reasons for doing away with the malice and matter of the earlier plays. I would like to know what these reasons are. I am curious, above all, of Shakespeare's own idea of what his own play means.

There is not in the world either malice or matter to alter [this friendship]. Every word is true and yet the statement as a whole is misleading in regard to the long and happy life that it predicts for the friendship. Since the friendship is quickly altered, it must be altered by something other than malice or matter.

The line of Archimadus discreetly warns us about the very special nature of this play. This is Shakespeare's last meditation on jealousy and he does not want the subject to be spoiled this time. He does not want its full force to be diluted in the traditional fashion. *The Winter's Tale* is the only play which portrays the full horror of a passion that Shakespeare has often represented before, but always with some attenuation.

When a very old and close friendship or a happy marriage is destroyed, we automatically assume that the agent of their destruction must lie outside the relation. Either the friends and spouses listened to some malicious slander about one another, or some unex-

pected issue arose between them. On something of great importance they must differ importantly.

If the friendship is not destroyed from the outside and yet is destroyed, it must be destroyed *from the inside.* Archimadus sees quite correctly that the catastrophe cannot come from outside and he concludes incorrectly that it will not come at all. He does not even mention the most disturbing possibility; he simply cannot imagine it. His statement is true *as far as it goes,* but it does not go far enough and it becomes misleading because of the very truth it contains.

This is what a tragic oracle should be: a statement about the future that sounds misleadingly reassuring because of some truth in it, a pleasant enough reality that seems to exclude a quite unpleasant possibility, the fulfillment of which has been anticipated with some concern: The oracle shows up just in time to alleviate this concern and facilitate the catastrophe by putting the listeners to sleep when they should be on their guard.

In reality there is no incompatibility between the pleasant reality and the unpleasant possibility. The second follows from the first both logically and chronologically. Far from affording the protection that it seems to afford, the absence of *malice* and *matter* secretly prepares and facilitates the internal destruction of the friendship.

Archimadus' statement is the tragic oracle at the entrance of *The Winter's Tale,* a superb example of the genre since it relies on our fundamental misunderstanding of human relations rather than on mere wordplay, as the oracles in *Macbeth* for instance. If we look for irrelevant excuses and do not want to face up to the tragic possibilities of even the most harmonious human relations, we, too, will fall into the trap. Just like Archimadus himself. To this urbane and optimistic gentleman, a friendship invulnerable to *malice* and *matter* has nothing to fear.

The Archimaduses of this world never foresee the serpent in the Garden of Eden. All around them, friendships crumble; allies of long standing go to war; the most stable associations dissolve; lovers separate; spouses divorce, but every time they react as if no such thing had ever happened before. They greet each new catastrophe as an unheard of exception, a miracle in reverse that shall never occur again. Here is an event, they say to one another, that contradicts the natural order of the universe.

The critics with no affinity for the tragic fall into the oracular trap and clamor for the *malice* and the *matter* that Shakespeare, this time, will not give them. *Malice* and *matter* are the lame excuses and scapegoats that, in the face of shattered loves and friendships, a certain love of mankind requires in order to maintain its faith in the intrinsic goodness of man.

There is another clue to the author's intentions, and it confirms our interpretation of Archimadus' statement. The literary source of *The Winter's Tale* is *Pandolfo* by Robert Green. The hero of this novel has conventional motives for being jealous. They are gone from *The Winter's Tale*. If Shakespeare had not been himself when he wrote the play, or too uninterested in his hero to provide him with credible motives, in all probability they would still be there. I cannot believe that they disappeared accidentally; they had to be discarded on purpose, and the most important task of a critic of the play is to identify that purpose.

Let us overcome the oracular ambiguity of Archimadus and regard his statement as an invitation to rise above *malice* and *matter*. Let us reflect on the mystery of a jealousy that dispenses for the first time with the conventional motives to which Shakespeare had always resorted before, even in as great a play as *Othello*.

In the second scene, we learn how a trusting friend and loving husband can suddenly be metamorphosed into a wild beast. Everybody is on stage. Polixenes announces that, after nine months with Leontes and Hermione, he must return without delay to his family and the affairs of Bohemia; an additional motive is the burden that his presence might be to Leontes.

Leontes insists that Polixenes could never stay long enough to tire him and he begs his friend to wait some more, even if only a week. Several critics have questioned his sincerity. Can a man that close to an almost insane fit of jealousy seriously attempt to prevent the departure of his presumed rival? These critics assume that the suspicion of Leontes must antedate the beginning of the play. If he is serious about wanting Polixenes to stay, he must already be planning to have him murdered.

This is the wrong approach. Shakespeare is not writing a detective story. He first portrays Leontes as a man genuinely distressed at the prospect of losing his friend, and we must assume that this distress is real. With an almost childlike petulance, Leontes begs Polixenes to stay a little longer. He needs to prepare himself for a future without his friend. He cannot find the right words. Hermione stands at his side, silent. No more than two minutes, perhaps, after Polixenes' announcement, Leontes, brusquely, turns to her:

> Tongue-tied our queen? speak you.

The only "tongue-tied" character is Leontes himself. He knows how charming and eloquent his wife can be and he wants her to plead his case with Polixenes. He wishes that she had intervened without being asked. He is as dependent on her as he is on his friend. The two most precious people in his life now seem to be going their separate ways, deserting him

simultaneously . . . Sensing his disarray, Hermione intervenes and the first thing she does is to answer the implicit reproach of her husband:

> I had thought, sir, to have held my peace until
> You had drawn oaths from him not to stay.
>   You, sir,
> Charge him too coldly.

She then proceeds to do precisely what Leontes has requested; in an always dignified and humorous manner, she "charges" Polixenes warmly and eloquently; Leontes is highly pleased. Twice he repeats "well said, Hermione."

To call Hermione to the rescue was the right move. Victory crowns her efforts; Polixenes will stay a while longer. I detect no resentment in Leontes' congratulations, only admiration and gratitude:

> At my request he would not.
> Hermione, my dearest, thou never spok'st
> To better purpose.

A playful Hermione now asks her husband if he really means his last statement. In the same lighthearted way, he answers that, on one other occasion only, she spoke as well as she just has; it was the day when she said "yes" to his marriage proposal. She then recapitulates the observations of her husband:

> . . . I have spoke to th' purpose twice:
> The one, for ever earn'd a royal husband;
> Th' other, for some while a friend. [*Giving*
>   *her hand to Polixenes*]

As he hears these words and sees his wife hold hands with Polixenes, Leontes feels overwhelmed with jealousy:

> LEONTES:
> [Aside] Too hot, too hot!
> To mingle friendship far, is mingling bloods.
> I have *tremor cordis* on me: my heart dances,
> But not for joy—not joy.

Occurring as it does *in front of him,* this display of affection means strictly nothing. Leontes is too intelligent not to be aware of the possibility:

> This entertainment
> May a free face put on, derive a liberty
> From heartiness, from bounty, fertile bosom,
> And well become the agent; it may—I grant.

And yet he cannot help regard the innocent gesture of his wife as solid proof of adultery. His perverse interpretation can seem credible only in the hypothesis of a long-standing affair between Hermione and Polixenes, to which he alone would have remained blind. The deluded husband is always the last to know his own disgrace. The lovers must regard him as a man be-yond enlightenment, and they have thrown precautions to the wind. They no longer hesitate to display their mutual affection in public, even in his own presence.

> But to paddling palms and pinching fingers,
> As now they are, and making practic'd smiles,
> As in a looking-glass; and then to sigh, as
>   'twere
> The mort o' th' deer—O, that is entertainment
> My bosom likes not, nor my brows!

The words of Hermione and her physical contact with Polixenes are the two stones that produce the spark that sets off the explosion. We can see the spark and we can hear the explosion, but where is the dynamite?

Hermione was not first to place her marriage on the same footing as her friendship with Polixenes. Leontes himself used the word "earned" apropos of the two. A little before he had also asked: "Is he won yet?" mean-ing Polixenes. Hermione then adopted his metaphor; she follows every lead of her husband; she *imitates* him in everything.

Why should Leontes react as he does to this innocent mimicry? A moment before, he had interpreted Hermione's nonintervention in his debate with Polixenes as a rebuff to himself. He found her too cold and now he finds her too hot. Between too little and too much friendship is there a perfect point that would satisfy Leontes? Obviously not. Leontes puts his wife and his friend in a double bind. If they seem uninter-ested in each other, he feels betrayed, but as soon as they seem interested, he feels betrayed all the more.

Hermione behaves like a docile instrument in the hands of her husband. Everything she says and does, she says and does because of him. The same is true of Polixenes, who postpones his departure for the sake of Leontes. Her insistence made him understand how important it is, but not to her, to him alone, that his friend should not leave too suddenly.

Does Leontes fail to grasp all this? We take for granted that he must. If he only perceived how eager his wife and his friend are to act in the manner he himself has suggested, he would acknowledge their innocence. What can his misguided jealousy amount to if not to a gross misapprehension of the available information? This is what our common sense assumes. Our common sense is wrong. This jealousy is more intelligent than we realize.

Until the fateful line 108, no doubt, Leontes was un-aware of his crucial role in the interaction of Polixenes and Hermione, but awareness has come to him in a flash of insight based on the information that we, the spectators, share with him, interpreted almost in the same way. Leontes realizes that he has been manipu-lating his wife for the sake of his friend. As long as he did not see this, he entertained no suspicion.

The morbidly sensitive Leontes feels hurt at the thought that his wife might not treat his best friend as her own best friend. He wants the two persons he loves most to feel toward one another the way he feels toward them. He desires a triangle of perfect love.

Until line 108, Leontes was continuing on the course that had been his during the entire visit of Polixenes. He was not suspicious in the slightest. His only prob-lem was that he found Polixenes and Hermione too indifferent to one another, and he was doing his best to change that. As he listens to Hermione and watches her hold hands with Polixenes, all of a sudden he thinks that he has succeeded beyond his wildest dreams.

Hermione has just said that she "earned" a friend in the same way that she "earned" a husband. Leontes recognizes his own feelings as well as his own words: he has always seen the two relations as equally impor-tant, almost equivalent, and a terrifying idea takes hold of him. He thinks that his insistence on too much friend-ship has driven Hermione into the arms of Polixenes. He has incited her to commit adultery. *To mingle friend-ship far, is mingling blood.*

Leontes sees himself as an involuntary go-between. He thinks that his own love has exerted a perverse *mimetic* influence on the pair and that they love one another *after his own example,* but in the wrong manner.

This interpretation is based on *mimetic desire,* or rather on Leontes' anticipation of mimetic desire, on his belief in a mimetic contagion that does not really exist but might exist. This reading may seem exces-sively subtle at first and yet it is Shakespeare's own. The readers do not have to take my word for it. Shakespeare himself made it completely explicit. He placed it in the mouth of the reliable Camillo, the character best informed of what Leontes is up to. This shrewd and honest counsellor diagnoses his master's condition in the manner that I do, and there is no reason to doubt that he is right:

> He thinks, nay, with all confidence he swears,
> As he had seen't, or *been an instrument*
> *To vice you to't,* that you have touch'd his
>   queen
> Forbiddenly. (414-17; italics mine)

Leontes sees himself as the *instrument* of his own cuckoldry. In the language of mimetic theory, which owes a lot to Dostoevsky, we might say that Leontes sees himself in the role of *The Eternal Husband*; but he reacts more violently than this antihero to a discov-ery that, in his case, is not even true. He thinks that he not only facilitated the love affair of Polixenes and Hermione, but that he first planted the desire in their hearts.

Camillo is present during the entire scene. When Leontes talks to him privately, he takes for granted that a man as intelligent as his advisor must have reached the same conclusion as himself. When he finds that Camillo still believes in the loyalty of Hermione, he becomes indignant and calls him "a bawd." He thinks that Camillo deliberately continues in the role that he, himself, was also playing before his illumination.

Another clue to the feelings of Leontes lies in his parting words to Hermione, when she leaves the stage with Polixenes:

> Hermione,
> How thou lov'st us, show in our brother's
>   welcome;
> Let what is dear in Sicily be cheap.
> Next to thyself and my young rover, he's
> Apparent to my heart.
>
> (I.ii.173-77)

These lines function both as an invitation to friendship and as an invitation to sexual promiscuity. For the love of me, Leontes says to his wife, show your love to Polixenes, fall in love with him. You, my wife, prove to me that my friend is the most desirable friend by desiring him as much as I do. And you, my friend, prove to me that my wife is the most desirable wife by desiring her as I also do.

Even the most banal words of civility can seem ambiguous in an ambiguous context. If a husband desires, quite innocently, to have his wife extend the proper hospitality to his best friend, he cannot help sounding as if he were encouraging her to commit adultery.

Leontes is satirical; he gives a caricature of his former language, during the entire nine months of Polixenes' visit, a language, he now thinks, that has been obeyed to the letter.

In order to show that he is no longer fooled, Leontes exaggerates what he now perceives as the rash imprudence of his invitation to cordiality. This parody of his former self is a bitter reproach: "When you took me at my word," really means "you turned me, the trusting husband, into an innocent tool of your perversity."

Leontes is merely imagining something that really happens in *The Two Gentlemen of Verona*. Proteus falls in love with Valentine's mistress, Silvia, for obeying too literally the too insistent suggestion of his old friend: For the love of me, Valentine keeps saying, fall in love with the woman I love!

A brief episode in Act Five confirms, I believe, this interpretation of Leontes' jealous desire. Sixteen years have elapsed; the son of Polixenes, Florizel, and Perdita, the long lost daughter of Leontes, not yet identified as such, have left Bohemia together to take refuge with Leontes. They claim that they are officially engaged and that Polixenes himself has sent them to his old friend Leontes. In reality, the king does not want his son to marry the humble shepherdess that Perdita seems to be, and the two lovers are feeling his rage.

In the midst of this first encounter with Leontes, the truth is publicly revealed, and the two young people throw themselves at the feet of their host, begging for his help. In an effort to awaken his sympathy, Florizel reminds him of his own past when he, too, was a young man in love:

> Beseech you, sir,
> Remember since you ow'd no more to time
> Than I do now. With thought of such affections,
> Step forth as mine advocate. At your request
> My father will grant precious things as trifles.

The answer of Leontes is astonishing, at least for a repentant sinner and an older man forever buried, he claims, in the remembrance of his supposedly dead wife:

> Would he do so, I'd beg your precious mistress,
> Which he counts as a trifle.

Leontes is thinking of Perdita as a possible spouse not for Florizel but *for himself*. His great grief, his sense of guilt, his daily visitations of the supposed tomb of Hermione, all seem forgotten. We can understand why the ever-watchful Paulina intervenes forcefully:

> Sir, my liege,
> Your eye hath too much youth in't. Not a
>   month
> 'Fore your queen died, she was more worth
>   such gazes
> Than what you look on now.
> LEONTES: I thought of her,
> Even in these looks I made.

The reason Leontes behaves as he does is not that he has forgotten his wife, but that he remembers her too vividly. Perdita looks so much like Hermione and Florizel looks so much like Polixenes that the past seems resurrected. From Leontes' standpoint, this is a perfect *repetition* of that past, not solely because of the physical resemblance between the actors, but also because the new ones display openly, this time, the mutual love that Leontes had wrongly attributed to Polixenes and Hermione.

Another circumstance that makes the scene a perfect repetition of the past is the role of go-between and protector of their love that Florizel and Perdita want Leontes to assume. In Act One, Leontes saw himself as the involuntary go-between of his wife and friend and the engineer of a love affair that did not exist. This time, everything is real. Florizel and Perdita really love each other and they really put Leontes in charge of their love. Every reason Leontes once thought he had to be jealous has come back to haunt him. His heroic efforts to convince himself that his jealous desire was pointless are powerfully challenged by what he sees. Shakespeare does not want to cast discredit on the repentance of Leontes. His purpose is to produce circumstances identical not to the original situation as it truly was but to Leontes' distorted interpretation of it. As a result, the old jealous desire overwhelms him once again, so powerfully that Leontes forgets everything else, at least for a moment.

The same insolent happiness radiates from Florizel and Perdita as from Hermione and Polixenes when they held hands in front of Leontes. This love makes a great show of being in need, in need of Leontes but, in reality, it needs nothing at all, nothing outside of itself. It seems divinely self-sufficient, and that is the reason Leontes, once again, feels the pangs of jealousy. The very perfection of the relationship makes him feel excluded from paradise.

This is exactly how he had felt the other time. He had been pushing Hermione and Polixenes toward each other in order to reinforce his own desire for them, mimetically, through the imitation of its own mimetic replicas reflected back from them as in a mirror. And he had really succeeded. Suddenly, Polixenes and Hermione had seemed superhuman and so suited to one another that they seemed bound to love one another exclusively; it seemed impossible that they might waste any love on anyone else, especially himself. That is the reason he had felt like an outcast. As his old feelings reassert themselves, once again he sees himself abandoned and humiliated, compelled, as a result, to espouse and imitate the beautiful desire that seems to deprive him of everything desirable.

What Paulina sees in the eyes of Leontes cannot be his own vanished youth; it must be borrowed from the two young people. It is not Leontes anymore but his own rendition of Florizel's desire for Perdita, of Perdita's desire for Florizel.

Being once again in a position of power, Leontes can choose his own role. He can be the complacent go-between who favors the illicit loves that he secretly admires or he can take advantage of the situation to satisfy his own desire at the expense of the young couple. At this point, he is tempted less to marry Perdita, perhaps, than to separate these lovers once and for all, to destroy the insolent happiness of which he has no share, as he had destroyed it in the case of Polixenes and Hermione.

If we read the episode until the end, we will find a line that confirms the mimetic nature of Leontes' reawakened jealousy. Leontes once again addresses Florizel:

> But your petition
> Is yet unanswer'd. I will to your father.
> Your honor not o'erthrown by your desires,
> *I am a friend to them and you.* (italics mine)

The last line does not seem particularly interesting at first. It obviously means: "I am your friend in every possible way and especially in those matters that relate to the interest of your desires. You want me to intervene with your father; I will ask him to permit your marriage to Perdita; I will be an honest go-between."

Leontes' brief personal crisis is over and the episode concludes on a positive note. A happy end is in sight for the two lovers. All this is obvious and we hardly give it a thought.

And yet the wording of our line is a little strange. It seems to suggest that: *I am a friend to them* (meaning *your desires*) does not necessarily imply: *I am your friend.* If the alternative is not a real one, the final *and you* is pointless; it merely repeats what Leontes has already said. We are left wondering why Shakespeare should have ended the whole episode on a rather flat and uselessly redundant note.

How can we make the alternative real, so that the *and you* will not be redundant? We must explore the possibility that a friendship of the desires might not be synonymous with the friendship of the men whose desires they are. This is not as far-fetched as it seems at first. If desires are friends we may assume that they will feel like friends; they will share identical views about whatever seems important to them.

Nothing can be more important to a desire than the object that it pursues *as desire,* in its own energetic and single-minded fashion. If there are two desires with a single mind, it is probable, it is almost inevitable that they will pursue one and the same object "with the soul of desire," the *same* object for both men at once. If our two desires pursue this object single-mindedly, the same Perdita for instance, will not each desire insist on the exclusive possession of it, will they not stubbornly refuse to share it with even the friendliest desire?

They certainly will. We can see, therefore, that the friendship of men and the friendship of their desires are not at all one and the same thing. The friendship of the men means harmony and peace and the friendship of their desires means jealousy and war.

Without the addition of the final *and you,* nothing prevents the first part of the line, *I am a friend to your desires,* from harboring the dark possibilities of mimetic rivalry, of a new tragedy, in other words. The two friendships become equivalent only retrospectively, after the *and you* has been added.

To be a friend to Florizel or to be a friend to his desires . . . that is the question Leontes has been debating, and it is not an idle question. The beginning of our line still reflects a hesitation that is resolved only with the final *and you,* uttered perhaps with a sigh of regret. Only then does Leontes finally triumph over his last temptation.

If we read the line carefully, we will see that it alludes to a major Shakespearean problem, which is the problem of *The Winter's Tale* at least as much as jealousy is, the problem of the archetypal brothers or friends. Why do they invariably become the worst of enemies?

The ambiguousness of a friendship that makes the desires of the friends too much the same, and therefore turns them into rivals, is what our line suggests. This is made unquestionable, I feel, by Leontes' first reaction to the request by Florizel. He was immediately tempted to seek Perdita as a wife not for the young man but for himself.

The two possible meanings of *I am a friend to your desires* are clearly present in our text and the phrase must allude to both; its ambivalence cannot be fortuitous.

This line also reflects the temporality of Leontes' experience. The disquieting interpretation of the first six words is only half-glimpsed and it is quickly suppressed by the reassuring certainty of *and you.* As soon as Leontes has surmounted his temptation, we almost doubt that it ever was there. We almost doubt that once again he was tempted to rebel against the thankless role of the empty-handed go-between. He had never played that role before, I repeat, but now he is really asked to play it, and in circumstances so reminiscent of his old illusion that we can well understand why, at least for a minute, he would fall again under its horrible spell.

The use of such words as "friend," "friendship" for the mimetic affinity between desires is particularly appropriate in view of the insidious nature of mimetic rivalry, of its tendency to creep up on friends and brothers when their intentions seem most pure, when they have no other conscious purpose than to lend a helping hand. Many men think they are still friends to other men when, in fact, they are friends to their desires exclusively. There is a world of difference between the two, but the shift is so easy that the difference, most of the time, remains unseen. A man can "honestly" believe that he is acting in the interests of a friend when his allegiance has already shifted to the latter's desires and the friendship is already betrayed. The extreme pertinence of the word "friend" makes the wordplay almost invisible as wordplay.

This ambiguous use of "friend" does not occur in *The Winter's Tale* only, and a comparison with other plays, notably *A Midsummer Night's Dream,* confirms the deliberateness of the ambivalence.

When they lyrically rehash the traditional reasons why "true love" always runs into trouble, Lysander and Hermia enumerate all sorts of mythical obstacles, such as oppressive fathers and omnipotent tyrants, but they fail to mention the only relevant source of disturbance which is themselves. They keep "crossing" each other's desires because they keep imitating these same desires. We only have to observe the lovers' behavior in order to perceive the imitation that their ideology of "true love" will not acknowledge, and we only have to pay attention to their words to understand that, unwittingly, they keep defining their own mimetic desire:

> LYSANDER:
> Or else *it [desire] stood upon the choice of friends*
> HERMIA:
> O hell! To choose love with another's eyes!

The first emotion of Leontes when he meets Florizel and Perdita is sympathy for the young couple, but that sympathy immediately extends to their desires. As his need for sympathetic participation increases, he feels compelled to espouse these desires, to make them his own, through a process of imitation so encompassing that it includes even the *youth* in the eyes of the old man, the youth of Florizel and Perdita, no doubt, reflected in the eyes of their imitator.

The line we just read makes the presence and the effects of mimetic desire completely transparent to those willing to acknowledge this constant source of conflictual ambivalence in Shakespeare but, to those not so willing, this same desire remains completely invisible. The technique of the passages we have just read, the discretion in the handling of the crucial themes is most appropriate to the subject matter, of course, but it also amounts to a strategy of selective revelation.

The diabolical ambivalence of *a friend to your desires* can be regarded as a case of overreading since it turns out to mean exactly the same thing in the end as a friend of yours. A spectator interested only in light entertainment never suspects anything of the whole complex of themes I call mimetic desire. After everything is over, the surface of the text appears perfectly smooth and not a trace remains of what has just disappeared.

If we want to know the truth, Shakespeare will help us and he will hide nothing. If we do not want to know, if we want to be kept in the dark regarding the operation of our desires, which is the case with most men, we will see absolutely nothing. At the end of our episode, everything we just discovered has vanished and the banal meaning seems so limpid and obvious that not a trace can be found of the possibilities we only half-glimpsed.

If we belong to the group of those who want to see nothing, we will feel perfectly comfortable; the disquieting possibility that unsuspected depths remain to be explored and that we might have missed something will never enter our mind.

The jealousy of Leontes proves baseless in *The Winter's Tale,* but it would make a good deal of sense in the context of many earlier plays of Shakespeare.

Everywhere in Shakespeare a certain type of character keeps recurring: a man—more rarely a woman—has a spouse, or a friend of the opposite sex as well as a friend, or a brother of the same sex. Instead of a friend, it can be an esteemed associate, or a revered superior; it can even be a total stranger, the Iachomo of *Cymbeline.*

For one reason or another, the man brings the woman into his relationship with the male friend (in the *Sonnets*), or he brings his male friend into his relationship with the woman (in a number of plays). His official reason may be that he needs a helping hand in his courtship of the woman; he does not have enough self-confidence to approach her single-handedly. In other instances, he has too much self-confidence; he is in a "boastful" mood; he yearns *for the envious looks of another man for the purpose of bolstering* his own desire. Would he need this kind of reinforcement if he were as sure of himself as he seems to be?

The two types are less far apart than they seem. They are the two phases of the same personality, one that tends to oscillate between too much and too little self-confidence, the *mimetic* personality *par excellence.*

Whatever his motives, our man works assiduously at effecting a rapprochment of the two friends. He wants to foster the same close relations between them as he already entertains with each separately. He does not seem to realize that his behavior may push the two friends into each other's arms. This often turns out to be the case in Shakespeare.

I already briefly mentioned a first example of this theme, that of Valentine and Proteus in *The Two Gentlemen of Verona.* I will now give a few more, beginning with the one closest to Leontes in chronological order, the Posthumus of *Cymbeline.* This hero boasts about the beauty and virtue of his young wife, Imogen, in front of a Roman dandy named Iachomo, instilling into him an intense desire to try his luck with this wonderful woman. Posthumus wagers that Iachomo will fail and then, quixotically, facilitates his rival's enterprise by giving him a letter of introduction to Imogen. When Iachomo returns with some spurious evidence that Imogen has succumbed to his courtship, Posthumus'

loss of confidence in her is as rash, unbalanced, and unfair to this virtuous wife as the *macho* bragging of the previous phase.

Troilus is another illustration of the type. Not unlike Posthumus, he is prone to bragging, but he is quite insecure underneath. When he praises the superior worldliness and charm of the Greek warriors, he does not realize the impact of his words on Cressida. His mimetic envy of "the merry Greeks" suggests to the woman he has unwittingly humiliated not only that a Greek lover might be enjoyable, but that it could help her regain the upper hand with her Trojan lover. Troilus displayed the most callous indifference toward Cressida after spending only one single night in her bed.

A little later, one of the Greeks, Diomed, is taking charge of Cressida and the incorrigible Troilus loudly praises the young woman in front of him. First Troilus stupidly channeled Cressida's mimetic desire in the direction of the Greeks, and then, apparently eager to complete the job so neatly begun with his mistress, he channels Diomed's desire in her direction; he arouses the Greek warrior's vigorous sense of mimetic emulation with the Trojans. Diomed, needless to say, becomes the second lover of Cressida.

Even more than Pandarus, Troilus is Cressida's "bawd," but unlike Pandarus, he is not even aware of contributing to the process of her mimetic corruption. He has no remembrance of having been spiritually unfaithful to her before she becomes physically unfaithful to him. Since he gets hooked a second time before he has had an opportunity to succumb to a temptation similar to hers, he is sincerely convinced, as have been numerous generations of critics who have vigorously applauded him for his steadfast virtue, that he occupies the high moral ground in the whole affair. He still passes for "the only positive hero" in an otherwise distressingly cynical play.

Troilus must be regarded just as responsible as Pandarus for the prostitution of Cressida, if not more so. Were *Troilus and Cressida* a French play, it might be entitled *L'école des putains;* in this School for Whores, all the teachers are former lovers or would-be lovers of their students.

The Silvius of *As You Like It* is a variation on the same archetype: he carries the love letter of his cruel mistress to another man, Ganymede (in reality a woman, Rosalind), in the absurd hope that his abject submissiveness will improve his chances with the author of the letters, Phebe, who is bound to despise this spineless man. His submissiveness repels Phebe not because she differs from him to a significant extent, but because she does not. Most of these Shakespearean lovers in the comedies resemble one another enormously. They are as "masochistic" with their persecutors as they are "sadistic" with their victims, and Phebe will prove as servile as Silvius, as soon as someone shows up, Rosalind, who treats her as harshly as she does Silvius.

Another good example is Orsino, the duke of *Twelfth Night,* who finds the young Cesario (Viola) so charming that he dispatches him (or her) posthaste to the cruel Olivia, loaded with his own messages of love. Piqued by Viola's indifference to her, Olivia, naturally, falls in love with the ambassador.

The theme of the man who invites cuckoldry by praising his mistress or wife in public, exhibiting her as a fashion designer would his best model, dispatching possible lovers to her, acting as her go-between with other men, or otherwise making it difficult for her to remain faithful, recurs too frequently and prominently in the theater of Shakespeare to be dismissed as an inconsequential trick, an external device, alien to the sublime aspects of the noble bard, unrelated to the themes truly worthy of our critical attention.

Unless we perceive the process of these mimetically inflammable men who become "infected" (the word has a quasi-technical sense in this theater) with the desire of a boastful husband or lover, we have no grasp of dramatic interaction in the comedies. When we see that the phenomenon has its exact counterpart in the realm of power—with the Ulysses of *Troilus and Cressida*—we realize how widespread it is. The truth is that indirect desire, second-hand desire, desire borrowed from a friend, mimetic desire, constitutes the strongest kind of desire in the Shakespearean corpus, and the only kind that really serves the purpose of the playwright because it provides him with an inexhaustible source of conflicts.

Our survey of the erotic landscape leaves no doubt regarding the nature of Leontes' suspicion and its legitimacy in the context of the early plays. Except for his own play and, to a more limited extent, some of the plays that come immediately before it, all triangular conjunctions of a cast similar to that of *The Winter's Tale* quickly produce the mimetic offspring, either in the man friend, or in the woman friend, or in both, that would make Leontes' jealousy well founded if he were the hero in one of these plays. On statistical grounds, this jealousy makes sense.

There is much self-defeating eroticism in Shakespeare and it bears an undeniable resemblance to the behavior of Leontes before he becomes jealous. The supposed mystery of Leontes' jealousy stems from our inability to recognize the unity of a Shakespearean archetype behind the diversity of the examples I have mentioned.

If characters such as Valentine, or Collatine, the husband of Lucrece, or Hermia, or Troilus, had come around to the jealous perspective of Leontes early enough, they would have saved themselves a great deal of trouble. Instead of regarding them as madmen, we would congratulate them for their shrewdness.

Why is Leontes so well informed about mimetic contagion, and why does he fear its effects so much? He had to observe it somewhere. The objects of his observation could not be Hermione or Polixenes, who are immune to it. Hermione in particular is admirably unaware of all the evils imagined by Leontes. The only mimetic contagion that her husband has observed is her innocent exhibition of friendship for Polixenes and he was the one who requested it. It was possible to misinterpret this friendship, of course, but, in order to do so, Leontes had to refer it not to its real source, which is the sincere affection of his wife for him, but to the perverted source in his own mimetic desire.

The cause of Leontes' jealousy is his own heart. He condemns his victims in function of what he finds in himself. That is why his mistake is so stubborn and remains unaffected by the external evidence.

Leontes implicitly acknowledges his own mimetic obsession since he sees himself as a source of virulent contamination. Observing in himself the self-defeating impulse that invites the perverse kind of imitation, he anticipates its effects in others and erroneously believes that Hermione must have come under its influence. She slavishly follows his suggestions, to be sure, but only because of her eagerness to please him.

The only desire Leontes can know firsthand is his own; his belief in a love affair between Hermione and Polixenes is an extrapolation of this self-understanding. Modern psychologists would call this a "projection." If the attribution of mimetic desire to others is essentially *projective,* should it not be dismissed as the fabrication of sick mind not solely in the case of Leontes but also systematically?

This, I believe, is one of the questions that lies behind the creation of Leontes. In the early works, and even more in the so-called "cynical" works of the middle period, such as *Troilus and Cressida,* the system of mimetic contamination operates so infallibly that it seems a law of nature. *The Winter's Tale* can be read as an implicit but radical critique of the "epistemology of desire" that underlies all these plays.

I see some radical self-criticism in *The Winter's Tale,* but one that is perfectly compatible with a sound interpretation of the mimetic theory and therefore does not overturn it. How is this possible?

If our knowledge of mimetic desire in others comes from mimetic desire in ourselves, it is indeed a projection. In the case of Leontes, this projection is exactly what the modern theory of projection leads us to expect, an illusion. I do not believe, however, that the play invalidates the mimetic theory. It does not even invalidate the possibility of a correct insight that would be based solely on the projection of mimetic desire itself.

This apparently impossible paradox will disappear if we take the mimetic nature of mimetic desire more fully into account. If desire is as "infectious" as Shakespeare normally represents it, it will reproduce itself in routine fashion. An individual made suspicious by his own propensity to mimetic desire will expect to encounter around himself what his pessimistic view of human nature leads him to expect, the perfect replicas of his own desire, and, as a rule, he will indeed encounter them. If they were not there in the first place, his own desire would generate them.

More often than not, the expectation of mimetic contamination by mimetic desire will be self-fulfilling; it will produce its own truth. Mimetic desire is the original self-fulfilling prophecy and it is the real force behind self-fulfilling prophecies of all kinds in countless areas of human endeavor.

If, in the case of Leontes, his projection of desire encounters nothing but the void, the reason lies with Hermione's immunity to mimetic contagion. With different characters, the same projection might have turned out differently. The modern idea of projection as *necessarily* deceptive is not applicable to mimetic desire any more than its counterpart, the rationalistic and psychoanalytical fallacy of a completely objective knowledge of desire, entirely divorced from the desire it seeks to know.

Considerations of this type seem too abstract, theoretical, and undramatic to figure in a play, and yet they are developed at some length in *The Winter's Tale;* desperate jealousy is a desperate search for the truth and it is understandable, after all, that a Leontes would bring up the subject at the moment of his greatest disarray, in a fashion that is faintly reminiscent of the Marcel Proust of *La prisonniére.*

The text I have in mind is Leontes famous soliloquy on *affection,* or desire. It does not make much sense either from a traditional or from a psychoanalytical viewpoint, but it will make sense to us as a reflection on how far the intuition of mimetic desire can be trusted, coming as it does from mimetic desire itself:

> LEONTES:
> Affection! thy intention stabs at the centre.
> Thou dost make possible things not so held,
> Communicat'st with dreams (how can this be?)
> With what's unreal thou co-active art,
> And fellow'st nothing. Then, 'tis very credent
> Thou mayst co-join with something, and
>   thou dost

> (And that beyond commission), and I find it
> (And that to the infection of my brains
> And hard'ning of my brows).
>
> (I. ii. 138-46)

Leontes first insists on the most misleading aspects of desire, on its overall unreality. Desire may think that it grasps something outside of itself when, in fact, it does not and clutches only at fantoms.

Two different modalities of linkage with the outside world seem to be involved. The first appears to be intellectual: Leontes obviously alludes to a kind of knowledge specific to desire; it can fail miserably, but it can also produce results. It fails when desire "fellows nothing" and, as a result, cannot compare itself to anything real. Desire may remain alone but it is not its nature that it always should. It may fasten on something that truly exists and, in that case, it may really apprehend and comprehend that something.

The second linkage seems to belong to desire itself, to its own affective dimension. Desire becomes really *coactive* this time and it *co-joins* with the desire that it has *fellowed,* when it does *fellow* something which can only be its own mimetic replica. Either a desire will be sterile in all respects and will produce no knowledge because it produces no duplicate of itself, or it will be fertile in all respects and will produce real knowledge because it has already produced the object of that knowledge. Desire understands its children just as it understands itself, for the simple reason that children resemble their parents.

The last lines of our text confirm this reading. If the communication and co-creation of desires that Leontes is talking about has really occurred between him, on the one hand, and Polixenes and Hermione, on the other, then it is "beyond commission." The two other partners of the triangle must already desire one another in the same way that Leontes desires them, and his jealous insight is unfortunately a real one. He has been irreparably cuckolded and the *hard'ning of his brows* coincides with *the infection of his brain,* with his ever-growing consumption and absorption of mimetic contamination.

Everything falls into place if we only assume that desire itself is the source of what we know about desire and, as a result, the knowledge of other people's desires is not impossible but carries no absolute certainty.

As Jean-Pierre Dupuy has observed, the only thing that mimetic theory makes predictable is the unpredictability of the mimetic contamination, from which the fallibility can be deduced of any anticipation that relies too much on its happening automatically, confusing it with a causal effect.

I have tried to distinguish between the affective and intellectual aspects that seem to be present in our text, but it cannot really be done: the distinction is contrary to the spirit of the text. Judging from the number and diversity of the words that express it, the main idea is the notion of desire as *communication,* as something that may or may not *co-join* with something else. All these essential words and, above all, the magnificent definition of desire as a *co-active art,* apply to both aspects at once. Taken together they account to a definition of mimetic desire that would not be complete if it did not include a definition of how we know about this desire in others as well as in ourselves. The knowledge is part of the mimetic process itself and therefore it can be true, if the mimetic contamination is reciprocal; and it can be false, if the original mimetic desire remains childless.

The idea that our own desire is the chief source of all our insights into desire itself is evident to Shakespeare but not to us, and it is largely responsible for the alleged unintelligibility of this text. We are accustomed to a complete separation between desire and its knowledge. This is a most stubborn intellectual presupposition and it coincides with the massive rationalistic blindness to the importance of mimetic contamination in human affairs. This blindness must be rooted in the platonic repression of conflictual *mimesis* and in the distinction of the sensible and the intelligible. It has persisted during the entire history of Western philosophy and is stronger than ever today.

Far from breaking new ground in this respect, Freud reinforces this fundamental prejudice. In the light of Shakespeare, the postulate of an "unconscious" that would be totally separated from our "consciousness" appear not as a rebellion but as a caricatural exaggeration of the old rationalism. The true knowledge of desire, if there is one, is always supposed to come from an uncontaminated source, which seeks to eliminate the role of introspection and projection in order to believe in its own "scientificity."

The text seems written hastily, but its chaotic appearance may be intended to reflect Leontes' chaotic state of mind and his permanent problem with language. And this time, the problem might well be Shakespeare's own, at least up to a point. The writer is trying to find the right words for a subject matter that does not yet exist . . .

The obscurity of this text disappears if we renounce the prejudice of an irreducible separation between the subjective or, as Lacan would say, the imaginary projections of desire on the one hand and, on the other, the truth of desire, a truth that should reach us through those non-human and therefore immaculate channels invented by our modern mythologists.

We can regard the speech on *Affection* as a valid expression of what Shakespeare himself believed at the time of *The Winter's Tale.* Our only knowledge of

mimetic desire is mimetic and its application to individual human beings is uncertain. Leontes himself illustrates this uncertainty. His theory is right but his application is wrong. Leontes sees a dissemination of mimetic desire that has not occurred, but his overall theory, incomplete and misleading as it may be, is not devoid of validity. It is ironic, of course, that a man as perceptive as he about desire in general could be so completely deluded in his evaluation of the people closest to him, but such is the fate of many a theorist!

Laurence Wright (essay date 1989)

SOURCE: "When Does the Tragi-Comic Disruption Start?: *The Winter's Tale* and Leontes' 'Affection'," in *English Studies,* Vol. 70, No. 2, April, 1989, pp. 225-32.

[*In the essay below, Wright argues that the controversy surrounding the beginning of Leontes' jealousy overshadows Shakespeare's own dramatic emphasis of the collapse of Leontes' rational nature.*]

In most accounts of *The Winter's Tale,* the question of when the tragi-comic disruption starts has generally been taken as synonymous with 'When does Leontes become jealous?'. The assumption may blur an interpretative crux of some importance and one which is actually signalled in the text.

Leontes's jealousy, which initiates *The Winter's Tale's* tragi-comic cycle, has proved a perennial problem for the critics mainly on account of its suddenness. Sir Arthur Quiller-Couch reached the notorious conclusion that 'Shakespeare *had* time, or could have found time, to make Leontes's jealousy far more credible than it is. I maintain that he bungled it'.[1] Dover Wilson was largely instrumental in promulgating the opposite view that Leontes should appear jealous from the outset.[2] That these positions are not in fact irreconcilable has been demonstrated by Roger J. Trienens, arguing that 'suddenness' is thoroughly appropriate to Shakespeare's dramatic purpose, but that vestigial clues are deliberately left to hint at the genesis of the jealousy along the lines recounted in Greene's *Pandosto.*[3] Modern productions tend to favour this composite approach, having Leontes smouldering away from his first entry; a menacing inflection to I.ii.87, 'At my request he would not'; and the raw passion becoming explicit for the audience at I.ii.108 ('Too hot, too hot!').[4]

However, this controversy over the inception and genesis of Leontes's jealousy, though intriguing in itself, has tended to obscure Shakespeare's own dramatic emphasis, which is not on how and when the jealousy comes into being but on the moment of its triumph— the moment when Leontes's rational nature collapses. This is the crisis during which the disruptive force is unleashed. There is nothing in *Pandosto* to suggest the dramatic pointing Shakespeare gives to the episode, and to understand it we must look to psychological models which make no appearance in Greene.

The crucial speech is I.ii.137-46, given in F as follows:

> Most dear'st, my Collop: Can thy Dam, may't be
> Affection? thy Intention stabs the Center.
> Thou do'st make possible things not so held,
> Communicat'st with Dreames (how can this be?)
> With what's vnreall: thou coactiue art,
> And fellow'st nothing. Then 'tis very credent,
> Thou may'st co-ioyne with something, and thou do'st,
> (And that beyond Commission) and I find it,
> (And that to the infection of my Braines,
> And hardning of my Browes.)[5]

This apostrophe to Affection has always been regarded as a difficult speech. A fairly orthodox paraphrase is given by J. H. P. Pafford in his Arden Appendix of 1963:

> Can your mother (be faithless)? Is it possible? Lustful passions: your intensity penetrates to the very heart and soul of man. You make possible things normally held to be impossible just as dreams do [. . .]. How can this be? Lust causes one to associate in the mind with persons who are purely imaginary, who do not exist at all, therefore it is very credible that the most unthinkable lustful association can take place between real people: and lust, you have brought it about in this case, going beyond what is lawful—and I am the sufferer to such an extent that I am losing my senses and grow cuckold's horns.[6]

Pafford reads the speech as an impassioned outcry concerning mankind's general susceptibility to 'lustful passions', the case with which such passions turn sexual phantasy into actual infidelity, and the hurtful certainty that this is what has happened between Hermione and Polixenes. One objection to such an interpretation is that to some extent it denies the context, the presence and dramatic value of the young Mamillius. In line 136, Leontes is trying desperately to discern the innocency of the mother in the welkin eye of the son. The boy's looks are the concrete eugenic evidence of Hermione's past faithfulness, evidence which not even Leontes can gainsay. While it is possible (in the study, if not on stage) that Mamillius simply precipitates Leontes's festering suspicions with regard to the parentage of Hermione's unborn child, it is much more likely that the boy's manifestly innocent presence would substantiate the idea of his wife's fidelity and therefore cast doubt on the validity of Leontes's own suspicions. This seems to be the clear dramatic import of the child's presence.

Pafford's reading requires that Leontes abruptly deny the dramatic logic of the boy's presence and launch into a speech which asserts the capacity of 'lustful passions' to overwhelm Hermione's virtuous nature in respect of the second pregnancy. While this seems psychologically feasible, given Leontes's distraught state, it is not dramatically justified by the text. Surely the deft build-up from line 119 ('Mamillius/Art thou my boy?') to Leontes's tender but tortured recognition that the child is incontrovertibly his son cannot be thrown away so lightly? The dramatic logic is far stronger if it be allowed that the physical, visual 'argument' of Mamillius's presence on the stage causes Leontes to doubt, quite radically, the validity of his own underlying suspicions concerning Hermione.

Such a reading becomes possible once 'Affection' is no longer taken to mean simply 'lustful passions'.

Hallet Smith, building on the work of H. C. Goddard[7] and others, greatly clarified the sense of Leontes's speech when he proposed that 'Affection' might be the vernacular equivalent of the Latin affectio, as used by Cicero, and defined in Cooper's Thesaurus Linguae Romanae et Britannicae (1582 ed.) as follows:

> Affectio, Verbale. Cic. Affection: a disposition or mutation happening to bodie or minde: trouble of minde. Impetus, commotio, affectioque animi. Cic.[8]

Hallet Smith observes:

> Munroe and all the other editors think 'Affection' means love or lust, the feeling Hermione has for Polixenes (supposedly). I maintain that 'Affection' here means Affectio, that is, a sudden mental seizure, and that the passage describes the feeling of Leontes, his own suspicion or jealousy, and not his wife's supposed feeling at all.[9]

Hallet Smith's view has since been elaborated to the point where John Erskine Hankins, drawing on the vocabulary of Aquinas, Ficino and others, sets the entire speech in the context of specific psychological terminology.[10] Hankins thinks 'Intention' refers to a secondary image formed by the phantasy or imagination on the basis of a primary image supplied to the common sense by the external senses. Emphasising OED 11 rather than OED 8, this modifies, but does not controvert, the more usual reading of 'intensity' or 'intentness'.[11] Similarly 'Communicat'st', another formal psychological term, carries its original meaning of 'impart, share, hold in common' (as in OED 5). Used here, the term would imply that the Affection, working through its Intention, might have the power to delude Leontes in the same fashion that dreams can 'make possible things not so held'. While the plain meaning of the words is not disturbed, Hankins also supplies psychological contexts for (modernising the spelling) 'co-active', 'co-join', and less problematically, 'infection', thereby sharpening our sense of the intellectual and social sophistication of the Sicilian court, and heightening the contest between intellect and passion in Leontes himself. Following Goddard and Hallet Smith, Hankins regards this elaborate vein of overwrought psychological commentary as Leontes's effort at self-diagnosis, the convention of the dramatic soliloquy expressing the struggle of the rational man to examine and comprehend his own state of being.[12]

Such a reading gains support from instances of contemporary psychological discussion where this special sense of 'affection' appears in contexts which help elucidate Leontes's important speech. Timothy Bright's *A Treatise of Melancholie* (1586) gives a trenchant account of such unnatural perturbations. He writes that 'if the brayne be altered, and the object not rightly apprehended then is it deliuered otherwise then it standeth in nature, and so the hart moued to a disorderly passion'.[13] In terms of *The Winter's Tale*, the 'object not rightly apprehended' would be Hermione's innocent social flirtation with Polixenes. Furthermore, Leontes's interjection at I.ii.108 ('Too hot, Too hot!') becomes decidedly ambiguous. Is the 'heat', which Leontes thinks he detects in his wife's behaviour, really in his own metabolism? Bright details the effects of excessive heat in the human system as follows:

> Now particularly the spirite of the humour being subtiler, thinner, and hoter than is meete, maketh the apprehension quicker then it should be, and the discretion more hasty, then is meete for the vpright deliuery to the hart, what to embrace or to refuse: this causeth pronenes to anger, when we are offended without cause, commonly called teastines, and frowardnes. If the humour also with this spirite possesse the brayne, then are these passions of longer continuance: humour being of a more sollid nature then the spirite, and so not easily dispersed, which causeth fittes of such passõs to be of longer continuance: and thus the hart may be abused from the brayne . . . [14]

This account certainly seems to underwrite aspects of Leontes's behaviour. Bright stresses that the perturbation affects principally two organs, brain and heart, and that the affection is *communicated* from brain to heart (where the word carries the psychological sense implied in I.ii 140: 'Communicat'st with Dreames . . . '):

> Of all partes of the body, in ech perturbation, two are chiefly affected: first the brayne, that both apprehendeth the offensive or pleasaunt object, & iudgeth of the same in like sort, and communicateth it with the harte, which is the second part affected: these being troubled carie with them all the rest of the partes into a simpathy, they of all the rest being in respecte of affection of most importance.[15]

Robert Burton's version of the phenomenon (based partly on Bright) is rather more sedate, and lays greater emphasis on the power of imagination to exacerbate the mental turmoil. The following passage is particularly interesting because it implies the formation of an exaggerated or misleading secondary image based on a primary image 'residing in the former [foremost] part of the brain', and also includes the notions both of 'intentness' or 'intensity' and of 'communication':

> To our imagination commeth by the outward sense or memory, some object to be knowne (residing in the former part of the Braine) which he mis-conceauing or amplifying, presently commun-icates to the Heart, the Seat of all affections. . . . If the Imagination be very apprehensive, intent, and violent, it sends great store of spirits to or from the Heart, and makes a deeper impression, and greater tumult, . . . [16]

Such a conception calls to mind Leontes's cry at I.ii.110:

> I have *tremor cordis* on me: my heart dances,
> But not for joy—not joy.

If these examples do accurately suggest an appropriate psychological background for the upheaval dramatised in Leontes's speech, this may have important implications for our sense of the dramatic genre and structure of the play and specifically for the question of when the disruption actually starts. A figure striving (and failing) to maintain faith and integrity while seized by an insidious attack of jealousy is, at least in potential, an inhabitant of a tragic universe such as those of *Othello* and *Macbeth*. However, Leontes is overcome, not by the machinations of an Iago[17] or the supernatural seductions of witchcraft, but by a psychological aberration which overwhelms his rationality[18] and has no evident moral significance at all—except, of course, in its consequences. This moral arbitrariness points in two (congruent) directions: towards the self-conscious artifice of the theatrical experience, and towards the larger, more disturbing, notion of life as a tragi-comic artifice presided over by whimsical playwright gods who orchestrate human affairs for their own delectation, even at the cost of much human pain and confusion. As Barbara Mowat has noted, 'the undermining of the "tragic world" of Sicilia with comic distortions and exaggerations gives us a world uninformed by tragic universality, one which produces an effect approaching the grotesque . . . '.[19] It obviously will not do to read Leontes's predicament as a tame reworking of Othello's, especially when the arbitrary violence of the attack on Leontes' rationality is subtly dramatised in the apostrophe to 'Affection'. A man struggling rationally with an onslaught of jealousy remains a potentially tragic figure. But once the rational faculty is swamped in *this* way—a moment which is indicated in line 142—the play moves decisively into the painful, yet tender and illuminating world of tragicomedy.

Until this point (line 42) Leontes has been engaged in a turbulent but admirably rigorous effort of self-analysis. He has before him the hypothesis that his jealousy may be entirely unfounded, the effect of an 'Affection'. The Affection is brought on by an image (an 'Intention' or, later, a 'Dreame') which seems to attest unequivocally Hermione's adultery with Polixenes. This Intention 'stabs the Center': it goes to the heart of the frantic doubts and speculations which have been obsessing Leontes.[20] In so doing it necessarily stabs the emotional, passional 'Center' for, as Burton has it, the heart is 'the Seat of all affections'.[21] The violence here is complex. Natural relief at attaining intellectual certainty (comparable to the elation of 'hitting the white', 'the Center', in archery)[22] is savagely counterpointed by the emotional agony of supposing Hermione guilty. The violence also suggests the perceptual disfunction which precipitates this kind of perturbation. Not only does the Affection present itself with overwhelming intensity but it gains direct access to Leontes's inner being. In normal circumstances the submissions of the phantasy and the imagination would be modified by the judgement.[23] Here man's rational nature is simply by-passed, so the violent impact of the Intention indirectly conveys the violence done to Leontes' identity as a rational being.

As the conventional comparison with dreams shows, Leontes knows that such an Affection can make things which judgement, memory and experience affirm to be impossible seem possible: 'things' such as the absurd notion that Hermione should be unfaithful, above all with his trusted friend Polixenes. But at the very point where he seems about to diagnose the delusory nature of his jealousy, the Affection overwhelms Leontes's intellect:

> With what's vnreal: thou coactiue art,
> And fellow'st nothing. Then 'tis very
>   credent [142]
> Thou may'st co-ioyne with something, and
>   thou do'st,

The caesura in line 142 marks the moment of crisis. 'Then' purports to be a logical connective, but there is no logical passage from the conventional wisdom surrounding the untrustworthiness of the Affection, to the possibility that the Intention may indeed be properly grounded in reality. Before the break Leontes's judgement appears to be winning the struggle: he is acknowledging that his overwrought state may be largely the product of an imagination untempered by reality. Thereafter his rationality is suborned by the psychologically imperative Affection. The very intensity of his passion convinces Leontes of its basis in reality. No longer attempting to weigh the Intention against the testimony of his judgement, Leontes reasons from the premise of the Intention towards his experience of the world with disastrous consequences: if Affections usually co-operate with illusions, they may also, *a fortiori*, co-join with reality. Significantly, his state of mind now becomes public knowledge for the first time. Such is the violence of Leontes's mental turmoil that

it can no longer be concealed (I.ii.146-50) and hereafter the Court of Sicilia is subject to the tyranny of unreason. As Hermione later puts it (III.ii.81): 'My life stands in the level of your dreams'.

We have, then, to distinguish between the inception of Leontes's jealousy and the start of the tragi-comic disruption—a distinction which has obvious implications for the shape and pace of the play in performance. Whatever conclusion is reached as to how and when the jealousy initially comes into being, the tragic-comic disruption commences at the moment when Leontes's intellect succumbs to a perceptual aberration, a moment which is clearly implied in the text.

The cruel suddenness of this capitulation is in keeping with the extreme self-conscious theatricality of the play as a whole. C. O. Gardner has noted the importance of the word 'strike' in establishing that almost brutal disregard for naturalistic propriety which weighs so heavily in our experience of the play.[24] 'Strike' occurs at each of three crises in the story of Leontes. When jealousy overwhelms him, he says of Hermione's supposed infidelity:

> Physic for't there's none;
> It is a bawdy planet, that will strike
> Where 'tis predominant;—
>
> (I.ii.200-2)

Then immediately after his son's death he cries out:

> Apollo's angry, and the heavens themselves
> Do strike at my injustice.
>
> (III.ii.146-7)

Finally, at the miraculous moment of Hermione's 'resurrection' we have:

> Music, awake her, strike!
>
> (V.iii.98)

This is the *coup de théâtre* which is to 'Strike all that look upon with marvel' (V.iii.100). It is therefore appropriate that this theatrical cycle, in which disaster and miracle 'strike' with terrifying precipitateness and splendour, should be inaugurated by Leontes' speech on Affection, dominated as it is by the brutal verb 'stab': 'Affection? thy Intention stabs the Center'. This is the cruel theatrical blow by means of which the playwright-gods of tragi-comedy take hold both of the Sicilian court, and the audience in the theatre.

Notes

[1] Sir Arthur Quiller-Couch, *Shakespeare's Workmanship* (London, 1918), p. 290.

[2] New Cambridge Shakespeare, *The Winter's Tale* (Cambridge, 1931), n. 9-10, p. 131.

[3] Roger J. Trienens, 'The Inception of Leontes' Jealousy in *The Winter's Tale*', *Shakespeare Quarterly*, 4 (1953), pp. 321-6.

[4] J. L. Styan has recently summarised some of the production history and many of the practical problems surrounding Leontes's entry: 'Some moments in Shakespeare we may never fully understand, no matter how many versions of them we see. The shape and form to be taken by Leontes's jealousy at the beginning of *The Winter's Tale* is one of these dramatic enigmas. Presumably not wanting to repeat the long, slow growth of the green-eyed sickness he had demonstrated in *Othello* ten years before, Shakespeare now chose to show jealousy descending on the King of Sicilia like a bolt from hell. The effect is so quick that it is an embarrassment to any actor who must play the part and appear to be the least realistic. Following the suggestion of John Dover Wilson, John Gielgud in 1951 decided to make Leontes jealous from the start, got up a head of steam offstage and stormed on to the astonishment of all. Not having seen the character before, the audience wondered about the cause of his bad temper: had he stubbed his toe as he came in? In 1969, newly inheriting all the apparatus of the Stratford Memorial Theatre, Trevor Nunn decided to play a strobe light on the Leontes of Barrie Ingham perhaps to suggest the telescoping of time; he succeeded only in suggesting that the King was having a fit. In 1981, Ronald Eyre's production for the RSC permitted Patrick Stewart, who had recently been playing a psychiatrist on television, to apply his new learning to Shakespeare and play Leontes as a schizophrenic; he did a brilliant job of making the disjointed lines seem to fit the dual personality. The only trouble was that no one in the audience could feel a jot of sympathy with a madman. Which half of the dual personality do we identify with?' J. L. Styan, 'Understanding Shakespeare in Performance', *Shakespeare in Southern Africa*, 1 (1987), 21.

[5] Reproduced from Appendix I of the Arden edition, ed. J. H. P. Pafford (London, 1963), p. 165. Unless otherwise specified, all references are to this edition.

[6] *Ibid.*, p. 166.

[7] Harold C. Goddard, *The Meaning of Shakespeare*, 2 (2 vols.; Chicago, 1951), pp. 264-5.

[8] Hallett Smith, 'Leontes' Affectio', *Shakespeare Quarterly*, 14 (1963), pp. 163-6.

[9] *Ibid.*, p. 163 (footnote 6). Other noteworthy usages occur in *MV* IV.i.35-62, and *Ant.* I.v.12ff. However, both suggest a wilful indulgence of 'affection', whereas Leontes's predicament lacks entirely this element of deliberate choice.

[10] John Erskine Hankins, *Backgrounds of Shakespeare's Thought* (Hassocks, 1978), pp. 98-101.

[11] See *The Winter's Tale*, A New Variorum Edition of Shakespeare, ed. Horace Howard Furness (6th ed.: Philadelphia, 1898), pp. 27-30.

[12] Hallett Smith (*op. cit.*, p. 164) draws attention to the comparison with *Mac.* I.iv.137-42: Present Feares

> Are lesse then horrible Imaginings:
> My Thought, whose Murther yet is but
>   fantasticall,
> Shakes so my single state of Man,
> That Function is smother'd in surmise,
> And nothing is, but what is not.

Smith comments: 'the device of having the tempted man ironically express the way to his own salvation though he does not recognise it or follow it is used in both plays'. A crucial difference is that (as argued below) Leontes' soliloquy actually renders the collapse of the rational faculty, whereas Macbeth, though plagued by "horrible Imaginings", remains coldly rational throughout.

[13] Timothy Bright, *A Treatise of Melancholie* (1586), p. 93.

[14] *Ibid.*, p. 94.

[15] *Ibid.*, p. 93.

[16] Robert Burton, *The Anatomy of Melancholy* (Oxford, 1621), p. 121.

[17] There is an interesting comparison to be made between Leontes's agonised musings at I.ii.115/6 ('But to be paddling palms, and pinching fingers,/As now they are . . . ') and Iago's tempting of Roderigo at II.i.251-259:

> Iago. . . . Didst thou not see her paddle with the palm of his hand?
> Rod. Yes, but that was but courtesy.
> Iago. Lechery, by this hand: an index and prologue to the history of lust and foul thoughts: they met so near with their lips, that their breaths embrac'd together. When these mutualities so marshall the way, hard at hand comes the main exercise, the incorporate conclusion.

Leontes has no need of an external tempter; the jealous fictions are internalised and proliferating unaided. That the common lexical set should recur from Roderigo's facile love story rather than Othello's grand passion perhaps suggests something of Leontes's lack of true tragic stature.

[18] Reason is conventionally the faculty pitted against affection in unnatural peturbations of the kind attributed to Leontes. For instance, Erasmus recounts the

views of Diogenes as follows: ' . . . he is reported to have used this saying also, that to matche against fortune, he sette alwayes the confidence or stoutnesse of courage: against the law, he sette nature: against affeccions, mociõus, or wilfull pangues of the minde, reason. . . . For by these three thynges is purchased and mainteined the tranquillitee of menne.' Erasmus, *Apophthegmes,* trans. Nicolas Udall (1542), 92 verso.

[19] Barbara A. Mowat, *The Dramaturgy of Shakespeare's Romances* (Athens, 1976), 20.

[20] This 'Intention' is not necessarily rooted in the particular flirtation implied at I.ii.108: 'Too hot, Too hot!' (though to an audience it may well appear so). I.ii.115-17 and 284-96 suggest that Leontes's jealousy has undergone at least some period of gestation, as in *Pandosto.* Perhaps the necessary distinction is that between a private gestation and a public manifestation: *The Winter's Tale* dramatises a sudden, uncontrollable eruption (in public) of a festering private jealousy.

[21] Burton, *op. cit.*

[22] The reference to archery is noted by R. G. White (see New Variorum, ed. Furness, p. 28). Many commentators have picked up a correspondence between microcosm and macrocosm in the word 'Center'. The likelihood is borne out by Leontes's speech at I.ii.200:

> Physic for't there's none;
> It is a bawdy planet. . . .

[23] 'The understanding . . . had to sift the evidence of the senses already organised by the common sense, to summon up the right material from memory, and on its own account to lay up the greatest possible store of knowledge and wisdom. It was for the will to make the just decision on the evidence presented to it by the understanding.' E. M. W. Tillyard, *The Elizabethan World Picture,* 1943 (Harmondsworth, 1963), p. 91.

[24] C. O. Gardner, 'Three Notes on *The Winter's Tale*', *Theoria,* 54 (May, 1980), pp. 51-66.

Martha Ronk (essay date 1990)

SOURCE: "Recasting Jealousy: A Reading of *The Winter's Tale*," in *Literature and Psychology,* Vol. XXXVI, Nos. 1 and 2, 1990, pp. 50-77.

[*In the following essay, Ronk compares Leontes to Othello, and demonstrates that the function of elapsed time in* The Winter's Tale *allows a psychological shift in Leontes which does not occur in Othello.*]

In the middle of *The Winter's Tale* the character Time announces that Leontes disappears for sixteen years,

only a piece of an evening in stage time, but symbolically crucial for positing the opportunity for change, for turning tragedy to romance, destructive obsession to grace. As in so many other Shakespeare plays, obliteration—here not just metaphorical but of an actual figure on stage—argues for possibility. Leontes takes on years of penance, following Paulina's prescribed routine, and finally, although she says otherwise here, moves the gods to forgive him:

> Therefore betake thee
> To nothing but despair. A thousand knees,
> Ten thousand years together, naked, fasting,
> Upon a barren mountain, and still winter
> In storm perpetual, could not move the gods
> To look that way thou wert.
>
> (III, ii, 207-212)[1]

Having created jealousy out of nothing (cf. his repetition of this word at I, ii, 292-296), Leontes must now strip himself back and become "nothing but despair," his voice completely silenced. Like Paulina who vows to say nothing (III, iii, 229-230), he too says nothing at all. This is important not only because of the value of silence in other Shakespearean contexts—a particular type of knowledge associated with the non-verbal—but also because it signals a retreat from the conscious to some unconscious realm prior to language.[2]

Yet this period in which the major character of the play is absent is one of the most fertile in a play itself filled with images of procreation, pregnancy, and fertility, for it allows Leontes to reimagine the characters and scenes of the tragic opening of the play, giving us in Part II the comic pastoral and the miraculous rebirth of Hermione. Like Hamlet who disappears off-stage and is threatened by death before he can imagine the necessary end of his play, Leontes moves off-stage into the house of death, penance, and a kind of psychological winter (this aspect of the play's title) in order to rework himself and his dreams.

What I want to demonstrate here, using Othello as a kind of foil, is that although the two heroes are alike in uncanny ways, the structural maneuver at the center of *The Winter's Tale* not only allows a generic shift from tragedy to romance,[3] but also provides a psychological basis for Leontes' change. Critics have already noted the similarities in Othello and Leontes: both are irrationally jealous of innocent wives; both are unable to accept mature sexuality and the loss of male intimacy; both tend to see the world and its creatures as entirely idealized or debased; once affected, both characters view the world in a paranoid and distorted way— everything becomes suggestive of copulation and cuckoldry; both appear destined for tragedy and death. What happens to each character in relation to a similar situation is, however, quite different, and it is this difference, especially Leontes' crucial time off-stage—a time not available to Othello—that I wish to examine here.

Why might Shakespeare have designed the play in what appears so awkward a fashion, and how can we come to "know" what happens in places we cannot see; what relationship does Time, both as character and as passing years, have to do with penance; what is there about the nature of penance that prevents it from being seen? What is the relationship between what we see on-stage and what we imagine as occurring off-stage; and what is the nature of the relationship between penance and Bohemia?[4]

Shakespeare might have presented Leontes in some conventional pose as the penitent described by Paulina: kneeling, weeping, flagellating himself, praying—but does not. What is gained then as a result is that Leontes is defined as different from an emblematic figure of Penance; whatever changes are occurring to Leontes are not those which would be visible to the eye, an important fact in a play that has already demonstrated the fallibility of the eye as trustworthy witness; rather the essential changes are within and involve the restructuring of Leontes' psyche and way of being. Although as audience we remain keenly aware of this missing figure, aware of absence and what it means as well, we do not see him, nor could we see the changes which Luther, for example, details as necessary for attaining grace. The sorts of bodily punishments which Leontes vows to undergo would mean nothing without the unseen operation of faith in a man's heart, an operation which his physical absence implies:

> Just as faith alone gives us the spirit and the desire for doing works that are plainly good, so unbelief is the sole cause of sin: it exalts the flesh, and gives the desire to do works that are plainly wrong, as happened in the case of Adam and Eve in the Garden of Eden. Genesis 3:6[5]

Another important aspect of penance, beyond its invisibility, is that it requires time; although Leontes has destroyed his family and world by a momentary madness, he must spend years atoning for his crime, indeed a lifetime, and it is therefore appropriate that Time should announce his whereabouts and efforts. Moreover, Leontes must manage his penance in silence. Shakespeare removes him from the stage: no action and no words can demonstrate true penance, especially since his actions and words have been in error and quite at odds with what he should have known about the loyalty of his wife and of his friend. Like Lear, who also should have known of Cordelia's love and loyalty through years of demonstrated affection, Leontes ought also to know, although he does not. He accuses and rants and rails, even against the words of the oracle, and now he is appropriately silent.

Diana Wynyard as Hermione and John Gielgud as Leontes in Act V, scene iii of Peter Brook's Phoenix Theatre production.

Also, as we know from overhearing Claudius' prayers for forgiveness, a speech or gesture can seem convincing (and in this instance does to Hamlet) although one's heart is not in it; thus Shakespeare chooses another theatrical convention to represent Leontes' genuine penance. As Greek theater represented crucial dramatic events such as suicide and death as occurring off-stage, so here Leontes loses one sort of life in exchange for another, off-stage. The most significant and mysterious actions cannot be seen; moreover, because we do not see Leontes we are not tempted to judge his efforts as imperfect or inauthentic.

Thus the central character disappears and, although the relationship between on-stage and off-stage events over the course of theatrical history is too large a topic for this paper, in this case, as in others, we learn obliquely about Leontes from the images that appear on-stage. Like Oliver in *As You Like It,* Leontes is converted off-stage and while we witness other miraculous changes in a timeless pastoral world containing significant gestures of love, generosity, faith: the Duke, for example offers food to Orlando and Adam, and Perdita offers abundant flowers with her love. Only by withdrawing into silence and into a visual discourse prior to speech can Leontes hope to effect change; Shakespeare removes Leontes and in his place presents Bohemia, a visual representation of regeneration, possibility and growth, an Eden found for the one, as Luther mentions, lost.

In his famous discussion of archetypes, Northrop Frye argues that comic romances provide their characters with a green world, a pastoral world of healing, imagination, and rearrangements so that they may return to court rejuvenated and strong. In *The Winter's Tale* the mythical sea-coasted Bohemia serves as this green world, and "has analogies, not only to the fertile world of ritual, but to the dream world that we create out of our own desire."[6] Interestingly, however, in this play we see a green world that does not include the central character; it is his world, but he is missing from it. He is not present as a participant or as a spectator on a balcony—certainly a possible staging—though Bohemia is surely his in some important way beyond the appearance of his stand-in daughter.

But the notion of a green world is not quite enough to explain how regeneration operates in this particular play, because unlike the more innocent characters of the early comedies, Leontes is not a part of this world; a decidedly fallen and tragic figure, Leontes is outside Bohemia even as it is potentially his. Secondly, the changes that occur in other green worlds happen far more quickly; here sixteen years pass between Leontes' vow of penance and the presentation of a world that contains within it the next (innocent) generation. As chorus Time refers to the metaphor of dreaming that dominates the play and asks that the audience accept the passing of years, "as you had slept between"; and thus in the play's own terms, it is as if Leontes' work of penance is coincident with dreamwork, as if Leontes has slept out the sixteen years in order to dream anew.[7] Phenomenologically, what happens on stage is like something taking place in his unconscious; it is dreamlike and illusory, but also profoundly true, literal, and recognizable.

Moreover, the green world is not, as in earlier comedies, a stage to be passed through in order to learn enough to return to the real world, but a Romantic and mythical stage to be re-attained as if innocence could be re-imagined. Like the Romantic heroines in the film comedies of remarriage, Leontes has lost his sexual innocence—the point is emphasized—but as Stanley Cavell says in *Pursuits of Happiness,* "if we are to continue to provide ourselves with the pleasure of romantic comedies, with this imagination of happiness, we are going to require narratives that do not depend on the physics of virginity but rather upon the metaphysics of innocence."[8]

The second half of the play, parallel in so many obvious ways to the first half, reads like wish-fulfillment, Leontes' reworking of unconscious material in order to produce the right dream. Although both of Leontes' dreams are embodiments of similar obsessions, they differ radically. Leontes' original encounter with his own repressed unconscious material results in rage and death. At first his "dream"—that which he imagines is a vision of betrayal—is regressive and destructive,[9] as Leontes sees Hermione's actions not as existing in their own right, out in the world and separate from his own state of mind, but as enactments of his own paranoia. As Hermione says, "You speak a language that I understand not / My life stands in the level of your dreams / Which I'll lay down" (III, ii, 78-79). Leontes' second and overwhelming dream comes, however, as a result of his conscious choice of penance; and in withdrawing to an inner life he creates the wish he expresses when he first glimpses his error: "Apollo, pardon / My great profaneness 'gainst thine oracle. / I'll reconcile me to Polixenes / New woo my queen, recall the good Camillo (III, ii, 150ff.). At this moment in the play, however, Leontes' wish is unearned, for it is the sixteen years when he believes his wife dead and when he is dead to stage life which provide the necessary rearrangements and shifts of material that enable romance to assert itself. There are several ways in which the processes of penance and dreaming overlap here, and several reasons why I see a close relationship between Leontes' penance off-stage and the dreaming which visualizes Bohemia. Both are intense internal activities in which the psyche is freed as a result of the body's removal from daily life by sleep, mortification of the flesh, entombment in darkness and solitude. Both concern what one is behind the facades and theatricalities of life—and also what one was originally, in early childhood or in being born, having one's origins in sin. Penance can be effected by meditation of visual images as Louis L. Martz argues in *The Poetry of Meditation,*[10] and certainly dreams are powerfully visual (preceding the fall into language). Both are generated by a strong desire or wish (in Leontes' case for oneness with the feminine, his family, and the divine), and both demand belief of some sort, at the very least a belief in the reality of the experience itself. In *The Interpretation of Dreams,* Freud describes dreams as wishes visualized:

> Here we have the most general and the most striking psychological characteristic of the process of dreaming: a thought, and as a rule a thought of something that is wished, is objectified in the dream, is represented as a scene, or as it seems to us, is experienced.[11]

Moreover, penance obviously requires a belief in the divine and in powers beyond one's own control; although a person can kneel and pray, it is not solely in his or her power to experience penance without some intervening grace. In Luther's words:

Faith . . . is something that God effects in us . . .
Faith puts the old Adam to death and makes us
quite different men in heart, in mind, and in all our
powers . . . what a living, creative, active powerful
thing it is.[12]

Likewise in dreaming, something unconscious and
beyond one's control produces the images encountered.
Leontes' dream of Bohemia bears witness to his alteration; for without a change in his psyche he could not
have had such a dream. Having lost his faith in his life
previously, a loss signaled by his loss of a wife and
son, his dream of Bohemia signals a new creative faith.
Since what is at stake in this play is also how to interpret what one sees—Leontes having so badly misinter-
preted his wife's hospitality towards Polixenes—the
particular presentation of Bohemia lets the audience
know that Leontes has suffered towards good ends,
that he knows finally how to read his dreams.

In this context it is also useful to think of Victor
Turner's description of liminal states as states of transition;[13] such a place as Paulina's chapel would be a
"betwixt and between" stage of institutionalized transition. Yet since it is a transitional threshold, between
one place and another, it cannot be seen any more than
the passage of time can be seen. Such liminal states
are, according to Turner, characterized by transition,
anonymity, absence of status and its accordant rites
and obligations, sexual continence, humility, sacredness, silence, reference to mystical powers, acceptance
of pain, and obedience. Leontes partakes of all these,
giving up all his public functions in order to unmake
himself, as if he had to strip himself (to become nothing) in order to remake himself as a new man. Leontes
must lose his ego in order to be capable of the sort of
renewal as a result of which Hermione's life indeed
stands at the level of his dreams. That is, the profound
change which Paulina effects makes possible the awakening of Hermione at the end; she does stand before
him as a living statue, but for him—at least to begin
with—she seems a dream of his own making. Miraculously, he gets exactly what he has wished for, both a
new wife (life) and an emblem of the old: Hermione
both unchanged and wrinkled by age.

What I would also argue is that, although the play does
not specifically locate Leontes for the time he is off-
stage, it is appropriate to imagine him in a chapel which,
if not identical to, is one which at least participates in
or blurs with the chapel located in Paulina's house.
Although Leontes indicates as he arrives to see the
statue in Act V that he has not visited the place before,
he also has several other contradictory experiences in
this scene: his wife is dead and lives; his daughter is
not lost but found; sixteen years have passed and none;
stone is flesh. Moreover, he has been in a long and
extreme state of mourning—a mourning that has stimulated the desire to restore what is lost—and if not

entirely rapt and confused, certainly "so far gone" as
to be absent from the stage. Does he really know, one
might ask, where he has been? Since his efforts in one
"place" create the miracle in the other, they are bound
to collapse into one another for an audience which
sees but one chapel although two are mentioned.
Moreover, the residing spirit in each chapel is Paulina
who effects the change in Leontes which makes possible the change in Hermione. Paulina herself is a liminal figure (representative of St. Paul) who is maternal,
paternal, forgiving, judgmental, old enough for wisdom and a husband and children, and young enough to
join the others in (re)marriage at the end of the play.
Like other Shakespearean figures such as Falstaff,
Rosalind, and Portia, who aid in transforming male
character, Paulina functions to embrace opposite aspects of gender and generation, not as dangerously
collapsed, but as signalling a Tiresian-like wisdom.
More importantly, perhaps, she witnesses (to the extent that it is possible) Leontes' penance; in Luther's
schema, one Christian confessing to another effects
the peace of mercy.

The "place" where Leontes is located then is representative of the unconscious mind, as Leontes is remembering, withdrawn into himself, out of all action. Thus,
as the withdrawal is symbolic of Leontes' withdrawal
into himself, we come to understand what occurs to
him by what occurs on-stage, each aspect of his internal struggle dramatized by what we do see. In his book,
Shakespeare and the Artist, W.M. Merchant argues that
Shakespeare's staging is always symbolic, following
the medieval principles of simultaneity and symbolic
presentation. Since the arts of music, architecture,
painting and verse were not separated from one another, he argues, a witty interchange of ideoms and
methods was used to transfer significance from one
medium to another: "drama adopted the essential qualities of the well-tried simultaneous setting in its most
allusive and flexible form and it achieved ease of
multiple reference by employing conceit, most obviously in the verse, but equally richly in the music
employed and in the relationship of the architectural
setting to the witty movement of the plot."[14] An important way then of understanding Leontes' motivation
and behavior, both early and at this moment in the
play, is to examine what does appear in language,
metaphors, staging, the embodiment of what cannot be
seen and heard by what can be, by looking at his
"dream" to understand his mind as Freud suggests:
"The interpretation of dreams is the royal road to a
knowledge of the unconscious activities of the mind."[15]

A. The Consequences of Jealousy: Leontes and Othello

Before examining Leontes' final dream and the ways
in which Leontes' escape from the stage allows for the
dream of romance and allows the audience to follow
his psychological shifts, I want to return to the starting

points of *The Winter's Tale* and *Othello* to describe the similarities between the two characters in order to understand more completely the radical differences of the endings and the radical introduction in *The Winter's Tale* of the gap of time. Critics have often noted that both Leontes and Othello suffer from the same sort of projective paranoid jealousy as a defense against homosexual attraction; both are described as losing themselves to the irrational forces of the unconscious. As Murray Schwartz argues in his essay on Leontes, such men suffer a paranoia derived from homosexual desire (thus the formula: I do not love him, she does), and from a deeply ambivalent relationship towards both the maternal and paternal, the sexual and sacred: "In *The Winter's Tale,* jealousy and the sacred and dialectical terms; each implies the other, as separation implies union or winter spring."[16] Schwartz further describes paranoia as a psychic imprisonment, the sort which traps Othello throughout, but the opposite of the bodily imprisonment which Leontes undergoes as he works to free his psyche:

> Paranoia is a form of psychic imprisonment in which the loss of ego boundaries makes the external world *nothing but* a confluence of symbols, selected according to subjective and ambivalent wishes and fears. For the paranoid, others become what D.W. Winnicott has called "subjective objects," embodiments of psychic realities that exist only in relation to the subject. Others lose their otherness. In this sense, paranoia can be seen as a radical denial of separation, a perversion of the mutuality of the boyhood myth which shares with it a crucial element. In his delusions Leontes identifies with both Hermione and Polixenes and tries desperately to exclude himself from the fantasies he projects on them.[17]

What occurs in each play as a result of initial paranoia is, however, quite different. What happens to Othello is that his unconscious material becomes, in Freud's words, fixed, even as he is spatially trapped on the stage, not allowed to leave its confines for long enough. In speaking of patients with obsessional neuroses, Freud says that they are "fixed to a particular point in their past that they do not know how to release themselves from, and are consequently alienated from both present and future."[18] Othello's experiences with the horrors of his unconscious is thus given no chance for revision. The consummation of his marriage, occurring off-stage and at some indeterminate time, triggers the release of unconscious material which Othello is never allowed time to rework. He is goaded by Iago, rushed by war and sword fights, pressed by his wife. He is kept in a state of permanent madness until he sees no way out of his nightmare but to still the flesh and blood which arouses him.

What most especially fixes Othello and holds him fixated on sexual consummation and its attendant confusion and horror is the overwhelming presence of the absent handkerchief, emblematic of his wedding sheets. The discrepancy between the ideal he has constructed of Desdemona and the real experience of marriage including both blood and passion, is more than he can bear. Moreover, Iago knows how to mirror his anxiety and to establish a male bond more powerful, familiar, and reassuring than the marriage bond; Othello is never permitted to dream again, but is instead kept by Iago ever crazed, ever in a state of frustrated excitation, his sleep and sexual performance interrupted, until finally he enacts such anxiety in a fit, and moves to rid himself of it by murder and suicide. Othello comes undone not only physically, but also, as others have noted, verbally[19] as he loses his ability to proceed in a linear, narrative way, a horror for one who relies so heavily upon storytelling to construct his character. The mad Othello catches, repeats, makes "lie" (falsehood) into the "lie" of sexual hysteria, and "zounds" (God's wounds) into the fulsome female wound central to his madness. The divine Desdemona is no longer a pure diety to him, but a woman wounded:

> Lie with her? Lie on her?—We say lie on her when they belie her.—Lie with her! Zounds, that's fulsome.—Handkerchief—confessions—handkerchief! (IV, i, 36ff.)

Leontes' fit of jealousy is quite similar. Like Othello's, his jealousy has its origin in a mistaken sense of his wife's behavior and it also surges up seemingly out of nowhere, in part in reaction to an ideal vision, for Leontes of his childhood past as described by Polixenes. It was a past without wives, as he says, without adult sexuality and without children:

> We were as twinned lambs, that did frisk i'th'sun, And bleat the one at th'other; what we changed Was innocence for innocence; we knew not The doctrine of ill-doing, nor dreamed That any did; had we pursued that life, And our weak spirits ne'er been higher reared With higher blood, we should have answered heaven Boldly, "not guilty;" the imposition cleared, Hereditary ours. (I, i, 67ff.)

Out of this "dream" of childhood innocence, Leontes extracts the crazed "dream" of betrayal discussed by Schwartz and others[20] as Leontes converts his sexual tie to Polixenes into a perverse relationship between Polixenes and Hermione.[21] One might also argue that as "twins" the two are competing for maternal love (emblemized by the pregnant Hermione) and that Leontes is hence catapulted into an infantile paranoid state in which ego boundaries are completely dissolved and other people become figures without external reality.[22] Gazing at the two together, Leontes' aside reveals the crazed state of his mind: "Too hot, too hot! / To mingle friendship far is mingling bloods. / I have tremor cordis on me; my heart dances, / But not for joy, not joy." (I, ii, 109-111) In this diffuse state—

"muddy," "unsettled" the mingling of friendship which Leontes has projected onto his wife and friend creates all manner of mingling: of sexes, of characters, of generations.[23] Leontes sees himself as merging with Polixenes who has usurped his role; with Mamillus who is like him in his boyishness (his desire to be "boy eternal"), as like him as one egg is to another; and with Hermione as he identifies with the female, envisioning both of them with their "gates" forced open. Although he begins by identifying with the cuckolds,[24] and seeing all neighbors as adulterers (as all neighbors blend into a disembodied "smile"), his imagery of ponds and gates becomes both female and ambiguously referential. Moreover, "Sir Smile" is a free floating image that draws attention not only to the neighbor's oily falsity, but to both a slit and an erection (by shape), and to male (Sir)/female (orifice) confusion:

> And his pond fished by his next door
>   neighbor, by
> Sir Smile, his neighbor; nay, there's comfort
>   in't,
> Whiles other men have gates, and those
>   gates opened,
> As mine, against their will.
>
>   (I, ii, 194-7)

Most obviously, Leontes conflates his wife and his friend, blending their bodies into what for him is a terrifying image of male and female parts overlapping until there is no distinction between cheek and cheek, lip and lip, nose and nose, breath and breath (and as he moves into animal imagery, between "neb" and mouth). He defies Camillo's assertion of their innocence by anatomizing, by reducing each whole being to a small part:

> Is whispering nothing?
> Is leaning cheek to cheek? Is meeting noses?
> Kissing with inside lip? Stopping the career
> Of laughter with sigh (a note infallible
> Of breaking honesty)?
>
>   (I, ii, 285-89)

Once boundaries between people are broken in Leontes' mad dream, the boundaries between life and death are also broken and Perdita is sent to die and Mamillius does die.[25] In the case of Hermione the boundaries are blurred if not actually broken, since her death remains a seeming truth throughout most of the play. Each loss thus prepares him for the necessary loss of himself to himself and to the audience, and teaches him his tragic error. First, in losing touch with the world around him and specifically with the female in it, he loses both the nurturing and protective female (the pregnant Hermione) and the female as a potential force for courtesy, gracefulness, and grace (Perdita).[26] Although he describes Antigonus as dreading his wife, it seems rather as if Leontes has projected such fear onto him. It is Leontes who seems to dread all that is female, for

when Paulina lays his child before him, he speaks in an hysterical fashion that merges female as whore and female as infant. He wants both "out":

> Out!
> A mankind witch! Hence with her, out o'door!
> A most intelligencing bawd! (III, iii, 65-67)

But it is his other child whom he loses forever. As Richard Wheeler remarks, the loss of Mamillius in the actual world confirms its independent existence and wakes Leontes from his deluded "dream."[27] Leontes cannot have his boyhood, mirrored in Mamillius, again. Certainly he can never return to the boyhood Polixenes describes in Act I in which the two were without guilt, sin, or women. They were, as he says, "unfledged," without the plumage symbolic of adult sexuality, and untried. Thus in killing Mamillius, Leontes kills not only his son, but his own boyhood, and the living proof of his adult sexuality. In denying (as he denies the truth of the oracle) the truth of the psychosexual stages he has already passed through, in wanting to be, "boy eternal," Leontes must return to an unconscious state and begin again to construct himself.

Leontes also loses Antigonus, a loss which can be understood symbolically both as Antigonus represents both the larger world which is devastated by the king's madness, and as he represents an aspect of Leontes' own sick psyche. His name splits into parts (anti-go-nad) indicating yet again male fear of sexuality. His speeches about his wife and daughters are also ugly in the extreme and match Leontes' imagination in their cruelty and male paranoia. Although his daughters are only five, nine, and eleven years old, he offers them up as sacrifices if Hermione proves false. He will keep them "girls eternal" and will castrate himself. Although he appears to be exaggerating only for the rhetorical effect of asserting Hermione's innocence, his language nonetheless reveals his similar obsession with betrayal and fear:

> By mine honor,
> I'll geld 'em all; fourteen they shall not see
> To bring false generations. They are co-heirs,
> And I had rather glib myself than they
> Should not produce fair issue.
>
>   (II, i, 146-50)

Murray Schwartz comments that in this passage Antigonus confuses his own potency with masculine honor and duplicates the disease he repudiates: "He becomes, therefore, the surrogate for his master and the carrier of Paulina's curse (II, ii, 76-79), the vehicle for Shakespeare's displaced exorcism of Leontes' jealousy."[29] Sent to the seacoast with Leontes' child, Antigonus hears the name "Perdita." Having lost faith in Hermione's innocence, and believing falsely that she is dead, he dreams that Hermione appears before him, telling him to name the lost baby Perdita, but, of course, it is he himself, not the baby, who is lost, whom nature destroys.

Many readers have noted the parallels between the first and second parts of the play;[28] for example, in both parts a king has an irrational outburst, someone longs to return home by sea, a woman represents fertility, a pastoral scene is described or appears, gods reveal the truth. Critics have also noted that the romances are in many ways revisions of the tragedies; *The Winter's Tale* is of particular interest as it demonstrates the revision mid-way in a single play, and as it offers Leontes an experience denied Othello or Macbeth or Lear. Unlike these equally maddened figures, Leontes is allowed to settle and be still. Unlike Lear's frail, deluded dream of being imprisoned with Cordelia, Leontes' dream also growing out of imprisonment and total immersion in the self, proves robust and fruitful. In spite of the powerful conclusion, however, the vision of death is never quite expunged; perhaps indeed it contributes to Leontes' (and our) awe at the preciousness and cost of life returned as those that remain appear on stage together.

B. Recasting

The process which culminates in Leontes' time off-stage and his new dream begins with his becoming nothing, and we know this as early as the courtroom scene in which Leontes is so certain of his accusations that he defies Apollo. According to Cleomenes' description of his own experience, one that Leontes is soon to replicate, the oracle manifests itself first as overpowering thunder and only then as clear words setting forth Hermione's innocence:

> But of all, the burst
> And the ear-deaf'ning voice o'th'oracle,
> Kin to Jove's thunder, so surprised my sense,
> That I was nothing.
>
> (III, i, 8-11)

It is this very experience of "nothing" which Leontes must come to know as Lear does on the heath; he must come to know that his suspicions were as he himself named them, "nothing," and that he created them out of nothing, and must therefore experience complete loss and nothingness. David Willbern in his wonderfully suggestive article on "Shakespeare's Nothing," gives a description of Leontes' destructive abilities; his essay does not explore, but does suggest that the awareness of nothing can be creative as well:

> Psychoanalytic theories of the origins and acquisition of language, of perception, or reality testing, of the capacity to symbolize or to interact creatively with an environment, all start from the primary fact of absence, separation, loss. The loss of an immediate,

felt relationship: to bring things symbolically to mind when they are not really present, or to make them present through some communicative act (like a cry). *Awareness of absence thus results in imagined or reenacted presence: a recollecting or remembering of what was lost* (my emphasis).[30]

The scene in which Antigonus is pursued by a bear and in which the clown describes the tearing of Antigonus to bits (anatomized even as Leontes has anatomized Hermione and Polixenes) has frequently been described as grotesquely comic, a scene in which genres and tones are audaciously mixed. At the threshold of sea and land, sea and sky, as the ship bores the moon with her main mast, this coast presents those at the thresholds of life and death: Perdita, Antigonus, and the seamen. Yet in the midst of the clown's jumbled stories of destruction come the suggestions of miracle, the discovery of the baby and the idea of charity. It is tempting to read the clown's description as a description of the (re)birth of Perdita. Since Leontes cannot look upon the original birth, convinced that his wife is a whore and the child a bastard, we get it, like so much else in Part II of the play, a second time; and the clown's words seem in this context to describe not only the drowning but also intercourse, the yeasty rising of a pregnant belly, and finally crowning, birth, and the mother's cries of pain: "O, the most piteous cry of the poor souls! Sometimes to see 'em, and not to see 'em; now the ship boring the moon with her main mast, and anon swallowed with yeast and froth, as you'd thrust a cork into a hogshead" (III, iii, 89-93). Although the shepherd cannot save the men on board (to do so, as the clown says, would mean being able to walk on water), the two can value and care for the baby—which they do even before they discover that the baby's value is also measured in gold. This wrenching seacoast scene is analogous to Leontes' unconscious, off-stage wrestling with his own past as discordant elements are tossed up together. Many critics have noted the composite and unsettling nature of the seacoast scene, how like a dream it seems. In *The Interpretation of Dreams,* Freud writes:

> The possibility of creating composite structures stands foremost among the characteristics which so often lend dreams a fantastic appearance, for it introduces into the concept of dreams elements which could never have been objects of actual perception.[31]

In this scene from *The Winter's Tale,* the common element comparable to the common element Freud describes as the organizing principle of a dream is the element of thresholds. Importantly, it is the scene that occurs immediately after Leontes announces that tears shall be his recreation: "Come, and lead me / To these sorrows" (III, ii, 240-41). Although Leontes cannot know it at this point, buried in his words is the hope of re-creation. The *OED* defines "recreation" as a restoration of vigor and health, and as a new creation, the re-creation necessary to make the old Adam into the new; "As in the creation he could have made all at once, but he would take days for it: so in our recreation by grace, Bp. Hall, 1611." Clearly this is the direction Leontes has been working towards during his time off-stage. The logic of romance almost requires an experience of death (often in association with water leading to new life). Out of his watery tears (presented on stage in images of the sea) comes the miraculous possibility of change, dependent, of course, on the image of Jesus which stands behind the shepherd and the reference to walking on water. Likewise, Hermione's initial tears of sorrow, the spouts of Antigonus' dream, become in her final speech, waters from the gods; both Leontes and Hermione are made anew, recreated out of something dead:

> You gods look down
> And from your sacred vials pour your graces
> Upon my daughter's head.
>
> (V, iii, 122-24)

The recreation allowed Leontes in *The Winter's Tale* is not allowed Othello. Like other critics of the play, I read Othello as one who in marrying loses his sense of separate identity as a self-defined soldier and story-teller, one whose past and character do not prepare him for marriage and specifically for sexuality in marriage.[32] Oddly, Othello announces his own lack of appetite as he tells the Venetian senators of his modesty; one must wonder why he makes his private affairs so public and what he is defending against, what worries have slipped out in so inappropriate a setting when he says, "the young affects / in me defunct." How different this is from Desdemona's straightforward request to accompany her husband to Cyprus: "that I love the Moor to live with him."[33] Although Othello woos Desdemona with story, addresses her in fine language, and wishes to perceive her as alabaster, pure, and chaste, he is drawn not only by Iago, but by his own private vision of her "topped" into a morass of overwhelming feelings and confusions that he cannot sustain. It is Othello who has had the vision which Iago describes as the most horrible and which, were there not a murder, the audience too would be forced to witness in Act V; Iago cries:

> Would you, the supervisor, grossly gape on?
> Behold her topped?
>
> (III, iii, 393-93)

The consequent state of chaos, jealousy and sexual fantasy into which Othello plunges, literally undoes him as he falls to the ground in a trance. Once in this state, Othello, like Leontes, perceives an amorphous world of his own making in which "chaos is come again," and in which his vision of Desdemona merges with a picture of a whore. This double vision of her

and his inability to imagine a woman of both delicacy and appetite is revealed throughout in language similar to Leontes' of anatomizing and splitting: "O curse of marriage, / That we can call these delicate creatures ours / And not their appetites" (III, iii, 268-69). It is also important to note here, as other critics have done, that dissolutions affect Othello's sentences as well as his perception and that it is not until the murder of Desdemona is complete that he again stands cloaked in fine phrases, a story of his own making, speeches appropriate to his image of himself as hero. The various ways in which Othello's language fails him or in which he merges with image are both odd and telling. For example, he conflates not Desdemona and Diana, goddess of the moon and chastity, but himself and the virgin Dian: "I think my wife be honest, and think she is not . . . / I'll have some proof. My name, that was as fresh / as Dian's visage, is now begrimed and black / As mine own face" (III, iii, 383-85). It is, as he reveals, the fact that he is black that disturbs him; and I would add that the character Othello is disturbing to the audience precisely because he does not totally break a slanderous stereotype: a black man, he is both sexually obsessed and threatening to the white world, a murderer.

In his farewell speech, Othello also creates an odd substitution which is revealing of how he sees himself. He begins the speech by asserting that he could have stood his situation, even if Desdemona had been tasted by the entire camp of soldiers, if only he had not known. Yet when he comes to list what he must say goodbye to, he moves from the logic of "Farewell the tranquil mind," to a list of farewells that is not, as one might expect, of bliss or contentment or Desdemona, but of troops, wars, steeds, banners, all manner of military items. What he has lost in suspecting Desdemona of adultery, it seems, is war; yet this makes psychological if not logical sense only if Othello has been "unmanned" (weakened like a virginal girl), only if what he has lost by his immersion in his sexual union with Desdemona is his sense of himself as potent soldier.

Unlike Leontes, Othello is unable to escape the state he has created. For one, this play has a villain, an embodiment of Othello's imagination presented in an exterior character who keeps Othello in a state of paranoid delusion and anxiety; each echoing "indeed" or "think" from Iago prevents Othello from recasting his perceptions, from recreating his initial vision: "To be once in doubt / Is to be resolved" (III, iii, 179-80). Moreover, it is Iago who interrupts Othello each time in the play that he is in bed with Desdemona; although it is impossible in the play to discover exactly when sexual consummation takes place (it seems to occur and not to occur throughout) it is possible to note that when Othello and Desdemona move toward an off-stage bedroom, what we witness on stage as an emblem for what happens off-stage is a riot of shouting male figures, swords, moneybags, in essence a "nightbrawl." One might therefore assume that Othello finds it difficult to prevent sexuality from becoming violent, that for him sexual battle and battle merge; or that his image for the manly is so allied to soldiering that in trying to cast off the soldier, he finds himself unmanned as well. And yet, if there were a place which might offer the hope of Othello's revising his initial vision of sexual horror, it might very well be this bed, not as a place of impotence, but as a place of fertility, playfulness, the timelessness of sexual pleasure, dream.

Rather what seems to occur in the play is that Othello's initial horror is fixed in place, reified by Iago whose imagination of women, goats, and monkeys replicates his own, and by the emblem of the handkerchief and the image of the "beast with two backs." That is, in the play Othello's vision of a world without differentiation is given emblematic existence by the emblem-maker, ensign Iago who carries the army's flag and who waves this red and white flag of a handkerchief. The bit of cloth dyed in mummy gotten from the hearts of dead maidens is passed from hand to hand, from mother to Othello to Desdemona, to Emilia to Iago to Cassio to Bianca, and it seems in its passage across generations, genders, and classes to indicate a pervasive—albeit unconscious—obsession with the fearful destructiveness of sexuality.[34] It is as if the dominating vision is a bed, "lust-stained," spotted with "lust's blood" (V, i, 36). Othello's superstitions seem to touch everyone, even Desdemona who wishes she had never seen the handkerchief with magic in its web, but who also asks Emilia to put the wedding sheets on her bed. Perhaps this request is not exactly superstitious, but it does cause one to wonder what she knows, suspects, or fears, and what exactly she means when she says to Emilia that Othello will return to her at once, "incontinent." This word appears earlier as well when Iago attempts to pacify the eager Roderigo by telling him to "go to bed and sleep." Roderigo replies, "I will incontinently drown myself" (I, iii, 300). If Othello has been unable to control his ejaculation and his fears of violence before, Desdemona must suspect she will encounter the same sort of man in her death bed as she did in her marriage bed.

The handkerchief is, moreover, an emblem exactly suggestive of stained marriage sheets,[35] and it is therefore threatening to Othello in any scenario of off-stage action one might try to envision (although it seems to me that it is exactly this effort to envision and the equally forceful avoidance of it that makes the audience anxious even as the central character is anxious). Even in his final speeches Othello speaks in an equivocal and metaphoric way about Desdemona's body, his fear of marring her perfect alabaster skin with blood, his fear of penetration: "When I have plucked the rose, / I cannot give it vital growth again; It needs must wither" (V. ii, 14-16).

The other image, although one not given concrete realization, that dominates the play is the image of the two-backed beast, thrown up by Iago to Brabantio in Act I, Scene i.[36] The image is obviously designed by Iago to incite mischief, and it does. Moreover, reason and evidence to the contrary, it continues to live in memory, so that like the stain on the handkerchief it haunts the play, even if one is uncertain how to place it, how to understand it. The image is a false one. That is, we have no evidence that Desdemona and Othello are in bed together at the outset of the play, and in fact the play presents evidence to the contrary: Othello and Desdemona arrive at the council chamber where Brabantio will accuse them, not together but separately; and it is not until Cyprus that Othello gives a speech in seeming anticipation of their union: "The purchase is made, the fruit's are to ensue, / That profit's yet to come 'tween me and you" (II, ii, 9-10). The image can also be seen as false in its utter fearfulness and in its creation of a composite figure in which male and female, human and beast, front and back are merged into a deformed being with two backs. Yet, of course, it is just such a vision that is appropriate to Othello's crazed imagination, one way of understanding—via Iago—what drives the Moor to slay the woman to whom he is joined, who creates him a "beast" rather than a "perfect soul."

Once caught in this web, Othello is unable to escape, and indeed is kept from a return to the unconscious that might have created a new fate for himself. Rather, he becomes a rigid, almost caricatured version of the noble Moor, speaking his own praise by means of story (cf. V, ii, 334-352); he gets to be what he wants and needs: by killing Desdemona he makes her the rigid, cold, statue-like figure he originally adored, and he makes himself the separate, exotic figure he recognizes and understands.

In *The Winter's Tale* the wrenching that makes change possible is not easy or pleasant. If one views the seacoast scene as the scene that effects change, one can see that it is painful, discomforting, upsetting, not only for those on stage, but also for Leontes whose psyche is represented by the events as he remains in darkness, and who must acknowledge, as Prospero must, that darkness and all its evils belong to him ("this thing of darkness I acknowledge mine"). In so many of Shakespeare's plays, it seems that the path to revision lies through darkness, and when Freud describes the battle within a patient's unconscious as the patient tries through analysis to effect recovery, or when a Christian describes the battle between the old Adam and the new, they also describe something like the action of romance.[37]

C. The New World

The revised world in Part II contains, as many have noted, parallel elements to Part I. It begins, for ex-

ample, with Camillo, yet again the faithful helper, wanting to return home even as Polixenes wanted to leave
court to return home at the outset of the play; his eventual leaving is the first of two sea voyages in Part II
paralleling two voyages in Part I. In Part I Camillo speaks
of Mamillius, the child who "makes all hearts fresh"
(and who now must be, as Polixenes says, "afresh lamented") and in Part II he speaks of Prince Florizel.
Instead of the robbing of honor Leontes imagines in
Part I, Part II offers the robbery of sheets and Autolycus'
robbery of the clown's pockets, closely related, but
comic. Like Leontes, Autolycus robs himself although
he does it by design, for controlled effect; and even his
speech in which he confuses virtue and vice in a courtroom scene, echoes in miniature the earlier confusion in
Sicilia's court of justice as Leontes makes Hermione's
virtue into vice. Autolycus describes himself as having
been whipped out of court for his virtues; the clown's
correction is comic here, but reminds us nevertheless of
Hermione's treatment in Part I: "His vices, you would
say; there's no virtue whipped out of court" (V, iii, 91).

In Part II Polixenes calls his son too base to be acknowledged (IV, iv, 422) as Leontes refuses his daughter in Part I: "This brat is none of mine" (I, iii, 91).
Yet of course, Polixenes' refusal is brief and completely transformed by the joyful reunions that dominate the ending of the play. Again, Polixenes breaks
into an angry fit at the sheepshearing and threatens to
scratch Perdita's face with briers. Although this is like
Leontes' fury in Part I, it is here deflected, contained,
immediately undone by the opening of the fardel, like
the opening of a second oracle speaking truth from
some hidden time and place in the written voice of
Antigonus, his letters wrapped in Hermione's cloak.

Many of the same elements are presented in Part II,
but they have been transmogrified into song and dance;
art keeps us at some distance from the sharp experience itself and nothing is finally harmful. In fact, one
might argue that Part II, including the revival of
Hermione in which art and nature are conjoined, is a
demonstration of the necessity of art for the success of
romance. Thus the servant can describe Autolycus'
songs as filled with that which horrified Leontes and
no one is afraid: "He has the prettiest love songs for
maids, so with bawdry, which is strange; with such
delicate burdens of dildos and fadings; 'Jump her, and
thump her'" (IV, iv, 194 ff.). Autolycus picks pockets
and sings of "pins and poking sticks of steel; / What
maids lack from head to heel" and the world does not
come undone. The dance of the satyrs, emblematic of
lust, who have "danced before the King," might be
seen as a version of King Leontes' own animal rage of
projected desire; yet here such raw energy is confined
to a ritual for celebration.

The second half of the play is also, like the first part,
dominated by the imagery of dreams, but here of course
the dreams come true, and as the shepherd says, Perdita
will bring Doricles "that which he not dreams of." The
second half also refers to important issues of faith,
echoing Leontes' loss of faith and parodying his inability to believe in something so obvious as his wife's
virtue and his own paternity by presenting Autolycus'
song about the woman turned fish "for she would not
exchange flesh with one that loved her." "The ballad"
Autolycus asserts, "is very pitiful, and as true". (IV,
iv, 281 ff.). The ballad also gives a low comic version
in its description of woman turned fish of the miraculous high comic change of statue into woman. And
both transformations are dependent not only on faith
but on the presence of witnesses. According to
Autolycus, "Five justices' hands at it, and witnesses
more than my pack will hold," and in the chapel many
are the "lookers-on," including those the audience, who
witness Hermione dead become Hermione living.

The entire pastoral is a wonderful emblem of the "betwixt and between" state of the play that reigns until
the final unveiling scene; the sheepshearing occurs
between two seasons, "Not yet on summer's death, or
on the birth / Of trembling winter," and it offers mixed
flowers, mixed costumes, a mixture of classes and stations, a mixture of the high and the low in style and
language.[38] As a revised projection from Leontes' own
psyche, the pastoral is crucially different from the initial pastoral scene in which Leontes and Polixenes
romped as twinned lambs, longing to be "boy eternal."
This time the eternal aspect of this world is not in
fixity, but in process, a process that goes on forever.
Florizel praises Perdita by wishing that she would ever
speak, sing, buy and sell, give alms, dance:

> When you do dance, I wish you
> A wave o'th'sea, that you might ever do
> Nothing but that—move still so,
> And own no other function.
>
> (IV, iv, 140-43)

Most importantly, this time the pastoral world is popu-
lated with a boy and a girl instead of two boys, a
match which makes union and generation possible as
it was not before.

If there is a single character in the midst of this pastoral who represents flexibility, changeability, potential and mirth, it is Autolycus. According to the servant, his songs transform the most mundane of objects
into something divine: "why, she sings 'em over, as
they were gods or goddesses; you would think a smock
were a she-angel." Moreover, there is a way in which
Autolycus replaces the absent Leontes and signals his
change; while the major character is off-stage, this onstage figure represents and enacts the other. As Freud
asserts, every dream treats of oneself, one's ego often
hidden behind a strange person.[39] Both Autolycus and
Leontes see themselves as victims, Autolycus' false

pleas as victim literalizing Leontes' false pleas as cuck-old, the difference between them being that Autolycus knows he is playing both the parts, whereas Leontes has to learn that he is. Like Leontes Autolycus is turned in on himself, even his name is self-referential, and like Leontes he can pull from his bag all manner of tricks and dreams—some destructive and some recre-ative, though all in a comic jumble. He is, moreover, that aspect of Leontes which remains "boy eternal." True only to himself, childishly selfish, he is the play's version of his puppet show character, the Prodigal Son, who unlike Leontes never grows up, never marries, but who will try, as he says in his last speech, to be-come the "tall fellow" the clown describes him as being. Here the clown declares his faith in one he knows to be false, because, one can only assume, of affection and his own essentially good nature, and this simple declaration takes us forward to the end and to Leontes' own declaration of faith and love.[40]

Autolycus also provides the parody of torture in his story of how the clown will be tortured; although Autolycus' account of what never takes place is not verbally similar to what happens at some off-stage place to Leontes, as he talks we know that Leontes has also been suffering pen-ance and sorrow. Yet again, Part II of The Winter's Tale has removed a painful human experience to a story and has thus presented and also protected us from it, has turned a "tragic" moment to a comic one: "He has a son," says Autolycus to the clownish son, "who shall be flayed alive." Although the death of a son has occurred in Part I, we are now about to enter the changed world not only of Leontes' psyche, but of the conscious world of the court as the character Leontes appears on stage, rather a miracle in and of itself.[41]

Finally, Autolycus represents the impulse towards and the enactment of change that Leontes has worked long years in isolation to achieve; Autolycus himself is never still, flitting from place to place, changing costume, service, tone, and position. He moves, for example, from the seeming perpetrator of action in urging the clown and shepherd onto the boat bound for Sicilia to the receptive audience who hears from the first gentle-man what occurred when the shepherd opened the fardel. Like Leontes he exerts effort, but must await the ultimate fulfilling. His overflowing bag represents the possibilities of the mind, the possiblities which Leontes' immersion in the unconscious bring forth.

In the final act of the play Leontes is taken to the chapel to see a statue of his wife. The paranoic fixity that completely dominates Othello and keeps his mind rigid, his jealousy aroused and frozen in position, has in The Winter's Tale produced several deaths and has turned a warm, living, witty, sexual woman into a statue; even as Othello, unable to endure his wife's sexual nature, turns her by means of imagery and murder into a statue-like figure as well:[42]

> Yet I'll not shed her blood,
> Not scar that whiter skin of hers than snow,
> And smooth as monumental alabaster.
> Yet she must die.
>
> (V, ii, 3-6)

Yet The Winter's Tale will move from marble to flesh as we begin to know through the story of Perdita, the child whose flesh bears the imprint of both mother and father. When Perdita hears of her mother's death, she weeps and sighs, and, as the third gentleman reports, "Who was most marble there changed color." As Hermione comes alive, she does so in parts; when Leontes went about to slay her, he did so by anatomiz-ing her. Here in the chapel, first she appears, then she seems to breathe, her veins to bear blood, then she moves, and her hand and Leontes' hand meet, and fi-nally she descends to embrace him in a silence analo-gous to their sixteen years of mutual silence. Each of the senses is awakened one by one. The parts become whole again. Unlike Othello who wants to cut off the air that gives Desdemona life, who fears her breath as countering the justice of his deed, Leontes longs for it, seems to breathe life into Hermione by wanting breath from her:

> Still, methinks,
> There is an air comes from her. What fine chisel
> Could ever yet cut breath? Let no man
>   mock me,
> For I will kiss her.
>
> (V, iii, 75ff.)

This is a miracle of many sorts, of the seasons, of faith, of birth, of life itself. It is the celebration of process over fixity, and as Leontes admires what is before him, his words echo those of Florizel gazing at and admiring Perdita, singing, dancing, doing what-ever she does (IV, iv, 135.): "What you can make her do, / I am content to look on." (V, iii, 92-93). But it is also a miracle of wish-fulfillment out of which Leontes is shown to produce not just a dream of de-struction, but also a dream of memory and rejoining—the entire family brought together as he says, after a wide gap of time, "since first / We were disserved."[43] Although Leontes is off-stage for a long period of the play, we in the audience are keenly aware of his ab-sence. He is the central character, the missing figure we remember. His being is kept vivid, as I have ar-gued by parallel figures and speeches on stage during this second half, and by the presence of his daughter, an exact copy of the father: "although the print be little, the whole matter / And copy of the father," a mirroring that can be underscored in a production by careful casting, costumes, gesture, rhythms of speech. The plotting also keeps us in obvious suspense waiting for Leontes' reappearance . . . and aware of his ab-sence. As Florizel and Perdita play at king and queen of the festival we await the royal couple. When

Polixenes "discovers himself" to Florizel, we anticipate the other king's reappearance. When Florizel argues that his union with Perdita cannot fail "but by / The violation of my faith" (IV, iv, 480-81), we think of the person who is demonstrating, albeit off-stage, his own faith, as it turns out, not only in his sins but also in (re)union. As the play moves with the powerful logic of romance, a quest through ritual death towards a final scene of recognition and life, we remember Leontes and what he is doing as the absent participant. In playing his part in off-stage darkness, he moves to reunite with his old role and his queen; according to Frye:

> Translated into dream terms, the quest-romance is the search of the libido or desiring self for a fulfillment that will deliver it from the anxieties of reality but will still contain that reality . . . Translated into ritual terms, the quest-romance is the victory of fertility over the waste land. Fertility means food and drink, bread and wine, body and blood, the union of the male and female.[44]

Leontes' dream can thus be seen as behind the ending of the play. In taking on a mock-death by his absence, moving to the innermost stage of being, Leontes produces on-stage that which uses elements of the past (Part I of the play) to produce the future. Dreams, says Freud, are derived from the past in every sense:

> Nevertheless the ancient belief that dreams foretell the future is not wholly devoid of the truth. By picturing our wishes as fulfilled, dreams are after all leading us into the future. But this future, which the dreamer pictures as the present, has been moulded by his indestructible wish into a perfect likeness of the past.[45]

Leontes as the hero of romance grafts life onto that which would otherwise be stone. Perdita lives. The earth lives after winter. Hermione lives in a perfect likeness of the past. As his unconscious dreams are realized both in the stage action while he is absent and in the chapel scenes where he is present, he becomes both the creator and the witness—since he is dependent on divine and psychological elements beyond his total control—of that which is more wonderous and powerful than even he could have dreamed possible.

Notes

[1] All references to the plays are to the Signet Classic Shakespeare edition, *The Winter's Tale*, ed. Frank Kermode, and *Othello*, ed. Alvan Kernan (N.Y.: NAL, 1963).

[2] David J. Gordon, *Literary Art and the Unconscious* (Baton Rouge: Louisiana State University Press, 1976), p. xxii: "If, as seems reasonable, we identify consciousness and verbal language, then we must postulate some

sort of mental activity or preverbal language anterior to consciousness, and we must think of creation as taking place, to some extent, at the Threshold of Consciousness."

[3] Many recent studies focus on the issue of genre in Shakespeare. See, for example, Stephen Orgel, "Shakespeare and the Kinds of Drama," *Critical Inquiry* (Autumn, 1979), 107-123; Rosalie Colie, *The Resources of Kind* (Berkeley: University of California Press, 1973); Norman Rabkin, *Shakespeare and the Problem of Meaning* (Chicago: University of Chicago Press, 1981); David Young, *The Heart's Forest* (New Haven: Yale University Press, 1972).

[4] Especially here, but throughout, I am grateful for the probing questions and critical insights of Professor Robert Byer.

[5] Martin Luther, "Preface to The Epistle of St. Paul to The Romans," *Martin Luther Selections,* ed. John Dillenberger (Garden City: Doubleday, 1961), p. 22.

[6] Northrop Frye, *Anatomy of Criticism* (Princeton, New Jersey: Princeton University Press, 1957), p. 183.

[7] Sigmund Freud, "A Dream is the Fulfillment of a Wish," *The Interpretation of Dreams,* trans. James Strachey (N.Y.: Avon Books, 1965), pp. 155-168.

[8] Stanley Cavell, *Pursuits of Happiness* (Cambridge, Mass.: Harvard University Press, 1981), p. 54.

[9] Freud, *Interpretation of Dreams*, p. 583.

[10] Louis L. Mantz, *The Poetry of Meditation* (New Haven: Yale University Press, 1954): "It is this habit of feeling theological issues as a part of a concrete, dramatic scene that the meditative writers . . . stress as all important for the beginning of a meditation."

[11] Freud, *Interpretation of Dreams,* p. 572.

[12] Luther, p. 24.

[13] Victor Turner, "Betwixt and Between: The Liminal Period," *The Forest of Symbols* (Ithaca: Cornell University Press, 1967).

[14] W.M. Merchant, *Shakespeare and the Artist* (London: Oxford University Press, 1959), p. 7.

[15] Freud, *Dreams,* p. 647. Cf. also the insights of Madelon (Gohlke) Springnether, "'I wooed thee with my sword': Shakespeare's Tragic Paradigms," *Representing Shakespeare* (Baltimore: The Johns Hopkins Press, 1980), p. 171. In the same volume, cf. Murray Schwartz, "Shakespeare Through Contemporary Psychoanalysis," and Meredith Skura, "Interpreting

Posthumus' Dream from Above and Below: Families, Psychoanalysts, and Literary Critics."

[16] Murray Schwartz, "Leontes' Jealousy in *The Winter's Tale,*" *American Imago,* XXX (1973), 260.

[17] *Ibid.,* 262.

[18] Sigmund Freud, *A General Introduction to Psychoanalysis,* trans. Joan Riviere (New York: Pocket Books, 1969), p. 284.

[19] Many critics have commented on this. See, for example, Rosalie Colie, *Shakespeare's Living Art* (Princeton: Princeton Univ. Press, 1974) pp. 164-167; and on *The Winter's Tale,* Carol Thomas Neeley, "*The Winter's Tale:* The Triumph of Speech, *SEL,* XV (1975), 321-38.

[20] Murray Schwartz, 250-73. J.I.M. Steward, *Character and Motive in Shakespeare* (London, 1949), pp. 30-39. C.L. Barber, "'Thou that beget'st him that did thee beget': Transformations in *Pericles* and *The Winter's Tale,*" *Shakespeare Survey,* 22 (1969), 59-67. Stephen Reid, "Othello's Jealousy," *American Imago,* 25 (1968), 274-93.

[21] Schwartz, p. 251.

[22] Schwartz, p. 262. Schwartz is here using the theories of D.W. Winnicott.

[23] Richard Wheeler, *Shakespeare's Development and the Problem Comedies, Turn and Counter-turn* (Berkeley: University of California Press, 1981). This book influenced my reading especially in its emphasis on the psychological need for autonomy and fear of merger in Shakespeare's plays.

[24] For a discussion of male fear of sexuality, cuckoldry, and loss of boundaries in many Shakespeare plays, see Coppelia Kahn, *Man's Estate* (Berkeley: University of California Press, 1981).

[5] Joel Fineman, "Fratricide and Cuckoldry: Shakespeare's Doubles," *Representing Shakespeare,* ed. Kahn and Schwartz (Baltimore: The Johns Hopkins Press, 1980), p. 86. Fineman uses Girard's theory to discuss the horrors of "no difference" between twin-like characters in Shakespeare's plays.

[26] Several recent articles and books focus on gender and its misuse in Shakespeare. See Kahn, Fineman, and also essays by Janet Adelman, "Anger's My Meat," Madelon Gohlke, "I wooed thee with my sword," C.L. Barber, "The Family in Shakespeare's Development," all in *Representing Shakespeare.* See also Marjorie Garber, *Coming of Age in Shakespeare* (New York: Methuen, 1981)

[27] Wheeler, p. 217.

[28] Ernest Schanzer, "The Structural Pattern in *The Winter's Tale,*" *REL* 5.2 (1964), 72-78. Richard Proudfoot, "Verbal Reminiscence and the Two-Part Structure of *The Winter's Tale,*" *Shakespeare Survey,* 29 (1976), 67-78.

[29] Schwartz, p. 260. I am a bit hesitant to equate characters with aspects of the psyche, and indeed in emphasizing the psychological aspects of the play in total exclusion of the religious, for it does seem to me that the play can also be read, as Frye for one reads it, as a Christian play in which Leontes' penance leads to grace. See Northrop Frye, "Recognition in *The Winter's Tale,*" *Essays in Shakespearian Criticism,* ed. Calderwood and Toliver (Englewood Cliffs, NJ: Prentice-Hall, 1970). See also Robert Hunter, *Shakespeare and The Comedy of Forgiveness* (New York: Columbia University Press, 1965); and of the sonnets, Martha Lifson, "The Rhetoric of Consolation," *Assays* (Pittsburgh: Pittsburgh University Press, 1982).

[30] David Wilbern, "Shakespeare's Nothing," *Representing Shakespeare,* p. 250.

[31] Freud, *Interpretation of Dreams,* p. 359.

[32] Stanley Cavell, *The Claim of Reason* (New York: Oxford University Press, 1979), pp. 481-96. Throughout, I am indebted to this fine reading.

[33] Carol Neeley, "Women and Men in *Othello,*" *Shakespeare Survey,* 10 (1977), 138.

[34] Schwartz, p. 225.

[35] Majorie Garber, *Coming of Age in Shakespeare,* p. 137. I wrote this during Professor Garber's NEH faculty seminar at Harvard, 1984, and am indebted to her insights and crucial comments on this work.

[36] Another powerful image of "no difference" in the play is the image of men eating men, the cannibals whom Othello mentions in his original stories: "And of the Cannibals that each other eat / The Anthropod, and men whose heads / Grew beneath their shoulders" (I, iii, 142-44). I would urge that these powerful images of frightening merger dominate Othello's and hence our imagination during the course of the play.

[37] Freud, *A General Introduction to Psychoanalysis,* p. 445.

[38] Peter Lindenbaum, "Time, Sexual Love, and the Uses of Pastoral in *The Winter's Tale,*" *MLQ,* 33 (1972), 3-23, argues that it is actually June, and that this speech simply explains why Perdita doesn't have certain flowers available to give.

[39] Joan Hartwig, "Cloten, Autolycus, and Caliban: Bearers of Parodic Burdens," *Shakespeare's Romances Reconsidered,* ed. Kay and Jacobs (Lincoln: University of Nebraska Press, 1978), pp. 98-100; and Freud, *The Basic Writings,* ed. Brill, p. 349.

[40] Lee S. Cox, "The Role of Autolycus in *The Winter's Tale,*" *SEL,* IX (1969), 283-301, discusses the significance of swearing and saying the play and focuses on this exchange between the clown and Autolycus, and makes similar points to mine.

[41] In the movement from Act IV to Act V, it is amusing to note that the word "bear" occurs, reminding us of the real bear on the seacoast and again providing the transitional object cluing the shift; proposing to bribe his way out of torture, the clown says, "though authority be a stubborn bear, yet he is oft lead by the nose with gold" (IV, iv, 809-10). Such a detail underscores the care by which the play has been structured; even transitional movements are made parallel.

[42] Cavell, *The Claim of Reason,* pp. 481-96.

[43] Recent critics on the family in Shakespeare remain centrally indebted to C.L. Barber's work; see "The Family in Shakespeare's Development: Tragedy and Sacredness," *Representing Shakespeare.*

[44] Frye, *Anatomy of Criticism,* p. 193.

[45] Freud, *Interpretation of Dreams,* p. 660.

STRUCTURE

Alastair Fowler (essay date 1978)

SOURCE: "Leontes' Contrition and the Repair of Nature," in *Essays and Studies,* Vol. 31, 1978, pp. 36-64.

[*In the following essay, Fowler discusses the allegorical relations in* The Winter's Tale, *maintaining that the pastoral scenes symbolically reveal Leontes' transition from sin to repentance.*]

The Winter's Tale and *Measure for Measure* fall each into distinct sections written in different fictive modes. In *Measure for Measure,* the early, potentially tragic scenes of naturalism have been contrasted with the subsequent allegorical black comedy, which is supposed to show a 'falling off'. In *The Winter's Tale,* the contrast between the first three acts (again largely naturalistic) and the pastoral-comical continuation is too sharp, and the writing too good, to seem anything but intentional. Still, the marvels and unconvincing deaths have been regretted. And Rosalie Colie, doing what she could for a 'conspicu-

ously ill-made' play,[1] has presented it as an extreme generic experiment: an essay in *genera mixta* that has perhaps not quite come off. Its tragic and comic portions are 'not articulated' but merely juxtaposed; so that genre is 'forced' (pp. 267-8), with contrary generic tendencies allowed to confront one another. *The Winter's Tale* becomes in fine a play about the problems of tragi-comedy. Now, Shakespeare was probably aware of these problems (as any literary man would be, at a time when they were the subject of prolonged controversy). But he did a good deal to articulate the disparate members. The genres may confront one another through the grotesque indecorum of the clown's nuntius speech; but other passages and brief touches—the name Sicilia, early allusions to shepherds, anticipations of the image of the storm—show an approach less abrupt. As Colie herself noticed, the oracle in Act III, Scene ii is a characteristic motif of pastoral romance.[2] But it is also a tragic motif: it serves in fact as a generically ambiguous feature, allowing a shading of tragedy into romance. Moreover, the play's thematic continuity is also far stronger than most current criticism supposes. Only, the continuous strands are symbolic and mythological in character. Modern audiences being less at home with the non-naturalistic connections, they have not been much explored. But in the Renaissance the deepest treatments of passions and of ideas were quite likely to take a romance or symbolic form. This is not to say that Shakespeare expresses his meaning through personification allegory like that of *Old Fortunatus.* But the symbols of *The Winter's Tale* depend on allegorical relations and even on scraps of narrative allegory. And we shall not understand the play until we glimpse something of these allegorical lines. Their continued metaphors dominate the last three acts, and have profound implications for their staging.

The Winter's Tale is about a man's jealousy and rage; his gradual contrition; and his eventual repentance. We call the man Leontes; although properly Leontes symbolizes only part of the experience, as Polixenes symbolizes another. Both commit the sins of jealousy and of self-righteousness. But they do so in complementary ways: Leontes' jealousy of a wife is expressed tyrannously, against the opinion of his court; Polixenes' jealousy of a son takes a more disguised, perhaps more socially acceptable, form. Jealousy bulks large in Shakespeare's work, as in the mind of his time. But in this play it seems to figure mainly as a representative sin to be repented. The focus is less on the experience of jealousy itself (although this is evoked, in the first two acts, with the plausible verisimilitude of Shakespeare's art at its best) than on its consequences. The difficulty of repentance, we may say, is the play's subject.

Leontes' jealousy soon leads to estrangement from Hermione and to her loss. As Shakespeare's choice of her name suggests, this has a symbolic force. The name is not from *Pandosto,* or from Plutarch. Hermione was anciently the daughter of Menelaus and Helen.[3] But by one of those heuristic confusions which make Renaissance mythology subtly yet profoundly different from its pagan counterpart, she was identified by Stephanus and others with Harmonia, daughter of Jupiter and Electra (or of Mars and Venus). The two names became alternative forms; so that Milton could make Hermione, not Harmonia, the wife of Cadmus.[4] At their marriage, he tells us, 'all the choirs of heaven sang in concert'.[5] This universal celebration was appropriate because Renaissance interpreters took Hermione-Harmonia to refer to the Pythagorean harmony of the moral or cosmic order. The way in which Hermione was thought of in the early seventeenth century is probably well exemplified by George Sandys's Commentary on Ovid *Metamorphoses* IV:

> Cadmus, after so many difficulties, advanced to a flourishing kingdom (Honour is to be courted with sweat and blood, and not with perfumes and garlands) now seemeth happy in his exile: having besides Harmione to wife; whose nuptials were honoured by the presence of the Gods, and their bountiful endowments. So beloved of them is the harmony of exterior and interior beauty espoused to Virtue. She is said to be the daughter of Mars and Venus; in that music not only recreates the mind with a sweet oblivion of former misfortunes, but also inflames it with courage . . . [6]

If Hermione signifies the soul's harmony, her loss would aptly symbolize Leontes' sinful state of psychological discord. The cosmic significance, the order of nature, is implied in the original righteousness whose loss the individual sin recapitulates. To find so large a meaning in Hermione's absence seems not unreasonable, in view of the play's many universalizing speeches with religious overtones:

> They looked as they had heard of a world ransomed, or one destroyed . . .
>
> (V.ii.14-15)

> if all the world could have seen't, the woe had been universal.
>
> (V.ii.90-1)

To regard such speeches merely as burlesque of court hyperbole is to underestimate the closeness of construction. A series of such overtones—not all from First and Second Gentlemen—culminates with the statue's movement, when it is music that brings Hermione's recovery; 'Music awake her; strike' (V.ii.98). These words of Paulina's, which are far more than a conventional adjunct of the transformationscene, imply the operation of magical or moral music, the ordering principle that in Shakespeare regularly opposes the destructive storm.[7] Moral harmony has been recovered.

The juncture at which Leontes loses Hermione is when he first realizes something of his guilt. Previously,

throughout the trial, he has been self-righteous. Only when he hears the oracle ('Hermione is chaste . . . Leontes a jealous tyrant') and having denied it finds it immediately confirmed by Mamillius' death, does he recognize his fault: 'Apollo's angry, and the heavens themselves / Do strike at my injustice' (III.ii.146-7). Meanwhile Hermione is 'dying', as the next speech, Paulina's, tells us: 'This news is mortal to the queen: look down / And see what death is doing'. Subsequently we learn that she fainted before hearing all of the oracle.[8] This sequence of events is intelligible enough as fable: the good news of the oracle's first words has been too much for Hermione. (So, when Bellaria hears the oracle in *Pandosto* she is 'surcharged . . . with extreme joy'.) The sequence is also highly meaningful, however, in allegorical terms; alluding to a Pauline doctrine that profoundly influenced thinking about sin and repentance, and that was reflected in other literary works of the period.[9] St Paul's fullest statement is at Rom. 7.7-13:

> I knew not what sin meant, but by the law. . . . I once lived without law. But when the commandment came, sin revived and I was dead. And the very same commandment which was ordained unto life, was found to be unto me an occasion of death.

This Pauline idea of a sinner's virtual death at the coming of the divine commandment may well underlie Hermione's 'death' at the report of the 'ear-deafening voice o' the oracle'.[10] It is, after all, a divine commandment judging Leontes guilty. True, it is Hermione who 'dies' and not Leontes himself. But we should recall how closely Shakespeare identifies Hermione with Leontes' honour—'The sacred honour of himself, his queen's'[11]—and even with his innocent soul. There is more than one sense in which Leontes may say to Hermione 'Your actions are my dreams'.[12]

Before the oracle, the topic of innocence is developed both in relation to Hermione and Leontes. In Act II, Scene i, for example, Antigonus and others defend Hermione's spotless innocence at some length. But innocence is also attributed to Leontes, and not only by himself:

> POL. We were as twinned lambs that did frisk
>   i' th' sun,
> And bleat the one at th' other: what we
>   changed
> Was innocence for innocence: we knew not
> The doctrine of ill-doing, nor dreamed
> That any did. Had we pursued that life,
> And our weak spirits ne'er been higher reared
> With stronger blood, we should have answered
>   heaven
> Boldly 'not guilty', the imposition cleared
> Hereditary ours.
>
> (I.ii.67-75)

Polixenes playfully attributes temptation to womankind: 'Temptations have since then been born to's: for / In those unfledged days was my wife a girl' (I.ii.77-8). And behind this amiable flirtation, we might catch a hint of nostalgia for male friendship, a dubious innocence of 'twinned lambs', a simple concord before the disturbance of heterosexuality. Moreover, it is a mistaken application of Hermione's reply ('If you first sinned with us . . . that you slipped not / With any but with us'), to Polixenes alone rather than to the generality of husbands including himself, that in all probability occasions Leontes' jealousy; so that his sinful action may begin with illusory innocence. Moreover, possessive love of his friend seems to occasion pique in Leontes when it is Hermione who persuades Polixenes to stay in Sicilia.[13] And Paulina's remark about 'Fancies too weak for boys, too green and idle / For girls of nine' (III.ii.181-2) also implies immaturity. But little can be made of such motivation, since Shakespeare focuses on consequences, not aetiology. Leontes' madness is an 'infection', like 'the imposition . . . Hereditary ours'—original sin—of which the dramatist clearly takes a more serious view than Polixenes.

Two distinct allegories about Leontes' sin might be disengaged: (1) an allegory about harmony, with Hermione representing a state of mind lost and recovered; and (2) an allegory about guilt's virtual death, with Hermione as the soul that dies. These meanings are not logically compatible. But then, *The Winter's Tale* is not simple allegory. Its symbolism can imply both aspects of sin (if no more) without contradiction.

Besides the apparent death of Hermione, Leontes' sin and judgment are accompanied by a series of unreversed mortalities: the dwindling death of Mamillius, the sudden death of Antigonus, the drowning of the mariners who carried Perdita to Bohemia. Northrop Frye treats the deaths as sacrificial.[14] But they are more intelligible if we regard them as objectifying particular aspects of sin. Thus, news of Mamillius' death marks the beginning of Leontes' remorse. Apollo's revelations seem at first to leave Leontes unaffected ('There is no truth at all i' th' Oracle'); but knowledge of Mamillius' death instantly brings guilt ('Apollo's angry'). Leontes realizes, that is to say, the loss of innocence. The circumstances of the death confirm this interpretation. Mamillius died, according to Leontes,

> Conceiving the dishonour of his mother!
> He straight declined, dropped, took it deeply,
> Fastened and fixed the shame on 't in himself,
> Threw off his spirit, his appetite, his sleep,
> And downright languished.
>
> (II.iii.13-17)

And according to a servant Mamillius died 'with mere conceit [thought] and fear' of the verdict on Hermione (III.ii.144-5). While these explanations are not impos-

sible, the death is more eloquent as a symbolic statement: innocence dwindles with growing consciousness of sin. Mamillius' touching innocence, particularly in his scene with the ladies (II.i), is his main trait. But he also incorporates Leontes' dynastic hopes of natural perpetuity. As his heir, an 'unspeakable comfort', he 'physics' the nation with 'the hopes of him' (I.i.34 ff.). More than once, he is called a 'hopeful' prince (III.ii.41; cf.II.iii.85). But when Leontes loses the best of his natural life (the first-born), his hope of immortality is gone. He is himself under judgment of death.

The loss of an entire ship's company in the storm of III.iii seems more cut-and-dried allegory. Yet this disaster has been called 'morally and dramatically unnecessary': unsporting, so to say, on Shakespeare's part.[15] We are assured that 'in performance their deaths hardly evoke pity or terror'. Certainly the clown's narration encourages neither: he cuts with breathless gusto from sea tragedy to land tragedy, making the heaped disasters tragi-comic by mere excess. But Shakespeare subsequently glosses the catastrophe at V.ii, where Third Gentleman remarks that 'all the instruments which aided to expose the child were even then lost when it was found' (V.ii.70-2). In short, the mariners are 'instruments', or instrumental causes, of Leontes' sinful rejection of grace.[16] More specifically, the finding of grace for contrition requires destruction of sin's instrumental causes; so that if Perdita has not been found the mariners need not have died. Hence Shakespeare's repeated close connection of 'things dying' with 'things new-born' (III.iii.113): they are related aspects of repentance. And the vividly described storm that kills the mariners is allegorically identical with the 'storm perpetual' of Leontes' penance, which according to Paulina will be insufficient to move the gods. Even this episode, however, is not simply allegorical: shipwreck was too familiar an emblem of moral failure not to have something of this sense, in a scene immediately after judgment on Leontes.

Antigonus, who is simultaneously eliminated, must also be categorized as an instrumental cause, albeit reluctant, of Perdita's rejection. Indeed, his very name ('against offspring') implies a less than favourable destiny, in a play where innocence and grace are identified with the new life of Leontes' children. However, Antigonus' character is sufficiently developed, and the means of his death bizarre enough, for him to merit separate treatment. His pursuit by the bear, whose dinner he later provides, is indeed an interpretative crux. Opportunistic use of a tame bear, conveniently available at the Southwark bear-pit (Quiller-Couch); transition from tragedy to comedy through a frisson of horror succeeded by laughter at a disguised clown (Coghill); abandonment of the usual dramatic persuasion to belief, and shift to 'an entirely different mode, that of romance' (Colie): prolonged debate has not produced a solution worthy of the dramatist. An initial frisson of horror, well achieved in the 1969 R.S.C. production, may be the right effect for the bear. It surely draws, like the 'ever-angry bears' of *The Tempest* I.ii.289, on a common emblem of rage.[17] As such, it is yet another 'cause' of Leontes' sin: the formal (i.e. his sin takes the *form* of jealous rage). It too must therefore be eliminated. Thus, the bear does not merely happen by, but is being hunted—'This is the chase' (III.iii.57). To arrange for the bear to kill Antigonus *en passant* is economical plotting, and not at all the unnecessary complication Quiller-Couch thought it. But the arrangement is also ironic; since Antigonus earlier expressed a naïve trust in nature's kindness, when he accepted Leontes' commission:

> Some powerful spirit instruct the kites and
>   ravens
> To be thy nurses! Wolves and bears, they say,
> Casting their savageness aside, have done
> Like offices of pity.
>
> (II.iii.185-8)

The bear, sometimes a symbol of the dangerous aspect of *prima materia*,[18] could figure as an emblem of nature, considered in opposition to man's constructive efforts. It is thus related to themes of nature and art that some have seen as the play's main concern.

The prayer of Antigonus may be a pious allusion to the story of Elisha and the ravens. But it is also more distinctly an allusion by Shakespeare himself, with a very different implication, to a later verse in 2 Kgs.2. Verse 24 relates how at Elisha's curse 'there came forth two she bears out of the wood, and tare forty and two children of them'. Following St Jerome (in Ps. 108) and St Isidore (*Glossa ordinaria*), commentators interpreted this passage as referring to God's expectation of repentance by the Jews, after the death of Christ, for 42 years. Only then, when conversion was not forthcoming, did he send the Roman Vespasian and Titus to destroy Jerusalem. The bear, then, specifically symbolizes God's judgment on reluctance to repent.

Antigonus' pietism and his (rather *ex parte*) application of the Bible should not mislead us into thinking him a martyr, or an example of true faith. On the contrary, Shakespeare repeatedly contrasts him with Paulina and Camillo in this regard. Kindly but ineffectual, Antigonus has a conventional inclination to obey his sovereign right or wrong. Of course Shakespeare exploits the comic possibilities of a weak husband impotent to silence his wife, and involves the audience on Antigonus' side ('Hang all the husbands / That cannot . . . '). But this should not conceal Antigonus' fault in *trying* to silence Paulina. Moreover, he is prepared to buy the tyrant off with promises. In a sense he is even accessory to Leontes' crimes. The way in which he echoes Leontes' errors (though in a harmless form) comes out in his ludicrous but revealing response to

the idea of Hermione's guilt. If she is 'honour-flawed', his own daughters will suffer for it, he promises, in lines that substantiate his sinister name:

> By mine honour
> I'll geld 'em all; fourteen they shall not see
> To bring false generations: they are co-heirs,
> And I had rather glib myself, than they
> Should not produce fair issue.
>
> (II.i.146-50)

It is a coarse, comic horsey transposition of the same obsession with honour and 'fair issue' that Leontes—and Polixenes—display. Later, Antigonus acts 'against generation'—and against faith in Hermione's innocence—when a vision convinces him of her guilt, and he accepts its directive to expose the baby 'upon the earth/ Of its right father' Polixenes (III.iii.45-6). This scene sifts the quality of the audience's faith too: they have every reason, almost, for saying with Antigonus 'I do believe/Hermione hath suffered death', and to that extent interpreting the vision similarly. Only the simply devout, perhaps, are untroubled, content to have seen providence in the dream's selection of Bohemia.

Eventually Antigonus is succeeded as Paulina's spouse by a very different 'honourable husband'. Camillo resembles Antigonus in being kind. And he is repeatedly connected with the idea of honour.[19] But his honesty strikes us as altogether deeper and more severe. It is also more uncompromising. Camillo's 'policy' contrasts sharply with Antigonus' compliant propitiation of Leontes. *He* would have known how to break a promise to do evil.[20]

Just as the play's deaths adumbrate allegorical suggestions, so does the intrigue—for that is what it amounts to—of Paulina. As in *Measure for Measure,* the final reconciliation is elaborately stage-managed so as to bring the characters who are in the dark to a very particular spiritual state. Paulina conceals Hermione for sixteen years, and then reveals her in the form of a statue whose coming to life precipitates the *denouement,* in the play's climactic, and arguably its strongest, scene.

Hermione's concealment and vivification make a strikingly discontinuous fable. The audience is never precisely told why Hermione should allow Leontes to mourn her death, year after year, for sixteen years. Of course any rapid switch to easy reconciliation would have been unthinkable—

> When you shall come to clearer knowledge . . .
> You scarce can right me throughly, then, to say
> You did mistake.
>
> (II.i.97-100)

But to make this a motive for sentencing Leontes to sixteen years' grief and penance would be to make Hermione a monster. And to say that a major part of any cure for her must consist of the knowledge that Leontes had been purified. . . . Forgiveness must be won: it cannot be given where there is any suspicion of unworthiness[21]

is theologically unsound (no man is worthy) and in any case inconsistent with Hermione's character. Such a grudging censorious calculation of worthiness is not in her free nature. (Leontes speaks of her at I.ii.102-5 as having been stiff in courtship; but that is probably only Shakespeare's conventional sign of her virtue.) Nor does it seem like Hermione to stand as a statue withholding every sign of emotion, during Leontes' exclamations. The enlivening of the statue is presented as a miracle requiring faith (V.iii.95); so that we should perhaps not expect a full explanation. There may even be a sense in which Hermione has been dead and brought to life again. After all, for many of the audience the evidence that she died has been firm and uncontroverted. Indeed, Paulina almost affirms it on oath at III.ii.203: 'I say she's dead: I'll swear 't. If word nor oath/Prevail not, go and see'.[22] Few notice that she does not actually swear. And it is hard to think of anything in the subtext that can have emptied such speeches of their weight. Hermione never appears during the interval between her faint and the transformation—after which Leontes remains baffled: 'I saw her,/As I thought, dead'. In fact, the discontinuity is so marked, the undramatic irony so extreme, that the audience are 'as . . . mocked with art'.

The possibility that Shakespeare was indifferent to continuity has not deterred those bent on finding psychological causes. Coleridge remarked that

> it seems a mere indolence of the great bard not to have provided in the oracular response . . . some ground for Hermione's seeming death and fifteen [sic] years' voluntary concealment. This might have been easily effected by some obscure sentence of the oracle, as for example:—'Nor shall he ever recover an heir, if he have a wife before that recovery.[23]

Quiller-Couch followed Coleridge, and others such as Gervinus, over-ingenious in their naturalism, went a step further and imagined the change in the oracle actually effected. So now it is often supposed that Hermione's motive really is a wish not to offend Apollo, or not to spoil Leontes' chance of an heir.[24] We need to remind ourselves of the oracle as Shakespeare gives it: merely that 'the king shall live without an heir, if that which is lost be not found' (III.ii.134-6). Nothing about Leontes and Hermione cohabiting. As for Hermione's 'explanation', all that she says is:

> thou shalt hear that I,
> Knowing by Paulina that the Oracle
> Gave hope thou wast in being, have preserved
> Myself to see the issue.[25]

This by no means explains why she did not reveal herself earlier (even if Leontes and she had to avoid conceiving an heir).

The apparently cruel intrigue might be more amenable to explanation in generic terms. *The Winter's Tale* has many romance features (as its name leads us to expect);[26] and romances after all are full of extreme, irrational actions, unmotivated or inadequately motivated. Behaviour in them may seem to us almost psychopathological; as when, to cite a familiar instance, the Count of Ponthieu's daughter, having been raped, tries to murder her quite innocent husband, who has been defending her. Such actions were beyond the reach of rational understanding, but not necessarily of fiction and of wisdom. From this point of view Hermione's long seclusion might indicate the depth of her humiliation and the strength of her hatred of Leontes for 'publishing' her dishonour. But even in Elizabethan romance people should be in character, unless some powerful reason overrides the fable.

However, the last three acts of *The Winter's Tale* are allegorical romance, or a blend of pastoral romance and morality. In such a form, continuity sometimes depends entirely on the *significatio* or allegory. And in morality terms, the story is exclusively one of Leontes' repentance. There can be no question of Paulina's and Hermione's waiting for him to seem worthy—'There is none worthy,/Respecting her that's gone' (V.i.34)—for the delay is not theirs but Leontes'. It is he who cannot recover his inner harmony until he has repented fully. It is he who is spiritually 'dead'. Thus Hermione withdraws without any motive, involuntarily. Indeed, as Leontes' internal harmony, she simply does not exist, until the final scene. Her non-existence or virtual death, during the 'wide gap' of time (IV.i.7), obviates motive. The duration of the gap says nothing about Hermione: it has the effect, rather, of amplifying the difficulty of repentance.

Shakespeare treats Leontes' repentance with unusual fulness; unfolding it by slow stages of attrition, contrition and repentance.[27] Throughout, the sinner is directed by Paulina, who operates as a presiding genius of justification by faith. Her ascendancy—at first violent, but soon repentantly softened—begins with Leontes' first admission of guilt, at the news of Mamillius' death. Leontes' response might be thought repentant: so Pafford says 'he immediately repents' (p.lxviii); while Hunter has it that Leontes 'immediately experiences contrition'. If his first response is mere 'attrition', or horror of judgment ('the heavens . . . Do strike'), surely his later public confession and promise to make amends (III.ii.153-72: 'I'll reconcile me to Polixenes, / New woo my queen . . . ') amount to 'contrition', or full sorrow? Yet when Paulina returns from sequestering the queen, she continues the stage of attrition; wearing Leontes down with reminders of judgment and counsels of despair:

Do not repent these things, for they are heavier Than
all thy woes can stir: therefore betake thee To
nothing but despair.

(III.ii.208-10)

Has Leontes been too glib in his remorse? Certainly
Shakespeare makes much of Paulina's memorial function; giving it comic development when she repeatedly
breaks her promise not to remind Leontes of his losses:
'I'll not remember you of my own lord/(Who is lost
too)' (III.ii.230-1). After sixteen years she is still tact-
lessly reminding him—as at V.i.15 ('she you killed')—
when events trap her in having to steer him away from
a second marriage. But then, after sixteen years his reconciliation with Polixenes remains theoretical: the visit
that he 'justly owes' (I.i.6-7) has never been made.
Besides, it may be wrong to think of Paulina as keeping
Hermione from Leontes. She encouraged him from the
beginning to visit, even to kiss, the 'dead' Hermione:
'go and see: if you can bring/Tincture, or lustre in her
lip, her eye' (III.ii.204-5). Perhaps it is precisely Leontes'
slowness to accept the invitation, and to rouse his soul,
that delays reunion. Even in the transformation scene,
he shows such hesitancy that Paulina must chide him
(V.iii.107). It is as if he repented only intellectually or
formally in Act III. The ordering and moving of the
emotions, however, require repeated symbolic statements
and enactments that progressively involve Leontes and
the audience more and more, until the strange ritual of
the transformation brings release. This long and painful
process accords with the gravity of Shakespeare's treatment of repentance in other late plays, and contrasts
with the instant conversions in such contemporary tragicomedies as *Philaster*.

The final stage of Leontes' repentance coincides with
the animation of Hermione: an episode in the tradition
of epiphanic unveiling of statues in sixteenth-century
tableaux vivants (itself related to the religious veneration of statues). An old form for an old tale; although
it would scarcely be possible to find an earlier statue
that *moved*.[28] The preceding comment scene, rightly
prized by Coghill, gives a lead in to the symbolism of
the transformation scene itself. Third Gentleman says
that when Perdita heard Hermione's death

bravely confessed and lamented by the king . . . she
did . . . I would fain say, bleed tears, for I am sure
my heart wept blood. Who was most marble, there
changed colour; some swooned, all sorrowed: if all
the world could have seen't, the woe had been
universal. (V.ii.87-91)

In this shared movement of feeling, even in those 'most
marble', the softening of stone is the softening of hard
stony hearts. We are led to expect similar emotion in
connection with the statue. When he sees it, Leontes
applies Third Gentleman's metaphor to his own
stoniness: 'I am ashamed: does not the stone rebuke

me/ For being more stone than it?' (V.iii.37-8). the
Biblical allusion[29] is to the same text that underlies
Paradise Lost XI.3-5:

Prevenient grace descending had removed
The stony from their hearts, and made new flesh
Regenerate grow instead, that sighs now
    breathed . . .

For Leontes, then, the movable statue signifies a po-
tentiality of repentant emotion (*movere*). Since the death
of Antigonus—who could not weep, in spite of
Hermione's injunction, in his vision, that he should do
so (III.iii.32 and 51)—the heart has been ready to soften.
But it never does, until Leontes visits Paulina's house.
The significance of the occasion is emphasized by the
use of religious words, which only have to be taken
literally to disclose the allegorical meaning. Paulina
describes the visit, in the language of the court, as 'a
surplus of grace' (V.iii.7). Later, when the animation
is to be attempted, she calls for spiritual response from
Leontes: 'It is required/You do awake your faith'
(V.iii.94-5). By now the softened Hermione is weeping, as her first speech shows:

You gods, look down,
And from your sacred vials pour your graces
Upon my daughter's head!

—and the audience should know, by the movement of
their own feelings, that Leontes' contrition is complete. He has at last responded to the grace of
repentence, and is reconciled.

Leontes' all-important condescending visit to Paulina's
house, we should notice, has little to do with his volition. Its occasion is Perdita's wish to learn through
Giulio Romano's art what her mother was like.[30] It
depends, therefore, on her return. Leontes' recovery of
Perdita precedes the softening of his heart and the
animation of Hermione, just as the rejection of Perdita
preceded the hardening of his heart and Hermione's
death. The oracle is explained: what Leontes has found
is grace, prevenient grace, grace to repent. Both Perdita
and Hermione are repeatedly associated with grace.
But their allegorical aspects are distinct. Perdita is
Hermione's daughter, as the descendant or successor
of original righteousness is grace to repent—'Dear
queen' says Perdita, 'that ended when I but began'
(V.iii.45). However, the soul reanimated by repentance
cannot recover its original innocence—'You scarce can
right me throughly'. The twice-born Hermione is not
'tender/As infancy and grace' (V.iii.27) but an experienced, wrinkled form.

The transformation scene has been faulted for its contrivance, staginess and inadequacy of dramatic means.
But Coghill has rightly defended its fine stagecraft;
especially the exquisite delay in discovering the statue's

nature—which continues in a hesitation just before her first movement.[31] For Coghill, the naming of Giulio Romano as the sculptor is to borrow authenticity from the 'real' cultural world: to 'confer a special statueishness'. And Rosalie Colie reminds us of Giulio's contemporary reputation for 'miraculous illusionism'.[32] Shakespeare's own art shows its capacity for illusionism in Paulina's references to the fresh paint of the statue. This wet paint is cosmetic art in the actor's real world, Giulio's art in the second-order fictive world of Hermione's charade, but real tears in her own. (It is characteristic of Shakespeare to turn possible shortcomings of an actor to good account—imperfect stillness of the statue passes as a *vraisemblable* sign of Hermione's emotion.) But the *paragone* of arts, or of nature and art, is abandoned at a crucial point. Hermione's wrinkles are less a *tour de force* of realism (Giulio's and Shakespeare's own) than an acknowledgment of the limits of art, the claims of reality. As Rosalie Colie finely puts it, the pathos of the wrinkles makes all questions about mimesis seem trivial; and 'by calling attention to the *vraisemblable* wrinkles, the playwright underscores his *invraisemblable,* and turns us back to rethink the convention of the "marvelous" in pastoral drama, the taming of a miracle to literary device' (p. 281). At the same time, the wrinkles are also an occasion of comedy: Leontes' noticing them obliges Paulina to think on her feet:

> So much the more our carver's excellence,
> Which lets go by some sixteen years and
>   makes her
> As she lived now.
>
>   (V.iii.30-2)

We are not to dwell too lugubriously on the reflection that the most excellent art shows most of nature's faults.

Shakespeare has already taken us beyond the *paragone* of nature and art to the idea of 'art/That nature makes' (IV.iv.91-2). But to understand the function of art in the transformation, we must go beyond even Polixenes' sophisticated naturalism, to a deeper view of art's place in a fallen world. This view was quite orthodox in Shakespeare's time. And it can be illustrated from a work he certainly knew, Thomas Wilson's *Art of Rhetoric*. After the Fall, writes Wilson,

> whereas man through reason might have used order: man through folly fell into error. And thus for lack of skill, and for want of grace evil so prevailed, that the devil was most esteemed. . . . Even now when man was thus past all hope of amendment, God still tendering his own workmanship, stirring up his faithful and elect, to persuade with reason all men to society . . . being somewhat drawn, and delighted with the pleasantness of reason, and the sweetness of utterance.[33]

Wilson represents 'art and eloquence' as drawing men back to the original order of human nature. Since the dramatist's art similarly worked to repair nature, the artificial character of the transformation scene is perhaps thematic in an unsuspected way. Hermione turned statue may be soul restored by art. To move, after all, is the perfection of the sculptor's Pygmalion art. The transformation would in that case be no 'outrageous device' (Colie) but moving drama—a scene meant to move the audience themselves. A common Elizabethan defence of the stage was to instance criminals and tyrants (such as Alexander of Pherae) brought to sudden repentance by a tragedy. From Leontes' point of view, moreover, the dramatist's art symbolizes that of repentance, whose *paragone* is with wrinkles—sufferings never to be made up for without grace beyond the natural. The shortcomings of art, even the possibility of excessive artificiality, are not forgotten. Too much art could be seen as impeding Hermione's movement; just as Leontes, encouraged by Paulina, takes his penitence to what Cleomenes considers are excessive lengths.[34]

Leontes' sixteen-year repentance takes place off stage; being narrated in Time's prologue speech, Act IV, Scene i. This used also to be regarded as a clumsy 'device' (Quiller-Couch), a mere programme note, 'not central at all' (Bethell). But as *Pericles* shows, Shakespeare could leap over wide gaps of time without apology, when he wished. And Inga-Stina Ewbank has argued that Time presents himself more significantly, as a 'principle and power'.[35] This power goes beyond the revealing of truth—the aspect of time treated, nominally, in Shakespeare's main source *Pandosto* (subtitled *The Triumph of Time*. . . . Temporis filia veritas).[36] From Leontes' point of view, Time's revealing movement has so far been destructive, though just. But, as William Blisset has taught us to see, *The Winter's Tale* has the structure of a diptych, with the devouring Time of the first panel exactly matched by the redeeming Time of the second; with the turning point at the centre, Act III, Scene iii, where the devouring beast and storm symbolize 'a time of tyranny and the tyranny of time'.[37] And now, beyond the worst, beyond tragedy, Time says:

> Your patience this allowing,
> I turn my glass, and give my scene such
>   growing
> As you had slept between:
>
>   (IV.i.15-17)

We have to learn patience as well as Leontes.[38] As we do, we begin to see a different movement: construction and growth and change: 'things new born' replacing 'things dying' (III.iii.112-13). Time prepares us to understand this by his presenter's speech. For example, he three times mentions 'growth' as modified by art. It is as if the natural course of events, 'growth untried', could be replaced by, or grafted in with, a new order.

Indeed, Time (and not only the dramatist) claims just such a power 'To o'erthrow law, and in one self-born hour/To plant and o'erwhelm custom' (IV.i.8-9). It would be paltry to take these lines merely as Shakespeare's defiance of the unities. They refer to Time as a means of change: change that can replace the order of law— the customary, the habitual, the rigid, the hereditary world of the reprobate Old Man—with a new order of grace. Time's 'tale' might seem old-fashioned, or 'stale', to the taste of Shakespeare's contemporaries ('the glister-ing of this present') in that the device of a presenter was becoming obsolete. But in the course of the play 'the old tale' comes to represent an object of belief, not unlike the 'old old story' of revivalists.[39] Thus the truth that Time eventually fathers is a vindication of faith. Indeed, in a sense Time brings forth the faithful soul itself by a process of *conversio*: 'truth' often meant 'troth' or faithfulness.

The subtle *simplesse* of Time's presenter's speech finds matching form in sixteen couplets corresponding to the sixteen years of 'swift passage'. We can choose to patronize this as another clumsy device, an outmoded manner of decorum. But if we can be patient with number symbolism, it has much to tell about the play's structure. Of course probability dictates that Time's gap should be more or less sixteen years: Perdita must grow to marriageable age. But the specific choice is particularly apt for several reasons. Precisely sixteen was given by Plato as the optimal lower marriage age. Moreover, in certain schemes of the Ages of Man it would bring Perdita to a stage of transition between *pueritia* and *adolescentia*.[40] (In the same Varronian tradition, Leontes would also reach a transition. After the 'wide gap' he is 44 or 45, and changing from *jun-ior* to *senior*.)[41] These references to the Ages of Man do more than glance at one of Time's measures. Tran-sition between Ages, or phases of life, is a way of changing nature—'growth'. The Ages were a subject of profound meditations, such as that of Plutarch on the Varronian scheme: 'dead is the man of yesterday, for he is passed into the man of today'.[42]

But the number sixteen had also a more abstract fit-ness to the wide gap. As a square number, and espe-cially as the square on the tetrad, it symbolized virtue and justice. Particularly, it meant the ordering of the psyche ('Proportioned equally by seven and nine')[43] through composition of its mortal feminine part (seven) and its immortal masculine part (nine), to produce the harmony of the double octave.[44] Thus the measure of Leontes' sixteen-year repentance represents the moral *Harmonia* that he recovers. Leontes himself speaks of his repentance in a similar mathematical metaphor when he says to Paulina 'O, that ever I/Had squared me to thy counsel!'[45]

Other measures of Time are represented by more de-veloped forms, in both the imagery and the action of the pastoral scenes; suggesting many intermingled pro-cesses of nature and art, or nature and grace.[46] Thus Perdita makes 'four-and-twenty nosegays for the shearers' (IV.iii.41). And the herdsmen's dance at the sheep-shearing feast is a dance of months or signs, almost in the symbolic manner of *ballets de cour* or masque dances. Indeed, it probably borrows the antimasque of satyrs from Jonson's *Masque of Oberon*.[47] Its mixture of nature and art could hardly therefore be more thorough: rustics disguised by art as natural satyrs perform an art-dance far from 'coun-try art'. Shakespeare makes his added meaning obvi-ous enough for the popular stage by repeating the numbers, under the excuse of a servant's comic pro-lixity: 'three carters, three shepherds, three neat-herds, three swine-herds' (IV.iv.325-6). Polixenes' amused recapitulation, 'four threes of herdsmen' makes sure that we catch the reference to months disposed in their seasons or signs in their humour-governing tri-plicities. Time is now ordered in its parts and cer-emonially composed, where earlier it was torn apart, as between the ship's destruction and the *sparagmos* of Antigonus.

If some of the pastoral measures represent natural change, others associated with Perdita express the ac-tion of grace. Perdita describes herself here as like a player in a 'Whitsun pastoral' (IV.iv.133)—the feast of Pentecost, the descent of the Holy Spirit. And most critics, including those least sympathetic to allegory,[48] agree that she embodies 'grace'; even if they take the latter as a secular analogy of grace in the Christian sense, or merely as 'gracefulness'. Florizel's praise marvellously evokes her gracefulness, 'so singular in each particular' (IV.iv.144). But this seems to me the outward form of a distinct spiritual role that she con-sistently enacts throughout the overall allegory. So when Time tells us that Perdita has 'grown in grace' (IV.i.24) he implies that grace comes through a process of natu-ral change. From this point of view Perdita's moral and spiritual value finds a highly significant reflection in her presentation of flowers at the sheepshearing feast. This ceremony too has its measures: Perdita names just sixteen species.[49]

Shakespeare further develops Perdita's meaning in terms of poetic theology. As several mythologizing critics have shown, he connects her with Proserpina, particularly in the imagery of the flower presentation.[50] Indeed, he makes Perdita apostrophize the goddess: 'O Proserpina,/For the flowers now that, frighted, thou let'st fall/From Dis's waggon!' (IV.iv.116-18). The loss and qualified return of Proserpina was a seasonal myth; but also (because of the identity of Demeter and Proserpina as different phases of growth) a theological one—a myth of death and resurrection.[51] However, another mythological *persona* of Perdita's, that seems not to have been previously discussed, is in some ways a more developed role.

Just as Hermione plays a stony-hearted statue of herself, so Perdita plays a definite part at the sheep-shearing feast: 'Flora/Peering in April's front' (IV.iv.1-2). In the Ovidian myth, which received Neoplatonic interpretations, Flora was a metamorphosis of the nymph Chloris ('Green') after her rape by Zephyrus, the quickening spirit of spring.[52] After her subsequent marriage, flowers from her garden dower, gifts of the queen of flowers, are culled by the three Horae, associated with the Graces. Perdita enacts part of this myth of the natural cycle when she presents flowers of the three ancient seasons (Horae) to her guests. From a naturalistic standpoint, this many-seasoned passage has been baffling.[53] But in its own terms there is no uncertainty of season. The whole year is in effect covered by three groups of flowers: the 'flowers of winter' (IV.iv.79) given to Polixenes and Camillo; the 'flowers of middle summer' (IV.iv.108) given to men of middle age; and the 'flowers o' th' spring' (IV.iv.113) desiderated for Florizel, Mopsa, and the girls, who still wear upon their 'virgin branches'—branches of honour, as it were—their 'maidenheads growing'. Schemes of the Four Ages of Man related each age to a season, in just this way.[54] Shakespeare alludes to the idea unambiguously in his identification of spring with Florizel's youth (*pueritia* or *adolescentia*), summer with *virilitas* and winter with *senecta*; although he leaves the sequence incomplete, so that it could refer to three- or five-age schemes also. Spring flowers are inaccessible (IV.iv.113: 'I would I had some flowers o' th' spring, that might/Become your time of day') for the practical reason that spring is past at sheepshearing time. But there is a more touching reason, which explains some of Perdita's melancholy at the feast. She associates flowers with girls throughout—

> primroses,
> That die unmarried, ere they can behold
> Bright Phoebus in his strength (a malady
> Most incident to maids);

—just as she herself is referred to as 'blossom' (III.iii.46). And at sixteen, Perdita is growing away from girlhood to *adolescentia* (16-30): her girlish time of day is past, and her state must change. Of course, co-presence of all the seasons would not be impossible in some earthly paradises. But in *The Winter's Tale* (unlike many pastorals) Flora's spring is conspicuously missed, and spring flowers regretted. The sense is not merely that of a vegetation myth of cyclic repair. Perdita's ritual of presentations symbolizes not only the process of natural growth, but growth associated with the *Gratiae*, with grace: 'Grace and remembrance be to you both'.[55] And it is no accident that the gracious Perdita should be assisted by a shepherdess called Dorcas, after the woman 'full of good works' in Acts 9.36-9.

The other components of the pastoral scenes similarly develop themes of repair and change in the natural

order and beyond it. This is obviously true of Perdita's and Polixenes' debate (IV.iv. 85-103) about the gillyflower, Puttenham's example of the power of art to 'mend nature—change it rather'.[56] Perdita's phrase 'nature's bastards' has rightly been referred to Wisd. 4.3-6, 'the multiplying brood of the ungodly shall not thrive, nor take deep rooting from bastard slips'. But the whole debate must also be seen in the context of St Paul's far more familiar development of this passage, in Rom. II, as an allegory of election by grace and incorporation in Christ through repentance—'God is able to graff them in again'.[57] An abstract debate for country chat, it inextricably mingles art with nature, and nature with grace, in its paradoxes and nuances.

Contrary to the professed sides, as has often been pointed out, Polixenes is emotionally opposed to mixture of court and country, the grafted Perdita inclined to practise it. What matters in such things is not the side we profess. In any case, Polixenes' supposed profundity, in perceiving that horticultural art is a natural creation ('an art that nature makes'), is in reality a splendid commonplace.[58] And although Perdita seems put down, her immovable loyalty to simple original nature reaches a deeper spiritual level, where grace, not art, must amend. At the same time she represents in her own person an unsearchably complex grafting, in that she is intelligently innocent and simply or 'naturally' good. By nature royal, by nurture rustic, by festal art semi-divine, and by betrothal royal again, what is she when *by disguise* she becomes an African princess?[59] By contrast, Polixenes' behaviour represents a more confused, less satisfactory mixture. His disguise has an ulterior motive. And he seems to confuse Nature's bastards with those of human irregularity: valuing honour so excessively as to put it in effect above righteousness. His deficiency appears repeatedly: subtly in his suspicion that Florizel may not be 'gracious' (IV.ii.28), grossly in his tyrant's threat to torture Perdita. In fact, his scenes with Perdita and Florizel restate the theme of jealous rage, varied now by extension across the generation gap. (The analogy between Polixenes and Leontes is elaborate; extending to Camillo's similar ameliorations, and to such details as importunate jealous hospitality.)[60] It comes as a shock when gracefulness is attributed to Polixenes by the generously repentant Leontes (V.i.170).[61] Although he feels her attractiveness himself, Polixenes is an opponent of the simple, pure 'gracious' love that makes Perdita a blessing to her community.

Even the popular Autolycus, unexpectedly, is related to the same thematic complex. His suggestions are mythological—'My father named me Autolycus; who, being as I am, littered under Mercury, was likewise a snapper-up of unconsidered trifles' (IV.iii.24-6). Anciently, Autolycus was not merely an astrological 'child of Mercury' but Mercury's son. Shakespeare's Autolycus conforms to the mercurial archetype in his ingenious thefts, his eloquence and his music (he sings five of the six songs solo, and leads in a sixth). Centuries before Mann's Felix Krull he is a representative of the cultural process; a parasitic improviser; a snapper-up, taking material from simple nature and exploiting the rustics with sophisticated and amoral arts—not least the tragi-comic art of the rogue-pastoral ballad.[62] Yet exploitation of nature is only a part of Autolycus' meaning. He is also a mercurial genius presiding over the many disguises of the last two acts. To say nothing of Autolycus' own Biblical disguise in search of a good Samaritan, Polixenes and Camillo disguise to spy; Perdita dresses up first as Flora, then in Autolycus' hat, an attribute of Mercury[63] that comes to her via Florizel, and finally as a Libyan princess; and Florizel becomes a shepherd, and then, by changing clothes with Autolycus, a ruined courtier. (Moreover, the metamorphoses of the Clown and the old Shepherd to gentlemen is strictly supervised by Autolycus.) Mercury was also a god of deeper changes; so that the disguises (as often in Renaissance literature) externalize character transformation.[64] Perdita herself says: 'sure this robe of mine/Does change my disposition' (IV.iv.134-5). In part Autolycus contributes the spontaneous creativity of ordinary mundane social roles. But disguise has also a negative aspect, of deception; so that Florizel must set aside the Autolycus *persona*, and the instability of the Age of Mercury, before the action can reach its happy resolution.[65] Finally, in the concluding scene, the most profound transformation of all, the shedding of Hermione's disguise of stone, is achieved without Autolycus' arts.

The pastoral scenes, then, develop in metaphorical terms the 'hidden growth' that changes the character of Leontes. Far from being a mere interlude, they present symbols of the repair of nature; of the civilizing effect of art; of the gentling effect of time; of the interplay between nature and grace (as in Perdita's pageant of Flora); and of integration (as in the measurement of time, an emblem of temperance). Perdita's grace is not conceived as something super-added to nature, but as totally implicit; perfect mixture. Hence the placement of the Bohemian idyll: its natural phase allows time for grace to permeate and transform, edifying and growing a new nature. It is in the depths of ordinary goodness that the soul's life is to be recovered, it seems. Yet Bohemia is no 'merely' natural realm, but a mercurial place of mixture, where character transformation—under such common symbols as disguises and changing Ages—seems to happen all the time. And it is only after the Bohemian act that Cleomenes the oracle's messenger pronounces Leontes penitent: 'Sir, you have done enough' (V.i.1).

Notes

[1] Rosalie L. Colie, *Shakespeare's Living Art* (Princeton University Press, 1974), 266.

[2] *Ibid.* 270 (for documentation see J. H. P. Pafford's note in the New Arden edn (Methuen and Harvard University Press, 1963), which I have used for *Winter's Tale* quotations and references). Earlier pastoral features include the place name *Sicilia*; similes from shepherding such as I.ii.I ff. ('the shepherd's note') and I.ii.67 ff. ('twinned lambs'). Romance features include the bear, exposure of Perdita and the shipwreck (III.iii).

[3] Hermione was also a town with a famous cult of Ceres and Proserpina. On the statue of special importance in Ceres' cult, see Vicenzo Cartari, *Imagini delli Dei de gl' Antichi* (Venice, 1647), 121, 125.

[4] *Paradise Lost,* IX.503-6, 'not those that in Illyria changed/Hermione and Cadmus'. On the confusion of Hermione and Harmonia, see D. T. Starnes and E. W. Talbert, *Classical Myth and Legend in Renaissance Dictionaries* (University of North Carolina, 1955), 243.

[5] *Prolusion* 2; Yale Prose Milton, 1.238. See, e.g., Diodorus Siculus, V.49; Ovid *Met.*, III.132; Apollodorus, *Bibliotheca*, III.iv.2; Natale Conti, *Mythologiae*, IX.14.

[6] George Sandys, *Ovid's Metamorphosis Englished, Mythologized and Represented in Figures* (1632), 99.

[7] See Northrop Frye, 'Recognition in *The Winter's Tale*', reptd in *Fables of Identity* (New York: Harcourt, Brace & World, 1963), 117.

[8] III.ii.148-9 (no s.d. in Folio); cf. V.iii.126-7, where Hermione explains that she only learnt the rest of the oracle from Paulina.

[9] See further my 'The Image of Mortality: *The Faerie Queene*, II.i-ii', *HLQ* 24 (1961), 91-110. S. L. Bethell, *'The Winter's Tale': A Study* (Staples, 1947), 74, suggests that the Pauline doctrine of baptism may be involved, without going into detail.

[10] III.i.9. See Bethell 83-4 on Shakespeare's amplification of the oracle's sanctity.

[11] II.iii.84; cf. III.ii.43, 45, 51.

[12] III.ii.82; cf. 81, where Hermione says 'My life stands in the level of your dreams', meaning 'within the range of your aggressive delusions', but perhaps with a punning implication. See Nevill Coghill, 'Six Points of Stage-craft' in *Shakespeare 'The Winter's Tale': A Casebook*, ed. K. Muir (Macmillan, 1968), 212.

[13] See the balanced consideration of motives in A. D. Nuttall, *Shakespeare: 'The Winter's Tale'*, Studies in English Literature, 26 (Arnold, 1966), 24, *et pass.*

[14] 'Recognition in *The Winter's Tale'*, 112.

[15] Pafford lix, note 4.

[16] On the 'causes' of sin in seventeenth-century logic, see Leon Howard, ' "The Invention" of Milton's "Great Argument": A Study of the Logic of "God's Ways to Men"', *HLQ* 9 (1945).

[17] See Pierio Valeriano, *Hieroglyphica* (Lyons, 1595), 106. Cf. Peele *Old Wives' Tale,* 196-202, 'he with his chanting spells/Did turn me straight unto an ugly bear . . . And all the day I sit, as now you see,/And speak in riddles, all inspired with rage,/Seeming an old and miserable man:/And yet I am in April of my age'; Nashe, *The Unfortunate Traveller,* in *Works,* ed. McKerrow and Wilson, (Oxford: Blackwell, 1958), 240, 'a bear (which is the most cruelest of all beasts)'. The comedy of the scene is no argument (*pace* Pafford 72 note) against its having allegorical contents; particularly in view of the didactic theory that favoured incongruous fables. On the use of bizarre images, see E. H. Gombrich, *Symbolic Images* (Phaidon, 1972), 123-95: 'Icones symbolicae'. R. G. Hunter, *Shakespeare and the Comedy of Forgiveness* (New York and London: Columbia, 1965), 192, 196 notices the iconographical appropriateness of the bear, but sees no allegory.

[18] C. G. Jung, *Psychology and Alchemy* (Routledge, 1953), 179.

[19] III.ii.165-70 'He (most humane/And filled with honour) . . . himself commended,/No richer than his honour'; cf. I.ii.310,407,410,442; II.ii.188; IV.iv.511; V.i.193.

[20] Hunter 195 shows that according to the moral theology of Shakespeare's time Antigonus would not be thought bound by an evil oath.

[21] Pafford lxix.

[22] Many passages confirm the impression: e.g. III.iii.16-46 (Antigonus' vision of Hermione's ghost, which leads him to say 'I do believe/Hermione hath suffered death') and V.iii.115-17: 'That she is living,/Were it but told you, should be hooted at/Like an old tale'; III.ii.201; III.iii.42; V.i.80; V.iii.140.

[23] *Shakespearean Criticism,* ed. T. M. Raysor, 2 vols. (Dent, 1960), I.119.

[24] G. G. Gervinus, *Shakespeare Commentaries,* tr. F. E. Bunnett (1883), 811; Bethell 87, 102.

[25] v.iii.125-8; This is treated by Pafford as a loose end, since Hermione was present herself to hear the oracle; but see n. 8 above on the timing of Hermione's faint. The speech is probably allegorical: Hermione knew by

Paulina's theological instruction that there was hope of grace (i.e., of Perdita's recovery).

[26] Frye 107 takes 'winter's tale' to refer to the dark first part of the play. But *winter's tale* seems to have been used either as a generic term for a fairy-tale or romance; or else in the sense 'fantastic, idle tale'. So examples in *OED* s.v. *Winter* 5: 'A mere winter-story without any ground or reason'; 'Old wives' fables and winter tales'; 'Such winter tales as it were too great a mispence of time and words to refute them'.

[27] *OED* s.v. *Attrition* cites Tucker: 'Three stages in the passage from vice to virtue: attrition, contrition, and repentance'. Hooker defines attrition as 'horror of sin through fear of punishment, without any loving sense, or taste of God's mercy'. Its sorrow for sin was incomplete; so that Bradford (1555) made it 'one of the differences between contrition and attrition', that in the former there was 'just and full' sorrow (*Works,* Parker Soc., p. 46). Shakespeare's use of semi-technical theological terms is noticeable: see e.g. III.ii.223 'affliction'; III.ii.240-1 'recreation', 'exercise'; V.iii.145 'justified'.

[28] George R. Kernodle, *From Art to Theatre* (Univ. of Chicago, 1944), 62; Inga-Stina Ewbank, 'The Triumph of Time', in Muir, 115, n. 15 (suggesting that Shakespeare may have started a fashion for moving statues in masques). There is a *speaking* statue in Peele's *Old Wives' Tale.*

[29] Ezek.11-19: 'And I will give them one heart, and I will put a new spirit within you; and I will take the stony heart out of their flesh, and will give them an heart of flesh'. Hab. 2.10-11, the text usually cited, is also apt: 'Thou hast . . . sinned against thy soul. For the stone shall cry out of the wall, and the beam out of the timber shall answer it.'

[30] V.ii.93-103; V.iii.13-14.

[31] Coghill 212.

[32] *Shakespeare's Living Art* 280.

[33] Ed. G. H. Mair (Oxford: Clarendon, 1909), 'The Preface'; cf. Frye 117.

[34] V.i.1-23. Cf. F. D. Hoeniger 'The Meaning of *The Winter's Tale'*, *UTQ* 20 (1950), 25 on the ambivalence of art, as a source both of decadence and of creation.

[35] 'The Triumph of Time', esp. 104 ff.

[36] *Pandosto. The Triumph of Time. Wherein is discovered by a pleasant History, / that although by the means of sinister fortune, Truth may be concealed yet by Time in spite of fortune it is most manifestly revealed. Pleasant for age to avoid drowsy thoughts, profitable for*

youth to eschew other wanton pastimes, and bringing to both a desired content. Temporis filia veritas. . . . On Time as a revealer, see Erwin Panofsky, *Studies in Iconology.* (New York: Harper, 1962), 82-3; Fritz Saxl, *'Veritas Filia Temporis'* in *Philosophy and History: Essays Presented to Ernst Cassirer,* ed. R. Klibansky and H. J. Paton (1936), 197-222.

[37] W. Blisset, 'This Wide Gap of Time: *The Winter's Tale'*, *ELR* 1(1971), 52-69, esp. 56-9, 63.

[38] See John Taylor, 'The Patience of *The Winter's Tale'*, *EC* 23 (1973), 333-56.

[39] V.ii.28; V.ii.62; V.iii.115 17. Cf. Pafford liii.

[40] *De legibus* 6; see Pietro Bongo, *Numerorum mysteria* (Bergamo, 1591), 412. Valeriano (358), partly following Varro and Censorinus, gives the five ages as: I *infantia* (0 to 5), II *pueritia* (to 15 or 16), III *adolescentes* (to 30), IV *iuniores* (to 45), V *seniores*(from 46). Samuel C. Chew, *The Pilgrimage of Life* (Port Washington, N.Y.: Kennikat, 1973), discusses the five age scheme at 160-2, 218-19, giving examples from Palingenius, Raleigh and John Davies of Hereford.

[41] For the calculation of Leontes' age, see F. W. Bateson, below, p. 70. The repeated appearance of the number 23, to which Mr Bateson draws attention, may be an intentional number symbolism. Bongo (442) comments that 'by this number can be signified the completing and perfecting of human salvation, which is brought about especially by true faith and good works. Perfect faith is denoted by the triad, which mystically implies faith in the Holy Trinity; while the perfection of works consists in observation of God's commandments, which is expressed through the number 20, in accordance with the double dyad, in that the decalogue is handed down through the Old Testament, and declared more fully in the New.'

[42] *De E apud Delph.* 292 D-E. On the general significance of the Ages of Man schemes, see Raymond Klibansky *et al., Saturn and Melancholy* (Nelson, 1964), a study of the Four Ages, and the only adequate treatment of any of the schemes.

[43] Spenser, *F. Q.* II.ix.22.

[44] See my *Spenser and the Numbers of Time* (Routledge, 1964), App., esp 284 n.; also (with Douglas Brooks) 'The Structure of Dryden's *A Song for St Cecilia's Day, 1687'* in *Silent Poetry,* ed. Alastair Fowler (Routledge, 1970), 195-6, citing Macrobius, Pico and Athanasius Kircher.

[45] V.i.51-2; see *Spenser and the Numbers of Time,* 280, 287 n. Antigonus too intends to 'be squared' (regu-

lated) by his vision's instructions (III.iii.41). But in the case of the Old Man, allegorically Leontes' sinful part, this will mean elimination.

[46] Number symbolism was a conventional feature of pastoral: see Helen Cooper, 'The Goat and the Eclogue', *PQ* 53 (1974), 372 and cf. my *Triumphal Forms* (Cambridge Univ., 1970), 139.

[47] Enid Welsford, *The Court Masque* (reissued New York: Russell & Russell, 1962), 283-4.

[48] Such as Pafford (lxxviii).

[49] IV.iv.74-127: rosemary, rue, carnation, gillyflower, lavender, mint, savory, marjoram, marigold, daffodil, violet, primrose, oxlip, crown imperial, lily, iris.

[50] E.g. Hoeniger 22; E. A. J. Honigmann 'Secondary Sources of *The Winter's Tale'*, *PQ* 34 (1955), 34-5.

[51] Conti V.14; X; Sandys 193. Cf. Hunter 198.

[52] *Fasti* V.195 ff. See Edgar Wind, *Pagan Mysteries in the Renaissance* (Faber, 1968), 115-17 esp. 117: 'the progression Zephyr-Chloris-Flora spells out the familiar dialectic of love. . . . ' Flora's desire to count the flower colours in her garden ('saepe ego digestos volui numerare colores/nec potui') was a constant challenge to numerological imitation. On the connection of the primroses at IV.iv.122-5 with chlorosis, see Pafford 172.

[53] As it is to Pafford (lxix, note). But he rightly rejects the popular error that the pastoral scenes take place in spring. On this point IV.iv.79, 107 and 113 are decisive. See Ewbank 108.

[54] Klibansky 293-4.

[55] 'Remembrance' perhaps in a specific sense: 'Rosemary and rue signified respectively remembrance (friendship) and grace (repentance). Rue is known as 'herb grace' (Pafford). Cf. Robert Greene *Upstart Courtier* (1871), 4: 'some of them smiled and said "rue was called herb *grace*" which though they scorned in their youth, they might wear in their age, and it was never too late to say *miserere'*.

[56] *The Art of English Poesy,* ed. Gladys D. Willcock and Alice Walker (Cambridge Univ., 1936), 303-4; cf. Frye 114. The gillyflower had two other relevant associations: it was a term for a loose woman (*OED* s.v. *Gillyflower* 2b, late examples only); and it was an emblem of gentleness (e.g. *A Handful of Pleasant Delights* (1584), ed. H.E. Rollins (New York: Dover, 1965), 5: 'Gillyflowers is for gentleness,/which in me shall remain:/Hoping that no sedition shall,/Depart our hearts in twain.')

[57] Cf. Herrick's use of the Wisdom and Romans passages, *The Poetical Works of Robert Herrick,* ed. L. C. Martin (Oxford: Clarendon, 1968), 278, 'To His Friend, Master J. Jincks': 'The bastard slips may droop and die/Wanting both root, and earth; but thy/Immortal self, shall boldly trust. . . . '

[58] Polixenes' grandiloquence, from the very start, is noted in M. M. Mahood, *'The Winter's Tale'* in Muir 214. On Polixenes as a Baconian improver, see Colie 275.

[59] Cf. *ibid.* 253 n. and 254; Bethell 93, 94; Nuttall 47-9 (on Perdita's civilized innocence).

[60] IV.ii.1-3; 10-20; cf. I.ii.I ff.

[61] Cf. Mahood 228.

[62] 'Doleful matter merrily set down', as the Clown says (IV.iv.190). See Taylor 333 for instances of boisterous pastoral.

[63] For Mercury's hat, see Jean Seznec, *The Survival of the Pagan Gods,* tr. Barbara F. Sessions, Bollingen Series 38 (New York: Pantheon, 1953), 211 etc.; Guy de Tervarent, *Attributs et symboles dans l'art profane 1450-1600,* Travaux d'humanisme et renaissance 29 (Geneva: Droz, 1958), col. 70.

[64] See Norman Holland, 'Disguise, Comic and Cosmic' in *The First Modern Comedies* (Cambridge, Mass.: Harvard, 1959), 45-63. On Marsilio Ficino's theory of Mercury's part in *conversio,* see Wind 123; on Mercury's relation to Flora, *ibid.* 126 n. Ficino's *In vita coelitus comparanda* III.5 discusses the neutral Mercury's moderating role in character formation. On Mercury as a god of mixture, see Ficino, *In Platonis Timaeum,* chs. XIX-XX.

[65] In the five-age as in the commoner (Ptolemaic) seven-age scheme, Mercury presided over the second age, *pueritia* (6-16 and 5-14 respectively): see Ptolemy, *Tetrabiblos,* IV.10 and consult Chew 163-9, Klibansky 149, n. 74, Franz Boll, 'Die Lebensalter', *Neue Jahrbücher für das klassische Altertum* 16 (1913), 89-154.

On Mercury's changeable influence, see Valeriano 358, on the five ages: assigning *pueritia* to Mercury, he continues: 'undeillud eius aetatis studium rerum plurimarum, et mutabilitas, et inconstantia, ut modo hoc, modo illud appetant . . . '

Charles W. Hieatt (essay date 1978)

SOURCE: "The Function of Structure in *The Winter's Tale,*" in *The Yearbook of English Studies,* Vol. 8, 1978, pp. 238-48.

[*In the essay below, Hieatt examines "the adherence of mortals to a standard of ideal behaviour" as the shaping principle which forms a coherent basis of the play's structural segments.*]

I

That *The Winter's Tale* presents an experimental, two-part structure has been generally agreed since the time of Thomas Price, a late Victorian critic who described the play as 'a genuine diptych', the first part of which is 'a tragedy and the second a comedy'.[1] On the other hand, opinion of the success of this structure has changed radically, the once maligned gap in time between Acts III and IV now being regarded as less a flaw than an index of Shakespeare's over-all design. Whereas Price found that 'in passing from part to part, the mind loses grasp of the artistic unity',[2] Nevil Coghill sees the end of Act III as 'a kind of dramaturgical hinge, a moment of planned structural antithesis'.[3] And while Northrop Frye also calls the play a diptych, he finds coherence in an arrangement 'of parallel and contrasting actions, one dealing with age, winter, and the jealousy of Leontes, the other with youth, summer, and the love of Florizel'.[4] Thus, in the modern view, Shakespeare achieves unity through a significant balance of elements on either side of Time's central chorus: events such as Perdita's two ocean voyages and the attempts to stay the departures of Polixenes and Camillo in Acts I and IV would appear to establish a certain architectural symmetry, while others would seem to join the two parts in the cross-referential manner of the Elizabethan double plot.[5] As Dr Tillyard pointed out, 'Florizel and Perdita re-enact the marriage of Leontes and Hermione, but with better success'.[6] Moreover, as Frye has observed, these contrasting illustrations of imperfect and perfect love develop complementary views of the same theme.

> Florizel's love for Perdita, which transcends his duty to his father and his social responsibilities as a prince, is a state of mind above reason. He is advised, he says, by his 'fancy':
>
> If my reason
> Will thereto be obedient, I have reason;
> If not, my senses, better pleased with madness,
> Do bid it welcome.
>
> Leontes' jealousy is a fantasy below reason, and hence a parody of Florizel's state.[7]

It is clear that the play presents contrasting illustrations of the effects of sinful as opposed to virtuous fantasy, and the behaviour of Leontes in the first three acts supports Frye's claim of a mutual theme of reason overcome by passion. While partly agreeing with this modern approach, however, I am convinced that both the theory of a bilateral structure and the current idea

of the unifying function of parallel action are erroneous. Recently, Philip Weinstein has questioned the merit
of Florizel's behaviour, finding his idealism inadequate
to the occasion, his irrational love to some extent an
echo of Leontes's jealousy; Weinstein observes that
the motifs of symbolic regeneration are not resolved at
the end of the Pastoral Scene and claims that 'to the
degree that such motifs remain unresolved, the scene
will mirror, not redeem, life as we have seen it in that
fatal country Sicilia'.[8] So disparaging a view of Florizel
is unfounded. It is true that irrational passion twice
leads to Perdita's exile, but this does not mean that the
young lovers, like Leontes, are morally at fault; indeed, a comic conclusion to the play depends upon
Florizel's behaving as he does, and, from the audience's
point of view, a resolution to the young lovers' difficulties is all but promised at the end of the Pastoral
Scene when Camillo directs them to Sicily. But
Weinstein's point that the Pastoral Scene reproduces
an earlier pattern is none the less a valuable one. Regardless of its significance, the action in Bohemia *does*
mirror that in Sicily, and the similarity between the
first three and the fourth Acts suggests that a two-part
view of the play accounts for only a portion of a larger,
more complicated scheme. As for the alleged unifying
function of parallel action, the linear development of
The Winter's Tale denies that its structural segments
are linked primarily by cross-reference. Events are
arranged chronologically throughout and, unlike those
of the double plot, bear not only a comparative but a
sequential, cause-and-effect relationship. Thus, despite
their disjunctive nature, the structural segments will
cohere on the basis of an over-all shaping principle,
while their parallel action will have the secondary
function of underscoring and redefining this principle
in terms of theme.

II

To deny the modern theory of unity in *The Winter's
Tale* is to re-confront the old complaints of fragmen-
tation and an inappropriate mixture of tragedy and
comedy. In seeking an over-all shaping principle, one
might therefore look to the implications of the play's
comic reversal, which occurs in Act III when a providential intelligence wrests control from Leontes and
shows itself responsive to human desire. The forces of
moral order in Shakespearian tragedy remain in the
background and allow a kind of roughshod and unpo-
etic justice to take its course, but the death of Mamillius
immediately following the oracle's announcement that
'the king shall live without an heir'[9] confirms the presence of a supernal being who had foreseen the wilfulness of Leontes and planned to punish him accordingly. Furthermore, if Apollo can punish he can also
forgive, and the possibility that 'that which is lost'
may be 'found' suggests to an experienced audience
the promise of a brighter future. Subsequently, Perdita's
escape and imminent return at the end of Act IV antici-

*Richard Gale as Florizel and Virginia McKenna as Perdita in
Act IV, scene iv of Peter Brook's production.*

pate the accuracy of this suggestion, and evidence of
divine ordination seems even greater on Hermione's
resurrection near the end of Act V. Her unexpected
awakening momentarily implies that the tale is a comic
myth, a story in which the Divine is both controller
and hero, with the unlikelihood of tragedy turned to
comedy explained as being a result of providential
power and mercy.

Inherent, then, is a strong sense of allegory, and a
pattern of sin, penance, and forgiveness has led a number of critics to describe the play in terms of Christian
doctrine.[10] Weinstein, on the other hand, sees 'great
creating nature' as the agent of a controlling power
that remains undefined,[11] while still others have seen
Nature herself as a force whose cyclical benediction
renews life through the springtime love of Florizel and
Perdita. But to emphasize an other than human element in this way is to disregard the essentially mundane forces that govern the play's outcome. Mamillius's
death may well represent divine punishment, and
Hermione's resurrection need not be an actual return
from the dead to symbolize miraculous intervention. In
the end, however, Shakespeare reveals that her death

and resurrection were illusory, though he might easily, and perhaps more credibly, have presented them as real. By the same token, the reconciling power of love in the Pastoral Scene is not joined with nature, as C. L. Barber illustrates is the case in Shakespeare's middle comedies, in a 'compelling rhythm that orders men's affairs'.[12] Seasonal imagery, festivity, and mistaken identity are all evident, but these things do not signify confusion or lack of self-control on the part of the young lovers, who, like all of the principal characters, have a share in effecting a comic ending. What allows the play to proceed beyond Act III is not so much Apollo's intervention as that of Paulina, whose shrewish courage in Act II introduces a note of humour, and whose intimidation of Leontes first suggests that he is something less, and more, than the irreconcilable tragic hero. The possibility of development from 'tragedy' to comedy is gained by Leontes's partial response to good advice in allowing Perdita to live, and thus the possibility of his redemption may be traced to his own actions, while redemption itself will also require something more than Apollo's mercy. Although the oracle suggests a brighter prospect to an audience, it predicts alternatives that depend on human behaviour and therefore claims for the gods only a limited control within the fictional world. That 'the king shall live without an heir, if that which is lost be not found' gives the mortals primary responsibility for effecting a happy ending: Hermione must remain hidden from her husband, as her earlier disclosure would signify an intention to produce an heir; for the same reason, Leontes must not remarry but remain contrite and faithful to the memory of his queen until their daughter returns; the younger couple must place their love above fear of reprisal if Perdita is to leave Bohemia; and Camillo must retain his love for Leontes if he is to direct Perdita homeward.

In so far as the oracle is understood by the fictional characters, of course, it constitutes a direct command and therefore imposes a measure of control over them; but in no sense is it a covenant guaranteeing reward for specified behaviour, nor is it obeyed primarily from a regard for religious duty. Paulina argues that Leontes's remarriage would disobey the 'tenor' of Apollo's words and 'to the heavens be contrary' (v. I. 38, 45), but Leontes at this point has already declined his counsellors' advice in memory of his love for Hermione. Hermione, in her greater awareness, is more directly responsive to the oracle; as she says, it 'gave hope' that her daughter was alive, and she remained hidden in order 'to see the issue' (v.3.127, 128). But she has no assurance of finding Perdita, and, like that of Leontes, her continued celibacy depends on enduring fidelity rather than dutiful obedience or the certainty of coming reward. Hence the principal characters reunite themselves by independently preserving what Leontes had allowed his passion to destroy, and their combined efforts cohere with the 'tragic' action in a continuous illustration of the results of imperfect and

perfect love.[13] To be sure, Apollo aids a desirable outcome: a timely dream causes Antigonus to abandon Perdita where she will be protected by shepherds and later discovered by Florizel. But if serious romance can admit the supernatural, its shaping principle is the adherence of mortals to a standard of ideal behaviour; while divine justice and mercy are part of the scheme, the play, like Arthurian and Renaissance epic romance, takes primary meaning from a demonstration of human influence over human destiny.

III

The relationship of structure to this shaping principle is most easily approached through a comparison of *The Winter's Tale* with its source, Robert Greene's *Pandosto*. In the first section of the original story, Pandosto's jealousy of his childhood friend, Egistus, results in the exile of his daughter, Fawnia, and the death of his son and wife. Subsequently, the scene changes to Egistus's realm where Fawnia is found and brought up by shepherds, is courted by Prince Dorastus, and for the second time escapes a king's wrath as she flees with her lover. Finally, the scene shifts again to Pandosto's court, where Fawnia is unsuccessfully wooed by her lustful father before she is identified and the joy of her return and marriage to Dorastus is offset by Pandosto's guilt-inspired suicide. Thus the major difference in the two plots is in their endings: in Greene a comic outcome involves the mortification of the evil Pandosto, in Shakespeare the restoration of Leontes and Hermione to their former felicity. Despite these different conclusions, however, the fundamental pattern of the two stories is identical, and the play therefore presents a more complex structure than is generally recognized. The first movement in both works constitutes a discrete segment of fictional time, a single 'organic action' (to use Bernard Beckerman's terminology of dramatic structure),[14] in which a king's passion runs its dreadful course and the initial dramatic conflict is brought to a standstill. But in contrast with this 'tragic', falling action, the events rising to comic reconciliation in both play and novel comprise two integral movements, the one dealing with young love, the other chiefly with the further adventures of Pandosto and Leontes. The dramatic conflict in the first part of *The Winter's Tale* is, in effect, re-enacted between the young lovers and Polixenes, and matters are again brought to a standstill with the removal of those accused of conspiring against the king's interests. Furthermore, this second organic action is also followed by a major shift in time and place, which in turn precipitates another organic action ending with the return of Hermione. Thus, rather than symmetrical events on either side of Time's chorus, Perdita's two ocean voyages are structural interruptions that precede and initiate second and third movements, much as Polixenes's voyage to Sicily initiates the first. Like Greene, Shakespeare employs a three-part structure, each part having its separate setting and grouping of characters, its individual reversals of fortune and mood, its discrete increment of fictional time.[15]

This is not to deny the pivotal effect that is enhanced by Time's chorus at the centre of *The Winter's Tale;* as Emrys Jones points out, the Shakespearian pattern of equally apportioned action and reaction that A. C. Bradley noted in the tragedies is clearly present here.[16] At the same time, however, Shakespeare develops fully his usual comic pattern of oppression, mistaken identity, and final clarification in a series of structural segments that in combination make up the whole. Moreover, if the conspicuousness of the central break between Acts III and IV has tended to obscure this tripartite structure, it has likewise drawn attention from a coinciding triptych of parallel actions and language that Shakespeare also shares with Greene. Acting under false assumptions, Pandosto allows his 'reason' to be 'suppressed with rage' (p. 190) and passes an unlawful judgement upon his wife, and this series of impelling circumstances is twice repeated: in the second part as Dorastus finds that his unlawful love for the unidentified Fawnia is 'not to be suppressed by wisdom, because not to be comprehended by reason' (p. 205), and in the third as Pandosto is also attracted by a mere shepherdess and vainly seeks 'by reason and wisdom to suppress this frantic affection' (p. 219). Similarly, *The Winter's Tale* presents three occasions on which a prince labouring under false assumptions approaches the daughter of a king to deny both reason and law in judging the propriety of her outward appearance and her suitability as a bride. In Act I Leontes illogically claims that Hermione's strayed 'affection . . . dost make possible things not so held' (2.138-9), his illegal judgement of her ironically foreshadowing the central events of Act IV, where Florizel also ignores a counsel of 'reason' in favour of 'madness' and 'fancy' and finds himself 'heir to my affection' (4.482 ff.). And so, too, in the ceremonial Statue Scene at the end of the play, passion and reason are once again dramatically opposed as the king steps forward to judge the merits of a queenly guise. Having exhibited what is assumed to be a mere counterfeit of Hermione, Paulina turns to Leontes (l. 56) and offers to close the curtain and thereby end the ceremony. Leontes twice rejects this and, responding to her alleged fear that his 'fancy' will belie reality, adopts Florizel's earlier attitude: 'No settled senses of the world can match / The pleasure of that madness' (ll. 72-3). Paulina then mentions that she could 'afflict' him further, to which Leontes agrees, and having addressed the statue he attempts to kiss it. Finally, her last offer to close the curtain (l. 83) is followed by her announcement that, although it may seem 'unlawful', she can make the statue move, and the assent of Leontes completes a third judgement in which fantasy has been preferred to reason.

So close a resemblance between plot, structure, and cross-referential technique, moreover, suggests that the two authors have the identical intention of illustrating varied qualities and effects of motivating passion. In both stories jealousy is ugly and self-defeating, but love enlists our sympathy and predicates creative rather than destructive results; and although the endings differ, they would appear to demonstrate the same governing principle: Pandosto's suicide contrasting with the triumphant marriage of Dorastus, and the fidelity of Leontes and Florizel bringing its similar rewards. But if this is Greene's purpose, he fails to realize it, primarily because the implications of the parallel action in *Pandosto* conflict with the principles of heroic romance. Fawnia owes her safe conduct back and forth across stormy seas to an arbitrary and capricious 'Fortune', and any evidence of human control over the course of the plot is denied by the inability of Greene's characters to control themselves. Dorastus refrains from imposing his will on Fawnia, and his eventual oath of loyalty in trothplight is also commendable (p. 212); but the central conflict in Greene's pastoral scene is Dorastus's interior struggle between prudent disgust for so demeaning a marriage and what proves to be overwhelming sexual desire. Like Pandosto, he caroms helplessly between the dictates of reason and passion, and his surrender to Fawnia's charms implies no pertinent alternative to Pandosto's jealousy and lust, but merely proves that he, too, is passion's victim rather than its lord. Despite a surface of fashionable moralizing, the overriding point in Greene's story is the similarity of crucial events whose governing principle is the mysterious power of the emotions to 'perplex' and subdue the mind. Consequently, although a single theme illustrated in similar circumstances imparts a certain unity to the tale, an inherent disavowal of human responsibility deprives its three parts of further rationale for their juxtaposition, either as contrasting moral exempla or as a continuous demonstration of human influence over human destiny.

These contradictions are resolved in *The Winter's Tale,* chiefly through a far more elaborate use of cross-referential action to redefine the theme of motivating passion. Shakespeare omits Dorastus's anxious soliloquies that show love victorious over reason, as he does the events that explain and nearly justify Pandosto's suspicion of his wife, the point being that reason is neither a necessary prologue to jealousy and love nor always a suitable means for confronting them: like all humankind, Leontes and Florizel on attaining sexual maturity unavoidably became subject to that 'stronger blood' that Polixenes implies is 'heriditary ours' (I.2.73, 75), and neither man can support his behaviour on the basis of circumstantial evidence. But while an implied comparison shows the fallibility of passion and reason, it also shows that one's actions should none the less be based on unhampered judgement and a recognition of prior commitments. Unlike Dorastus, Florizel has no qualms about his loved one's social status, and his intuitive perception of Perdita's merit condemns

Leontes's biased judgement of her. Moreover, in Shakespeare's version of the story the young lovers have already dared to 'mingle faith' (IV.4.461), thereby entering into a formal contract that raises their relationship above the illusive sway of the affections; like Leontes and Hermione, they are pledged from their first appearance in eternal trothplight,[17] and thus a comparison of the two men's behaviour is morally significant. Having succumbed to passion, Leontes eclipses his 'faith' with his 'folly' (I.2.429, 430); but while Florizel acknowledges himself heir to his affection, he nevertheless rejects both passion and reason as unreliable guides to be transcended, according to his 'oath' and his 'honour', in view of his 'faith' (IV.4.33-5, 478, 492). His state of mind, as Frye says, is above rather than below reason; moreover, it is above passion as well, and it therefore redefines Leontes's irrational jealousy as a lack of constancy in love.

Confined to Florizel and Leontes, however, the comparison is incomplete and somewhat misleading. If Florizel has sworn allegiance to Perdita, he is also bound in duty to his father, and that the latter obligation predates the former would seem to lend support to Philip Weinstein's argument for Florizel's culpability. But the point here is that the dramatic conflict between father and son that Shakespeare brings to the tale repeats the formal judgement scene of Act III from a different perspective. As king and magistrate, Polixenes gathers what appears to be incontrovertible evidence of Florizel's guilt, and his verdict, though given in anger, is measurably justified. As an enemy to love, however, he ignores the primacy of honourable trothplight because he finds his own 'honour' in jeopardy (IV.4.437). Like Leontes, he misjudges Perdita, debases his own offspring (IV.4.419-20), and discovers an illicit relationship where none exists. Thus, although Weinstein is correct in saying that the Pastoral Scene mirrors 'life as we have seen it in that fatal country Sicilia', the echo of Leontes's jealousy that he hears in Florizel is in fact sounded by Polixenes, the implication being that the young prince stands between two irreconcilable claims to choose the greater. Although exile is 'desperate' Florizel 'needs must think it honesty' (IV.4.488) and, in rejecting his father's appeal to reason, he actually employs reason to choose the more honourable course.

Furthermore, implication is followed by proof when at the end of the Pastoral Scene the method of Shakespeare's alterations is fully revealed. In retrospect, one can see that the second movement imitates the sequential development of the first, passing from a stayed departure, to suspicion of sexual treachery, to a picture of the impassioned lover, controversial views of Perdita, a climactic judgement scene, and exile. But exile results from different causes, and it elicits different responses from the gods, whose actions as an integral part of the parallel sequence are morally defini-

tive. Blinded by anger, Leontes orders that his child be burnt and, although this sentence is modified by the influence of Paulina, Antigonus dutifully abandons Perdita to chance and probable death. But Leontes's judgement is overruled when Perdita is inadvertently conveyed to safety, and his punishment is confirmed when Antigonus dies for his obedience and the shepherds resolve to suppress her identity. Impelled by love, Florizel also causes Perdita's exile, and again a 'ponderous and settled project' is modified by courageous advice. But Florizel acts against misused authority, and his contrasting behaviour causes what had been arranged by the gods as an equally contrasting response. Whereas Antigonus's dream of the weeping Hermione had directed Perdita to Bohemia, Camillo's vision of Leontes's joyful welcome redirects her homeward (IV.4.548), and whereas the shepherds had unknowingly condemned Leontes, the decision to reveal their secret endorses Florizel's behaviour by anticipating his reward.

Shakespeare continues this technique in the third movement, employing the pre-established sequence and varying the individual action to demonstrate a varied result. The plea of Cleomenes and Dion at the beginning of Act V, that Leontes remarry and produce an heir, is to be compared with the stayed departures of Polixenes and Camillo in Acts I and IV. Alike in their brevity and expositional function, each of these occasions presents a character who is urged to neglect a primary duty to someone he loves, and thus a series of initiating motifs emphasizes the tripartite structure and calls attention to the theme of fidelity under stress. In the third movement, however, this motif coincidentally advances the parallel sequence, the whole of which will now have a dual reference. In remaining true to his vow to revere Hermione, Leontes reverses his initial behaviour and, in taking an oath not to remarry until she returns, he stands, as had Florizel, between private and public obligations to choose the greater. Next, Perdita's worth is once again defended and then denied, and again a king becomes suspicious of sexual treachery. Leontes's question, 'Is this the daughter of a King?', is ominously iterative, as is his remark that Florizel has broken from 'where you were tied in duty' (V.1.207, 212). But on this occasion the judge is amenable. Whom he once would have burnt and Polixenes have scratched with briars, Leontes now can wish to have for himself; where Polixenes had found only dishonour, Leontes finds a more important bond than filial duty, so long as 'honour' is 'not o'erthrown by your desires' (V.1.229); and whereas a disregard for the sanctity of trothplight had caused dishonour and confusion, the willingness of Leontes to intercede on the lovers' behalf is immediately followed by the discovery of Perdita's true identity.

Hence, the sequence to this point represents a corrected re-enactment of the past. Leontes's present fidelity to Hermione would have forestalled the unhappy consequences of his passion, and with a proper judgement of Florizel's behaviour Polixenes's objections to the match disappear. At the same time, Leontes's imitation of Florizel also indicates that Perdita's return has been a joint enterprise. While Florizel is responsible for initiating the chain of events that led her homeward, these events are allowed to occur because Leontes has remained constant to his own trothplight in the face of similar demands that he recognize his duty to the state. Moreover, Leontes's reversal of his behaviour as lover and magistrate provides both cause and model for his further redemption. In the Statue Scene Paulina assumes Polixenes's former role as she interrogates the lover surreptitiously, urging prudence while disguising her ability to react to his decision. But Paulina is aware of the gods' secret purposes, and her response, like theirs, will be compliant and morally definitive. Overwhelmed by the statue's authenticity, Leontes fancies that it is truly his queen and accepts responsibility for Paulina's bringing it to life, an act that, as she says, may appear 'wicked' and 'unlawful'. Furthermore, Paulina draws attention to the full meaning of his decision when she says that 'It is required / You do awake your faith' (ll. 94-5). Here, again, 'faith' assumes its literal meaning, denoting the fidelity mutually sworn in anticipation of formal wedlock; as elsewhere in *The Winter's Tale,* the term is synonymous with 'trothplight' and 'contract'[18] and represents an ideal whose violation sets man against himself and his society, but whose veneration effects integration and harmony. Leontes is required to reaffirm his faith in order to recover his bride, and with his command to 'proceed', Paulina beckons Hermione from her pedestal in a final demonstration of the power of fidelity to make possible things not so held.

While repeating both theme and pattern, moreover, parallel action in this last movement is made to carry an additional burden, the index to which is a calculated challenge to our credulity. Because Florizel and Leontes have already earned their rewards, events follow one another with little sense of cause and effect, and the third movement becomes progressively more artificial as we encounter the sheer unlikelihood of the Statue Scene. That Paulina and Hermione would subject their king to so elaborate a reconciliation is quite improbable, and for withholding the true state of affairs from his audience Shakespeare has been accused of sacrificing credibility to an expedient bravura ending. Furthermore, this departure from previous standards of versimilitude is not to be explained in terms of generic convention. Improbability is sometimes meant to be tolerated by an audience as a part of the comic spirit, and, as Leo Salingar has pointed out, conspicuous artifice at the end of Shakespeare's comedies often provides a contrast with what has gone before and thereby enhances and 'testifies to a reality within the spec-

tacle'.[19] But in *The Winter's Tale* terminating artifice imitates an established sequence of events, and although these events are obviously improbable they are to be seriously regarded as a part of the reality of the spectacle.

Unaware that Hermione is alive, we no longer share the author's Olympian point of view in the Statue Scene and are enjoined with Leontes to expect the impossible. But our experience, though similar, is qualitatively different. As in the first movement, Leontes must choose between love and reason, and a willingness to renew his trothplight is only one of several indications of his continued devotion and the true lover's denial of reason. As onlookers, however, we do not undergo a trial of allegiance to Hermione, and thus we hear in Paulina's call for faith overtones of the word's religious usage, which signifies objective trust in a merciful, all-powerful deity, and which is favoured by the allegorical critics.[20] But the word as addressed to the audience merely borrows from its religious meaning, Paulina's stipulation, as Frye points out, being a call for the 'imaginative faith' necessary to grasp the truth that art has to offer.[21] The several references to developments in the play as being like an 'old tale' raise the question of the ability of art to reproduce nature and anticipate our own reaction to an analogous but more complicated set of circumstances. Having witnessed the means of Perdita's escape and return, we do not share the amazement of the fictional characters on learning her true identity; what to them seems miraculous is to us the final result of a series of independent actions. But in the Statue Scene we are equally nonplussed on being told that Hermione can return to life, while at the same time our memory of a parallel sequence strongly suggests that she will,[22] and thus an apparent conflict between art and reality in the minds of the audience requires that we, like Leontes, undergo a trial of faith. While referring to black magic, Paulina's denial that she is about 'unlawful business' also indicates our obligation to continue to suspend our disbelief and trust in the verity of the artistic illusion. Like Time, she asks that we 'impute it not a crime' if the usual 'law' and 'custom' of dramatic probability are temporarily overthrown, but, unlike Time's, her tone is imperative and implies that we, too, must deny reason and momentarily accept, not only that the impossible will occur on the stage, but that its occurrence will represent an accurate imitation of life. Without a personal commitment to fidelity as a guide more valuable than reason, we are not qualified to appreciate the truth of the Statue Scene and do not deserve to share in Leontes's reward. Like him, we should regard Hermione's awakening as an 'art lawful as eating', and hence we are required to acknowledge our trust in the power of love to achieve and art to represent what we do not yet understand, or else to rise early from our places and leave the theatre.

Notes

[1] Thomas R. Price, 'The Construction of *A Winter's Tale*', in *Shakespeariana,* VII (1890); quoted from *'The Winter's Tale': A Casebook,* edited by Kenneth Muir (London, 1968), p. 44.

[2] Price, p. 45.

[3] 'Six Points of Stage-craft in *The Winter's Tale*', *Shakespeare Survey,* 11 (1958), p. 53.

[4] 'Recognition in *The Winter's Tale*', in *Essays on Shakespeare and Elizabethan Drama,* edited by Richard Hosley (London, 1963), p. 235.

[5] See Ernest Schanzer, 'The Structural Pattern of *The Winter's Tale*', *Review of English Literature,* 5, No. 2 (April, 1964), 72-82 (pp. 78 ff.).

[6] E. M. W. Tillyard, *Shakespeare's Last Plays* (London, 1938), p. 22.

[7] 'Recognition in *The Winter's Tale*', pp. 236-7.

[8] 'An Interpretation of Pastoral in *The Winter's Tale*', *SQ,* 22 (1971), 97-109 (pp. 97, 102).

[9] *The Winter's Tale,* edited by J. H. P. Pafford (London, 1963), III.2.134-5. For convenience, quotations in my text from both *The Winter's Tale* and Robert Greene's *Pandosto* are taken from this Arden edition, with page references to the latter work which appears there as an appendix to the play.

[10] See, for example, S. L. Bethell, *'The Winter's Tale': A Study* (London, 1947), and Jerry Bryant, 'Shakespeare's Allegory: *The Winter's Tale*', *Sewanee Review,* 63 (1955), 202-22.

[11] 'An Interpretation of Pastoral in *The Winter's Tale*', p. 109.

[12] *Shakespeare's Festive Comedy* (Princeton, 1959), p. 9.

[13] For a similar view of the play as an illustration of the power of love rather than 'an allegory of resurrection', see *Narrative and Dramatic Sources of Shakespeare,* edited by Geoffrey Bullough, 6 vols (London, 1966-75), VI, 153.

[14] *Dynamics of Drama* (New York, 1970), pp. 41-2.

[15] Pafford recognizes a three-part structure but does not argue the point; see *The Winter's Tale,* p. liv.

[16] See Bradley's *Shakespearean Tragedy* (1904; reprinted London, 1960), p. 51, and Emrys Jones, *Scenic Form in Shakespeare* (Oxford, 1971), pp. 68-9.

[17] Shakespeare most often employs 'faith' with its literal meaning of 'trust, observance of trust, pledge', or 'troth' (see *OED* and *Barlett's Concordance*), and the words 'faith' and 'trothplight' are virtually interchangeable throughout the play. Florizel refers to his trothplight as early as IV.4.49-51, and, although it is not yet celebrated publicly, it is recognized as valid by Leontes in V.3.149-51.

[18] For a discussion of Shakespeare's use of the two terms and of the legality of the trothplight, see Pafford's note, *The Winter's Tale,* I.2.278.

[19] *Shakespeare and the Traditions of Comedy* (Cambridge, 1974), p. 23.

[20] See Derek Traversi, *Shakespeare: The Last Phase* (London, 1954), pp. 190-91, and Bryant, 'Shakespeare's Allegory', pp. 217-18.

[21] Northrop Frye, *A Natural Perspective* (New York, 1965), pp. 18-19.

[22] Though it is not necessary that one's memory be precise; as William Empson says of the double plot, parallel action 'does not depend on being noticed for its operation'. See *Some Versions of Pastoral* (London, 1935), p. 25.

Joseph M. Lenz (essay date 1986)

SOURCE: "'We Are Mock'd With Art': *The Winter's Tale*," in *The Promised End: Romance Closure in the Gawain-poet, Malory, Spenser, and Shakespeare,* Peter Lang, 1986, pp. 89-117.

[*In this essay, Lenz divides the play into three distinct sections, associating each with a certain genre and outlining the steps of the "prepared surprise" as a structural unit.*]

Romance, like all modes, creates and maintains a consistent fictive world, an other world with laws unto itself, so events in *The Winter's Tale* can fall out "like an old tale," differently than they would in "real life." Because that other world does not behave according to "normal" expectations, romance asks that we adjust our vision to meet its own. In fact, romance closure, the sense of eucatastrophic achievement, depends upon the confirmation of its vision, as we have seen in *Sir Gawain and the Green Knight* and *The Faerie Queene.* The author must therefore assist his readers to make the necessary adjustment. Medieval romance's literary ancestry gives the author the various ethical systems that complicate the action, setting one knight in conflict with another and sometimes with himself. By watching which system (knight) prevails we recognize that story's values. In an art romance, one that imitates the medieval version, the author more deliberately toys with generic conventions. The encyclopedic *Faerie Queene* contains epic, chivalric romance, chronicle, historical allegory, pastoral, and myth, Spenser using them to enrich his make-believe world, to provide a background for his knights, and to facilitate our understanding of his vision by presenting something familiar: poetry teaches us what we already know. Our participation in romance does not rely on the other world's similarity to the "real" world; it relies on our familiarity with other literary genres.

Walter F. Eggers, who examines how "traditional generic distinctions function in a reader's or audience's experience," describes how the reader discovers a given text's genre: "we inevitably make successive, unsatisfactory guesses about the nature of a work as a whole, until, to satisfy ourselves, we make a last guess at its 'intrinsic' genre."[1] The language ourselves, we make a last guess at its 'intrinsic' genre."[1] The language recalls our discussions of closure. It too is a "last guess" about the "nature of the work as a whole," a guess confirmed by a revelation: the *Gawain*-poet's envoi, Malory's explicit, Chaucer's palinode, and, most notably, Spenser's Mutabilitie Cantos, each breaks the fiction's bounds by revealing its artificiality. Since romance's generic catholicity makes it perhaps the most artificial mode, it requires this sort of acknowledgment to close, to identify its otherness. In other words, regardless of the ordering principle, whether narrative, spatial, or revelatory, revelation is inherent in romance closure. *The Winter's Tale* offers a prime example of romance as a revelatory mode.

Partly because of its ending, partly because of its beginning, we are not quite sure what to label *The Winter's Tale*. Eggers describes too well our critical experience. We make "successive, unsatisfactory guesses about the nature" of the play, for it is protean, changing its shape before our eyes. The play owes much of its elusiveness to its allusiveness. It belongs to tragedy, comedy, tragicomedy, pastoral, and romance—or, rather, all of these belong to the play.[2] The fascination with identifying each and every genre in it bears out Eggers' contention that we are not comfortable with a fiction until we know its nature.

Despite the recognition that *The Winter's Tale* presents Polonius' rare combination of "tragical-comical-historical-pastoral" or Quince's "very tragical mirth" (a recognition of its literary origins), there seems to be an irresistible tendency to discuss the similarity between Shakespeare's creation and the "real world." Howard Felperin, one of the latest and best of the play's commentators, focuses on the "lifelike characterization" which, to some extent, is effected by the play's varied descent from Greek romance, chivalric romance, and the mystery and morality plays.[3] "The best romance," he writes, "manages to pass itself off as the

image of the real" by "shadowing or qualifying or problemetizing the triumphs it presents."[4] A touch of tragedy, like Mamillius' death, makes romance seem more "real." Likewise, for Fitzroy Plye, "Shakespeare's Romances are the comedies of a man who having written the tragedies is not prepared to cut the material of life to the customary measure of comedy."[5] Again we have the generic blend and again we have the confusion of literary and "real" worlds. What these critics describe as the "lifelike" quality of *The Winter's Tale* results from the density achieved by Shakespeare's combining several generic intentions and expectations. Just as the epic context of *The Faerie Queene* contributes a sense of narrative progress, the record of the hero's trials which informs the final realization of his quest, so too the dramatic context of *The Winter's Tale* forces the romance to accommodate the theatre's demands. Unlike narrative, where episode follows episode and where the reader is free to pick up and put down the book at will, drama assumes an immediate ending. Since drama is performance oriented, the play must be presented within certain prescribed time limits, hence the popularity of the unity of time, in which the plot time should concur with the performance time. Thus the dramatic structure itself, the plot, can reflect the impending conclusion. In *The Tempest,* for instance, Prospero names the hours between two and six as the time needed to complete his scheme, and he repeatedly measures the time left to him. If nothing else, a stop to the action and an epilogue tell us the play is over. Ideally, however, drama shares with romance the self-fulfilling prophecy. From the beginning the playwright sets his dominoes so that in the last act he can tip one to make the whole line fall, revealing the discrete units to be part of a unified, coherent design. Long ago Aristotle defined the complex plot, one which provided an end that both reversed the situation and provoked a recognition, as the best possible dramatic design. For Aristotle, drama, especially tragedy, must always work towards an end: "the structure of events, the plot, is the goal of tragedy, and the goal is the greatest thing of all."[6]

Still, drama is more than a narrative: it is a representation. Sir Philip Sidney explains the difference "betwixt reporting and representing": "As, for example, I may speak (though I am hereof Peru, and in speech digress from that to the description of Calicut); but in action I cannot represent it without Pacolet's horse." And he complains about too much reporting being done on the stage: "you shall have Asia of the one side, and Afric of the other, and so many other under-kingdoms, that the player, when he cometh in, must ever begin by telling where he is, or the tale will not be conceived."[7] Anyone would think that he had just seen *Antony and Cleopatra*. Nevertheless, dramatists are cautious about "representing" without a warning that their show is only pretense. So much does Bottom worry about his audience's gullibility (or, more likely, his own ability) that he asks Quince to "Write me a prologue, and let that prologue seem to say, we will do no harm with our swords." "This," he concludes, "will put them out of fear" (*MND,* 3.1.16-21).[8] We may smile at Bottom's simplicity, but dramatists possess a cabinet of tranquilizers to put their audiences out of fear. Stages, costumes, actors and acting, sets, asides, apostrophes, prologues, epilogues, all blatantly advertise the play's fictiveness. In drama we are especially challenged to suspend our disbelief because we are so often reminded of the need for belief.

Drama's self-reflexive or self-revelatory conventions complement romance's penchant for calling attention to itself, especially as it reaches its end. In the previous chapter we noted how Spenser develops the correspondence between the knight's quest and the poet's as Book Six draws to its close, making Calidore, as well as Colin, a figure for the poet. A tale's open admission of its literariness does not necessarily undermine its acceptability. In fact, William Nelson, who traces the debate between fact and fiction during the Renaissance, sees self-consciousness as a rhetorical trick played by romancers to escape the classical, humanist, and moral charges against them for lying:

> But the proper relationship between the author and his audience required a mutual understanding that the story was neither history told 'for true' nor a childish confusion of make-believe with real, but a transparent device calculated to appeal to a less-than-serious aspect of human nature.[9]

When a writer admits his tale is a fiction, he asks that we do not impose sense on the tale; in time the tale will make its own sense to us, and its sense, as Spenser insists in Book Six's final stanza, is to give pleasure. The romance writer, like Bottom, does not want his audience to fear a live lion when they should enjoy a make-believe one, or, more pertinently, to confuse a real bear with a stage bear.

But the point where having fun becomes making fun is difficult to establish precisely. Self-consciousness in a story can turn too easily from a "device calculated to appeal to the less-than-serious aspect of human nature" to a device calculated to ridicule. Here drama is particularly dangerous to romance. The very fact that we can see the characters limits the range of their actions. To produce on stage Redcrosse's fight with the dragon, as Spenser describes it and with the same effect, is of course impossible. We expect human actors to behave according to normal human motivations and within certain boundaries of action, time, and space.[10] This mimetic expectation makes drama a natural form to satirize romance fantasies, as it does in *The Old Wive's Tale* and *The Knight of the Burning Pestle.*

In *The Winter's Tale* Shakespeare uses drama to test the credibility of his romance vision. Throughout the

play he alternates between representation and report, between dramatic performance and tall story telling, an alternation evidenced in the play's structure. It divides into three distinct sections, each associated with a specific genre and each reflecting one means by which closure can be attained. Part One (Acts I, II, III) uses a causal narrative reminiscent of tragic plot to order events; Part Two (Act IV) establishes an enclosed space on the pastoral Bohemian island and alters the narrative to an analogical order; Part Three (Act V) presents the statue scene, the eucatastrophe which reveals the play's true kind, a miraculous balance between dramatic belief and romance incredibility.

I

While certainly not a satire, *The Winter's Tale* demonstrates how drama alters romance material and how the intercourse between the two satisfies and frustrates audience expectations of both. The legitimacy of Leontes' much debated jealousy affords a fine example. Critics divide into two schools on this matter: those, like Northrop Frye, for whom "the jealousy explodes without warning"; and those, like Neville Coghill, who see the "fuse already burning early in I.ii."[11] The first group regards the jealousy as romantic or incredible, the second as dramatic or credible. Both are correct.

The suddenness and ferocity of Leontes' jealousy *are* surprising, and Shakespeare alters his source, Robert Greene's *Pandosto,* to accent the surprise. Although Greene outlines the plot, "Wherein Pandosto (furiously incensed by causelesse Jealousie) procured the death of his most loving and loyall wife," he does take pains to show there is *some* cause for Pandosto's suspicion: the constant companionship between Bellaria and Egistus, their secret meetings in the garden, and Bellaria's provocative habit of "coming her selfe into his [Egistus'] bed chamber to see that nothing should be amis to mislike him."[12] Yet, despite appearances, we have Greene's assurance that Pandosto's jealousy is causeless.

In *The Winter's Tale,* however, we have no general announcement of plot. All of our early information concerning Leontes and Polixenes details their long friendship, their alliance, Leontes' promised visit, and the extension of Polixenes' present stay. Just prior to admitting his jealousy, Leontes and Hermione recall their courtship, when

> Three crabbed months had sour'd themselves
> to death
> Ere I could make thee open thy white hand
> And clap thyself my love.
>
> (I.ii.102-04)

Leontes' marital suspicion contrasts sharply, and unexpectedly, with his premarital hopes. In his extreme

passion he turns his suspicion against the most innocent party present, Mamillius:

> Art thou my boy? (I.ii.120)

> Art thou my calf? (127)

> Most dear'st! my collop! Can thy dam?—may't be?
> (127)

He subsequently makes his plans to murder Polixenes,
his lifelong friend. The sheer irrationality of Leontes'
behavior tells us he is mistaken, just as surely as if
Shakespeare had followed Greene's example by explaining the plot in a prologue. Greene sets jealousy
against a background of suspicious actions; Shakespeare
sets jealousy against a background of long established
mutual amity—"They were trained together in their
childhoods; and there rooted between them such affection, which cannot choose but branch now" (I.i.22-24).
The eruption of Leontes' jealousy in the face of "such
affection" shocks us. Where we accept Pandosto's jealousy, partly because it seems more rational, we take
exception to Leontes' sudden outburst.

Yet, as Coghill has shown, careful analysis of I.ii reveals that we are prepared for Leontes' explosion.
Leontes' efforts to persuade Polixenes to extend his
visit are terse and perfunctory, to the point that
Hermione scolds, "You, sir, / Charge him too coldy"
(29-30). Leontes' cold manner, his silence while
Hermione and Polixenes banter, and his possible sarcasm—"Is he won yet?" (86)—all indicate something
is amiss. Leontes promptly identifies that something:

> But to be paddling palms and pinching
>   fingers,
> As they are now, and making practiced smiles
> As in a looking-glass, and then to sigh, as
>   'twere
> The mort o' th' deer—O, that is entertainment
> My bosom likes not, nor my brows.
>
> (115-19)

Leontes' confession of jealousy invites us to reinterpret the earlier dialogue. Camillo's remark about the
friendship "which cannot choose but branch now" takes
on a double-meaning: that which was united must now
divide, an ominous prediction of the succeeding action. We can even trace the logic that leads Leontes to
conclude he has been cuckolded. Hermione insists that
Polixenes stay, and persuades him to do so after Leontes
has failed—"At my request he would not" (87). When
the topic is courtship and sexual temptation, Hermione
confuses (for Leontes at least) who sinned with whom:

> Th' offenses we have made you do we'll
>   answer,
> If you first sinned with us and that with us

> You did continue fault and that you slipped not
> With any but with us.
>
> (83-86)

Her statement is triply ambiguous. She could mean
"you" (Polixenes and Leontes) sinned with "us"
(Polixenes' wife and Hermione); or "you" (Polixenes)
with "us" (his wife and Hermione); or "you" (Polixenes)
with "us" (Hermione, using the royal plural). The
ambiguity increases when Hermione teases, "I have
spoken to the purpose twice":

> The one for ever earned a royal husband,
> The other for some while a friend.
>
> (106-08)

The parallel clauses encourage Leontes to equate the
two purposes. Hermione's payment to the "earned" (the
correct verb to fill the ellipsis) friend is the same as her
payment to the "earned" husband: the marriage bed.

What surprises us about Leontes' jealousy is that it
makes sense, despite its sharp contrast to former friendship and love. Like Greene, Shakespeare provides
evidence, or the suggestion of evidence, to make his
protagonist's jealousy plausible. Unlike Greene, whose
continual exclamations of Bellaria's innocence and
Pandosto's "causelesse Jealousie" force sympathy for
her and antipathy for him, Shakespeare allows the
drama itself to guide our responses. The pastoral tran-
quility which fosters friendship and love is subtly
undercut by hints of discord. The opposition is focused
when Leontes admits his jealousy, as much a recognition for us as it is for him. Coghill calls this the technique of the "prepared surprise."[13] The audience is given
an expectation that the dramatist can play upon and
later confirm. Frank Kermode, we remember, defines
this ironic process as *peripeteia,* the falsification of
expectations which discovers "something real." By
reversing the flow of our naive expectations an author
can provoke our recognition of the true course of events.
In Leontes' case, we believe that all is well in Sicilia,
that Leontes, Hermione, and Polixenes dwell in mutual
friendship and harmony. Leontes upsets this belief when
his jealousy erupts. But because that jealousy concurs
with bits of information embedded in the dialogue, we
can accept it as plausible, even if it conflicts with our
original beliefs and even if we think Leontes mistaken.

The "prepared surprise" constitutes the basic structural
unit of *The Winter's Tale.* We can identify a set formula which the "surprise" follows: a prophetic statement; a series of remarks, actions and events that substantiate the prophecy; and the ironic fulfillment of the
original statement. This pattern, which recalls romance
closure through prophetic fulfillment, can be found in
the play's plot skeleton. There is the oracle about finding that which is lost, the scenes devoted to the lost
one, Perdita, and her eventual restoration to her father,

each step corresponding to a section of the play as I have divided it: prediction (Part One), substantiation (Part Two), fulfillment (Part Three). Curiously, Shakespeare takes even greater care to ground his scenes' trueness as the play develops and as the action becomes more dramatically preposterous.

Let us take for example Antigonus' unfortunate demise, which concludes Part One. Shakespeare's most famous stage direction distresses some and delights others. "The deep damnation of his taking off," so detestable to Arthur Quiller-Couch, evokes peals of laughter from Coghill, at least as he would stage it.[14] In the bear scene S. L. Bethel hears the "deliberate creaking of stage machinery" which "draws attention to the play as play by obtruding matters of technique upon the audience."[15] As we have noticed, the deliberate advertisement of the play as play distances the audience from the action, permitting them to view it with that "less-than-serious aspect of human nature." Whether he used a real bear or a man in costume, Shakespeare does not want to affright the ladies.

As he does with Leontes' jealousy, which surprises because it makes subtle sense against the tenor of the opening scene, Shakespeare carefully prepares us for the bear's entrance. Antigonus predicts his own death when he begs Leontes to save the baby's life: "I'll pawn the little blood I have left / To save the innocent" (II.iii.166-67). The statement is reinforced by Leontes' curt "It shall be possible" (168) and by his charging Antigonus to abandon the baby "On thy soul's peril and thy body's torture" (181). Later, when cataloging the suffering caused by Leontes, but before Antigonus lands in Bohemia, Paulina mourns "my own lord, / who is lost too" (III.ii.230-1). And, just prior to leaving the baby, Antigonus reflects on his dream in which Hermione warns "thou ne'er shalt see / Thy wife Paulina more" (III.iii.35-36). Thus, Antigonus' death is heralded from several quarters. Even the manner of his death has its harbingers. When he accepts Leontes' charge Antigonus prays that "Wolves and bears" will show the baby mercy (II.iii.187). When they arrive in Bohemia, the Mariner cautions that "this place is famous for the creatures / of prey that keep upon't" (III.iii.12-13). The timing of these statements, one following Antigonus' pawning his life for Perdita's, the other preceding the actual exchange, underscores the irony inherent in the bear's fulfillment of the predictive statements. Rather than being a haphazard or lazy stage trick, "Exit pursued by a bear" belongs to the basic structural pattern of the play, initiated by Leontes' jealousy and completed by the statue.

In *The Winter's Tale* Shakespeare makes his metaphors literal. The friendship cannot choose but branch now, and does. Antigonus names "that which is lost" Perdita. When he first takes up the baby Antigonus hopes that Nature will show it mercy:

> Come on, poor babe.
> Some powerful spirit instruct the kites and
>   ravens
> To be thy nurses. Wolves and bears, they say,
> Casting their savageness aside, have done
> Like offices of pity.
>
> (II.iii.184-88)

He is thinking of rumors, stories, myths, like that of Daphnis and Chloe, in which beasts act more humanely toward abandoned babies than the bestial humans who abandoned them. But Antigonus does not really believe such a thing will—or even can—happen; he merely wishes for it to be so. Without casting its savageness aside the bear does perform an office of pity. It pursues Antigonus instead of falling upon the helpless Perdita, evidently preferring old goat to lamb. "They are never curst but when they are hungry," the Clown asserts. With its belly full of Antigonus the bear poses no threat to Perdita, thus saving her to be found by the Shepherd. We experience the same surprise or irony here that we do when we realize the plausibility of Leontes' jealousy. Events fall out in nearly the exact terms that Antigonus predicts: he does pawn his life for Perdita's and a bear does perform a peculiar office of pity.

Not only does the episode provide another example of the prepared surprise, it also punctuates the first part of the play without closing it. The bear scene makes the transition from prediction to substantiation, from Sicilia to Bohemia, from court to country, from tragedy to pastoral, without breaking the play at the seams. Because it occupies the last scene of the first major section of the play, the bear reflects back on the previous action as well as forecasts subsequent events.

The bear scene completes a series of predictions about Antigonus' death. It also begins to substantiate Apollo's oracle: "the king shall live without an heir if that which is lost be not found" (III.ii.134-36). "That which is lost," Perdita, is found by the Shepherd while the bear dines on Antigonus. The scene also rehearses much of the action. After his dream, Antigonus correctly names the baby but mistakenly deduces that Hermione did sin with Polixenes, recalling for us the original cause for his presence in Bohemia. The rehearsal continues with the Shepherd's entrance, his opening lines summarizing the plot so far:

> I would there were no age between ten and
> three-and-twenty, or that youth would sleep
>   out the rest;
> for there is nothing in the between but
>   getting wenches
> with child, wronging the ancientry, stealing,
>   fighting.
>
> (III.iii.58-61)

A woman got with child has delivered her baby, ancient friends, traditions, and gods have been wronged, reputations and lives have been stolen, friend and friend, king and subject, husband and wife have all fought.

In the first section Shakespeare seems to strive for lifelike characterization and for action that imitates nature. His characters remember things past and lost. They are conscious of time's passing—Polixenes is nine months in Sicilia, his sailors have expected his departure for two days, he quibbles with Leontes about staying another week or month, the messengers take twenty-three days to journey to Delphos and back. His characters weep, take sick, give birth, get angry and jealous, make mistakes, repent, die: they represent that illusion of reality once described as "rounded" characters. Shakespeare moves his plot from scene to scene and act to act with an expedience fit for tragedy. *The Winter's Tale* opens with a brief history of Leontes, Polixenes, and Hermione, presents Leontes' jealousy, and develops, in quick succession, the immediate consequences of his jealousy—Camillo's defection and Polixenes' fight, Hermione's trial, Perdita's birth and the queen's "death," all without a single digression. Messengers are sent to Delphos; therefore we have a scene (III.i) showing their return, introduced by a servant in II.iii and followed by the delivery of the oracle in III.ii. The sequence of events is ordered by cause-effect logic. The first section of the *The Winter's Tale* contains an economic, concentrated tragedy, Shakespeare demonstrating that he can observe the unities of action and place.

The bear, however, chases tragedy from the scene. Even while reminding us of the previous action III.iii alters our perspective on that action. The change of locale from Sicilia to Bohemia changes the tragic vision to comic. In Sicilia we witness Othello-like jealousy and the cost of that jealousy—estranged friends, a dead son, a supposedly dead wife, an exiled daughter. In Bohemia life is different. It is a place where a shepherd believes in fairies ("It was told me I would be rich by the fairies. This is some changling"), a place where a man's dream comes true (Antigonus does not see Paulina again), a place "famous for the beasts of prey that keep upon't" where myth ("Wolves and bears, *they say*") is realized. In the very act of recording yet another casualty to Leontes' tyranny Shakespeare asserts the significance of the new locale.[16] We are startled to see a bear chase a man across the stage, startled, I think, to laughter. Shakespeare confirms this response by following the bear with the Shepherd and the Clown. The Clown's description of the shipwreck and the bear's dinner, his comparison of the tossed ship to a cork in a hogshead, his inability, like Dogberry's, to keep track of his points, are all genuinely humorous. By making light of the twin disasters, which are a direct result of the tragic action in the first section, at the conclusion of that section, Shakespeare transmutes the tragedy into comedy.

Yet even this generic exchange has its preparation. Veins of comedy course through the first part of *The Winter's Tale*. For one thing Shakespeare bases his characters on stock comedy personnel. Antigonus, for instance, is the harassed husband, a Noah with a nagging wife. Throughout Paulina's attempt to persuade the King to accept Hermione's baby (II.iii), Leontes rails at Antigonus:

> What, canst thou rule her? (46)

> Thou dotard, thou art woman-tired, unroosted
> By the Dame Partlet here
>
> (74-75)

> He dreads his wife. (79)

> And, lozel, thou art worthy to be hanged
> That wilt not stay her tongue.
>
> (108-09)

If Antigonus is the hen-pecked husband, Paulina is the pecking hen: "Dame Partlet," "Lady Margery," "A callat of boundless tongue, who late hath beat her husband" (91-92). But these insults flow from Leontes, the imaginary cuckold, the petty tyrant who out-Herods Herod. His exaggerated jealously and irrationality make him an object of humor too, as he himself realizes: "Camillo and Polixenes / Laugh at me, make their pastime at my sorrow" (II.ii.23-24).[17] Antigonus, the touchstone used to detect Leontes' true metal, agrees: his king's behavior will raise us "To laughter, as I take it, if the good truth were known" (II.i.198-99). Similarly, he reduces Leontes' threat to hang all husbands who cannot quiet their wives to its logical absurdity:

> Hang all the husbands
> That cannot do that feat, you'll leave yourself
> Hardly one subject.
>
> (II.iii.110-12)

The king, in fact, would probably hang himself, for, as far as he knows, he cannot keep his wife faithful, let alone quiet. Such nuggets scattered over the first part of the play hint at the wealth to be mined in the second.

With the entrance of the Shepherd and the Clown, obvious representatives of pastoral and comedy, we recognize, if we had not already, that the "rounded" participants in the domestic tragedy belong to stock comedy after all. Now we see Leontes' dark suspicions through the shepherd's eyes: "This has been some stairwork, some trunk-work, some behind-door-work" (III.iii.73-75). The pastoral setting that ends this section links up with the pastoral descriptions that begin the play, thus encasing the intervening tragic action in, as Florizel will say, "a swain's wearing." The tragic impact is mitigated by these comic and pastoral elements, bringing about a re-cognition of the first section. We begin to get at "the good truth."

In its reassessment of certain thematic structures, this end functions like the close of a complete work. But because the play is only at its midpoint Shakespeare must leave some strings untied. Our romance expectations call for Leontes and Perdita's reunion. The oracle reinforces that expectation and opens the possibility that Leontes' question, "Shall I live on to see this bastard kneel / And call me father?"—needs to be answered. The Shepherd's promise to take up the baby "for pity" (and for fairy gold) requires depiction. Finally, although we do not know it yet, the Clown's report of the twin disasters—

> how the poor souls roared, and the sea mocked
> them, and how the poor gentleman roared, and
> the bear mocked him, both roaring louder than the
> sea or weather

(III.ii.94-97)—

anticipates the close of the play, when Leontes will remark how "we are mock'd with art."

II

At the end of Part One Shakespeare transfers his scene to Bohemia, a place where dreams, myths, and oracles come true. He begins the Bohemian interlude with that iconic anachronism, Father Time, using him to bridge the "wide gap" between the play's parts; he ends it by returning his cast to Sicilia, once more dislocating the action. Thus the play's second part is confined to that idyllic enclosed space, the pastoral island, a space delineated in the play itself. This new locale allows Shakespeare to continue the comic trend from the previous scene, strengthened by a new narrative order, and to explore dramatically pastoral's reflexive landscape—the outward show that mirrors an inner reality.

At his simplest Father Time makes a transition from Leontes to Perdita, from prediction to substantiation; on a more complex level, he reminds the audience about who controls the play. Time emblemmatizes, literally, the joining of the dramatic and the romantic. Using him Shakespeare leaps over place and time, committing the fault that so annoyed Sidney:

> Impute it not a crime
> To me, or to my swift passage, that I slide
> O'er sixteen years and leave the growth untried
> Of that wide gap, since it is in my pow'r
> To o'erthrow law, and in one self-born hour
> To plant and o'erwhelm custom.

(IV.i.4-9)

He ushers a player on stage to report the change in years, leaving "the growth untried" or unrepresented. As hundreds of years of commentary tells us, dramatic "law" and "custom" argue against such practice, but

Time is Shakespeare's "Pacolet's horse." Shakespeare defies one dramatic custom, the unity of time, by employing another, the chorus. What's more, Time knows he is a character in a play. He steps from one kind of fiction, the emblem book, onto another, the stage. He is both a "chorus" addressing "Gentle Spectators" and the symbol for time, winged, carrying a glass, identifying himself in riddles:

> I, that please some, try all, both in joy and
>   terror
> Of good and bad, that makes and unfolds error,
> Now take upon me, in the name of Time,
> To use my wings.

(1-4)

The obvious—and yet ambiguous—riddle can be applied to the author as well, for he too pleases some and tries all. To demonstrate his power over law, Time passes from Leontes, definitely a tried man whose error has been made and unfolded and who has tasted the terror of badness, to Perdita, whom Time hints will enjoy goodness.

In a sense, Time is the playwright.[18] By calling attention to his own conventionality Time shows the other conventional characters in bold relief: the shepherd, the Clown, the cuckold, the shrew, "a son o' th' King's," and "A shepherd's daughter." He claims the play as "my tale." He even predicts, in general terms, the remaining plot:

> A shepherd's daughter
> And what to her adheres, which follows after,
> is the argument of Time.

(27-29)

The most telltale sign, however, is his instruction to the audience:

> imagine me,
> Gentle Spectator, that I now may be
> In fair Bohemia, and remember well,
> I mentioned a son o'th'King's which Florizel
> I now name to you.

(19-23)

We remember well that this is Father Time's first appearance, and that only Polixenes and Leontes have mentioned the king's son, back when these characters were first introduced. Time here speaks for the playwright, with whom he shares a "self-born" power. Like Puck, Rosalynde, and Prospero, who beg for applause at the ends of their plays, and most like Gower, who acts as guide through *Pericles,* Father Time interrupts *The Winter's Tale* to arrange the play and reassure the audience. We may also remember the subtitle of Shakespeare's source: "The Triumph of Time." At its start, then, the second part's outward show reveals a truth, the playwright's debt to both dramatic and narrative custom.

The triumph that follows—and there is something processional about Act IV—exhibits a narrative order different from causation. It follows a method more familiar in Shakespeare's comedies, that of introducing several characters or character groups in a series of scenes, with little apparent regard for unity of action, and then weaving them all together. The lovers, fairies, and mechanicals of *A Midsummer Night's Dream* provide an ideal example. Shakespeare presents each group in a series of scenes (I.i, I.ii, II.i) in which the groups announce their reasons for going to the forest on midsummer night. The scenes do not logically advance the supposed main plot, the marriage of Theseus and Hippolyta. However, the scenes do explore the play's subject matter—marital love—by replacing Theseus and Hippolyta with three very different versions of their relationship: the Athenian quartet's premarital misadventures, Pyramus and Thisbe's tragic elopement, and Oberon and Titania's marital quarrel. At the play's end, when each group has had intercourse, of one kind or another, with the others we recognize the matter that holds the plots together. This development of a comedy by thematic variation and association approximates romance's analogical narrative, for both contain multiple plots unified by their "matter."

So it is with Father Time, Polixenes and Camillo, and Autolycus and the Clown, who appear in scenes i, ii, and iii, respectively. Part One's direct narrative, together with the clues about what comes next, leads us to expect Perdita as the next order of business. Instead, Shakespeare introduces new characters. Father Time and Autolycus each makes his first appearance, and two others, Polixenes and Camillo, have not been seen since I.ii. Only the Clown, who does not appear until the third scene, belongs to the set of characters who end Part One. Further, the action of each scene seemingly bears little relation to the others: Father Time tells us Perdita is next, but she does not appear; instead Camillo talks of returning to Sicilia while Polixenes plans to spy on his son's affairs; then Autolycus enters to rob the Clown. The scenes are only tangentially related by their reference to Perdita, just as the wood connects the groups in *A Midsummer Night's Dream*. However, they do triangulate on scene iv, the sheep shearing festival, where Shakespeare collects the first three scenes together by repeating their order: Perdita and Florizel wooing, as Time hints; Polixenes testing his son; and Autolycus again duping rustics. True, the section does follow a general plot line—"A shepherd's daughter/And what to her adheres"—but it is the scenes' thematic unity that really binds them together.

The fourth act consists of four scenes that adhere to Perdita, but the main plot is secondary to the matter of identity. "Any well constructed comedy," writes Northrop Frye, will contain three phases: a Period of Preparation (the initial social block—parental interference, exile, and so on); a Period of License (loss of identity), and a Period of Festivity (discovery of identity).[19] Each phase can be associated with successive scenes in Part Two. Polixenes prepares to interfere with his son (ii). Autolycus adopts a new identity to separate the Clown from his purse (iii). Polixenes discovers himself to Florizel, and Perdita is thought to be something more than she seems (iv). But the loss of identity, a matter closely tied to the finding of Perdita, the next step needed to substantiate the oracle, predominates over the action. We are not faced with one lost identity, we are faced with many. Polixenes and Camillo, the king and his counsellor, disguise themselves as gentlemen. Autolycus, a displaced courtier, becomes a robbed traveller, a peddler, and a courtier again. Prince Florizel transforms from swain to prince to peddler. And Perdita, the lost Princess who thinks she is a shepherdess, changes from festival queen to something anonymous.[20] The last exchange of clothes between Florizel, Perdita, and Autolycus (IV.iv.624-59) integrates the trickster, who has thus far interacted only with the rustics, into the main plot. We should note that he becomes involved in the lovers' escape, not by an accident of plot (being in the right place at the right time), but by their ability, like his own, to shape-shift. Perdita may well speak for Autolycus—and everyone else—when she remarks,

> I see the play so lies
> That I must bear a part.
>
> (655-56)

The lost identities, shown by all the costume changing, particularly those done openly on stage, follows Time's lead and flaunts a dramatic truth.

I earlier described *The Winter's Tale* as protean, changing before our eyes like its characters who slip in and out of costume. This shape-shifting or metamorphosis—the realized potential—is basic to the romance world, where revelation, whether of a knight's identity or of a story's kind, depends so much on adaptability, on the knight's and thus the reader's ability to keep his balance and discern the truth amidst myriad possibilities. In the fourth act of his own old tale Shakespeare represents several variations on the theme of change. Father Time initiates it by changing the subject from Leontes to Perdita. Camillo and Polixenes complicate it by donning disguises. Autolycus, the chamelion who changes color to fit his setting, amplifies it. But the theme does not reach its fullest orchestration until the fourth scene. Indeed, the word "change" and its synonyms—"transformation," "alters," "exchange"—occur fifteen times in that one scene alone. There we see or hear of transformations at nearly every level, divine, human, chronological, animal, vegetable, each one a deliberate show and each one revealing a hidden truth.

Like any proper pastoral lover Florizel is a disguised prince and to defend his "swain's wearing" he invokes divine practice:

> The gods themselves
> (Humbling their deities to love) have taken
> The shapes of beasts upon them. Jupiter
> Became a bull and bellow'd; the green Neptune
> A ram and bleated; and the fire-rob'd god,
> Golden Apollo, a poor humble swain,
> As I seem now.
>
> (IV.iv.25-31)

If the great Jove can become an animal, Florizel sees no reason why a prince cannot masquerade as a shepherd. He fittingly selects Ovid's stories as his text, alluding to one of Shakespeare's own sources and advertising the "magic" behind his change. Later in the scene Autolycus satirizes these metamorphoses in his coarse ballads:[21]

> Here's another ballad, of a fish that appear'd upon the coast on Wed'n'sday the fourscore of April, forty thousand fadom above water, and sung this ballad against the hard hearts of maids. It was thought she was a woman and was turn'd into a cold fish for she would not exchange flesh with one that lov'd her. The ballad is very pitiful, and as true.
>
> (275-86)

Autolycus' puns realize another change: a woman who does not "exchange flesh" with her lover is of course a cold fish. Shakespeare includes Sylvius and Phebe in *As You Like It* to parody and authenticate the conventionality of Orlando and Roslynde's love. That is, by demonstrating the absurdity of romantic love Shakespeare makes it palpable. So, too, he parodies mythological transformations and pastoral disguises with folk ballad. If Jove can change into a bull and bellow, then why cannot a woman turned fish appear on the "fourscore of April, forty thousand fadom above water"? Both fictions are "very pitiful, and true."

The trueness of change is indeed a matter of deep concern to pastoral romance writers. As we saw in the previous chapter, Spenser combines the pastoral's predilection for debate or contest with the artist's desire for permanence, following Book Six with an allegorical *debat* about permanence and change. Like a proper pastoralist Shakespeare too addresses the question of mutability in the brief exchange—a debate—between Perdita and Polixenes.

Appropriate to the topic, Perdita repeats the progress followed by Spenser's Mutabilitie, speaking in terms of the cyclic year:

> Sir, the year growing ancient,
> Not yet at summer's death, nor on the birth

Of trembling winter, the fairest flow'rs o'th' season
Are our carnations and streak'd gillyvors
(Which some call Nature's bastards).

> (79-82)

Perdita strives for a natural decorum. To the visiting gentlemen, "men of middle age," she matches flowers "Of middle summer" (107); to Florizel, "I would I had some flow'rs o' th' spring" (113). She talks of "the blasts of January" (111), "the winds of March" (120), and even of "the gods that control natural cycles": Proserpina, Cytherea, and Phoebus. Although she seems attuned to Nature's contrary ways, Perdita distrusts contradiction. She would plant the bastard gillyflowers, "No more than were I painted I would wish / This youth should say 'twere well, and only therefore / Desire to breed by me" (101-03). The irony, of course, is that she herself is contrary. Moments before, this pranked up girl and her prince did desire to breed, hoping for "that nuptial, which / We two have sworn shall come" (50-51), and she readily admits to being painted:

> You see, sweet maid, we marry
> A gentle scion to the wildest stock,
> And make conceive a bark of baser kind
> By bud of nobler race. This is an art
> Which does mend Nature—change it rather; but
> The art itself is Nature.
>
> (92-97)

Polixenes believes that the gardener actually changes Nature, just as Perdita supposes that her costume alters her character. And, again like Perdita, Polixenes sets up his own contradictory disposition.[22] He will forbid his royal son ever to enter "These rural latches" again, an injunction which ignores his horticultural advice of marrying "A gentle scion to the wildest stock." Thus both disguised characters exhibit contradictory behavior, but a behavior which, paradoxically, hints at the eventual truth: Perdita will marry Florizel with Polixenes' full approval.

To appreciate fully the ironies in this episode we should remember Nature's judgment of Mutabilitie:

> I well consider all that ye have sayd,
> And find that all things stedfastness do hate
> And changed be: yet being rightly wayd
> They are not changed from their first estate;
> But by their change their being doe dilate:
> And turning to themselves at length againe,
> Do worke their own perfection so by fate:
> Then ouer them Change doth not rule and raigne;
> But they raigne ouer change, and doe ther states maintaine.
>
> (*FQ*, VII.58)

We could do worse than choose Spenser's words as a gloss for *The Winter's Tale*. The alteration in the appearance of a thing *elucidates* its nature, a truth just as basic to drama as it is to romance. Polixenes is wrong to suppose that the gardener's art changes Nature: the flower is still a flower for all its piedness. Jove may metamorphose into a bull, but he is no less Jove; the change illustrates his divine prerogative. Perdita desires to breed by a prince because she is a princess. Polixenes forbids the marriage because romantic comedy demands a blocking parent. Both of them act as they do in Whitsun pastorals because they *are* actors in a pastoral: "I see the play so lies that I must bear a part." All of the central characters in Act IV adopt several parts, each part revealing, not disguising, something new (or true) about them.

Camillo and Autolycus, especially, "worke their own perfection." The act ends with two parallel scenes. In the first, Camillo directs the lovers' costume change and their escape to Sicilia. In the second, Autolycus manages the Shepherd and Clown's passage, as well as his own. These twin episodes answer the section's earlier scenes, the desires of Camillo to return home, of Polixenes to check his son, of Autolycus to fatten his purse, and echo Part One by shipping Perdita to sea again. Further, the congregational flight to Sicilia associates all the characters in one course of action, the central plot of finding that which was lost. Camillo can prophesy:

> Methinks I see
> Leontes opening his free arms, and weeping
> His welcomes forth; asks thee, son, forgiveness,
> As 'twere i' th' fathers business; kisses the
>   hands
> Of your fresh princess; o'er and o'er divides
>   him
> 'Twixt his unkindness and his kindness: th' one
> He chides to hell, and bids the other grow
> Faster than thought or time.
>   (548-54)

He envisions his plot's end, an end, as we shall see, coincident with the play's end, when it too discovers its kind-ness. The Shepherd's decision to reveal his truth about Perdita, a reminder of Part One's end, sets *The Winter's Tale*'s final stage.

Thus it is that the plotting, scheming, planning, disguising, changing, all belong to returning Perdita—and everything else, the play included—to the proper estate. Like the players who don costume after costume, the play itself passes through several stages, each one a new revelation, each one provoking another guess at its true nature. Despite the altered appearance of *The Winter's Tale* brought off in Part Two, the stock characters, the pastoral setting, the comic plot, the new age, even a different world order, the substance of the

play remains the same. Time turns his glass; he does not trade it for another.

In some ways the second section serves as an analogue of the first. For instance, the comic pattern of preparation-license-festivity mocks the prepared surprise pattern found in Part One, mocks because so little surprises in Part Two. Polixenes can make his plans, adopt his disguises and reveal himself at the proper time, with few subtle hints or hidden meanings. Act IV, scenes ii, iii, and iv ridicule Leontes' behavior through Acts I, II, III. His admission of jealousy pairs with Polixenes' proposal to spy, his attempts to convince the court of Hermione's guilt become Autolycus' deception of the Clown, and Apollo's oracle is mimicked by Camillo's prophecy. Once more analogy dominates over the structure of events. The first and second parts are unified by their thematic structure, their matter. In Sicilia we see the tragic implications of mistaken identity and deception; in Bohemia we witness the comic portrayal of disguise and deceit.

A king's mistaken jealousy rules in Sicilia. Although Leontes claims to base his suspicion on appearances, "paddling palms and pinching fingers," once that jealousy gains credibility, at least for himself, he loses all faith in reason. He dismisses past love of and for his wife and friend. He ignores the entire court's protestations. He denies the physical evidence of the baby's likeness to himself. He repudiates Apollo's oracle. In short, Leontes imposes a personal fiction, an internal doubt (witness the number of his asides), on the Sicilian reality. In Bohemia Shakespeare turns Leontes' self-deception outward. We have already noted how the characters broadcast roles make a comedy of their lives. Polixenes openly plans to watch his son. Autolycus openly tricks the Clown. Florizel openly admits his rustic disguise. Perdita openly plays the festival queen. Camillo openly plots his return to Sicilia. In this second section the audience knows something else as well. Every character supposes that Perdita is either a shepherd's daughter or an abandoned bastard, and all their poses and counterposes (except Autolycus') are based on that supposition. They are, of course, mistaken. In this case a Bohemian fiction imposes on their personal realities.

III

With the return to Sicilia we should recognize the legitimacy of the three part division of *The Winter's Tale*. The change of locale once more predicates an alteration in genre and narrative technique. The play that begins as a tragedy, laced with comedy and pastoral, and turns to pastoral, informed by comedy and romance, finishes as a romance. Perhaps Fitzroy Pyle, in his book-length study of the play, best describes Part Three:

The last act is tightly packed. It has a great deal to do and little space to do it in. It has rapidly to reinstate the thesis figure, Leontes, bring the antithesis into relation with the thesis, and introduce a synthesis. For this purpose it divides into three scenes— interrelated, like the movements of the play itself.[23]

Pyle reduces the play to a telling dialectical syllogism, bespeaking his awareness of the play's structure and identifying the final act as instrumental in clinching that structure. Scene one, which begins with unhappy memories and the Bohemian's arrival, fits section one, which starts with happy memories and ends with the flight to Bohemia. Scene two, which reports the joy and betrothal of a verily identified girl, matches section two, which portrays the tribulations of a variously identified girl. And scene three, the statue's metamorphosis, represents the third section itself, a final "movement" (a happy choice) that integrates the world orders of Sicilia and Bohemia, tragic plot and comic plot, mimetic representation and romantic sensation, personal fiction and public display.

Because they interrelate with the play's major divisions, the last three scenes can be associated with stages in the dramatic surprise formula. Leontes' vow to remarry only with Paulina's permission (V.i.69-70) predicts the final outcome, a remarriage. Perdita's return substantiates the oracle's condition that prohibits Leontes from marrying again until "that which is lost be found." The restoration of Hermione to Leontes provides the ironic twist to his remarriage: he indeed marries again, but his new wife is his old wife, thus maintaining the proper estate. The remarriage symbolizes on a mundane level the ending's cosmic implications: "The recognition toward which romance moves is more than a matter of stripping away a few diguises or sorting out a few cases of mistaken identity; it is an epiphany of Apollinian order, clarity, and harmony in the universe."[24] Shakespeare shares his vision of an Apollinian order with other romancers, notably Longus, Chaucer, and Spenser, though with one important distinction: Shakespeare achieves his on the stage, where physical limitation prohibits ascending to the eighth sphere or contemplating Revelations. Hermione's surprise re-appearance is the eucatastrophe, a deliberately artificial representation that mirrors the play's magic.

Referring to this scene, Adrien Bonjour says that, "we enjoy the effect produced on the characters of the play much better than if we received at the same time with them the shock of the *complete* surprise."[25] We are not, I think, *completely* surprised by the plot's ending. Shakespeare takes us into his confidence; we share a more omniscient view, possessing a superior knowledge than that of the purblind characters. Shakespeare drops hints like Hansel and Gretel dropping bread crumbs: the path is easily found. Yet the last scene does have special impact, partly because, like the bear

scene, it so literally fulfills the predictions, and partly because Shakespeare obscures his destination by not following a well-known trail.

He makes Hermione's return more affecting by downplaying Perdita's reunion with her father. All of our romance experience points to the necessary ending, the reunion of child and father, and the whole of *The Winter's Tale* supports that expectation. From the moment Leontes asks, in the first section, "Shall I live to see this bastard kneel / And call me father?", we fix our attention on Perdita, awaiting the inevitable moment when she does kneel and claim her father. In order for events to end happily the oracle demands that she be found. We follow Perdita from Sicilia to Bohemia and back to Sicilia again. Time's argument for Act IV involves "what adheres" to Perdita. By the end of the second section, with Camillo bent on forcing Leontes and Polixenes together and the Shepherd bent on producing the heirlooms, we know Perdita's recognition will be swift and sure. Shakespeare even teases us further at the opening of the final part. Seeing Florizel and Perdita together reminds Leontes that, "I lost a couple, that 'twixt heaven and earth / Might thus have stood, begetting wonder" (V.i.132-33). The announcement of Polixenes' arrival momentarily creates tension, until we remember that the Shepherd stands ready with the trinkets. The moment is at hand.

But we do not see it. At the climactic moment, when her ascending star has reached its zenith, Perdita all but disappears from the play. She speaks only twice in the entire fifth act. True, her presence on stage is important, but her importance is relative to Hermione. The first, and perhaps most surprising, twist at the close of *The Winter's Tale* is that Perdita plays a supporting role to her mother. Her beauty is remarkable, but only insofar as it reminds Leontes of his wife. Her reunion with her father is joyful, but it is counterbalanced by the loss of Hermione: "Our king, being ready to leap out of himself for joy of his found daughter, as if that joy were now become a loss, cries, 'O, thy mother, thy mother!'" (V.ii.49-52). Even her return, supposedly the solution to the play, is important in terms of Hermione, as the queen herself admits:

> for thou shalt hear that I,
> Knowing by Paulina that the oracle
> Gave hope thou wast in being, have preserv'd
> Myself to see the issue.
>
> (V.iii.125-28)

Shakespeare goes beyond mere comparisons, however. He emphasizes Perdita's subsidiary role by withdrawing her "scene" from the play. Directors often complain that the long, drawn-out description of all that joy and all that sorrow is unplayable. Of course it is: that is the point. The Gentleman can remark, ironically, that: "The dignity of this act was worth the audience of kings and princes, for by such was it acted" (V.ii.79-81). Obviously so, for we are none of us kings and princes, and none of us is in that audience. The scene is one which we have often seen acted, even (or especially) in Shakespeare. He gives us romantic versions in *As You Like It* and *Pericles,* and a tragic version in *King Lear.* Shakespeare readily admits the conventionality of the reunion: the news is "like an old tale" (28), "like an old tale still" (61). The Gentlemen repeatedly complain of their inability to describe it: "I make a broken delivery of the business" (9); "Then you have lost a sight which was to be seen, cannot be spoken of" (42-3); "I have never heard of such another encounter, which lames report to follow it, and undoes description to do it" (56-58). Evidently our familiarity with father-daughter reunions makes another one unnecessary: it does not have to be seen to be believed.

The ironic means of *reporting* Perdita's return is the surest sign that Shakespeare will offer something else, something better, some greater miracle with which to close his fiction.[26] Frank Kermode, we remember, instructs that our sense of an ending is strengthened when "the fiction under consideration is one of those which, by upsetting the ordinary balance of our naive expectations, is finding something out for us, something *real.*" To be sure, our naive expectations have been upset, but we have not found out "something real." In fact, Shakespeare makes the reunion as unreal as possible. We merely overhear courtiers' gossip. The news is like an old tale. "Such a deal of wonder is broken out within this hour that ballad makers cannot be able to express it" (23-25). The reunion between father and daughter is such a fiction that one gentleman regards the event with a critic's eye:

> One of the prettiest touches of all, and that which angled for mine eyes (caught the water though not the fish), was when, at the relation of the Queen's death (with the manner how she came to't bravely confessed and lamented by the King), how attentiveness wounded his daughter, till (from one sign of dolor to another) she did (with an "Alas!"), I would fain say, bleed tears; for I am sure my heart wept blood. Who was not marble there chang'd color; some swounded, all sorrow'd. If all the world could have seen't, the woe had been universal.
> (82-92)

Perdita's reception of her mother's death is "the prettiest touch," one "bravely" acted, that angles for attention. It is a special effect, in which the Gentleman "would fain say" Perdita bled tears. The touch is so affecting that "some swounded, all sorrow'd. If all the world had seen't, the woe had been universal." The Gentleman's conditional statements turn his report into another fiction. Perdita receives rave would-be reviews for a would-be scene.

While evaluating Perdita's performance the Gentleman introduces an even prettier touch. He identifies a num-

ber of transformations and indicates the next turn of events. Perdita, for instance, is again linked to the gillyflower: she gets pied in the face, changing "from one sign of dolor to another." Her histrionics angled at eyes and "caught water though not the fish." Autolycus previously sang of a spurning woman turned into a cold fish. Hermione, we next discover, is a spurned woman turned into cold stone. "The revelation of the Queen's death" is, like Autolycus's ballad, a tale "very pitiful, and as true," or so thinks the Gentleman: "Who was not marble there changed color."

Thus, if we are acute, we are prepared for Hermione's transformation. Autolycus's ballad parodies the metamorphoses invoked by Florizel to defend his costume. Ovid's stories also include the tale of Pygmalion, the woman turned to life from stone. That Romano's lifelike statue follows so quickly upon the heels of the recalled transformations and fills so conveniently the void left by Perdita's unseen performance ought to be enough to arouse our suspicions. Even if we are not acute, the accumulation of poses assumed, masks donned, and parts played should have taught us the simple lesson about outward show. Hence Leontes' refrain that "we are mocked with art." Fitzroy Pyle quite mistakenly insists that the audience must believe, with the characters on stage, they are actually witnessing a statue come to life. He is correct, though, to stress the dramatic quality of the statue scene:

> The events related in V.ii were, considered in the context of the play, all the more effective for being reported as contrived, posed, arranged as though performed on stage. This event, on the other hand, is and must be performed upon the stage. It must be seen to be believed.[27]

Shakespeare reverses the procedure followed in V.ii. Where he first narrates a familiar, dramatic scene, he now dramatizes a rare, narrative scene. He audaciously attempts to produce on stage a romance wonder—and he succeeds.

Shakespeare encloses the statue scene within an opposing set of terms, the lifelike and the marvellous, the realistic and the magical. The statue is admired for its perfect imitation of Hermione's "natural posture." One stands before her in hope of answer. We are told to prepare "To see the life as lively mock'd as ever / Still sleep mock'd death" (V.ii.19-20). Leontes can ask, "Would you not deem it breath'd?" (64), and Polixenes can agree, "The very life seems warm upon her lip" (66). Far from a mundane response, however, this mimetic masterpiece by that "rare Italian" who, like Father Time and the playwright, "would beguile Nature of her custom, so perfectly is he her ape" (V.ii.99-100), strikes awe into its audience. They regard it as a "wonder" (22), an "amazement" (87), a "marvel" (100). Leontes apostrophizes:

O royal piece,
There's magic in thy majesty, which has
My evils conjur'd to remembrance.

(38-40)

And indeed, Paulina does turn to conjuring to transform the inanimate statue into animate woman, her incantation rousing Leontes to proclaim, "If this be magic, let it be an art/Lawful as eating." (110-11)

We are mocked with art because the whole episode is a charade. Hermione never was dead, never a statue, except to pretense. She merely has "preserv'd" herself these sixteen years. Paulina pretends to be a magician, producing a play, setting the stage, preparing the audience, building suspense, displaying her final trick, one done, I am tempted to add, with mirrors. Her art is lawful, for it is a literary art. The "magic" needed for her play's success is audience belief: "It is requir'd / You do awake your faith" (94-95).[28] Once Leontes admits his desire for Hermione, Paulina need only show the statue, tease about wet paint, and announce her power to "make the statue move" to apprehend Leontes' fixed attention: "Proceed, / No foot shall stir" (97-98). He will see the statue alive, regardless of "wicked powers" or "unlawful business." His willingness to believe Hermione adulterous begins the play; his belief in her rebirth ends it. In the interim, as Birnam Wood to Dunsinane, Bohemia has come to Sicilia, complete with its faith in fairies and its predilection for play, and Leontes realizes his, and his wife's, comic potential. Perhaps the final and most telling irony of *The Winter's Tale* is that no one objects to Paulina's joke. That Hermione has been alive, at court, for sixteen years bothers Leontes not in the least. Our characters, each of whom stages his own little play, appreciate a finely wrought fiction. Like Tinkerbell, art cannot be sustained without attention, without its audience's faith, and, again like Tinkerbell, it begs for it.

As we should expect from previous romance experience, the eucatastrophe does not resolve the play's conflicts, real or imaginary. F. R. Foakes believes that the final scene "holds the paradoxes in suspension, for they cannot be resolved."[29] Shakespeare chooses that moment when the play reaches its fullest, densest, and yet clearest statement of generic identity to dissolve his fiction. To compose his final arrangement he combines opposites. The mimetic and the marvellous we have noted, but others can be added, Camillo listing several in one speech:[30]

My lord, your sorrow was too sore laid on
Which sixteen winters cannot blow away,
So many summers dry. Scarce any joy
Did ever so long live; no sorrow
But kill'd much sooner.

(49-53)

The oppositions belong to nature, emotion, time: winter/summer, live/kill'd, joy/sorrow, so long/much sooner—all of which resonate through the play. The sentence structure yokes antithetical phrases, yet, through parallelism, balances their meaning, and as with all balanced oppositions, the terms are cancelled. Thus, when Paulina contrives her little drama about a mythical metamorphosis, when she mocks Shakespeare's transformation of *Pandosto* into *The Winter's Tale,* the play made from prophecy and surprise, tragic consequences and pastoral license, the credible and the incredible, prepares to make its end.

Leontes' last speech empties the stage. Complemented by his queen and flushed with his renewed role of King, Leontes now assumes the functions of stage manager and epilogue. He forbids Paulina her intended role as pathetic widow ("I, an old turtle, / Will wing me to some wither'd bow") and forces the demands of genre upon her. He summarizes the plot, begging forgiveness from both Hermione and Polixenes for his "ill-suspicion" and verifying Florizel and Perdita's troth-plight. More importantly, he draws a final, emphatic line between the worlds of the play and the world outside the play:

Good Paulina,
Lead us from hence, where we may leisurely
Each one demand and answer to his part

The ending has met the beginning. "Since first we were dissever'd" connects with Camillo's opening observation about the friendship "which cannot choose but branch now," not to mention the original severance of "play" time and "real" time. "This wide gap of time" directly refers to Father Time's prologue, as well as alludes to the time expired during which each of these actors "his part / Perform'd." The characters are, after all, only characters; they exist only in stories, and to keep themselves alive they exit to swap tales, revealing the wooden O, the enclosed space that literally shapes the play, and leaving it vacant.

The Winter's Tale is about winter's tales, tall stories about wonderfull successes achieved against impossible odds. We remember the references to tales and tale-telling, plays and playwrighting, and know that Shakespeare "wrights" a play about romance. He takes a prose romance for a source, transforming its narrative order of fulfilled prophecy into the dramatic prepared surprise. He uses the stage as the space that encloses the other world, a space mirrored by the pastoral island. He pours the heart's blood of romance, mutability, the principle that all things must pass, into the play. The characters change their clothes, change their roles, change their locales, change their hearts. They allude to divine, natural, human, and literary change. They debate the ethics of change. They believe in change, the play ending with the players producing a scene modelled on an Ovidian metamorphosis. When all is said and done, when even the play has shifted genres, *The Winter's Tale* works its own perfection and does its state maintain.

Like many others before him, Shakespeare addresses mutability by making a fiction about it; yet in the end the fiction itself is transitory. Where others seek the permanence of print for their stories, Shakespeare chooses to dramatize his. We must think a moment of the implications. We need only flip Malory's book over to begin again, to turn from apocalypse to creation. The theatre audience lacks that option. We can come again another night, but as everyone knows, as Shakespeare knew, another performance means another play. Our experience of a closed dramatic romance is a golden age, unique, permanent, inviolate, ephemeral, never to be had again.

Notes

[1] Walter F. Eggers, Jr., "Genre and Affective Distance—The Example of *The Winter's Tale*," *Genre*, 10 (1977), 30-31. For more complete discussions of genre identification, see E. D. Hirsch's chapter, "The Concept of Genre," in *Validity in Interpretation* (New Haven: Yale UP, 1967), and Rosalie Colie, *The Resources of Kind* (Berkeley: Univ. of California Press, 1973).

[2] The two standard discussions of the pastoral, romance, and tragicomic backgrounds to *The Winter's Tale* are E. C. Pettet, *Shakespeare and the Romantic Tradition* (London: Staples Press, 1949), especially chapter one, and Hallett Smith, *Shakespeare's Romances* (San Marino: Huntington Library, 1974. Also consult Rosalie Colie, *Shakespeare's Living Art* (Princeton: Princeton UP, 1974), 243-83.

[3] Howard Felperin, *Shakespearean Romance* (Princeton: Princeton UP, 1972), 10-16, 212-16. The legacy of Greek romance has been studied by Samuel Lee Woolf, *The Greek Romances and Elizabethan Prose Fiction* (New York: Press of the New Era Printing Co., 1912) and Carol Gesner, *Shakespeare and the Greek Romance* (Lexington: Univ. of Kentucky Press, 1970).

[4] Felperin, 52.

[5] Fitzroy Pyle, *The Winter's Tale: A Commentary on the Structure* (London: Routledge & Kegan Paul, 1969), 149.

[6] *Aristotle's Poetics,* trans. Leon Golden, commentary O. B. Hardison (Englewood Cliffs, NJ: Prentice-Hall, 1968), 27.

[7] Sir Philip Sidney, *A Defence of Poetry*, ed. J. A. Van Dorsten (1966; rpt. London: Oxford UP, 1973), 65-67. For an excellent survey of the interpretation and application of the unities of time, place, and action in Re-

naissance critical theory, see Bernard Weinberg, *A History of Literary Criticism in the Italian Renaissance*, 2 vols. (Chicago: Univ. of Chicago Press, 1961).

[8] All references made to Shakespeare's plays are to *The Riverside Shakespeare*, ed. G. Blakemore Evans (Boston: Houghton Mifflin, 1974).

[9] William Nelson, *Fact or Fiction: The Dilemma of the Renaissance Storyteller* (Cambridge, Mass.: Harvard UP, 1973), 59. Richard Lanham, in a thoughtul study, characterizes Western man as a combination of "serious" man, epitomized by Plato, and "rhetorical" or playful man, epitomized by Ovid; he then traces the expression of Ovidian man in several Renaissance works: *Motives of Eloquence* (New Haven: Yale UP, 1976). F. A. Foakes, *Shakespeare: The Dark Comedies to the Last Plays* (Charlottesville: Univ. of Virginia Press, 1971), notices that Shakespeare distances the action and the characters of *The Winter's Tale* "by making us continually aware of the incredible fictiveness of the action, by exposing what he is doing with a conscious and often blatant theatricality" (78).

[10] The disparity between descriptions of characters and events and their presentation has been studied by Janet Adelmen, "Character and Knowledge," *Twentieth Century Interpretations of Antony and Cleopatra*, ed. Mark Rose (Englewood Cliffs, NJ: Prentice Hall, Inc., 1977) 118-25.

[11] Northrop Frye, "Recognition in *The Winter's Tale*," in *Essays on Shakespeare and Elizabethan Drama in Honour of Hardin Craig*, ed. Richard Hosley (London: Routledge & Kegan Paul, 1963), 241. Among those who agree with Frye are Hallett Smith, who calls the eruption "a sudden seizure, a perturbation of the mind" (101-02), and G. Wilson Knight, *The Crown of Life* (London: Oxford UP, 1947), 94, who claims Leontes "has allowed himself to be temporarily possessed." On the other side are Neville Coghill, "Six Points of Stagecraft," *Shakespeare, The Winter's Tale: A Casebook*, ed. Kenneth Muir (London: Macmillan, 1968), 199-202, and John Lawlor, "*Pandosto* and the Nature of Dramatic Romance," *PQ*, 41 (1962), 96-113.

[12] Robert Greene, *Pandosto* in *Narrative and Dramatic Sources of Shakespeare*, VIII, ed. Geoffrey Bullough (London: Routledge & Kegan Paul, 1975), 156-58.

[13] Coghill's essay examines how "contrivance works" in six key scenes—Leontes' jealousy, the bear, Father Time, the exchange of clothes between Perdita, Florizel, and Autolycus, the report of Perdita's return, and the statue (198-213).

[14] Sir Arthur Quiller-Couch and John Dover Wilson, eds., *The Winter's Tale* (1931; rpt. Cambridge: Cambridge UP, 1959), xx; Coghill, 202-05; in basic agree-

ment with Coghill is Dennis Biggins, " 'Exit Pursued by a Beare': A Problem in *The Winter's Tale*," *Shakespeare Quarterly*, 13 (1962), 8.

[15] *The Winter's Tale: A Study* (London: Staples Press, 1947), 52.

[16] Colie, *Living Art*, 248, explains that the pastoral elegy "offers a marvellous rationale for death," a fusion of the shepherd-poet and his inspiration, a creation of a "world of imagination in which, depending on his temperment, he could live as he would." In a sense the pastoral world offers both an after-life and an alter-life. It is at the moment of Antigonus' death, Colie notices (268), that the pastoral in *The Winter's Tale* begins. As we shall see, the pastoral elements start much earlier, but it certainly takes over at this point.

[17] Knight, 86, and Bethel, 59-61, both mention the comic possibilities of Leontes' jealousy.

[18] Norman Rabkin writes that Shakespeare's romances call "attention to the fact that what we are experiencing is art, not life, whether by the use of such awkward playwright surrogates as Time or Gower, or the incessant allusions to stage performance, or the drama of real characters in fairy-tale gardens, or sudden changes from tragedy to comedy, or in *The Tempest* the clear implication that Prospero is in some way to be thought of as analogous to the author of the play": "The Holy Sinner and the Confidence Man: Illusion in Shakespeare's Romances," in *Four Essays on Romance*, ed. Herschel Baker (Cambridge, Mass.: Harvard UP, 1971) 36-37. Two studies more fully investigate the matter of self-reflexivity in Shakespeare's art and, more particularly, of the various persona adopted by the playwright: James Calderwood, *Shakespearean Metadrama* (Minneapolis: Univ. of Minnesota Press, 1971) and, more recently, Alvin B Kernan, *The Playwright as Magician* (New Haven: Yale UP, 1979).

[19] *A Natural Perspective* (New York: Columbia UP, 1965, 92.

[20] In Act IV, Foakes aptly remarks, "clothes seem to make the man." He sees the series of disguises as transformations that culminate in the statue scene (134-135).

[21] Rabkin, 50-53

[22] Of this debate Rosalie Colie has written: "With these literary or generic or social mixes, comes also moral mixture, a mixture of ways of life set in actual or implied contradistinction or even contradiction" (*Living Art*, 253). We note that the mixture of roles, "ways of life," within a character, not between them, creates the conflicts, much as it does in chivalric romance.

[23] Pyle, 153. Compare Pyle's statement to the following quotation from Guarini, *Il Pastor Fido e il compendio della poesia tragicomica*, ed. Gioachino Brognoligo (Bari, 1914), 282:

> Now this untying has three parts worthy of consideration: the first is employed in the preparation of the matter, and is the most important of all; the second is the act itself by which the untying of the knot and the reversal of the action takes place; the third is entirely filled with delight and joy, according to the true end of tragicomic poetry.

Found in May Elizabeth Campbell, *The Winters Tale: A Study in Shakespeare's Late Plays with Special Reference to Guarini's Theory of Tragicomedy*, Diss. University of North Carolina 1970 (Ann Arbor: University Microfilms, 1971). Campbell's translation.

[24] Felperin, 25.

[25] "The Final Scene of *The Winter's Tale*," *English Studies*, 33 (1952), 198-201.

[26] Felperin, 17: "It is the central place that Shakespearean comedy and romance accords to the extraordinary in experience which distinguishes it from the other tradition of comedy that presents, in Sidney's phrase, 'the common errors of our life,' and which enables it to add the effect of 'wonder' to the 'delight' of most comedy."

[27] Pyle argues that in the last scene "the effect aimed at is that of a statue coming to life, not of a woman pretending to be a statue and pretending to come to life" (122-23). In keeping with the theatrical bravura of the play, I rather think the final scene should have the flavor of an amateur production, one not much more refined than Quince's. We ought to see a woman pretending to be a statue and pretending to come to life.

[28] Frye cautions against investigating too deeply the credibility of the statue scene, for it is more on the level of wish fulfillment (like Bottom's dream) than 'historical' event. He draws a distinction between actual belief and the desire to believe: "The world we are looking at in the conclusion of *The Winter's Tale* is not an object of belief so much as an object of desire." He links this world to that of Leontes' jealousy: "the world of Leontes' jealousy does not exist at all; only the consequences of believing in it exist" (*Natural Perspective*, 117). Shakespeare blurs this distinction; when we awake our faith we lend any fiction credibility.

[29] Foakes, 144.

[30] Traversi, 108, notes that Camillo also opens the play with a speech (I.i.21-32) that combines "under one set of images two processes apparently contradictory—that

of natural unified development existing side by side with widening division." That Camillo should combine opposites at the close of the play is no accident.

FURTHER READING

Barber, Charles. "*The Winter's Tale* and Jacobean Society." In *Shakespeare In A Changing World*, edited by Arnold Kettle, pp. 233-52. London: Lawrence & Wishart, 1964.

    Compares themes of the play to problems in seventeenth-century English society, especially in the contrast between court life and country life.

Bellette, A. F. "Truth and Utterance in *The Winter's Tale.*" *Shakespeare Survey* 3 (1978): 65-75.

    Examines the capacity of words to accurately represent truth, how words are used in relationships, and Leontes's failure to understand others or himself.

Bergeron, David M. "Hermione's Trial in *The Winter's Tale.*" *Essays in Theater* 3, No. 1 (November 1984): 3-12.

    Focuses on Hermione's courageous defense of herself in her trial, and how it contrasts with Leontes's irrational passion.

Blisset, William. "This Wide Gap of Time: *The Winter's Tale.*" *English Literary Renaissance* 1 (Winter 1971): 52-70.

    Discusses the symmetry of the play's two halves in terms of dramatic irony.

Cohen, Derek. "Patriarchy and Jealousy in *Othello* and *The Winter's Tale.*" *Modern Language Quarterly* 48, No. 3 (September 1987): 207-23.

    Describes the perceived role of female fidelity in maintaining social order, and compares the motives for and growth of jealousy in Othello and Leontes.

Cuvelier, Elaine. "'Perspective' in *The Winter's Tale.*" *Cahiers Elisabethains*, No. 23 (April 1983): 35-46.

    Examines the basis of Leontes's jealousy from a Jacobean perspective.

Dawson, Anthony B. "*King Lear, Antony and Cleopatra,* and *The Winter's Tale.*" In *Indirections: Shakespeare and the Art of Illusion*, pp. 129-55. Toronto: University of Toronto Press, 1978.

    Compares *The Winter's Tale* to *King Lear* and *Anthony and Cleopatra*, and discusses the metaphor of "seeing" in all three plays.

Felperin, Howard. "Our Carver's Excellence: *The Winter's Tale.*" In *Shakespearean Romance,* pp. 211-45. Princeton: Princeton University Press, 1972.

    Compares *The Winter's Tale* with Shakespeare's other romances and argues that its combination of romance and realism makes it one of his greatest works.

Foster, Verna A. "The Death of Hermione: Tragicomic Dramaturgy in *The Winter's Tale.*" *Cahiers Elisabethains*, No. 43 (April 1993): 43-56.

    Describes the subtle methods by which Shakespeare prepares his audience emotionally for the resurrection of Hermione.

Hartwig, Joan. "*The Winter's Tale*: 'The Pleasure of That Madness.'" In *Shakespeare's Tragicomic Vision*, pp. 104-36. Baton Rouge: Louisiana State University Press, 1972.

    Considers the methods by which Leontes is protected from the immediate condemnation of the audience, and examines the relationship of Leontes and Paulina and the roles they fill for each other.

Lindenbaum, Peter. "Time, Sexual Love, and the Uses of Pastoral in *The Winter's Tale.*" *Modern Language Quarterly* 33, No. 1, (March 1972): 3-22.

    Discusses two patterns of development in the scheme of the play: fall and redemption, and a gradual development from disease to health.

Ludwig, Jay B. "Shakespearean Decorum: An Essay on *The Winter's Tale.*" *Style* 8, No. 2 (Spring 1974): 365-404.

    Describes a pattern of "merged opposites" in *The Winter's Tale*, as revealed in the language of the characters, and the structures and themes of the play.

McCandless, David. "'Verily Bearing Blood': Pornography, Sexual Love, and the Reclaimed Feminine in *The Winter's Tale.*" *Essays in Theatre* 9, No. 1 (November 1990): 61-81.

    Compares Leontes's jealous delusion to a type of pornographic fantasy replaying the archetypal female deceit—the Fall of Eve—and the rehabilitating power of the female characters to transform Leontes and preserve the patriarchy.

Morse, William R. "Metacriticism and Materiality: The Case of Shakespeare's *The Winter's Tale.*" *ELH* 58, No. 2 (Summer 1991): 283-304.

    Considers the role contemporary political forces played in shaping *The Winter's Tale*, and conversely, the role of Shakespeare's dramas in shaping audience atttitudes towards the absolutist culture of the royal court.

Palmer, Daryl W. "Entertainment, Hospitality, and Family in *The Winter's Tale.*" *Iowa State Journal of Research* 59, No. 3 (February 1985): 253-61.

    Explores the relationship between the extended family and hospitality or entertainment in Jacobean England, extending the discussion to the families of *The Winter's Tale*, and demonstrating that the fractured relationships begin to heal only once Leontes reexercises hospitality.

Schalkwyk, David. "'A Lady's 'Verily' Is as Potent as a Lord's': Women, Word, and Witchcraft in *The Winter's Tale.*" *ELH* 22, No. 2 (Spring 1992): 242-72.

Examines the influence of women's language in the play, and the challenge it presents to men's power.

Smith, Hallett D. "*The Winter's Tale* and *Pandosto*." In *Shakespeare's Romances: A Study of Some Ways of the Imagination*, pp. 95-121. San Marino: Huntington Library, 1972.

Considers the sources which inform *The Winter's Tale* and other plays by Shakespeare, most notably Robert Greene's *Pandosto*.

Sokol, B. J. *Art and Illusion in 'The Winter's Tale'*. Manchester: Manchester University Press, 1994, 283 p.

Discusses the influences of Renaissance art on *The Winter's Tale*, and Shakespeare as an artist himself.

Taylor, Michael. "Innocence in *The Winter's Tale*." *Shakespeare Studies* 15 (1982): 227-42.

Describes Leontes's actions in terms of a childish innocence, claiming that such hysterical behavior is akin to that of a spoiled child; however, he argues, the play concludes with a new innocence, ushered in by the confident female characters and Leontes's own personal growth.

Ziegler, Georgianna. "Parents, Daughters and 'That Rare Italian Master': A New Source for *The Winter's Tale*." *Shakespeare Quarterly* 36, No. 2 (Summer 1985): 204-12.

Reviews sources from which Shakespeare possibly could have learned of Julio Romano, the "rare Italian master."

Cumulative Index to Topics

The Cumulative Index to Topics identifies the principal topics of discussion in the criticism of each play and non-dramatic poem. The topics are arranged alphabetically. Page references indicate the beginning page number of each essay containing substantial commentary on that topic.

Topic Index

Topic Index

Topic Index

Topic Index

credibility **1:** 540, 542, 543, 554, 562, 581, 587
Elizabethan culture, relation to **1:** 549, 553, 555, 563, 581, 587, 620; **16:** 53; **19:** 42, 78; **26:** 357; **28:** 1; **34:** 323, 330
fancy **1:** 543, 546
Feste
   characterization **1:** 558, 655, 658; **26:** 233, 364
   role in play **1:** 546, 551, 553, 566, 570, 571, 579, 635, 658
   song **1:** 543, 548, 561, 563, 566, 570, 572, 603, 620, 642
gender issues **19:** 78; **34:** 344
homosexuality **22:** 69
language and imagery **1:** 570, 650, 664; **22:** 12; **28:** 9; **34:** 293
love **1:** 543, 546, 573, 580, 587, 595, 600, 603, 610, 660; **19:** 78; **26:** 257, 364; **34:** 270, 293, 323
madness **1:** 554, 639, 656; **26:** 371
Malvolio
   characterization **1:** 540, 544, 545, 548, 550, 554, 558, 567, 575, 577, 615; **26:** 207, 233, 273
   forged letter **16:** 372; **28:** 1
   punishment **1:** 539, 544, 548, 549, 554, 555, 558, 563, 577, 590, 632, 645
   as Puritan **1:** 549, 551, 555, 558, 561, 563; **25:** 47
   role in play **1:** 545, 548, 549, 553, 555, 563, 567, 575, 577, 588, 610, 615, 632, 645; **26:** 337, 374
music **1:** 543, 566, 596
Olivia **1:** 540, 543, 545
order **1:** 563, 596; **34:** 330
philosophical issues **1:** 560, 563, 596; **34:** 301, 316
Puritanism **1:** 549, 553, 555, 632; **16:** 53; **25:** 47
Saturnalian elements **1:** 554, 571, 603, 620, 642; **16:** 53
self-deception **1:** 554, 561, 591, 625
self-indulgence **1:** 563, 615, 635
sexual ambiguity and sexual deception **1:** 540, 562, 620, 621, 639, 645; **22:** 69; **34:** 311, 344
Shakespeare's canon, place in **1:** 543, 548, 557, 569, 575, 580, 621, 635, 638
Shakespeare's other plays, relation to **34:** 270
sources **1:** 539, 540, 603; **34:** 301, 323, 344
staging issues **26:** 219, 233, 257, 337, 342, 346, 357, 359, 360, 364, 366, 371, 374
structure **1:** 539, 542, 543, 546, 551, 553, 563, 570, 571, 590, 600, 660; **26:** 374; **34:** 281, 287
tragic elements **1:** 557, 569, 572, 575, 580, 599, 621, 635, 638, 639, 645, 654, 656; **26:** 342
Viola **26:** 308

The Two Gentlemen of Verona

absurdities, inconsistencies, and shortcomings **6:** 435, 436, 437, 439, 464, 507, 541, 560
appearance vs. reality **6:** 494, 502, 511, 519, 529, 532, 549, 560
audience vs. character perceptions **6:** 499, 519, 524
authorship, question of **6:** 435, 436, 437, 438, 439, 449, 466, 476
characterization **6:** 438, 442, 445, 447, 449, 458,

462, 560; **12:** 458
Christian elements **6:** 438, 494, 514, 532, 555, 564
education **6:** 490, 494, 504, 526, 532, 555, 568
Elizabethan setting **12:** 463, 485
forest **6:** 450, 456, 492, 514, 547, 555, 564; 568
friendship vs. love **6:** 439, 449, 450, 458, 460, 465, 468, 471, 476, 480
genre **6:** 460, 468, 472, 516
identity **6:** 494, 511, 529, 532, 547, 560, 564, 568; **19:** 34
ironic or parodic elements **6:** 447, 472, 478, 484, 502, 504, 509, 516, 529, 549; **13:** 12
Julia or Silvia **6:** 450, 453, 458, 476, 494, 499, 516, 519, 549, 564
language and imagery **6:** 437, 438, 439, 445, 449, 490, 504, 519, 529, 541; **28:** 9
Launce and Speed, comic function of **6:** 438, 439, 442, 456, 458, 460, 462, 472, 476, 478, 484, 502, 504, 507, 509, 516, 519, 549
love **6:** 442, 445, 456, 479, 488, 492, 494, 502, 509, 516, 519, 549; **13:** 12
mimetic rivalry **13:** 12
morality **6:** 438, 492, 494, 514, 532, 555, 564
Proteus **6:** 439, 450, 458, 480, 490, 511
repentance and forgiveness **6:** 450, 514, 516, 555, 564
resolution **6:** 435, 436, 439, 445, 449, 453, 458, 460, 462, 465, 466, 468, 471, 476, 480, 486, 494, 509, 514, 516, 519, 529, 532, 541, 549; **19:** 34
romantic and courtly conventions **6:** 438, 460, 472, 478, 484, 486, 488, 502, 507, 509, 529, 541, 549, 560, 568; **12:** 460, 462
setting **12:** 463, 465, 485
sources and influences **6:** 436, 460, 462, 468, 476, 480, 490, 511, 547; **19:** 34
staging **12:** 457, 464
structure **6:** 445, 450, 460, 462, 504, 526
youth **6:** 439, 450, 464, 514, 568

The Two Noble Kinsmen

amorality, question of **9:** 447, 460, 492
authorship
   Shakespeare not a co-author **9:** 445, 447, 455, 461
   Shakespearean portions of the text **9:** 446, 447, 448, 455, 456, 457, 460, 462, 463, 471, 479, 486
   Shakespeare's part in the overall conception or design **9:** 444, 446, 448, 456, 457, 460, 480, 481, 486, 490
ceremonies and rituals, importance of **9:** 492, 498
characterization **9:** 457, 461, 471, 474
Emilia **9:** 460, 470, 471, 479, 481; **19:** 394
free will vs. fate **9:** 474, 481, 486, 492, 498
friendship **9:** 448, 463, 470, 474, 479, 481, 486, 490; **19:** 394
innocence to experience **9:** 481, 502; **19:** 394
irony or satire **9:** 463, 481, 486
the jailer's daughter **9:** 457, 460, 479, 481, 486, 502
language and imagery **9:** 445, 446, 447, 448, 456, 461, 462, 463, 469, 471, 498, 502
love **9:** 479, 481, 490, 498

masque elements **9:** 490
Palamon and Arcite **9:** 474, 481, 490, 492, 502
sources **19:** 394

Venus and Adonis

Adonis **10:** 411, 420, 424, 427, 429, 434, 439, 442, 451, 454, 459, 466, 473, 489; **25:** 305, 328; **28:** 355; **33:** 309, 321, 330, 347, 352, 357, 363, 370, 377
allegorical elements **10:** 427, 434, 439, 449, 454, 462, 480; **28:** 355; **33:** 309, 330
ambiguity and paradox **10:** 434, 454, 459, 462, 466, 473, 480, 486, 489; **33:** 352
beauty **10:** 420, 423, 427, 434, 454, 480; **33:** 330, 352
the boar **10:** 416, 451, 454, 466, 473; **33:** 339, 347, 370
the courser and the jennet **10:** 418, 439, 466; **33:** 309, 339, 347, 352
death and nature's destructiveness **10:** 419, 427, 434, 451, 454, 462, 466, 473, 480, 489; **25:** 305; **33:** 309, 321, 347, 352, 363, 370
dramatic elements **10:** 459, 462, 486
eroticism or sensuality **10:** 410, 411, 418, 419, 427, 428, 429, 442, 448, 454, 459, 466, 473; **25:** 305, 328; **28:** 355; **33:** 321, 339, 347, 352, 363, 370
Faerie Queene (Edmund Spenser), compared with **33:** 339
Hero and Leander (Christopher Marlowe), compared with **10:** 419, 424, 429; **33:** 309, 357
humorous or parodic elements **10:** 429, 434, 439, 442, 459, 462, 489; **33:** 352
hunt motif **10:** 434, 451, 466, 473; **33:** 357, 370
imagery **10:** 414, 415, 416, 420, 429, 434, 449, 459, 466, 473, 480; **25:** 328; **28:** 355; **33:** 321, 339, 352, 363, 370, 377
love vs. lust **10:** 418, 420, 427, 434, 439, 448, 449, 454, 462, 466, 473, 480, 489; **25:** 305; **28:** 355; **33:** 309, 330, 339, 347, 357, 363, 370
morality **10:** 411, 412, 414, 416, 418, 419, 420, 423, 427, 428, 439, 442, 448, 449, 454, 459, 466; **33:** 330
negative appraisals **10:** 410, 411, 415, 418, 419, 424, 429
Ovid, compared with **32:** 352
pictorial elements **10:** 414, 415, 419, 420, 423, 480; **33:** 339
popularity **10:** 410, 412, 418, 427; **25:** 328
procreation **10:** 439, 449, 466; **33:** 321, 377
reason **10:** 427, 439, 449, 459, 462, 466; **28:** 355; **33:** 309, 330
rhetoric **33:** 377
Shakespeare's plays, compared with **10:** 412, 414, 415, 434, 459, 462
Shakespeare's sonnets, compared with **33:** 377
sources and influences **10:** 410, 412, 420, 424, 429, 434, 439, 451, 454, 466, 473, 480, 486, 489; **16:** 452; **25:** 305; **28:** 355; **33:** 309, 321, 330, 339, 347, 352, 357, 370, 377
structure **10:** 434, 442, 480, 486, 489; **33:** 357, 377
style **10:** 411, 412, 414, 415, 416, 418, 419, 420, 423, 424, 428, 429, 439, 442, 480, 486, 489; **16:** 452
Venus **10:** 427, 429, 434, 439, 442, 448, 449,

Topic Index